57th Annual Edition

Gun Digest®
2003

Edited by
Ken Ramage

—GUN DIGEST STAFF—

EDITOR
Ken Ramage

CONTRIBUTING EDITORS

Bob Bell – *Scopes & Mounts*

Holt Bodinson – *Ammunition, Ballistics & Components; Web Directory*

Raymond Caranta – *The Guns of Europe*

J. W. "Doc" Carlson – *Blackpowder Review*

John Haviland – *Shotgun Review*

John Malloy – *Handuns Today: Autoloaders*

Layne Simpson – *Rifle Review*

Larry S. Sterett – *Handloading Update*

John Taffin – *Handguns Today: Sixguns & Others*

Editorial Comments and Suggestions

We're always looking for feedback on our books. Please let us know what you like about this edition. If you have suggestions for articles you'd like to see in future editions, please contact.

Ken Ramage/Gun Digest
700 East State St.
Iola, WI 54990
email: ramagek@krause.com

Manuscripts, contributions and inquiries, including first class return postage, should be sent to the GUN DIGEST Editorial Offices, Krause Publications, 700 E. State Street, Iola, WI 54990-0001. All materials received will receive reasonable care, but we will not be responsible for their safe return. Material accepted is subject to our requirements for editing and revisions. Author payment covers all rights and title to the accepted material, including photos, drawings and other illustrations. Payment is at our current rates.

CAUTION: Technical data presented here, particularly technical data on the handloading and on firearms adjustment and alteration, inevitably reflects individual experience with particular equipment and components under specific circumstances the reader cannot duplicate exactly. Such data presentations therefore should be used for guidance only and with caution. Krause Publications, Inc., accepts no responsibility for results obtained using this data.

Published by

krause publications

700 E. State Street • Iola, WI 54990-0001
Telephone: 715/445-2214
Web: www.krause.com

Please call or write for our free catalog of publications. Our toll-free number to place an order or obtain a free catalog is 800-258-0929 or please use our regular business telephone, 715-445-2214.

Library of Congress Catalog Number: 44-32588
ISBN: 0-87349-481-4

JOHN T. AMBER LITERARY AWARD

Christopher Bartocci

Chris Bartocci has won the prestigious John T. Amber Award for his article *"AK47: The Path of a Legend,"* a work meticulously researched over a number of years and published in the GUN DIGEST 2002, 56th Edition.

Christopher Bartocci is currently a forensic firearms examiner with the Wisconsin Department of Justice State Crime Laboratory in Milwaukee, Wisconsin. He researches and writes about subjects related to firearms forensics and is published in the *AFTE* (Association of Firearm and Toolmark Examiners) *Journal*. Bartocci's background includes engineering and development of laser handgun sights, test and evaluation/destruction of firearms and ammunition, firearms instruction, gunsmithing, attendance of numerous armorer schools—as well as service in the U.S. Army. In his spare time, he enjoys researching the intricacies of modern military assault rifles, pistols and ammunition.

"The AR-15/M-16-series rifles have always interested me. I found there was still a serious misunderstanding of what happened to the M-16 rifle in Vietnam, giving the rifle a bad reputation through no fault of it's own. My goal was to research and present—as best as I could—a thorough and truthful account of the M-16's problems in Vietnam. This article was the result of more than four years of research.

"My interest in—and growing passion for—the subject lead me in this work and I always encountered people anxious to help. Colt's Manufacturing, Diemaco, Knight's Manufacturing and Bushmaster all supported my research and development of this article and made contributions to it. An article of this historical significance could not be possible without such help."

The only juried literary award in the firearms field, the John T. Amber Award replaced the Townsend Whelen Award, originated by the late John T. Amber and re-named in his honor. Now, a $1,000 prize goes to the winner of this annual award.

Nominations for the competition are made by the GUN DIGEST editor and are judged by a distinguished panel of editors experienced in the firearms field. Entries are evaluated for felicity of expression and illustration, originality and scholarship, and subject importance to the firearms field.

This year's Amber Award nominees, in addition to Bartocci, were: Ken Aiken, *"The Water-Proof Rifle"*

R. W. Ballou, *"Tubular Magazines... ARE Safe"*

Jerry Burke, *"The Mysterious Makarov"*

Jim Foral, *" The Model 1910 Ross: 'The Best Rifle in the World' "*

R. C. House, *"Old Eli & Old Sam: My Life's Companions"*

Steve Hurst, *"The Family Colt"*

George J. Layman, *"Remington's Number Three Hepburn"*

John Malloy, *"The H&R Defender"*

Harvey T. Pennington, *"Homemade 'Express' Bullets for the 40/65 Winchester"*

Rocky Raab, *"Most Needed Revolver Wildcat?"*

R. H. VanDenburg, Jr., *"The Evolution of Remington Autoloading Shotguns"*

Serving as judges for this year's competition were John D. Acquilino, editor of *Inside Gun News*; James W. Bequette, executive editor of *Shooting Times*; David Brennan, editor of *Precision Shooting*, Sharon Cunningham, director of Pioneer Press; Pete Dickey, former technical editor of *American Rifleman*; Jack Lewis, former editor and publisher of *Gun World*; Bill Parkerson, former editor of *American Rifleman*, now director of research and information for the National Rifle Association; Dave Petzal, executive editor of *Field & Stream,* and Ken Warner, former editor-in-chief of GUN DIGEST and KNIVES.

Introduction

There is good news to report regarding our shooting sports manufacturers and importers. As I edited the post-SHOT Show new product reports from the GUN DIGEST field editors, I was again struck by the growing array of interesting firearms and airguns available to us. Certain of our major arms companies who were languishing–like Colt and Smith & Wesson–have greatly improved their business health and are enjoying strong sales. Blount Sporting Equipment Division, a conglomerate better known by the companies held: Federal Cartridge, RCBS, CCI/Speer, Outers, Weaver, Redfield and Simmons – was acquired by ATK, parent corporation of Alliant Powder.

You'll notice two new names on the contributing editors' masthead: John Haviland, who joined us last year as contributing editor for shotguns, replacing Bill Hanus who ably stepped in after Don Zutz passed away. And, in this 57th edition, John Taffin follows Hal Swiggett and the late George Nonte as contributing editor for revolvers, single-shot and other handguns. I've had the pleasure of being acquainted with Hal for most of my 30 years in the shooting sports industry. Hal, thanks for your contribution to these pages over the years, and our very best wishes. John Taffin is a familiar name to sixgunners across the country and around the world–and we welcome him to GUN DIGEST.

Over 20 years ago, a new book title was derived from the GUN DIGEST. This fall, the 23rd edition of the KNIVES annual will be published. In case you are not familiar with the title, the subject of the book is–predominantly–custom knives and the craftsmen and artisans who make them. Each edition contains relevant articles of interest and heavily-illustrated sections of custom cutlery, followed by a variety of directories updated annually. The commercial sporting cutlery industry has grown, and offers an increasing number of new and interesting products to the outdoorsman. So we created a new book title, focused exclusively on the commercial sporting and collectible cutlery.

The new book is called SPORTING KNIVES, and the second edition has just been published. Contents are organized along the lines of GUN DIGEST, to include authoritative articles, new product reports on major categories, an illustrated catalog section and useful reference section. There's even a web site directory. If you have an interest in fixed- or folding-blade knives, tactical or survival blades, pocket knives – and more, you'll find them all in this book. Check with your favorite bookseller.

Within this edition of GUN DIGEST, we have a wide range of articles for your reading pleasure. I found myself considering adding to my S&W K-frame inventory after reading Hollis Flint's article. Just as that urge was subsiding, Tom Schiffer's article rekindled my interest in certain replica muzzleloaders. And I don't know if I can continue to do without one of the USRAC Model 9410s!

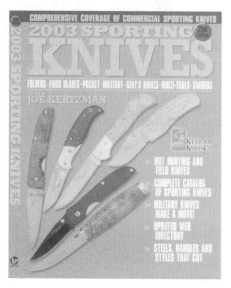

We once again have an editorial color section and use part of it to display pages of beautifully photographed custom and engraved guns. Appearing on our covers, thanks to our friends at the American Custom Gunmakers Guild and the Firearms Engravers Guild, are some examples of the beautiful work done by custom gunmakers and engravers.

We hope you enjoy this 57th edition of GUN DIGEST. Comments are always welcome.

Ken Ramage, Editor

About Our Covers...

Front Cover:

Our front cover displays one view of the latest in a series of custom-made rifles crafted by the artisans of the American Custom Gunmakers Guild and the Firearms Engravers Guild of America–then offered by raffle to any interested party. Here's a description of the work:

To commemorate the 100th anniversary of the 1903 Springfield rifle, members of the American Custom Gunmakers Guild have created a very special one-of-a-kind sporting version of this American favorite.

The Guild members involved decided to pay tribute not only to the Springfield but also to some of the people who made it

a classic sporter of choice. With this in mind, they chose to style it after the great pre-war Griffin & Howe-built rifles and to chamber it for the famous 35 Whelen cartridge.

Edward LaPour performed the metalwork on the ACGG #18. Ed welded the rear receiver bridge over and machined it into a square bridge configuration. The left side of the action, where the bolt stop normally lies, was welded to create a smooth surface for engraving and to allow a new, handmade bolt stop to sit flush with the surface when the bolt stop is closed. Ed then made a new bolt stop pivot pin, spring and plunger system to hold the bolt stop in its open and closed positions. He welded a Griffin & Howe side mount

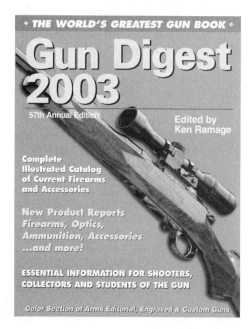

scope base to the side of the receiver. He facilitated the later stocking by extending the weld rearward over the ejector mount area, creating a flat side from the base to the end of the receiver. A new bolt handle was fabricated and welded on to clear a low mounted scope. To create a more pure sport look, Ed welded up all signs of the military clip charger slots and installed a Canjar trigger mechanism with a new "classic" trigger shoe. Although he did install a new three-position safety, he kept the Springfield 1903 cocking knob. Jim Wisner of Precise Metalsmithing Enterprises, Chehalis, Washington, supplied a one-piece trigger guard/floorplate assembly. In keeping with the style of the overall project, the team chose to use an Austrian Kahles 4x scope with 26mm tube from the period. This required new scope rings for the Griffin & Howe single-lever mount. John Krieger supplied the 35-caliber oversized barrel blank that Ed fashioned into a medium sporter contour with an integral barrel band sling swivel and an integral banded rear sight ramp with a secondary recoil lug underneath. The rear sight ramp carries sight blades with one standing and two folding leaves calibrated for 50, 100 and 200 yards and so engraved. The front sight ramp is a barrel band type provided by Precise Metalsmithing Enterprises with a custom hood.

From the moment the U.S. 1903 Springfield Rifle became available to the sportsmen of this country, gunsmiths and stockmakers began transforming it not only into plain hunting rifles but also into one-of-a-kind custom rifles. Many early stockmakers had a hand in creating what we call the "American classic gunstock" and many of them did it using the Springfield. Names such as Wundhammer, Shellhammer, Linden, Owen, and Griffin & Howe come to mind.

With this in mind, the stock for the 2003 ACGG Rifle was designed to fit with this period. Bruce Farman chose a quarter-sawn piece of California English walnut with fiddleback from end to end. The lines of the stock are "softer" than today's stocks tend to be but are typical of stocks from the pre-war period. The cheek piece carries the English style of rounded ends and has a beaded shadow line following the circumference, one at the top and another at the bottom, with a convex area in between. Bruce fashioned light fluting along each side of the comb nose. The buttstock ends with a steel buttplate typical of pre-war sporters. The forend is tipped with Ebony. The grip cap

is steel and is of a style used by Wesley Richards during this era. The rear sling swivel is a two-screw style inletted into the toe line and compliments the barrel band front swivel. Bruce finished the stock with traditional hand rubbed tung oil and checkered it 24 lines per inch in a point pattern with a fine-line border to accent the points.

Master engraver Robert Evans used a style called "blackleaf" which is similar to engraving done by Arnold Griebel in the 1930s. Bob also included a modest amount of gold highlights. The metal was blued and then the engraved areas were French grayed.

Unlike previous Guild raffle projects that have included a leather covered display case, the 2003 project is displayed in a French-fitted display stand by Ralph Powell of Beaverton, Oregon. Ralph fashioned this lovely piece of furniture from walnut with exotic maple marquetry inlays. The legs are removable and store in a compartment under the rifle. The interior is lined with blue ultra-suede and has compartments for the oil bottles, turn screws, brush, and cleaning rod. All handles and other fittings are solid brass.

Tickets at $20 each are available from Jan Billeb, ACGG, 22 Vista View Drive, Cody, WY 82414 (307) 587-4297 or through the ACGG web site www.acgg.com. Ticket sales are limited to 4,000 and the winner does not have to be present at the drawing in Reno on February 2, 2003.

The Makers:

Edward La Pour, *(member, the American Custom Gunmakers Guild)*
908 Hayward Ave., Bremerton, WA 98310/360-479-4966

Bruce Farman, *(member, the American Custom Gunmakers Guild)*
2563 NE Wm. E Sutton Ave., Bremerton, WA 98311/360-692-4188

Robert Evans, *(member, the Firearms Engravers Guild of America)*
332 Vine Street, Oregon City, OR 97045/403-656-5693

Case by:
Ralph Powell
Powell's Custom Presentation Cases
13595 S.W. Hazel, Beaverton, OR 97005

Photography: Turk's Head Productions, Inc.

Back Cover:

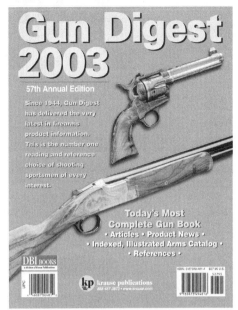

The back cover features *(top)* a Colt Single Action Army chambered for the 44 Special cartridge. This revolver was part of the ACGG's #12 Special Sporting Set. This was a wood-cased set that included, besides the SAA, a single-shot rifle, bowie knife and sheath, and accessories such as turnscrews, cleaning rod and oil bottle. Artisans contributing to the project were Robert J. Snapp, metalsmith; Steven Dodd Hughes, stockmaker and Frank E. Hendricks, engraver. The case was made by Marvin Huey. Photography by Mustafa Bilal, Turk's Head Productions, Inc.

Beneath the SAA is the Guild's #15 firearm, the 'Game Gun.' This is a 20-gauge Belgian Browning Superposed shotgun with 28-inch barrels choked Modified and Full. The metalwork was extensively upgraded to include sideplates, a solid hand-matted rib, beaded-edge trigger guard and checkered trigger, and gold-plated internal parts. Engraved games scenes are framed in fine English scroll and border.

The stock is a fine piece of English walnut with a diamond-shaped straight grip, detailed moldings around the metalwork and a gold oval fitted in the toe line. The checkering is in a 28-lpi point pattern with mullered borders. The recoil pad is covered in pigskin leather.

Artisans contributing to the 'Game Gun' project were Dennis Potter, metalwork; Hugh P. de Pentheny O'Kelly, stockwork and Ed Kane, engraving. The fitted and accessorized case furnished by Marvin Huey. Photography by Mustafa Bilal, Turk's Head Productions, Inc.

Gun Digest 2003

The World's Greatest Gun Book

CONTENTS

Page 11

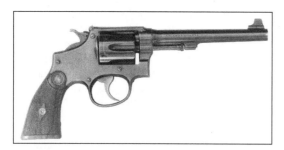

Page 24

Here Is The Gun You Have Been Waiting For

The New Colt .22 Automatic Target Pistol

Specifications:—Capacity of Magazine, 10 shots; Length of Barrel, 6¼ inches; Length over All, 10½ inches; Weight, 28 ounces; Finish, Full Blued; checked English Walnut stocks; Sights, Bead Front Sight, adjustable for elevation; Rear Sight, with adjusting screw, adjustable for windage; Distance between sights, 9 inches; Cartridge, .22 Long Rifle rim fire (greased cartridges only) either lesmok, semi-smokeless or smokeless. Note—"Greased" cartridges may be used provided shells are slightly lubricated.

Get One Quick and Without Cost to You

Years ago the Editors of Outer's Book recognized the need for an Automatic Target Pistol of small caliber. They pounded away at the manufacturers until, at last, it has been produced. They know what pleasure the little gun will afford and they want every Outer's Book Gunman to have one. Therefore the Outer's Book has arranged to offer it as a premium before it is even on the market, and this announcement is made so that clubs can be forming while the gun is being distributed. *It will be given for thirty-four new subscriptions at the club rate of $1.00.* The guns will be delivered just as soon as the manufacturers can furnish them. Get busy with a club and secure this great little gun as soon as it is out.

Premium Department, Outer's Book Company, Chicago, Ill.

Page 41

REPORTS FROM THE FIELD:

Page 84

Page 106

CATALOG OF ARMS AND ACCESSORIES

AK47

Lawrence Ventura.

Path of a Legend

The first Soviet Avtomat *(assault rifle), the definitive AK47. While technically the AK49, the true AK47 used the original stamped receiver design. Notice the milled receiver identified by the elongated groove above the magazine.*

by Christopher R. Bartocci

FEW STUDENTS OF firearms have not heard of the AK47. The rifle is legendary, ranking with the most influential firearms of the post-World War II era. Many know the name, but few know it's origins or just how it earned the reputation it did. The story of the AK47 was one of changing times and necessity. In the post-World War II battlefield, there was little use for a full-powered battle cartridge, such as the 7.62x54R, fired in a bolt-action rifle. The German style of mechanized/maneuver warfare was here to stay and, from that time on, emphasis would be on machine guns, pistols and the new "Assault Rifle." The infantry's range of engagement–previously 1,000 meters–would be greatly reduced, to 300 meters. The Soviet Army needed to upgrade its weapons to accommodate this new type of warfare.

The Beginning

During World War II, the Soviets had a serious shortage of small arms with which to equip their soldiers. The mechanized/maneuver warfare they encountered on their Eastern Front took a serious toll on the Red Army. Casualties averaged one dead *Wehrmacht* soldier for every 15 Soviet soldiers. At the time, the main battle rifle of the

Soviet Army was the Mosin-Nagant bolt-action rifle firing the 7.62x54R Russian round, no match for the MP38, MP40, StG44, MG34 and MG42. The high volume of full-auto fire put out by the Germans was too much for the Russians.

For the first time, the Soviets encountered the newest weapon in the German arsenal, one that would redefine the whole concept of the modern battle rifle. The German soldiers were equipped with the new StG44 *Sturmgewehr*, or Assault Rifle.

This rifle was remarkable and revolutionary for two reasons, the first being its cartridge. The StG44 fired the new 7.92x33mm Kurz (Short) intermediate cartridge. The cartridge ranked in power between the full-powered 7.92x57mm rifle round and the 9x19mm pistol round (*theory being that you would obtain the best of both worlds–the controllability of the sub-machine gun with the range of the battle rifle*). With the new tactics of warfare, a maximum range of approximately 300 to 400 meters was required and this new cartridge filled the bill.

The second revolutionary idea was that the rifle was a selective-fire weapon. At the shooter's discretion, he could fire either semi-automatic or full-automatic. A large-capacity magazine held 30 rounds. All features combined, greatly increased firepower was now available on the individual level.

Being on the receiving end of this new rifle, the Soviets learned of the excellent merits of the intermediate cartridge, as well as the new rifle and concept. They wanted their own intermediate-range cartridge. It is unconfirmed, but Soviet sources claim that the development of the 7.62x39mm round began in 1939 (*not adopted until 1943*)—just two years after the development of the 7.92x33mm *Kurz* round and one year after the first German MP43/MP44/StG44 rifles went into service. The new 7.62x39mm Soviet round was a 122-grain full metal jacket boattail bullet fired at a muzzle velocity of 2,300 feet per second, compared to the full-powered 7.62x54mm cartridge, firing a 150-grain bullet at 2,800 feet per second. The change resulted in a major decrease in weight and, most importantly, in recoil. The Soviets had their intermediate-powered cartridge. Now all they needed was a weapon to fire it.

General Mikhail Timofeyevich Kalashnikov, the designer of the AK-series rifle. Known as one of the most influential small arms designers of the post-World War II era. *Valery Shilin, IZHMASH Company, Russia.*

The SKS

You cannot discuss the history of the AK47 without first discussing the SKS rifle. The first weapon adopted to fire this new intermediate 7.62x39mm cartridge was the SKS45 (*Samozaryadnya Karabin Siminova 1945*), developed by Sergei Simonov. This rifle was outdated, however, at the time of adoption. It is claimed by some that the decision to adopt the SKS was political rather than based on its merits. It fired semi-automatic only and had a 10-round fixed magazine. The Soviets had great success with submachine guns during World War II. The future in military small arms was clearly the select-fire assault rifle. Mass-controlled full-auto bursts were now essential on the modern battlefield. The Soviets were looking for their own assault rifle, which set the stage for the AK47.

The Birth of the AK47

Mikhail Timofeyevich Kalashnikov was born on 10 November, 1919, to a poor family in Kurja—a small village in the Altay District, Russian Federation. He was fascinated by machines from a young age. He entered the Soviet Army in 1938, where he wound up in the

Tank Corps. He was sent to a technical school for armorers following his basic training. There he made his first invention: A device to measure and record the mileage of tanks, to differentiate between the mileage a tank traveled and the time it ran idle.

In June of 1941, the German invasion of the Soviet Union caused Kalashnikov to leave school. He was given command of his own tank. During action, Senior Sergeant Kalashnikov was seriously wounded and sent to a military hospital for treatment. While in the hospital, he heard stories from veterans about how Germans armed with automatic weapons were overwhelming the poorly armed Soviet troops. Now he started heavily researching the development of small arms. He was given six months' convalescent leave from the Army to recover from his wounds—but he did not go to rest.

He entered an Army-sponsored competition for a new submachine gun. In three months' time, he produced a working prototype in a railroad machine shop. His design was rejected, but it got him noticed by the Red Army and he was sent to the Small Arms Proving Ground at Ensk. At the time Kalashnikov worked on his first design, the SKS45 was adopted, but the next-generation Soviet battle rifle was in the making.

In 1945-46, Kalashnikov worked diligently on his assault rifle, instead of working in a railroad machine shop. He had professional technical support to perfect his design at the Tula Weapons Factory. In 1947, his design was adopted by the Soviet Union as their new assault rifle and the AK47 (*Avtomat Kalashnikova 1947*) was born. It was not until 1949 to 1950 that the AK47 went into production. There was a good four years of refinement and improvement before it was fielded on any large scale–unlike the U.S. M-16, which was rushed into service. The development was highly classified and kept very quiet; however, the actual model that went into full production was the AK49.

The first Soviet rifle adopted to fire the new 7.62x39mm cartridge was the SKS-45 (*Samozaryadnya Karabin Siminova 1945*). Note the 10-round fixed magazine. *Lawrence Ventura.*

The true AK47 was the rifle with the stamped receiver that went out of production in 1951. The AK49 was the model in production from 1951 until the late 1950s, when the AKM was introduced. The main difference between the AK47 and the AK49 is that the AK47 used the original stamped receiver and the AK49 used the conventional milled receiver. Those outside the Soviet Union did not get the first look at the new weapon until 1956, when Soviet troops carried them during the Hungarian Revolt.

Method of Operation

The AK47 is a selective-fire, gas-operated, air-cooled, magazine-fed assault rifle. It weighs approximately 9.56 pounds, with an overall length of approximately 34.25 inches and a barrel length of 16.34 inches.

The first AK47 rifles had a stamped receiver; however, since the industrial resources of the Soviet Union were not equipped to do such stamping operations in a timely fashion, the rifle was switched to a milled receiver. The AK47 exhibits an elongated milled groove above the magazine. The magazine is cammed into the receiver, and the magazine release is in front of the trigger guard. The selector lever sits on the right side of the firearm. When in the safe position, the selector acts as a dust cover, which the cocking handle follows on its backward motion. Drop the lever down one notch, and you are in the full-auto mode; down one more, and you are in the semi-automatic mode. There is a cleaning rod attached to the bottom of the barrel. The rear sight has elevation adjustments up to 800 meters. The rifle has a very short sight radius and a maximum practical effective range of 250 to 300 meters.

Operation of the AK47:

When the trigger is pulled, a claw on the trigger releases the hammer. The hammer strikes the firing pin, discharging the cartridge. As the bullet travels down the barrel, it passes through the gas port. Gas is bled into the piston chamber, driving the piston rearward. As the bolt carrier moves rearward, the rotating bolt unlocks. The continuing rearward motion extracts and ejects the fired cartridge case. The hammer is caught by the disconnect. When the hammer is all the way down, the auto-sear engages the hammer. The recoil spring then drives the bolt forward, stripping a round from the magazine, and feeds the round

into the chamber. When the bolt moves into the locked position, the bolt trips the auto-sear, releasing the hammer to the disconnector. When the trigger is released, the hammer is engaged to the trigger. When firing in the full-auto mode, the only difference is that the auto-sear will not release the hammer to the disconnector; it will release the hammer to strike the firing pin.

THE AKM

Around 1954, the industrial situation changed in the Soviet Union. Their manufacturing capabilities improved, and they returned to the original stamped receiver, decreasing the rifle's weight by approximately 2.5 pounds, to approximately 7.92 pounds. This third-generation rifle was called the AKM (*Avtomat Kalashnikova sistemi Modernizirovanniyi*), or Modernized Kalashnikov Assault Rifle, and ultimately became the most-produced of the AK-type rifles.

Sergeant Vladimir Maximov at the 40th anniversary of the Soviet armed forces in 1958. He carries the AK47. *Collector Grade Publications.*

Other changes: The addition of a simple 45-degree muzzle compensator to reduce muzzle climb. The rear sight of the AKM was made adjustable to 1,000 meters, the front sight assembly lightened, and the gas tube was changed. The exhaust portholes on the original AK47 were on the gas tube, but on the new AKM there are radial gas ports on the rifle itself, which reduce the chance of dirt getting in the gas piston assembly. There are grasping rails on the lower forearm grip and new Bakelite polymer magazines were introduced to replace the heavy steel magazines.

Another modification the Soviets made was to the trigger group itself. Because of the lighter receiver, the cyclic rate of fire increased. To slow the rate of fire, a decelerator was added to the trigger group to offer "drag" to the hammer, slightly retarding the rate of fire. The decelerator also gives the rifle's bolt some extra time to lock up before the next round is fired. Interesting to note that most AKM rifles use this decelerator; the main exception being the Chinese AKM rifles. The largest number of AK-type rifles produced was the AKM type.

Another requirement was for a rifle that would be more compact—one that could be used by paratroopers, tankers and any other unit requiring a more compact rifle. The AKS47 (*Avtomat Kalashnikova Skladyvauyushchimsya Prikladom 1947*) was developed. The AKS47 was a standard AK47 with an under-folding metal stock, virtually identical to that of the German MP38/MP40 machine pistols, and had a milled receiver. Later came the AKMS (*Avtomat Kalashnikova sistemi Modernizirovanniyi Skladyvauyushchimsya*), which was merely the stamped receiver version. The overall length of the AKMS, stock folded, is approximately 26 inches.

The RPK, the Soviet SAW

The Soviets also found the need for a magazine-fed squad automatic weapon. Interchangeability of parts was a concern so they developed the RPK (*Ruchnoi Pulemet Kalashnikova*). The RPK was basically an AK47, with modifications to make it more suitable as a squad automatic weapon. The receiver was built stronger, to withstand more constant automatic fire. The barrel was made heavier and longer, approximately 23.2 inches in length. The RPK weighs approximately 11 pounds. They equipped the RPK with basically the same sights as the AK47, and made the rear sight windage-adjustable. A bipod was added. The stock has a different shape, and the bottom handguard has been beefed up. With the exception of the aforementioned parts, the rest are interchangeable with the AK47. The RPK mainly uses a 40-round box magazine, but can use a 75-round drum and the standard

The post-World War II Soviet battle cartridges. The 7.62x54R (*left*), the 7.62x39mm (*middle*) and the 5.45x39mm (*right*). Lawrence Ventura.

The world's first assault rifle, the German StG44 firing the 7.92x33mm *Kurz* cartridge (*top*), and the Soviet AK47 firing the 7.62x39mm Soviet cartridge (*bottom*). The lineage of the StG44 in the AK47 is undeniable. Lawrence Ventura.

The AK47 (*top*) and the AKM (*bottom*). Notice the milled receiver of the AK47, and the return to the stamped receiver of the AKM. The AKM is the most mass-produced of all of the Kalashnikov assault rifles. *Lawrence Ventura.*

30-round AK47 magazine—all magazines are interchangeable.

The Reputation

The AK47 has seen action in every climate on the planet—from the freezing Siberian mountains to the sands of the Middle East—but the true proving grounds for the AK47/AKM were the jungles of Southeast Asia. The Soviet Union, as well as China, was supplying rifles to the North Vietnamese Army and the Vietcong. The jungles prove to be most trying on small arms. The combination of heat, humidity, mud and water represented the most hostile operating conditions. The NVA and VC were known to poorly maintain their weapons, which were carried in muddy tunnels and through wet rice paddies without proper cleaning. In spite of this abuse and neglect, the rifle would still fire with utter reliability when called upon.

Designer Mikhail Kalashnikov claims the secret to the AK47's reliability is its simplicity. The tolerances on the moving parts of the rifle are extremely loose. Most military rifles have much closer tolerances to increase accuracy. The AK47, on the other hand, had loose tolerances—so loose that one could throw sand into the action, and the weapon would still fire. There is,

however, a consequence to having loose tolerances: reduced accuracy. The AK-series rifles have always been known for reliability, never for accuracy. Practical maximum effec- tive range of an AKM on a human sil- houette is approxi- mately 250 meters. Those familiar with the M-16A2 know that it can reliably engage human targets at well over 500 meters and area targets at 800 meters. A high-quality AK-type rifle will deliver 6- to 8-MOA accuracy at 100 meters. A stock M-16 rifle will deliver 1- to 4-MOA at the same distance.

The right side of a Romanian-made AKM assault rifle. Notice the selector lever that also acts as a dust cover; while in the uppermost position the rifle is in the (*S*) Safe mode. Dropping the lever down one notch (*A*) is the full-automatic position and dropping it down one more (*R*) is the semi-automatic position. Also note the magazine release in front of the trigger. *Lawrence Ventura.*

The AKS47 (*top*) and the AKMS (*bottom*). The folding stock "para-trooper" model. The stock is nearly identical to that of the German MP38 and MP40 submachine gun. Notice the 45-degree muzzle brake on the AKMS, standard on most AKM rifles. *Lawrence Ventura.*

The AK74—the Soviet Answer to the M-16

In 1974, the concept of the assault rifle changed once more for the AK-series rifle. The Soviets had seen how much more effective a small-caliber high-velocity cartridge is on enemy personnel, compared to the 30-caliber cartridge. The experience with the M-16 rifle and its new 5.56x45mm cartridge had proven this in the jungles of Southeast Asia. The Soviets wanted their own high-velocity bullet, so the birth of the 5.45x39mm Soviet round came. Mikhail Kalashnikov was adamantly opposed to this reduction in caliber. He felt that the 7.62x39mm cartridge was much better suited for the Soviet Army. The rifle that would shoot this new round would be the proven Kalashnikov design, the AK74. The AK74 is identical to the AKM, the only differences being a new compensator and magazines made of black or orange polymer. The AK74 also has a folding-stock model, the AKS74. The major difference between that and the AKMS was that the stock was a side-folding skeleton stock instead of the under-folding style. There is also an RPK74 that is very similar to the standard RPK but fires the 5.45x39mm round and uses a 45-round magazine. Few parts were actually interchangeable between the AKM and the AK74. The AK74 was first put into service in the Soviet war in Afghanistan. The new 5.45x39mm cartridge acquired quite a reputation among the *Mujahidin* for absolutely devastating wounds.

Galen Geer of *Soldier of Fortune* magazine brought the new rifle and its cartridge to the attention of Western intelligence for the first time while on assignment in Afghanistan in 1980. Subsequently, the new rifle and ammunition made their public debut in the October 1980, edition of *Soldier of Fortune* magazine.

The AK47/AKM Production Abroad

The Soviet Union, during the off-set of the Cold War, began to equip its allies with the new Kalashnikov rifles. At first, the Soviet Union sold the rifles or gave them away. Soon demand grew to the point that allies were visiting Soviet arsenals to gain experience in AK production. The Soviet engineers went to these allied countries to assist in building factories to produce the rifles.

The first countries to produce the AK47 were Poland and China, in 1956. Both countries still produce and issue AK-type rifles. The Chinese, with their Type 56, have been one of the largest producers of the AK weapon system and have produced both the AK47 and the AKM designs. However, they did not switch to the entire AKM weapon system. Instead, they modified their current rifle. Basically, all that changed was converting from a milled to a stamped receiver and addition of the compensator. Unlike the model Soviet AKM, the Chinese ignored the modified trigger group with the decelerator, the new reinforced receiver cover and the new gas tube. It is said the Chinese wanted to keep parts interchangeable, and many of the modified parts are not interchangeable

The field-stripped AK-type rifle breaks down into 7 basic components: The main rifle, magazine, bolt, gas tube, bolt carrier/gas piston, recoil/action spring and the receiver cover. Very easy to maintain in the field. *Lawrence Ventura.*

The RPK (*Ruchnoi Pulemet Kalashnikova*), the Soviet squad automatic weapon. The rifle has a 40-round magazine inserted and a 75-round drum to the right. There is a bipod mounted on the longer and heavier barrel. Notice the reinforced receiver for constant full-automatic fire. *Lawrence Ventura.*

between the AK47 and AKM. Poland produces its PMK version of the AK47. The PMK-DGN60 rifle is equipped to fire grenades and includes a recoil boot, grenade-launching sight, grenade launcher and gas cut-off valve.

In 1958, Hungary and North Korea began production of the AK47. Both eventually switched over to the AKM. The Hungarian AKM-63 and the AMD-65 rifles are in use today. The AMD-65 differs in that the barrel is shorter, with a unique two-port muzzlebrake. The rifle has a folding single-strut (*T-shaped*) stock and, instead of an exposed wood fore-grip, there is a forward pistol grip. North Korea produces the Type 68.

In 1959, production began in Bulgaria and East Germany. In Bulgaria, both AK47 and AKM rifles were made. In the former East Germany, the MPiKM (*Maschinen Pistole Kalashnikova Modern*) was an AKM with the fixed stock. Most common were polymer stocks. The MPiKMS-72 was the carbine version, which used a side-folding single-strut stock. This is one of the best quality AK-type rifles. In 1964, Yugoslavia began to produce AK-type rifles. The Yugoslavian M64 was a copy of the AK47, and the M70 is the copy of the AKM. The M70 is built on an RPK-style reinforced receiver and comes standard with factory night sights. This is another of the extremely high quality AK47-type rifles.

The Chinese Type 56 AKM rifles. The Chinese are one of the largest producers of AK-type rifles in the world. Their AKM (*top*) and their AKMS (*bottom*). *Lawrence Ventura.*

The Finnish M76 Valmet assault rifle. One of the finest AK rifles ever produced. Notice the rear sight sits at the rear of the receiver cover, giving a much longer sight radius. The rifle also has a very effective flash suppressor. *Lawrence Ventura.*

The Finnish Defense Force uses a modified AK47 as its main battle rifle. The M60/M76, made by Valmet, is known as the "Cadillac" of AK-type rifles. They still use the milled receiver; they have a flash suppressor on the muzzle and make use of polymer stocks. One of the

unique modifications to the Valmet is that the rear sight sits at the back of the receiver cover rather than on the trunion block, giving a much longer sight radius. They also make use of fixed, as well as folding, metal stocks. The current issue rifle is the A-90, a refined M76 still based on the Kalashnikov weapon system.

One of the most refined of all AK designs is the Israeli Galil assault rifle. During its development, Finnish receivers were used as the base of the rifle and, when looking at the rifle, you can easily see the Finnish influence. The Israelis took the best features of the Valmet and added some of their own innovations, such as the rifle's being chambered in 5.56x45mm NATO, a thumb-actuated safety lever which worked the selector lever on the right side of the rifle and an M-16-style flash suppressor. Galil rifles are produced in both 5.56x45mm NATO and 7.62x51mm NATO chamberings. This design was so well received that the South African military and

The Yugoslavian AKM. Another one of the finest AK-type rifles. This rifle comes with factory night sights installed and the RPK-style reinforced receiver. *Lawrence Ventura.*

The Israeli Galil, perhaps the most refined of all AK-type rifles. The Galil uses an M-16-style flash suppressor and a Finnish Valmet-type receiver. There is a thumb-actuated safety on the left side of the rifle that will manipulate the selector lever on the right side of the rifle. Galil rifles are mainly chambered in the 5.56x45mm NATO cartridge and also the 7.62x51mm NATO cartridge. *Lawrence Ventura.*

the military of India use rifles very similar to the Galil.

Some of the other countries known to produce AK-type rifles are Egypt, Romania and Iraq. Many of the AKM and RPK rifles captured from the Iraqi Army during the Gulf War were of Romanian origin. The switchover from the 7.62x39mm to the 5.45x39mm by the former Soviet Union caused a chain reaction in the Warsaw-Pact countries. Currently, Russia, Romania, Poland and Bulgaria use the 5.45x39mm service round in their own versions of the AK74. Prior to Germany re-uniting, the former East Germany used the 5.45x39mm cartridge in its own version of the AK74, the MPi-AK74N and the folding-stock MPi-AKS74N. Poland produces the wz/88 'Tanatal' version of the AK74.

The Future

The AK47 has had an extremely successful career, spanning more than a half-century, and served with distinction wherever it was employed. As with all things, it's reign has ended. The future combat rifle for Russia is no longer based on the Kalashnikov design.

The successor to the AK74 is the highly advanced AN94 (*Avtomat Nikonova 1994*) firing the 5.45x39mm cartridge. Designed by Gennady Nikonov, the AN94, some arms experts claim, is the most advanced assault rifle in the world. The only things that the AN94 shares with the AK74 are the magazine, pistol grip, cleaning kit, optical

sight base and stock hinge. (*I would like to thank Mr. Valery N. Shilin of IZHMASH Open Joint Stock Company of Izhevsk, Russia, for his technical help regarding the AN94. IZHMASH is one of the largest small-arms production facilities in all of Russia. They have produced AK-type rifles for many years and now produce the AN94 for the Russian Army.*)

The AN94 is a unique weapon. The AN94 uses a new method of operation that is best described as a combination of both recoil operation and gas operation. Mr. Shilin

Valery Shilin of the IZHMASH Company in Russia firing the new highly advanced AN94 (*Avtomat Nikonova 1994*). In 1994 the AN94 officially replaced the AK74 as the standard small arm of the Russian Army, ending the nearly half-century service of Kalashnikov-based firearms. *Valery Shilin, IZHMASH Company, Russia.*

described it as *Gas-Operated Blow-back Shifted Pulse.* The main purpose of this operating mechanism is to delay felt recoil until the first two rounds have left the barrel, supposedly resulting in increased accuracy. Mr. Shilin stated the barrel is integrated with the receiver, making the "firing mechanism," which travels inside the carrier-stock made of black glass-fiber reinforced plastic. The most fascinating thing about this rifle is that it has two cyclic rates of fire. Whether the rifle is fired on two-round burst or on full-auto, the first two rounds will fire at the incredible rate of 1,800 rounds per minute, and then subsequent rounds will fire at a decreased rate of 600 rounds per minute as long as the trigger is held to the rear. Mr. Shilin stated that, in one full travel of the barrel assembly, the carrier performs two cycles inside the receiver, giving the two-round rate of fire (1800 rpm) before the assembly travels to its fully rearward position. Then, the rifle slows to the 600-rpm rate of fire. The barrel and receiver assembly are then synchronized, giving one full stroke per shot. There is a piston connected to the bolt/bolt carrier assembly and the rifle uses gas operation to work the bolt assembly.

The Soviet answer to the M-16. The AK74, firing the new 5.45x39mm Soviet high-velocity cartridge. Notice the muzzle brake, one of the best in the world. The rifle is equipped with a Bakelite 30-round magazine. This marks the final evolution in the Kalashnikov weapon system. *Lawrence Ventura.*

The right side view of the AN94. Notice the use of modern polymer furniture and the muzzle brake. The rifle uses a standard AK74 magazine. *Valery Shilin, IZHMASH Company, Russia.*

Another interesting feature on the AN94 is the use of a cable-and-pulley mechanism that enables feeding of the round in two stages. This, in turn, shortens the chambering cycle timing by preloading the round onto a feed tray and keeps the bolt from having to extend fully past the rear of the magazine to pick up a live cartridge.

The rifle weighs a light 8.47 pounds due to use of black fiber-glass-reinforced polyamide stock assembly. The stock on the AN94 is collapsible and folds to the right side of the rifle. With the stock extended, the rifle overall length is approximately 37.1 inches; stock folded, approximately 28.6 inches. The barrel is approximately 15.9 inches long with a chrome-plated bore and chamber. The rifle has three modes of fire: semi-automatic, two-shot burst and full-auto. The rifle accepts the standard 30-round magazine used in the AK74, as well as the 45-round RPK74 magazine. The AN94 also uses the newly developed 60-round box magazine (with four columns rather than the standard two). In other words, instead of the magazine's having two columns of 15 rounds each, it has four columns of 15 rounds each. Testing of the AN94 by the Russians determined that even though the AN94 is more complex than the AK74, it is far more reliable than the Kalashnikov rifle. The mean number of rounds fired between failures is 40,000 with the AN94 compared to approximately 30,000 with the AK74 – but keep in mind the AN94 has yet to be battle-proven.

It will take many years for the AN94 to completely replace the AK74 rifle in Russia, even though they are producing them as fast as their limited resources will allow. You can rest assured, however, that the AK47/AKM/AK74 will be encountered on the battlefield for many years to come.

Specifications				
	AK47	**AKM**	**AK74**	**AN94**
Cartridge	7.62x39	7.62x39	5.45x39	5.45x39
Overall length	34.21 in	34.49 in	36.53 in	37.1 in
Barrel Length	16.34 in	16.34 in	15.75 in	15.9 in
Weight	9lb. 7oz.	8lb. 7oz.	8lb.8oz	8lb. 8oz.
Operating Method	Gas	Gas	Gas	*GOBBSP
Mag Cap	30,40, 75	30,40,75	30,45	30,45,60
Receiver	Machined	Stamped	Stamped	Polymer
Cyclic Rate of Fire	600 RPM	600 RPM	600 RPM	1800 and 600 RPM

* Gas Operated Blow Back Shifted Pulse

Ammunition Specifications				
	7.92x33	**7.62x39**	**5.45x39**	**5.56x45**
Weight of Bullet	125 grs.	122 grs	53 grs.	62 grs.
Muzzle Velocity	2,240 fps	2,300 fps	2,953 fps	3,100 fps
Muzzle Energy	1,408 fpe	1,470 fpe	1,045 fpe	1,325 fpe

Some 66 years ago, a 12-year old boy made his first hunt for deer, his rifle an old Winchester 38-40. Black bears were an unexpected bonus!

WHITETAILED DEER
WITH
BLACK POWDER
by Jack McPhee

Thanks, Jack McPhee !

Jack McPhee's article in the 1974 edition of GUN DIGEST inspired the author's purchase of an 1892 Winchester, and a subsequent deer-hunting trip to Maine

by Harvey Pennington

WHEN THE FRONT sight settled just behind the buck's shoulder, I pressed the trigger. Then came the soft boom of the old 44-40, and the target was momentarily obscured by a small cloud of blackpowder smoke. As the smoke began to dissipate, I could see the deer was down—lying in the snow of northern Maine.

The above accurately describes the climax of a hunt I had a few years ago. The hunt, with my good friend Arville Allen, was inspired by a man whom I have never personally known. In all probability, I suppose the man who provided that

inspiration passed to his reward many years before our hunt. Regretfully, I know that man only through his writings and a couple of photographs. His name was Jack McPhee.

Most of us who enjoy hunting, reloading, and both competitive and informal shooting, read a great deal about these subjects that we find so fascinating. For me, the *best* of these articles have one thing in common—they *inspire* the reader to do something he might not otherwise have done.

A few years ago, an article written by Jack McPhee caused me to

buy a certain old repeating rifle, learn new reloading techniques, and take one of my most enjoyable hunts—in a section of our country then totally unfamiliar to me. For the inspiration that single article gave me, and for its lasting influence in the types of hunting rifles I now enjoy, I will forever be indebted to that fine author.

Let me explain how all this came about. Some years ago, I set out to complete my collection of the GUN DIGEST, and one of my new acquisitions was the 1974 edition. On page 269 was McPhee's article entitled

"Whitetailed Deer with Black Powder." When I began reading it, the detail was so explicit, the setting so compelling, and the story so fascinating that I felt as if I were an observer of the hunt (*which took place in Michigan in 1907*), not just one who was reading about it. In addition, the rifle McPhee (*then a boy of just 12 years of age*) hunted with was a Model 1892 Winchester, chambered for 38 WCF (38-40 Win.), which had a Marble tang peep sight and an ivory bead front sight. In an sidebar on page 272, McPhee explained in detail about his loading tools and

low who had a '92 Winchester rifle in 38-40. The rifle, manufactured in 1900, had a 24-inch octagon barrel. Its metal had a patinaed finish and the stock had a few dings but, otherwise, it appeared to be in sound condition. The owner offered the old rifle at a very reasonable price; I felt lucky as I took it home.

Author's 44-40 Model 1892 Winchester, manufactured in 1900, effectively used cast bullet loads with blackpowder in old Remington/UMC "folded-head" cases.

The original Marble tang sight was added to author's '92 Winchester prior to the Maine hunt.

technique; the alloy of his bullet; the mixture of the bullet lubricant; and the brand, granulation and weight of the blackpowder charge used. McPhee managed to take a couple of whitetail bucks with his 38-40 on that trip and reported no deficiency in the rifle's ability.

I was hooked. I already had a natural love for Winchester lever rifles; I had acquired my first (a Model 71, 348 Win.) in 1965 and had taken a black bear and a couple of deer with it. And I already used cast bullets for deer—in the 348 and in a 38-55 single-shot rifle, which I had built using a Falling Block Works action and a Douglas barrel. But the idea of using the much smaller 38-40 cartridge, with its traditional blackpowder loads and soft lead bullet, in the handy little Model 1892 Winchester, had an overwhelming nostalgic appeal to me — an appeal that would have to be satisfied.

The first step, of course, was to come up with a rifle. I started my search before the current "cowboy action shooting" sport had become popular, and an 1892 Winchester did not then bear the higher price tag that it seems to demand today. At any rate, through the help of a local gun dealer, I was introduced to a fel-

Bullets for the hunt were cast in Lyman's #42798 mould and lubed with a mixture consisting of three-parts sheep tallow to one-part beeswax.

I fired some of the then-available factory jacketed-bullet ammunition in the rifle while waiting on my Lyman mould to arrive, and it shot quite well. However, when the mould (Lyman #40143) did arrive, I was hugely disappointed to discover the 38-40's bore was too worn to shoot cast bullets with any reasonable degree of accuracy. At this point, I decided to have it rebored to 44-40 Winchester (44 WCF), and sent it off to Bob Snapp's gun shop in Michigan to have this work done. In a few months, the rifle was

returned; it was now a 44-40, but the bore was slick as a whistle—and accurate, with bullets cast in Lyman's #42798 mould. (*Today, I would have the rifle's bore relined to the original 38-40 caliber; at that time, I knew nothing about relining and did not realize it to be an option.*)

Obviously, the differences in those two cartridges are very minor. Bullet diameter of the 38-40 is .401-inch, and the normal bullet weight is 180 grains, versus a bullet diameter of about .428-inch for the 44-40, and a bullet weight of 200 grains. The only variance in the cases of those two cartridges is the smaller neck diameter of the 38-40. Each case has virtually the same powder capacity as the other. On game the size of deer, any difference in field performance of the 38-40 or 44-40 would be based more upon the perception of the individual hunter rather than any practical, ballistic difference between the two cartridges.

As I began the process of learning to load the 44-40 with blackpowder and cast bullets, I was lucky enough to have a friend, Bud Salyer, who gave me about 50 original factory Remington (UMC) blackpowder cartridges for the 44-40. I immediately disassembled a few of those loads and found that the cases were the old "balloon-head" or "folded-head" type. They were loaded with, on average, about 36 grains of what appeared to be FFg blackpowder, and the bullets appeared to be pure lead. Of course, I had no way of knowing the exact content of the bullets' lubricant but, in reviewing McPhee's article, I was reminded that he had used a mixture of "beeswax and tallow" on his bullets. Since no ratio was given, I began researching in some of the older books in my home library for more information on the bullet-lubricant issue.

One of the sources I referred to was Gerald O. Kelver's *100 Years of Shooters and Gunmakers of Single Shot Rifles* (copyright 1975). Mr. Kelver included a very comprehensive list of bullet lubes in that book, and one of those was "Three parts tallow to one part beeswax." This was the formula I decided to try.

I was spared the task of rendering the tallow I needed when a friend gave me a small coffee can of mutton tallow that he used to grease his boots from time to time. The beeswax was obtained at a local craft store. I slowly melted the ingredients for the 3:1 ratio in a homemade kind of "double boiler"— one pot of water was allowed to heat up on the stove while a second pot (*containing the tallow and beeswax*) was floating in the water of the first pot. This method allows the lube to be melted without the possibility of scorching. Once the lube was melted, mixed and allowed to cool, it was ready to be applied to the cast bullets.

Perhaps this is a good place to pass along a precaution. Bullet lube containing tallow can be harmful to a rifle barrel unless the bore is thoroughly cleaned at the end of the shooting session, since tallow naturally contains salt. It is best to use

this type of lube only when shooting blackpowder loads since shooters clean the firearm quickly due to the corrosive nature of blackpowder residue. This cleaning also removes the salty residue left by the tallow. Most shooters who use smokeless powder do not clean as promptly.

Of course, there are many commercially-marketed, first-rate blackpowder bullet lubes on the market today which are not independently corrosive; but, this project was to be as traditional as possible, hence the tallow/beeswax lube.

In his GUN DIGEST article, Mr. McPhee explained the alloy he used for his bullets was one part tin to sixteen parts lead. I felt that, considering the low velocity of the 44-40, I should be able to use a softer

Left to right: Author's reloads used original Remington-UMC "folded-head" 44-40 (44 W.C.F.) cases; Lyman #42798 bullet was cast with 1:40 alloy; completed 44-40 cartridge used 36 grains of blackpowder; and author's partner on the hunt used a 30-30 Winchester loaded with the Lyman #31141 cast bullet and 27 grains of IMR 4895.

alloy with equally good results. I also remembered that the old factory UMC ammo appeared to be loaded with a pure lead bullet. After a little experimenting, my choice for an alloy was one part tin to forty parts lead. It shot well and did not lead the barrel.

The 1:40 bullets cast in my #42798 mould dropped out with a diameter of .431-inch. This was fine for the new bore of my Model '92, which had a groove diameter of .429-inch.

The bullets were loaded as-cast (*without sizing*) and the lube was applied by placing the bullets (*base down*) in a shallow, flat pie pan and pouring the melted lube in the pan until the top lube groove of the bullets was covered. After allowing time for the lube to cool, the hardened lube (complete with the bullets) was pried out of the pan after running a dull kitchen knife completely around the outside edge of the lube and "popping" it out. The bullets were then pushed out; base first, one at a time. When this is properly accomplished, the result is a bullet still as perfect as when it was cast, with the lubricant evenly applied in the bullet's grooves.

My cases were resized and reloaded using RCBS dies. The only problem associated with reloading the 44-40 was related to the one inherent problem with that case– the necks are thin. The person who does his first reloading for that cartridge gets a practical lesson about this thinness after crumpling the necks on a couple of cases by not taking time to carefully align the cases with the resizing die. So it was with myself. After losing several of those precious old folded-

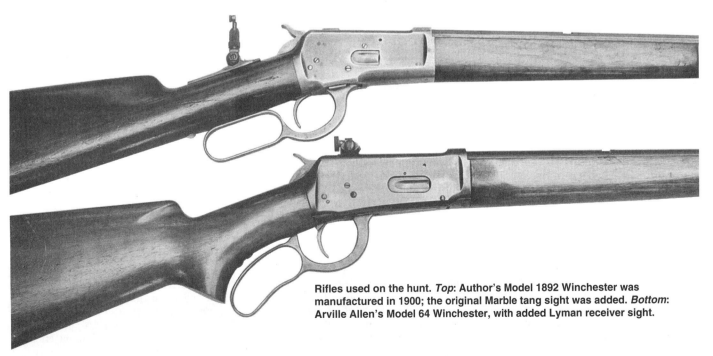

Rifles used on the hunt. *Top*: Author's Model 1892 Winchester was manufactured in 1900; the original Marble tang sight was added. *Bottom*: Arville Allen's Model 64 Winchester, with added Lyman receiver sight.

head UMC cases, I learned to slow down during the resizing procedure and to make sure those case mouths were not touching the edge of the sizing die as they entered it. Problem solved!

On the exact weight and granulation of the powder charge to be used, I deferred to the expertise of those who loaded the original Remington-UMC factory loads that I had examined. I loaded 36 grains of Du Pont (now GOEX) FFg blackpowder.

My Lyman #42798 cast bullet was a copy of the original factory 44-40 bullet design, and I adjusted my seating die so the mouth of the case was crimped over the bullet's top driving band. Since the 44-40 was created in the days when blackpowder was the sole propellant for cartridge rifles, there was no need for a crimping groove on the bullet to prevent it from receding into the case. In blackpowder loads, the base of the bullet is seated on the powder charge, slightly compressing it, making it virtually impossible for the bullet to be driven back into the case while in a rifle's tubular magazine. Neither the force of the magazine spring against the cartridge nor the recoil of the rifle could cause the bullet to move rearward.

The overall cartridge length of my loads was kept at the recommended length of 1.59 inches. There is no room for compromise here when dealing with the Model 1892 Winchester or any other tubular-magazine lever-action rifles. Any significant variance from the recommended length for the cartridge will surely affect the rifle's ability to feed properly, and clearing a jammed lever-action rifle can be a cumbersome and time-consuming process. That overall length also slightly compressed the 36-grain powder charge, just as it should have.

Primers for my 44-40 loads were the standard (non-magnum) CCI 300, large pistol primers. Do not forget the 44-40 was, originally, a pistol round and its primer pocket is the correct depth for pistol primers only. Of course, large pistol magnum primers can also be used, and may provide more complete combustion of the blackpowder charge—but the standard primers gave satisfactory performance in my rifle.

When I began firing the blackpowder loads, one of the first things I did was to chronograph them. The average velocity was 1219 fps from my 24-inch barrel. Interestingly, I had earlier chronographed a few of the original Remington-UMC factory loads which had averaged an almost identical 1220 fps.

Nights were cold on this hunt, but the mornings were warmed, in part, by biscuits baked in a Coleman oven.

The author (*left*) and Arville Allen with their deer hanging in camp. (*Arville Allen photo*)

The assembled loads were certainly accurate enough for the deer hunting I had in mind. Five-shot groups fired at 100 yards averaged about 2-1/2 inches. No barrel cleaning was performed between shots of the same group.

Since this rifle was meant for hunting, I would have to carry a means of cleaning the rifle in the field. For this purpose, I used a pull-through cleaner made from a bootlace cord. On one end of the cord, using nylon thread, I sewed a loop about 3/4-inch in diameter. On the other end, a simple knot was tied (*at the end of the length of the cord I would need*) and the excess length was cut off. I then took a small, thin, flat piece of lead (*a rectangular piece about 1/2-inch wide and 1-1/2 inches long*), bent it around the cord above the knot, and crimped it onto the cord with pliers.

To use, cleaning patches are placed in the loop-end of the cord and the weighted end is dropped into the chamber of the rifle. The patches are pulled out through the muzzle. First, a few wet patches are pulled through to remove the fouling; those are followed by a few dry patches to remove remaining moisture; then, when the barrel is thoroughly dry, an oily patch is pulled through.

This type of cleaner is convenient in the field and can be carried in a pocket or simply tied around the hunter's neck. When my rifle is put away, I tie the pull-through cleaner

Arville Allen's 30-30 Model 64 Winchester used cast bullets and smokeless powder hunting loads.

around the tang of the stock, where it stays until the rifle is next used. McPhee mentioned using a cleaner such as this, but stated that he later started using a jointed cleaning rod that he carried in his hunting bag.

By this time, I had acquired an original Marble tang peep sight (*like McPhee's*) for my rifle, from Buckingham's in Tennessee. Peep sights were nothing new to me; my very first deer was taken (*when I was a junior in high school*) using a Williams 5-D receiver peep sight that I had mounted on a 303 British SMLE military rifle which I had "sporterized." After that experience, peep sights (*both for receiver and tang*) found their way onto almost every hunting rifle I owned. But there was something special about the Marble sight. It belonged on that old Model '92. It appeared to be as much a part of the rifle as the finger lever itself. Somehow, I believe McPhee probably felt the same way about his.

Consulting with my long-time hunting buddy, Arville Allen, plans for the anticipated hunt began to take shape. Arv and I agreed this hunt should be somewhere in the 'North Woods' and, somewhere along the line, we decided that northern Maine would be the area that we to hunt. We had learned that Maine's deer season ran the full month of November and that there were huge areas owned by lumber companies where hunting was allowed for a modest fee. Besides, neither Arv nor I had ever been to Maine, and we were just looking for something different.

Arv was taking a new rifle on this hunt also. A couple of months before the trip, he ran into a good buy on a

beautiful Model 64 Winchester lever rifle chambered for the 30 WCF (30-30). The rifle had been manufactured in 1948, and was in terrific shape. It had a 24-inch barrel, three-quarter-length tubular magazine, and pistol-grip stock. Arv equipped it with a Lyman receiver sight and a "sourdough" post front sight with gold insert. He needed little persuasion to use a cast-bullet load for the hunt and chose to use the Lyman #31141 gas-check bullet, cast from a 1:15 alloy. With a powder charge of 27 grains of IMR 4895, he had an accurate, powerful load. Velocity from this load was about 1900 feet per second.

When the time came to leave, Arv and I happily piled into his pickup and headed north from our eastern Kentucky hills. When we finally set up the borrowed 8x10-foot wall tent, we were at the northern tip of Maine, 5 miles and 15 miles, respectively, from the Canadian provinces of New Brunswick and Quebec.

After we got situated, Arv was the first out of the tent. Almost immediately, he gave a shout of surprise. When I stuck my head out of the tent door, I could see the south end of a big bull moose heading into the woods! That was a nice bonus, since we Kentucky boys aren't all that accustomed to seeing moose.

Well, with the moose that easy to see, we figured finding deer in this place would be a veritable piece of cake. Of course, we were wrong. Moose were there, as were ruffed

grouse, but the deer were conspicuous only by their absence.

And it got cold. We had taken the precaution of bringing a Kerosun heater along. With that heater, a Coleman lantern and cooking stove, Arv and I could get that little wall tent uncomfortably, smotheringly hot. But, when we turned off those appliances, and retired to our sleeping bags at night, the cold came in silently and made itself at home. In the mornings following those long, cold mid-November nights, somehow our shaking hands would manage to light the lantern, heater and cooking stove. The heat would begin to build within the tent and soon the smell of coffee, bacon, eggs and (*sometimes*) biscuits would fill the air. Life was good again.

Our hunting luck changed for the better as soon as we started hunting some hardwood ridges a couple of miles from our camp. A logging road provided access and our first excursion revealed deer trails in the snow and several scrapes where rutting bucks had pawed.

Arv was the first to strike. After hunting a couple of hours one morning, he returned to the pickup to grab a bite for lunch and warm up. A buck suddenly appeared at the edge of the logging road about 50 yards away, then disappeared back into the timber. Arv got his rifle, concealed himself at the edge of the road, and waited.

I was about 300 yards away when I heard the shot from Arv's 30-30, startling in the frozen stillness on the ridge that morning. By the time I reached my old hunting buddy, my pulse had returned to a normal rate.

There was Arv, pleased as punch, with a nice, plump 4-point buck at his feet. His Model 64 Winchester leaned against a nearby tree. The deer had reappeared after only a few minutes, and Arv had taken the shot from about 75 yards. The 176-grain cast bullet had struck the deer, broadside, in the spine above the chest, and my friend had his venison.

On the last morning, I still hadn't had a shot with the little 44-40, and the loud, crunchy, crusted snow on the ridge didn't boost my confidence. Someone (*I believe it was Frances Sell*) had written another article about trying to hunt in conditions like these. His solution, I remembered, was to walk like a deer–with a measured, even pace–hoping nearby deer might interpret the noise as the approach of another deer. Made sense to me! What did I have to lose? At least the wind was in my favor.

So, there I went, crunching my way forward toward the area where I had seen the most deer sign. It was a *snort* that finally stopped me in my tracks. Definitely—it was a snort! I peered through the trees and dimness ahead, and saw the

Arville Allen with his 4-point buck taken with a cast bullet from his 30-30.

This spike buck was taken on the last day of the hunt with one shot from author's 44-40. (*Arville Allen photo*)

deer—a spike buck, certainly large enough for me on the final morning of the hunt. But, could I manage to get a shot? The deer was looking straight at me, and my rifle was not yet up to my shoulder.

I brought that rifle up as slowly as possible and, finally, felt the crescent buttplate of the '92 Winchester nestle against my shoulder. I drew a quiet breath, tried to relax, and put the top of the front sight in the middle of the faint shadow of the aperture of the Marble sight, and then placed the front sight behind the deer's shoulder.

For those who have never heard the report of a 44-40 loaded with blackpowder, I can only describe the sound that rolled off the hardwood ridge in Maine that morning as a soft, round *boom*. Wanting to save my old, UMC folded-head case, I placed my hand on top of my rifle's receiver and caught the empty, smoking hull as it was ejected–just as the deer regained his feet and dashed out of sight. He went only about 20 yards, however, and piled up for good.

When Arv drove up the ridge that morning, I already had the deer field-dressed and lying next to the logging road. After the usual smiles, congratulations and hand-shaking, we took my deer back to camp and hung it alongside Arv's 4-point.

The most important thing that anyone can take away from a hunt is the memory of it, and this hunt in Maine, which took place in 1981, will always be near the top of my list.

There is no doubt that this wonderful hunt would never have taken place were it not for Jack McPhee's

fine article in the 1974 GUN DIGEST. Very possibly, in the absence of that article, I may not have come to appreciate Winchester's Model 1892, or sought to produce traditional blackpowder cast-bullet loads for the 44-40 and experienced the effectiveness of those loads in the field. I may never have developed my present interest in single-shot blackpowder cartridge rifles, with which I now hunt and compete–and I may never have gone to Maine.

McPhee's article had a magical quality about it that led me back in time. And, sometimes, backward is not a bad direction to take.

POSTSCRIPT

For those readers who may wish to review other articles by Jack McPhee, I am aware of only three: "The Caribou of Alaska," 1969 Edition of GUN DIGEST, page 147; "Cast Bullets on Game," 1963 edition of GUN DIGEST, page 143; and "Sea Otter Hunting," 1962 edition of GUN DIGEST, page 213.

Only two published photographs of McPhee are known to me; one accompanies his above-mentioned article "Cast Bullets on Game," and the other can be found on page 122 of Elmer Keith's book SIXGUNS (copyright 1961, published by Bonanza Books). The photograph in SIXGUNS is very interesting. McPhee, whose address was then given as "Fairbanks, Alaska," is shown aiming a revolver. In that picture, he is standing, wearing snowshoes strapped to his boots, a sash tied around his coat, and his hair– by then–was white. ●

Smith & Wesson

K-Frame 38 Special Target Revolvers

by Hollis M. Flint

"But among all of Smith & Wesson's contributions, there is one that stands head and shoulders above all others: the 38 Military and Police Model and the 38 S&W Special cartridge designed to be used in this model."

Roy Jinks, Smith & Wesson Historian

THE SUCCESS OF the 1854 partnership of Horace Smith (1808-1893) and Daniel Wesson (1825-1906) was due to their sustained contributions to handgun design. The primal combination of Wesson's 22-caliber rimfire cartridge with the bored-through cylinder, secured from Rollin White, lead to a series of popular Civil War-era rimfire revolvers of tip-up frame design. The continued success of Smith & Wesson was assured with the advent of their Model 3 top-break centerfire revolver in 1869. The new top-break design was used in all Smith & Wesson revolvers from 1869 to 1896 and endured well into the 20th century. However, events were to force Smith & Wesson to new designs at the end of the nineteenth century.

Smith & Wesson needed a solid-frame hand-ejector design to compete with Colt. Colt had the lead in solid-frame revolvers with their swing-out cylinder hand-ejector design of 1887. Colt's Models 1889 Navy and 1892 Army and Navy revolvers sold in good quantity to military and civilian markets. Smith & Wesson undertook development of their own hand-ejector design. Daniel Wesson settled on two frame sizes in 1894. The I and K-frames were designed for 32- and 38-caliber centerfire cartridges, respectively. The I-frame revolver, introduced in 1896, was chambered for the new 32 Smith & Wesson Long cartridge. The Model 1896 revolver had a four-screw sideplate located on the right side of the frame while the cylinder swung to the left and rotated coun-

terclockwise, characteristics of future Smith & Wesson hand-ejector revolvers. However, the K-frame for 38-caliber cartridges did not debut until 1899.

The K-frame Model 1899 was improved over the I-frame Model 1896. Unlatching the cylinder was accomplished with a thumb-piece on the left side of the frame, rather than pulling forward on the ejector rod. The cylinder stop was located at the bottom, rather than the top, of the frame window. Both designs shared leaf-type main and trigger-return springs. The Model 1899 was chambered for the 38 Long Colt (military contracts), 32-20 Winchester and the new 38 Smith & Wesson Special cartridge. Smith & Wesson initially called their new revolver the Military Model and later, the Military and Police Model. They would go on to produce nearly nine million K-frame revolvers, more than all their other revolvers combined.

Smith & Wesson produced K-frame 38 Special revolvers from 1899 to the present. The K-frame revolver saw many changes over the years but it has always served with distinction in a variety of applications. The K-frame 38 Special target revolver with adjustable sights was an option from the beginning. The 32-20 chambering was also an option in both standard and target versions until 1940. The base Model 1899 Military revolver originally sold for $14.50. For $1.75 more you could order target sights.

Target shooting with handguns was well established by the end of

the nineteenth century. Smith & Wesson was already well known for its large frame top-break target revolvers. The new Military and Police revolver was adopted by noted shooters of the day. The names of some of these shooters could be listed, but few would be recognized today. Walter Winans might be one you've heard of.

Walter Winans, born in Baltimore and resident of Great Britain, was an internationally known Olympic target shooter of the period. Winans was an advocate of the Military and Police target revolver. He cited the front and rear cylinder lockup, precision cylinder boring and hardened steel cylinder stop inserts that provided concentric barrel and chamber alignment. Winans, in his 1911 book *The Art of Revolver Shooting* states *"It is not too much to say that I have never shot any revolver of any other make which I can so safely trust not to give me a wild shot."* Roy Jinks, Smith & Wesson historian, quotes from the 1900 Smith & Wesson catalog: *"The new Military and Police revolver, while it has not been on the market long enough to become well known, is certain to rank with the best as a target weapon when fitted with target sights."* Continuing, *"Fully ninety-nine percent of the expert target shots of this country use Smith & Wesson arms."* In this case Smith & Wesson was referring to the records being set with their New Model 3 top-break target revolvers and 22 single-shot pistol. Jinks adds, *"It did not take long*

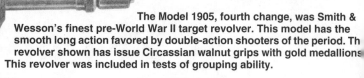

The Model 1905, fourth change, was Smith & Wesson's finest pre-World War II target revolver. This model has the smooth long action favored by double-action shooters of the period. Th revolver shown has issue Circassian walnut grips with gold medallions This revolver was included in tests of grouping ability.

before the Military and Police target revolver became the standard target revolver for most competitive shooters." According to Jinks, Smith & Wesson's records indicate that the Smith & Wesson target revolver held 27 of 40 United States Revolver Association (USRA) records in 1913. The USRA, founded in 1900, conducted slow fire 50-shot matches at 50 yards for revolvers and single-shot 22 pistols. The smooth double-action trigger pull of the Military and Police revolver was relatively unimportant to these target shooters. It remained for a Montanan named Ed McGivern to highlight this feature.

Ed McGivern did things with handguns in the first half of the last century that still seem impossible. Conventional target shooter, trick shooter and fast draw expert, McGivern did it all. Today he is most remembered for his five shots in two-fifths of a second, double action, all shots in a playing card at 12 feet. The loads used were Peters full power, with 158-grain lead bullets. McGivern's Military and Police target revolver, serial number 640792, had his special bead front sight mounted on a six-inch barrel. McGivern "*tickled the trigger*" in January 1934, at the armory in Lewistown, Montana. The revolver was presented to Douglas B. Wesson, his friend and supporter, in 1935. Douglas B. Wesson, vice president of Smith & Wesson, was instrumental in the birth of the 357 Magnum that same year. Wesson, in the 1938 edition of his book *Burning Powder*, notes "*The 38 caliber Military and Police is a wonderful target arm and a standard in Police Departments throughout the country.*" Many of McGivern's fans and students were in law enforcement.

McGivern used many handguns but his favorites were the Military and Police model and the N-frame Heavy Duty and 357 Magnum revolvers. He used them unmodified except for sights and, occasionally, grips. McGivern built machines to test the double-action pull and speed of revolvers. His results revealed that the Smith & Wesson 357 Magnum revolver "*has one of the smoothest and lightest operating double-action mechanisms available.*" The Military and Police model was not far behind. Both could be mechanically cycled double action faster than any other revolver and faster than McGivern could shoot them. McGivern, writing in Wesson's book, states "*The Double-Action 38 S. & W. Special target revolver, with 6-inch barrel, having a gold bead front sight, is the best all-around gun for this work.*" Many of the pictures in McGivern's 1938 book *Fast and Fancy Revolver Shooting* show him with a Military and Police target revolver in either or both hands. The revolver he used to set his record was the Model of 1905, fourth change, as it is known to collectors. You can build a substantial collection of the variations of the Military and Police revolver.

Close to one million Smith & Wesson Military and Police revolvers encompassing several

variations were produced prior to World War II. The models and changes in the Military and Police revolvers and corresponding target versions prior to World War II may be summarized briefly. The Model of 1902 followed the Model of 1899 and incorporated changes in lockwork as well as the addition of a barrel lug for forward locking of the ejector rod and cylinder. This provided front and rear cylinder lock-up which has been a Smith & Wesson feature ever since. The first change of the Model 1902 occurred in 1903 and increased the diameter of the barrel shank and frame for added strength. Chafing bushings were added to the trigger and hammer to protect the case hardened finish on these parts. The square-butt grip frame became available in 1904 at serial number 58000 as a variation in the Model 1902, first change, production. According to Roy Jinks, the round-butt revolvers advertised as Model of 1902 by Smith & Wesson after 1905 were round-butt Model 1905 revolvers. The square-butt Model of 1905 was the first five-screw frame with the addition of the trigger guard screw to contain the cylinder stop spring. The Model 1905 revolver went through several changes in lockwork before the enduring Model 1905, fourth change, emerged in 1915.

The evolution of 38-caliber revolver cartridges include the 38 Short rimfire (ca. 1865), 38 Short Colt (ca. 1875), 38 Long Colt (1875), 38 Smith & Wesson (1879), 38 Smith & Wesson Special (1899) and 357 Smith & Wesson Magnum (1935). Unlike the 38 Short Colt, which functions in the 38 Long Colt chamber, the 38 Smith & Wesson will not enter the 38 Smith & Wesson Special chamber.

Cylinders of Military and Police revolvers received heat treatment for additional strength beginning in 1919 at serial number 316648. Target models were made with grooved front and rear tangs and grooved triggers beginning in 1923. An improved leaf-spring hammer block mounted in a groove in the sideplate was installed in service revolvers in 1915 and in target revolvers in 1926. Barrel lengths the 1899-1940 period included 2, 4, 5, 6, 6 1/2 and 8 inches. The 8-inch barrel was dropped from production in 1902, followed by the 6 1/2-inch barrel in 1909. The two-inch barrel was added to the line in 1933. Roy Jinks states *"The 38 Military and Police series of revolvers could be ordered with target sights in any barrel length manufactured by Smith & Wesson at the time of the order."* Jinks has seen all barrel lengths with target sights, but the 2-inch version is very rare. The number of Military and Police revolvers produced with target sights cannot be provided because they were serial numbered with the standard models.

From 1915 to 1942 the Military and Police revolver and its target version were not changed, except as noted above. However, two notable K-frame target revolvers were added. The K-22, called the Outdoorsman, and the K-32 were added to the line in 1931 and 1936, respectively. Both new target revolvers were brought into production following Colt's lead with their 22 and 32 Officers Model Target revolvers, which had attained popularity with target shooters. The K-22 and K-32 were serial numbered with the Military and Police 38 Special revolvers. The second model K-22 was introduced at serial number 682420 in 1940. The second model K-22 had an improved short hammer fall action and new *"click"* micrometer sights

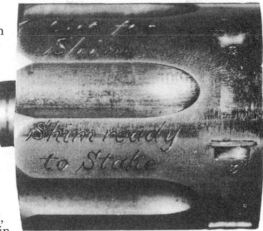

Smith & Wesson used hardened steel inserts in the cylinder stop notches of their Model 1899 through the Model 1905, second change, revolvers in 1909. The insert prevented peening of the cylinder stop notch. The insert shown has yet to be staked in place and polished to the contour of the cylinder. Photograph from Neal and Jinks Smith & Wesson 1857-1945.

with self-locking adjustment screws, features to be incorporated in Smith & Wesson target revolvers after the approaching war. Smith & Wesson called their new revolver the K-22 Masterpiece.

The new short action introduced in the K-22 Masterpiece became the action of all K-frame Smith & Wesson revolvers in the late 1940s. Smith & Wesson described the short action as *"redesigned for even easier, faster handling."* Featuring faster lock time, the short action was readily accepted by single-action target shooters, the intended market. Fanciers of double-action shooting were less enthusiastic. A formidable critic was Bob Nichols, former shooting editor of *Field and Stream* magazine. Bob was a disciple of Ed McGivern—right down to the long-action Military and Police revolver. Nichols, in his

1950 book *The Secrets of Double-Action Shooting*, criticized the new short action as lacking the smooth and light trigger pull of the original long action. Nichols states *"The new Smith & Wesson short action double action revolver, at least in my hand, does not offer the easy and sure control of the older standard long action S & W model."* However, Nichols adds, *"The current Smith & Wesson short action double action revolver is a better double action revolver than the Colt."* Always good for an opinion, Elmer Keith states *"There is no comparison between the smooth, effortless, pull of the Smith & Wesson double action [long action] as compared to the Colts."* Furthermore, *"To sum up the whole picture, I agree with McGivern and Nichols that the Smith & Wesson double action with magna or target grip is the best possible choice for fast double action shooting."* This from Keith's chapter on "Double Action Shooting" in his book *Sixguns.*

World War II brought an end to production of revolvers for the civilian market. Incredibly, from 1940 to 1945 Smith & Wesson produced its second million Military and Police revolvers. An improved hammer-block safety was incorporated into the lockwork during the war and was indicated by an additional 'S' added as a serial number prefix. While the Smith & Wesson factory was busy with wartime production they were planning a complete redesign of the K-frame target revolvers. The new line of target revolvers, called the Masterpiece series, included the K-22, K-32 and K-38. These revolvers were to all feature the short action and micrometer sights introduced by the prewar K-22 Masterpiece. In addition, a heavy ribbed barrel was added to increase weight and improve balance for target shooting.

Smith & Wesson resumed commercial production in September 1945, beginning with the Military and Police Model with the original long action. In a full-page ad in the December 1946 issue of the *American Rifleman* Smith & Wesson proclaimed *"We are working night and day to speed up the day when your dealer will have the new K-Masterpieces."* Production of the K-22 Masterpiece began in 1946. The new Masterpiece line had its own serial number series, beginning with a K-prefix. The first K-22 was serial

Chafing bushings were first installed in the Model 1902 revolvers to prevent cosmetic wear to the case hardened finish of hammers and triggers. The bushings were deleted in 1915 with the advent of the Model 1905, fourth change, revolver. The two bushings on the hammer and one on the trigger average .0025-inch protrusion.

numbered K101. The K-38 and K-32 soon followed. The K-38 Masterpiece revolvers began with serial number K1661. All the Masterpiece target revolvers came with magna grips, introduced in 1935 on the N-frame 357 Magnum. Magna grips extend up around the rear of the frame to provide additional support for the web of hand. In 1949 the K-32 and K-38 revolvers received wider and heavier barrel ribs to compensate for weight lost due to their larger bore diameters. The three Masterpiece revolvers now had identical loaded weights of 38 1/2 ounces. Not accidentally, this was close to the 39 to 43 ounce weight of the Colt Officers Model Target revolvers in these calibers. Colt's extra weight had gained them the edge with target shooters prior to World War II. Both the original and wider rib barrels were made for a few years and then the lighter barrels were discontinued. Barrel lengths were 6 inches for all models until 1959 when the 8 3/8-inch length become an option.

The 8 3/8-inch barrel length was the maximum possible under the USRA rules calling for no more than 10 inches between front and rear sights in *"Any Revolver"* competition. Interestingly, the USRA classification *"38 Revolver League"* revolvers were limited to the early Smith & Wesson 6 1/2-inch barrel length. Target hammers and grips are shown as options for the Masterpiece line in 1950 catalogs, five and three years ahead of the N-frame revolvers, respectively. Target triggers show up in 1957. The K-22, K-32 and K-38 Masterpiece revolvers became Models 17, 16, and 14, respectively, when Smith & Wesson designated model numbers in 1957. The diamond around the grip screw escutcheons on checkered walnut grips, standard on Smith & Wesson revolvers since the 1880s, was deleted in 1969. Barrels of all Smith & Wesson K-frame revolvers were pinned until about 1982. Chambers of Smith & Wesson revolvers were never recessed, except in 22 and magnum calibers. Recessed chambers on magnums were discontinued about 1982. The chambers of 22 rimfire revolvers remain recessed to support the thin cartridge rim.

The K-prefix series subsequently expanded to include 11 target-sighted revolvers in 22 through 357 Magnum calibers in blue, nickel and stainless steel. Many of the new K-frame revolvers, such as the Model 19 357 Combat Magnum and its stainless steel counterpart, the

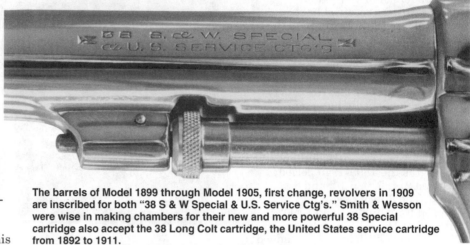

The barrels of Model 1899 through Model 1905, first change, revolvers in 1909 are inscribed for both "38 S & W Special & U.S. Service Ctg's." Smith & Wesson were wise in making chambers for their new and more powerful 38 Special cartridge also accept the 38 Long Colt cartridge, the United States service cartridge from 1892 to 1911.

The new "micrometer click" rear sight of 1940 abandoned the idea that fine rear sight notches and corresponding narrow post or fine-bead front sights were best for target shooting. The early rear sight blade is simply pushed back and forth by two opposing screws.

Model 66, became quite popular with both law enforcement and sportsmen. However, the change to autoloaders by law enforcement agencies eventually caused Smith & Wesson's revolver sales to be reduced as sales of their autoloaders expanded. According to Jinks, Smith & Wesson's sales of revolvers still exceed sales of autoloaders: *"Revolvers are still the best sellers and the company's bread and butter."* The original K-32 passed away in 1973. The K-38 followed in 1982. Finally, the K-22 passed into history in 1989. All were killed by insufficient sales. Various reincarnations of these models have appeared over the years but none are comparable to the original Masterpiece series, in my opinion. The originals are now classics.

Insufficient sales of the K-frame target revolvers were largely due to changes in handgun competition. The target revolver ruled the USRA matches during the early part of the last century. Initially USRA matches

were shot *"shoulder to shoulder."* Later, the USRA matches were shot on home ranges and the targets sent in the national headquarters for scoring and recording. Until the mid-'teens, the USRA conducted the only indoor and outdoor national matches. About 1915, the National Rifle Association (NRA) added handgun competition to rifle competition at Camp Perry. The NRA *"Camp Perry Course"* consisted of slow, timed, and rapid-fire stages with 22, centerfire and 45 calibers. The NRA conducted regional and national matches shoulder-to-shoulder, in contrast to the home range concept of the USRA. The USRA held on fairly well until World War II. After the war, the USRA simply lost out to the larger organization and its more popular program. Also, post-war handgun technology convinced target shooters that they could do better with a battery of autoloaders. I recently found out the USRA conducts a wide variety of indoor and

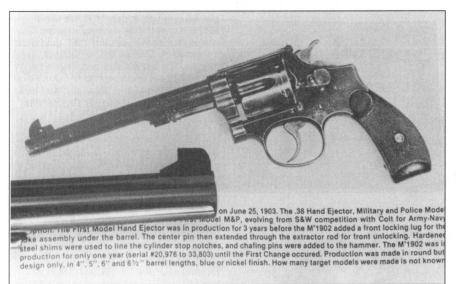

on June 25, 1903. The .38 Hand Ejector, Military and Police Model ...st Model M&P, evolving from S&W competition with Colt for Army-Navy ...ption. The First Model Hand Ejector was in production for 3 years before the M'1902 added a front locking lug for the ...ke assembly under the barrel. The center pin then extended through the extractor rod for front unlocking. Hardened ...steel shims were used to line the cylinder stop notches, and chafing pins were added to the hammer. The M'1902 was i... production for only one year (serial #20,976 to 33,803) until the First Change occured. Production was made in round but... design only, in 4", 5", 6" and 6½" barrel lengths, blue or nickel finish. How many target models were made is not known...

Post-World War II Smith & Wesson target revolvers come with Patridge square-notch rear and 1/10 (discontinued 1952) or 1/8-inch wide post front sights. Shown in the background is a photograph of Mr. E. E. Patridge's Model 1902 38 Special revolver equipped with his sights. Patridge sights are the universal choice of target shooters today. The photograph is from Killip and Furnishs' article "E. E. Patridge."

outdoor handgun matches and accepts autoloaders for all but a special double-action revolver match.

A survey of 35 of *"the finest target pistol competitors in this country"* published in the *American Rifleman* in July 1949, exemplifies the postwar choices of handguns for competition. All shooters in the 45 classification used Colt Model 1911 autoloaders. Centerfire classification yielded three shooters with Smith & Wesson revolvers while the remaining shooters selected the Colt Officer's Model Target revolver. There were 14 shooters of High Standard autoloaders and 25 shooters of Colt Match Target Woodsman autoloaders in the 22 classification. It is my guess that Smith & Wesson's postwar target revolvers never regained prominence in target shooting.

The Model 14 revolver reappeared in 1991 in a full-lug barrel version but is no longer listed in Smith & Wesson catalogs. In their 2001 catalog Smith & Wesson shows only the heavy barrel version of the Military and Police revolver, the Model 10, in 38 special. It is the last blued steel K-frame revolver in the Smith & Wesson line.

A brief explanation of the post-World War II variations of the K-38 / Model 14 revolvers may be of interest since these revolvers are most commonly encountered. The post-war K-38 five-screw frame became a four-screw frame with the deletion of the upper sideplate screw in 1955. The K-38 became the Model 14 in 1957. In 1959 the right-hand thread of the extractor rod was changed to left-hand thread to prevent backing out of the extractor rod due to cylinder rotation: Model 14-1. In 1961 the screw in the front of the trigger guard retaining the cylinder stop spring and plunger were deleted. The now three-screw frame was designated Model 14-2. Model 14-3 in 1967 marked the relocation of the rear sight leaf screw away from the gas-cutting area on the top strap. The Model 14-4 designation indicates the 1977 change from machined gas ring on the yolk to an insert gas ring in the front of the cylinder. The Model 14-4 was discontinued in 1982. The heavy full-lug barrel version of 1991 was designated Model 14-5. The change to round-butt grip frame, synthetic grips, drilling and tapping of the frame for scope mounting and other small alterations came together in the Model 14-6 of 1994. The Model 14-7, of 1998, had further changes to the frame and lockwork. The Model 14-7 was discontinued November, 1999. Roy Jinks states *"I am sure that it* [the Model 14] *will be manufactured from time to time as a special order as distributors look for various products to sell."*

Jinks provides additional information on the demise of the Model 14 in 1982: *"The reason for dropping the Model 14 was to consolidate it into the Model 15 line to eliminate a frame."* The Models 14 and 15 differ in frame dimensions related to barrel weight and rib width. The Model 15 line, introduced as the K-38 Combat Masterpiece in 1949, was expanded in 1985 to include 6- and 8 3/8-inch barrels. In effect the Model 15 took over the target revolver role of the Model 14. Jinks adds: *"The reason that the Model 15 was retained and not the Model 14 was it was a model heavily used by police and many countries specify the Model 15 in their bids."*

The 'star' marking on the rear of the cylinder of the Model 1902, first change, revolver indicates work done by the factory. A star was stamped adjacent to the serial number on revolvers returned to the factory for work. The star marking was used into the 1960s.

The markings stamped on the grip frame of the Model 1902, first change, revolver indicates two trips back to the factory. The first, in February 1914, probably resulted in the later type post front sight and/or other work. In December 1979, the revolver was returned to the factory and refinished-nickel (R-N).

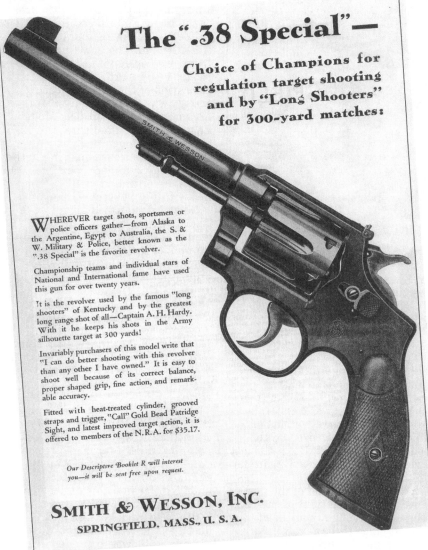

The ".38 Special"—

Choice of Champions for regulation target shooting and by "Long Shooters" for 300-yard matches:

WHEREVER target shots, sportsmen or police officers gather—from Alaska to the Argentine, Egypt to Australia, the S. & W. Military & Police, better known as the ".38 Special" is the favorite revolver.

Championship teams and individual stars of National and International fame have used this gun for over twenty years.

It is the revolver used by the famous "long shooters" of Kentucky and by the greatest long range shot of all—Captain A. H. Hardy. With it he keeps his shots in the Army silhouette target at 300 yards!

Invariably purchasers of this model write that "I can do better shooting with this revolver than any other I have owned." It is easy to shoot well because of its correct balance, proper shaped grip, fine action, and remarkable accuracy.

Fitted with heat-treated cylinder, grooved straps and trigger, "Call" Gold Bead Patridge Sight, and latest improved target action, it is offered to members of the N.R.A. for $35.17.

Our Descriptive Booklet R will interest you—it will be sent free upon request.

SMITH & WESSON, INC.
SPRINGFIELD. MASS., U. S. A.

Smith & Wesson in the mid-1950s. Blocks of 90 and 230 K-38 Masterpiece revolvers with 5-inch barrels were shipped to the Illinois state police in 1957. Serial numbers were in the K304XXX range.

A special order of K-38 target revolvers with 4-inch barrels, serial numbers in the K623XXX range, was shipped from the factory in 1965. During the period 1965 to 1968, Smith & Wesson produced an additional 2038 K-38 target revolvers with 4-inch barrels. These K-38 target revolvers were produced for Dayton Gun Headquarters in Dayton, Ohio. All were marked Model 14-2 and had Baughman quick-draw front sights. They came in blue or nickel finish with various combinations of target accessories. These revolvers have the heavy barrel of the target revolver and are not to be confused with the K-38 Combat Masterpiece revolver (Model 15) with its lighter 4-inch barrel. Small lots of 4-inch full-lug barrel Models 14-5 and 14-6 revolvers were produced in the 1990s for law enforcement and specialty outlets. I am sure there are other uncataloged small lot variations of the K-38/Model 14 revolvers.

A cataloged variation of the K-38 is the single-action version produced from 1961 to 1982. Pulling the trigger double action rotates the cylinder but does not cock the hammer. Thumb-cocking the hammer rotates the cylinder and sets up a very nice single-action trigger pull. Hammer fall is even shorter than the double-action K-38. I bought Smith & Wesson's conversion kit consisting of hammer, trigger and rebound slide spring and installed it in one of my K-38 revolv-

The weight of the 6-inch barrel Model 15 is listed at 35 ounces, 3 1/2 ounces lighter than the Model 14 it replaced. However, this weight is very close to the 36-ounce weight of the original K-38 Masterpiece with narrow rib. The long-barreled versions of the Model 15 were discontinued about 1991 when the Model 14 with full-lug barrel was reintroduced. All versions of the Model 15 were discontinued in 1999. Jinks feels that the K-38 Combat Masterpiece/Model 15 series were a very important contribution to the K-frame target line.

There are some post-war variations of the K-38 target revolver that are of special interest. During the period November 1945, to December 1946, Smith & Wesson produced 2091 hybrid 38 Special target revolvers. These revolvers used pre-war unribbed barrels and long actions with the 'S' hammer block. However, the revolvers had the post-war micrometer sights and magna grips. Serial numbers ranged from S5812000 to S5817000.

Most of these "*38 Military and Police Target Model of 1946*" revolvers were shipped to Mexico.

A collector friend of mine once owned a K-38 Masterpiece target revolver with a 5-inch barrel. This revolver, K156XXX, was part of two groups of K-38 target revolvers with 5-inch barrels shipped from the factory in November 1952. The Missouri Highway Patrol purchased 5-inch barrel K-38 revolvers from

Specifications of Tested K-Frame 38 Special Target Revolvers					
Model	Serial number	Year produced	Single-action pull (lbs.)	Barrel/ cylinder gap (in.)	Weight empty (oz.)
1902-1	45XXX	1904	4.5	0.003	32.1
1905-4	247XXX	1916	3.4	0.005	32.2
K-38	K225XXX	1954	3.4	0.006	38.6
14-2	K831XXX[a]	1968	4.2	0.005	39.4
14-4	22KOXXX	1977	3.5	0.004	38.8

[a]Produced in 1968, thus should be a Model 14-3. It has the relocated rear sight leaf screw of the 14-3. Mis-marking happens.

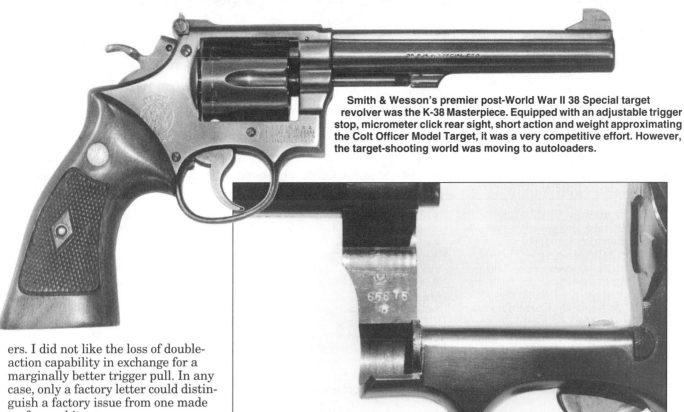

Smith & Wesson's premier post-World War II 38 Special target revolver was the K-38 Masterpiece. Equipped with an adjustable trigger stop, micrometer click rear sight, short action and weight approximating the Colt Officer Model Target, it was a very competitive effort. However, the target-shooting world was moving to autoloaders.

The highlighted number inside the yoke cut of the 1954 K-38 revolver is an assembly number. The model and serial number are found in this location after about 1957. The serial number is always found on the butt of K-frame revolvers.

ers. I did not like the loss of double-action capability in exchange for a marginally better trigger pull. In any case, only a factory letter could distinguish a factory issue from one made up from a kit.

The factory letter is a great aid to Smith & Wesson owners who wish to verify the original features and history of a particular revolver. Requests for factory letters should be addressed to Mr. Roy Jinks, Smith & Wesson Historian, Smith & Wesson, P.O. Box 2208, Springfield, MA 01102-2208. Provide complete information on the revolver including serial number and markings. Enclose a money order for 30 dollars for each revolver to be researched. Roy Jink's book *The History of Smith & Wesson* and Jim Supica and Richard Nahas' *The Standard Catalog of Smith & Wesson* are essential for the study of Smith & Wesson handguns. A wealth of information on Smith & Wesson revolvers is available through the Smith & Wesson Collectors Association.

The 38 Special Cartridge

There is no doubt that a large measure of the success of the K-frame revolver is due to the 38 Special cartridge. Circumstances might have led to a different chambering for the K-frame. The original choice for the K-frame when it was conceived in 1894 was the 38 Long Colt service cartridge. The delay of five years between conception and production of the K-frame revolver provided a change in circumstances. The Spanish-American War and the ensuing Philippine insurrection proved the 38 Long Colt cartridge lacked stopping power. Daniel Wesson decided to chamber his new

Smith & Wesson K-Frame 38 Special Target Revolvers are Found Within the Blocks of Serial Numbers Shown Below		
Model [a]	**Produced**	**Serial number range**
1899 Military	1899-1902	1-20975
1902 Military & Police	1902-1903	20976-33803
1902 First change	1903-1905	33804-62449
1905 Military & Police	1905-1906	62450-73250
1905 First change	1906-1909	73251-120000
1905 Second change	1906-1909	120001-146899
1905 third change	1909-1915	146900-241703
1905 Fourth change	1915-1942	241704-1000000
K-38 Masterpiece [b]	1946-1957	K1661-K317822
14	1957-1959	K288989-K386804
14-1	1959-1961	K350548-K468098
14-2	1961-1967	K429895-K779162
14-3	1967-1977	K715997-24K9999
14-4	1977-1982	10K0001-269K999
14-5 [c]	1991-1994	BFW3337-CBDXXXX
14-6	1994-1998	CBDXXXX-CCWXXXX
14-7	1998-1999	CCWXXXX-CDRXXXX

a. Target model revolver serial numbers are intermingled with standard Military and Police revolver serial numbers until allotted their own K-prefix serial numbers beginning in 1946.

b. Eleven models of K-frame revolvers with adjustable sights are numbered in the K-prefix series.

c. The Model 14-5 has a full-length barrel lug and is the last of the square-butt K-frame target revolvers.

revolver for a more potent cartridge in view of its intended sale to the military. Wesson lengthened the Colt case 1/8 inch, increased the charge of blackpowder from 18 to 21 1/2 grains and increased the bullet weight from 150 to 158 grains. Ballistics for the new 38 Smith and Wesson Special cartridge were 960 fps and 320 fpe (810 and 250 for the 38 Long Colt, respectively). The change to smokeless powder at the turn of the century reduced the 38 Special ballistics to 860 fps and 260 fpe. However, 38-caliber ballistics were by then irrelevant to the military, as a return to the 45 caliber was mandated. Fortunately, the 38 Special proved useful for target shooters, sportsmen and law enforcement agencies.

Frank Barnes sums up the 38 Special in his book, *Cartridges of the World*: "*The 38 Special is considered one of the best balanced, all around handgun cartridges ever designed. It is also one of the most accurate. Because of its moderate recoil, the average person can learn to shoot well with it.*" The 38 Special is at its best in a target revolver.

The 38 Special Test Revolvers

I thought it would be of interest to readers to test the grouping ability of two early K-frame 38 Special target revolvers, the Models 1902, first change, and 1905, fourth change, and three post-World War II K-frame target revolvers, the Models K-38 Masterpiece, 14-2 and 14-4. These revolvers are representative of the Smith & Wesson 38 Special target revolver line from 1904 to 1977.

The Model 1902, first change, revolver was shipped from the Smith & Wesson factory on August 29, 1904. The receiver was Fuqua Hardware Company, Baton Rouge, Louisiana. The factory records show that the revolver was shipped with 6 1/2-inch barrel, nickel finish, adjustable rear target sight and checkered black hard rubber grips. The frame is the pre-five-screw four-screw used prior to the Model 1905. The markings on the left grip frame beneath the grip indicate that the revolver was returned to the factory for work in 1914 and 1979. A '*star*' marking was added adjacent to the serial number on the barrel and cylinder in 1914. The star marking indicates factory work and was used as late as the 1960s. The factory letter further indicates that the post-type front sight of this revolver was probably added in 1914, as it was not available in 1904. The barrel of the revolver, with original serial number, shows sharp rifling and no pitting.

The Model 1905, fourth change, revolver was shipped from the factory on January 19, 1916, and delivered to Mr. F. M. Kelley. The revolver was shipped with a six-inch barrel, blue finish, adjustable rear target sight and checkered walnut grips. The frame is the five-screw version used from 1905 to 1955. The revolver is in near-new condition with clean, sharp rifling showing no pitting. Both early revolvers have a shallow "U" notch rear sight and flat-top semi-post front sight.

The 1954 K-38 Masterpiece revolver has a standard trigger, target hammer and walnut grips with the uncheckered diamond surrounding the grip escutcheons. The frame is the five-screw version of the Model 1905. The serial number is stamped on the barrel, extractor star, cylinder and butt of the grip frame. The numbers found on the yoke, sideplate and frame beneath the yoke are assembly numbers used to keep fitted pieces together during production. They are not serial numbers. The finish of this revolver is Smith & Wesson blue with low gloss.

The 1968 revolver, Model 14-2, has target hammer, trigger and special target grips fitted by the author during his target shooting days. The aftermarket "*Fitz*" grips are superior to the Smith & Wesson target grips, particularly in placing the thumb for hammer cocking in timed and rapid fire. The frame is marked with the model number and serial number beneath the yoke. Assembly numbers are found on the yoke and inside the sideplate and frame. The frame is the three-screw version used from about 1961 through current K-frame production. The 1977 revolver, Model 14-4, is essentially the same as the 1968 revolver but still has its factory walnut target grips. Both of these revolvers have a blue finish closer to Smith & Wesson's bright blue reserved for their premium models. The three K-38 revolvers have six-inch barrels, short actions, micrometer rear sights with square notches and 1/8-inch wide Patridge front sights. All are in near-new condition.

Shooting the Test Revolvers

The Ransom rest was set up at a sheltered outdoor range with a heavy bench designed for machine-rest testing. Five settling shots were fired from each revolver after tightening the insert blocks around the grip frame. The revolver was targeted on the top of a large sheet of target paper at 50 yards. I fired a set of four test groups on each target paper. Changes of impact were obtained by lowering the elevation of the Ransom rest approximately one-quarter turn of adjusting wheel between groups. Each revolver was tested for grouping with all ammunition during one set-up of the Ransom Rest. Five fouling shots were taken with each ammunition type before firing for record.

I loaded a cylinder full of six cartridges for each group, to include all

Grouping of K-Frame 38 Special Target Revolvers Held in a Ransom Rest			
Model	**Velocity in fps and group size in inches for indicated load**[a]		
	Win. 148 WC	**Fed. 158 LRN**	**Speer 158 TMJ+P**
1902-1	808 ±15 2.65 ± .2	816 ± 17 3.37 ± .3	
1905-4	759 ± 13 2.90 ± .4	798 ± 12 3.40 ± .5[b]	
K-38	765 ± 20 2.17 ± .3	778 ± 14 2.92 ± .3	761 ± 34 3.27 ± .5
14-2	777 ± 12 1.78 ± .3	795 ± 09 2.24 ± .4	844 ± 16 2.83 ± .5
14-4	770 ± 08 1.60 ± .4	793 ± 09 3.11 ± .2	846 ± 22 3.34 ± .9

a. Average velocity for 18 shots at five feet from the muzzle. Average group size for four six-shot groups at 50 yards. Standard deviations are provided.

b. One shot of each group noticeably out of main group at 7 o'clock. Excluding this shot from each group yielded an average five-shot group size of 2.21 inches.

The best group obtained during tests was this 1.18-inch, 50-yard group fired by the Model 14-4. Winchester Super Match 148-grain wadcutter ammunition was used. Other groups fired by this revolver and ammunition measured 1.91, 1.44 and 1.89 inches.

chambers in the group. Four groups were fired for each of three 38 Special factory loads: Winchester Super Match 148-grain wadcutter, Federal 158-grain lead round nose and Speer 158-grain total metal jacket +P. The two early revolvers with unhardened cylinders were excused from the +P load. A Beta Chrony chronograph set five feet from the muzzle recorded velocities of the first 18 shots with each ammunition. Each group was measured with a micrometer from the centers of the two widest shots.

Results and Conclusions

The velocities obtained with 148-grain wadcutter and 158-grain lead round nose loads, 759-808 and 778-816 fps, respectively, were greater than the published velocities of 710 and 755 fps. However, the published velocities are for four-inch vented test barrels. The longer barrels of the revolvers should

The Ransom Rest, with a variety of grip inserts available, is a most useful tool for evaluating the accuracy of handguns and loads. Manufacturer instructions must be closely followed for optimum results.

explain the greater velocities obtained. The Model 1902 revolver gave apparently greater velocities with these two loads than the other revolvers. I attribute this to the 1/2-inch longer barrel and tight .003-inch barrel/cylinder gap.

The 158-grain total metal jacket +P load, listed at 890 fps from a four-inch vented barrel, did not achieve this velocity in the three late revolvers. Further, the K-38 produced conspicuously less average velocity, 761 fps, than the average of 845 fps for the two Model 14 revolvers. The K-38 also had an unusually large spread in extreme of velocities for the +P load: 684 to 798 fps.

Grouping, however, was similar to the two Model 14 revolvers. I have no explanation for the low velocity of the +P load in the K-38.

I was initially disappointed with the grouping of the test revolvers, particularly the two early revolvers. I somehow had the idea they would all shoot X-ring size groups! The NRA 50-yard pistol target has, by my measurement, a 1.7-inch X-ring and 3.36-inch 10-ring. None of the test revolvers could be counted on to stay inside the X-ring with the match ammunition tested. The best numerical average grouping, that of the Model 14-4, was 1.6 inches. Add the standard deviation of 0.36 inches and you find that 95 percent of all shots should fall within 1.96 inches at 50 yards. Even if you held perfectly, you could not be sure of a full X-count. But you would be less than perfect if you didn't get a '10' on every shot. Four of the revolvers should stay in the 10-ring at 50 yards with the match load tested. The Model 1905 was borderline with 95 percent of its shots going into 3.30 inches.

The Model 1905 revolver had one chamber that routinely threw a shot out of the main group at 7 o'clock. The fault was most noticeable with the Federal 158-grain load. The off-chamber undoubtedly contributed to the relatively poor grouping with the match load. I did not sort out the cause of problem. Most of us would not recognize the problem unless a machine rest was used in testing. I also found a surprising amount of variation in consecutive groups fired under apparently identical conditions. Six-shot groups

My favorite K-38 is the version with 8 3/8-inch barrel. The revolver shown was produced in 1959, the first year of production. It is very accurate with my favorite load of five grains of Unique behind a 158-grain semi-wadcutter bullet.

with the Federal 158-grain load in the Model 1905 ranged from 2.66 to 3.87 inches, for example.

Target revolver accuracy has not changed much over the years. Al Barr, writing in the May 1949 issue of the *American Rifleman*, found that machine-rest groups from a six-inch barrel Colt Officers Model Target revolver, with a variety of loads, averaged 2.73 inches at 50 yards. Barr tested four factory match loads fired in 10-shot groups. The best load, Western's 146-grain mid-range wadcutter, provided an average group size of 2.29 inches, with extreme group sizes of 1.13 and 2.92 inches. The contemporary 1954 K-38 I tested produced an almost identical average group size of 2.17 inches with Winchester 148-grain wadcutter ammunition. Colt, at the time, was advertising the 38 Special Officer's Model as "*A revolver with ten ring accuracy!*" It was. So was its longtime rival, the Smith & Wesson K-frame target revolver.

Skeeter Skelton, writing on the Masterpiece series in the May, 1978, issue of *Shooting Times*, found the K-38 and Remington wadcutter ammunition grouped six shots into .6- to .7-inch at 20 yards from a Ransom Rest. Skelton noted "*I had expected the K-22 with its match stuff to steal the show. It didn't. The queen of the ball was the K-38.*" In 1978 the Colt Officers Model was history and the K-38 soon would be.

The K-frame revolver was produced throughout the 20th century and continues in Smith & Wesson's line. The target version of the K-frame was once the latest technology and ruled the target ranges around the world for nearly half the century. Smith & Wesson made major changes in their target revolver line after World War II but new technology sidelined their efforts. The world moved on to autoloaders. Target revolvers are now relegated to shooters of nostalgia matches and remaining diehard revolver fans. That's a shame because the new generation of handgunners is missing out on a lot of shooting satisfaction. Any dedicated handgunner should own a few accurate double-action revolvers. The classic K-38 should be your second choice. It comes after you have a K-22. Then you'll probably decide there are other Smith & Wesson revolvers you need. ●

Acknowlegement

I thank Roy Jinks for critical review of this manuscript. No man has done more to make the history of Smith & Wesson available to the enthusiast.

Bibliography

Barr, Al. Handgun Handloads. *American Rifleman*. May, 1949.

Dickey, Pete. S & W's Model of 1899 and its Heirs. Part 1. *American Rifleman*. February, 1989.

Dickey, Pete. S & W's Model of 1899 and its Heirs. Part 2. *American Rifleman*. April, 1989.

Foral, Jim. The Long Shooters of Pewee Valley. *GUN DIGEST*. Krause Publications Inc., Iola, Wisconsin. 1997.

Jinks, Roy. G. How Do You Spell Success? K-Frame. *Smith & Wesson Handguns 99*. (catalog). Smith & Wesson. Springfield, Massachusetts. 1999.

Jinks, Roy G. Smith & Wesson K-Frame Target Model. *Smith & Wesson Collectors Association Journal*. Vol. 33, Spring 1999

Jinks, Roy G. Smith & Wesson Military and Police Revolvers K-Frames. Part 1.

Smith & Wesson Collectors Association Journal. Vol. 32, Spring 1998.

Jinks, Roy G. *The History of Smith & Wesson*. Beinfield Publishing Incorporated, North Hollywood, California. Eleventh Edition 1992.

Keith, Elmer. *Sixguns*. Bonanza Books, New York, New York. 1961.

Libasci, A. M. What Makes a Pistol Champion? *American Rifleman*. July, 1949.

Killip, Devore E. and Furnish, William M. E. E. Patridge. *Smith & Wesson Collectors Association Journal*. Vol. 15, Winter 1983.

McGivern, Ed. *Fast and Fancy Revolver Shooting*. Reprint of 1938 edition. New Win Publishing, Incorporated, Clinton, New Jersey. 1984.

McHenry, Roy C. and Roper, Walter G. *Smith & Wesson Handguns*. Reprint of 1945 Edition. Wolfe Publishing Company, Prescott, Arizona. 1994.

Neal, Robert J. and Jinks, Roy G. *The History of Smith & Wesson 1857-1945*. R & R Books, Livonia, New York. 1966.

Nichols, Bob. *The Secrets of Double Action Shooting*. G. P. Putnam's Sons, New York. 1950.

Roper, Walter F. *Pistol and Revolver Shooting*. The MacMillan Company, New York, New York. 1945.

Skelton, Skeeter. S & W's Masterpieces. Over 30 Years and Still Going Strong. *Shooting Times*. May, 1978.

Smith & Wesson Collectors Association. Miscellaneous publications. For association information contact Administrative Assistant, P. O. Box 32, Great Bend, Kansas 67530. On line at: swca @ greatbend.com.

Smith & Wesson on line at www.smithwesson.com for current product information, news releases and history.

Supica, Jim and Nahas, Richard. *Standard Catalog of Smith & Wesson*. Krause Publications, Iola, Wisconsin. Second Edition 2001.

United States Revolver Association. 49 River Street, Quincy, MA 02169

Wesson, Douglas B. *Burning Powder*. Sixth edition. Smith & Wesson, Springfield, Massachusetts. 1938.

Winans, Walter. *The Art of Revolver Shooting*. G. P. Putnam's Sons. New York and London. 1911.

BACK IN TIME FOR
YOUR NEXT HUNT...

RUGER
NEW MODEL
SUPER BLACKHAWK HUNTER
KS47NH

.44 Mag.

Suggested retail price of $639.00.

scope rings included

*The Ruger New Model
Super Blackhawk Hunter is designed
to accept your favorite pistol scope.
(scope not included)*

THE
RETURN OF THE
HUNTER

Back by popular demand, the New Model Super
Blackhawk Hunter offers a no-compromise
fusion of traditional single-action style,
simplicity and strength with the desirable option
of easily mounting your favorite pistol scope.
Crafted of heat-treated 400-series stainless steel,
the Hunter features a 7 ½" heavy barrel with an
integral full-length solid rib, factory machined
to accommodate the 1" Ruger stainless scope
rings supplied. Fully adjustable Ruger open sights
are, of course, standard equipment, so you can
choose what's best for your own hunting
requirements. Wherever you hunt, whatever
the weather, the Hunter is a partner you
can always rely on.

FREE instruction manuals for all
Ruger firearms available on request.
Please specify model for which you require a manual.

STURM, RUGER and Company, Inc.

Southport, CT 06490, U.S.A. • www.ruger.com

All RUGER firearms are designed and manufactured in our own factories in the United States of America

— Arms Makers for Responsible Citizens —

Owners of "Old Model" (three screw) single-action revolvers manufactured from 1953-1972, and Bearcats
with serial numbers below 93-00000 should contact us for details about FREE safety conversions.

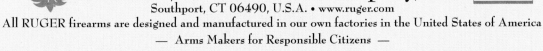

WANTED:

A 22 AUTOMATIC PISTOL

by Jim Foral

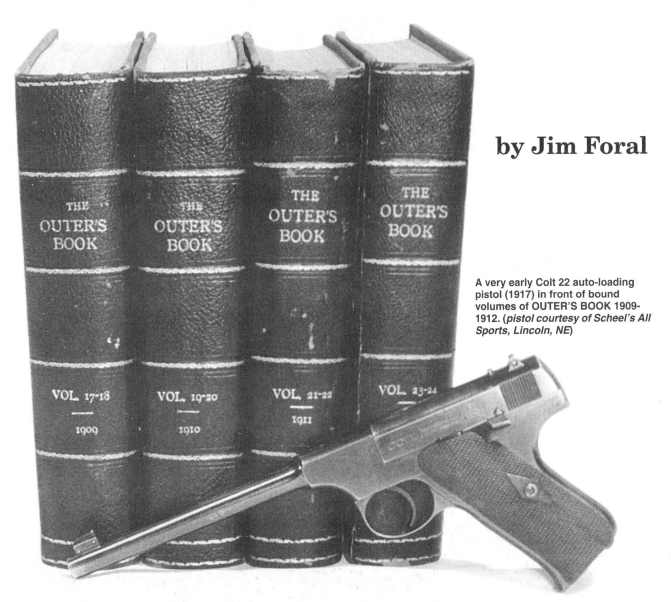

A very early Colt 22 auto-loading pistol (1917) in front of bound volumes of OUTER'S BOOK 1909-1912. (*pistol courtesy of Scheel's All Sports, Lincoln, NE*)

To THE GUN buyer of turn-of-the-century America, the oft-spoken Biblical passage *"ask and ye shall receive"* was just a hollow cliché. As an axiom, the adage *"the squeaky wheel gets the grease,"* was equally imprecise. The average consumer, in the main, was perfectly contented selecting an ordinary 'issue' gun from the manufacturer's catalog. For the individual flush enough to personalize or dress up a standard model on special order, the giant arms companies were extraordinarily accommodating. But there has always been a contingent of malcontents unreasonably insisting upon an entirely revamped model or a dream gun based upon a completely new mechanism. They considered the special item to be their entitlement, and the arm needed to be instantly developed and speedily marketed, simply because they wanted one. There was little likelihood, however, that the grumblings of a scattered few could gain corporate receptivity, much less a commitment. This fringe of noisemakers lacked both the numbers and the unity and, by themselves, represented a wheel not worthy of the greasing.

During the first Roosevelt's administration, emerging technology–coupled with an increasingly equipment-savvy populace–forced sweeping changes in the sporting scene, and this was reflected in the outdoorsman's press. Late in 1908, *OUTER'S BOOK*, an enormously popular sportsman's magazine, recognized the need to update its lifeless, behind-the-times format.

Just the right man was found to fill the vacancy of gun column editor. Bob Kane was a regular contributor who'd demonstrated an unusual brightness, together with a thorough grasp of sporting arms of all types. He was a remarkably articulate and well-rounded gun crank. Indeed, E. C. Crossman, never accused of being a habitual dispenser of compliments, wrote that his contemporary was *"the foremost authority in the U.S. on the pistol."*

Instantly, Kane's *'Arms and Ammunition'* column became the model of progress. His editorial guidance transformed the *OUTER'S* section from a dry-as-dust muddle of unsolicited letters from readers and other entry-level drivel into a lively dozen pages directed at the thinking man's passion for knowledge. The mission now was to edu-

cate and be of service. Kane had structured his column for reader discussion, as a clearinghouse for 'cranky' ideas, and a space for the exchange of experience and opinion. Each noteworthy viewpoint was accommodated hospitably, and this engendered a spirit of kinship among the readers.

In 1907, one W.W. McQueen of Menominee, Michigan indulged himself in a reoccurring daydream about an autoloading pistol shooting 22-rimfire cartridges. He conveyed this concept privately to Mr. Kane, two years prior to his signing on with the magazine. The idea had picked up minor local support, but never advanced beyond fanciful notion status.

Kane himself became interested and recognized that a 22-caliber semi-automatic pistol would be a cause worthy of the championing. If properly exposed and promoted nationally through his column, there was a possibility of bringing it about.

OUTER'S stood ready to sponsor the movement, and future editions of the journal were promised to contain much of interest on the subject. Having stated this, Bob Kane took the lid off, and welcomed courteous and sensible discussion of the matter and the 'Arms and Ammunition' pages would be the space to watch for developments. The enthusiasm was infectious as the staff and readership applied themselves to the task.

It was A.W. Loudermilk, an *OUTER'S* regular, who suggested that those sufficiently interested in a 22 automatic start by agreeing on the main points wanted and submit a consolidated sketch for inspection and evaluation of the gunmakers. Then, the chances of action being

taken by a manufacturer would likely be increased, he reasoned.

Diversity in what qualified as a "main point" made the recommendation impractical. Loudermilk's own outline of such a specimen, promised to be shared in a future column, never materialized. This didn't prevent others from advancing their own ideas. Initial input from the OUTER'S community focused on points deemed desirable in a rimfire automatic. They listed both rigid specifications and loose guidelines. A naive few figured existing semi-automatics could be compared, gleaning from them their attributes, and assembling these features into a perfected hybrid gun. Most recognized, however, that

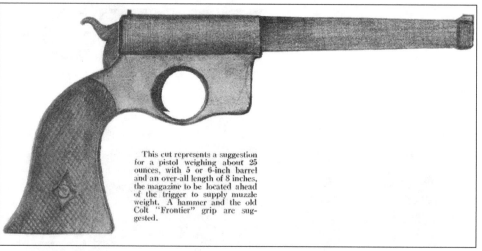

This cut represents a suggestion for a pistol weighing about 25 ounces, with 5 or 6-inch barrel and an over-all length of 8 inches, the magazine to be located ahead of the trigger to supply muzzle weight. A hammer and the old Colt "Frontier" grip are suggested.

Bob Kane's first design appeared in the October '09 issue of *OUTER'S*.

the proposed 22–from stern to bow– needed to be a new design with civilized dimensions on an intermediate-sized frame. It was intended to occupy an entirely new field, after all, and a compromise modification resembling a 25- or 32-caliber vest pocket auto simply wouldn't do. Eliminating the dead metal typically burdening the popular automatics foreign armorers turned out was seen as necessary. Some weight forward of the trigger would aid balance and steady aiming, as well as streamline the arm. First thoughts on weight established an indefinite *"not too heavy, not too light"* standard, and designers were cautioned not to err in either direction. The knowing estimated a weight of 25-29 oz. to be *'about right.'*

Many of the centerfire automatics suffered from an unsightly overhang to the rear of the gun, and this was to be avoided.

Progressive, up-to-the-minute types bucked at an outside hammer, but realized that a hammerless

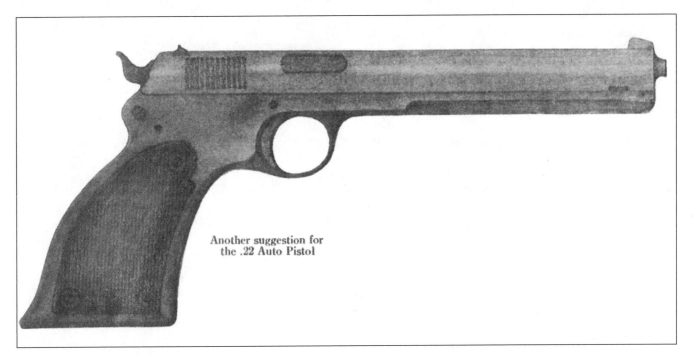

Another suggestion for
the .22 Auto Pistol

Kane's second design appeared in the November '09 issue of *OUTER'S*.

style required a safety lever, or grip safety. The hammerless should be a bit safer, and easier to look at, too.

Boosters for the holdover external hammer made a lot of noise, but the hammerless advocates were in the majority. Barrel length was mostly a matter of personal preference, but no shorter than six inches and no longer than eight was the consensus. Opinions varied on the location of the magazine, and divided those concerned into two camps; in the grip or ahead of the trigger guard. An issue awaiting being reasoned out was the correct grip-to-barrel angle. Without bothering to drag out the protractors, *OUTER'S* readers agreed that it must be *"just right."* The sights were to be adjustable, of course. Gun architects were advised to consider these points and give them the attention they merited.

The indulgent editor Kane urged a letter-writing segment of his campaign, and *OUTER'S* fans responded by mercilessly pounding Colt and Smith & Wesson with mail insisting that their call be met. Winchester, curiously, got more than their expected share, and the marketability of a 22 auto-pistol was repeatedly pointed out to the Stevens people, too.

In November of 1909, editor Kane contributed a description and a 'cut' of a 22 automatic of his own devising. It was his column, after all, and he was entitled. Obviously, the Colt-Browning pattern was the source of his inspiration. Mr. Kane neglected to include the details of his gun's function. Presumably, it

was blowback-operated. Weight in proportion to caliber was Kane's aim. Towards this end, the slide was streamlined somewhat and its added length was promised to increase balance and give the gun the characteristics of a natural pointer. Kane's shapely grip was a simulation of the Colt Single Action's, and the spurred hammer was copied from the same serviceable weapon. The arm's clean and racy lines were unspoiled by projections or encumbrances such as safeties, locks, or magazine releases. Kane regarded a safety as something else to fumble with, and his safety notch cut into the hammer simplified things. Recognizing that the truly progressive must be truly receptive to censure, Kane stood ready to receive his critics. A few found fault with the outside hammer, but all in all, it was considered a good plan.

The editor's diagram was closely followed by another, this one illustrating Kane's ideas centering on ideal weight distribution and balance. The improved version purposefully placed the magazine in front of the trigger guard so that an already muzzle-heavy pistol would be even more so. Mr. Kane calculated the finished weight to be in the 25-ounce range. Retained were the favored and time-proven Peacemaker handle and hammer. The Kane spur was criticized constructively. When the hammer came back, there was no better way to gash nastily the flesh 'twixt thumb and forefinger than with this dangerous appendage. A hump on the

grip would prevent such a skinning, but the more practical solution would be to eliminate the spur.

By 1909, semi-automatic guns were, as they used to say, *"all the go"*. These were the wave of the future, and every literate gun crank abreast of the times had surrendered to the fact. The faster pace of the 20th century, machinery-mad America, and our *"craze for speed in everything,"* explains the measure of demand for automatic sporting weapons. The semi-automatic shotgun had been perfected, and more or less accepted. The self-loading rifle, though somewhat underpowered, had been virtually fool-proofed and was almost totally reliable. Refinement of the automatic pistol, for various reasons, hadn't kept pace with the long guns.

In sixty years, the outmoded revolver principle hadn't been rid of its faults or bettered appreciably, and the automatic pistol–still full of flaws–threatened to soon supplant the slow-loading, gas-leaking six-gun. Seemingly insurmountable obstacles confronted automatic pistol inventors. Making it less of a gadget would be a step in the right direction and improve on its durability and certainty of function. There was a desperate need for breakthroughs in the beauty and balance departments, too.

Prior to 1900, there had been a steady demand for a high quality 22-caliber revolver. Smith and Wesson–as well as Colt–pointed to the dainty, spur-triggered models in their lines and considered the call answered. This response failed to

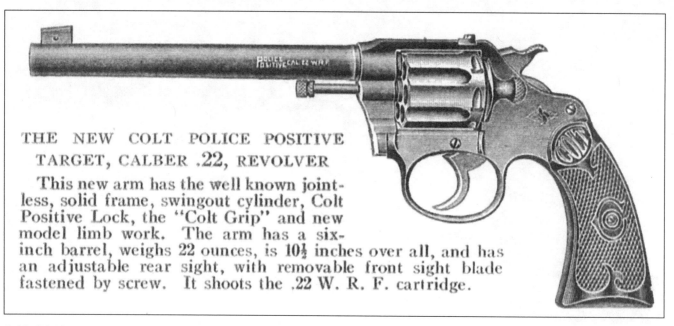

THE NEW COLT POLICE POSITIVE
TARGET, CALBER .22, REVOLVER

This new arm has the well known joint-
less, solid frame, swingout cylinder, Colt
Positive Lock, the "Colt Grip" and new
model limb work. The arm has a six-
inch barrel, weighs 22 ounces, is 10½ inches over all, and has
an adjustable rear sight, with removable front sight blade
fastened by screw. It shoots the .22 W. R. F. cartridge.

Colt's DA 22 revolver.

THE NEW SMITH & WESSON WITH SIX-INCH BARREL

Smith & Wesson's DA 22 revolver, 1910.

take the edge off the desire, but again each firm managed to defuse the malcontents. Colt obliged by supplying the massive Single Action chambered in 22 rimfire, while S&W slipped in a 22 single-shot target handgun. Both were wholly unsuited to the needs of the agitators.

Rival *OUTDOOR LIFE* magazine conducted a similar, but more realistic—in terms of expected success—crusade. Its readers petitioned for either a 22 revolver or an automatic, but by an overwhelming margin preferred a six-shot revolver built on a man-sized frame. Giving them what they wanted, *OL* readers rationalized, was a simple matter amounting to turning in a 22-caliber barrel into an already-existing frame, reaming somewhat smaller chambers in a standard cylinder, and substituting a rimfire hammer.

A letter-writing campaign was initiated, and much of the mail arriving on the desks of Hartford and Springfield decision-makers in 1909 were penny postcards insisting upon a 22 double-action revolver. Meantime, activity in the gun column of the *Magazine of the West* kept the rally vibrant. Finally, by the summer of 1910, both New England gunmakers were ready with the goods, and the *OUTDOOR LIFE* crowd was pacified. The common denominator of the new 22 six-guns was a beefy 32-caliber frame; S&W based theirs on the familiar Hand Ejector receiver while Colt used the 32 New Police frame for its 22 Police Positive Target. Each firm's gun was furnished with a 6-inch barrel, and both models were target-sighted, as had been specified. The successful *OUTDOOR LIFE* clan congratulated themselves for having been such an important factor in influencing the creation of these arms. Placing an order for one of the new 22 double actions, the magazine's editor reminded everyone, was the proper way of showing support and appreciation.

As the 22 revolvers became well distributed by late 1910, discouraging accounts reached the *OUTER'S BOOK* Milwaukee publishing offices. Difficult extraction, hard-turning cylinders, and poor targets were common complaints that were objectively and impartially shared with the magazine's vast readership. Very likely, some of the failure was traceable to the use of dirty-shooting blackpowder ammunition. Soured now to the revolvers in varying degrees, the *OUTER's* bunch pressed on with their automatic crusade with a renewed vigor, and continued to pester Colt and Smith & Wesson executives.

The apprehension of the gun builder to immediately satisfy these crusaders can be readily appreciated. Bringing out the 22 revolvers had tied up considerable capital, and now the arms makers were expected to abandon that proposition for a new and equally risky departure, based solely on the united whim of a few handsful of automatic pistol zealots. To determine if the 22 automatic pistol was yet another passing fancy of the fickle consumer, the gun company leaders adopted a wait-and-see stance—but wisely kept an eye on Bob Kane's column.

If the size of the mailbags was any gauge, supplementary evidence as to the growing demand for a 22 automatic was not wanting. The *OUTER'S BOOK* publishing office was deluged with postcards and letters—from every corner of the Republic and all 46 states—written by like-minded individuals who found the proposed gun extremely alluring.

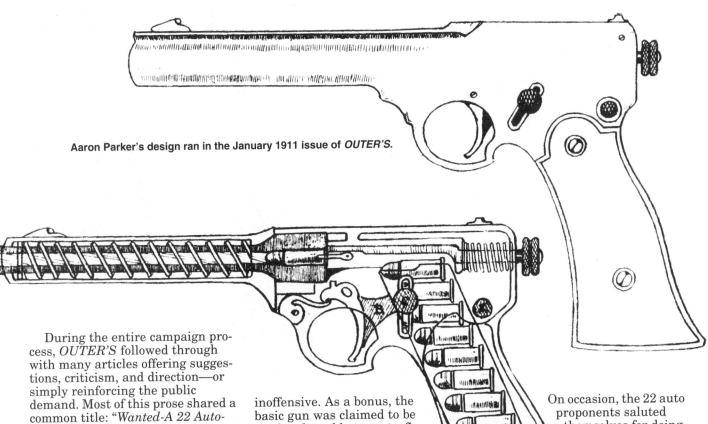

Aaron Parker's design ran in the January 1911 issue of *OUTER'S*.

During the entire campaign process, *OUTER'S* followed through with many articles offering suggestions, criticism, and direction—or simply reinforcing the public demand. Most of this prose shared a common title: *"Wanted-A 22 Automatic Pistol"*.

To this sum of 22 automatic suggestions, Aaron Parker of Michigan added his interesting submission and exposed it in January of 1911 for the approval of his fellow *OUTER'S* readers. Parker whittled out a wooden model, *ala* Sam Colt. In the process, he expended considerable effort testing and adjusting the grip for the most natural aiming position. The proper grip contour, by the way, was a disputable preoccupation taking up much magazine space, disproportionate to its importance, perhaps. Parker's blowback mechanism was a combination of ideas borrowed from the Remington semi-automatic rifle and Savage pistol action. The barrel moved front and back in a stationary jacket. Located in the slot cut into the frame was the sliding safety button, positioned where trial and error determined its manipulation was easiest. Unsightly as was the protuberance at the rear of the gun, people were pleased to learn it wasn't a hammer.

Maintaining the creative tempo was J.J. Reifgraber, who displayed an obvious flair for invention with his modern-looking Model 1910 automatic pistol. His design, published in November of 1911, was a single and double-action, break-open, gas- and recoil-operated self-loader employing no slides or toggles. The few moving parts were contained within the frame, and the spurless hammer was relatively

inoffensive. As a bonus, the basic gun was claimed to be easily adaptable to centerfire cartridges of any caliber. Another point of merit, at least in the eyes of the inventor, was that this small-bore repeater could be operated with one hand. Reifgraber's Model 1910 looked good on paper.

The question as to which of the rimfire cartridges to use quite naturally arose, and the accurate, cheap, familiar, and universally available outside-lubricated 22 Long Rifle was the instinctive pick. Most of those protesting this seemingly sensible choice objected to the Long Rifle shell simply because its wax coating made it a lint 'magnet.' A better selection, in the minds of many, was the more powerful 22 WRF, Winchester's clean and inside-lubricated rifle cartridge. Though the ammunition was more expensive, the added benefits were said to be worth the extra cost. The 22 Winchester Automatic—the 45-grain cartridge for the Model 1903 Autoloader—also had a band of adherents that talked sense. At one point, a reloadable centerfire 22 was suggested, an approach which failed to satisfy the established criteria for economy of shooting. One citizen was brash enough to recommend the 25 ACP case be necked to 22 and adapted to the proposed automatic.

That the fabrication of a 22 autoloader, from the ground up, involved a considerable investment in an armsmaker's time and resources was a universally recognized fact.

On occasion, the 22 auto proponents saluted themselves for doing the armorers a favor by pointing out the obvious–that alteration of an existing automatic pistol to handle a rimfire cartridge might be practicable. Presumably, the gunmakers considering adding a 22 automatic to their lines had already eliminated this compromising approach, but we'll never know. Company spokesmen refused to publicly participate in the fray.

One man took a hard look at the German Luger, and saw no good reason why it could not be contrived to shoot 22s reliably. A twenty-dollar bill was the calculated retail price of such an item. He tried to stimulate his *OUTER'S* fellows by concluding: *"So let's get together and boost this thing and we will get it."*

Another envisioned the self-pointing Savage 32 Autoloader frame fitted with a longer 22-caliber barrel and slide, a repositioned firing pin, a properly scaled magazine holding ten rimfire shots–and the other necessary "minor" modifications. The engineering and manufacturing obstacle, he argued, was the raw receiver–and Savage already had theirs forged by the hundreds.

Foremost among the progressive spirits actively thinking and working to promote the automatic movement was Arthur T. Ward. He was

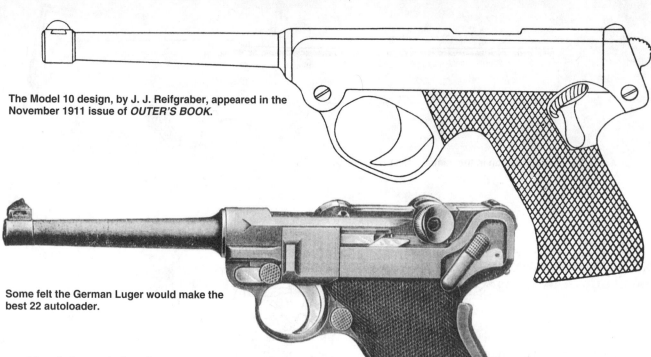

The Model 10 design, by J. J. Reifgraber, appeared in the November 1911 issue of *OUTER'S BOOK*.

Some felt the German Luger would make the best 22 autoloader.

considered the period authority on the subject of autoloading pistols and routinely reviewed them for the magazines. Ward's byline was a powerful lure to the 'Arms and Ammunition' column of *OUTER'S BOOK*. Late in 1911, Mr. Ward readied the design of his own 22 *self-functioner* for publication, and used his appointed space in the February 1912 number of *OUTER'S* to explain how any proposed 22 autoloader should work. The only principle of operation really suitable to the low-powered rimfire, Ward ably explained to his *OUTER'S* comrades, was the blowback principle which used the recoil pressures directly back against the unlocked breech. Recoil from a locked breech-type of action would simply be insufficient to operate the mechanism. Also ruled out was the overly delicate gas-operating system. Though highly successful with high-power cartridges, it was ill-adapted to the low volume rimfire cases. Included in the essay was the diagram of a 22 automatic pistol that the author regarded as simple and workable. The clip-fed blowback hammer gun was conceived, designed, and artfully sketched at the drawing board of Arthur Ward.

At first glance, one is reminded of one of the Bergmann models, which the Ward plan resembles in profile. A stationary barrel was among its good points. The magazine well, which held a five-shot clip, was positioned ahead of the trigger guard. A revolver-shaped grip was formed for comfort and a natural, non-contortive reach for the hammer. Internal parts were accessible through a removable sideplate. Most of *OUTER'S* readers objected to the

location of the magazine and the protruding hammer. Still, the Ward blowback satisfied its share of admirers who demanded its immediate adoption—but their enthusiasm failed to last.

In the autumn of 1912, another popular *OUTER'S BOOK* contributor, Dr. S.J. Fort, convincingly made a case for his pet notion, and pointed out the advantages. Dr. Fort suggested that a 22 automatic, built on exactly the same lines as the military 45-caliber Model 1911, might prove to be a practical and economical understudy with application for both soldier and civilian. Such a replica would allow National Guardsmen, having shot up their stingy annual allotment of 45 ACP cartridges, to continue to practice on indoor ranges during the off-season. As a bonus, it could double as a plinker and a field gun. Dr. Fort's seemingly reasonable solution wouldn't catch fire for almost twenty more years when Colt would introduced their Ace Target pistol, the 22-rimfire conversion of the 1911 45 Auto.

For those despairing and in need of hope, America's foremost amateur ballistician wrote a heartening message in *OUTER'S* December 1912 column. Chas. Newton's mouthful of a title — *"Is There A Demand for a 22 Caliber Automatic Pistol?"* — posed the question, which he succinctly answered with the opening sentence — *"Yes."* He continued with a wordy elaboration which, in essence, was an examination of fundamental economics.

To install the expensive tooling necessary to produce an article in

sufficient quantities to make it affordable to a great many consumers was a cost-intensive undertaking, Newton explained. Still, Colt had taken the gamble with their pocket automatics and the venerable institution was not thrown into bankruptcy. The new double-action 22 revolvers had become instantly popular, and by then both were paying propositions. In addition, the fact that a 22 six-shooter was finally in dealers' stockrooms, and its merits demonstrated, would certainly create a demand had none already existed—but the unexampled call for one constituted an actual, *bona-fide* demand. As surely as the skeptics accepted the self-loading shotgun, rifle, and big-bore pistols, it followed just as surely that the 22 auto pistol would sell well. Newton concluded with this encouragement: *"So, we might as well begin now to prepare for its reception."*

Some minor notice of the 22 automatic project was taken in the contemporary rabbit and squirrel shooter's press—and from time to time the discussion migrated onto the pages of *OUTDOOR LIFE*. In the main, though, the matter was the brainchild and mission of *OUTER's BOOK* fraternity of readers.

Chauncey Thomas, an *OUTDOOR LIFE* staffer and occasional *OUTER'S* contributor, touched upon the deficiencies of the 22 revolvers in *OUTER'S* for November 1912. To begin with, tolerances wouldn't allow for a perfect cylinder/barrel alignment. Big holes are somewhat forgiving, the 22 much less so.

Unavoidably, there was some play, some shaved lead, and some 'stung' bystanders. The rimfire cartridge itself was the weak link in the chain. The unsupported head of the soft copper-cased 22 Long Rifle oftentimes burst when fired in a revolver. Thomas told tales of shooters being injured by wayward gas and metal. These soft cases were also responsible for difficult extraction. Also, a consideration was the loss of power, calculated to be 18 percent of potential, due to propellant gases leaking out the cylinder gap. Only by fencing in all sides of the rimfire case in an automatic's chamber could the repeating handgun be made safe and efficient. *"The 22-caliber automatic pistol can never be a man-killing gun, but for practice, amusement, and small game hunting, we need it, and need it right now,"* pulpiteer Thomas declared.

Ultimately, it was a foreign maker that first took an interest in what the American public desired. To meet the demand occasioned by

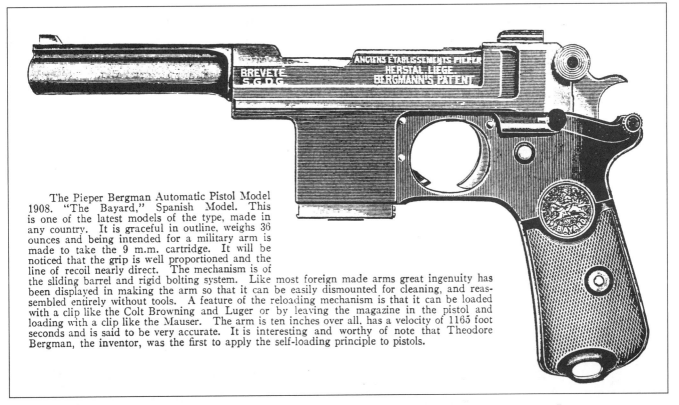

Many felt the Savage automatic could easily be converted to the rimfire cartridge.

the popularity of miniature rifle shooting in England, the British firm of Webley and Scott brought out a boxy-looking, blowback-operated 22 automatic late in 1912. With a 9-inch fixed barrel, target-style sights, and a magazine in the grip, the Webley & Scott embodied

The Pieper Bergman Automatic Pistol Model 1908. "The Bayard," Spanish Model. This is one of the latest models of the type, made in any country. It is graceful in outline, weighs 36 ounces and being intended for a military arm is made to take the 9 m.m. cartridge. It will be noticed that the grip is well proportioned and the line of recoil nearly direct. The mechanism is of the sliding barrel and rigid bolting system. Like most foreign made arms great ingenuity has been displayed in making the arm so that it can be easily dismounted for cleaning, and reassembled entirely without tools. A feature of the reloading mechanism is that it can be loaded with a clip like the Colt Browning and Luger or by leaving the magazine in the pistol and loading with a clip like the Mauser. The arm is ten inches over all, has a velocity of 1165 foot seconds and is said to be very accurate. It is interesting and worthy of note that Theodore Bergman, the inventor, was the first to apply the self-loading principle to pistols.

The magazine location on the Bergman Model 1908 interested some of the 22 automatic designers.

many of the points Americans had campaigned for. There was considerable objection to the external hammer, though. There were importation and distribution difficulties with the Webley, and few of these guns found their way across the Atlantic. Still, the import did not stifle the insistent cry for a domestically-produced 22 automatic pistol.

Unavoidably, rumors of a forthcoming 22 autoloader made their way into the columns of the sporting press. In 1911, Dr. E. F. Conyngham, a Montana physician and familiar name to *OUTDOOR LIFE* subscribers, visited the Browning's store in Ogden, Utah and became privy to some confidential industry scuttlebutt. Here a clerk leaned over the counter and whispered that a 22 auto pistol would be out the next Spring, and advised that folks best begin to save up the asking price. Later that same year, N. Pugh, displaying a measure of inside knowledge–but bound by a confidence not to divulge the maker–leaked that a 22 lead-slinger would be seen before the year was out. 1912 came and went without the anticipated announcement. Dr. S. J. Fort was a source close to an unspecified firm experimenting with various models of self-loading rimfire pistols. In March of 1913, Dr. Fort published that he had reason to speculate that a 22 auto would be on the market "*in a short time.*" The balance of 1913, and the

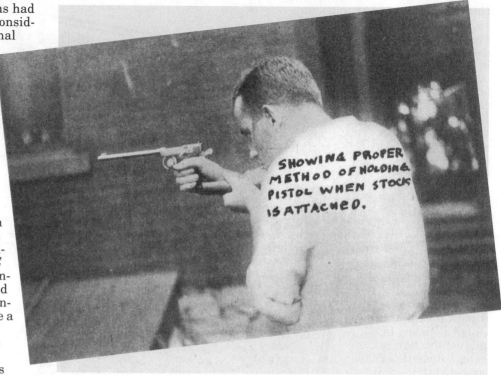

A. T. Ward shoots the Webley & Scott 22 auto in 1912.

whole of the following year, passed without the materialization of a 22 pistol. Disheartened by the reality, the persistent gossip nevertheless gave the automatic advocates encouragement that the seat of corporate reason had been penetrated.

During 1913, the sporadic editorial reflection on the campaign's progress in the course of the intervening years did little to give the people hope. Meanwhile, Mr. W. W. MacQueen chimed in, reminding everyone that he was the original

"baby" who had first cried for a 22 automatic pistol.

The next year, the rumor mills were again active and generated hearsay that Colt had distributed a handful of salesman's samples of an automatic rimfire handgun. As things turned out, there was some foundation to this talk. Indeed, there had been one in the works, but Colt had remained closed-mouthed about the project until shortly before first factory shipments were ready. In answer to the

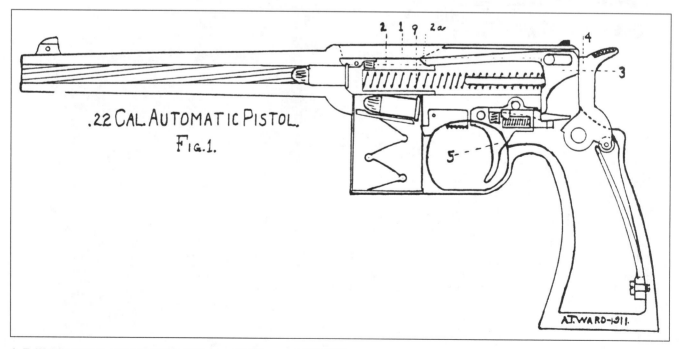

A. T. Ward's design appeared in the February 1912 issue of *OUTER'S*.

At last. Colt announced their new Automatic Target Pistol in early 1915. This advertisement appeared in the September 1915 issue of the *OUTER'S BOOK*.

demand *OUTER'S* staff and readership had proven to exist, executives in Hartford formally announced the Colt Caliber 22 Automatic Target Pistol. The new arm, born of the commonsensical genius of John Browning, incorporated many features suggested by its agitators. The 6 1/2-inch barrel was the prescribed length, the lines were slick and clean, sights were adjustable, and the weight was within the ordained range. Overall, the proportions, balance, and grip geometry certainly looked and felt "*right.*"

After the press released the news in the Spring of 1915, the smug supporters of the *OUTER'S* movement were quite pleased with themselves, and fell into a self-congratulating swoon. Colt had every right and reason to expect a readymade and receptive group of consumers–and they were not disappointed. The continual galling and grating emanating from the wheels associated with *OUTER'S BOOK* finally culminated in a rightful anointing.

A new Colt automatic was shipped to Chas. Askins Sr., this country's leading shotgun authority, for his evaluation. Askins filed a cold and clinical report that might have been expected from a shotgun buff. It appeared in *OUTER'S*

April, 1916 issue. The use of an ancient one hundred-round lot of Winchester 'Lesmok' cartridges resulted in two empties stuck in the chamber. After switching to fresh UMC Long Rifle ammunition, Askins Senior rattled off 700 rounds "*without a wobble.*" Despite efforts to do so, he was unable to get the magazine to "*choke*" or fail to feed the UMC shells.

At the 60-foot target, the Colt printed its shots closer than the deliberate shooter could hold. The 22 was then turned on starlings, tin cans, and other targets of opportunity. There was considerable *whanging away* at the Oklahoma jackrabbit, and it was all pure fun, the ordinarily dry writer confessed. "*I am convinced that the average man will have no trouble whatever with this pistol,*" he concluded.

Ashley Haines, the *OUTDOOR LIFE* reviewer, would have preferred another 22 revolver, but welcomed the automatic with an uncharacteristic enthusiasm. He marveled at the correctly-angled grip, the nice balance, and pronounced the pistol to be "*king of all the one-hand arms that have thus far left the Colt factory.*" In summary, Haines conveyed the impres-

sion that his time with the Colt 22 had been a lark when he wrote: "*To be perfectly happy, the owner of one of these little gems should have a half dozen extra magazines, as many assistants as might be required to keep them filled, the output of a cartridge factory at his disposal, and nothing more serious in life to do than shoot ten solid hours per day the year round.*"

The American gun-buying public was immediately receptive to the newest in the Colt line. In terms of popularity and sales, it was successful from the beginning. After 1927, the Colt 22 Automatic Pistol came to be known as the Woodsman, a beloved arm that became familiar to generations of gun enthusiasts. For 62 years, the Colt Woodsman was in continuous production. It was, and still is, regarded as among the finest handguns ever to be turned out in New England.

OUTER'S BOOK combined with *RECREATION* in 1918—and both were absorbed by competitor *OUTDOOR LIFE* nine years later. And nearly lost in the mists of time is the tale of the magazine's unflagging determination, combined with the united effort of its readers, to fill an unacceptably vacant niche in the battery of the American gun crank. •

The Brown-Merrill Bolt Action

.......Premier Mystery of a Single-Shot Rifle

by George J. Layman

"A New Military Arm, unequalled for strength, simplicity, durability and fewness of parts-pronounced in every instance, on inspection by Army Officers, to be the best Military Gun ever made. A thorough examination and comparison with any other system is solicited."

SUCH WAS THE introduction in the 1869 Brown Manufacturing Company catalog that introduced the "Brown Military Breech-Loading Gun." It has always been remembered that this organization

The author is pondering the question of which U.S. state militias had been issued the Brown-Merrill military rifle. The March 20, 1872, article in the *Newburyport Herald* was very convincing in that the Brown Mfg. Co. had a contract for the conversion of 2,000 Enfield muzzleloaders. The question is, just who contracted with them? Was it state militias exclusively, or were there foreign contracts formulated as well? Up to this point, it has been determined that the state of New Hampshire had at least one known militia unit having been issued a very small number of the Brown-Merrill rifles.

was the last manufacturer of the Ballard rifle in Massachusetts, lasting a mere 3 1/2 years in business. During its tenure in the arms manufacturing trade, the Newburyport, Massachusetts-based Brown company was certainly anxious to impress the industry with an expanded product line compared to its predecessor, the Merrimack Arms Manufacturing Co. Of course, the Ballard rifle and the Southerner derringer were the two main firearms that were carried over from Edward Bray's old Merrimack company line and retained by the new organization. However, once the first Brown company catalog introduced a radically different military single-shot rifle, a whole set of different priorities were in store. Remember this was the post-Civil War era where nations across the Atlantic were increasingly ill at ease with their neighbors and were in the market for good serviceable breech-loading arms to replace the muzzleloader.

By the end of the 1860s, there were already several established military-style metallic breech-loading designs–the Remington rolling block, the Peabody, the Sharps, and several others. The Brown Manufacturing Company was incorporated on February 18, 1869, and obtained control of all stocks from its predecessor, the Merrimack Arms Mfg. Co. One Charles S. Brown became president, with George Merrill as secretary. In this inaugural year of the Brown Manufacturing Company, many were quite surprised to note that a bolt-action single-shot military rifle became part of the new line. The illustrated 1869 Brown Mfg. Co. catalog is, up to this point, the only known catalog issued by the company prior its shutdown in 1873. Pages 12 to 15 feature the new "Brown Military Breech-Loader" which is given a major introduction in both line illustration and text. The mysterious circumstances that surround this very early–if not actually the first–American-made bolt-action rifle, leave a whole host of questions and speculation that, to this day, continue to mystify researchers of antique firearms. I became interested in the particulars of the Brown bolt-action single-shot rifle many years ago, but

The Brown Manufacturing Company of Newburyport, Massachusetts, certainly took quite a chance in attempting to interest the U.S. firearms market in a new bolt-action rifle. Though the original design is credited to S.F. Van Choate, it was the improved Merrill patent variation which had been manufactured in the largest production figures. The Brown-Merrill is shown with the Enfield-type angular bayonet, an optional accessory sold with the rifle.

failed to obtain one until a short while ago. Over the past thirty years, I have been able to examine a mere eight to ten examples of the Brown-Merrill, in varying degrees of condition, in private collections.

Recently I was very fortunate and purchased a specimen that is likely the finest piece observed to date. The rifle is in 58 Berdan centerfire, with a 34-inch barrel, and is essentially a converted 1853 Pattern 577 British Enfield muzzleloader with the Merrill action added. It has a well-executed alteration of the stock, with the sidelock and screw bases removed and all recesses precisely inlaid - and finished flush - with matching walnut. The barrel is a deep brown, with the action–like all examined so far–having been left in the white, as its patina is much lighter compared to

the barrel and its furniture. The short, straight bolt handle on this rifle lifts upward quite briskly and, when pulled back, cocks the centrally-hung exposed hammer–which has a 'half-cock' as well and can be manually operated if necessary. One of the most salient features of the bolt is its heavy and very solid construction, together with the twin, machined locking lugs at the rear.

It is a quite advanced system for its period in time and is indeed a much stronger than required action for such a low-pressure blackpowder number as the 58 Berdan cartridge. The overall appearance of the rifle, from the rear sight to the muzzle, is distinctly Enfield–but according to the 1869 Brown catalog, (under the "Transformations" heading)..."*United States Springfield, or the Enfield Rifles, can be converted to this System at a small expense (sic)...* " No one (*to my knowledge*) has yet seen a U. S. Springfield converted to the Brown-Merrill system, and there are a number of contradictions which continue to plague the researcher on these rifles.

It has been written, by several Depression-era arms authors, that the Brown-Merrill rifle was, in essence, the Van Choate rifle–sometimes known as the "Prince Rifle" (*there was one N.E. Prince who was a witness at Merrill's patent signing*), which was chambered for the 45-70 Van Choate cartridge. This same speculation also includes a so-called "58 Van Choate" cartridge that I have yet to actually see. They noted that the Van Choate was produced in 1872 by the Brown Manufacturing Company. Phil Sharpe, in his book "*The Rifle in America,*" notes the state of New York tested the Brown-manufactured Van Choate rifle but, in actuality, this may have been the Brown-Merrill rifle.

Before and after. Shown is an original Pattern 1853 Enfield muzzle-loading rifle-musket (*top*) as compared to the converted Brown-Merrill breech-loading system (*bottom*) after its transformation. It can plainly be seen that much wood was removed in the receiver area by the Brown factory in fitting the new action, which somewhat weakened the stock in the vicinity of the wrist. Note the screw sockets on the Brown-Merrill were neatly filled by matching walnut filler panels.

Long ago it should have been acclaimed as the first modern U.S.-designed bolt action; perhaps it's hybrid British/American appearance has influenced the general view of it being one of the more uninteresting single-shot breechloaders.

In either case, however, the rifle failed to win approval by New York state and was a heavy financial loss for the Brown company. A mortgage was placed upon the Brown Mfg. Co. on May 8, 1871, reflecting the company's dire financial straits.

The Brown-Merrill single-shot rifle has a patent date of October 17, 1871 on the top of the bolt. This was patent # 119,939 and # 119,940–both issued to George Merrill of East Orange, NJ. The 1869 Brown catalog, however, offered the rifle before the patent was issued, meaning it was likely in production already. Extolling the virtues of the Brown military rifle was part of a hopeful ad campaign to convince U.S. state militias, or foreign powers, to convert their muzzle-loading arms to the new Brown-Merrill breech-loading system.

But how does the Van Choate fit into this? Silvanus Frederick Van Choate of Boston, Mass. received four patents on breech-loading firearms: two in 1869, one in 1871, and another in 1872–all within the Brown bolt-action production era. Was the basic action of the Brown-Merrill originally patented by Van Choate, and is it

the rifle pictured in the 1869 Brown catalog? The early line drawings are, to a degree, similar my own Brown-Merrill rifle. However, the example in the catalog is devoid of the lever-type safety on the rear of the right frame–as well as having the trigger guard, hammer, and mainspring all joined as one. Perhaps George Merrill's October, 1871 patent is the addition of the safety to the Van Choate action, together with the hammer, trigger and mainspring assembly joined to the action as most surviving specimens show.

Or it could well be that Van Choate sold his rights to Brown about this time and they became the sole proprietors and had Merrill work over the action even further (?). Additionally, the drawing in the 1869 Brown catalog appears slightly different from an Enfield, having two barrel bands, whereas all Brown-Merrill rifles examined so far have had three. It is difficult to understand this possible connection between Van Choate and Merrill. I feel the Brown Mfg. Co. may have built the Van Choate rifle for the Ordnance tests, and even a few for commercial purposes. However, they did not advertise or incorporate the rifle into their line,

acting merely as sub-contractors–which may be the reason that writers and collectors have been confused by seeing Brown markings on another bolt-action rifle, such as the Van Choate.

An interesting marking found on the lower portion of the stock on Brown-Merrill conversions of the Enfield, and most other unconverted Enfields as well, are those of Cooper & Goodman. It is found that one Joseph Rock Cooper of Birmingham, England, was granted U.S. patent # 84,938 on December 15, 1868. He was a partner with John Dent Goodman and both men were principal shareholders of the Birmingham Small Arms Company. Having never seen an example of the Cooper breech-loading action, there seems to be some speculation that the Brown-Merrill action may have had some sort of a connection. I speculate, to a degree, that Cooper and Goodman attempted to act as an import agent selling surplus

A close-up of the Birmingham Small Arms Trade *cartouche* on the author's Brown-Merrill rifle. Why the Brown Mfg. Co. left the BSA *cartouche* intact on the rifles is a mystery. Most manufacturers would not wish to leave any evidence of surplus parts usage on a newly-introduced product.

As well-proportioned and strong as the Remington rolling block or Sharps action, it is perhaps the hybrid British/American appearance of the Brown-Merrill-Enfield which turned off many U.S. customers. As far as overall durability is concerned, the wrist of the stock is the weakest area of the entire rifle. Had the Enfield stock been replaced or redesigned, the rifle might have received more serious consideration by prospective military customers.

The Cooper and Goodman marking is another question–why? Perhaps there may have been an arrangement with the British govt. regarding testing for possible adoption by the British Army. Remember, Cooper and Goodman were both major shareholders with BSA. Anything could have been 'in the works' as they were individuals with substantial influence in high places.

Enfield muzzle-loading rifles to the Brown company for conversion, and then as an export agent for the Brown-Merrill rifle in an attempt to interest the British government. With the absence of any factory records, which likely were acquired by Schoverling and Daly at the Brown company foreclosure in July 1873, we'll probably never know. It is an established fact, however, that the Brown-Merrill was entered as No.83 in the 1872 U.S. Army Ordnance Board tests but was not recommended for further production, or issue for field trials. The U.S. Army's test specimen was chambered for the 50-70 Govt. cartridge. In Charles Winthrop Sawyer's reference book *Our Rifles* (published 1920), he presents a photo plate and narrative that appears to indicate both the Brown-Merrill *and* the Van Choate were evaluated during U.S. Ordnance tests. The photo in this book displays two different actions, and the test version of the Brown-

Merrill is a carbine with double triggers. In the original George Merrill patent, one of the features, which makes his design quite advanced for the day, was the firing pin that retracted upon opening the action. Sawyer's book, on page 239, has this feature listed as well under the Van Choate's basic specifications.... contradictions abound!

The specimen I obtained came with an Enfield-type bayonet and remnants of the original sling, and appears to have had some type of military affiliation. An interesting aspect, long shrouded in controversy, may be a connection to the Fenian troubles of the late 1860s. In 1866 when the secret Irish Fenian organization was planning to execute raids on the northern New England-Canadian border region, concerned Canadian farmers from the St. Armand region were worried for their safety. They formed their own militia group, known as the "red sashes," and ultimately sent

two representatives to the Merrimack Arms Company in Newburyport, Massachusetts, to purchase 40 Ballard sporting rifles with 30-inch barrels. This was some three years prior to the Brown-Merrill bolt-action rifle's appearance in 1869, from the successor of the Merrimack company.

Colonel John O'Neill, a former U.S. officer during the Civil War, was a leader of one of the Fenian brigades since 1866. After several invasions along the border, he was readying for another in the spring of 1870. Establishing a base near Franklin, Vermont, he cached his store of 15,000 weapons and about 3 million rounds of cartridges. When the Fenian attack force advanced on May 25th, few of O'Neill's comrades showed up for the ill-fated invasion. As luck would have it, the group was surprised by a superior Canadian military force, ultimately scattered and the survivors fled.

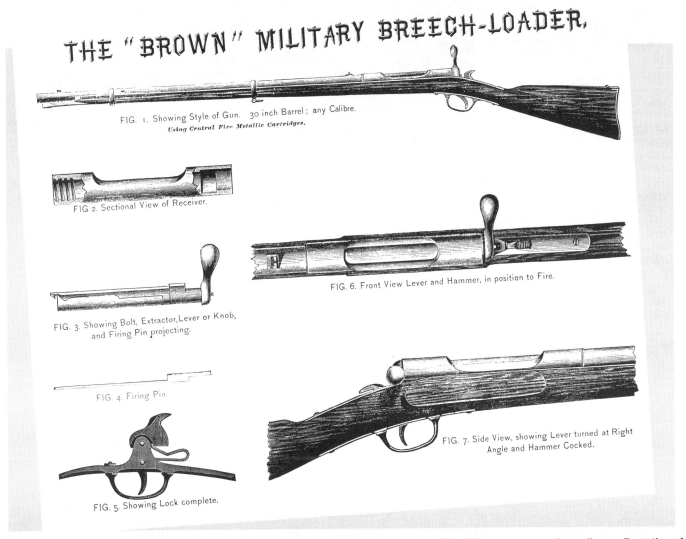

THE "BROWN" MILITARY BREECH-LOADER.

FIG. 1. Showing Style of Gun. 30 inch Barrel; any Calibre.
Using Central Fire Metallic Cartridges.

FIG 2. Sectional View of Receiver.

FIG. 3. Showing Bolt, Extractor, Lever or Knob, and Firing Pin projecting.

FIG. 4. Firing Pin.

FIG. 5. Showing Lock complete.

FIG. 6. Front View Lever and Hammer, in position to Fire.

FIG. 7. Side View, showing Lever turned at Right Angle and Hammer Cocked.

This illustration, from the 1869 Brown catalog, clearly indicates the differences between Merrill's patent versus the earlier configuration of the Van Choate version as found in the catalog. Note the one-piece lock assembly that is combined with the trigger guard. The bolt, in the drawing, differs as well by having an externally-mounted extractor and (*apparently*) a single locking lug. There were no updated versions of this catalog which featured the Merrill patent variant of the Brown Military Gun.

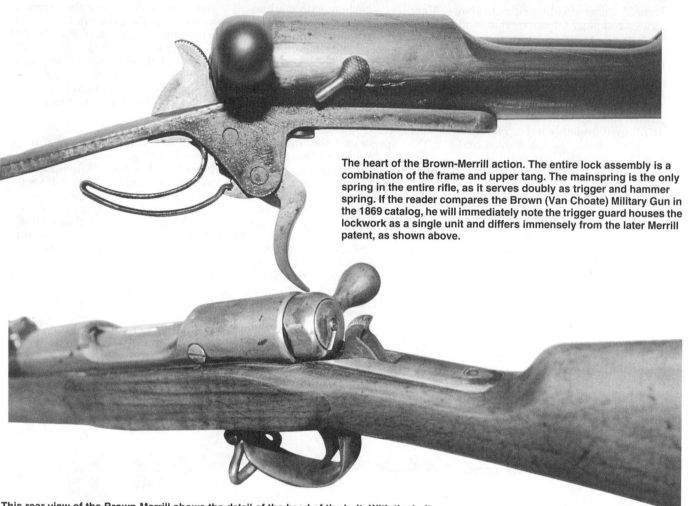

The heart of the Brown-Merrill action. The entire lock assembly is a combination of the frame and upper tang. The mainspring is the only spring in the entire rifle, as it serves doubly as trigger and hammer spring. If the reader compares the Brown (Van Choate) Military Gun in the 1869 catalog, he will immediately note the trigger guard houses the lockwork as a single unit and differs immensely from the later Merrill patent, as shown above.

This rear view of the Brown-Merrill shows the detail of the head of the bolt. With the bolt closed, the firing pin is in the free-floating position. The simple construction of the bolt allows it to be disassembled by removing the slotted-head screw. All three pieces are internally stamped with s/n 998.

Externally, there are no serial numbers on the Brown-Merrill military rifle. When disassembled, however, they can be found on the inner trigger guard flat (*as shown*), on the barrel, the inner recess of the stock beneath the barrel, and inside of the bolt. Each part of the bolt is serialized, to include the firing pin.

With the barrel and action removed, the serial number of 998 is also found on the front of the stock, within the recess adjacent to where the barrel is seated.

U.S. marshals later located O'Neill and arrested him for violation of the 1818 U.S. neutrality laws. Most of the 15,000 arms were confiscated by both United States and Canadian authorities.

How does the Brown-Merrill rifle fit into this? The 1927 Bannerman catalog of military goods, on page 49, lists for sale "*Fenian Raiders Brown B/L Rifle. Price $8.75.*" Did O'Neill make a substantial purchase of these bolt-action rifles in the 1869-1870 period, in preparation for the final raid, through a clandestine purchase from the Brown company? No concrete data as yet. We do know the Needham conversions were definitely Fenian arms, but many facts about the Brown connection have yet to surface; locating other issues of Bannerman catalogs may shed further light, as they always provided interesting footnotes on much of their military ordnance.

L.D. Satterlee's 1927 edition of "*A Catalog of Firearms for the Collector*" brings to light one other question about the Brown-Merrill. Satterlee notes there was a Brown bolt action in 58 caliber, in 50 (50-70 Govt.) caliber, and also mentions a bolt-action carbine. The carbine, he states, is 577 caliber with a 21-inch barrel, which he noted was cut down from an Enfield muzzle-loading rifle. (*Mention is also made that the secretary of the Brown company, G. Merrill, patented a carving machine on Sept. 15, 1868.*) A carbine in this system has yet to be seen by anyone. Phil Sharpe notes Satterlee's observation in his own book, believes it to have a different action from the Brown-Merrill, and that the carbine took a 58 Van Choate cartridge. Sharpe also concludes that "*... the absence of details makes this somewhat confusing.*"

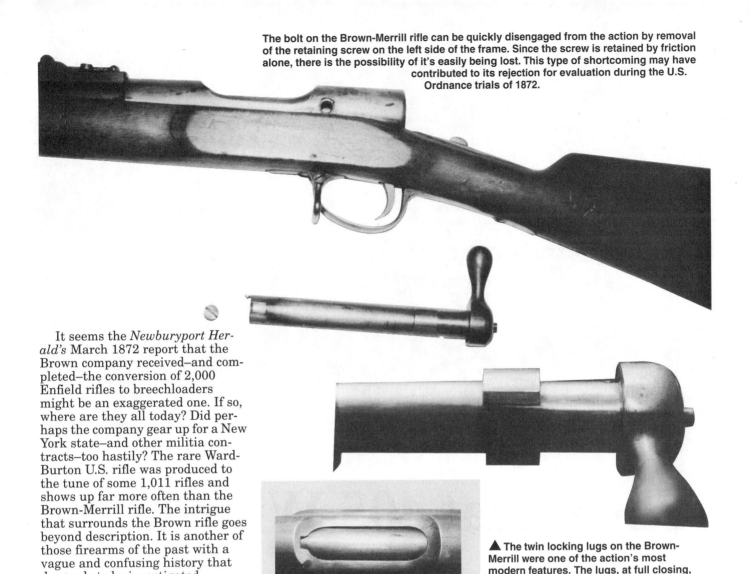

The bolt on the Brown-Merrill rifle can be quickly disengaged from the action by removal of the retaining screw on the left side of the frame. Since the screw is retained by friction alone, there is the possibility of it's easily being lost. This type of shortcoming may have contributed to its rejection for evaluation during the U.S. Ordnance trials of 1872.

▲ The twin locking lugs on the Brown-Merrill were one of the action's most modern features. The lugs, at full closing, lock into a vertical position and were strong enough for the largest blackpowder cartridges of the day.

The top of the bolt is marked with the Brown Mfg. Co. address, together with the Merrill patent date of October 17, 1871.

It seems the *Newburyport Herald's* March 1872 report that the Brown company received–and completed–the conversion of 2,000 Enfield rifles to breechloaders might be an exaggerated one. If so, where are they all today? Did perhaps the company gear up for a New York state–and other militia contracts–too hastily? The rare Ward-Burton U.S. rifle was produced to the tune of some 1,011 rifles and shows up far more often than the Brown-Merrill rifle. The intrigue that surrounds the Brown rifle goes beyond description. It is another of those firearms of the past with a vague and confusing history that demands to be investigated.

The overall construction of the Brown-Merrill is quite practical and is very simple. The lock has only three pieces: the hammer, trigger, and the mainspring. The rifle chambers newly manufactured 58 Berdan centerfire cases precisely. None of those observed have ever had a readily visible serial number; however, after disassembling my own, most of the new internal parts produced by the Brown company have the number '988' in various places, including the inner flat of the trigger guard. The bolt is marked only with the Brown Mfg. Co. address and the patent date.

There is, in fact, evidence of one Brown-Merrill having Western usage by a settler in the Pike's Peak area in the 1870s; that rifle is now displayed in a museum in Colorado. For the Ballard fan, one of these would be appropriate in a collection since the last pre-Marlin Ballard manufacturer produced the Brown-Merrill. It might also be stated the reason that doomed the Brown Manufacturing Company to fiscal failure was not only slow sales of the Ballard rifle, but also their hav-

ing excessive confidence in a rifle of such radical design as the Brown-Merrill. The contradictions abound, and the correlation between Van Choate and George Merrill requires further in-depth research; and, as well, determination of the Fenian connection.

From a reenactment standpoint, it would definitely cause a sensation to pack one of these early bolt-action rifles into a single-shot military match, or cowboy action shoot for entry into a side event, and watch the other shooters look on with awe and amazement. Few

shooters, collectors or firearms dealers have ever had a chance to examine one of these and, perhaps, many who are not single-shot rifle students do not even know of the Brown-Merrill's existence during the latter part of the Westward venture. I am certain that several more may have been sold by western dealers, such as Lower and others, after Schoverling and Daly liquidated the inventory from the Brown company after the foreclosure auction.

The Brown-Merrill is truly one of those single-shot rifles that seldom shows its face. It ought to be remembered as the father of the modern American bolt-action centerfire rifle. It also should be considered the rifle that put the last Massachusetts manufacturer of the Ballard rifle out of business. Had this not occurred, we may never have seen the Ballard rifle blossom into one of John Marlin's greatest success stories.

●

The Great 405 Winchester

by Dennis W. Confer

IN THE 1800s, the various 45- and 50-caliber cartridges were popular. Velocities of most were similar– 1100 to 1300 fps–the limit of the blackpowder propellant. The only way to increase potency was to increase bullet weight and diameter. Along came smokeless powder, and with it higher velocities and energy levels. Many shooters back then felt the developing 40 caliber was better than the 45s and 50s. Trajectories were somewhat flatter, recoil was less—and although they may not have known about "sectional density" or "ballistic coefficients" back then—they realized the smaller-diameter, but longer, bullet was effective and delivered deep penetration. There were many 40-caliber cartridges. *Cartridges of the World* listed 26 different 40-caliber cartridges, but only 11 different 45s in the obsolete cartridge section of the book – 40s were indeed popular.

The 405 cartridge was introduced in 1904 for the 1895 Winchester. It fired a 300-grain bullet at over

2,200 fps for over 3,200 fpe – more energy than the great 30/03/06, and with a much heavier bullet. *Cartridges of the World, 6th Edition* states "i*t is only slightly less powerful than the 375 H&H."* This is an exaggeration, but the 405 proved effective even on buffalo, rhinoceros and elephant. It is no wonder that Teddy Roosevelt adopted it as his "*big medicine"* on lions. Major Townsend Whelen said the 405 was "*the best American cartridge for bear and moose, and the one least likely to require a second shot."*

Today, there is renewed interest in the 405 Winchester. U.S. Repeating Arms Company (USRAC) reintroduced the unique 1895 Winchester rifle (*Browning's last lever action*) for the 405. I love old guns: especially Winchester, Marlin and Savage lever actions, and the

Above cartridge boxes. *Bottom:* 405 Winchester (300 grain), red & yellow boxes. *Top (l. to r.)*: 405 Winchester (300 grain), orange label; 405 UMC Remington (red and white box).

cartridges made for them. I love powerful guns, too—and the 405 is powerful.

The 1895 Winchester was a unique and well-made gun. The design incorporated a box magazine (*likely to help secure military contracts*) that allowed use of the flatter-shooting spitzer bullet, since tubular magazines required use of the less-efficient flat-nose bullet. The first cartridge chambered in the '95 was the 30 U.S. — also known as the 30 Army, or 30/ 40 Krag. It was also chambered for the 303 British, 30/03, 30/06 and 7.62 Russian (*similar to the 30/06*) military rounds. Sporting cartridge chamberings were the 38/72, 40/72, 35 WCF, and 405 Winchester. Over 425,000 1895s were produced; nearly 300,000 for Russian military use.

Some were used by the U.S. Army and other governmental organizations, like the Texas Rangers. Lyman supplied a unique quick-adjustable receiver peep sight right from the

Left side of author's Model '95 shows the adjustable Lyman aperture sight as well as the small forend schnabel and the crescent buttplate.

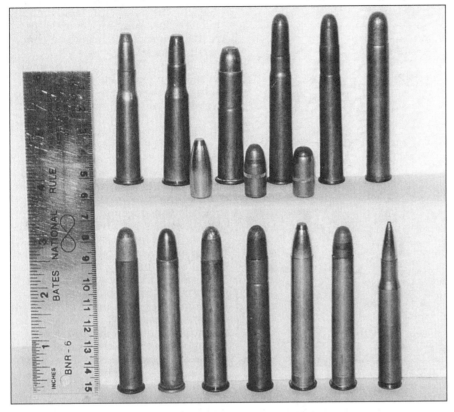

Cartridges & bullets for author's lever guns [(*F*) = factory; (*RL*) = reload]:
Bottom row (left to right): F – early Winchester; F – early Remington; F – later Winchester; RL – Rearden; RL – Barnes 40/72; F – 30/06.
Top row (left to right): Winchester cartridges: 33, 348, 45/70, 35 WCF, 38/72, 405. Bullets (left to right): Barnes, Rearden, DKT

of Alaska–as well as quite a few Alaskans (*and guides*) –are fond of lever actions for that reason. Witness the popularity of the new commercial 45/70 loads and the new Guide Model guns by Marlin. If something must be stopped, it must be stopped now–and large-caliber guns will do that. The 405 Winchester will do it.

The reintroduction of the Model 1895 chambered for the 405 Winchester satisfied demand for the rifle/cartridge combo, but USRAC did not produce ammunition for it! Finding ammunition was a problem, until recently. There is some old ammunition around but it has attained "collector" status and is very expensive. I have quite a few boxes myself that I am not about to shoot or sell. Fortunately, Hornady is now producing cartridges, and bullets for reloading. Other bullet-makers are adding 405 Winchester bullets to their offerings, and it appears USRAC will offer another run of 405 Winchesters.

When my wife gave me a Winchester 1895/405, I had to have ammunition to shoot so I had to resort to reloading,

beginning. The rear sight's elevation travel of about 1 1/4 inches allowed shooting to 1,000 yards, obviously not a sporting requirement.

The 405 was the most powerful American cartridge of the day. Winchester's 1895 405s were furnished with a curved steel buttplate that some felt accented recoil. (*To me, the recoil is very tolerable with that buttplate.*) A shotgun-style buttplate was also available. The 405 still is more powerful than the 30/06, 348 Winchester, 350 Remington

Magnum, 35 Whelen, 444 Marlin, 45/70 and 450 Marlin. Energies (fpe) from factory loads are (*cartridge and bullet weight*): 30/06 (200 gr.) – 2830 fpe; 348 (250 gr.) –

3060 fpe; 350 Remington Magnum (200 gr.) – 3261 fpe; 35 Whelen (250 gr.) – 3197 fpe; 444 Marlin (240 gr.) – 3069 fpe; 45/70 (405 gr.) – 1570 fpe and the 450 Marlin (350 gr.) – 2891 fpe. The 405 Winchester can generate from 3200 to over 3500 fpe.

There is a lot to be said for lever actions, especially when dangerous game is involved. Two or three fast shots are usually better than only one from a bolt action. The natives

which I love. Finding new cases was not a problem. Powders were not a problem. Bullets were a problem, but I finally came up with solutions. My best solutions in 1993 were Frank Rearden of Chippewa Falls, Wisconsin, Barnes Bullets, and DKT bullets. Frank Rearden passed away in January, 2001 and Barnes no longer supplies soft-point bullets of .411-inch diameter. Today, DKT and others like Alaska Bullet Works, Cast Performance Bullets, Custom Bullets, Hawk, Hornady, Huntingtons, Old Western Scrounger, and Woodleigh supply appropriate bullets specifically for the 405. Lyman has discontinued moulds for .411- or .412-inch bullets, but NEI Handtools and SAECO have suitable moulds. Other bullet-makers have become aware of, and are filling, the growing need for 405 Winchester bullets.

Winchester's Model 1895, chambered for the 405 Winchester. Graceful lines complement the unique design that includes a box magazine.

One writer tried cast bullets without much success, but every gun is an individual and it might be worth trying NEI moulds or Cast Performance Bullet Company for cast bullets. Bullets for the 41 Magnum revolver can be used for deer, but not for bigger game. Loads for some are listed in *Ken Waters Pet Loads* book. You will find it interesting and have lots of fun working up loads for today's new bullets

Is the 405 obsolete? Obsolete can mean: *no longer in general use, not used, outmoded, out-of-date*. The 405 cartridge and the 1895 Winchester are being used today. Many 75 year-old guns, cartridges—and guys—are useful today and even held in high esteem by many. I became interested in the 405/1895 when I learned of its power and reputation because, as an Alaskan hunter and outfitter, I was interested in a gun and cartridge that would be reliable and trustworthy on brown bear and moose—both of which are often shot at under 100 yards.

I carried a new model 1895 Marlin loaded to maximum as a backup gun for bears for over 10 years. It was to take care of wounded bear at close range and I trusted it, even though I never had to use it. I love and use mainly bolt actions in all calibers for my hunting, but wanted a repeater for that rare encounter at 5 to 20 feet. With a bolt action you will probably get only one shot on a charging bear at that range.

I shot a big muskox with my 405 Winchester in February, 1994. I called it *Murphy's Muskox* as most things went wrong. Group after group of the animals would not form their usual defense ring, with the mature muskox facing outwards protecting their young. Instead, they would huddle like a

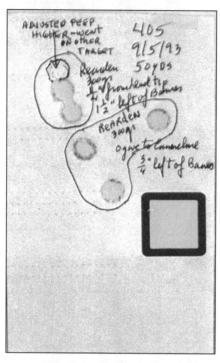

Three bullet ogive variations were fired on this target, while experimenting with the modification of the Rearden bullet design, to find the configuration that worked best.

football team–heads in, backsides out–so I couldn't judge the bulls. When the bulls came out of the huddle, they and the rest would stampede off in the distance a few miles but the wind blew their tracks away quickly; perhaps the 35 to 40 mph winds made them nervous. I know the minus 170 degree-plus wind-chill factor made me nervous. You quickly learn to restrict your coffee intake on that sort of a hunt!

I went up the "umpteenth" knoll to spot, not expecting to see anything. On the other side, I surprised a group of about 15 muskox that immediately went into their 'huddle' about 90 yards away. I got so excited that I wrenched my slung 405 off my shoulder and over my head. In my haste, the sling pulled off both my glasses and beaver skin hat. I caught my glasses but the right lens popped out (*I see poorly without glasses.*)! The muskox were a blur. I put my Zeiss binoculars on them just as a bull backed out of the huddle. Fortunately, my taxidermist had taught me how to judge them (*very difficult, but I was smart enough to ask*) and this was the bull I wanted. I noted which end was the front and mounted my 405. Everything was a blur – sights and muskox. Looking through the peep, I pulled the blurry front sight down on the blurry, furry shoulder and fired. The bull took five steps and collapsed.

Unfortunately, muskox stiffened up fast before help arrived to take good photos. In Alaska, moose shot in the winter are often dismantled with a chainsaw, using vegetable oil for the chain lubricant. Someday, maybe I'll shoot a big moose with the 405.

Author's favorite guns (*top to bottom*): Model 1892 (25/20) made in 1903; outstanding shooter with tang peep. Model 1886 (33 Winchester) made in 1907; very accurate. Model 1895 (405 Winchester) made in 1913; author's favorite. Model 71 (348 Winchester) made in 1938; maple stock by Hal Hartley, bolt peep–an outstanding shooter.

The 405 did a great job! Bullet penetration and expansion were great – my shot placement was fortunate. He stiffened up quickly before good field photos could be taken, and froze solid in about two hours. Although it is grainy and looks like it would be tough, muskox meat is outstanding in flavor but must be cooked quickly to be tender.

Other "oldies" that I love are the 1892, 1886, and 71 Winchesters.

My 1892, a 25/20 with the tang peep, was made in 1903 and has put five shots into less than 3/4-inch at 50 yards several times. I have several 25/20s – they are all great shooters even with open sights. All,

The fruits of a successful hunt. The muskox is now a welcome addition to the author's family room décor.

Author with muskox horns in his yard after the hunt. If entered, he would have been #135 of 204 muskox in the *Boone & Crockett Recordbook, 9th Edition*, (1988). He is probably #1 for muskox shot by a blind man using a 405 Winchester!

Table of Loads

#1 – #3 used Bertram cases, CCI 200 primers and *(except #1)* 300-grain bullets.

Bullet Maker	Bullet Diameter	Jacket Thickness	Powder	Load/grs.	Velocity fps	Energy fpe	Use
Barnes (1)	.411	.049	IMR 4198	46.7	2274	3393	Anything
DKT (2)	.412	.020	IMR 4895	58.5	2189	3192	Deer
Rearden (3)	.411	.034	IMR 4198	46.5	2250	3373	Anything
Rearden (3)	.411	.034	RL-7	53.0	2314	3568	Anything
Rearden (3)	.411	.034	IMR 3031	57.0	2250	3380	Anything
Factory	—	—	—		2200	3220	—
Hornady factory (4)	—	—	—	—	2225	—	Anything

1. The Barnes bullet was a soft-nose spitzer that I shortened to a flat nose so it would fit in the magazine and be held firmly in the case neck. Actual weight after shortening was 295.5 grains. This bullet is not available today. Barnes has a .411-inch "X" bullet that probably would not be satisfactory in the 405 because of length.

2. This was all the IMR 4895 that would fit into the thick-walled Bertram cases so velocity is lower but this, or a lighter load, would be good for deer, considering the thinner jacket.

3. Frank Rearden of Chippewa Falls, WI made these bullets up for me in 1993. They were great bullets for the 405. Frank passed away in January, 2001.

4. New factory load available today.

** The best source of reloading data that I know is *Ken Waters' Pet Loads, Volume II* – 1980.

Disclaimer: These loads were safe in my gun but every gun is an individual. To be safe, start with loads 10% under those shown and work upwards while observing pressure signs.

including a Marlin 27S pump and a Remington 25 pump, will keep five shots under one inch at 50 yards. Although the 25/20 cartridge generates only 500-plus fpe, it has reportedly accounted for many elk and deer. I think of it as one of the best survival guns, as ammunition is light and easily reloadable. It is great for small game.

The 1886 is a 33 Winchester made in 1907. It shoots almost three inches high at 50 yards, as the open sights were designed, which puts it dead on at 100 yards. It gives 2423 fps with 47 grains of IMR 4895 and a 200-grain Hornady, for 2629 fpe.

The Model 71 replaced the 1886. My 71 was made in 1938 and will shoot into two inches at 100 yards using its bolt peep. Hal Hartley *(deceased)*, one of the greatest stock makers, stocked it in maple. The 348 is a powerful round producing over 3,000 fpe with a 250-grain bullet.

Another favorite of mine today (*I have so many favorites*) is an 1892 Marlin that handles both 32 rimfire and 32 centerfire (called the 32 Long Rifle) with quick-interchangeable firing pins. It fires the 32 Colt with great accuracy, produces about 200 fpe and is an excellent small game gun.

I have owned at least one of every Winchester, Marlin and Savage lever gun model ever made—and I shot them all. Every one I bought, or was gifted by my wife, had an excellent trigger pull. Back then, arms makers could — and did — take the time to do things right without having to fear litigation. Common sense was the rule then.

There are so many good "oldies," all good honest guns. Have fun — take an oldster hunting. •

Current 405 Winchester Supply Sources

(Prices rounded to even dollars and do not include shipping.)

Alaska Bullet Works, (907) 349-4999: bullets (50) @ $42.

Ammo Depot, IL (618) 455-2666: bullets and loaded cartridges, no cases.

Cast Performance Bullet Co., PO Box 153, Riverton, WY 82501

DKT, 14623 Vera Drive, Union, MI 49103: bullets (.412").

Hawk, NJ (609) 299-2800: bullets (50) @ $32, two jacket thickness'.

Hornady, 1-800-338-3220, PO Box 1848, Grand Island, NE 68802; newly-loaded cartridges, and bullets for reloading.

Huntingtons, CA (530) 534-1210: Bertram cases (20) @ $31; Woodleigh.

Bullets (50) @ $56; Custom Bullets (50) @ $33 and SAECO moulds.

NEI Handtools, OR (503) 543-6776: moulds.

Old Western Scrounger, CA 1-800-877-2666: loaded cartridges (20) @ $70.

SAECO, CA (*moulds through Huntingtons, above*)

Reference Books:

Big Bore Rifles & Cartridges, Wolfe Publishing, 1991.

Cartridges of the World, 6th Edition, by Frank C. Barnes, 1989.

Ken Waters' Pet Loads, Volume II from Wolfe Publishing, 1980.

The Winchester Book, by George Madis, 1985.

Winchester – An American Legend, by R.L. Wilson, 1991.

Practical Accuracy Of 22 LR Ammunition

by Mike Thomas

CONTEMPORARY RIMFIRE ACCURACY enthusiasts have a remarkable choice when it comes to ammunition selection. It seems the only limiting factor is price—upwards of ten dollars per box of fifty rounds for the shooter desiring the very best available. Aside from the serious competitor, few enthusiasts can justify such an expense.

It is important to remember that, quite often, the difference in accuracy (*group size*) between the cheapest 22 Long Rifle ammo and the more expensive may be very small indeed. That's not to imply that premium match ammunition is of questionable quality. Rather, it is indicative of the exceptional quality of today's inexpensive rimfire cartridges. Anyway, the slight difference can often be traced to a particular barrel that simply lacks any true accuracy potential.

Shooting cans at twenty-five yards would probably indicate no practical difference in accuracy, regardless of the ammunition/gun combination used. Informal fifty-yard bulls-eye target shooting will probably display a measurable difference, yet it may be rather small. Hunting small game at various ranges may be successfully done with discount store "brick" ammo. In this scenario, few could tell if the accuracy level of the inexpensive stuff was any different from that of the pricey stuff.

Please bear in mind the author is not advocating a general acceptance of mediocrity here. For serious competitors, or others requiring the very best ammunition regardless of price, obviously "premium" ammo is the only way to go.

As mentioned previously, price and quality of cartridges don't mean much for any gun that is fundamentally inaccurate. If 2-inch, benchrested groups at 50 yards are the best to be had from a particular

The 24 types of 22 Long Rifle rimfire ammunition used in author's testing more than adequately represents the ammo used by the vast majority of rimfire shooters. Five 5-shot groups were fired, with each ammunition type, in six firearms.

Rifles used in this project include (*left to right*): Ruger 10-22T with Burris 6x HBR (Hunter Bench Rest) scope; open-sighted Winchester Model 63 reproduction, and the Browning Model 52 with 4x Leupold scope.

rifle; several versions of the inexpensive stuff will extract all the practical accuracy from the gun. For handguns, increase the arbitrary maximum group size to around 3 inches and reduce the range to 25 yards. Again, a steady benchrest is required for meaningful analysis.

Fortunately, many rifles and handguns are quite accurate 'as-is' and will easily best the minimum accuracy figures mentioned. It is not at all unusual to find a utility-grade 22 rifle, with a rough blue job and a stock that appears to have been made from laminated cardboard, that will easily shoot groups under an inch at fifty yards; this with the cheapest ammunition one can find.

Finding out what works best does require some effort, however. In preparing for this article, I selected three rifles and three handguns that are fairly representative for the intended comparisons of ammunition. Rifles included one of the late reproduction Browning Model 52 Winchester bolt-action sporters with a 24-inch barrel and 4x Leupold scope; a Ruger 10-22T semi-automatic, 20-inch factory heavy barrel and a 6x Burris HBR (Hunter Bench Rest) scope, and a Winchester Model 63 reproduction semi-automatic with a 23-inch barrel and open sights.

Handguns used in this project were the following: Ruger Mark II semi-automatic Government Model with a 6 7/8-inch bull barrel; a Smith & Wesson Model 17 revolver with a 6-inch barrel; and a Rossi Model 84 revolver with a 4-inch barrel.

Ammunition? Considering the utilitarian aspects of the project, I chose to use neither "ultra" high-velocity cartridges nor true premium "match" ammunition. Why eliminate these from the testing? Because they are of a very specialized nature and/or may be comparatively expensive. Most of us use such ammunition infrequently, if at all.

I did select 24 different rimfire ammunitions produced by the major makers of such products: CCI, Federal, PMC (Eldorado Cartridge Corporation), Remington, and Winchester. This is the same ammunition many of us use on a regular basis and the list includes standard and high-velocity loadings, solid bullets and hollow-points.

While our 22 rimfire guns may be of fine quality and not necessarily inexpensive, they are generally not specialized "target" arms, either. We don't test specific lots of ammunition for accuracy potential. Nor do we sort cartridges by weight, dimensions–or some other gauging technique that will - reportedly - all but ensure uniformity and consistency from one cartridge to the next. More to the point, we enjoy shooting and prefer not to transform ammo selection into a huge and tedious chore.

In the real world we purchase ammunition several boxes, or a brick of ten boxes, at a time–quite often from a discount store. Price likely influences our selection more than it should. Such decisions notwithstanding, "cheap" ammo will often shoot very well in a number of guns and, conversely, it will perform quite dismally far more often than the more expensive stuff will.

Now, the big ammunition manufacturers all market what they refer to as "target" ammo. While this is not the same thing as the true match-grade product, more often than not it is rather accurate in many guns. These cartridges are always standard velocity and loaded with a 40-grain solid bullet. Should it be exceptionally accurate in any firearm, it may be a real bargain. While it is usually more expensive than other rimfire ammo, the difference is often not very great.

More on ammunition selection... nothing listed in the tables retails for more than about $3.00 (maximum) per box of fifty rounds. Shopping around (*and not overlooking the various mail-order outfits*), one will likely find all the ammo used in this project priced significantly under the $3.00-per-box figure.

Much shooting was done to compile the results set forth in the accompanying tables. The average of five 5-shot groups (25 rounds) with twenty-four ammunition brands & types in six firearms was recorded. Listed group sizes are to the nearest quarter-inch. For the purposes of this article I could see no need for more exacting measurements. I simply added five group sizes on a calculator and divided by five, hence the figures shown to a decimal point. While I consider these numbers to be valid and useful, I am not a statistician or math expert, so perhaps there is room for error with my methods. Hopefully, I have kept that margin small.

What the figures do very clearly show is what can be reasonably expected from "regular, everyday" rimfire rifles and handguns using "regular, everyday" rimfire ammunition. This also serves to - at least - partially satisfy the curiosity aspect

Table 1:
Average Group Size (inches) Per Ammunition Specific To Each Of Six Test Firearms

RIFLES

Ammunition:	Browning M52	Ruger 10/22T	Winchester M63	*Average*
Winchester HV	.75	85	1.70	1.10
PMC Scoremaster	1.00	.90	1.80	1.23
CCI Blazer	.75	.80	2.15	1.23
Winchester Wildcat	.75	.90	2.15	1.26
Federal HV	1.05	1.00	1.80	1.28
PMC Sidewinder	.70	1.20	1.95	1.28
CCI Std. Velocity	.75	.90	2.30	1.32
CCI MiniMag	.95	1.10	2.00	1.35
Fed. HV HP	.95	.65	2.45	1.35
CCI MiniMag HP	.90	1.05	2.15	1.36
PMC Zapper HP	.95	1.35	1.95	1.41
Federal Lightning	.85	1.60	1.85	1.43
Fed. American Eagle	.80	1.15	2.35	1.43
PMC Zapper	1.05	1.45	1.90	1.46
Win. Power Point HP		.95	2.55	1.47
Remington Cyclone HP	.95	1.25	2.20	1.47
Win. T22 Target	.75	1.15	2.60	1.50
Rem. Subsonic HP	.75	1.10	2.65	1.50
Remington Target	.85	1.20	2.50	1.51
Winchester HV HP	65	1.10	2.80	1.51
Remington HV HP	1.20	1.05	2.40	1.55
Federal Target	.95	1.10	3.00	1.68
Remington HV	1.30	1.15	2.80	1.75
Rem. Thunderbolt	1.15	1.30	2.95	1.80
Average, Each Rifle	**.904"**	**1.09"**	**2.29"**	**—**

HANDGUNS

Ammunition:	Ruger Gov't.	Smith & Wesson M17	Rossi M84	*Average*
Winchester HV	1.65	1.65	2.20	1.83
Federal Target	1.35	1.95	2.20	1.83
CCI MiniMag HP	1.50	2.00	2.20	1.90
Remington HV HP	1.55	1.65	2.50	1.90
Remington Subsonic HP	1.75	1.95	2.15	1.95
Federal HV HP	1.45	2.05	2.55	2.01
Win. T22 Target	2.00	1.80	2.25	2.02
Winchester Wildcat	1.75	1.90	2.40	2.02
CCI MiniMag	1.85	1.75	2.65	2.08
Winchester HV HP	1.95	1.65	2.70	2.10
Federal HV	1.75	1.80	2.90	2.15
CCI Standard Vel.	1.65	2.10	2.75	2.17
Fed. American Eagle	1.90	2.00	2.65	2.18
CCI Blazer	2.25	1.80	2.65	2.23
Win. Power Point HP	1.80	2.10	3.10	2.33
Remington HV	1.60	2.15	3.45	2.40
Remington Cyclone HP	2.20	2.00	3.10	2.43
PMC Scoremaster	2.25	2.35	2.90	2.50
PMC Zapper HP	1.90	2.75	2.90	2.52
Remington Target	1.60	2.70	3.30	2.53
Federal Lightning	2.20	2.45	3.00	2.55
PMC Zapper	2.70	1.95	3.10	2.58
PMC Sidewinder	1.95	2.55	3.40	2.63
Rem. Thunderbolt	2.75	2.85	3.85	3.15
Average, Each Handgun	**1.88"**	**2.08"**	**2.79"**	**—**

These handguns (*top to bottom*) were used to compile the data listed in the tables: Ruger Mark II Government model, 6 7/8-inch bull barrel. Rossi Model 84, 4-inch barrel. Smith & Wesson Model 17 with 6-inch barrel. All carry adjustable sights.

This is the manner in which the handguns were rested by the author for test firing. Though not visible in the photograph, revolver butt is not touching the sandbag.

AMMUNITION ACCURACY RANKING
In Inches, Based On Overall Average Group Size

RIFLES		HANDGUNS	
1. Winchester HV	1.10	**1.** Winchester HV	1.83
2. CCI Blazer	1.23	**2.** Federal Target	1.83
3. PMC Scoremaster	1.23	**3.** CCI MiniMag HP	1.90
4. Winchester Wildcat	1.26	**4.** Remington HV HP	1.90
5. PMC Sidewinder	1.28	**5.** Rem. Subsonic HP	1.95
6. Federal HV	1.28	**6.** Federal HV HP	2.01
7. CCI Std. Vel.	1.32	**7.** Win. T22 Target	2.02
8. Federal HV HP	1.35	**8.** Winchester Wildcat	2.02
9. CCI MiniMag	1.35	**9.** CCI MiniMag	2.08
10. CCI MiniMag HP	1.36	**10.** Winchester HV HP	2.10
11. PMC Zapper HP	1.41	**11.** Federal HV	2.15
12. Federal Lightning	1.43	**12.** CCI Std. Vel.	2.17
13. Fed. American Eagle	1.43	**13.** Fed. American Eagle	2.18
14. PMC Zapper	1.46	**14.** CCI Blazer	2.23
15. Rem. Cyclone HP	1.47	**15.** Win. Power Point HP	2.33
16. Win. Power Point HP	1.47	**16.** Remington HV	2.40
17. Win. T22 Target	1.50	**17.** Remington Cyclone HP	2.43
18. Rem. Subsonic HP	1.50	**18.** PMC Scoremaster	2.50
19. Win. HV HP	1.51	**19.** PMC Zapper HP	2.52
20. Remington Target	1.51	**20.** Remington Target	2.53
21. Remington HV H	1.55	**21.** Federal Lightning	2.55
22. Federal Target	1.68	**22.** PMC Zapper	2.58
23. Remington HV	1.75	**23.** PMC Sidewinder	2.63
24. Rem. Thunderbolt	1.80	**24.** Rem. Thunderbolt	3.15

1. Refer to text for specs on test firearms. **2.** All group size averages for test rifles are based on five 5-shot 50-yard groups fired from a solid benchrest. **3.** All group size averages for test handguns are based on five 5-shot 25-yard groups fired from a solid benchrest. **4.** Group sizes were measured to the nearest quarter-inch and averaged on a calculator. **5.** Cartridges with bullets of hollowpoint design are designated in the data tables with an "HP." **6.** Hollowpoint bullets have a nominal weight of between 36 and 40 grains, depending on manufacturer. Nominal muzzle velocities from rifles are in the range of 1255-1280 feet per second (fps), depending on manufacturer. **7.** All solid bullets weigh 40 grains, regardless of manufacturer. Those loaded to standard velocities have nominal rifle muzzle velocities in the range of 1070 -1150 fps, depending on manufacturer. **8.** An "HV" designation indicates a high-velocity loading; high-velocity solid bullet loads have nominal rifle muzzle velocities between 1250 and 1260 fps, depending on manufacturer. **9.** The Remington Subsonic cartridge is loaded with a 38-grain HP bullet and has a rifle muzzle velocity of 1050 fps. **10.** All test work was done over a period of several months with ambient temperatures varying from approximately 80º Fahrenheit to 100º Fahrenheit. **11.** Any group fired for record that included a known, shooter-induced "flyer" was eliminated from the data and re-fired before tabulation.

as well. Enough variables come into play with test work of this sort that results might be markedly different with the same ammunition in different firearms than those I used. They might be. As far as averages go, overall results with six other firearms should turn up figures relatively close to my own. Testing of this sort is not often done because it is very time-consuming, requires much measuring and note-taking–and one needs quite a pile of ammunition.

An interesting and beneficial part of this project was that the overall average group size recorded with the three rifles when using Winchester High Velocity 40-grain solid ammunition was 1.10 inches. Per table data, this was the most accurate in two of the three rifles. One of these just happened to be the Model 63 Winchester reproduction. This rifle, as one can glean from the tables, can hardly be called accurate, however. Regarding the three handguns, the same Winchester HV 40-grain solid again produced the best average group size: 1.83 inches at 25 yards.

With several different firearms and many different types of ammunition, I believe this to be more than mere coincidence. I am not touting this ammunition as having any mystical qualities, *BUT*— if I pulled six more guns and repeated this project, I would keep a close eye on the HV Winchester solids just to see if there was a repetition of the initial results. Perhaps this particular cartridge would be a good bet for initial testing of any 22 rimfire with an unproven (*unknown*) accuracy potential. Ultimately, this is information worth having. Other useful correlations can be made by studying the data tables. ●

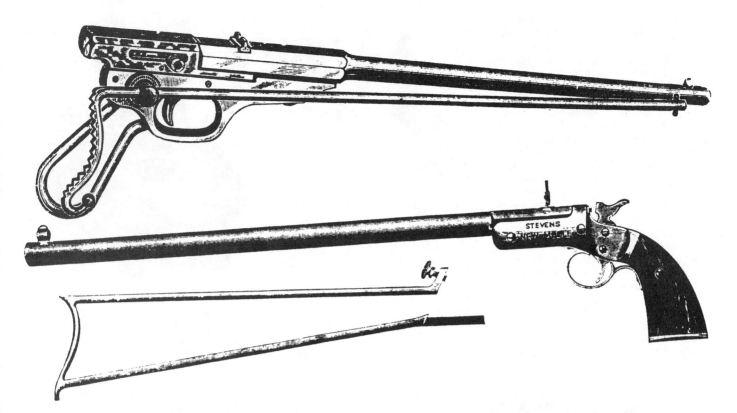

When Grandpa Walked Abroad

by Ralph Hurne

AS TOWNSHIPS BEGAN to spread around the turn of the last century and easy access to shooting country shrank, so did gun calibers of town and city shooters. The bigger game and opportunities got farther away. City crime, too, was getting more sophisticated.

Moreover, the day of the openly-carried six-shooter had already begun to wane, with smaller, lighter 38-caliber revolvers becoming more general in parts of the U.S., and even smaller guns in Europe. Yet, of course, men still liked to carry a gun, and a knife, to "*have something handy.*"

The convenient autoloading pistol era was only just beginning, with the 1900 Browning 32 ACP catching a lot of that market. So what best to slip into the pocket or bag, or attach to the bicycle? The absurdly-named Saturday Night Special revolver

Typical tip-up pistol fired 22 Shorts or CB caps.

was widespread, as were plenty of superior pocket revolvers – mostly 32s, with 22, 25, short 38s and 41 calibers comprising the balance.

Colt's New Line offering provided a good selection, S&W not offering quite the same array of calibers and sizes even though their 32s and 38s were justifiably popular, particularly their Lemon Squeezer and New Model 1 1/2. Pocket revolvers put out by Forehand & Wadsworth and Merwin Hulbert also found a niche in the

Above: Quackenbush (*top*) and Stevens New Model (*bottom*) pocket or bicycle rifles.

market, as did Remington's No. 3, 4 and Smoot models. In addition, imports from Britain and Europe were coming into America, helping to create a buyers' market. For years, makes like Tranter and the popular Webley Bulldog had been available.

Yet the day of the derringer had not diminished, the over/under 41 Remington was popular then and remained so for many years to come. Colt's neat No. 3 derringer was still widespread, the earlier and bulkier No. 1 and No. 2 rapidly finding their way to the back of a cupboard. Here again were many manufacturers, and what many of the derringers supplied was extreme smallness that few revolvers could match. The vast majority were 41 rimfire; 32, 30, and 22 calibers trailing. For some reason 38 caliber was ignored, although I would have thought the

38 Short a better choice than the puny 41. Although both had a 130-grain bullet, the 38 was pushed by 15-18 grains of blackpowder against the 41's 10-13 grains.

Although Frank Wesson's derringers started out as single-shot 22s, he moved into the two-shot world with a nice over/under line in both 22 and 32 calibers. The succeeding shot was obtained by hand-rotating the twin barrels. By 1870 he had broadened the offering to include 41RF. The Wesson "Fob Watch" was a small version of the 22, the name derived from the large aperture in the hammer spur whereby the pistol could be attached to a watch chain. Even more interesting are the Wessons which incorporate a small sliding blade alongside the barrels, pushed forward with the thumb to an 'open' position. The Marstons also utilized a sliding blade on their 3-shot superimposed derringers. On these, the hammer nose moved up

Cyclists' pocket revolvers in 5mm pinfire. Options included plain or checkered walnut grips, engraving, fitted case and nickel plate.

liked to have a gun handy in case he saw the chance of a possible shot, the detachable- or folding-stock pistol was the answer. Here Stevens monopolized the market, producing a wide choice… from the small to the large. Their only real challenge (*and not a strong one*) came from Wesson, although a few others ventured into this field, notably Quackenbush, Remington and Bay State.

Such was the craze for cycling at the close of the century and beyond

collector. The majority were Belgian-made and although cleverly disguised to a point where the gun function can't be detected, most were not of high quality. Some sticks, especially those with bit of a kick, often came with a detachable skeleton stock of wood or steel. Without a stock, the cane-gun fluttered between being a very long pistol or an unsteady longarm. But as extended range was never their intended role, either usage was sufficient to bowl a rabbit at 25 yards.

Noise could sometimes be a problem. The pneumatic air-cane overcame this snag even though the cane itself did not exactly resemble a *bona fide* walking stick, being rather on the fat side. I have seen one rifled cartridge cane-gun – and this was many years ago – which incorporated a silencer and was indistinguishable from an ordinary walking stick. Today's do-gooders would have a fit! Moreover, it had neat folding sights worked into the floral design-work and was chambered for the 230 Long Morris cartridge.

Out of sheer practicality cane-guns were never powerful, 20 and 28 bores being about the limit. Far more common and ideal is the .410 bore. Equally common were the 7mm, 9mm and 12mm centerfires for which special walking-stick cartridges were made. These were, of course, very mild. Other bores were the 9mm (no. 3) rimfires and the centerfire 360, shot or ball. The barrels were little more than a length of tubing sheathed in wood or leather, but they seemed sufficient to cope with the blackpowder charge. Usually a silver band, which turned and let a small trigger appear, or a stud trigger was exposed. A turn/twist-type of bolt action was the most common, although other clever mechanisms

Improved English Air Canes.

159.
161.
162.

Trade No.			Best Quality.	Second Quality.	Third Quality.	Fourth Quality.
*159.	**Air Cane,** with Rifle and Shot Barrels	each	210/-	170/-	128/-	114/-
160.	" " with Rifle or Smooth Bore Barrel for Shot	"	186/-	150/-	108/-	96/-
161.	" " with Rifle Barrel (Breech-loading)	"	206/-	162/-	120/-	110/-
*162.	**Bent Air Cane,** with Rifle and Shot Barrels to use from Shoulder	"	220/-	182/-	140/-	130/-
163.	" " " with Rifle Barrel (Breech-loading)	"	216/-	176/-	134/-	126/-

Brass Bullet Moulds, to cast 6 Bullets, 24/-; 4 Bullets, 15/-

* If Breech-loading, 20/- extra.

Prices include all accessories. Bore of rifle barrels are 140 (about), of the shot barrel 60 (about).

and down to discharge the shots; a neat *0-1-2-3* indicator on the right side let you know where you were.

The tiniest pistols were found among the single shots. Chambering them for 22 Shorts, makers such as Allen, Eclipse and Newbury produced them as "vest pocket" or "for ladies." Most were about four inches overall with 2-inch barrels, possibly the smallest being the Hopkins and Allen 'Baby,' which was still selling into the 1920s.

For the more sporting shooter who did not necessarily want to carry a light rifle or shotgun, but

that the "bicycle rifle" became accepted. Special leather or canvas carriers were made to fit the bicycle frame so the rider could carry the gun. A distant jackrabbit would give the rider chance to 'snap the firearm ready' and try his hand at stalking.

While not so widespread as in Europe and Britain, the walking-stick gun must have had its adherents in the U. S. because the Remington walking-stick gun presumably sold quite well. And doubtless many made outside the U. S. found their way into the country, today providing an interesting subject for the

were employed. Those with fancy handles of stag or ivory were most attractive.

A sturdier variety was also widespread, made entirely of steel and painted, blued or japanned. Often in .410, but invariably in 28 or 20 bore; mostly with attachable stocks. These were practical shotguns, yet — strangely — ones in 22 rimfire are rare.

Pneumatic canes held the compressed air either in the hollow rear portion or in an attachable steel ball beneath the action. The stock or ball was unscrewed, and then screwed into a foot pump supplied with the gun. The hopeful shooter then exhausted himself and ruined his back putting enough air in to reach a pressure level that can be described as '*dangerous*.' However, because of the better quality of these arms, bursts were rare. Usually, air-canes were cocked by inserting a key into the action and turning it. Again the trigger was simply a pop-out stud. When pressed, it released a "firing pin" to touch the valve and release a stab of pent-up pressure sufficient to drive the projectile; something like touching the valve stem of a fully-inflated car tire. On a 'full pump' the power was considerable, sufficient shatter a ball to pieces. As the air pressure got used from successive shots, so the velocity weakened and the trajectory got steeper. But many shots could be fired before this happened. Pneumatic guns were silent, accurate, recoil-less, powerful and clean—and only axed by various law changes when interesting possibilities were seen for knocking off some passing dignitary. When some were used by Austrians against Napoleon they were seen a secret weapon and captured sharpshooters were harshly dealt with.

Thick-gauge steel was needed to withstand the air pressure, resulting in air-canes being heavy and less slender. With the gun (with polygroove rifling) came the pump and bullet mould, generally around 32 caliber. Some were breech-loading, some muzzle-loading, and an additional smoothbore insert could be had. The sights were very small and fixed, a U-rear and a 'button' front. Prominent English makers made most of them. Ones with a bend in them to give the shooter the feel of a stock are sometimes encountered.

Perhaps the most bizarre walking-stick gun was one that had no firing mechanism, as such. It loaded in the normal way, with a bolt-action twist. However, the rear half was simply a hollow tube that housed a floating striker. The top

Walking Stick Guns.
Breech-Loading.

Trade No.			Each
145.	**Malacca Cane covered**, gun metal barrel, steel chamber, crooked handle, 7 mm.	.. .. ..	£1 5 6
147.	**Malacca Cane covered**, steel barrel, horn handle, secret trigger, 7 mm. ..	.. ..	£1 12 0
148.	,, ,, ,, steel barrel, black horn handle, 9 mm., secret trigger	..	£1 17 0
149.	,, ,, ,, steel barrel, black handle, 410 bore, secret trigger	.. ..	£2 4 0
151.	**Malacca covered**, dismounting action, Irish horn handle, 410 bore	.. ..	£2 14 0
152.	**Selected Irish horn Handle**, secret trigger, picked Malacca cane, 9 mm.	.. ..	£2 14 0
144.	**Malacca covered**, dismounting action, invisible trigger, fine quality, 410 bore	.. ..	£3 6 0
153.	**Original English make**, black steel barrels, with safety bolt and attachable stock, 410 bore	..	£4 0 0
154.	As above in 28 bore	.. ..	£5 0 0
155.	,, in 20 bore	.. .. ..	£5 10 0

Walking Stick Gun Parts :—
Ferrules—7 mm., 9 mm., and 12 mm. £0 2 0
Black Horn Handles—7 mm., **3/4** ; 9 mm., **4/-** ; 12 mm., **5/-** each.

Walking-Stick Gun Metallic Cartridges.

7 mm. 9 mm. 12 mm. 12 mm.

		Per 1,00
Gauge 7 mm. **Ball** in Boxes of 50		£2 6
Shot ,, ,, ...		£3 0
Gauge 9 mm. **Ball** ,, ,, ...		£3 5
Shot ,, ,, ...		£4 0
Gauge 12 mm. **Ball** ,, ,, ...		£3 10
Shot ,, ...		£4 0

The embossed sheaths on these Sheffield-made daggers were made of a hard card material covered with a thin leather veneer. Tips and throats of coin silver, stud for attachment to a belt frog (seldom used). Their fragility prompted many owners to employ a saddlemaker to enclose the embossed work inside a strong leather outer sheath.

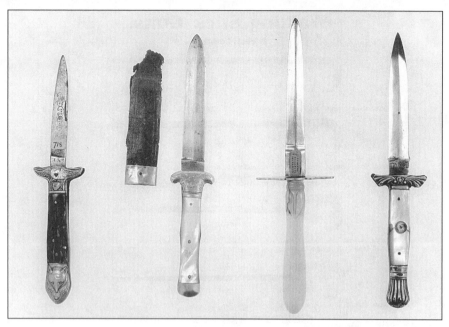

Mid-nineteenth century daggers. A handy concealable defense in settled communities; they often replaced larger, heavier knives carried in wilder areas as the efficient cartridge revolver replaces slow-loading percussion pistols. Blade lengths generally ran 5 to 6 inches.

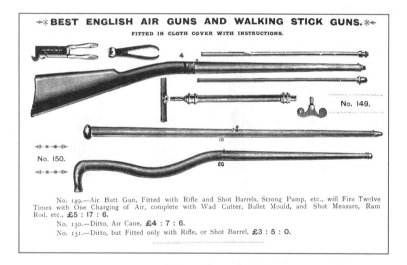

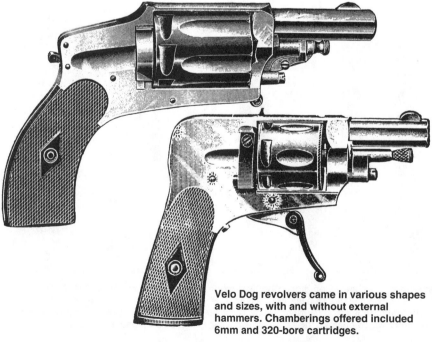

Velo Dog revolvers came in various shapes and sizes, with and without external hammers. Chamberings offered included 6mm and 320-bore cartridges.

portion of the silver knob handle unscrewed to expose a trombone-like mouthpiece. Once the cartridge was in place, you tilted the stick so that the striker fell to the rear. To fire, you blew hard into the mouthpiece, sending the striker zooming up to hit the primer. A dentist's dream gun, surely?

Many a grandpa must have carried a knife also. Just as the big bowie got smaller with the advent of the cartridge six-gun, the knife also came down in size. In the period covered here it was mainly the dirk or dagger that predominated, along with the locking folder. A photo exists of a group of Texas Rangers in 1887, still with holstered six-guns, yet all visible knives a dirk, not bowies.

The knife-pistol survived the percussion era well into the rimfire world, Unwin & Rogers being the chief manufacturer. Interesting they may be, yet neither the pistol role nor the knife function were very impressive as defense weapon. And for their bulk/weight a smaller, lighter revolver would seem a much better defense proposition.

With the coming of the larger areas of habitation came the curse of the fierce, wandering dog, showing a particular taste for the passing cyclist. This problem must have reached sufficient proportion to cause manufacturers to produce a surprisingly larger numbers of cartridges for the Velo Dog revolver. Even today these little handguns appear regularly on the market. S&W themselves put out a 2-inch barrel model in their break-open line, naming it a cyclists' revolver.

Using a long 5.5mm (5.75-inch) centerfire case and jacketed 43-grain bullet coming out the business end at 672 fps, it had no real advantage over the standard 22 rimfire.

Some of these Velo Dogs had outside or shrouded hammers, but mostly concealed-hammer models were typical. Their function was simply to carry in the pocket and, if attacked by a Baskerville look-alike, to grab and fire double action before the rabid beast sent you on your way looking like the phantom of the opera. With no trigger guard and a folding trigger, even a gloved hand could quickly get off a couple of shots – pronto. Fiocchi, whom may the gods preserve, still makes the ammunition.

Such was the problem that a European maker put out a 5mm pinfire or 22 rimfire in the shape of a handlebar grip so that the weapon could be jerked free for immediate use.

All a far cry from today's pocket blasters!

TURKEY RIFLES

Past

and Present

by Steve Gash

TURKEY HUNTING HAS almost gained the status of a religion these days. Specialized shotguns abound – from models Whelen with stubby, ported barrels to those covered with special camo finishes that match the terrain, almost by state. Calls, decoys, and other gear approach the sublime. Turkey hunters attend seminars and study the birds like grad students. State game departments cater to the hunter with Spring and (*sometimes*) Fall seasons. Small wonder. Turkeys are all over the place. They're fun to hunt, and they're tasty.

But one subject that doesn't get a lot of press these days is the turkey rifle. Rifle, you say? You bet!

In the wide-open spaces of the American West, turkeys are really "big game birds," so hunting them

Above, the Savage M-219B in 22 Hornet (*top*). After 45 years of service, it will still do the job. Below it, the Ruger M-77/22VHZ in 22 Hornet with 6x Tasco WC scope.

like big game seems appropriate. Rifles are legal for turkeys in several western states. I hunted the wily birds with a rifle many years ago in Colorado and Wyoming, with varying degrees of success.

The hunter can take a couple of approaches to the turkey rifle. One is to use a (*relatively*) high-powered rimfire round. The other is to load down a centerfire rifle so as to not tear up much meat. This approach utilizes an expanding or FMJ bullet with a reduced powder charge for a low velocity. Let's take a look at the possibilities.

22 Winchester Magnum Rimfire (WMR)

The standard turkey rimfire rifle for the last 40 years has been the 22 Winchester Magnum Rimfire (WMR). With 40- or 50-grain hunting bullets to choose from, in either FMJ or HP styles, the round is plenty of medicine for turkey within its range, about 100 yards or so. The 40-grain bullets are usually listed by the factories at 1910 fps, but CCI's 40-grain HP ammo chronographed 1799 fps out of my Marlin M-783. The Federal 50-grain JHP is my favorite 22 WMR load. It is listed at 1650, and clocks 1554 in the Marlin. I have never plugged a turkey with a 22 WMR, but enough people have to prove its worth as a viable gobbler-getter.

5mm Remington Rimfire Magnum

There was another rimfire alternative in years past, one with which I actually harvested two Wyoming turkeys. This was the 5mm Remington Rimfire Magnum (RFM).

Announced by Remington in 1969, but not actually available until 1970, the 5mm RFM was produced in the M-591 (box magazine) and M-592 (tubular magazine) bolt-action rifles. The cartridge was a cute little bottleneck number with an odd .2045-inch bore. The round had impressive ballistics. In order to pump up the velocity, the bullet weight was lowered to 38 grains, from the then-standard 22 WMR weight of 40 grains. The little 5mm hollowpoint zipped right along at a cataloged velocity of 2100 fps, or a bit faster than the 22 WMR. The smaller-diameter bullet had a little better sectional density, too. This, and the higher velocity, flattened the trajectory somewhat. These facts were not lost on the marketing folks, of course.

The Remington M-591 and M-592 rifles were themselves unique. The action was a multi-lug design, similar to the firm's M-788 centerfire rifle, which was noted for its strength and accuracy. The rifles were consequently very strong for a rimfire, as required by the high-pressure 5mm RFM cartridge.

Because of the much higher pressures of the 5mm RFM, the rifle's extractors were not made with the usual angled cut into the side of the barrel at the chamber. Instead, the extractor was a piece of spring-steel attached to the outside of the bolt that cammed out from the side of the chamber as the bolt was closed. This left a solid ring of steel around the chamber. Then, as the bolt was opened, the extractor hook moved in and (*hopefully*) grabbed onto the cartridge rim, and pulled the case from the chamber.

The extractors were prone to breakage, and the fired cartridges sometimes stuck, so a functional extractor – or a cleaning rod with which to poke out the empties – was a must. While this design left no cutout in the side of the chamber, it also led to some problems.

As I mentioned, I took two gobblers in successive years in Wyoming with a 5mm RFM. Each bird took two shots. On each bird, the spring-steel extractor on my M-591 broke on the second shot, and rendered the rifle inoperable. Fortunately, the birds in each case were in the bag. I soon tired of this malady, and sold my M-591 rifle and remaining ammo to a 5mm aficionado in Texas. I hope they're happy together.

The 5mm RFM did not exactly set the sales charts on fire. Only about 27,000 M-591s and 25,000 M-592s were made, and the rifles were discontinued in 1974. Ammunition was produced for a few years longer; it is listed in the 1983 GUN DIGEST, but not in the 1984 edition. The discontinuance of the non-reloadable rimfire ammo did not endear Remington to the 52,000 or so customers who had bought their rifles, and at the time elicited a hue and cry from the masses. But to no avail. The late Frank C. Barnes noted that "The 5mm RFM is another good idea that didn't catch on." No kidding.

On the centerfire front, there is a plethora of fine choices. I will discuss the basic parameters, which are the same. The reloader can easily adapt the principles to another cartridge. The earlier editions of the Speer and Hornady loading manuals have reduced loads for many cartridges with appropriate bullets.

22 Hornet

The venerable Hornet is almost a perfect turkey cartridge as-is, and really doesn't need to be loaded down. About all that is required is to find an accurate load, and stick with it.

In years past, I used a Savage M-219B single-shot 22 Hornet with factory 45-grain loads at 2677 fps. This combination worked, but bullet performance left something to be desired. The factory 45-grain loads are excellent groundhog-getters out to about 150 yards, but to me always seemed a little too explosive on edible critters. This problem can be easily solved by handloading, however.

Nowadays, my working Hornet is a Ruger M-77/22VHZ. In it I use Sierra 40-grain high-velocity HP bullets (#1385) over 12.0 grains of

Effective turkey cartridges, with their bullets (*from left*): 22 Hornet with 45-grain factory load and 40-grain Sierra HP, 222 Remington with 55-grain Speer FMJ, and 220 Slow with 50-grain Sierra SP.

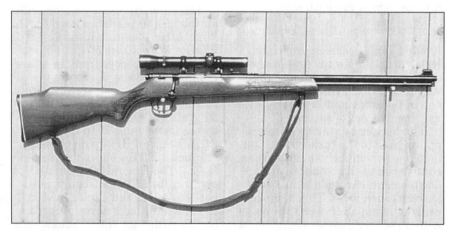

The rimfire leader in turkey armament – Marlin M-783 in 22 Winchester Magnum Rimfire with Weaver K-3 scope.

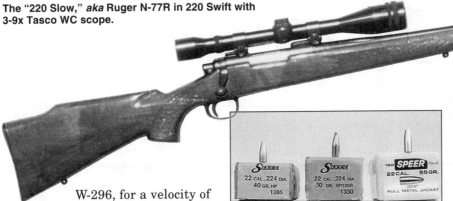

The "220 Slow," *aka* Ruger N-77R in 220 Swift with 3-9x Tasco WC scope.

W-296, for a velocity of 2920 fps. Sierra notes in its loading manual that this bullet is designed to withstand 4000 fps velocity. At Hornet velocities, this tough little pill just bores through a turkey's wing-butts with little meat damage. Absent a FMJ bullet in a weight suitable for the Hornet, this is about as good as it gets for the old round.

222 Remington

I have always had a soft spot for the 222 Remington. Introduced in 1950, it reigned supreme on the benchrest circuit until the PPC cartridges arrived. The 222 is still a

Suitable turkey bullets include (*from left*): the Sierra 40-grain HP, Sierra 50-grain SP, and the Speer 55-grain FMJ.

terrific little cartridge, despite the inroads made by the omnipresent 223 Remington. I bought a M-700 ADL in 222 back in 1979. It is extremely accurate. (*As an aside, I have a SAKO 6PPC-USA single shot with a 24x benchrest scope on it. On a good day, it will sometimes outshoot the old 222.*)

For years, Speer made a 22-caliber 55-grain FMJ bullet (#1045).

This bullet is not listed in the latest Speer bullet catalog, nor are data for it to be found in the *No. 13 Speer Manual.* Older editions have loading data for it, however. I tried various military-style 55-grain FMJ-BT bullets designed for 223 semi-autos, and even the 50-grain Remington FMJ, but I could never get the accuracy necessary in my rifles for the precise bullet placement required for successful rifle turkey hunting. Speer currently lists two 22-caliber FMJ bullets — a 55-grain (#1044) and a 62-grain (#1050). Both are boattail designs with a cannelure. Hornady also offers a 55-grain FMJ-BT (#2267). One of these FMJ bullets might work just fine in your rifles. Try 'em. I have never tried loading the 40-grain Sierra HP bullet down to sedate velocities in the larger 22 centerfires, but if the accuracy is there, I'm sure that it would be as effective in them as it is in the 22 Hornet.

The Speer 55-grain #1045 bullet is perfect for turkeys. In the M-700

Table 1. Turkey Rifle Loads

Cartridge	Rifle	Barrel Length	Bullet Weight, Brand & Type		Powder Number	Powder Charge	Vel.
22 Win. Mag. RF	Marlin M-783	22	40-grain CCI HP		factory	load	1799
			50-grain Fed. HP		factory	load	1554
5mm Rem. Mag.	Remington M-591	24	38-grain Rem. HP		factory	load	2100*
22 Hornet	Savage M-219B	26	45-grain Peters HP		factory	load	2677
	Ruger M-77/22VHZ	24	40-grain Sierra HP		W-296	12.0	2920
222 Remington	Remington M-700	24	55-grain Speer FMJ		SR-4759	8.8	1768
220 Slow	Ruger M-77R	24	50-grain Sierra SP		H-4227	12.0	1850
			50-grain Rem. FMJ		SR-4759	12.0	1697
					H-4227	12.0	1840
			55-grain Speer FMJ		H-4227	12.0	1911
					SR-4759	12.0	1956
					SR-4759	13.0	2034
			55-grain Hor. FMJBT		H-4227	12.0	1862
					SR-4759	13.0	2023
243 Winchester	Win. M-70 (1)	22	80-grain Hor. FMJ		SR-4759	16.8	2100
	Ruger M-77R (2)		90-grain Speer FMJ		IMR-4198	17.0	1766
6mm Remington	Rem. M-700 (1)	22	80-grain	Hor. FMJ	SR-4759	19.4	2100
	Rem. M-700 (2)		90-grain	Speer FMJ	IMR-4198	17.0	1770

*factory published velocity

(1) Hornady Handbook Third Edition data

(2) Speer Reloading Manual No. 11 data

Remington M-700ADL in 222 Remington with vintage Weaver K8 scope.

222, I use 8.8 grains of SR-4759 for a velocity of 1768 fps. It groups into about 0.5-inch at 100 yards. This load would, of course, be a snap to duplicate in the ubiquitous 223 Remington. I hunted turkeys with this 222 load in the M-700 in Wyoming for a number of years, but the bullet and a turkey never connected, at least from this rifle.

One year, I used a then-new Valmet M-412 over/under combination gun with a 12-gauge barrel on top, and a 222 on the bottom. I mounted a 2.5x Bushnell scope on the gun. It was, I surmised, the perfect turkey rig.

My hunting partner and I huffed and puffed up Wyoming hill after Wyoming hill. Eventually, we spied a flock of turkeys in a sage-covered draw, and the stalk was on. Finally, a reasonable shot presented itself, and I took a crack at a big turkey at about 100 yards. After I shot, the turkey just stood there, unconcerned. He then walked around in a circle a couple of times, and nonchalantly strolled off. I was sure that I'd I missed. But I proceeded slowly and quietly after him through the waist-high sagebrush. Suddenly, at about 20 yards, a red head popped up out of the sage. I don't know which one of us was more startled. A load of magnum #2s from the upper Valmet barrel finished the job. Upon inspection, I discovered the 222 bullet had only lightly nicked the bird in the tail; I used to cut myself worst than that shaving. Not exactly an awe-inspiring performance. But I did get a Wyoming gobbler with this bullet with a rifle of another chambering – a 220 Swift.

220 Swift

Now, before you get all lathered up, and scoff at the use of the premier varmint cartridge on turkeys,

let me explain. I have two 220 Swifts. One is a Ruger 1973 flat-bolt M-77V heavy-barrel that is loaded to the gills for various varmints. The other is a 1989-vintage Ruger M-77 sporter in which I use reduced loads. Thus, I refer to it as my "220 Slow" and have worked up two loads for it.

My favorite load is 12.0 grains of H-4227 and the 50-grain Sierra SP bullet (#1330). Sierra describes this bullet as a "high-velocity spitzer," and it is certainly tough enough for this application. This load groups under an inch at 100 yards. With a velocity of 1850 fps, it is nigh on to perfect. As with the 40-grain Sierra HP, there is just enough expansion to do the job. I can highly recommend this load.

Another good "220 Slow" load is the same powder charge under the aforementioned Speer 55-grain FMJ bullet. This gives a velocity of 1911 fps, groups consistently into less than one inch at 100 yards, and drops turkeys like a rock – without much meat damage. I also tried 12.0 grains of SR-4759 for a velocity of 1956 fps. While a good load, in my 220 Slow it just didn't measure up to the accuracy of the H-4227 load. Of course, loads of these levels could easily be developed for the wonderful 22-250 Remington or a similar cartridge.

The 6 Millimeter Cartridges

Famed gunwriter Layne Simpson, whose work graces these pages, once wrote a magazine article entitled (*I think*) "The 6mms - Good For Varmints, Good For Deer, Good For Nothing?" I am definitely in the last category of opinion when it comes to the 24-bores, having always preferred the 250 Savage and 257 Roberts as a "small-medium" bore rifle. Oh, I have owned several 6mms, but none of them found a permanent

place in either my heart or gun safe. But since the 6mms are so popular, it is only fitting that we include turkey loads for them, too.

The 243 Winchester was introduced in 1955 and has become, by far, the most popular round in its class. Along with the 6mm Remington, they pretty much have the 24-caliber market cornered. Hornady makes an 6mm 80-grain FMJ bullet (#2430). In the 243, their lightest load is 16.8 grains of SR-4759 for a velocity of 2100 fps. Switching to the 6mm Remington, it takes 19.4 grains of the same powder to give 2100 fps. At these relatively sedate velocities, both should make a fine turkey load.

Speer's 6mm FMJ weighs 90 grains. I have used this bullet in various 6mm Remingtons, and it was plenty accurate, even at low velocities. Speer's lowest-velocity load for the 243 is 17.0 grains of IMR-4198 for a velocity of 1766 fps. For the 6mm Remington, the same 17.0-grain charge gives 1770 fps.

With the 22 and 6mm loads of this power class, a shot at the wing-butts misses the breast and is essentially a "lung shot" on the big birds. At the hit, the birds usually waddle off a few paces, and pitch beak down into the dirt. I have never had one fly off. As for trajectories of these loads, they are all pretty similar. With a 100-yard zero, the bullet is about 1.3 inches high at 50 yards, making precise hits at intermediate ranges relatively easy. Check out your load at the range to be sure.

Hunting turkeys with this rifle isn't for everyone; the shotgun purists are probably offended. It is not legal in all states – check your state game laws – but the technique will certainly add some spice to your days afield and, just maybe, put a roast turkey on the table. ●

Issue 45s
of the
Twentieth Century

By John L. Marshall

IN THE TWENTIETH century, one handgun caliber was the *AMERICAN* caliber, and it served our United States armed forces well throughout the century. Having their origins in the nineteenth century and extending the tradition into the twenty-first, handguns with a bore diameter of 0.45-inch have consistently been favored by our armed forces.

The beginnings of our 45-caliber legacy came about in the early 1870s, when the Model 1873 Colt Single Action Army was adopted as our standard service handgun. It was chambered for the new and soon-to-be-legendary 45 Colt cartridge. It was quickly appreciated that the big gun and its massive cartridge made a man-stopping combination that got the job done with dispatch. A slightly shortened version of the cartridge was used in the Smith & Wesson "Schofield" revolver, and this modified cartridge could also be used in the Colt revolvers. Soon, the 45 caliber became popular in the civilian sector as well, and many 45 Colt and S&W revolvers were sold to those desiring an argument-stopping means of personal protection.

However, in the waning years of the 1800s, the U.S. armed services took a step backward and adopted a 38-caliber cartridge, chambered in double-action Colt and Smith & Wesson revolvers. While the new round had less recoil and allowed more ammo to be carried, it came up lacking as a man-stopper. This prompted many in the service to insist upon personal retention of the old single-action 45s when doing battle. This was common during the Spanish-American War, and even though supposedly "obsolete,"

the 45 single-action saw service and acquitted itself well.

As the twentieth century dawned, our troops in the Philippines soon learned anew that a 38-caliber handgun was far short of what was required. Drug-crazed Moro warriors would bind themselves with rags that acted as before-the-fact tourniquets, and charge the American lines wielding their fierce kris knives, bolos and machetes. Even the 30-caliber Krag-Jorgensen rifles would often fail to down these fanatical assailants. But the old 45-caliber 1873 revolvers seemed to be in a class apart for close-in efficiency, and soon the cry arose: *"Give us back our 45s!"*

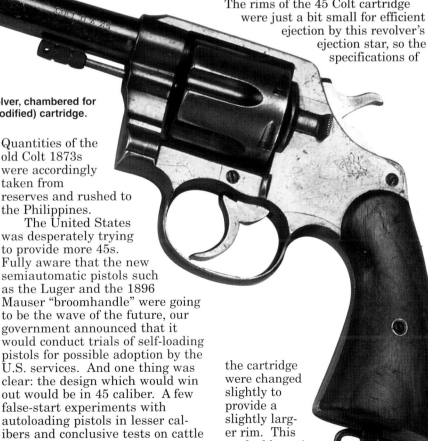

1909 Colt revolver, chambered for the 45 Colt (modified) cartridge.

Quantities of the old Colt 1873s were accordingly taken from reserves and rushed to the Philippines.

The United States was desperately trying to provide more 45s. Fully aware that the new semiautomatic pistols such as the Luger and the 1896 Mauser "broomhandle" were going to be the wave of the future, our government announced that it would conduct trials of self-loading pistols for possible adoption by the U.S. services. And one thing was clear: the design which would win out would be in 45 caliber. A few false-start experiments with autoloading pistols in lesser calibers and conclusive tests on cattle and cadavers showed that larger was better. The 45 caliber was

deemed optimally effective for both power and the ability of its user to control it.

Still, until a new 45-autoloading pistol could be adopted, something had to be done to fill the immediate need for a more modern man-stopping handgun for the troops. And thus was born the first 45-caliber service handgun of the twentieth century.

The Model 1909 Colt Revolver

The U.S. government put out an emergency call for a large double-action revolver chambered for the 45 Colt cartridge that had served so well in the past. Colt's responded with its new "New Service" revolver. The rims of the 45 Colt cartridge were just a bit small for efficient ejection by this revolver's ejection star, so the specifications of the cartridge were changed slightly to provide a slightly larger rim. This worked beautifully, and the new revolver and modified cartridge was soon in production and being sent to the needy troops. The larger-rimmed cartridge could not be used in the older 1873 revolvers, but the small-rimmed variety could be used in both, so the original version "stuck" and is the standard round today. The large-rimmed 45 Colt cartridge is a collector's item today.

The big revolver was indeed impressive. It measured 10.75 inches in length. The double-action mechanism allowed for a "panic" double-action close-range shot, or a more precise thumb-cocked single-action shot at longer range. The newer swing-out cylinder design allowed for simultaneous ejection of the fired cases, something the old 1873 Colt could not do. Its solid frame was superior in strength to the break-open design of the Schofield revolver. It was blued, with the hammer left "in the bright." The stocks were of smooth walnut, and the butt was equipped with a lanyard ring. The 5.5-inch barrel was topped with a "shark fin" front sight, and it was the same diameter throughout from the muzzle right up to the frame. The rear sight was a groove cut in the top-strap. Colt serial numbers were on the butt, the crane and the frame for all U.S. Army models. These were also marked "U.S. ARMY MODEL 1909" on the butt. On guns made for the Navy and Marines, the Colt serial number will be found on the crane and frame only. For these handguns, special serial numbers were placed on the butt: "USN 1" to "USN 1000" and "USMC 1" to "USMC 1,300." The initials of Rinaldo A. Carr (R.A.C.), the Colt's company ordnance sub-inspector, were placed on the right side above the grip on all variations.

With production beginning in 1909 and continuing through 1911, the big Colt was a hot item and almost all of the production run of nearly 22,000 handguns went directly to the Philippines for service. The Model 1909 was immensely popular with the troops, and gave the fine service its reliable action and proven cartridge promised. It became the new standard for a service handgun. The troops finally had a handgun they could swear by instead of swear at!

From 11:30 o'clock, clockwise: 1909 Colt, 1911 Colt, 1911 Springfield Armory, 1911 Remington-UMC, 1917 Colt, 1917 Smith & Wesson, 1911 A.J. Savage-Slide rework, 1911A1 Colt, 1911A1 Union Switch & Signal, 1911A1 Remington-Rand, 1911A1 Ithaca, Mark 23 SOCOM, and *(center)* the F.P. 45 "Liberator."

A group of 1911 pistols with an original 1913 swivel holster, web belt and magazine pouch. *Upper left:* Colt. *Upper right:* Springfield Armory. *Lower left:* Remington-UMC. *Lower right:* A.J. Savage-slide rework.

Because nearly all Model 1909s went straight to overseas service, finding a good specimen for a collection today can be difficult. Most saw extensive service in a humid and harsh climate, and most were never rotated home to the U.S. Many saw service as late as WWII, and quite a few were lost in the Japanese occupation of the Philippines during that fracas. So a reasonable-condition Model 1909 is a prize in any U.S. service handgun collection. It was the first 45-caliber handgun to be adopted by our services in the twentieth century, and as such is the "granddaddy" of all the 45s to follow.

As good a handgun as it was, the Model 1909's official service life was brief. Beginning in the early part of the twentieth century, a savvy Utah gunsmith was experimenting with self-loading pistol designs. In 1905, Colt's Patent Firearms Mfg. Co. put his first 45-caliber design into production. Enter John Moses Browning and the beginning of a handgun legend.

The Model 1911 Colt semiautomatic pistol

John Browning was an acknowledged genius. Let's just start with that. He, in partnership with Colt's, had designed and

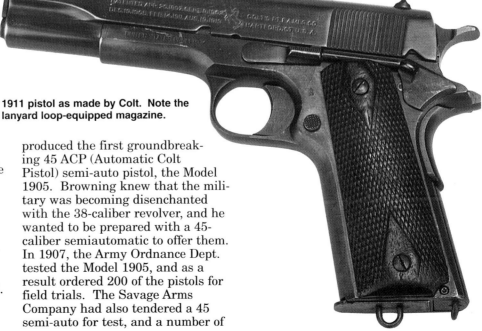

1911 pistol as made by Colt. Note the lanyard loop-equipped magazine.

produced the first groundbreaking 45 ACP (Automatic Colt Pistol) semi-auto pistol, the Model 1905. Browning knew that the military was becoming disenchanted with the 38-caliber revolver, and he wanted to be prepared with a 45-caliber semiautomatic to offer them. In 1907, the Army Ordnance Dept. tested the Model 1905, and as a result ordered 200 of the pistols for field trials. The Savage Arms Company had also tendered a 45 semi-auto for test, and a number of

these pistols were also ordered for field trials. The Colt 45s, unfortunately, did not fare well, suffering jams and parts breakage during the trials. One soldier testing the arm was even struck by a slide that had flown off the frame of the pistol he was shooting! The silver lining to this cloud over the Colt was that the Savage pistols also performed poorly. Soldiers shooting the Savages apparently didn't like them much. They complained of heavy recoil, frequent parts breakage, and constant jams. Many of the Savage pistols dumped their magazines when the pistols were fired.

Browning went to work improving his basic pistol. In August of 1909, his improved 45 semi-auto design had shown great promise, and a very small number of pilot-series pistols was manufactured. Some of these pistols hit the road with Colt's Vice President Frank Nichols and Colt's marksman Gus Reising. Together, these two men visited a number of Army posts and demonstrated the improved pistol to Army officers. They hoped to counter the bad publicity generated by earlier field trials. In this, they were successful. The 1909 prototype was a hit with the officers to whom it was demonstrated. Most of them became converts to and champions of the pistol within the Army. Lt. Col. John T. Thompson (*later the father of the Thompson submachine gun*) was so impressed with these pistols that he

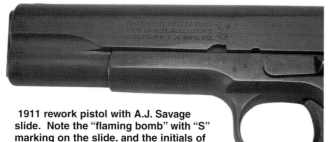

1911 pistol as made by Springfield Armory.

set up special tests at Springfield Armory to see if they could be further improved upon. These special tests were, in effect, dress rehearsals for the official Army trials of 1910.

1911 rework pistol with A.J. Savage slide. Note the "flaming bomb" with "S" marking on the slide, and the initials of the rework facility, Augusta Arsenal, in front of the slide stop on the frame.

In November of 1910, yet another improved Browning/Colt prototype, forged as a result of the unofficial tests at Springfield Armory, was entered in the official Army trials. Its main competitor was another entry from Savage. The Colt bore a remarkable likeness to the eventual Model 1911 in almost all respects, and had the features desired by both infantry and cavalry, such as a manual safety and a grip safety. However, when the firing stopped, neither the Colt nor the Savage got approval. Reliability of both the pistols was still not satisfactory. While the Colt malfunctioned less

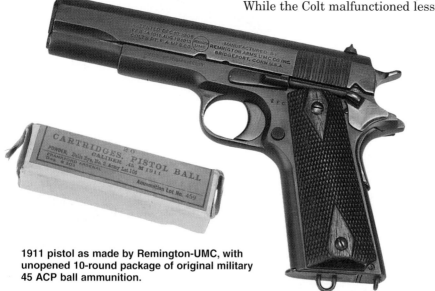

1911 pistol as made by Remington-UMC, with unopened 10-round package of original military 45 ACP ball ammunition.

often than the Savage, some metal fatigue cracks in the barrel and frame were induced under extended test firing. The Army Chief of Ordnance, General William Crozier, told Colt's president that except for those cracks, the gun might have succeeded in being adopted as the new Army sidearm.

Disappointed but at the same time encouraged, John Browning went back to the drawing board at Colt's and worked feverishly to improve what was already an impressively promising design. A new round of tests was scheduled for March 1911, and Savage was also working around the clock to prepare.

What came out of this redesign effort at Colt's was the "Model of 1911 Special Army." Approximately 15 pistols were produced under the watchful eye of John Browning himself, and he wanted them to be the most flawless and perfect 45-caliber pistols possible. In tests within Colt's, Browning picked one pistol out of the initial six made as the most reliable of all available. This was the gun that could win all the marbles for Colt's.

The rest, as they say, is history. That pistol, in the March, 1911 tests, fired 6,000 full-power loads without a malfunction of any kind. Browning and the people at Colt's were jubilant. On March 28, 1911, the word went forth: The U.S. Army had formally adopted the Colt

A 1917 Colt on the left, and a 1917 Smith & Wesson on the right. Note the WWI issue half-moon clip pouch, which held 18 rounds of 45 ACP ammo in clips. Note also the clips with ammo inserted.

Model 1911 semiautomatic pistol. Colt's was awarded a contract for 31,344 pistols. The income from that contract was to equal more than one-third of the company's revenues in the previous year!

The Model 1911 became the standard by which all combat pistols came to be eventually judged. Its configuration is familiar to all. It is a big locked-breech recoil-operated pistol, nine inches long, with a 5-inch barrel. Its magazine holds 7 rounds, and the gun propels a 230-grain full-metal-jacketed projectile at about 830 feet per second. A single-action design, it must be thumb-cocked (or slide-cocked) for the first shot. A manual safety blocks the sear, and a grip safety blocks the trigger. The swinging-link drop-barrel unlocking system designed by Browning is widely copied in principle even today. It has a positive disconnector that prevents more than one shot per trigger pull, and a "floating" firing pin shorter than its channel that must be struck a positive blow by the hammer to inertially hit the primer of the cartridge in the chamber. The slide locks back on the last shot, indicating the need to reload with a fresh magazine. The grip angle and circumference have been praised as being "just right" for most people. Model 1911s were blued, and sported the beautiful and now traditional "double diamond" checkered grips. Initial pistols were equipped with magazines that featured a lanyard loop, although this nicety was later dropped in favor of a flat-bottomed design. The pistol itself had a lanyard loop at the bottom of the flat-style mainspring housing. Parkerized 1911s are often encountered today. Typically, these are arms that were reconditioned and upgraded when pressed into service during WWII, and are usually marked with the initials of the reworking arsenal. The Parkerizing finish is the result of a process that leaves a distinctive non-reflecting matte gray, black or gray-green appearance on the firearm. It resists rust far better than the earlier bluing. No 1911s were ever originally manufactured with this finish, however.

The Model 1911 saw service in the Punitive Expedition to Mexico in 1916 commanded by General John Pershing, and was the standard handgun of our services during WWI. It figured in numerous exploits during the war in the hands of such men as Medal of Honor winners Cpl. Alvin York and Lt. Frank Luke Jr. Corporal York's marksmanship with both pistol and rifle was exemplary against the enemy, and he was proud to herd a large number of German prisoners back to our lines single-handedly, keeping his big Colt trained on them for insurance. Lieutenant Luke, the Arizona "Balloon Buster" ace aviator, was shot up by ground fire after having a field day in the air and was forced to land his Spad behind enemy lines. He refused to

1917 S&W revolver, with clip pouch and ammo on half-moon clip.

1917 Colt revolver, with two half-moon clips holding 45 ACP ammo.

be captured and died blazing away at his antagonists with his only personal armament, a Model 1911. He was given a solemn soldier's burial by the Germans in honor of his exceptional spirit and bravery.

In addition to being made by Colt's, the Model 1911 was produced by Springfield Armory *(the government arsenal, not the modern commercial facility)*, and Remington-UMC. A contract was let to North American Arms in Canada during WWI, but only a few pistols were produced and none were accepted in the service. A.J. Savage also got a WWI contract, but no pistols were produced. A number of slides bearing an "S" within an ordnance bomb as a marking are believed to have been produced by A.J. Savage. Arsenal-reworked pistols utilizing these slides, usually on Colt frames, are known to exist and are quite collectable. Good examples of Model 1911s as made before and during WWI are prized collector's items today, with those made by Springfield and Remington-UMC meriting a premium based on their lower production totals.

The Model 1917 Colt Revolver

As America entered WWI in 1917, it was obvious that the number of Model 1911 pistols being produced was not going to be enough to satisfy the ravenous demand of our troops for sidearms. Interestingly, Colt's still retained the tooling for the New Service

Model of 1909 revolver, and without too much trouble could adapt that revolver for the now standard 45 ACP cartridge. All that was required, other than a cylinder chambered for the newer cartridge, was the utilization of two 3-shot clips that had been developed by Smith & Wesson. These clips enabled ejection of the rimless rounds and quick loading of the cylinder. So the Model 1917 Colt revolver was born. Externally, it was a dead ringer for the Model 1909, with just a few differences. The straight barrel of the Model 1909 was abandoned for one that flared up to a larger diameter just before it met the frame. The cylinder was shorter and left space for the clipped cartridges.

The 1911A1 pistol as made by Colt during WWII.

The blued finish and smooth walnut grips of the Model 1909 were retained, as was the lanyard loop on the butt. Early Colt Model 1917s had cylinders in which the chambers were bored straight through. These absolutely required the use of the 3-round "half-moon" clips. Later production featured chambers that had an internal headspace ledge, allowing use of individual cartridges. Of course, these could not be ejected in the normal manner, but could be plucked out of the cylinder with the fingers or poked out with a pencil or similar instru-

ment. "UNITED STATES PROPERTY" *(including the quotation marks)* is marked on the underside of the barrel. I suspect some simple oaf was instructed in writing to put this marking on, and he assumed that the quotation marks used in his instructions were to be used also. On top of the barrel will be found the markings "COLT'S PT.FA.MFG.CO. HARTFORD CT.U.SA." over "PAT'D AUG. 5, 1884. JUNE 5, 1900.JULY 4, 1905." On the left rear of the frame near the rear sight area will be found the inspection mark of Major Gilbert H. Stewart (GHS), Lt. Col. John M. Gilbert (JMG), or an eagle's head with a number. As with the 1909 revolver, the hammer was left unblued and bright. The military serial number will be found on the butt, along with "U.S. ARMY MODEL 1917." Colt's commercial serial numbers, which do not match the military serial number, are inside the cylinder crane recess and on the inside surface of the crane. Nearly 155,000 Colt Model 1917 revolvers were made from October 1917 to February 1919. The Model 1917s gave good service during WWI; there is a picture extant of Army Artillery Captain Harry Truman, the future president, with one on his belt during the war. Many were brought out of storage and reconditioned for WWII; these were usually Parkerized in the process. Model 1917 Colts are still fairly plentiful for collectors, but their prices are in an ever-escalating spiral.

The Model 1917 Smith & Wesson Revolver

The heavy demand for sidearms during WWI was also responded to by Smith & Wesson, which had a large ("N-frame") revolver ready to be adapted to the 45 ACP cartridge. Similar in size to the Colt, it featured a cylinder release that had to be pushed instead of pulled, and an ejection rod that locked into a stud on the barrel. Its grips were smaller than on the Colt, but were also smooth walnut. The standard finish was blue, and the barrel was topped with a two-step rounded front sight instead of the "shark fin" of the Colt. The bluing was finer than on the Colt, and the trigger and hammer were color case-hardened. All Smith & Wesson 1917s had the head-spacing ledge in the chambers of the cylinder, and could be used with or without the 3-round clips, with the understanding that not using the clips meant manual ejection of the empties. The same quotation mark-framed "UNITED STATES PROPERTY" as on the Colt was placed on the bottom of the barrel in front of the ejector rod stud. The top of the barrel was marked: "SMITH & WESSON SPRINGFIELD MASS.U.S.A" over "PATENTED DEC. 17,1901.FEB.6, 1906. SEP.14, 1909." The serial number will be stamped on the bottom of the butt, along with the marking "U.S. ARMY MODEL 1917." Inspection markings found on the left rear of the frame near the rear sight area will be GHS (Major Gilbert H. Stewart), a "flaming bomb," or an eagle's head with a number. Nearly 170,000 revolvers were manufactured from September 1917 to January 1919. Like the Colt, these big revolvers gave excellent service during WWI, and many were brought out of mothballs and refurbished for use during WWII. Many of these had the standard WWII Parkerizing finish applied during the reconditioning process, along with the initials of the arsenal doing the work.

The 1911A1 pistol as made by Union Switch and Signal during WWII. Note the "Du-Lite" finish as opposed to Parkerizing, and a 50-round box of G.I. ball ammo.

The Smith & Wesson Model 1917, like the Colt, is still fairly available for collectors, but escalating in price. Good original specimens are getting harder to find.

Both Colt and Smith & Wesson Model 1917 revolvers gave long service, and some surplus M1917s were even issued to the U.S. Postal Service and the Border Patrol.

The Model 1911A1 Semiautomatic Pistol

In the interim period between WWI and WWII, a few minor changes were made to the basic Model 1911 design, based on comments received from its users.

lengthened in an attempt to help prevent "hammer bite" in which the tip of the hammer pinched a fleshy hand against the grip safety. The "ears" on the hammer were eliminated and the sides machined flat and flush with the shank of the hammer. The front and rear sights were altered for better visibility – a thicker front sight blade and a wider, deeper notch in the rear sight. The fine bluing that was used on the WWI 1911s gradually gave way to either Parkerizing or "Du-Lite" bluing over a sand-blast preparation. While early grips were of wood, the 1911A1 grips were almost always molded checkered plastic. The elegant "double-dia-

The 1911A1 pistol as made by Ithaca during WWII.

The changes were formalized in 1923, and handguns designated as the Model 1911A1 began to appear around 1926. Machined into the frame on each side in back of the trigger was a half-moon "cutout" designed to allow easier access to the trigger. The trigger itself was shortened, allowing better use with gloves and easier access for those with smaller fingers. The mainspring housing was arched to give a bit more angle to the grip. The grip safety was

mond" checkering design faded into history and full checkering was utilized on all 1911A1 grips, either wood or plastic.

During the WWII period, contracts were let for production of the M1911A1 to Colt's,

had an ordnance escutcheon inletted. General officers to whom this pistol was

The 1911A1 pistol as made by Remington-Rand. Remington-Rand made more 1911A1 pistols than any other maker during WWII.

Remington-Rand, Inc., Ithaca Gun Company, and the Union Switch and Signal Company. All produced sizable quantities of pistols, with Remington-Rand making the most, followed by Colt's, Ithaca, and Union Switch and Signal, in that order. Slides were appropriately marked with the manufacturer's name. Frames were not so marked, but serial number ranges were assigned to each manufacturer, and lists are readily available which should pin down the manufacturer of a particular frame. I highly recommend the book *U.S. Pistols & Revolvers* by J.C. Harrison, which contains these listings. The Singer Sewing Machine Company was awarded an experimental contract, and it made only 500 finely-finished and blued pistols. These were reportedly all issued to the U.S. Army Air Force. If you find an authentic Singer pistol today, be prepared to mortgage your home to own it! The government decided Singer did such a terrific job that it was better suited to making other precision parts for the war effort, which it did. I've seen only one Singer in my lifetime, and it was definitely not for sale.

A sub-category of the M1911A1 pistol was the M15 General Officer's pistol. Beginning in 1973, Rock Island Arsenal began customizing some M1911A1s for issue to general officers. In the process, the slide and barrel were shortened, high-visibility fixed sights added, a full-length recoil spring guide fitted, and the pistols were given a high-polish blue. The frontstrap of the grip was checkered. Special walnut stocks were used, with the left side panel having a brass plate inletted so the general could have his name engraved. The right-hand panel

issued had the option to buy the sidearm upon retirement. These pistols were very limited issue, and are collector's items usually obtained only from the estates of the deceased officers.

Good, as-issued, authentic 1911A1s are getting increasingly scarce. Most were reconditioned by the government after WWII, and as a result will show the use of mixed parts from many manufacturers. The reconditioning arsenals did not respect maker integrity, and as a result, you may find a Colt frame with an Ithaca slide, and so on. Small parts were freely switched, as well. The Model 1911 and the Model 1911A1 pistols served as our official sidearms for over 70 years. They are still in use in the service today, demanded in lieu of 9mm pistols by those professionals whose lives particularly depend on a hard-hitting man-stopper of a cartridge!

The F.P. 45 "Liberator" Pistol

One of the weirdest (and scarcest) 45s issued by our country during the twentieth century was this pistol. During WWII, the O.S.S. (Office of Strategic Services), forerunner of the Central Intelligence Agency, decided that it would be useful to have a really cheap single-shot pistol available for air-dropping to resistance forces in both the European and Pacific theatres of operation. The idea was that an allied resistance fighter could slay a German or Japanese soldier at close range with one of these, and then take his weapon to use. If the enemy discovered the weapons, they would be virtually useless as war materiel to them. The Chief of Military Intelligence

requested one million pistols be made for appropriate distribution. A design team went into high gear, and a contract was let to the Guide Lamp Division of General Motors to produce the pistol. The barrel was seamless unrifled tubing; the frame was welded, stamped and riveted sheet metal, and the firing mechanism consisted of a few springs, a cast firing pin knob and stampings. The breech was a flat metal plate that slid up and down to admit the 45 ACP cartridge. The fired cartridge had to be poked out with a pencil or stick through the muzzle. The name "Liberator" was not used until after the war. The official designation for the pistol was "F.P. 45," which ostensibly stood for "Flare Pistol, Model 45." The whole project was done in secret, and even those working on the subassemblies and parts of the pistol did not know what they were making. All parts and blueprints were mislabeled with generic designations in the interest of secrecy. For example, the striker/firing pin was called a "control rod" and the barrel was simply called a "tube." Within 30 days, one million pistols were completed in the fall of 1942, and the cost was $1.72 per pistol. The pistol was packaged in a cardboard box with a wax coating, a length of dowel for poking out the empties, and 10 rounds of 45 ACP ammo that would fit in the butt of the pistol for storage. Also included was a wordless "comic strip" instruction sheet for operation, which could be understood regardless of the native language of the recipient.

The Liberator pistol, sometimes called the "Woolworth gun" for its five-and-dime store appearance, or the "Kangaroo gun" because it was once smuggled into areas by Australian submarines, was not a very significant contribution to the war effort. Few were actually delivered to occupied Europe. The Army didn't have much use for them, and so gave them back to the O.S.S. Some were delivered to the

The rare F.P. 45 "Liberator" single-shot pistol, designed to be dropped to partisans behind enemy lines in WWII.

China-Burma-India theatre, and to the Philippines. After the war, the Philippine Constabulary used some of them as issue sidearms. Quite a number had been sent to Britain, and after the war the British Steel Corporation in Wales disposed of most of these as scrap. Some of these pistols, predictably, were taken home in lunch pails from the steel mill, and some were given to children in the area as cap pistols! The authorities put the kibosh on this when it was found that the "toys" were actually guns that could fire!

Few Liberator pistols have survived today, making them one of the rarest and most valuable of the U.S. 45-caliber handguns. I'm fortunate enough to have fired one, and at short range, the bullet key-holed through the target, not surprising in view of its unrifled barrel. These relics of World War II had best be left as collectible curiosities, however, as repeated firing is only sure to destroy a pistol that was only designed to fire a few shots and then be discarded.

The Mk 23 Mod 0 SOCOM semiautomatic pistol

When the Beretta Model 92F 9mm pistol was adopted as the new U.S. service handgun in 1985 as the M9, it certainly didn't please everyone. Many moaned *(does this remind you of the early twentieth century?)* that such an anemic caliber had no business on the battlefield. Still, the 9mm was NATO standard, and almost pre-ordained. The real professionals, however, thought that they needed, and deserved, a 45-caliber handgun that could be used by special operations personnel such as the Navy's

SEALS, the Army's Special Forces (Green Berets) and Delta Force. The concept was a serious "offensive pistol." They appealed to SOCOM (the joint services Special Operations Command) to get a pistol for them that would be selective single/double action, and capable of firing +P 45 ACP jacketed hollow-point ammo. They wanted this pistol to have a high-capacity magazine, a de-cocker, an ambidextrous safety, a threaded barrel to accept a sound suppressor, and to be able to accept a laser/visible light/infrared light module. It should be absolutely reliable, extremely accurate, and impervious as possible to the elements. It should be easily field-stripped for cleaning and as lightweight as possible given its probable size.

Those were tough specifications. In the early 1990s, both Colt's and Heckler and Koch of Germany submitted samples for trial by Special Operations Command. After extensive testing, the H&K pistol was adopted for issue within SOCOM for special operations usually involving counter-terrorism. A spin-off of the highly successful H&K USP (Universal Service Pistol) design, the Mk 23 pistol is massive and intimidating. It measures 9.65 inches in length,

and carries a 5.87-inch barrel. The barrel itself has a polymer O-ring which mates with the opening for the barrel in the slide, giving a tight seal and excellent accuracy. The recoil spring is two-stage and soaks up recoil well, giving the gun an extended service life. The frame itself is polymer, the same as used in the USP pistol. The sights are mounted high to clear a special sound suppressor designed for use on the pistol, and are adjustable for windage. The barrel is threaded for the suppressor. The pistol is equipped with a decocker on the left side of the frame, and an ambidextrous safety mounted in the same location as that on the 1911 pistol. The magazine carries a staggered-column 12

A rear view of the Liberator pistol with its action open. Note the smooth, unrifled bore.

rounds, giving a total capacity of 13. The pistol operates on the time-honored drop-barrel principle designed by John Browning so many years ago. The barrel's cam surface mates with a matching one on the recoil spring guide rod. Removal of the conventional slide stop allows quick field-stripping; the pistol breaks down into six assemblies/parts: the barrel, the slide, the frame, the recoil spring assembly, the slide stop, and the magazine. Exterior metal surfaces are coated with a marine finish that is highly resistant to salt water and spray. In tests, the pistol proved to be incredibly reliable and accurate. It is designed to have a service life of over 30,000 rounds. The O-ring on the barrel is operator-replaceable in a few moments. Because of the polymer frame, the pistol is surprisingly light and soaks

The Mark 23 SOCOM pistol with dummy suppressor attached.

single-action mode; when used double-action, there is no need for a safety; that function being superceded by the heavier double-action pull. The sidearm is grooved for a dedicated laser/visible light/infrared light module, which attaches in an instant. The sound suppressor is specially made for the pistol and is amazingly efficient. The gun will cycle normally with this specially-engineered item. The pistol is issued in a ballistic nylon camouflage-pattern case holding the pistol, two spare magazines, the suppressor,

The Mark 23 SOCOM pistol, with a display dummy suppressor, legal for unrestricted ownership by civilians. Note the threaded barrel which accommodates the suppressor.

(not Mk 23) by H&K, and is marked as such on the slide. It also comes with the special case, absent the suppressor and module, and, of course, two politically-correct 10-round magazines. A few 12-round magazines made their way into the civilian market before the hi-capacity magazine ban; these have now reached astronomical prices on the collector circuit. The guns themselves are quite expensive and in very short supply. It is reputed that they will not be available forever.

So there you have it. A century of 45-caliber handguns – the red, white and blue AMERICAN caliber, still in use today by our armed services. The 9mm may be the "official" handgun cartridge, but the love affair that the American services have for the good old 45 will probably never die until vaporizer pistols become standard issue. For students of the handgun and collectors, the issue 45-caliber handguns of our armed services hold great and absorbing fascination!

up recoil very well. The Mk 23 is calibrated for 185-grain +P jacketed truncated-cone or hollow-point ammo, but will feed and function with virtually any 45 ACP ammo on the market. The manual safety can be applied only when the pistol is in

and the laser/light module. A thigh-mounted Kydex holster is specially made for the pistol by Bianchi.

The SOCOM pistol has an equivalent that can be purchased by civilians for collector *(and shooting!)* purposes. It's called the Mark 23

Engraved and Custom Gun Review

by Tom Turpin

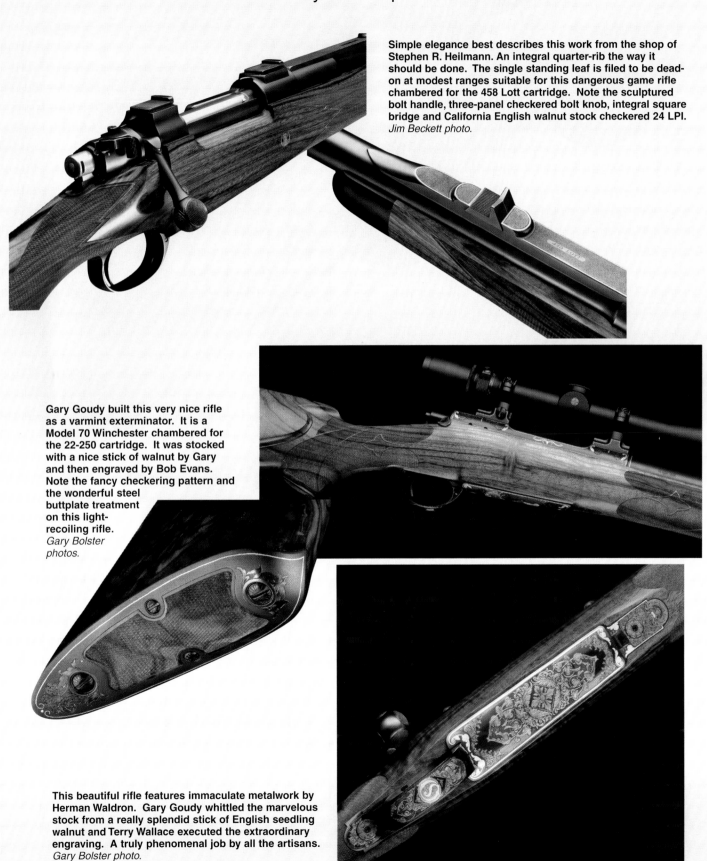

Simple elegance best describes this work from the shop of Stephen R. Heilmann. An integral quarter-rib the way it should be done. The single standing leaf is filed to be dead-on at modest ranges suitable for this dangerous game rifle chambered for the 458 Lott cartridge. Note the sculptured bolt handle, three-panel checkered bolt knob, integral square bridge and California English walnut stock checkered 24 LPI. *Jim Beckett photo.*

Gary Goudy built this very nice rifle as a varmint exterminator. It is a Model 70 Winchester chambered for the 22-250 cartridge. It was stocked with a nice stick of walnut by Gary and then engraved by Bob Evans. Note the fancy checkering pattern and the wonderful steel buttplate treatment on this light-recoiling rifle. *Gary Bolster photos.*

This beautiful rifle features immaculate metalwork by Herman Waldron. Gary Goudy whittled the marvelous stock from a really splendid stick of English seedling walnut and Terry Wallace executed the extraordinary engraving. A truly phenomenal job by all the artisans. *Gary Bolster photo.*

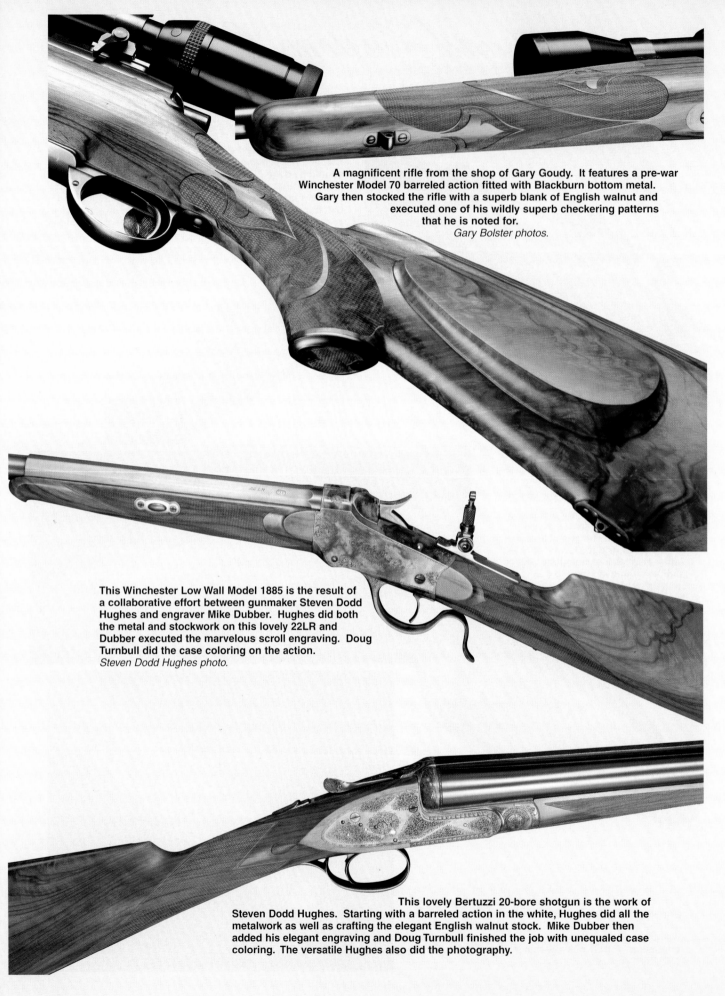

A magnificent rifle from the shop of Gary Goudy. It features a pre-war Winchester Model 70 barreled action fitted with Blackburn bottom metal. Gary then stocked the rifle with a superb blank of English walnut and executed one of his wildly superb checkering patterns that he is noted for.
Gary Bolster photos.

This Winchester Low Wall Model 1885 is the result of a collaborative effort between gunmaker Steven Dodd Hughes and engraver Mike Dubber. Hughes did both the metal and stockwork on this lovely 22LR and Dubber executed the marvelous scroll engraving. Doug Turnbull did the case coloring on the action.
Steven Dodd Hughes photo.

This lovely Bertuzzi 20-bore shotgun is the work of Steven Dodd Hughes. Starting with a barreled action in the white, Hughes did all the metalwork as well as crafting the elegant English walnut stock. Mike Dubber then added his elegant engraving and Doug Turnbull finished the job with unequaled case coloring. The versatile Hughes also did the photography.

This floorplate is on a wonderful little rifle built on a shortened Mauser action by Stephen R. Heilmann. Steven did all the metalwork on the rifle, Darwin Hensley crafted the stock, Pete Mazur did the metal finishing and Sam Welch did the wonderful engraving and gold inlay. The rifle was an award winner at the annual American Custom Gunmakers Guild/Firearms Engravers Guild of American combined Exhibition.
Sam Welch photo.

Sam Welch engraved this bottom metal from a custom 375 H&H with metalwork by Ross Billingsley and custom stock by Darwin Hensley. The rifle was intended for use on safari in Africa, hence the Big Five motif in the engraving.
Sam Welch photo.

This floorplate is from a custom Model 70 rifle built by Sharmon Smith. Sam Welch added the wonderful engraving. Sam's scroll styling is rather unique and easily recognizable to those familiar with his work.
Sam Welch photo.

A stunning little 250-3000 Improved-chambered Mauser from the shop of Stephen R. Heilmann. Steve accomplished not only the extensive metalwork on the rifle, but also crafted the classic-styled stock.
Stephen Dodd Hughes photo.

One of our very best makers is Gene Simillion of Gunnison, Colorado. This Model 70 300 Winchester Magnum is a good example of his work. His execution is superb and his styling is right in line with this scribe's idea of classic styling. *Steven Dodd Hughes photos.*

A very unusual custom rifle from the very talented and artistic Stephen R. Heilmann. This rifle is a Springfield M-22, 22LR, the only one I've ever seen in custom guise. All the metalwork and the fine custom stock were accomplished by Steve Heilmann. *Steven Dodd Hughes photos.*

An absolutely magnificent Winchester Low Wall Model 1885 22LR. All the metalwork and stock were executed by Montana maker Steven Dodd Hughes. The metal is adorned by the splendid engraving of William Gamradt. *Steven Dodd Hughes photos.*

The maker is a relative newcomer to the craft but is doing wonderful work. This Mauser is a good example of his artistry. The rifle is chambered for the 416 Nitro Express cartridge, a wildcat based on the 404 Jeffrey case that is ballistically similar to the 416 Remington. Another relative newcomer, Lee Griffith, executed the engraving. We will, I believe, be hearing much from these comparative youngsters in the future.
Steven Dodd Hughes photos.

The scenes engraved on this German-made drilling are very unusual. Apparently the customer wanted scenes from his past replicated on his hunting gun. German master engraver Hendrik Frühauf of Schleusingen, Germany, followed his instructions wonderfully.
Photos courtesy of Hendrik Frühauf.

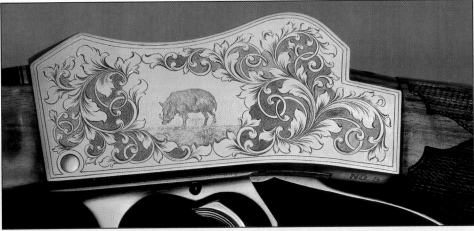

A close-up of the engraving of Ed DeLorge. This work adorns one of Ed's custom Martini-action rifles built completely in his Louisiana shop.
Ed DeLorge photo.

This German-built double rifle is obviously intended for African hunting. German master engraver Hendrik Frühauf adorned the gun with scenes of the Big Five game animals of Africa. These bulino scenes are magnificently executed.
Photos courtesy of Hendrik Frühauf.

Three views of a magnificent Parker shotgun that has been engraved, inlaid and carved by Joe Rundell. I first learned of Joe's talent's through his carving. I had seen several stocks that he had carved but had no idea that he was also an engraver. The first of his engraving jobs that I saw really blew my mind. His work is superb.
Weyer of Toledo photo.

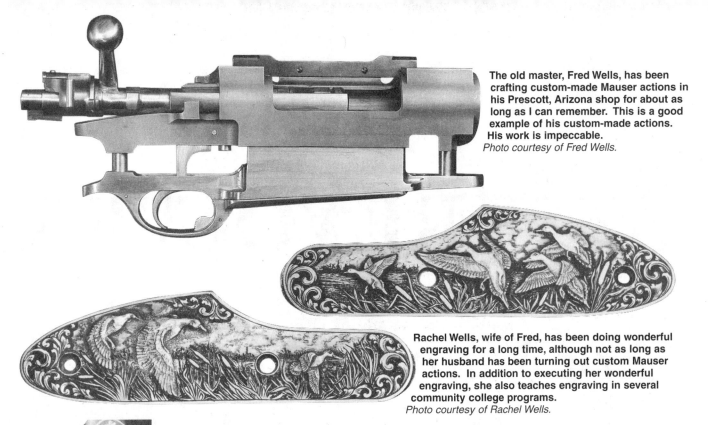

The old master, Fred Wells, has been crafting custom-made Mauser actions in his Prescott, Arizona shop for about as long as I can remember. This is a good example of his custom-made actions. His work is impeccable.
Photo courtesy of Fred Wells.

Rachel Wells, wife of Fred, has been doing wonderful engraving for a long time, although not as long as her husband has been turning out custom Mauser actions. In addition to executing her wonderful engraving, she also teaches engraving in several community college programs.
Photo courtesy of Rachel Wells.

Using a Fred Wells custom rifle built on a prototype 'cap' action as a canvas, engraver Mark Swanson embellished the rifle magnificently. His work on this piece is second to none.
Photos courtesy of Mark Swanson.

In my youth, I chased Mr. Bob behind an English setter and English pointer, very much like the two depicted on the bottom of this 28-bore Parker. Master engraver Geoffroy Gournet of Easton, Pa. has captured the scene exquisitely.
Photo courtesy of Mr. Gournet.

THE 32-20 REVOLVER

Not Your Ordinary 32!

by Marshall R. Williams

I RECENTLY ACQUIRED an old Smith & Wesson "K-frame" target model revolver in 32-20. It had an insignificant ring bulge in the barrel and some previous owner had replaced the front sight with one made from a copper penny. Since the 90-year old gun remained serviceable, I determined to shoot it and to do some reloading for it.

The 32-20 in revolvers was no ordinary 32, at least not in the 32 S&W or 32 Short Colt sense. It offered penetration equal to, or superior to, the big-bore blackpowder revolvers of its day, had a "large-bore" reputation—and it was popular. As surprising as it may seem, Colt and S&W total production of 32-20 revolvers appears to exceed the total made for all larger bores except 38 S&W, 38 Special—and possibly the 38 Long Colt.

Although the 32-20 was a very good revolver cartridge, it did not start out as one. Winchester introduced the 32-20 in 1882 as a new offering for their popular Model 73 rifle and carbine. Winchester advertised the cartridge as suitable for Eastern deer hunting, but we all know better.

Or, maybe we don't. Many years ago, one of my friends bought a Model 1892 Winchester in 32-20 from an elderly gentleman who was moving into a nursing home and had no further use for it. Part of the

deal was an old box of cartridges missing seven rounds. My friend asked about the missing rounds. The old man said that he had killed five deer and two turkeys. Not a bad run for an unsuitable gun.

The original 32-20 load appears to have been a 115-grain lead bullet driven by 20 grains of blackpowder, hence the name. The '32' designates the nominal caliber, and '20' designates the grains of blackpowder comprising the proper load. Rifle velocity was on the order of 1200 fps, and energy would have been around 365 fpe. In more recent times, bullet weights have been 100 grains and 80 grains.

Reviewing old ammunition lists reveals the cartridge listed as the 32 Winchester, the 32 WCF (Winchester Center Fire), the 32 CLMR (Colt Lightning Magazine Rifle), the 32 Winchester, Marlin and Remington. The high-velocity version is sometimes designated "32 Winchester M/92 Special." No doubt several of these names created confusion with the much larger 32 Winchester Special.

There have been both standard velocity and high velocity versions of the cartridge. According to "*Handloading*," (Wm. C. Davis, NRA, 1981), the standard chamber pressure limit was 16,000 psi and the high pressure limit was 26,000 psi. The standard velocity is loaded to

pressures considered to be suitable for the 1873 Winchester and revolvers; the high velocity loading is loaded to pressures suitable for the Winchester Model 1892 (*which has a much stronger action than the '73*) and "similarly strong rifle actions." Which other rifle actions are similarly strong is matter of discretion.

Again relying on old ammo lists, the standard velocity smokeless powder versions of both the 100-grain and the 115-grain versions achieved a rifle velocity of about 1290 fps. This velocity gave the 100-grain bullet a muzzle energy of 369 fpe and the 115-grain bullet a muzzle energy of 425 fpe. The high velocity 115-grain version achieved a velocity of about 1600 fps and a muzzle energy of 654 fpe The high velocity 100-grain version achieved a velocity of about 1670 fps and a muzzle energy of about 619 fpe. The 80-grain bullet, which appears to have been loaded only in high velocity form, got up to 2130 fps with a muzzle energy of 805 fpe in some versions. These loads nearly double the cartridge's muzzle energy and noticeably flatten its trajectory.

In addition to the Winchester Model 1873 and 1892, many other lever-action, slide-action, bolt-action, and single-shot rifles have chambered the cartridge, and, before the advent of the high-speed 22-caliber centerfire cartridges, the

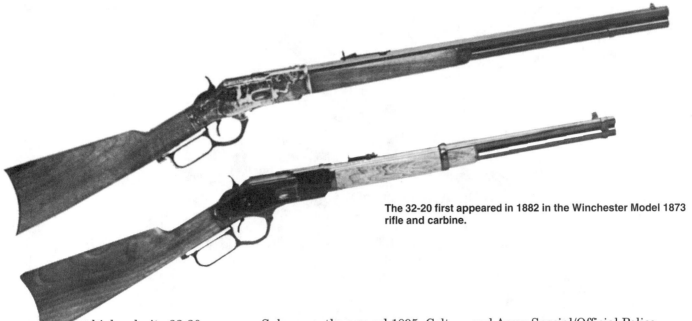

The 32-20 first appeared in 1882 in the Winchester Model 1873 rifle and carbine.

high velocity 32-20 was a popular varmint and groundhog cartridge.

In 1884, two years after Winchester introduced the 32-20 as a rifle cartridge, Colt added the 32-20 to its revolver line in both the Single Action Army and the Model 1878 Double Action revolver. This made the 32-20 a combination rifle-pistol cartridge after the fashion of the 44-40. The big advantage to this was that a frontiersman—or farmer, for that matter—could buy just one type of ammunition for both his rifle and revolver.

The combination advantage is always mentioned by modern writers but, based on my reading, the advantage seems to have been ignored by many of the very people who should have benefited from it. I have read a number of accounts of Westerners who carried a Colt 45-caliber revolver and a Winchester 44-caliber rifle, but only one account by an old-timer who obtained a 44 revolver to match the caliber of his rifle. He quickly traded off his revolver for a Colt 45 because the 44-40 revolver locked up when he fired rifle ammunition in it.

Ultimately more than 29,000 SAAs would chamber the 32-20, making it the fourth most popular chambering in that arm, exceeded by the 45 Colt, the 44-40, and the 38-40. The Model 1878 DA was not a big seller in Colt's line, being quickly replaced by more modern designs, but Doug Wickland of the National Firearms Museum states that 933 of the 1878 DAs chambered the 32-20. Colt offered the Bisley in 32-20 throughout its production (1894-1912) and, curiously, it was the most popular cartridge in the Bisley, with over 13,000 so chambered.

Subsequently, around 1895, Colt added the 32-20 to their offerings on the 41 frame-size New Model of the Army and Navy. In 1908, this became the Army Special, and still later, in 1926, it became the Official Police. In about 1907, Colt also offered the smaller-frame Police Positive Special in 32-20.

Starting in 1899, Smith & Wesson offered its "K-frame" guns in 32-20 and made more than 144,000 before it was discontinued. During the same period, S&W made nearly 1,000,000 M&Ps in 38 Special, establishing roughly a 1:7 ratio of 32-20s to 38 Specials. The target model S&W differed from the regular version only in the matter of having an adjustable rear sight; the front sight is a standard blade. The 32-20 Target Model appears to be rare.

I could find no information to indicate how many 32-20s Colt made in the Police Positive Special and Army Special/Official Police models. I speculate their production percentages ran parallel to those of Smith & Wesson's. If so, the combined (Colt and S&W) production of all 32-20 revolvers probably exceeded 330,000 guns. To put that number in perspective, it about equals the number of American revolvers chambered in 45 Colt and considerably exceeds the number made in 38-40, 44-40, 44 Russian and 44 Special. The 32-20 was a popular cartridge.

I have seen no references to target-model Colts in this chambering except the SAA and Bisley. That leads me to believe that a target model Police Positive Special or Army Special in this caliber also would be rare.

Both Colt and Smith & Wesson discontinued all revolvers in 32-20 by about 1939 and, discounting modern copies of the Colt Single

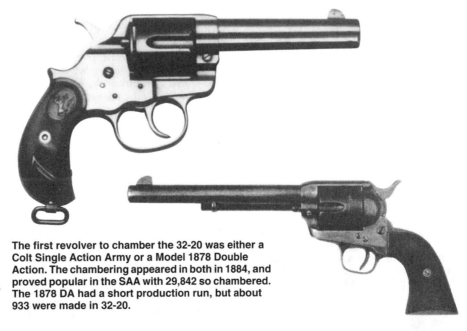

The first revolver to chamber the 32-20 was either a Colt Single Action Army or a Model 1878 Double Action. The chambering appeared in both in 1884, and proved popular in the SAA with 29,842 so chambered. The 1878 DA had a short production run, but about 933 were made in 32-20.

An interesting old piece, a Smith & Wesson 32-20 Target Model. By current standards, the adjustable sights are miserable, a narrow notch and a very thin homemade copper replacement front sight, and tiny screws with no clicks. Fortunately, they are adjusted correctly. The group was shot off-hand at 25 yards with new WW cartridges loaded with 100-grain lead bullets.

The 32-20 was the most common chambering in the Colt Bisley (13,422), narrowly edging out the 41 Long Colt (13,183) and the 38-40 (12,261). Curiously, the number of Bisleys in each of these calibers greatly exceed the total of Bisleys in 45 Colt (8,102) and 44-40 (6,881).

Action Army and small runs of Ruger Blackhawk convertibles and Dan Wesson revolvers, the only other 32-20 revolvers (of which I am aware) are Belgian and Spanish copies of the Colt and S&W medium-frame designs.

According to late 1930s ammo lists, both the standard velocity 100-grain bullet and the standard velocity 115-grain bullet gave 1030 fps from a six-inch barrel. The 100-grain bullet developed a muzzle energy of 230 fpe while the 115-grain bullet increased muzzle energy to 271 fpe

All boxes of high-velocity ammunition, at least all that I have seen, are clearly marked "Do not use in revolvers or 1873 Winchester." Revolver shooters should heed the warning. While the 26,000 psi limit

for the high-velocity load appears only slightly above +P+ 38 Special levels, I have seen two Colt Army Specials that clearly had been damaged by high-pressure ammunition.

Nevertheless, to those foolish enough to ignore the warnings on the box, the high-speed stuff must have been spectacular. It was "magnum" class, comparable to the 30 Carbine in a Ruger Blackhawk, accompanied by appropriate sound and fury. All of the old-time gun writers who tried this complained of the loud, sharp, and disagreeable muzzle blast.

Perhaps the closest comparison to the 32-20 is the pre-1930 38 Special. Both the 32-20 and the 38 Special were available in the same models: the S&W K-frame, Colt Official Police, Police Positive Special, and the old single actions. At that time, the standard 38 Special load was a 158-grain bullet at 870 fps from a 6-inch barrel, developing a respectable muzzle energy of 266 fpe. Nevertheless, the 32-20 shot its

115-grain bullet at 1030 fps from a 6-inch barrel, developed 271 fpe of muzzle energy and recoiled 16 percent less. Impressive.

For those of us who were weaned on the 357 Magnum, which did not arrive until 1935, these loads don't sound so hot. However, before passing judgment, recall that from 1884 until 1930, when the first high-velocity 38 Special was developed, the 32-20 was the highest velocity revolver[1] cartridge in the U.S. The pre-1930 38 Special load had a muzzle velocity of 870 fps. The fastest of the big-frame revolver cartridges was a tie between the 38-40 and the 44-40, with both advertised as delivering 975 fps. At 1030 fps, the 32-20 was fastest of all.

The 32-20 penetrates just like the big bores. According to the old ammo lists, at revolver velocities the 32-20 would penetrate six 7/8-inch pine boards. This equals the penetration of the 45 Colt, and the 38-40 and 44-40 from revolvers.

According to the formula for penetration in 20-percent gelatin, the 32-20 should at least equal the larger cartridges. Assuming round-nose bullets and advertised velocities, the old 38 Special would penetrate 23 inches, the 45 Colt would

1. Several auto rounds were faster. These include the 30 Luger, 30 Mauser, 9mm Luger, and 38 ACP and Super. However, in the United States in 1940, no pistols had ever been manufactured for the first three cartridges, and the 38 ACP and Super were not especially popular.

Ballistics Of Some Common Revolver Calibers Available In 1884.			
Cartridge	**Bullet Weight**	**Velocity**	**Energy**
32 Short Colt	80 gr.	800 fps	117 fpe
32 Long Colt	82	800	117
32 S&W	85	720	98
32-20	**115**	**1030**	**270**
38 Short Colt	130	770	171
38 Long Colt	150	785	205
38 S&W	145	745	179
38-40	**180**	**975**	**380***
41 Long Colt	200	745	247
44 American	205	682	212
44 Colt	225	640	207
44 Russian	**246**	**745**	**303***
44-40	**200**	**975**	**422***
45 Schofield	230	730	276
45 Colt	**255**	**870**	**429***

penetrate 23.6 inches, and both the 38-40 and the 44-40 would penetrate 24.5 inches of flesh. The 100-grain 32-20 would penetrate 23 inches and the 115-grain 32-20 would penetrate 26 inches. Few animals (*or gelatin blocks*) will notice a difference.

Penetration gives us a strong hint at comparative effectiveness. When solid lead bullets travel at pedestrian velocities, depth of penetration is the single most significant factor in wounding. Note that I said

"single most significant factor," not "only factor." But, since skin and flesh are quite elastic, the permanent hole made by a 38-40 bullet or by a 44-40 bullet is but little larger than the permanent hole made by a 32-20 bullet. For that reason, the effectiveness of non-expanding bullets is related more closely to how deeply the bullet penetrates rather than to the diameter of the penetrating bullet.

Both Colt and S&W discontinued all 32-20 revolvers just before

A vintage 1919 nickel-plated S&W M&P in 38 Special with six-inch barrel above the vintage 1906 S&W 32-20 Target Model with five-inch barrel. Prior to the introduction of the high-speed 38 Special in 1930, the 32-20 was the highest velocity revolver cartridge available. The 115-grain loading developed slightly more energy than the standard 38 Special. By curious coincidence, both of these guns have a small ring bulge in their barrels, probably from firing a shot with a bullet lodged in the barrels. Nevertheless, both remain accurate.

Colt's Army Special in 32-30 appeared in about 1895 and Colt's Police Positive Special in 32-20 in about 1907. The 32-20 remained available in these models until about 1939, and they account for the great bulk of the American revolvers chambered for the 32-20. Author estimates total American production to be in the neighborhood of 330,000 revolvers, a number which greatly exceeds the total of 38-40s, 44-40s, and 44 S&W Specials revolvers, and matches or exceeds even the total production of the 44 Russian and 45 Long Colt.

WWII. In 1930, the 38-44, first of the high-velocity 38 Specials, appeared and quickly overshadowed the 32-20. In fact, the 38 Special not only replaced the 32-20 as high-velocity revolver champion, it developed more energy, more penetration, and more versatility than the 38-40, 44-40, 44 Special and 45 Colt and substantially displaced these larger revolver calibers as well. Of these four big bores, only the 44 Special survived World War II, and that just barely. However, that is another story. The point is that after 1930, the high-speed 38 Special stole the 32-20's thunder, and in less than ten years 32-20 revolvers were discontinued.

Officially, the 32-20 employs a bullet diameter of .310"-.311". That is a smidgen smaller than most 32s and a smidgen larger than most 30s. I have used no bullets with a diameter of .310", but bullets with a diameter of .311"-.314" work well.

The only commercial 32-20 loads still catalogued use the 100-grain lead bullet, and both Remington and Winchester still list it. I pulled a lead bullet from a new Winchester 32-20 cartridge and it "miked" .313-.314-inch. The powder charge weighed four grains and consisted of a round flake powder looking more like Unique than any Olin Ball powder. Four grains of Unique would be a light load for the 32-20, with 100-grain bullet.

The factories currently advertise the 32-20's velocity as 1210 fps in a 24-inch rifle barrel. Five rounds of fresh Winchester 32-20s from a new Marlin Model 1894 with 21-inch barrel averaged 1135 fps at ten feet for a rather anemic 286 fpe of energy.

I can find no recent representations as to revolver velocities. In the five-inch barrel of the old Smith & Wesson, six cartridges from the same fresh box of Winchester 32-20 ammo averaged a disappointing 855 fps. Nevertheless, this load would give a muzzle energy of 162 fpe, only a little less than the current listings for the standard 38 Special. Among the six shots, extreme spread was 100 fps (811-911 fps), suggesting that the powder charge is light for its burning rate in this application.

Notwithstanding the velocity spread, the accuracy of the old Smith & Wesson was very good, especially considering the awful sights and the aging eyes of the operator. The six shots grouped into 3 inches at 25 yards. Spread was mostly horizontal.

The sights deserve some comment. This is a S&W 32-20 Target Model with a 1905 state-of-the-art adjustable rear sight. Actually, it looks much like a modern S&W adjustable rear sight, but the elevation screw is tiny, like those on eyeglass hinges, and it has no "clicks." There are two equally tiny, dual-opposed, windage screws that "jam lock" the sight in place. The notch in the rear sight blade is square and tiny, about 1/16-inch wide and 1/32-inch deep. *Tiny.* The original front sight, which was formed integral with the barrel, has been replaced with a copper one made from a penny. Under close scrutiny, the date "1936" is legible. Following a custom of some target shooters of long ago, it has been filed to extreme thinness, no more than .05-inch.

Reloading the 32-20 presents some informational problems for the reloader. Many of the pioneer handloaders used very heavy loads in the 32-20 revolvers. Commentators complained of the painfully loud crack of their reloads, suggesting magnum-level performance. Elmer Keith estimated that his favorite load using Hercules 2400 powder gave a velocity of 1500 fps. (*I do not think he actually chronographed the load.*) But clearly these reloaders worked at pressure levels much higher than the standard for the cartridge.

There is little modern pressure-tested data for the 32-20, and older data is suspect whenever there is no indication whether the data was developed for strong rifles or for general-purpose use. To add to the confusion, the Thompson-Center Contender is available chambered for the 32-20 cartridge but uses a .308-inch groove diameter barrel.

The original bullets for the 115-grain 32-20, the 180-grain 38-40, and the 200-grain 44-40 looked like these. Seen in this way, it is obvious why, at similar blackpowder velocities, the 32-20 penetrates as well as either of the other two cartridges.

Data developed for this strong single-shot pistol are not suitable for revolvers or for weak rifle designs like the Winchester 1873. With all these factors, plus developments in tort law, little modern information is available–except for the weakest and safest loads.

The 32-20 also presents the handloader with some mechanical problems not encountered in reloading modern straight-cased cartridges like the 357 Magnum. I despise lubricating cases and favor carbide dies for handgun reloading. Such dies are not available for the 32-20 because it has a necked case with a barely perceptible shoulder.

The brass of the 32-20 case is very thin, compared to modern revolver designs. Each time you run a case into any die, whether resizing, mouth expanding, bullet seating, or crimping – you must take care not to collapse the case mouth or shoulder. Because conventional crimping is the step most likely to collapse the shoulder, I purchased a Lee Factory Crimp Die along with their excellent three-die pistol set for the 32-20. Lee's factory crimp die crimps by compressing the case mouth in a collet rather than pushing down on the case mouth as does a conventional crimp die. This eliminates the danger of collapsing the shoulder when crimping a bullet in place. I found it particularly useful when crimping the new Hornady XTP bullets and swaged SWCs. I highly recommend it.

As factory-loaded, the modern 32 H&R Magnum develops similar energies to those developed by the old 32-20, but at higher chamber pressures.

Components for reloading the 32-20 are readily available, although I had to go to four gun stores before I found one with a box of factory ammunition on hand. All suppliers of new unprimed cases should have 32-20 brass.

All my reloading data sources indicate that the correct primer for the 32-20, even when intended for pistols, is the standard small rifle primer. However, for standard-pressure revolver ammunition, I would expect a standard small pistol primer to work just as well. I would also note that most primer manufacturers offer two types of small rifle primers, one for use in the high-pressure 222-223 class of cartridges and another for use in all other small rifle cases. I would avoid the 223-type primer for revolvers.

Any bullets of proper weight having a diameter of about .310-.314 inches should be suitable for reloading the 32-20. I note many more bullets suitable for reloading all 32s are now available than could be found just a few years ago. These include modern jacketed hollow-point bullets that can be found in weights of 60 grains, 85 grains, and 100 grains. The 71-, 74-, and 77-grain jacketed solids for the 32 ACP also work, and swaged and cast lead bullets can be obtained in a number of useful designs.

All powders suitable for non-magnum revolver cartridges, plus several which are suitable for magnums, seem to work quite well in the 32-20. Alliant (*formerly Hercules*) Unique is a traditional powder and remains one of the best. However, because it is very traditional, it also is the powder for which the most untested data are available. Therefore, anyone choosing Unique for his 32-20 reloads

Reloading the 32-20 (*and the 38-40 and 44-40*) requires special care. Many old blackpowder cartridge designs involve cases with thin brass that is easily crumpled.

The 32-20 is *NOT* your ordinary 32. *Left to right*, a 32 S&W, the 32-20, and the 38 Special.

should make doubly sure of the pressure level of the reloading data.

For my first reloads, I turned to the very good selection of data that came with the Lee dies. These data suggest that Hodgdon HS-7 would work well with jacketed bullets. I tried 7.9 grains of HS-7, a .312-inch diameter Hornady 85-grain XTP hollow point. For this and all subsequent loads, I used CCI #400 small rifle primers and new unprimed Remington brass. The chronograph said the bullet was traveling 1062 fps, which would give 213 fpe of energy. Not bad. It equals the advertised performance of the 32 H&R Magnum and the accuracy seemed good.

Thinking a heavier bullet might improve things, I tried 7.4 grains of HS-7 under a .312-inch diameter Hornady 100 grain XTP bullet with the CCI #400 and R-P brass. Velocity averaged just 929 fps for a muzzle energy of 192 fpe. Well, not so impressive as the lighter bullet, but accuracy remained good. And to give the 32-20 its due, the energy level equals current standard velocity 38 Special factory loads.

For a light load, I tried 4.4 grains of Unique with Hornady's .314-inch diameter 90-grain SWC, CCI's #400 primer and R-P brass. Velocity averaged 958 fps and energy was 183 fpe. Although I have shot nothing with it, I think this would make a very good rabbit and small game load. Incidentally, this bullet has given excellent accuracy in every 32 in which I have tried it, including the old 32 S&W, the 32 S&W long, and the 32 H&R magnum. It excelled in the old S&W 32-20.

I also tried blackpowder. Curious to see exactly what the old timers saw when they used the first 32-20s, I loaded a few rounds with 115-grain cast lead bullets and GOEX FFg blackpowder. Twenty grains would not conveniently fit into the modern solid-head cases, so I used 16.7 grains instead. This load gave me all the smoke I could wish for—each shot completely obscured the target for a moment, but the chronograph disappointed. Velocity from the old S&W's five-inch barrel averaged just 752 fps, for muzzle energy of just 144 fpe. This still exceeds the best levels of any other 32 revolver cartridge, but I had expected more and questioned whether the originals lived up to their advertising.

All of this was well and good, but I wanted to duplicate the old ammo lists' 115-grain bullet at 1030 fps or, actually, a little less. The original ballistics were taken in a six-inch barrel, and my gun has a five-inch barrel. Accordingly, I obtained some

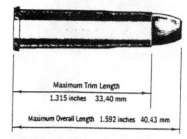

32/20 WCF
BULLET DIAMETER
.312 inches   7,92 mm

Maximum Trim Length
1.315 inches   33,40 mm

Maximum Overall Length 1.592 inches   40,43 mm

SMALL RIFLE PRIMERS

Reloading Data For Revolvers

The following 32-20 reloading data, provided by the respective powder manufacturers, is thought to be safe for revolvers and Model 1873-type rifles. Velocities shown are for maximum loads and have been developed in different types of test equipment and performance may vary in another gun. When using maximum loads, the minimum overall length of the loaded cartridge must be at least 1.54 inches. Where only a single powder charge is indicated, it should be treated as a maximum charge.

Bullet/Powder	Start Load	Max Load	Velocity
74-grain Jacketed			
Bullseye	3.6 grains	4.0 grains	1145 fps
80-grain Jacketed			
Unique	5.3	5.9	1220
85-grain Jacketed			
HS7	7.2	8	1205
HS6	6.3	7	1182
Unique	5.2	5.8	1160
Bullseye	3.2	3.6	1060
HP38	4	4.5	1050
90-grain Jacketed			
HS7	7	7.8	1172
HS6	6.1	6.8	1081
Accur 1680	14.4	14.4	1039
HP38	3.9	4.3	1023
Accur #9	—	7.3	986
Accur #7	6.1	6.1	937
Accur #5	4.9	5	906
Accur 2015BR	15	15	874
100-grain Jacketed			
Win 630	6.3	7.5	1215
Unique	4.9	5.5	1065
HS7	6.8	7.6	993
HS6	5.9	6.6	992
HP38	3.7	4.1	992
Accur 1680	11.1	12.5	975
Bullseye	3.1	3.4	955
Accur #9	6.2	7	927
Accur #7	5.4	5.8	887
Accur 2015BR	12.1	14	846
Accur #5	4.3	4.7	844
110-grain Jacketed			
HS7	6.7	7.5	998
HS6	5.8	6.5	988
HP38	3.6	4	869
115-grain Jacketed			
Unique	4	4.5	925
Bullseye	2.8	3.1	850

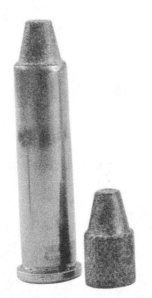

Left to right, 32-20 reloads using the Hornady 90-grain SWC, a 115-grain cast bullet of traditional design, and a 100-grain Hornady XTP. Last is a factory WW 100-grain lead bullet load for comparison.

commercial cast lead bullets. They weighed 114.5 grains and had an average diameter of .313-inches.

I tried 4.7 grains of Unique with the 115-grain cast bullet. This gave an average of 976 fps for an energy of 243 fpe. However, one round gave a very low velocity. Without it, the average was 984 fps and 247 fpe. This was quite close to what I wanted, so I tried 4.9 grains of Unique. This load averaged 992 fps, but again I got one round much below the average. Without the low round, the average was 1007 fps, and the resulting energy was 259 fpe. These loads seem to get about as much out of the 32-20 as was intended, and that is all I sought.

While pressures of all of these loads appeared quite benign in my gun, the heavier Unique loads should be approached with caution. I would point out that after reviewing data from a large number of sources, 5 grains of Unique appears to be the maximum acceptable revolver load with the 115-grain cast lead bullet.

Many people might wonder why I would be interested in a 32-20 revolver when the 32 H&R Magnum equals it ballistically and provides a more modern case. As it happens, I have a very nice little 32 Magnum, a S&W Model 631 with four-inch barrel and adjustable sights, and I reload for it as well. It appears to me that with the 85-grain bullet, the 32 H&R Magnum can easily match the recommended loads for the 32-20 in a revolver. Probably, it can do so with the 100-grain bullets, although I have little experience with that weight in the 32 Magnum. However, I cannot match the 115-

grain bullet's performance without exceeding recommended pressures. In a modern revolver, made of modern steels and intended for high pressures, a 32-20 "Magnum" would leave the 32 H&R Magnum even farther behind.

I once wrote to S&W suggesting they chamber the Model 19 in 30 Carbine. Although never put into production, S&W actually developed a 30 Carbine revolver during WWII. However, a 32-20 loaded to the same pressure levels would be better. After all, it is a rimmed cartridge, better suited to a revolver than the rimless 30 Carbine that would require half-moon or full-moon clips for efficient use. The 32-20 also has a slight advantage in total case capacity: 24 grains of water for the 32-20 vs. 22 grains for the 30 Carbine case, and a 2 1/2 percent larger bore area. All other things being equal, both of these factors would permit slightly better performance at a given pressure level.

The problem with such a cartridge is not in the design. Rather, there would appear to be a very limited market for it. Judging by what I read in shooting publications, small bores don't have wide appeal among gun writers. But even that is not the greatest problem for a modern American manufacturer. The greatest problem is that, sooner or later, someone would get such a cartridge in a totally unsuitable old gun and an expensive lawsuit would result. Factories don't invite that kind of trouble.

Once upon a more sensible time, Americans, like people throughout the rest of the world, were responsible for assuming the risk of their

carelessness or foolishness. Of course, for Americans at least, those unenlightened times are long past, and, notwithstanding the self-evident economic evils of the practice, manufacturers sometimes find themselves strictly liable for the foolishness of improvident people who misuse their products.

Like many people before me, including big-bore advocates Elmer Keith and Skeeter Skelton, I think a medium-frame revolver capable of handling the high-speed 32-20 would be a good thing. However, I don't intend to develop this ancient S&W into one. It appears that Dan Wesson actually made a 32-20 revolver on their standard-size frame. I have never seen one, but the Dan Wesson is a very strong modern design manufactured with modern steels and intended for the highest-pressure modern revolver cartridges. It should easily contain the highest pressures recommended for the 32-20. I also think it would be a simple matter to rechamber a modern 32 H&R Magnum S&W Model 16, the one with the full underlug barrel, to the cartridge. Unfortunately, that gun has been discontinued. Still, I occasionally see them in used gun cases. If I were to find a used one priced cheaply enough, I just might try it.

Elmer Keith killed three mule deer and an elk with a 32-20 Colt SAA. He encountered some problems with soft-nosed jacketed bullets that expanded too quickly, and he recommended high-speed reloads with cast lead bullets for such work. Skeeter Skelton had a friend who armed himself with a Colt Police Positive Special in 32-20 and went away to Alaska where he killed moose. Both also endorsed the cartridge for self-defense, by the way.

Personally, I don't see the 32-20 as a big-game cartridge. (*I also don't see the 44-40 as a big-game cartridge, but it probably killed more American buffalo than any other cartridge.*) Instead, I hanker to shoot groundhogs using the 85-grain Hornady 32-caliber XTP bullet at the highest possible velocity. It should be a powerful groundhog suppressant and a very pleasant cartridge to shoot. •

Upland Scatterguns Is LESS... More?

by Thomas C. Tabor

Lıke many youngsters I began my obsession with shotgunning and hunting with a small gauge single-shot shotgun. There were pheasants to challenge my young farm boy eyes—even the occasional cottontail. Though I faced these challenges with the vigor common to young farm kids I was plagued by two serious handicaps. First, I was young and inexperienced and, second, the bolt-action 20 gauge, handed down to me by my brother, had seen better days. At one time that relic could have been termed a "repeater", but no longer. The clip had been broken and repaired too many times. Further, the maple stock had severely cracked at the pistol grip. Repairs were attempted (*involving glue, baling wire and lots of black electrical tape*), but eventually the stock was replaced by an amateur stockmaker – me, at age 15, in wood shop class. Upon completion, my mother told it looked "real good," but I knew better.

I learned to hate that old 20, dreaming of someday owning a real adult gun, a man-sized 12-gauge pump action… and eventually that dream came true. I got my 12, then another, and another, and on like that until my gun cabinet was overflowing into virtually every corner of the house.

I hunted for a lot of years using various 12s before it ever entered

The author's SKB over/under did a fine job in collecting a mixed bag of chukar partridge, Hungarian partridge and California valley quail.

my mind to use any other gauge. But the day finally came when another 20 worked its way into my life. This time it was a lightweight, older Ithaca pump. But, the bad experiences of my childhood continued to plague me. I put the 20 in the rig for several hunting trips, but it never came out of the case until one day, chukar hunting. I'd burned a lot of ammo that day, much more than I like to admit, but finally I was only two birds away from my 6-bird limit. What better opportunity, I thought, to give that 20 a try. Marveling at how light it felt in my hands, I headed out once again. Within moments a covey burst from their scrub-hiding place in true chukar fashion, fast to the wing and hugging the curves of the rimrock as they frantically attempted their escape. Remarkably, I was on the first bird in an instant. With a puff of feathers it was destined for my game pouch. I swung to the next closest bird and—"puff"—it was down as well. It seemed that both birds were on the ground before the 12 gauge could have touched my shoulder.

I recounted that story many times, to myself as well as to my

The three choices of the perfect upland bird gauges consist of: (*l to r*) the 28 gauge, the 2 3/4-inch 20 gauge and the 3-inch 20 gauge.

shooting buddies. I even (*jokingly*) told a few friends that I just might put that shotgun on the shelf and never shoot it again, because it never missed and that took some of the fun out of shooting. Undoubtedly, that experience was the turning point in the way I viewed upland bird guns.

It is understandable for some reader to be a little skeptical of how a "lesser" shotgun could be considered a better choice in any hunting situation. How could a shotgun that puts less lead in the air (*typically, at a lower velocity*) ever be a better option? Well, let's just see.

Every shotgun has its place, even the heavy 3 1/2-inch 10 gauge. If you are looking to sky-bust long-range Canada geese coming out of the north wearing a full armored suit of winter feathers and thick down, the 10 may be the best call. But shooting steel shot for waterfowl is a different ballgame and, as a result, calls for a set of shotgun characteristics different from those of the upland bird gun.

For comparison purposes, pick up that 10 gauge—or for that matter a magnum 12 gauge—and try to get it moving. In either case, it takes a lot to just get the gun to your shoulder, let alone get it moving toward a target. True, these examples are the extreme opposite to the handling of a petite little 20 or 28 gauge that may be 6 or 8 inches shorter in the barrel and weigh half as much. Nevertheless, when we make a comparison involving a normal 8- or 9-pound 12 gauge to its smaller pipsqueak cousins, it is quite obvious which will react quicker in an upland hunting situation.

The 20 gauge enjoyed a burst of popularity in the 1960s and '70s when manufacturers began turning out 3-inch chambered models in earnest. The 3-inch 20-gauge guns were often touted as ballistically equivalent to the 12 gauge, with an overall lighter weight. In reality, as far as down-range energy goes, the 3-inch 20s can't really compete with even the 2 3/4 inch-chambered 12 gauge. Even though the longer version of the 20 can hold an additional 1/4-ounce of lead over that of the 2 3/4-inch 20, it still falls short when compared with the 12 gauge. The maximum muzzle velocities of the 3-inch 20 do not come close to the potential of the 12.

If we make a comparison between the 2 3/4-inch 20 and its 3-inch counterpart we are able to increase the shot charge from a

At first glance, the outward appearance between the 28 gauge (*left*) and the 20 gauge (*right*) is not all that noteworthy.

A good mixed bag of game birds can be had using a pip-squeak 2 3/4-inch 20 gauge like the author's Ithaca 37 pump. Note that steel shot must be used in the case of hunting waterfowl species.

maximum of 1-1/8 to 1-1/4 ounce, and realize a slight increase in muzzle velocity. But, when we look closely at the actual differences in performance we find that any benefit in shooting the longer 20 is minor. A shooter that reloads his ammunition can further narrow any gap between these two shells through careful load selection.

Unfortunately, the slightly smaller 28 gauge has never been a popular choice of hunters—and continues to suffer today. Actually, the 28 could have easily disappeared completely, like the 24 and 32 gauges, if it wasn't for the Skeet shooters. But that does not mean the 28 gauge isn't a terrific choice for the upland bird hunter. Only slightly less powerful than the 2 3/4-inch 20 gauge, the 28 gauge is truly a fine choice for most upland bird hunting situations. The often-unappreciated 28 is capable of sending a 3/4-ounce shot charge out the muzzle at well over 1,300 fps.

We would be remiss if we didn't at least discuss the 16 gauge and .410 bore. I'm sure what I am about to say will anger the few diehard

The new screw-in choke tube systems, as on the author's SKB 20-gauge over/under, provide a great deal of flexibility for the small-gauge shooter.

Patterning a shotgun is an important way of check performance, but a shooter should still understand how the shot string plays an important role in development of the pattern.

16-gauge fans, but in my estimation the 16 is only a 12 gauge in disguise. The vast majority of 16-gauge shotguns are nearly as heavy and unwieldy as a 12 gauge. Often manufacturers build their 16s on the exact same frame as the 12, which amounts to the shooter reducing his ballistic effectiveness without realizing a handling advantage. In contrast, the vast majority of today's 20s and 28s are appropriately scaled down to match the shell's reduced power.

As far as the pipsqueak .410 goes, it is best left on the Skeet range. It simply does not have the capability to be consistently effective on most game birds.

The distinct advantages of the lighter 20 and 28 gauges should have a great deal of appeal to any bird hunter; a shotgun weighing 5 or 6 pounds comes to the shoulder quicker and swings faster than a heavier one. Obviously, this puts the shooter on the target faster. In some instances, getting on the target quicker can shave the range upwards of 5 to 10 yards on fast-

Many states offer off-season small-gauge shooting fun in the way of crow hunting. The author is using his SKB 20 gauge over/under.

traveling birds intent on putting a lot of distance between themselves and the shooter. But the advantages of the smaller-gauge shotguns don't stop there.

In order to be effective in shotgunning, it is important that all shooters understand how the shot charge interacts with the target. A common misapprehension is that the shot pattern arrives on target like a flat pancake, with all the pellets making contact at precisely at the same instant. I suppose this assumption is a natural one. After all, that is how the pattern appears on paper. But what we see when we look at a patterning board is a "stop-frame" image formed after all the shot has impacted. On the contrary, this is not how the shot flies or arrives at its destination. As the shot charge leaves the muzzle of the barrel, it disperses more longitudinally than laterally. As it travels toward the target it takes on a shape of an elongated egg that stretches to as much as 15 or 16 feet in length. The actual length of the shot string will vary, based on a number of conditions and characteristics. One significant factor strongly affecting the length of shot string is how long the

shot column is to begin with. Because a larger-gauge shotshell has a larger bore diameter, its column of shot is shorter than that of the smaller gauges. For this reason, a 12-gauge shotgun will generally produce a shorter shot string in flight than a 20 gauge, and a 20 gauge will produce a shorter string than a 28 gauge, especially if equal shot charges are fired.

Table 1 provides an idea of how the length of the shot column varies with the size of the gauge. The measurements in this particular chart were based on #6 shot. Slight variations in shot column length will occur, depending on shot size.

You might ask, "*Is the shot string length important and if so, what is best - a short shot string or a long one?*" Without question, the length of the shot string will affect shooting performance, particularly when the shooter is trying to intercept a fast-moving crossing target. Whether it is best to have a long - or short - shot string is a matter of personal preference. In most cases when a target is flying perpendicular to the shooter only some of the shot will strike the target, even when the shot is precisely

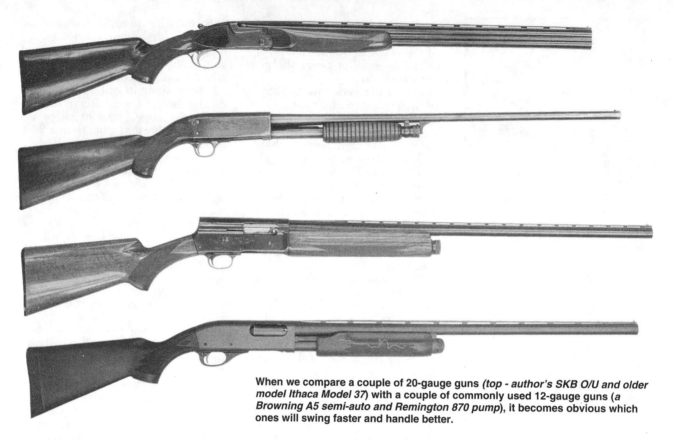

When we compare a couple of 20-gauge guns *(top - author's SKB O/U and older model Ithaca Model 37)* with a couple of commonly used 12-gauge guns (*a Browning A5 semi-auto and Remington 870 pump*), it becomes obvious which ones will swing faster and handle better.

aligned with the bird. Because the shot is strung out in flight over several yards some of it will likely pass in front of, or behind the bird. To what degree this happens will partially depend on how accurately the shooter judged the target speed, and the amount of lead required.

The advantage of a short shot string (versus a longer string) is that possibly more shot pellets will make contact with the target. The disadvantage of a short shot string is that it requires more precise shooting in order to hit a crossing target. Consequently, I believe that, like a more open-choked barrel, a longer shot string will benefit the vast majority of shooters since it provides a certain "fudge factor" when it comes to lead on a crossing target. Remember, you must first hit the target before you can put a bird in your game pouch!

If you've ever fired a box or two of heavy 12-gauge field loads you will soon learn to appreciate the reduced recoil associated with the 20 or 28 gauge. Even with the typical reduced gun weight of the smaller gauges, the difference in recoil is somewhat similar to the difference in packing out a quarter of an elk on your back, versus a quarter of a deer.

If we look at recoil and how to reduce it, we find that while gun weight is an important consideration — it is not necessarily the most important one. How we perceive the effects of recoil is a complicated matter that could stimulate substantial discussion. For simplicity's sake let's just say that 'free' recoil can be calculated mathematically, whereas how the recoil feels to you ('felt' recoil) the shooter, is a bit harder to assess numerically. Many

physical factors go into felt recoil, including the design and configuration of the stock, how the stock fits the shooter, whether the shotgun is equipped with a good recoil pad or not, etc. As far as free recoil goes, if we increase gun weight by 10 percent it will reduce the free recoil about the same percentage. On the contrary, if we reduce the muzzle velocity or shot weight, the free recoil, as well as the felt recoil, will be reduced by a greater percentage. For example, a 10-percent reduction in muzzle velocity — from a 1,200 fps load to a 1,080 fps load — will decrease the free recoil not by an equal 10 percent, but by almost 20 percent. In addition, the same applies to shot charge weight. If you decrease the shot load from 1 1/8 ounce to 1 ounce (about 11 percent) —you will reduce free recoil by around 19 percent. While not always an exact 2:1 reduction — it is close enough to know that if you reduce muzzle velocity and shot charge weight you will get more recoil reduction than by simply using a heavier gun.

Now, let's use this recoil information to compare and contrast small-gauge and large-gauge shotguns. Usually the larger-gauge shotguns are heavier, reducing both free and felt recoil. Often these bigger guns carry heavier shot payloads and, in many cases, they send their shot out the barrel faster. The smaller gauges are usually lighter-weight

TABLE 1			
Length of Shot Column			
__Shot Charge__	__28 Ga.__	__20 Ga.__	__12 Ga.__
3/4 oz.	7/8 inch	5/8 inch	1/2 inch
1 oz.	N/A	15/16 inch	3/4 inch
1 1/8 oz.	N/A	1 1/16 inch	13/16 inch
1 1/4 oz.	N/A	1 3/16 inch	1 inch

TABLE 2

Pellet Energy *(Foot-Pounds/fpe)* at Field Distances

#4 SHOT

Muzzle Velocity	Muzzle Energy	20 Yards	40 Yards	60 Yards
1,330	12.73	7.34	4.78	3.38
1,295	12.07	7.12	4.60	3.28
1,255	11.33	6.70	4.49	3.23
1,200	10.36	6.29	4.21	3.04
1,155	9.66	5.89	3.99	2.86

#6 SHOT

Muzzle Velocity	Muzzle Energy	20 Yards	40 Yards	60 Yards
1,330	7.62	4.05	2.52	1.74
1,295	7.23	3.89	2.42	1.68
1,255	6.77	3.73	2.36	1.66
1,200	6.20	3.49	2.23	1.55
1,155	5.75	3.30	2.11	1.47

#7 1/2 SHOT

Muzzle Velocity	Muzzle Energy	20 Yards	40 Yards	60 Yards
1,330	4.91	2.40	1.42	0.93
1,295	4.63	2.30	1.38	0.92
1,255	4.37	2.20	1.34	0.90
1,200	4.00	2.08	1.26	0.86
1,155	3.71	1.97	1.20	0.83

TABLE 3

Shot Velocities *(Feet Per Second)* at Field Distances

#4 SHOT

Muzzle Velocity	20 Yards	40 Yards	60 Yards
1,330	1,010	815	685
1,295	990	800	675
1,255	965	790	670
1,200	935	765	650
1,155	905	745	630

#6 SHOT

Muzzle Velocity	20 Yards	40 Yards	60 Yards
1,330	970	765	635
1,295	950	750	625
1,255	930	740	620
1,200	900	720	600
1,155	875	700	585

#7 1/2 SHOT

Muzzle Velocity	20 Yards	40 Yards	60 Yards
1,330	930	715	580
1,295	910	705	575
1,240	885	690	565
1,200	865	675	555
1,155	840	659	546

firearms that typically shoot lighter shot charges at lower muzzle velocities. Certainly the shooter of a large-gauge shotgun can opt to shoot lighter loads. Nevertheless, the potential of reduced recoil is already built in for the small-gauge user. Even though the 20s and 28s usually are lighter firearms, reduced recoil will be realized thanks to their characteristic lower velocities and lighter shot charges.

Not all advantages automatically indicate the use of a 20 or 28. No shooter should expect the smaller-gauge shotguns to be capable of reaching out quite as far — or as forcefully — as the larger bores, though on several occasions I have been amazed at just how well these little guns perform. Several times I have had to bring down birds for a 12-gauge-firing partner when a wounded bird was fleeing the scene. On one occasion my little 2 3/4-inch 20 gauge, loaded with #7 1/2 shot,

The author with his SKB 20-gauge over/ under and a partial bag of chukar partridge taken in Washington state.

A diverse bag of game birds that fell during a day's small-gauge shooting.

Favorite Loads For The 20 And 28 Gauge

20 Gauge 2 3/4 inch

Hull:	Winchester-Western Plastic AA type hull (Compression Formed)
Powder:	Alliant Herco 20.5 grains
Wad:	Remington RP-20
Primer:	Winchester 209
Shot:	1 1/8 ounce of #7 1/2 shot
Velocity:	1,220 fps

Author's Note: Data reference can be found in "*Speer Manual For Reloading Ammunition Number 8*" page 423.

28 Gauge 2 3/4 inch

Hull:	Winchester - Western Plastic AA type hull (Compression Formed)
Powder:	Alliant Unique 13.0 grains
Wad:	Winchester WAA28
Primer:	Winchester 209
Shot:	3/4 ounce of #8 or #7 1/2 shot
Velocity:	1,200 fps

Author's Note: Data reference can be found on Alliant's web page http://www.alliant.powder.com and/or in the publication pamphlet "*Reloader's Guide for Hercules Smokeless Powders*" 200-277B 11-81 250m.

crumpled a chukar while my partner had no choice but to watch, holding his emptied 12 gauge. He had pounded the bird several times with his 12 gauge, but was unable to bring it down. Another time, my 1 1/8-ounce of copper-plated #6s brought to bag a crippled pheasant rooster that my friend couldn't stop with his 12 gauge. In both cases the biggest casualty was the pride of the 12-gauge owner.

Normally, however, the shooter of a small-gauge shotgun should accept that he won't be able to reach out quite as far as the bigger guns. It seems commonly accepted that the maximum consistent killing

Chronographing various shotshells will help the shooter select the best hunting loads.

range for a 12 gauge is around 40 to 50 yards. In reality, however, 90 percent of all game birds are killed at 30 yards or less. Remember, too, that a light-weight, fast-handling gun will have the advantage of putting you on the target sooner. So, do you really need the extra range the larger bores can provide, considering most birds are killed at 30 yards or less? Generally speaking, if the maximum range for a lead-shoot-

ing 12 gauge is considered 40 or 50 yards, the maximum range of a 20 or 28 gauge should be around 30 yards. Of course these figures will vary somewhat depending on shot size, choke constriction and, to a lesser degree, other factors.

You can also narrow any difference in killing range by choosing

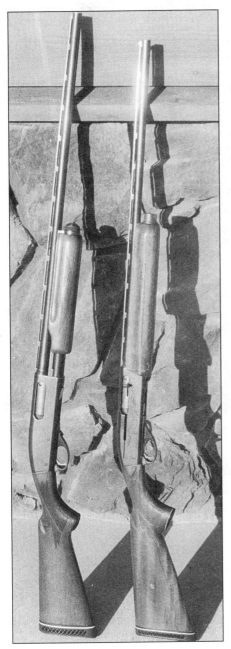

Remington has a great selection of small-gauge shotguns. On the left is a Remington 870 20 gauge; on the right a Remington 1100 semi-auto 28 gauge. Either would make an excellent upland bird scattergun.

your loads carefully. For most hunting situations where larger game birds are encountered, this means shooting near-maximum lead shot weights at the highest velocity possible in the smaller gauges. In addition, select the shot size very carefully. Possibly more #6 shot is fired by 12-gauge bird hunters than all other shot sizes combined. But, while #6s may be a great choice for the big-bore crowd, it may not be the best choice for a 20- or 28-gauge user. With the reduced payload of shot in the smaller gauges, #6 shot sometimes produces a pretty thin pattern. This does not

mean you should abandon #6s completely. Late season cornfield pheasants sometimes require a little heavier shot to penetrate the thick winter feathers and when the birds are spooky, the shots are on the long side. It is always hard to generalize, but the smaller #7 1/2 shot, or if you are lucky enough to locate some scarce #7s, are a better choice for general use. In the case of smaller game, like doves and quail, #8 shot can be used for a denser pattern.

Retained velocity and energy are as important in shotgunning as they are in rifle shooting. In order to make consistent kills you must penetrate deep enough to end the life of the target, or at least render it incapable of getting away. Tables 2 and 3 provide an idea of how the different sizes of shot will perform at various yardages, and different starting velocities. In every situation there are always trade-offs. Larger shot will retain its energy and velocity better than smaller shot; shot started at higher velocities will also deliver better long-range performance. Each shooter will have to judge what is best for his particular situation.

Birds have a tendency to get harder to kill in late season. The reason for this is two-fold: First, if they have been hunted a lot, the birds will get spooky and flush farther from the hunters, so the shots will be at longer range. Second, feathers get thicker with the coming of winter and those thick, dense feathers require higher pellet energy to penetrate them. Consequently, the perfect shot size and velocity in early season may not necessarily remain 'perfect' as the season progresses.

Proper choke selection is extremely important no matter what gauge you choose to shoot. A short-barreled, lightweight gun will provide the most benefit when it contains a more open choke. An Improved Cylinder or Modified choke will usually produce more kills in the field than a tighter choke. In some cases, when the vast majority of your targets are within 20 yards, it might even call for the use of a Skeet choke. With the advent of the new screw-in choke systems, the small-gauge shooter has the advantage of switching to a tighter - or more open - choke if the situation calls for it. If, however, you shoot a fixed-choke shotgun it is best to select the more open choke. First preference in most hunting situations is either an Improved Cylinder or Modified choke.

At no time in our history have Americans had a better selection of quality shotguns to choose from. While the selection of 28-gauge guns is still on the sparse side, if you look hard you will find them from many current manufacturers. As far as the 20s go - they can be found in the vast majority of models.

Watch the weight when selecting a small-gauge gun. Even today there are a few manufacturers that persist in producing 20s that weigh nearly as much as a 12 gauge. Select 'light' for the best in handling ease and upland effectiveness. Browning's BPS (Browning Pump Shotgun) weighs around 7 pounds, as do the newly-manufactured Ithaca Model 37s of similar bottom-ejection design. Older Ithaca 37s can sometimes be found that are considerably lighter in weight than the new ones. Remington's pump Model 870s are always very popular with hunters and are available in 20 gauge at slightly over 6 pounds, while their 28 gauge tips the scales at a slim 6 pounds. Both Remington's Model 1100 and 11-87 come in a little heavier at 6 3/4 and 6 1/2 pounds, respectively. Winchester's 1300 pumps are 6 5/8 pounds and up.

If you lean more toward double guns you will find a good selection of both imports and American-made over/unders. Side-by-sides have dwindled in popularity in America and are a bit harder to find. While some doubles are a bit heavy, the stack-barreled Ruger Red Label weighs a meager 5 7/8 to 6 pounds in 28 gauge; 6 3/4 pounds in 20 gauge.

Both the side-by-sides and over/unders provide the added advantage of an overall shorter gun length for the same barrel length as the pumps or semi-auto shotguns. It is necessary in the case of the semi-autos and pumps to dedicate around 3 inches of the receiver to their action works. For this reason you may be able to go with a little longer barrel on your O/U or SxS, for a slight edge on velocity, and still have a quick-handling firearm. In addition, doubles provide the distinct advantage of having two different chokes immediately at hand.

Over the years I have seen many hunters shelving their 12s to hunt with a 20 or 28 gauge. Like me, they have learned that 'more' is not necessarily 'better' when it comes to shotguns. And, it always seems that once the switch is made they find it very hard to switch back to the heavy-frame, slower-moving 12 gauge. If you haven't switched yet - give it a try. See what you've been missing. ●

SELLING THE AMERICAN 303

by Jim Foral

THE PHASE-OUT OF the one-shot muzzleloader and the advent of the repeating breechloader simply marked transitional stages in the mechanical evolution of firearms. Change is necessary in the march of progress. The good must surrender to the better and the weaker force must yield to the stronger.

In the time of the muzzleloader, a man kept the same gun for a lifetime and passed it to a favorite son or grandson. The continual improvement of the breechloader,

however, activated a trend to remain up-to-date, and the sportsman's compulsion was to fall in line and try to keep up with the procession, lest he be ridiculed for shooting a "*back number.*" This accelerated course of arms development culminated in the early 1890s, when the small-bore military rifle, using jacketed bullets and smokeless powder, was ushered in. New

Above, an 1896 advertisement for the Savage Repeating Rifle.

England armsmakers again adjusted to the times and scurried to furnish their latest.

By 1895, conditions were right and the market was ready for a lever-action rifle strong enough to contain the higher chamber pressures associated with the new smokeless powders. In June of that year, Arthur W. Savage, a Jamaican-born mechanic of some ability, who'd already developed several machines used in textile production and a highly successful torpedo, was prepared to add such a rifle to his list of inventions. The Savage Repeating Arms Co. was organized in Utica, New York, to manufacture the uniquely simple Model 1895, a strong and light repeater with decidedly clean and practical lines. In the minds of many, Savage's hammerless feature represented the apex of nineteenth century rifle design.

Just as novel, and just as noticeable, was the new rifle's ammunition. On the face of it, the 30-caliber Savage was just another rifle shell, though a curious one.

The Savage 303 rifle.

The pronounced bottleneck was unusual, but more striking was the departure in caliber. Typically, sportsmen were accustomed to seeing straight-walled cases topped with fat leaden slugs, and the metal-cased bullet in this runty Savage round was uncommonly smaller than standard. First impressions are often lasting ones, and the instinct of many was that this cartridge was too pipsqueaky-appearing to be the powerful package purported. Speaking presumably for the mainstream, a *FOREST AND STREAM* contributor wrote in early 1896: *"This is going to take a lot of selling if I am going to buy one."*

In 1895, the 303 Savage was more than a cartridge; it was a concept. Militarily, smokeless powder cartridges had been around for a number of years and all the major armies of the planet were arming their troops with this new class of ammunition. On the sporting scene, the cartridges of the 1870s and 1880s were overdue for retirement, and it was just a matter of time before the next newfangled step was undertaken by the arms trade.

Convincing a skeptical, yet receptive public to try his commercially untested combination of unique particulars – smokeless powder, jacketed bullet, and bottle-shaped shell – was the challenge before Arthur Savage. Fortunately, salesmanship was among his *fortes*. He realized the success of his rifle depended substantially upon how well the cartridge was accepted, and there was a critical need to entice the shooting public to try the Savage system. Towards this end, Savage devised a battle plan, and in the process, demonstrated adeptness at creating interest in his product.

To begin with, ordinary-looking columns in the sporting bi-weeklies were naturally gathered to be press releases, reviewer's contributions, or unbiased coverage. The fine print identified them as Savage advertisements in disguise. The introduction and complete description of the new rifle in June of 1895 was the first of many examples of a tactic Arthur Savage had mastered.

Magazine advertisements helped, and Savage ads pervaded the commercial sections of the sporting media. One, run in 1896, *"The new rifle you've heard so much about."* illustrating the rifle and its shell, was precisely what the public needed to see. Thoroughly weary of the Gay '90s overuse of superlatives, consumers generally resisted being influenced by the *"Acme of perfection"* approach, though a stunning Savage rifle was pictured. The *"ne plus ultra in repeating rifles"* ad was of dubious effectiveness in selling the rifle, but the contrast of an unfired and expanded 190-grain softpoint opened the eyes of a generation. Another scheme was to raise suspicions about a person's antiquated deer gun. "The 20th Century Arm" was Savage's claim well before 1900. The slogan, *"years ahead of any other repeating rifle,"* compelled some to "keep up with the times" as another Savage ad challenged. Throughout the promotion of the cartridge, much space was devoted to depicting triumphant hunters posed with moose, bears, and other assorted four-leggers, each efficiently slain by the 303 Savage.

When the inaugural Savage catalog went to press in the spring of 1895, glowing testimonials from satisfied customers were understandably in short supply. Substituted were excerpts from *SCRIBNER'S, LONDON FIELD,* and other journals detailing results secured with *"303-caliber smokeless powder military rifles."* Armed with 303 British or 8mm Mannlicher arsenal rifles, or sporters based upon them, British and German officers and civilian adventurers fearlessly faced the great beasts of the world. Moose, tigers, rhinos, and elephants fell to the small bore, and the accounts of these men were presented initially as passable examples of the 303 Savage principle.

In 1893, the 303's developer drew first blood during the New York open deer season. The first 303 Savage bullet fired at game pierced both ears of a whitetail doe at 200 yards, and the follow-up shot blew off a jaw. A softpoint to the throat finished the animal. The second deer allowed on Savage's license, a buck, was hit in the spine and killed instantly. "Taurus," an immense slaughterhouse bull, was then sacrificed at the altar of commerce. Shot in the forehead, the bullet demolished heavy neck bones and came to rest near the kidneys. A group of Adirondack guides, assembled to witness the display,

Dall DeWeese with his 303 elk, 1898.

Keep Up With the Times

Do not buy a rifle until you have examined into the merits of the

SAVAGE

which is the **TWENTIETH CENTURY ARM.** Only hammerless, repeating rifle in the world. **Absolutely Safe, Strongest Shooter, Flattest Trajectory,** also neatest and most effective rifle manufactured. **Highest Development of Sporting Rifles.** Constructed to shoot **Six Different Cartridges,** or may be used as a single shot without the slightest change in the mechanism. Adapted for large and small game. .303 and 30-30 calibres.

Every rifle thoroughly guaranteed.

Awarded Grand Gold Medal at Paris, in competition with all other styles of repeating rifles.

Write for new illustrated catalogue M.

Manufacturers of **SAVAGE** Magazine and Magnetic Hammers. Send for circular.

Savage Arms Co.

Utica, New York, U. S. A.

BAKER & HAMILTON,
San Francisco and Sacramento, Cal.,
Pacific Coast Agents.

Result of a Single Shot from a .303 **SAVAGE** Expanding Bullet

Savage Arms Company advertisement, 1900.

stood slack-jawed at the penetration and destruction wrought by such a tiny missile.

Savage recognized the importance of legitimate testimonials, from sportsmen with recognizable names, to the success of his mission. Towards that end, Savage recruited Dall De Weese, the well-known hunter/columnist from Canyon City, Colorado. By 1899, De Weese had run up a 25-year string of annual major North American hunts, and his readers looked forward to his yearly report. He was shipped a rifle and the record elk he'd 303'd in 1897 was featured in magazine ads. The next year, Dall conducted a five-month specimen collecting expedition underwritten by the Smithsonian. Three large Alaskan bull moose and five Dall rams fell to his 303 Savage. In his letter to the factory, subsequently reprinted everywhere, he wrote: *"Your rifle is a killer. In fact, the moose were simply paralyzed with the first shot and, if hit anywhere about the shoulders,*

one ball was sufficient. I used a metal-patch, soft-nose." Alaskan hunter and explorer Cpt. F.E. Kleinschmidt slew every species of Alaskan big game with a 303 Savage and told the tales to turn-of-the-century readers of *OUTDOOR LIFE.* Harry Story's 303 killed elephant, hippo, lion–and all the lesser African plains game. Story's endorsements were instrumental in documenting the deadliness of the 30-caliber Savage.

Versatility was an important element injected into the futuristic 303 Savage equation. Magazine ads professed *"for Grizzly or Grouse, the 303 Savage is equally adaptable."* Savage's 1895 catalog offered four types of cartridges to adapt to nearly any conceivable sporting application. There was a 190-grain full-patch load, together with an expanding bullet counterpart: both with a muzzle velocity of 2,000 feet per second. For the unconverted throwbacks, a full power 180-grain blackpowder loading was thoughtfully provided.

Rounding out the first year's line-up was a low-powered gallery/small game cartridge loaded with five grains of #2 Savage smokeless and a 100-grain lead bullet.

Two new loads were detailed in the 1897 catalog. Another reduced load with a 100-grain full-patch bullet in front of 15 grains of smokeless, the metal-covered miniature, as it came to be known, was useful to trappers running their lines, shooting furbearers, and for polishing off wounded big game. It became a practice for 303 users to carry a few in a pants pocket. A specialized 185-grain "Schuetzen Target" load allowed 303 Savage owners to compete in the sport dominated by the precision single-shot rifles. Styled after traditional Schuetzen bullets, the Savage 185-grain projectile was paper-patched. The 1895 Savage rifle actually saw limited use in important matches, and ten paper-patched bullets would reportedly stay in a six-inch circle at two hundred yards. If a casual shooter had

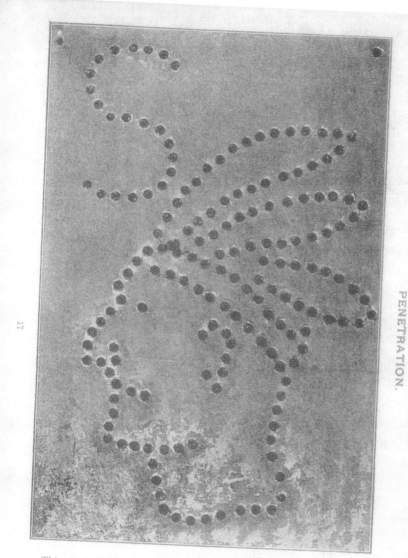

PENETRATION.

This steel plate is ⅟₁₆ inch thick. The perforations were made by the .303 expanding bullet and regular charge of smokeless powder, fired from a Savage magazine rifle at a distance of thirty feet. The holes are one-half inch in diameter, while the bullet is only .303 or about .30 caliber: this is caused by the expanding of the bullet on the first impact. The penetration of the regular metal covered bullet in pine is about 50 inches.

The "penetration" demonstration appeared in both the 1900 and 1903 Savage catalogs.

the nerve to show up on line with a lever action amid a field of Ballards, Stevens, and Winchester single shots, he could be assured that his outfit was competitive.

When the trendy lubricated wire-patched bullet was all the rage, there was a rush by the period's up-to-the-minute types to buy them. Savage was the first in 1900 to offer 160-, 180-, and 200-grain variations loaded into factory cartridges, fueled with either smokeless or black powder.

Several advantages were connected with the extraordinary 2,000 fps Savage velocity against the 1,200-1,500 fps level of the old-fash-ioned heavily-loaded blackpowder rounds. Foremost among these was the dramatic increase in the not-easily definable quality variously termed *killing, stopping, shocking*, or *"bruising"* power attributed to the Savage expanding bullet. The secret to its deadliness lay in a simple and well-known mechanical principle best demonstrated by shooting into sealed water-filled cans. Savage's first catalog offered a wordy explanation of the phenomenon—which boils down to the effect we recognize as 'hydraulic shock.'

Obviously, the lighter bullet translated to less recoil, an impor-tant consideration to the many who were using a Winchester equipped with one of those cruel crescent buttplates.

As another consequence, trajectory was remarkable—and marketably flat. The path of a 190-grain 303 bullet, when zeroed at fifty yards, dropped only 2.5 inches at 200 yards. In contrast, the blackpowder cartridges so commonly in use in 1895, typically fell two feet or more at this range. Savage's 1895 catalog insisted the customary holdover could be disregarded out to 250 yards, and the extension of sensible game shooting ranges was the practical result. Only sixty years previously, the British soldier had been instructed to hold 120 feet over a man 600 yards distant if he wished to hit him. Most people agreed that the Savage trajectory was a certifiable breakthrough.

The 303's use of the new smokeless powder brought the easily-seen benefits buzzed about in military circles for a few years, but which were just becoming apparent to the civilian sportsman. To begin with, the absence of a fog of blackpowder smoke was appealing. Nitro charges and jacketed bullet proportions made for a concentrated unit, and therefore the 303 ammunition was comparatively light, compact and clean. Because the clean-burning smokeless didn't build up a cakey and corrosive fouling, bore cleaning automatically became a less crucial concern. In addition, the spent shells didn't require the boiling ritual after firing, and were fully reloadable.

During the fall of 1896, the small-bore suspicious sat on the sidelines waiting for his brother sportsman to advise him if the 303 was a certifiable wonder—or a gimmick, pumped up by the fancy talk of the ad writer. Meanwhile, the 303 Savage tryout began in earnest. Animals of all descriptions were unfailingly reduced to possession with the Savage hammerless and it's radical ammunition. There was a verified account of an Alaskan harvesting a whale of some description with Savage softpoints. A hunter in Wyoming flattened a bull elk in its tracks, and an antelope—though 480 paces from the Savage muzzle—dropped dead at the 303's report. His account, filed in an October, 1896 number of *FOREST AND STREAM*, concluded with the message: *"This may be interesting to your readers, as it is practice, not theory."* Many other similar reports helped to lay the public's uncertainty to rest.

SAVAGE CARTRIDGES, Manufactured by the Savage Arms Co. CALIBER .303. CASES CONTAIN 1,000 CARTRIDGES.

Cartridges sold in quantities of 20 and upward.
Cartridges are packed 20 in a box.
It is not always necessary to use long-range cartridges in the Savage rifle; Cartridges Nos. 4 and 6 are excellent for short range or small game.

1 SAVAGE .303. SMOKELESS.
REGULAR SMOKELESS POWDER CARTRIDGE.
REGULAR BULLET. Lead with Nickel Cover.

2 SAVAGE .303. EXPANDING.
EXPANDING SMOKELESS POWDER CARTRIDGE.
EXPANDING BULLET. Lead, with Partial Nickel Cover.

3 SAVAGE .303. BLACK
BLACK POWDER CARTRIDGE. Forty Grains Black Powder.
REGULAR BULLET. Lead, with Nickel Cover.

4 SAVAGE .303. MINIATURE
MINIATURE SMOKELESS CARTRIDGE. Grooved Shell.
MINIATURE BULLET. Lead.

5 SAVAGE .303 PAPER PATCHED.
PAPER-PATCHED SCHUETZEN TARGET CARTRIDGE.
PAPER-PATCHED BULLET. Lead.

6 SAVAGE .303. COVERED MINIATURE.
MINIATURE METAL-COVERED CARTRIDGE.
MIN. METAL-COVERED BULLET. Lead, with Metal Cover.

Cartridge.	Price per M Loaded Cartridges.	Price per M Bullets.	Price per M Primed Shells.		Grains Bullet.	
	$ C.	$ C.	$ C.			
Regular	38.00	10.50	18.50		180	
Expanding	38.00	10.50	18.50		190	
Black	32.00	10.50	18.50	Powder charges given on the cans.	180	All the indicated six Cartridges can be used in the .303 Savage Magazine Rifle or the Savage Carbine without any change being made in the arm, excepting the necessary adjustment of the sights. The metal coverings of the different bullets are made of a soft alloy, which does not injure or wear the rifling of the barrel.
Miniature	30.00	3.00	18.50		100	
Paper Patched	38.00	10.00	18.50		185	
Miniature Metal Covered	35.00	5.00	18.50		100	

36

Savage 303 ammunition offering, from the 1903 catalog.

Right from the start, accounts filtered in from the field about the unexpected penetration of the 190-grain Savage bullet. The reports told tales of bullets traversing rump through brisket on straightaway deer; they even zipped the interior length of moose, elk, and foreign game. The word spread quickly, along with rampant misconceptions, and the 303 Savage became defined by these mistaken beliefs. The rumor circulated that the 303 Savage bullet had a range of four and a half miles and was, to a surprising extent, swallowed as gospel. In the minds of multitudes, an exaggerated mental picture of the 303's potency formed. The full-patch bullet, it was repeatedly written, could easily penetrate a twelve-inch oak, and a hunter contentedly sitting behind a tree in the next county was still not safe from a stray bullet.

During the Winter of 1896, it was the sentiment in some localities to question the wisdom of allowing the use of "such a dangerous engine." In Minnesota, there was actually a movement to bar, by statute, the 30-caliber smokeless menace before some innocent wandering the forest was struck by a wayward 303 ball. Edwyn Sandys and Caspar Whitney, both with *OUTING*, editorialized their agreement with the Minnesotan's stance, as did a goodly number of *FIELD AND STREAM* correspondents. The effect of this mini-hysteria, of course, was to intensify the reputation and appeal of the 303. As a bonus, there was considerable no-cost advertising for the gunmaker along with an increase in sales of the lever-action Savage.

The peak years of the 303 Savage was a time of transition – an old and new world coming into a clear and direct contrast with one another. It is important to remember the new small calibers were still being met with a great deal of resistance and the popular press did little to ease this inevitable passage. Caspar Whitney, the very influential editor of *OUTING* magazine, benefited from the experience of years and travel. He witnessed a lot of game fairly hit with the 30-caliber Savage and Krag escape wounded, and he was convinced these rounds lacked the "smashing power" to make them suitable to kill moose-sized animals. For caribou on up, Whitney had no end of confidence in his 45-90 and 50-110 Winchesters. "*I want a club rather than a rapier,*" he preached in his 1900-era columns.

The Sportsman's Expo was a high-flown industry affair held at Madison Square Garden each spring – the Gay '90s version of the SHOT Show. If a gun manufacturer had any hope of being taken seriously, his presence at the Expo was essential. At the 1896 show, Arthur Savage himself manned the company's booth, exhibiting the only gun in his line, and the assortment of cartridges, on slanted silk-covered tables. Getting their fair share of attention at the Savage space were two items, which rather forcefully demonstrated the power of the new 303. The first of these was a 3/8-inch steel plate with bullet holes tracing the letter S. Arthur Savage did the perforating from a distance of thirty feet with metal-jacketed bullets fired from a "Savage Repeating Rifle." Secondly, a hemlock log split lengthwise to expose two captured bullets represented a striking visual comparison of the wood penetrating capacity of the Savage

TELLING HOW 'TWAS DONE

The Savage 303: preferred rifle of the experienced hunter, as implied in this photograph appearing in the December 1904 issue of *RECREATION*.

smokeless 303 and a typical black-powder cartridge, in this case the ordinary 38-55. The 255-grain blackpowder bullet buried itself only 5 3/8-inches into the timber while 32 inches were needed to stop the 220-grain 30 caliber. These two props were also featured promi-nently in the Savage 1895 catalog. An easily overlooked caption speci-fied that the 220-grain hemlock penetrator was launched by 36 grains of nitro powder. Elsewhere in the catalog, we find the recom-mended charge for the standard 190-grain 303 bullet as being 30 grains of smokeless, and 36 grains of gray powder for the 30-40 Krag shell. The inference here was that it was the 303 Savage ammunition that had been put to the test against a rather feeble blackpow-der target cartridge. Catalog data tends to prove otherwise, and men have been hung on lesser evidence. It is highly suspected that the steel was punched by the Krag bullet, too. Savage was hopeful of military

contracts, and a handful of 30-40 Krag Model 1895s were produced for government trials.

In his zeal to gild the 303 lily, Mr. Savage seems to have departed from the advertising straight and narrow. Though not a lie in the strictest sense, the catalog captions have all the appearances of being deliberately misleading. The fact-twisting incident deserves to be recorded among the more blatant deceptions ever foisted on the Amer-ican gun buyer. Savage may have counted on the general under-sophistication of this era's gun crank to pull it off. In any event, he got away with it for over a century.

A different steel plate traveled to the Sportsmen's Expo in 1899 and 1900. The profile of an Indian head outlined with 303 softpoints through 5/16-inch boilerplate now illustrated the steel penetration of the cartridge. Sporting journal cov-erage of the Expo fails to mention the earlier evidence of wood pierc-ing being on display.

A visitor to the Savage booth had a chat with the fledgling gunmaker concerning the trajectory of the flat-shooting 303. Mr. Savage assured the man that the rifle would shoot "point-blank" at 200 yards, though advertising circulars indicated the drop of the bullet at this range was eight inches. As this individual pon-dered the apparent discrepancy, a feeling that he had been deceived was being formed in his mind. In his haste to blame Savage, the man who used the initials *H.B.S.* as his signa-ture enlarged without restraint upon his peevish complaint in a letter printed in *FOREST AND STREAM* a month later. This mean-spirited communication did not escape the notice of potential gun buyers and dealt Savage at least some damage, precisely when he could not afford any negative ink.

One can't ignore the element of exclusivity contributing to the 303 appeal. There has always been a certain attraction or pride in own-ing the technologically latest as

A GOOD, CLEAN KILLING SHOT.

A clean kill by the Savage 303, ca 1909.

30 did it," the Winchester ad was a fresh and trusted reinforcement of the Savage message, and the perception it generated was mutually beneficial to both concerns.

Savage's intention was to be the single-source supplier of 303 Savage ammunition, handloading components, and Savage-brand Smokeless powder. He made the plan work – for a while. Under contract, Union Metallic Cartridge Company loaded the 303 with Savage-provided smokeless powder for the first three years. In 1899, an alliance known as the Big Three (U.M.C., Winchester Repeating Arms, and the U.S. Cartridge Co.) threatened to shut off the essential ammunition flow entirely, unless they could be assured a piece of the lucrative action, forcing Savage to break ground on his own cartridge works. Because the title "303 Savage" was given protection by trademark, the familiar Ideal tong tool for reloading the Savage proprietary round could only be purchased through the sales office at Savage's Utica plant. This continued until 1903.

It could be where Savage really missed the boat, at least in a marketing sense, was his failure to develop an out-of-the-ordinary expanding bullet to complement the 303. An express style–or other distinctively Savage design–properly advertised in conjunction with the cartridge, would not only have set apart the Savage projectile from the generic exposed lead softpoint, but would have added yet another enticing aspect to the Savage pattern.

Over the years, other aspiring rifle merchants have come along. Sir Charles Ross, Chas. Newton, and Roy Weatherby each professed to offer a breakthrough in sporting arms development. Complementing their ultra-modern rifles was a cartridge–or series of cartridges–touted as the ultimate ballistic achievement. The marketing philosophy and technique of each individual didn't vary markedly from the proven Savage approach. Pushing the rifle went hand in hand with the smart promotion of the cartridges headstamped with their name.

In terms of establishment, Lazzeroni Arms Co. seems to be in a position paralleling Savage Repeating Arms Co. of the late 1890s. John Lazzeroni, in a recent letter, unwittingly paraphrased A. Savage's

soon as it became available. Among the snobs and elitists, there was a race to be the first to show up at the 1896 deer camp with a 303 hammerless. This factor alone sold many 1895 rifles, as well as the necessary supply of 303 ammunition. Savage's magazine ads cunningly nourished the impulse.

The industry's nearest counterpart to the 303 Savage was Winchester's new 1895 model in 30-40 Krag chambering, released for public distribution in March of 1895. The 30-30 WCF was thrown into the mix a year later. Surprisingly, both arrived with little fanfare, in terms of magazine advertising. However, a nicely-done *Big Red W* ad of 1897 depicted one '95-armed sport pointing out to another the entrance hole in a defunct wapiti. Captioned "*the*

The Savage 303 could do it all, according to this advertisement appearing in the October 1911 issue of *NATIONAL SPORTSMAN*.

statement of a hundred years prior: "*I want to build the cartridge that will be used for hunting in the next century.*" By the way of contrast, a 180-grain bullet started from John's 7.82 Warbird at 3,500 fps, generates a kinetic energy that doesn't fall below the 303 Savage's muzzle energy level of 1,190 ft/lbs (fpe) until it has passed the 850-yard mark. Others belonging to the current crop of beltless 30-caliber magnums deliver much the same numbers. This is how far we've come between 30-caliber hotrocks on extreme ends of a century.

By 1905, Townsend Whelen and others had broadcast the reality, that rather than a supernatural ray of death, the 303 Savage was actually quite a mundane number more properly belonging to the "*30-30 class of cartridges.*" By that time, the public's fascination had worn off, and the Savage 303 was yesterday's news.

Between 1912 and 1915, bullet speeds were taking monumental strides upwards, and a new "*some speed is good, more is better*" mood was astir. Savage's latest wonder, the 22 Hi-Power, made its appearance–

and the 250-3000 was not far behind. Both were promoted with the same aggressive vigor and tactics that had puffed up the 303 nearly twenty years earlier. The sudden rush to try these out overloaded the factory with orders. In the spring of 1913, those who couldn't live without owning the Imp were faced with a two-month wait.

Men who clung to their trusted 303s all those years abandoned them *en masse* in favor of the new thing, and the used gun market was saturated with second-hand 303s at bargain prices. In 1922, a half-hearted 303 revival was attempted. Savage Arms reissued 1900 ads with the Montana bear hunter's wager: "*I'll bet I can shoot through a grizzly endwise with my 303 Savage.*" No one was interested anymore.

With the Model 1895 rifle as the foundation and the 303 cartridges as the cornerstone, the enterprising Arthur Savage built up an extensive and successful business in a remarkably short time. Before the 1899 calendars were thrown away, he'd solidly established his firm as an active player in the global arms trade. By the Spring of 1900, the factory had been

expanded. In April of that year, Mr. Savage sailed to Europe for the important Paris Exposition where he displayed the most modern and lavish lever actions on the planet. Five weeks later, he returned to Utica with the Grand Gold Medal for the finest firearms at the Expo. That summer, the new three-story cartridge plant was finally in operation, cranking out Savage-brand 303 ammunition. In October, Savage Arms Co. sold more guns – 900 of them – than any month in its existence. One of these was an ultra-fancy 303 ordered by Russian Grand Duke Michael, who could have just as easily ordered a Winchester. When the need arose to equip the Alaska Expedition in June of 1901, the U.S. government chose the 30-caliber lever rifle Arthur Savage advertised as "*years ahead of any other repeating rifle.*"

Darwin was right; it is survival of the fittest. In the Darwinian struggle to endure, the cartridge failed, though not before it established a reputation of its own and accomplished its mission. The reception of the 303 Savage, together with Arthur Savage's astute presentation and the rifleman's eagerness to adjust to the times, brought the Model 99 permanently into the public eye. ●

The Irish and American teams practicing at Creedmoor, L. I., N. Y. on the day before the 1874 International Rifle Match. *The American Rifleman*, Robert Uhl, July 1954.

Long-Range Muzzleloading Rifles

by Thomas D. Schiffer

THERE IS A series of rifles that defined long-range shooting, beginning over one hundred and fifty years ago. These rifles had, and continue to have, a strong appeal to those attracted to functional design, purity of line and excellent workmanship. Other than the newly-made rifles, the specimens shown here came out of collections, musty closets, and attics in response to a series of long-range rifle matches introduced by the National Muzzle Loading Rifle Association (NMLRA) that started over ten years ago. Other matches for these rifles, in other places, have sprung up since.

There is an old story, perhaps true, that illustrates an important point. As the story goes, Christopher Columbus was listening to some chatter at table minimizing what he, Columbus, had accomplished... after all, his dining companions were saying, everyone knew the word was round, etc. After listening awhile, he challenged them to stand a hen's egg on its small end. They all set to work at once. As imagination and skill became exhausted and frustration took a strong hold on them, they declared it could not be done. Seizing one of the eggs in his fist, Columbus brought it down point first on the table top with sufficient force to crush the end into a small flat... gently unfolding his fingers, the egg stood obediently on end.

"*Now that you've seen it done,*" he said. "*... any of you can do it!*"

If Columbus discovered the New World, so did Joseph Whitworth discover a whole new world of accurate long-range shooting. In so doing, he created a weapons system that provided his home country with a unique means of defense. The great expense of a large standing army had caused England to look to its citizens for a pool of effective riflemen to defend its shores, and the Empire. Thus, the Volunteer Rifle Brigade system was born in the mid-1850s, a system roughly akin to the U.S. National Guard and militia, focusing heavily upon rifle marksmanship. In typical fashion, it did not gather

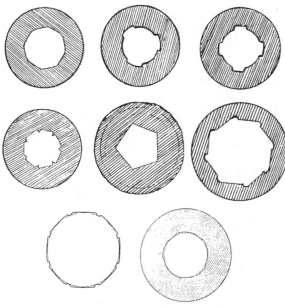

Types of Rifling: Top Row, No. 1, Octagon Bore used by Numerous Old-time Rifle-makers. No. 2, Enfield, English, 3-grooved Model about 1853. Also U. S. Springfield Rifles Models 1873 to 1888. No. 3, 4-Grooved Rifling used by various makers.
Center Row. No. 1, British, Henry type Rifling. No. 2, "5-Square Rifling" used by many Old-time Rifle-makers. No. 3, Major Nuthall's, British, "Rachet Rifling," about 1850. Bottom: No. 1, Pope Rifling. No. 2, Chas. Newton "Parabolic Rifling."

Various forms of rifling. *Muzzle Loading Caplock Rifle,* by Ned Roberts.

momentum until fear of a French invasion jarred things off dead-center in the late 1850s.

Earlier, in 1852, Lord Hardinge, then English Master General of Ordnance, asked Joseph Whitworth, the foremost mechanical engineer of his day, to find out why some government muskets shot well and others did not. Whitworth immediately launched an investigation into the science of musketry. He was restricted to the 530 grains of lead and 70 grains of powder used in the service ammunition of that day. After a detailed scientific investigation he determined a bore size of .451-inch worked far better with 70 grains of powder than the .577-inch bore of the government's musket. Reducing the bore size to 45 caliber required a much longer bullet to weigh 530 grains. He then empirically determined that a much faster twist rate was necessary to keep the bullet stable in flight. He increased the rate of spin from one turn in 78 inches to one turn in 20 inches. This essentially defines all the rifles you see here. All (*except one of the Alexander Henrys*) are of 45 caliber and all have the 1:20 rate of twist–or very close to it.

Two things that define Whitworth's rifle work in most people's minds... to me, the least important... was his adoption of the hexagonal bore, which he patented, and the mechanically-fitted bullet. When others made rifles under his system, they either obtained barrels from Whitworth or devised their own form of rifling. The Alexander Henry rifling is but a variation of the hexagonal bore and Harry Pope's rifling but a variation of the Henry. As to the mechanically-fitted bullet, it was found that properly designed bore-sized bullets (*not groove-diameter bullets*) of the correct hardness, 'bumped up' sufficiently to fill the barrel with a bullet exactly the shape and size of the rifling grooves. Franklin Mann, a half-century later, demonstrated that bore-sized pure lead bullets delivered accuracy superior to other bullet types tried in his exhaustive experiments with blackpowder rifles. See *The Bullet's Flight From Powder To Target,* by F. W. Mann. But as to the 45-caliber bore and twist rate, makers of the Volunteer rifles followed the leader closely. Bullets of approximately 530 grains and powder charges of 70 to 90 grains — or greater — were used.

Tests at the Hythe School of Musketry in 1857 compared the accuracy of Whitworth's system to that of the current service rifle. The best service rifle, made at Enfield Lock, produced a 20-shot 'pattern' over six feet in diameter at 500 yards. This would certainly make life interesting for an artillery crew at that range. However, the Whitworth rifle, tested under the same conditions, produced a 20-shot group measuring slightly over one foot in diameter. While this looks like a ratio of 1:6, consider that a circle enclosing the Enfield bullets has an area of nearly 50 square feet, whereas the area of a circle enclosing the Whitworth bullets would be a little over three-quarters of one square foot. That is a ratio greater than 50:1!

As long as blackpowder was the propellant, Whitworth's findings remained valid, and remain so today. The rifles designed by Whitworth anticipated the ballistics of all blackpowder military cartridges, until the end of the century when smokeless propellants opened an entirely new set of possibilities. The Martini/Henry, the 45-70, the 43 Spanish–and the rest of the blackpowder military cartridges– exhibited exterior ballistics nearly identical to those of the Whitworth.

The British government never did embrace Whitworth's system for its service rifle for a number of good and bad reasons–mostly bad, in my opinion. However, the Volunteer rifle brigades took to the system with a vengeance and rifles of the type were ordered in sizable numbers. In addition, Whitworth and Kerr rifles were exported to the Confederate States of America where they established a reputation for deadly accuracy at great distances.

English, Irish and Scottish makers of note–and many you have never heard of–made rifles on this system. All the rifles generally looked alike, within the four or five different types produced: military, military/target, military/target/ sporting, target and sporting/target rifles. Within this genre, defined by varying match requirements, they differed in refinement of detail, workmanship, style, sights and embellishment, as the owner's wishes might dictate and the depth of his purse allow.

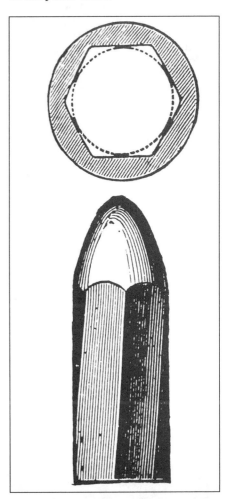

Cut of Whitworth bullet showing how it fit the rifling. Note the 1:20 rifling twist is also incorporated into the fitted bullet. *The Gun,* **by Greener.**

The National Rifle Association of Great Britain was established in 1869 to promote rifle shooting and competition for the Queen's Prize. This resulted in increased participation in long-range rifle shooting. Two of the rifles shown here were prize rifles... one a Kerr from an 1864 competition and the other a Whitworth from the 1860 competition at Wimbledon.

The British NRA produced many rifle matches between teams and individuals throughout the empire, as far away as Canada and Australia. The first NRA competition was held in 1860 at Wimbledon Common for the Queen's Prize. These and other matches were hotly contested, producing reams of copy for the newspapers, magazines and sporting journals that, in turn, helped create intense popular interest.

The Elcho Shield competition was a team event. At stake was the Championship of the Empire. In 1873 an Irish rifle team using Rigby muzzleloading rifles won the Elcho Shield with a record score. The Irish, in turn, challenged "the world" to a rifle match.

The Amateur Rifle Club of the United States picked up this challenge, which was contested at Creedmoor on Long Island, New York in 1874. It may be of interest that the U. S. team used Sharps and Remington breechloaders. The Rigbys outscored the breechloaders, but, since the Irish team member Millner scored a bullseye on the wrong target (*scored under the rules*

THE QUEEN'S OWN !

Caricature of English long-range shooter. *Currier & Ives*, 1875.

as a miss), the Americans won by three points instead of losing by one point. These well-known matches at Creedmoor, Long Island in 1874 led to a series of long-range matches in the U.S. The Wimbledon Cup and the Leech Cup are–to this day–contested for among U.S. long-range shooters with modern rifles, and owe their origins to the long-range muzzleloading matches of long ago.

Quite aside from the original military aspects, long-range rifle shoot-

ing with muzzleloaders was, and is, a fascinating sport in itself. A relatively small but dedicated group of shooters has taken up this activity and the number of adherents is growing slowly but surely.

You might ask if this was, and is, a lost art? The answer is both *no* and *yes*. *No* in that there are scattered examples of the original gunmaker's art that are not only suitable for firing, but are being fired in competition at distances from 220 to 1000 yards. This last distance is well over a half-mile. The 'black' area of the 1000-yard target, which measures over three and a half feet in diameter, looks like a pinhead at that distance. The answer is *yes* in that we do not know nearly as much about how they were loaded and fired, as we might like. Powders of the time are no longer available and the precise methods used by some of the original shooters are not known. But new rifles are being made today that rival, if not equal, the accuracy of the original arms. One of the reasons the sport is growing slowly is that rifles suitable for competition are neither inexpensive nor commonly available. Long-distance ranges for practice and competition are few and far between. The Creedmoor range long ago became a hospital for the mentally ill–and many other ranges are now housing developments.

Parker Hale of Birmingham, England reintroduced the Whitworth and the Volunteer rifles back in the 1970s. They sold fairly well–but not well enough–and that firm no longer makes them. Rifles with

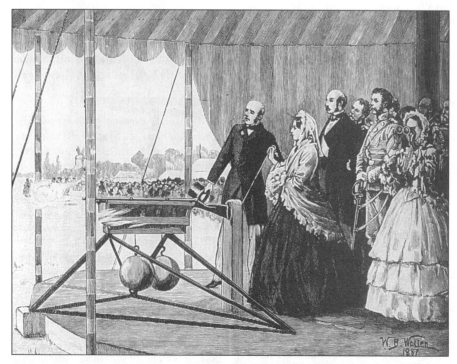

Queen Victoria, firing the first shot at the first annual meeting of the British N.R.A. on Wimbledon Common, July 1860. *The Gun*, by Greener.

the Parker Hale name are now made in Italy and have been for some time. In my opinion, most original buyers of Parker Hale rifles simply did not know how to manage them to best advantage and they were soon relegated to the back of the gun cabinet. The Birmingham-made Parker Hale rifles, the only ones I know anything about are, in my opinion, competitive with the original rifles, providing they are properly set up with match sights, a platinum-lined nipple and given proper loading. The barrels of the Birmingham Parker Hales were hammer-forged; the Whitworth copied the original hexagonal bore and the Volunteer models featured Alexander Henry rifling.

Newly-made rifles on the old pattern... and that is the only thing we are talking about here... utilize 45-caliber barrels of good quality to excellent advantage. Restorations of old rifles have been effected using both liners and replacement barrels–again, with excellent results. However, this restoration work must be done in a sensitive and skillful manner, to justify any attempt at all. While the mechanical skills may be well in hand, no attempt should begin until all aspects of the originals are well understood, as well as implications to the present and future collector value of the rifle. I do not know of many qualified to do this work, and many of those who do qualify will not attempt work for others. None of it is likely to come cheaply or quickly. Makers who have done this kind of work are Don Brown, Bob Woodfill and Mark Silver. There are no doubt others unknown to me. It will be a real plus if your rifle-building candidate actually shoots at long range with blackpowder rifles.

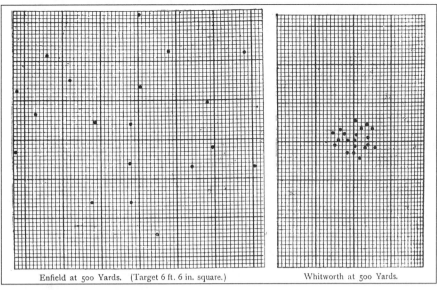

Enfield at 500 Yards. (Target 6 ft. 6 in. square.) Whitworth at 500 Yards.

This shows the accuracy of the Whitworth rifle contrasted to that of the Enfield at 500 yards. *The Gun*, by Greener.

How well did — and do — they shoot? While somewhat better scores were made later, John Rigby placed fifteen consecutive shots in a group measuring about 45 inches at 1000 yards during the great International Match of 1874. We have done a bit better (43 inches)–but with only ten shots–and we used cross-sticks to rest the barrel of the rifle. Rigby shot from the conventional prone position in that match, with no rest at all.

John Rigby went on to become Superintendent of the Royal Small Arms Factory. It was under Rigby that the Lee Metford rifle was adopted. Rigby also invented a method of making cartridges from coiled sheet brass that was adopted later by Colonel Boxer in the Boxer service cartridge for the Snider rifle.

W. W. Greener was a well-known maker of fine arms, as was his

father before him. He talked about target shooting in general in his great book, *The Gun and its Development*, published from 1881 to 1910. He had this to say about long-range shooting:

"Long range shooting is the most difficult, requiring finer training, wide-knowledge, steadier nerve, and better physique than that demanded by any other sport. The long range match rifle is not the superior of the military rifle as a weapon, but as a shooting instrument is considerably ahead of any arm produced."

Loading Long-Range Muzzleloading Rifles

Loading long-range rifles is not too complicated if certain criteria are observed. Perhaps the most important is selection of a bullet that will meet the criterion for bore-

Birds-eye view of the Historic Creedmoor Rifle Range during the September 1874 International Match. *The American Rifleman*, Robert Uhl, June 1954.

sized bullets. Note we are talking about bore-diameter, not groove-diameter, bullets here. Modern cartridge reloading technique, where groove-diameter (*or larger*) cast bullets are favored, has confused many who attempt shooting these rifles.

These are *upsettage* loads wherein bullets of, or slightly over, bore diameter are used. Upon firing, the action of the powder on the base of the bullet 'bumps' the bullet up to groove diameter. Many barrels in the old days had a groove diameter of .457/.458-inch. This is typical of many modern-made barrels, as well, and you will find many of the bore diameters are .451-inch. Some are so marked on the barrel because the bore size was, and is, the key dimension. You are looking for a finished bullet that is a bit tighter than a 'slip fit' in the bore.

Other considerations: Short (*say, pistol-length*) bullets, weighing approximately 250 grains, may not 'upset' reliably since they may well not supply enough inertia to allow the powder gases to expand the bullet to fill the grooves. To ensure reliable expansion you need a bullet of at least 400 grains.

There are other techniques that can be employed to cause the bullet to expand. Soft bullet metal is one and a hollow-base bullet design is another. Pure lead plainbase bullets, weighing 475 grains, have expanded reliably ahead of as little as 65 grains of FFFg powder. Bullets do not get any softer than when made of pure lead. They will exhibit a Brinell hardness of from 4.5 to 5. Any alloy you are likely to use will introduce some hardness. I have used pure lead bullets in both breech-loading rifles and muzzle-

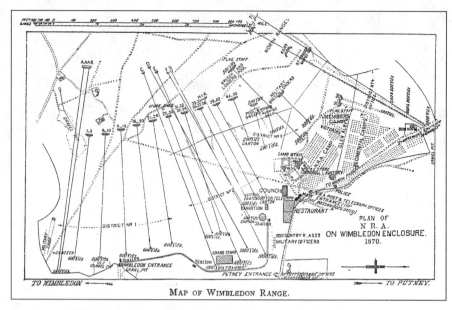

Rare map of Wimbledon Range. *Handbook for Riflemen*, by **FOREST and STREAM**.

loaders with excellent results and NO leading at the blackpowder velocities I employ.

Alloy bullets also have a greater or lesser propensity to age harden. They may work well when first cast - and refuse to upset a month or so later, opening groups. Stay away from alloy bullets unless you are using 'fitted' bullets... discussed later.

Pure lead bullets are not as easy to cast as the common alloys usually used. Keep in mind the bullet mould and the melt must be *HOT* to make good pure lead bullets. Some are surprised that pure lead had a melt temperature higher than the harder alloys commonly used in bullet casting. Adding a bit of tin to pure lead—say a 50:1 alloy—will not harden the bullet appreciably and will make it easier to cast.

Quality bullets must have a well filled-out base, uniformly sharp all the way around. Weight variations of a grain or two are less important than a well filled-out base. Keep in mind that a nose-pour mould has a plate on the other end against which the base of the bullet is formed. That thin plate will cool faster than the common mould blocks and it is important to keep that plate hot via a steady and fairly rapid cadence of casting in order to keep bullet bases well filled-out. The base-pour mould has the bottom plate as the sprue plate, which is re-heated by the incoming melt.

Alloy bullets, being harder than pure lead, may need a hollow base to upset properly upon ignition. Because of age-hardening, as well as loss of hardness over time, I do not recommend alloy bullets unless you are willing to experiment with them. Casting with pure lead will avoid varying hardness in *upsettage* projectiles, arguably the most sensitive component in your load.

Keep in mind a bullet mould will throw larger-diameter bullets when casting with an alloy than it will if pure lead is used. If you are special-ordering a mould, you need to tell the maker the bullet metal you intend to use and the diameter of bullet you need—which means you need to know your bore diameter. A bullet of the correct diameter should enter the rifle's muzzle easily with only finger pressure, but not be small enough to fall down the bore under it's own weight. While the loose bullet might shoot OK, the poor fit may allow the bullet to slip forward off the powder charge, if the muzzle is pointed down. The resulting airspace is usually detrimental

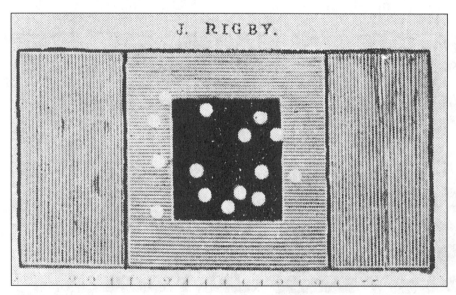

1000-yard Creedmoor target of Irish Team member, John Rigby that was fired in the International Match of 1874. *The Muzzle-Loading Caplock Rifle*, by Ned Roberts.

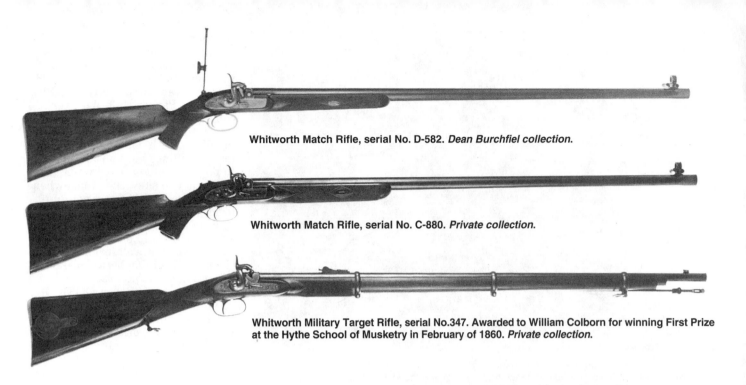

Whitworth Match Rifle, serial No. D-582. *Dean Burchfiel collection*.

Whitworth Match Rifle, serial No. C-880. *Private collection*.

Whitworth Military Target Rifle, serial No.347. Awarded to William Colborn for winning First Prize at the Hythe School of Musketry in February of 1860. *Private collection*.

Prize inscription on capbox lid of Whitworth Rifle No. 347: "Hythe School of Musketry, First Prize, Feby 1860, William Colburn" *Private collection*.

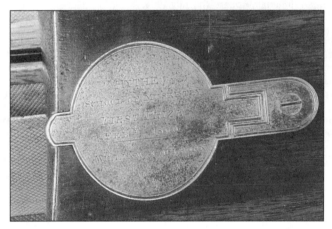

Whitworth Military Rifle, 2 band, serial No. C-465. Whitworth rifles were made at Manchester. *Tom Neigebauer collection*.

Whitworth Military Target Rifle, 3 band, serial No. 915. *Dean Burchfiel collection*.

Whitworth Military Sporting, Target Rifle, serial No. C-775. *Dean Burchfiel collection*.

Irish Rifle Team after the 1874 International Match. John Rigby is on the left, standing. Can you guess which one fired on the wrong target, giving the victory to the Americans? *The American Rifleman*, Robert Uhl, July 1954.

to accuracy and can be disastrous to the barrel, bulging or bursting it. Larger bullets can be sized down to fit the bore and will be more 'round' than the as-cast bullets, but many feel that sizing reduces accuracy. If I had an otherwise good mould and a proper sizing die, I would certainly try sizing before ordering a new mould.

Flat-nosed 475-grain bullets cast of pure lead give excellent accuracy out to 600 yards, in my experience. At 1000 yards, a more streamlined bullet does better. A sharper, rounder nose–with a minimal flat at the tip and a weight in excess of 500 grains–will do better.

My current favorite 1000-yard bullet is 1.325 inches long, weighs 519 grains in pure lead and has a bearing length of nearly .900-inch. It has five generous lube grooves over .600-inch of the bearing length. Pure lead bullets shorten about 1/16-inch upon firing; the bullet

being 'upset' to fill out the rifling. I have captured fired bullets in snow and this inertial shortening effect can be clearly seen. Snow does not deform the bullets unless it is slushy/icy. Finding the fired bullets is a hand-numbing experience, but rewarding in terms of learning what goes on shortly after the trigger is pulled. Sometimes I have simply placed newspapers under the snow piles and waited for a thaw to deposit my prize on the paper. It has been many years, but I seem to remember that about

thirteen feet of packed snow was required to stop a 45/100 bullet.

In my loads with plain-based pure lead bullets I have used a 1/8-inch felt wad successfully. In a Birmingham Parker Hale Whitworth copy, I used the hexagonal wad punch that came with the rifle. In my Rigby, with a more conventional form of rifling, I use a round punch to produce snugly-fitted wads. It is quite easy to skew the punch when cutting the wad and any non-uniform wads should be rejected.

Pure lead bullets lubricated with a "messy" lube like Ox Yoke Wonder Lube have shot well for me without cleaning or wiping between shots when using certain brands and granulations of powder. GOEX FFFg powder has worked well in loadings from 65 to 75 grains; Wano FFFg has also worked well. Swiss powder in FFFg granulation in similar loads required cleaning between shots. The fouling is light with the Swiss, but seems harder.

Many long-range riflemen use CCI Magnum #11 caps and a platinum-lined nipple. The platinum-lined nipple seems to resist erosion almost indefinitely. There are other nipples available that feature ceramic or other erosion-resistant materials, which may do as well. The military rifles have musket nipples. A friend who owns the Thomas

Contemporary loading box on firing line at Oak Ridge, Tennessee. Note vials of pre-weighed powder charges.

Turner rifle pictured here uses a platinum-lined nipple and a #11 cap. The big hammer and strong spring, seemingly designed to crush rock, has not caused any trouble - to date - with the small nipple… and ignition seems just fine, too.

Now, let's talk about fitted bullets. A 'fitted' bullet, by definition, is a bullet pre-formed to fit the bore rather exactly, with enough clearance to allow it to be rammed down the barrel. The fitted bullet can be formed in several ways. Whitworth extruded his bullets through a die and machined the nose and tail. It seems a shame to shoot a bullet with that much work lavished on it. The body of the bullet had the rifling twist incorporated in it, too! Bill Roberts has successfully made such "corkscrew" bullets and they - predictably - shoot very well. Don't expect to pick up a box or two of them at the gun store on the way home, however. Incidentally, these bullets are then paper-patched. In other words, the lead bullets have to be made eight or ten thousandths of an inch smaller than the barrel; the paper patching brings them up to the correct diameter.

Moving to an easier method to get a fitted bullet, some use a piece of cut-off barrel in newly-made rifles. You won't catch any of us cutting an old barrel in order to do this. The cut-off portion is then machined so that a groove-diameter bullet can be forced through it in such a way as to form a negative impression of the rifling on the bearing surface of the bullet. The die can be machined to form a lubricating die as well. Some skillful machine work is required to produce bullets, straight with the axis of the barrel, which

ERIN GO BRAGH !

Caricature of Irish Rifleman. *Currier & Ives*, 1875

have to be free to rotate as they are engraved by the rifling in the forming operation. In this system, the hardness of the bullet is not as critical. It is written in the literature that in the old days, fitted bullets were preferred because harder bullets, which resisted deformation, could be employed. Gibbs Metford used this fitted bullet, as did Whitworth before him, with excellent results.

While I have no personal experience with fitted bullets, Ted Greer has used them in our matches with telling effect. His forming die was made from a piece of the Douglas

barrel with which his rifle is fitted. He uses a Lyman mould; I believe #457124, a grooved, lubricated bullet. Ted wipes the barrel between shots to keep loading easy. When fitted bullets are done properly, they are as accurate as anything we can devise. More recently, Ted has used a false muzzle to start his pure lead groove-diameter bullet, with equal success.

Now we come to paper-patched bullets. I have not used paper-patched bullets in muzzleloaders, but did some paper-patch cartridge work about 25 years ago with a Rigby-barreled Ballard rifle in 45/100/550. The patching method can be the same for a muzzle-loading rifle and identical bullets can be used. In my method, I decided what

▲ Thomas Turner Match Rifle started life as a military rifle; later modified by Thomas Turner (Birmingham) into this configuration. Note the large military Enfield-style lock and hammer. Rifle has no serial number.
Gary Freking collection.

Action detail of Thomas Turner Match Rifle. *Gary Freking collection.*

Section of an old original platinum lined nipple. The platinum is the light-colored material threaded into the bottom of the nipple. Some have the platinum silver-soldered in...not threaded. *Rick Weber.*

paper I wanted to use. As I remember, it was .0025-inch bond paper. Working backwards from the desired size, in this case the .451-inch bore diameter of the Rigby barrel, I found I needed a naked lead bullet of .441-inch. Chucking up a piece of 1/2-inch drill rod in my lathe, I turned the shape of bullet that I wanted. I turned the body portion about a 1/2-inch or so longer, leaving about a 2-inch shank for chucking purposes. I then carefully hacksawed half of the "bullet" away lengthwise, filed clearance and relief into it, hardened it with a torch and quenched in water. I drew it back to a straw color and had an effective "half reamer."

Taking a 1-1/2 inch diameter piece of Stressproof free-machining steel for a die body, I chucked approximately a 3-inch length of it in the headstock and hogged out much of the steel with a drill bit. I then centered and drilled a 1/16-inch 'bleed' hole out the other end. Chucking the reamer in the tailstock, I formed the fin-

ished interior of the die with the half-reamer. A base punch was then made to closely fit the die body, and easily adaptable to form most bullet sizes. By altering the simple base punch, you can change the base configuration. I used lead wire to make my bullets. I cut off a piece of 3/8-inch lead wire about ten grains over the desired bullet weight, lubed it very lightly with STP and dropped it into my unhardened die. Putting the base punch in behind it, I squeezed the base punch into the die in my 4-inch bench vise. The base punch would stop when it hit the shoulder provided as a 'stop' for the punch. The punch and die would nicely form the bullet and force the excess lead out the 1/16-inch vent hole in the die's nose. Removing the base punch, the bullet could be pushed out with a pin punch directed through the bleed hole. After cutting off the bleed section with a pair of sharp side cutters, I had a perfectly formed bullet, ready for the paper patching.

Lyman made some paper-patch moulds about a century ago. The cavity was smooth inside, with a spring-loaded nose punch and a sprue plate fitted to the base. The lead was poured, the sprue plate swung aside and the nose plunger tapped to eject the solid bullet. I have only one in my collection and it fits a 32-40, or one of its kin.

Now the fun begins. Suitable paper is not easily identified and you will not get much help from your local stationary store. You are looking for a paper with high rag content for strength. I have not been in the marketplace for 25 years and do not know what might be available today. I used Southworth Bond paper back then, and liked it.

Once you get the paper, you will need a wooden cutting board, a sharp single-edge razor blade or

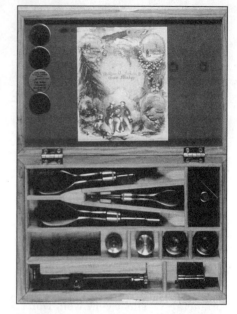

Sight case with turnscrew, nipple wrench, sights and inserts for the front sight; disc for rear sight. Fine workmanship is not dead. William A. Roberts Jr. recently made this quarter-sawn oak case and implements.

Xacto knife. First, identify the length of patching needed to wrap twice around the bullet. Make two full turns and a little more with a dummy strip of the paper you wish to use, and cut through them with your razor blade just behind the ogive. This is a mark only. Unrolling

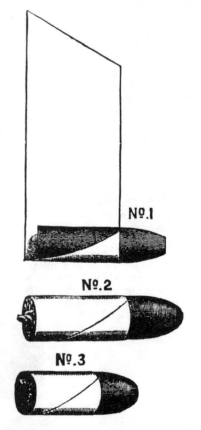

Page from Lyman Handbook No.15. *Lyman Products.*

Three bullets successfully used in 45-caliber muzzle loading rifles. *L-R*: Brooks, 516 grain; Lyman #451112, 475 grain; Pedersoli 518-grain from Dixie Gun Works.

Kerr military rifle, London Armoury, Second Model, serial No. 643. *Tom Neigebauer collection.*

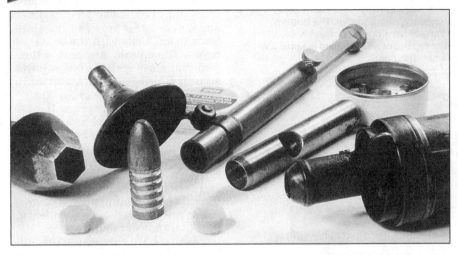

Hexagonal wad punch, powder measure, round wad punch and powder flask surround cylindrical bullet successfully used in a Whitworth.

the paper, you can accurately measure the length of strip needed to make up precut patches. About ten thousandths of an inch - or a little more - should be subtracted from this length to avoid any lump where the paper butts up against itself after two wraps. You will need a strip wide enough to reach from where the ogive of the bullet is tangent to the cylindrical portion to the base - plus enough to wrap around the base. The usual practice is to cut the end lines on an angle of 30 to 45 degrees. A template can then be filed from shim stock and used, with the razor blade, to cut patches.

Paper has a definite grain structure. By tearing the paper, you can see which way the grain is running. Cut your patches so the grain runs around the bullet. Wrap the paper around the bullet such that the diagonal cut is across the line that the rifling will cut into the bullet. I

put all my patches on damp (not wet). Once you get the proper amount of dampness and the hang of doing it, the patch can be given a half-turn around the bullet, laid on a flat surface and rolled the length of one finger and have it all come where you want it. Perfection won't be realized the first time you try this, but stay with it. The excess paper projecting past the base is then wrapped around the base with a twisting motion and the bullet set aside, base-down, until the paper dries. With dry paper, the weight of the bullet holds things in place after they are placed in their hole in a styrene foam cartridge block or something similar. With hollow-base bullets, the excess paper is often twisted into a knot and pushed into the base. (*I did not like this*

because I have found this twist still neatly tucked into some of my recovered bullets.) The bulk of the patching material will land a little forward of the muzzle after the gasses blast it off. Damp patches shrink tightly to the bullet but there is no real bonding to the bullet. I never had any trouble having the majority of the paper come off at the muzzle; none at all with plain-based bullets. (*Bill Roberts puts his paper on dry and it works fine that way. He then rolls the dry-patched bullets on a pad lubricated with artificial sperm oil–just a light coating–immediately before loading.*)

Dig enough paper-patched bullets out of a clay bank or a snow pile and you will see something else I did not like about paper patching. There was the mute evidence that every fold of the paper patch, where it wrapped around the base, was ironed into the lead by the powder gasses. A well-patched bullet with a full, sharp base became somewhat mutilated some milliseconds before exiting the muzzle, where a smooth even base is all-important. Hardened bullets would have more resistance to this deformation, but would be harder to upset... requiring a hollow base and thereby providing the twisted tail of the paper patch a place to ride (*sometimes*) to the target. Not good!

But performance, not crackbrained theory, is the bottom line. I never

▲ **Kerr military rifle, London Armoury, Third Model, serial No. 775. *Matthew Middleton collection.***

▶ **Presentation disc in stock of Kerr rifle serial No. 775. *Matthew Middleton collection.***

Fired paper patched bullets. Note the paper creases "ironed" into the base of the lower right bullet. That bullet started life with a cylindrical body, now fully upset into hexagonal shape by firing in a Whitworth. Note paper wad patch tail jammed into the base of the bulleton the left. You can see the impression of the rifling, which came through the patch paper on the top bullet (*from a 38-caliber schuetzen rifle*). Under it is a piece of recovered patch paper showing rifling marks. The bottom bullets were dug out of a clay bank. The top bullet was stopped in snow and is not deformed.

met a firearm in my life that seemed to care what I thought about why it did or did not shoot to my standards. Some of the best shooting ever done with blackpowder rifles was done with factory paper-patched bullets.

Groove-diameter bullets, either paper patched or lubricated, can be used in these rifles, with the added inconvenience of using a false muzzle or other means of engraving the rifling on the bullet. This entails using some force, not necessarily extreme, to do the engraving. Toggle levers, mallets and other means have been employed to accomplish

this. All the practitioners I know wipe carefully between shots.

Now we come to the issue of wads. The justification for wads is sealing the bore against 'young' gas leakage before the bullet itself can bump up to seal the bore. Leaking gas can cut deeply into the side of the bullet; any hope for best accuracy departs with the gas and

eroded lead. Recovered bullets sometimes show a deep groove cut into the side of the bullet. The lead spray, melted by the hot gasses, collects on the surface of the bore.

It is difficult to use a wad effectively with any but a plain-based bullet. Any suggestion of a boattail or hollow base on the bullet complicates things excessively. Boattails and hollow bases provide places for wads to tag along with the bullet beyond the muzzle. Any part of the wad that stays with the bullet hurts accuracy. Also, jamming a wad into a hollow base also tends to pull the periphery away from sealing the bore... not good. A wad beneath a plain-base paper-patch bullet tends to keep the tail from being blasted away from the bullet upon exiting the muzzle... also not good.

There is a reason, quite aside from its bore-sealing propensities, to use a wad. Most of us soon learn that blackpowder fouling concentrates in a hard ring where the bullet rested against the powder. This hard ring tends to mutilate the next bullet seated there. The use of a proper wad will cause the ring to form at the base of the wad– not at the base of the bullet. If the wad is thick enough, it will hold the next bullet away from that ring. Lubrication on the wad, or a lube 'cookie,' tends to keep fouling soft enough that it will do no harm. In the old rifle accessories, we find several kinds of "lubricators," wads having a lubricant and

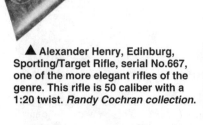

▲ Alexander Henry, Edinburg, Sporting/Target Rifle, serial No.667, one of the more elegant rifles of the genre. This rifle is 50 caliber with a 1:20 twist. *Randy Cochran collection.*

▲ Alexander Henry, Edinburg, Sporting/Target Rifle, serial No.667, note the fine engraving. *Randy Cochran collection.*

John Rigby, Dublin & London, Target Rifle, serial No. 13,835. Note provision for mounting rear sight on the wrist of the stock or on the heel of the butt.

John Rigby, Dublin & London, Target or Match Rifle, serial No. 12601. Rigby Holdings, Ltd. indicate from their factory records that the original rifle was delivered on October 26, 1865 to Trent Cunningham. This rifle had been extensively rebuilt, the only original part is the barrel.

THE HIGHLAND FLING.

Caricature of Scotsman shooting at long range. *Currier & Ives*, 1875.

a hard, dry face to seat against the powder. It is generally considered bad form to allow lube to wet the powder... causing it to not burn. Lube also has a tendency to cause the wad to stick to the bullet... not good. Perhaps a lube 'cookie' sandwiched between two hard wads?

I use a 1/8-inch wad of felt with no lubricant and it seems to work well. I have not yet tried variations on that theme. A bad feature of wads is that they are yet another item to deal with on the firing line... *let's see now, that last shot went low... did I forget to put a wad in for that last shot??*

As far as specific loads are concerned, I will give you two recipes. One for grooved, lubricated bullets and the other for paper-patched bullets. Before deciding either will not work, make absolutely sure you have followed the instructions to the letter... not always an easy matter. My best load to date consists of a Brooks 516-grain bullet with the Cochran modification to the forepart cast of pure lead and lubricated with Ox Yoke Wonder Lube, ahead of 70 grains weight of GOEX FFFg or Wano FFFg powder and a 1/8-inch thick U.S. Felt Co. F-1 felt wad. The wad needs to be hexagonal if used in the Whitworth boring, or round

and snugly-fitted in the others. Parker Hale furnished a hexagonal punch with their Whitworth rifles. I use CCI magnum No. 11 caps with the above load. Seat the bullet with uniform pressure and assure the bullet is down on the powder. I shoot the above load "dirty," not cleaning or wiping the bore between shots. Dixie

Gun Works sells a Lyman mould (#457121), and a similar Pedersoli mould, for these rifles. In my experience they work very well through 600 yards, but not as good as the Brooks at 1000 yards. While I feel the above load works well, I will be surprised if I have not changed it, one way or another, by the time you read this.

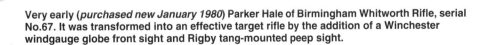

Very early (*purchased new January 1980*) Parker Hale of Birmingham Whitworth Rifle, serial No.67. It was transformed into an effective target rifle by the addition of a Winchester windgauge globe front sight and Rigby tang-mounted peep sight.

Early Parker Hale of Birmingham 2-band Volunteer Rifle, serial No. 809. The front sight has been replaced and a rear tang sight added. The white sticker on the stock is a National Muzzle Loading Rifle Association match inspection sticker, attesting to correct overall weight and trigger pull weight. *Gary Freking collection.*

Bill Roberts and others use paper-patch bullets with excellent results. I will let him tell you how: *"Use of the paper-patch bullet requires that the bore be wiped between shots with a lightly moistened cloth patch. Before loading, the muzzle is pointed downward (at the firing line) and a cap snapped to remove any loose fouling in the small ignition passages in the breech. Powder is poured through a brass tube to the powder chamber to prevent moisture in the bore from coming in contact with the powder. Bullets are swaged in tooling I made and then dry paper-patched with two wraps of onionskin paper similar to air mail stationery. The bullet is lightly oiled on a felt pad saturated with artificial sperm oil right before loading. No wad is used because the swaged bullets have a cavity in the base for twisting the tail of the paper into. Wads used with base-cavity bullets impair accuracy, per my experiments. Both Elephant and Swiss powder in the FFg granulation are used. Using the same lot of powder for your shooting is very important."*

You can see there is endless room for variation and likely no two of us load our rifles exactly alike. However, I have tried to appraise you of the important things...the rest is up to you, your rifle, the mirage, and the wind at 1000 yards.

Shooting Long-Range Muzzleloading Rifles

The shooter turns from the loading procedure and notes the wind flags on the range. The one on the butts at 1000 yards is lifting up about 45 degrees and to the right, over toward 3 o'clock. The flag at the 600-yard line is fluttering and falling. The flag at the firing line points to 9 o'clock with as much gusto as the one at the butts points to three o'clock... nothing is changed from the last shot which looked good when it broke cleanly when the sights drifted

minutely to the right. The shot had been flagged back a '10' at 9 o'clock.

Based on that, the shooter adjusted the front sight windage a bit to the left (*which will move the bullet to the right*). The shooter quickly gets into the prone position on the shooting mat, checks the wind flags have not changed, puts the spirit level bubble

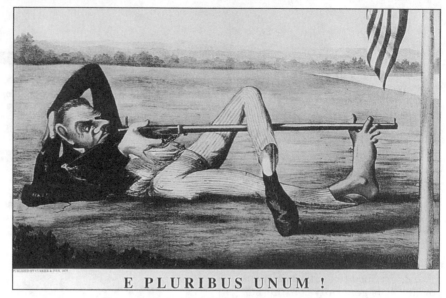

E PLURIBUS UNUM !

Caricature of United States long-range rifleman. *Currier & Ives.*

Detail of hollow-base Whitworth bullet made recently by William A. Roberts Jr. Don't expect to find these for sale in your local gun shop. That is a hexagonal wad under the base. *Author's collection.*

◄ This match rifle is a marriage of old and new, performed by William A. Roberts Jr. It consists of an orphan barrel made by George Gibbs, Bristol, and an orphan Whitworth, Manchester, buttstock. Much hardware is newly made, in the spirit of the original. The appearance and shooting ability of this rifle (*and that of its current owner*) might well cause the ghosts of the original builders to dance. *William A. Roberts collection.*

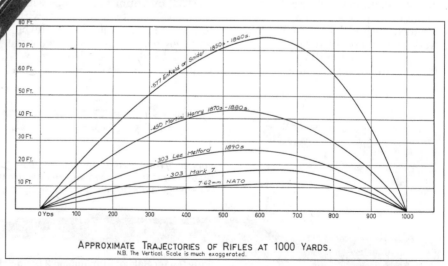

APPROXIMATE TRAJECTORIES OF RIFLES AT 1000 YARDS.
N.B. The Vertical Scale is much exaggerated.

Trajectory curves of old-time black powder rifles contrasted with the "modern" rifles (*bottom two*). The 577/450 Martini Henry curve is practically identical to that of the Whitworth and its Volunteer progeny. *The Target Rifle in Australia*, J. E. Corcoran.

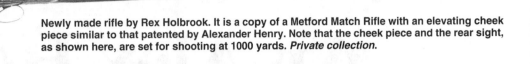

Newly made rifle by Rex Holbrook. It is a copy of a Metford Match Rifle with an elevating cheek piece similar to that patented by Alexander Henry. Note that the cheek piece and the rear sight, as shown here, are set for shooting at 1000 yards. *Private collection.*

Birmingham Small Arms (B.S. A.) Whitworth Target Rifle, serial No. F507. This rifle was given a new (Douglas) barrel by William A. Roberts Jr. and has won its share of matches. *William A. Roberts Jr. collection.*

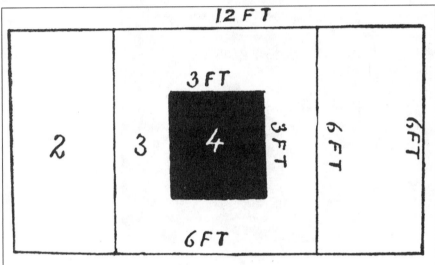

Fig. 170. — Old Creedmoor Targets.

Creedmoor 1000 yard target used in the 1874 International match. *Modern American Rifles*, A. C. Gould.

'to sleep' where it belongs (*the middle of the vial on the front sight*) carefully but quickly aligns the sights on the target and squeezes off a shot. The rifle comes down out of recoil and the shooter knows the sights drifted ever so slightly to the left this time and sees that the target is still there. As the apprehension mounts, the target finally disappears into the pit. It took the bullet more than three seconds to get there and another three or four seconds for the pit crew to react to the hit. It seems an eternity, since the shooter knows the target will stay up if the bullet misses the target.

Meanwhile, the shooter rises to reload the rifle. The powder is already in the rifle before the pit crew returns the target to the firing position. The spotter reports a close '9' at 9 o'clock. About what the shot looked like when it broke. The shooter returns to the loading procedure feeling that the rifle was now well-zeroed for the prevailing conditions; if only the conditions hold...

The above vignette illustrates the typical usage of the long-range rifles. If an event like that happened over a century ago you would be not be hearing about '9s' and '10s', but 'centers' and 'bullseyes' instead. Shooting like this took place a century and a half ago, but it also may have happened just the other day. And it will happen again.

If you shoot long-range rifles, at times you will be greeted by an agreeable score from the pit, or you will swear the rotation of the earth caused your miss on that last shot... other times you may just swear! I cannot tell you what it feels like when the pit flags back a 10X, but some say the earth really does move!! Good luck!

Thousand-yard targets at Oak Ridge, Tennessee. There are three targets up; the others are down in the pits for scoring. The light-colored line beneath are the target frame numbers.

My English Sharps ... An Alex Henry!

by Bill Pace

OR PERHAPS I should call it a Scottish Sharps, since Henry's shop was in Edinburgh, Scotland. Sometime in the late 1950s, I fell in love with my first Alex Henry... just could not put it down! It was a graceful little 360 x 2-1/4" Black Powder Express "Rook rifle." With its pistol-grip stock of dense English walnut, an octagon barrel, and fine engraving, it was a true beauty! This rifle had a left-hand lock which made for

easy loading from the right side, the safety bolt was behind the hammer and convenient to manipulate with the right thumb. I hunted with this rifle for several years, handloading some expanded 38-55 cases. Its light weight, coupled with its looks and fit, made it a real joy to carry in our East Texas woods.

Alas! In a moment of madness I traded it for another *"gotta have it"* gun that I can't even remember now.

Fortunately that Alex Henry resides in the collection of a friend – who consistently rejects my efforts to reacquire it... oh well, maybe some day.

For those not familiar with the fine rifles of Mr. Henry, I enthusiastically recommend Wal Winfer's fine book, *British Single Shot Rifles Vol. I.* It outlines the basics of Henry's superb rifles and gear much better than I can. In it, we learn that Henry was an excellent shooting

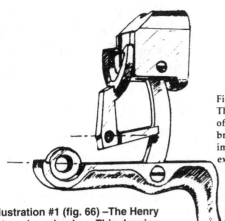

Fig. 66—Henry Internal Mechanism
This drawing illustrates the relationship of the major parts. Clearly shown is the breechblock and how, on lowering, it impinges on the extended legs of the extractor.

Illustration #1 (fig. 66) –The Henry internal mechanism. This drawing illustrates the relationship of the major parts. Clearly shown is the breechblock and how, on lowering, it impinges on the extended legs of the extractor.

competitor, as well as the maker of outstanding arms. In addition to his high quality rifle and shotgun production, he was also a tireless experimenter and inventor; one item being the "snap caps" that we use today!

With all due respect to Mr. Sharps, it takes only a moment with a Henry in your hands to understand this article title. Henry took the Sharps action and converted it into a "silk purse." The concept of a dropping block, under-lever controlled, with a side hammer, is all there, but so graceful and flowing that it's hard to grasp the relationship at first. Henry's actions are smaller, more rounded, locks are English "Best" and on the larger calibers, 'cranked' or curved inward at the wrist in such a way as to produce a slender, very comfortable grip. I feel the description of the locks in Henry's rifles that Winfer has in his book is so good that it bears quoting:

"The locks will show the highest workmanship and, if rust has not penetrated, will show faultless flat polishing and will sneak through its sear bents with the sweetness of a violin. "....the collector will notice the strong mainspring as he draws the hammer up from the fired position. As the lock slides past the half-cock notch he will be aware of a softening of the spring's tension until the hammer reaches full cock. At this point the mainspring is quite light, thus guaranteeing a light, safe and enduring trigger pull as well as a hammer increasing in energy as it falls."

Winfer has done the best job I've read of describing the unique feel of those superb locks. The lever is locked to the shotgun-like trigger guard, but easily released with a simple push button. No loose levers here, everything fits so smoothly that you can reload in total silence. In my opinion though, the best changes from the Sharps are the powerful extractor and hammer/firing pin mechanics. Instead of the trouble-causing Sharps side extractor with its penchant for getting behind an inserted cartridge, Henry's extractor engages both sides of a cartridge for sure extraction. The simple, direct, one-piece firing pin is coupled with excellent hammer power. I've never had a misfire. The extractor on my current Henry (*yep, I had to have another*) is his Martini style – very powerful, no stuck cases ever! See illustrations 1, 2, and 3 (*figs. 66, 67, and 72 from Winfer's book*) for a clear picture of the workings of his action, firing pin, and extractor.

Shortly after my brain-dead trade, I fell into a supposed 450 x 3-1/4" BPE that was a plain unengraved sporter. After much bore slugging and chamber casting, I returned this piece because neither our local "experts" nor I could figure out what the chambering really was. Better informed today, my guess is that it may have been chambered for one of the early paper-cased cartridges with very generous tolerances. Wish I'd kept it now!

My next Henry cost me dearly. I traded an early Remington Creedmore for this rifle! Oh, how passion can control our better judgment! My undoing this time was a first quality take-down sporter in 450 x 3-1/4" BPE, with a perfect bore. Extensively engraved, it was a beautiful piece. I struggled for five years to get it to shoot consistently... nothing

I tried worked! This gun is similar to the one pictured on page 83 of Winfer's book, with the same take-down arrangement. Looking back, I'm sure there was an awful lot of pilot error in those loading attempts. My experience loading blackpowder cartridges is much more extensive today and I feel certain I could now make it shoot well. The serial number of this rifle was #5708, just in case a reader has it.

At a Houston, Texas gun show I found two Henrys on a dealer's table, one, a 500 x 3" BPE, was nicely engraved and, though showing lots of use, still a fine rifle. The other rifle was in better condition but the 500 BPE felt so good as it came to my shoulder. Light, graceful, and with a lovely honey-colored buttstock, it became hard to put down. After returning to touch and feel several times, lust got the better of me! I was already loading for this cartridge so a little haggling later I traded the 450 for the 500.

Illustration #2 (fig. 67) –Henry breechblock and link. Also shown is firing pin, spring and nipple. This block shows the rarely-found rebate in its face for a cartridge's rim.

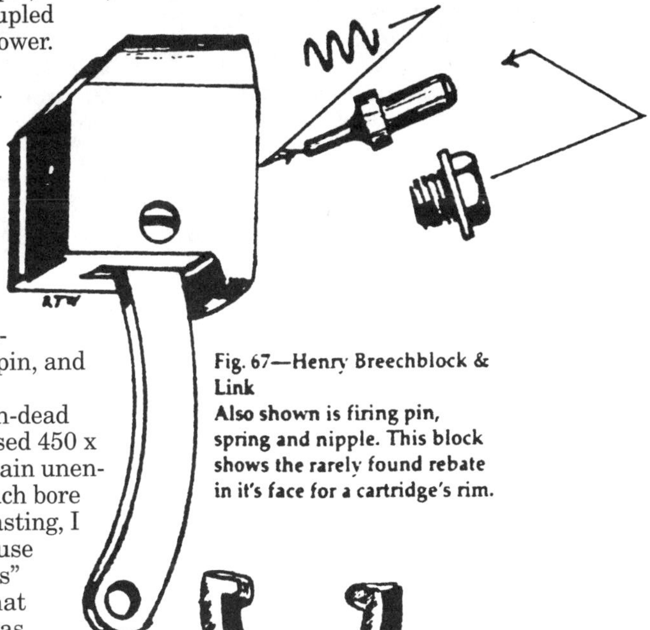

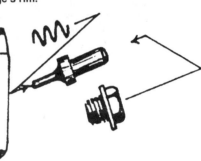

Fig. 67—Henry Breechblock & Link
Also shown is firing pin, spring and nipple. This block shows the rarely found rebate in it's face for a cartridge's rim.

Fig. 72—Henry Extractor Martini type.

Illustration #3 (fig. 72) – The Henry extractor, Martini type.

Well... the light in the Astro Hall is never all that good and the bore was heavily greased and when I got home – in better light and after cleaning – I found the bore to be quite worn. It had that very gray appearance that results from many rounds of blackpowder cartridges. Someone had used it in the game fields a bunch. Boy! If this piece could tell its story! Nonetheless it was a quality piece and felt like Henry had made it just for me. Why is it that those English stocks fit so well?

Amazingly, I've owned four of Henry's fine sporting rifles, more amazing when you realize that he only produced about 2,500 of them! That realization makes me feel especially blessed. Mine all came fairly dear, not so easy as one of my friends. While wandering the Houston HGCA gun show, Gordon Bailey noticed an odd-looking barreled action lying on a table. Close inspection confirmed it was indeed an Alex Henry in 450 x 3-1/4" BPE with an excellent bore! A few questions later and the lock was produced. A complete barreled action and lock... no wood! What a travesty for someone to rob the stocks! A hundred-dollar bill changed hands and Gordon brought his prize to my attention. *Drat the luck... where was I that day!*

A comparison confirmed that my stocks were essentially identical to the originals on his piece, so off (*very carefully*) came my butt and fore

stocks, and on to C.P.A. Corp. in Pennsylvania, where Paul Shuttlesworth did his usual careful job of copying the stocks with no damage to mine. Then Gordon did a fine job of fitting and finishing... now Alex Henry #4398 had a new life. I'm sure, in Gordon's care, that it will be a long one. Just to make me feel worse about his finding it first, he regales me with stories about its accuracy.

The 500 x 3" BPE cartridge is one of the easy-to-load rounds and despite the worn bore (*groove diameter of .518" plus*) it shot fairly well – as do all Henrys with their unique rifling

Illustration #4 (fig. 82) – The Henry rifling design, showing the similarities to the Whitworth style of rifling. Henry added an additional land where the corners were in the Whitworth style.

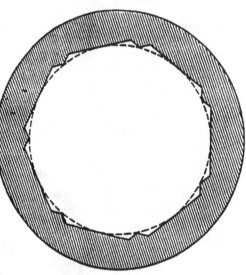

Fig. 82—Henry's Rifling
This shows similarities to the Whitworth style of rifling. Henry added an additional land where the corners were in the Whitworth style.

Henry's Patent Rifling

that grips bullets so effectively. A glance at Illustration #4 shows the great controlling surfaces of Henry's rifling. No wonder the British used his barrels on the Martini action to comprise the Martini-Henry that we know today. Illustration #5, a photo of the muzzle of my rifle, will give a better feel for this rifling. I prefer bright crisp bores though, and this bore was like a pebble in my shoe, a constant small irritant; I kept wishing for a way to improve it.

Despite carrying this rifle in the field many times, no big bucks came

Illustration #6 – The first three rounds from the rebarreled Henry, kneeling, at 60 yards – without forend.

my way. My only kill, until recently, was a large javelina that wandered too close. At 50 yards, I tagged him in the right shoulder, with the bullet exiting the left hip and on into the cactus. Mr. Javelina never quivered... a clean, merciful shot. He made great barbecue.

In a conversation with Bill Loos of Rochester, N.Y., the well-known purveyor of obsolete reloading tools, he told me about his newest acquisition, a Peabody with a lousy bore. He was planning to have Ron Snover re-line the bore. Knowing that Peabody used Henry rifling, I asked if Ron could actually duplicate Henry's rifling... "Oh yeah! He can do anything" was the reply! Thinking of a liner, too, I made a quick call to Snover. "What caliber did you say? Hold just a minute" was Ron's response. I heard metal clinking in the background. I wasn't prepared for his next statement; it really stunned me! "In my hand, as I speak, I hold an original Henry barrel in 500 BPE that's never been fired!"

After I got my chin up off the floor, I managed to ask how, when and where he got it. Seems Ron had bought several British rifles in the white and, in order to sell the Henry, had rebarreled it. He went on to say "I've just been waiting for you to call, Bill!" My response was "send it to me quick!"

When the barrel arrived it was everything Ron had said; more importantly, it looked just like the one on my rifle. The bore was pristine and dimensionally correct. Henry serial-numbered actions and barrels separately, so it was possible to estimate it to be late 1890s' production. My rifle had been produced in the early 1870s, 20 years before. Could it fit? Close measurements convinced me that it was possible. Though the two barrels were similar, it would be necessary to make a new forend since the barrel lug was in a different position and the barrel ten-thousandths larger in diameter than mine. Thankfully, the rear sight slid perfectly into place.

Back to Snover went my rifle and the new barrel with instructions to make the swap, if he could do it without damage to the old barrel and forend. I wanted to keep them with the piece so some future owner could return it to original if desired. Not to worry, Snover's reputation for quality work was well earned, not a scratch on either piece.

Snover did have one unanticipated problem. Henry had two methods of

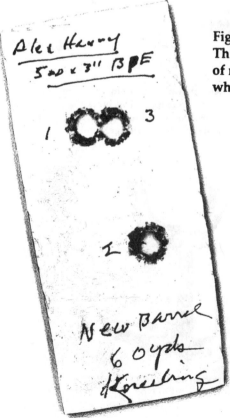

Alex Henry
500 x 3" BPE

1   3

I

New Barrel
60 yds
Kneeling

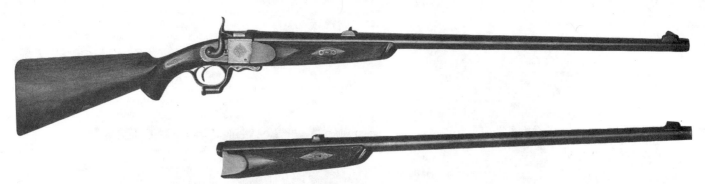

Illustration #7 – The completed rifle, with original barrel and forend.

dealing with the counter-bore for cartridge rims. One, most common, was to counter-bore the end of the chamber; the other a rebate in the face of the breech block (*look closely at Illustration #2, fig. 67 in the book*). You guessed it... the new barrel had the chamber counter-bore, my rifle the rebated block! To remedy this excessive headspace and the problems of setting the barrel back, re-threading, re-indexing, re-chambering, and cutting new extractor slots, he fitted a washer that filled the chamber counter-bore. This left the cartridge supported by the face of the breechblock. Unorthodox, but it has proved to be a safe and effective remedy.

When the Henry came back with its new partner, I was so anxious to try it that I couldn't wait to fit a new forend. I stuck the side of a cardboard box into a log pile at my place in East Texas and fired three rounds "*as is*." Illustration #6 shows the results at 60 yards from kneeling. It will shoot!

Paul Shuttlesworth furnished a nice slab of English walnut for the forend and I proceeded to pretend that I was a Scot in Henry's shop (*Pace being a Scots name*). To be honest, it was as challenging a job of inletting as any I've tried. The discipline to do as good a piece of work as the original was a major test of my self-control. After I had inletted and shaped the forend, I sawed out the side escutcheons for the cross-key that secures the forend to the barrel and then filed and tightly fitted them into the wood. Chris Hirsch, well known for his ability to do magic in restoring damaged antique firearms, did the engraving on the escutcheons, copying the original engraving on the escutcheons and key extremely well. The original forend had been much darker in color and tone than the honey-colored buttstock, so I was pretty careful in staining for a match. It had been years since I had done any checkering and I didn't trust these old eyes, so the job went to David Beasley in Conroe, Texas. David used the old forend pattern as a guide in masterful fashion. Finally

Illustration #5 – Close-up of rifle's muzzle clearly shows the Henry rifling form.

finished (with a little help from my friends!), I think you'll agree that it turned out well (*see Illustration #7*). Mr. Henry was now ready for a hunt!

The population of feral hogs has exploded across Texas with some weighing in the 200 to 400 pound range. I was anxious to see how my new toy would perform on a solid big pig. In early January 2001, I was deer hunting with my son near San Saba, Texas. The last evening I climbed a small oak tree overlooking a clearing with a multitude of tracks. Just at "ghost time" light, a big boar moved into the opening. Mr. Henry came to my shoulder very slowly, I quietly cocked the hammer... when he spoke to the pig, I was momentarily blinded by the muzzle flash and smoke. When it cleared, there was a large black hulk, unmoving, on the ground. Though I had aimed for the base of his ear, the shot took him about four inches back, exiting behind the right shoulder. He had literally dropped in his tracks! This boar weighed 250 pounds, or more. Full of hormones, he went to the "tamale man" in San Saba instead of to chops and sausage. The new barrel had done its job well.

As stated earlier, I'll keep the original barrel and forend with this rifle so it can be returned to original if a future owner desires it. It's my hope that they'll appreciate it as I do and, more importantly, that they take it to the woods and use it often. It was meant to spend its life in service; its earlier owner obviously used it often and well. So to the next owner, I'll pen these words: "*love it ... shoot it ... and keep it healthy for its next shooting partner!*"

For the moment though, until I cross the river, I have a honey of a Sharps...oops! Henry...with a perfect bore! ●

Acknowledgements & References:

British Single Shot Rifles - Vol. #1 by Wal Winfer. Illustrations 1, 2, 3, and 4

Bill Loos - 295 Lake Breeze Park, Rochester, NY 14622

David Beasley

Chris Hirsch - Tel.# 281-491-1680 Houston, TX.

Steve DeHart - Tel.# 713-690-9404 Houston, TX; photographer.

Ron Snover - 1245 Delta Valley Rd., Greeneville, TN 37745

C.P.A. Corp. - R.R#2 Box 1012, Dingmans Ferry, PA 18328

Stress Elimination In Scope Mounting

by Norman E. Johnson

ACCURACY IS THE perplexing part of shooting that often means different things to different people. The average big-game hunter may be quite content in placing a bullet in an animal's vital area at any reasonable distance. These hunters may rationalize that pursuing better accuracy isn't all that important since most rifles will deliver a bullet far more accurately than they can hold the rifle, anyway. In many shooting situations this undoubtedly is true. But where does this leave the big-game hunter who has spent big bucks and long hours for that one critical, long shot of the season... or those serious varmint or target shooters who have come to expect–and rely on–the full accuracy potential from their rifles?

Accurate shooting at any range is becoming increasingly more important to many. In my case, I realized the importance of the highly accurate rifle when in pursuit of distant canine predators. At a time when red fox pelts brought nearly a hundred dollars, well-placed shots at extremely long range required good planning along with an accurate, well-zeroed rifle. Trying to squeeze the last quarter-inch of accuracy from a rifle consumed a great deal of my time back then, and little has changed today. I became keenly aware of how the enjoyment derived from my rifles was made possible through the scope sight. The rifleman cannot truly appreciate the full potential of his rifle without a good scope and

A dependably accurate rifle begins here, with a stress-free scope mounting system that will withstand heavy recoil and remain 'zeroed' from shot-to-shot.

a good mounting system beneath it. Many long hours have been spent at my firearms test range mounting and sighting-in rifles. Many hunters and shooters have their guns sighted-in here at the range, and each year I see more of these guns equipped with scope sights.

Unfortunately, scope sights, along with the various mounting systems, have inherent problems directly related to the deliverable accuracy potential of any rifle. Relatively few shooters are aware of this, and few scopes and mounting systems are immune to fault. Shooters are sometimes bewildered when their rifle is perfectly sighted-in one day, only to shoot well off target the next time they use it. It happens; but there is always some underlying cause... very often the scope mounting system itself.

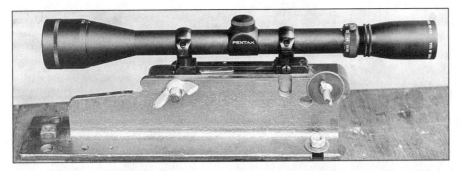

As part of a test series to evaluate scopes and mounts, author used rigid device to secure scope to shooting bench and learned a great deal about stress-free scope mounting.

Additional tests, using a third scope ring and dial indicator, reveal stresses inherent in scope rings as base is tightened down.

The scope base, or bases, is the solid foundation between scope rings and gun receiver, which must be solidly attached and in true alignment for a stress-free mounting job. Here, underside of base is seen after light lapping with abrasive paper on receiver. Note irregular surface at rear underside of scope base.

Several years ago I conducted extensive research and testing, including both the internal and external aspects of scope adjustment problems, as well as factors produced by external forces directly related to sighting and bullet impact changes. For the purpose of these tests I designed a unit with scope base and rings attached that enabled me to solidly hold any type of scope for adjusting and viewing. This work was published in 1992.

Following this, my primary focus shifted to the scope mount. I had known for some time there often was measurable stress within the entire scope mounting system. This included the scope base-to-receiver interface, as well as the scope rings and related parts. It became apparent this was a major cause for a rifle being sighted-in one day, only to later shift its point of impact for no apparent reason. While there are fewer corrective actions possible within the scope, *per se*, in keeping the rifle sighted-in, there are positive steps that can be taken during scope mounting for maintaining better accuracy and more reliable rifle 'zero.'

A frequent problem in scope mounting is the projected axes of the scope rings not coinciding. Alignment between these projected ring axes can be bad: either up or down or from side to side, or both, depending on the type of mounting system used and the method or skill of installation. In such cases, scope-to-mount stresses are inevitable, usually resulting in a scope that will not remain sighted-in. As mentioned, an important factor here is the precision fit (*or lack of same*) between the scope base and the rifle receiver–where problems in mounting can originate. This critical link interfacing the scope rings to the rifle receiver is often overlooked. Both the rifle receiver and the scope base may fail to meet exact industry standards in manufacturing tolerance.

Evaluating Scope Mounting Problems

A way to identify problems, as well as a way to determine true scope ring alignment, is important in the scope mounting trouble-shooting process. Brownell's offers a tool to accurately show misalignment of scope rings. The principle involves a pair of sleeved alignment rods. The sleeves are stepped to fit both 1-inch and 30mm scope rings. When held in the sleeves, the two pointed rods give a very close approximation of scope ring alignment. Then, as a positive test for absolutely coincident axes, the longer, pointed rod is slid through both sleeves. When this degree of alignment can be accomplished, perfect axial congruency is assured. Non-sleeved rods would make this test impossible.

Stress-Free Scope Mounting

Tests have shown that most mounted scope bases and rings will have some degree of stress and axial deviation. This is directly traceable to the scope base (or bases) and rings.

Much of this deviation can be reduced or eliminated through a careful mounting procedure using the sleeved alignment rods as a guide. Further correction can be made through scope base shimming or planing, or scope ring lapping.

If you use the following scope-mounting routine, it is easy to identify scope-mounting stresses, and reduce or eliminate them entirely. The procedure is simple and straightforward. Begin by attaching the scope base or bases to the receiver after manually checking them for receiver contact. If there is any doubt about precise contact, simply place a sheet of fine grit

Enlarging receiver base screw hole in converting from 6-48 to 8-40 screw size.

Tapping the new hole, converting from 6-48 to 8-40 screw size.

The final, positive test in stress-free ring mounting is made here if one alignment rod can be passed through both mounted sleeves. Very few mounting jobs pass this test until adjustments are made. Ring lapping or reversal will sometimes help attain true alignment.

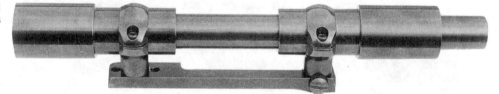

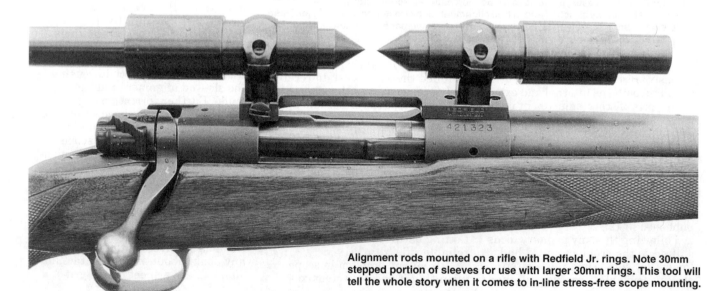

Alignment rods mounted on a rifle with Redfield Jr. rings. Note 30mm stepped portion of sleeves for use with larger 30mm rings. This tool will tell the whole story when it comes to in-line stress-free scope mounting.

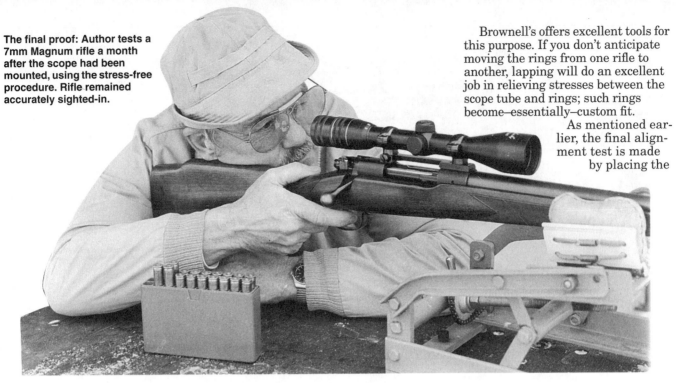

The final proof: Author tests a 7mm Magnum rifle a month after the scope had been mounted, using the stress-free procedure. Rifle remained accurately sighted-in.

paper (*400-grit paper works fine*) over the receiver and carefully press down with the scope base and slide it back and forth under moderate downward pressure. This maneuver will show base-to-receiver defects by periodic inspection of the underside of the base during the fitting process; actual lapping can be accomplished. Then, with the scope base system in full contact with the receiver and mounted firmly in place, the rings can be tested for alignment: simply mount the base and rings according to instructions and place the alignment sleeves into the rings.

Now, insert both alignment rods with pointers toward each other. If everything is normal, there will be no in-line deviation between the pointers as they are brought together; not usually the case.

If the pointers are not in line, simply reversing one or both of the rings may do the job. Reversing the rings end-for-end also may

Fox and coyote shot by author using the ultimate in long-range shooting equipment. Scope must remain absolutely zeroed to attain this performance.

have some corrective influence, depending on the type of mounting system being used. The scope base controls ring position and coaxial ring alignment. If the alignment rods are projected parallel, but one above the other, look to base height for the cause. Rifle receivers can also vary from 'standard.' Shimming the base or lapping it into position by moving it forth and back over abrasive paper will often solve the problem.

Ring lapping or reaming is yet another way to attain a better fit and alignment between rings.

Brownell's offers excellent tools for this purpose. If you don't anticipate moving the rings from one rifle to another, lapping will do an excellent job in relieving stresses between the scope tube and rings; such rings become—essentially–custom fit.

As mentioned earlier, the final alignment test is made by placing the stepped alignment sleeves back into the lapped or adjusted rings, and testing for pointer contact. If pointers appear to touch, remove the shorter of the two pointed rods and again attempt to slide the longer rod from one sleeve into the other sleeve. If this can be accomplished, absolute ring congruity exists and you can be assured of a stress-free, scope-mounting job where your rifle will remain sighted-in.

Any rifle, particularly those with heavy recoil, also will benefit by having the scope base attached more securely to the receiver. A base that slides around or works loose is a major reason for a rifle to shift its point-of-impact and Brownell's offers a further means of stabilizing the scope-mounting system. Their 8-40 scope base conversion kit enables the shooter to replace the standard 6-48 base screws. The average moderately handy person can install this kit quite easily.

When given the choice, there are few shooters who wouldn't prefer to have their rifles solidly zeroed. I don't believe we should ever become too dispassionate about our shooting. Not that we should have things so mechanically perfect that we minimize the importance of the human element in making a hit—but when we pull a trigger, the gun should go *bang*, and if we've done our part in correctly mounting the scope and sighting-in the rifle, the bullet should land where we intended–and the rifle should maintain that 'zero'. ●

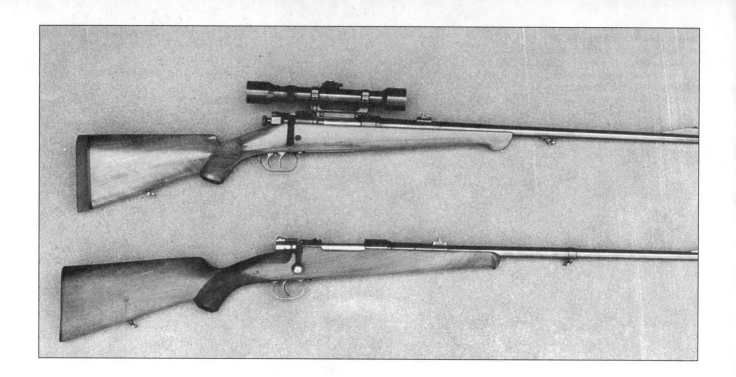

The Germanic Rifle

by Danny Arnold

I HAVE A confession to make. You see, I actually like "Germanic" styling; the short forend ending a schnabel tip, the barrel-mounted sling swivel, set triggers in their graceful bows–and even the clunky side-mounted rifle scope with the invariable "picket" post and crosshair reticle. I like it all. I can even tolerate the fish-scale checkering and deeply chiseled carvings in both metal and wood that German gun makers were so fond of.

Just as the British deeply influenced, or as some would say -'perfected' - the side-by-side shotgun, the rifle-shooting world owes a debt to the Germans. Most are not aware of it, but German gunmakers have had a huge influence upon the evolution of the hunting rifle. German "Jaeger" rifles, along with German gunsmiths, accompanied the colonists to the new world and spawned

(Above) Author's "German-03" (*top*) and Swedish Mauser sporter.

the "Pennsylvania" and "Kentucky" rifles of the American frontier a generation later. Some features of those rifles, such as the crescent buttplate and the "set trigger," would continue until the era of modern cartridge arms. Over two hundred years later, Paul Mauser, another German, would perfect the ultimate bolt-action rifle, a design little changed since 1898. From that beginning, the "Germanic" style would reach its zenith in 1938, propelled by a host of factories and countless custom gunmakers in central Europe.

The "Germanic" rifle would eventually have the following characteristics: A stock with a short, slender forend graced with a schnabel tip or fully-stocked to the muzzle in the

Mannlicher style. Either stock would have noticeably more drop than contemporary American rifles and would usually have an egg-shaped cheek piece. The front sling swivel would be attached to the barrel by a band, or screwed directly to the barrel. Rear sights would be mounted directly to the barrel and consist of a fixed blade, or a series of folding blades of different heights which correspond to different distances, but usually not farther than 300 yards/meters. Triggers would be either a modified military trigger in a factory bow or set triggers in a shotgun-style bow. Scopes, often as not, were absent. If one was attached, it would include some version of the European "picket post" reticle and rest in a detachable side-mount, or claw mounts attached to the receiver. In some instances, the scope mount would have been permanently attached to the scope by brazing. I like these attributes. Thus, those who don't know me well regard me as something of an eccentric. My friends know better because I have let them shoot my rifles.

The Germans are considered to be a very practical people. I believe this is true. It is certainly reflected in the blend of practicality and aesthetics exhibited in most of their rifles. Take for instance the shorter, thinner forend and schnabel tip. The resulting stock is a bit lighter and requires a slightly smaller blank to produce. In its finished form, you will note that if you shoulder the rifle while standing, it fits very comfortably. Once shouldered, you can look through the scope or iron sights with your head erect, in a very natural position. There is no "scrunching" to get behind the scope or iron sights, and the rifle swings like a fine shotgun for running shots.

The schnabel tip in its various forms is pleasing to the eye and the shape keeps your hand from sliding forward off the stock. The barrel-mounted sling swivel not only allows you to carry the rifle in a lower position relative to your body, thus preventing your barrel from being caught in low-hanging branches, but it also keeps the sling swivel from gouging the web of your hand in the heavier-recoiling calibers. The standard blade rear sights are fine for most shots taken at deer, and the ability to change sight settings for longer shots with the flick of a thumb leads me to wonder why this isn't a standard item on rifles today.

Set triggers can be a boon, so long as one takes the time to become proficient in their use. The "unset" front trigger usually has a pull weight of about four pounds, which is about right for those times you get surprised by deer that you aren't expecting. Pulling the rear trigger firmly "sets" the front trigger to release at between two and eight ounces. This is far too light for snap-shooting, but perfect for deliberate shots.

At first, the "picket post" reticle felt strange to me until I realized I was just looking at a rather large front sight blade. After that, it was no problem. At ranges out to two hundred yards it is perfectly adequate, and in low light or on running shots it far surpasses the standard "American" duplex reticle.

This blend of practicality and aesthetics makes perfect sense if you consider the type of hunting available in central Europe during

The 30-06 round (*left*) and the 9.3x57mm round (*right*). Each is effective, but have dissimilar ballistics.

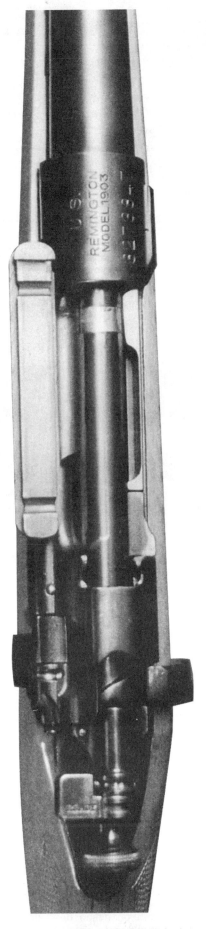

There's no mistaking that action. Remington made Springfield 1903 actions for just over a year, beginning in November 1941.

this time period. The game available ranged from wild boar to moose, and was hunted by various means including the use of blinds, stalking, and drives. We also have to remember that the Europeans didn't have the expansive prairies that we enjoy in the United States; they had forests that were dense enough to preclude shots farther than 200 yards. The majority of the shots fired were at considerably shorter distances than that due to the density of the cover and were, therefore, fired from the standing position while "stalking" or "still hunting," as we call it. The game was usually moving, possibly running at full speed away from you—or toward you, in the case of a drive. That is where the well-fitting, light rifle, with good open sights or a scope featuring a broad "picket post" reticle, really shines. This is also the type of hunting that much of America enjoys today. If a European hunter was fortunate, he or she might enjoy a blind equipped with a small stool to sit on. In this case the distances were still short, so the sighting equipment on most rifles was still adequate. Since the hunter would be making a deliberate and, hopefully, well-placed shot, the set-trigger would come into play. This is exactly the type of hunting I do from time to time as I suspect many of us do.

My love affair with the "Germanic" style started early, fueled only by pictures in books and the occasional rifles seen at gun shows. I say 'occasional' because Mauser only turned out about 126,000 sporter rifles from 1898 until 1945, therefore an original Mauser

A close look at the '03 action. The scope itself is adjustable only for elevation; windage adjustments are done on the mount. The shotgun-style trigger bow accommodates the two triggers. The factory floorplate and magazine box were retained.

Left side of the action showing the double-lever release for the scope mount. The scope slides on and off smoothly; returns to perfect zero each time.

sporter is relatively rare and, of course, costly. Many similar rifles were turned out by factories in other countries as well as custom gun makers, but the years have not been kind. Nowadays it is unusual to see one of these rifles outside of the largest gun shows or specialty dealers. I was resigned to being an admirer until a fair October morning, when fate would place me in the proper place at the proper time to indulge two of my loves.

It sat in a corner of the gun rack, apart from the other rifles because it was an outcast amongst the Remingtons and Winchesters or because, with its scope and stock dimensions, it didn't fit in the rack quite right. I couldn't be sure, but it caught my eye immediately: the schnabel tip, the slender barrel, the 'butterknife' bolt

handle. I practically levitated to that end of the counter. The burly fellow behind the counter asked if I wanted to look at anything. Trying to act non-chalant and probably failing, I replied that yes, I wanted to look at the rifle over there on the end. As he picked it up, I saw the cocking piece. There is only one rifle with a cocking piece like that. A 1903 Springfield. I should mention at this point that I also collect 1903 Springfields.

The rifle was somewhat mysterious. The action was a Model 1903, made by Remington. Remington made 1903 rifles from November, 1941 until December, 1942 when production was changed to the 1903A3. None of those rifles were made for commercial sale or sent to Germany, so the rifle probably assumed its present form sometime

after World War II. Perhaps a GI in the occupation forces wanted a rifle made up to take home. I'm afraid I'll never know. A decal was affixed to the stock immediately aft of the pistol grip cap indicating the name of the maker or retailer - F. Biebl - and his four-digit telephone number in Berchtesgaden, Germany. The metalwork and the scope were almost totally devoid of wear.

Unfortunately, the same couldn't be said for the stock—it was a wreck. There was a longitudinal crack beginning behind the action tang and extending into the pistol grip. The forend had numerous gouges and scratches, which looked exactly as if someone had rested the rifle directly on the top of a metal fence post and fired two or three boxes of ammunition. Worse, the

The epitome of Germanic styling, form and function: the butterknife bolt handle, schnabel, two-leaf sight and set triggers.

The scope slides off its mount effortlessly and returns to perfect zero. Perfect for those days when the weather is too bad for a scope.

forend had warped, and now there was a gap of almost 1/2-inch between barrel and forend.

Still, it looked salvageable—it had the styling, it came from Germany, and it was also a Remington '03. Serious negotiations ensued, and that afternoon I walked out of the shop with the rifle.

Further examination revealed another problem. There was no cross bolt in the stock for a recoil lug and years of shooting, combined with ill-fitting inletting had allowed the recoil shoulder in the stock to

crack. I decided to turn to a friend for help at this point.

Gary took a look at the rifle and muttered something unintelligible, then looked again, twisted the stock, squeezed the action area in a padded vice, looked some more and pronounced it fixable. Good to his word, he returned it to me about two months later. A long screw now extends from inside the action inletting through the pistol grip. Another screw goes through the stock from left to right and forms a recoil lug. Lots of epoxy holds everything together, as well as fully bedding the action. He also fitted another recoil pad to replace the crumbling one installed by a previous owner. Gary pronounced his repairs longer-lasting than the stock itself. I would tend to agree. The best part is that despite the complexity of the work he did, the only visible part is the screw that forms the recoil lug. Now it was my turn.

Why the stock was in such poor condition was a question that I believe I have finally answered. The stock is walnut but I believe it was from an immature tree, and improp-

erly seasoned. Europe, as a whole, has used much of its walnut for the production of gunstocks from the earliest times. Manufacturing the quantity of gunstocks required to arm the soldiers of World War I stretched their capacity dangerously thin. Remember the laminated beech stocks of the World War II Model 98K? That was a reaction to the scarcity of walnut. Beech was available, and by using laminates, more of the tree could be used. Immediately after World War II walnut would still have been in short supply, and out of necessity a gunmaker would have to make do with what he had available.

The forend turned out to be easier than I expected. All that was necessary was some steam and a couple of weeks in an improvised jig to take the bend out of the forend. Touching up the checkering was tedious, to say the least, but well worth the effort. Many, many coats of oil, all hand-rubbed, completed the finishing of the stock. Unfortunately, the maker's decal couldn't be saved.

All in all, I am delighted with the rifle. The Hensoldt-Wetzlar 4X scope is clear and sharp, and resides

Author's 9.3x57mm Swedish Mauser typifies the "Germanic" style and duplicates early Mauser factory sporters.

The action of the Swedish Mauser sporter is the standard Model 1896; right down to the clip-loading slot and cut-out in the left lug raceway.

in a detachable, side-mounted, windage-adjustable mount. The 1903 action lives up to its reputation as one of the smoothest actions ever designed, and the butterknife bolt handle makes for a much trimmer rifle overall. The rifle has set triggers, the front trigger releasing at 3.5 pounds, unset. Pulling the rear trigger "sets" the front trigger audibly, and enables a release of eight ounces–perfect for sighting in at the bench or hunting out of a stand. The barrel looks like a standard wartime Remington four-groove with the outside polished to remove the tooling marks left when the rear sight was removed. There is no Ordnance bomb insignia on the barrel, that having been polished off along with the tooling marks. The bore appears to be a bit smoother than most wartime barrels made by Remington. Perhaps the gunmaker lapped it. It is, of course, a 30-06. Using Hornady 180-grain bullets, it will keep them all inside of two inches at 100 yards.

Best of all, the rifle fits me like a surgeon's glove. This past deer season, a friend and I flushed a doe out of a shallow gully in an unused field overgrown with knee- to thigh-high grasses and weeds. The doe bolted for an adjacent field, presenting a right-to-left shot as she ran perpendicular to me. At about sixty yards, I brought the "picket post" across her body from behind and fired as it reached her nose. My companion said he could hear the slap of the bullet connecting. Sure enough, about 100 yards further along we

found her, shot through both lungs. The 180-grain Hornady had passed completely through. I can still see that "picket post" touching her nose in my mind. The shot was so fluid it was almost effortless. I can only credit good stock design and optics. Doing it with a German-03 just makes it better.

My other "Germanic" rifle hails not from Germany, but from Sweden. It is a 9.3x57mm built by Husqvarna Vapenfabriks using a Model 1896 action sans the usual checkered cocking piece of the military model. The action does share the stripper clip slot, cutout in the left side rail, proof marks, and two-stage trigger of the military version. There the similarities end. The stock is beech, which seems strange to Americans but makes perfect sense when you consider the Swedish climate, is of slender proportions and ends in a schnabel tip. The grip cap and the buttplate, embossed with the Husqvarna logo, are made of plastic. There is no scope–or will there ever be one, and there is only a single fixed sight leaf which is set for 100 yards. The ballistics for the 9.3x57mm cartridge are not terribly impressive: a 286-grain bullet driven between 2000 and 2100 fps. A look at the trajectory table evokes visions of a rainbow, but at 100 yards it reliably shoots three-inch groups using the superb Nosler partition bullet.

The same attributes that endear me to my German-03 apply to the Husqvarna as well. It handles like a fine shotgun, it is light, and it is the absolutely perfect rifle to use in the dense woods and creek bottoms that late-season deer frequent. Shots in this type of cover are never over 100 yards and the open sights allow for fast shooting. The 9.3x57 may seem

anemic to the uninitiated, but at 100 yards a 286-grain Nosler partition makes a 366-caliber hole going in, and an even larger one leaving. This round was extremely popular in Europe at the turn of the century, being simply the 8x57mm Mauser round necked up to 9.3mm. The Swedes used it with great success to hunt moose, so I feel confident when deer hunting.

When I bought the rifle I also got two boxes of Norma brass and some Hornady reloading dies to go with it. If I hadn't gotten any 9.3x57 brass I could have easily expanded the necks on some 8x57 brass. Norma, Nosler, Swift, and Barnes all make 9.3mm bullets so it was easy to put together ammunition. One thing I have found about the European calibers is that most of them are - or were - relatively popular and getting brass and bullets is only a matter of checking some catalogs. Some of the more exotic cartridges may require forming brass, which is a chore, but I would look into doing that before I re-chambered a rifle. Not only does rechambering detract from the rifle's value, but those cartridges were developed for a reason, and most of them work pretty well.

Fit, form, and functionality are the reasons I like my rifles. Perhaps there is something deeper, though. Perhaps it is a connection to a time— before CNC machines, stampings, and synthetics—when men used scrapers and chisels, checkering tools and files to produce rifles numbering in the hundreds or thousands, rather than in the millions. Somehow I suspect those old craftsmen would be pleased to know that, years later, a man from another time, living in another land, and speaking a different language would use and appreciate the rifles they made. ●

The Merkel 96K Drilling

by Bernard H. DiGiacobbe

WHILE THREE-BARREL combination guns, usually called 'drillings,' are most commonly encountered in Europe, they have a small but dedicated following here in the United States—especially among turkey hunters. Combination guns are obviously most useful in those states that allow both big game and small game to be hunted simultaneously. For example, in my native Pennsylvania, black bear season falls at the end of small game season and therefore, a combination gun with its big-game rifle capabilities and shotgun for grouse has its advantages.

Although three-barrel combination guns have been constructed in all conceivable configurations, the vast majority–like the Merkel 96K Drilling imported by GSI–are configured as a side-by-side shotgun over a single-shot rifle. Successfully integrating the conflicting requirements of a rifle and its firing mechanism into the tight spatial constraints of a side-by-side shotgun is one of those seemingly impossible tasks that German and Austrian gunsmiths seem to enjoy. To compensate for the weight of the extra rifle barrel, it usually is of minimal diameter. The 30-06 rifle barrel on this drilling measures less than .450-inch at the muzzle. While this may seem rather flimsy, the three cold-hammer-forged barrels are actually quite rigid when soldered together into one unit.

The short barrels and extra thickness belie the gun's handling qualities. Shooters were generally enthusiastic about the gun's "feel."

While such a thin rifle barrel heats up rather quickly at the target range, this is a situation not likely to be encountered when hunting. To bring the balance back (pun intended), a drilling's barrels are frequently shorter than those on conventional doubles, and the barrels on this drilling measure a short 23-5/8 inches in length. While this and the extra depth of the gun make it appear clumsy, it is actually quite well-balanced and ideally suited for hunting in thickets. As with other drillings and many European side-by-side doubles, this drilling is equipped with double triggers. These are canted to the midline and faced at an angle, allowing instantaneous acquisition in selection for a right-handed shooter, even when wearing gloves. The front trigger breaks at a clean 5.5 lbs. and the rear at 6 lbs. The extra weight of the second trigger, of course, takes into account the rather hurried nature of the follow-up shot. Actually, as the triggers break quite cleanly with no perceptible creep, the pulls seem significantly lighter. For the sake of safety, Merkel got it right - since light trigger pulls are not advantageous on field guns.

Now, with two triggers and three barrels, some sort of selector mechanism is required and this was the major flaw of most older drillings. They almost invariably had the selector located on the top tang, just where most shooters' thumbs expect to find the 'normal' safety. The small and difficult-to-release safety was then usually placed (inconveniently) on the left side of the head of the stock. To add to the confusion, the top selector was usually shaped like a conventional top safety. The safety was difficult to manipulate under the best of circumstances and nearly impossible for use on snap shots. Fortunately, on this Merkel 96K Drilling, the system is much improved and even includes a few innovative features. The safety and selector are integrated into one easy-to-use unit. Like a conventional safety, it is released by pushing it forward (actually, down and forward). The slight downward force is necessary to release a small button/lock protruding through the top of the safety. Pushing the safety an additional 3/4-inch forward simultaneously cocks the rifle's firing mechanism and readies the front trigger to fire the rifle barrel. Because of the button/lock in the safety, it will not function as an automatic safety and it needs to be reset to the 'safe' position by the shooter. With the large size and ergrometic shape of the safety/selector, it is convenient to use, even with gloves. In addition, this system allows the shooter the assurance of having the rifle barrel uncocked when the gun is used as a shotgun. Having hunted with numerous drillings over the years, and suffering through various systems, I'm convinced that this is the best design available. On most older drillings, pushing the "conventional" top selector forward also raised the rear sight from its recess in the barrel's top rib.

This open view with snap caps (courtesy Brownells) demonstrates how the two-piece extractor facilitates removal at the rifle cartridge. This feature is especially useful when removing small cases with gloved fingers.

No, it wasn't magic, there was a longitudinal rod located within the top rib. Somewhat atypical for a drilling, the pivoting rear sight on this gun has two different configurations, neither of which folds flat into the half-inch wide top rib. The larger semi-circular notch is well suited for "snap shots" with slugs, or the rifle barrel. Incidentally, the iron sights were "dead on" at 100 yards with the rifle barrel.

As with other drillings and many German doubles for that matter, this drilling is built on a trigger plate action. The firing mechanism is mounted at the top of the trigger plate, behind the frame. So while it looks like a boxlock externally, it more closely resembles a sidelock, both in terms of strength and ease of disassembly. It should be noted that sidelock drillings are, however, available from Merkel through the importer. Like a sidelock, the inletting of the blitz mechanism into the head of the stock weakens the stock significantly. To compensate for this potential weakness, this drilling, unlike many others, is fitted with an unobtrusive, but not insignificant cross pin that reinforces the stock.

If multiple bolting is important for containing the higher pressure of the rifle cartridge, it is imperative for maintaining accuracy with the rifle barrel. Any looseness that develops

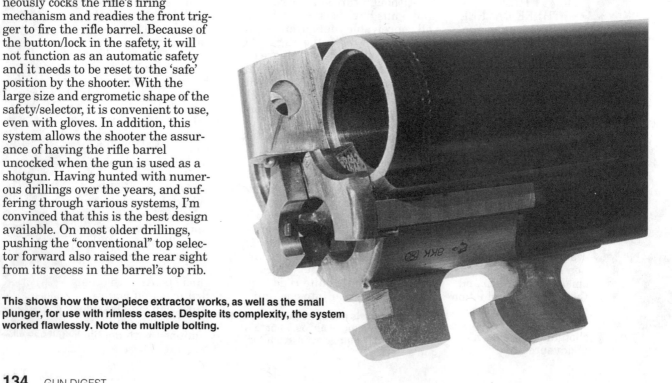

This shows how the two-piece extractor works, as well as the small plunger, for use with rimless cases. Despite its complexity, the system worked flawlessly. Note the multiple bolting.

between the barrels and the frame will be greatly magnified in downrange accuracy. So this gun is fitted with double underlugs to keep it closed and a Greener cross bolt to keep the barrels tightly pinned to the action face at the instant of firing. In addition to all this, the stylish sculpting at the angle of the frame actually adds extra metal/strength at this inherently weak part of any double's frame.

As a further indication of quality, all three firing pins are bushed. This allows them to be removed from the face of the action–without removing the stock–for maintenance or occasional cleaning. It also means that the firing pins are inserted from the front and thus circumferentially shouldered against the rear of their passageway. Thus, in the event of a catastrophic failure of a cartridge, the firing pins will not be driven rearward in the direction of the shooter's face! There are even two cocking indicators, readily seen or felt, protruding through the top of the frame. The position of the selector, of course, serves as cocking indicator for the rifle barrel.

Perhaps the greatest indication of quality is the precise fitting of the metal components with seams that disappear once the gun is closed. Opening and closing the gun demonstrates a certain stiffness that is far from being a nuisance–but a joy to behold for most enthusiasts. The metal finish of the case-colored frame–as well as the metal finish of the barrels–is flawless. The fancy inletting of the head of the stock into the rear of the frame is perhaps a sort of trademark that both enhances the appearance and increases the strength of the joint; it can be compared to a mortise tenon joint.

Accuracy testing any rifle with iron sights is a better test of the shooter than the gun. A shooter with better eyes than mine, Phil Maceno, had no trouble (from the bench) in placing five Remington 165-grain bullets into a 2-inch circle at 100 yards. With the rifle's set trigger and forward weight balance, Phil did almost as well off-hand, at that same distance. Accuracy was no doubt aided by the gun's blade front sight, as opposed to the usual bead front sight found on other drillings. Incidentally, the rear face of this 0.1-inch wide blade sight has a brass insert, which should be ideal in dim lighting usually associated with woodland hunting. With an available scope and quick-detachable claw mount–and selected ammunition–this gun could prove to be a real "tack driver."

While some shooters maintain that only rimmed cartridges should be used in break-open guns, the small extractor plunger functioned flawlessly. There is, however, a wide range of rimmed–as well as rimless–chamberings available. Manual extraction of the rimless cartridge was aided by the rather unique two-piece extractor design. Unlike other drillings with a single one-piece extractor, the extractor on this drilling was split like a conventional double with an ejector. However, unlike a conventional ejector, the left side is retracted slightly higher to facilitate manual extraction of the cartridge. Still, with gloves, manual extraction is a bit cumbersome. With a rimmed cartridge, of course, the gun could be tipped upward allowing the cartridge to fall out.

While the Merkel drilling on the bottom is brand new, the Merkel drilling above it was manufactured well before WWII.

The various shooters that handled the gun were impressed with its overall feel. The gun weighs approximately 7-1/2 pounds, with a slightly forward weight balance that most handlers found ideal. Those who prefer a lighter gun may opt for the (available) smaller 16- or 20-gauge versions. With its narrow forend, cheekpiece and arched comb, the stock has a definite European flair. Because of the arch configuration of the stock, the figures of the drop-at-the comb and -heel of 1-3/4 and 2-7/8 inches respectively, and a length-of-pull of 14-1/4 inches are somewhat misleading. A more accu-

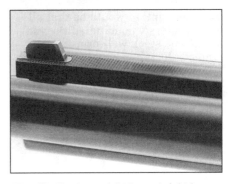

The rifle-like front sight has a bright brass insert on its rear face, making it useful for the dim lighting usually associated with woodland hunting. A small detail, but important.

Close-up view of the rear sight with its choice of two different notch widths. Sometimes it's the little details that make all the difference between a hit and a miss–and this drilling abounds with attention to all those little details.

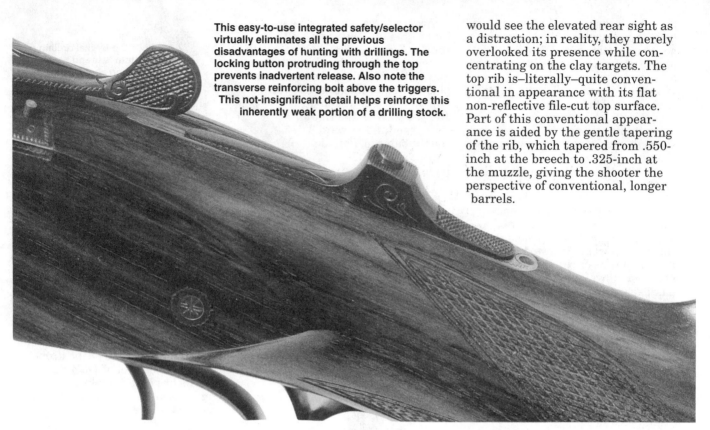

This easy-to-use integrated safety/selector virtually eliminates all the previous disadvantages of hunting with drillings. The locking button protruding through the top prevents inadvertent release. Also note the transverse reinforcing bolt above the triggers. This not-insignificant detail helps reinforce this inherently weak portion of a drilling stock.

would see the elevated rear sight as a distraction; in reality, they merely overlooked its presence while concentrating on the clay targets. The top rib is—literally—quite conventional in appearance with its flat non-reflective file-cut top surface. Part of this conventional appearance is aided by the gentle tapering of the rib, which tapered from .550-inch at the breech to .325-inch at the muzzle, giving the shooter the perspective of conventional, longer barrels.

rate description would be that all the shooters who handled the gun found the stock well-proportioned and comfortable.

The shotgun barrels were choked Modified and Full and delivered patterns that were both uniform and to the same point of impact at 40 yards. The patterns were centered a bit above the line of sight,

just as they should be. As the shooter knows to lead a bird, the gun knows to lead the upward path of a rising bird. As the only birds in season were clay birds when I had this firearm to review, the gun was taken to the skeet range where it performed as well as any tightly choked field grade side-by-side. While I thought the various users

While the inletting is generally flawless, shooters that demand fancy grain and checkering patterns will no doubt be disappointed with the gun's rather plainly-finished and straight-grained stock. This is consistent with Merkel's preference for the inherent strength of a straight-grain stock, which is perhaps a wise move considering the considerable amount of wood that needs to be removed at the head of the stock to accommodate the mechanism. However, to those who can afford it, custom stocks with carvings, fish-scale or basket-weave checkering, are available—as well as engraved receivers.

With the gun's list price at $6,495 a hunter could alternately purchase several other hunting guns, some of which would be better suited for specific hunting situations. Yet, as every hunter knows, the only gun that counts is the one you have with you when the opportunity arises. And this is the one that can handle any reasonable opportunity at big game and small game—in the same season. •

Additional information:
GSI, Inc.
108 Morrow Avenue
P.O. Box 129
Trussville, AL 35173
205-655-8299

All three firing pins are bushed to facilitate maintenance and provide an extra measure of safety. The "brass" pins protruding through the top of the back of the receiver are, of course, the cocking indicators.

R & D Gunshop's Conversion Cylinder

by Butch Winter

SOON AFTER THE War Between the States, and before the Rollin White patent for the "bored-through" cylinder expired, various and sundry "conversions" of percussion revolvers to fire a metallic cartridge were developed. Colt, perhaps the best-known gun maker in the nation had three: the Richards, Richards-Mason, and Thuer conversions.

Remington's 44-caliber New Model Army, in addition to its 36-caliber Navy models were also converted to metallic cartridges by manufacturing cylinders that would accept 46-caliber rimfire, 44-caliber or 38-caliber rimfire, or centerfire cartridges, respectively.

There were other home-grown conversions to both Colt and Remingtons, but in most cases, when a revolver was converted from percussion to metallic it was a permanent conversion. A very few allowed the use of both cylinders, percussion or metallic.

Ken Howell of R & D Gunshop came up with a conversion cylinder that is the best of both worlds. In the space of just a few seconds a percussion revolver can be converted to fire a metallic cartridge merely by dropping out the percussion cylinder and dropping in a cylinder filled with metallic cartridges.

Since the replica 1858 Remington "44s" have an actual bore diameter of .451-inch and the nominal diameter of the 45 Colt cartridge is .452-inch,

The Pietta 1858 Remington Revolver is one of the most popular reproduction revolvers on the market.

While this can't be called a "bragging" group, it demonstrates the positive function and potential accuracy of the Pietta 1858 Remington reproduction percussion revolver fitted with the R & D Gunshop conversion cylinder.

this cartridge is a perfect match for these revolvers.

R & D Gunshop's solution to the problem of using the percussion hammer to fire the metallic cartridge is a two-piece cylinder. The upper portion of the cylinder consists of a ring with six firing pins. This ring is removed and each chamber is loaded with 45 Colt cartridges (45 Schofield cartridges can also be used) and the ring is replaced.

A stud on the cylinder fits into a hole on the ring to assure proper alignment. All, as you may imagine, is machined so that the fit is perfect.

The percussion cylinder is removed by placing the revolver on half-cock, unlatching the loading lever and pulling the cylinder pin forward out of the frame. The hammer must be positioned so that the hand disengages from the back of the cylinder and the cylinder can be rotated out of the gun.

Loading the R & D cylinder into the revolver is as simple as rotating the cylinder into the frame, making sure the hand is disengaged. The cylinder pin is pushed back into place, the loading lever latched back to the barrel and the gun is ready to fire. With practice, replacing a loaded cylinder with an unloaded one is much faster than punching out the empties and reloading a fired cylinder from an 1873 Colt, 1875 Remington or any similar single-action revolver.

While what we have used here is a 44 Remington reproduction by Pietta, R & D also offers conversion cylinders for Uberti and Armi San Marco reproductions.

The reason for the R & D conversion cylinders is to offer an alternative to the percussion revolver shooter who wants to compete in cowboy action shooting, but doesn't want

Put revolver on half-cock.

Unlatch and lower the loading lever and pull the cylinder pin forward, out of the frame.

Rotate percussion cylinder out of contact with the hand and then out of the revolver's frame.

The percussion cylinder removed from the frame. Note nipples for the percussion caps.

The conversion cylinder. Note individual firing pins for each chamber.

to purchase another revolver. Or who wants to use the same revolver in both percussion and metallic cartridge matches. These cylinders are also handy for the individual who isn't interested in springing for a centerfire revolver when he can obtain one of these cylinders for considerably less.

The R & D replacement cylinders are designed to be fired with the reduced smokeless loads used in cowboy action shooting, Black Hills ammunition, and blackpowder or a blackpowder substitute such as Pyrodex, Clean Shot, etc.

Cartridges were loaded with 22 grains of FFFg blackpowder and a 250-grain lead bullet and fired for function only. No attempt was made to "work-up" an accurate load, but it was nice to see that the out-of-the-box Pietta revolver shot to the point of aim. A comparable load of 22 grains of Clean Shot and the same 250-grain bullet went into the same group. Most reproduction percussion revolvers are notorious for shooting high and wide. Blame the rather large group shown here on the shooter who used over-the-hill eyes in poor light.

It needs to be pointed out that some of the Pietta revolvers will require that the frame be relieved at the front of the cylinder. The Pietta I used was one of those. I did it with a file, free hand, on the range, and within a half-hour of filing and fitting had everything working flawlessly.

The replacement cylinders are priced at just over $200, which I think represents one heck of a bargain. Here is the opportunity to take a percussion revolver you already have and turn it into a metallic cartridge gun while retaining its percussion capabilities. Or purchasing a percussion revolver and turning it into a cartridge revolver at less than the cost—and none of the hassle—of purchasing a reproduction 1873 Colt, 1875 or 1890 Remington.

Here is the best of both worlds... just a letter or phone call away. Contact Taylor's, Inc. 304 Lenoir Drive, Winchester, VA 22603 (540)-722-2017 or info@taylorsfirearms.com. Taylor's & Co. handles the R & D cylinders for the 44-caliber percussion reproductions. Other conversion cylinders and full-blown conversion revolvers are available from R & D Gunshop, RR1 Box 283 Beloit, WI 53511. ●

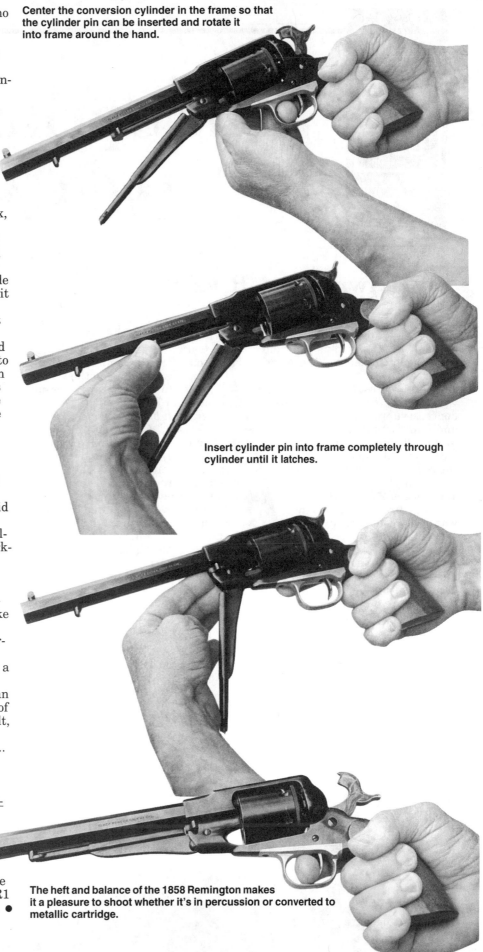

Center the conversion cylinder in the frame so that the cylinder pin can be inserted and rotate it into frame around the hand.

Insert cylinder pin into frame completely through cylinder until it latches.

The heft and balance of the 1858 Remington makes it a pleasure to shoot whether it's in percussion or converted to metallic cartridge.

ONE GOOD GUN

The Springfield 1903-A3

by Lawrence J. Rivard

THE 50th ANNIVERSARY of WWII, celebrated over the last decade, have many of us admiring the accomplishments of the generation of Americans—now referred to as " The Greatest Generation"—that won the war. There is ample evidence to support that contention, and I am fortunate enough to own a rifle built during that era, a Springfield 1903-A3 made by the Smith Corona Typewriter Company of Syracuse New York, one of 236,831 they manufactured to support the war effort, and a dandy job they did.

Ironically, this old campaigner came to me because of my great admiration for the renowned semi-auto that replaced the '03 Springfield - the M1 Garand. I guess that I am not too different from many other shooters born during the war, in that I lusted for years after one of what Patton called *"The greatest battle implement ever devised."* All those war movies on early TV must have burned the picture of a Garand into my mind. When I got to shoot a few rounds through one in Navy boot camp, it was great fun.

In any event, I wanted one and decided to buy it through the Director of Civilian Marksmanship (DCM). At the time, the DCM rules said you had to compete in several conventional high-power rifle matches to qualify to purchase the M1. I had never shot a rifle match of any kind, a few conventional pistol matches being the extent of my experience. A little investigation indicated I would need a centerfire rifle with iron sights, capable of holding a minimum of five rounds, which could be reloaded quickly. Nothing in my meager arsenal filled the bill. I was thinking about installing a peep sight on my Winchester Model 88 deer rifle when a friend invited me to attend a gun show with him.

Wandering the rows of firearms without any real purchase objective in mind, I happened to spot a clean-looking M1903-A3 Springfield. The stock was pretty dark from years of soaking up Cosmoline, but the Parkerizing showed very little wear. Not an unfired, mint condition piece, but real nice. The odd-looking scant stock seemed to fit me well, bringing the sights up to my eye properly when I shouldered the rifle. *Hmm, clip-slotted for quick loading. Holds five in the magazine. Iron sights, adjustable for windage and elevation. And chambered in 30-06, with cheap brass galore. This thing might get me my Garand!*

So, Smith Corona #4820390 followed me home. It took me a while to clean the rifle, there was still Cosmoline in a few out-of-the-way corners, and a while longer to fix a little glitch in the feeding. But the first trip to the range, shooting some old hunting ammo I had on the shelf for a 30-06 Mauser, really opened my eyes. This old girl could shoot! The groups I got weren't much different than what I was used to seeing from a scope-sighted hunting rifle.

I worked up a load using the Sierra 125-grain bullet to hold the recoil down, and went after that Garand. Got it, too. I even had big plans to accurize the Garand for conventional high-power competition,

The '03-A3 and author's personal high-power match equipment.

Sierra's 155-grain Palma bullet and H414 combine to deliver 10-ring accuracy.

shot for score at 100 and 200 yards on the NRA decimal targets: MR31 at one 100 and MR52 at 200. The ten-ring of the MR 31 is 1-3/4 inches in diameter. The Smith Corona produced a '99' score on this target at the first match, with one shot just leaking into the 9-ring at 6 o'clock. Remarkably, the other nine shots were all in the bottom half of the 10-ring! This was with the Sierra 155-grain Palma bullet and a case full of H414 powder. I believe this old rifle shoots better than I can hold, and surely better than my aging eyes can cope with issue iron sights.

The serial number on my sweetheart shows it was made during the last couple of months of production, within 26,000 or so of the end, in 1944. The barrel date is 10–43, but a stock cartouche shows an Ogden Utah arsenal rework, so the barrel may not be original. It is a four-groove barrel, but it does not have the manufacturer's mark from High Standard, who supplied most of the Smith Corona barrels. When I first started shooting conventional high-power with this rifle I was pleased with how well it shot, but aghast at the heavy copper fouling that accumulated in the barrel. It would take weeks of scrubbing with Sweets 7.62 solvent to get it all out. The grooves were quite smooth, but the tops of the lands were rough, as though cut by a dull reamer that had been pushed too fast.

I wrote to the NRA's technical division for advice, and got back an essay on how to lap a barrel, composed and signed by Roy Dunlap, a nice keepsake in and of itself. I never did lap that barrel. By the time I got the reply I had fallen under the influence of Merrill Martin, a frequent contributor to the benchrest press, who espoused a method of cleaning factory barrels for Hunter class benchrest match shooting that worked just dandy for the old Springfield. This involves a couple of patches of good solvent, ten passes each way with a patch soaked in RemClean, a couple of dry patches and an oily patch, and don't worry about the copper still in the bore. Works for me.

The old Smith Corona handles 125- to 220-grain bullets well. It has been on deer and elk hunts as a backup rifle many times, and has racked up a ton of mileage behind the seat of a pickup. It would be my first choice for a survival rifle, yet it remains a serious competitor in a lot of very enjoyable rifle matches.

Brother, that's One Good Gun! ●

but never did. It is still as it came from the DCM, because by that time, the old Smith Corona had me hooked on shooting bolt rifles. I stuck with conventional high-power–and with the Smith Corona–for quite a while, eventually switching to a couple of Model 70 Winchester match rifles gussied up with target sights, adjustable combs, butt-plates and what all. Funny thing is, I don't score all that much better than I did with the 03-A3.

The sportsman's club in Oakdale California has a monthly rifle match, a multi-class affair with an event to accommodate about anything a guy can bring to the range, all shot off the bench. For a while, one of the categories contested was Military Rifle, shot prone, later changed to shoot off the bench. The Smith Corona has won these matches many times, and has been a strong contender every time out. Oakdale's match spawned similar matches run by the Modesto, California Rifle Club. These take two forms, a conventional high-power position match for issue bolt rifles, and a series of benchrest matches open to single-shot, manual repeating, and semi-auto military rifles, with classes for both iron sights and scopes.

The Smith Corona has taken second overall in the position match twice, and won the issue rifle class outright in the first of the benchrest matches. These benchrest matches are

Well-made, dependable–and accurate. In the right hands, the 1903-A3 is a match-winner as well as a reliable field rifle.

by JOHN MALLOY

HANDGUNS TODAY:

AUTOLOADERS

*F*OR MOST OF the year 2001, the firearms industry, in particular the segment that offered autoloading handguns, looked as if it were in trouble.

The anti-gun policies of the previous Clinton administration had brought about a marked decrease in the number of U. S. gun dealers, and restrictions against purchasers had cut down the number of people buying firearms. Lawsuits by municipalities had driven some small manufacturers out of business, and some others stopped offering handguns.

A single event can make a great difference in people's perceptions.

On September 11, 2001, terrorists carried out a devastating attack against the World Trade Center towers in New York and the Pentagon in Washington. Things were very different afterwards, in many ways.

The United States economy, already in a slump, went into a tailspin. The economy made a recovery, but for the first few weeks, the only things selling well were American flags, gas masks, Bibles ...and firearms.

As this is written, the majority of firearms companies seem to have a new, although cautious, optimism. There are still signs of the old uncertainty, though. Some companies that made semiautomatic pistols are now out of business, but some new ones have been started to make similar products.

A number of trends seem evident.

Certain states require mechanical safety devices on handguns. So, some manufacturers have introduced new safety arrangements so that they can sell their products in those areas.

The 45 ACP seems to be the leading cartridge for new pistols being introduced. Many of the new pistol offerings are of the time-tested 1911 Colt/Browning design, but some are very different. The 1911 design still interests a vast number of shooters,

and many new variations are available. The military-style 1911A1, as used during World War II, has caught the fancy of many, and several companies have introduced similar pistols.

Pistols chambered for the 22 rimfire are always of interest and several different new concepts, in the general class of plinking pistols, are now offered.

New cartridges for semiautomatic handguns have been introduced. In past years, most new pistol cartridges have been big boomers of 40 to 50 caliber, but now the smaller end of the scale is getting attention. All the recent new cartridges have been small-caliber bottleneck rounds.

The concealed-carry market continues to grow. Reportedly, applications for concealed-weapons licenses reached record levels after the

tragedy of September 11, 2001. Almost all handgun manufacturers make something to appeal to those wanting a pistol for personal protection. Polymer frames continue to be popular, and new pistols with polymer frames are now available.

More and more, companies involved with autoloading handguns realize the value of electronic communication, and maintain websites. Websites for the various companies are again included in the following discussion. However, this publication's Web Directory is becoming so useful that this separate listing may well not be needed in the future.

Semiautomatic pistols are of interest to competitive shooters, to plinkers, to hunters, to those who desire personal protection... and to those anti-gun forces who would restrict or ban their possession. In this framework, there is much happening in the world of autoloading handguns.

With all this in mind, let's take a look at what the companies are doing:

Alchemy

The Alchemy Arms Spectre pistol, introduced in 2000 as a new design for personal protection or as a service sidearm, has undergone some modifications. The manual safety has been redesigned for comfort of use, and the safety now will lock the slide.

The new sights are big and wide, allowing the shooter's eye to achieve a sight picture quickly. A new frame incorporates an accessory rail. However, the pistol is also available without a rail.

The Alchemy Spectre was initially available in 45 ACP. The original design had a 4 1/2-inch barrel and measured about 5x7 inches. A new 4-inch "Commander" variant has now joined it. By about August 2002, 9mm and 40 S&W versions were scheduled to be available.

www.alchemy.com

Malloy tries out a pre-production specimen of Beretta's new plinking 22, the U22 NEOS pistol, on the firing line.

Beretta

Beretta has introduced a number of new pistols. Most are modifications of pistols previously in the line, but one is a completely new offering.

Previously, Beretta had offered a number of 22-caliber pistols, but never one that could really be called a plinking pistol. They were either small pocket pistols or precision target pistols. Now, the brand-new U22 "NEOS" pistol is a new 22-caliber pistol designed as an affordable entry-level plinking pistol that could be put to more precise uses. Its moulded grip with its 'slanty' angle, and its turn-screw barrel removal, will remind long-time shooters of the old High Standard Dura-Matic of the '50s and '60s. However, Beretta has incorporated modern concepts. The magazine release is located on the right, above the trigger, so it can be operated by the right index finger. Thus, the grip frame can be easily replaced with alternate frames to be offered by Beretta. The adjustable sights are contained within a full-length top rail attached to the barrel, a rail that will accept optical or electronic sights. The NEOS is an interesting addition to Beretta's line.

The compact polymer 9000S is now available with a new B-Lok system. This optional key-lock blocks the movement of the hammer.

Recall that the Model 92 pistols are 9mm and the Model 96 pistols are 40 caliber. The new 92/96 Vertec has a reshaped "vertical" *(well, more-nearly vertical)* grip frame. There are a large number of shooters who believe the 1911 Colt has the best 'feel' of any pistol. So, Beretta has shaped their grip frame on these variants to feel more like…well…a 1911. A "short-reach" trigger and thin grip panels add to this effect. Vertec pistols use the same magazines as do the standard 92 and 96 variants.

To commemorate the military operation against terrorism, Beretta has introduced a new Model 92 "Enduring Freedom" variant. It will be manufactured in five versions, honoring the U. S. Army, Marines, Navy, Air Force and Coast Guard.

Many shooters add laser sights to pistols as aftermarket items. Beretta now offers the Model 92 FS, a 9mm pistol that comes from the factory with a laser sight installed. The laser sight, with its battery power and its beam generator, is contained entirely within the grips, and is provided by Crimson Trace. The Crimson Trace company has been building excellent grip-mounted lasers since June 1994, and was a logical choice to provide the laser sight for the new 92 FS.
www.berettausa.com

Bernardelli

Bernardelli, a name in firearms manufacturing since 1721, has been absent from the shooting world for a time. The company has been reorganized and some guns went back into production in November 2001.

All previous lines, including Bernardelli pistols in 22 Short, 22 Long, 22 Long Rifle (22 LR), 25 ACP, 32 ACP, 7.65mm Parabellum, 380, 9mm, 9x21 and 40 S&W, were scheduled for production to be resumed by June 2002. This will be quite a lineup. Some of the former small Bernardellis, however, will not be available in the United States, due to U. S. import restrictions.

A totally new design of 9mm pistol was scheduled for introduction in 2002, but details were not available at the 2002 SHOT Show. However, there were suggestions that it may be a polymer-frame double-action (DA) pistol.
www.bernardelli.com

Browning

What? Did Browning discontinue their 9mm pistols? No, but the 9mm section was inadvertently left out of the 2002 catalog by the printer. Hopefully, revised catalogs will be available by the time you read this.

One item not in the catalog is the "Forest Camper" 22 pistol. It is a variant of the Camper 22 pistol, introduced on these pages several years ago, but with a green anodized frame and multicolored laminated grips. It will be made in limited numbers for special distribution.

The 40 S&W chambering is back for the "High Power" pistol. Last year, only the 9mm variant was made.
www.browning.com

Century International

Century International Arms' "Blue Thunder" line of 45-caliber 1911-style pistols was introduced last year and is in full production. One small change has been made in current-production pistols. Early guns had grip screws of shank and head diameters larger than

No surprises—the mechanics of the Century Blue Thunder are straight 1911.

The Bernardelli company has reorganized, and Bernardelli pistols have returned to the shooting world. Seda Tural Emir holds a stainless steel Bernardelli P.ONE pistol.

Century International Arms imports the Blue Thunder line of 1911-type 45 pistols. Century has initiated a small change that allows Colt and aftermarket grips to be easily installed.

Those who like the P38 design will be interested in Century International's importation of West German police P1 pistols.

Colt offers a mixture of old and new designs, and has reintroduced its Series 70 Government Model.

those of original Colt screws. Thus, Colt and most aftermarket grips would not fit without modification. Now they will, for the screws of current pistols are of the correct size to use Colt-type grips. This is a small change, but important to those who want to use different grips, or specialty grips, such as laser-sight grips. A polymer-frame double-stack 45 variant is in the works, but details had not been worked out at press time.

Century is now importing P1 pistols. This is the original Walther P38 design with an aluminum frame, as used by the West German police. The guns come with a holster and an extra magazine. The P38 pistol design is highly regarded by many who would like to see some company undertake new production. These excellent P1 variants should serve nicely.

www.centuryarms.com

Cobra

Cobra Enterprises is a new name that offers some familiar designs. When Davis Industries, Republic Arms and Talon Industries went out of business recently, Cobra bought all the existing inventory and tooling of the three companies, and set up the new company headquarters in Salt Lake City, Utah.

Cobra Enterprises now handles pistol designs previously made by Republic, Talon and Davis. Doug and Leslie Skillman of Cobra hold some of the varieties of pistols the new company offers.

The Cobra line consists of a polymer-frame double-action-only (DAO) 45 pistol (Republic), a polymer-frame DAO 9mm pistol (Talon) and 32- and 380-caliber single-action semi-auto pistols (Davis). Derringers formerly made under the Davis brand are also included in the Cobra line. It is good to see these affordable pistols continue to be available.

Some small improvements have been made on pistols carrying the Cobra name. Still, Cobra will do warranty and repair work for pistols made by the previous manufacturers.

www.cobrapistols.com

Colt

Colt offers a new Defender Plus pistol, a 45 with a 3-inch barrel and full-size lightweight aluminum frame. Thus, it has full capacity in a lightweight package. The new Colt has a burr hammer, skeletonized trigger, beavertail grip safety and finger-groove rubber grips, things that seem to be in vogue now.

Colt's other new offerings are a mixture of old and new. The Blue Government Model has the construction and slide markings of the old pre-1970 Government Model, with modern niceties such as a burr hammer, ambidextrous safety and skeletonized trigger added.

The Series 70 Government Blue pistol likewise has the slide markings and construction of the original Series 70 guns, and comes with "big diamond" wood grips.

All new Colt 45-caliber semiautomatic pistols now come with two magazines.

www.colt.com

CZ

Too new for their 2002 catalog, CZ-USA has introduced the CZ-P.01 Police pistol. This is a conventional double-action pistol with a nice two-stage decocker. Offered in 9mm, it has an accessory rail. Designed to Czech police specifications, it is tightly fitted, but all parts are completely interchangeable from one specimen to another without additional fitting.

www.cz-usa.com

Bill Jeffery of Dan Wesson introduces the new Patriot pistol at the 2002 SHOT Show.

Dan Wesson

Dan Wesson has introduced a new line of 1911-type pistols as a lower-cost "Patriot" line. The new pistols have a "Series 70" mechanism with a forged slide and frame. Most notable new feature is the external extractor, which makes it obvious something is different from the original 1911 design. Patriot pistols are offered with traditional rounded-top slides, dovetail front sights, Chip McCormick 8-round magazines, and Cocobolo big-diamond grips. At first, they will be available in 45 ACP only, with initial deliveries scheduled for May 2002. Dan Wesson sees the Patriot as a way of getting

Dan Wesson's new Patriot series can be recognized as the company's first pistol with an external extractor.

Kathy Gilliam of Excel Industries displays the company's new 45-caliber pistols, one all stainless steel, the other with a polymer frame.

more new people interested in competition shooting.

The company's mainstay Pointman pistols, introduced in 2000, have the traditional internal extractor. Slides have a solid rib on top, and the front sight is dovetailed into it. Chamberings offered are 9mm, 40 and 10mm, as well as 45. 38 Super may soon be added.

The original Dan Wesson company was founded on the idea of interchangeable components for its revolvers, and a new kit extends this concept to their Pointman autoloaders. The kit contains three 'top ends' in 9mm, 40 S&W and 10mm.

A new Pointman Guardian ("Commander-size"), with a 4 1/4-inch barrel, has also been added to the line.
www.danwessonfirearms.com

Davis

Davis Industries of Chino, CA, the maker of affordable semi-auto pistols and derringers, has gone out of business, after being with us 20 years. Stock and tooling have been acquired by Cobra Enterprises, a company that will continue production of the line. (See Cobra)

DPMS / Panther Arms

This company (Defense Procurement Manufacturing Services),

a maker of AR-15-type rifles and accessories, had a prototype 1911A1-type 45 pistol at the February 2002 SHOT Show. It was basically a military-style 1911A1, but with a skeletonized trigger, big-diamond grips and a checkered flat mainspring housing.

The pistol will tentatively be called the Model 45P (Panther 45). Production was scheduled for mid-November 2002.
www.dpmsinc.com

EAA

European American Armory is now handling a line of Israeli-made BUL 1911-style pistols. These will be polymer-frame double-column guns in three barrel sizes—the five-inch "Government," the four-inch "Commander," and the three-inch "Stinger." Slides can be provided with blued or stainless finishes. All variants have a beavertail grip safety, skeletonized trigger and hammer, and extended thumb safety lever.
www.eaacorp.com

One of the new Excel Arms 45 pistols is the XP-45, a 10+1 capacity version with a polymer frame.

This is the prototype of a new DPMS / Panther Arms 45, scheduled for introduction in late 2002. It is roughly of WWII GI configuration, with a few details changed.

Excel Arms has introduced a new CP-45, a stainless-steel compact with 6+1 capacity. This specimen is serial number 000001.

Excel Industries

Excel Industries, the maker of the Accu-Tek line of pistols, has brought out two new pistols under the Excel Arms name. The new handguns are both in 45 ACP, a departure from the existing Accu-Tek line of 380 and 9mm chamberings.

A new double-action 45-caliber compact pistol has been introduced under the Firestorm name.

The new 45s are single-action subcompacts. Two variants have been introduced. The CP-45 is a stainless-steel gun with a single-column magazine, providing 6+1 capacity. The XP-45 has a polymer frame with a double-column magazine and a 10+1 capacity. This 3 1/2-inch-barrel polymer version tips the scales at 25 ounces.

Pre-production specimens of both types were displayed at the February 2002 SHOT Show. Availability of production models was scheduled for May 2002. The new Excel 45s will come with a lock and cleaning kit, and carry a lifetime warranty.

www.accu-tekfirearms.com

Firestorm

A new Firestorm 45 pistol was offered for 2002. A distinct design apart from the existing line of single-action 45s, the new pistol is a conventional double-action, with a decocker. Last year, Firestorm introduced these features in its "Mini-Firestorm" 9mm and 40 DA pistols. Now, the line is expanded to include the 45 ACP variant. The new Mini-Firestorm 45 is a 7-shot DA pistol. It features an ambidextrous manual safety and—a nice touch—an ambidextrous manual slide release. Finishes are matte black, satin nickel and duo-tone.

www.Firestorm-sgs.com

FNH USA

The formation of a new United States company, FNH USA, Inc., was formally announced in February 2002. This is an American subsidiary of FN Herstal, the Belgian firearms manufacturer, and will produce firearms for U. S. law enforcement and commercial customers, and for the military market.

A number of pistols are in the FNH lineup. Among them are the "High Power" pistols similar to those otherwise available under the Browning name. These include single-action, double-action and double-action-only variants.

Two new pistols are not similar to anything in the Browning line. The FN Model Forty-Nine was anticipated on these pages last year, and is now available in 9mm and 40 S&W. It is a polymer-frame DAO pistol with a revolver-type trigger pulling around 8 to 10 pounds. It weighs 26 ounces, and measures 5 3/4 x 7 3/4 inches, with a 4 1/4-inch barrel. The slide can be furnished in stainless steel or with a black semi-gloss finish. It has some interesting features, some hardly noticeable, such as a flat-coil recoil spring to allow greater compression.

The new FN Model Five-seveN is for law-enforcement and military sales only. With a 4.8-inch barrel and 8 1/4-inch overall length, it is a big polymer DAO pistol with a very light weight of only 22 ounces. Perhaps the most interesting feature is the cartridge for which it is chambered. The cartridge is a special 22-caliber bottleneck round, the 5.7x28mm, about 1.6 inches long. It is thus long for a pistol cartridge. *(It is actually the same round used in the FN P90 submachine gun).* However, the cartridge is only .310" in diameter (only slightly wider than a 30-caliber bullet) and, so, 20 rounds can be easily carried in the pistol's magazine. The cartridge is loaded with a 31-grain bullet that achieves 2133 feet per second from the pistol barrel. Because of the light bullet, it is said to have 30 percent less recoil than would be generated shooting a 9mm cartridge in a pistol of equal weight.

It is interesting to note the names of these two pistols feature the letters "FN" and designate the calibers for which they are chambered.

www.fnherstal.com

This is the FN Five-seveN, a 20-shot polymer pistol for military and law-enforcement sales. Chambering is 5.7x28mm, a high-velocity 22-caliber bottleneck cartridge.

The FN Forty-Nine feels good in the hand, and the DAO pistol is suitable for left-hand use.

The new FN DAO pistol has a cam-actuated tilting-barrel locking system. The captive recoil spring is a flat-coil spring to allow greater compression.

High Standard's Alan Aronstein displays a new GI Model pistol, made in the classic WWII style. Behind the gun is an original M1911 instruction manual, a copy of which will be included with each pistol sold.

The FN 5.7x28mm cartridge is shown with a 9mm Parabellum cartridge for comparison. The 5.7 is longer, but its small case diameter allows large magazine capacity.

Malloy fires a 9mm FN Forty-Nine pistol using a two-handed hold.

Glock

Glock had developed prototype specimens of a new safety locking system last year, and final working specimens were on display in February 2002. The system uses a special dimpled key inserted into the rear portion of the grip, behind the magazine well. When locked, a projection extends rearward from the grip and is obvious, by sight or feel, to a shooter gripping the pistol. The new locking system was scheduled for availability in early 2002.

Glock has made a run of "America's Heroes" pistols to commemorate the police and firefighters on the scene during the September 11, 2001 tragedy.
www.glock.com

Heckler & Koch

New in HK's USP line is the USP Compact 40 S&W LEM (Law Enforcement Modification) pistol. The action has been described as a hybrid double-action/single-action system that uses an internal "pre-cock" for reduced trigger pull. The trigger retains the longer DA trigger movement, but it has a fairly light—about 7 pounds—pull. In case of a misfire, the trigger can be pulled again for a second strike. The pistol is available in 40 S&W.

A brand-new pistol, too new for the 2002 catalog, is the P2000, a 9mm offering. The mechanism is said to be similar to that of the 40 S&W LEM, but the 9mm is conventional DA and is equipped with a decocker.
www.hecklerkoch-usa.com

High Standard

A GI Model 45 is new in High Standard's line. The pistols are made in the classic World War II style, and the finish is military-specification Parkerizing. On the left side of the slide, the guns will be marked "Model of 1911 A1." On the right of the slide, "Hi-Standard" will appear.

Each pistol will come with a reprint of an original military instruction manual, "Description of the Automatic Pistol, caliber .45, Model of 1911." All the information in the manual is still valid.
www.highstandard.com

Hi-Point

Hi-Point continues to modify and improve its line of low-cost pistols with little fanfare. The large-frame 40- and 45-caliber Hi-Point pistols will be phasing in polymer frames during 2002. A prototype of the new design was displayed at the 2002 SHOT Show.

The new frame will provide a slightly different grip shape and be slightly lighter than the present aluminum frames. The new pistols will offer an accessory rail, pushbutton magazine release and last-round hold-open features.

Hi-Point plans to eventually offer adjustable sights on all pistols, and all adjustable-sight models now come with an additional aperture sight.

Hi-Point likes to stress that their guns are made to be shot, and that their No-Questions-Asked warranty covers repairs.
www.hi-pointfirearms.com

The new Kahr PM9 is a subcompact polymer-frame 9mm with a shortened grip. The new little Kahr has ball-and-bar sights.

Kahr

Kahr got its start with a nicely designed small pistol, and its line has consisted of subcompact 9mm and 40-caliber pistols. At the 2002 SHOT Show, Kahr displayed a larger prototype "Target Model" pistol with a long grip frame and a longer 4-inch barrel. The construction was stainless steel, with wood grips. Most who handled it liked the feel of the pistol—it would be a nice holster gun for those who don't need a subcompact.

For those whose desires run to subcompacts, though, Kahr has added a new model. The new PM9 (Polymer Micro 9mm) is a small (MK9-size) pistol with a shorter polymer grip frame. It has a 3-inch barrel with

Kahr's Auto-Ordnance line of full-size 1911 pistols now has a shorter 4 1/4-inch barrel "Mid-Size" variant.

Here is a peek at Kahr's prototype large-frame 40 S&W "Target Model" pistol, exhibited for the first time at the 2002 SHOT Show.

polygonal rifling. The little gun weighs 15.9 ounces and measures 4 x 5.3 inches. Sights consist of a white ball front and white bar rear for fast alignment. The new little Kahr comes with two magazines—a flush 6-rounder or an extension 7-rounder; all Kahr 9mm magazines, however, including the longer ones, will work in the PM9. The frame is black polymer with steel inserts, and the slide is matte stainless steel.

Recall that Kahr now offers the Auto-Ordnance line of 1911-type pistols. New in that line is a "Commander-size" 45 (Kahr calls it a "Mid-size"), with a 4 1/4-inch barrel.

All Kahr pistols come with a lifetime warranty.
www.kahr.com

Kel-Tec

The little 6 1/2-ounce 32 ACP P-32 pistol, introduced in 1999, has been well-received. As of early 2002, well over 70,000 had been made. A new 10-round magazine is now available for the P-32. It adds some bulk, but feels good in the hand. For practice shooting, it provides more grip. I suspect those who carry the P-32 concealed, but also like to carry an extra magazine, may choose to carry the original 7-rounder in the pistol, with the 10-shot as a spare. The P-32 has gained surprising acceptance in the American West—the spring clip allows it to be conveniently carried as a boot pistol.
www.kel-tec.com

Kimber

The Kimber Ultra Ten II was introduced last year, and has been revised slightly. The final version was scheduled for production by the second quarter of 2002. Recall that the "II" designation indicated the new safety locking mechanism. Beginning in 2002,

Some people just want to have a pistol with the current 10+1 "legal limit" of cartridges. Kel-Tec now offers a 10-shot magazine for their P-32 that includes a grip extension. Makes the pistol bigger, but feels pretty good.

Kimber's Donna Logan displays the striking-looking Kimber Eclipse Target II pistol. The Eclipse line is stainless steel, blackened, with the sides polished bright.

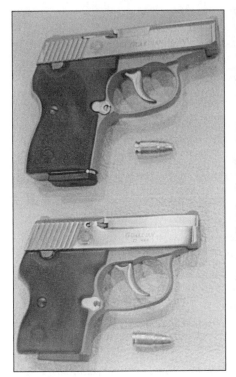

North American Arms has introduced two new Guardian pistols for two new cartridges. The larger-frame Guardian (*top*) uses the 32 NAA, essentially the 380 necked down to 32 caliber. The original smaller-frame version is now offered in 25 NAA, the 32 ACP necked down to 25.

North American Arms' new cartridges and the original rounds from which they were derived: *from left*, the 25 NAA, its parent 32 ACP, the 32 NAA, and the parent 380.

all Kimber pistols will have the lock and are thus considered Series II pistols.

The striking-looking Eclipse pistols—stainless steel, covered black, then the sides polished bright—were Custom Shop items last year. They proved so popular they are now full-time in the line as standard catalog items.

A Stainless Target pistol is now available for the first time chambered in 38 Super.

Kimber is proud to be a sponsor of the U. S. Olympic Shooting Team.
www.kimberamerica.com

Malloy examines an Olympic Arms OA-98, a large pistol chambered for the 223 Remington. Parts have been skeletonized to reduce weight.

Magnum Research

Magnum Research is now handling the new IMI (Israeli Military Industries) Barak 45-caliber pistol. The 30-ounce pistol has a polymer frame with an accessory rail. It is a hammer-fired design and is conventional double-action (DA), with a decocker. Locking is by a cam-actuated tilting-barrel system. The 3.9-inch barrel has polygonal rifling, and the pistol measures 5.4 x 7.4 inches. Capacity is 10+1. The Barak has a rounded slide that might lead one to suspect that the recoil spring was around the barrel. However, it actually uses two separate springs on rods beneath the barrel.
www.magnumresearch.com

North American

The little 32 ACP Guardian pistol, introduced a few years ago, proved popular and led North American Arms to introduce a new 380 Guardian last year. Now the company has introduced two new Guardian pistols for two new cartridges.

The new cartridges are the 25 NAA—essentially the 32 ACP necked down to 25 caliber, and the 32 NAA—the 380 necked down to 32 caliber. Cor-Bon will produce the ammunition, and preliminary velocity figures promise to be pretty zippy. The 380-frame Guardian will be offered in the 32 NAA, and the smaller 32-frame Guardian will be available in 25 NAA.

The Guardian pistols will be provided with a new internal safety lock.
www.naaminis.com

Olympic

For people who like big pistols, Olympic Arms now offers the OA-98. It is an AR-15 type pistol, chambered for the 223 Remington (5.56mm) cartridge. Pistols of this sort must weigh under 50 ounces to be "civilian legal," so the OA-98 has a skeletonized grip, magazine well and shield to reduce weight.

The OA-98 has been under development for some time, and is now in full production.
www.olyarms.com

Para-Ordnance

Para-Ordnance now offers the Para Carry (Model C6.45 LDA) and the Para Companion (Model C7.45 LDA). They are small 45-caliber single-column carry pistols with the company's "Light Double Action" mechanism. These all-steel guns were introduced last year on these pages, and are now in full production.

The Para Carry, with its three-inch barrel, measures 4 3/4 x 6 1/2 inches, weighs 30 ounces and offers 6 + 1 capacity. The Para Companion is slightly larger, with a 3 1/2-inch barrel

The new Para Carry is a small single-column 45 with a 3-inch barrel, and offers 6+1 capacity.

The Para-Ordnance new 45-caliber single-column Para Companion has a 3 1/2-inch barrel with 7+1 capacity.

This is the prototype of the new Rohrbaugh 9mm all-metal subcompact pistol. The 14-ounce DAO pistol will be available in a version with a magnetic safety.

The frame is 7075 aircraft aluminum; all other parts are 17-4 stainless steel. The grips on the prototype were of aluminum, but wood and other materials will be offered.

The little pistol is a short-recoil locked-breech design with a cam-operated tilting-barrel locking system. The barrel is free-bored for a quarter-inch, and the pistol will handle all standard 9mm loads.

Two models will be available. The MS-9 will have a magnetic safety. With this system, the shooter wears a Neodymium magnetic ring that opens an internal block to allow the trigger to operate. Another model, the R-9, will be made without the magnetic safety. Production was scheduled for July 2002.
API380@aol.com

Sarsilmaz

A name generally connected with shotguns, the Turkish Sarsilmaz firm plans to introduce a line of 9mm semiautomatic pistols. The catalog offered in February 2002 featured the pistols, but actual specimens were not available to examine. From the catalog illustrations, the guns looked to be based on the CZ-75 design. A polymer-frame variant may be made under the Bernardelli name. Timing of the introduction of the new pistols was uncertain at press time.
www.sarsilmaz.com

Sigarms

Sigarms has introduced two new handguns. The P226 Sport ST will be made in a limited run for competitive shooters. It is a stainless-steel pistol with a heavy barrel, adjustable sights and extended controls. It will be available in 9mm chambering only.

The P226 ST is now also offered as a stainless-steel duty gun. Availability at present is in 9mm, and versions in 40 S&W and 357 SIG are anticipated.

Sigarms is now handling Sig-Sauer, Sig Pro, Blaser, Sauer, Hammerli and Mauser arms, and is projecting more expansion into the hunting field.
www.sigarms.com

Smith & Wesson

Smith & Wesson has introduced a new pistol, the model 952. The new item is a 9mm target pistol. It is similar to the former Model 52 of long ago, which was chambered for the 38 Special wadcutter cartridge. The 952 barrel bushing is of titanium nitride and is fitted closely. The pistol has a decocker, and uses a "grip safety" device to release the firing pin block, so that trigger pull is unaffected.

Seven models of S&W pistols are now available with the "Saf-T-Trigger" mechanical trigger lock. The American firm, Saf-T-Hammer, originator of the

and measuring about 5 x 7 inches. The slightly longer grip frame gives the pistol a 7 + 1 capacity.
www.paraord.com

Republic

Republic Arms, of Chino, California, maker of a 20-ounce polymer 45, has gone out of business. Inventory and tooling have been acquired by Cobra Enterprises, and that new company will continue production of the pistol. (See Cobra)

Rohrbaugh

A prototype of the new Rohrbaugh pistol was displayed at the February 2002 SHOT Show. The little gun is an all-metal 14-ounce DAO pistol, chambered for the 9mm cartridge. With a 2.7-inch barrel, it measures 3.6 x 4.9 inches. Thus, it will stick out a little from under a 3x5 note card, but not much. Thickness is a little over 3/4-inch.

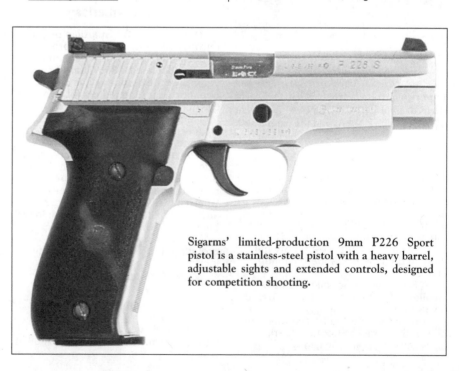

Sigarms' limited-production 9mm P226 Sport pistol is a stainless-steel pistol with a heavy barrel, adjustable sights and extended controls, designed for competition shooting.

The new Sphinx Model 3000 pistol.

Susanne Seiler holds a Sphinx Model 3000 pistol. The Swiss-made pistol has a machined titanium frame.

new trigger lock mechanism, is the new owner of Smith & Wesson. After the bad publicity generated while the company was under British ownership by the Tomkins group, S&W is capitalizing on this with their new "American Made – American Owned" slogan.

All S&W hammers are now made by the Metal Injection Moulding (MIM) process, and are somewhat lighter than previous hammers.

www.smith-wesson.com

Sphinx

We may still think of the Swiss as gunmakers, but Sphinx is the last remaining firearms manufacturer in Switzerland. Sphinx pistols are high-end pistols; made primarily for military, law enforcement and competition use. They are based on the CZ-75 design, and are available in either conventional DA or double-action-only (DAO) configuration. The Swiss Sphinx offerings now include pistols made with titanium frames.

The Model 3000 has an all-titanium frame. It is the top-of-the-line pistol, chambered in 9mm, 9x21, 40 and 45. Barrel options are 4 1/2 or 3 3/4 inches. The CNC-machined titanium frame has a beavertail tang, squared trigger guard and accessory rail.

The Model 2000 now comes with a titanium layer on the frame. It also features an accessory rail on its traditional frame. The same barrel lengths are offered as on the 3000. Cartridges chambered are 9mm, 9x21 and 40; the 45 chambering is not available.

www.sphinxarms.com

Springfield

Big news from Springfield is their new line of X-treme Duty (XD) polymer-frame pistols. The new pistols are available in 4- and 5-inch barrel variants. The chamberings offered are 9mm, 40 S&W and 357 SIG. Safety features include a grip safety (an uncommon feature on a polymer-frame pistol); a trigger safety and an internal firing-pin-block drop safety. The slide will not unlock unless the grip safety is pressed in. The XD pistol also has loaded chamber and cocking indicators. Takedown is simple and essentially foolproof.

Regular readers of these pages will recognize that HS America introduced a similar pistol in 2000. With minor modifications, the pistol is now part of the Springfield line. This nice design should benefit from the company's established distribution system.

Springfield's new XD pistol (X-treme Duty) is a polymer-frame gun in 9mm and 40 caliber. This is a variant with a 4-inch barrel.

Cindy Griffin, production coordinator for Springfield, displays the company's new offering, the polymer-frame XD (X-treme Duty) pistol. This variant is a version with a five-inch barrel.

The Taurus PT 145 is here disassembled to show the cam-actuated tilting-barrel system and the two recoil springs; one inside and one outside the guide rod.

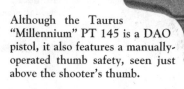

Although the Taurus "Millennium" PT 145 is a DAO pistol, it also features a manually-operated thumb safety, seen just above the shooter's thumb.

will continue to offer paid service on Steyr firearms as long as their parts supply lasts.

At least some Steyr guns will remain in production, and Dynamit Nobel RWS, Inc, operating from Closter, NJ, will be the new importer. More details could not be had by press time.

The recently-introduced Steyr pistols had begun to develop a following, and we hope this interesting design will continue to be available.
www.dnrws.com

Talon

Talon Industries, of Ennis, MT, had introduced a line of low-cost polymer-frame 380 and 9mm pistols just last year, but now has gone out of business. Inventory and tooling have been acquired by

Cobra Enterprises, a company that will continue production. **(See Cobra)**

Taurus

Taurus believes there is always room for a new 22-caliber plinking pistol, and has introduced the PT 922. It is a large-frame 22LR pistol with a 6-inch barrel, based on the PT 92, but is a blowback design. At first glance, the protruding barrel makes it look a bit like a Walther P38 or one of the Walther PP Sport pistols. The PT 922 has 10+1

Everyone can use a 22-caliber plinking pistol, and Millie Matias is pleased to display Taurus' new offering, the PT 922.

In addition, Springfield has introduced the Micro Compact 45. The smallest pistol in the company's 1911 lineup, it has a 3-inch barrel and weighs just 24 ounces. Slimline Cocobolo grips keep the pistol thin, and all sharp edges are rounded off.

All Springfield pistols, including the new XD pistols, are covered by a lifetime warranty.
www.springfield-armory.com

Steyr

Last year, rumors circulated that the plant in which Steyr pistols were being made was being taken over for other uses. By September 2001, Austria's Creditensalt bank, then the owner of Steyr, had apparently sold the land on which the Steyr factory was located to BMW for automotive production.

By February 2002, GSI of Trussville, AL, the U. S. importer for Steyr firearms, confirmed that Steyr was under new ownership, and that GSI would no longer be the importer. GSI

The Taurus PT 145, a 10+1 compact polymer-frame 45, is now in full production.

Taurus' new Model PT 922 pistol is a nice 22-caliber plinker with a 6-inch barrel.

Volquartsen's new Cheeta pistol will be offered in several rimfire cartridge chamberings. *From the left*, the 22 Long Rifle, the 22 Winchester Magnum Rimfire and the 17 Hornady Magnum Rimfire. The 17 Aguila is also scheduled.

A 5-inch "Target" model of the Walther P22 is available. The P22 pistols have 10+1 capacity and weigh about 20 ounces.

The Walther P22 is now in production. This version, with a 3.4-inch barrel, is a compact little plinking pistol.

capacity and a three-position safety. The safety acts as a manual safety and also as a decocking lever. The PT 922 will have the key-operated Taurus Security System. The new pistol was scheduled for late summer 2002 availability.

The Taurus PT 145, announced back in 2000, ran into production delays, only recently resolved. The pistol has now come into full production. This new 45 ACP pistol is the biggest-caliber offering in Taurus' polymer-frame Millennium series. It has a 3 1/4-inch barrel and the locking mechanism is a cam-operated tilting-barrel system. Trigger is DAO, and the pistol also has a manual thumb safety, an uncommon feature on a DAO pistol. Two recoil springs of different diameters operate on the inside and outside of a hollow

The big new long-range Volquartsen rimfire pistol, the Cheeta, is displayed by Jarod Menke.

spring guide. The magazine is a staggered-column type and holds 10 rounds. A Taurus-made magazine loader is provided to get them all in, making the PT 145 a pistol of 10+1 capacity. The PT 145 weighs just 23 ounces and measures 5 x 6 1/4 inches in overall size. All the Taurus Millennium pistols, including the new 45, have the key-lock Taurus Security System.

www.taurususa.com

Volquartsen

Volquartsen has made high-grade Custom 22-caliber semi-auto pistols based on the Ruger Mark II for some time. In early 2002, however, Volquartsen introduced a completely new design of rimfire semiautomatic pistol. The new "Cheeta" has a separate rear-mounted grip, and has the magazine forward of the trigger. Designed for long-range shooting, it has an integral scope base.

The barrel is bimetallic—a titanium sleeve over a steel barrel. The grip is

ambidextrous, and the safety can be operated from either the right or left side.

Volquartsen reports that the new pistol has produced groups under one inch at 100 yards in tests. In what caliber? Ah, there is an interesting situation. The Cheeta is scheduled to be available in four rimfire chamberings. As one might expect, the 22 Long Rifle and 22 Winchester Magnum Rimfire are two of them. One of the other two, the 17 Hornady Magnum Rimfire *(essentially the 22 WMR necked down to 17 caliber)* was designed for Marlin and Ruger bolt-action rifles, but Volquartsen has successfully adapted it to the Cheeta autoloading pistol. The 17 Aguila *(the 22 LR necked down to 17 caliber)* was introduced by the Aguila ammunition firm for much the same use, and is on the list for Cheeta chamberings.

The Volquartsen Cheeta was scheduled for April 2002 availablity. www.volquartsen.com

Walther

As of early 2002, Walther was starting to deliver the neat little P22 pistols it introduced last year. The P22 looks like a small P99, but is a hammer-fired conventional DA blowback. The pistols will be available with interchangeable "backstraps" (rear grip inserts); barrel-length options are 3.4 or 5 inches. The P22 pistols weigh about 20 ounces and have 10+1 capacity.

Recall that the classic PPK/S design was undergoing a slight revision. The new PPK/S in 380 ACP was scheduled for February 2002 availability. The same pistol in 32 ACP will be offered some time later.

www.walther-usa.com

Wilson

Wilson Combat has introduced a new Tactical Carry Pistol (TCP). The new 1911-style pistol has a Kevlar-reinforced polymer frame with stainless-steel inserts. The frame was designed specifically for a staggered 10-round magazine *(not a plugged higher-capacity one)*, which allowed the polymer frame to actually be slightly narrower across the grips than

The redesigned Walther PPK/S is available in 380 ACP now, with the 32 ACP version scheduled later.

POSTSCRIPT

Many of us remember when the misguided "Assault Weapons" bill was passed into law in 1994. Perhaps the most lasting effect of that act was to restrict firearms magazine capacity to 10 rounds for ordinary citizens, while the police could continue to use high-capacity magazines.

Forgotten by many is that the 1994 law has a 10-year duration and will expire in 2004–not all that long from now. Contact your senators and representatives and line up support to defeat it at the designated time. Then, we can all keep our plugged magazines to remind us to remain active in the future.

Wilson Combat has introduced a compact polymer-frame TCP with a 4-inch barrel and 9+1 capacity.

a traditional 1911. The new TCP has been designed with an external extractor.

Two variants are offered, in full-size and compact configurations. The full-size TCP weighs 31 ounces and measures 5 1/2 by 8 5/8 inches, and sports a 5-inch barrel. The compact has a 4.1-inch barrel, an overall size of 5 1/4 by 8 inches and weighs 29 ounces. The shortened grip frame of the compact holds one round less, giving it a 9+1 capacity.

Wilson's TCP pistols are guaranteed to shoot within 1 1/2 inches at 25 yards. www.wilsoncombat.com

The new Wilson polymer-frame full-size Tactical Carry Pistol is a slim 10+1 pistol.

by JOHN TAFFIN

HANDGUNS TODAY:

SIXGUNS & OTHERS

those found on the 19th-century Colt Single Action Army. The top-of-the-line model is the Peacekeeper, which adds a factory-tuned action, 11-degree forcing cone, 1st Generation-style cylinder flutes, and bone/charcoal case-hardened frame.

There is a definite difference between the case coloring found on the Longhorn and the Peacekeeper; the latter's being much more brilliant, and the bluing seems a little deeper, too. Both models feature a beveled ejector-rod housing to keep the metal from digging into the leather on a tight holster, and both models can be had in nickel finish. The Peacekeeper can also be ordered with the "blackpowder frame" that uses an angled screw in the front of the frame to hold the cylinder pin in place rather than the spring-loaded cross-pin style of the later SAA frame design.

Chamberings include 45 Colt, 44-40, 357 Magnum, and 44 Special. I expect both the 38-40 and 32-20 to be offered eventually. In addition to the Longhorn

*S*INCE I WAS a teenager, I always looked forward to the release of the latest *GUN DIGEST*–and the first section I always turned to was this one. For the past 23 years this annual report has been written by my dear friend, Hal Swiggett, and before him, the late George Nonte handled the reporting of the latest handgun developments. Two pistoleros *of renown, to be sure. Now the mantle has passed to me and I hope my work meets with their approval.*

A beautiful rendition of the Single Action Army is AWA's Peacekeeper.

American Derringer

For more than 150 years, a most popular concealed weapon has been the derringer. A multitude of companies have offered both single-shot and double-shot easy-to-hideaway pistols to be used in a time or situation we hope never occurs. Many of these little guns have been poorly made and lacking in accuracy. The derringers from American Derringer go against the grain–being of high-quality and more than adequate accuracy. The lovely Elizabeth Saunders, *aka* Lady Derringer, offers shooters a full line of both single-action and double-action

two-shooters in chamberings from 22 rimfire to 380 ACP to 44 Magnum to 45 Colt–even 45-70 (*ouch*!)–and a multiple of calibers in between. The stainless steel M-1, for example is offered in 24 chamberings with the original, and my favorite, being the 45 Colt.

The traditional M-1 looks much like the old 41 Remington, though slightly larger and definitely stronger. In addition to the 24 chamberings currently cataloged, it can also be special-ordered with each of the two barrels in a different chambering. I have used the M-1 45 Colt for over a decade, carried in a Thad Rybka pocket holster which also holds two extra 45 Colt rounds, and the M-1 is safe to carry in the pocket as it is equipped with a hammer-block safety that automatically disengages when the hammer is cocked. American Derringer offers a whole line of custom finishes, engraving, holsters, and custom grips.

American Western Arms (AWA)

AWA imports Armi San Marco parts, which are then assembled in this country and the firearms finished–resulting in a beautiful Single Action Army replica, in two basic versions. The standard model is the Longhorn with a color case-hardened frame and hammer, blue finish, and one-piece walnut grips. Both the front sight and hammer checkering are based upon

and Peacekeeper six-guns, American Western Arms also markets a large selection of custom grips and western-style leather.

AWA had a couple of shaky starts but they are now under new ownership and turning out many variations as well as high-grade, fully-engraved, ivory- or pearl-handled six-guns. At Tin Star Ranch in November 2001, I pointed out to Chris Harrison of AWA that they needed to do a better job of radiusing the rounded curve at the backstrap area where it meets the back of the hammer—all three should have the same smooth radius. At the SHOT Show in February 2002, the six-guns on display indicated this problem has been addressed.

Cimarron Firearms

Mike Harvey of Cimarron has been one of the primary forces in upgrading replica six-guns from the "Spaghetti Western-style" of the 1960s to the highly authentic replicas of both percussion and fixed ammunition six-guns we have today. Cimarron's lineup includes the Model P, a near-perfect copy of the 1st Generation Colt Single Action Army, including old model-style frames–often referred to as blackpowder style–that were in use from 1873 to the mid-1880s, and the new model frame that arrived in 1896.

One of the best derringers ever offered is the American Derringer M-1, especially when chambered in 45 Colt.

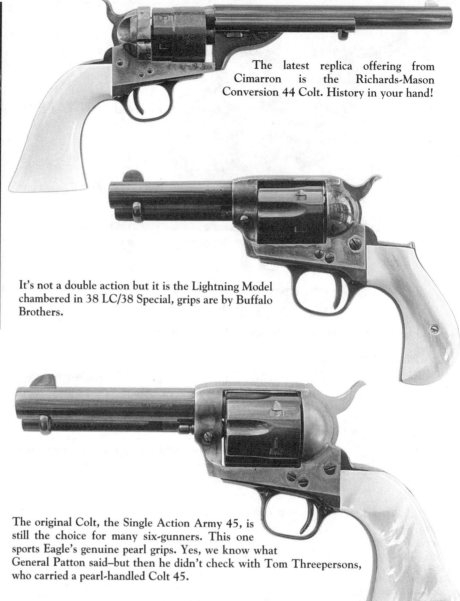

The latest replica offering from Cimarron is the Richards-Mason Conversion 44 Colt. History in your hand!

It's not a double action but it is the Lightning Model chambered in 38 LC/38 Special, grips are by Buffalo Brothers.

The original Colt, the Single Action Army 45, is still the choice for many six-gunners. This one sports Eagle's genuine pearl grips. Yes, we know what General Patton said—but then he didn't check with Tom Threepersons, who carried a pearl-handled Colt 45.

Harvey Lane of Cimarron Firearms with the new Wyatt Earp Model P.

Cimarron now offers the Frontier Six-Shooter, totally assembled and finished in this country using European parts. In addition to these authentic "Colt" models, CFA also provides shooters with the Bisley Model, Flat-Top Target Models from the 1890s, and the Thunderer and Lightning–two single actions utilizing the grip shape of Colt's 1877 double actions.

Moving deeper into six-gun history, we find the Model 1872 Open-Top, immediate predecessor of the Colt Single Action Army; the Richards-Mason Conversion (*new this year*), which enabled percussion revolvers to use fixed ammunition–and every cap-and-ball revolver offered by Colt from the original 1836 Paterson through the Walker, Dragoon, Navy, and Army models. Nearly every single action offered by Cimarron is not only available in the original blue and case-colored style but also in what Cimarron refers to as their 'original' finish, a 'distressed' finish that makes the six-gun appear to have been used - but not abused - for over 100 years. Cimarron's custom shop also offers a full line of custom finishes, grips, and engraving.

One of the most spectacular and eye-catching six-guns offered by Cimarron is the Wyatt Earp Buntline. This 10-inch-barreled 45 Colt six-gun is offered in blue/case-coloring, or original finish, and is the same six-gun used by Kurt Russell in his memorable performance as Wyatt Earp in the movie "Tombstone." Each is equipped with authentic one-piece walnut stocks, with a sterling silver shield inlaid in the right-side grip commemorating the presentation of the long-barreled Colt to Wyatt Earp by "the Grateful People of Dodge City." I've ordered mine in the standard blue/case-colored finish.

The Colt Single Action has dropped over $400 in suggested retail price and is now offered in blue/case-colored or nickel, 4 3/4- or 5 1/2-inch barrels, and in 45 Colt, 44-40, and 357 Magnum.

Two welcome returnees to the Colt stable, the stainless steel Anaconda and the blued Python.

Colt

Colt has new management once again, and this time it looks good! General William "Bill" Keys is now the president and has pledged to get Colt completely back on track. As a start, the Anaconda is back–not only in the original 44 Magnum and 45 Colt chamberings, but 41 Magnum as well. Colt's 'Cadillac' double-action revolver, the Python, has returned and is available in both stainless steel and the beautiful Royal Blue finish. General Keys also plans to return such longtime favorite as the Detective Special and the Official Police to the product line.

The most stunning announcement - and most welcome - from the General, is his hope to return the New Service to production. This was Colt's large-frame double action produced from the 1890s up to the start of World War II. If Colt can return the New Service, with no major modifications, and having the same look and feel of the magnificent New Service and New Service Target Models of the 1930s chambered in 44 Special, 45 Colt, and 45 ACP–and do so at an affordable price, they will certainly sell all they can produce.

Speaking of price, the near-impossible has happened! Colt has actually lowered the price on their Single Action Army!! At the 2001 SHOT Show the retail price on an SAA was a staggering $1968. One year later the price has been reduced - not by just a few dollars, but by $438 - resulting in a new retail price of $1530. That puts it not all that far above some of the high-dollar replicas being offered. Colt has also added the 357 Magnum as a standard chambering, along with 45 Colt and 44-40. All models are available in both 4 3/4-inch and 5 1/2-inch barrel lengths, and either blue/case-hardened or nickel finishes.

In addition to lowering the price of the Single Action Army, many custom shop services have also been lowered in price. One can now have their Single Action Army converted to 357 Magnum, 38-40, 44-40, 44 Special, or 45 Colt using new barrels and cylinders–at a very reasonable price. Colt is once again listening to shooters.

Early & Modern Firearms (EMF)

EMF holds the distinction of being the first to offer replica Colt Single Actions. 'Way back in the 1950s, EMF was a distributor of the Great Western line of frontier six-shooters. These were the very first replicas ever offered and were unique in that they were not manufactured overseas, but actually produced — of all-American parts — in Los Angeles. Great Western disappeared in the 1960s, however. EMF continues to offer a complete line of 19th-century firearms of both fixed ammunition and percussion style.

EMF's top-of-the-line Single Action Army is the Premier Hartford Model with a special deluxe finish, blue and case-colored, Colt-style rubber grips, and chambered in 45 Colt. I have long used several Hartford Models from EMF for *CAS*, including a pair of consecutively-numbered 7 1/2-inch, nickel-plated 44-40s with Colt-style grips. The nickel plating really eases the chore of cleaning up after using blackpowder. One of the most accurate replica six-guns I have ever shot, whether with blackpowder or smokeless, is a 7 1/2-inch Hartford Model in 38-40.

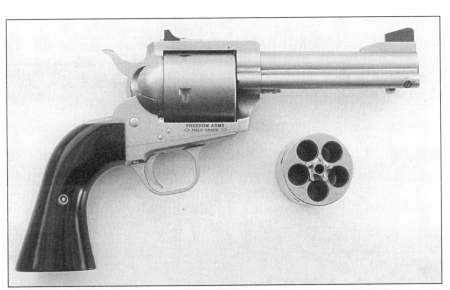

With the advent of the new Ruger cartridge, this Freedom Arms 475 Linebaugh has been fitted with a second cylinder in 480 Ruger.

Freedom Arms' latest offering is the Model 97 22 rimfire, displayed by President Bob Baker.

First really big critter to fall to the 480 Ruger, my 1200-pound buffalo taken with Buffalo Bore's 410 hard-cast load in the Freedom Arms 4 3/4-inch Model 83.

Newest chambering from Freedom Arms is the Model 97 in 22 LR and 22 Magnum.

Freedom Arms

For two decades now, Freedom Arms has been offering the finest single actions ever produced by any factory at any time. Beginning with the 454 Casull in 1983, Freedom has gone on to offer their first six-gun, albeit a five-shooter, in 44 Magnum, 357 Magnum, 41 Magnum, 50 Action Express, 22 LR and 22 Magnum, and - quite recently - in 475 Linebaugh. No matter what the caliber, every Freedom Arms revolver is meticulously crafted, with most chamberings available in either a fixed-sight or adjustable-sight version and barrel lengths of 4 3/4, 6, 7 1/2, and 10 inches. The adjustable-sight version also accepts a scope mount. For the first time this year, the Model 83 is offered in a 10-inch 475 Linebaugh. With the advent of the 480 Ruger cartridge, I had a 4 3/4-inch 475 Model 83 fitted with a 480 cylinder. Using Buffalo Bore's 410 Hard Cast load at 1100 fps from this short-barreled revolver, I took a 1200-pound bull bison in December of 2001. Penetration was complete on a broadside shot at 35 yards and, as far as I know, this was the largest game taken with the 480 Ruger up to that time.

In 1997 Freedom Arms downsized their revolver, introducing the Model 97, which is only slightly smaller than the Colt Single Action Army. This mid-framed six-gun was first offered in 357 Magnum, in either fixed or adjustable

sight versions, and in barrel lengths of 5 1/2 or 7 1/2 inches, with a 4 1/4-inch length now added. This was also the first six-shot Freedom Arms revolver and, as such, the first taken to heart by cowboy action shooters. Following the 357 Magnum Model 97 were five-shooters in 45 Colt and 41 Magnum– the latter two chamberings place the Model 97 in the "near-perfect packin' pistol" category. Although smaller than the Colt Single Action Army, the 45 Colt Model 97 will handle loads much heavier than should ever be used in the Colt.

The newest revolver from Freedom Arms is the long-awaited 22 rimfire Model 97. This will be the most expensive - and also the finest - 22 rimfire revolver ever offered to shooters. By the time you read this it will be available in barrel lengths of 4 1/4, 5 1/2, 7 1/2 and 10 inches, with an extra cylinder for 22 Magnum available through the custom shop. Imagine what a tack-driver the 10-inch Model 97 should be!

Magnum Research

Long known for the superbly accurate Desert Eagle semi-auto pistol, Magnum Research also offers hunters a traditionally-styled single-action revolver, the BFR. Previously offered in standard cylinder length versions in 22 Hornet and 454 Casull; and long-frame, long-cylinder five-shooters in 45-70, 444 Marlin, 450 Marlin - and a special 45 Colt that also accepts .410 shotgun shells. The BFR line now includes two of the newest and most powerful six-gun chamberings: 480 Ruger and the 475 Linebaugh.

The BFR is constructed of 17.4 PH stainless-steel with a cut-rifled 416-R stainless-steel barrel; is offered in 6 1/2- and 7 1/2-inch barrel lengths, 10-inch in 22 Hornet, 444 and 450 Marlin, and 45-70; and features a free-wheeling cylinder that rotates forwards or backwards as desired when the loading gate is open. Sights are a fully adjustable rear mated with an orange front, and the revolver is also designed to accept a Leupold scope mount base.

Magnum Research's BFR is offered for rifle cartridges, such as the 444 Marlin and 45-70.

Grips are rubber wraparound style. With a suggested retail price of $999, this is the least expensive way to get into a single-action six-gun chambered in 454 or 475, and the only six-gun I know of currently chambered in the lever-gun cartridges: 444 Marlin, 450 Marlin, and 45-70.

M.O.A.

For two decades, Richard Mertz of M.O.A. has been offering superbly accurate single-shot pistols of the falling-block style, using a one-piece receiver fitted with a Douglas barrel. Although equipped with precisely adjustable sights, most hunters will opt for the use of scopes and the receivers are drilled and tapped to accept M.O.A. bases.

The M.O.A. Maximum is strong enough to handle about any cartridge that one might wish to hold onto—and some I wouldn't care to shoot, such as the 375 H&H! Any M.O.A. chambered for what is normally a bolt-action rifle cartridge should be fitted with a muzzle brake. Barrels are interchangeable on the M.O.A. action and are free-floating, with no pressure from the forearm. Safety is paramount with the M.O.A. and it can only be loaded or unloaded with the transfer bar button in the "SAFE" position.

Navy Arms

Val Forgett of Navy Arms, who has been providing shooters with quality replicas for nearly a half-century, truly deserves the title "Father of the Modern Replica Firearms Industry." I purchased my first Navy Arms revolver, an 1858 Remington, sometime around 1960. It wasn't the last. Not only can we thank Navy Arms for Colt and Remington centerfire and cap-and-ball replicas, they were the first to bring us a copy of the Smith & Wesson single-action six-gun. First came the Schofield, now offered in a 7-inch Cavalry Model, a 5-inch Wells Fargo Model, and a 3 1/2-inch Hideout Model, all in 45 Colt and 44-40; and now we have the New Model Russian chambered in 44 Russian.

The New Model Russian, a favorite of Buffalo Bill, is a finely-detailed replica of the same six-gun that Smith & Wesson sold by the thousands to the Imperial Russian Army in the 1870s. The Navy Arms version features a blue finish, walnut stocks, and case-colored hammer, trigger, and locking latch. The New Model Russian also features a spur on the rear portion of the trigger guard. Placing your middle finger on this spur provides a very steady hold for accurate shooting.

Ruger

Great news for handgun hunters from Ruger. The Super Blackhawk Hunter model is back! Dropped in 1992 due to the barrel loosening (*rarely*) when a scope was mounted, that problem has been solved and hunters once again reap the benefits. The 7 1/2-inch stainless steel Hunter model

The Navy Arms Model #3 Russian with Eagle's UltraIvory grips (*top*) is a faithful reproduction of this original six-gun from 1874.

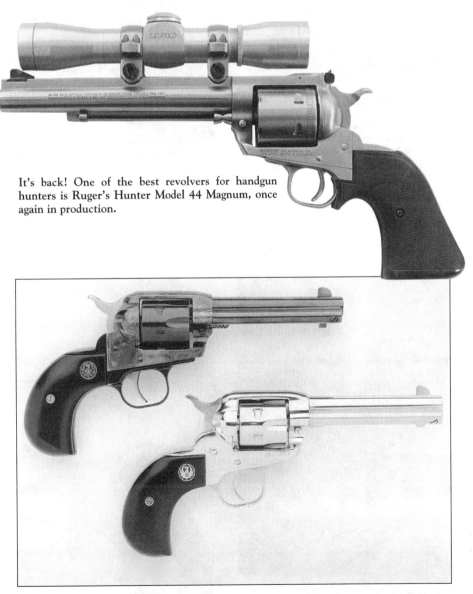

It's back! One of the best revolvers for handgun hunters is Ruger's Hunter Model 44 Magnum, once again in production.

Ruger has not only resurrected the 32 Magnum Single-Six, it is also now available as a miniaturized Vaquero with a round-butt grip frame; in blue or stainless steel finishes.

differs from the standard Super Blackhawk in having a rounded trigger guard, a heavyweight full-ribbed barrel, scallops on the barrel that accept provided Ruger scope rings, an interchangeable front sight system, and an ejector rod and housing that is approximately 3/4 inch longer for more positive ejection of fired cases. A scope can be mounted without removing the iron sights, making it possible to switch back and forth between scope and iron sights with a tool no more sophisticated than a 50-cent piece to loosen the Ruger scope rings. This is one of the best-designed six-guns ever offered for handgun hunters, and its return is heartily welcomed.

Ruger captured a major portion of the cowboy action market when they introduced the Vaquero 10 years ago. First offered in a 45 Colt blued/case-colored version, it was soon joined by a stainless steel counterpart, as well as those chambered in 44-40, 44 Magnum, and 357 Magnum. Then came the Bisley Vaquero, the same basic six-gun with the Bisley Model grip frame, hammer, and trigger. All versions and calibers have been extremely popular with both CAS participants and outdoorsmen. Last year, Ruger introduced the 45 Colt Vaquero in a "Sheriff's Model" version with 3 3/4-inch barrel and a bird's-head grip frame. This popular offering has now been joined by a smaller version in 32 H&R Magnum. This variation of the Single-Six has fixed sights, blue/case-color or stainless steel finish, and either a shortened standard grip frame or the bird's-head style. An excellent choice for shooters with small hands.

Ruger's big-bore Super Redhawk trio consists of the 44 Magnum, the 454

Irony of ironies! Jerry Miculek holds the new McGivern Model from Smith & Wesson.

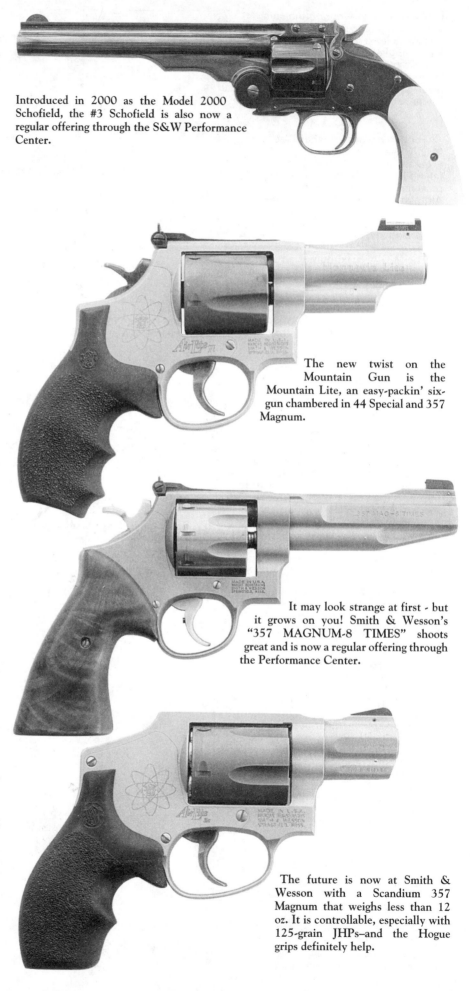

Introduced in 2000 as the Model 2000 Schofield, the #3 Schofield is also now a regular offering through the S&W Performance Center.

The new twist on the Mountain Gun is the Mountain Lite, an easy-packin' six-gun chambered in 44 Special and 357 Magnum.

It may look strange at first - but it grows on you! Smith & Wesson's "357 MAGNUM-8 TIMES" shoots great and is now a regular offering through the Performance Center.

The future is now at Smith & Wesson with a Scandium 357 Magnum that weighs less than 12 oz. It is controllable, especially with 125-grain JHPs—and the Hogue grips definitely help.

Casull, and the 480 Ruger. Scope-ready, stainless steel, and in 7 1/2- or 9 1/2-inch barreled models, all Super Redhawks come equipped with recoil-reducing cushioned rubber grips. Very popular with hunters, the 454 Super Redhawk sold 15,000 units its first year of production, which has now been equaled by the first year of the 480 Ruger Super Redhawk.

One of most popular Ruger six-guns has been the 22 Bearcat. First made from 1958-1973, it was my son's first handgun, purchased for him on his 10th birthday in 1973. Twenty years later, the Bearcat was reintroduced - only to be dropped again - and then brought back in 1996. Finally, the Bearcat is in production and this year the standard blued model has been joined by the stainless steel version. All new Bearcats feature Ruger's transfer bar system. All the stainless steel version needs to make it the perfect 'kit gun' is adjustable sights.

Smith & Wesson

It looks like a great year! Not only is Colt getting back on track, Smith & Wesson is already there with new ownership and new management. For the first time in several decades Smith & Wesson is once again American-owned. Bob Scott, a former vice-president of S&W, and president of Saf-T-Hammer, is the leader of the group that purchased Smith and is also the new president. Everyone I have talked to at Smith & Wesson is totally upbeat and ready to go forward.

New products abound from Smith & Wesson this year. The old classics–such as the original Model 27, 19, and 29–may be gone; however, a new generation of lightweight revolvers is here. Who would have thought we would ever see an 11 oz. 357 Magnum? It's here–the AirLite Sc series of "J-frames" with major components manufactured of Scandium. These are offered in the 340 Centennial hammerless-style, and the Model 360 with a standard hammer. The 340 Sc is the first five-shot revolver that can be carried in complete comfort in a jeans pocket. For those that prefer a slightly larger - but still lightweight 357 Magnum - there is the 386

MountainLite, a 3 1/8-inch seven-shooter that weighs 18.5 oz. The MountainLite comes equipped with a HiViz fiber-optic front sight, found on many new models and which can be retrofitted by the factory to older models.

Other new revolvers from Smith & Wesson this year include the 6 1/2-inch Model 629 44 Magnum with the HiViz front sight, which Smith & Wesson assured me will stand up to the recoil of the 44 Magnum; and the very popular Model 625 45 ACP is not only available as a standard catalog item with a 4-inch barrel, but is also available through the Performance Center with a shortened cylinder custom-made to fit the length of the 45 ACP and 45 Auto Rim. Custom gunsmiths built revolvers with shortened cylinders and the barrel extending further back through the frame back in the 1950s. However, this is the first factory offering I've heard of. To complement the short-cylinder 45, the Performance Center also offers the same basic six-gun with a 5 1/2-inch barrel and the cylinder chambering eight 38 Super rounds in a full-moon clip. All Smith & Wesson revolvers now feature an internal lock activated by inserting a special key in a very small opening above the cylinder latch release.

Two S&W revolvers formerly offered exclusively by select distributors are now standard Performance Center offerings. One is the stainless steel, eight-shot Model 627 with the distinctive, slab-sided 5-inch barrel marked ".357 MAG-8 TIMES." Smith & Wesson had to do some serious modification of the frame and barrel to modify a basic Model 27 to accept an eight-shot cylinder. However, it was accomplished and is one of the better ideas carried out in 357 Magnum. In 2000, Smith & Wesson offered the Model 2000 Schofield on a limited basis. This recreation of the original 1875 Schofield chambered in 45 S&W is now a standard item as the 7-inch-barreled Model 3 Schofield. Thank you, Smith & Wesson - on both counts.

The Schofield started the manufacturing of nostalgic six-guns at Smith & Wesson and it has now been joined by the Heritage Series. The first in this series last year was the HEG, a revolver reminiscent of the old First Model Hand Ejector or, as better known by most shooters, the Triple-Lock. With its slim tapered 6-inch barrel, adjustable sights with a flat black post front sight with a McGivern gold bead and traditional blue finish, the HEG 45 Colt transported us, spiritually speaking in a six-gun sense, back to simpler days.

Now that original Heritage Series offering has been joined by the same basic revolver offered in either 44 Special with a case-colored frame, and a nickel-plated 44 Magnum, both with slim tapered barrels. Rounding out the N-frame Heritage Series is a new rendition of the 1917 Army Model as used in World War I. Beautiful six-guns

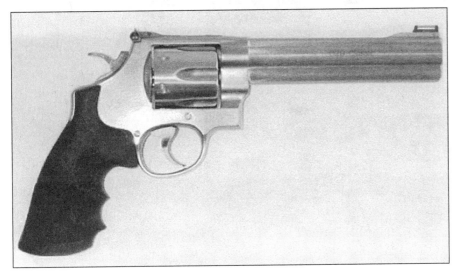

Smith & Wesson's 629 44 Magnum now comes with a Hi-Viz front sight.

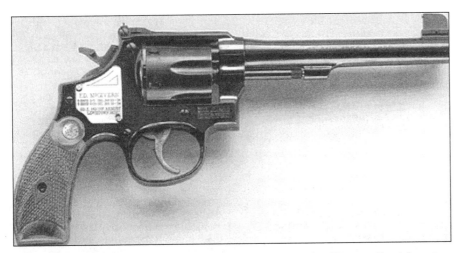

An exceptionally attractive little six-gun is the Military & Police Heritage Special version, the McGivern Model.

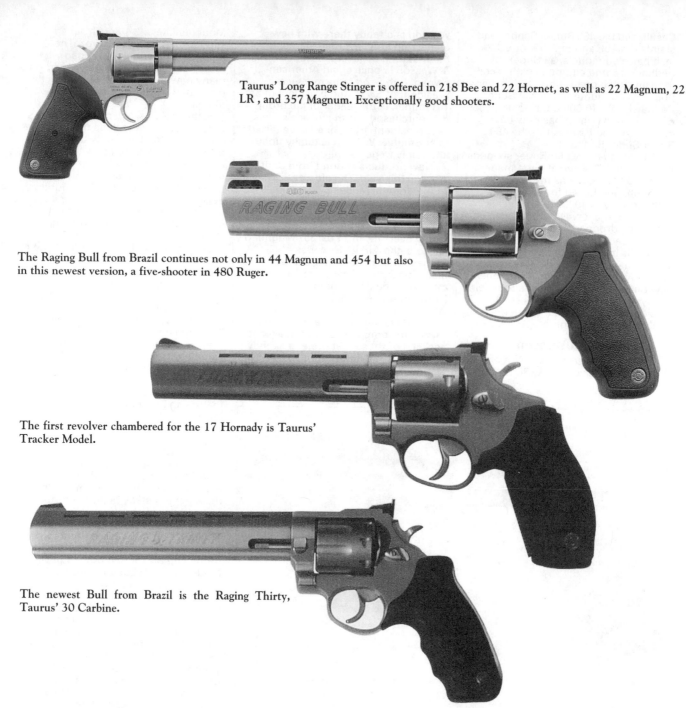

Taurus' Long Range Stinger is offered in 218 Bee and 22 Hornet, as well as 22 Magnum, 22 LR , and 357 Magnum. Exceptionally good shooters.

The Raging Bull from Brazil continues not only in 44 Magnum and 454 but also in this newest version, a five-shooter in 480 Ruger.

The first revolver chambered for the 17 Hornady is Taurus' Tracker Model.

The newest Bull from Brazil is the Raging Thirty, Taurus' 30 Carbine.

all, but I have saved the best for last. The latest member of the Heritage Series is the McGivern Model 15. Ed McGivern's favorite revolver for speed shooting was the Smith & Wesson Military & Police 38 Special. As he set new shooting records, a miniature metal plaque was appropriately inscribed and placed on the sideplate of the M&P 38 Special. This is a faithful recreation of a 1930s Military & Police, complete with a facsimile of the sideplate plaque commemorating the record that was set and, as well, a post front sight with the McGivern gold bead. The only departure of any consequence from the original revolver is the fact that (as on all Heritage Series revolvers) the grip frames are round instead of square. Normally, I reserve round butts for short-barreled revolvers; however, they do feel good on these 5-inch

M&Ps. Three finishes are available, Bright Blue, Nickel, or Blue with a case-colored frame. These are beautiful revolvers!

Taurus

Taurus is one company that never lets any grass grow under its feet. While other companies have been touting the 17 Hornady Rimfire Magnum as a rifle cartridge, Taurus is the first company to offer this new cartridge in a handgun. The latest Tracker from Taurus is an eight-shot 17 HRM. Other new Trackers include a 6-inch 45 Colt and a 4-inch 45 ACP–both holding five rounds. The little Trackers, with their "Ribber" grips, are easy packin' and powerful.

Sometimes six-guns are very serious and other times they simply just need to be fun. The new silhouette

guns from Taurus certainly fall into the 'fun' category. These revolvers, with 12-inch barrels, were first offered in 22 LR and 22 Magnum and now have been joined by a 357 Magnum–as well as two "Stingers," the 22 Hornet and 218 Bee.

On a more serious side, at least for big game hunters, is the Taurus Raging Bull. First offered as a six-shot 44 Magnum, it was soon joined by a 5-shot 454 Casull, and then last year by a Raging Bull chambered in 480 Ruger. The Raging Bulls are offered with heavy full-underlug and ported barrels and specially-cushioned rubber finger-grooved grips, all of which help dampen felt recoil. Barrel lengths available are 5 inch, 6 1/2 inch, and 8 3/8 inch - in both blue and stainless finishes.

Fans of the 41 Magnum will be happy to know the Raging Bull is now

The Thompson/Center Contender has been upgraded to the G2, shown here by Ken French.

offered in 41. This cartridge, once pronounced dead by so many "experts," has in recent years been chambered by Freedom Arms and now by both Colt and Taurus. Joining the big-bore Raging Bulls is the Raging Thirty, an eight-shot 30 Carbine. And finally, from Taurus we have the new Protector, in both 38 Special and 357 Magnum. The hammer on the Protector is shrouded on both sides but still allows for manual cocking, and the rear sight - while adjustable - has also been de-horned. This 2-inch pocket pistol is a five-shooter with finger-groove rubber grips and is offered in stainless steel, blue steel, or titanium. All Taurus revolvers feature the built-in security system that allows the action to be locked.

The newest revolver from Dan Wesson is the Model 360DW chambered in 360DW, a slightly elongated 357. Accurate, and pleasant to shoot.

Herrett's stocks, and personalized engraving on the barrel, highlight this Dan Wesson 460 that shoots 460 Rowland, 45 Winchester Magnum, 45 ACP, and 45 Auto Rim–all from the same cylinder.

After several false starts under previous owners, the New Dan Wesson 414 SuperMag is finally a reality.

Thompson/Center

Thirty-five years ago Thompson/Center introduced the single-shot Contender to handgunners. First chambered in 22 Long Rifle and 38 Special, it did not take long for Thompson/Center to realize the Contender was capable of handling the pressures normally associated with lever-guns and Magnum revolvers and we soon had Contenders for cartridges such as 30-30, 35 Remington, and 44 Magnum. Hunters found that Contenders were often more accurate, when chambered for rifle cartridges, than many rifles.

The Contender had been offered in dozens of factory chamberings over the years, and J. D. Jones of SSK Industries led the way in wildcatting the Contender with - literally - hundreds of both standard and wildcat offerings. If it can be done safely, Jones has probably offered it. Two of the best (*in my hunting experience*) from SSK have been the 6.5 JDJ and the 375 JDJ. Together, they cover all the bases.

As good as the Contender is, it has two major shortcomings. It is quite often difficult to break open - sometimes requiring two hands to release the action, or worse, requiring one to strike the operating lever sharply karate-style with the edge of the hand. The other "problem" has been that once the Contender was

The Contender has been upgraded to the G2. Barrels and forearms interchange with the original, grips do not.

cocked to fire, and one decided not to fire, the hammer had to be carefully let down; then it was necessary to open the action before the gun could be cocked and ready to fire again.

Thompson/Center addressed both of these problems with the introduction of the Encore single-shot pistol a few years back. In addition to an easy-opening feature and also a hammer safety–which allowed the hammer to be re-cocked without opening the action–the Encore is also a larger, stronger pistol with the ability to handle cartridges normally chambered in bolt-action rifles. Wouldn't it be wonderful if the features of the Encore could be incorporated into the smaller Contender?

The answer is 'yes,' and the new Contender is the G2. Not only has Thompson/Center succeeded in upgrading the original Contender with the easy-opening and hammer safety features of the Encore, they have also ensured the G2 will accept any T/C barrels. It will also take the same forearm as the original Contender. The grips, however, are not interchangeable and shooters will find the new grip has a slightly different angle - and is more comfortable. A new handgun-hunting chapter begins with the Thompson/Center G2.

Dan Wesson Firearms

In 1968, Dan Wesson brought his better ideas to shooters. Three of his ideas were radical to say the least. Instead of a grip frame, Dan Wesson revolvers featured a stud that accepted a one-piece wooden grip bolted on at the bottom, allowing for great latitude in grip shape and size. Second, all Dan Wesson six-guns came with interchangeable front sights. Both of these features have been picked up by other manufacturers. The most radical of his ideas was the interchangeable barrel system. Instead of a solid barrel, Wesson used a slim barrel within a shroud. A special tool removed a nut at the end of the barrel, which then allowed the shroud to be removed, and the barrel could then be easily unthreaded by hand. What was designed to be a convenient way to change barrel lengths also resulted in superb accuracy.

Dan Wesson revolvers soon became the favorite of six-gun silhouetters and Dan Wesson rode that crest for several years. When that market went down, Dan Wesson experienced financial difficulties and soon closed it's doors. That's the bad news. The good news is that Dan Wesson was purchased by Bob Serva in 1996, moved to New York and equipped with all-new machinery - resulting in the best Dan Wessons ever manufactured. In the past, Dan Wessons were often plagued with rough chambers and a barrel/cylinder gap that was often uneven. All that has changed. The new Dan Wessons, thanks to the all-new machinery, come from the factory with extremely smooth cylinder chambers and perfectly parallel barrel/cylinder spacing.

In addition to all the standard models, Dan Wesson has reintroduced the Alaskan Guide series, a compensated 445 SuperMag with a 4-inch barrel; the rarely-seen 414 SuperMag (*before 1996*) is now a standard model; new chamberings such as the 460 Rowland and 45 WinMag have been introduced; and a totally new cartridge - the 360 DW - is chambered in the New Generation large-frame series. This cartridge is longer than the 357 Magnum, which is offered on the New Generation small frame, and shorter than the 357 SuperMag, which is found in the New Generation SuperMag frame series.

United States Fire Arms Mfg. Co. (USFA)

From 1873 until 1941, the 1st Generation Colt Single Actions were manufactured in the original Colt factory, under the trademark rampant colt dome. Today, in that same building, USFA is turning out single actions produced and finished as carefully as those original Colts. USFA informs us that all their single actions feature American-made barrels and cylinders and that they provide many of the services and custom touches offered on the originals.

The Single Action Army (or Bisley Model), for example, comes in the three standard barrel lengths of 4 3/4, 5 1/2, and 7 1/2 inches, with other lengths available as a custom feature. Chamberings are 45 Colt, 44 WCF, 38 WCF, 32 WCF, 41 LC, 38 Special, and 44 Special. The metal finish is 'Old Army Bone Case' on frame and hammer, the balance finished in 'Dome Blue,' or full-nickel plating. Standard stocks are one-piece walnut, with hard rubber, pearl, ivory, or stag optional. A 1890s Flat-Top Target revolver is also available, as is a 16-inch barreled Buntline Special, complete with flip-up rear sight and skeleton shoulder stock.

The newest offerings from USFA include the Rodeo, a basic no-frills, satin-finish 45 Colt single action designed for cowboy shooters, and the Omni-Potent, a Bisley-style six-gun with a grip frame reminiscent of the Colt Double Action Model of 1878, complete with a lanyard ring. USFA also offers a complete line of custom features including all levels of engraving, custom stocks, special serial numbers–and even replacement cylinders and barrels for original 1st Generation Colts in the above-mentioned calibers.

Raj Singh of Eagle Grips with the new Heritage (S&W "Coke bottle") Grips.

Eagle Grips

Eagle has furnished shooters with custom grips of ivory, stag, pearl, and exotic woods for several decades. During that time we have seen grips on factory double-action revolvers go from highly useable wood... to poorly-shaped wood... to rubber. The latter is functional but not aesthetically pleasing. Many of us search the tables at gun shows to find the old Smith & Wesson 'coke-bottle' grips with the diamond in the center for both N- and K-frames. Now Eagle has stepped into the breach and is offering their Heritage Grips, a faithful reproduction of the old Smith grips - right down to the center diamond. Grips are rosewood and feel and look great.

Shooters have had a hard time getting staghorn grips because of the exportation ban, so Eagle has filled a need by offering stag grips of elkhorn. They polish out nicely, with good color. Also from Eagle are the Ultralvory grips that are about one-third the cost of the real thing–and several light-years ahead of the plastics and polymers offered as "ivory." Instead of being molded as one set of grips, Ultralvory comes in large pieces that are first 'slabbed' and then cut into grip shapes. They have good grain and color in them and most folks would have hard time telling them from the real thing.

It looks like a great year for six-gunners!

by RAYMOND CARANTA

THE GUNS OF EUROPE

KORTH

Workmanship supreme!

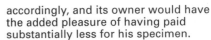

FEW AMERICAN READERS are acquainted with this German company from Ratzeburg, a charming town located on an island in the Schaale River, about 12 miles from Lubeck. However, Ratzeburg is where some of the finest European handguns have been carefully handcrafted since 1964.

While famous among Europeans for their high quality, Korth revolvers and semi-automatic pistols are relatively unknown to the majority of American shooters. Production is limited, and the cost is extremely high, due to the many hours of skilled labor required. Thus, most of us admire the samples displayed in catalogs, at international gun shows, or in the windows of the most famous arms retailers–but only a happy few actually own and shoot them.

- The investment.

Nevertheless, perhaps it is time for the American handgunner to invest in such pieces of art, as the U.S. dollar has recently gained ground, compared to European currencies. As a matter of fact, while the dollar was the equivalent of .76 Euro ca. 1995, now it is the Euro that is equivalent to .85 dollar approximately (in June 2001) – a 60 percent variance in six years! What was very expensive–just a few years ago– is now a bargain...

If today's currency exchange is clearly favorable to American handgunners considering the basic models, it is even better for the engraved and gold-inlaid

versions—and will only improve. After all, Korth revolvers are rare items, of a recognized original design, executed with the very best workmanship.

Should the exchange rate reverse itself, the Korth's value on the American market would increase

accordingly, and its owner would have the added pleasure of having paid substantially less for his specimen.

Of course, as far as target shooting is concerned, a 'perfect' score is the same, whether made by the cheapest South American or the most expensive German revolver.

However, in the latter case, we are dealing with a fine weapon, intended for a true connoisseur looking for absolute perfection–and willing to pay for it–much the same as the person who purchases an Aston-Martin "DB7", Lotus "Esprit" or Lamborghini "Diablo" coupe...

In this vein, while visiting an Italian friend in Turin many years ago, I was surprised to see a brand new Ferrari "Daytona" in the courtyard, and the red nose of an older model "365" protruding from an open door. After congratulating him for owning such exceptional cars, I asked if he would dispose of the oldest.

He answered, "*Well, Raymond, it is already a pity that such mechanical wonders are purchased with money... Therefore, when you are lucky enough to have one, it is only your duty to keep her for your whole life!*"

Right side view of the 6-inch barrel Korth "Sport" revolver.

- About Willi Korth.

During the immediate post-war years, when Ferdinand Porsche was in Gmund, Austria, 'nursing' his outstanding "356" car fitted with the Volkswagen engine, and Fritz Walther was manufacturing calculating machines in Niederstotzingen, Willi Korth, a railway engineer passionately fond of shooting and hunting, was designing the action of his future revolvers. Being German, he could not be satisfied taking advantage of lower European manufacturing costs, while copying the best American designs, as many others did. He had to excel on his own terms.

This drive motivated him, when he founded his company in 1954, at the age of forty-one, to select the best available steel–that from MG-34 machine guns scraped at the end of the war. Nowadays, such scrap steel no longer exists, and modern Korth handguns, including the revolver sideplates, cylinder cranes, cylinders, triggers and hammers—or pistol slides and receivers—are machined from forgings made of the most appropriate modern steels: 1,700 psi tensile strength, heat-treated to Rockwell 58 C.

The Allied forces occupied post-war Germany, and the manufacture of bullet-firing firearms was prohibited.

Willi Korth started his business, in a modest Ratzeburg cellar, by producing alarm revolvers he had designed in 1953. This enabled him to profit from the design of his basic action and to develop the strict quality standards, which would later be applied to his conventional revolvers. The German alarm revolver market being particularly price-sensitive, Willi Korth was nevertheless able to compete, thanks to his innovative ideas, without diminishing the final product quality. These first Korth alarm revolvers fired gas cartridges, which used German cases and a specific mixture developed by the small company. Korth produced 20,000 of these alarm revolvers in the ten years from 1954 to 1964. Their success was such, notwithstanding a high price (*for the time*) of 90 DM, that the inventor was soon obliged to abandon his cellar!

Today, a half-century later, Korth products are no longer produced in a cellar, but in a modern factory. All revolver components are individually hand-finished by a highly qualified staff, resulting in exceptionally close parts tolerances, a prime requisite for precision revolving firearms. Currently, 30 percent of Korth revolver manufacturing operations are carried out on machine tools and the remaining 70 percent is accomplished by manual operations, involving component shaping and fitting, quality control and final assembly.

- The German sporting revolvers.

Following relaxation of the German law and opening of the international market, a niche appeared for German sporting revolvers.

Through the 'Fifties, Europe was dominated by the semi-auto pistol and, in her shooting ranges, was ruled by the I.S.U. regulations. Lugers, chambered for the 7.65mm and 9mm cartridges and featuring skillfully reworked triggers with crisp let-offs, were mostly used for the popular "Sport Handgun" event.

The softening of European customs regulations ca. 1960 permitted new generations of shooters to discover the virtues of the American 38 Special cartridge. We were soon flooded with Colt and Smith & Wesson revolvers, significantly more reliable than our old Luger pistols, and with much better triggers.

It was time for the leaders of the new German sporting arms industry to act.

Among them, Hermann Weihrauch, was able to establish himself with his economical, but sturdy and accurate, Arminius revolvers. Willi Korth, on the other hand, reached the pinnacle of sporting revolver technology in 1964– both for the quality of materials and for superior workmanship.

- The Korth revolvers design.

Theoretically, any fixed-barrel revolver properly installed in an appropriate holding fixture securely mounted on a sturdy bench is able, with good ammunition, to make 100/ 100 groupings at 25 meters on the ISU "Sporting Handgun" target featuring a 2-inch ten-ring (the current European standard), provided the

Willi Korth (July 11, 1913 - October 10, 1982), the founder of the company, was a talented gunmaker who launched the German revolver revival.

▼The fast-operating cylinder latch of the Korth revolver.

◀The basic 4-inch barrel version of the Korth "Combat" revolver is a double-action six-shooter, weighing 36-oz. empty, available in 22 LR, 22 WRM, 32 S&W Long, 38 Special and 357 Magnum. This model was also made as a 5-shot revolver, in 38 Special or 357 Magnum, from 1966 to 1968.

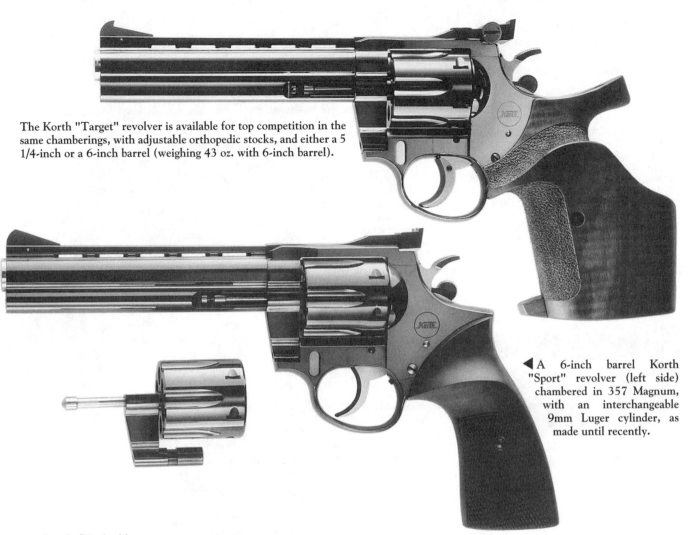

The Korth "Target" revolver is available for top competition in the same chamberings, with adjustable orthopedic stocks, and either a 5 1/4-inch or a 6-inch barrel (weighing 43 oz. with 6-inch barrel).

◀ A 6-inch barrel Korth "Sport" revolver (left side) chambered in 357 Magnum, with an interchangeable 9mm Luger cylinder, as made until recently.

revolver is fitted with a properly bored and rifled barrel.

However, the matter becomes more complicated, when considering the cylinder fitting, boring and concentricity–thus requiring top-quality steels perfectly heat-treated, precisely machined and meticulously hand-fitted–quality available only from the leading international arms specialists.

When such criteria are extended to a thirty-round course of fire, as is the case under the ISU "Slow Fire" regulation, one can easily imagine the quality level required! Moreover, the one-hand, extended-arm shooting position regulation requires perfect single-action let-offs, attainable only by custom gunsmithing.

For double-action revolvers, such as those made by Korth, the action must be powerful, but soft and smooth, with a short DA-cocking cycle absolutely free of vibration when the hammer breaks, to prevent flinching in rapid fire. Then, handling qualities and balance must be considered, together with reliability and ease of cartridge case extraction, indicative of the uniform quality and interior finish of all chambers. Finally, the purist will not be satisfied with a poorly finished exterior or marred, poorly fitted parts.

Revolver components ready for assembly.

▲ A compact "Combat" Korth 3-inch barrel revolver, made in 1976.

Besides these basic considerations, let us mention the exceptional smoothness of the Korth revolvers in double action, their adjustable let-offs with over-travel stop, the telescopic mainsprings, similar to the "MP-38" submachine gun recoil spring, the original indexing of the easily-interchangeable cylinders, the special cylinder latch design–parallel to the hammer for fast opening–and their axial double locking.

It is the well-executed combination of all these design elements that justify the cost... and explain the success of Korth revolvers for some forty years.

The current Korth 9mm Luger semi-auto pistol. In March 2001, a new single-action-only version was released with a 2.4/2.6-pound trigger pull and a mere .06-inch trigger travel.

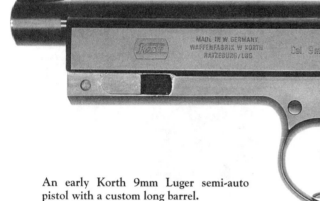

An early Korth 9mm Luger semi-auto pistol with a custom long barrel.

- The Korth semi-automatic pistol.

Currently chambered in 9mm Luger, 9x21 IMI, 357 SIG and 40 S&W, this semi-auto pistol was announced in March 1982, in 9mm Luger, but was actually first available in 1985, as a limited production single-action gun featuring an exceptionally crisp let-off, in direct competition with the SIG "P210" pistol.

The final double-action version was first marketed in France in 1987. It cost then, in my country, the equivalent of $3,400! This first batch was numbered from 1 to 100. Nowadays, production samples of this pistol cost, in the United States, from $4,900 to $5,500, according to the finish selected.

As with the Korth revolvers, this axial short-recoil semi-automatic pistol (*typically German*!) is a mechanical perfection, without 'play' between the barrel and the receiver (*even without recoil spring tension*), to the pivoting trigger. The slide is very smooth to operate, with minimal operating 'play.' Bearing and external surfaces are highly polished, with perfect edges.

The single-action pull of the sample we fire-tested in 1987 was very clean, at 4 pounds, with a .2-inch long first-stage pull at 25 oz. and almost non-existent backlash, measuring less than .04-inch. The trigger breaks at 3.3 pounds in single action and at about 11 pounds, in double action.

A special single-action-only version, with shorter trigger travel and crisp let-off, is also available on request. Safety devices consist of an automatic firing pin safety, rebounding hammer and loaded chamber indicator. A thumb-operated safety is optional. The sturdy swiveling barrel lock is located under the barrel, near the muzzle.

- Korth Germany GmbH, today.

Recently (April, 2000) the Korth company was purchased by Freylinger & Co., gunsmiths in Levange, Grand Duchy of Luxemburg, who have infused new blood in the undertaking and are developing its activities.

As an early initiative, Korth Company GmbH has created, for the millennium, a limited batch of ten commemorative "Combat" 357 Magnum 4-inch barrel revolvers, designated "Anno Domini 2000" and numbered from 2000-1 to 2000-10. These richly finished revolvers are treated with gold-tone PVD plasma coating (like spacecraft), deeply engraved, and decorated with thorns. Grips are made of exquisite ambonia wood.

Willi Korth is no more, but his works endure! ●

KORTH GERMANY GmbH
Robert Bosch Strasse, 11
D-23909
RATZEBURG, Germany
www.korthwaffen.de
Fax: (04.541).84.05.35

by LAYNE SIMPSON

RIFLE REVIEW

Anschutz

ONE OF THE most handsome rifles I've seen lately is the special edition Model 1710 DKL in 22 Long Rifle from Anschutz. Fancy wood, elaborate engraving, hand-cut checkering, it has it all. Another nice thing about Anschutz rifles is they always shoot as good as they look. As for standard-production hunting, varminting and plinking rifles, about two dozen are available in 22 rimfire, 22 Hornet, 222 Remington and the new 17 HMR–all offered in standard and heavy-barrel variants. In case anyone out there is interested, my favorite Anschutz is the Classic; I especially like the heavy-barrel version.

A-Square

A-Square is back and under new ownership, although company founder Art Alphin is still there. Hannibal, Hamilcar and Genghis Khan model rifles are in the works and just as they always have been, all are built on highly modified 1917 Enfield actions. Loaded ammunition ranging from the 7mm STW (*which A-Square was first to load years ago*) to the 700 Nitro Express is available, as is a complete selection of solid and soft-nose bullets in many calibers and weights. I have taken a few Cape buffalo with A-Square's monolithic solids and Dead Tough soft-nose bullets and their performance has always been flawless.

Browning

Browning is chambering several versions of its A-Bolt for Winchester's new 270 WSM and 7mm WSM. It might be of interest to note that Winchester has changed dimensions slightly on its short 7mm magnum cartridge. Whereas the 270 WSM is simply the 300 WSM necked down for .277-inch bullets, the 7mm WSM is the 300 WSM necked down but with its shoulder moved forward a bit. This dimensional change will prevent the inadvertent chambering of a 7mm WSM cartridge in a rifle chambered for the 270 WSM. Sounds a lot like the old 280 Remington/270 Winchester story. I used the A-Bolt Stainless Stalker in 270 WSM on an expedition for nilgai that took place on the 850,000 acre King Ranch in south Texas during early 2002 and one shot at 170 yards with the 140-grain Fail Safe load did the trick. On that same hunt I took another nilgai at about 60 yards with one round of Winchester's 200-grain Silvertip loading of the 348 Winchester fired in my 1950s-vintage Model 71 lever action. Which just goes to prove that getting close with something old works just as well as shooting from afar with something new.

Through the years I have taken around 20 nilgai and consider it to be, pound for pound, the toughest game animal walking the North American continent. Only five of the animals I shot dropped in their tracks, and those were taken with (*interestingly enough*)

Winchester ammo. In addition to the pair taken with the 270 WSM and the 348, there were a couple taken with the 160-grain Fail Safe loading of the 7mm STW and another with the 260-grain Partition Gold loading of the 454 Casull, the latter in a 7 1/2-inch Freedom Arms revolver. All the others, including two shot with the 416 Remington Magnum, reacted to my shots exactly as nilgai are programmed to do; they ran 50 to 60 yards before discovering they were dead.

The new Dura-Touch coating was designed to improve the feel of a rifle stock and is available first on the A-Bolt Varmint Stalker in 223 and 22-250. The stock feels velvety smooth, offers a no-slip grip to cold, wet hands and has a very high durability rating as synthetic stock finishes go. Equally new in the 2002 Browning catalog is the BAR Lightweight Stalker made up of blued steel and synthetic. Chambering options now include Winchesters 300 WSM.

Charles Daly

The name Charles Daly has been used by several different companies through the years and this time it is out of Harrisburg, Pa. This company offers a variety of shotguns and handguns as well as various models of rifles built around commercial 1898 Mauser actions. The Field grade is available with blued or stainless steel barreled action, both housed in black synthetic stocks. Offered only in blued steel, the walnut-stocked Superior Grade is available in standard and mini actions, the latter a perfectly scaled-down '98 Mauser action in 223 and 7.62x39mm Russian. All rifles have staggered magazines with hinged floorplates except for the mini-Mauser in 22 Hornet with its detachable five-round magazine. You can also buy the actions alone or barreled actions chambered for cartridges ranging from 22 Hornet to 458 Winchester Magnum. Rimfires range from a single-shot youth gun in 22 LR to the fancy Superior with a quick-detach magazine. This same basic rifle is also available in 22 Hornet.

CZ USA

One of the most fun guns I have shot lately is a CZ 527 in 7.62x39mm Russian. Combine this one with factory ammo or handloads with expanding bullets weighing in the neighborhood of 125 grains and you have a lightweight, low-recoil rifle suitable for taking deer out to 100 yards or so. While I don't see the 30 Russian listed in their latest catalog, it should be

A-Bolt Varmint Stalker with the Dura-Touch stock coating.

available on special order. As new rifles go, the 527 Varmint has a Kevlar stock and is chambered for the 223 Remington cartridge.

Flodman Guns

One of the more interesting rifles I examined at this year's SHOT Show was an over-under double built by the Swedish firm of Flodman Arms. For now at least, it is available in 7x57R, 7x65R and 9.3x62mm but others are slated for future introduction. Over-under barrels with one of those chamberings down below and the 12 gauge up top are also available. The receiver of this gun is quite shallow, making it extremely comfortable to carry with one hand.

Gibbs Rifle Company

What can you do to the old British Enfield that hasn't already been done many times? Well, you could rebarrel it to 45-70 and convert its detachable magazine so it will hold three of those big, fat cartridges. This, along with outfitting the No. 4 with a new hardwood stock replete with cut checkering, is exactly what Gibbs has done. Called the Summit, the new rifle with an old action wearing a barrel chambered for an even older cartridge weighs 8-1/2 pounds and has an 18 1/2-inch barrel.

Kimber

A downsized version of the standard Kimber 22, the new Youth with its 12 1/4-inch length of pull, 5-1/4 pound weight and 18 1/4-inch barrel is built just for kids–and what kid wouldn't just love to own one. Overall length is 35 1/2 inches. Kimber has pledged to donate $50 from the sale of each rifle to the NRA's Youth Education Endowment, something more companies should do. Other new variations of Kimber's magnificent 22 are the Hunter and Classic which look the same to me except the latter seems to have a bit more figure in its stock. Like all Kimbers, those two do not leave the factory until they shoot five bullets into .400 inch at 50 yards. The actual test target packaged with each rifle is proof enough of its capability.

Last time we sat by the old campfire I mentioned an upcoming hunt for red stag in New Zealand with the new Kimber Model 84M rifle. What a grand adventure in a most beautiful country it turned out to be. Both my hunting buddy and I used rifles in 308 Winchester and a handload I cooked up with W748 powder and the Nosler 165-grain Ballistic Tip bullet. We each bagged red stag, fallow deer and sika deer, all free-ranging animals and all

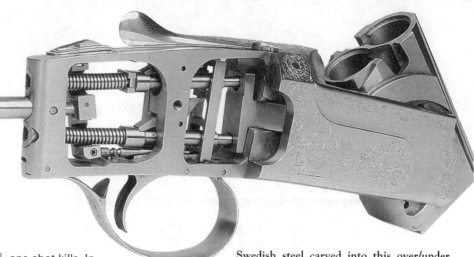

Swedish steel carved into this over/under action eventually becomes a complete rifle from Flodman Guns.

one-shot kills. In fact, the red stag I harvested was the best my outfitter, Adrian Moody, had ever taken. What a great mountain rifle Kimber's Model 84M is. The one I hunted with weighed only an ounce over seven pounds, including a 2.5-8X scope. As I write this, the 308 Winchester is its only available chambering but the 243 Winchester, 260 Remington and 7mm-08 Remington should be just around the corner. Prior to taking it on a prairie dog shoot, I bench-tested the varmint version of this same rifle with a medium-heavy, 26-inch barrel in 22-250 and its average 100-yard group was 0.94 inch. The most accurate load, 36.0 grains of Hodgdon's Varget behind Ed Shilen's 52-grain hollowpoint, averaged 0.54 inch for five shots. Among various factory loads tried, ammo with the horse and rider on the box won the accuracy contest with a 0.76-inch average for its 40-grain Ballistic Silvertip load. That ammo, by the way, averaged a rather speedy 4083 feet per second on my Oehler chronograph. At any rate, Kimber is now offering three versions of its Model 84M rifle. In addition to the Classic and Varmint I have hunted with, there is the 10-pound LongMaster VT with its 26-inch, fluted stainless steel barrel in 22-250 and laminated wood stock replete with high rollover cheekpiece and wide beavertail-style forearm.

Legacy Sports International

Latest variation of the Howa Model 1500 rifle is the Ultralight with a 20-inch barrel in 243 Winchester and a weight of 6-1/2 pounds. It has a blued steel action and black synthetic stock and is sure to become available in 260 Remington, 7mm-08 Remington and 308 Winchester in the not too distant future. The Supreme lineup with

I took this magnificent red stag in New Zealand with Kimber's new Model 84M in 308 Winchester.

classic-, thumbhole- and varminter-style stocks–all of laminated wood–is available in a variety of chamberings from 223 Remington to 338 Winchester Magnum. The Classic and Thumbhole Sporter have stainless steel barreled actions while the Classic is blued. New chamberings of the Puma lineup of

Howa Ultralight M1500, from Legacy Sports.

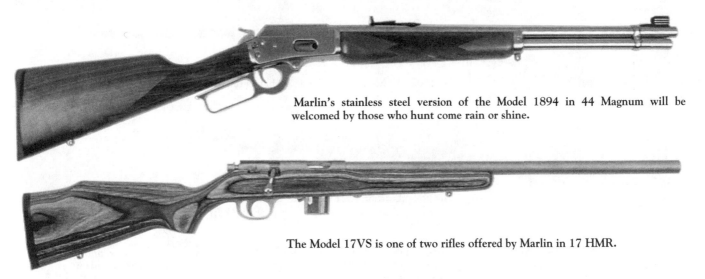

Marlin's stainless steel version of the Model 1894 in 44 Magnum will be welcomed by those who hunt come rain or shine.

The Model 17VS is one of two rifles offered by Marlin in 17 HMR.

lever-action Winchester look-alikes is the 45 Colt and 454 Casull, the latter sure to be a great choice in lever-action carbines for shooting game up to the size of elk and moose at woods ranges. Rifling twist rate of the 454 barrel is 1:9 inches while barrels in 38 Special/357 Magnum, 44 Magnum and 45 Colt are 1:10.

Marlin

As you might guess from their 17VS and 17V model designations, Marlin's time-proven Model 17 bolt action is now available in 17 Magnum. A combination of hardwood and blued steel, the six-pound 17V has a 22-inch, heavy-contour barrel with a 1:9-inch rifling twist rate. Switch to stainless steel for the barreled action and a laminated wood stock and you have the 17VS at seven pounds. The stocks of both rifles are protected from hard knocks by Marlin's tough Mar-Shield finish.

Rainy day deer hunters who have yearned for a stainless steel lever-action carbine in 44 Remington Magnum will yearn no more because the Model 1894SS has a 20-inch barrel chambered for that cartridge. It also has Ballard-style rifling with a twist rate of 1:38 inches, a 10-round magazine, squared finger lever, straight-wrist buttstock replete with cut checkering and (*thank goodness*) quick-detachable sling swivel posts. Also new are the Model 1894 Cowboy Competition with 20-inch octagon barrel in 38 Special and the Model 1897 Texan version of the 22 caliber Golden 39A with 20-inch tapered octagon barrel and a magazine long enough to hold 21 Shorts, 16 Longs or 14 Long Rifles. This is one of the prettiest little rifles Marlin has ever

The Versa-Pack from H&R/Marlin is a kid-sized firearm with barrels in 22 rimfire and .410-bore shotshell.

built. Two other new stainless steel rifles are Marlin's unsinkable autoloader called Model 795SS and a kid-sized single shot that goes by the name of Model 15YS.

A couple of months after writing this I'll be stalking a 400-pound black bear on Vancouver Island and have about decided to hunt with the Model 336 Cowboy in 38-55 Winchester equipped with a Marble tang sight Frank Brownell sent to me. Out of respect for the old Ballard and Stevens single shots and other vintage rifles, Winchester loads its factory ammo to original blackpowder velocities. Since the Model 336 is strong enough to handle the later high-velocity smokeless loads, which are no longer

available, I'll handload either the Winchester or Barnes 255-grain bullet to about 1850 fps and head for the hills. Such a load should handle any black bear Canada has to offer. I'll let you know for sure next time we meet.

Biggest news from H&R 1871 (*which is owned by Marlin*) is the 50-caliber Huntsman single-shot muzzleloader with an extra barrel chambered for 243 Winchester or 12 gauge. Also available is the Versa-Pak, a youth-size single-shooter with .410 bore and 22 rimfire barrels. Incidentally, this same gun is also available in 28 gauge, an excellent choice for a youngster's first shotgun. But then, as I proved many times a few years ago when I was just a kid, so is the .410 bore.

The Remington Model 710; improved and arguably *the* "best buy" big-game rifle.

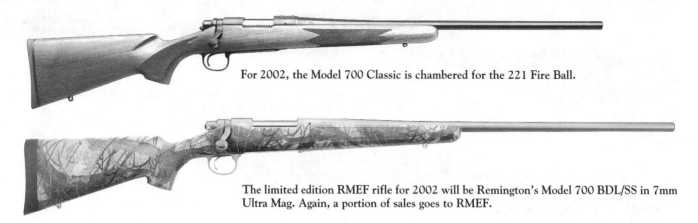

For 2002, the Model 700 Classic is chambered for the 221 Fire Ball.

The limited edition RMEF rifle for 2002 will be Remington's Model 700 BDL/SS in 7mm Ultra Mag. Again, a portion of sales goes to RMEF.

Montana Rifleman

This relatively new shop does not offer complete rifles but buying its Model 1999 action should be a great first step toward having one built. Available in standard and long lengths with .473- or .534-inch bolt faces and a 3.650-inch magazine box length, some of its other features include a three-position Model 70-style safety, non-rotating Mauser-type extractor, one-piece steel trigger guard/floor plate assembly, bridge-mounted bolt release and Mauser '98 style breeching. You can buy one of these in 4140 chrome moly or 415 stainless steel.

Remington

Remington's short versions of its 7mm and 300 Ultra Mag are designed to work in the short-action Model 700 and the Model Seven as well. Called the Short Action Ultra Mags (SAM for short), first to be introduced are 7mm and 300 versions which are capable of duplicating the 7mm Remington Magnum and 300 Winchester Magnum. Ballistically, they will also do anything that can be done with Winchester's 7mm WSM and 300 WSM. For 1992, both will be available in three versions of the Model Seven, LS Magnum with blued steel barreled action and laminated wood stock, SS Magnum with stainless steel barrel and black synthetic stock, and from Remington's custom shop, the AWR with stainless barrel and action and black composite stock. Nominal weights range from 6-1/8 pounds for the AWR to a pound more for the other two. All have 22-inch barrels. The LS Magnum in 7mm SAM and Remington ammo loaded with the equally new 140-grain Ultra Core-Lokt I hauled to Newfoundland during late 2001 worked fine on caribou.

My license was good for two bulls so I took the second one with a rolling-block rifle in 45-70 from Remington's custom shop. What fun! Since the rifle wore target sights and since I burned up several hundred rounds of ammo establishing zeroes in 50-yard increments out to 300 yards, one shot at a laser-ranged 236 yards was all I needed. I used Remington factory ammo with the 300-grain hollowpoint bullet, which had averaged six to seven inches for five-shot groups at 300 yards back home.

The Model 710 bolt-action centerfire has been with us for about a year now and because demand has far exceeded Remington's capacity to build it, available chamberings will remain limited to 30-06 and 270 Winchester for 2002. I have not shot the latest version but am told that it is improved considerably over the first ones produced. In my opinion, the 710 is one of the best buys in big-game rifles ever designed. It isn't pretty but it gets the job done at a very affordable price.

Remington's classic chambering for the limited-production Model 700 Classic for 2002 is the 221 Fire Ball. Along with the rifle Remington is breathing new life into a once discontinued cartridge by loading it with the 50-grain V-Max bullet at 2650 fps in a 10-inch XP-100 (*which is not being reintroduced*) and 2995 fps in the 24-inch barrel of the Model 700 Classic. I once owned a Kimber rifle in 221 Fire Ball (*and still own a XP-100*) and find the little cartridge capable of treading closely on the heels of the great 222 Remington. In a good rifle the Fire Ball delivers excellent accuracy whether loaded full throttle or reined back to 22 Hornet performance.

Remington sold enough limited edition Model 700 BDL/SS rifles in 300 Ultra Mag during 2001 to enable them to contribute over $30,000 to the Rocky Mountain Elk Foundation. So successful was the program that the same rifle in 7mm Ultra Mag will be available during 2002. Features include stainless steel barreled action, synthetic stock with Realtree Hardwoods camo finish and RMEF etched into the stock. Weight is just over 7-1/2 pounds. And speaking of pounds, there are only 5-1/4 in the Model 700 Titanium and the short-action version is now available in 308 Winchester.

Reimer Johannsen, Inc.

Of all the really serious big-game rifles I have looked at and fondled thus far this year, the one I'd like most to have taken home was the Express from Johannsen. All three models are copies of the old English-built express rifles built on the single and double square-bridge Mauser actions. Rather than go into the various differences of the Classic Safari, the Safari and the Tradition versions, I'll just say any rifle lover would be proud to have any of the three reposing in his gun cabinet. Standard magazine capacities are four for standard belted magnums such as the 375 Holland & Holland and 300 Weatherby, and three for bigger cartridges such as the 338-378 Weatherby Magnum, 416 Rigby, and 500 Jeffery. The optional dropped magazine holds an additional cartridge. Extra cost options include a Holland & Holland-style night sight up front, peep sight mounted on the cocking piece (*I'd have to have both*), three-position Model 70-style safety (*in lieu of the standard Mauser two-position safety*) and quick-detach scope mount. Takedown rifles are also available.

Rogue River Rifle Co.

I hate to use the word 'cute' in describing a rifle but cannot think of a more descriptive word for the Chipmunk. Scaled down in every direction for kids, the one in 22 Long Rifle I own has been shot by more youngsters through the years than I can recall. Its latest chambering, the 17

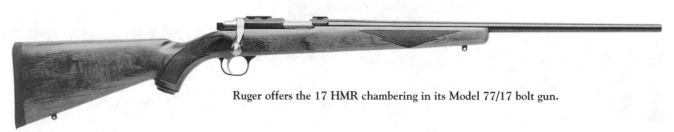

Ruger offers the 17 HMR chambering in its Model 77/17 bolt gun.

Tikka Whitetail Hunter.

HMR, will be fun to play with but the new version I am excited about is chambered for the .410 shotshell. A manually cocked single shot with a turn-bolt action, it has a walnut stock with a 11-1/2 inch pull length and a 18 1/4-inch barrel. The little scattergun weighs approximately 3-1/4 pounds and measures 33 inches overall. Also new is the Target Model with 18-inch heavy barrel and walnut stock with accessory rail and adjustable pull length (11-1/2 to 13-3/4 inches).

Ruger

Latest from Ruger is a No. 1 single-shot rifle with a stainless steel barreled action fitted to a buttstock and forearm carved from black laminated wood. Ruger's news release shows the same retail price for the Tropical version in 416 Rigby and the Standard version in 308 Winchester. New chamberings for six variations of the Model 77 Mark II are the 7mm and 300 Remington SAM. I find it interesting that Ruger chose to go with Remington's short-action magnums even though Winchester's versions were on the market first. The Mark II Compact is now available in 7mm-08 Remington in both blued and stainless steel. Last and most certainly least, Ruger has hopped aboard the 17 HMR bandwagon by offering its bolt-action rimfire rifle for that cartridge. Called the Model 77/17, it has an American walnut stock replete

with cut checkering and a 1:9 twist, 22-inch barrel. Nominal weight is 6-1/2 pounds and the rotary magazine holds eight rounds.

Sako

The big news from Sako this year is that one of my favorite rifles, the Model 75 Deluxe, is now available in Remington's 7mm Ultra Mag and 300 Ultra Mag chamberings. Sako offers more different action lengths (four) than any other company so I won't be surprised to see the new breed of short magnums from Remington and Winchester discussed here next year. In the target rifle department, the new TRG 22 rifles in 308 Winchester and 338 Lapua Magnum should live up to Sako's reputation for superb accuracy. Hunters who like laminated wood stocks (*and I am one of them*) should take a close look at the Tikka Whitetail Hunter with its stainless steel barreled action and five standard and magnum chamberings. Another rifle I'd like to have taken home this year is Sako's 80th anniversary model. Available only in 375 H&H Magnum, it comes in a beautiful hard leather case and is a sight to behold at just under $16,000, or a month's salary for our editor.

Savage

Savage is introducing what the company calls its Package Series of

bolt-action centerfires. Built around the old Model 110 action, each comes with a scope already mounted. The Varmint Package, as an example, is outfitted with a Burris 6-18X and is packaged in an aluminum hard case. Six variations will be offered, from the Model 12VSS-XP varmint rifle with stainless steel barreled action and laminated wood stock to the Model 111FCXP3 with blued steel and plastic. Both short and long actions are available in a variety of chamberings including the 223 Remington, 7mm STW and 300 WSM.

New to the Weather Warrior series is the Model 16BSS with stainless barreled action and laminated wood stock, along with new chamberings such as Remington's 7mm SAM and 300 SAM.

The new Law Enforcement series contains four members with the top-of-line Model 10FPXP-LE equipped at the factory with a Burris 3.5-10 scope and a Harris folding bipod. Other new variations added to the Savage lineup are two on the Model 64 autoloading action, one on the Model 93 bolt gun and three on the Mark I bolt gun.

Tristar Sporting Arms

Tristar's catalog gets bigger each year. Latest to catch my eye is the Sharps 1874 Sporting Rifle in 45-70 Government. Standard features include 28-, 32- or 34-inch octagon barrel, double-set triggers, ladder-style adjustable rear sight, cut-checkered walnut buttstock and forearm and case-colored receiver. It weighs 9-3/4 pounds and anyone who decides to buy it would be wise to include the Creedmore sight set from Tristar. Also new is the 1885 Winchester reproduction with a 28-inch barrel in 45-70. A very nice rifle for the price. Then we have the Italian-built lever actions, which do a good job of replicating the 1860 Henry, and 1866 and 1873 Winchesters. Their chamberings are 44-40 and 45 Colt and Tristar offers a very nice tang sight for them as well. Just in case our shotgun man overlooks it, I'll mention Tristar's reproduction of the Winchester Model 1887 lever-action smoothbore. Made in Australia and available in 12 gauge only, it has a 22-inch barrel, weighs 8-3/4 pounds and is sure to have cowboy action shooters stampeding to buy it.

USRAC

Quite a bit of new Winchester stuff from U.S. Repeating Arms Company this year. New chamberings for the Model 70 are the 270 and 7mm WSM. I bagged a very nice nilgai bull in south Texas with a Browning A-Bolt

Of the various hunts I participated in during 2001, one of the most enjoyable was taking this Newfoundland caribou with a rolling-block rifle chambered for the 45/70 Government.

Winchester's Model 9410 Packer is new this year.

The 480 Ruger is now chambered in the Model 94 Traditional.

Winchester's Heritage Edition *One of One Thousand* Model 94.

chambered for the 270 WSM and was greatly impressed by how flat it shot and how hard it hit. Both new chamberings are available in the Featherweight, Classic Stainless and Laminated versions of the Model 70.

In the lever-action category, the Model 9410 simply refuses to go away. This year you can buy one called the Packer Shotgun. It has a 20-inch barrel, curved grip, two-thirds magazine and quick-detach sling swivel posts. Then we have the Model 94 Traditional in 480 Ruger, which should be just about right for taking on deer, black bear and wild hogs out to 100 yards or so. The new Heritage Edition One Of One Thousand is one of the most handsome Model 94s I have ever seen. Chambered for the 38-55 Winchester, it has a 26-inch half-octagon, half-round barrel, full-length magazine, steel forearm cap, curved steel buttplate, gold-plate engraving (*the old Winchester #3 pattern*), and fancy walnut replete with cut checkering. As the name implies, only a thousand will be built. Add more of the same along with Winchester's historic #2 engraving pattern and quite a bit more money and you have the One Of One Hundred rifle.

USRAC officials have promised delivery on new Model 1895 rifles in 405 Winchester during 2002. The Grade I will have a blued receiver while the receiver of the Grade II is left in the white and engraved with hunting scenes. Both have 24-inch barrels and four-round magazines.

Weatherby

Weighing only 5-3/4 pounds, the Super Big GameMaster is just the ticket for hunting big game where the country is steep and the shots are long. Think of Weatherby's Super VarmintMaster

made light enough for toting in the high country and you've got this one. The bore of its Krieger 24-inch stainless steel barrel is hand-lapped for smoothness and the muzzle wears an 11-degree parabolic crown. The barrel is fluted for lightness and its black exterior coating cuts down on light reflection in the field. The trigger is fine-tuned at the factory with sear engagement set at .012- to .015-inch and an average pull weight of four pounds. The action rests in an aluminum bedding block which is hand-bedded into a composite stock made up of Arimid, graphite and glass fibers–all finished in a pleasing-to-the eye tan coloration. A Pachmayr Decelerator pad out back soaks up a good bit of the recoil generated by its 15 available chamberings which include such favorites as the 270 (Winchester and Weatherby), 25-06, 280, 7mm Magnum (Weatherby and Remington), 300 Magnum (Weatherby and Winchester) and the 338-06 A-Square. Rifles chambered for various Weatherby, Remington and Winchester magnums have 26-inch barrels and weigh 6-3/4 pounds.

For the first time in its history (*as far as I know*), Weatherby has entered the law enforcement market. Called the Threat Response Rifle (TRR), this one comes with a number of accuracy-enhancing features that meet various requirements of law enforcement tactical units and military applications as well. Built around the famous Mark V action, it is available in three versions, one being the standard TRR with a 22-inch barrel in 223 Remington or 308 Winchester. The TRR Magnum is available in a number of magnum chamberings with the 26-inch barrels of two of them, the 30-378 and 338-378 Weatherby Magnum, equipped with Weatherby's Accubrake for muzzle

jump and recoil reduction. The third variation, called TRR Magnum Custom, is the same except its stock is fully adjustable for a custom fit to various body sizes.

Incidentally, the most accurate factory rifle I tested during 2001 was a Weatherby Super VarmintMaster in 220 Swift. I liked everything about that rifle, from the tan coloration of its synthetic stock to its 26-inch Krieger barrel to its single-shot action. I tried one handload and seven factory loads in that rifle and, incredible as it might seem, each and every one averaged less than an inch for five shots at 100 long paces. Overall average was 0.72-inch for 32 five-shot groups. The Shilen 52-grain hollowpoint pushed out the muzzle at 3812 fps by 39.0 grains of Reloder 15 was most accurate at 0.49-inch and in a virtual tie for first place was Remington's 55-grain Power-Lokt load at 0.48-inch.

Last from Atascadero, California but certainly not least is the Mark V Royal Custom. Sit down and list all of the custom features you have always wanted in a Weatherby rifle and chances are good this one has most of them. For starters, the Monte Carlo-style stock is carved from fancy Claro walnut, the contrasting figure of which is highlighted by a high-gloss finish. The stock also has cut checkering, as does the knob of the bolt handle. The bolt body and follower have a jeweled finish. The receiver, bolt sleeve and floorplate are engraved with a scroll pattern. If you want to really outshine your hunting pals you can opt for a gold deer, elk, sheep, bear or moose on the floorplate. The Mark V Royal Custom wears a 26-inch No. 2 contour barrel and is available in five Weatherby magnum chamberings: 257, 270, 7mm, 300 and 340. ●

THE 2003 GUN DIGEST WEB DIRECTORY

by Holt Bodinson

WHILE THE "DOT-coms" may have hit the skids on Wall Street, the World Wide Web continues to branch out to become an increasingly essential source of information and e-commerce for the firearms community.

This year the U.S. Commerce Department reported that 143 million Americans, or 54% of the country, were regularly using the Internet--an increase of 26% over the previous year. It is estimated that each month 2 million more Americans hook-up to cruise the Web. The future looks even brighter with 90% of young Americans between the ages of five and 17 currently using computers.

The *Gun Digest* Web Directory is in its fourth year of publication. The trend is clear. More and more firearm-related businesses are striking out and creating their own discrete web pages, and it's never been easier with the inexpensive software programs now available.

The Internet is a dynamic environment and, since our last edition, there have been many changes. Companies have consolidated and adopted a new owner's website address. Many of the smaller, specialized collector forums are now grouped and thriving at **www.gunandknife.com/forums**. New companies have appeared and old companies have disappeared. Search engines are now more powerful than ever and seem to root out even the most obscure reference to a product name or manufacturer.

The following index of current Web addresses is offered to our readers as a convenient jumping-off point. Half the fun is just exploring what's out there. Considering that most of the Web pages have hot links to other firearm-related Web pages, the Internet trail just goes on-and-on once you've taken the initial step to go online.

Here are a few pointers:

If the website you desire is not listed, try using the full name of the company or product, typed without spaces, between www.-and-.com, for example, **www.krause.com**. Probably 95% of current websites are based on this simple, self-explanatory format.

Try a variety of search engines like *Microsoft Internet Explorer*, *Metacrawler*, *GoTo.com*, *Yahoo*, *HotBot*, *AltaVista*, *Lycos*, *Excite*, *InfoSeek*, *Looksmart*, *Google*, and *WebCrawler* while using key words such as gun, firearm, rifle, pistol, blackpowder, shooting, hunting— frankly, any word that relates to the sport. Each search engine seems to comb through the World Wide Web in a different fashion and produces different results. We find *Metacrawler* to be among the best. Accessing the various search engines is simple. Just type **www.metacrawler.com** for example, and you're on your way.

Welcome to the digital world of the Web. Enjoy our Directory!

WEB DIRECTORY

AMMUNITION AND COMPONENTS

3-D Ammunition www.3dammo.com
Accurate Arms Co. Inc www.accuratepowder.com
ADCO/Nobel Sport Powder www.adcosales.com
Aguila Ammunition www.aguilaammo.com
All Purpose Ammunition www.dragonbreath.com
Alliant Powder www.alliantpowder.com
Ammo Depot www.ammodepot.com
Arizona Ammunition, Inc. www.arizonaammunition.com
A-Zoom Ammo www.a-zoom.com
Ballard Rifle & Cartridge LLC www.ballardrifles.com
Ballistic Products, Inc. www.ballisticproducts.com
Barnes Bullets www.barnesbullets.com
Baschieri & Pellagri www.baschieri-pellagri.com
Beartooth Bullets www.beartoothbullets.com
Bell Brass www.bellbrass.com
Berger Bullets, Ltd. www.bergerbullets.com
Berry's Mfg., Inc. www.berrysmfg.com
Big Bore Bullets of Alaska www.awloo.com/bbb/index.htm
Big Bore Express www.bigbore.com
Bismuth Cartridge Co. www.bismuth-notox.com
Black Hills Ammunition, Inc. www.black-hills.com
Brenneke of America Ltd. www.brennekeusa.com
Buffalo Arms www.buffaloarms.com
Bull-X inc. www.bull-x.com
Calhoon, James, Bullets www.jamescalhoon.com
Cast Performance Bullet www.castperformance.com
CCI www.cci-ammunition.com
Century Arms www.centuryarms.com
Cheaper Than Dirt www.cheaperthandirt.com
Cheddite France www.cheddite.com
Claybuster Wads www.claybuster.com
Clean Shot Powder www.cleanshot.com
Cole Distributing www.cole-distributing.com
Cor-Bon www.cor-bon.com
Denver Bullet Co. denbullets@aol.com
Dillon Precision www.dillonprecision.com
DKT, Inc. www.dktinc.com
Dynamit Nobel RWS Inc. www.dnrws.com
Elephant/Swiss Black Powder www.elephantblackpowder.com
Eley Ammunition www.remington.com
Eley Hawk Ltd. www.eleyhawk.com
Eley Limited www.eley.co.uk
Federal Cartridge Co. www.federalcartridge.com
Fiocchi of America www.fiocchiusa.com
Fowler Bullets www.benchrest.com/fowler
Garrett Cartridges www.garrettcartridges.com
Glaser Safety Slug, Inc. www.safetyslug.com
GOEX Inc. www.goexpowder.com
Graf & Sons www.grafs.com
Hawk Bullets www.hawkbullets.com
Hevi.Shot www.hevishot.com
Hi-Tech Ammunition www.iidbs.com/hitech
Hodgdon Powder www.hodgdon.com
Hornady www.hornady.com
Hull Cartridge www.hullcartridge.com
Huntington Reloading Products www.huntingtons.com
Impact Bullets www.impactbullets.com
IMR Smokeless Powders www.imrpowder.com
Kent Cartridge America www.kentgamebore.com

Kynoch Ammunition www.kynochammunition.com
Lapua www.lapua.com
Lawrence Brand Shot www.metalico.com
Lazzeroni Arms Co. www.lazzeroni.com
Lightfield Ammunition Corp www.lightfield-ammo.com
Lomont Precision Bullets www.klomont.com/kent
Lost River Ballistic Technologies, Inc. www.lostriverballistic.com
Lyman www.lymanproducts.com
Magnus Bullets www.magnusbullets.com
MagSafe Ammunition www.realpages.com/magsafeammo
Magtech www.magtechammunition.com
Mast Technology www.bellammo.com
Masterclass Bullet Co. www.mastercast.com
Meister Bullets www.meisterbullets.com
Midway USA www.midwayusa.com
Miltex,Inc. www.miltexusa.com
MK Ballistic Systems www.mkballistics.com
Mullins Ammunition www.mullinsammunition.com
National Bullet Co. www.nationalbullet.com
Nobel Sport www.adcosales.com
Nobel Sport www.snpe.com
Norma www.norma.cc
Nosler Bullets Inc www.nosler.com
Old Western Scrounger www.ows-ammunition.com
Oregon Trail/Trueshot www.trueshotbullets.com
   (formerly Laser-Cast)
Pattern Control www.patterncontrol.com
PMC-Eldorado Cartridge www.pmcammo.com
Polywad www.polywad.com
Pro Load Ammunition www.proload.com
Rainier Ballistics www.rainierballistics.com
Ram Shot Powder www.ramshot.com
Reloading Specialties Inc. www.reloadingspecialties.com
Remington www.remington.com
Sauvestre Slug kengsfirearms@mindspring.com
Sellier & Bellot USA inc. www.sb-usa.com
Shilen www.shilen.com
Sierra www.sierrabullets.com
Speer Bullets www.speer-bullets.com
Sporting Supplies Int'l Inc. www.ssiintl.com
Starline www.starlinebrass.com
Triton Cartridge www.triton-ammo.com
Tru-Tracer www.trutracer.com
Vihtavuori Lapua www.lapua.com
West Coast Bullets www.westcoastbullet.com
Western Powders Inc. www.westernpowders.com
Widener's Reloading & Shooters Supply www.wideners.com
Winchester Ammunition www.winchester.com
Wolf Ammunition www.wolfammo.com
Woodleigh Bullets www.woodleighbullets.com.au
Zanders Sporting Goods www.gzanders.com

CASES, SAFES, GUN LOCKS, AND CABINETS

Ace Case Co. www.acecase.com
AG English Sales Co. www.agenglish.com
All Americas' Outdoors www.innernet.net/gunsafe
Alpine Cases www.alpinecases.com
Aluma Sport by Dee Zee www.deezee.com
American Security Products www.amsecusa.com
Americase www.americase.com

Avery Outdoors, Inc. **www.averyoutdoors.com**
Bear Track Cases **www.beartrackcases.com**
Boyt Harness Co. **www.boytharness.com**
Bulldog Gun Safe Co. **www.gardall.com**
Cannon Safe Co. **www.cannonsafe.com**
CCL Security Products **www.cclsecurity.com**
Concept Development Corp. **www.saf-t-blok.com**
Fort Knox Safes **www.ftknox.com**
Franzen Security Products **www.securecase.com**
Frontier Safe Co. **www.frontiersafe.com**
Granite Security Products **www.granitesafe.com**
Gunlocker Phoenix USA Inc. **www.gunlocker.com**
GunVault **www.gunvault.com**
Hakuba USA Inc. **www.hakubausa.com**
Heritage Safe Co. **www.heritagesafecompany.com**
Hide-A-Gun **www.hide-a-gun.com**
Hunter Company **www.huntercompany.com**
Knouff & Knouff, Inc. **www.kkair.com**
Kolpin Mfg. Co. **www.kolpin.com**
Liberty Safe & Security **www.libertysafe.com**
New Innovative Products **www.starlightcases**
Noble Security Systems Inc. **www.noble.co.ll**
Phoenix USA Inc. **www.gunlocker.com**
Rhino Gun Cases **www.rhinoguns.com**
Rocky Mountain Safe Inc. **www.rockymountainsafe.com**
Safe Tech, Inc. **www.safrgun.com**
Saf-T-Hammer **www.saf-t-hammer.com**
Saf-T-Lok Corp. **www.saf-t-lok.com**
San Angelo All-Aluminum Products Inc. **sasptuld@x.netcom.com**
Securecase **www.securecase.com**
Shot Lock Corp. **www.shotlock.com**
Smart Lock Technology Inc. **www.smartlock.com**
Sportsmans Steel Safe Co. **www.sportsmansteelsafes.com**
Stack-On Products Co. **www.stack-on.com**
T.Z. Case Int'l **www.tz-case.com**
Treadlock Security Safes **www.treadlok.com**
Versatile Rack Co. **www.versatilegunrack.com**
V-Line Industries **www.vlineind.com**
Winchester Safes **www.fireking.com**
Ziegel Engineering **www.ziegeleng.com**

CHOKE DEVICES, RECOIL REDUCERS, AND ACCURACY DEVICES

100 Straight Products **www.100straight.com**
Answer Products Co. **www.answerrifles.com**
Briley Mfg **www.briley.com**
Carlson's **www.carlsonschokes.com**
Colonial Arms **www.colonialarms.com**
Comp-N-Choke **www.comp-n-choke.com**
Hastings **www.hastingsbarrels.com**
Mag-Na-Port Int'l Inc. **www.magnaport.com**
Truglo **www.truglo.com**

CHRONOGRAPHS

Competitive Edge Dynamics **www.cedhk.com**
Oehler Research Inc. **www.oehler-research.com**
PACT **www.pact.com**
ProChrony **www.competitionelectronics.com**
Shooting Chrony Inc **www.chrony.ca**

CLEANING PRODUCTS

Accupro **www.accupro.com**
Ballistol USA **www.ballistol.com**
Birchwood Casey **www.birchwoodcasey.com**
Bore Tech **www.boretech.com**
Break-Free, Inc. **www.break-free.com**
Bruno Shooters Supply **www.brunoshooters.com**
Butch's Bore Shine **www.lymanproducts.com**
Clenzoil **www.clenzoil.com**
Corrosion Technologies **www.corrosionx.com**
Dewey Mfg. **www.deweyrods.com**
Eezox Inc. **www.xmission.com**
G 96 **www.g96.com**
Hoppes **www.hoppes.com**
Hydrosorbent Products **www.dehumidify.com**
Iosso Products **www.iosso.com**
KG Industries **www.kgproducts.com**
Kleen-Bore Inc. **www.kleen-bore.com**
L&R Mfg. **www.lrultrasonics.com**
Mpro7 Gun Care **www.mp7.com**
Otis Technology, Inc. **www.otisgun.com**
Outers **www.outers-guncare.com**
Ox-Yoke Originals Inc. **www.oxyoke.com**
Parker-Hale Ltd. **www.parker-hale.com**
Prolix Lubricant **www.prolixlubricant.com**
ProShot Products **www.proshotproducts.com**
ProTec Lubricants **www.proteclubricants.com**
Rusteprufe Labs **www.rusteprufe.com**
Sagebrush Products **www.sagebrushproducts.com**
Sentry Solutions Ltd. **www.sentrysolutions.com**
Shooters Choice Gun Care **www.shooters-choice.com**
Silencio **www.silencio.com**
Stony Point Products **www.stoneypoint.com**
Tetra Gun **www.tetraproducts.com**
World's Fastest Gun Bore Cleaner **www.michaels-oregon.com**

FIREARM MANUFACTURERS AND IMPORTERS

AAR, Inc. **www.iar-arms.com**
Accuracy Int'l North America **www.accuracyinternational.org**
Accuracy Rifle Systems **www.mini-14.net**
Ace Custom 45's **www.acecustom45.com**
Advanced Weapons Technology **www.AWT-Zastava.com**
AIM **www.aimsurplus.com**
AirForce Airguns **www.airforceguns.com**
Airguns of Arizona **www.airgunsofarizona.com**
Airgun Express **www.airgunexpress.com**
Alchemy Arms **www.alchemyltd.com**
Alexander Arms **www.alexanderarms.com**
American Derringer Corp. **www.amderringer.com**
AMT **www.amtguns.com**
Answer Products Co. **www.answerrifles.com**
AR-7 Industries,LLC **www.ar-7.com**
Armalite **www.armalite.com**
Armscorp USA Inc. **www.armscorpusa.com**
Arnold Arms **www.arnoldarms.com**
Arthur Brown Co. **www.eabco.com**
Austin & Halleck **www.austinhalleck.com**
Autauga Arms,Inc. **www.autaugaarms.com**
Auto-Ordnance Corp. **www.auto-ordnance.com**

WEB DIRECTORY

AWA Int'l www.awaguns.com
Axtell Rifle Co. www.riflesmith.com
Aya www.webstudio.net/aya
Ballard Rifle & Cartridge LLC www.ballardrifles.com
Barrett Firearms Mfg. www.barrettrifles.com
Beeman Precision Airguns www.beeman.com
Benelli USA Corp. www.benelliusa.com
Benjamin Sheridan www.crosman.com
Beretta U.S.A. Corp. www.berettausa.com
Bill Hanus Birdguns www.billhanusbirdguns.com
Bond Arms www.bondarms.com
Borden's Rifles, Inc. www.bordensrifles.com
Bowen Classic Arms www.bowenclassicarms.com
Briley Mfg www.briley.com
BRNO Arms www.zbrojouka.com
Brown, Ed Products www.edbrown.com
Browning www.browning.com
Bushmaster Firearms/Quality Parts www.bushmaster.com
Cape Outfitters www.doublegun.com
Carbon 15 www.professional-ordnance.com
Caspian Arms, Ltd. www.caspianarmsltd.8m.com
Casull Arms Corp. www.casullarms.com
Century Arms www.centuryarms.com
Chadick's Ltd. www.chadicks-ltd.com
Champlin Firearms www.champlinarms.com
Charles Daly www.charlesdaly.com
Charter2000, Inc. www.charterfirearms.com
Christensen Arms www.christensenarms.com
Cimarron Firearms Co. www.cimarron-firearms.com
Clark Custom Guns www.clarkcustomguns.com
Cobra Enterprises www.cobrapistols.com
Colt Mfg Co. www.colt.com
Compasseco, Inc. www.compasseco.com
Connecticut Valley Arms www.cva.com
Cooper Firearms www.cooperfirearms.com
Crosman www.crosman.com
Crossfire, L.L.C. www.crossfirelle.com
C. Sharp Arms Co. www.csharparms.com
CZ USA www.cz-usa.com
Daisy Mfg Co. www.daisy.com
Dakota Arms Inc. www.dakotaarms.com
Dan Wesson Firearms www.danwessonfirearms.com
Davis Industries www.davisindguns.com
Dixie Gun Works www.dixiegun.com
Dlask Arms Corp. www.dlask.com
D.S. Arms, Inc. www.dsarms.com
Dynamit Noble www.dnrws.com
DZ Arms www.tool-fix.com/dzarms.html
Eagle Imports, Inc. www.bersa-llama.com
EDM Arms www.edmarms.com
E.M.F. Co. www.emf-company.com
Enterprise Arms www.enterprise.com
European American Armory Corp. www.eaacorp.com
Fabarm www.fabarm.com
Firestorm www.firestorm-sgs.com
Flodman Guns www.flodman.com
FN Herstal www.fnherstal.com
Franchi www.franchiusa.com
Freedom Arms www.freedomarms.com
Gambo Renato www.renatogamba.it
Gamo www.gamo.com

Gary Reeder Custom Guns www.reeder-customguns.com
Gibbs Rifle Company www.gibbsrifle.com
Glock www.glock.com
Griffin & Howe www.griffinhowe.com
Griffon USA, Inc. griffonusa@aol.com
Grizzly Big Boar Rifle www.largrizzly.com
GSI Inc. www.gsifirearms.com
Hammerli www.hammerli.com
Heavy Express, Inc. www.heavyexpress.com
Heckler and Koch www.hecklerkoch-usa.com
Henry Repeating Arms Co. www.henryrepeating.com
Heym www.heym-waffenfabrik.de
High Standard Mfg. www.highstandard.com
Hi-Point Firearms www.hi-pointfirearms.com
H&R Firearms www.marlinfirearms.com
H-S Precision www.hsprecision.com
IAR Inc. www.iar-arms.com
Imperial Miniature Armory www.1800miniature.com
Inter Ordnance www.interordnance.com
Intrac Arms International LLC www.hsarms.com
Israel Arms www.israelarms.com
Ithaca Gun Co. www.ithacagun.com
Izhevsky Mekhanichesky Zavod www.baikalinc.ru
JP Enterprises, Inc. www.jpar15.com
Kahr Arms/Auto-Ordnance www.kahr.com
K.B.I. www.kbi-inc.com
Kel-Tec CNC Ind., Inc. www.kel-tec.com
Kimber www.kimberamerica.com
Knight's Mfg. Co. kacsr25@aol.com
Knight Rifles www.knightrifles.com
Korth www.korthwaffen.de
Krieghoff GmbH www.krieghoff.de
Krieghoff Int'l www.krieghoff.com
L.A.R Mfg www.largrizzly.com
Lazzeroni Arms Co. www.lazzeroni.com
Les Baer Custom, Inc. www.lesbaer.com
Lone Star Rifle Co. www.lonestarrifle.com
Magnum Research www.magnumresearch.com
Markesbery Muzzleloaders www.markesbery.com
Marksman Products www.marksman.com
Marlin www.marlinfirearms.com
McMillan Bros Rifle Co. www.mcfamily.com
Merkel www.gsifirearms.com
Miltech www.miltecharms.com
Miltex, Inc. www.miltexusa.com
Montana Rifle Co. www.montanarifleman.com
Navy Arms www.navyarms.com
Nesika Actions www.nesika.com
New England Arms Corp. www.newenglandarms.com
New England Custom Gun Svc, Ltd.
    www.newenglandcustomgun.com
New Ultra Light Arms www.newultralight.com
North American Arms www.naaminis.com
Nowlin Mfg. Inc. www.nowlinguns.com
O.F. Mossberg & Sons www.mossberg.com
Olympic Arms www.olyarms.com
Panther Arms www.dpmsinc.com
Para-Ordnance www.paraord.com
Pedersoli Davide & Co. www.davide-pedersoli.com
Power Custom www.powercustom.com
Remington www.remington.com

WEB DIRECTORY

Republic Arms Inc. www.republicarmsinc.com
Rizzini Di Rizzini www.rizzini.it
Robar Companies, Inc. www.robarguns.com
Robinson Armament Co. www.robarm.com
Rock River Arms, Inc. www.rockriverarms.com
Rogue Rifle Co. Inc. www.chipmunkrifle.com
Rossi Arms www.rossiusa.com
RPM www.rpmxlpistols.com
RWS www.dnrws.com
Sabatti SpA info@sabatti.it
Saco Defense www.sacoinc.com
Safari Arms www.olyarms.com
Sako www.berettausa.com
Samco Global Arms Inc. www.samcoglobal.com
Sarco Inc. www.sarcoinc.com
Savage Arms Inc. www.savagearms.com
Scattergun Technologies Inc. www.wilsoncombat.com
SIG Arms,Inc. www.sigarms.com
Simpson Ltd. www.simpsonltd.com
SKB Shotguns www.skbshotguns.com
Smith & Wesson www.smith-wesson.com
Sphinx System www.sphinxarms.com
Springfield Armory www.springfield-armory.com
SSK Industries www.sskindustries.com
Steyr Mannlicher www.gsifirearms.com
STI Int'l sales@sti-guns.com
Strayer-Voigt Inc. www.sviguns.com
Sturm, Ruger & Company www.ruger-firearms.com
Tar-Hunt Slug Guns, Inc. www.tar-hunt.com
Taser Int'l www.taser.com
Taurus www.taurususa.com
Tennessee Guns www.tennesseeguns.com
The 1877 Sharps Co. www.1877sharps.com
Thompson Center Arms www.tcarms.com
Traditions www.traditionsfirearms.com
Uberti USA,Inc. www.uberti.com
U.S. Firearms Mfg. Co. www.usfirearms.com
U.S. Repeating Arms Co. www.winchester-guns.com
Vektor USA www.vektorusa@series2000.com
Volquartsen Custom Ltd. www.volquartsen.com
Walther USA www.walther-usa.com
Weatherby www.weatherby.com
Webley and Scott Ltd. www.webley.co.uk
Wild West Guns www.wildwestguns.com
William Larkin Moore & Co. www.doublegun.com
Wilson's Gun Shop Inc. www.wilsoncombat.com
Winchester Firearms www.winchester-guns.com

GUN PARTS, BARRELS, AFTER-MARKET ACCESSORIES

300 Below www.300below.com
Accuracy Speaks, Inc. www.accuracyspeaks.com
American Spirit Arms Corp. www.gunkits.com
Badger Barrels, Inc. www.badgerbarrels.com
Bar-Sto Precision Machine www.barsto.com
Belt Mountain Enterprises www.beltmountain.com
Brownells www.brownells.com
Buffer Technologies www.buffertech.com
Bullberry Barrel Works www.bullberry.com
Bushmaster Firearms/Quality Parts www.bushmaster.com

Butler Creek Corp www.butler-creek.com
Cape Outfitters Inc. www.capeoutfitters.com
Caspian Arms Ltd. www.caspianarmsltd.8m.com
Cheaper Than Dirt www.cheaperthandirt.com
Chesnut Ridge www.chestnutridge.com/
Chip McCormick Corp www.chipmccormickcorp.com
Colonial Arms www.colonialarms.com
Cylinder & Slide Shop www.cylinder-slide.com
Dixie Gun Works www.dixiegun.com
DPMS www.dpmsinc.com
D.S. Arms, Inc. www.dsarms.com
Ed Brown Products www.edbrown.com
EFK Marketing/Fire Dragon Pistol Accessories www.flmfire.com
Federal Arms www.fedarms.com
Forrest Inc. www.gunmags.com
Gentry, David www.gentrycustom.com
Gun Parts Corp. www.e-gunparts.com
Harris Barrels wwharris@msn.com
Hart Rifle Barrels www.hartbarrels.com
Hastings Barrels www.hastingsbarrels.com
Heinie Specialty Products www.heinie.com
100 Straight Products www.100straight.com
I.M.A. www.ima-usa.com
Jarvis, Inc. www.jarvis-custom.com
J&T Distributing www.jtdistributing.com
Jonathan Arthur Ciener, Inc. www.22lrconversions.com
JP Enterprises www.jpar15.com
King's Gunworks www.kingsgunworks.com
Krieger Barrels www.kriegerbarrels.com
Les Baer Custom, Inc. www.lesbaer.com
Lilja Barrels www.riflebarrels.com
Lone Star Rifle Co. www.lonestarrifles.com
Lone Wolf Dist. www.lonewolfdist.com
Lothar Walther Precision Tools Inc. www.lothar-walther.de
M&A Parts, Inc. www.m-aparts.com
Marvel Products, Inc. www.marvelprod.com
MEC-GAR SrL www.mec-gar.it
Michaels of Oregon Co. www.michaels-oregon.com
Numrich Gun Parts Corp. www.e-gunparts.com
Pachmayr www.pachmayr.com
Pac-Nor Barrels www.pac-nor.com
Para Ordinance Pro Shop www.ltms.com
Point Tech Inc. pointec@ibm.net
Promag Industries www.promagindustries.com
Power Custom, Inc. www.powercustom.com
Rocky Mountain Arms www.rockymountainarms.com
Royal Arms Int'l www.royalarms.com
R.W. Hart www.rwhart.com
Sarco Inc. www.sarcoinc.com
Scattergun Technologies Inc. www.wilsoncombat.com
Shilen www.shilen.com
Smith & Alexander Inc. www.smithandalexander.com
Speed Shooters Int'l www.shooternet.com/ssi
Sprinco USA Inc. sprinco@primenet.com
S&S Firearms www.ssfirearms.com
SSK Industries www.sskindustries.com
Tapco www.tapco.com
Trapdoors Galore www.trapdoors.com
Triple K Manufacturing Co. Inc. www.triplek.com
U.S.A. Magazines Inc. www.usa-magazines.com
Verney-Carron SA www.verney-carron.com

WEB DIRECTORY

Volquartsen Custom Ltd. **www.volquartsen.com**
W.C. Wolff Co. **www.gunsprings.com**
Waller & Son **www.wallerandson.com**
Weigand Combat Handguns **www.weigandcombat.com**
Western Gun Parts **www.westerngunparts.com**
Wilson Combat **www.wilsoncombat.com**
Wisner's Inc. **www.gunpartsspecialist.com**
Z-M Weapons **www.zmweapons.com/home.htm**

GUNSMITHING SUPPLIES AND INSTRUCTION

American Gunsmithing Institute **www.americangunsmith.com**
Battenfeld Technologies **www.battenfeldtechnologies.com**
Brownells, Inc. **www.brownells.com**
B-Square Co. **www.b-square.com**
Clymer Mfg. Co. **www.clymertool.com**
Craftguard Metal Finishing **crftgrd@aol.com**
Dem-Bart **www.dembartco.com**
Du-Lite Corp. **www.dulite.com**
Dvorak Instruments **www.dvorakinstruments.com**
Gradiant Lens Corp. **www.gradientlens.com**
Gunline Tools **www.gunline.com**
JGS Precision Tool Mfg. LLC **www.jgstools.com**
Manson Precision Reamers **www.mansonreamers.com**
Midway **www.midwayusa.com**
Olympus America Inc. **www.olympus.com**

HANDGUN GRIPS

Ajax Custom Grips, Inc. **www.ajaxgrips.com**
Altamont Co. **altamont@net66.com**
Badger Grips **www.pistolgrips.com**
Barami Corp. **www.hipgrip.com**
Crimson Trace Corp. **www.crimsontrace.com**
Eagle Grips **www.eaglegrips.com**
Fitz Pistol Grip Co. **johnpaul@snowcrest.net**
Hogue Grips **www.getgrip.com**
Lett Custom Grips **www.lettgrips.com**
Pachmayr **www.pachmayr.com**
Pearce Grips **www.pearcegrip.com**
Trausch Grips Int.Co. **www.trausch.com**
Uncle Mike's: **www.uncle-mikes.com**

HOLSTERS AND LEATHER PRODUCTS

Aker Leather Products **www.akerleather.com**
Alessi Distributor R&F Inc. **www.alessiholsters.com**
Alfonso's of Hollywood **www.alfonsogunleather.com**
Armor Holdings **www.holsters.com**
Bagmaster **www.bagmaster.com**
Bianchi **www.bianchiint.com**
Blackhills Leather **www.blackhillsleather.com**
BodyHugger Holsters **www.nikolais.com**
Boyt Harness Co. **www.boytharness.com**
Brigade Gun Leather **www.brigadegunleather.com**
Chimere **www.chimere.com**
Classic Old West Styles **www.cows.com**
Conceal It **www.conceal-it.com**
Concealment Shop Inc. **www.theconcealmentshop.com**
Coronado Leather Co. **www.coronadoleather.com**

Creedmoor Sports, Inc. **www.creedmoorsports.com**
Custom Leather Wear **www.customleatherwear.com**
Defense Security Products **www.thunderwear.com**
Dennis Yoder **www.yodercustomleather.com**
DeSantis Holster **www.desantisholster.com**
Dillon Precision **www.dillonprecision.com**
Don Hume Leathergoods, Inc. **www.donhume.com**
Ernie Hill International **www.erniehill.com**
Fist **www.fist-inc.com**
Fobus USA **www.fobusholster.com**
Front Line Ltd. **frontlin@internet-zahav.net**
Galco **www.usgalco.com**
Gilmore's Sports Concepts **www.gilmoresports.com**
Gould & Goodrich **www.goulduse.com**
Gunmate Products **www.gun-mate.com**
Hellweg Ltd. **www.hellwegltd.com**
Hide-A-Gun **www.hide-a-gun.com**
Holsters.Com **www.holsters.com**
Horseshoe Leather Products **www.horseshoe.co.uk**
Hunter Co. **www.huntercompany.com**
Kirkpatrick Leather Company **www.kirkpatrickleather.com**
Kramer Leather **www.kramerleather.com**
Law Concealment Systems **www.handgunconcealment.com**
Levy's Leathers Ltd. **www.levysleathers.com**
Michaels of Oregon Co. **www.michaels-oregon.com**
Milt Sparks Leather **www.miltsparks.com**
Mitch Rosen Extraordinary Gunleather **www.mitchrosen.com**
Old World Leather **www.gun-mate.com**
Pager Pal **www.pagerpal.com**
Phalanx Corp. **www.phalanxarms.com**
PWL **www.pwlusa.com**
Rumanya Inc. **www.rumanya.com**
S.A. Gunleather **www.elpasoleather.com**
Safariland Ltd. Inc. **www.safariland.com**
Shooting Systems Group Inc. **www.shootingsystems.com**
Strictly Anything Inc. **www.strictlyanything.com**
Strong Holster Co. **www.strong-holster.com**
The Belt Co. **www.conceal-it.com**
The Leather Factory Inc. **lflandry@flash.net**
The Outdoor Connection **www.outdoorconnection.com**
Top-Line USA inc. **www.toplineusa.com**
Triple K Manufacturing Co. **www.triplek.com**
Wilson Combat **www.wilsoncombat.com**

MISCELLANEOUS SHOOTING PRODUCTS

10X Products Group **www.10Xwear.com**
Aero Peltor **www.aearo.com**
Beartooth **www.beartoothproducts.com**
Dalloz Safety **www.cdalloz.com**
Deben Group Industries Inc. **www.deben.com**
Decot Hy-Wyd Sport Glasses **www.decot.com**
E.A.R., Inc. **www.earinc.com**
Johnny Stewart Wildlife Calls **www.hunterspec.com**
North Safety Products **www.northsafety-brea.com**
Second Chance Body Armor Inc. **www.secondchance.com**
Silencio **www.silencio.com**
Smart Lock Technologies **www.smartlock.com**
Walker's Game Ear Inc. **www.walkersgameear.com**

WEB DIRECTORY

MUZZLELOADING FIREARMS AND PRODUCTS

Austin & Halleck, Inc. **www.austinhalleck.com**
CVA **www.cva.com**
Davis, Vernon C. & Co. **www.mygunroom/vcdavis&co/**
Dixie Gun Works, Inc. **www.dixiegun.com**
Elephant/Swiss Black Powder **www.elephantblackpowder.com**
Goex Black Powder **www.goexpowder.com**
Jedediah Starr Trading Co. **www.jedediah-starr.com**
Jim Chambers Flintlocks **www.flintlocks.com**
Knight Rifles **www.knightrifles.com**
Log Cabin Shop **www.logcabinshop.com**
Lyman **www.lymanproducts.com**
Millennium Designed Muzzleloaders
   www.m2kmuzzleloaders.com
Mountain State Muzzleloading
   www.mtnstatemuzzleloading.com
MSM, Inc. **www.msmfg.com**
Muzzleloading Technologies, Inc. **www.mtimuzzleloading.com**
Navy Arms **www.navyarms.com**
October Country Muzzleloading **www.oct-country.com**
Ox-Yoke Originals Inc. **www.oxyoke.com**
Rightnour Mfg. Co. Inc. **www.rmcsports.com**
The Rifle Shop **trshoppe@aol.com**
Thompson Center Arms **www.tcarms.com**
Traditions Performance Muzzleloading
   www.traditionsfirearms.com

PUBLICATIONS, VIDEOS, AND CD'S

Airgun Letter **www.airgunletter.com**
American Firearms Industry **www.amfire.com**
American Handgunner **www.americanhandgunner.com**
American Hunter **www.americanhunter.org**
American Shooting Magazine **www.americanshooting.com**
Blacksmith **bcbooks@glasscity.net**
Blackpowder Hunting **www.blackpowderhunting.org**
Black Powder Journal **www.blackpowderjournal.com**
Blue Book Publications **www.bluebookinc.com**
Combat Handguns **www.combathandguns.com**
Countrywide Press **www.countrysport.com**
DBI Books/Krause Publications **www.krause.com**
Delta Force **www.infogo.com/delta**
Discount Gun Books **www.discountgunbooks.com**
Gun List **www.gunlist.com**
Gun Video **www.gunvideo.com**
GUNS Magazine **www.gunsmagazine.com**
Guns & Ammo **www.gunsandammomag.com**
Gunweb Magazine WWW Links **www.imags.com**
Harris Publications **www.harrispublications.com**
Heritage Gun Books **www.gunbooks.com**
Krause Publications **www.krause.com**
Moose Lake Publishing **MooselakeP@aol.com**
Munden Enterprises Inc. **www.bob-munden.com**
Outdoor Videos **www.outdoorvideos.com**
Precision Shooting **www.precisionshooting.com**
Rifle and Handloader Magazines **www.riflemagazine.com**
Safari Press Inc. **www.safaripress.com**
Shooters News **www.shootersnews.com**
Shooting Industry **www.shootingindustry.com**
Shooting Sports Retailer **ssretailer@ad.com**

Shotgun News **www.shotgunnews.com**
Shotgun Report **www.shotgunreport.com**
Shotgun Sports Magazine **www.shotgun-sports.com**
Small Arms Review **www.smallarmsreview.com**
Sporting Clays Web Edition **www.sportingclays.com**
Sports Afield **www.sportsafield.comm**
Sports Trend **www.sportstrend.com**
Sportsmen on Film **www.sportsmenonfilm.com**
The Gun Journal **www.shooters.com**
The Shootin Iron **www.off-road.com/4x4web/si/si.html**
The Single Shot Exchange Magazine **singleshot@earthlink.net**
Voyageur Press **www.voyageurpress.com**
VSP Publications **www.gunbooks.com**
Vulcan Outdoors Inc. **www.vulcanpub.com**

RELOADING TOOLS AND SUPPLIES

Ballisti-Cast Mfg. **www.powderandbow.com/ballist**
Bruno Shooters Supply **www.brunoshooters.com**
CH Tool & Die **www.cdhd.com**
Corbin Mfg & Supply Co. **www.corbins.com**
Dillon Precision **www.dillonprecision.com**
Forster Precision Products **www.forsterproducts.com**
Hanned Line **www.hanned.com**
Harrell's Precision **www.harrellsprec.com**
Hornady **www.hornady.com**
Huntington Reloading Products **www.huntingtons.com**
J & J Products Co. **www.jandjproducts.com**
Lee Precision,Inc. **www.leeprecision.com**
Littleton Shotmaker **www.leadshotmaker.com**
Lyman **www.lymanproducts.com**
Magma Engineering **www.magmaengr.com**
Mayville Engineering Co. (MEC) **www.mecreloaders.com**
Midway **www.midwayusa.com**
Moly-Bore **www.molybore.com**
MTM Case-Guard **www.mtmcase-guard.com**
NECO **www.neconos.com**
NEI Handtools Inc. **www.neihandtools.com**
Neil Jones Custom Products **www.neiljones.com**
Ponsness/Warren **www.reloaders.com**
Ranger Products
   www.pages.prodigy.com/rangerproducts.home.htm
Rapine Bullet Mold Mfg Co. **www.bulletmolds.com**
RCBS **www.rcbs.com**
Redding Reloading Equipment **www.redding-reloading.com**
Russ Haydon's Shooting Supplies **www.shooters-supply.com**
Sinclair Int'l Inc. **www.sinclairintl.com**
Stoney Point Products Inc **www.stoneypoint.com**
Thompson Bullet Lube Co. **www.thompsonbulletlube.com**
Wilson (L.E. Wilson) **www.lewilson.com**

RESTS—BENCH, PORTABLE, ATTACHABLE

B-Square **www.b-square.com**
Bullshooter **www.bullshootersightingin.com**
Desert Mountain Mfg. **www.bench-master.com**
Harris Engineering Inc. **www.cyberteklabs.com/harris/main/htm**
Kramer Designs **www.snipepod.com**
L Thomas Rifle Support **www.ltsupport.com**
Level-Lok **www.levellok.com**
Midway **www.midwayusa.com**

Ransom International **www.ransom-intl.com**
R.W. Hart **www.rwhart.com**
Sinclair Intl, Inc. **www.sinclairintl.com**
Stoney Point Products **www.stoneypoint.com**
Target Shooting **www.targetshooting.com**
Varmint Masters **www.varmintmasters.com**
Versa-Pod **www.versa-pod.com**

SCOPES, SIGHTS, MOUNTS AND ACCESSORIES

Accusight **www.accusight.com**
ADCO **www.shooters.com/adco/index/htm**
Aimpoint **www.aimpoint.com**
Aim Shot, Inc. **www.3aimshot.com**
Aimtech Mount Systems **www.aimtech-mounts.com**
Alpec Team, Inc. **www.alpec.com**
American Technologies Network, Corp. **www.atncorp.com**
AmeriGlo, LLC **www.ameriglo.net**
AO Sight Systems Inc. **www.aosights.com**
Ashley Outdoors, Inc. **www.ashleyoutdoors.com**
ATN **www.atncorp.com**
BSA Optics **www.bsaoptics.com**
B-Square Company, Inc. **www.b-square.com**
Burris **www.burrisoptics.com**
Bushnell Corp. **www.bushnell.com**
Carl Zeiss Optical Inc. **www.zeiss.com**
C-More Systems **www.cmore.com**
Conetrol Scope Mounts **www.conetrol.com**
Crimson Trace Corp. **www.crimsontrace.com**
Crossfire L.L.C. **www.amfire.com/hesco/html**
DCG Supply Inc. **www.dcgsupply.com**
EasyHit, Inc. **www.easyhit.com**
EAW **www.eaw.de**
Electro-Optics Technologies **www.eotechmdc.com/holosight**
Europtik Ltd. **www.europtik.com**
Gilmore Sports **www.gilmoresports.com**
Hakko Co. Ltd. **www.hakko-japan.co.jp**
Hesco **www.hescosights.com**
Hitek Industries **www.nightsight.com**
HIVIZ **www.hivizsights.com**
Horus Vision **www.horusvision.com**
Innovative Weaponry,Inc. **www.ptnightsights.com**
Ironsighter Co. **www.ironsighter.com**
ITT Night Vision **www.ittnightvision.com**
Kahles **www.kahlesoptik.com**
Kowa Optimed Inc. **www.kowascope.com**
Laser Bore Sight **www.laserboresight.com**
Laser Devices Inc. **www.laserdevices.com**
Lasergrips **www.crimsontrace.com**
LaserLyte **www.laserlyte.com**
LaserMax Inc. **www.lasermax-inc.com**
Laser Products **www.surefire.com**
Leapers, Inc. **www.leapers.com**
Leica Camera Inc. **www.leica-camera.com/usa**
Leupold **www.leupold.com**
LightForce/NightForce USA **www.nightforcescopes.com**
Lyman **www.lymanproducts.com**
Marble's Outdoors **www.marblesoutdoors.com**
Meprolight **www.kimberamerica.com**
Micro Sight Co. **www.microsight.com**
Millett **www.millettsights.com**

Miniature Machine Corp. **www.mmcsight.com**
Montana Vintage Arms **www.montanavintagearms.com**
NAIT **www.nait.com**
Newcon International Ltd. **newconsales@newcon-optik.com**
Night Owl Optics **www.nightowloptics.com**
Nikon Inc. **www.nikonusa.com**
North American Integrated Technologies **www.nait.com**
O.K. Weber, Inc. **www.okweber.com**
Pentax Corp. **www.pentaxlightseeker.com**
Premier Reticle **www.premierreticles.com**
Redfield **www.redfieldoptics.com**
R&R Int'l Trade **www.nightoptic.com**
Schmidt & Bender **www.schmidt-bender.com**
Scopecoat **www.scopecoat.com**
Scopelevel **www.scopelevel.com**
Segway Industries **www.segway-industries.com**
Shepherd Scope Ltd. **www.shepherdscopes.com**
Sightron **www.sightron.com**
Simmons **www.simmonsoptics.com**
S&K **www.scopemounts.com**
Springfield Armory **www.springfield-armory.com**
Sure-Fire **www.surefire.com**
Swarovski/Kahles **www.swarovskioptik.com**
Swift Instruments Inc. **www.swift-optics.com**
Tasco **www.tascosales.com**
Trijicon Inc. **www.trijicon-inc.com**
Truglo Inc. **www.truglo.com**
U.S. Optics Technologies Inc. **www.usoptics.com**
Valdada-IOR Optics **www.valdada.com**
Warne **www.warnescopemounts.com**
Weaver-Blount **www.blount.com**
Wilcox Industries Corp **www.wilcoxind.com**
Williams Gun Sight Co. **www.williamsgunsight.com**
Zeiss **www.zeiss.com**

SHOOTING ORGANIZATIONS, SCHOOLS AND RANGES

Amateur Trapshooting Assoc. **www.shootata.com**
American Custom Gunmakers Guild **www.acgg.org**
American Gunsmithing Institute **www.americangunsmith.com**
American Pistolsmiths Guild **www.americanpistol.com**
American Shooting Sports Council **www.assc.com**
Assoc. of Firearm & Tool Mark Examiners **www.afte.org**
BATF **www.atf.ustreas.gov**
Blackwater Lodge and Training Center
    www.blackwaterlodge.com
Boone and Crockett Club **www.boone-crockett.org**
Buckmasters, Ltd. **www.buckmasters.com**
Citizens Committee for the Right to Keep & Bear Arms
    www.ccrkba.org
Civilian Marksmanship Program **www.odcmp.com**
Colorado School of Trades **www.gunsmith-school.com**
Ducks Unlimited **www.ducks.org**
Fifty Caliber Shooters Assoc. **www.fcsa.org**
Firearms Coalition **www.nealknox.com**
Front Sight Firearms Training Institute **www.frontsight.com**
German Gun Collectors Assoc. **www.germanguns.com**
Gun Clubs **www.associatedgunclubs.org**

WEB DIRECTORY

Gun Owners' Action League **www.goal.org**
Gun Owners of America **www.gunowners.org**
Gun Trade Asssoc. Ltd. **www.brucepub.com/gta**
Gunsite Training Center,Inc. **www.gunsite.com**
International Defense Pistol Assoc. **www.idpa.com**
International Handgun Metallic Silhouette Assoc. **www.ihmsa.org**
International Hunter Education Assoc. **www.ihea.com**
Murray State College(gunsmithing) **darnold@msc.cc.ok.us**
National 4-H Shooting Sports **kesabo@nmsu.edu**
National Benchrest Shooters Assoc. **www.benchrest.com**
National Muzzle Loading Rifle Assoc. **www.nmlra.org**
National Reloading Manufacturers Assoc **www.reload-nrma.com**
National Rifle Assoc. **www.nra.org**
National Rifle Assoc. ILA **www.nraila.org**
National Shooting Sports Foundation **www.nssf.org**
National Skeet Shooters Association **www.nssa-nsca.com**
National Sporting Clays Assoc. **www.nssa-nsca.com**
National Wild Turkey Federation **www.nwtf.com**
North American Hunting Club **www.huntingclub.com**
Pennsylvania Gunsmith School **www.pagunsmith.com**
Quail Unlimited **www.qu.org**
Right To Keep and Bear Arms **www.rkba.org**
Rocky Mountain Elk Foundation **www.rmef.org**
SAAMI **www.saami.org**
Second Amendment Foundation **www.saf.org**
Shooting Ranges Int'l **www.shootingranges.com**
Single Action Shooting Society **www.sassnet.com**
S&W Academy and Nat'l Firearms Trng. Center
   www.sw-academy.com
Ted Nugent United Sportsmen of America **www.tnugent.com**
Thunder Ranch **www.thunderranchinc.com**
Trapshooters Homepage **www.trapshooters.com**
Trinidad State Junior College **www.tsjc.cccoes.edu**
U.S. Int'l Clay Target Assoc. **www.usicta.com**
United States Fish and Wildlife Service **www.fws.gov**
U.S. Practical Shooting Assoc. **www.uspsa.org**
USA Shooting **www.usashooting.com**
Varmint Hunters Assoc. **www.varminthunter.org**
Wildlife Legislative Fund of America **www.wlfa.org**
Women's Shooting Sports Foundation **www.wssf.org**

STOCKS

Advanced Technology **www.atigunstocks.com**
Bell & Carlson, Inc. **www.bellandcarlson.com**
Boyd's Gunstock Industries, Inc. **www.boydboys.com**
Butler Creek Corp **www.butler-creek.com**
Calico Hardwoods, Inc. **www.calicohardwoods.com**
Choate Machine **www.riflestock.com**
Elk Ridge Stocks **www.reamerrentals.com/elk_ridge.htm**
Great American Gunstocks **www.gunstocks.com**
Lone Wolf **www.lonewolfriflestocks.com**
McMillan Fiberglass Stocks **www.mcmfamily.com**
MPI Stocks **www.mpistocks.com**
Ram-Line- Blount Inc. **www.blount.com**
Rimrock Rifle Stock **www.rimrockstocks.com**
Royal Arms Gunstocks **www.imt.net/~royalarms**
Tiger-Hunt Curly Maple Gunstocks **www.gunstockwood.com**
Wenig Custom Gunstocks Inc. **www.wenig.com**

TARGETS AND RANGE EQUIPMENT

Action Target Co. **www.actiontarget.com**
Advanced Interactive Systems **www.ais-sim.com**
Birchwood Casey **www.birchwoodcasey.com**
Caswell Detroit Armor Companies **www.caswellintl.com**
MTM Products **www.mtmcase-gard.com**
National Target Co. **www.nationaltarget.com**
Newbold Target Systems **www.newboldtargets.com**
Range Management Services Inc. **www.casewellintl.com**
Range Systems **www.shootingrangeproducts.com**
Reactive Target Systems Inc. **chrts@primenet.com**
Super Trap Bullet Containment Systems **www.supertrap.com**
Thompson Target Technology
   www.cantorweb.com/thompsontargets
Visible Impact Targets **www.crosman.com**
White Flyer **www.whiteflyer.com**

TRAP AND SKEET SHOOTING EQUIPMENT AND ACCESSORIES

Auto-Sporter Industries **www.auto-sporter.com**
10X Products Group **www.10Xwear.com**
Claymaster Traps **www.claymaster.com**
Do-All Traps, Inc. **www.do-alltraps.com**
Laporte USA **www.laporte-shooting.com**
Outers **www.blount.com**
Trius Products Inc. **www.triustraps.com**
White Flyer **www.whiteflyer.com**

TRIGGERS

Brownells **www.brownells.com**
Shilen **www.shilen.com**
Timney Triggers **www.timneytrigger.com**

MAJOR SHOOTING WEB SITES AND LINKS

Alphabetic Index of Links **www.gunsgunsguns.com**
Auction Arms **www.auctionarms.com**
For The Hunt **www.forthehunt.com**
Gun and Knife Forums **www.gunandknife.com/forums**
Gun Broker Auctions **www.gunbroker.com**
Gun Index **www.gunindex.com**
Gun Industry **www.gunindustry.com**
GunLinks **www.gunlinks.com**
Guns For Sale **www.gunsamerica.com**
Gun Show Auction **www.gunshowauction.com**
GunXchange **www.gunxchange.com**
Hunting Digest **www.huntingdigest.com**
Hunting Information(NSSF) **www.huntinfo.org**
Hunting Network **www.huntingnetwork.com**
Outdoor Yellow Pages **www.outdoorsyp.com**
Real Guns **www.realguns.com/links/glinks.htm**
Rec.Guns **www.recguns.com**
Shooters' Gun Calendar **www.guncalendar.com/index.cfm**
Shooter's Online Services **www.shooters.com**
Shooters Search **www.shooterssearch.com**
Shotgun Sports Resource Guide **www.shotgunsports.com**
Sixgunner **www.sixgunner.com**
Sportsman's Web **www.sportsmansweb.com**
Where To Shoot **www.wheretoshoot.com**

by JOHN HAVILAND

SHOTGUN REVIEW

*I*N THIS LESS *than stellar economic year, many shotgun models have remained unchanged or received only decorative changes, like engraving and fancier wood, or accessories like multiple choke tubes and carrying cases. A few new guns have been introduced, though, mostly lightweight side-by-sides in 12 gauge with a few new 16-gauge guns.*

Let's see exactly what is new.

Benelli

Benelli has covered its M1 Field 12 and 20 gauge, Nova pump 20 gauge and Super Black Eagle 12 gauge with Advantage Timber High Definition camouflage to play hide and shoot with turkeys and waterfowl. Replacement

stocks and forearms in the camo are also available if your current Benelli feels underdressed without the camo.

Beretta

Beretta has refined its 686 and 687 line of over/under guns.

The 686 field-grade Quail Unlimited 20- and 28-gauge guns feature gold-filled flushing quail engraved on the sides. Each Quail Unlimited includes a carrying case and five choke tubes.

The 686 Silver Pigeon S 12, 20 and 28 gauges feature high-grade walnut, checkered on the grip and forearm. Scroll engraving covers the silver receiver.

The 686 E Sporting 12 and 20sare made over with high-grade wood, checkering and gold-plated triggers.

The four variations of the 687 Pigeon competition guns feature enhanced engraving.

Browning

The 525 is Browning's newest version of its Citori. The 525 Sporting, Golden Clays and Field models in 12 and 20 gauge are stocked with tightly curved grips, pronounced palm swells and checkered with a "Euro" pattern. The barrels are thinner, for lighter weight, and are ported in the Sporting and Golden Clays models. *"A racy gun,"* notes Browning's Scott Grange. The 525's trigger system has been redesigned for less overtravel and

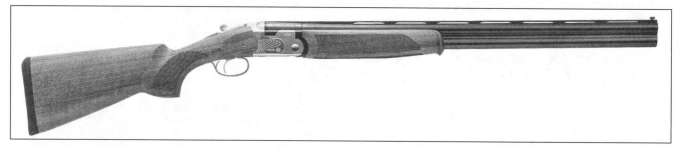

The 686 Silver Pigeon S 12, 20 and 28 gauges feature high-grade walnut checkered on the grip and forearm. Scroll engraving covers the silver receiver.

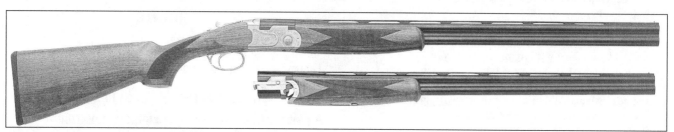

The 686 E Sporting 12 and 20s are made over with high-grade wood, checkering and gold-plated triggers.

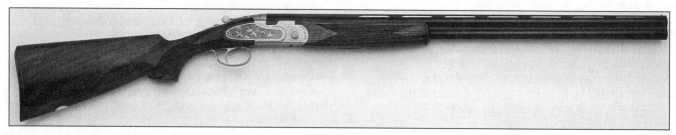

The four variations of the 687 Pigeon competition guns feature enhanced engraving.

Browning 525 over/under 12 gauge.

Browning 525 over/under 20 gauge.

Browning's Little Skeeters gauge reducers are only slightly longer than the shells they accept. At $50 retail they are much less expensive than full-length insert tubes.

expensive than full-length tubes. The tubes fit a:
* 10 gauge to fire 12 and 20 gauge shells.
* 12 gauge to fire 20, 28, and .410.
* 16 gauge to hold 20, 28 and .410.
* 20 gauge to hold 28 and .410.

I wondered if all the powder gas would blow right past a 20, 28 or .410 wad rattling down a 12-gauge bore. But I hit just as many clay targets when I shot a 12-gauge Citori with inserts to hold 20- and 28-gauge shells as I did with regular Winchester 12-gauge 1 1/8-ounce loads. Talk about back-bored!

Franchi

Advantage Timber High Definition camouflage is also new on the Franchi Model 912 and 620 autoloaders. A satin-finished walnut stock is also available for hunters who prefer a traditional look.

The Franchi VarioSystem on these guns consists of a collar on the magazine tube that can be set to regulate the bleed-off of powder gas to ensure functioning of light loads and to reduce the felt recoil of magnum shells.

The 48 AL Deluxe semi-auto and Veloce over/under 20 gauge now come with straight-grip stocks, in addition to the standard curved grips.

The Alcione Titanium over/under 3-inch 12- and 20-gauge guns shave nearly 10 ounces off the weight of the steel-receiver Alcione Field guns. Both the 12- and 20-gauge guns weigh about 6.8 pounds. The Titanium is made with an aluminum receiver with titanium inserts in high impact areas. The Titanium is etched with gold-filled scenes of pheasant and quail, and carries a gold trigger. A choice of 28- or 26-inch barrels is available, threaded for Improved Cylinder, Modified and Full choke tubes. Twelve-gauge guns accept optional 20-gauge barrels. The whole works fit in a supplied hard case.

features three interchangeable triggers that allow adjustment of length of pull by plus-or-minus 1/8 inch. A high-grade Golden Clays has a fancy walnut stock and forearm. Engraving depicts the transition of a game bird into a clay bird, all highlighted in 24-karat gold.

The Citori Superlight Feather 12 gauge shaves 11 ounces off the weight of the similar Citori Lightning Feather by going to a straight-grip stock and slimmer forearm. The 20-gauge Superlight weighs eight ounces less than the comparable Lightning Feather.

The Citori XS Pro-Comp 12 gauge is a full-blown target gun. It features ported barrels, adjustable comb, beavertail forearm, right-hand palm swell grip and interchangeable triggers that allow adjustment of length of pull. A GraCoil system reduces recoil. A tungsten alloy weight on the forearm

further reduces recoil and adds weight to the gun.

The sideplates of the Citori Esprit are removable and accept plates with five engraving patterns, from scrollwork to gold-enhanced pointers and game birds.

The Gold Fusion 12 gauge was a hit last year and, this year, is available in 20 gauge. The 20-gauge Fusion is about seven ounces lighter than the standard Gold Classic Hunter.

The 20-gauge Gold Classic High Grade is dressed up with a nickel-plated receiver with a motif depicting doves and quail. A slight 'hump' to the receiver reminds you of the old Auto-5.

A great accessory for open-breech guns like the Citori is Browning's Little Skeeters. These gauge reducers are only slightly longer than the shells they accept. At $50 retail they are much less

The Citori 525 Sporting, Golden Clays and Field models in 12 and 20 gauge are stocked with tightly curved grips, pronounced palm swells and checkered with a "Euro" pattern. The barrels are thinner, for lighter weight, and are ported in the Sporting and Golden Clays models.

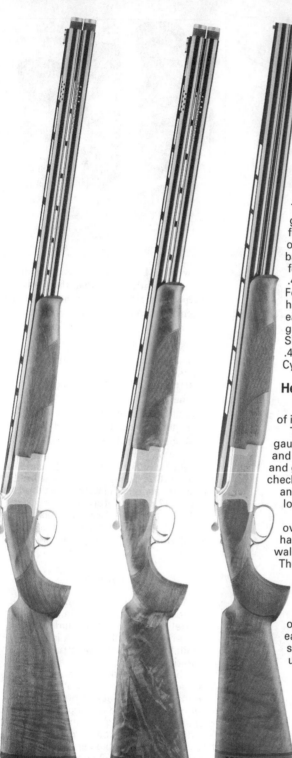

Bill Hanus Birdguns

Bill Hanus Birdguns side-by-sides are made by AYA in 16, 20 and 28 gauge. This year Hanus is offering a 28/.410 combination side-by-side. The gun is built on a 28-gauge receiver and weighs five pounds and a few ounces with the 28-gauge barrels. The gun weighs a few more ounces with the .410 barrels installed. Forearm and leather handguards come with each barrel set. The 28-gauge barrels are choked Skeet 1 and 2, while the .410 is bored Improved Cylinder and Modified.

Heckler & Koch FABARM

H&K has dressed up three of its FABARM shotguns.

The Red Lion semi-auto 12 gauge shows off with a black-and silver-finished receiver and gold inlaid engraving. A checkered Turkish walnut stock and forearm enhances its looks.

The Max Lion Paradox over/under features a case-hardened receiver and fancy walnut stock and forearm. The last six inches of the bottom barrel is rifled with a 1:14-inch twist to produce a spreader pattern. I guess that's okay. But wouldn't it be easier to just chamber a spreader load when close-up shots are expected?

The Classic Lion Elite side-by-side has a color case-hardened receiver. Its walnut stock and forearm are sealed with decals that give a deep and marbled look to the wood.

Ithaca

The Ithaca Model 37 pump QUAD Bore 20-gauge Turkeyslayer has four individual borings, that make the barrel a single long constriction, to provide incredibly tight patterns. The first diameter is overbore, while the next three steps taper to the final choke tube constriction. All this treats the shot column gently to reduce shot deformation. The barrel is ported to reduce recoil. A set of fully adjustable TRUGLO sights is standard and the receiver is factory drilled and tapped to accept a scope base. All the metal is steel, finished in matte blue.

The UltraFeatherlight Model 37 "Premier Edition" in 16 gauge is limited to 400 guns. The UltraFeatherlight's light weight of 5.5 pounds comes from an aluminum receiver. The 26-inch barrel has a ventilated top rib with an extended forcing cone and three interchangeable choke tubes. A hard rubber butt plate reminiscent of the 1930s is also available.

The Ruffed Grouse Society Conservation Edition shotgun is a Model 37 20-gauge Ultra Featherlight. It features a 22- or 24-inch barrel with interchangeable choke tubes, a ventilated rib and American black walnut stock and forearm. The stock is laser-engraved with a ruffed grouse feather and the legend "Ruffed Grouse Society Conservation Edition." Ithaca will make a donation from the sale of each gun to the Ruffed Grouse Society to assist them in their conservation work.

The Model 37 Homeland Security Model is made to its original U.S. military specifications. The Homeland Security features all-steel construction, 18 1/2-inch Cylinder-bore barrel with 3-inch chamber, oil-finished American black walnut stock and forearm, and matte-blue finish

The Model 37 Field Classic is a faithful reproduction of the standard 12-gauge field gun of the 1940s and 50s. The polished steel receiver supports a plain 28-inch Modified-

The Citori Superlight Feather 12 gauge shaves 11 ounces off the weight of the similar Citori Lightning Feather by going to a straight-grip stock and slimmer forearm.

The Citori XS Pro-Comp 12 gauge features ported barrels, adjustable comb, beavertail forearm and interchangeable triggers. A GraCoil shock absorber system reduces recoil.

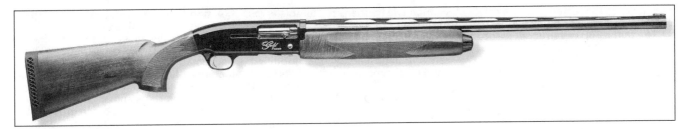

Browning's Gold Fusion 20 gauge is about seven ounces lighter than the standard Gold Classic Hunter.

choked barrel. The stock, with hard rubber buttplate, and ringtail forearm are American black walnut, uncheckered.

H&R

Marlin Firearm's subsidiary H&R 1871 has a new gun based on the New England Firearms single-barrel hinge-action design. Four versions of the Huntsman gun include two barrels chambered for different cartridges and one with a single shotgun barrel. The ones that include shotgun barrels are the:

* Pardner with a 28-inch 12-gauge barrel and 24-inch 50-caliber muzzleloader barrel.
* Pardner with a 12-gauge 3 1/2-inch chamber, all decked out in Mossy Oak Break-Up camo.

Mountains. But then you consider the prairie surrounding Augusta is full of sharp-tailed grouse, Hungarian partridge, mourning doves and pheasants--and west of town, where the prairie butts up against the mountain wilderness, live blue, ruffed and spruce grouse.

The Kimber Augusta is made in four configurations; all based on a boxlock action, oversized bores of .736 inches, one-inch Decelerator recoil pad, adjustable and removable trigger assembly and unusually tight-curved grip. All the guns have a slight cast-off at the stock heel and toe. Kimber's Ryan Busse says any style and dimension stock can be ordered through Kimber's custom shop.

* The Sporting model features a point checkering pattern and a schnabel tip forearm.
* The Field includes a beavertail forearm and optional straight-grip stock, fancy walnut and engraving.
* The Trap features a raised comb and varying lengths of barrels and engraved sideplates.
* The Skeet is similar to the Trap, but sans the raised comb.

Legacy Sports

Legacy Sports (the old Interarms company) imports a whole line of rifles, which include Mauser, Howa and

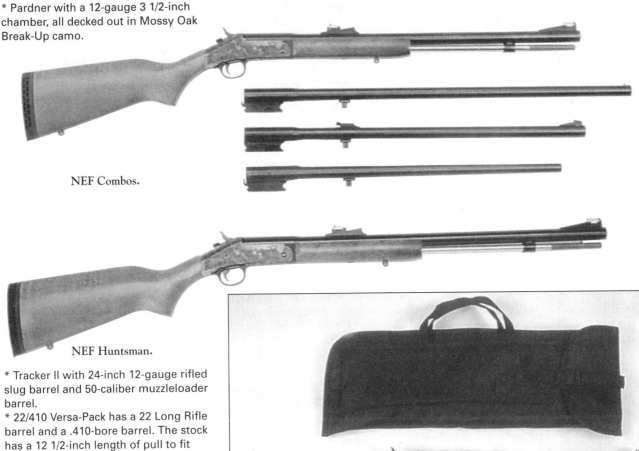

NEF Combos.

NEF Huntsman.

* Tracker II with 24-inch 12-gauge rifled slug barrel and 50-caliber muzzleloader barrel.
* 22/410 Versa-Pack has a 22 Long Rifle barrel and a .410-bore barrel. The stock has a 12 1/2-inch length of pull to fit young shooters.

Kimber

At first it seems strange that Kimber would name its new Augusta Italian-made over/under 12 gauge after a dusty and windy cow town along Montana's Eastern Front of the Rocky

NEF Versa-Pack.

Puma. We're interested in Legacy's Escort and Silma shotguns.

The Silma 70EJ over/under made in Italy is available in Standard, Deluxe and Deluxe Superlight models. The 12-gauge version weighs 7.6 pounds (5.6 pounds with an aluminum receiver in the Superlight) and features a single trigger, ventilated rib on a 28-inch barrel, screw-in chokes, automatic ejectors and safety, and a recoil pad. The 12 gauge is chambered to accept 3 1/2-inch shells, just in case you want to shoot a few to find out what it's like to get in a car wreck. Actually, the 3 1/2's long chamber is a good idea for shooting shorter shells because it acts like an extra-long forcing cone. The 20-, 28-gauge and .410-bore guns weigh in at 6.9 pounds.

Standard grade guns are engraved with a mallard on one receiver flat and a quail on the other side. The Deluxe is engraved with a pheasant and woodcock on the flats and a mallard on the receiver bottom.

The autoloading Escort offers a Turkish walnut stock (AS) or black polymer stock (PS). The gun has several nice features. One is the adjustment screw at the front right of the forearm that adjusts the amount of gas bleed to ensure cycling of 2 3/4-inch target loads to three-inch magnum shells. A magazine cutoff button at the front right of the receiver allows pulling out the shell in the chamber and replacing it with another round when a goose flies over your duck decoys. In case the Escort shoots a bit high or low for you, two shims are included to adjust stock drop. An extension readily attaches to the magazine tube in case

The Kimber Augusta over/under 12 gauge made in Italy.

your beagle happens to stumble across a warren of rabbits.

Normal features on the Escort include a threaded muzzle that accepts screw-in Improved Cylinder, Modified and Full chokes, a ventilated rib, chrome-lined bores, shock-absorbing bolt sleeve and a cushy recoil pad.

Merkel

Merkel's new 1620EL side-by-side is a beautiful gun with barrels that rest on a sculptured receiver ledge, a silver-grayed receiver with hand-engraved hunting scenes and borders, and a high-grade walnut straight-grip stock. Best of all, the gun is chambered in 16 gauge. The 1620EL two-barrel set comes with barrels chambered for the three-inch 20 gauge and attached forearm. However, once you've seen how much better the 16 gauge patterns 1 1/8- and 1 1/4-ounce loads you'll most likely use the 20-gauge barrels for a lamp stem.

The 1620 EL features an Anson and Deeley boxlock action, which locks with a cross-bolt and under-barrel double lugs. The automatic safety is located on the top of the tang. Merkel believes the easiest and most reliable way to select which barrel to shoot is with double triggers.

The 28-inch barrels are choked Improved Cylinder and Modified. Briley Manufacturing, of Houston, Texas, can install screw-in chokes as an after-market service. The gun weighs 5.9 pounds.

The Model 16/20SL sidelock chambered in 16 gauge and the 16/20SL with 16- and 20-gauge barrels will be available later this year.

The Merkel Model 280 is a similar side-by-side chambered in 28 gauge, but with less ornamentation and a case-hardened receiver with its border engraved in an Arabesque pattern. The gun weighs 5.2 pounds.

The Merkel Model 360 is the same gun chambered in three-inch .410 bore.

The Model 280/360 is one receiver with a two-barrel set, one chambered for the 28 and the other the .410.

Mossberg

To realize the best accuracy with today's sabot slugs, like the Winchester Partition Gold and Remington Copper Solid, you need the tight lockup of a bolt-action gun. The Mossberg 695 Bolt

Action Slug Gun is one such gun. The gun has a fully rifled barrel with a 1:36-inch twist, which is ported to reduce the recoil. A choice of TRUGLO adjustable fiber-optic sights or regular open sights comes on the gun. A scope base is also mounted on the receiver to hold scope rings and a scope. Mossberg claims 1 1/2-inch groups at 100 yards are not unusual for the 695.

Remington

In keeping with the rising popularity in the 16 gauge, Remington has once again chambered the 16 in its Model 870 Wingmaster, 870 Express and 870 Express Youth Synthetic. All three variations of the 870 have ventilated ribs and screw-in chokes (Improved Cylinder, Modified and Full). The Wingmaster is the fancy one with a checkered American walnut stock and polished blue metal. The light-contour barrel is either 26 or 28 inches. Because the gun is based on the 12-gauge receiver, it actually weighs seven pounds, compared to 6 3/4 pounds for the comparable 12-gauge Wingmaster.

The 16-gauge Wingmaster my youngest son shoots was bought in the early 1960s and has been passed down through the hands of six hunters. It has weathered hard use every year. A few years back the gun's firing pin broke after having shot untold cases of ammunition. A call to the Remington service department secured a new firing pin, for three dollars and change—including postage. The 870 is such a simple mechanism that I had the broken pin out and the new one installed in ten minutes. The gun is ready for another 40 years.

The 870 Express 16 comes with a 28-inch barrel equipped with a Modified screw-in choke. The stock is either hardwood with pressed checkering or black synthetic to match the tough matte-black finish.

The Express Youth sticks with the black synthetic stock and sports an easier to carry 23-inch barrel and 1 1/2-inch shorter length of pull, at 13 inches.

Now if Remington would offer a 16-gauge waterfowl load with its new nontoxic Hevi-Shot, the 16 would be the all-around gauge it once was.

Remington is hoping its past success during the 1930s with its Model 32 over/under will sell today in its updated version Model 332.

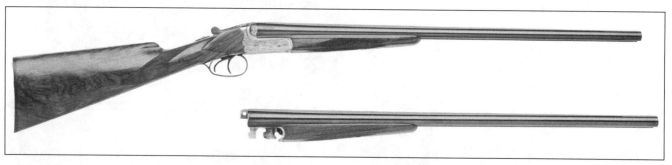

The Merkel 1620EL side-by-side two-barrel set comes with barrels chambered for the 16 gauge and the three-inch 20 gauge and attached forearms. However, once you've seen how much better the 16 gauge patterns 1 1/8- and 1 1/4-ounce loads you'll most likely use the 20-gauge barrels for a lamp stem.

This nearly 40 year-old Model 870 16 gauge has passed through the hands of six hunters.

By all accounts, Remington made the best-stocked and balanced over/under in America in the ten years between 1932 and 1942. Remington hopes American's shotgun tastes have remained unchanged because its new over/under Model 332 is practically a copy of the old Model 32. According to Remington, the new Model 332 has the same stock dimensions, contour, balance point and checkering and engraving patterns as the Model 32 of 70 years ago. The only differences between the guns are the 332's upgraded lock design and utilization of today's manufacturing technology. Barrels are available in 26-, 28- and 30-inch lengths. Screw-in chokes include Improved Cylinder, Modified and Full. Time will tell if tastes still favor the 332's restrained appearance as a functional field gun, or if they have been won over to bulbous forearms, humped combs and bright metal.

Rotary Round

I had to stare a minute the first time I saw a Rotary Round gun. It looked like an over/under, but it wasn't a boxlock and certainly not a sidelock. I picked up the gun and found no levers to open it.

"Rotate the barrel and receiver ring a quarter-turn to the right, then pull the barrels forward," instructed George Hoenig.

The action opened at the twist and fell open when I pulled the barrels forward. The inside of the action looked like nothing I had ever seen. Hoenig, from Boise, Idaho (208-375-1116), said 40 years of his gunsmithing experience went into designing the Rotary Round.

Hoenig explained that the hinge of a conventional break-action gun eventually works loose after repeated firing. By developing a rotary locking system, Hoenig felt he could make a strong and rigid double-gun action.

The breech of the Rotary Round contains the strikers, safety, trigger and hinge and two large locking lugs that are directly in line with the chambers. The forward part of the receiver contains recesses for the locking lugs and the extractors. The extractor utilizes the sliding weight of the barrels to pull cases from the chamber. Because the barrels turn on opening, loading and unloading is like with a side-by-side. Sliding the extractor past its normal position separates the barrels from the breech.

The first gun, completed in 1996, was chambered for the 9.3x74R rifle cartridge. The gun will accept rimmed cartridges up to 470 Nitro Express and is also available in 28 gauge.

The shotgun is available with 26- or 28-inch barrels choked in any combination of Improved Cylinder, Modified or Full. Stocks are English walnut and feature elaborate checkering.

Ruger

The Ruger Gold Label side-by-side 12 gauge has the shotgun industry asking, *"How did Ruger do that?"*

"From the beginning of the Gold Label's design, Bill Ruger Jr. insisted it have the looks and light weight of a traditional side-by-side," says Syl Wiley, the marketing manager for Sturm, Ruger and Company.

One seemingly minor feature is the thin wrist of the Gold Label's straight or curved grip that shows Ruger has followed the British and European idea of the correct double gun. No American shotgun on the low side of $5,000 has ever incorporated such a thin wrist. Americans were believed to be so primitive that they needed thick heavy stocks in case they had to swing their gun like a club, or use it to wedge open a gate. When I first handled the Gold Label, the slender wrist and splinter forearm lay deep in the palms of my hands, the comb rose to my cheek and I was looking slightly above the steel rib.

Examination of the Gold Label revealed no exposed pin or screw heads, just a clean round-bottom receiver of stainless steel with the receiver ledges blending into the double barrels.

Ruger states the Gold Label weighs 6 1/3 pounds with 28 inch barrels that accept screw-in Improved Cylinder, Skeet, Modified and Full chokes. The boxlock action includes a single trigger, internal hammer interrupters, an assisted-opening cocking system, safety/barrel selector and selective ejectors.

Sarsilmaz

Sarsilmaz was founded in 1880 in Turkey and makes a line of autoloading handguns and pump, over/under and autoloading shotguns.

New this year is the Trap 2000 over/under in 12 gauge. The autoloading Classic and Autumn now feature camo stocks and forearms. The Jaws is based on the same autoloading action with a

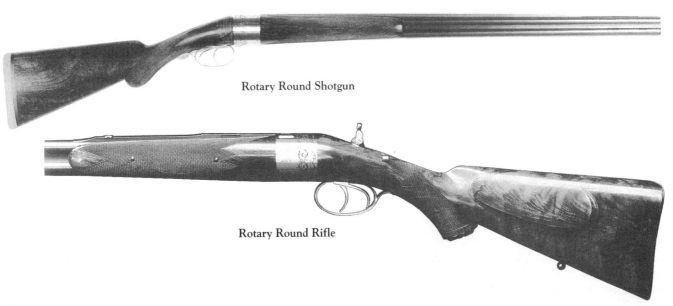

Rotary Round Shotgun

Rotary Round Rifle

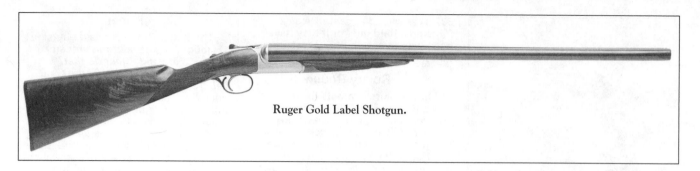

Ruger Gold Label Shotgun.

black polymer stock and fiber-optic sights. A Jaws model with a folding stock, pistol grip handle and extended magazine is also available.

SKB

SKB has started to phase out its 585 model over/unders and to replace them with the 85TSS Target. The new Super Sport over/under models include Sporting Clays, Skeet and Trap—and barrel sets of different gauges for each model. The Sporting Clays is chambered in 12, 20, 28 and .410 bore in 28-, 30- or 32-inch barrels. Barrel sets include 30-inch barrels in 12 and 20, 20 and 28 and 20, 28 and .410. The Skeet model is chambered in 12, 20 and 28 in 28- or 30-inch barrels and .410 in 28-inch barrels. Three-barrel sets come in 28-inch barrels chambered for the 20, 28 and .410. The Trap over/under models wear choices of 30- or 32-inch barrels. The Trap Combo has over/under barrels or single barrel from 30 to 34 inches.

All these models feature chrome-lined chambers and bores, ventilated top ribs, vented ribs between barrels, Hi-Viz fiber-optic sights and a selection of Briley choke tubes.

Stoeger

The Stoeger Model 2000 autoloading 12-gauge shotgun has been dressed up (or down) with a black synthetic stock and Advantage Timber High Definition camouflage. A smoothbore slug barrel comes either as part of a package with the synthetic gun, or as an option.

The Condor Special 12- and 20-gauge over/unders feature a matte-nickel receiver, in place of the regular blued receiver. Screw-in chokes, ventilated rib and hardwood stocks are still standard.

The Stoeger Upland Special is the fourth in the Uplander series of side-by-side guns. The Special is set apart from the other guns by its matte nickel receiver and checkered straight-grip stock of Brazilian hardwood. The 12-, 20- and 28-gauge guns have 24- or 26-inch barrels and weigh slightly over seven pounds.

The Silverado Coach Gun side-by-side is for guarding the strongbox on the stagecoach and doing in the bad guys wearing big black hats during cowboy action shooting. The Silverado has a nickel matte finish on its receiver and 20-inch barrel. The gun is chambered in 12, 20 and .410 bore. A straight-grip version is chambered in 12 and 20 gauge.

Traditions

The Fausti Stefano shotguns made in Italy are marketed by Traditions in America.

The Traditions Classic Series Sporting Clay III over/under in 12 and 20 gauge is an upgrade. It features a schnabel forearm and palm-swell grip—two features that for some reason must be included on a sporting clays gun. The 28- or 30-inch barrels have ventilated top and middle ribs and a red fiber-optic front bead. The porting rows behind the muzzles reduce muzzle jump to keep the gun pointing for the second clay of a fast double. The supplied Skeet, Improved Cylinder, Modified and Full choke screw-in tubes are knurled and extend past the muzzle for quick removal and replacement without having to search in your vest pockets for a wrench.

The ALS 2100 semi-auto 12-gauge Hunter Combo comes with two barrels to accommodate feathers and fur. The 28-inch smoothbore barrel accepts furnished Improved Cylinder, Modified and Full screw-in choke tubes. The second barrel is a 24-inch fully rifled barrel for slugs. The rifled barrel has either TRUGLO fiber-optic front adjustable sights or a cantilever (scope-mounting) base attached to the barrel. The base accepts Weaver-style rings for mounting a scope or other optical

sight. Stocks come in either walnut or synthetic. The ALS 2100 weighs 6 to 6 1/2 pounds with the rifled barrel installed, which is rather light for a three-inch 12 gauge.

The rifled barrel, with sights or cantilever mount, is also available as the ALS 2100 Slug Hunter Cantilever.

The ALS 2100 Turkey Hunter is fitted with a ventilated rib 26-inch barrel threaded for screw-in chokes. Chokes included are Improved Cylinder, Modified and Full. The whole gun is covered in Mossy Oak Break-Up camo.

The ALS 2100 Home Security wears a black synthetic stock and 20-inch barrel with a wide open bore.

Verona

Eldorado Cartridge Company (PMC) imports the Verona line of shotguns.

The Verona LX501 over/under is now available with two barrel sets; the 28-inch barrels in three-inch 20 gauge and 2 3/4-inch 28 gauge, or 28-gauge and .410-bore barrels. These guns weigh about 6 1/4 pounds and accept screw-in chokes in three constrictions.

The fancier LX692G Field also comes with barrel sets chambered for 28 gauge and .410.

The LX680TC Gold Trap Combo barrel sets allow shooting a 12-gauge over/under with 30-inch barrels and five Briley screw-in choke tubes. The other barrel of the set is a single, 32 inches in length. The LX680GTSB-12 is the same outfit, but with just the single barrel. All Gold Competition 12-gauge guns feature an adjustable length of pull, single selective trigger, extended forcing cones and ported barrels.

The LX702GCT-20 Gold Competition Trap is the little brother to the 12-gauge Competition guns. The 20-gauge version weighs 1 1/4 pounds less than the 12 and carries the same features, except the adjustable comb. It features a slightly thicker comb, beavertail forearm, palm-swell grip and an

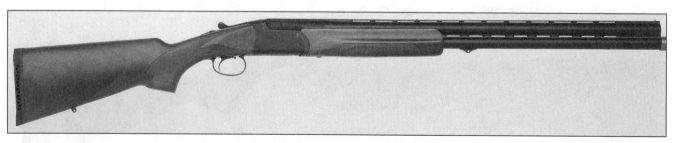

The ALS 2100 semi-auto 12-gauge Hunter Combo comes with two barrels to accommodate feathers and fur. The 28-inch smoothbore barrel accepts furnished Improved Cylinder, Modified screw-in choke tubes. The second barrel is a 24-inch fully rifled barrel for slugs.

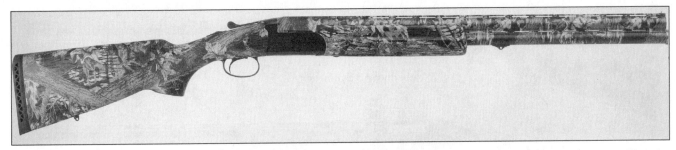

The ALS 2100 Turkey Hunter in Mossy Oak Break-Up camo. The ventilated rib 26-inch barrel is threaded for screw-in chokes.

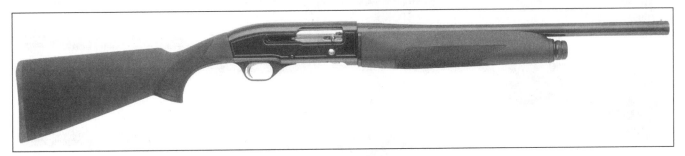

The ALS 2100 Home Security wears a black synthetic stock and 20-inch barrel with a wide open bore.

engraved receiver with gold-inlaid bird hunting scenes.

The LX792GCT-20/28 is the same 20 over/under, but with a 28-gauge barrel set and forearm.

The Verona semiautomatic SX401-12 offers a choice of a 26-, 28- or 30-inch barrel. A red dot Doctersight is also available.

Just the name "MX301-12 Pump Action Police" scares me. This shotgun packs six shells in its magazine under an 18 1/2-inch barrel and stores four more rounds in tubes in the stock. The whole gun is dressed in Parkerized metal and black synthetic stock and forearm.

Winchester

During an elk hunt last fall, we finally noticed the elk were someplace else. However, ruffed grouse were thick along the creek bottoms and in the quaking aspen groves. After the third day a friend and I said the heck with the elk and headed out with a Winchester Model 9410 and a box of Winchester Super-X .410 shells loaded with 1/2-ounce of #7 1/2 shot. We shot grouse as they pecked along the ground and flew through the brush. In an hour we had our limits without firing all nine shots in one magazine load.

This year the Model 9410 is available in the Packer model with a 20-inch barrel and 3/4-length magazine that holds four cartridges. The Packer has a curved grip, forearm cap and swivel studs for a sling for the long haul. The Packer has a Cylinder bore, but Winchester states the gun still produces full-choke patterns at 25 yards.

Winchester has added a Dura-Touch surface to its Super X2 3 1/2-inch and calls it the Greenhead. The surface on the composite stock provides a positive grip in cold and wet weather. The Greenhead protective applied over the finish results in the same deep green to purple sheen of a drake mallard's head feathers.

The Super X2 Universal Hunter 3 1/2-inch is intended for turkey hunters with its synthetic stock covered in Mossy Oak Break-Up camo. The gun has a 26-inch barrel with a selection of screw-in chokes including an Invector-Plus Extra Full choke tube. TRUGLO front and rear sights quickly detach from the gun's ventilated rib.

The Super X2 Cantilever Deer features a 22-inch fully rifled barrel to

Winchester Model 9410.

Weatherby SAS Shadow Grass.

Weatherby SAS Field.

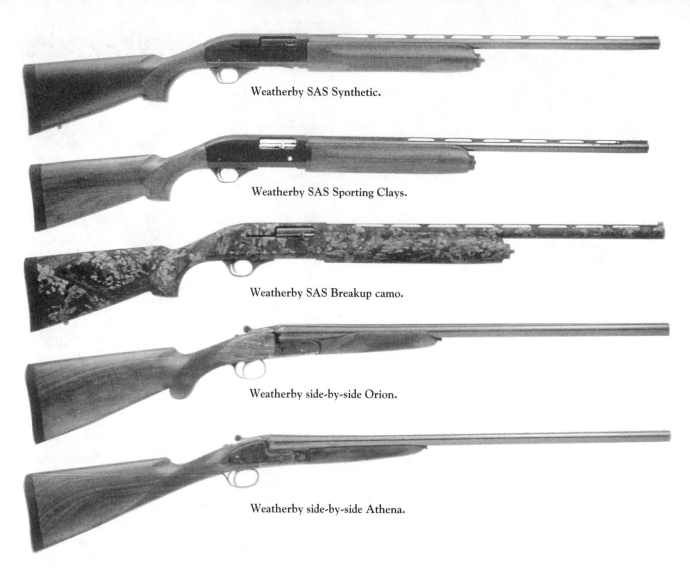

Weatherby SAS Synthetic.

Weatherby SAS Sporting Clays.

Weatherby SAS Breakup camo.

Weatherby side-by-side Orion.

Weatherby side-by-side Athena.

handle rifled slugs or sabot-encased bullets, like the Winchester Partition Gold. The cantilever mount, attached to the barrel, keeps sights aligned with the barrel. An adjustable rear sight on the cantilever aligns with the fiber-optic front sight. The rear sight folds down so a scope, or electronic sight like a Bushnell HOLO sight, can be mounted on the rail that extends over the top of the receiver.

The SX2 Practical Mk II is made for quickly blowing competition targets flat. The gun is built around a Super X2 three-inch 12-gauge action and a 22-inch barrel with a cantilever sight mount. A ghost ring rear sight quickly mounts and dismounts. An eight-round extended magazine makes sure bowling pins are quickly reduced to kindling.

The Winchester Model 1300 12-gauge Sporting/Field covers all the bases. The gun's features include a thick recoil pad, mid-bead and TRUGLO TRU-BEAD front sight with interchangeable fiber-optic inserts of different colors. Five Winchoke tubes screw into the 28-inch barrel. A compact version has a 24-inch barrel, a shorter stock with a 13-inch length of pull and a slimmer forearm.

The Model 1300 NWTF Buck and Tom is covered in Mossy Oak Break-Up camo. Its 22-inch barrel is threaded to accept both the Hi-Density Winchoke

Extra-Full Turkey tube and an extended Rifle choke tube that come with it. Adjustable TRUGLO fiber-optics sights put the shot or slug on target. The receiver is ready to accept scope bases to mount a scope or other optic sights. "Team NWTF" is printed on the side of the stock to let others know you support the good work of the National Wild Turkey Federation.

The Model 1300 NWTF Short Turkey is a similar gun with an 18-inch barrel that accepts furnished Extra-Long and Extra-Full Extended Turkey tubes.

The Model 1300 Coastal Marine has an aluminum receiver, a plated magazine tube and 18-inch barrel to weather salt water. The eight-shot magazine, Cylinder bore and TRUGLO front sight will provide all sorts of protection in coastal bear country and against sharks that want to eat your dingy. A pistol grip is also available.

Weatherby

Weatherby has two grades of shotguns based on its new side-by-side made in Spain. The Athena 12 and 20 gauge sports a Turkish walnut stock with a straight grip and splinter forearm checkered in 22 lines per inch. The boxlock action has a single trigger. Scroll and rose engraving decorates

the false sideplates. A variety of screw-in chokes are included for the 26- or 28-inch barrels. *"The response to this gun has been unbelievable,"* says Weatherby's Brad Ruddell. *"Everybody wants to get their hands on one."*

The Orion is a bit plainer gun, although still very attractive. The curved, half-round grip and semi-beavertail forearm fit the hands well. The Orion is chambered in 12, 20, 28 and .410–and 16 gauge through Weatherby's custom shop.

The Weatherby gas-operated Semi-Auto Shotguns (SAS) are made in Italy. Five styles include the Field with a 26- or 28-inch barrel and walnut stock, Sporting Clays with walnut stock and 28-inch barrel, and 26-inch barrel synthetic-stocked guns with either black, Shadow Grass or Break-Up camouflage.

All the models share common features. The trigger assembly drops out for cleaning and to provide access to the inside of the aluminum receiver. The gas system comes apart for cleaning and easily reassembles. A variety of Briley stainless steel screw-in chokes come with each gun. Four spacers allow changing stock cast and comb height. Everything stores in a hard plastic case.

by DOC CARLSON

BLACKPOWDER REVIEW

GIVEN THE CATASTROPHIC events of the past year, coupled with the "gloom and doom" concerning the economy, one would expect any recreational product category - such as blackpowder firearms and accessories - that depends on the so-called "extra" income would be in disarray. However, such is not the case. Not only is the blackpowder firearms industry in pretty good shape, it is offering a wide range of new products this year. Lines are expanding and becoming more sophisticated. The inline-action firearm is still the most popular style of gun, although the traditional-type arms are also in demand. New powders, projectiles and firearms make the coming year an interesting one for the muzzle-loading and blackpowder enthusiast.

Thompson/Center

Thompson/Center, a name well known to blackpowder shooters and hunters, is marketing a brand new rifle design, based upon an inline-type action with a center-hung hammer. Called the Omega 50, this rifle incorporates a unique swinging-block lever action. The closed-breech design utilizes a lever on the trigger guard which, when pushed forward, swings the breech block downward, exposing the breech end of the barrel and the recess for the #209 primer. When the #209 primer is in place, the lever is pulled to the rear, seating the breechblock tightly against the breech plug, with its installed primer. The fit is weather tight, giving an effective sealed breech system.

To fire the rifle, the hammer is merely cocked to the rear and the trigger pulled. The patented hammer and trigger mechanism permits the hammer to make contact with the primer only when the trigger is pulled fully to the rear. This virtually eliminates accidental firing by bumping the hammer. The entire action contains only four moving parts. The non-adjustable trigger is very light, with no creep, and a let-off of around 3 or 4 pounds.

The Omega 50 has the capability to handle three Pyrodex 50-grain pellets or a 150-grain load of loose blackpowder or Pyrodex. The 28-inch barrel burns these heavier charges efficiently, delivering higher velocities and flatter trajectories downrange. The barrel incorporates the T/C Quick Load Accurizer muzzle system. This system is essentially a deep countersink at the muzzle–an updated version of the old-time "coned muzzle" that facilitates loading of projectiles without the use of a short starter.

Sights are an adjustable rear with a ramp front, both of steel and both with Tru-Glo fiber-optic inserts. The Tru-Glo sights greatly improve sight pictures, especially in poor light or for "over-40" eyes. The top flat of the barrel is drilled and tapped for scope mounts, if you are so inclined. An aluminum ramrod hangs under the barrel. This solid metal rod accepts standard 10x32 accessories. There are 1 1/2 inches of serrations on the gripping end of the rod to improve gripping ability–another simple thing, but a great boon to the hunter with cold hands.

The Omega 50 is a snap to clean. The action lever is pushed ahead, dropping the block and revealing the breech plug. The breech plug is unscrewed, using a furnished special wrench, and the rifle can cleaned from the breech end with no further take down required. The stock doesn't need to be taken off, something that helps keep the point of impact the same from one shooting session to the next.

This new rifle is available in three stock types: Black composite, Realtree Hardwoods camo and gray laminated wood. Metal work can be had in either stainless steel or blued. The stocks feature a high comb for use with open sights or scope, a rubber recoil pad, pistol grip with cap and sling swivels.

The new Omega 50-caliber rifle, from Thompson/Center Arms.

The New England Firearms/Marlin Huntsman rifle.

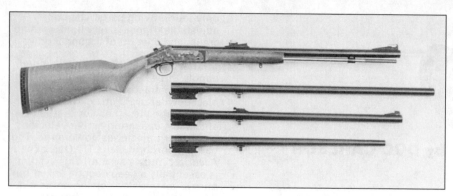

The basic Huntsman and various additional barrels are marketed as several different 'combo' offerings.

H&R 1871/New England Firearms

H&R 1871 and New England Firearms, both now under the Marlin Firearms Company banner, have announced a new muzzleloader based upon the venerable single-barrel, top-break design. Called the Huntsman, the gun can be had in several different calibers and combinations. The basic rifle is available in 45 and 50 caliber with a blued 24-inch barrel with adjustable fiber-optic Fire Sights and a unique, telescoping brass ramrod with a hardwood handle. The frame is color case-hardened and the hardwood stock has a walnut finish.

The gun is opened like a single-shot shotgun, exposing the breech plug and recess for a #209 primer. When the breech is closed, the primer is protected from weather and possible loss. To clean, the breech is opened, the breech plug removed with the provided wrench, and the barrel easily swabbed from the breech to the muzzle. The hammer fall is short to speed lock time, providing improved accuracy potential. The hammer/trigger uses a transfer bar system so the hammer cannot hit the firing pin unless the trigger is pulled fully to the rear; a good safety feature.

The gun is available in various barrel combinations. The Pardner is available with a 50-caliber barrel combined with a 12-gauge muzzleloading barrel with a Modified choke. The Tracker II combines the 50-caliber M/L barrel with a 12-gauge 24-inch rifled slug barrel. In the Handi-Rifle/Huntsman, the 24-inch 50-caliber muzzleloading barrel is paired with a 22-inch 243 Winchester centerfire cartridge barrel with a scope mount— and no iron sights. All these combinations make this a very versatile outfit for the hunter. I suspect this will be a popular addition to the hunters' arsenal.

H&R also has a couple of cartridge rifles of interest to the blackpowder *aficionado*. The same top-break action is barreled for a couple of cartridges from the past. The Buffalo Classic rifle features a checkered, straight-grip American walnut stock with a color case-hardened buttplate to match the case-hardened receiver. The blued 32-inch round barrel sports a Williams receiver aperture rear sight and a Lyman front with 8 inserts. The chambering is, of course, the 45/70 Government. The length of pull is 14 inches and the rifle weighs 8 pounds.

For those who prefer a lighter-recoiling rifle for target work, etc., the same rifle is chambered in the respected 38/55. Called the Target Model, this gun utilizes a shorter, 28-inch heavy target barrel with the same sighting system. It weighs 7 1/2 pounds. Both these rifles provide a reasonably priced alternative to those who like to shoot these old cartridges. Accuracy is pretty darn good, I'm told.

MDM Ltd.

Another rifle based on a top-break, single-barrel system is offered by MDM Ltd. They offer a wide range of stocks and finishes, plus - new this year - an interchangeable barrel system that covers a wide range of hunting situations. The new addition to the line comes from their custom shop and includes three barrels: Two rifle barrels in 50 caliber with a 1:24 inch twist and the other in 45 Nitro Magnum, with a 1:20 inch twist—along with a 12-gauge shotgun barrel. All barrels interchange on the same action and have their own ramrod.

Ramrods, made of space-age synthetics, are darn near indestructible and have a cleaning jag with concealed patch and bullet puller on one end, which will unscrew to accept other 8x32 accessories. The opposite end is threaded for 10x32 rod tools. Given the use of both thread sizes by makers of ramrod accessories, this is a welcome feature. Ignition is via #209 primers. Sights on the rifle barrels are a Williams fully-adjustable rear with a ghost-ring aperture, and ramp front with the Williams Fire Sight. The barrels are also drilled and tapped for scope installation. The shotgun barrel features a screw-in choke system, ivory bead front sight and is drilled and tapped for scope mounting.

The action of this firearm system, equipped with a transfer bar that prevents firing pin contact unless the trigger is pulled to the rear, can't be opened or closed with the center-hung hammer cocked unless the trigger is pulled to the rear. Another versatile reasonably priced firearms system for the hunter.

Split Fire Sporting Goods, LLC

Split Fire Sporting Goods, LLC, the outfit that markets the White Rifle line, has created a new bolt-action rifle called the Thunderbolt. The new rifle uses the White rifling system, combined with a 26-inch barrel, to effectively burn powder charges up to 150 grains. The bolt closes tightly against the #209 primer in the breech plug to provide better weather protection. The lock time is exceedingly fast, contributing to accuracy. Sights are adjustable rear and ramp front; both of steel and featuring Tru-Glo fiber-optic inserts. The action is also drilled and tapped for scope mounting, of course.

White rifles all use a wide recoil lug, welded close to the center axis of the bore, that transmits recoil evenly through the stock to reduce felt recoil and enhance accuracy. The action is held in the black laminate stock by two receiver screws. The trigger is fully adjustable and is factory-set at a crisp

MDM's multi-use offering, with interchangeable barrels in 45 and 50 caliber as well as 12 gauge.

Winchester's Model X-150 rifle.

4 pounds. The primary safety completely locks and blocks the trigger.

The new gun is available in 45 caliber with a 1:20-inch twist and 50 caliber with a 1:24-inch twist. Both calibers are matched to the White bullets for the White Shooting System but can be used with any of the projectiles on the market of appropriate caliber.

In addition to full charges of blackpowder, Pyrodex or Pyrodex pellets, the rifle will also handle recommended smokeless powder loads, due to the tight seal of the bolt face against the #209 primer and breech-plug face. Whatever your opinion about smokeless powder in muzzle-loading arms, it appears it is going to become a factor in muzzleloading. **Never use smokeless powder in a muzzle-loading firearm not specifically designed for it.**

Savage Arms

Speaking of smokeless powder in muzzleloaders, Savage Arms, who caused a considerable stir a year or so ago when they came out with the first muzzle-loading arm recommended for smokeless powder, has updated and improved their bolt-action "modern" gun. The original offering used a so-called "primer module" that held the #209 primer and fit tightly into a corresponding cavity in the breech plug. This module, which showed centerfire cartridge parentage, sealed the breech on firing and made the use of smokeless powder possible. Savage has eliminated the module and now ues the #209 primer alone to do this job. The face of the bolt forces the soft rim of the primer against the breech plug face, effectively sealing the system. The removable breech plug and vent liner are replaceable if burnout occurs after many shots. This new system remedies one of the complaints about the previous gun—the necessity of having extra primer modules on hand, because if the module was lost, the gun was inoperable. With this new system, the #209 primer is inserted into the bolt face recess and the bolt is closed. When the bolt is opened, the fired primer is extracted. Simple.

Called the Model 10ML II, the rifle is available in black synthetic, Realtree Hardwoods synthetic camo or brown-laminate wood stocks with recoil pad and sling swivel studs standard. The synthetic stocks have moulded-in checkering on the forend and pistol grip. The M-10ML can be had in either stainless steel or blued metal finish. The 24-inch heavy contour barrel uses a 1:24-inch twist and is topped with adjustable fiber-optic open sights. The receiver is drilled and tapped for scope mounting. The gun weighs a respectable 7 3/4 pounds.

Both this gun and its predecessor have shown very good accuracy and down-range energy with smokeless powder, as well as blackpowder and Pyrodex. Fouling is non-existent when using smokeless powder, eliminating the need to wipe between shots; cleaning is greatly simplified.

Winchester

There's a very familiar name appearing in the muzzle-loading market place this year. Winchester is the latest of the "Big Names" to arrive in blackpowder circles. Their offering is called the Model X-150, a bolt-action design built in the same factory as the Connecticut Valley Arms line of guns. The rifle action is stainless steel and the bolt removes without tools for easy takedown and cleaning. The metal can be had in either stainless steel or blued finish. Stocks are solid composite - not hollow - and are offered in black fleck (with stainless barrel), gray fleck (with blued barrel), High Definition Advantage Timber camo or High Definition Hardwoods finish. The stock has a hand-filling palm swell, beavertail forend and Monte Carlo butt with recoil pad.

Calibers are either 45 or 50 with a 1:28-inch twist. Sights are fully adjustable fiber optic, and the receiver is drilled and tapped for scope mounting. Ramrod is synthetic and equipped with standard jag and 10x32 thread for other accessories. The trigger is nonadjustable and factory-set at about 3 pounds. The gun handles and points well.

Knight Rifles

Knight Rifles brought out their disc rifle in 1997. The idea, that the plastic disc would hold a #209 primer and be squeezed between the breech plug and bolt face to seal the system against weather, worked well. The one drawback was that the discs were rather small and easily dropped - especially with cold hands. Knight has now updated this system.

The new plastic disc system is called a Full Plastic Jacket, and is larger than the old disc with a projection on the front end that fits over a nipple-like projection in the breech plug. As the bolt is closed on the Full Plastic Jacket, the breech is sealed against weather, even to the point of being able to immerse the breech in water with no leakage. The larger plastic jacket is easier to load, also. Just drop it in and close the bolt.

The Knight Disc Extreme, the rifle made to handle this new disc system, is a bolt action. It is available with a walnut, laminated wood or a thumbhole synthetic stock. It can be had with a 50-caliber barrel, either blued or stainless, or a 45-caliber fluted barrel in blue or stainless. Barrel length is 26 inches, allowing full burn of heavy charges. The twist is 1:30 inches for 45 caliber and 1:28 inches for the 50. Sights are fully adjustable steel with Tru-Glo inserts. The trigger is also fully adjustable for creep and weight of pull. Truly a hunter's rifle.

Connecticut Valley Arms

In the more traditional type of rifle, Connecticut Valley Arms offers a wide range of all types of rifle, but the star of the line is, in my opinion, the Mountain

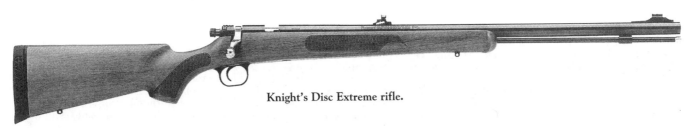

Knight's Disc Extreme rifle.

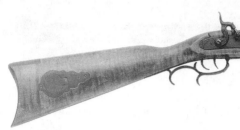

CVA's Mountain Rifle returns in two versions, the Classic (*shown*) and the less expensive Mountain Hunter.

Rifle. Referred to as the Mountain Rifle Classic, this nice reproduction gun is offered in 50 caliber with a 1:66-inch twist for patched round ball. The percussion lock is the old Maslin style. All hardware is browned steel except for the barrel key escutcheons, which are German silver. The barrel is held in the nicely figured American hard maple half-stock by two keys. The 32-inch barrel is octagonal, fitted with silver blade front and adjustable rear sight with an old-time look. The ramrod is hickory with brass ends, tapped 10x32. A browned steel cap box adorns the buttstock.

The Classic Mountain Rifle was actually put back in the line after a hiatus of several years. It has been upgraded a bit this year with better wood. This is a nice-looking rifle that shoots very well. Traditional shooters will be happy with this one.

A more economical version of the Classic Mountain Rifle is also offered. Called the Mountain Hunter Rifle, this is basically the same gun as the Mountain Rifle except with a blued barrel and hardware. The 50-caliber barrel utilizes a 1:48-inch twist for use with either conical projectiles or patched round ball. The stock is UltraGrain Finish hardwood. This is a "skin" finish over the hardwood that looks more like a highly-figured expensive wood stock than the actual thing - this finish is truly unbelievable. It successfully mimics a burl walnut stock of the highest quality. This reasonably priced rifle looks and handles well. It will do very well with the hunter, shooter or re-enactor looking for a good-looking, lower-priced rifle.

Austin & Halleck

Austin & Halleck has long been known for top-drawer inline muzzle-loading firearms. Their high-grade wood stocks and highly polished blued metal have led many to call them the Weatherby of muzzleloaders. This well-known company has now added a traditional rifle to their line.

The Austin & Halleck Mountain Rifle is a half-stock rifle with lines reminiscent of southern mountain rifles. The steel buttplate and trigger guard are similar to those found on the famous Hawken rifles. They are stocked in curly maple with an oil-type finish. Metal work and barrels are rust browned. The 1-inch octagon barrel is 32 inches long, 50 caliber, in a 1:66-inch twist for round ball or a 1:48-inch twist for both round ball and conical projectiles. Barrels are held to the half-stock by one barrel key with German silver escutcheons. Locks are well designed and reliable in both flint and percussion. A nicely shaped set of double-set triggers completes the firing mechanism.

The Mountain Rifle can be had in three forms: The Percussion Standard with nice wood, fixed-rear buckhorn sight and silver-blade front, the Flintlock or the Percussion Select. The Select grade includes a higher grade of wood, adjustable rear buckhorn sight and silver blade front. All three are fine-looking guns equally at home in a primitive re-enactors' camp, the hunting field or shooting range.

Traditions, Inc.

Traditions, Inc. now has a flintlock rifle set up to shoot the Pyrodex pellets. In this they join Thompson/Center in providing the only two rifles of flintlock persuasion that will handle these handy-loading charges. The gun is a half-stock design with either hardwood, synthetic black or synthetic Mossy Oak Break Up camo stocks. A non-slip recoil pad and sling swivels are standard. The 26-inch barrel is bored 50 caliber with a 1:48-inch twist for the use of round ball or conical projectiles. Barrels, available blued or nickel-plated, are topped by a Tru-Glo fiber-optic adjustable sight system.

Ignition is via a "Super Flint" lock that has a large frizzen combined with a deeper-than-normal pan for sure, quick ignition when using Pyrodex pellets. A single, crisp hunting trigger fires the gun. The rifle is also available in a left-hand version with wood stock only.

Takedown and cleaning is very simple. The single barrel key is driven out, the barrel pulled forward out of the stock and the breech plug removed, using the wrench supplied with the gun. The barrel can then be cleaned from the breech, as with inline guns. The solid-aluminum ramrod, tapped on both ends, is supplied with a cleaning/loading jag of brass.

Those shooters and hunters who shoot flintlocks, either because of hunting regulations or preference, now have another flint rifle that will handle the easily acquired Pyrodex pellets, or loose powder.

Dixie Gun Works

For those who enjoy replica firearms, I think the ultimate replica may be on the way. Dixie Gun Works is going to have a replica of the Colt Revolving Percussion Musket of the Civil War era. It appears it will be available as the two-band, rifled musket model–probably in 44 caliber–with a steel ramrod and sling swivels. This is something I would enjoy shooting. Originals are too rare and valuable to shoot but this new replica will give those of us with an itch to try this venerable rifle a chance to scratch.

Dixie also has a couple of knives that will interest the re-enactors.

The first is a wood-handled, utility-type knife made of old circular saw blades. These knives are of a shape that would look right with any era outfit—from first settlement of the Eastern Seaboard right through the cowboy era—even as a modern hunting knife. The 6-inch blade is well-shaped and the handle fits the hand. Good knife design never goes out of date. These knives are supplied without a sheath.

The other knife is a replica of the Rio Grande Camp Knife popular during the Civil War era. John Wilkes Booth carried one of these when he shot President Lincoln. After leaping down onto the stage, he brandished it over his head, shouting, "*Sic Semper Tyrannus.*" The original knives were made in Sheffield, England; the repro is U.S.-made. The massive spear-point blade is 1 1/2 inches wide and 10 inches long. The bone handle has a tapered tang. A sheath of top-grain leather is available for this one.

Back when I used to backpack, I carried a similar knife lashed to my pack frame. It did good duty around camp, filling the role of machete, hatchet, bacon slicer and spatula. This one should be popular with Civil War re-enactors and cowboy action shooters.

Taylor, Inc.

Last year I had a chance to look at the prototype of Taylor, Inc.'s reproduction of the Civil War Spencer Repeating Rifle: "That damn Yankee rifle that you load on Sunday and shoot all week!" The gun is now in production and in stock.

The Taylor Spencer is the 1865 Carbine model, the successor to the original 1860 model. The 1865 incorporated modifications to correct some inherent flaws in the original design. The result is a very high-quality reproduction that will proudly take its place among the favorite arms of Civil War re-enactors and Cowboy Action Shooters.

The Spencer is offered in centerfire only, a departure from the original. Reloadable cartridges are definitely required in today's world. Chamberings are the original 56/50 (*in centerfire, not rimfire*), 44 Russian and 45 Schofield. The little carbine loads through the buttplate, as the originals did, and the

Blakeslee six-tube cartridge box is available as an accessory. Taylor's authentic Blakeslee Box is a leather cartridge carrier with a wood insert that holds six cartridge-filled tubes for quick reloading of the Spencer tubular magazine. The Spencer features walnut stocks, blued 20-inch barrel, and casehardened frame. The overall length is 37 inches. It carries sling swivels, as did the originals. This gun is a meticulously made copy of the original and joins Taylor's fine line of reproduction firearms.

Green Mountain Rifle Barrels

Green Mountain rifle barrels are well known in muzzle-loading circles as match winners. They have long been a top choice among rifle builders, available in straight octagon only. This has changed. Green Mountain is now making muzzle-loading barrels in a variety of calibers–in both tapered and swamped profiles. This is good news to rifle builders. They are also making tapered octagon barrels for black-powder cartridge firearms, both single-shot and repeating types. The single-shot patterns have breech ends sized for the various actions: Sharps, Remington Rolling Block–or whatever. These barrels are available in various calibers from 22 through 50, with the correct twists for blackpowder cartridge shooting. Tapered octagon barrels for various lever actions are available in calibers from 22 to 45, with correspondingly correct twists.

These barrels are in addition to their regular line of drop-in barrels for many of the commercially available muzzle-loading rifles out there. They will, of course, continue to offer straight octagon and round barrels for both blackpowder cartridge and muzzle-loading shooters.

Hodgdon Powder Company

Hodgdon Powder Company, who brought the first replica blackpowder - Pyrodex - to muzzle-loading shooters, has done it again. They have a new blackpowder substitute called 777 (*Triple Seven*) that can be shipped as smokeless powder, as is Pyrodex. This makes it available in areas where blackpowder is difficult to get.

Pyrodex is known for having less fouling than regular blackpowder, something many appreciate. It does, however, foul just enough to make a second or third shot hard to load, when using sabotted bullets or conical slugs. The new powder addresses this problem, leaving little or no fouling. It gives pressures in the blackpowder range when loaded volume-for-volume with black or Pyrodex. After shooting, cleanup is accomplished with plain water - no solvents needed. Because it contains no sulfur, there is no "sewer gas" smell associated with cleaning, something many will appreciate since it may eliminate some of the odd looks that blackpowder shooters often get because of the 'aroma' that surrounds them.

The new powder gives somewhat-higher velocities than either blackpowder or Pyrodex, with similar loadings. Velocity variations, shot-to-shot, are minimal—something conducive to accuracy.

The greatest selling point of this new powder, however, will be the lack of fouling… which contributes to ease of loading repeat shots with sabots and such. I loaded 22 consecutive shots through a popular inline model, using the new powder and sabotted bullets–with no wiping between shots. The last shot loaded nearly as easily as the first. There was a slight fouling buildup in the first half-inch or so of the muzzle but nothing that required use of a short starter—all loading was done with ramrod alone. This eliminates one of my major complaints about the use of sabots and conical bullets–the difficulty of loading down a fouled bore.

The new powder, priced roughly the same as Pyrodex Select, is now in production and should be on dealers' shelves. The 777 name came about because, I'm told, this was the 777th formula tried in the search for the qualities Hodgdon wanted in a blackpowder substitute. It's not available in pellet form yet, although Hodgdon is working on it. It looks like the Hodgdon folks have another winner. •

Hodgdon's new 777 – all the benefits of Pyrodex, plus greatly reduced fouling.

by BOB BELL

SCOPES AND MOUNTS

AFTER SPENDING MOST of a long life shooting, hunting and reading about such things, it's inevitable that certain statements from long ago stick in my mind. One of these dates back to the mid-'30s when some gun writer, whose name I've long forgotten, said that when anyone looked into the rear end of a scope, he didn't look out the front end. This was a striking statement to a 10-year-old who at that time had never even seen a scope, but it never occurred to me to question anything that a well-known authority wrote in a national magazine.

As I became older, I occasionally thought about that statement, though, and I didn't agree with it. As a comment intended to startle the reader a bit–and thus grab his attention–it was good, but truth is, a shooter doesn't look into the rear end of a scope in the first place. He just raises his rifle to interpose the scope between his eye and whatever is beyond, and the incoming light rays–from either an incandescent source or reflected off whatever is out there–pass through the scope. Their paths are altered by the lenses and enter through the pupil of the user's eye. They excite nerve endings on the retina, and impulses are transmitted through the optic nerve to the brain, which somehow—nobody really knows how—creates images that let us say we are "seeing."

The interesting thing is that we don't see anything out yonder where it actually is, but only images within our brains. So to repeat—the light comes into us, we don't "see out" to the object. And since it takes time for the incoming light to travel from any object (*even at a speed of 186,000+ miles per second, which ain't too lackadaisical!*), anything we see is actually a representation of how an object looked some time in the past, not very long before, but nevertheless in the past. In other words, we have only an idea of how it used to be, and can never be absolutely certain that's how it is *right now*.

I kinda recall reading about some old Irish priest who decided that since we never have more than an idea of what's out there anyway, we should dispense with the common sense belief in a material reality and face up to his conclusion that the universe (*which includes you and me and everything else!*) is only a figment of God's imagination.

I'm not positive I remember that story correctly, and don't really agree with it anyway, but it does show how some people think about the vagaries of light. And since light is what makes scopes work and this article is about scopes, maybe there's a connection. And if some *GUN DIGEST* readers have never heard about such an old theory as this, maybe they've never even heard some of the basic facts about scopes, which make them the most popular additions to new rifles. That's not to say that a shooter needs to know the inner workings of his scope in order to use it. Nobody has to be a mechanic to drive a car either, but situations are always arising when it's better to know something than not to know.

To begin with, a scope is simply a metal tube containing a series of lenses and an aiming point (reticle). The reticle can be adjusted so the shooter can get his line of sight close to the bullet's path. (*It isn't practical to change the bullet's path to align with the reticle.*) An instant after the bullet leaves the gun muzzle it becomes subject to gravity and starts to fall, so it's necessary to tilt the bore slightly upward to overcome gravity's downward acceleration and extend the distance where line of sight and the bullet's path are close enough together to hit a target. The line of sight is straight but the bullet's path is curved, so there are two points where they will intersect. With most modern cartridges, having the scope mounted 1 1/2 inches above the bore's centerline, as is normal, if zeroed at 25 yards, bullet impact will be a couple of inches high

at 100. This should be fine-tuned by actual firing, but once known, it will often prove convenient, for at most outfitters' camps 97 bush plane miles from nowhere, it's usually much easier to find a place to check your zero at 25 yards than 100.

Scopes provide a brighter image than the unaided eye because they "gather" light. Some people ask how this can be done, but it's simple. The objective lens is invariably larger in diameter than the eye's pupil, and incoming light strikes its entire surface. As it progresses through the various lenses, all of this light is compressed into what is called the **exit pupil**, which is the beam of light that enters the eye. The diameter of the exit pupil is equal to the scope's objective lens diameter in millimeters divided by its magnification. A 4x28mm scope, for instance, has a 7mm exit pupil, which equals the maximum diameter of the eye pupil even under dark conditions. This means that all of the light that struck the 28mm scope lens now enters the eye. Even if the scope's light transmission rating is only 85 percent, say, that's still far greater than would enter an unaided eye.

Also, since lenses are installed at certain distances from one another, they produce a magnified image, which is the main reason most hunters use a scope, so shooters commonly think of lenses as the most important parts of a riflescope. Actually, each part is indispensable, but scopes wouldn't exist without lenses, so a brief look at them might be worthwhile.

The front lens is called the **objective** (*because it's the one nearest the object being viewed*). The rearmost lens is the **ocular** or eyepiece (it's nearest the eye), and the ratio between the focal lengths of these two largely determines the magnification of the scope, though other lenses can have some effect.

Erector, **collector** and **field** lenses are precisely positioned between the objective and ocular. All are commonly referred to as single lenses—the objective, for instance—but many are actually doublets or triplets—units consisting of two or three individual lenses of various shapes. So riflescopes have upwards of a dozen individual lenses in total.

Most riflescope lenses are "positive"—that is, they cause the light rays to converge rather than scatter, as a "negative" lens would do. Their surfaces are ground and polished to incredible accuracy, less than 1/100,000 of an inch in the better makes. The ingredients 'recipe' of the glass from which they're made are accurate to at least three decimal places. Because their surfaces are normally compound curves, each lens refracts light at a slightly different angle, which results in a tiny aberration because the rays do not focus on exactly the same plane. This is one reason several lenses are combined to form, for example, the objective unit; each succeeding lens corrects some of the aberrations of the preceding one. It introduces its own aberrations, of course, but the final product is a high-grade image.

The objective unit produces a target image in the first focal plane. But because of the way that lens refracts the light rays, this image is upside down and reversed left to right. This has no importance in an astronomical telescope (*there's really no "up" or "down" when looking at a star*), but it would be extremely annoying to a hunter if the deer he was aiming at seemed to be reversed. So after the light rays continue on through the first focal plane, they pass through a set of erector lenses. These reverse the already-reversed image and focus it on the second focal plane, where it now appears normal to the user.

The two focal planes, plus the *immediately* adjacent areas, are the only places within a scope that anything can be seen. Therefore, the reticle must be placed precisely in one of them. (*It's a good idea for the shooter to be able to see the reticle!*) If the reticle is slightly ahead of or behind the focal plane, and the position of the aiming eye varies a trifle from shot to shot, the reticle is seen at a slightly different angle to the focal plane and seems to jump. This movement is called **parallax**, and causes a tiny displacement of the bullet's point of impact. In low magnification hunting scopes this is an insignificant amount, so they are made without a method of focusing for different ranges. Such scopes often are said to have universal focus. This isn't true, but it's close enough for all practical purposes.

Shooters who use high-power 'scopes in competitive rifle matches, or for small varmints at long distances, insist on eliminating all error possible, so focus precisely for range. This means they get the target image and reticle in exactly the same plane. This is done by screwing the objective unit in or out, or by moving the erector system via a mechanism that's integral with the w. and e. adjustment turret. Now, no parallax can occur no matter how the eye is moved.

Which focal plane is used for the reticle also is important in variable power scopes. If the reticle is placed in the front plane—the position that's always been popular in Europe—it subtends the same amount of the target, regardless of magnification. Shifting the positions of the erector lenses makes any magnification power change. Since the erectors are located behind the front focal plane, the reticle is magnified right along with the target. As scope power goes up, both target and reticle are enlarged. Or as power goes down, both get smaller.

Most Americans don't like the heavy look of the reticle at high power. Even though it doesn't subtend any more of the target than at low power, it's annoyingly conspicuous. So in this country most scopemakers install the reticle in the second focal plane. Now the erectors are in front of the reticle, so any magnification change that is made by shifting them affects only the target image, not the reticle image. So when the target is enlarged and the reticle is not, the reticle seems to get smaller because it subtends less of the target. Therefore a variable-power scope is adaptable for big game at the lower powers and for varmints at top power.

Well, space is limited, so we'd better knock off for now. Should tell you that info from Leica indicates they have discontinued the manufacture of riflescopes. Too bad, for Leica has long been—and still is, as far as binoculars, spotting scopes, and other optical items go—one of the world's top manufacturers.

Here, in random order, is the dope on this year's new scopes:

Bushnell

Bushnell's Elite 4200 and 3200 lines now feature hammer-forged titanium-reinforced tubes that are half again as strong as previous models. New 4200s are a 4-16x40 AO at less than 16 in. and 22 oz., and a 2.5-10x50 with red dot reticle at 13 1/2 in. and 16 oz. The former has eighth-minute clicks; the latter, quarter-minute. New 3200s are a 3-9x40, 3-9x50, and 10x40 Mil Dot. All have fast-focus eyepieces.

All Elite scopes have RainGuard coating on objective and eyepiece external lenses, to maintain optical efficiency in the rain, snow or cold that's common to big-game seasons... and to help stupid hunters like me who occasionally breathe on scope lenses. They are also recoil-tested to the equivalent of 1,000 375 H&H shots, which is more punishment than most of us will subject them to... or even want to think about.

For high-velocity airgun shooters, whose number seems to grow constantly, Bushnell now makes a 3-9x32 Sportsman Airgun Scope. It has a 50-ft. parallax adjustment, coated optics, 1/4-moa adjustments, and 3 inches of eye relief. And it's built to take the double-shuffle effect of airguns.

There are a couple of new Trophy scopes too, a 3-9x40 Tactical model with mil-dot reticle and a 1x28 Red Dot scope with four dial-in interchangeable reticles. At 9x the centers of the dots are 3.6 minutes apart, and so can be used as a rangefinder.

Bushnell has been making a variety of small, lightweight laser rangefinders for some years now, and they're highly popular with riflemen as different as Pennsylvania 'chuck shooters and professional hunters in Africa. A recent upgraded model is the Yardage Pro Legend. It's 100-percent waterproof, which can be a definite plus on some hunts. It's small enough to fit into a jacket pocket, weighs only 7 oz. and has a 6x eyepiece.

This 3-9x40 Bushnell is in their Elite 3200 series.

Bushnell's Yardage Pro Legend laser rangefinder is waterproof, can be used with one hand.

This 2.5-10x40 Bushnell is a perfect match for stainless rifles.

Nikon

Nikon has a number of new items this year, including a 3.3-10x44 AO for their Monarch line. This good-size objective provides greater light gathering ability than their standard 40mm, yet permits the use of medium rings to keep the scope mounted low, as it should be.

Other new Monarchs are the 6.5-20x44 with 1/8-min. clicks and a 3.5-10x50 with Nikoplex or Mil-Dot reticle. These can be used black, or illuminated red or green, to give the best contrast with given backgrounds. Then there's a 6x42 Monarch, for the long-range deer or pronghorn hunter who wants the simplicity of a straight-power scope. This one obviously delivers a 7mm exit pupil and therefore all the light that the eye can take in, no matter how dark it is. It's only 12 inches long and weighs an ounce per inch.

For the cops or military use, Tactical 2.5-10x44 and 4-16x50 models built on 30mm tubes with side-focus parallax adjustments are offered this year, and for handgun hunters there's a 2.5-8x28 built to take the recoil of today's powerful pistols.

All these new Nikons have Ultra Clear coating, for light transmission in the 95 percent range, which wasn't even dreamed of a few years ago.

Bushnell's Elite 4200 4-16x40 has a strong titanium-reinforced tube and 1/8-moa clicks.

Straight power 6x42 Nikon Monarch makes fine long-range scope for Western deer and pronghorn hunters.

The 6.5-20x44 AO Monarch from Nikon has 1/8-moa clicks for precise long-range shooting.

The 2.5-8x28 is a sturdy offering from Nikon for magnum handguns.

Nikon's 3.3-10x has a 44mm objective for good light transmission but still doesn't require high mounting rings.

Swarovski Optic

Swarovski Optic has been making top-grade scopes in several lines for many years, the Habicht AV (American variables) having features especially liked on this side of the Atlantic, 1-inch mounting tube diameter, reticle in second focal plane, etc. They're still available, of course, as are models with European characteristics.

New this year are two "Dangerous Game" scopes, 1.25-4x24 and 1.5-6x42. Scopes of these sizes can be mounted low on the rifle, which permits solid cheeking of the stock when aiming, as experienced hunters prefer. The objective bell, 30mm middle mounting tube, turret housing and ocular bell connection are all machined out of one solid piece of bar stock, either steel or hardened aluminum. Light transmission is high, and there's a choice of illuminated reticles for a dim-light opportunity on a half-visible bait-chomping leopard on the last evening of an expensive hunt, say. The internal optical system uses a 4-point coil spring suspension to ensure the accuracy of reticle adjustments, with one click in the 1.24-4x being valued at 1/2 moa and in the 1.5-6x at 1/3 minute.

Daniel Swarovski, who patented a precision grinder for precious stones, founded this company in 1892. In 1935 his eldest son William developed the prototype of a binocular, which was the beginning of the firm's award-winning optics department. Since Daniel and William, two more generations of Swarovskis have come along and are deeply involved in the company. Swarovski now makes binoculars, observation and spotting scopes, and accessories for these units, as well as riflescopes.

Leupold

Leupold had almost fifty scopes listed in last year's GD, and that should be enough for anyone to find something to suit him. But if it wasn't, this year they've added four lines; the Competition series, the VX-1 and VX-2 lines, and the Mark 4 CQ/T (Close Quarter/Tactical). Admittedly, the M4 CQ/T is but a single tactical scope for the AR-15 and M-16, so is intended

Swarovski's new 1.5-6x42 and 1.25-4x24 are called "Dangerous Game" scopes, because that's what they're intended for.

primarily for military and police use. A 1-3x14 with Illuminated Circle Dot reticle, it's designed for rapid use on multiple targets at close range.

Of more interest to civilian riflemen are the Competition models, made in 35x, 40x, and 45x, all with 45mm objectives. These scopes were created in response to what competitive riflemen—benchresters and target shooters—told Leupold they wanted. In other words, Leupold surveyed many of them and considered their wants and needs before building these scopes, not waiting for their comments and criticisms after scopes were in production.

The Competitions all have 1/8-moa clicks, with an ocular adjustment range of -2.0 to +1.0. A 30mm main tube gives room for at least 38 moa of w. and e. adjustment travel. Reticle is either fine CH or 1/8-minute dot, and there's 3.2 inches of eye relief. Instead of focusing for different ranges by screwing the objective in or out, there is a capped dial on the left side of the adjustment turret, so the shooter can make changes without getting out of position. These scopes are 15.9 inches long and weigh 21.5 oz.

Early Competition scopes were used by Jim Carmichel, Tony Boyer and Dwight Scott in last year's National Benchrest Rifle Championships. Collectively, they took eight 1st places, one 2nd, one 4th, and one 5th. How'd you like to shoot against that trio?

Leupold's Competition scopes are made in 35x, 40x, and 45x—all with 45mm objectives and 1/8-moa clicks.

Leupold's VX-2 line is an update of the Vari-X II series; this one's a 3-9x50.

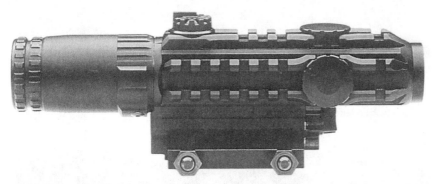

Here's Leupold's Mark 4 CO/T, a 1-3x14 for close combat use.

Leupold's VX-1 series, like this 3-9x40, has friction adjustments.

Anyway, now you can have one of these Competitions too. Remember, though, a 45x scope having a 45mm objective has only a 1mm exit pupil, so on a dim day there won't be a lot of light transmitted to the eye. A large target image makes up for some loss of light, but there comes a point when high magnification means you get only a large dull target.

Leupold's VX lines offer solid quality for those who don't want to pay for Vari-X IIIs. The VX-1 scopes have Duplex reticles, non-click adjustments, magnesium fluoride coating, and are made in 2-7x33 (*my choice for all-around big-game hunting*), 3-9x40 (*the choice of most hunters*), and 4-12x40, a reasonable choice for routine big game and varmint hunting.

The VX-2 line is sort of an update of the long-popular Vari-X II series. There's a 1-4x20, 2-7x33, 3-9x40, 3-9x50, 4-12x40 and 6-18x40, the last two with adjustable objectives. The VX-2s have quarter-minute clicks, a choice of seven reticles, and Multicoat 4 coating on external lenses. Like all Leupolds, the VXs are waterproof.

BSA Optics

BSA Optics introduced its Catseye scopes some time back, for hunters who get out before first light and stay until quitting time, even if the weather is dark and nasty. Now they've added the Big Cat series, with longer eye relief and more layers of lens coating—fourteen!

Big Cat scopes are not really big. Lengths range from less than ten inches for the 2-7x42 to less than thirteen for the adjustable objective 4.5-14x52. A 3.5-10x42 is also offered, along with three 30mm models in 1.5-4.5x42, 3.5-10x42 and 3-9x42. All have 5-inch eye relief. This is helpful on hard-recoiling rifles, but some mounts don't permit taking advantage of it, so give thought to your mounting system.

Simmons

Simmons has expanded their Prohunter SE line extensively with eight new models, one straight-power 4x32 and seven variables, the 2-7x32, 3-9x40, 4-12x40, 4-12/50, 6-18x40, 6-18x50 and 3.5-10x50. The last five all have adjustable objectives. The entire line has one-piece body tube construction and black matte finish, with quarter-minute clicks. All are waterproof, fogproof and shockproof, of course.

T. K. Lee

T. K. Lee, nicknamed "Tackhole" because of the tiny groups he shot in competition, was the originator of the famous Floating Dot reticle back in the mid-'30s. His successor, Dan Glenn, retired years ago and dots are now installed by Mike O'Donnell. Mike can put them in most scopes, any size or spacing you want, and he can install multiple dots to coincide with the bullet drop of your favorite load, if you tell him the points of impact at various ranges. Or he can install dots of a consistent spacing (*like a mil-dot*) as Lee did generations ago.

Multiple dots obviously have advantages for precisely aimed shots at long-distance targets, but for routine hunting at normal ranges nothing is simpler or more natural to use than a single Floating Dot. It just seems the most normal thing in the world to paste it on a critter and squeeze. I've been doing that with Lee dots in a number of scopes since just after World War II.

Don't get a dot too small, though, for big game if you like it to subtend 4 minutes of angle in a 4x scope. That size won't cover a deer's shoulders even at 400 yards, but can be seen well in the woods. Higher magnification scopes can use smaller dots, and lower powers larger ones, say 1-minute in 10x or 12x varmint scopes or 6 minutes in 2 1/2x models. Benchresters using extremely high powers can use quarter- or even 1/8-minute dots.

Competitive shooters often find dots give less eyestrain than crosswires, when used for long periods.

Kahles

Kahles is one of the oldest optical companies in the world, dating from 1898, which is more than a century. I haven't been using their scopes quite that long, but for several decades one of my favorite woods outfits has been a Mannlicher-stocked 9x57 Mauser topped with an older Kahles, featuring a European-style 3-post reticle. I've had great results with it in brushy deer country, and I'm glad I've got it, for I don't think they're making this model anymore.

But Kahles, which is based in Vienna and is now in the Swarovski Group, does make many 1-inch scopes, and they have a new line on hardened aluminum 30mm tubes—1.1-4x24, 1.5-6x42, 2.5-10x50 and 3-12x56. Obviously these cover all the needs of the big-game hunter and most of the varminter's.

Also new in the American Hunter series is a 2-7x36 built on a 1-inch main tube for top-quality 22 rimfires. They'd better be top quality, for this scope costs over five hundred bucks! That does include a set of Talley mount rings and a brick of Winchester Super-X ammo, though. Also, there's a 3.5-10x50 for hunters whose shots tend to be long ones, and a 3-9x42 intended for in-line muzzleloaders. This 3-9x features one of T.D. Smith's special reticles having horizontal bars to indicate impacts at 125, 150, 175 and 200 yards, when zeroed at 100.

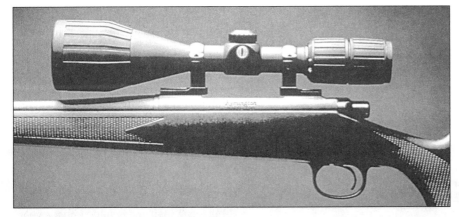

Big Cat scope from BSA has 14 coating layers.

These four new scopes from Kahles are built on 30mm mounting tubes.

Schmidt & Bender's hunting scope.

The Police/Marksman II, from Schmidt & Bender

Redfield

Redfield's well-known Illuminator line is now offered in 6.5-20x with a 50mm objective. It's made with a choice of three finishes—silver, black matte or gloss—and has 1/8-moa clicks. Also new is their ESD (Electronic Sighting Device), with a variable reticle pattern or Vari-dot (4, 8, 12 and 16 moa). It's intended for handgun action shooters, of course, and there are new twin-dovetail bases and rings for solid mounting on even magnum-caliber handguns.

Schmidt & Bender

Schmidt & Bender is a small company compared to some scopemakers—about 60 employees— and less than a half-century old, and they began their operation in a converted stable. Bit it's safe to say they've had a big impact on the field, for everyone I know who's used an S&B scope ranks it with the best. In fact, other companies around the world contract with Schmidt & Bender for precision optical components.

So they don't feel it's necessary to bring out new models every year when their line already covers any hunter's needs, as well as those of SWAT teams or military snipers. Straight powers from 4x to 10x are offered, as well as variables from 1.25-4x20 (*a particular favorite of mine*) to 4-16x50, and of course there are numerous reticle designs. One of these is the P-1 designed by SWAT team member Robert Bryant; it has numerous features of known subtension to allow quick range estimation.

Schmidt & Bender is located in Biebertall, Germany, and does not have a U. S. distributor as this report is written.

Warne

Warne's Maxima series sintered-steel mount line, introduced last year, has been expanded to fit rifles having mount bases integral with the actions, such as Ruger, Sako, Tikka and Brno/CZ. Such a mount/receiver interface eliminates the weakest feature in installing a scope—having to rely on a few small screws to resist the shearing effect of heavy recoil—especially with one of today's heavy glass sights. These mounts are made in two diameters, 1-inch and 30mm, and two styles, either a return-to-zero, lever-activated, quick-detachable design or permanently attached. Both are made in three heights and three finishes.

And new this year is the 7.3 series of rings to fit Warne's Premier and Weaver-style bases. By removing the detachable recoil key, which engages the base's cross-slot, the 7.3s also fit grooved-receiver 22 rifles.

Weaver

Weaver scopes are so numerous and varied, ranging in size from current iterations of the early K2.5 and K4 up to the 36x T-model for benchresters, that it's hard to squeeze in a new one. So they didn't even attempt to, this year. But they are now offering the high-magnification Grand Slam models with black-accented silver finish to better match the stainless barrels of benchrest and varmint shooters.

Weaver also has new pistol scope bases for numerous handguns. A steel yoke design allows easy installation without drilling or tapping, and there's a lug to absorb recoil. Bases accept either 1-inch or 30mm Weaver or Redfield/Weaver style rings.

This is probably as good a place as any to mention that Blount International, who has been supplying Weaver and other make scopes for years, has sold their Sporting Equipment Group to Alliant Techsystems, located in Lewiston, ID.

Shepherd

Shepherd's 6-18x40 Varmint/Target scope was mentioned here last year, but since then we've had almost a year

Riflemen who have high-grade 22 rimfires should like this Kahles 22 RF 2-7x36.

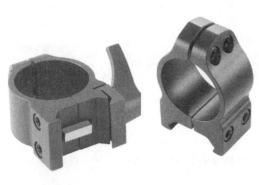

Warne Maxima mounts are now made for actions having integral bases, such as Ruger and Sako. The new 7.3 rings are easily adapted to grooved-receiver 22s.

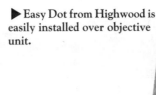

▶ Easy Dot from Highwood is easily installed over objective unit.

Highwood Special Products

Highwood Special Products (1531 E. Highwood, Pontiac, MI 48340) is the American supplier for an interesting European gizmo that will aid aiming with many scopes. Called the Easy Dot, this unit slips onto the objective unit of any scope whose outside diameter there is a half millimeter of 45, 48, 54, 57, or 61.5mm. It provides a bright red dot at the reticle intersection, adjustable to ten levels of intensity, for aiming in bad light. It does not shorten eye relief or affect focus adjustment.

Swift

Swift has four new scopes this year, the 680M series which includes a 3-9x40, 1.5-6x40, 4-12x50, and 2-7x32. The last is designed for modern airgun use, the other three for centerfires. All are waterproof and fully coated, and all have Swift's Speed Focus feature. The centerfire scopes have variable-intensity illuminated reticles, and a CR-2032 lithium battery is included.

Nightforce

Nightforce scopes, noted for their optical and mechanical excellence, are now made in their Precision Benchrest and NXS (Extreme Performance) series. All have 30mm tubes.

The PBs come in 8-32x56 and 12-42x56, with adjustable objectives, 1/8-minute clicks, and 3-inch eye relief. The NXS models are made in 3.5-15x with 50mm or 56mm objectives, 5.5-22x56, 8-32x56 and 12-42x56. They have 4-inch eye relief, 1/4-moa clicks, and a side dial to remove parallax.

Nightforce scopes have a choice of eight illuminated reticles, from a fine crosshair to a complex unit with ranging scale for deliberate long-range aiming. New is a modified mil-dot. It's of conventional layout, with the centers of adjacent dots on the vertical and horizontal lines separated by 1 mil (3.6 in. at 100 yards); but instead of solid dots, the Nightforce design has open, see-through circles with a tiny dot centered in each. Posts are also just outlines, so the target is not obstructed in any significant way.

to shoot it on a Hart-barreled 22-250. Quite a rig. This scope's reticle has aiming circles of decreasing size, each enclosing 18 inches at succeeding 100-yd. intervals to 1000. I almost never shoot beyond 400—maybe 500—yards, and I still have misses out yonder. But none that I can blame on the scope or rifle or load. Wind still makes most of my problems.

Shepherd also now offers rifle rests, binoculars, spotting scopes and related gear. Get their catalog.

Pentax

Pentax has added a 3-9x50 and a 6.5-20x50mm to their Whitetails Unlimited line. This size objective gives excellent light transmission but the scope isn't so big that high mount rings are necessary as with a 56mm. Part of the price of every scope in this series goes to Whitetails Unlimited Inc. to improve environment for this species of deer.

Mitchell Optics

Mitchell Optics continues to make traditional, externally-adjusted target scopes of

the type made famous in past decades by Unertl, Fecker, Lyman and others. The Mitchells were described in last year's *GUN DIGEST*. Barrel-mounted scopes of this style were long-popular with both large- and small-bore competitive riflemen, early benchresters, American snipers in various wars, varmint hunters, etc. I'm still using one from long ago. Mitchell scopes are made with 1 1/2-, 2-, or 2 1/2-in. objectives, so some are even larger than the early ones, and their mounts are sturdier. Magnifications from 12x to 52x are now available.

Conetrol

Conetrol honcho George Miller advises that their new windage-adjustable AQD (Adjustable Quick-Detach) mount should be available before you read these lines. Lateral movement is accomplished by a screwdriver-type hex driver (provided with each base). With this unit, a jam screw forces the mount ring back to its original position each time the scope is reattached, which makes accurate return to zero normal. Adjustment for wear is also automatic when the screw is tightened.

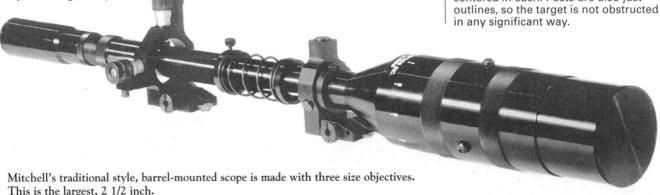

Mitchell's traditional style, barrel-mounted scope is made with three size objectives. This is the largest, 2 1/2 inch.

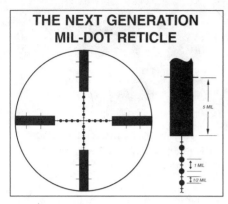

THE NEXT GENERATION MIL-DOT RETICLE

5 MIL

1 MIL

1/2 MIL

The GEN 2 Mil-Dot is Premier's update of this popular reticle, gives 1/2-mil aiming points.

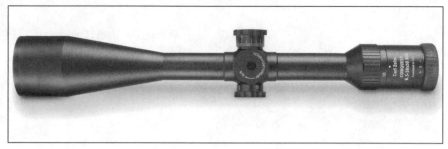

The 6.5-20x Conquest is the latest export from Zeiss to America and will do for varmints at any distance as well as long-range big game.

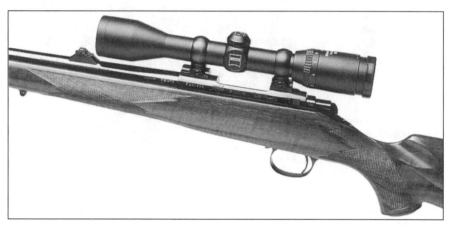

Conetrol's DapTar mounts were used by Zeiss to make this neat hunting rig.

Trijicon

Trijicon is perhaps best known for their Tactical scopes such as the ACOG (Advanced Combat Optical Gunsight), but they also have two AccuPoint scopes, a 3-9x40 and 1.2-4x24. Both are of an advanced design that features battery-free, dual-illumination technology for aiming in low light at dawn or dusk. There's a triangular-shaped tritium aiming point and also a fiber-optic light collector that automatically adjusts reticle brightness to existing light conditions.

Premier Reticles

Premier Reticles, started by the late Robert Thomas just after World War II, is still a family organization, headed up now by son Dick and grandson Chris. In the late '40s I had what I believe was then called a Tommy Dot put into a 2-1/2x Norman-Ford Texan. I still have that scope, but for years now Premier Reticles have been put in only Leupold scopes. Most shooters think only of center dots when they consider Premiers, but actually more than a dozen styles of reticle are available, from the early German 3-post design to the new Generation 2 mil-dot.

Called the GEN 2, this reticle includes short hash marks between the dots to provide half-mil gradients. These marks, which are .15 mil, or about one-half minute long, allow very accurate range estimating and windage holdoff, and make precise aiming points.

A free 18-page booklet describes in detail all items available from Premier.

Cabela's

Cabela's, the well-known hunter/shooter outfitter, just started supplying scopes under their own name, and oddly enough they're called the Outfitter Series. All scopes have 40mm objective units and, interestingly, the medium-power variables such as the 3-9x and 4-12x have half-minute adjustments, which is reasonable on a big-game scope. The 6-20x40, intended for small long-range targets, has 1/8-minute clicks.

Sightron

Sightron has for years offered their extensive SII variables running from 1.5-6x to 6.5-25x, target/competition models of 4-16x to 36x, tacticals, compacts, shotgun and handgun scopes in conventional powers, all on 1-inch tubes with enlarged objectives, plus two SIIIs on 30mm mounting tubes. Now they've added a pair of SI scopes (*don't ask me why the newest models seem to have the lowest numbered series*), a 3-9x40 and a 1x20. The latter is called a Black Powder Scope, which shows what it was designed for, but with its 111-ft. field it will also make a fine choice for any big-game hunter who haunts the dark, brushy hollows where shots come at feet instead of yards, so doesn't need high magnification but does need a big bright field and conspicuous reticle.

Speaking of reticles, for some time now I've been using Sightron's 2.5-7x32 with Double Diamond reticle on my old 7x61 S&H. The maker calls this a Shotgun scope, but the DD gives multiple aiming points for deliberate long-range shooting, and it's conspicuous enough for fast short-range work, while still providing a sort of "transparent" look overall. So maybe it was designed for shotguns, but it also works fine on a rifle.

Zeiss

Zeiss continues to lure American shooters. Their latest Conquest is the 6.5-20x50 MC. With a 1-inch center tube diameter, it can be used with most American mounts, and eye relief is 3 1/2 in. at all powers, enough to keep the rear end of the tube away from your eyebrow if properly mounted, even on a heavy-recoiling rifle. This scope is 15 1/2 in. long and weighs 21+ oz. There's a choice of quarter-minute or eighth-minute clicks, it has a turret-mounted parallax adjustment, and its 50mm objective gives a twilight factor of 18 to 31, depending on magnification. (*Incidentally, the TF is calculated by taking the square root of the power multiplied by the unobstructed diameter of the objective lens in millimeters. This is a system developed in Europe decades ago to let a potential scope buyer compare different scopes for poor light use. A high TF number means it's possible to make out target detail even when ambient light is poor.*)

This 6.5-20x Conquest is the highest magnification scope I remember Zeiss manufacturing, at least for export. It's obviously intended for precise long-range shooting, especially on varmints. But its reasonable size and weight should make it a fine choice for pronghorns or distant deer, especially on super-accurate, high-velocity bolt actions, such as are preferred by riflemen who locate their game with binoculars or spotting scopes, determine its distance with laser rangefinders, come up the required clicks, then squeeze. ●

by LARRY S. STERETT

HANDLOADING UPDATE

*W*HEN THE FIRST edition of the *GUN DIGEST* was published, loading presses were relatively small C-types or handheld and the number of reloading manuals–Belding & Mull, Lyman, NRA, etc.–and components limited. Shotshell reloading was done using straight-line tools, and progressives were still in the future. Synthetics were not plentiful, and reloads were often placed back in the original boxes. The number of accessories available was minimal. Not so today. Some of the old-line firms are gone, but there are many new products available to the handloader.

Barnes Bullets

Barnes' Reloading Manual No. 3 was mentioned in the last edition, as was the new Barnes Ballistics Program Version 2.0. Currently the firm is busy keeping up with production of bullets, including the new Taurus HEX Copper Bullets.

Battenfeld Technologies

Battenfeld has a new lightweight hand-held Vibra-Prime Automatic Primer Tube Filler that's a gem. Battery operated; it will fill primer tubes, large or small rifle or pistol, in seconds for transferring to Dillon or RCBS progressive presses. Place the primers in the tray, jiggle until the primers have flipped, open the gate and pull the trigger. It's simple and it's fast.

Berry's Manufacturing

Berry's is known for its plastic ammo boxes, powder funnels, ammo trays, and plated swaged bullets for reloading. In addition to a couple of new round nose bullet designs, one each for the 9x18mm Makarov and 45-70 Govt., the firm has a new Deluxe Bullet Puller. Featuring an overmolded head and large rubberized grip, the Puller comes complete with three collets, and will handle most cartridges when a bullet has to be pulled to check a powder charge.

Corbin Manufacturing & Supply

Long known as the swaging people, Corbin Manufacturing & Supply has a new high precision, all-steel reloading and bullet-making press. Designed to eliminate the need for an arbor press often used with straight-line dies in precision reloading, the new S-Press features four sets of Torrington needle-bearings in the linkage to provide smooth operation. The S-Press weighs 22 pounds, and accepts standard 7/8 x 14 dies and RCBS-type button shellholders. *(Optional arbor press anvils will permit the press to use non-threaded dies if desired.)* Supplied with a side-vented primer port, a primer catcher tray that travels with the ram, and a CNC-style floating punch holder for bullet swaging punches, the S-Press replaces the 1980s Corbin Series II-style swaging press. With a 4-inch ram stoke for reloading and a 2-inch high-powered swaging stroke, the new O-frame press has an 180,000-psi tensile strength and is capable of swaging bullets up to .458-inch diameter. Finished with a gold and black metal polymer powder coat to resist heat, abrasion, wear and most chemical solvents, the S-Press is a professional-quality tool suitable for reloading or

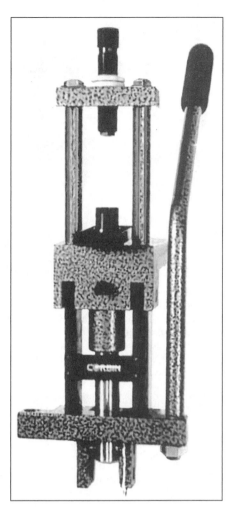

Corbin's new S-Press is specifically designed for reloading metallic cartridges using regular 7/8 x 14 dies, but is capable of swaging bullets up to .458 size.

---

swaging. It will handle most cartridges, but the ram travel is not long enough to handle the 50 BMG, nor will it accept dies for this cartridge.

Berry's new inertia Deluxe Bullet Puller features a rubberized grip and comes with three collets.

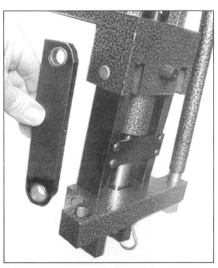

One of the links on the Corbin S-press showing the location of the roller bearings at both ends of the link.

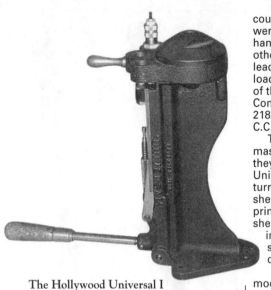

The Hollywood Universal I loading press can be changed to a 12-station turret press by changing the die head, and by adding other parts the single shellholder can be increased to four different sizes. Hollywood parts are again available, in addition to new Senior and Turret presses.

Forster Precision Products

The Lanark, Illinois, firm has six new chamberings added to their Bench Rest die set line, plus an optical 'short-throw' handle for the Co-Ax loading press. The new cartridges covered include 300 Winchester Short Mag, the 338 Lapua, and the 7mm and 300 Remington Short Ultra Mag and the 7mm and 375 Remington Ultra Mag cartridges. Complete die sets - or individual dies - are available, including the Ultra Seating dies. A Kwik-Fill Sandbag Filler, with long drop tube, is also available to help fill the bags needed to check out those handloads.

Hollywood Engineering

Handloaders who have been around for a while will recall the ultimate reloading presses were those produced by Lyle S. Corcoran of the Hollywood Gun Shop. A half-century ago they had the Senior, "Junior," Universal I, II, and III, and later an automatic 12-gauge model that could churn out 1,800 loaded shotshells per hour ... provided the hoppers and magazines

could be kept filled. Bullet swaging dies were available in most popular rifle and handgun calibers, and so were many other loading items, powder measures, lead core cutters, and a multitude of loading dies–including the 23 calibers of the Wildcat C.C.C. (Controlled Combustion Cartridge) series from the 218 Bee C.C.C. to the 375 Magnum C.C.C.

The Hollywood presses were massive and almost indestructible, but they were not low-priced. The Universal III, which had a 12-station turret die head, four-position shellholder head and four-position primer rod head, minus dies, shellholders or primer rods was $88.50 in 1952, and worth it, while the single-stage Senior with one set of dies was priced at $37.50.

Over the years some of the press models, such as the Junior and Universal (a couple were renamed the A and B models.), were discontinued and the names changed. By the mid-1960s the firm was still at the same address in Hollywood, but was now Hollywood Reloading, Inc. Only the Senior, which had doubled in price without the dies, a Senior Turret model, and an automatic at $895.00 for metallics–plus two shotshell tools in a choice of 20, 16, or 12 gauge–were available. All the loading die sets, including the 50 BMG at $35.00 and most of the big British calibers from the 360 No. 2 up to the 600 Nitro Express for $25.00-$35.00 were still available.

The good news is some Hollywood tools are again available. It's now Hollywood Engineering and the firm is in Sun Valley, not Hollywood. Only the Senior and Senior Turret presses are available, but parts for the older models—Universal, etc.—are still available as are swaging dies, lead core cutters, loading die sets, including those of the C.C.C. and 50 BMG cartridge. For handloaders owning an older Hollywood press who have lost their instructions, copies are available for a fee, and old tools can be reconditioned and repaired. (The Hollywood was unique for its time in featuring 1-1/2 x 12 threaded die stations with bushings to handle regular 7/8 x 14 die sets. The larger holes permitting the use of shotshell dies, big-bore English caliber or 50 BMG die sets, or regular 7/8 x 14 die

The Collet Resizing Die from Innovative Technologies will work on more than 15 belted cartridge cases, ironing out the pre-belt bulge and extending the reloading life of the case.

sets using the bushings. It's good to have them available again.)

Hornady Manufacturing

The big news from Hornady was the introduction of the exciting new 17 HMR rimfire cartridge, plus 405 Winchester and 458 Lott loads, and a more powerful 444 Marlin load in their ammunition line, in addition to some other new loads. However, the firm hasn't forgotten handloaders and has added several new chamberings to their line of loading dies. In the two-die Custom Grade Series I, the 270 WSM, 7mm WSM, 300 WSM, 7mm Remington SA Ultra, 7mm Rem. Ultra Mag., 300 Rem. SA Ultra, 375 Rem. Ultra Mag. calibers have been added, while in the Series II three-die sets, the 405 Winchester and 458 Lott have been added. Shell holders have been added for the 405 Winchester and the 338 Lapua cartridges.

For maximum accuracy all metallic cases require trimming to the correct length and the Hornady Cam-Lock Trimmer makes the job easy. Now a Cam-Lock Premium Extra Cutter can be obtained. With a Cam-Lock Trimmer,

Hornady's Cam-Lock Trimmer makes the job of trimming brass cartridge cases much easier, and extra cutters can be obtained.

Lyman's new Pro Magnum Tumbler will handle up to 900 38 Special cases at a time, or a smaller number of larger cases.

pilots, Premium Cutter, and a Neck Turning Tool with micro-adjustable cutter, a handloader should be set to handle all case trimming needs.

Innovative Technologies

Handloaders who reload several different cartridges based on the 300/375 H & H Magnum belted case head size may find the Magnum Collet Resizing Die manufactured by Innovative Technologies (1480 Guinevere Drive, Dept GDH, Casselberry, FL 32707) useful. Conventional resizing dies do not always fully restore belted cases to their original size, resulting in a 'bulge' above the belt. This die uses a collet, which fits over the cartridge case up to the belt. The collet, with case, is then inserted into the sizing die where the top of the die serves as a gauge to determine when "complete" brass resizing is required. By allowing the case to go farther into the die the 'bulge' can be reduced, permitting up to 20 firings per case. This unit will work on more than 15 different belted magnum calibers, and can even resize loaded ammunition according to the manufacturer. Currently available only from the manufacturer, the die is not inexpensive, costing just under a C-note, delivered.

King & Co.

Handloaders wanting a specific set of loading dies and not being able to find it may want to contact King & Co. (P. O. Box 1242, Dept. GDH,

Bloomington, IL 61702). This firm states it is the nation's largest die service, buying and selling and even trading 7/8 x 14 dies, new and used. It could be well worth the price of a letter and a SASE (self-addressed, stamped envelope).

Lee Precision, Inc.

Lee Precision has four new bullet moulds available, all flat-nose designs, including a 158-grain 38, a 200-grain 45, a 300-grain 45 for the 454 Casull and a 400-grain for the 480 Ruger and 475 Linebaugh cartridges. The Lee Turret Press is now available with a four-hole turret, and updating kits are available, as are extra four-hole turrets. Owners of Lee turret presses with the three-hole turret can change them to four-hole. The Lee three-die carbide pistol die set has been upgraded to a Deluxe Pistol Die Set in six calibers by including a free crimp die along with the free shellholder. The cartridges for which the Deluxe dies are available include the 9mm Luger, 38 Special, 40 S & W, 44 Special, 45 Colt, and 45 ACP. Others may be added later.

Lyman Products

Lyman Products has been in the reloading business longer than most of the firms covered in this report, starting back in the days of blackpowder and Ideal 'tong' tools. Among the latest

from Lyman is the Pro Magnum Tumbler, which features a two-gallon capacity capable of handling up to 900 38 Special cases at a time. Available in two versions, 110 or 220 volts, it has a heavy-duty motor designed to deliver fast cleaning.

Three new chamberings, 300 SWM, 7mm Rem Ultra Mag and 375 Remington Ultra Mag, have been added to the Lyman line of 2-die sets, with three taper-crimp dies added to the blackpowder die line. Blackpowder cartridges require charge compression for proper ignition. The Taper Crimp dies, available in .40, .45 Short and .45 Long sizes, will provide the firm neck tension required for such blackpowder cartridges as the 40-65, 45-70, 45-100, 45-110 and 45-120. Neck-size dies in the same three calibers, plus 38-55, are also available. These dies allow the case neck to be sized to retain the bullet, without overworking the case body. *(Cases that are repeatedly fired in the same rifle tend to provide better accuracy when neck-sized only.)*

Magma Engineering Company

Magma Engineering, the firm that produces the Master Caster and Mark 6 Bullet Master casting machines, the Lube Master, the Case Master Rimless

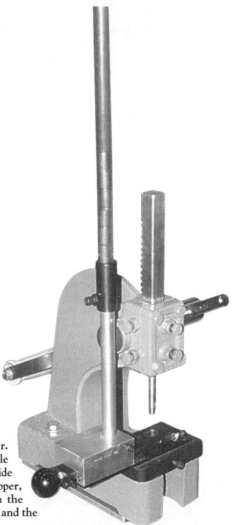

Magma Engineering's new Case Master Jr. Rimless Case Sizer features a shovel handle for easy operation and the hopper will provide a continuous supply of case. With a full hopper, just push and release the plunger head on the left, move the handle to its stop, and return, and the case is sized to the original head size.

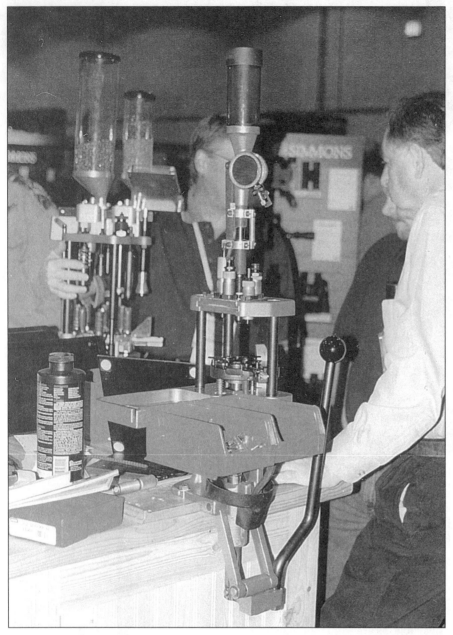

The RCBS Piggyback III can increase loaded metallic output by a factor of eight by simply changing a single-stage press into a five-station, manual-indexing progressive unit, as shown in the foreground.

and each features thick-wall construction, heavy-duty latches, padlock tabs, crush-proof O-ring sealing, handles, and a hands-free nylon carrying strap.

RCBS

RCBS has a couple of new 'big' units, one each for metallic reloaders and shotshell loaders. Piggyback units have been available before, but the latest, Piggyback III, is a conversion unit that can increase loaded cartridge output from 50 rounds per hour to over 400 by changing a single-stage press into a 5-station, manual-indexing, progressive unit which allows the use of a separate crimp die, a powder checker, etc. It will handle all handgun cases from 32 and up, and rifle cases up to the 223 Remington. Case insertion and removal can be performed at each station. Interchangeable die plates permit fast and simple cartridge conversions and the Piggyback III utilizes the APS Priming System. The kit comes with a bullet tray, loaded cartridge box and empty case box, ready for easy installation.

Shotshell reloaders will appreciate the new RCBS Grand press, available in 12 and 20 gauges, with Conversion Units available to permit loading both gauges on the same press, *(the Grand has a lifetime warranty.)* The shot and powder hoppers hold 25 pounds of shot and 1-1/2 pounds of powder respectively, and both have convenient forward drains for rapid component removal or changing. The powder station is directly in front of the press, and powder and shot bushings can be changed in less than one minute when needed.

The massive green-colored frame is large and open, permitting easy access to all 8 stations. Both the powder and shot systems are case-activated. No hull? Then no powder or shot; no need to manually shut off either of these stations–no spillage of powder or shot can occur. Cases can be removed at any station, and universal case holders allow the case to be sized down to the rim using a steel sizing ring. Primers are fed one at a time, and fired primers drop down a tube into an easily emptied container. The wad guide tilts out for convenient feeding of wads. Progression of the hull through the stations is automatic, but it can easily be altered to permit manual indexing, if desired.

Redding Reloading Equipment

Redding has several new items, including a 'Big Boss' reloading press and a T-7 Turret press. Both presses feature cast iron frames and one-inch diameter rams with nearly four inches of travel. The 'Big Boss' frame has 36 degrees of offset to provide easy access and an offset ball handle for ease of operation. It and the T-7 are also designed to accept the new optional Slide Bar Automatic Primer Feeding System *(which comes with a safety shield and tubes for small and*

Case Sizer, and more than 100 styles of bullet moulds, now has a Case Master Jr. Rimless Case Sizer. Manually operated, the Jr. features a shovel-style handle for ease of operation. The cases pass completely through the carbide die, insuring a completely round circumference.

Magma has five new bullet moulds, mainly for shooters handloading for cowboy action shooting, with one each in the 32-20, 38-40, 41, 44, and 45-caliber sizes. One, for the 38-40, is a round-nose design, the other four produce flat-nose bullets. Cast bullet handloaders could also benefit from the Meister Slug kits Magma features. Available in six sizes, from .30 to .45, each kit contains soft lead slugs, driving pins, forceps, and lubricant to permit determining the barrel bore groove diameter. For reloading, the shooter should then

select a bullet that matches, or is one thousandth over the slug diameter.

MTM Molded Products Co.

MTM is known to handloaders for its line of molded plastic ammunition boxes in which to store their reloaded rifle, handgun or shotgun cartridges. The firm also produces loading blocks or trays, primer flippers, powder funnels, a handloaders log, load labels, and boxes to hold die sets. For handloaders who take a small press, powder measure, and components, etc. to the range with them, one of the new MTM Utility Plus Dry Boxes may be just the answer. Six models are available, and the SPUD 6 or 7 models should be about right. These boxes offer a top-access lid compartment, a lift-out tray, plenty of depth for a small press, etc.–

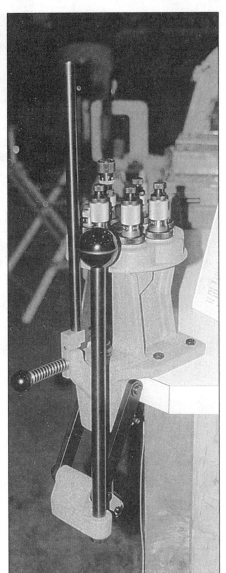

Redding's T-7 Turret press with the Redding Slide Bar Automatic Primer Feeding System.

The new RCBS Grand shotshell press is available in 12 or 20 gauge, and a conversion unit is available. The powder and shot stations are case-activated.

large primers.). Both presses feature compound linkage for additional power, and the new seventh station on the T-7 allows for a powder measure or an additional die. (The Big Boss press will be available as an option in the latest Redding Reloading Kits, Pro-Pak or Deluxe.)

Other new Redding products include "E-Z Feed" shellholders featuring a tapered design to permit easier case entry, and a knurled exterior for ease in handling. The E-Zs are available individually, or in a set of six of the most popular sizes, and will fit Redding presses or most other popular brands.

Redding is now packaging Type S bushing dies with their Competition seating dies. Either a full-size or neck-size is packaged, depending on the die set selected. A deluxe version of the Pro Series die sets, known as the "Competition Pro series," is now

available for use in progressive reloading presses. This three-die set includes a Titanium Carbide sizing die, Competition seating die, and a Profile Crimp die that headspaces on the case mouth.

Reloading Innovations, Inc.

Reloading Innovations has a new system that's ideal for shotshell reloaders who shoot skeet, trap, etc. extensively. Called the Ultimate Loading System, it consists of a special angled metal loading stand to hold the Shell Caddy line of reusable plastic 25-round shell boxes, a Shell Caddy pouch which holds a box of shells, plus some spare rounds and a few accessories, and the Shell Caddy 'Shooters Carrying Case,' which will hold ten boxes of shells, up to 200 empty hulls, and additional accessories. It's available as

a complete system, or the loading (stacking) stand and Shell Caddy boxes can be purchased separately per pack of ten. The stands are available in a choice of red or black, and the Shell Caddy boxes in red, black, or green–each with space provided on which load information may be written.

It's not new, but with many surplus bolt-action military rifles in 6.5mm Carcano, 7.35mm Terni, 7.5mm French, and 7.5mm Swiss being available in the past few years, why isn't a plentiful supply of Boxer-primed reloadable brass available? Norma has brass in some of these calibers, but not all, and Norma brass is not always easy to locate. Back in 1959 the Pasadena, California, firm of Santa Fe had virgin unprimed Boxer cases available in 30-06, 7.5mm Swiss, and 6.5mm Swedish, with the 6.5mm Carcano, 7.35mm Terni, etc. scheduled for 1960. Unfortunately, it never came to pass, but the demand is still there, and especially for the French 7.5mm, Italian 6.5mm and 7.35mm, Russian

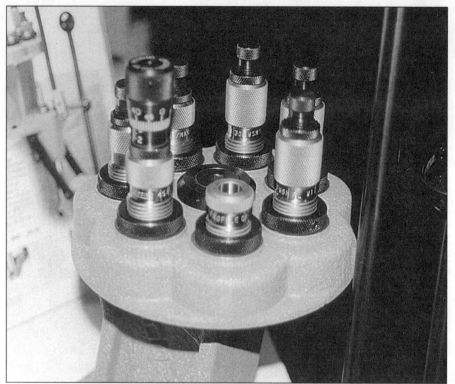

The head or turret of Redding's new T-7 press will hold seven dies, as shown, or a powder measure and six dies, or even three 2-die sets.

7.62x54mm, and the Swiss 7.5mm. It would enable owners of such rifles to do considerably more shooting.

Sinclair International

Handloaders concerned with maximum accuracy from their rifle and handgun reloads realize the flash holes in the case primer pockets can make a difference, especially on cases such as the 220 Russian, 6mm BR, etc. These cases have small flash holes (approximately 0.060-inch) and the decapping pins can stick in them. Sinclair International has a new reamer which will open the flash holes just enough to reduce the sticky pin problem. Consisting of a reamer holder and a guide sleeve, this stainless steel tool is knurled for easy turning to make each flash hole the same diameter. Sinclair also has a new handle for their DB-1000 Flashhole Deburring Tool, making it more comfortable to use when a lot of cases are being deburred. The handle will fit all the Sinclair Deburring Tools in this series, whether it is standard (0.080-inch), small (0.060-inch) or on one of the 17-caliber cases.

Swift Bullet Company

Swift, manufacturer of the famed A-Frame and Scirocco bonded bullets, has a new hardbound loading manual, their first. Contained within the more than 400 pages is loading data and ballistics information on 47 popular hunting cartridges. Each cartridge will be provided a dimensioned drawing, plus a sectioned loaded cartridge illustration, and a big game sketch.

Swift currently produces more than a dozen different caliber A-Frame bullets from .25 to .470, in 32 different weights from 100 to 500 grains. The Scirocco rifle line currently includes three calibers, 270, 7mm, and 30. Swift also has two calibers of hollowpoint A-Frame handgun bullets from 240 to 325

grains, with four of these included in their saboted muzzleloading bullet line. The new manual includes the test components used with each of the cartridges for which loading data is provided.

Versatile Rack Co.

Shotshell reloaders who have a problem keeping the empty hulls and wads orderly on the loading bench may want to check into the Pail Hopper at their local dealer. Versatile Rack Co. has a kit that converts those plentiful five-gallon plastic pails, often available for a dollar or two each at discount stores, into a handy hopper holding enough hulls or wads–or even metallic cases–for several hours reloading. The pails can even be used to transport empties from the range, and a patent-pending flow pan ensures a constant flow of the components. Having the hulls in a hopper on one side and a hopper full of wads on the other side for a progressive shotshell reloader should definitely save time.

Hood

Benchrest shooters and some other handloaders often feel the need for a compact, lightweight, portable loading press to take to the range with them. Such a press is the Hood model, available in two sizes and three variations. The more compact version features a 2-1/2" stroke, weighs 6-1/2 pounds, and folds into a 1-1/2" x 4" x 10-1/4" package for transporting. It's available to accommodate Wilson-type inline seater and neck dies, or regular full length 7/8 x 14 dies, or with one 7/8 x 14 station, and one blank station for use with a Wilson-type seater die.

The Shell Caddy by Reloading Innovations is a method of stacking and storing those shotshell reloads in neat 25round, reusable plastic boxes.

Sinclair's Bullet Comparator is manufactured using actual rifle throating reamers to allow more accurate measurement. The six-caliber stainless steel comparator shown will handle 17-, 22-, 6mm, 30-, 27-, and 33-caliber bullets.

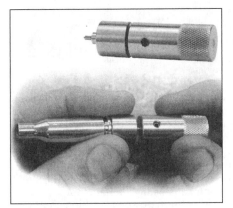

Sinclair's new Flashhole Reamer will open the flash holes in PPC and BR brass cases just enough to permit the decapping pin to pass through without sticking.

Extremely rigid for its size, its portability can be surpassed by few other table presses and possibly only by such hand tools as the Lee Hand Press and Lyman Tong Tool.

New & Noteworthy Reloading Information

With new bullets, powders, wads, and other components being introduced, handloaders never have enough information. However, there is an abundance of loading data available, much of it free for the asking.

One of the most interesting new handloading volumes this handloader has used in some time is the *Manual of Reloading No. 5*, by Rene Malfatti. This large *(as tall as the GUN DIGEST, but not quite as thick)*, softbound manual contains more 160 pages of loading data and even more pages of textual material on handloading. Each of the cartridges for which data is provided is illustrated with a photograph, along with the specifications, a history, and comments. The rifle cartridges covered range from the 17 Remington to the 50 BMG, with handgun calibers from the 32 ACP to the 50 A. E. Among the cartridges not always found in other current reloading manuals are the 5.6x57mm, 6x62mm Freres, 6.5x57mm,

Swift's new *Reloading Manual, Number 1*, is a hardbound volume that provides reloading data on 47 popular hunting cartridges.

7x64mm, 30-284, 32 Remington, 8x60mmS, 351 Winchester SL, 7.65mm Long (Re: 1918 Pedersen device, the French M1935 pistols, etc.), 8mm Nambu, 41 A.E., and 11mm M1873. Components are, for the most part, those with which U. S. handloaders are familiar: CCI, Federal, Hirtenberger, Lapua, Norma, Remington, R.W.S., Sierra, Speer, and Winchester—although the powders are principally Vectan varieties.

The textual portion is lavishly illustrated with photographs, drawings and tables. Many of the photos and drawings present sectioned views of cartridges, dies, bullets, primers, etc. The coverage of handloading is extensively thorough, and among the many topics discussed are primers, differences of Boxer and Berdan primers, powders, comparison of powders—Accurate Vectan, IMR, Hodgdon, W.W., Norma, R.W.S., VithaVuori, —pressures, exterior ballistics, tools for reloading, bullet casting, and much more. In addition projectiles (bullets)—European and

U.S.– cast, swaged and jacketed are listed and illustrated. Most, if not all, known loading die calibers are listed, including the French Lynx and the Australian Simplex brands. Many cartridge cases that are not currently available as factory-loaded ammunition are listed and illustrated, including such oldies as the 11mm Werndl, 10.75x58R Berdan, 11mm Gras, 450 Webley, 350 Rigby, and 600/577 REWA. *(These have Boxer primer pockets and include the Le Hussard and Bertram Bullet brands.)*

Completing this volume are tables of conversion units, including grain/gramme, bushing volumes, a bibliography, listings of photographs, cartridges, accessories and eight tables listing the dimensions of both metric and English caliber metallic cartridges, handgun and rifle. Shotshells, reloading or otherwise, are not covered in this manual.

Available direct from the publisher, Editions Crepin-Leblond, any U.S. bookstore handling foreign books, and possibly from your local book dealer, this is a worthy addition to the handloader's reference shelf. The text is in French, but most of the loading data is in English and can easily be deciphered.

Thompson/Center Arms is the manufacturer of the most famous single-shot pistol of all times, the T/C Contender. Most reloading manuals now devote space to loading data for the many cartridges for which the Contender is, and has been, chambered. Loading data specially for the Contender is featured in a spiral-bound T/C manual that features over 5,197 tested and proven loads for Contender cartridges, from the 17 Bumble Bee to the 45-70 Gov't. All for the price of less than three sawbucks.

VihtaVuori has a new 60-page reloading guide available that provides loading data for two-dozen handgun

The Pail Hopper by Versatile Rack solves the problem of how to handle the mass of empty hulls and wads necessary to do some serious shotshell reloading. The kit can be used to convert the plentiful five-gallon buckets into hoppers.

The latest VihtaVuori *Reloading Manual*, No 3, has reloading data for nearly nine dozen handgun and rifle cartridges, including a few not often seen in the U. S., such as the 7x33mm SAKO and the 9.3x53R Finnish.

cartridges (from the 7mm TCU to the 50 A.E.) and four-dozen rifle cartridges (from the 17 Remington to the 50 BMG). A burning rate chart for 108 different powders is provided, along with a discussion on powders, storage recommendations, and other useful information. The regular hardbound *Reloading Manual, 3rd Edition*, can be purchased at most gun shops handling handloading supplies and the VihtaVuori line of powders. The first six of the total eleven chapters in this volume cover VihtaVuori powders, rifle and handgun competition, VihtaVuori Powders for Small Arms, Reloading Components and Cartridge Properties, Exterior Ballistics, and Reloading Process. Chapters 9-11 are devoted to Ballistic Measuring System, and Unit Conversions, ending with an excellent illustrated Glossary followed by several pages for notes. Chapters 8 and 9 provide reloading data for nearly six dozen rifle cartridges, from the 17 Remington to the 50 BMG, and 28 handgun cartridges from the 25 ACP to the 50 E. C. Most of the rifle cartridges are familiar, but some on which reloading data is not often found include the 5.6x35R Vierling, 220 Russian, 5.6x57mm, 6.3x53R Finnish, 6.5x57R, 7x33mm SAKO, 7x54mm Finnish, 8.2x53R Finnish, and 9.3x53R Finnish. Each cartridge has a dimensioned drawing, followed by specs and a few paragraphs of history. The test components are listed preceding the actual loading data, which includes both Starting Load and Maximum Load columns.

The data for handgun cartridges does not include any but current

There's a plentiful supply of 'comp' loading data manuals and guides available to handloaders for the asking. Your local gun dealer should have several of these, if not all. The amount of data presented varies from a few calibers or gauges to rather extensive coverage–and it's all useful.

production cartridges, including the 9x21mm and the 9x23mm Winchester cartridges. Format is the same as with the rifle cartridge loading data. There is no data on handloading of shotshells.

Micro Tech, LLC., the Duster Wads firm, has a 28-page guide of loads using their wads in 12-, 20-, and 28-gauge shotguns, plus .410-bore *(no 16-gauge loads in this guide)*. Major hull, primer and powder brands are included, and there are several useful tables, such as the one illustrating the space occupied by one ounce of shot in the various shells, from the .410-bore to the 12 gauge.

Nosler, the Ballistic Tip and Partition bullet manufacturer, has a new *Reloading Guide*, their number five, available. Featuring the newest bullets and the latest cartridges *(as of the date the Guide went to press)*, this hardbound volume is a welcome addition to the wealth of data available to handloaders.

Graf & Sons, Inc., distributors of the Rex line of Hungarian smokeless powders, has a 16-page booklet of loading data featuring Rex, Alliant, and Hodgdon powders. Data is provided for five handgun calibers, and the 12, 16, 20, and 28 gauges, plus .410-bore. There are only four 16-gauge loads listed and only with Universal powder in Cheddite hulls, but it's better than no data. Three 'recommended bushings' tables for use with Rex powders are also provided, along with other miscellaneous information.

Western Powders has a new 64-page *Handloading Guide, Edition II*, featuring Ramshot powders. Featured are nine handgun calibers from the 9mm Luger to the 54 Casull, and 23 rifles calibers from the 222 Remington

to the 45-70 Gov't. Several pages are devoted to loads for the 12-gauge shotshells using the Ramshot Competition powder. Bushing charts for MEC, Hornady, and P/W also provided, along with a number of blank tables and worksheets for the reloader to record his or her own data; these sheets are thorough, providing spaces for not only the components used, but location, temperature, humidity, wind, maximum group size, comments, etc.

Hodgdon has the most extensive line of complimentary "reloader's manuals," with at least three: *Pyrodex*, *Cowboy Action 4th Edition*, and *Basic 2002*. They also have their more comprehensive *2001 Shotshell Manual* and *No. 27 Data Manual*, which are available for purchase. The cowboy action manual features data for the new Triple Seven powder, plus regular smokeless and Pyrodex loads for the more common chamberings used in CAS handgun, rifle, and shotgun events. The thin Pyrodex loading guide deals mainly with the use of pellets and loose powders in muzzle-loading arms, but does provide data for the use of pellets in four 44 and 45 metallic cartridges, along with lots of other useful information.

The handy 76-page *Basic* manual is divided approximately into two parts: metallic cartridges and shotshells. The first half provides data for reloading over six dozen rifle cartridges and more than three dozen handgun cartridges. The rifle calibers range from the 17 Remington to the 50 BMG, including the 338-06, 356 Winchester and 376 Steyr, while the handgun calibers covered range from the 223 Remington to the 500 Linebaugh and include the 9mm Makarov, 44 Auto Mag, 460

Handloaders who like to reload at the range should find the Hood press to their liking. The unit weighs 6 1/2 pounds and is shown here operating with two different die types: *(left)* a Wilson-type straight-line die and, *(top)* in the center die station, a standard 7/8 x 14 die.

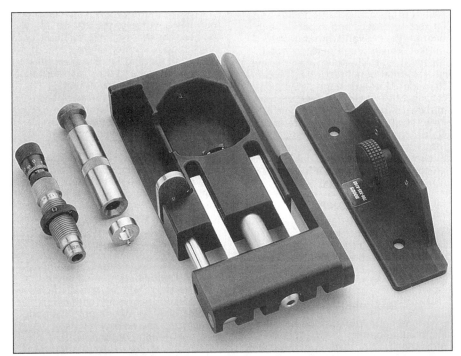

Dismantled and folded for transport, the two-piece Hood press weighs 6 1/2 pounds and measures a compact 10-1/4 x 4 x 1-1/2 inches. Integral workstations support two types of die systems: 7/8 x 14 *(left)* and straight-line *(right)*.

Rowland, and 480 Ruger. The second half covers shotshells, from the 10 gauge to the .410-bore, and includes the 16 gauge. Bushings tables for Lee, MEC, P/W and Hornady/Spolar are provided, along with a chilled shot table, shot chart, powder reference table, wad chart, and some excellent notes on recoil.

Accurate Arms' 2002 *Reloaders Guide* features 64 pages of data based on the Accurate line of powders. The guide is thumb-tabbed in black for handy reference in seven categories, from *Introduction* to *Shotshell*. Loading data is provided for 29 handgun cartridges, including the 300 Whisper, 357 SIG, and 50 A.E., and 13 cowboy cartridges. *(The 480 Ruger didn't make this edition.)* In the rifle section data is provided for 54 different cartridges, from the 17 Remington to the 50 BMG, including 450 Marlin, 45/120 Sharps 3 1/4", and 50/140 Sharps 3 1/4". Under the Shotshell Data section, in addition to cowboy action loads, charts on MEC, Lee, Hornady, and P/W bushings for the respective presses, load data is provided on regular--field and target-- 12, 16, 20 and 28 gauge shells, plus the .410-bore. There are also Quick Guides to shotshell primers and wads and wad assemblies.

Alliant Powder's large magazine-size *Reloaders' Guide* features shotshell reloading data for the 10, 12, 16, 20 and 28 gauges, plus the .410-bore for the various Alliant powders, plus 12 gauge data with the Promo powder, which is available in 8-pound containers only. Sections are also devoted to 12-gauge International loads, steel shot loads, buckshot loads, and rifled slug loads. Loading data is provided for 23 regular handgun cartridges from the 25 Auto to the 454 Casull, with separate sections covering cowboy action and silhouette calibers. Centerfire rifle reloading data is provided for nearly five-dozen cartridges from the 17 Remington to the 458 Winchester Magnum–but there are some missing, such as the 30-40 Krag and 450 Marlin. *(Data for the 458 Lott, which is now factory-loaded by Hornady, is not covered in any of the 'comp' manuals.)* There are also several pages of useful reference data and precautions provided, including tables on shot sizes, the number of shells which can be loaded per pound of powder, bore diameters, choke definitions, ballistic data, etc.

Just as new and improved components for reloading become available, so too do new products— tools, accessories, manuals, etc.— designed to make handloading safer, faster, and even more enjoyable... and the resulting cartridges and shotshells more accurate to bag more game, break more clays and produce smaller groups. Handloading has come a long way from the era of the tong tool, casting bullets over an open fire, and waterglassing or paraffinning the top wad in a brass shotshell. ●

by HOLT BODINSON

AMMUNITION, BALLISTICS & COMPONENTS

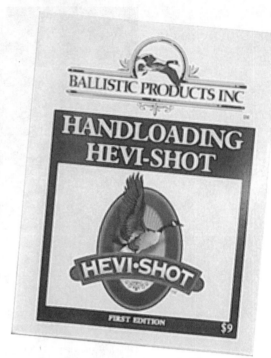

*T*HE SHORT MAGNUM race is heating up in earnest with the introduction of Winchester's new 270 and 7mm Winchester Short Magnums (WSM) and Remington's 7mm and 300 Short Action Ultra Magnums. Federal joined in with two loadings for the 300 WSM and it's our understanding that Norma, too, will be loading the short magnums shortly. Winchester's short magnum case offers slightly more capacity and velocity than Remington's so the choice between the two seems to be coming down to what brand of rifle the shooter favors. Faster still are the 7mm and 300 Lazzeroni short magnums that continue to carve out a niche all of their own in the hunting community.

At the other end of the ballistics scale is the appearance of a remarkable small-game round, the 17 Hornady Rimfire Magnum. Designed to compete with the 22 Win. Mag., the new 17 HRM should be just the ticket for suburban and farmland varminting. Better quality premium bullets continue to appear across all rifle and pistol lines while Hevi.Shot has finally found a commercial home and is being loaded by Remington in some sensational waterfowl, turkey and upland game offerings. The year wouldn't be complete without the reintroduction of some oldies but goodies, and Hornady has done just that with its new 405 Win. and 458 Lott loadings. The quality and selection of sporting ammunition has never been better. Here are the latest developments.

Accurate Arms

The appearance and growing popularity of the short magnum rifle cartridges have spurred on the powder companies to develop and market a compatible line of high-performance propellants. MAGPRO is Accurate

Arms' response in the form of a ball powder with a burn rate tailored specifically to the fat, squat little magnums. From the loading data we've seen on the 300 WSM, MAGPRO is capable of delivering factory-level velocities. www.accuratepowder.com

Alliant Powder

Possibly the biggest news of the year was Alliant Technologies' acquisition of Federal Cartridge, CCI/Speer, Estate Cartridge, RCBS, Weaver, Simmons, Redfield, Ram-Line and Outers from Blount. As the largest supplier of ammunition in the world, Alliant is uniquely positioned to bring its vast resources and experience to bear on the civilian ammunition market. This is a company to watch. Meanwhile at Alliant Powder, there is a new varmint/benchrest rifle powder — Reloader 10X — designed specifically for the 223 and similar-sized varmint and target cartridges. Don't miss Alliant Powder's latest, free "Reloader's Guide" that includes updated data for the short magnums, the full spectrum of shotshells, and additional sections on cowboy action and silhouette loads. www.alliantpowder.com

A-Square

A-Square is under new ownership and management. The company's up-beat president, James Smith, assures us that the complete A-Square line of cartridges, cases and bullets is back in production.

Ballistic Products

Here's the mother lode for shotshell reloaders. If a wad, case, projectile, tool or loading manual isn't contained within the 60 or so pages of their entertaining catalog, it probably doesn't exist, nor have a right to. Always on the cutting edge, the

Hevi.Shot is in-- Ballistic Products has bundled some great recipes in their new reloading manual.

company now offers bulk Hevi.Shot in #s BB, 2,4,6, 7 1/2 and 9, plus special 10- and 12-gauge wads, and, most importantly, a well-researched and informative loading manual entitled "Handloading Hevi.Shot." The new Hevi.Shot manual joins the company's already excellent series of manuals on handloading non-toxic steel and Bismuth shot. There's even data on loading non-toxic shells for the English 2-, 2 1/4- and 2 1/2-inch shells.

Promised this year are specialized manuals devoted to the 20 and 28 gauges. These folks have manuals on everything from the "Mighty Ten Gauge" to loading for "Fine Doubles and Vintagers," and they're essential reading. There's a new universal spreader wad being offered this year, called the "X-stream," that fits into the shot column of every gauge from 20 through 10. Remember the Alcan "Air Wedge" wad? Ballistic Products has its own version--the GS2 Air Wedge. This is a 1/4-inch spacer/sealer wad, for the 12-gauge shell, that facilitates adjustment of wad columns. If you load shotshells, go to www.ballisticproducts.com

Barnes

Barnes new "Reloading Manual #3" is what a reloading manual should be. Pictures of suitable bullets accompany each cartridge together with clear graphic displays of comparative bullet trajectories and energy levels, recommended powder data, and application preferences. In addition, each caliber chapter, such as the 6mms, is followed by a complete ballistics section for all available Barnes bullets. The new manual also includes never-before-published reloading data for their lines of dry film-lubricated "X" bullets (XLC) and copper-jacketed, lead-core varmint bullets (VLC). There's even a thread-pitch table for every brand of seating die that equates degrees of seating stem rotation with thousandths of an inch. Neat!

New in the bullet line this year are a 168-grain .308 XLC modeled after a match bullet; two, hot varmint bullets, a 58- and a 72-grain 6mm VLC; and a 195-grain .458 Expander muzzleloader bullet. www.barnesbullets.com

Bismuth

Looking for environmentally friendly ammo? Look no further than Bismuth's "Eco Ammo." Offered in 12- and 20-gauge field loads, Eco Ammo features biodegradable paper cases, fiber wads, brass-plated steel heads and, of course, a charge of non-toxic Bismuth shot. Also new this year is a 12-gauge 3-inch buffered turkey load consisting of 1 5/8 oz. of #4,5 or 6 shot. Safe for older barrels, Bismuth is still an ideal load for fine double guns.
www.bismuth-notox.com

Black Hills Ammunition

From the hills of South Dakota come a number of new loadings this year, particularly interesting is the 338 Lapua matched with a 250-grain Sierra MatchKing at 2950 fps. Black Hills' line

Barnes new reloading manual includes new data for the company's XLC and VLC bullets.

Bismuth's new "Eco Ammo" features biodegradable paper cases, fiber wads, brass-plated steel heads and non-toxic Bismuth shot.

of 223 cartridges has been upgraded with the addition of a 40-grain Nosler BT at 3600 fps; a 69-grain Sierra MatchKing at 2850 fps; and a 73-grain Berger BTHP at 2750 fps. Great ammo — great folks. www.black-hills.com

Cast Performance Bullet Company

Looking for an LBT bullet design, an odd caliber bullet, a lead bullet sized to different diameters, or a 500-grain Springfield Trapdoor bullet cast from a 20:1 alloy? Cast Performance probably can supply it. These are quality hand-cast products. In fact, they're so good, Cast Performance bullets are factory-loaded by Federal in its Cast Core Premium Handgun Hunting Cartridge line. www.castperformance.com

CCI-Speer

Now part of the Alliant Ammunition Group, CCI-Speer has developed some intriguing products for the new year. CCI's "Velocitor" is the world's fastest 40-grain 22 LR round. How fast? 1435 fps fast, plus the HP bullet is based on CCI's Gold Dot technology that ensures exacting controlled expansion. Speaking of bullets, Speer is now offering the complete line of Trophy Bonded Bear Claw bullets in diameters from .224 to .458, plus 165- and 180-grain .308 Deep-Shok bullets. Previous to this, both bullet lines were loaded exclusively by Federal and unavailable as separate components. With the increasing popularity of the 454 Casull, 50 Action Express, 475 Linebaugh and 480 Ruger in handgun hunting circles, Speer is offering a 300-grain HP .45; 300-grain HP .50; and a 325-grain SP .475 in its Gold Dot component line-up this year. Speer's Gold Dot handgun ammunition line has been expanded with a 124-grain HP 9mm+P at 1220 fps and a 325-grain SP 480 Ruger at 1350 fps. Finally, Speer's truly non-leading, dry-film lubricant has been added to all of their extensive lead bullet designs.
www.cci-ammunition.com & www.speer-bullets.com

Federal

Another member of Alliant's Ammunition Group, Federal has been particularly active in the shotshell end of the business. New this year are some Premium Grand Slam Turkey loads featuring buffered, copper-plated shot in #s 4,5 and 6 for the 10- and 12-gauge 3 1/2"; 12-gauge/3" and 20-gauge/3". A portion of the proceeds from the sales of these shells will be donated to the National Wild Turkey Federation.

Steel shot velocities keep getting pumped up annually by the major manufacturers and Federal is releasing a series of new loads in their Classic Steel-Heavy High Velocity line. Available in a 1 1/4 oz. loading of #s T, BBB, BB, 1, 2, 3, 4, and 6, the 12-gauge/3-inch case is pushing 1450 fps while the 2 3/4-inch cartridge is not far behind at 1350 fps.

In their metallic lines, Federal has added the 300 WSM with either a

180-grain Trophy Bonded Bear Claw or 180-grain Speer Grand Slam at 2970 fps. plus a 125-grain FMJ 357 SIG loading at 1350 fps and a 200-grain Expanding FMJ 45 Auto load clocking 1035 fps. www.federalcartridge.com

Fiocchi

Paper cases are coming back in vogue. Fiocchi is adding 12-gauge skeet, trap and sporting clays loads loaded with 1 1/8 oz of #s 7 1/2 or 8 in paper hulls. Their hard-hitting Golden Pheasant line carrying nickel-plated shot has been expanded to include a 16-gauge shell loaded with 1 1/8 oz. of #s 5,6,and 7 1/2 ripping along at 1310 fps and a 20-gauge 2 3/4-inch load carrying 1 oz. of #5s at 1245 fps.

Sporting clays competition is getting a big boost with the introduction of the company's 12-gauge Nickel Rino shell loaded with 1 1/8 oz. of nickel-plated #s 7 1/2 and 8. For new shooters, there's even a new ultra-low recoil load for the 20-gauge 2 3/4-inch shell featuring 3/4 oz. of #7 1/2s at a mild-paced 1075 fps. www.fiocchiusa.com

Garrett Cartridge

Known for their superior penetrating cast bullet line, Garrett is adding a new 44 Magnum load featuring a 255-grain LBT bullet with a wide flat nose at 1000 fps and a SAAMI pressure-compliant 45-70 loading pushing a 420-grain Hammerhead bullet at 1650 fps, making it ideal for the T/C Contender, C. Sharps rifles, BFR revolver and Kodiak Mk IV. www.garrettcartridge.com

GPA

This is a new monolithic copper alloy, HP or solid bullet that was announced at the SHOT Show by ROC Import. According to their literature, it will be available in every caliber from 6mm to .600. See them at www.roc-import.com

Graf & Sons

This popular handloader's heaven is importing a new line of shotgun/pistol powders manufactured in Hungary by Nitrokemia under the trade name "REX." Presently the REX line is available in four burn rates corresponding roughly to Bullseye through Universal. www.grfs.com

Hodgdon

What powder powers the new 17 HRM? It's Hodgdon's Lil' Gun. Never at a loss to give handloaders a new propellant, Hodgdon is introducing RETUMBO magnum rifle powder for super-big capacity cases like the 30-378 Weatherby. The loading data looks exciting, with very high velocities at sane pressures in the big boomers. If you're into muzzleloading, you'll enjoy Hodgdon's new TRIPLE SEVEN powder that contains no sulfur, is odorless, cleans up completely with one to three water-soaked patches and, volume-for-volume, delivers velocities that exceed all other blackpowder substitutes. If

you're more traditional and shoot a 45-caliber muzzle stuffer, there's a new Pyrodex 45-caliber/50-grain pellet available for you. Finally, Hodgdon has produced a new 81-page shotshell manual that covers all gauges from .410 through 10, including the 2- and 2 1/2-inch cases for English 12-gauge doubles. www.hodgdon.com

Hornady

Hornady's novel 17 HRM (Hornady Rimfire Magnum) simply stole the show this year. Pushing an explosive, 17-grain V-Max bullet at 2550 fps and currently chambered by Ruger, Marlin, H&R, and Anschutz, the 17 HRM will find a warm spot with varmint hunters and, frankly, with any rifleman who

Hodgdon's TRIPLE SEVEN muzzleloading propellant contains no sulfur, produces high velocities and cleans up quickly with water.

wants less noise and flatter trajectories than the venerable 22 Magnum offers.

From its roots in the component business, the company has evolved into a major, innovative ammunition manufacturer, and this year has added the 458 Lott with a 500-grain RN at 2300 fps; the 405 Win. loaded with a 300-grain SP at 2200 fps; and a "Light/Heavy Magnum" loading for the 444 Marlin featuring a 265-grain FP at 2335 fps.

Hornady's line of SST (Super Shock Tipped) game bullets has been expanded with the addition of nine new

Hodgdon's RETUMBO propellant is formulated to bring out the best in the largest capacity magnum cases.

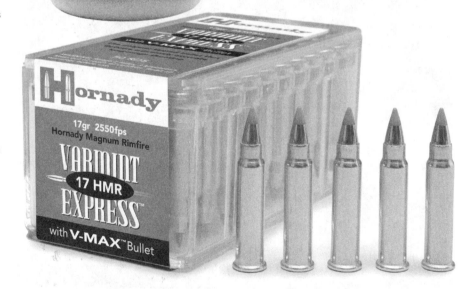

Hornady's 17 Rimfire magnum is quieter and flatter shooting than the 22 Magnum and should prove ideal for varmint hunting in suburbia or densely-populated farming areas.

Lyman's "Black Powder Handbook and Loading Manual" is the most comprehensive treatment of the subject ever published.

bullets from 6mm to .338 while there are nine new ammunition offerings featuring the SST projectiles. Other new handloading components include a 300-grain .411 FP bullet for the 405 Winchester and a .475 gas check. www.hornady.com

Huntington

Looking for a unique or hard-to-find reloading component? Huntington is the place to find it. Do you need 22 Rem. Jet, 6.5 Rem. Mag., 30 Rem., or

Noted for their quality, Norma reloading products should be more plentiful in 2003.

416 Rem. Mag. cases? Huntington commissioned Remington to make special runs of these great, but often neglected, cartridges this year. From quality brass makers like Hirtenberger and Horneber, Huntington has secured ample supplies of cases for the 5.6x50mm, 5.6x50R, 6.5x57mm, 6.5x68S, 8x68S, 5.6x35R, 6.5x61mm, 7x66 Vom Hofe, 7x72R, 280 Ross, 8mm Lebel, 8x56 MS, 9x56 MS, 9x57mm, 9.3x64mm, 9.5x57 MS, 10.75x68mm, 11.2x72 Schuler and any classic English big-game case you can think of. There's also a fresh supply of 8mm Nambu cases on hand. I'm just touching the tip of the iceberg. See them at www.huntingtons.com

Lapua/Vihtavuori

Lapua's debuting a number of new products including a subsonic, match quality, 22 LR cartridge named "Signum" that sports a high-tech bullet lubricant that eliminates leading and decreases pressure, resulting in less bullet base deformation and improved accuracy; 750-grain and 800-grain "Bullex-N" match bullets for 50 BMG shooters; brass and a wide selection of hunting and match bullets for the 338 Lapua Magnum; and five new VihtaVuori high-energy powders for shotshell reloading under the "Total Knockdown" label. www.lapua.com

Lyman

Lyman's series of handloading manuals have always been among the most original and invaluable references in the field. Not tied to any particular brand of powder or projectile, Lyman manuals have a breadth of data that is refreshingly unique. This year's release of the 2nd Edition Black Powder Handbook & Loading Manual carries on the tradition, covering not only every possible aspect of muzzleloading but blackpowder cartridges as well. The loading and ballistics data section contains thousands of combinations for every caliber, barrel length and barrel twist typically available. The powders tested include GOEX, Elephant and Pyrodex. Don't miss this manual. It's that good. www.lymanproducts.com

MAST Technology

Here's the home of the famous Bell Brass. The two new commercial offerings this year are 11mm(43) Mauser and 338 Lapua. If you follow military matters, MAST was just awarded the contract to manufacture M-781, 40mm practice grenade ammunition at the Lake City Army Ammunition Plant. See their complete list of tough brass cases at www.bellammo.com.

Norma

Norma's upping the ante with their announcement of the release of the Oryx hunting bullet. The Oryx is a flat-based, semi-spitzer, bonded-core bullet with a gilding metal jacket to reduce fouling. The company indicates fired weight retention runs 90-95 percent. Oryx bullets are already

Norma's new Oryx big-game bullet features a bonded core and is available in Norma ammunition or as a reloading component.

loaded in Norma ammunition and will be available this year as components in: 6.5mm/156 grain; 7mm/156 grain; .308/180 and 200 grain; 8mm/196 grain; and 9.3mm/286 grain. www.norma.cc

Northern Precision

Northern Precision is the place to look for a unique variety of .308, .358, .375, .429, .416 and .458 handmade bullets. They include a 198-grain .416 or 265-grain .458 "Varminter;" bonded-core big-game bullets; and more recently a full line of .358-inch diameter projectiles. Catalogued this year are even primer-propelled .375 "poly balls" for short-range indoor target shooting with your Holland & Holland. Tel: (315) 493-1711

Nosler

Have a 375 H&H languishing in the gun cabinet? Filling in their ever-expanding line of terrific performing Ballistic Tips, Nosler has released a 260-grain .375 BT specifically designed for light to medium big game. With a ballistic coefficient of .473, the new .375 BT combines flat trajectory with tremendous down-range energy. For the smaller-bore enthusiast, there's a new 95-grain .243 BT designed

Made with benchrest-quality J4 jackets, Nosler's 69-grain .224 match bullet is ideal for high-power and service rifle events.

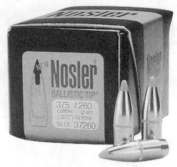

Have a 375 H&H languishing in the closet? Nosler's 260-grain .375 BT is specifically designed for light- and medium-size big game.

Nosler's expanding Ballistic Tip line now includes a 95-grain .243 BT that should bring out the best in the 6mms.

Win. Mag., and 308 Win. There's even a 385-grain 12-gauge Core-Lokt Ultra bonded sabot slug at 1900 fps from the 2 3/4-inch case.

Remington continues to work with Eley on the development of target-grade 22 RF ammo. This year there are three different grades—Match EPS, Club Xtra and Target Rifle—all loaded with a 40-grain bullet at 1085 fps. And the little 221 Fireball has returned to favor, being chambered in the annual Classic Model 700.

www.remington.com

Schroeder Bullets

Having trouble locating old or odd-size bullets and brass? Then send for

specifically for light big game in the deer and antelope class. And for the high-power and service rifle competitor, there are new 69-grain and 80-grain .224 match bullets made on benchrest-quality J4 jackets. Both bullets are hollowpoint boattail low-drag designs with ballistic coefficients of .359 and .440 respectively. A 1:9 twist is recommended for the 69-grain, and a 1:7 for the 80-grain bullet. www.nosler.com

Oregon Trail/Trueshot

Offering a wide selection of pistol and rifle bullets cast from a great alloy, sized and lubricated correctly, Oregon Trail has earned an enviable reputation in the shooting community. Their former line of "Laser-Cast" gas-checked and plain-based rifle and pistol bullets is now called "Trueshot." It includes such specialized designs as gas-checked 310-grain 44-caliber and 360-grain 45-caliber revolver bullets as well as exceptionally accurate 30- and 32-caliber rifle bullets.

Responding to a request from dedicated IDPA and Limited shooters for a 40-caliber bullet that would feed reliably in 1911 autoloaders and meet major power factors with safe pressure margins, Trueshot has developed the solution--the 40-1911 185-grain RN SWC. The new bullet feeds flawlessly in

10mm and 40 S&W guns without having to resort to freeboring. See them at www.trueshotbullets.com.

Remington

Big Green was busy this year. Possibly the most interesting development is the adoption of Hevi.Shot in their waterfowl, turkey and upland game shotshells. An alloy of tungsten-nickel and iron, Hevi.Shot is 10 percent denser than lead and is noted for delivering dense patterns and exceptional penetration. With interest in short-action, beltless magnums growing, Remington brought out two: the 7mm and 300 Rem. Short Action Ultra Mags.

The old faithful Core-Lokt bullet was upgraded this year with a new bonded-core and jacket design. Named the Core-Lokt Ultra, it will be loaded in the 270 Win., 7mm Rem. Mag., 30-06, 300

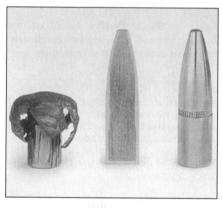

Remington's classic Core-Lokt bullet has been improved with the addition of a bonded-core and redesigned jacket. It's the new Core-Lokt Ultra.

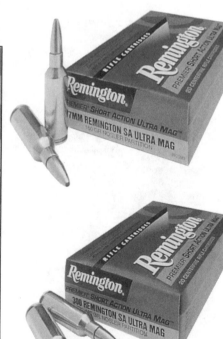

Remington's 7mm and 300 Short Action Ultra Magnum cartridges bring magnum performance to their light, portable short-action rifle models.

Responding to the needs of IDPA and Limited competitors, Oregon Trail designed a 185-grain 40-caliber bullet that works flawlessly in the Model 1911.

"Trueshot" is Oregon Trails' latest line of high quality gas-checked and plain-based handgun and rifle bullets.

Remington's 385-grain 12-gauge Core-Lokt Ultra bonded sabot slug is a hot performer at 1900 fps from a 2 3/4-inch case.

Winchester's 270 WSM is faster and flatter than the 270 Win. and ideally mated to today's lighter-weight, compact, short-action rifles.

For the first time, Remington has chambered the compact and efficient 221 Fireball in a Model 700 rifle.

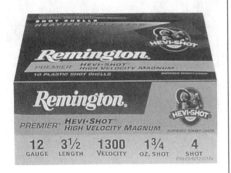

Remington has added Hevi.Shot to its waterfowl, turkey and upland game loads.

Schroeder's new catalog. In it is everything from .287-inch diameter 280 Ross bullets to 6mm Lee Navy brass. And if you really want a wildcat, try Schroeder's 5mm centerfire conversion kit for the Remington Model 591/592

5mm Rimfire Magnum. It makes into the perfect urban varminter.
Tel: (619) 423-8124.

Sierra

If you enjoy shooting the 8mm in any guise, you'll find Sierra's new 200-grain 8mm HPBT MatchKing a sterling performer. Designed originally for the 8x57mm and marketed exclusively in Europe, the new MatchKing is being made available to any aficionado who wants to wring out the best from an 8mm case. Periodically, Sierra publishes a very informative and technical newsletter called the "X-Ring" that any handloader will find useful. The current issue, as well as back issues, is available at the company's web site: www.sierrabullets.com

Swift Bullets

The bonded-core, polymer-tipped Scirocco line is being expanded this year with the addition of a 130-grain .270 bullet with a ballistic coefficient of .430, and just possibly a 210-grain .338 as well. Finally Swift is issuing a handloading guide for their complete lines of premium bullets. The first edition, that covers 50 popular hunting cartridges, will be published as a hardbound limited edition, so get your orders in early. Tel: (785) 754-3959.

Taurus

One of the surprise announcements of the year was that Taurus was getting into the handgun ammunition business. Planned for this year are the 9mm, 40 S&W, 45 ACP, 357 Mag., 41 Mag., 44 Mag., 454 Casull, and 480 Ruger. The new brand will appear under the Taurus name and be loaded with a solid copper alloy HP bullet, by Barnes, called the "HEX." www.taurususa.com

Widener's

This is a great catalog supply house for components and ammunition--some of which are unique. They always stock a wide selection of surplus military bullets, powder, and loaded ammunition with extensive listings of Israel Military Industries products. Excellent prices — good service. www.wideners.com

Winchester Ammunition

They had to do it! Winchester finally awarded their classic caliber - the 270 - Winchester Short Magnum status, and then went on to grant it to the 7mm as well. The new 270 WSM kicks out a 130-grain Ballistic Silvertip at 3275 fps and the 7mm WSM, a 140-grain Ballistic Silvertip at 3225 fps. The 270 WSM really performs, and it was my cartridge of choice this past fall for antelope. Both the short 270 and 7mm is being factory loaded with Winchester's proprietary Fail Safe and Power-Point bullets as well.

There's a new line of Supreme products this year under the "Platinum Tip Hollow Point Hunting Ammunition" label consisting of a 400-grain 12-gauge Platinum Tip sabot slug with a muzzle velocity of 1700 fps and a saboted 260-grain 50-caliber muzzle-loading projectile.

Sierra's 200-grain 8mm HPBT MatchKing is designed to deliver target accuracy in the 8x57mm and other 8mms.

Giving more punch to the 28 gauge for sporting clays competition, Winchester boosted the velocity of this 3/4 oz./#8 AA load to 1200 fps.

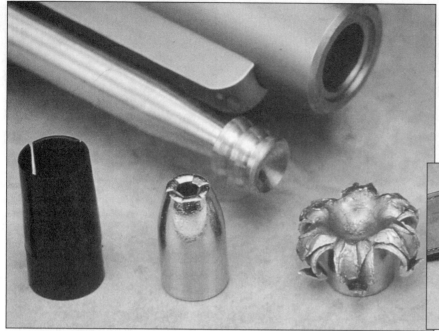

Winchester's new "Platinum Hollow Point Hunting Ammunition" line includes a 400-grain 12-gauge sabot slug loaded to 1700 fps. and a 260-grain 50-caliber sabot projectile for muzzleloaders.

Winchester is adding 38 Special, 44 Special, 44-40 and 45 Colt, low velocity, lead cowboy action loads to its competitively priced USA line.

Winchester's new Supreme High Velocity Field load for the 12-gauge 2 3/4-inch chambering offers 1400 fps with 1 1/4 oz. of #s 4,5,6 & 7 1/2.

For the cowboy action shooters, Winchester is adding low velocity, lead bullet loads for the 38 Special, 44 Special, 44-40, and 45 Colt to its competitively priced USA line.

There are lots of new components this year, including all of the WSM cases and bullets; 9x23mm and 454 Casull brass; and the Platinum Tip shotgun and muzzle-loading sabot projectiles. www.winchester.com

WOLF AMMUNITION

Importing ammunition from Russia, Wolf is introducing a rather complete line of 20- and 12-gauge shotshells. www.wolfammo.com ●

To give more punch to the 20 and 28 gauges for sporting clays use, Winchester has developed some high-velocity AA target loads. The 20-gauge shell carries 7/8 oz. of #s 7 1/2 and 8 at 1275 fps and the 28-gauge shell holds 3/4 oz. of #s 8 and 9 with a muzzle velocity of 1200 fps. Speaking about velocity, there's a new Supreme High Velocity Field load for the 2 2/4-inch 12 gauge producing 1400 fps with 1 1/4 oz. of #s 4,5,6, and 7 1/2. Similarly, two 1550 fps loadings have been added to the Super-X Drylok Super Steel line –- a 3 1/2-inch 12-gauge shell with 1 1/4 oz. of #s BB and 2 and a 3-inch 12-gauge shell with 1 1/8 oz. of #s 2 and 3.

AVERAGE CENTERFIRE RIFLE CARTRIDGE BALLISTICS AND PRICES

Many manufacturers do not supply suggested retail prices. Others did not get their pricing to us before press time. All pricing can vary dependent on the exact brand and style of ammo selected and/or the retail outlet from which you make your purchase. Pricing has been rounded to the nearest dollar and represents our best estimate of average pricing. An * after the cartridge means these loads are available with Nosler Partition or Swift A-Frame bullets. Listed pricing may or may not reflect this bullet type. ** = these are packed 50 to box, all others are 20 to box. Wea. Mag.= Weatherby Magnum. Spfd. = Springfield. A-A-Sq. = A-Square. N.E.=Nitro Express.

Cartridge	Bullet Weight Grains	VELOCITY (fps)					ENERGY (ft. lbs.)					TRAJ. (in.)				Est. Price/box
		Muzzle	100 yds.	200 yds.	300 yds.	400 yds.	Muzzle	100 yds.	200 yds.	300 yds.	400 yds.	100 yds.	200 yds.	300 yds.	400 yds.	
17 Remington	25	4040	3284	2644	2086	1606	906	599	388	242	143	+2.0	+1.7	-4.0	-17.0	$17
221 Fireball	50	2800	2137	1580	1180	988	870	507	277	155	109	+0.0	-7.0	-28.0	NA	$14
22 Hornet	34	3050	2132	1415	1017	852	700	343	151	78	55	+0.0	-6.6	-15.5	-29.9	NA
22 Hornet	35	3100	2278	1601	1135	929	747	403	199	100	67	+2.75	0.0	-16.9	-60.4	NA
22 Hornet	45	2690	2042	1502	1128	948	723	417	225	127	90	+0.0	-7.7	-31.0	NA	$27**
218 Bee	46	2760	2102	1550	1155	961	788	451	245	136	94	+0.0	-7.2	-29.0	NA	$46**
222 Remington	40	3600	3117	2673	2269	1911	1151	863	634	457	324	++1.07	0.0	-6.13	-18.9	NA
222 Remington	50	3140	2602	2123	1700	1350	1094	752	500	321	202	++2.0	-0.4	-11.0	-33.0	$11
222 Remington	55	3020	2562	2147	1773	1451	1114	801	563	384	257	+2.0	-0.4	-11.0	-33.0	$12
22 PPC	52	3400	2930	2510	2130	NA	1335	990	730	525	NA	+2.0	1.4	-5.0	NA	NA
223 Remington	40	3650	3010	2450	1950	1530	1185	805	535	340	265	+2.0	+1.0	-6.0	-22.0	$14
223 Remington	40	3800	3305	2845	2424	2044	1282	970	719	522	371	0.84	0.0	-5.34	-16.6	NA
223 Remington	50	3300	2874	2484	2130	1809	1209	917	685	504	363	1.37	0.0	-7.05	-21.8	NA
223 Remington	52/53	3330	2882	2477	2106	1770	1305	978	722	522	369	+2.0	+0.6	-6.5	-21.5	$14
223 Remington	55	3240	2748	2305	1906	1556	1282	922	649	444	296	+2.0	-0.2	-9.0	-27.0	$12
223 Remington	60	3100	2712	2355	2026	1726	1280	979	739	547	397	+2.0	+0.2	-8.0	-24.7	$16
223 Remington	64	3020	2621	2256	1920	1619	1296	977	723	524	373	+2.0	-0.2	-9.3	-23.0	$14
223 Remington	69	3000	2720	2460	2210	1980	1380	1135	925	750	600	+2.0	+0.8	-5.8	-17.5	$15
223 Remington	75	2790	2554	2330	2119	1926	1296	1086	904	747	617	2.37	0.0	-8.75	-25.1	NA
223 Remington	77	2750	2584	2354	2169	1992	1293	1110	948	804	679	1.93	0.0	-8.2	-23.8	NA
222 Rem. Mag.	55	3240	2748	2305	1906	1556	1282	922	649	444	296	+2.0	-0.2	-9.0	-27.0	$14
225 Winchester	55	3570	3066	2616	2208	1838	1556	1148	836	595	412	+2.0	+1.0	-5.0	-20.0	$19
224 Wea. Mag.	55	3650	3192	2780	2403	2057	1627	1244	943	705	516	+2.0	+1.2	-4.0	-17.0	$32
22-250 Rem.	40	4000	3320	2720	2200	1740	1420	980	660	430	265	+2.0	+1.8	-3.0	-16.0	$14
22-250 Rem.	50	3725	3264	2641	2455	2103	1540	1183	896	669	491	0.89	0.0	-5.23	-16.3	NA
22-250 Rem.	52/55	3680	3137	2656	2222	1832	1654	1201	861	603	410	+2.0	+1.3	-4.0	-17.0	$13
22-250 Rem.	60	3600	3195	2826	2485	2169	1727	1360	1064	823	627	+2.0	+2.0	-2.4	-12.3	$19
220 Swift	40	4200	3678	3190	2739	2329	1566	1201	904	666	482	+0.51	0.0	-4.0	-12.9	NA
220 Swift	50	3780	3158	2617	2135	1710	1586	1107	760	506	325	+2.0	+1.4	-4.4	-17.9	$20
220 Swift	50	3850	3396	2970	2576	2215	1645	1280	979	736	545	0.74	0.0	-4.84	-15.1	NA
220 Swift	55	3800	3370	2990	2630	2310	1765	1390	1090	850	650	0.8	0.0	-4.7	-14.4	NA
220 Swift	55	3650	3194	2772	2384	2035	1627	1246	939	694	506	+2.0	+2.0	-2.6	-13.4	$19
220 Swift	60	3600	3199	2824	2475	2156	1727	1364	1063	816	619	+2.0	+1.6	-4.1	-13.1	$19
22 Savage H.P.	71	2790	2340	1930	1570	1280	1225	860	585	390	190	+2.0	-1.0	-10.4	-35.7	NA
6mm BR Rem.	100	2550	2310	2083	1870	1671	1444	1185	963	776	620	+2.5	-0.6	-11.8	NA	$22
6mm Norma BR	107	2822	2667	2517	2372	2229	1893	1690	1506	1337	1181	+1.73	0.0	-7.24	-20.6	NA
6mm PPC	70	3140	2750	2400	2070	NA	1535	1175	895	665	NA	+2.0	+1.4	-5.0	NA	NA
243 Winchester	55	4025	3597	3209	2853	2525	1978	1579	1257	994	779	+0.6	0.00	-4.0	-12.2	NA
243 Winchester	60	3600	3110	2660	2260	1890	1725	1285	945	680	475	+2.0	+1.8	-3.3	-15.5	$17
243 Winchester	70	3400	3040	2700	2390	2100	1795	1435	1135	890	685	1.1	0.0	-5.9	-18.0	NA
243 Winchester	75/80	3350	2955	2593	2259	1951	1993	1551	1194	906	676	+2.0	+0.9	-5.0	-19.0	$16
243 Winchester	85	3320	3070	2830	2600	2380	2080	1770	1510	1280	1070	+2.0	+1.2	-4.0	-14.0	$18
243 Winchester	90	3120	2871	2635	2411	2199	1946	1647	1388	1162	966	1.4	0.0	-6.4	-18.8	NA
243 Winchester*	100	2960	2697	2449	2215	1993	1945	1615	1332	1089	882	+2.5	+1.2	-6.0	-20.0	$16
243 Winchester	105	2920	2689	2470	2261	2062	1988	1686	1422	1192	992	+2.5	+1.6	-5.0	-18.4	$21
243 Light Mag.	100	3100	2839	2592	2358	2138	2133	1790	1491	1235	1014	+1.5	0.0	-6.8	-19.8	NA
6mm Remington	80	3470	3064	2694	2352	2036	2139	1667	1289	982	736	+2.0	+1.1	-5.0	-17.0	$16
6mm Remington	100	3100	2829	2573	2332	2104	2133	1777	1470	1207	983	+2.5	+1.6	-5.0	-17.0	$16
6mm Remington	105	3060	2822	2596	2381	2177	2105	1788	1512	1270	1059	+2.5	+1.1	-3.3	-15.0	$21
6mm Rem. Light Mag.	100	3250	2997	2756	2528	2311	2345	1995	1687	1418	1186	1.59	0.0	-6.33	-18.3	NA
6.17(.243) Spitfire	100	3350	3122	2905	2698	2501	2493	2164	1874	1617	1389	2.4	3.20	0	-8	NA
240 Wea. Mag.	87	3500	3202	2924	2663	2416	2366	1980	1651	1370	1127	+2.0	+2.0	-2.0	-12.0	$32
240 Wea. Mag.	100	3395	3106	2835	2581	2339	2559	2142	1785	1478	1215	+2.5	+2.8	-2.0	-11.0	$43
25-20 Win.	86	1460	1194	1030	931	858	407	272	203	165	141	0.0	-23.5	NA	NA	$32**
25-35 Win.	117	2230	1866	1545	1282	1097	1292	904	620	427	313	+2.5	-4.2	-26.0	NA	$24
250 Savage	100	2820	2504	2210	1936	1684	1765	1392	1084	832	630	+2.5	+0.4	-9.0	-28.0	$17

17
22
6mm (24)
25

Cartridge	Bullet Weight Grains	VELOCITY (fps)					ENERGY (ft. lbs.)					TRAJ. (in.)				Est. Price/ box
		Muzzle	100 yds.	200 yds.	300 yds.	400 yds.	Muzzle	100 yds.	200 yds.	300 yds.	400 yds.	100 yds.	200 yds.	300 yds.	400 yds.	
25 257 Roberts	100	2980	2661	2363	2085	1827	1972	1572	1240	965	741	+2.5	-0.8	-5.2	-21.6	$20
257 Roberts+P	117	2780	2411	2071	1761	1488	2009	1511	1115	806	576	+2.5	-0.2	-10.2	-32.6	$18
257 Roberts+P	120	2780	2560	2360	2160	1970	2060	1750	1480	1240	1030	+2.5	+1.2	-6.4	-23.6	$22
257 Roberts	122	2600	2331	2078	1842	1625	1831	1472	1169	919	715	+2.5	0.0	-10.6	-31.4	$21
257 Light Mag.	117	2940	2694	2460	2240	2031	2245	1885	1572	1303	1071	+1.7	0.0	-7.6	-21.8	NA
25-06 Rem.	87	3440	2995	2591	2222	1884	2286	1733	1297	954	686	+2.0	+1.1	-2.5	-14.4	$17
25-06 Rem.	90	3440	3043	2680	2344	2034	2364	1850	1435	1098	827	+2.0	+1.8	-3.3	-15.6	$17
25-06 Rem.	100	3230	2893	2580	2287	2014	2316	1858	1478	1161	901	+2.0	+0.8	-5.7	-18.9	$17
25-06 Rem.	117	2990	2770	2570	2370	2190	2320	2000	1715	1465	1246	+2.5	+1.0	-7.9	-26.6	$19
25-06 Rem.*	120	2990	2730	2484	2252	2032	2382	1985	1644	1351	1100	+2.5	+1.2	-5.3	-19.6	$17
25-06 Rem.	122	2930	2706	2492	2289	2095	2325	1983	1683	1419	1189	+2.5	+1.8	-4.5	-17.5	$23
257 Wea. Mag.	87	3825	3456	3118	2805	2513	2826	2308	1870	1520	1220	+2.0	+2.7	-0.3	-7.6	$32
257 Wea. Mag.	100	3555	3237	2941	2665	2404	2806	2326	1920	1576	1283	+2.5	+3.2	0.0	-8.0	$32
257 Scramjet	100	3745	3450	3173	2912	2666	3114	2643	2235	1883	1578	+2.1	+2.77	0.0	-6.93	NA
6.5 6.5x50mm Jap.	139	2360	2160	1970	1790	1620	1720	1440	1195	985	810	+2.5	-1.0	-13.5	NA	NA
6.5x50mm Jap.	156	2070	1830	1610	1430	1260	1475	1155	900	695	550	+2.5	-4.0	-23.8	NA	NA
6.5x52mm Car.	139	2580	2360	2160	1970	1790	2045	1725	1440	1195	985	+2.5	0.0	-9.9	-29.0	NA
6.5x52mm Car.	156	2430	2170	1930	1700	1500	2045	1630	1285	1005	780	+2.5	-1.0	-13.9	NA	NA
6.5x55mm Light Mag.	129	2750	2549	2355	2171	1994	2166	1860	1589	1350	1139	+2.0	0.0	-8.2	-23.9	NA
6.5x55mm Swe.	140	2550	NA	NA	NA	NA	2020	NA	NA	NA	NA	NA	NA	NA	NA	$18
6.5x55mm Swe.*	139/140	2850	2640	2440	2250	2070	2525	2170	1855	1575	1330	+2.5	+1.6	-5.4	-18.9	$18
6.5x55mm Swe.	156	2650	2370	2110	1870	1650	2425	1950	1550	1215	945	+2.5	0.0	-10.3	-30.6	NA
260 Remington	125	2875	2669	2473	2285	2105	2294	1977	1697	1449	1230	1.71	0.0	-7.4	-21.4	NA
260 Remington	140	2750	2544	2347	2158	1979	2351	2011	1712	1448	1217	+2.2	0.0	-8.6	-24.6	NA
6.5-284 Norma	142	3025	2890	2758	2631	2507	2886	2634	2400	2183	1982	1.13	0.0	-5.7	-16.4	NA
6.71 (264) Phantom	120	3150	2929	2718	2517	2325	2645	2286	1969	1698	1440	+1.3	0.0	-6.0	-17.5	NA
6.5 Rem. Mag.	120	3210	2905	2621	2353	2102	2745	2248	1830	1475	1177	+2.5	+1.7	-4.1	-16.3	Disc.
264 Win. Mag.	140	3030	2782	2548	2326	2114	2854	2406	2018	1682	1389	+2.5	+1.4	-5.1	-18.0	$24
6.71 (264) Blackbird	140	3480	3261	3053	2855	2665	3766	3307	2899	2534	2208	+2.4	+3.1	0.0	-7.4	NA
27 270 Winchester	100	3430	3021	2649	2305	1988	2612	2027	1557	1179	877	+2.0	+1.0	-4.9	-17.5	$17
270 Winchester	130	3060	2776	2510	2259	2022	2702	2225	1818	1472	1180	+2.5	+1.4	-5.3	-18.2	$17
270 Win. Supreme	130	3150	2881	2628	2388	2161	2865	2396	1993	1646	1348	1.3	0.0	-6.4	-18.9	NA
270 Winchester	135	3000	2780	2570	2369	2178	2697	2315	1979	1682	1421	+2.5	+1.4	-6.0	-17.6	$23
270 Winchester*	140	2940	2700	2480	2260	2060	2685	2270	1905	1590	1315	+2.5	+1.8	-4.6	-17.9	$20
270 Win. Light Magnum	130	3215	2998	2790	2590	2400	2983	2594	2246	1936	1662	1.21	0.0	-5.83	-17.0	NA
270 Winchester*	150	2850	2585	2336	2100	1879	2705	2226	1817	1468	1175	+2.5	+1.2	-6.5	-22.0	$17
270 Win. Supreme	150	2930	2693	2468	2254	2051	2860	2416	2030	1693	1402	1.7	0.0	-7.4	-21.6	NA
270 WSM	130	3275	3041	2820	2609	2408	3096	2669	2295	1564	1673	1.1	0.00	-5.5	-16.1	
270 WSM	140	3125	2865	2619	2386	2165	3035	2559	2132	1769	1457	1.4	0.00	-6.5	-19.0	
270 Wea. Mag.	100	3760	3380	3033	2712	2412	3139	2537	2042	1633	1292	+2.0	+2.4	-1.2	-10.1	$32
270 Wea. Mag.	130	3375	3119	2878	2649	2432	3287	2808	2390	2026	1707	+2.5	-2.9	-0.9	-9.9	$32
270 Wea. Mag.*	150	3245	3036	2837	2647	2465	3507	3070	2681	2334	2023	+2.5	+2.6	-1.8	-11.4	$47
7mm 7mm BR	140	2216	2012	1821	1643	1481	1525	1259	1031	839	681	+2.0	-3.7	-20.0	NA	$23
7mm Mauser*	139/140	2660	2435	2221	2018	1827	2199	1843	1533	1266	1037	+2.5	0.0	-9.6	-27.7	$17
7mm Mauser	145	2690	2442	2206	1985	1777	2334	1920	1568	1268	1017	+2.5	+0.1	-9.6	-28.3	$18
7mm Mauser	154	2690	2490	2300	2120	1940	2475	2120	1810	1530	1285	+2.5	+0.8	-7.5	-23.5	$17
7mm Mauser	175	2440	2137	1857	1603	1382	2313	1774	1340	998	742	+2.5	-1.7	-16.1	NA	$17
7x57 Light Mag.	139	2970	2730	2503	2287	2082	2722	2301	1933	1614	1337	+1.6	0.0	-7.2	-21.0	NA
7x30 Waters	120	2700	2300	1930	1600	1330	1940	1405	990	685	470	+2.5	-0.2	-12.3	NA	$18
7mm-08 Rem.	120	3000	2725	2467	2223	1992	2398	1979	1621	1316	1058	+2.0	0.0	-7.6	-22.3	$18
7mm-08 Rem.*	140	2860	2625	2402	2189	1988	2542	2142	1793	1490	1228	+2.5	+0.8	-6.9	-21.9	$18
7mm-08 Rem.	154	2715	2510	2315	2128	1950	2520	2155	1832	1548	1300	+2.5	+1.0	-7.0	-22.7	$23
7mm-08 Light Mag.	139	3000	2790	2590	2399	2216	2777	2403	2071	1776	1515	+1.5	0.0	-6.7	-19.4	NA
7x64mm Bren.	140				Not Yet Announced											$17
7x64mm Bren.	154	2820	2610	2420	2230	2050	2720	2335	1995	1695	1430	+2.5	+1.4	-5.7	-19.9	NA
7x64mm Bren.*	160	2850	2669	2495	2327	2166	2885	2530	2211	1924	1667	+2.5	+1.6	-4.8	-17.8	$24
7x64mm Bren.	175				Not Yet Announced											$17
284 Winchester	150	2860	2595	2344	2108	1886	2724	2243	1830	1480	1185	+2.5	+0.8	-7.3	-23.2	$24
280 Remington	120	3150	2866	2599	2348	2110	2643	2188	1800	1468	1186	+2.0	+0.6	-6.0	-17.9	$17
280 Remington	140	3000	2758	2528	2309	2102	2797	2363	1986	1657	1373	+2.5	+1.4	-5.2	-18.3	$17
280 Remington*	150	2890	2624	2373	2135	1912	2781	2293	1875	1518	1217	+2.5	+0.8	-7.1	-22.6	$17

Cartridge	Bullet Weight Grains	VELOCITY (fps)					ENERGY (ft. lbs.)					TRAJ. (in.)				Est. Price/box
		Muzzle	100 yds.	200 yds.	300 yds.	400 yds.	Muzzle	100 yds.	200 yds.	300 yds.	400 yds.	100 yds.	200 yds.	300 yds.	400 yds.	
280 Remington	160	2840	2637	2442	2556	2078	2866	2471	2120	1809	1535	+2.5	+0.8	-6.7	-21.0	$20
280 Remington	165	2820	2510	2220	1950	1701	2913	2308	1805	1393	1060	+2.5	+0.4	-8.8	-26.5	$17
7x61mm S&H Sup.	154	3060	2720	2400	2100	1820	3200	2520	1965	1505	1135	+2.5	+1.8	-5.0	-19.8	NA
7mm Dakota	160	3200	3001	2811	2630	2455	3637	3200	2808	2456	2140	+2.1	+1.9	-2.8	-12.5	NA
7mm Rem. Mag.*	139/140	3150	2930	2710	2510	2320	3085	2660	2290	1960	1670	+2.5	+2.4	-2.4	-12.7	$21
7mm Rem. Mag.	150/154	3110	2830	2568	2320	2085	3221	2667	2196	1792	1448	+2.5	+1.6	-4.6	-16.5	$21
7mm Rem. Mag.*	160/162	2950	2730	2520	2320	2120	3090	2650	2250	1910	1600	+2.5	+1.8	-4.4	-17.8	$34
7mm Rem. Mag.	165	2900	2699	2507	2324	2147	3081	2669	2303	1978	1689	+2.5	+1.2	-5.9	-19.0	$28
7mm Rem Mag.	175	2860	2645	2440	2244	2057	3178	2718	2313	1956	1644	+2.5	+1.0	-6.5	-20.7	$21
7mm Rem. SA ULTRA MAG	140	3175	2934	2707	2490	2283	3033	2676	2277	1927	1620	1.3	0.00	-6	-17.7	
7mm Rem. SA ULTRA MAG	150	3110	2828	2563	2313	2077	3221	2663	2188	1782	1437	2.5	2.10	-3.6	-15.8	
7mm Rem. SA ULTRA MAG	160	2960	2762	2572	2390	2215	3112	2709	2350	2029	1743	2.6	2.20	-3.6	-15.4	
7mm Rem. WSM	140	3225	3008	2801	2603	2414	3233	2812	2438	2106	1812	1.2	0.00	-5.6	-16.4	
7mm Rem. WSM	160	2990	2744	2512	2081	1883	3176	2675	2241	1864	1538	1.6	0	-7.1	-20.8	
7mm Wea. Mag.	140	3225	2970	2729	2501	2283	3233	2741	2315	1943	1621	+2.5	+2.0	-3.2	-14.0	$35
7mm Wea. Mag.	154	3260	3023	2799	2586	2382	3539	3044	2609	2227	1890	+2.5	+2.8	-1.5	-10.8	$32
7mm Wea. Mag.*	160	3200	3004	2816	2637	2464	3637	3205	2817	2469	2156	+2.5	+2.7	-1.5	-10.6	$47
7mm Wea. Mag.	165	2950	2747	2553	2367	2189	3188	2765	2388	2053	1756	+2.5	+1.8	-4.2	-16.4	$43
7mm Wea. Mag.	175	2910	2693	2486	2288	2098	3293	2818	2401	2033	1711	+2.5	+1.2	-5.9	-19.4	$35
7.21(.284) Tomahawk	140	3300	3118	2943	2774	2612	3386	3022	2693	2393	2122	2.3	3.20	0.0	-7.7	NA
7mm STW	140	3325	3064	2818	2585	2364	3436	2918	2468	2077	1737	+2.3	+1.8	-3.0	-13.1	NA
7mm STW Supreme	160	3150	2894	2652	2422	2204	3526	2976	2499	2085	1727	1.3	0.0	-6.3	-18.5	NA
7mm Rem. Ultra Mag.	140	3425	3184	2956	2740	2534	3646	3151	2715	2333	1995	1.7	1.60	-2.6	-11.4	NA
7mm Firehawk	140	3625	3373	3135	2909	2695	4084	3536	3054	2631	2258	+2.2	+2.9	0.0	-7.03	NA
7.21 (.284) Firebird	140	3750	3522	3306	3101	2905	4372	3857	3399	2990	2625	1.6	2.4	0.0	-6	NA
30 Carbine	110	1990	1567	1236	1035	923	977	600	373	262	208	0.0	-13.5	NA	NA	$28**
303 Savage	190	1890	1612	1327	1183	1055	1507	1096	794	591	469	+2.5	-7.6	NA	NA	$24
30 Remington	170	2120	1822	1555	1328	1153	1696	1253	913	666	502	+2.5	-4.7	-26.3	NA	$20
7.62x39mm Rus.	123/125	2300	2030	1780	1550	1350	1445	1125	860	655	500	+2.5	-2.0	-17.5	NA	$13
30-30 Win.	55	3400	2693	2085	1570	1187	1412	886	521	301	172	+2.0	0.0	-10.2	-35.0	$18
30-30 Win.	125	2570	2090	1660	1320	1080	1830	1210	770	480	320	-2.0	-2.6	-19.9	NA	$13
30-30 Win.	150	2390	1973	1605	1303	1095	1902	1296	858	565	399	+2.5	-3.2	-22.5	NA	$13
30-30 Win. Supreme	150	2480	2095	1747	1446	1209	2049	1462	1017	697	487	0.0	-6.5	-24.5		NA
30-30 Win.	160	2300	1997	1719	1473	1268	1879	1416	1050	771	571	+2.5	-2.9	-20.2	NA	$18
30-30 PMC Cowboy	170	1300	1198	1121			638	474				0.0	-27.0			NA
30-30 Win.*	170	2200	1895	1619	1381	1191	1827	1355	989	720	535	+2.5	-5.8	-23.6	NA	$13
300 Savage	150	2630	2354	2094	1853	1631	2303	1845	1462	1143	886	+2.5	-0.4	-10.1	-30.7	$17
300 Savage	180	2350	2137	1935	1754	1570	2207	1825	1496	1217	985	+2.5	-1.6	-15.2	NA	$17
30-40 Krag	180	2430	2213	2007	1813	1632	2360	1957	1610	1314	1064	+2.5	-1.4	-13.8	NA	$18
7.65x53mm Arg.	180	2590	2390	2200	2010	1830	2685	2280	1925	1615	1345	+2.5	0.0	-27.6	NA	NA
307 Winchester	150	2760	2321	1924	1575	1289	2530	1795	1233	826	554	+2.5	-1.5	-13.6	NA	Disc.
307 Winchester	180	2510	2179	1874	1599	1362	2519	1898	1404	1022	742	+2.5	-1.6	-15.6	NA	$20
7.5x55 Swiss	180	2650	2450	2250	2060	1880	2805	2390	2020	1700	1415	+2.5	+0.6	-8.1	-24.9	NA
308 Winchester	55	3770	3215	2726	2286	1888	1735	1262	907	638	435	-2.0	+1.4	-3.8	-15.8	$22
308 Winchester	150	2820	2533	2263	2009	1774	2648	2137	1705	1344	1048	+2.5	+0.4	-8.5	-26.1	$17
308 Winchester	165	2700	2440	2194	1963	1748	2670	2180	1763	1411	1199	+2.5	0.0	-9.7	-28.5	$20
308 Winchester	168	2680	2493	2314	2143	1979	2678	2318	1998	1713	1460	+2.5	0.0	-8.9	-25.3	$18
308 Winchester	178	2620	2415	2220	2034	1857	2713	2306	1948	1635	1363	+2.5	0.0	-9.6	-27.6	$23
308 Winchester*	180	2620	2393	2178	1974	1782	2743	2288	1896	1557	1269	+2.5	-0.2	-10.2	-28.5	$17
308 Light Mag.*	150	2980	2703	2442	2195	1964	2959	2433	1986	1606	1285	+1.6	0.0	-7.5	-22.2	NA
308 Light Mag.	165	2870	2658	2456	2263	2078	3019	2589	2211	1877	1583	+1.7	0.0	-7.5	-21.8	NA
308 High Energy	165	2870	2600	2350	2120	1890	3020	2485	2030	1640	1310	+1.8	0.0	-8.2	-24.0	NA
308 Light Mag.	168	2870	2658	2456	2263	2078	3019	2589	2211	1877	1583	+1.7	0.0	-7.5	-21.8	NA
308 High Energy	180	2740	2550	2370	2200	2030	3000	2600	2245	1925	1645	+1.9	0.0	-8.2	-23.5	NA
30-06 Spfd.	55	4080	3485	2965	2502	2083	2033	1483	1074	764	530	+2.0	+1.9	-2.1	-11.7	$22
30-06 Spfd.	125	3140	2780	2447	2138	1853	2736	2145	1662	1279	953	+2.0	+1.0	-6.2	-21.0	$17
30-06 Spfd.	150	2910	2617	2342	2083	1853	2820	2281	1827	1445	1135	+2.5	+0.8	-7.2	-23.4	$17
30-06 Spfd.	152	2910	2654	2413	2184	1968	2858	2378	1965	1610	1307	+2.5	+1.0	-6.6	-21.3	$23
30-06 Spfd.*	165	2800	2534	2283	2047	1825	2872	2352	1909	1534	1220	+2.5	+0.4	-8.4	-25.5	$17

7mm

30

Cartridge	Bullet Weight Grains	VELOCITY (fps)					ENERGY (ft. lbs.)					TRAJ. (in.)				Est. Price/box
		Muzzle	100 yds.	200 yds.	300 yds.	400 yds.	Muzzle	100 yds.	200 yds.	300 yds.	400 yds.	100 yds.	200 yds.	300 yds.	400 yds.	
30-06 Spfd.	168	2710	2522	2346	2169	2003	2739	2372	2045	1754	1497	+2.5	+0.4	-8.0	-23.5	$18
30-06 Spfd.	178	2720	2511	2311	2121	1939	2924	2491	2111	1777	1486	+2.5	+0.4	-8.2	-24.6	$23
30-06 Spfd.*	180	2700	2469	2250	2042	1846	2913	2436	2023	1666	1362	-2.5	0.0	-9.3	-27.0	$17
30-06 Spfd.	220	2410	2130	1870	1632	1422	2837	2216	1708	1301	988	+2.5	-1.7	-18.0	NA	$17
30-06 Light Mag.	150	3100	2815	2548	2295	2058	3200	2639	2161	1755	1410	+1.4	0.0	-6.8	-20.3	NA
30-06 Light Mag.	180	2880	2676	2480	2293	2114	3316	2862	2459	2102	1786	+1.7	0.0	-7.3	-21.3	NA
30-06 High Energy	180	2880	2690	2500	2320	2150	3315	2880	2495	2150	1845	+1.7	0.0	-7.2	-21.0	NA
300 REM SA ULTRA MAG	150	3200	2901	2622	2359	2112	3410	2803	2290	1854	1485	1.3	0.00	-6.4	-19.1	
300 REM SA ULTRA MAG	165	3075	2792	2527	2276	2040	3464	2856	2339	1898	1525	1.5	0.00	-7	-20.7	
300 REM SA ULTRA MAG	180	2960	2761	2571	2389	2214	3501	3047	2642	2280	1959	2.6	2.20	-3.6	-15.4	
7.82 (308) Patriot	150	3250	2999	2762	2537	2323	3519	2997	2542	2145	1798	+1.2	0.0	-5.8	-16.9	NA
300 WSM	150	3300	3061	2834	2619	2414	3628	3121	2676	2285	1941	1.1	0.0	-5.4	-15.9	NA
300 WSM	180	2970	2741	2524	2317	2120	3526	3005	2547	2147	1797	1.6	0.0	-7.0	-20.5	NA
308 Norma Mag.	180	3020	2820	2630	2440	2270	3645	3175	2755	2385	2050	+2.5	+2.0	-3.5	-14.8	NA
300 Dakota	200	3000	2824	2656	2493	2336	3996	3542	3131	2760	2423	+2.2	+1.5	-4.0	-15.2	NA
300 H&H Magnum*	180	2880	2640	2412	2196	1990	3315	2785	2325	1927	1583	+0.8	-6.8	-21.7		$24
300 H&H Magnum	220	2550	2267	2002	1757	NA	3167	2510	1958	1508	NA	-2.5	-0.4	-12.0	NA	
300 Peterson	180	3500	3319	3145	2978	2817	4896	4401	3953	3544	3172	+2.3	+2.9	0.0	-6.8	NA
300 Win. Mag.	150	3290	2951	2636	2342	2068	3605	2900	2314	1827	1424	+2.5	+1.9	-3.8	-15.8	$22
300 Win. Mag.	165	3100	2877	2665	2462	2269	3522	3033	2603	2221	1897	+2.5	+2.4	-3.0	-16.9	$24
300 Win. Mag.	178	2900	2760	2568	2375	2191	3509	3030	2606	2230	1897	+2.5	+1.4	-5.0	-17.6	$29
300 Win. Mag.*	180	2960	2745	2540	2344	2157	3501	3011	2578	2196	1859	+2.5	+1.2	-5.5	-18.5	$22
300 W.M. High Energy	180	3100	2830	2580	2340	2110	3840	3205	2660	2190	1790	+1.4	0.0	-6.6	-19.7	NA
300 W.M. Light Mag.	180	3100	2879	2668	2467	2275	3840	3313	2845	2431	2068	+1.39	0.0	-6.45	-18.7	NA
300 Win. Mag.	190	2885	1691	2506	2327	2156	3511	3055	2648	2285	1961	+2.5	+1.2	-5.7	-19.0	$26
300 W.M. High Energy	200	2930	2740	2550	2370	2200	3810	3325	2885	2495	2145	+1.6	0.0	-6.9	-20.1	NA
300 Win. Mag.*	200	2825	2595	2376	2167	1970	3545	2991	2508	2086	1742	-2.5	+1.6	-4.7	-17.2	$36
300 Win. Mag.	220	2680	2448	2228	2020	1823	3508	2927	2424	1993	1623	+2.5	0.0	-9.5	-27.5	$23
300 Rem. Ultra Mag.	150	3450	3208	2980	2762	2556	3964	3427	2956	2541	2175	1.7	1.5	-2.6	-11.2	NA
300 Rem. Ultra Mag.	180	3250	3037	2834	2640	2454	4221	3686	3201	2786	2407	2.4		-3.0	-12.7	NA
300 Rem. Ultra Mag.	200	3025	2826	2636	2454	2279	4063	3547	3086	2673	2308	2.4		-3.4	-14.6	NA
300 Wea. Mag.	100	3900	3441	3038	2652	2305	3714	2891	2239	1717	1297	+2.0	+2.6	-0.6	-8.7	$32
300 Wea. Mag.	150	3600	3307	3033	2776	2533	4316	3642	3064	2566	2137	+2.5	+3.2	0.0	-8.1	$32
300 Wea. Mag.	165	3450	3210	3000	2792	2593	4360	3796	3297	2855	2464	+2.5	+3.2	0.0	-7.8	NA
300 Wea. Mag.	178	3120	2902	2695	2497	2308	3847	3329	2870	2464	2104	+2.5	-1.7	-3.6	-14.7	$43
300 Wea. Mag.	180	3330	3110	2910	2710	2520	4430	3875	3375	2935	2540	+1.0	0.0	-5.2	-15.1	NA
300 Wea. Mag.	190	3030	2830	2638	2455	2279	3873	3378	2936	2542	2190	+2.5	+1.6	-4.3	-16.0	$38
300 Wea. Mag.	220	2850	2541	2283	1964	1736	3967	3155	2480	1922	1471	+2.5	+0.4	-8.5	-26.4	$35
300 Warbird	180	3400	3180	2971	2772	2582	4620	4042	3528	3071	2664	+2.59	+3.25	0.0	-7.95	NA
300 Pegasus	180	3500	3319	3145	2978	2817	4896	4401	3953	3544	3172	+2.28	+2.89	0.0	-6.79	NA
32-20 Win.	100	1210	1021	913	834	769	325	231	185	154	131	0.0	-32.3	NA	NA	$23**
303 British	150	2685	2441	2210	1992	1787	2401	1984	1627	1321	1064	+2.5	+0.6	-8.4	-26.2	$18
303 British	180	2460	2124	1817	1542	1311	2418	1803	1319	950	687	+2.5	-1.8	-16.8	NA	$18
303 Light Mag.	150	2830	2570	2325	2094	1884	2667	2199	1800	1461	1185	+2.0	0.0	-8.4	-24.6	NA
7.62x54mm Rus.	146	2950	2730	2520	2320	NA	2820	2415	2055	1740	NA	+2.5	+2.0	-4.4	-17.7	NA
7.62x54mm Rus.	180	2580	2370	2180	2000	1820	2650	2250	1900	1590	1100	+2.5	0.0	-9.8	-28.5	NA
7.7x58mm Jap.	180	2500	2300	2100	1920	1750	2490	2105	1770	1475	1225	+2.5	0.0	-10.4	-30.2	NA
8x57mm JS Mau.	165	2850	2520	2210	1930	1670	2965	2330	1795	1360	1015	+2.5	+1.0	-7.7	NA	NA
32 Win. Special	170	2250	1921	1626	1372	1175	1911	1393	998	710	521	+2.5	-3.5	-22.9	NA	$14
8mm Mauser	170	2360	1969	1622	1333	1123	2102	1464	993	671	476	+2.5	-3.1	-22.2	NA	$18
8mm Rem. Mag.	185	3080	2761	2464	2186	1927	3896	3131	2494	1963	1525	+2.5	+1.4	-5.5	-19.7	$30
8mm Rem. Mag.	220	2830	2581	2346	2123	1913	3912	3254	2688	2201	1787	+0.6	-7.6	-23.5		Disc.
338-06	200	2750	2553	2364	2184	2011	3358	2894	2482	2118	1796	+1.9	0.0	-8.22	-23.6	NA
330 Dakota	250	2900	2719	2545	2378	2217	4668	4103	3595	3138	2727	+2.5	+1.3	-5.0	-17.5	NA
338 Lapua	250	2963	2795	2640	2493	NA	4842	4341	3881	3458	NA	+1.9	0.0	-7.9	NA	NA
338 Win. Mag.	200	2960	2658	2375	2110	1862	3890	3137	2505	1977	1539	+2.5	+1.0	-6.7	-22.3	$27
338 Win. Mag.*	210	2830	2590	2370	2150	1940	3735	3130	2610	2155	1760	+2.5	+1.4	-6.0	-20.9	$33
338 Win. Mag.*	225	2785	2517	2266	2029	1808	3871	3165	2565	2057	1633	+2.5	+0.4	-8.5	-25.9	$27
338 W.M. Heavy Mag.	225	2920	2678	2449	2232	2027	4259	3583	2996	2489	2053	+1.75	0.0	-7.65	-22.0	NA
338 W.M. High Energy	225	2940	2690	2450	2230	2010	4320	3610	3000	2475	2025	+1.7	0.0	-7.5	-22.0	NA
338 Win. Mag.	230	2780	2573	2375	2186	2005	3948	3382	2881	2441	2054	+2.5	+1.2	-6.3	-21.0	$40

Cartridge	Bullet Weight Grains	VELOCITY (fps)					ENERGY (ft. lbs.)					TRAJ. (in.)				Est. Price/box
		Muzzle	100 yds.	200 yds.	300 yds.	400 yds.	Muzzle	100 yds.	200 yds.	300 yds.	400 yds.	100 yds.	200 yds.	300 yds.	400 yds.	
338 Win. Mag.*	250	2660	2456	2261	2075	1898	3927	3348	2837	2389	1999	+2.5	+0.2	-9.0	-26.2	$27
338 W.M. High Energy	250	2800	2610	2420	2250	2080	4350	3775	3260	2805	2395	+1.8	0.0	-7.8	-22.5	NA
338 Ultra Mag.	250	2860	2645	2440	2244	2057	4540	3882	3303	2794	2347	1.7	0.0	-7.6	-22.1	NA
8.59(.338) Galaxy	200	3100	2899	2707	2524	2347	4269	3734	3256	2829	2446	3	3.80	0.0	-9.3	NA
340 Wea. Mag.*	210	3250	2991	2746	2515	2295	4924	4170	3516	2948	2455	+2.5	+1.9	-1.8	-11.8	$56
340 Wea. Mag.*	250	3000	2806	2621	2443	2272	4995	4371	3812	3311	2864	+2.5	+2.0	-3.5	-14.8	$56
338 A-Square	250	3120	2799	2500	2220	1958	5403	4348	3469	2736	2128	+2.5	+2.7	-1.5	-10.5	NA
338-378 Wea. Mag.	225	3180	2974	2778	2591	2410	5052	4420	3856	3353	2902	3.1	3.80	0.0	-8.9	NA
338 Titan	225	3230	3010	2800	2600	2409	5211	4524	3916	3377	2898	+3.07	+3.80	0.0	-8.95	NA
338 Excalibur	200	3600	3361	3134	2920	2715	5755	5015	4363	3785	3274	+2.23	+2.87	0.0	-6.99	NA
338 Excalibur	250	3250	2922	2618	2333	2066	5863	4740	3804	3021	2370	+1.3	0.0	-6.35	-19.2	NA
348 Winchester	200	2520	2215	1931	1672	1443	2820	2178	1656	1241	925	+2.5	-1.4	-14.7	NA	$42
357 Magnum	158	1830	1427	1138	980	883	1175	715	454	337	274	0.0	-16.2	-33.1	NA	$25**
35 Remington	150	2300	1874	1506	1218	1039	1762	1169	755	494	359	+2.5	-4.1	-26.3	NA	$16
35 Remington	200	2080	1698	1376	1140	1001	1921	1280	841	577	445	+2.5	-6.3	-17.1	-33.6	$16
356 Winchester	200	2460	2114	1797	1517	1284	2688	1985	1434	1022	732	+2.5	-1.8	-15.1	NA	$31
356 Winchester	250	2160	1911	1682	1476	1299	2591	2028	1571	1210	937	+2.5	-3.7	-22.2	NA	$31
358 Winchester	200	2490	2171	1876	1619	1379	2753	2093	1563	1151	844	+2.5	-1.6	-15.6	NA	$31
358 STA	275	2850	2562	2292	2039	NA	4958	4009	3208	2539	NA	+1.9	0.0	-8.6	NA	NA
350 Rem. Mag.	200	2710	2410	2130	1870	1631	3261	2579	2014	1553	1181	+2.5	-0.2	-10.0	-30.1	$33
35 Whelen	200	2675	2378	2100	1842	1606	3177	2510	1958	1506	1145	+2.5	-0.2	-10.3	-31.1	$20
35 Whelen	225	2500	2300	2110	1930	1770	3120	2650	2235	1870	1560	+2.6	0.0	-10.2	-29.9	NA
35 Whelen	250	2400	2197	2005	1823	1652	3197	2680	2230	1844	1515	+2.5	-1.2	-13.7	NA	$20
358 Norma Mag.	250	2800	2510	2230	1970	1730	4350	3480	2750	2145	1655	+1.0	0.0	-8.58	-26.1	NA
358 STA	275	2850	2562	229*2	2039	1764	4959	4009	3208	2539	1899	+1.9	0.0	-8.58	-26.1	NA
9.3x57mm Mau.	286	2070	1810	1590	1390	1110	2710	2090	1600	1220	955	+2.5	-2.6	-22.5	NA	NA
9.3x62mm Mau.	286	2360	2089	1844	1623	NA	3538	2771	2157	1670	1260	+2.5	-1.6	-21.0	NA	NA
9.3x64mm	286	2700	2505	2318	2139	1968	4629	3984	3411	2906	2460	+2.5	+2.7	-4.5	-19.2	NA
9.3x74Rmm	286	2360	2089	1844	1623	NA	3538	2771	2157	1670	NA	+2.5	-2.0	-11.0	NA	NA
38-55 Win.	255	1320	1190	1091	1018	963	987	802	674	587	525	0.0	-23.4	NA	NA	$25
375 Winchester	200	2200	1841	1526	1268	1089	2150	1506	1034	714	527	+2.5	-4.0	-26.2	NA	$27
375 Winchester	250	1900	1647	1424	1239	1103	2005	1506	1126	852	676	+2.5	-6.9	-33.3	NA	$27
376 Steyr	225	2600	2331	2078	1842	1625	3377	2714	2157	1694	1319	2.5	0.0	-10.6	-31.4	NA
376 Steyr	270	2600	2372	2156	1951	1759	4052	3373	2787	2283	1855	2.3	0.0	-9.9	-28.9	NA
375 Dakota	300	2600	2316	2051	1804	1579	4502	3573	2800	2167	1661	+2.4	0.0	-11.0	-32.7	NA
375 N.E. 2-1/2"	270	2000	1740	1507	1310	NA	2398	1815	1362	1026	NA	+2.5	-6.0	-30.0	NA	NA
375 Flanged	300	2450	2150	1886	1640	NA	3998	3102	2369	1790	NA	+2.5	-2.4	-17.0	NA	NA
375 H&H Magnum	250	2670	2450	2240	2040	1850	3955	3335	2790	2315	1905	+2.5	-0.4	-10.2	-28.4	NA
375 H&H Magnum	270	2690	2420	2166	1928	1707	4337	3510	2812	2228	1747	+2.5	0.0	-10.0	-29.4	$28
375 H&H Magnum*	300	2530	2245	1979	1733	1512	4263	3357	2608	2001	1523	+2.5	-1.0	-10.5	-33.6	$28
375 H&H Hvy. Mag.	270	2870	2628	2399	2182	1976	4937	4141	3451	2150	1845	+1.7	0.0	-7.2	-21.0	NA
375 H&H Hvy. Mag.	300	2705	2386	2090	1816	1568	4873	3793	2908	2195	1637	+2.3	0.0	-10.4	-31.4	NA
375 Rem. Ultra Mag.	270	2900	2558	2241	1947	1678	5041	3922	3010	2272	1689	1.9	2.7	-8.9	-27	NA
375 Rem. Ultra Mag.	300	2760	2505	2263	2035	1822	5073	4178	3412	2759	2210	2.0	0.0	-8.8	-26.1	NA
375 Wea. Mag.	300	2700	2420	2157	1911	1685	4856	3901	3100	2432	1891	+2.5	-.04	-10.7	-	NA
378 Wea. Mag.	270	3180	2976	2781	2594	2415	6062	5308	4635	4034	3495	+2.5	+2.6	-1.8	-11.3	$71
378 Wea. Mag.	300	2929	2576	2252	1952	1680	5698	4419	3379	2538	1881	+2.5	+1.2	-7.0	-24.5	$77
375 A-Square	300	2920	2626	2351	2093	1850	5679	4594	3681	2917	2281	+2.5	+1.4	-6.0	-21.0	NA
38-40 Win.	180	1160	999	901	827	764	538	399	324	273	233	0.0	-33.9	NA	NA	$42**
405 WIN	300	2200	1851	1545	1296		3224	2282	1589	1119		4.6	0.00	-19.5		NA
450/400-3"	400	2150	1932	1730	1545	1379	4105	3316	2659	2119	1689	+2.5	-4.0	-9.5	-30.0	NA
416 Dakota	400	2450	2294	2143	1998	1859	5330	4671	4077	3544	3068	+2.5	-0.2	-10.5	-29.4	NA
416 Taylor	400	2350	2117	1896	1693	NA	4905	3980	3194	2547	NA	+2.5	-1.2	15.0	NA	NA
416 Hoffman	400	2380	2145	1923	1718	1529	5031	4087	3285	2620	2077	+2.5	-1.0	-14.1	NA	NA
416 Rigby	350	2600	2449	2303	2162	2026	5253	4661	4122	3632	3189	+2.5	-1.8	-10.2	-26.0	NA
416 Rigby	400	2370	2210	2050	1900	NA	4990	4315	3720	3185	NA	+2.5	-0.7	-12.1	NA	NA
416 Rigby	410	2370	2110	1870	1640	NA	5115	4050	3165	2455	NA	+2.5	-2.4	-17.3	NA	$110
416 Rem. Mag.*	350	2520	2270	2034	1814	1611	4935	4004	3216	2557	2017	+2.5	-0.8	-12.6	-35.0	$82
416 Rem. Mag.*	400	2400	2175	1962	1763	1579	5115	4201	3419	2760	2214	+2.5	-1.5	-14.6	NA	$80
416 Wea. Mag.*	400	2700	2397	2115	1852	1613	6474	5104	3971	3047	2310	+2.5	0.0	-10.1	-30.4	$96
10.57 (416) Meteor	400	2730	2532	2342	2161	1987	6621	5695	4874	4147	3508	+1.9	0.0	-8.3	-24.0	NA
404 Jeffrey	400	2150	1924	1716	1525	NA	4105	3289	2614	2064	NA	+2.5	-4.0	-22.1	NA	NA

33

34
35

9.3 mm

375

40
41

Cartridge	Bullet Weight Grains	VELOCITY (fps)					ENERGY (ft. lbs.)					TRAJ. (in.)				Est. Price/box
		Muzzle	100 yds.	200 yds.	300 yds.	400 yds.	Muzzle	100 yds.	200 yds.	300 yds.	400 yds.	100 yds.	200 yds.	300 yds.	400 yds.	
425 425 Express	400	2400	2160	1934	1725	NA	5115	4145	3322	2641	NA	+2.5	-1.0	-14.0	NA	NA
44 44-40 Win.	200	1190	1006	900	822	756	629	449	360	300	254	0.0	-33.3	NA	NA	$36**
44 Rem. Mag.	210	1920	1477	1155	982	880	1719	1017	622	450	361	0.0	-17.6	NA	NA	$14
44 Rem. Mag.	240	1760	1380	1114	970	878	1650	1015	661	501	411	0.0	-17.6	NA	NA	$13
444 Marlin	240	2350	1815	1377	1087	941	2942	1753	1001	630	472	+2.5	-15.1	-31.0	NA	$22
444 Marlin	265	2120	1733	1405	1160	1012	2644	1768	1162	791	603	+2.5	-6.0	-32.2	NA	Disc.
444 Marlin Light Mag	265	2335	1913	1551	1266		3208	2153	1415	943		2	-4.90	-26.5		
45 45-70 Govt.	300	1810	1497	1244	1073	969	2182	1492	1031	767	625	0.0	-14.8	NA	NA	$21
45-70 Govt. Supreme	300	1880	1558	1292	1103	988	2355	1616	1112	811	651	0.0	-12.9	-46.0	-105	NA
45-70 Govt. CorBon	350	1800	1526	1296			2519	1810	1307			0.0	-14.6			NA
45-70 Govt.	405	1330	1168	1055	977	918	1590	1227	1001	858	758	0.0	-24.6	NA	NA	$21
45-70 Govt. PMC Cowboy	405	1550	1193				1639	1280				0.0	-23.9			NA
45-70 Govt. Garrett	415	1850					3150					3.0	-7.0			NA
45-70 Govt. Garrett	530	1550	1343	1178	1062	982	2828	2123	1633	1327	1135	0.0	-17.8			NA
450 Marlin	350	2100	1774	1488	1254	1089	3427	2446	1720	1222	922	0.0	-9.7	-35.2		NA
458 Win. Magnum	350	2470	1990	1570	1250	1060	4740	3065	1915	1205	870	+2.5	-2.5	-21.6	NA	$43
458 Win. Magnum	400	2380	2170	1960	1770	NA	5030	4165	3415	2785	NA	+2.5	-0.4	-13.4	NA	$73
458 Win. Magnum	465	2220	1999	1791	1601	NA	5088	4127	3312	2646	NA	+2.5	-2.0	-17.7	NA	NA
458 Win. Magnum	500	2040	1823	1623	1442	1237	4620	3689	2924	2308	1839	+2.5	-3.5	-22.0	NA	$61
458 Win. Magnum	510	2040	1770	1527	1319	1157	4712	3547	2640	1970	1516	+2.5	-4.1	-25.0	NA	$41
450 Dakota	500	2450	2235	2030	1838	1658	6663	5544	4576	3748	3051	+2.5	-0.6	-12.0	-33.8	NA
450 N.E. 3-1/4"	465	2190	1970	1765	1577	NA	4952	4009	3216	2567	NA	+2.5	-3.0	-20.0	NA	NA
450 N.E. 3-1/4"	500	2150	1920	1708	1514	NA	5132	4093	3238	2544	NA	+2.5	-4.0	-22.9	NA	NA
450 No. 2	465	2190	1970	1765	1577	NA	4952	4009	3216	2567	NA	+2.5	-3.0	-20.0	NA	NA
450 No. 2	500	2150	1920	1708	1514	NA	5132	4093	3238	2544	NA	+2.5	-4.0	-22.9	NA	NA
458 Lott	465	2380	2150	1932	1730	NA	5848	4773	3855	3091	NA	+2.5	-1.0	-14.0	NA	NA
458 Lott	500	2300	2062	1838	1633	NA	5873	4719	3748	2960	NA	+2.5	-1.6	-16.4	NA	NA
450 Ackley Mag.	465	2400	2169	1950	1747	NA	5947	4857	3927	3150	NA	+2.5	-1.0	-13.7	NA	NA
450 Ackley Mag.	500	2320	2081	1855	1649	NA	5975	4085	3820	3018	NA	+2.5	-1.2	-15.0	NA	NA
460 Short A-Sq.	500	2420	2175	1943	1729	NA	6501	5250	4193	3319	NA	+2.5	-0.8	-12.8	-	NA
460 Wea. Mag.	500	2700	2404	2128	1869	1635	8092	6416	5026	3878	2969	+2.5	+0.6	-8.9	-28.0	$72
475 500/465 N.E.	480	2150	1917	1703	1507	NA	4926	3917	3089	2419	NA	+2.5	-4.0	-22.2	-	NA
470 Rigby	500	2150	1940	1740	1560	NA	5130	4170	3360	2695	NA	+2.5	-2.8	-19.4	NA	NA
470 Nitro Ex.	480	2190	1954	1735	1536	NA	5111	4070	3210	2515	NA	+2.5	-3.5	-20.8	NA	NA
470 Nitro Ex.	500	2150	1890	1650	1440	1270	5130	3965	3040	2310	1790	+2.5	-4.3	-24.0	NA	$177
475 No. 2	500	2200	1955	1728	1522	NA	5375	4243	3316	2573	NA	+2.5	-3.2	-20.9	NA	NA
50 **58** 505 Gibbs	525	2300	2063	1840	1637		6166	4922	3948	3122	NA	+2.5	-3.0	-18.0	NA	NA
500 N.E.-3"	570	2150	1928	1722	1533	NA	5850	4703	3752	2975	NA	+2.5	-3.7	-22.0	NA	NA
500 N.E.-3"	600	2150	1927	1721	1531	NA	6158	4947	3944	3124	NA	+2.5	-4.0	-22.0	NA	NA
495 A-Square	570	2350	2117	1896	1693	NA	5850	4703	3752	2975	NA	+2.5	-1.0	-14.5	NA	NA
495 A-Square	600	2280	2050	1833	1635	NA	6925	5598	4478	3562	NA	+2.5	-2.0	-17.0	NA	NA
500 A-Square	600	2380	2144	1922	1766	NA	7546	6126	4920	3922	NA	+2.5	-3.0	-17.0	NA	NA
500 A-Square	707	2250	2040	1841	1567	NA	7947	6530	5318	4311	NA	+2.5	-2.0	-17.0	NA	NA
500 BMG PMC	660	3080	2854	2639	2444	2248	13688			500 yd. zero		+3.1	+3.90	+4.7	+2.8	NA
577 Nitro Ex.	750	2050	1793	1562	1360	NA	6990	5356	4065	3079	NA	+2.5	-5.0	-26.0	NA	NA
577 Tyrannosaur	750	2400	2141	1898	1675	NA	9591	7633	5996	4671	NA	+3.0	0.0	-12.9	NA	NA
600 **700** 600 N.E.	900	1950	1680	1452	NA	NA	7596	5634	4212	NA	NA	+5.6	0.0	NA	NA	NA
700 N.E.	1200	1900	1676	1472	NA	NA	9618	7480	5774	NA	NA	+5.7	0.0	NA	NA	NA

CENTERFIRE HANDGUN CARTRIDGES — BALLISTICS & PRICES

Notes: Blanks are available in 32 S&W, 38 S&W and 38 Special. "V" after barrel length indicates test barrel was vented to produce ballistics similar to a revolver with a normal barrel-to-cylinder gap. Ammo prices are per 50 rounds except when marked with an ** which signifies a 20 round box; *** signifies a 25-round box. Not all loads are available from all ammo manufacturers. Listed loads are those made by Remington, Winchester, Federal, and others. DISC. is a discontinued load. Prices are rounded to nearest whole dollar and will vary with brand and retail outlet. † = new bullet weight this year; "c" indicates a change in data.

Cartridge	Bullet Wgt. Grs.	VELOCITY (fps)			ENERGY (ft. lbs.)			Mid-Range Traj. (in.)		Bbl. Lgth. (in).	Est. Price/ box
		Muzzle	50 yds.	100 yds.	Muzzle	50 yds.	100 yds.	50 yds.	100 yds.		
221 Rem. Fireball	50	2650	2380	2130	780	630	505	0.2	0.8	10.5"	$15
25 Automatic	35	900	813	742	63	51	43	NA	NA	2"	$18
25 Automatic	45	815	730	655	65	55	40	1.8	7.7	2"	$21
25 Automatic	50	760	705	660	65	55	50	2.0	8.7	2"	$17
7.5mm Swiss	107	1010	NA	NA	240	NA	NA	NA	NA	NA	NEW
7.62mmTokarev	87	1390	NA	NA	365	NA	NA	0.6	NA	4.5"	NA
7.62 Nagant	97	1080	NA	NA	350	NA	NA	NA	NA	NA	NEW
7.63 Mauser	88	1440	NA	NA	405	NA	NA	NA	NA	NA	NEW
30 Luger	93†	1220	1110	1040	305	255	225	0.9	3.5	4.5"	$34
30 Carbine	110	1790	1600	1430	785	625	500	0.4	1.7	10"	$28
30-357 AeT	123	1992	NA	NA	1084	NA	NA	NA	NA	10"	NA
32 S&W	88	680	645	610	90	80	75	2.5	10.5	3"	$17
32 S&W Long	98	705	670	635	115	100	90	2.3	10.5	4"	$17
32 Short Colt	80	745	665	590	100	80	60	2.2	9.9	4"	$19
32 H&R Magnum	85	1100	1020	930	230	195	165	1.0	4.3	4.5"	$21
32 H&R Magnum	95	1030	940	900	225	190	170	1.1	4.7	4.5"	$19
32 Automatic	60	970	895	835	125	105	95	1.3	5.4	4"	$22
32 Automatic	60	1000	917	849	133	112	96			4"	NA
32 Automatic	65	950	890	830	130	115	100	1.3	5.6	NA	NA
32 Automatic	71	905	855	810	130	115	95	1.4	5.8	4"	$19
8mm Lebel Pistol	111	850	NA	NA	180	NA	NA	NA	NA	NA	NEW
8mm Steyr	112	1080	NA	NA	290	NA	NA	NA	NA	NA	NEW
8mm Gasser	126	850	NA	NA	200	NA	NA	NA	NA	NA	NEW
380 Automatic	60	1130	960	NA	170	120	NA	1.0	NA	NA	NA
380 Automatic	85/88	990	920	870	190	165	145	1.2	5.1	4"	$20
380 Automatic	90	1000	890	800	200	160	130	1.2	5.5	3.75"	$10
380 Automatic	95/100	955	865	785	190	160	130	1.4	5.9	4"	$20
38 Super Auto +P	115	1300	1145	1040	430	335	275	0.7	3.3	5"	$26
38 Super Auto +P	125/130	1215	1100	1015	425	350	300	0.8	3.6	5"	$26
38 Super Auto +P	147	1100	1050	1000	395	355	325	0.9	4.0	5"	NA
9x18mm Makarov	95	1000	NA	NA	NA	NA	NA	NA	NA	NA	NEW
9x18mm Ultra	100	1050	NA	NA	240	NA	NA	NA	NA	NA	NEW
9x23mm Largo	124	1190	1055	966	390	306	257	0.7	3.7	4"	NA
9x23mm Win.	125	1450	1249	1103	583	433	338	0.6	2.8	NA	NA
9mm Steyr	115	1180	NA	NA	350	NA	NA	NA	NA	NA	NEW
9mm Luger	88	1500	1190	1010	440	275	200	0.6	3.1	4"	$24
9mm Luger	90	1360	1112	978	370	247	191	NA	NA	4"	$26
9mm Luger	95	1300	1140	1010	350	275	215	0.8	3.4	4"	NA
9mm Luger	100	1180	1080	NA	305	255	NA	0.9	NA	4"	NA
9mm Luger	115	1155	1045	970	340	280	240	0.9	3.9	4"	$21
9mm Luger	123/125	1110	1030	970	340	290	260	1.0	4.0	4"	$23
9mm Luger	140	935	890	850	270	245	225	1.3	5.5	4"	$23
9mm Luger	147	990	940	900	320	290	265	1.1	4.9	4"	$26
9mm Luger +P	90	1475	NA	NA	437	NA	NA	NA	NA	NA	NA
9mm Luger +P	115	1250	1113	1019	399	316	265	0.8	3.5	4"	$27
9mm Federal	115	1280	1130	1040	420	330	280	0.7	3.3	4"V	$24
9mm Luger Vector	115	1155	1047	971	341	280	241	NA	NA	4"	NA
9mm Luger +P	124	1180	1089	1021	384	327	287	0.8	3.8	4"	NA
38 S&W	146	685	650	620	150	135	125	2.4	10.0	4"	$19
38 Short Colt	125	730	685	645	150	130	115	2.2	9.4	6"	$19
39 Special	100	950	900	NA	200	180	NA	1.3	NA	4"V	NA
38 Special	110	945	895	850	220	195	175	1.3	5.4	4"V	$23

Notes: Blanks are available in 32 S&W, 38 S&W and 38 Special. "V" after barrel length indicates test barrel was vented to produce ballistics similar to a revolver with a normal barrel-to-cylinder gap. Ammo prices are per 50 rounds except when marked with an ** which signifies a 20 round box; *** signifies a 25-round box. Not all loads are available from all ammo manufacturers. Listed loads are those made by Remington, Winchester, Federal, and others. DISC. is a discontinued load. Prices are rounded to nearest whole dollar and will vary with brand and retail outlet. † = new bullet weight this year; "c" indicates a change in data.

Cartridge	Bullet Wgt. Grs.	VELOCITY (fps)			ENERGY (ft. lbs.)			Mid-Range Traj. (in.)		Bbl. Lgth. (in).	Est. Price/ box
		Muzzle	50 yds.	100 yds.	Muzzle	50 yds.	100 yds.	50 yds.	100 yds.		
38 Special	110	945	895	850	220	195	175	1.3	5.4	4"V	$23
38 Special	130	775	745	710	175	160	120	1.9	7.9	4"V	$22
38 Special Cowboy	140	800	767	735	199	183	168			7.5" V	NA
38 (Multi-Ball)	140	830	730	505	215	130	80	2.0	10.6	4"V	$10**
38 Special	148	710	635	565	165	130	105	2.4	10.6	4"V	$17
38 Special	158	755	725	690	200	185	170	2.0	8.3	4"V	$18
38 Special +P	95	1175	1045	960	290	230	195	0.9	3.9	4"V	$23
38 Special +P	110	995	925	870	240	210	185	1.2	5.1	4"V	$23
38 Special +P	125	975	929	885	264	238	218	1	5.2	4"	NA
38 Special +P	125	945	900	860	250	225	205	1.3	5.4	4"V	#23
38 Special +P	129	945	910	870	255	235	215	1.3	5.3	4"V	$11
38 Special +P	130	925	887	852	247	227	210	1.3	5.50	4"V	NA
38 Special +P	147/150(c)	884	NA	NA	264	NA	NA	NA	NA	4"V	$27
38 Special +P	158	890	855	825	280	255	240	1.4	6.0	4"V	$20
357 SIG	115	1520	NA	NA	593	NA	NA	NA	NA	NA	NA
357 SIG	124	1450	NA	NA	578	NA	NA	NA	NA	NA	NA
357 SIG	125	1350	1190	1080	510	395	325	0.7	3.1	4"	NA
357 SIG	150	1130	1030	970	420	355	310	0.9	4.0	NA	NA
356 TSW	115	1520	NA	NA	593	NA	NA	NA	NA	NA	NA
356 TSW	124	1450	NA	NA	578	NA	NA	NA	NA	NA	NA
356 TSW	135	1280	1120	1010	490	375	310	0.8	3.50	NA	NA
356 TSW	147	1220	1120	1040	485	410	355	0.8	3.5	5"	NA
357 Mag., Super Clean	105	1650									NA
357 Magnum	110	1295	1095	975	410	290	230	0.8	3.5	4"V	$25
357 (Med.Vel.)	125	1220	1075	985	415	315	270	0.8	3.7	4"V	$25
357 Magnum	125	1450	1240	1090	585	425	330	0.6	2.8	4"V	$25
357 (Multi-Ball)	140	1155	830	665	420	215	135	1.2	6.4	4"V	$11**
357 Magnum	140	1360	1195	1075	575	445	360	0.7	3.0	4"V	$25
357 Magnum	145	1290	1155	1060	535	430	360	0.8	3.5	4"V	$26
357 Magnum	150/158	1235	1105	1015	535	430	360	0.8	3.5	4"V	$25
357 Mag. Cowboy	158	800	761	725	225	203	185				NA
357 Magnum	165	1290	1189	1108	610	518	450	0.7	3.1	8-3/8"	NA
357 Magnum	180	1145	1055	985	525	445	390	0.9	3.9	4"V	$25
357 Magnum	180	1180	1088	1020	557	473	416	0.8	3.6	8"V	NA
357 Mag. CorBon F.A.	180	1650	1512	1386	1088	913	767	1.66	0.0		NA
357 Mag. CorBon	200	1200	1123	1061	640	560	500	3.19	0.0		NA
357 Rem. Maximum	158	1825	1590	1380	1170	885	670	0.4	1.7	10.5"	$14**
40 S&W	135	1140	1070	NA	390	345	NA	0.9	NA	4"	NA
40 S&W	155	1140	1026	958	447	362	309	0.9	4.1	4"	$14***
40 S&W	165	1150	NA	NA	485	NA	NA	NA	NA	4"	$18***
40 S&W	180	985	936	893	388	350	319	1.4	5.0	4"	$14***
40 S&W	180	1015	960	914	412	368	334	1.3	4.5	4"	NA
400 Cor-Bon	135	1450	NA	NA	630	NA	NA	NA	NA	5"	NA
10mm Automatic	155	1125	1046	986	436	377	335	0.9	3.9	5"	$26
10mm Automatic	170	1340	1165	1145	680	510	415	0.7	3.2	5"	$31
10mm Automatic	175	1290	1140	1035	650	505	420	0.7	3.3	5.5"	$11**
10mm Auto. (FBI)	180	950	905	865	361	327	299	1.5	5.4	4"	$16**
10mm Automatic	180	1030	970	920	425	375	340	1.1	4.7	5"	$16**
10mm Auto H.V.	180†	1240	1124	1037	618	504	430	0.8	3.4	5"	$27
10mm Automatic	200	1160	1070	1010	495	510	430	0.9	3.8	5"	$14**
10.4mm Italian	177	950	NA	NA	360	NA	NA	NA	NA	NA	NEW

38 cont.

357

40, 10mm

Notes: Blanks are available in 32 S&W, 38 S&W and 38 Special. "V" after barrel length indicates test barrel was vented to produce ballistics similar to a revolver with a normal barrel-to-cylinder gap. Ammo prices are per 50 rounds except when marked with an ** which signifies a 20 round box; *** signifies a 25-round box. Not all loads are available from all ammo manufacturers. Listed loads are those made by Remington, Winchester, Federal, and others. DISC. is a discontinued load. Prices are rounded to nearest whole dollar and will vary with brand and retail outlet. † = new bullet weight this year; "c" indicates a change in data.

| Cartridge | Bullet Wgt. Grs. | VELOCITY (fps) | | | ENERGY (ft. lbs.) | | | Mid-Range Traj. (in.) | | Bbl. Lgth. (in). | Est. Price/ box |
		Muzzle	50 yds.	100 yds.	Muzzle	50 yds.	100 yds.	50 yds.	100 yds.		
41 Action Exp.	180	1000	947	903	400	359	326	0.5	4.2	5"	$13**
41 Rem. Magnum	170	1420	1165	1015	760	515	390	0.7	3.2	4"V	$33
41 Rem. Magnum	175	1250	1120	1030	605	490	410	0.8	3.4	4"V	$14**
41 (Med. Vel.)	210	965	900	840	435	375	330	1.3	5.4	4"V	$30
41 Rem. Magnum	210	1300	1160	1060	790	630	535	0.7	3.2	4"V	$33
44 S&W Russian	247	780	NA	NA	335	NA	NA	NA	NA	NA	NA
44 S&W Special	180	980	NA	NA	383	NA	NA	NA	NA	6.5"	NA
44 S&W Special	180	1000	935	882	400	350	311	NA	NA	7.5"V	NA
44 S&W Special	200†	875	825	780	340	302	270	1.2	6.0	6"	$13**
44 S&W Special	200	1035	940	865	475	390	335	1.1	4.9	6.5"	$13**
44 S&W Special	240/246	755	725	695	310	285	265	2.0	8.3	6.5"	$26
44-40 Win. Cowboy	225	750	723	695	281	261	242				NA
44 Rem. Magnum	180	1610	1365	1175	1035	745	550	0.5	2.3	4"V	$18**
44 Rem. Magnum	200	1400	1192	1053	870	630	492	0.6	NA	6.5"	$20
44 Rem. Magnum	210	1495	1310	1165	1040	805	635	0.6	2.5	6.5"	$18**
44 (Med. Vel.)	240	1000	945	900	535	475	435	1.1	4.8	6.5"	$17
44 R.M. (Jacketed)	240	1180	1080	1010	740	625	545	0.9	3.7	4"V	$18**
44 R.M. (Lead)	240	1350	1185	1070	970	750	610	0.7	3.1	4"V	$29
44 Rem. Magnum	250	1180	1100	1040	775	670	600	0.8	3.6	6.5"V	$21
44 Rem. Magnum	250	1230	1132	1057	840	711	620	0.8	2.9	6.5"V	NA
44 Rem. Magnum	275	1235	1142	1070	931	797	699	0.8	3.3	6.5"	NA
44 Rem. Magnum	300	1200	1100	1026	959	806	702	NA	NA	7.5"	$17
44 Rem. Magnum	330	1385	1297	1220	1406	1234	1090	1.83	0.00	NA	NA
440 CorBon	260	1700	1544	1403	1669	1377	1136	1.58	NA	10"	NA
450 Short Colt/450 Revolver	226	830	NA	NA	350	NA	NA	NA	NA	NA	NEW
45 S&W Schofield	180	730	NA	NA	213	NA	NA	NA	NA	NA	NA
45 S&W Schofield	230	730	NA	NA	272	NA	NA	na			
45 Automatic	165	1030	930	NA	385	315	NA	1.2	NA	5"	NA
45 Automatic	185	1000	940	890	410	360	325	1.1	4.9	5"	$28
45 Auto. (Match)	185	770	705	650	245	204	175	2.0	8.7	5"	$28
45 Auto. (Match)	200	940	890	840	392	352	312	2.0	8.6	5"	$20
45 Automatic	200	975	917	860	421	372	328	1.4	5.0	5"	$18
45 Automatic	230	830	800	675	355	325	300	1.6	6.8	5"	$27
45 Automatic	230	880	846	816	396	366	340	1.5	6.1	5"	NA
45 Automatic +P	165	1250	NA	NA	573	NA	NA	NA	NA	NA	NA
45 Automatic +P	185	1140	1040	970	535	445	385	0.9	4.0	5"	$31
45 Automatic +P	200	1055	982	925	494	428	380	NA	NA	5"	NA
45 Super	185	1300	1190	1108	694	582	504	NA	NA	5"	NA
45 Win. Magnum	230	1400	1230	1105	1000	775	635	0.6	2.8	5"	$14**
45 Win. Magnum	260	1250	1137	1053	902	746	640	0.8	3.3	5"	$16**
45 Win. Mag. CorBon	320	1150	1080	1025	940	830	747	3.47			NA
455 Webley MKII	262	850	NA	NA	420	NA	NA	NA	NA	NA	NA
45 Colt	200	1000	938	889	444	391	351	1.3	4.8	5.5"	$21
45 Colt	225	960	890	830	460	395	345	1.3	5.5	5.5"	$22
45 Colt + P CorBon	265	1350	1225	1126	1073	884	746	2.65	0.0		NA
45 Colt + P CorBon	300	1300	1197	1114	1126	956	827	2.78	0.0		NA
45 Colt	250/255	860	820	780	410	375	340	1.6	6.6	5.5"	$27
454 Casull	250	1300	1151	1047	938	735	608	0.7	3.2	7.5"V	NA
454 Casull	260	1800	1577	1381	1871	1436	1101	0.4	1.8	7.5"V	NA
454 Casull	300	1625	1451	1308	1759	1413	1141	0.5	2.0	7.5"V	NA
454 Casull CorBon	360	1500	1387	1286	1800	1640	1323	2.01	0.0		NA
475 Linebaugh	400	1350	1217	1119	1618	1315	1112	NA	NA	NA	NA
480 Ruger	325	1350	1191	1076	1315	1023	835	2.6	0.0	7.5"	NA
50 Action Exp.	325	1400	1209	1075	1414	1055	835	0.2	2.3	6"	$24**

40, 10mm cont.

44

45, 50

Note: The actual ballistics obtained with your firearm can vary considerably from the advertised ballistics. Also, ballistics can vary from lot to lot with the same brand and type load.

Cartridge	Bullet Wt. Grs.	Velocity (fps) 22-1/2" Bbl.		Energy (ft. lbs.) 22-1/2" Bbl.		Mid-Range Traj. (in.)	Muzzle Velocity
		Muzzle	100 yds.	Muzzle	100 yds.	100 yds.	6" Bbl.
17 Aguila	20	1850	NA	NA	NA	NA	NA
17 HMR	17	2550	1902	245	136	NA	NA
22 Short Blank	—	—	—	—	—	—	—
22 Short CB	29	727	610	33	24	NA	706
22 Short Target	29	830	695	44	31	6.8	786
22 Short HP	27	1164	920	81	50	4.3	1077
22 Colibri	20	375	183	6	1	NA	NA
22 Super Colibri	20	500	441	11	9	NA	NA
22 Long CB	29	727	610	33	24	NA	706
22 Long HV	29	1180	946	90	57	4.1	1031
22 LR Ballistician	25	1100	760	65	30	NA	NA
22 LR Pistol Match	40	1070	890	100	70	4.6	940
22 LR Sub Sonic HP	38	1050	901	93	69	4.7	NA
22 LR Standard Velocity	40	1070	890	100	70	4.6	940
22 LR HV	40	1255	1016	140	92	3.6	1060
22 LR Silhoutte	42	1220	1003	139	94	3.6	1025
22 SSS	60	950	802	120	86	NA	NA
22 LR HV HP	40	1280	1001	146	89	3.5	1085
22 Velocitor GDHP	40	1435	0	0	0	NA	NA
22 LR Hyper HP	32/33/34	1500	1075	165	85	2.8	NA
22 LR Stinger HP	32	1640	1132	191	91	2.6	1395
22 LR Hyper Vel	30	1750	1191	204	93	NA	NA
22 LR Shot #12	31	950	NA	NA	NA	NA	NA
22 WRF JHP	45	1300	1015	169	103	3	NA
22 Win. Mag.	30	2200	1373	322	127	1.4	1610
22 Win. Mag. V-Max BT	33	2000	1495	293	164	0.60	NA
22 Win. Mag. JHP	34	2120	1435	338	155	1.4	NA
22 Win. Mag. JHP	40	1910	1326	324	156	1.7	1480
22 Win. Mag. FMJ	40	1910	1326	324	156	1.7	1480
22 Win. Mag. JHP	50	1650	1280	300	180	1.3	NA
22 Win. Mag. Shot #11	52	1000	—	NA	—	—	NA

NOTES: * = 10 rounds per box. ** = 5 rounds per box. Pricing variations and number of rounds per box can occur with type and brand of ammunition. Listed pricing is the average nominal cost for load style and box quantity shown. Not every brand is available in all shot size variations. Some manufacturers do not provide suggested list prices. All prices rounded to nearest whole dollar. The price you pay will vary dependent upon outlet of purchase. # = new load spec this year; "C" indicates a change in data.

Dram Equiv.	Shot Ozs.	Load Style	Shot Sizes	Brands	Avg. Price/box	Velocity (fps)
10 Gauge 3-1/2" Magnum						
4-1/2	2-1/4	premium	BB, 2, 4, 5, 6	Win., Fed., Rem.	$33	1205
Max	2	premium	4, 5, 6	Fed., Win.	NA	1300
4-1/4	2	high velocity	BB, 2, 4	Rem.	$22	1210
4-1/2	2-1/4	duplex	4x6	Rem.	$14*	1205
Max	18 pellets	premium	00 buck	Fed., Win.	$7**	1100
Max	1-7/8	Bismuth	BB, 2, 4	Win., Bis.	NA	1225
Max	1-3/4	Tungsten-Polymer	4, 6	Fed.	NA	1325
Max	1-3/4	hevi. shot	2, 4	Rem.	NA	1300
4-1/4	1-3/4	steel	TT, T, BBB, BB, 1, 2, 3	Win., Rem.	$27	1260
Mag	1-5/8	steel	T, BBB	Win.	$27	1285
4-5/8	1-5/8	steel	F, T, BBB	Fed.	$26	1350
Max	1-5/8	Tungsten - Iron	BBB, BB, 2, 4	Fed.		1300
Max	1-5/8	Bismuth	BB, 2, 4	Bismuth	NA	1375
Max	1-1/2	Tungsten - Iron & steel	2xBB	Fed.	NA	1375
Max	1-3/8	steel	T, BBB, BB, 2	Fed., Win.	NA	1450
Max	1-3/8	Tungsten - Iron	BBB, BB, 2, 4	Fed.		1450
Max	1-3/4	slug, rifled	slug	Fed.	NA	1280
Max	24 Pellets	Buckshot	1 Buck	Fed.	NA	1100
Max	54 pellets	Super-X	4 Buck	Win.	NA	1150
12 Gauge 3-1/2" Magnum						
Max	2-1/4	premium	4, 5, 6	Fed., Rem., Win.	$13*	1150
Max	2	Lead	4, 5, 6	Fed.	NA	1275
Max	2	Copper plated turkey	4, 5	Rem.	NA	1300
Max	18 pellets	premium	00 buck	Fed., Win., Rem.	$7**	1100
Max	1-7/8	Bismuth	BB, 2, 4	Win., Bis.	NA	1225
Max	1-7/8	hevi. shot	4, 5, 6	Rem.	NA	1225
Max	1-3/4	Tungsten-Polymer	4, 6	Fed.	NA	1275
Max	1-3/4	hevi. shot	2, 4, 5, 6	Rem.	NA	1300
4-1/8	1-9/16	steel	TT, F, T, BBB, BB, 1, 2	Rem., Win., Fed.	$22	1335
Max	1-3/8	steel	T, BBB, BB, 2, 4	Fed., Win.	NA	1450
Max	1-3/8	Tungsten - Iron	BBB, BB, 2, 4	Fed.	NA	1450
Max	1-3/8	Tungsten - Iron & steel	2xBB	Fed.	NA	1375
Max	24 pellets	Premium	1 Buck	Fed.	NA	1100
Max	54 pellets	Super-X	4 Buck	Win.	NA	1050
12 Gauge 3" Magnum						
4	2	premium	BB, 2, 4, 5, 6	Win., Fed., Rem.	$9*	1175
4	2	duplex	4x6	Rem.	$10	1175
4	1-7/8	premium	BB, 2, 4, 6	Win., Fed., Rem.	$19	1210
4	1-7/8	duplex	4x6	Rem., Fio.	$9*	1210
Max	1-3/4	turkey	4, 5, 6	Fed., Fio., Win., Rem.	NA	1300
4	1-3/4	duplex	2x4, 4x6	Fio.	NA	1150
4	1-5/8	premium	2, 4, 5, 6	Win., Fed., Rem.	$18	1290
Max	1-5/8	Bismuth	BB, 2, 4, 5, 6	Win., Bis.	NA	1250
Max	1-5/8	hevi. shot	4, 5, 6	Rem.	NA	1225
4	24 pellets	buffered	1 buck	Win., Fed., Rem.	$5**	1040
Max	1-1/2	hevi. shot	2, 4, 5, 6	Rem.	NA	1300
4	15 pellets	buffered	00 buck	Win., Fed., Rem.	$6**	1210
4	10 pellets	buffered	000 buck	Win., Fed., Rem.	$6**	1225

Dram Equiv.	Shot Ozs.	Load Style	Shot Sizes	Brands	Avg. Price/box	Velocity (fps)
12 Gauge 3" Magnum (cont.)						
4	41 pellets	buffered	4 buck	Win., Fed., Rem.	$6**	1210
Max	1-3/8	Tungsten - Polymer	4, 6	Fed.	NA	1330
Max	1-3/8	Tungsten-Iron	4	Fed.	NA	1300
Max	1-1/4	Tungsten - Iron & steel	4x2, 4x4	Fed.	NA	1400
Max	1-3/8	slug	slug	Bren.	NA	1476
Max	1-1/4	slug, rifled	slug	Fed.	NA	1600
Max	1-3/16	saboted slug	copper slug	Rem.	NA	1500
Max	1-1/8	Tungsten - Iron	BBB, BB, 2, 4	Fed.	NA	1400
Max	1	steel	4, 6	Fed.		1330
Max	1	slug, rifled	slug, magnum	Win., Rem.	$5**	1760
Max	1	saboted slug	slug	Rem., Win., Fed.	$10**	1550
3-5/8	1-3/8	steel	TT, F, T, BBB, BB, 1, 2, 3, 4	Win., Fed., Rem.	$19	1275
Max	1-1/8	steel	T, BBB, BB, 2, 4, 5, 6	Fed., Win.	NA	1450
Max	1-1/8	steel	BB, 2	Fed.	NA	1400
4	1-1/4	steel	TT, F, T, BBB, BB, 1, 2, 3, 4, 6	Win., Fed., Rem.	$18	1375
Max	1-1/4	Tungsten-Iron and Steel	4x2	Fed.	NA	1400
Max	1-1/8	Tungsten-Polymer	4, 6	Fed.	NA	1375
Max	1-3/8	Tungsten-Polymer	4, 6	Fed.	NA	1330
12 Gauge 2-3/4"						
Max	1-5/8	magnum	4, 5, 6	Win., Fed.	$8*	1250
Max	1-3/8	turkey	4, 5, 6	Fio.	NA	1250
Max	1-3/8	duplex	2x4, 4x6	Fio.	NA	1200
Max	1-3/8	Bismuth	BB, 2, 4, 5, 6	Win., Bis.	NA	1280
Max	1-3/8	hevi. shot	4, 5, 6	Rem.	NA	1250
3-3/4	1-1/2	magnum	BB, 2, 4, 5, 6	Win., Fed., Rem.	$16	1260
3-3/4	1-1/2	duplex	BBx4, 2x4, 4x6	Rem., Fio.	$9*	1260
Max	1-1/4	Supreme H-V	4, 5, 6, 7-1/2	Win. Rem.	NA	1400
3-3/4	1-1/4	high velocity	BB, 2, 4, 5, 6, 7-1/2, 8, 9	Win., Fed., Rem., Fio.	$13	1330
Max	1-1/4	Tungsten - Polymer	4, 6	Fed.	NA	1330
Max	1-1/4	hevi. shot	4, 6, 7-1/2	Rem.	NA	1325
3-1/2	1-1/4	mid-velocity	7, 8, 9	Win.	Disc.	1275
3-1/4	1-1/4	standard velocity	6, 7-1/2, 8, 9	Win., Fed., Rem., Fio.	$11	1220
Max	1-1/4	Bismuth	4, 6	Win.		1220
3-1/4	1-1/8	standard velocity	4, 6, 7-1/2, 8, 9	Win., Fed., Rem., Fio.	$9	1255
Max	1	steel	BB, 2	Fed.	NA	1450
Max	1	Tungsten - Iron	BB, 2, 4	Fed.	NA	1450
3-1/4	1	standard velocity	6, 7-1/2, 8	Rem., Fed., Fio., Win.	$6	1290
3-1/4	1-1/4	target	7-1/2, 8, 9	Win., Fed., Rem.	$10	1220
3	1-1/8	spreader	7-1/2, 8, 8-1/2, 9	Fio.	NA	1200
3	1-1/8	target	7-1/2, 8, 9, 7-1/2x8	Win., Fed., Rem., Fio.	$7	1200
2-3/4	1-1/8	target	7-1/2, 8, 8-1/2, 9, 7-1/2x8	Win., Fed., Rem., Fio.	$7	1145
2-3/4	1-1/8	low recoil	7-1/2, 8	Rem.	NA	1145
2-1/2	26 grams	low recoil	8	Win.	NA	980
2-1/4	1-1/8	target	7-1/2, 8, 8-1/2, 9	Rem., Fed.	$7	1080
Max	1	spreader	7-1/2, 8, 8-1/2, 9	Fio.	NA	1300

SHOTSHELL LOADS & PRICES, *continued*

Dram Equiv.	Shot Ozs.	Load Style	Shot Sizes	Brands	Avg. Price/box	Velocity (fps)
12 Gauge 2-3/4" (cont.)						
3-1/4	28 grams (1 oz)	target	7-1/2, 8, 9	Win., Fed., Rem., Fio.	$8	1290
3	1	target	7-1/2, 8, 8-1/2, 9	Win., Fio.	NA	1235
2-3/4	1	target	7-1/2, 8, 8-1/2, 9	Fed., Rem., Fio.	NA	1180
3-1/4	24 grams	target	7-1/2, 8, 9	Fed., Win., Fio.	NA	1325
3	7/8	light	8	Fio.	NA	1200
3-3/4	8 pellets	buffered	000 buck	Win., Fed., Rem.	$4**	1325
4	12 pellets	premium	00 buck	Win., Fed., Rem.	$5**	1290
3-3/4	9 pellets	buffered	00 buck	Win., Fed., Rem., Fio.	$19	1325
3-3/4	12 pellets	buffered	0 buck	Win., Fed., Rem.	$4**	1275
4	20 pellets	buffered	1 buck	Win., Fed., Rem.	$4**	1075
3-3/4	16 pellets	buffered	1 buck	Win., Fed., Rem.	$4**	1250
4	34 pellets	premium	4 buck	Fed., Rem.	$5**	1250
3-3/4	27 pellets	buffered	4 buck	Win., Fed., Rem., Fio.	$4**	1325
Max	1	saboted slug	slug	Win., Fed., Rem.	$10**	1450
Max	1-1/4	slug, rifled	slug	Fed.	NA	1520
Max	1-1/4	slug	slug	Lightfield		1440
Max	1	slug, rifled	slug, magnum	Rem., Fio.	$5**	1680
Max	1	slug, rifled	slug	Win., Fed., Rem.	$4**	1610
Max	1	sabot slug	slug	Sauvestre		1640
Max	400	plat. tip	sabot slug	Win.	NA	1700
Max	385 grains	Partition Gold Slug	slug	Win.	NA	1900
Max	385 grains	Core-Lokt bonded	sabot slug	Rem.	NA	1900
Max	325 grains	Barnes Sabot	slug	Fed.	NA	1900
3	1-1/8	steel target	6-1/2, 7	Rem.	NA	1200
2-3/4	1-1/8	steel target	7	Rem.	NA	1145
3	1#	steel	7	Win.	$11	1235
3-1/2	1-1/4	steel	T, BBB, BB, 1, 2, 3, 4, 5, 6	Win., Fed., Rem.	$18	1275
3-3/4	1-1/8	steel	BB, 1, 2, 3, 4, 5, 6	Win., Fed., Rem., Fio.	$16	1365
3-3/4	1	steel	2, 3, 4, 5, 6, 7	Win., Fed., Rem., Fio.	$13	1390
Max	7/8	steel	7	Fio.	NA	1440
16 Gauge 2-3/4"						
3-1/4	1-1/4	magnum	2, 4, 6	Fed., Rem.	$16	1260
3-1/4	1-1/8	high velocity	4, 6, 7-1/2	Win., Fed., Rem., Fio.	$12	1295
Max	1-1/8	Bismuth	4, 5	Win., Bis.	NA	1200
2-3/4	1-1/8	standard velocity	6, 7-1/2, 8	Fed., Rem., Fio.	$9	1185
2-1/2	1	dove	6, 7-1/2, 8, 9	Fio., Win.	NA	1165
2-3/4	1		6, 7-1/2, 8	Fio.	NA	1200
Max	15/16	steel	2, 4	Fed., Rem.	NA	1300
Max	7/8	steel	2, 4	Win.	$16	1300
3	12 pellets	buffered	1 buck	Win., Fed., Rem.	$4**	1225
Max	4/5	slug, rifled	slug	Win., Fed., Rem.	$4**	1570
Max	.92	sabot slug	slug	Sauvestre		1560
20 Gauge 3" Magnum						
3	1-1/4	premium	2, 4, 5, 6, 7-1/2	Win., Fed., Rem.	$15	1185
Max	1-1/4	Tungsten-Polymer	4, 6	Fed.	NA	1185
3	1-1/4	turkey	4, 6	Fio.	NA	1200
Max	1-1/8	hevi. Shot	4, 6, 7-1/2	Rem.	NA	1300
20 Gauge 3" Magnum (cont.)						
Max	18 pellets	buck shot	2 buck	Fed.	NA	1200
Max	24 pellets	buffered	3 buck	Win.	$5**	1150
2-3/4	20 pellets	buck	3 buck	Rem.	$4**	1200
3-1/4	1	steel	1, 2, 3, 4, 5, 6	Win., Fed., Rem.	$15	1330
Max	1-1/16	Bismuth	2, 4, 5, 6	Bismuth	NA	1250
Max	7/8	Tungsten - Iron	2, 4	Fed.	NA	1375
Mag	5/8	saboted slug	275 gr.	Fed.	NA	1450
20 Gauge 2-3/4"						
2-3/4	1-1/8	magnum	4, 6, 7-1/2	Win., Fed., Rem.	$14	1175
Max	1-1/8	Tungsten-Polymer	4, 6	Fed.	NA	1175
2-3/4	1	high velocity	4, 5, 6, 7-1/2, 8, 9	Win., Fed., Rem., Fio.	$12	1220
Max	1	Bismuth	4, 6	Win., Bis.	NA	1200
Max	1	Supreme H-V	4, 6, 7-1/2	Win. Rem.	NA	1300
Max	7/8	Steel	2, 3, 4	Fio.	NA	1500
2-1/2	1	standard velocity	6, 7-1/2, 8	Win., Rem., Fed., Fio.	$6	1165
2-1/2	7/8	clays	8	Rem.	NA	1200
2-1/2	7/8	promotional	6, 7-1/2, 8	Win., Rem., Fio.	$6	1210
2-1/2	1	target	8, 9	Win., Rem.	$8	1165
Max	7/8	clays	7-1/2, 8	Win.	NA	1275
2-1/2	7/8	target	8, 9	Win., Fed., Rem.	$8	1200
2-1/2	7/8	steel - target	7	Rem.		1200
Max	5/8	Saboted Slug	Copper Slug	Rem.	NA	1500
Max	20 pellets	buffered	3 buck	Win., Fed.	$4	1200
Max	5/8	slug, saboted	slug	Win.,	$9**	1400
2-3/4	5/8	slug, rifled	slug	Rem.	$4**	1580
Max	3/4	saboted slug	copper slug	Fed., Rem.	NA	1450
Max	3/4	slug, rifled	slug	Win., Fed., Rem., Fio.	$4**	1570
Max	.9	sabot slug	slug	Sauvestre		1480
Max	260 grains	Partition Gold Slug	slug	Win.	NA	1900
Max	3/4	steel	2, 3, 4, 6	Win., Fed., Rem.	$14	1425
28 Gauge 2-3/4"						
2	1	high velocity	6, 7-1/2, 8	Win.	$12	1125
2-1/4	3/4	high velocity	6, 7-1/2, 8, 9	Win., Fed., Rem., Fio.	$11	1295
2	3/4	target	8, 9	Win., Fed., Rem.	$9	1200
Max	5/8	Bismuth	4, 6	Win., Bis.	NA	1250
410 Bore 3"						
Max	11/16	high velocity	4, 5, 6, 7-1/2, 8, 9	Win., Fed., Rem., Fio.	$10	1135
Max	9/16	Bismuth	4	Win., Bis.	NA	1175
410 Bore 2-1/2"						
Max	1/2	high velocity	4, 6, 7-1/2	Win., Fed., Rem.	$9	1245
Max	1/5	slug, rifled	slug	Win., Fed., Rem.	$4**	1815
1-1/2	1/2	target	8, 8-1/2, 9	Win., Fed., Rem., Fio.	$8	1200

SHOOTER'S MARKETPLACE

INTERESTING PRODUCT NEWS FOR THE ACTIVE SHOOTING SPORTSMAN

The companies represented on the following pages will be happy to provide additional information – feel free to contact them.

NYLON COATED GUN CLEANING RODS

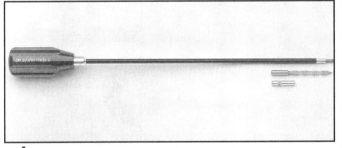

J. Dewey cleaning rods have been used by the U.S. Olympic shooting team and the benchrest community for over 20 years. These one-piece, spring-tempered, steel-base rods will not gall delicate rifling or damage the muzzle area of front-cleaned firearms. The nylon coating elmininates the problem of abrasives adhering to the rod during the cleaning operation. Each rod comes with a hard non-breakable plastic handle supported by ball-bearings, top and bottom, for ease of cleaning.

The brass cleaning jags are designed to pierce the center of the cleaning patch or wrap around the knurled end to keep the patch centered in the bore.

Coated rods are available from 17-caliber to shotgun bore size in several lengths to meet the needs of any shooter. Write for more information.

J. DEWEY MFG. CO., INC.
P.O. Box 2014, Southbury, CT 06488
Phone: 203-264-3064 • Fax: 203-262-6907
Web: www.deweyrods.com

HIGH QUALITY OPTICS

One of the best indicators of quality is a scope's resolution number. The smaller the number, the better. Our scope has a resolution number of 2.8 seconds of angle. This number is about 20% smaller (better) than other well-known scopes costing much more. It means that two .22 caliber bullets can be a hair's breadth apart and edges of each still be clearly seen. With a Shepherd at 800 yards, you will be able to tell a four inch antler from a four inch ear and a burrowing owl from a prairie dog. Bird watchers will be able to distinguish a Tufted Titmouse from a Ticked-Off Field Mouse. Send for free catalog.

SHEPHERD ENTERPRISES, INC.
Box 189, Waterloo, NE 68069
Phone: 402-779-2424 • Fax: 402-779-4010
E-mail: shepherd@shepherdscopes.com • Web: www.shepherdscopes.com

SHOOTER'S MARKETPLACE

COMBINATION RIFLE AND OPTICS REST

The Magna-Pod weighs less than two pounds, yet firmly supports more than most expensive tripods. It will hold 50 pounds at its low 9-inch height and over 10 pounds extended to 17 inches. It sets up in seconds where there is neither time nor space for a tripod and keeps your expensive equipment safe from knock-overs by kids, pets, pedestrians, or even high winds. It makes a great mono-pod for camcorders, etc., and its carrying box is less than 13" x 13" x 3 1/4" high for easy storage and access.

Attached to its triangle base it becomes an extremely stable table pod or rifle bench rest. The rifle yoke pictured in photo is included.

It's 5 pods in 1: Magna-Pod, Mono-Pod, Table-Pod, Shoulder-Pod and Rifle Rest. Send for free catalog.

SHEPHERD ENTERPRISES, INC.
Box 189, Waterloo, NE 68069
Phone: 402-779-2424 • Fax: 402-779-4010
E-mail: shepherd@shepherdscopes.com • Web: www.shepherdscopes.com

RUGGED TOMMI & JOUNI FOLDER

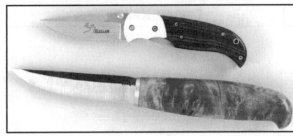

From a harsh and challenging environment, Finns have learned to make tools they can rely on for their survival. In this tradition, Kellam Knives Co. continues to provide knives today – reliable and razor sharp.

Jouni Kellokoski, president of Kellam Knives, designed the FJ1 knife as his optimal personal carry folder. Custom made quality. From tuxedo to jeans, it's handsome and elegant, yet ready for many rugged tasks. Cocobolo wood and ivory micarta handle with an AUS-8 stainless 2.5" blade. Razor sharp.

Since 1610 the KP Smithy family has been hammering with the ultimate knowledge of knifemaking. The smith pounds steel hundreds of times with a hammer to make razor sharp knives. The tradition still continues. No compromise is made with workmanship or materials. Hand hammered and progression tempered razor sharp blades up to 62 Rc hardness with handles of rare root burl of raita wood.

902 S. Dixie Hwy., Lantana, FL 33462
Phone: 561-588-3185
or 800-390-6918
Fax: 561-588-3186
Web: www.kellamknives.com
Email: info@kellamknives.com

6x18x40 VARMINT/TARGET SCOPE

Send for Free Catalog

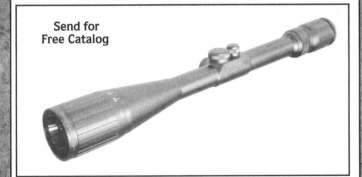

The Shepherd 6x18x40 Varmint/Target Scope makes long-range varmint and target shooting child's play. Just pick the ranging circle that best fits your target (be it prairie dogs, coyotes or paper varmints) and Shepherd's exclusive, patented Dual Reticle Down Range System does the rest. You won't believe how far you can accurately shoot, even with rimfire rifles.

Shepherd's superior lens coating mean superior light transmission and tack-sharp resolution.

This new shockproof, waterproof scope features 1/4 minute-of-angle clicks on the ranging circles and friction adjustments on the crosshairs that allow fine-tuning to 0.001 MOA. A 40mm adjustable objective provides a 5.5-foot field of view at 100 yards (16x setting). 16.5 FOV @ 6X.

SHEPHERD ENTERPRISES, INC.
Box 189, Waterloo, NE 68069
Phone: 402-779-2424 • Fax: 402-779-4010
E-mail: shepherd@shepherdscopes.com • Web: www.shepherdscopes.com

PRESSURE ♦ VELOCITY ♦ ACCURACY

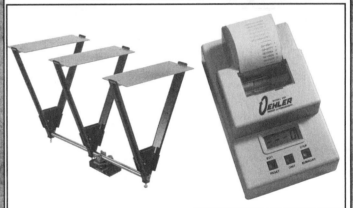

You must know all three. For over thirty years, Oehler ballistic test equipment and software have been the standard for precision measurements. We invite comparison. and even make our systems compare to themselves. The patented *Proof Channel*™ uses three screens to make two velocity measurements on each shot. The Model 43 Personal Ballistics Lab provides shooters with accurate measurements of pressure, velocity, ballistic coefficient, and target information. Oehler instruments are used by military proving grounds and all major ammunition makers.

Phone for free catalog or technical help.

OEHLER RESEARCH, INC.
P.O. Box 9135, Austin, TX 78766
Phone: 800-531-5125 or 512-327-6900
Web: www.oehler-research.com

SHOOTER'S MARKETPLACE

CUSTOM KNIVES

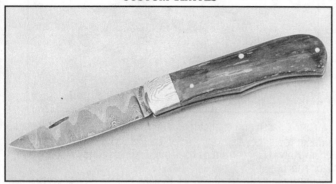

Knife pictured has Damascus blade made of 480 layers of 1095-203E steels in Mr. Hawes' shimmed ladder pattern. Bolster made of mokume from Sakmar. Handles are mammoth ivory. Truly a one-of-a-kind gem that will also function as a utility knife if you desire.

Hawes Forge specializes in high carbon, Damascus steel that are not just for show, they are made to stand up to use and will hold a superior edge. Let Hawes Forge provide you with a knife you can be proud of from their designs or yours.

HAWES FORGE

P.O. Box 176, Weldon, IL 61882
Phone: 217-736-2479

FOR THE SERIOUS RELOADER...

Rooster Labs' line of top-quality, innovative products...for individual and commercial reloaders...now includes:
- **ZAMBINI** 220° Pistol Bullet Lubricant (1x4 & 2x6)
- **HVR** 220° High Velocity Rifle Bullet Lube (1x4)
- **ROOSTER JACKET** Water-based Liquid Bullet Film Lube
- **ROOSTER BRIGHT** Brass Case Polish...Brilliant!
- **CFL-56** Radical Case Forming Lube...for the Wildcatter
- **PDQ-21** Spray Case Sizing Lube...quick, no contamination
- **BP-7 BLACK POWDER** Bullet Lube (1x4 hollow)

 Rooster LABORATORIES®
P.O. Box 414605, Kansas City, MO 64141
Phone: 816-474-1622 • Fax: 816-474-7622
E-mail: roosterlabs@aol.com

RUGER 10-22® COMPETITION HAMMER

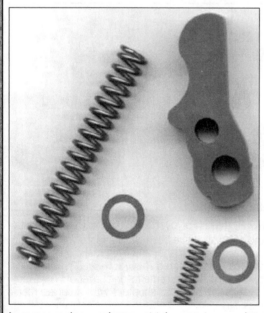

Precision EDM/CNC machined custom hammer for your Ruger 10-22®. Machined from a solid billet of steel. Case hardened to RC-58-60. Drop in designed to lighten your trigger pull to a crisp 2-1/4 lbs. Precision ground with Vapor hand honed engagement surfaces. Includes Wolff Extra Power hammer spring, replacement trigger return spring, and 2 hammer shims.

Price $29.99 plus $3.85 Priority mail.

POWER CUSTOM, INC.

29739 Hwy. J, Dept. KP, Gravois Mills, MO 65037
Phone: 1-573-372-5684 • Fax: 1-573-372-5799
Web: www.powercustom.com • E-mail: rwpowers@laurie.net

FOLDING BIPODS

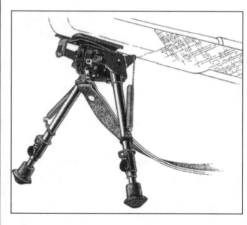

Harris Bipods clamp securely to most stud-equipped bolt-action rifles and are quick-detachable. With adapters, they will fit some other guns. On all models except the Model LM, folding legs have completely adjustable spring-return extensions. The sling swivel attaches to the clamp. This time-proven design is manufactured with heat-treated steel and hard alloys and has a black anodized finish.

Series S Bipods rotate 35° for instant leveling on uneven ground. Hinged base has tension adjustment and buffer springs to eliminate tremor or looseness in crotch area of bipod. They are otherwise similar to non-rotating Series 1A2.

Thirteen models are available from Harris Engineering; literature is free.

HARRIS ENGINEERING INC.

Dept: GD54, Barlow, KY 42024
Phone: 270-334-3633 • Fax: 270-334-3000

SHOOTER'S MARKETPLACE

SWIFT EXTENDS THE HUNT FROM DAWN TO DUSK

Swift Instruments, Inc., extends the hunt with three new illuminated reticle rifle scopes. All three are waterproof, shock tested and have multi-coated lenses that provide for a brighter, sharper, glare-free image from dawn to dusk. Add to this variable intensity illuminated red cross hairs in the center of the reticle that adjust to increase or decrease to your needs to make getting on target easier in low light situations. All three of these new rifle scopes offer fast focusing with Swift *Speed Focus* feature.

Model 680M Swift: 3-9X, 40mm
Model 681M Swift: 1.5-6X, 40mm
Model 682M Swift: 4-12X, 50mm

SWIFT INSTRUMENTS, INC.
952 Dorchester Avenue, Boston, MA 02125
Phone: 617-436-2960 • Fax: 617-436-3232
Web: www.swift-optics.com

ALASKAN HUNTER

Gary Reeder Custom Guns, builder of full custom guns, including custom cowboy guns, hunting handguns, African hunting rifles, custom Encores and Encore barrels, has a free brochure available or you can check out the large Web site at www.reedercustomguns.com. One of our most popular series is our Alaskan Hunter. This beefy 5-shot 454 Casull is for the serious handgun hunter and joins our 475 Linebaugh and 500 Linebaugh as our most popular hunting handguns. For more information contact:

GARY REEDER CUSTOM GUNS
2601 E. 7th Avenue, Flagstaff, AZ 86004
Phone: 928-527-4100 or 928-526-3313

BLACK HILLS GOLD AMMUNITION

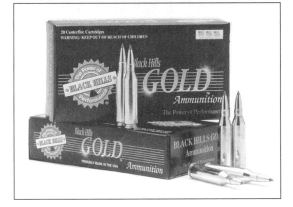

Black Hills Ammunition has introduced a new line of premium performance rifle ammunition. Calibers available in the Black Hills Gold Line are .243, .270, .308, .30-06, and .300 Win Mag. This line is designed for top performance in a wide range of hunting situations. Bullets used in this ammunition are the Barnes X-Bullet with XLC coating and the highly accurate Nosler Ballistic-Tip™.

Black Hills Ammunition is sold dealer direct. The Gold line is packaged in 20 rounds per box, 10 boxes per case. Black Hills pays all freight to dealers in the continental United States. Minimum dealer order is only one case.

BLACK HILLS AMMUNITION
P.O. Box 3090, Rapid City, SD 57709
Phone: 1-605-348-5150 • Fax: 1-605-348-9827
Web: www.black-hills.com

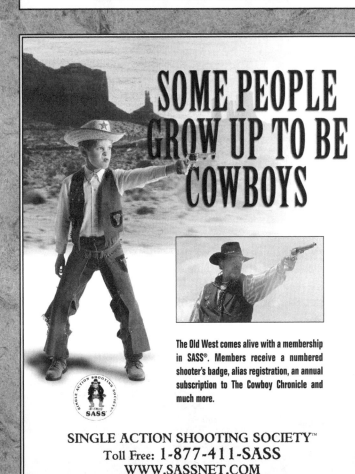

SOME PEOPLE GROW UP TO BE COWBOYS

The Old West comes alive with a membership in SASS®. Members receive a numbered shooter's badge, alias registration, an annual subscription to The Cowboy Chronicle and much more.

SINGLE ACTION SHOOTING SOCIETY™
Toll Free: **1-877-411-SASS**
WWW.SASSNET.COM

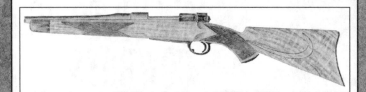
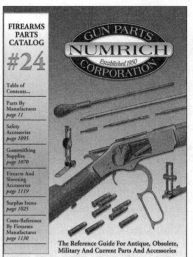

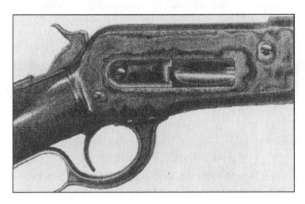

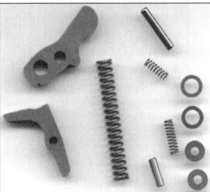

SHOOTER'S MARKETPLACE

CUSTOM COWBOY HANDGUNS

Gary Reeder Custom Guns, builder of full-custom guns, hunting handguns, custom Contenders and Contender barrels and custom Encores and Encore barrels, would be happy to build a custom gun for you. See our Web site at www.reedercustomguns.com, or call Gary Reeder. One of our most popular cowboy guns since 1991 has been our Tombstone Classic. This little beauty has our own birdshead grip, comes in full hi-polished stainless, Black Chromex finish or two-toned. The Tombstone is fully engraved and highly slicked up inside, and is only one of a series of close to 20 custom cowboy guns.

GARY REEDER CUSTOM GUNS
2601 E. 7th Avenue, Flagstaff, AZ 86004
Phone: 928-527-4100 or 928-526-3313

DETACHABLE RINGS & BASES

A.R.M.S.® #22 Throw Lever Rings

All steel 30mm ring, secured with A.R.M.S.® dovetail system to an extruded aluminum platform. Built in no-mar patented buffer pads. Available in Low, Medium, and High height. Low height measures .925". Medium height measures 1.150". High height measures 1.450". Height is measured from the center of the optic to the bottom of the base.

Sugg. Retail $99.00
U.S. Patent No. 5,276,988 & 4,845,871
Item #37 to convert 30mm to 1",
   Suggested Retail $29.00

Call for dealer or distributor in your area.

A.R.M.S., INC.
230 W. Center St., West Bridgewater, MA 02379
Phone: (508) 584-7816 • Fax: (508) 588-8045
E-mail: sswan37176@aol.com • Web: www.armsmounts.com

NEW MANUAL AVAILABLE

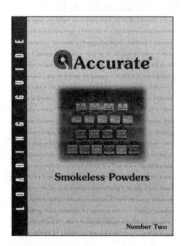

Accurate Powder's newest manual, Number Two, contains new data on powders XMR 4064 and XMP 5744, as well as a special section on Cowboy Action Shooting. In addition, the 400-page manual has loads for new cartridges, such as the .260 Rem., .300 Rem. Ultra Mag., .338 Rem. Ultra Mag., .357 Sig., .300 Whisper, .400 Corbon and more. It also includes many new bullets for the most popular cartridges as well as data for sabots in selected calibers. The price for the book is $16.95, plus $3.00 for shipping and handling in the continental U.S. To order a copy, call or write to:

ACCURATE ARMS
5891 Hwy. 230 W., McEwen, TN 37101
Phone: 1-931-729-4207 • Web: www.accuratepowder.com

QUALITY GUNSTOCK BLANKS

Cali'co Hardwoods has been cutting superior-quality shotgun and rifle blanks for more than 31 years. Cali'co supplies blanks to many of the major manufacturers—Browning, Weatherby, Ruger, Holland & Holland, to name a few—as well as custom gunsmiths the world over.

Profiled rifle blanks are available, ready for inletting and sanding. Cali'co sells superior California hardwoods in Claro walnut, French walnut, Bastogne, maple and myrtle.

Cali'co offers good, serviceable blanks and some of the finest exhibition blanks available. Satisfaction guaranteed.

Color catalog, retail and dealer price list (FFL required) free upon request.

CALI'CO HARDWOODS, INC.
3580 Westwind Blvd., Santa Rosa, CA 95403
Phone: 707-546-4045 • Fax: 707-546-4027

SHOOTER'S MARKETPLACE

LaserMax
TOTALLY INTERNAL LASER SIGHTS FOR SEMIAUTO HANDGUNS

LaserMax's rugged laser sight is a favorite for police and self-defense. Most lethal force encounters occur between dusk and dawn. The LaserMax® increases shooting accuracy in low light or from behind cover/concealment, improves aiming speed and reduces assailant aggression.

LaserMax goes inside the recoil spring, has deliberate activation from the take-down lever (ambidextrous). User installed (no smithing). Maintains alignment always. Beam is as close to the bullet trajectory as physically possible, point of aim and bullet are center of mass from 0 to 20 yds. Flashing beam is scientifically proven to be more noticeable than continuous-on beams. For all Glocks, M1911s, SigArms, Berettas, and more. Fits all holsters. Use with your favorite grips and tactical lights.

New low prices. Police discounts and training programs available.

LASERMAX, INC.
3495 Winton Place, Rochester, NY 14623-2807
Toll-free Phone: (800) LASER-03 • Fax: (585) 272-5427
E-mail: webmaster@lasermax-inc.com • Web: www.lasermax-inc.com

MODULAR RUBBER GRIP SYSTEM

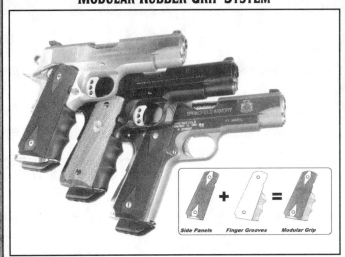

Side Panels   Finger Grooves   Modular Grip

Pearce Grip, Inc., originators of the popular ModularGrip™ for the full size Government Model 1911 style pistols, introduces the Officer's Model Series of this unique grip concept. These grips are a three-piece system which includes finger grooves and side panels. The finger grooves can also be used with other manufacturers exotic wood or other specialty side panel grips. The rubber side panels can be used independently of the finger grooves or combined as a complete set for an ultra slim wrap-around rubber grip.

PEARCE GRIP, INC.
P.O. Box 40367, Fort Worth, TX 76140
Phone: 800-390-9420 • Fax: 817-568-9707

QUALITY OPTICS

Deutsche Optik is the world's leading mail order catalogue specializing in unique and collectible high-end optics and instruments. Long recognized for carrying Cold War era and Eastern Block binoculars, Deutsche Optik has made available a limited quantity of Swiss Military Rangefinders built by Wild. Used by Swiss Alpine troops, this highly accurate Rangefinder is coincident configured and provides 12x power for viewing from 30-20,000 meters. No batteries to worry about...no "ideal conditions" required...no gentle handling necessary. Tough, rugged and easy to use, each Rangefinder includes a lathe board, tripod and snipping canister.

Price reduced to $499. Limited quantity.

DEUTSCHE OPTIK
P.O. Box 601114, San Diego, CA 92160
Phone: 800-225-9407 • Fax: 619-287-9869
Web: www.deutscheoptik.com • e-mail: info@deutscheoptik.com

2003 Sporting Knives
2nd Edition
edited by Joe Kertzman

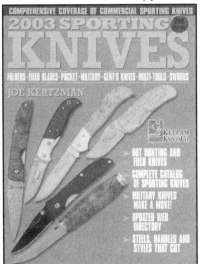

More than 60 cutlery companies reveal over 300 models of available sporting knives, complete with large, clear photos and detailed specifications and retail prices. The catalog covers knives from commercial sporting cutlery companies such as Browning, Buck, Case, Columbia River, and Spyderco. Enjoy new feature articles and reports from the field on knife trends, the latest blade materials, and the newest commercial knife designs. An updated reference directory lets you directly contact manufacturers and dealers. Often described as the factory version of the Knives annual, this is a perfect companion to Knives 2002, which showcases custom knives.

Softcover • 8-1/2 x 11 • 256 pages
700 b&w photos
Item# DGK02 • $22.95

To order call **800-258-0929**
Offer GNB2
M-F 7am - 8pm • Sat 8am - 2pm, CST

Krause Publications
Offer GNB2
P.O. Box 5009, Iola WI 54945-5009
www.krausebooks.com

Shipping & Handling: $4.00 first book, $2.25 each additional. Non-US addresses $20.95 first book, $5.95 each additional.
Sales Tax: CA, IA, IL, NJ, PA, TN, VA, WI residents please add appropriate sales tax.

2003 GUN DIGEST Complete Compact CATALOG

GUNDEX

HANDGUNS

RIFLES

SHOTGUNS

BLACKPOWDER

AIRGUNS

ACCESSORIES

REFERENCE

DIRECTORY OF THE ARMS TRADE

GUNDEX

Includes models suitable for several forms of competition and other sporting purposes.

Accu-Tek AT-380

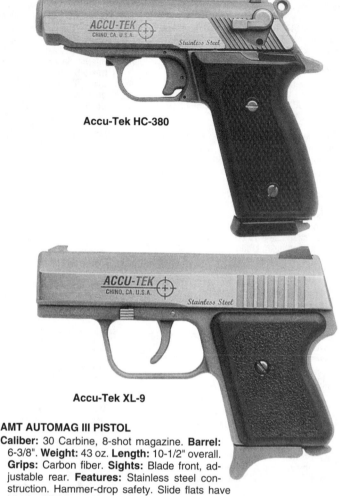

Accu-Tek HC-380

Accu-Tek XL-9

ACCU-TEK MODEL AT-380 AUTO PISTOL

Caliber: 380 ACP, 5-shot magazine. **Barrel:** 2.75". **Weight:** 20 oz. **Length:** 5.6" overall. **Grips:** Grooved black composition. **Sights:** Blade front, rear adjustable for windage. **Features:** Stainless steel frame and slide. External hammer; manual thumb safety; firing pin block, trigger disconnect. Introduced 1991. Price includes cleaning kit and gun lock. Made in U.S.A. by Accu-Tek.
Price: Satin stainless **$239.00**

Accu-Tek Model AT-32SS Auto Pistol

Same as the AT-380SS except chambered for 32 ACP. Introduced 1991. Price includes cleaning kit and gun lock.
Price: Satin stainless **$239.00**

ACCU-TEK MODEL HC-380 AUTO PISTOL

Caliber: 380 ACP, 10-shot magazine. **Barrel:** 2.75". **Weight:** 26 oz. **Length:** 6" overall. **Grips:** Checkered black composition. **Sights:** Blade front, rear adjustable for windage. **Features:** External hammer; manual thumb safety with firing pin and trigger disconnect; bottom magazine release. Stainless steel construction. Introduced 1993. Price includes cleaning kit and gun lock. Made in U.S.A. by Accu-Tek.
Price: Satin stainless **$249.00**

ACCU-TEK XL-9 AUTO PISTOL

Caliber: 9mm Para., 5-shot magazine. **Barrel:** 3". **Weight:** 24 oz. **Length:** 5.6" overall. **Grips:** Black pebble composition. **Sights:** Three-dot system; rear adjustable for windage. **Features:** Stainless steel construction; double-action-only mechanism. Introduced 1999. Price includes cleaning kit and gun lock, two magazines. Made in U.S.A. by Accu-Tek.
Price: **$267.00**

AMERICAN ARMS MATEBA AUTO/REVOLVER

Caliber: 357 Mag., 6-shot. **Barrel:** 4", 6", 8". **Weight:** 2.75 lbs. **Length:** 8.77" overall. **Grips:** Smooth walnut. **Sights:** Blade on ramp front, adjustable rear. **Features:** Double or single action. Cylinder and slide recoil together upon firing. All-steel construction with polished blue finish. Introduced 1995. Imported from Italy by American Arms, Inc.
Price: **$1,295.00**
Price: 6" **$1,349.00**

AMT AUTOMAG II AUTO PISTOL

Caliber: 22 WMR, 9-shot magazine (7-shot with 3-3/8" barrel). **Barrel:** 3-3/8", 4-1/2", 6". **Weight:** About 32 oz. **Length:** 9-3/8" overall. **Grips:** Grooved carbon fiber. **Sights:** Blade front, adjustable rear. **Features:** Made of stainless steel. Gas-assisted action. Exposed hammer. Slide flats have brushed finish, rest is sandblast. Squared trigger guard. Introduced 1986. From Galena Industries, Inc.
Price: **$429.00**

AMT AUTOMAG III PISTOL

Caliber: 30 Carbine, 8-shot magazine. **Barrel:** 6-3/8". **Weight:** 43 oz. **Length:** 10-1/2" overall. **Grips:** Carbon fiber. **Sights:** Blade front, adjustable rear. **Features:** Stainless steel construction. Hammer-drop safety. Slide flats have brushed finish, rest is sandblasted. Introduced 1989. From Galena Industries, Inc.
Price: **$529.00**

AMT AUTOMAG IV PISTOL

Caliber: 45 Winchester Magnum, 6-shot magazine. **Barrel:** 6.5". **Weight:** 46 oz. **Length:** 10.5" overall. **Grips:** Carbon fiber. **Sights:** Blade front, adjustable rear. **Features:** Made of stainless steel with brushed finish. Introduced 1990. Made in U.S.A. by Galena Industries, Inc.
Price: **$599.00**

AMT 45 ACP HARDBALLER II

Caliber: 45 ACP. **Barrel:** 5". **Weight:** 39 oz. **Length:** 8-1/2" overall. **Grips:** Wrap-around rubber. **Sights:** Adjustable. **Features:** Extended combat safety, serrated matte slide rib, loaded chamber indicator, long grip safety, beveled magazine well, adjustable target trigger. All stainless steel. From Galena Industries, Inc.
Price: **$425.00**
Price: Government model (as above except no rib, fixed sights) . **$399.00**
Price: 400 Accelerator (400 Cor-Bon, 7" barrel) **$549.00**
Price: Commando (40 S&W, Government Model frame) **$435.00**

AMT 45 ACP HARDBALLER LONG SLIDE

Caliber: 45 ACP. **Barrel:** 7". **Length:** 10-1/2" overall. **Grips:** Wrap-around rubber. **Sights:** Fully adjustable rear sight. **Features:** Slide and barrel are 2" longer than the standard 45, giving less recoil, added velocity, longer sight radius. Has extended combat safety, serrated matte rib, loaded chamber indicator, wide adjustable trigger. From Galena Industries, Inc.
Price: **$529.00**

HANDGUNS

AMT Backup

Auto-Ordnance Deluxe

Auto-Ordnance 1911A1 Standard

Baer Custom Carry

Baer Premium II

AMT BACKUP PISTOL
Caliber: 357 SIG (5-shot); 38 Super, 9mm Para. (6-shot); 40 S&W, 400 Cor-Bon; 45 ACP (5-shot). **Barrel:** 3". **Weight:** 23 oz. **Length:** 5-3/4" overall. **Grips:** Checkered black synthetic. **Sights:** None. **Features:** Stainless steel construction; double-action-only trigger; dust cover over the trigger transfer bar; extended magazine; titanium nitride finish. Introduced 1992. Made in U.S.A. by Galena Industries.
Price: 9mm, 40 S&W, 45 ACP **$319.00**
Price: 38 Super, 357 SIG, 400 Cor-Bon **$369.00**

AMT 380 DAO Small Frame Backup
Similar to DAO Backup except smaller frame, 2-1/2" barrel, weighs 18 oz., and is 5" overall. Has 5-shot magazine, matte/stainless finish. Made in U.S.A. by Galena Industries.
Price: **$319.00**

AUTO-ORDNANCE 1911A1 AUTOMATIC PISTOL
Caliber: 45 ACP, 7-shot magazine. **Barrel:** 5". **Weight:** 39 oz. **Length:** 8-1/2" overall. **Grips:** Checkered plastic with medallion. **Sights:** Blade front, rear adjustable for windage. **Features:** Same specs as 1911A1 military guns—parts interchangeable. Frame and slide blued; each radius has non-glare finish. Made in U.S.A. by Auto-Ordnance Corp.
Price: 45 ACP, blue. **$511.00**
Price: 45 ACP, Parkerized **$515.00**
Price: 45 ACP Deluxe (three-dot sights, textured rubber
wraparound grips). **$525.00**

AUTAUGA 32 AUTO PISTOL
Caliber: 32 ACP, 6-shot magazine. **Barrel:** 2". **Weight:** 11.3 oz. **Length:** 4.3" overall. **Grips:** Black polymer. **Sights:** Fixed. **Features:** Double-action-only mechanism. Stainless steel construction. Uses Winchester Silver Tip ammunition.
Price: . . . . **NA**

BAER 1911 CUSTOM CARRY AUTO PISTOL
Caliber: 45 ACP, 7- or 10-shot magazine. **Barrel:** 5". **Weight:** 37 oz. **Length:** 8.5" overall. **Grips:** Checkered walnut. **Sights:** Baer improved ramp-style dovetailed front, Novak low-mount rear. **Features:** Baer forged NM frame, slide and barrel with stainless bushing; fitted slide to frame; double serrated slide (full-size only); Baer speed trigger with 4-lb. pull; Baer deluxe hammer and sear, tactical-style extended ambidextrous safety, beveled magazine well; polished feed ramp and throated barrel; tuned extractor; Baer extended ejector, checkered slide stop; lowered and flared ejection port, full-length recoil guide rod; recoil buff. Partial listing shown. Made in U.S.A. by Les Baer Custom, Inc.
Price: Standard size, blued **$1,640.00**
Price: Standard size, stainless **$1,690.00**
Price: Comanche size, blued **$1,640.00**
Price: Comanche size, stainless **$1,690.00**
Price: Comanche size, aluminum frame, blued slide **$1,923.00**
Price: Comanche size, aluminum frame, stainless slide **$1,995.00**

BAER 1911 PREMIER II AUTO PISTOL
Caliber: 9x23, 38 Super, 400 Cor-Bon, 45 ACP, 7- or 10-shot magazine. **Barrel:** 5". **Weight:** 37 oz. **Length:** 8.5" overall. **Grips:** Checkered rosewood, double diamond pattern. **Sights:** Baer dovetailed front, low-mount

Beretta 92 Billennium

Beretta 950 Jetfire

Beretta 96

Bo-Mar rear with hidden leaf. **Features:** Baer NM forged steel frame and barrel with stainless bushing; slide fitted to frame; double serrated slide; lowered, flared ejection port; tuned, polished extractor; Baer extended ejector, checkered slide stop, aluminum speed trigger with 4-lb. pull, deluxe Commander hammer and sear, beavertail grip safety with pad, beveled magazine well, extended ambidextrous safety; flat mainspring housing; polished feed ramp and throated barrel; 30 lpi checkered front strap. Made in U.S.A. by Les Baer Custom, Inc.

Price: Blued **$1,428.00**
Price: Stainless **$1,558.00**
Price: 6" model, blued, from **$1,595.00**

BAER 1911 S.R.P. PISTOL

Caliber: 45 ACP. **Barrel:** 5". **Weight:** 37 oz. **Length:** 8.5" overall. **Grips:** Checkered walnut. **Sights:** Trijicon night sights. **Features:** Similar to the F.B.I. contract gun except uses Baer forged steel frame. Has Baer match barrel with supported chamber, Wolff springs, complete tactical action job. All parts Mag-na-fluxed; deburred for tactical carry. Has Baer Ultra Coat finish. Tuned for reliability. Contact Baer for complete details. Introduced 1996. Made in U.S.A. by Les Baer Custom, Inc.

Price: Government or Comanche length **$2,240.00**

BERETTA MODEL 92 BILLENNIUM LIMITED EDITION

Caliber: 9mm. **Grips:** Carbon fiber. **Sights:** 3 dot. **Features:** Single action. Semiauto. Steel frame, frame mounted safety. Only 2000 made worldwide.

Price: **$1,357.00**

BERETTA MODEL 92FS PISTOL

Caliber: 9mm Para., 10-shot magazine. **Barrel:** 4.9". **Weight:** 34 oz. **Length:** 8.5" overall. **Grips:** Checkered black plastic. **Sights:** Blade front, rear adjustable for windage. Tritium night sights available. **Features:** Double action. Extractor acts as chamber loaded indicator, squared trigger guard, grooved front- and backstraps, inertia firing pin. Matte or blued finish. Introduced 1977. Made in U.S.A. and imported from Italy by Beretta U.S.A.

Price: With plastic grips **$676.00**
Price: Vertech with access rail **$712.00**
Price: Vertech Inox **$762.00**

Beretta Model 92FS/96 Brigadier Pistols

Similar to the Model 92FS/96 except with a heavier slide to reduce felt recoil and allow mounting removable front sight. Wrap-around rubber grips. Three-dot sights dovetailed to the slide, adjustable for windage. Weighs 35.3 oz. Introduced 1999.

Price: 9mm or 40 S&W, 10-shot **$716.00**
Price: Inox models (stainless steel) **$771.00**

Beretta Model 92FS Compact and Compact Type M Pistol

Similar to the Model 92FS except more compact and lighter: overall length 7.8"; 4.3" barrel; weighs 30.9 oz. Has Bruniton finish, chrome-lined bore, combat trigger guard, ambidextrous safety/decock lever. Single column 8-shot magazine (Type M), or double column 10-shot (Compact), 9mm only. Introduced 1998. Imported from Italy by Beretta U.S.A.

Price: Compact (10-shot) **$676.00**
Price: Compact Type M (8-shot) **$676.00**
Price: Compact Inox (stainless) **$734.00**
Price: Compact Type M Inox (stainless) **$721.00**

Beretta Model 96 Pistol

Same as the Model 92FS except chambered for 40 S&W. Ambidextrous safety mechanism with passive firing pin catch, slide safety/decocking lever, trigger bar disconnect. Has 10-shot magazine. Available with three-dot sights. Introduced 1992.

Price: Model 96, plastic grips **$676.00**
Price: Stainless, rubber grips **$734.00**
Price: Vertech with access rail **$712.00**
Price: Vertech Inox **$762.00**

BERETTA MODEL 80 CHEETAH SERIES DA PISTOLS

Caliber: 380 ACP, 10-shot magazine (M84); 8-shot (M85); 22 LR, 7-shot (M87). **Barrel:** 3.82". **Weight:** About 23 oz. (M84/85); 20.8 oz. (M87). **Length:** 6.8" overall. **Grips:** Glossy black plastic (wood optional at extra cost). **Sights:** Fixed front, drift-adjustable rear. **Features:** Double action, quick takedown, convenient magazine release. Introduced 1977. Imported from Italy by Beretta U.S.A.

Price: Model 84 Cheetah, plastic grips **$589.00**
Price: Model 84 Cheetah, wood grips, nickel finish **$652.00**
Price: Model 85 Cheetah, plastic grips, 8-shot **$556.00**
Price: Model 85 Cheetah, wood grips, nickel, 8-shot **$609.00**
Price: Model 87 Cheetah, wood, 22 LR, 7-shot **$589.00**
Price: Model 87 Target, plastic grips **$669.00**

Beretta Model 86 Cheetah

Similar to the 380-caliber Model 85 except has tip-up barrel for first-round loading. Barrel length is 4.4", overall length of 7.33". Has 8-shot magazine, walnut grips. Introduced 1989.

Price: **$591.00**

BERETTA MODEL 950 JETFIRE AUTO PISTOL

Caliber: 25 ACP, 8-shot. **Barrel:** 2.4". **Weight:** 9.9 oz. **Length:** 4.7" overall. **Grips:** Checkered black plastic or walnut. **Sights:** Fixed. **Features:** Single action, thumb safety; tip-up barrel for direct loading/unloading, cleaning. From Beretta U.S.A.

Price: Jetfire plastic, matte finish **$226.00**
Price: Jetfire plastic, stainless **$267.00**

Beretta M8000/8040 Cougar

Beretta U22 Neos

Bersa Thunder 380

Beretta Model 21 Bobcat Pistol

Similar to the Model 950 BS. Chambered for 22 LR or 25 ACP. Both double action. Has 2.4" barrel, 4.9" overall length; 7-round magazine on 22 cal.; 8 rounds in 25 ACP, 9.9 oz., available in nickel, matte, engraved or blue finish. Plastic grips. Introduced in 1985.

Price: Bobcat, 22 or 25, blue **$285.00**
Price: Bobcat, 22, stainless **$307.00**
Price: Bobcat, 22 or 25, matte **$252.00**

BERETTA MODEL 3032 TOMCAT PISTOL

Caliber: 32 ACP, 7-shot magazine. **Barrel:** 2.45". **Weight:** 14.5 oz. **Length:** 5" overall. **Grips:** Checkered black plastic. **Sights:** Blade front, drift-adjustable rear. **Features:** Double action with exposed hammer; tip-up barrel for direct loading/unloading; thumb safety; polished or matte blue finish. Imported from Italy by Beretta U.S.A. Introduced 1996.

Price: Blue $370.00
Price: Matte $340.00
Price: Stainless. $418.00
Price: Titanium $572.00

BERETTA MODEL 8000/8040/8045 COUGAR PISTOL

Caliber: 9mm Para., 10-shot, 40 S&W, 10-shot magazine; 45 ACP, 8-shot. **Barrel:** 3.6". **Weight:** 33.5 oz. **Length:** 7" overall. **Grips:** Checkered plastic. **Sights:** Blade front, rear drift adjustable for windage. **Features:** Slide-mounted safety; rotating barrel; exposed hammer. Matte black Bruniton finish. Announced 1994. Imported from Italy by Beretta U.S.A.

Price: $709.00
Price: D model, 9mm, 40 S&W. $739.00
Price: D model, 45 ACP $739.00

BERETTA MODEL 9000S COMPACT PISTOL

Caliber: 9mm Para., 40 S&W; 10-shot magazine. **Barrel:** 3.4". **Weight:** 26.8 oz. **Length:** 6.6". **Grips:** Soft polymer. **Sights:** Windage-adjustable white-dot rear, white-dot blade front. **Features:** Glass-reinforced polymer frame; patented tilt-barrel, open-slide locking system; chrome-lined barrel; external serrated hammer; automatic firing pin and manual safeties. Introduced 2000. Imported from Italy by Beretta USA.

Price: 9000S Type F (single and double action, external
hammer) $551.00
Price: 9000S Type D (double-action only, no external
hammer or safety). $551.00

Beretta Model 8000/8040/8045 Mini Cougar

Similar to the Model 8000/8040 Cougar except has shorter grip frame and weighs 27.6 oz. Introduced 1998. Imported from Italy by Beretta U.S.A.

Price: 9mm or 40 S&W. $709.00
Price: 9mm or 40 S&W, DAO $739.00
Price: 45 ACP, 6-shot $739.00
Price: 45 ACP DAO $739.00

BERETTA MODEL U22 NEOS

Caliber: 22 LR, 10-shot magazine. **Barrel:** 4.2"; 6". **Weight:** 32 oz.; 36 oz. **Length:** 8.8"; 10.3". **Sights:** Target. **Features:** Intregral rail for standard scope mounts, light, perfectly weighted, 100% American made by Beretta.

Price: $256.00
Price: Inox $299.00

BERSA THUNDER 380 AUTO PISTOLS

Caliber: 380 ACP, 7-shot (Thunder 380 Lite), 9-shot magazine (Thunder 380 DLX). **Barrel:** 3.5". **Weight:** 23 oz. **Length:** 6.6" overall. **Grips:** Black polymer. **Sights:** Blade front, notch rear adjustable for windage; three-dot system. **Features:** Double action; firing pin and magazine safeties. Available in blue or nickel. Introduced 1995. Distributed by Eagle Imports, Inc.

Price: Thunder 380, 7-shot, deep blue finish $256.95
Price: Thunder 380 Deluxe, 9-shot, satin nickel. $291.95

BLUE THUNDER/COMMODORE 1911-STYLE AUTO PISTOLS

Caliber: 45 ACP, 7-shot magazine. **Barrel:** 4-1/4", 5". **Weight:** NA. **Length:** NA. **Grips:** Checkered hardwood. **Sights:** Blade front, drift-adjustable rear. **Features:** Extended slide release and safety, spring guide rod, skeletonized hammer and trigger, magazine bumper, beavertail grip safety. Imported from the Philippines by Century International Arms Inc.

Price: . . . . $464.80 to $484.80

BROWNING HI-POWER 9mm AUTOMATIC PISTOL

Caliber: 9mm Para.,10-shot magazine. **Barrel:** 4-21/32". **Weight:** 32 oz. **Length:** 7-3/4" overall. **Grips:** Walnut, hand checkered, or black Polyamide. **Sights:** 1/8" blade front; rear screw-adjustable for windage and elevation. Also available with fixed rear (drift-adjustable for windage). **Features:** External hammer with half-cock and thumb safeties. A blow on the hammer cannot discharge a cartridge; cannot be fired with magazine removed. Fixed rear sight model available. Includes gun lock. Imported from Belgium by Browning.

Price: Fixed sight model, walnut grips $680.00
Price: Fully adjustable rear sight, walnut grips $730.00
Price: Mark III, standard matte black finish, fixed sight, moulded grips,
ambidextrous safety $662.00

Browning Micro Buck Mark Standard

Calico M-110

Browning Buck Mark Challenge

Carbon-15

Browning Hi-Power Practical Pistol

Similar to the standard Hi-Power except has silver-chromed frame with blued slide, wrap-around Pachmayr rubber grips, round-style serrated hammer and removable front sight, fixed rear (drift-adjustable for windage). Available in 9mm Para. Includes gun lock. Introduced 1991.
Price: **$717.00**

BROWNING BUCK MARK STANDARD 22 PISTOL

Caliber: 22 LR, 10-shot magazine. **Barrel:** 5-1/2". **Weight:** 32 oz. **Length:** 9-1/2" overall. **Grips:** Black moulded composite with checkering. **Sights:** Ramp front, Browning Pro Target rear adjustable for windage and elevation. **Features:** All steel, matte blue finish or nickel, gold-colored trigger. Buck Mark Plus has laminated wood grips. Includes gun lock. Made in U.S.A. Introduced 1985. From Browning.
Price: Buck Mark Standard, blue **$286.00**
Price: Buck Mark Nickel, nickel finish with contoured rubber grips **$338.00**
Price: Buck Mark Plus, matte blue with laminated wood grips . . . **$350.00**
Price: Buck Mark Plus Nickel, nickel finish, laminated wood grips **$383.00**

Browning Buck Mark Camper

Similar to the Buck Mark except 5-1/2" bull barrel. Weight is 34 oz. Matte blue finish, molded composite grips. Introduced 1999. From Browning.
Price: **$258.00**
Price: Camper Nickel, nickel finish, molded composite grips **$287.00**

Browning Buck Mark Challenge

Similar to the Buck Mark except has a lightweight barrel and smaller grip diameter. Barrel length is 5-1/2", weight is 25 oz. Introduced 1999. From Browning.
Price: **$320.00**

Browning Buck Mark Micro

Same as the Buck Mark Standard and Buck Mark Plus except has 4" barrel. Available in blue or nickel. Has 16-click Pro Target rear sight. Introduced 1992.
Price: Micro Standard, matte blue finish. **$286.00**
Price: Micro Nickel, nickel finish. **$338.00**
Price: Buck Mark Micro Plus, matte blue, lam. wood grips. **$350.00**
Price: Buck Mark Micro Plus Nickel **$383.00**

Browning Buck Mark Bullseye

Same as the Buck Mark Standard except has 7-1/4" fluted barrel, matte blue finish. Weighs 36 oz.
Price: Bullseye Standard, molded composite grips **$420.00**
Price: Bullseye Target, contoured rosewood grips **$541.00**

Browning Buck Mark 5.5

Same as the Buck Mark Standard except has a 5-1/2" bull barrel with integral scope mount, matte blue finish.
Price: 5.5 Field, Pro-Target adj. rear sight, contoured walnut grips **$459.00**
Price: 5.5 Target, hooded adj. target sights, contoured walnut grips
. . . . **$459.00**

Buck Mark Commemorative

Same as the Buck Mark Standard except has a 6-3/4" Challenger-style barrel, matte blue finish and scrimshaw-style, bonded ivory grips. Includes pistol rug. Limited to 1,000 guns.
Price: Commemorative. **$437.00**

CALICO M-110 AUTO PISTOL

Caliber: 22 LR. **Barrel:** 6". **Weight:** 3.7 lbs. (loaded). **Length:** 17.9" overall. **Grips:** Moulded composition. **Sights:** Adjustable post front, notch rear. **Features:** Aluminum alloy frame; compensator; pistol grip compartment; ambidextrous safety. Uses same helical-feed magazine as M-100 Carbine. Introduced 1986. Made in U.S.A. From Calico.
Price: **$570.00**

CARBON-15 (Type 97) PISTOL

Caliber: 223, 10-shot magazine. **Barrel:** 7.25". **Weight:** 46 oz. **Length:** 20" overall. **Stock:** Checkered composite. **Sights:** Ghost ring. **Features:** Semi-automatic, gas-operated, rotating bolt action. Carbon fiber upper and lower receiver; chromemoly bolt carrier; fluted stainless match barrel; mil. spec. optics mounting base; uses AR-15-type magazines. Introduced 1992. From Professional Ordnance, Inc.
Price: **$1,600.00**
Price: Type 20 pistol (light-profile barrel, no compensator,
weighs 40 oz.). **$1,500.00**

Charles Daly M-1911-A1P

Colt XSE Model O Commander

Colt 1991 Model O Compact

Colt XSE Lightweight Commander

Colt Lightweight Commander

CHARLES DALY M-1911-A1P AUTOLOADING PISTOL

Caliber: 45 ACP, 7- or 10-shot magazine. **Barrel:** 5". **Weight:** 38 oz. **Length:** 8-3/4" overall. **Grips:** Checkered. **Sights:** Blade front, rear drift adjustable for windage; three-dot system. **Features:** Skeletonized combat hammer and trigger; beavertail grip safety; extended slide release; oversize thumb safety; Parkerized finish. Introduced 1996. Imported from the Philippines by K.B.I., Inc.

Price: **$469.95**

COLT MODEL 1991 MODEL O AUTO PISTOL

Caliber: 45 ACP, 7-shot magazine. **Barrel:** 5". **Weight:** 38 oz. **Length:** 8.5" overall. **Grips:** Checkered black composition. **Sights:** Ramped blade front, fixed square notch rear, high profile. **Features:** Matte finish. Continuation of serial number range used on original G.I. 1911 A1 guns. Comes with one magazine and moulded carrying case. Introduced 1991.

Price: **$645.00**
Price: Stainless. **$800.00**

Colt Model 1991 Model O Commander Auto Pistol

Similar to the Model 1991 A1 except has 4-1/4" barrel. Overall length is 7-3/4". Comes with one 7-shot magazine, molded case.

Price: Blue **$645.00**
Price: Stainless steel **$800.00**

COLT XSE SERIES MODEL O AUTO PISTOLS

Caliber: 45 ACP, 8-shot magazine. **Barrel:** 4.25", 5". **Grips:** Checkered, double diamond rosewood. **Sights:** Drift-adjustable three-dot combat. **Features:** Brushed stainless finish; adjustable, two-cut aluminum trigger; extended ambidextrous thumb safety; upswept beavertail with palm swell; elongated slot hammer; beveled magazine well. Introduced 1999. From Colt's Manufacturing Co., Inc.

Price: XSE Government (5" barrel) **$950.00**
Price: XSE Commander (4.25" barrel) **$950.00**

COLT XSE LIGHTWEIGHT COMMANDER AUTO PISTOL

Caliber: 45 ACP, 8-shot. **Barrel:** 4-1/4". **Weight:** 26 oz. **Length:** 7-3/4" overall. **Grips:** Double diamond checkered rosewood. **Sights:** Fixed, glare-proofed blade front, square notch rear; three-dot system. **Features:** Brushed stainless slide, nickeled aluminum frame; McCormick elongated-slot enhanced hammer, McCormick two-cut adjustable aluminum hammer. Made in U.S.A. by Colt's Mfg. Co., Inc.

Price: 45, stainless **$950.00**

COLT DEFENDER

Caliber: 40 S&W, 45 ACP, 7-shot magazine. **Barrel:** 3". **Weight:** 22-1/2 oz. **Length:** 6-3/4" overall. **Grips:** Pebble-finish rubber wraparound with finger grooves. **Sights:** White dot front, snag-free Colt competition rear. **Features:** Stainless finish; aluminum frame; combat-style hammer; Hi Ride grip safety, extended manual safety, disconnect safety. Introduced 1998. Made in U.S.A. by Colt's Mfg. Co.

Price: **$773.00**

Colt Defender

CZ 75B 9mm

Coonan 357 Magnum

CZ 75B Decocker

COONAN 357 MAGNUM, 41 MAGNUM PISTOLS

Caliber: 357 Mag., 41 Magnum, 7-shot magazine. **Barrel:** 5". **Weight:** 42 oz. **Length:** 8.3" overall. **Grips:** Smooth walnut. **Sights:** Interchangeable ramp front, rear adjustable for windage. **Features:** Stainless steel construction. Unique barrel hood improves accuracy and reliability. Link-less barrel. Many parts interchange with Colt autos. Has grip, hammer, half-cock safeties, extended slide latch. Made in U.S.A. by Coonan Arms, Inc.

Price: 5" barrel, from. **$735.00**
Price: 6" barrel, from. **$768.00**
Price: With 6" compensated barrel. **$1,014.00**
Price: Classic model (Teflon black two-tone finish, 8-shot magazine, fully adjustable rear sight, integral compensated barrel) **$1,400.00**
Price: 41 Magnum Model, from **$825.00**

Coonan Compact Cadet 357 Magnum Pistol

Similar to the 357 Magnum full-size gun except has 3.9" barrel, shorter frame, 6-shot magazine. Weight is 39 oz., overall length 7.8". Linkless bull barrel, full-length recoil spring guide rod, extended slide latch. Introduced 1993. Made in U.S.A. by Coonan Arms, Inc.

Price: **$855.00**

CZ 75B AUTO PISTOL

Caliber: 9mm Para., 40 S&W, 10-shot magazine. **Barrel:** 4.7". **Weight:** 34.3 oz. **Length:** 8.1" overall. **Grips:** High impact checkered plastic. **Sights:** Square post front, rear adjustable for windage; three-dot system. **Features:** Single action/double action design; firing pin block safety; choice of black polymer, matte or high-polish blue finishes. All-steel frame. Imported from the Czech Republic by CZ-USA.

Price: Black polymer. **$472.00**
Price: Glossy blue. **$486.00**
Price: Dual tone or satin nickel. **$486.00**
Price: 22 LR conversion unit. **$279.00**

CZ 75D Compact

CZ 75B Decocker

Similar to the CZ 75B except has a decocking lever in place of the safety lever. All other specifications are the same. Introduced 1999. Imported from the Czech Republic by CZ-USA.

Price: 9mm, black polymer. **$467.00**
New! **Price:** 40 S&W. **$481.00**

CZ 75B Compact Auto Pistol

Similar to the CZ 75 except has 10-shot magazine, 3.9" barrel and weighs 32 oz. Has removable front sight, non-glare ribbed slide top. Trigger guard is squared and serrated; combat hammer. Introduced 1993. Imported from the Czech Republic by CZ-USA.

Price: 9mm, black polymer. **$499.00**
Price: Dual tone or satin nickel. **$513.00**
Price: D Compact, black polymer. **$526.00**

CZ 85

CZ 83B

CZ 97B

CZ 75/85 Kadet

CZ 75M IPSC Auto Pistol

Similar to the CZ 75B except has a longer frame and slide, slightly larger grip to accommodate new heavy-duty magazine. Ambidextrous thumb safety, safety notch on hammer; two-port in-frame compensator; slide racker; frame-mounted Firepoint red dot sight. Introduced 2001. Imported from the Czech Republic by CZ USA.

Price: 40 S&W, 10-shot mag. **$1,498.00**
Price: CZ 75 Standard IPSC (40 S&W, adj. sights) **$1,038.00**

CZ 85B Auto Pistol

Same gun as the CZ 75 except has ambidextrous slide release and safety-levers; non-glare, ribbed slide top; squared, serrated trigger guard; trigger stop to prevent overtravel. Introduced 1986. Imported from the Czech Republic by CZ-USA.

Price: Black polymer. **$483.00**
Price: Combat, black polymer. **$540.00**
Price: Combat, dual tone **$487.00**
Price: Combat, glossy blue. **$499.00**

CZ 85 Combat

Similar to the CZ 85B (9mm only) except has an adjustable rear sight, adjustable trigger for overtravel, free-fall magazine, extended magazine catch. Does not have the firing pin block safety. Introduced 1999. Imported from the Czech Republic by CZ-USA.

Price: 9mm, black polymer **$540.00**
Price: 9mm, glossy blue **$561.00**
Price: 9mm, dual tone or satin nickel **$561.00**

CZ 83B DOUBLE-ACTION PISTOL

Caliber: 9mm Makarov, 32 ACP, 380 ACP, 10-shot magazine. **Barrel:** 3.8". **Weight:** 26.2 oz. **Length:** 6.8" overall. **Grips:** High impact checkered plastic. **Sights:** Removable square post front, rear adjustable for windage;

three-dot system. **Features:** Single action/double action; ambidextrous magazine release and safety. Blue finish; non-glare ribbed slide top. Imported from the Czech Republic by CZ-USA.

Price: Blue **$378.00**
Price: Nickel **$378.00**

CZ 97B AUTO PISTOL

Caliber: 45 ACP, 10-shot magazine. **Barrel:** 4.85". **Weight:** 40 oz. **Length:** 8.34" overall. **Grips:** Checkered walnut. **Sights:** Fixed. **Features:** Single action/double action; full-length slide rails; screw-in barrel bushing; linkless barrel; all-steel construction; chamber loaded indicator; dual transfer bars. Introduced 1999. Imported from the Czech Republic by CZ-USA.

Price: Black polymer. **$607.00**
Price: Glossy blue **$621.00**

CZ 75/85 KADET AUTO PISTOL

Caliber: 22 LR, 10-shot magazine. **Barrel:** 4.88". **Weight:** 36 oz. **Grips:** High impact checkered plastic. **Sights:** Blade front, fully adjustable rear. **Features:** Single action/double action mechanism; all-steel construction. Duplicates weight, balance and function of the CZ 75 pistol. Introduced 1999. Imported from the Czech Republic by CZ-USA.

Price: Black polymer. **$486.00**

CZ 100 AUTO PISTOL

Caliber: 9mm Para., 40 S&W, 10-shot magazine. **Barrel:** 3.7". **Weight:** 24 oz. **Length:** 6.9" overall. **Grips:** Grooved polymer. **Sights:** Blade front with dot, white outline rear drift adjustable for windage. **Features:** Double action only with firing pin block; polymer frame, steel slide; has laser sight mount. Introduced 1996. Imported from the Czech Republic by CZ-USA.

Price: 9mm Para. **$405.00**
Price: 40 S&W **$405.00**

CZ 100

Davis P-380

Davis P-32

Desert Eagle Mark XIX

Desert Eagle Baby Eagle

DAVIS P-380 AUTO PISTOL

Caliber: 380 ACP, 5-shot magazine. **Barrel:** 2.8". **Weight:** 22 oz. **Length:** 5.4" overall. **Grips:** Black composition. **Sights:** Fixed. **Features:** Choice of chrome or black Teflon finish. Introduced 1991. Made in U.S.A. by Davis Industries.
Price: **$98.00**

DAVIS P-32 AUTO PISTOL

Caliber: 32 ACP, 6-shot magazine. **Barrel:** 2.8". **Weight:** 22 oz. **Length:** 5.4" overall. **Grips:** Laminated wood. **Sights:** Fixed. **Features:** Choice of black Teflon or chrome finish. Announced 1986. Made in U.S.A. by Davis Industries.
Price: **$107.00**

DESERT EAGLE MARK XIX PISTOL

Caliber: 357 Mag., 9-shot; 44 Mag., 8-shot; 50 Magnum, 7-shot. **Barrel:** 6", 10", interchangeable. **Weight:** 357 Mag.—62 oz.; 44 Mag.—69 oz.; 50 Mag.— 72 oz. **Length:** 10-1/4" overall (6" bbl.). **Grips:** Rubber. **Sights:** Blade on ramp front, combat-style rear. Adjustable available. **Features:** Interchangeable barrels; rotating three-lug bolt; ambidextrous safety; adjustable trigger. Military epoxy finish. Satin, bright nickel, hard chrome, polished and blued finishes available. 10" barrel extra. Imported from Israel by Magnum Research, Inc.
Price: 357, 6" bbl., standard pistol **$1,199.00**
Price: 44 Mag., 6", standard pistol **$1,199.00**
Price: 50 Magnum, 6" bbl., standard pistol **$1,199.00**

DESERT EAGLE BABY EAGLE PISTOLS

Caliber: 9mm Para., 40 S&W, 45 ACP, 10-round magazine. **Barrel:** 3.5", 3.7", 4.72". **Weight:** NA. **Length:** 7.25" to 8.25" overall. **Grips:** Polymer. **Sights:** Drift-adjustable rear, blade front. **Features:** Steel frame and slide; polygonal rifling to reduce barrel wear; slide safety; decocker. Reintroduced in 1999. Imported from Israel by Magnum Research Inc.
Price: Standard (9mm or 40 cal.; 4.72" barrel, 8.25" overall) . . . **$499.00**
Price: Semi-Compact (9mm, 40 or 45 cal.; 3.7" barrel,
7.75" overall) **$499.00**
Price: Compact (9mm or 40 cal.; 3.5" barrel, 7.25" overall) **$499.00**
Price: Polymer (9mm or 40 cal; polymer frame; 3.25" barrel,
7.25" overall) **$499.00**

EAA WITNESS DA AUTO PISTOL

Caliber: 9mm Para., 10-shot magazine; 38 Super, 40 S&W, 10-shot magazine; 45 ACP, 10-shot magazine. **Barrel:** 4.50". **Weight:** 35.33 oz. **Length:** 8.10" overall. **Grips:** Checkered rubber. **Sights:** Undercut blade front, open rear adjustable for windage. **Features:** Double-action trigger system; round trigger guard; frame-mounted safety. Introduced 1991. Imported from Italy by European American Armory.

EAA Witness

Entréprise Boxer P500

Entréprise Elite P500

Entréprise Tactical 500

Price: 9mm, blue. **$449.00**
Price: 9mm, Wonder finish **$459.00**
Price: 9mm Compact, blue, 10-shot **$449.00**
Price: As above, Wonder finish **$459.60**
Price: 40 S&W, blue **$449.60**
Price: As above, Wonder finish **$459.60**
Price: 40 S&W Compact, 9-shot, blue **$449.60**
Price: As above, Wonder finish **$459.60**
Price: 45 ACP, blue. **$449.00**
Price: As above, Wonder finish **$459.60**
Price: 45 ACP Compact, 8-shot, blue. **$449.00**
Price: As above, Wonder finish **$459.60**

EAA EUROPEAN MODEL AUTO PISTOLS
Caliber: 32 ACP or 380 ACP, 7-shot magazine. **Barrel:** 3.88". **Weight:** 26 oz. **Length:** 7-3/8" overall. **Grips:** European hardwood. **Sights:** Fixed blade front, rear drift-adjustable for windage. **Features:** Chrome or blue finish; magazine, thumb and firing pin safeties; external hammer; safety-lever takedown. Imported from Italy by European American Armory.
Price: Blue **$132.60**
Price: Wonder finish **$163.80**

EAA/BUL 1911 AUTO PISTOL
Caliber: 45 ACP. **Barrel:** 3", 4", 5". **Weight:** 24-30 oz. **Length:** 7-10". **Grips:** Full checkered. **Sights:** Tactical rear, dove tail front. **Features:** Lightweight polymer frame, extended beavertail, skeletonized trigger and hammer, beveled mag well.
Price: Blue **$559.00**
Price: Chrome. **$599.00**

ENTRÉPRISE ELITE P500 AUTO PISTOL
Caliber: 45 ACP, 10-shot magazine. **Barrel:** 5". **Weight:** 40 oz. **Length:** 8.5" overall. **Grips:** Black ultra-slim, double diamond, checkered synthetic. **Sights:** Dovetailed blade front, rear adjustable for windage;

three-dot system. **Features:** Reinforced dust cover; lowered and flared ejection port; squared trigger guard; adjustable match trigger; bolstered front strap; high grip cut; high ride beavertail grip safety; steel flat mainspring housing; extended thumb lock; skeletonized hammer, match grade sear, disconnector; Wolff springs. Introduced 1998. Made in U.S.A. by Entréprise Arms.
Price: **$739.90**

Entréprise Boxer P500 Auto Pistol
Similar to the Medalist model except has adjustable Competizione "melded" rear sight with dovetailed Patridge front; high mass chiseled slide with sweep cut; machined slide parallel rails; polished breech face and barrel channel. Introduced 1998. Made in U.S.A. by Entréprise Arms.
Price: **$1,399.00**

Entréprise Medalist P500 Auto Pistol
Similar to the Elite model except has adjustable Competizione "melded" rear sight with dovetailed Patridge front; machined slide parallel rails with polished breech face and barrel channel; front and rear slide serrations; lowered and flared ejection port; full-length one-piece guide rod with plug; National Match barrel and bushing; stainless firing pin; tuned match extractor; oversize firing pin stop; throated barrel and polished ramp; slide lapped to frame. Introduced 1998. Made in U.S.A. by Entréprise Arms.
Price: 45 ACP **$979.00**
Price: 40 S&W **$1,099.00**

Entréprise Tactical P500 Auto Pistol
Similar to the Elite model except has Tactical2 Ghost Ring sight or Novak lo-mount sight; ambidextrous thumb safety; front and rear slide serrations; full-length guide rod; throated barrel, polished ramp; tuned match extractor; fitted barrel and bushing; stainless firing pin; slide lapped to frame; dehorned. Introduced 1998. Made in U.S.A. by Entréprise Arms.
Price: **$979.90**
Price: Tactical Plus (full-size frame, Officer's slide) **$1,049.00**

FEG PJK-9HP

Firestorm Mini

Felk MTF 450

Firestorm Compact

Firestorm 45 Gov't

ERMA KGP68 AUTO PISTOL
Caliber: 32 ACP, 6-shot, 380 ACP, 5-shot. **Barrel:** 4". **Weight:** 22-1/2 oz. **Length:** 7-3/8" overall. **Grips:** Checkered plastic. **Sights:** Fixed. **Features:** Toggle action similar to original "Luger" pistol. Action stays open after last shot. Has magazine and sear disconnect safety systems.
Price: **$499.95**

FEG PJK-9HP AUTO PISTOL
Caliber: 9mm Para., 10-shot magazine. **Barrel:** 4.75". **Weight:** 32 oz. **Length:** 8" overall. **Grips:** Hand-checkered walnut. **Sights:** Blade front, rear adjustable for windage; three dot system. **Features:** Single action; polished blue or hard chrome finish; rounded combat-style serrated hammer. Comes with two magazines and cleaning rod. Imported from Hungary by K.B.I., Inc.
Price: Blue **$259.95**
Price: Hard chrome................................. **$259.95**

FEG SMC-380 AUTO PISTOL
Caliber: 380 ACP, 6-shot magazine. **Barrel:** 3.5". **Weight:** 18.5 oz. **Length:** 6.1" overall. **Grips:** Checkered composition with thumbrest. **Sights:** Blade front, rear adjustable for windage. **Features:** Patterned after the PPK pistol. Alloy frame, steel slide; double action. Blue finish. Comes with two magazines, cleaning rod. Imported from Hungary by K.B.I., Inc.
Price: **$224.95**

FELK MTF 450 AUTO PISTOL
Caliber: 9mm Para. (10-shot); 40 S&W (8-shot); 45 ACP (9-shot magazine). **Barrel:** 3.5". **Weight:** 19.9 oz. **Length:** 6.4" overall. **Grips:** Checkered. **Sights:** Blade front; adjustable rear. **Features:** Double-action-only trigger, striker fired; polymer frame; trigger safety, firing pin safety, trigger bar safety; adjustable trigger weight; fully interchangeable slide/barrel to change calibers. Introduced 1998. Imported by Felk Inc.
Price: **$395.00**
Price: 45 ACP pistol with 9mm and 40 S&W slide/barrel assemblies **$999.00**

FIRESTORM AUTO PISTOL
Features: 7 or 10 rd. double action pistols with matte, duotone or nickel finish. Distributed by SGS Importers International.
Price: 22 LR 10 rd, 380 7 rd. matte **$248.95**
Price: Duotone **$273.95**
Price: Mini 9mm, 40 S&W, 10 rd. matte **$366.95**
Price: Duotone **$374.95**
Price: Nickel **$391.95**
Price: Mini 9mm, 7 rd. matte **$374.95**
Price: Duotone **$387.95**
Price: Nickel **$399.95**
Price: 45 Government, Compact, 7 rd. matte............ **$314.95**
Price: Duotone **$324.95**
Price: Extra magazines **$29.95-49.95**

Glock 17C

Glock 22

Glock 26

Glock 30

GLOCK 17 AUTO PISTOL

Caliber: 9mm Para., 10-shot magazine. **Barrel:** 4.49". **Weight:** 22.04 oz. (without magazine). **Length:** 7.32" overall. **Grips:** Black polymer. **Sights:** Dot on front blade, white outline rear adjustable for windage. **Features:** Polymer frame, steel slide; double-action trigger with "Safe Action" system; mechanical firing pin safety, drop safety; simple takedown without tools; locked breech, recoil operated action. Adopted by Austrian armed forces 1983. NATO approved 1984. Imported from Austria by Glock, Inc.

Price: Fixed sight, with extra magazine, magazine loader, cleaning kit
.... **$641.00**
Price: Adjustable sight **$671.00**
Price: Model 17L (6" barrel) **$800.00**
Price: Model 17C, ported barrel (compensated) **$646.00**

Glock 19 Auto Pistol

Similar to the Glock 17 except has a 4" barrel, giving an overall length of 6.85" and weight of 20.99 oz. Magazine capacity is 10 rounds. Fixed or adjustable rear sight. Introduced 1988.
Price: Fixed sight **$641.00**
Price: Adjustable sight **$671.00**
Price: Model 19C, ported barrel **$646.00**

Glock 20 10mm Auto Pistol

Similar to the Glock Model 17 except chambered for 10mm Automatic cartridge. Barrel length is 4.60", overall length is 7.59", and weight is 26.3 oz. (without magazine). Magazine capacity is 10 rounds. Fixed or adjustable rear sight. Comes with an extra magazine, magazine loader, cleaning rod and brush. Introduced 1990. Imported from Austria by Glock, Inc.
Price: Fixed sight **$700.00**
Price: Adjustable sight **$730.00**

Glock 21 Auto Pistol

Similar to the Glock 17 except chambered for 45 ACP, 10-shot magazine. Overall length is 7.59", weight is 25.2 oz. (without magazine). Fixed or adjustable rear sight. Introduced 1991.
Price: Fixed sight **$700.00**
Price: Adjustable sight **$730.00**

Glock 22 Auto Pistol

Similar to the Glock 17 except chambered for 40 S&W, 10-shot magazine. Overall length is 7.28", weight is 22.3 oz. (without magazine). Fixed or adjustable rear sight. Introduced 1990.
Price: Fixed sight **$641.00**
Price: Adjustable sight **$671.00**
Price: Model 22C, ported barrel **$646.00**

Glock 23 Auto Pistol

Similar to the Glock 19 except chambered for 40 S&W, 10-shot magazine. Overall length is 6.85", weight is 20.6 oz. (without magazine). Fixed or adjustable rear sight. Introduced 1990.
Price: Fixed sight **$641.00**
Price: Model 23C, ported barrel **$646.00**
Price: Adjustable sight **$671.00**

GLOCK 26, 27 AUTO PISTOLS

Caliber: 9mm Para. (M26), 10-shot magazine; 40 S&W (M27), 9-shot magazine. **Barrel:** 3.46". **Weight:** 21.75 oz. **Length:** 6.29" overall. **Grips:** Integral. Stippled polymer. **Sights:** Dot on front blade, fixed or fully adjustable white outline rear. **Features:** Subcompact size. Polymer frame, steel slide; double-action trigger with "Safe Action" system, three safeties. Matte black Tenifer finish. Hammer-forged barrel. Imported from Austria by Glock, Inc. Introduced 1996.
Price: Fixed sight **$641.00**
Price: Adjustable sight **$671.00**

GLOCK 29, 30 AUTO PISTOLS

Caliber: 10mm (M29), 45 ACP (M30), 10-shot magazine. **Barrel:** 3.78". **Weight:** 24 oz. **Length:** 6.7" overall. **Grips:** Integral. Stippled polymer. **Sights:** Dot on front, fixed or fully adjustable white outline rear. **Features:** Compact size. Polymer frame steel slide; double-recoil spring reduces recoil; Safe Action system with three safeties; Tenifer finish. Two magazines supplied. Introduced 1997. Imported from Austria by Glock, Inc.
Price: Fixed sight **$700.00**
Price: Adjustable sight **$730.00**

Glock 31

Hammerli Trailside PL 22

Glock 35

Heckler & Koch USP Compact

Glock 31/31C Auto Pistols

Similar to the Glock 17 except chambered for 357 Auto cartridge; 10-shot magazine. Overall length is 7.32", weight is 23.28 oz. (without magazine). Fixed or adjustable sight. Imported from Austria by Glock, Inc.

Price: Fixed sight	**$641.00**
Price: Adjustable sight	**$671.00**
Price: Model 31C, ported barrel	**$646.00**

Glock 32/32C Auto Pistols

Similar to the Glock 19 except chambered for the 357 Auto cartridge; 10-shot magazine. Overall length is 6.85", weight is 21.52 oz. (without magazine). Fixed or adjustable sight. Imported from Austria by Glock, Inc.

Price: Fixed sight	**$616.00**
Price: Adjustable sight	**$644.00**
Price: Model 32C, ported barrel	**$646.00**

Glock 33 Auto Pistol

Similar to the Glock 26 except chambered for the 357 Auto cartridge; 9-shot magazine. Overall length is 6.29", weight is 19.75 oz. (without magazine). Fixed or adjustable sight. Imported from Austria by Glock, Inc.

Price: Fixed sight	**$641.00**
Price: Adjustable sight	**$671.00**

GLOCK 34, 35 AUTO PISTOLS

Caliber: 9mm Para. (M34), 40 S&W (M35), 10-shot magazine. **Barrel:** 5.32". **Weight:** 22.9 oz. **Length:** 8.15" overall. **Grips:** Integral. Stippled polymer. **Sights:** Dot on front, fully adjustable white outline rear. **Features:** Polymer frame, steel slide; double-action trigger with "Safe Action" system; three safeties; Tenifer finish. Imported from Austria by Glock, Inc.

Price: Model 34, 9mm.	**$770.00**
Price: Model 35, 40 S&W	**$770.00**

GLOCK 36 AUTO PISTOL

Caliber: 45 ACP, 6-shot magazine. **Barrel:** 3.78". **Weight:** 20.11 oz. **Length:** 6.77" overall. **Grips:** Integral. Stippled polymer. **Sights:** Dot on front, fully adjustable white outline rear. **Features:** Polymer frame, steel slide; double-action trigger with "Safe Action" system; three safeties; Tenifer finish. Imported from Austria by Glock, Inc.

Price: Fixed sight	**$700.00**
Price: Adj. sight	**$730.00**

HAMMERLI "TRAILSIDE" TARGET PISTOL

Caliber: 22 LR. **Barrel:** 4.5", 6". **Weight:** 28 oz. **Grips:** Synthetic. **Sights:** Fixed. **Features:** 10-shot magazine. Imported from Switzerland by Sigarms. Distributed by Hammerli U.S.A.

Price:	**$549.00**

HECKLER & KOCH USP AUTO PISTOL

Caliber: 9mm Para., 10-shot magazine, 40 S&W, 10-shot magazine. **Barrel:** 4.25". **Weight:** 28 oz. (USP40). **Length:** 6.9" overall. **Grips:** Non-slip stippled black polymer. **Sights:** Blade front, rear adjustable for windage. **Features:** New HK design with polymer frame, modified Browning action with recoil reduction system, single control lever. Special "hostile environment" finish on all metal parts. Available in SA/DA, DAO, left- and right-hand versions. Introduced 1993. Imported from Germany by Heckler & Koch, Inc.

Price: Right-hand	**$699.00**
Price: Left-hand	**$714.00**
Price: Stainless steel, right-hand	**$749.00**
Price: Stainless steel, left-hand	**$799.00**

Heckler & Koch USP Compact Auto Pistol

Similar to the USP except has 3.58" barrel, measures 6.81" overall, and weighs 1.60 lbs. (9mm). Available in 9mm Para. 357 SIG or 40 S&W with 10-shot magazine. Introduced 1996. Imported from Germany by Heckler & Koch, Inc.

Price: Blue	**$786.00**
Price: Blue with control lever on right	**$821.00**
Price: Stainless steel	**$849.00**
Price: Stainless steel with control lever on right	**$874.00**
New! Price: Same as USP Compact DAO, enhanced trigger performance	**$821.00**

Heckler & Koch USP45

Heckler & Koch USP Expert

Heckler & Koch USP45 Tactical

Heckler & Koch P7M8

Heckler & Koch USP45 Auto Pistol

Similar to the 9mm and 40 S&W USP except chambered for 45 ACP, 10-shot magazine. Has 4.13" barrel, overall length of 7.87" and weighs 30.4 oz. Has adjustable three-dot sight system. Available in SA/DA, DAO, left- and right-hand versions. Introduced 1995. Imported from Germany by Heckler & Koch, Inc.

Price: Right-hand **$827.00**
Price: Left-hand **$862.00**
Price: Stainless steel right-hand **$888.00**
Price: Stainless steel left-hand **$923.00**

Heckler & Koch USP45 Compact

Similar to the USP45 except has stainless slide; 8-shot magazine; modified and contoured slide and frame; extended slide release; 3.80" barrel, 7.09" overall length, weighs 1.75 lbs.; adjustable three-dot sights. Introduced 1998. Imported from Germany by Heckler & Koch, Inc.

Price: With control lever on left, stainless **$909.00**
Price: As above, blue **$857.00**
Price: With control lever on right, stainless **$944.00**
Price: As above, blue **$892.00**

HECKLER & KOCH USP45 TACTICAL PISTOL

Caliber: 45 ACP, 10-shot magazine. **Barrel:** 4.92". **Weight:** 2.24 lbs. **Length:** 8.64" overall. **Grips:** Non-slip stippled polymer. **Sights:** Blade front, fully adjustable target rear. **Features:** Has extended threaded barrel with rubber O-ring; adjustable trigger; extended magazine floorplate; adjustable trigger stop; polymer frame. Introduced 1998. Imported from Germany by Heckler & Koch, Inc.

Price: **$1,124.00**

HECKLER & KOCH MARK 23 SPECIAL OPERATIONS PISTOL

Caliber: 45 ACP, 10-shot magazine. **Barrel:** 5.87". **Weight:** 43 oz. **Length:** 9.65" overall. **Grips:** Integral with frame; black polymer. **Sights:** Blade front, rear drift adjustable for windage; three-dot. **Features:** Polymer frame; double action; exposed hammer; short recoil, modified Browning action. Civilian version of the SOCOM pistol. Introduced 1996. Imported from Germany by Heckler & Koch, Inc.

Price: **$2,444.00**

Heckler & Koch USP Expert Pistol

Combines features of the USP Tactical and HK Mark 23 pistols with a new slide design. Chambered for 45 ACP; 10-shot magazine. Has adjustable target sights, 5.20" barrel, 8.74" overall length, weighs 1.87 lbs. Match-grade single- and double-action trigger pull with adjustable stop; ambidextrous control levers; elongated target slide; barrel O-ring that seals and centers barrel. Suited to IPSC competition. Introduced 1999. Imported from Germany by Heckler & Koch, Inc.

Price: **$1,533.00**

HECKLER & KOCH P7M8 AUTO PISTOL

Caliber: 9mm Para., 8-shot magazine. **Barrel:** 4.13". **Weight:** 29 oz. **Length:** 6.73" overall. **Grips:** Stippled black plastic. **Sights:** Blade front, adjustable rear; three dot system. **Features:** Unique "squeeze cocker" in frontstrap cocks the action. Gas-retarded action. Squared combat-type trigger guard. Blue finish. Compact size. Imported from Germany by Heckler & Koch, Inc.

Price: P7M8, blued **$1,472.00**

Hi-Point 45 ACP

Hi-Point 9MM Comp

Kahr K9

HI-POINT FIREARMS 40 S&W AUTO

Caliber: 40 S&W, 8-shot magazine. **Barrel:** 4.5". **Weight:** 39 oz. **Length:** 7.72" overall. **Grips:** Checkered acetal resin. **Sights:** Adjustable; low profile. **Features:** Internal drop-safe mechanism; alloy frame. Introduced 1991. From MKS Supply, Inc.
Price: Matte black. $159.00

HI-POINT FIREARMS 45 CALIBER PISTOL

Caliber: 45 ACP, 7-shot magazine. **Barrel:** 4.5". **Weight:** 39 oz. **Length:** 7.95" overall. **Grips:** Checkered acetal resin. **Sights:** Adjustable; low profile. **Features:** Internal drop-safe mechanism; alloy frame. Introduced 1991. From MKS Supply, Inc.
Price: Matte black. $159.00
Price: Chrome slide, black frame $169.00

HI-POINT FIREARMS 9MM COMP PISTOL

Caliber: 9mm, Para., 10-shot magazine. **Barrel:** 4". **Weight:** 39 oz. **Length:** 7.72" overall. **Grips:** Textured acetal plastic. **Sights:** Adjustable; low profile. **Features:** Single-action design. Scratch-resistant, non-glare blue finish, alloy frame. Muzzle brake/compensator. Compensator is slotted for laser or flashlight mounting. Introduced 1998. From MKS Supply, Inc.
Price: Matte black. $159.00

HI-POINT FIREARMS MODEL 9MM COMPACT PISTOL

Caliber: 9mm Para., 8-shot magazine. **Barrel:** 3.5". **Weight:** 29 oz. **Length:** 6.7" overall. **Grips:** Textured acetal plastic. **Sights:** Combat-style adjustable three-dot system; low profile. **Features:** Single-action design; frame-mounted magazine release; polymer or alloy frame. Scratch-resistant matte finish. Introduced 1993. Made in U.S.A. by MKS Supply, Inc.
Price: Black, alloy frame $137.00
Price: With polymer frame (29 oz.), non-slip grips $137.00
Price: Aluminum with polymer frame $137.00

Hi-Point Firearms Model 380 Polymer Pistol

Similar to the 9mm Compact model except chambered for 380 ACP, 8-shot magazine, adjustable three-dot sights. Weighs 29 oz. Polymer frame. Introduced 1998. Made in U.S.A. by MKS Supply.
Price: $99.95

Hi-Point Firearms 380 Comp Pistol

Similar to the 380 Polymer Pistol except has a 4" barrel with muzzle compensator; action locks open after last shot. Includes a 10-shot and an 8-shot magazine; trigger lock. Introduced 2001. Made in U.S.A. by MKS Supply Inc.
Price: $125.00
Price: With laser sight. $190.00

HS AMERICA HS 2000 PISTOL

Caliber: 9mm Para., 357 SIG, 40 S&W, 10-shot magazine. **Barrel:** 4.08". **Weight:** 22.88 oz. **Length:** 7.2" overall. **Grips:** Integral black polymer. **Sights:** Drift-adjustable white dot rear, white dot blade front. **Features:** Incorporates trigger, firing pin, grip and out-of-battery safeties; firing-pin status and loaded chamber indicators; ambidextrous magazine release; dual-tension recoil spring with stand-off device; polymer frame; black finish with chrome-plated magazine. Imported from Croatia by HS America.
Price: $419.00

IAI M-2000 PISTOL

Caliber: 45 ACP, 8-shot. **Barrel:** 5", (Compact 4.25"). **Weight:** 36 oz. **Length:** 8.5", (6" Compact). **Grips:** Plastic or wood. **Sights:** Fixed. **Features:** 1911 Government U.S. Army-style. Steel frame and slide parkerized. GI grip safety. Beveled feed ramp barrel. By IAI, Inc.
Price: $465.00

KAHR K9, K40 DA AUTO PISTOLS

Caliber: 9mm Para., 7-shot, 40 S&W, 6-shot magazine. **Barrel:** 3.5". **Weight:** 25 oz. **Length:** 6" overall. **Grips:** Wrap-around textured soft polymer. **Sights:** Blade front, rear drift adjustable for windage; bar-dot combat style. **Features:** Trigger-cocking double-action mechanism with passive firing pin block. Made of 4140 ordnance steel with matte black finish. Contact maker for complete price list. Introduced 1994. Made in U.S.A. by Kahr Arms.
Price: E9, black matte finish. $425.00
Price: Matte black, night sights 9mm $668.00
Price: Matte stainless steel, 9mm. $638.00
Price: 40 S&W, matte black $580.00
Price: 40 S&W, matte black, night sights $668.00
Price: 40 S&W, matte stainless $638.00
Price: K9 Elite 98 (high-polish stainless slide flats, Kahr combat trigger), from $694.00
Price: As above, MK9 Elite 98, from. $694.00
Price: As above, K40 Elite 98, from $694.00
Price: Covert, black, stainless slide, short grip. $599.00
Price: Covert, black, tritium nite sights $689.00

Kahr K9 9mm Compact Polymer Pistol

Similar to K9 steel frame pistol except has polymer frame, matte stainless steel slide. Barrel length 3.5"; overall length 6"; weighs 17.9 oz. Includes two 7-shot magazines, hard polymer case, trigger lock. Introduced 2000. Made in U.S.A. by Kahr Arms.
Price: $599.00

HANDGUNS

Kahr MK40

Kel-Tec P-32

Kel-Tec P-11

Kimber Custom II

Kahr MK9/MK40 Micro Pistol

Similar to the K9/K40 except is 5.5" overall, 4" high, has a 3" barrel. Weighs 22 oz. Has snag-free bar-dot sights, polished feed ramp, dual recoil spring system, DA-only trigger. Comes with 6- and 7-shot magazines. Introduced 1998. Made in U.S.A. by Kahr Arms.

Price: Matte stainless **$638.00**
Price: Elite 98, polished stainless, tritium night sights **$791.00**

KAHR PM9 PISTOL

Caliber: 9x19. **Barrel:** 3", 1:10 twist. **Weight:** 15.9 oz. **Length:** 5.3" overall. **Features:** Lightweight black polymer frame, polygonal rifling, stainless steel slide, DAO with passive striker block, trigger lock, hard case, 6 and 7 rd. mags.

Price: Matte stainless slide **$622.00**
Price: Tritium night sights **$719.00**

KEL-TEC P-11 AUTO PISTOL

Caliber: 9mm Para., 10-shot magazine. **Barrel:** 3.1". **Weight:** 14 oz. **Length:** 5.6" overall. **Grips:** Checkered black polymer. **Sights:** Blade front, rear adjustable for windage. **Features:** Ordnance steel slide, aluminum frame. Double-action-only trigger mechanism. Introduced 1995. Made in U.S.A. by Kel-Tec CNC Industries, Inc.

Price: Blue **$314.00**
Price: Hard chrome **$368.00**
Price: Parkerized **$355.00**

KEL-TEC P-32 AUTO PISTOL

Caliber: 32 ACP, 7-shot magazine. **Barrel:** 2.68". **Weight:** 6.6 oz. **Length:** 5.07" overall. **Grips:** Checkered composite. **Sights:** Fixed. **Features:**

Double-action-only mechanism with 6-lb. pull; internal slide stop. Textured composite grip/frame. Made in U.S.A. by Kel-Tec CNC Industries, Inc.

Price: Blue **$300.00**
Price: Hard chrome **$340.00**
Price: Parkerized **$355.00**

KIMBER CUSTOM II AUTO PISTOL

Caliber: 45 ACP, 40 S&W, .38 Super. **Barrel:** 5", match grade, .40 S&W, .38 Super barrels ramped. **Weight:** 38 oz. **Length:** 8.7" overall. **Grips:** Checkered black rubber, walnut, rosewood. **Sights:** Dovetail front and rear, Kimber adjustable or fixed three dot (green) Meptrolight night sights. **Features:** Slide, frame and barrel machined from steel or stainless steel forgings. Match grade barrel, chamber and trigger group. Extended thumb safety, beveled magazine well, beveled front and rear slide serrations, high ride beavertail grip safety, checkered flat mainspring housing, kidney cut under trigger guard, high cut grip, match grade stainless steel berrel bushing, polished breech face, Commander-style hammer, lowered and flared ejection port, Wolff springs, bead blasted black oxide finish. Introduced in 1996. Made in U.S.A. by Kimber Mfg., Inc.

Price: Custom **$730.00**
Price: Custom Walnut (double-diamond walnut grips) **$752.00**
Price: Custom Stainless **$832.00**
Price: Custom Stainless 40 S&W **$870.00**
Price: Custom Stainless Target 45 ACP (stainless, adj. sight) . . . **$945.00**
Price: Custom Stainless Target 38 Super **$974.00**

Kimber Custom II Auto Pistol

Similar to Compact II, 4" bull barrel fitted directly to the stainless steel slide without a bushing, grip is .400" shorter than standard, no front serrations. Weighs 34 oz. 45 ACP only. Introduced in 1998. Made in U.S.A. by Kimber Mfg., Inc.

Price: **$870.00**

Kimber Compact II Custom

Kimber Ten II High Capacity Polymer

Kimber Ultra Carry II

Kimber CDP II

Kimber Pro Carry II Auto Pistol

Similar to Custom II, has aluminum frame, 4" bull barrel fitted directly to the slide without bushing. HD with stainless steel frame. Introduced 1998. Made in U.S.A. by Kimber Mfg., Inc.

Price: 45 ACP **$773.00**
Price: HD II **$879.00**
Price: Pro Carry HD II Stainless 45 ACP **$845.00**
Price: Pro Carry HD II Stainless 38 Spec. **$917.00**

Kimber Ultra Carry II Auto Pistol

Similar to Compact Stainless II, lightweight aluminum frame, 3" match grade bull barrel fitted to slide without bushing. Grips .400" shorter. Special slide stop. Low effort recoil. Weighs 25 oz. Introduced in 1999. Made in U.S.A. by Kimber Mfg., Inc.

Price: **$767.00**
Price: Stainless **$841.00**
Price: Stainless 40 S&W **$884.00**

Kimber Ten II High Capacity Polymer Pistol

NEW!

Similar to Custom II, Pro Carry II and Ultra Carry II depending on barrel length. Ten-round magazine capacity (double stack and flush fitting). Polymer grip frame molded over stainless steel or aluminum (Ultra Ten II only) frame insert. Checkered front strap and belly of trigger guard. All models have fixed sights except Gold Match Ten II, which has adjustable sight. Frame grip dimensions approximate that of the standard 1911 for natural aiming and better recoil control. Ultra Ten II weight is 24 oz. Others 32-34 oz. Additional 14-round magazines available where legal. All new for 2002. Much-improved version of the Kimber Polymer series. Made in U.S.A. by Kimber Mfg., Inc.

Price: Ultra Ten II **$850.00**
Price: Pro Carry Ten II **$828.00**
Price: Stainless Ten II **$812.00**

Kimber Gold Match II Auto Pistol

Similar to Custom II models. Includes stainless steel barrel with match grade chamber and barrel bushing, ambidextrous thumb safety, adjustable sight, premium aluminum trigger, hand-checkered double diamond rosewood grips. Barrel hand-fitted to bushing and slide for target accuracy. Made in U.S.A. by Kimber Mfg., Inc.

Price: Gold Match II **$1,169.00**
Price: Gold Match Stainless II 45 ACP **$1,315.00**
Price: Gold Match Stainless II 40 S&W **$1,345.00**

Kimber Gold Match Ten II Polymer Auto Pistol

Similar to Stainless Gold Match II. High capacity polymer frame with ten-round magazine. No ambi thumb safety. Polished flats add elegant look. Introduced 1999. Made in U.S.A. by Kimber Mfg., Inc.

Price: **$1,118.00**

Kimber Gold Combat II Auto Pistol

Similar to Gold Match II except designed for concealed carry. Extended and beveled magazine well, Meprolight tritium night sights; premium aluminum trigger; 30 lpi front strap checkering; special Custom Shop markings; Kim Pro premium finish. Introduced 1999. Made in U.S.A. by Kimber Mfg., Inc.

Price: 45 ACP **$1,682.00**
Price: Gold Combat Stainless (satin-finished stainless frame
and slide, special Custom Shop markings) **$1,623.00**

Kimber CDP II Series Auto Pistol

Similar to Custom II, but designed for concealed carry. Aluminum frame. Standard features include stainless steel slide, Meprolight tritium three dot (green) dovetail-mounted night sights, match grade barrel and chamber, 30 LPI front strap checkering, two tone finish, ambidextrous thumb safety, hand-checkered double diamond rosewood grips. Introduced in 2000. Made in U.S.A. by Kimber Mfg., Inc.

Price: Ultra CDP II 40 S&W **$1,120.00**
Price: Ultra CDP II (3 barrel, short grip) **$1,084.00**
Price: Compact CDP II (4 barrel, short grip) **$1,084.00**
Price: Pro CDP II (4 barrel, full length grip) **$1,084.00**
Price: Custom CDP II (5 barrel, full length grip) **$1,084.00**

Kimber Eclipse II

Kimber Eclipse Target II

Kimber LTP II

Llama Micromax

Llama Minimax

Kimber Eclipse II Series Auto Pistol

Similar to Custom II and other stainless Kimber pistol.s Stainless slide and frame, black anodized, two tone finish. Gray/black laminated grips. 30 LPI front strap checkering. All have night sights, with Target versions having Meprolight adjustable Bar/Dot version. New for 2002. Made in U.S.A. by Kimber Mfg., Inc.

Price: Eclipse Ultra II (3 barrel, short grip) **$1,052.00**
Price: Eclipse Pro II (4 barrel, full length grip) **$1,052.00**
Price: Eclipse Pro Target II (4 barrel, full length grip,
   adjustable sight) **$1,153.00**
Price: Eclipse Custom II (5 barrel, full length grip) **$1,071.00**
Price: Eclipse Target II (5 barrel, full length grip,
   adjustable sight) **$1,153.00**

Kimber LTP II Polymer Auto Pistol

Similar to Gold Match II. Built for Limited Ten competition. First Kimber pistol with new, innovative Kimber external extractor. KimPro premium finish. Stainless steel match grade barrel. Extended and beveled magazine well. Checkered front strap and trigger guard belly. Tungsten full length guide rod. Premium aluminum trigger. Ten-round single stack magazine. Wide ambidextrous thumb safety. New for 2002. Made in U.S.A. by Kimber Mfg., Inc.

Price: **$2,036.00**

Kimber Super Match II Auto Pistol

Similar to Gold Match II. Built for target and action shotting competition. Tested for accuracy. Target included. Stainless steel barrel and chamber. KimPro finish on stainless steel slide. Stainless steel frame. 30 LPI checkered front strap, premium aluminum trigger, Kimber adjustable sight. Introduced in 1999.

Price: **$1,926.00**

LLAMA MICROMAX 380 AUTO PISTOL

Caliber: 32 ACP, 8-shot, 380 ACP, 7-shot magazine. **Barrel:** 3-11/16". **Weight:** 23 oz. **Length:** 6-1/2" overall. **Grips:** Checkered high impact polymer. **Sights:** 3-dot combat. **Features:** Single-action design. Mini custom extended slide release; mini custom extended beavertail grip safety; combat-style hammer. Introduced 1997. Distributed by Import Sports, Inc.

Price: Matte blue **$281.95**
Price: Satin chrome (380 only) **$298.95**

LLAMA MINIMAX SERIES

Caliber: 40 S&W, 7-shot; 45 ACP, 6-shot magazine. **Barrel:** 3-1/2". **Weight:** 35 oz. **Length:** 7-1/3" overall. **Grips:** Checkered rubber. **Sights:** Three-dot combat. **Features:** Single action, skeletonized combat-style hammer, extended slide release, cone-style barrel, flared ejection port. Introduced 1996. Distributed by Import Sports, Inc.

Price: Blue **$324.95**
Price: Duo-Tone finish (45 only) **$333.95**
Price: Satin chrome **$341.95**

Llama Max-1 Government Deluxe

Para-Ordnance P12.45

**North American
Arms Guardian**

Para-Ordnance LDA

Llama Minimax Sub-Compact Auto Pistol

Similar to the Minimax except has 3.14" barrel, weighs 31 oz.; 6.8" overall length; has 10-shot magazine with finger extension; beavertail grip safety. Introduced 1999. Distributed by Import Sports, Inc.

Price: 45 ACP, matte blue **$341.95**
Price: As above, satin chrome **$358.95**
Price: Duo-Tone finish (45 only) **$349.95**

LLAMA MAX-I AUTO PISTOLS

Caliber: 45 ACP, 7-shot. **Barrel:** 5-1/8". **Weight:** 36 oz. **Length:** 8-1/2" overall. **Grips:** Black rubber. **Sights:** Blade front, rear adjustable for windage; three-dot system. **Features:** Single-action trigger; skeletonized combat-style hammer; steel frame; extended manual and grip safeties. Introduced 1995. Distributed by Import Sports, Inc.

Price: 45 ACP, 7-shot, Government model **$310.95**

NORTH AMERICAN ARMS GUARDIAN PISTOL

Caliber: 32 ACP, 6-shot magazine. **Barrel:** 2.1". **Weight:** 13.5 oz. **Length:** 4.36" overall. **Grips:** Black polymer. **Sights:** Fixed. **Features:** Double-action-only mechanism. All stainless steel construction; snag-free. Introduced 1998. Made in U.S.A. by North American Arms.

Price: **$359.00**

OLYMPIC ARMS OA-96 AR PISTOL

Caliber: 223. **Barrel:** 6", 8", 4140 chrome-moly steel. **Weight:** 5 lbs. **Length:** 15-3/4" overall. **Grips:** A2 stowaway pistol grip; no buttstock or receiver tube. **Sights:** Flat-top upper receiver, cut-down front sight base. **Features:** AR-15-type receivers with special bolt carrier; short aluminum hand guard; Vortex flash hider. Introduced 1996. Made in U.S.A. by Olympic Arms, Inc.

Price: **$858.00**

Olympic Arms OA-98 AR Pistol

Similar to the OA-93 except has removable 7-shot magazine, weighs 3 lbs. Introduced 1999. Made in U.S.A. by Olympic Arms, Inc.

Price: **$990.00**

PARA-ORDNANCE P-SERIES AUTO PISTOLS

Caliber: 9mm Para., 40 S&W, 45 ACP, 10-shot magazine. **Barrel:** 3", 3-1/2", 4-1/4", 5". **Weight:** From 24 oz. (alloy frame). **Length:** 8.5" overall. **Grips:** Textured composition. **Sights:** Blade front, rear adjustable for windage. High visibility three-dot system. **Features:** Available with alloy, steel or stainless steel frame with black finish (silver or stainless gun). Steel and stainless steel frame guns weigh 40 oz. (P14.45), 36 oz. (P13.45), 34 oz. (P12.45). Grooved match trigger, rounded combat-style hammer. Beveled magazine well. Manual thumb, grip and firing pin lock safeties. Solid barrel bushing. Contact maker for full details. Introduced 1990. Made in Canada by Para-Ordnance.

Price: Steel frame **$795.00**
Price: Alloy frame **$765.00**
Price: Stainless steel **$865.00**

Para-Ordnance Limited Pistols

Similar to the P-Series pistols except with full-length recoil guide system; fully adjustable rear sight; tuned trigger with overtravel stop; beavertail grip safety; competition hammer; front and rear slide serrations; ambidextrous safety; lowered ejection port; ramped match-grade barrel; dovetailed front sight. Introduced 1998. Made in Canada by Para-Ordnance.

Price: 9mm, 40 S&W, 45 ACP . . . . **$945.00 to $999.00**

Para-Ordnance LDA Auto Pistols

Similar to P-series except has double-action trigger mechanism. Steel frame with matte black finish, checkered composition grips. Available in 9mm Para., 40 S&W, 45 ACP. Introduced 1999. Made in Canada by Para-Ordnance.

Price: **$775.00**

**Para-Ordnance C5
45 LDA Para Carry**

Peters Stahl High Capacity

**Para-Ordnance C7
45 LDA Para Companion**

Peters Stahl Trophy Master

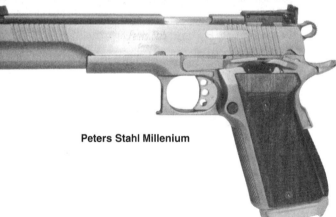

Peters Stahl Millenium

Para-Ordnance LDA Limited Pistols
Similar to LDA, has ambidextrous safety, adjustable rear sight, front slide serrations and full-length recoil guide system. Made in Canada by Para-Ordnance.
Price: Black finish **$975.00**
Price: Stainless **$1,049.00**

PARA-ORDNANCE P-SERIES AUTO PISTOLS
Caliber: 45 ACP. **Barrel:** 3", 6+1 shot. **Weight:** 30 oz. **Length:** 6.5". **Grips:** Double diamond checkered Cocobolo. **Features:** Stainless finish and receiver, "World's Smallest DAO .45 Auto." Major performance in micro package with Para LDA trigger system and safeties.
Price: **$899.00**

PARA-ORDNANCE C5 45 LDA PARA CARRY
Caliber: 45 ACP. **Barrel:** 3", 6+1 shot. **Weight:** 30 oz. **Length:** 6.5". **Grips:** Double diamond checkered Cocobolo. **Features:** Stainless finish and receiver, "world's smallest DAO 45 auto." Major performance in micro package wtih Para LDA trigger system and safeties.
Price: **$899.00**

PARA-ORDNANCE C7 45 LDA PARA COMPANION
Caliber: 45 ACP. **Barrel:** 3.5", 7+1 shot. **Weight:** 32 oz. **Length:** 7". **Grips:** Double diamond checkered Cocobolo. **Features:** Para LDA trigger system with Para LDA 3 safeties (slide lock, firing pin block and grip safety). Lightning speed, full size capacity.
Price: **$899.00**

PETERS STAHL AUTOLOADING PISTOLS
Caliber: 9mm Para., 45 ACP. **Barrel:** 5" or 6". **Grips:** Walnut or walnut with rubber wrap. **Sights:** Fully adjustable rear, blade front. **Features:** Stainless steel extended slide stop, safety and extended magazine release button; speed trigger with stop and approx. 3-lb. pull; polished ramp. Introduced 2000. Imported from Germany by Phillips & Rogers.
Price: High Capacity (accepts 15-shot magazines in 45 cal.; includes 10-shot magazine) **$1,695.00**
Price: Trophy Master (blued or stainless, 7-shot in 45, 8-shot in 9mm) **$1,995.00**
Price: Millenium Model (titanium coating on receiver and slide) **$2,195.00**

Phoenix Arms HP22

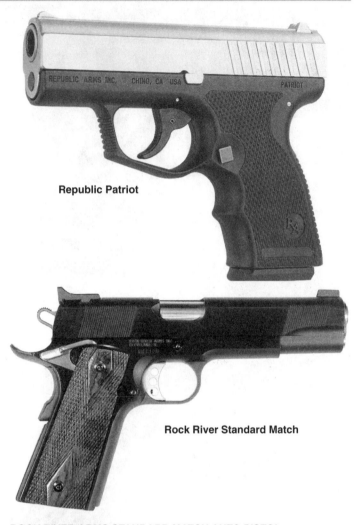

Republic Patriot

PSA-25 Auto

Rock River Standard Match

PHOENIX ARMS HP22, HP25 AUTO PISTOLS

Caliber: 22 LR, 10-shot (HP22), 25 ACP, 10-shot (HP25). **Barrel:** 3". **Weight:** 20 oz. **Length:** 5-1/2" overall. **Grips:** Checkered composition. **Sights:** Blade front, adjustable rear. **Features:** Single action, exposed hammer; manual hold-open; button magazine release. Available in satin nickel, polished blue finish. Introduced 1993. Made in U.S.A. by Phoenix Arms.

Price: With gun lock and cable lanyard **$128.00**
Price: HP Rangemaster kit with 5" bbl., locking case
and assessories **$169.00**
Price: HP Deluxe Rangemaster kit with 3" and 5" bbls.,
2 mags., case **$199.00**

PSA-25 AUTO POCKET PISTOL

Caliber: 25 ACP, 6-shot magazine. **Barrel:** 2-1/8". **Weight:** 9.5 oz. **Length:** 4-1/8" overall. **Grips:** Checkered black polymer, ivory, checkered transparent carbon fiber-filled polymer. **Sights:** Fixed. **Features:** All steel construction; striker fired; single action only; magazine disconnector; cocking indicator. Introduced 1987. Made in U.S.A. by Precision Small Arms, Inc.

Price: Traditional (polished black oxide).................... **$269.00**
Price: Nouveau-Satin (brushed nickel).................... **$269.00**
Price: Nouveau-Mirror (highly polished nickel)............. **$309.00**
Price: Featherweight (aluminum frame, nickel slide) **$405.00**
Price: Diplomat (black oxide with gold highlights, ivory grips) ... **$625.00**
Price: Montreaux (gold plated, ivory grips)................. **$692.00**
Price: Renaissance (hand engraved nickel, ivory grips)....... **$1,115.00**
Price: Imperiale (inlaid gold filigree over blue, scrimshawed
ivory grips) **$3,600.00**

REPUBLIC PATRIOT PISTOL

Caliber: 45 ACP, 6-shot magazine. **Barrel:** 3". **Weight:** 20 oz. **Length:** 6" overall. **Grips:** Checkered. **Sights:** Blade front, drift-adjustable rear. **Features:** Black polymer frame, stainless steel slide; double-action-only trigger system; squared trigger guard. Introduced 1997. Made in U.S.A. by Republic Arms, Inc.

Price: About **$325.00**

ROCK RIVER ARMS STANDARD MATCH AUTO PISTOL

Caliber: 45 ACP. **Barrel:** NA. **Weight:** NA. **Length:** NA. **Grips:** Cocobolo, checkered. **Sights:** Heine fixed rear, blade front. **Features:** Chrome-moly steel frame and slide; beavertail grip safety with raised pad; checkered slide stop; ambidextrous safety; polished feed ramp and extractor; aluminum speed trigger with 3.5 lb. pull. Made in U.S.A. From Rock River Arms.

Price: **$1,025.00**

ROCKY MOUNTAIN ARMS PATRIOT PISTOL

Caliber: 223, 10-shot magazine. **Barrel:** 7", with muzzle brake. **Weight:** 5 lbs. **Length:** 20.5" overall. **Grips:** Black composition. **Sights:** None furnished. **Features:** Milled upper receiver with enhanced Weaver base; milled lower receiver from billet plate; machined aluminum National Match handguard. Finished in DuPont Teflon-S matte black or NATO green. Comes with black nylon case, one magazine. Introduced 1993. From Rocky Mountain Arms, Inc.

Price: With A-2 handle top .... **$2,500.00 to $2,800.00**
Price: Flat top model .... **$3,000.00 to $3,500.00**

RUGER P89 AUTOLOADING PISTOL

Caliber: 9mm Para., 10-shot magazine. **Barrel:** 4.50". **Weight:** 32 oz. **Length:** 7.84" overall. **Grips:** Grooved black synthetic composition. **Sights:** Square post front, square notch rear adjustable for windage, both with white dot inserts. **Features:** Double action, ambidextrous slide-mounted safety-levers. Slide 4140 chrome-moly steel or 400-series stainless steel, frame lightweight aluminum alloy. Ambidextrous magazine release. Blue, stainless steel. Introduced 1986; stainless 1990.

Price: P89, blue, extra mag and mag loader, plastic case locks . **$475.00**
Price: KP89, stainless, extra mag and mag loader,
plastic case locks **$525.00**

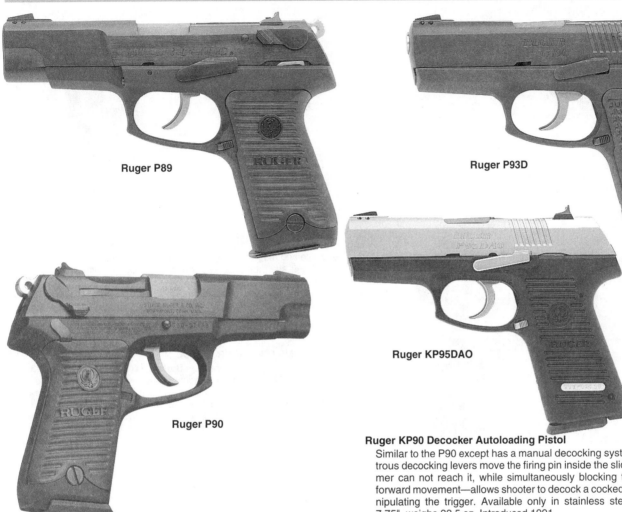

Ruger P89

Ruger P93D

Ruger P90

Ruger KP95DAO

Ruger P89D Decocker Autoloading Pistol

Similar to standard P89 except has ambidextrous decocking levers in place of regular slide-mounted safety. Decocking levers move firing pin inside slide where hammer can not reach, while simultaneously blocking firing pin from forward movement—allows shooter to decock cocked pistol without manipulating trigger. Conventional thumb decocking procedures are therefore unnecessary. Blue, stainless steel. Introduced 1990.

Price: P89D, blue, extra mag and mag loader, plastic case locks **$475.00**
Price: KP89D, stainless, extra mag and mag loader,
plastic case locks **$525.00**

Ruger P89 Double-Action-Only Autoloading Pistol

Same as KP89 except operates only in double-action mode. Has spurless hammer, gripping grooves on each side of rear slide; no external safety or decocking lever. Internal safety prevents forward movement of firing pin unless trigger is pulled. Available 9mm Para., stainless steel only. Introduced 1991.

Price: Lockable case, extra mag and mag loader **$525.00**

RUGER P90 MANUAL SAFETY MODEL AUTOLOADING PISTOL

Caliber: 45 ACP, 8-shot magazine. **Barrel:** 4.50". **Weight:** 33.5 oz. **Length:** 7.75" overall. **Grips:** Grooved black synthetic composition. **Sights:** Square post front, square notch rear adjustable for windage, both with white dot. **Features:** Double action ambidextrous slide-mounted safety-levers move firing pin inside slide where hammer can not reach, simultaneously blocking firing pin from forward movement. Stainless steel only. Introduced 1991.

Price: KP90 with extra mag, loader, case and gunlock **$565.00**
Price: P90 (blue). **$525.00**

Ruger KP90 Decocker Autoloading Pistol

Similar to the P90 except has a manual decocking system. The ambidextrous decocking levers move the firing pin inside the slide where the hammer can not reach it, while simultaneously blocking the firing pin from forward movement—allows shooter to decock a cocked pistol without manipulating the trigger. Available only in stainless steel. Overall length 7.75", weighs 33.5 oz. Introduced 1991.

Price: KP90D with case, extra mag and mag loading tool **$565.00**

RUGER P93 COMPACT AUTOLOADING PISTOL

Caliber: 9mm Para., 10-shot magazine. **Barrel:** 3.9". **Weight:** 31 oz. **Length:** 7.25" overall. **Grips:** Grooved black synthetic composition. **Sights:** Square post front, square notch rear adjustable for windage. **Features:** Front of slide crowned with convex curve; slide has seven finger grooves; trigger guard bow higher for better grip; 400-series stainless slide, lightweight alloy frame; also blue. Decocker-only or DAO-only. Includes hard case and lock. Introduced 1993. Made in U.S.A. by Sturm, Ruger & Co.

Price: KP93DAO, double-action-only **$575.00**
Price: KP93D ambidextrous decocker, stainless **$575.00**
Price: P93D, ambidextrous decocker, blue **$495.00**

Ruger KP94 Autoloading Pistol

Sized midway between full-size P-Series and compact P93. 4.25" barrel, 7.5" overall length, weighs about 33 oz. KP94 manual safety model; KP94DAO double-action-only (both 9mm Para., 10-shot magazine); KP94D is decocker-only in 40-caliber with 10-shot magazine. Slide gripping grooves roll over top of slide. KP94 has ambidextrous safety-levers; KP94DAO has no external safety, full-cock hammer position or decocking lever; KP94D has ambidextrous decocking levers. Matte finish stainless slide, barrel, alloy frame. Also blue. Includes hard case and lock. Introduced 1994. Made in U.S.A. by Sturm, Ruger & Co.

Price: P94, P944, blue (manual safety) **$495.00**
Price: KP94 (9mm), KP944 (40-caliber) (manual
safety-stainless) **$575.00**
Price: KP94DAO (9mm), KP944DAO (40-caliber) **$575.00**
Price: KP94D (9mm), KP944D (40-caliber)-decock only **$575.00**

Ruger KMK 4

Ruger KP512

Ruger 22/45-P4

RUGER P95 AUTOLOADING PISTOL

Caliber: 9mm Para., 10-shot magazine. **Barrel:** 3.9". **Weight:** 27 oz. **Length:** 7.25" overall. **Grips:** Grooved; integral with frame. **Sights:** Blade front, rear drift adjustable for windage; three-dot system. **Features:** Moulded polymer grip frame, stainless steel or chrome-moly slide. Suitable for +P+ ammunition. Safety model, decocker or DAO. Introduced 1996. Made in U.S.A. by Sturm, Ruger & Co. Comes with lockable plastic case, spare magazine, loader and lock.
Price: P95 DAO double-action-only **$425.00**
Price: P95D decocker only **$425.00**
Price: KP95D stainless steel decocker only **$475.00**
Price: KP95DAO double-action only, stainless steel **$475.00**
Price: KP95 safety model, stainless steel. **$475.00**
Price: P95 safety model, blued finish **$425.00**

RUGER P97 AUTOLOADING PISTOL

Caliber: 45ACP 8-shot magazine. **Barrel:** 4-1/8". **Weight:** 30-1/2 oz. **Length:** 7-1/4" overall. Grooved: Integral with frame. **Sights:** Blade front, rear drift adjustable for windage; three dot system. **Features:** Moulded polymer grip frame, stainless steel slide. Decocker or DAO. Introduced 1997. Made in U.S.A. by Sturm, Ruger & Co. Comes with lockable plastic case, spare magaline, loading tool.
Price: KP97D decocker only **$495.00**
Price: KP97DAO double-action only **$495.00**
Price: P97D decocker only, blued **$460.00**

RUGER MARK II STANDARD AUTOLOADING PISTOL

Caliber: 22 LR, 10-shot magazine. **Barrel:** 4-3/4" or 6". **Weight:** 35 oz. (4-3/4" bbl.). **Length:** 8-5/16" (4-3/4" bbl.). **Grips:** Checkered composition grip panels. **Sights:** Fixed, wide blade front, fixed rear. **Features:** Updated design of original Standard Auto. New bolt hold-open latch. 10-shot magazine, magazine catch, safety, trigger and new receiver contours. Introduced 1982.
Price: Blued (MK 4, MK 6) **$289.00**
Price: In stainless steel (KMK 4, KMK 6) **$379.00**

Ruger 22/45 Mark II Pistol

Similar to other 22 Mark II autos except has grip frame of Zytel that matches angle and magazine latch of Model 1911 45 ACP pistol. Available in 4" bull, 4-3/4" standard and 5-1/2" bull barrels. Comes with extra magazine, plastic case, lock. Introduced 1992.
Price: P4, 4" bull barrel, adjustable sights **$275.00**
Price: KP 4 (4-3/4" barrel), stainless steel, fixed sights **$305.00**
Price: KP512 (5-1/2" bull barrel), stainless steel, adj. sights **$359.00**
Price: P512 (5-1/2" bull barrel, all blue), adj. sights **$275.00**

SAFARI ARMS ENFORCER PISTOL

Caliber: 45 ACP, 6-shot magazine. **Barrel:** 3.8", stainless. **Weight:** 36 oz. **Length:** 7.3" overall. **Grips:** Smooth walnut with etched black widow spider logo. **Sights:** Ramped blade front, LPA adjustable rear. **Features:** Extended safety, extended slide release; Commander-style hammer; beavertail grip safety; throated, polished, tuned. Parkerized matte black or satin stainless steel finishes. Made in U.S.A. by Safari Arms.
Price: **$630.00**

SAFARI ARMS GI SAFARI PISTOL

Caliber: 45 ACP, 7-shot magazine. **Barrel:** 5", 416 stainless. **Weight:** 39.9 oz. **Length:** 8.5" overall. **Grips:** Checkered walnut. **Sights:** G.I.-style blade front, drift-adjustable rear. **Features:** Beavertail grip safety; extended thumb safety and slide release; Commander-style hammer. Parkerized finish. Reintroduced 1996.
Price: **$439.00**

SAFARI ARMS CARRIER PISTOL

Caliber: 45 ACP, 7-shot magazine. **Barrel:** 6", 416 stainless steel. **Weight:** 30 oz. **Length:** 9.5" overall. **Grips:** Wood. **Sights:** Ramped blade front, LPA adjustable rear. **Features:** Beavertail grip safety; extended controls; full-length recoil spring guide; Commander-style hammer. Throated, polished and tuned. Satin stainless steel finish. Introduced 1999. Made in U.S.A. by Safari Arms, Inc.
Price: **$714.00**

SAFARI ARMS COHORT PISTOL

Caliber: 45 ACP, 7-shot magazine. **Barrel:** 3.8", 416 stainless. **Weight:** 37 oz. **Length:** 8.5" overall. **Grips:** Smooth walnut with laser-etched black widow logo. **Sights:** Ramped blade front, LPA adjustable rear. **Features:** Combines the Enforcer model, slide and MatchMaster frame. Beavertail grip safety; extended thumb safety and slide release; Commander-style hammer. Throated, polished and tuned. Satin stainless finish. Introduced 1996. Made in U.S.A. by Safari Arms, Inc.
Price: **$654.00**

SAFARI ARMS MATCHMASTER PISTOL

Caliber: 45 ACP, 7-shot. **Barrel:** 5" or 6", 416 stainless steel. **Weight:** 38 oz. (5" barrel). **Length:** 8.5" overall. **Grips:** Smooth walnut. **Sights:** Ramped blade, LPA adjustable rear. **Features:** Beavertail grip safety; extended controls; Commander-style hammer; throated, polished, tuned. Parkerized matte-black or satin stainless steel. Made in U.S.A. by Olympic Arms, Inc.
Price: 5" barrel **$594.00**
Price: 6" barrel **$654.00**

SIG Sauer P220

SIG Arms Pro 2009

SIG Arms P245 Compact

Safari Arms Carry Comp Pistol

Similar to the Matchmaster except has Wil Schueman-designed hybrid compensator system. Made in U.S.A. by Olympic Arms, Inc.
Price: $1,067.00

SEECAMP LWS 32 STAINLESS DA AUTO

Caliber: 32 ACP Win. Silvertip, 6-shot magazine. **Barrel:** 2", integral with frame. **Weight:** 10.5 oz. **Length:** 4-1/8" overall. **Grips:** Glass-filled nylon. **Sights:** Smooth, no-snag, contoured slide and barrel top. **Features:** Aircraft quality 17-4 PH stainless steel. Inertia-operated firing pin. Hammer fired double-action-only. Hammer automatically follows slide down to safety rest position after each shot—no manual safety needed. Magazine safety disconnector. Polished stainless. Introduced 1985. From L.W. Seecamp.
Price: $425.00

SIG SAUER P220 SERVICE AUTO PISTOL

Caliber: 45 ACP, (7- or 8-shot magazine). **Barrel:** 4-3/8". **Weight:** 27.8 oz. **Length:** 7.8" overall. **Grips:** Checkered black plastic. **Sights:** Blade front, drift adjustable rear for windage. Optional Siglite nightsights. **Features:** Double action. Decocking lever permits lowering hammer onto locked firing pin. Squared combat-type trigger guard. Slide stays open after last shot. Imported from Germany by SIGARMS, Inc.
Price: Blue SA/DA or DAO $790.00
Price: Blue, Siglite night sights $880.00
Price: K-Kote or nickel slide $830.00
Price: K-Kote or nickel slide with Siglite night sights $930.00

SIG Sauer P220 Sport Auto Pistol

Similar to the P220 except has 4.9" barrel, ported compensator, all-stainless steel frame and slide, factory-tuned trigger, adjustable sights, extended competition controls. Overall length is 9.9", weighs 43.5 oz. Introduced 1999. From SIGARMS, Inc.
Price: $1,320.00

SIG Sauer P245 Compact Auto Pistol

Similar to the P220 except has 3.9" barrel, shorter grip, 6-shot magazine, 7.28" overall length, and weighs 27.5 oz. Introduced 1999. From SIG-ARMS, Inc.
Price: Blue $780.00
Price: Blue, with Siglite sights $850.00
Price: Two-tone $830.00
Price: Two-tone with Siglite sights $930.00
Price: With K-Kote finish. $830.00
Price: K-Kote with Siglite sights $930.00

SIG Sauer P229 DA Auto Pistol

Similar to the P228 except chambered for 9mm Para., 40 S&W, 357 SIG. Has 3.86" barrel, 7.08" overall length and 3.35" height. Weight is 30.5 oz. Introduced 1991. Frame made in Germany, stainless steel slide assembly made in U.S.; pistol assembled in U.S. From SIGARMS, Inc.
Price: $795.00
Price: With nickel slide $890.00
Price: Nickel slide Siglite night sights $935.00

SIG PRO AUTO PISTOL

Caliber: 9mm Para., 40 S&W, 10-shot magazine. **Barrel:** 3.86". **Weight:** 27.2 oz. **Length:** 7.36" overall. **Grips:** Composite and rubberized one-piece. **Sights:** Blade front, rear adjustable for windage. Optional Siglite night sights. **Features:** Polymer frame, stainless steel slide; integral frame accessory rail; replaceable steel frame rails; left- or right-handed magazine release. Introduced 1999. From SIGARMS, Inc.
Price: SP2340 (40 S&W) $596.00
Price: SP2009 (9mm Para.) $596.00
Price: As above with Siglite night sights $655.00

SIG Sauer P226 Service Pistol

Similar to the P220 pistol except has 4.4" barrel, and weighs 28.3 oz. 357 SIG or 40 S&W. Imported from Germany by SIGARMS, Inc.
Price: Blue SA/DA or DAO $830.00
Price: With Siglite night sights $930.00
Price: Blue, SA/DA or DAO 357 SIG $830.00
Price: With Siglite night sights $930.00
Price: K-Kote finish, 40 S&W only or nickel slide $830.00
Price: K-Kote or nickel slide Siglite night sights $930.00
Price: Nickel slide 357 SIG. $875.00
Price: Nickel slide, Siglite night sights $930.00

SIG Sauer P229 Sport Auto Pistol

Similar to the P229 except available in 357 SIG only; 4.8" heavy barrel; 8.6" overall length; weighs 40.6 oz.; vented compensator; adjustable target sights; rubber grips; extended slide latch and magazine release. Made of stainless steel. Introduced 1998. From SIGARMS, Inc.
Price: $1,320.00

SIG Sauer P229S

Smith & Wesson 457

SIG Sauer P232

Smith & Wesson 4013 TSW

SIG SAUER P232 PERSONAL SIZE PISTOL

Caliber: 380 ACP, 7-shot. **Barrel:** 3-3/4". **Weight:** 16 oz. **Length:** 6-1/2" overall. **Grips:** Checkered black composite. **Sights:** Blade front, rear adjustable for windage. **Features:** Double action/single action or DAO. Blowback operation, stationary barrel. Introduced 1997. Imported from Germany by SIGARMS, Inc.

Price: Blue SA/DA or DAO	**$505.00**
Price: In stainless steel	**$545.00**
Price: With stainless steel slide, blue frame	**$525.00**
Price: Stainless steel, Siglite night sights, Hogue grips	**$585.00**

SIG SAUER P239 PISTOL

Caliber: 9mm Para., 8-shot, 357 SIG 40 S&W, 7-shot magazine. **Barrel:** 3.6". **Weight:** 25.2 oz. **Length:** 6.6" overall. **Grips:** Checkered black composite. **Sights:** Blade front, rear adjustable for windage. Optional Siglite night sights. **Features:** SA/DA or DAO; blackened stainless steel slide, aluminum alloy frame. Introduced 1996. Made in U.S.A. by SIGARMS, Inc.

Price: SA/DA or DAO	**$620.00**
Price: SA/DA or DAO with Siglite night sights	**$720.00**
Price: Two-tone finish	**$665.00**
Price: Two-tone finish, Siglite sights	**$765.00**

SMITH & WESSON MODEL 22A SPORT PISTOL

Caliber: 22 LR, 10-shot magazine. **Barrel:** 4", 5-1/2", 7". **Weight:** 29 oz. **Length:** 8" overall. **Grips:** Two-piece polymer. **Sights:** Patridge front, fully adjustable rear. **Features:** Comes with a sight bridge with Weaver-style integral optics mount; alloy frame; .312" serrated trigger; stainless steel slide and barrel with matte blue finish. Introduced 1997. Made in U.S.A. by Smith & Wesson.

Price: 4"	**$264.00**
Price: 5-1/2"	**$292.00**
Price: 7"	**$331.00**

SMITH & WESSON MODEL 457 TDA AUTO PISTOL

Caliber: 45 ACP, 7-shot magazine. **Barrel:** 3-3/4". **Weight:** 29 oz. **Length:** 7-1/4" overall. **Grips:** One-piece Xenoy, wrap-around with straight backstrap.

Sights: Post front, fixed rear, three-dot system. **Features:** Aluminum alloy frame, matte blue carbon steel slide; bobbed hammer; smooth trigger. Introduced 1996. Made in U.S.A. by Smith & Wesson.

Price:	**$591.00**

SMITH & WESSON MODEL 908 AUTO PISTOL

Caliber: 9mm Para., 8-shot magazine. **Barrel:** 3-1/2". **Weight:** 26 oz. **Length:** 6-13/16". **Grips:** One-piece Xenoy, wrap-around with straight backstrap. **Sights:** Post front, fixed rear, three-dot system. **Features:** Aluminum alloy frame, matte blue carbon steel slide; bobbed hammer; smooth trigger. Introduced 1996. Made in U.S.A. by Smith & Wesson.

Price:	**$535.00**

SMITH & WESSON MODEL 4013, 4053 TSW AUTOS

Caliber: 40 S&W, 9-shot magazine. **Barrel:** 3-1/2". **Weight:** 26.4 oz. **Length:** 6-7/8" overall. **Grips:** Xenoy one-piece wrap-around. **Sights:** Novak three-dot system. **Features:** Traditional double-action system; stainless slide, alloy frame; fixed barrel bushing; ambidextrous decocker; reversible magazine catch, equipment rail. Introduced 1997. Made in U.S.A. by Smith & Wesson.

Price: Model 4013 TSW	**$886.00**
Price: Model 4053 TSW, double-action-only	**$886.00**

Smith & Wesson Model 22S Sport Pistols

Similar to the Model 22A Sport except with stainless steel frame. Available only with 5-1/2" or 7" barrel. Introduced 1997. Made in U.S.A. by Smith & Wesson.

Price: 5-1/2" standard barrel	**$358.00**
Price: 5-1/2" bull barrel, wood target stocks with thumbrest	**$434.00**
Price: 7" standard barrel	**$395.00**
Price: 5-1/2" bull barrel, two-piece target stocks with thumbrest	**$353.00**

Smith & Wesson 3913 TSW

Smith & Wesson
3913 LadySmith

Smith & Wesson 4006

SMITH & WESSON MODEL 410 DA AUTO PISTOL

Caliber: 40 S&W, 10-shot magazine. **Barrel:** 4".
Weight: 28.5 oz. **Length:** 7.5 oz. **Grips:** One-piece Xenoy, wrap-around with straight backstrap.
Sights: Post front, fixed rear; three-dot system. **Features:** Aluminum alloy frame; blued carbon steel slide; traditional double action with left-side slide-mounted decocking lever. Introduced 1996. Made in U.S.A. by Smith & Wesson.
Price: Model 410 . . . . **$591.00**
Price: Model 410, HiViz front sight **$612.00**

SMITH & WESSON MODEL 910 DA AUTO PISTOL

Caliber: 9mm Para., 10-shot magazine. **Barrel:** 4". **Weight:** 28 oz. **Length:** 7-3/8" overall. **Grips:** One-piece Xenoy, wrap-around with straight backstrap. **Sights:** Post front with white dot, fixed two-dot rear. **Features:** Alloy frame, blue carbon steel slide. Slide-mounted decocking lever. Introduced 1995.
Price: Model 910. . . . . **$535.00**
Price: Model 410, HiViz front sight **$535.00**

SMITH & WESSON MODEL 3913 TRADITIONAL DOUBLE ACTION

Caliber: 9mm Para., 8-shot magazine. **Barrel:** 3-1/2". **Weight:** 26 oz. **Length:** 6-13/16" overall. **Grips:** One-piece Delrin wrap-around, textured surface. **Sights:** Post front with white dot, Novak LoMount Carry with two dots. **Features:** Aluminum alloy frame, stainless slide (M3913) or blue steel slide (M3914). Bobbed hammer with no half-cock notch; smooth .304" trigger with rounded edges. Straight backstrap. Equipment rail. Extra magazine included. Introduced 1989.
Price: **$760.00**

Smith & Wesson Model 3913-LS LadySmith Auto

Similar to the standard Model 3913 except has frame that is upswept at the front, rounded trigger guard. Comes in frosted stainless steel with matching gray grips. Grips are ergonomically correct for a woman's hand. Novak LoMount Carry rear sight adjustable for windage, smooth edges for snag resistance. Extra magazine included. Introduced 1990.
Price: **$782.00**

Smith & Wesson Model 3953 DAO Pistol

Same as the Model 3913 except double-action-only. Model 3953 has stainless slide with alloy frame. Overall length 7"; weighs 25.5 oz. Extra magazine included. Equipment rail. Introduced 1990.
Price: **$760.00**

Smith & Wesson Model 3913TSW/3953TSW Auto Pistols

Similar to the Model 3913 and 3953 except TSW guns have tighter tolerances, ambidextrous manual safety/decocking lever, flush-fit magazine, delayed-unlock firing system; magazine disconnector. Compact alloy frame, stainless steel slide. Straight backstrap. Introduced 1998. Made in U.S.A. by Smith & Wesson.
Price: Single action/double action **$760.00**
Price: Double action only **$760.00**

SMITH & WESSON MODEL 4006 TDA AUTO

Caliber: 40 S&W, 10-shot magazine. **Barrel:** 4". **Weight:** 38.5 oz. **Length:** 7-7/8" overall. **Grips:** Xenoy wrap-around with checkered panels. **Sights:** Replaceable post front with white dot, Novak LoMount Carry fixed rear with two white dots, or micro. click adjustable rear with two white dots. **Features:** Stainless steel construction with non-reflective finish. Straight backstrap, quipment rail. Extra magazine included. Introduced 1990.
Price: With adjustable sights **$944.00**
Price: With fixed sight. **$907.00**
Price: With fixed night sights **$1,040.00**
Price: With Saf-T-Trigger, fixed sights **$927.00**

SMITH & WESSON MODEL 4006 TSW

Caliber: 40, 10-shot. **Barrel:** 4". **Grips:** Straight back strap grip. **Sights:** Fixed Novak LoMount Carry. **Features:** Traditional double action, ambidextrous safety, Saf-T-Trigger, equipment rail, satin stainless.
Price: **$927.00**

Smith & Wesson Model 4043, 4046 DA Pistols

Similar to the Model 4006 except is double-action-only. Has a semi-bobbed hammer, smooth trigger, 4" barrel; Novak LoMount Carry rear sight, post front with white dot. Overall length is 7-1/2", weighs 28 oz. Model 4043 has alloy frame, equipment rail. Extra magazine included. Introduced 1991.
Price: Model 4043 (alloy frame) **$886.00**
Price: Model 4046 (stainless frame). **$907.00**
Price: Model 4046 with fixed night sights **$1,040.00**

SMITH & WESSON MODEL 4500 SERIES AUTOS

Caliber: 45 ACP, 8-shot magazine. **Barrel:** 5" (M4506). **Weight:** 41 oz. (4506). **Length:** 8-1/2" overall. **Grips:** Xenoy one-piece wrap-around, arched or straight backstrap. **Sights:** Post front with white dot, adjustable or fixed Novak LoMount Carry on M4506. **Features:** M4506 has serrated hammer spur, equipment rail. All have two magazines. Contact Smith & Wesson for complete data. Introduced 1989.
Price: Model 4566 (stainless, 4-1/4", traditional DA, ambidextrous safety, fixed sight) **$942.00**
Price: Model 4586 (stainless, 4-1/4", DA only) **$942.00**
New!!! Price: Model 4566 (stainless, 4-1/4" with Saf-T-Trigger, fixed sight) **$961.00**

Smith & Wesson 4566 TSW

Smith & Wesson Sigma SW40V

Smith & Wesson 4553 TSW

Smith & Wesson 99

SMITH & WESSON MODEL 4513TSW/4553TSW PISTOLS

Caliber: 45 ACP, 7-shot magazine. **Barrel:** 3-3/4". **Weight:** 28 oz. (M4513TSW). **Length:** 6-7/8 overall. **Grips:** Checkered Xenoy; straight backstrap. **Sights:** White dot front, Novak LoMount Carry 2-Dot rear. **Features:** Model 4513TSW is traditional double action, Model 4553TSW is double action only. TSW series has tighter tolerances, ambidextrous manual safety/decocking lever, flush-fit magazine, delayed-unlock firing system; magazine disconnector. Compact alloy frame, stainless steel slide, equipment rail. Introduced 1998. Made in U.S.A. by Smith & Wesson.

Price: Model 4513TSW. **$924.00**
Price: Model 4553TSW. **$924.00**

SMITH & WESSON MODEL 4566 TSW

Caliber: 45 ACP. **Barrel:** 4-1/4", 8-shot . **Grips:** Straight back strap grip. **Sights:** Fixed Novak LoMount Carry. **Features:** Ambidextrous safety, equipment rail, Saf-T-Trigger, satin stainless finish. Traditional double action.

Price: **$961.00**

SMITH & WESSON MODEL 5900 SERIES AUTO PISTOLS

Caliber: 9mm Para., 10-shot magazine. **Barrel:** 4". **Weight:** 28-1/2 to 37-1/2 oz. (fixed sight); 38 oz. (adjustable sight). **Length:** 7-1/2" overall. **Grips:** Xenoy wrap-around with curved backstrap. **Sights:** Post front with white dot, fixed or fully adjustable with two white dots. **Features:** All stainless, stainless and alloy or carbon steel and alloy construction. Smooth .304" trigger, .260" serrated hammer. Equipment rail. Introduced 1989.

Price: Model 5906 (stainless, traditional DA, adjustable sight,
  ambidextrous safety). **$904.00**
Price: As above, fixed sight **$841.00**
Price: With fixed night sights **$995.00**
Price: With Saf-T-Trigger **$882.00**
Price: Model 5946 DAO (as above, stainless frame and slide) . . **$863.00**

SMITH & WESSON ENHANCED SIGMA SERIES DAO PISTOLS

Caliber: 9mm Para., 40 S&W, 10-shot magazine. **Barrel:** 4". **Weight:** 26 oz. **Length:** 7.4" overall. **Grips:** Integral. **Sights:** White dot front, fixed rear; three-dot system. Tritium night sights available. **Features:** Ergonomic polymer frame; low barrel centerline; internal striker firing system; corrosion-resistant slide; Teflon-filled, electroless-nickel coated magazine, equipment rail. Introduced 1994. Made in U.S.A. by Smith & Wesson.

Price: SW9E, 9mm, 4" barrel, black finish, fixed sights **$447.00**
Price: SW9V, 9mm, 4" barrel, satin stainless, fixed night sights. . **$447.00**
Price: SW9VE, 4" barrel, satin stainless, Saf-T-Trigger,
  fixed sights **$466.00**
Price: SW40E, 40 S&W, 4" barrel, black finish, fixed sights. **$657.00**
Price: SW40V, 40 S&W, 4" barrel, black polymer, fixed sights. . . **$447.00**
Price: SW40VE, 4" barrel, satin stainless, Saf-T-Trigger,
  fixed sights **$466.00**

SMITH & WESSON MODEL CS9 CHIEF'S SPECIAL AUTO

Caliber: 9mm Para., 7-shot magazine. **Barrel:** 3". **Weight:** 20.8 oz. **Length:** 6-1/4" overall. **Grips:** Hogue wrap-around rubber. **Sights:** White dot front, fixed two-dot rear. **Features:** Traditional double-action trigger mechanism. Alloy frame, stainless or blued slide. Ambidextrous safety. Introduced 1999. Made in U.S.A. by Smith & Wesson.

Price: Blue or stainless. **$680.00**

Smith & Wesson Model CS40 Chief's Special Auto

Similar to CS9, chambered for 40 S&W (7-shot magazine), 3-1/4" barrel, weighs 24.2 oz., measures 6-1/2" overall. Introduced 1999. Made in U.S.A. by Smith & Wesson.

Price: Blue or stainless. **$717.00**

Springfield 1911A1 Standard

Springfield TRP

Springfield Full-Size 1911A1

Springfield V10 Ultra Compact

Smith & Wesson Model CS45 Chief's Special Auto

Similar to CS40, chambered for 45 ACP, 6-shot magazine, weighs 23.9 oz. Introduced 1999. Made in U.S.A. by Smith & Wesson.
Price: Blue or stainless **$717.00**

SMITH & WESSON MODEL 99

Caliber: 9mm Para. 4" barrel; 40 S&W 4-1/8" barrel; 10-shot, adj. sights. **Features:** Traditional double action satin stainless, black polymer frame, equipment rail, Saf-T-Trigger.
Price: 4" barrel **$648.00**
Price: 4-1/8" barrel **$648.00**

SPRINGFIELD, INC. FULL-SIZE 1911A1 AUTO PISTOL

Caliber: 9mm Para., 9-shot; 38 Super, 9-shot; 40 S&W, 9-shot; 45 ACP, 7-shot. **Barrel:** 5". **Weight:** 35.6 oz. **Length:** 8-5/8" overall. **Grips:** Cocobolo. **Sights:** Fixed three-dot system. **Features:** Beveled magazine well; lowered and flared ejection port. All forged parts, including frame, barrel, slide. All new production. Introduced 1990. From Springfield, Inc.
Price: Mil-Spec 45 ACP, Parkerized **$559.00**
Price: Standard, 45 ACP, blued, Novak sights **$824.00**
Price: Standard, 45 ACP, stainless, Novak sights **$828.00**
Price: Lightweight 45 ACP (28.6 oz., matte finish, night sights) . . **$877.00**
Price: 40 S&W, stainless **$860.00**
Price: 9mm, stainless **$837.00**

Springfield, Inc. TRP Pistols

Similar to 1911A1 except 45 ACP only, checkered front strap and mainspring housing, Novak Night Sight combat rear sight and matching dovetailed front sight, tuned, polished extractor, oversize barrel link; lightweight speed trigger and combat action job, match barrel and bushing, extended ambidextrous thumb safety and fitted beavertail grip safety. Carry bevel on entire pistol; checkered cocobolo wood grips, comes with two Wilson 7-shot magazines. Frame is engraved "Tactical," both sides of frame with "TRP." Introduced 1998. From Springfield, Inc.
Price: Standard with Armory Kote finish **$1,395.00**
Price: Standard, stainless steel **$1,370.00**

Springfield, Inc. 1911A1 High Capacity Pistol

Similar to Standard 1911A1, available in 45 ACP with 10-shot magazine. Commander-style hammer, walnut grips, beveled magazine well, plastic carrying case. Introduced 1993. From Springfield, Inc.
Price: Mil-Spec 45 ACP **$807.00**
Price: 45 ACP Ultra Compact (3-1/2" bbl.) **$909.00**

Springfield, Inc. 1911A1 V-Series Ported Pistols

Similar to standard 1911A1, scalloped slides with 10, 12 or 16 matching barrel ports to redirect powder gasses and reduce recoil and muzzle flip. Adjustable rear sight, ambi thumb safety, Videki speed trigger, and beveled magazine well. Checkered walnut grips standard. Available in 45 ACP, stainless or bi-tone. Introduced 1992.
Price: V-16 Long Slide, stainless **$1,121.00**
Price: Target V-12, stainless **$878.00**
Price: V-10 (Ultra-Compact, bi-tone) **$853.00**
Price: V-10 stainless **$863.00**

Springfield, Inc. 1911A1 Champion Pistol

Similar to standard 1911A1, slide is 4". Novak Night Sights. Delta hammer and cocobolo grips. Available in 45 ACP only; Parkerized or stainless. Introduced 1989.
Price: Parkerized **$856.00**
Price: Stainless **$870.00**

Springfield Inc. Ultra Compact Pistol

Similar to 1911A1 Compact, shorter slide, 3.5" barrel, beavertail grip safety, beveled magazine well, Novak Low Mount or Novak Night Sights, Videki speed trigger, flared ejection port, stainless steel frame, blued slide, match grade barrel, rubber grips. Introduced 1996. From Springfield, Inc.
Price: Parkerized 45 ACP, Night Sights **$817.00**
Price: Stainless 45 ACP, Night Sights **$884.00**
Price: Lightweight, 9mm, stainless **$870.00**

Springfield X-Treme Duty

Taurus PT 22

Springfield Inc. Long Slide 1911 A1 Pistol

Similar to Full Size model, 6" barrel and slide for increased sight radius and higher velocity, fully adjustable sights, muzzle-forward weight distribution for reduced recoil and quicker shot-to-shot recovery. From Springfield Inc.

Price: Target, 45 ACP, stainless with Night Sights **$1,049.00**
Price: Trophy Match, stainless with adj. sights **$1,452.00**

NEW! SPRINGFIELD, INC. MICRO-COMPACT 1911A1 PISTOL

Caliber: 45 ACP, 6+1 capacity. **Barrel:** 3" 1:16 LH. **Weight:** 24 oz. **Length:** 5.7". **Sights:** Novak LoMount tritium. Dovetail front. **Features:** Forged frame and slide, ambi thumb safety, extreme carry bevel treatment, lockable plastic case, 2 magazines.

Price: **$1,060.00**

NEW! SPRINGFIELD, INC. X-TREME DUTY

Caliber: 9mm, 40 S&W, 357 Sig. **Barrel:** 4.08". **Weight:** 22.88 oz. **Length:** 7.2". **Sights:** Dovetail front and rear. **Features:** Lightweight, ultra high-impact polymer frame. Trigger, firing pink and grip safety. Two 10-rod steel easy glide magazines

Price: **$489.00**

STEYR M & S SERIES AUTO PISTOLS

Caliber: 9mm Para., 40 S&W, 357 SIG; 10-shot magazine. **Barrel:** 4" (3.58" for Model S). **Weight:** 28 oz. (22.5 oz. for Model S). **Length:** 7.05" overall (6.53" for Model S). **Grips:** Ultra-rigid polymer. **Sights:** Drift-adjustable, white-outline rear; white-triangle blade front. **Features:** Polymer frame; trigger-drop firing pin, manual and key-lock safeties; loaded chamber indicator; 5.5-lb. trigger pull; 111-degree grip angle enhances natural pointing. Introduced 2000. Imported from Austria by GSI Inc.

Price: Model M (full-sized frame with 4" barrel) **$609.95**
Price: Model S (compact frame with 3.58" barrel) **$609.95**
Price: Extra 10-shot magazines (Model M or S) **$39.00**

Taurus PT92B

TAURUS MODEL PT 22/PT 25 AUTO PISTOLS

Caliber: 22 LR, 8-shot (PT 22); 25 ACP, 9-shot (PT 25). **Barrel:** 2.75". **Weight:** 12.3 oz. **Length:** 5.25" overall. **Grips:** Smooth rosewood or mother-of-pearl. **Sights:** Fixed. **Features:** Double action. Tip-up barrel for loading, cleaning. Blue, nickel, duo-tone or blue with gold accents. Introduced 1992. Made in U.S.A. by Taurus International.

Price: 22 LR, 25 ACP, blue, nickel or with duo-tone finish
with rosewood grips **$215.00**
Price: 22 LR, 25 ACP, blue with gold trim, rosewood grips **$230.00**
Price: 22 LR, 25 ACP, blue, nickel or duotone finish with checkered
wood grips **$190.00**
Price: 22 LR, 25 ACP, blue with gold trim, mother of pearl grips . **$230.00**

TAURUS MODEL PT92B AUTO PISTOL

Caliber: 9mm Para., 10-shot mag. **Barrel:** 5". **Weight:** 34 oz. **Length:** 8.5" overall. **Grips:** Checkered rubber, rosewood, mother-of-pearl. **Sights:** Fixed notch rear. Three-dot sight system. Also offered with micrometer-click adjustable night sights. **Features:** Double action, ambidextrous 3-way hammer drop safety, allows cocked & locked carry. Blue, stainless steel, blue with gold highlights, stainless steel with gold highlights, forged aluminum frame, integral key-lock.

Price: Blue . . . . **$575.00 to $670.00**

Taurus Model PT99 Auto Pistol

Similar to PT92, fully adjustable rear sight.

Price: Blue . . . . **$575.00 to $670.00**
Price: 22 Conversion kit for PT 92 and PT99 (includes barrel and slide)
. . . . **$266.00**

TAURUS MODEL PT-100/101 AUTO PISTOL

Caliber: 40 S&W, 10-shot mag. **Barrel:** 5". **Weight:** 34 oz. **Length:** 8-1/2". **Grips:** Checkered rubber, rosewood, mother-of-pearl. **Sights:** 3-dot fixed or adjustable; night sights available. **Features:** Single/double action with three-position safety/decocker. Re-introduced in 2001. Imported by Taurus International.

Price: PT100. . . . . **$575.00 to $670.00**
Price: PT101. . . . . **$595.00 to $610.00**

TAURUS MODEL PT-111 MILLENNIUM AUTO PISTOL

Caliber: 9mm Para., 10-shot mag. **Barrel:** 3.25". **Weight:** 18.7 oz. **Length:** 6.0" overall. **Grips:** Polymer. **Sights:** 3-dot fixed; night sights available. Low profile, three-dot combat. **Features:** Double action only, polymer frame, matte stainless or blue steel slide, manual safety, integral key-lock. Deluxe models with wood grip inserts.

Price: . . . . **$425.00 to $550.00**

Taurus Model PT-111 Millennium Titanium Pistol

Similar to PT-111, titanium slide, night sights.

Price: **$585.00**

TAURUS PT-132 MILLENIUM AUTO PISTOL

Caliber: 32 ACP, 10-shot mag. **Barrel:** 3.25". **Weight:** 18.7 oz. **Grips:** Polymer. **Sights:** 3-dot fixed; night sights available. **Features:** Double action only, polymer frame, matte stainless or blue steel slide, manual safety, integral key-lock action. Introduced 2001.

Price: . . . . **$425.00 to $435.00**

Taurus PT-911

Taurus PT-940

Taurus PT-938

Taurus PT-945

Taurus PT-957

TAURUS PT-138 MILLENIUM SERIES
Caliber: 380 ACP, 10-shot mag. **Barrel:** 3.25". **Weight:** 18.7 oz. **Grips:** Polymer. **Sights:** Fixed 3-dot fixed. **Features:** Double action only, polymer frame, matte stainless or blue steel slide, manual safety, integral key-lock.
Price: .... $425.00 to $520.00

TAURUS PT-140 MILLENIUM AUTO PISTOL
Caliber: 40 S&W, 10-shot mag. **Barrel:** 3.25". **Weight:** 18.7 oz. **Grips:** Checkered polymer. **Sights:** 3-dot fixed; night sights available. **Features:** Double-action only; matte stainless or blue steel slide, black polymer frame, manual safety, integral key-lock action. From Taurus International.
Price: .... $455.00 to $605.00

TAURUS PT-145 MILLENIUM AUTO PISTOL
Caliber: 45 ACP, 10-shot mag. **Barrel:** 3.27". **Weight:** 23 oz. **Stock:** Checkered polymer. **Sights:** 3-dot fixed; night sights available. **Features:** Double-action only, matte stainless or blue steel slide, black polymer frame, manual safety, integral key-lock. From Taurus International.
Price: .... $490.00 to $575.00

TAURUS MODEL PT-911 AUTO PISTOL
Caliber: 9mm Para., 10-shot mag. **Barrel:** 4". **Weight:** 28.2 oz. **Length:** 7" overall. **Grips:** Checkered rubber, rosewood, mother-of-pearl. **Sights:** Fixed, three-dot blue or stainless; night sights optional. **Features:** Double action, semi-auto ambidextrous 3-way hammer drop safety, allows cocked and locked carry. Blue, stainless steel, blue with gold highlights, or stainless steel with gold highlights, forged aluminum frame, integral key-lock.
Price: .... $525.00 to $620.00

TAURUS MODEL PT-938 AUTO PISTOL
Caliber: 380 ACP, 10-shot mag. **Barrel:** 3.72". **Weight:** 27 oz. **Length:** 6.5" overall. **Grips:** Checkered rubber. **Sights:** Fixed, three-dot. **Features:** Double action, ambidextrous 3-way hammer drop allows cocked & locked carry. Forged aluminum frame. Integral key-lock. Imported by Taurus International.
Price: Blue $500.00
Price: Stainless...................................... $530.00

TAURUS MODEL PT-940 AUTO PISTOL
Caliber: 40 S&W, 10-shot mag. **Barrel:** 4". **Weight:** 28.2 oz. **Length:** 7.05" overall. **Grips:** Checkered rubber, rosewood or mother-of-pearl. **Sights:** Fixed, three-dot blue or stainless; night sights optional. **Features:** Double action, semi-auto ambidextrous 3-way hammer drop safety, allows cocked & locked carry. Blue, stainless steel, blue with gold highlights, or stainless steel with gold hightlights, forged aluminum frame, integral key-lock.
Price: .... $525.00 to $620.00

TAURUS MODEL PT-945 SERIES
Caliber: 45 ACP, 8-shot mag. **Barrel:** 4.25". **Weight:** 28.2/29.5 oz. **Length:** 7.48" overall. **Grips:** Checkered rubber, rosewood or mother-of-pearl. **Sights:** Fixed, three-dot; night sights optional. **Features:** Double-action with ambidextrous 3-way hammer drop safety allows cocked & locked carry. Forged aluminum frame, PT-945C has poarted barrel/slide. Blue, stainless, blue with gold highlights, stainless with gold highlights, integral key-lock. Introduced 1995. Imported by Taurus International.
Price: .... $560.00 to $655.00

Vektor SP1

Vektor Ultra with Tasco Scope

Walther PP

Walther PPK/S

TAURUS MODEL PT-957 AUTO PISTOL

Caliber: 357 SIG, 10-shot mag. **Barrel:** 4". **Weight:** 28 oz. **Length:** 7" overall. **Grips:** Checkered rubber, rosewood or mother-of-pearl. **Sights:** Fixed, three-dot blue or stainless; night sights optional. **Features:** Double-action, blue, stainless steel, blue with gold accents or stainless with gold accents, ported barrel/slide, three-position safety with decocking lever and ambidextrous safety. Forged aluminum frame, integral key-lock. Introduced 1999. Imported by Taurus International.
Price: . . . . **$525.00 to $620.00**
NEW! Price: Non-ported. . . . . **$525.00 to $535.00**

VEKTOR SP1 SPORT PISTOL

Caliber: 9mm Para., 10-shot mag. **Barrel:** 5 ". **Weight:** 38 oz. **Length:** 9-3/8" overall. **Grips:** Checkered black composition. **Sights:** Combat-type blade front, adjustable rear. **Features:** Single action only with adjustable trigger stop; three-chamber compensator; extended magazine release. Introduced 1999. Imported from South Africa by Vektor USA.
Price: **$829.95**

Vektor SP1 Tuned Sport Pistol

Similar to Vektor Sport, fully adjustable straight trigger, LPA three-dot sight system, and hard nickel finish. Introduced 1999. Imported from South Africa by Vektor USA.
Price: **$1,199.95**

Vektor SP1 Target Pistol

Similar to the Vektor Sport except has 5-7/8" barrel without compensator; weighs 40-1/2 oz.; has fully adjustable straight match trigger; black slide, bright frame. Introduced 1999. Imported from South Africa by Vektor USA.
Price: **$1,299.95**

Vektor SP1, SP2 Ultra Sport Pistols

Similar to the Vektor Target except has three-chamber compensator with three jet ports; strengthened frame with integral beavertail; lightweight polymer scope mount (Weaver rail). Overall length is 11", weighs 41-1/2 oz. Model SP2 is in 40 S&W. Introduced 1999. Imported from South Africa by Vektor USA.
Price: SP1 (9mm). **$2,149.95**
Price: SP2 (40 S&W) **$2,149.95**

VEKTOR SP1 AUTO PISTOL

Caliber: 9mm Para., 40 S&W (SP2), 10-shot magazine. **Barrel:** 4-5/8". **Weight:** 35 oz. **Length:** 8-1/4" overall. **Grips:** Checkered black composition. **Sights:** Combat-type fixed. **Features:** Alloy frame, steel slide; traditional double-action mechanism; matte black finish. Introduced 1999. Imported from South Africa by Vektor USA.
Price: SP1 (9mm). **$599.95**
Price: SP1 with nickel finish **$629.95**
Price: SP2 (40 S&W) **$649.95**

Vektor SP1, SP2 Compact General's Model Pistol

Similar to the 9mm Para. Vektor SP1 except has 4" barrel, weighs 31-1/2 oz., and is 7-1/2" overall. Recoil operated. Traditional double-action mechanism. SP2 model is chambered for 40 S&W. Introduced 1999. Imported from South Africa by Vektor USA.
Price: SP1 (9mm Para.) **$649.95**
Price: SP2 (40 S&W) **$649.95**

VEKTOR CP-1 COMPACT PISTOL

Caliber: 9mm Para., 10-shot magazine. **Barrel:** 4". **Weight:** 25.4 oz. **Length:** 7" overall. **Grips:** Textured polymer. **Sights:** Blade front adjustable for windage, fixed rear; adjustable sight optional. **Features:** Ergonomic grip frame shape; stainless steel barrel; delayed gas-buffered blowback action. Introduced 1999. Imported from South Africa by Vektor USA.
Price: With black slide **$479.95**
Price: With nickel slide **$499.95**
Price: With black slide, adjustable sight **$509.95**
Price: With nickel slide, adjustable sight **$529.95**

WALTHER PP AUTO PISTOL

Caliber: 380 ACP, 7-shot magazine. **Barrel:** 3.86". **Weight:** 23-1/2 oz. **Length:** 6.7" overall. **Grips:** Checkered plastic. **Sights:** Fixed, white markings. **Features:** Double action; manual safety blocks firing pin and drops hammer; chamber loaded indicator on 32 and 380; extra finger rest magazine provided. Imported from Germany by Carl Walther USA.
Price: 380 . . . . **$999.00**

Walther PPK/S American Auto Pistol

Similar to Walther PP except made entirely in the United States. Has 3.27" barrel with 6.1" length overall. Introduced 1980.
Price: 380 ACP only, blue. **$540.00**
Price: As above, 32 ACP or 380 ACP, stainless. **$540.00**

Walther PPK

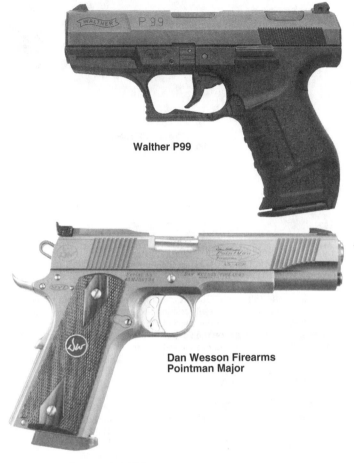

Walther P99

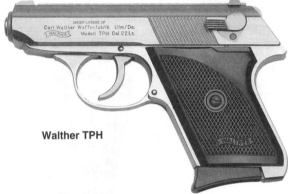

Walther TPH

Dan Wesson Firearms
Pointman Major

Walther PPK American Auto Pistol

Similar to Walther PPK/S except weighs 21 oz., has 6-shot capacity. Made in the U.S. Introduced 1986.

Price: Stainless, 32 ACP or 380 ACP..................... **$540.00**
Price: Blue, 380 ACP only **$540.00**

WALTHER MODEL TPH AUTO PISTOL

Caliber: 22 LR, 25 ACP, 6-shot magazine. **Barrel:** 2-1/4". **Weight:** 14 oz. **Length:** 5-3/8" overall. **Grips:** Checkered black composition. **Sights:** Blade front, rear drift-adjustable for windage. **Features:** Made of stainless steel. Scaled-down version of the Walther PP/PPK series. Made in U.S.A. Introduced 1987. From Carl Walther USA.

Price: Blue or stainless steel, 22 or 25 .... **$440.00**

WALTHER P88 COMPACT PISTOL

Caliber: 9mm Para., 10-shot magazine. **Barrel:** 3.93". **Weight:** 28 oz. **Grips:** Checkered black polymer. **Sights:** Blade front, drift adjustable rear. **Features:** Double action with ambidextrous decocking lever and magazine release; alloy frame; loaded chamber indicator; matte blue finish. Imported from Germany by Carl Walther USA.

Price: **$900.00**

WALTHER P99 AUTO PISTOL

Caliber: 9mm Para., 9x21, 40 S&W, 10-shot magazine. **Barrel:** 4". **Weight:** 25 oz. **Length:** 7" overall. **Grips:** Textured polymer. **Sights:** Blade front (comes with three interchangeable blades for elevation adjustment), micrometer rear adjustable for windage. **Features:** Double-action mechanism with trigger safety, decock safety, internal striker safety; chamber loaded indicator; ambidextrous magazine release levers; polymer frame with interchangeable backstrap inserts. Comes with two magazines. Introduced 1997. Imported from Germany by Carl Walther USA.

Price: **$799.00**

Walther P990 Auto Pistol

Similar to the P99 except is double action only. Available in blue or silver tenifer finish. Introduced 1999. Imported from Germany by Carl Walther USA.

Price: **$749.00**

WALTHER P-5 AUTO PISTOL

Caliber: 9mm Para., 8-shot magazine. **Barrel:** 3.62". **Weight:** 28 oz. **Length:** 7.10" overall. **Grips:** Checkered plastic. **Sights:** Blade front, adjustable rear. **Features:** Uses the basic Walther P-38 double-action mechanism. Blue finish. Imported from Germany by Carl Walther USA.

Price: **$900.00**

DAN WESSON FIREARMS POINTMAN MAJOR AUTO PISTOL

Caliber: 45 ACP. **Barrel:** 5". **Grips:** Rosewood checkered. **Sights: Features:** Blued or stainless steel frame and serrated slide; Chip McCormick match-grade trigger group, sear and disconnect; match-grade barrel; high-ride beavertail safety; checkered slide release; high rib; interchangeable sight system; laser engraved. Introduced 2000. Made in U.S.A. by Dan Wesson Firearms.

Price: Model PM1-B (blued)........................... **$799.00**
Price: Model PM1-S (stainless) **$799.00**

Dan Wesson Firearms Pointman Seven Auto Pistols

Similar to Pointman Major, dovetail adjustable target rear sight and dovetail target front sight. Available in blued or stainless finish. Introduced 2000. Made in U.S.A. by Dan Wesson Firearms.

Price: PM7 (blued frame and slide) **$999.00**
Price: PM7S (stainless finish)......................... **$1,099.00**

Dan Wesson Firearms Pointman Guardian Auto Pistols

Similar to Pointman Major, more compact frame with 4.25" barrel. Available in blued or stainless finish with fixed or adjustable sights. Introduced 2000. Made in U.S.A. by Dan Wesson Firearms.

Price: PMG-FS, all new frame (fixed sights) **$769.00**
Price: PMG-AS (blued frame and slide, adjustable sights) **$799.00**
Price: PMGD-FS Guardian Duce, all new frame (stainless frame and blued slide, fixed sights) **$829.00**
Price: PMGD-AS Guardian Duce (stainless frame and blued slide, adj. sights)... **$799.00**

Dan Wesson Firearms Major Aussie

Dan Wesson Firearms Patriot Marksman

Wilkinson Sherry

Dan Wesson Firearms Major Tri-Ops Packs

NEW!

Similar to Pointman Major. Complete frame assembly fitted to 3 match grade complete slide assemblied (9mm, 10mm, 40 S&W). Includes recoil springs and magazines that come in hard cases fashioned after high-grade European rifle case. Constructed of navy blue cordura stretched over hardwood with black leather trim and comfortable black leather wrapped handle. Brass corner protectors, dual combination locks, engraved presentation plate on the lid. Inside, the Tri-Ops Pack components are nested in precision die-cut closed cell foam and held sercurely in place by convoluted foam in the inside of the lid. Introduced 2002. Made in U.S.A. by Dan Wesson Firearms.

Price: TOP1B (blued), TOP1-S (stainless) **$2.459.00**

Dan Wesson Firearms Major Aussie

NEW!

Similar to Pointman Major. Available in 45 ACP. Features Bomar-style adjustable rear target sight, unique slide top configuration exclusive to this model (features radius from the flat side surfaces of the slide to a narrow flat on top and then a small redius and reveal ending in a flat, low (1/16" high) sight rib 3/8" wide with lengthwise serrations). Clearly identified by the Southern Cross flag emblem laser engraved on the sides of the slide (available in 45 ACP only). Introduced 2002. Made in U.S.A. by Dan Wesson Firearms.

Price: PMA-B (blued) **$999.00**
Price: PMA-S (stainless). **$1,099.00**

Dan Wesson Firearms Pointman Minor Auto Pistol

Similar to Pointman Major. Full size (5") entry level IDPA or action pistol model with blued carbon alloy frame and round top slide, bead blast matte finish on frame and slide top and radius, satin-brushed polished finish on sides of slide, chromed barrel, dovetail mount fixed rear target sight and tactical/target ramp front sight, match trigger, skeletonized target hammer, high ride beavertail, fitted extractor, serrations on thumb safety, slide release and mag release, lowered and relieved ejection port, beveled mag well, exotic hardwood grips, serrated mainspring housing, laser engraved. Introduced 2000. Made in U.S.A. by Dan Wesson Firearms.

Price: Model PM2-P **$599.00**

Dan Wesson Firearms Pointman Hi-Cap Auto Pistol

Similar to Pointman Minor, full-size high-capacity (10-shot) magazine with 5" chromed barrel, blued finish and dovetail fixed rear sight. Match adjustable trigger, ambidextrous extended thumb safety, beavertail safety. Introduced 2001. From Dan Wesson Firearms.

Price: PMHC (Pointman High-Cap) **$689.00**

Dan Wesson Firearms Pointman Dave Pruitt Signature Series

Similar to other full-sized Pointman models, customized by Master Pistolsmith and IDPA Grand Master Dave Pruitt. Alloy carbon-steel with black oxide bluing and bead-blast matte finish. Front and rear chevron cocking serrations, dovetail mount fixed rear target sight and tactical/target ramp front sight, ramped match barrel with fitted match bushing and link, Chip McCormick (or equivalent) match grade trigger group, serrated ambidextrous tactical/carry thumb safety, high ride beavertail, serrated slide release and checkered mag release, match grade sear and hammer, fitted

extractor, lowered and relieved ejection port, beveled mag well, full length 2-piece recoil spring guide rod, cocobolo double diamond checkered grips, serrated steel mainspring housing, special laser engraving. Introduced 2001. From Dan Wesson Firearms.

Price: PMDP (Pointman Dave Pruitt) **$899.00**

DAN WESSON FIREARMS PATRIOT 1911 PISTOL

NEW

Caliber: 45 ACP. **Grips:** Exotic exhibition grade cocobolo, double diamond hand cut checkering. **Sights:** New innovative combat/carry rear sight that completely encloses the dovetail. **Features:** The new Patriot Expert and Patriot Marksman are full size match grade series 70 1911s machined from steel forgings. Available in blued chome moly steel or stainless steel. Beveled mag well, lowered and flared ejection port, high sweep beavertail safety. Delivery begins in June 2002.

Price: Model PTM-B (blued) **$797.00**
Price: Model PTM-S (stainless) **$898.00**
Price: Model PTE-B (blued) **$864.00**
Price: Model PTE-S (stainless) **$971.00**

WILKINSON SHERRY AUTO PISTOL

Caliber: 22 LR, 8-shot magazine. **Barrel:** 2-1/8". **Weight:** 9-1/4 oz. **Length:** 4-3/8" overall. **Grips:** Checkered black plastic. **Sights:** Fixed, groove. **Features:** Cross-bolt safety locks the sear into the hammer. Available in all blue finish or blue slide and trigger with gold frame. Introduced 1985.

Price: **$280.00**

WILKINSON LINDA AUTO PISTOL

Caliber: 9mm Para. **Barrel:** 8-5/16". **Weight:** 4 lbs., 13 oz. **Length:** 12-1/4" overall. **Grips:** Checkered black plastic pistol grip, walnut forend. **Sights:** Protected blade front, aperture rear. **Features:** Fires from closed bolt. Semi-auto only. Straight blowback action. Cross-bolt safety. Removable barrel. From Wilkinson Arms.

Price: **$675.00**

Includes models suitable for several forms of competition and other sporting purposes.

Baer 1911 Ultimate Master

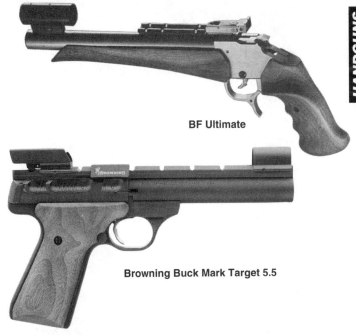

BF Ultimate

Baer 1911 Bullseye Wadcutter

Browning Buck Mark Target 5.5

BAER 1911 ULTIMATE MASTER COMBAT PISTOL

Caliber: 9x23, 38 Super, 400 Cor-Bon 45 ACP (others available), 10-shot magazine. **Barrel:** 5", 6"; Baer NM. **Weight:** 37 oz. **Length:** 8.5" overall. **Grips:** Checkered rosewood. **Sights:** Baer dovetail front, low-mount Bo-Mar rear with hidden leaf. **Features:** Full-house competition gun. Baer forged NM blued steel frame and double serrated slide; Baer triple port, tapered cone compensator; fitted slide to frame; lowered, flared ejection port; Baer reverse recoil plug; full-length guide rod; recoil buff; beveled magazine well; Baer Commander hammer, sear; Baer extended ambidextrous safety, extended ejector, checkered slide stop, beavertail grip safety with pad, extended magazine release button; Baer speed trigger. Made in U.S.A. by Les Baer Custom, Inc.
Price: Compensated, open sights. **$2,476.00**
Price: 6" Model 400 Cor-Bon **$2,541.00**

BAER 1911 NATIONAL MATCH HARDBALL PISTOL

Caliber: 45 ACP, 7-shot magazine. **Barrel:** 5". **Weight:** 37 oz. **Length:** 8.5" overall. **Grips:** Checkered walnut. **Sights:** Baer dovetail front with undercut post, low-mount Bo-Mar rear with hidden leaf. **Features:** Baer NM forged steel frame, double serrated slide and barrel with stainless bushing; slide fitted to frame; Baer match trigger with 4-lb. pull; polished feed ramp, throated barrel; checkered front strap, arched mainspring housing; Baer beveled magazine well; lowered, flared ejection port; tuned extractor; Baer extended ejector, checkered slide stop; recoil buff. Made in U.S.A. by Les Baer Custom, Inc.
Price: **$1,335.00**

Baer 1911 Bullseye Wadcutter Pistol

Similar to National Match Hardball except designed for wadcutter loads only. Polished feed ramp and barrel throat; Bo-Mar rib on slide; full-length recoil rod; Baer speed trigger with 3-1/2-lb. pull; Baer deluxe hammer and sear; Baer beavertail grip safety with pad; flat mainspring housing checkered 20 lpi. Blue finish; checkered walnut grips. Made in U.S.A. by Les Baer Custom, Inc.
Price: From. **$1,495.00**
Price: With 6" barrel, from **$1,690.00**

BF ULTIMATE SILHOUETTE HB SINGLE SHOT PISTOL

Caliber: 7mm U.S., 22 LR Match and 100 other chamberings. **Barrel:** 10.75" Heavy Match Grade with 11-degree target crown. **Weight:** 3 lbs., 15 oz. **Length:** 16" overall. **Grips:** Thumbrest target style. **Sights:** Bo-Mar/Bond ScopeRib I Combo with hooded post front adjustable for height and width, rear notch available in .032", .062", .080" and .100" widths; 1/2-MOA clicks. **Features:** Designed to meet maximum rules for IHMSA Production Gun. Falling block action gives rigid barrel-receiver mating. Hand fitted and headspaced. Etched receiver; gold-colored trigger. Introduced 1988. Made in U.S.A. by E. Arthur Brown Co. Inc.
Price: **$669.00**

Classic BF Hunting Pistol

Similar to BF Ultimate Silhouette HB Single Shot Pistol, except no sights; drilled and tapped for scope mount. Barrels from 8 to 15". Variety of options offered. Made in U.S.A. by E. Arthur Brown Co. Inc.
Price: **$599.00**

BROWNING BUCK MARK SILHOUETTE

Caliber: 22 LR, 10-shot magazine. **Barrel:** 9-7/8". **Weight:** 53 oz. **Length:** 14" overall. **Grips:** Smooth walnut stocks and forend, or finger-groove walnut. **Sights:** Post-type hooded front adjustable for blade width and height; Pro Target rear fully adjustable for windage and elevation. **Features:** Heavy barrel with .900" diameter; 12-1/2" sight radius. Special sighting plane forms scope base. Introduced 1987. Made in U.S.A. From Browning.
Price: **$448.00**

Browning Buck Mark Target 5.5

Same as Buck Mark Silhouette, 5-1/2" barrel with .900" diameter. Hooded sights mounted on scope base that accepts optical or reflex sight. Rear sight is Browning fully adjustable Pro Target, front sight is adjustable post that customizes to different widths, can be adjusted for height. Contoured walnut grips with thumbrest, or finger-groove walnut. Matte blue finish. Overall length is 9-5/8", weighs 35-1/2 oz. Has 10-shot magazine. Introduced 1990. From Browning.
Price: **$425.00**
Price: Target 5.5 Gold (as above with gold anodized frame and top rib) **$477.00**
Price: Target 5.5 Nickel (as above with nickel frame and top rib) **$477.00**

Browning Buck Mark Bullseye

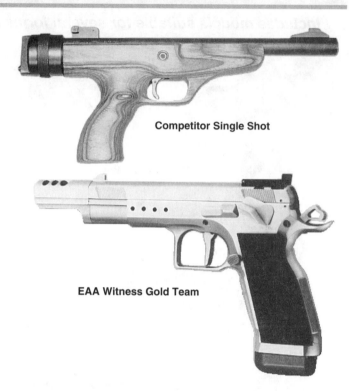

Competitor Single Shot

Colt Gold Cup Trophy

EAA Witness Gold Team

Browning Buck Mark Field 5.5
Same as Target 5.5, hoodless ramp-style front sight and low profile rear sight. Matte blue finish, contoured or finger-groove walnut stocks. Introduced 1991.
Price: **$425.00**

Browning Buck Mark Bullseye
Similar to Buck Mark Silhouette, 7-1/4" heavy barrel with three flutes per side; trigger adjusts from 2-1/2 to 5 lbs.; specially designed rosewood target or three-finger-groove stocks with competition-style heel rest, or with contoured rubber grip. Overall length 11-5/16", weighs 36 oz. Introduced 1996. Made in U.S.A. From Browning.
Price: With ambidextrous moulded composite stocks **$389.00**
Price: With rosewood stocks, or wrap-around finger groove **$500.00**

COLT GOLD CUP MODEL O PISTOL
Caliber: 45 ACP, 8-shot magazine. **Barrel:** 5", with new design bushing. **Weight:** 39 oz. **Length:** 8-1/2". **Grips:** Checkered rubber composite with silver-plated medallion. **Sights:** Patridge-style front, Bomar-style rear adjustable for windage and elevation, sight radius 6-3/4". **Features:** Arched or flat housing; wide, grooved trigger with adjustable stop; ribbed-top slide, hand fitted, with improved ejection port.
Price: Blue **$1,050.00**
Price: Stainless. **$1,116.00**

COMPETITOR SINGLE SHOT PISTOL
Caliber: 22 LR through 50 Action Express, including belted magnums. **Barrel:** 14" standard; 10.5" silhouette; 16" optional. **Weight:** About 59 oz. (14" bbl.). **Length:** 15.12" overall. **Grips:** Ambidextrous; synthetic (standard) or laminated or natural wood. **Sights:** Ramp front, adjustable rear. **Features:** Rotary canon-type action cocks on opening; cammed ejector; interchangeable barrels, ejectors. Adjustable single stage trigger, sliding thumb safety and trigger safety. Matte blue finish. Introduced 1988. From Competitor Corp., Inc.
Price: 14", standard calibers, synthetic grip **$414.95**
Price: Extra barrels, from **$159.95**

CZ 75 CHAMPION COMPETITION PISTOL
Caliber: 9mm Para., 9x21, 40 S&W, 10-shot mag. **Barrel:** 4.49". **Weight:** 35 oz. **Length:** 9.44" overall. **Grips:** Black rubber. **Sights:** Blade front, fully adjustable rear. **Features:** Single-action trigger mechanism; three-port compensator (40 S&W, 9mm have two port) full-length guide rod; extended magazine release; ambidextrous safety; flared magazine well; fully adjustable match trigger. Introduced 1999. Imported from the Czech Republic by CZ USA.
Price: 9mm Para., 9x21, 40 S&W, dual-tone finish **$1,484.00**

CZ 75 ST IPSC AUTO PISTOL
Caliber: 40 S&W, 10-shot magazine. **Barrel:** 5.12". **Weight:** 2.9 lbs. **Length:** 8.86" overall. **Grips:** Checkered walnut. **Sights:** Fully adjustable rear. **Features:** Single-action mechanism; extended slide release and ambidextrous safety; full-length slide rail; double slide serrations. Introduced 1999. Imported from the Czech Republic by CZ-USA.
Price: Dual-tone finish **$1,038.00**

EAA/BAIKAL IZH-35 AUTO PISTOL
Caliber: 22 LR, 5-shot mag. **Barrel:** 6". **Grips:** Walnut; fully adjustable right-hand target-style. **Sights:** Fully adjustable rear, blade front; detachable scope mount. **Features:** Hammer-forged target barrel; machined steel receiver; adjustable trigger; manual slide hold back, grip and manual trigger-bar disconnect safeties; cocking indicator. Introduced 2000. Imported from Russia by European American Armory.
Price: Blued finish. **$539.00**

EAA WITNESS GOLD TEAM AUTO
Caliber: 9mm Para., 9x21, 38 Super, 40 S&W, 45 ACP. **Barrel:** 5.1". **Weight:** 41.6 oz. **Length:** 9.6" overall. **Grips:** Checkered walnut, competition style. **Sights:** Square post front, fully adjustable rear. **Features:** Triple-chamber cone compensator; competition SA trigger; extended safety and magazine release; competition hammer; beveled magazine well; beavertail grip. Hand-fitted major components. Hard chrome finish. Match-grade barrel. From E.A.A. Custom Shop. Introduced 1992. From European American Armory.
Price: **$2,150.00**

EAA Witness Silver Team Auto
Similar to Witness Gold Team, double-chamber compensator, oval magazine release, black rubber grips, double-dip blue finish. Super Sight and drilled and tapped for scope mount. Built for the intermediate competition shooter. Introduced 1992. From European American Armory Custom Shop.
Price: 9mm Para., 9x21, 38 Super, 40 S&W, 45 ACP **$968.00**

Freedom Arms 8322 Silhouette Class

Hammerli SP 20

High Standard Trophy

High Standard Victor

ENTRÉPRISE TOURNAMENT SHOOTER MODEL I

Caliber: 45 ACP, 10-shot mag. **Barrel:** 6". **Weight:** 40 oz. **Length:** 8.5" overall. **Grips:** Black ultra-slim double diamond checkered synthetic. **Sights:** Dovetailed Patridge front, adjustable Competizione "melded" rear. **Features:** Oversized magazine release button; flared magazine well; fully machined parallel slide rails; front and rear slide serrations; serrated top of slide; stainless ramped bull barrel with fully supported chamber; full-length guide rod with plug; stainless firing pin; match extractor; polished ramp; tuned match extractor; black oxide. Introduced 1998. Made in U.S.A. by Entréprise Arms.
Price: **$2,300.00**
Price: TSMIII (Satin chrome finish, two-piece guide rod) **$2,700.00**

EXCEL INDUSTRIES CP-45, XP-45 AUTO PISTOL

Caliber: 45 ACP, 6-shot & 10-shot mags. **Barrel:** 3-1/4". **Weight:** 31 oz. & 25 oz. **Length:** 6-3/8" overall. **Grips:** Checkered black nylon. **Sights:** Fully adjustable rear. **Features:** Stainless steel frame and slide; single action with external hammer and firing pin block, manual thumb safety; last-shot hold open. Includes gun lock and cleaning kit. Introduced 2001. Made in U.S.A. by Excel Industries Inc.
Price: CP-45 . . . . **$425.00**
Price: XP-45 . . . . **$465.00**

FEINWERKEBAU AW93 TARGET PISTOL

Caliber: 22. **Barrel:** 6". **Grips:** Fully adjustable orthopaedic. **Sights:** Fully adjustable micrometer. **Features:** Advanced Russian design with German craftmanship. Imported from Germany by Nygord Precision Products.
Price: **$1,495.00**

FREEDOM ARMS MODEL 8322 FIELD GRADE SILHOUETTE CLASS

Caliber: 22 LR, 5-shot cylinder. **Barrel:** 10". **Weight:** 63 oz. **Length:** 15.5" overall. **Grips:** Black Micarta. **Sights:** Removable patridge front blade; Iron Sight Gun Works silhouette rear, click adjustable for windage and elevation (optional adj. front sight and hood). **Features:** Stainless steel, matte finish, manual sliding-bar safety system; dual firing pins, lightened hammer for fast lock time, pre-set trigger stop. Introduced 1991. Made in U.S.A. by Freedom Arms.
Price: Silhouette Class **$1,901.75**
Price: Extra fitted 22 WMR cylinder **$264.00**

FREEDOM ARMS MODEL 83 CENTERFIRE SILHOUETTE MODELS

Caliber: 357 Mag., 41 Mag., 44 Mag.; 5-shot cylinder. **Barrel:** 10", 9" (357 Mag. only). **Weight:** 63 oz. (41 Mag.). **Length:** 15.5", 14-1/2" (357 only). **Grips:** Pachmayr Presentation. **Sights:** Iron Sight Gun Works silhouette rear sight, replaceable adjustable front sight blade with hood. **Features:** Stainless steel, matte finish, manual sliding-bar safety system. Made in U.S.A. by Freedom Arms.
Price: Silhouette Models. **$1,634.85**

GAUCHER GP SILHOUETTE PISTOL

Caliber: 22 LR, single shot. **Barrel:** 10". **Weight:** 42.3 oz. **Length:** 15.5" overall. **Grips:** Stained hardwood. **Sights:** Hooded post on ramp front, open rear adjustable for windage and elevation. **Features:** Matte chrome barrel, blued bolt and sights. Other barrel lengths available on special order. Introduced 1991. Imported by Mandall Shooting Supplies.
Price: **$425.00**

HAMMERLI SP 20 TARGET PISTOL

Caliber: 22 LR, 32 S&W. **Barrel:** 4.6". **Weight:** 34.6-41.8 oz. **Length:** 11.8" overall. **Grips:** Anatomically shaped synthetic Hi-Grip available in five sizes. **Sights:** Integral front in three widths, adjustable rear with changeable notch widths. **Features:** Extremely low-level sight line; anatomically shaped trigger; adjustable JPS buffer system for different recoil characteristics. Receiver available in red, blue, gold, violet or black. Introduced 1998. Imported from Switzerland by SIGARMS, Inc and Hammerli Pistols USA.
Price: Hammerli 22 LR **$1,668.00**
Price: Hammerli 32 S&W **$1,743.00**

HARRIS GUNWORKS SIGNATURE JR. LONG RANGE PISTOL

Caliber: Any suitable caliber. **Barrel:** To customer specs. **Weight:** 5 lbs. **Stock:** Gunworks fiberglass. **Sights:** None furnished; comes with scope rings. **Features:** Right- or left-hand benchrest action of titanium or stainless steel; single shot or repeater. Comes with bipod. Introduced 1992. Made in U.S.A. by Harris Gunworks, Inc.
Price: **$2,700.00**

HIGH STANDARD TROPHY TARGET PISTOL

Caliber: 22 LR, 10-shot mag. **Barrel:** 5-1/2" bull or 7-1/4" fluted. **Weight:** 44 oz. **Length:** 9.5" overall. **Stock:** Checkered hardwood with thumbrest. **Sights:** Undercut ramp front, frame-mounted micro-click rear adjustable for windage and elevation; drilled and tapped for scope mounting. **Features:** Gold-plated trigger, slide lock, safety-lever and magazine release; stippled front grip and backstrap; adjustable trigger and sear. Barrel weights optional. From High Standard Manufacturing Co., Inc.
Price: 5-1/2", scope base **$540.00**
Price: 7.25" **$689.00**
Price: 7.25", scope base **$625.00**

HIGH STANDARD VICTOR TARGET PISTOL

Caliber: 22 LR, 10-shot magazine. **Barrel:** 4-1/2" or 5-1/2"; push-button takedown. **Weight:** 46 oz. **Length:** 9.5" overall. **Stock:** Checkered hardwood with thumbrest. **Sights:** Undercut ramp front, micro-click rear adjustable for windage and elevation. Also available with scope mount, rings, no sights. **Features:** Stainless steel construction. Full-length vent rib. Gold-plated trigger, slide lock, safety-lever and magazine release; stippled front grip and backstrap; polished slide; adjustable trigger and sear. Comes with barrel weight. From High Standard Manufacturing Co., Inc.
Price: 4-1/2" scope base **$564.00**
Price: 5-1/2", sights **$625.00**
Price: 5-1/2" scope base **$564.00**

HANDGUNS

Ruger Mark II Bull Barrel - MK10

Safari Arms Big Deuce

KIMBER SUPER MATCH AUTO PISTOL

Caliber: 45 ACP, 7-shot magazine. **Barrel:** 5". **Weight:** 38 oz. **Length:** 18.7" overall. **Sights:** Blade front, Kimber fully adjustable rear. **Features:** Guaranteed to have shot 3" group at 50 yards. Stainless steel frame, black KimPro slide; two-piece magazine well; premium aluminum match-grade trigger; 30 lpi front strap checkering; stainless match-grade barrel; ambidextrous safety; special Custom Shop markings. Introduced 1999. Made in U.S.A. by Kimber Mfg., Inc.
Price: **$1,927.00**

MORINI MODEL 84E FREE PISTOL

Caliber: 22 LR, single shot. **Barrel:** 11.4". **Weight:** 43.7 oz. **Length:** 19.4" overall. **Grips:** Adjustable match type with stippled surfaces. **Sights:** Interchangeable blade front, match-type fully adjustable rear. **Features:** Fully adjustable electronic trigger. Introduced 1995. Imported from Switzerland by Nygord Precision Products.
Price: **$1,450.00**

PARDINI MODEL SP, HP TARGET PISTOLS

Caliber: 22 LR, 32 S&W, 5-shot magazine. **Barrel:** 4.7". **Weight:** 38.9 oz. **Length:** 11.6" overall. **Grips:** Adjustable; stippled walnut; match type. **Sights:** Interchangeable blade front, interchangeable, fully adjustable rear. **Features:** Fully adjustable match trigger. Introduced 1995. Imported from Italy by Nygord Precision Products.
Price: Model SP (22 LR). **$950.00**
Price: Model HP (32 S&W). **$1,050.00**

PARDINI GP RAPID FIRE MATCH PISTOL

Caliber: 22 Short, 5-shot magazine. **Barrel:** 4.6". **Weight:** 43.3 oz. **Length:** 11.6" overall. **Grips:** Wrap-around stippled walnut. **Sights:** Interchangeable post front, fully adjustable match rear. **Features:** Model GP Schuman has extended rear sight for longer sight radius. Introduced 1995. Imported from Italy by Nygord Precision Products.
Price: Model GP **$1,095.00**
Price: Model GP Schuman. **$1,595.00**
New! Price: Model GP-E Electronic, has special parts **$1,595.00**

PARDINI K22 FREE PISTOL

Caliber: 22 LR, single shot. **Barrel:** 9.8". **Weight:** 34.6 oz. **Length:** 18.7" overall. **Grips:** Wrap-around walnut; adjustable match type. **Sights:** Interchangeable post front, fully adjustable match open rear. **Features:** Removable, adjustable match trigger. Toggle bolt pushes cartridge into chamber. Barrel weights mount above the barrel. New upgraded model introduced in 2002. Imported from Italy by Nygord Precision Products.
Price: **$1,295.00**

PARDINI GT45 TARGET PISTOL

Caliber: 45, 9mm, 40 S&W. **Barrel:** 5", 6". **Grips:** Checkered fore strap. **Sights:** Interchangeable post front, fully adjustable match open rear. **Features:** Ambi-safeties, trigger pull adjustable. Fits Helweg Glock holsters for defense shooters. Imported from Italy by Nygord Precision Products.
Price: 5" **$1,050.00**
Price: 6" **$1,125.00**
Price: Frame mount available. . . . . **$75.00 extra**
Price: Slide mount available . . . . **$35.00 extra**

PARDINI/NYGORD "MASTER" TARGET PISTOL

Caliber: 22 cal. **Barrel:** 5-1/2". **Grips:** Semi-wrap-around. **Sights:** Micrometer rear and red dot. **Features:** Elegant NRA "Bullseye" pistol. Superior balance of Pardini pistols. Revolutionary recirpcating internal weight barrel shroud. Imported from Italy by Nygord Precision Products.
Price: **$1,095.00**

RUGER MARK II TARGET MODEL AUTOLOADING PISTOL

Caliber: 22 LR, 10-shot magazine. **Barrel:** 6-7/8". **Weight:** 42 oz. **Length:** 11-1/8" overall. **Grips:** Checkered composition grip panels. **Sights:** .125" blade front, micro-click rear, adjustable for windage and elevation. Sight radius 9-3/8". Plastic case with lock included.
Features: Introduced 1982.
Price: Blued (MK-678) **$349.00**
Price: Stainless (KMK-678) **$439.00**

Ruger Mark II Government Target Model

Same gun as Mark II Target Model except has 6-7/8" barrel, higher sights and is roll marked "Government Target Model" on right side of receiver below rear sight. Identical in all aspects to military model used for training U.S. Armed Forces except for markings. Comes with factory test target, also lockable plastic case. Introduced 1987.
Price: Blued (MK-678G) **$425.00**
Price: Stainless (KMK-678G) **$509.00**

Ruger Stainless Competition Model Pistol

Similar to Mark II Government Target Model stainless pistol, 6-7/8" slab-sided barrel; receiver top is fitted with Ruger scope base of blued, chrome moly steel; has Ruger 1" stainless scope rings for mounting variety of optical sights; checkered laminated grip panels with right-hand thumbrest. Blued open sights with 9-1/4" radius. Overall length 11-1/8", weight 45 oz. Case and lock included. Introduced 1991.
Price: KMK-678GC. **$529.00**

Ruger Mark II Bull Barrel

Same gun as Target Model except has 5-1/2" or 10" heavy barrel (10" meets all IHMSA regulations). Weight with 5-1/2" barrel is 42 oz., with 10" barrel, 51 oz. Case with lock included.
Price: Blued (MK-512) **$349.00**
Price: Blued (MK-10) **$357.00**
Price: Stainless (KMK-10) **$445.00**
Price: Stainless (KMK-512) **$439.00**

SAFARI ARMS BIG DEUCE PISTOL

Caliber: 45 ACP, 7-shot magazine. **Barrel:** 6", 416 stainless steel. **Weight:** 40.3 oz. **Length:** 9.5" overall. **Grips:** Smooth walnut. **Sights:** Ramped blade front, LPA adjustable rear. **Features:** Beavertail grip safety; extended thumb safety and slide release; Commander-style hammer. Throated, polished and tuned. Parkerized matte black slide with satin stainless steel frame. Introduced 1995. Made in U.S.A. by Safari Arms, Inc.
Price: **$714.00**

SMITH & WESSON MODEL 41 TARGET

Caliber: 22 LR, 10-shot clip. **Barrel:** 5-1/2", 7". **Weight:** 44 oz. (5-1/2" barrel). **Length:** 9" overall (5-1/2" barrel). **Grips:** Checkered walnut with modified thumbrest, usable with either hand. **Sights:** 1/8" Patridge on ramp base; micro-click rear adjustable for windage and elevation. **Features:** 3/8" wide, grooved trigger; adjustable trigger stop drilled and tapped.
Price: S&W Bright Blue, either barrel **$958.00**

Smith & Wesson Model 41

Springfield 1911A1 Trophy Match

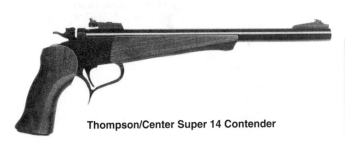

Thompson/Center Super 14 Contender

SMITH & WESSON MODEL 22A TARGET PISTOL
Caliber: 22 LR, 10-shot magazine. **Barrel:** 5-1/2" bull. **Weight:** 38.5 oz. **Length:** 9-1/2" overall. **Grips:** Dymondwood with ambidextrous thumbrests and flared bottom or rubber soft touch with thumbrest. **Sights:** Patridge front, fully adjustable rear. **Features:** Sight bridge with Weaver-style integral optics mount; alloy frame, stainless barrel and slide; blue finish. Introduced 1997. Made in U.S.A. by Smith & Wesson.
Price: **$367.00**
Price: HiViz front sight **$387.00**

Smith & Wesson Model 22S Target Pistol
Similar to the Model 22A except has stainless steel frame. Introduced 1997. Made in U.S.A. by Smith & Wesson.
Price: **$434.00**
Price: HiViz front sight **$453.00**

Springfield, Inc. 1911A1 Trophy Match Pistol
Similar to the 1911A1 except factory accurized, Videki speed trigger, delta hammer; has 4- to 5-1/2-lb. trigger pull, click adjustable rear sight, match-grade barrel and bushing. Comes with cocobolo grips. Introduced 1994. From Springfield, Inc.
Price: Blue **$1,148.00**
Price: Stainless steel **$1,219.00**

Springfield, Inc. Expert Pistol
Similar to the Competition Pistol except has triple-chamber tapered cone compensator on match barrel with dovetailed front sight; lowered and flared ejection port; fully tuned for reliability; fitted slide to frame; extended ambidextrous thumb safety, extended magazine release button; beavertail grip safety; Pachmayr wrap-around grips. Comes with two magazines, plastic carrying case. Introduced 1992. From Springfield, Inc.
Price: 45 ACP, Duotone finish **$1,724.00**
Price: Expert Ltd. (non-compensated) **$1,624.00**

Springfield, Inc. Distinguished Pistol
Has all the features of the 1911A1 Expert except is full-house pistol with deluxe Bo-Mar low-mounted adjustable rear sight; full-length recoil spring guide rod and recoil spring retainer; checkered frontstrap; S&A magazine well; walnut grips. Hard chrome finish. Comes with two magazines with slam pads, plastic carrying case. From Springfield, Inc.
Price: 45 ACP **$2,445.00**
Price: Distinguished Limited (non-compensated) **$2,345.00**

SPRINGFIELD, INC. 1911A1 BULLSEYE WADCUTTER PISTOL
Caliber: 38 Super, 45 ACP. **Barrel:** 5". **Weight:** 45 oz. **Length:** 8.59" overall (5" barrel). **Grips:** Checkered walnut. **Sights:** Bo-Mar rib with undercut blade front, fully adjustable rear. **Features:** Built for wadcutter loads only. Has full-length recoil spring guide rod, fitted Videki speed trigger with 3.5-lb. pull; match Commander hammer and sear; beavertail grip safety; lowered and flared ejection port; tuned extractor; fitted slide to frame; recoil buffer system; beveled and polished magazine well; checkered front strap and steel mainspring housing (flat housing standard); polished and throated National Match barrel and bushing. Comes with two magazines with slam pads, plastic carrying case, test target. Introduced 1992. From Springfield, Inc.
Price: **$1,499.00**

Springfield, Inc. Basic Competition Pistol
Has low-mounted Bo-Mar adjustable rear sight, undercut blade front; match throated barrel and bushing; polished feed ramp; lowered and flared ejection port; fitted Videki speed trigger with tuned 3.5-lb. pull; fitted slide to frame; recoil buffer system; checkered walnut grips; serrated, arched mainspring housing. Comes with two magazines with slam pads, plastic carrying case. Introduced 1992. From Springfield, Inc.
Price: 45 ACP, blue, 5" only **$1,295.00**

Springfield, Inc. 1911A1 N.M. Hardball Pistol
Has Bo-Mar adjustable rear sight with undercut front blade; fitted match Videki trigger with 4-lb. pull; fitted slide to frame; throated National Match barrel and bushing, polished feed ramp; recoil buffer system; tuned extractor; Herrett walnut grips. Comes with two magazines, plastic carrying case, test target. Introduced 1992. From Springfield, Inc.
Price: 45 ACP, blue **$1,336.00**

STI EAGLE 5.0 PISTOL
Caliber: 9mm, 38 & 40 Super, 40 S&W, 10mm, 45 ACP, 45 HP, 10-shot magazine. **Barrel:** 5", bull. **Weight:** 34.5 oz. **Length:** 8.62" overall. **Grips:** Checkered polymer. **Sights:** STI front, Novak or Heine rear. **Features:** Standard frames plus 7 others; adjustable match trigger; skeletonized hammer; extended grip safety with locator pad; match-grade fit of all parts. Many options available. Introduced 1994. Made in U.S.A. by STI International.
Price: **$1,794.00**

THOMPSON/CENTER SUPER 14 CONTENDER
Caliber: 22 LR, 222 Rem., 223 Rem., 7-30 Waters, 30-30 Win., 357 Rem. Maximum, 44 Mag., single shot. **Barrel:** 14". **Weight:** 45 oz. **Length:** 17-1/4" overall. **Grips:** T/C "Competitor Grip" (walnut and rubber). **Sights:** Fully adjustable target-type. **Features:** Break-open action with auto safety. Interchangeable barrels for both rimfire and centerfire calibers. Introduced 1978.
Price: Blued **$520.24**
Price: Stainless steel **$578.40**
Price: Extra barrels, blued **$251.06**
Price: Extra barrels, stainless steel **$278.68**

Thompson/Center Super 16 Contender
Same as the T/C Super 14 Contender except has 16-1/4" barrel. Rear sight can be mounted at mid-barrel position (10-3/4" radius) or moved to the rear (using scope mount position) for 14-3/4" radius. Overall length is 20-1/4". Comes with T/C Competitor Grip of walnut and rubber. Available in, 223 Rem., 45-70 Gov't. Also available with 16" vent rib barrel with internal choke, caliber 45 Colt/410 shotshell.

Unique D.E.S. 69U

Wichita Silhouette

Price: Blue **$525.95**
Price: 45-70 Gov't., blue **$531.52**
Price: Super 16 Vent Rib, blued **$559.70**
Price: Extra 16" barrel, blued **$245.61**
Price: Extra 45-70 barrel, blued **$251.08**
Price: Extra Super 16 vent rib barrel, blue **$278.73**

TOZ-35 FREE MATCH PISTOL

Caliber: 22 cal. **Barrel:** 11-1/2". **Grips:** Morini grips. **Sights:** Fully adjustable micrometer. **Features:** Pistol of choice for "Olympic Free Pistol" event. Single shot in wooden case with all tools and spare parts. No longer being made. Imported from Russia by Nygord Precision Products.
Price: **$950.00**

UNIQUE D.E.S. 32U TARGET PISTOL

Caliber: 32 S&W Long wadcutter. **Barrel:** 5.9". **Weight:** 40.2 oz. **Grips:** Anatomically shaped, adjustable stippled French walnut. **Sights:** Blade front, micrometer click rear. **Features:** Trigger adjustable for weight and position; dry firing mechanism; slide stop catch. Optional sleeve weights. Introduced 1990. Imported from France by Nygord Precision Products.
Price: Right-hand, about. **$1,350.00**
Price: Left-hand, about **$1,380.00**

UNIQUE D.E.S. 69U TARGET PISTOL

Caliber: 22 LR, 5-shot magazine. **Barrel:** 5.91". **Weight:** 35.3 oz. **Length:** 10.5" overall. **Grips:** French walnut target-style with thumbrest and adjustable shelf; hand-checkered panels. **Sights:** Ramp front, micro. adjustable rear mounted on frame; 8.66" sight radius. **Features:** Meets U.I.T. standards. Comes with 260-gram barrel weight; 100, 150, 350-gram weights available. Fully adjustable match trigger; dry-firing safety device. Imported from France by Nygord Precision Products.
Price: Right-hand, about. **$1,250.00**
Price: Left-hand, about **$1,290.00**

UNIQUE MODEL 96U TARGET PISTOL

Caliber: 22 LR, 5- or 6-shot magazine. **Barrel:** 5.9". **Weight:** 40.2 oz. **Length:** 11.2" overall. **Grips:** French walnut. Target style with thumbrest and adjustable shelf. **Sights:** Blade front, micrometer rear mounted on frame. **Features:** Designed for Sport Pistol and Standard U.I.T. shooting. External hammer; fully adjustable and movable trigger; dry-firing device. Introduced 1997. Imported from France by Nygord Precision Products.
Price: **$1,350.00**

WALTHER GSP MATCH PISTOL

Caliber: 22 LR, 32 S&W Long (GSP-C), 5-shot magazine. **Barrel:** 4.22". **Weight:** 44.8 oz. (22 LR), 49.4 oz. (32). **Length:** 11.8" overall. **Grips:** Walnut. **Sights:** Post front, match rear adjustable for windage and elevation. **Features:** Available with either 2.2-lb. (1000 gm) or 3-lb. (1360 gm) trigger. Spare magazine, barrel weight, tools supplied. Imported from Germany by Nygord Precision Products.
Price: GSP, with case. **$1,495.00**
Price: GSP-C, with case. **$1,595.00**

HANDGUNS — DOUBLE ACTION REVOLVERS, SERVICE & SPORT

Includes models suitable for hunting and competitive courses of fire, both police and international.

Armscor M-200DC

Comanche III

Medusa Model 47

ARMSCOR M-200DC REVOLVER
Caliber: 38 Spec., 6-shot cylinder. **Barrel:** 2-1/2", 4". **Weight:** 22 oz. (2-1/2" barrel). **Length:** 7-3/8" overall (2-1/2" barrel). **Grips:** Checkered rubber. **Sights:** Blade front, fixed notch rear. **Features:** All-steel construction; floating firing pin, transfer bar ignition; shrouded ejector rod; blue finish. Reintroduced 1996. Imported from the Philippines by K.B.I., Inc.
Price: 2-1/2" **$199.99**
Price: 4" **$205.00**

ARMSPORT MODEL 4540 REVOLVER
Caliber: 38 Special. **Barrel:** 4". **Weight:** 32 oz **Length:** 9" overall. **Sights:** Fixed rear, blade front. **Features:** Ventilated rib; blued finish. Imported from Argentina by Armsport Inc.
Price: **$140.00**

COMANCHE I, II, III DA REVOLVERS
Features: Adjustable sights. Blue or stainless finish. Distributed by SGS Importers.
Price: I 22 LR, 6" bbl, 9-shot, blue **$231.95**
Price: I 22LR, 6" bbl, 9-shot, stainless **$248.95**
Price: II 38 Special, 4" bbl, 6-shot, blue **$214.95**
Price: II 38 Special, 4" bbl, 6-shot, stainless **$231.95**
Price: III 357 Mag, 3", 4", 6" bbl, 6-shot, blue. **$248.95**
Price: III 357 Mag, 3", 4", 6" bbl, 6-shot, stainless **$264.95**

EAA STANDARD GRADE REVOLVERS
Caliber: 38 Spec., 6-shot; 357 magnum, 6-shot. **Barrel:** 2", 4". **Weight:** 38 oz. (22 rimfire, 4"). **Length:** 8.8" overall (4" bbl.). **Grips:** Rubber with finger grooves. **Sights:** Blade front, fixed or adjustable on rimfires; fixed only on 32, 38. **Features:** Swing-out cylinder; hammer block safety; blue finish. Introduced 1991. Imported from Germany by European American Armory.
Price: 38 Special 2" **$249.00**
Price: 38 Special, 4" **$259.00**
Price: 357 Magnum, 2" **$259.00**
Price: 357 Magnum, 4" **$279.00**

MEDUSA MODEL 47 REVOLVER
Caliber: Most 9mm, 38 and 357 caliber cartridges; 6-shot cylinder. **Barrel:** 2-1/2", 3", 4", 5", 6"; fluted. **Weight:** 39 oz. **Length:** 10" overall (4" barrel). **Grips:** Gripper-style rubber. **Sights:** Changeable front blades, fully adjustable rear. **Features:** Patented extractor allows gun to chamber, fire and extract over 25 different cartridges in the .355 to .357 range, without half-moon clips. Steel frame and cylinder; match quality barrel. Matte blue finish. Introduced 1996. Made in U.S.A. by Phillips & Rogers, Inc.
Price: **$899.00**

ROSSI MODEL 351/352 REVOLVERS
Caliber: 38 Special +P, 5-shot. **Barrel:** 2". **Weight:** 24 oz. **Length:** 6-1/2" overall. **Grips:** Rubber. **Sights:** Blade front, fixed rear. **Features:** Patented key-lock Taurus Security System; forged steel frame handles +P ammunition. Introduced 2001. Imported by BrazTech/Taurus.
Price: Model 351 (blued finish) **$298.00**
Price: Model 352 (stainless finish) **$345.00**

ROSSI MODEL 461/462 REVOLVERS
Caliber: 357 Magnum +P, 6-shot. **Barrel:** 2". **Weight:** 26 oz. **Length:** 6-1/2" overall. **Grips:** Rubber. **Sights:** Fixed. **Features:** Single/double action. Patented key-lock Taurus Security System; forged steel frame handles +P ammunition. Introduced 2001. Imported by BrazTech/Taurus.
Price: Model 461 (blued finish) **$298.00**
Price: Model 462 (stainless finish) **$345.00**

ROSSI MODEL 971/972 REVOLVERS
Caliber: 357 Magnum +P, 6-shot. **Barrel:** 4", 6". **Weight:** 40-44 oz. **Length:** 8-1/2" or 10-1/2" overall. **Grips:** Rubber. **Sights:** Fully adjustable. **Features:** Single/double action. Patented key-lock Taurus Security System; forged steel frame handles +P ammunition. Introduced 2001. Imported by BrazTech/Taurus.
Price: Model 971 (blued finish, 4" barrel) **$345.00**
Price: Model 972 (stainless steel finish, 6" barrel) **$391.00**

Rossi Model 851
Similar to Model 971/972, chambered for 38 Special +P. Blued finish, 4" barrel. Introduced 2001. From BrazTech/Taurus.
Price: **$298.00**

RUGER GP-100 REVOLVERS
Caliber: 38 Spec., 357 Mag., 6-shot. **Barrel:** 3", 3" full shroud, 4", 4" full shroud, 6", 6" full shroud. **Weight:** 3" barrel—35 oz., 3" full shroud—36 oz., 4" barrel—37 oz., 4" full shroud—38 oz. **Sights:** Fixed; adjustable on 4" full shroud, all 6" barrels. **Grips:** Ruger Santoprene Cushioned Grip with Goncalo Alves inserts. **Features:** Uses action, frame incorporating improvements and features of both the Security-Six and Redhawk revolvers. Full length, short ejector shroud. Satin blue and stainless steel.

Ruger GP161

Ruger KSRH-7

Ruger KSP-821

Smith & Wesson Model 10

Price: KSP-3231X (3-1/16", 32 H&R), 30 oz. **$482.00**
Price: KSP-321X (2-1/4", 357 Mag.). **$482.00**
Price: KSP331X (3-1/16", 357 Mag.) **$482.00**
Price: KSP3241X (32 Mag., 4" bbl) **$482.00**

RUGER REDHAWK

Caliber: 44 Rem. Mag., 45 Colt, 6-shot. **Barrel:** 5-1/2", 7-1/2". **Weight:** About 54 oz. (7-1/2" bbl.). **Length:** 13" overall (7-1/2" barrel). **Grips:** Square butt cushioned grip panels. **Sights:** Interchangeable Patridge-type front, rear adjustable for windage and elevation. **Features:** Stainless steel, brushed satin finish, blued ordnance steel. 9-1/2" sight radius. Introduced 1979.

Price: Blued, 44 Mag., 5-1/2" RH-445, 7-1/2" RH-44 . . . . **$585.00**
Price: Blued, 44 Mag., 7-1/2" RH44R, with scope mount, rings . . **$625.00**
Price: Stainless, 44 Mag., KRH445, 5-1/2", 7-1/2" KRH-44 . . . . . **$645.00**
Price: Stainless, 44 Mag., 7-1/2", with scope mount, rings
KRH-44R. **$685.00**
Price: Stainless, 45 Colt, KRH455, 5-1/2", 7-1/2" KRH-45 . . . . . . **$645.00**
Price: Stainless, 45 Colt, 7-1/2", with scope mount and rings
KRH-45R. **$685.00**

Price: GP-141 (357, 4" full shroud, adj. sights, blue) **$499.00**
Price: GP-160 (357, 6", adj. sights, blue) **$499.00**
Price: GP-161 (357, 6" full shroud, adj. sights, blue), 46 oz. **$499.00**
Price: GPF-331 (357, 3" full shroud) **$489.00**
Price: GPF-340 (357, 4") **$489.00**
Price: GPF-341 (357, 4" full shroud) **$489.00**
Price: KGP-141 (357, 4" full shroud, adj. sights, stainless) **$539.00**
Price: KGP-160 (357, 6", adj. sights, stainless), 43 oz. **$539.00**
Price: KGP-161 (357, 6" full shroud, adj. sights, stainless) 46 oz. **$539.00**
Price: KGPF-330 (357, 3", stainless) **$529.00**
Price: KGPF-331 (357, 3" full shroud, stainless) **$529.00**
Price: KGPF-340 (357, 4", stainless), KGPF-840 (38 Special) . . **$529.00**
Price: KGPF-341 (357, 4" full shroud, stainless) **$529.00**
Price: KGPF-840 (38 Special, 4", stainless). **$529.00**

Ruger SP101 Double-Action-Only Revolver

Similar to standard SP101 except double-action-only with no single-action sear notch. Spurless hammer for snag-free handling, floating firing pin and Ruger's patented transfer bar safety system. Available with 2-1/4" barrel in 357 Magnum. Weighs 25 oz., overall length 7.06". Natural brushed satin, high-polish stainless steel. Introduced 1993.
Price: KSP321XL (357 Mag.) **$482.00**

RUGER SP101 REVOLVERS

Caliber: 22 LR, 32 H&R Mag., 6-shot; 38 Spec. +P, 357 Mag., 5-shot. **Barrel:** 2-1/4", 3-1/16", 4". **Weight:** (38 & 357 mag models) 2-1/4"—25 oz.; 3-1/16"—27 oz. **Sights:** Adjustable on 22, 32, fixed on others. **Grips:** Ruger Cushioned Grip with inserts. **Features:** Incorporates improvements and features found in the GP-100 revolvers into a compact, small frame, double-action revolver. Full-length ejector shroud. Stainless steel only. Introduced 1988.
Price: KSP-821X (2-1/4", 38 Spec.) **$482.00**
Price: KSP-831X (3-1/16", 38 Spec.) **$482.00**
Price: KSP-241X (4" heavy bbl.), 22 LR), 34 oz. **$482.00**

Ruger Super Redhawk Revolver

Similar to standard Redhawk except has heavy extended frame with Ruger Integral Scope Mounting System on wide topstrap. Also available 454 Casull and 480 Ruger. Wide hammer spur lowered for better scope clearance. Incorporates mechanical design features and improvements of GP-100. Choice of 7-1/2" or 9-1/2" barrel, both ramp front sight base with Redhawk-style Interchangeable Insert sight blades, adjustable rear sight. Comes with Ruger "Cushioned Grip" panels with wood panels. Target gray stainless steel. Introduced 1987.
Price: KSRH-7 (7-1/2"), KSRH-9 (9-1/2"), 44 Mag **$685.00**
Price: KSRH-7454 (7-1/2") 454 Casull, 9-1/2 KSRH-9454 . . . . . . **$775.00**
Price: KSRH-7480 (7-1/2") 480 Ruger **$775.00**
Price: KSRH-9480 (9-1/2") 480 Ruger **$775.00**

SMITH & WESSON MODEL 10 M&P HB REVOLVER

Caliber: 38 Spec., 6-shot. **Barrel:** 4". **Weight:** 33.5 oz. **Length:** 9-5/16" overall. **Grips:** Uncle Mike's Combat soft rubber; square butt. **Sights:** Fixed; ramp front, square notch rear.
Price: Blue **$496.00**

Smith & Wesson Model 14

Smith & Wesson Model 36LS

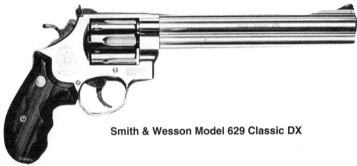

Smith & Wesson Model 629 Classic DX

Smith & Wesson Model 65LS

SMITH & WESSON COMMEMORATIVE MODEL 29

Features: Reflects original Model 29: 6-1/2" barrel, four-screw side plate, over-sized target grips, red vamp front and black blade rear sights, 150th Anniversary logo, engraved, gold-plated, blue, in wood presentation case. Limited.
Price: . . . . **NA**

SMITH & WESSON MODEL 629 REVOLVERS

Caliber: 44 Magnum, 44 S&W Special, 6-shot. **Barrel:** 5", 6", 8-3/8". **Weight:** 47 oz. (6" bbl.). **Length:** 11-3/8" overall (6" bbl.). **Grips:** Soft rubber; wood optional. **Sights:** 1/8" red ramp front, white outline rear, internal lock, adjustable for windage and elevation.
Price: Model 629, 4". **$717.00**
Price: Model 629, 6". **$739.00**
Price: Model 629, 8-3/8" barrel. **$756.00**

Smith & Wesson Model 629 Classic Revolver

Similar to standard Model 629, full-lug 5", 6-1/2" or 8-3/8" barrel, chamfered front of cylinder, interchangeable red ramp front sight with adjustable white outline rear, Hogue grips with S&W monogram, frame is drilled and tapped for scope mounting. Factory accurizing and endurance packages. Overall length with 5" barrel is 10-1/2"; weighs 51 oz. Introduced 1990.
Price: Model 629 Classic (stainless), 5", 6-1/2" **$768.00**
Price: As above, 8-3/8". **$793.00**
Price: Model 629 with HiViz front sight. **$814.00**

Smith & Wesson Model 629 Classic DX Revolver

Similar to Model 629 Classic, offered only with 6-1/2" or 8-3/8" full-lug barrel, five front sights: red ramp, black Patridge, black Patridge with gold bead, black ramp, black Patridge with white dot, white outline rear sight, adjustable sight, internal lock. Hogue combat-style and wood round butt grip. Introduced 1991.
Price: Model 629 Classic DX, 6-1/2" **$986.00**
Price: As above, 8-3/8". **$1,018.00**

SMITH & WESSON MODEL 37 CHIEF'S SPECIAL & AIRWEIGHT

Caliber: 38 Spec. +P, 5-shot. **Barrel:** 1-7/8". **Weight:** 19-1/2 oz. (2" bbl.); 13-1/2 oz. (Airweight). **Length:** 6-1/2" (round butt). **Grips:** Round butt soft rubber. **Sights:** Fixed, serrated ramp front, square notch rear. Glass beaded finish.
Price: Model 37. . . . . **$523.00**

Smith & Wesson Model 36LS, 60LS LadySmith

Similar to standard Model 36. 1-7/8" barrel, 38 Special. Smooth, contoured rosewood grips with S&W monogram. Speedloader cutout. Comes in a fitted carry/storage case. Introduced 1989.
Price: Model 36LS **$518.00**
Price: Model 60LS, 2-1/8" barrel stainless, 357 Magnum **$566.00**

SMITH & WESSON MODEL 60 CHIEF'S SPECIAL

Caliber: 357 Magnum, 5-shot. **Barrel:** 2-1/8" or 3". **Weight:** 24 oz. **Length:** 7-1/2 overall (3" barrel). **Grips:** Rounded butt synthetic grips. **Sights:** Fixed, serrated ramp front, square notch rear. **Features:** Stainless steel construction. 3" full lug barrel, adjustable sights, internal lock. Made in U.S.A. by Smith & Wesson.
Price: 2-1/8" barrel **$541.00**
Price: 3" barrel **$574.00**

SMITH & WESSON MODEL 65

Caliber: 357 Mag. and 38 Spec., 6-shot. **Barrel:** 4". **Weight:** 34 oz. **Length:** 9-5/16" overall (4" bbl.). **Grips:** Uncle Mike's Combat. **Sights:** 1/8" serrated ramp front, fixed square notch rear. **Features:** Heavy barrel. Stainless steel construction. Internal lock.
Price: **$531.00**

SMITH & WESSON
MODEL 317 AIRLITE, 317 LADYSMITH REVOLVERS

Caliber: 22 LR, 8-shot. **Barrel:** 1-7/8" 3". **Weight:** 9.9 oz. **Length:** 6-3/16" overall. **Grips:** Dymondwood Boot or Uncle Mike's Boot. **Sights:** Serrated ramp front, fixed notch rear. **Features:** Aluminum alloy, carbon and stainless steels, and titanium construction. Short spur hammer, smooth combat trigger. Clear Cote finish. Introduced 1997. Made in U.S.A. by Smith & Wesson.
Price: With Uncle Mike's Boot grip **$550.00**
Price: With DymondWood Boot grip, 3" barrel, HiViz front sight, internal lock. **$600.00**
Price: Model 317 LadySmith (DymondWood only, comes with display case) **$596.00**

**Smith & Wesson
Model 317 AirLite**

**Smith & Wesson Model 586,
686 Distinguished Combat**

Smith & Wesson Model 625

Smith & Wesson Model 637 Airweight Revolver

Similar to the Model 37 Airweight except has alloy frame, stainless steel barrel, cylinder and yoke; rated for 38 Spec. +P; Uncle Mike's Boot Grip. Weighs 15 oz. Introduced 1996. Made in U.S.A. by Smith & Wesson.

Price: **$548.00**

SMITH & WESSON MODEL 64 STAINLESS M&P

Caliber: 38 Spec. +P, 6-shot. **Barrel:** 2", 3", 4". **Weight:** 34 oz. **Length:** 9-5/16" overall. **Grips:** Soft rubber. **Sights:** Fixed, 1/8" serrated ramp front, square notch rear. **Features:** Satin finished stainless steel, square butt.

Price: 2" **$522.00**
Price: 3", 4" **$532.00**

SMITH & WESSON MODEL 65LS LADYSMITH

Caliber: 357 Magnum, 38 Spec. +P, 6-shot. **Barrel:** 3". **Weight:** 31 oz. **Length:** 7.94" overall. **Grips:** Rosewood, round butt. **Sights:** Serrated ramp front, fixed notch rear. **Features:** Stainless steel with frosted finish. Smooth combat trigger, service hammer, shrouded ejector rod. Comes with case. Introduced 1992.

Price: **$584.00**

SMITH & WESSON MODEL 66 STAINLESS COMBAT MAGNUM

Caliber: 357 Mag. and 38 Spec. +P, 6-shot. **Barrel:** 2-1/2", 4", 6". **Weight:** 36 oz. (4" barrel). **Length:** 9-9/16" overall. **Grips:** Soft rubber. **Sights:** Red ramp front, micro-click rear adjustable for windage and elevation. **Features:** Satin finish stainless steel. Internal lock.

Price: 2-1/2" **$590.00**
Price: 4" **$579.00**
Price: 6" **$608.00**

SMITH & WESSON MODEL 67 COMBAT MASTERPIECE

Caliber: 38 Special, 6-shot. **Barrel:** 4". **Weight:** 32 oz. **Length:** 9-5/16" overall. **Grips:** Soft rubber. **Sights:** Red ramp front, micro-click rear adjustable for windage and elevation. **Features:** Stainless steel with satin finish. Smooth combat trigger, semi-target hammer. Introduced 1994.

Price: **$585.00**

Smith & Wesson Model 686 Magnum PLUS Revolver

Similar to the Model 686 except has 7-shot cylinder, 2-1/2", 4" or 6" barrel. Weighs 34-1/2 oz., overall length 7-1/2" (2-1/2" barrel). Hogue rubber grips. Internal lock. Introduced 1996. Made in U.S.A. by Smith & Wesson.

Price: 2-1/2" barrel **$631.00**
Price: 4" barrel **$653.00**
Price: 6" barrel **$663.00**

SMITH & WESSON MODEL 625 REVOLVER

Caliber: 45 ACP, 6-shot. **Barrel:** 5". **Weight:** 46 oz. **Length:** 11.375" overall. **Grips:** Soft rubber; wood optional. **Sights:** Patridge front on ramp, S&W micrometer click rear adjustable for windage and elevation. **Features:** Stainless steel construction with .400" semi-target hammer, .312" smooth combat trigger; full lug barrel. Glass beaded finish. Introduced 1989.

Price: 5" **$745.00**
Price: 4" with internal lock **$745.00**

SMITH & WESSON MODEL 640 CENTENNIAL DA ONLY

Caliber: 357 Mag., 38 Spec. +P, 5-shot. **Barrel:** 2-1/8". **Weight:** 25 oz. **Length:** 6-3/4" overall. **Grips:** Uncle Mike's Boot Grip. **Sights:** Serrated ramp front, fixed notch rear. **Features:** Stainless steel. Fully concealed hammer, snag-proof smooth edges. Internal lock. Introduced 1995 in 357 Magnum.

Price: **$599.00**

SMITH & WESSON MODEL 617 K-22 MASTERPIECE

Caliber: 22 LR, 6- or 10-shot. **Barrel:** 4", 6", 8-3/8". **Weight:** 42 oz. (4" barrel). **Length:** NA. **Grips:** Soft rubber. **Sights:** Patridge front, adjustable rear. Drilled and tapped for scope mount. **Features:** Stainless steel with satin finish; 4" has .312" smooth trigger, .375" semi-target hammer; 6" has either .312" combat or .400" serrated trigger, .375" semi-target or .500" target hammer; 8-3/8" with .400" serrated trigger, .500" target hammer. Introduced 1990.

Price: 4" **$644.00**
Price: 6", target hammer, target trigger **$625.00**
Price: 6", 10-shot **$669.00**
Price: 8-3/8", 10 shot **$679.00**

SMITH & WESSON MODEL 610 CLASSIC HUNTER REVOLVER

Caliber: 10mm, 40 S&W, 6-shot cylinder. **Barrel:** 6-1/2" full lug. **Weight:** 52 oz. **Length:** 12" overall. **Grips:** Hogue rubber combat. **Sights:** Interchangeable blade front, micro-click rear adjustable for windage and elevation. **Features:** Stainless steel construction; target hammer, target trigger; unfluted cylinder; drilled and tapped for scope mounting. Introduced 1998.

Price: **$785.00**

SMITH & WESSON MODEL 340 PD AIRLITE Sc CENTENNIAL

Caliber: 357 Magnum, 38 Spec. +P, 5-shot. **Barrel:** 1-7/8". **Grips:** Rounded butt grip. **Sights:** HiViz front. **Features:** Synthetic grip, internal lock. Blue.

Price: **$799.00**

SMITH & WESSON MODEL 360 PD AIRLITE Sc CHIEF'S SPECIAL

Caliber: 357 Magnum, 38 Spec. +P, 5-shot. **Barrel:** 1-7/8". **Grips:** Rounded butt grip. **Sights:** Fixed. **Features:** Synthetic grip, internal lock. Stainless.

Price: Red ramp front **$767.00**
Price: HiViz front **$781.00**

Smith & Wesson
Model 340 PD Airlite Sc

Smith & Wesson Model
386 PD Airlite SC

Smith & Wesson Model 360 PD
Airlite SC Chief's Special

Smith & Wesson Model 442

SMITH & WESSON MODEL 386 PD AIRLITE Sc

Caliber: 357 Magnum, 38 Spec. +P, 7-shot. **Barrel:** 2-1/2". **Grips:** Rounded butt grip. **Sights:** Adjustable, HiViz front. **Features:** Synthetic grip, internal lock.
Price: Blue **$815.00**

SMITH & WESSON MODEL 331, 332 AIRLITE Ti REVOLVERS

Caliber: 32 H&R Mag., 6-shot. **Barrel:** 1-7/8". **Weight:** 11.2 oz. (with wood grip). **Length:** 6-15/16" overall. **Grips:** Uncle Mike's Boot or Dymondwood Boot. **Sights:** Black serrated ramp front, fixed notch rear. **Features:** Aluminum alloy frame, barrel shroud and yoke; titanium cylinder; stainless steel barrel liner. Matte finish. Introduced 1999. Made in U.S.A. by Smith & Wesson.
Price: Model 331 Chiefs **$716.00**
Price: Model 332, internal lock **$734.00**

SMITH & WESSON MODEL 337 CHIEF'S SPECIAL AIRLITE Ti

Caliber: 38 Spec. +P, 5-shot. **Barrel:** 1-7/8". **Weight:** 11.2 oz. (Dymondwood grips). **Length:** 6-5/16" overall. **Grips:** Uncle Mike's Boot or Dymondwood Boot. **Sights:** Black serrated front, fixed notch rear. **Features:** Aluminum alloy frame, barrel shroud and yoke; titanium cylinder; stainless steel barrel liner. Matte finish. Introduced 1999. Made in U.S.A. by Smith & Wesson.
Price: **$716.00**

SMITH & WESSON MODEL 342 CENTENNIAL AIRLITE Ti

Caliber: 38 Spec. +P, 5-shot. **Barrel:** 1-7/8". **Weight:** 11.3 oz. (Dymondwood stocks). **Length:** 6-15/16" overall. **Grips:** Uncle Mike's Boot or Dymondwood Boot. **Sights:** Black serrated ramp front, fixed notch rear. **Features:** Aluminum alloy frame, barrel shroud and yoke; titanium cylinder; stainless steel barrel liner. Shrouded hammer. Matte finish. Internal lock. Introduced 1999. Made in U.S.A. by Smith & Wesson.
Price: **$734.00**

Smith & Wesson Model 442 Centennial Airweight

Similar to Model 640 Centennial, alloy frame giving weighs 15.8 oz. Chambered for 38 Special +P, 1-7/8" carbon steel barrel; carbon steel cylinder; concealed hammer; Uncle Mike's Boot grip. Fixed square notch rear sight, serrated ramp front. DA only, glass beaded finish. Introduced 1993.
Price: Blue **$547.00**

SMITH & WESSON MODEL 638 AIRWEIGHT BODYGUARD

Caliber: 38 Spec. +P, 5-shot. **Barrel:** 1-7/8". **Weight:** 15 oz. **Length:** 6-15/16" overall. **Grips:** Uncle Mike's Boot grip. **Sights:** Serrated ramp front, fixed notch rear. **Features:** Alloy frame, stainless cylinder and barrel; shrouded hammer. Glass beaded finish. Introduced 1997. Made in U.S.A. by Smith & Wesson.
Price: With Uncle Mike's Boot grip **$564.00**

Smith & Wesson Model 642 Airweight Revolver

Similar to Model 442 Centennial Airweight, stainless steel barrel, cylinder and yoke with matte finish; Uncle Mike's Boot Grip; DA only; weighs 15.8 oz. Introduced 1996. Made in U.S.A. by Smith & Wesson.
Price: **$571.00**

Smith & Wesson Model 642LS LadySmith Revolver

Same as Model 642 except has smooth combat wood grips, comes with deluxe soft case; Dymondwood grip; aluminum alloy frame, stainless cylinder, barrel and yoke; frosted matte finish. Weighs 15.8 oz. Introduced 1996. Made in U.S.A. by Smith & Wesson.
Price: 1-7/8" **$597.00**

SMITH & WESSON MODEL 649 BODYGUARD REVOLVER

Caliber: 357 Mag., 38 Spec. +P, 5-shot. **Barrel:** 2-1/8". **Weight:** 20 oz. **Length:** 6-5/16" overall. **Grips:** Uncle Mike's Combat. **Sights:** Black pinned ramp front, fixed notch rear. **Features:** Stainless steel construction; shrouded hammer; smooth combat trigger. Internal lock. Made in U.S.A. by Smith & Wesson.
Price: **$594.00**

HANDGUNS

Smith & Wesson Model 649

Smith & Wesson Model 696

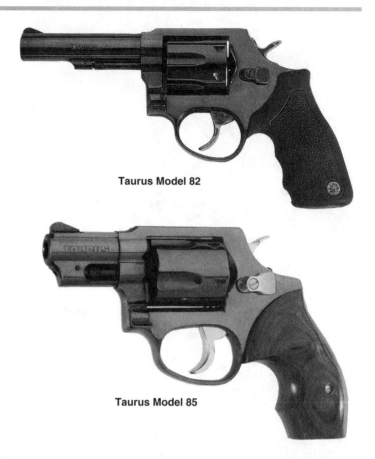

Taurus Model 82

Taurus Model 85

SMITH & WESSON MODEL 657 REVOLVER

Caliber: 41 Mag., 6-shot. **Barrel:** 7-1/2" full lug. **Weight:** 48 oz. **Grips:** Soft rubber. **Sights:** Pinned 1/8" red ramp front, micro-click rear adjustable for windage and elevation. Target hammer, drilled and tapped, unfluted cylinder. **Features:** Stainless steel construction.
Price: **$706.00**

SMITH & WESSON MODEL 696 REVOLVER

Caliber: 44 Spec., 5-shot. **Barrel:** 3". **Weight:** 35.5 oz. **Length:** 8-1/4" overall. **Grips:** Uncle Mike's Combat. **Sights:** Red ramp front, click adjustable white outline rear. **Features:** Stainless steel construction; round butt frame; satin finish. Introduced 1997. Made in U.S.A. by Smith & Wesson.
Price: **$620.00**

TAURUS MODEL 17 "TRACKER"

NEW! **Caliber:** 17 HMR, 7-shot. **Barrel:** 6". **Weight:** 45.8 oz. **Grips:** Rubber. **Sights:** Adjustable. **Features:** Double action, matte stainless, integral key-lock.
Price: **$391.00**

TAURUS MODEL 17-12 TARGET "SILHOUETTE"

NEW! **Caliber:** 17 HMR, 7-shot. **Barrel:** 12". **Weight:** 57.8 oz. **Grips:** Rubber. **Sights:** Adjustable. **Features:** Vent rib, double action, adjustable main spring and trigger stop. Matte stainless, integral key-lock.
Price: **$414.00**

TAURUS MODEL 63

NEW! **Caliber:** 22 LR, 10 + 1 shot. **Barrel:** 23". **Weight:** 97.9 oz. **Grips:** Premium hardwood. **Sights:** Adjustable. **Features:** Auto loading action, round barrel, manual firing pin block, integral security system lock, trigger guard mounted safety, blue or stainless finish.
Price: .... **$295.00 to $310.00**

TAURUS MODEL 65 REVOLVER

Caliber: 357 Mag., 6-shot. **Barrel:** 4". **Weight:** 38 oz. **Length:** 10-1/2" overall. **Grips:** Soft rubber. **Sights:** Fixed. **Features:** Double action, integral key-lock. Imported by Taurus International.
Price: Blue or matte stainless.................. **$345.00 to $435.00**

Taurus Model 66 Revolver

Similar to Model 65, 4" or 6" barrel, 7-shot cylinder, adjustable rear sight. Integral key-lock action. Imported by Taurus International.
Price: Blue or matte stainless.................. **$345.00 to $495.00**

Taurus Model 66 Silhouette Revolver

Similar to Model 6, 12" barrel, 7-shot cylinder, adjustable sight. Integral key-lock action, blue or matte stainless steel finish, rubber grips. Introduced 2001. Imported by Taurus International.
Price: ....**$414.00 to $461.00**

TAURUS MODEL 82 HEAVY BARREL REVOLVER

Caliber: 38 Spec., 6-shot. **Barrel:** 4", heavy. **Weight:** 36.5 oz. **Length:** 9-1/4" overall (4" bbl.). **Grips:** Soft black rubber. **Sights:** Serrated ramp front, square notch rear. **Features:** Double action, solid rib, integral key-lock. Imported by Taurus International.
Price: Blue or matte stainless.................. **$325.00 to $375.00**

TAURUS MODEL 85 REVOLVER

Caliber: 38 Spec., 5-shot. **Barrel:** 2". **Weight:** 17-24.5 oz., titanium 13.5-15.4 oz. **Grips:** Rubber, rosewood or mother-of-pearl. **Sights:** Ramp front, square notch rear. **Features:** Blue, matte stainless, blue with gold accents, stainless with gold accents; rated for +P ammo. Integral key-lock. Introduced 1980. Imported by Taurus International.
Price: ....**$345.00 to $460.00**
Price: Total Titanium................................ **$530.00**

TAURUS MODEL 94 REVOLVER

Caliber: 22 LR, 9-shot cylinder. **Barrel:** 2", 4", 5". **Weight:** 18.5-27.5 oz. **Grips:** Soft black rubber. **Sights:** Serrated ramp front, click-adjustable rear. **Features:** Double action, integral key-lock. Introduced 1989. Imported by Taurus International.
Price: Blue **$325.00**
Price: Matte stainless **$375.00**
Price: Model 94 UL, forged aluminum alloy, 18-18.5 oz. **$365.00**
Price: As above, stainless **$410.00**

Taurus Model 94UL

Taurus Model 44

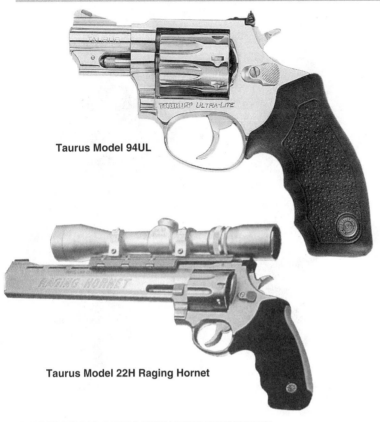

Taurus Model 22H Raging Hornet

Taurus Model 415

TAURUS MODEL 22H RAGING HORNET REVOLVER
Caliber: 22 Hornet, 8-shot. **Barrel:** 10". **Weight:** 50 oz. **Length:** 6.5" overall. **Grips:** Soft black rubber. **Sights:** Fully adjustable, scope mount base included. **Features:** Ventilated rib, stainless steel construction with matte finish. Double action, integral key-lock. Introduced 1999. Imported by Taurus International.
Price: **$898.00**

TAURUS MODEL 30C RAGING THIRTY
Caliber: 30 carbine, 8-shot. **Barrel:** 10". **Weight:** 72.3 oz. **Grips:** Soft black rubber. **Sights:** Adjustable. **Features:** Double action, ventilated rib, matte stainless, comes with five "Stellar" full-moon clips, integral key-lock.
Price: **$898.00**

TAURUS MODEL 44 REVOLVER
Caliber: 44 Mag., 6-shot. **Barrel:** 4", 6-1/2", 8-3/8". **Weight:** 44-3/4 oz. **Grips:** Rubber. **Sights:** Adjustable. **Features:** Double action. Integral key-lock. Introduced 1994. Imported by Taurus International.
Price: Blue or stainless steel .... **$445.00 to $575.00**

TAURUS MODEL 217 TARGET "SILHOUETTE"
Caliber: 218 Bee, 8-shot. **Barrel:** 12". **Weight:** 52.3 oz. **Grips:** Rubber. **Sights:** Adjustable. **Features:** Double action, ventilated rib, adjustable mainspring and trigger stop, matte stainless, integral key-lock.
Price: **$461.00**

TAURUS MODEL 218 RAGING BEE
Caliber: 218 Bee, 7-shot. **Barrel:** 10". **Weight:** 74.9 oz. **Grips:** Rubber. **Sights:** Adjustable rear. **Features:** Ventilated rib, adjustable action, matte stainless, integral key-lock.
Price: **$898.00**

TAURUS MODEL 415 REVOLVER
Caliber: 41 Mag., 5-shot. **Barrel:** 2-1/2". **Weight:** 30 oz. **Length:** 7-1/8" overall. **Grips:** Rubber. **Sights:** Fixed. **Features:** Stainless steel construction; matte finish; ported barrel. Double action. Integral key-lock. Introduced 1999. Imported by Taurus International.
Price: **$475.00**
Price: Total Titanium **$600.00**

TAURUS MODEL 425/627 TRACKER REVOLVERS
Caliber: 357 Mag., 7-shot; 41 Mag., 5-shot. **Barrel:** 4" and 6". **Weight:** 28.8-40 oz. (titanium) 24.3-28. (6"). **Grips:** Rubber. **Sights:** Fixed front, adjustable rear. **Features:** Double action stainless steel, Shadow Gray or Total Titanium; vent rib (steel models only); integral key-lock action. Imported by Taurus International.
Price: **$500.00**
Price: Total Titanium **$690.00**

TAURUS MODEL 445
Caliber: 44 Special, 5-shot. **Barrel:** 2". **Weight:** 20.3-28.25 oz. **Length:** 6-3/4" overall. **Grips:** Rubber. **Sights:** Ramp front, notch rear. **Features:** Blue or stainless steel. Standard or DAO concealed hammer, optional porting. Introduced 1997. Imported by Taurus International.
Price: .... **$345.00 to $500.00**
Price: Total Titanium 19.8 oz. **$600.00**

TAURUS MODEL 455 "STELLAR TRACKER"
Caliber: 45 ACP, 5-shot. **Barrel:** 2", 4", 6". **Weight:** 28/33/38.4 oz. **Grips:** Rubber. **Sights:** Adjustable. **Features:** Double action, matte stainless, includes five "Stellar" full-moon clips, integral key-lock.
Price: **$525.00**

TAURUS MODEL 460 "TRACKER"
Caliber: 45 Colt, 5-shot. **Barrel:** 4" or 6". **Weight:** 33/38.4 oz. **Grips:** Rubber. **Sights:** Adjustable. **Features:** Double action, ventilated rib, matte stainless steel, comes with five "Stellar" full-moon clips.
Price: **$525.00**

TAURUS MODEL 605 REVOLVER
Caliber: 357 Mag., 5-shot. **Barrel:** 2". **Weight:** 24 oz. **Grips:** Rubber. **Sights:** Fixed. **Features:** Double action, blue or stainless, concealed hammer models DAO, porting optional, integral key-lock. Introduced 1995. Imported by Taurus International.
Price: .... **$345.00 to $405.00**

HANDGUNS

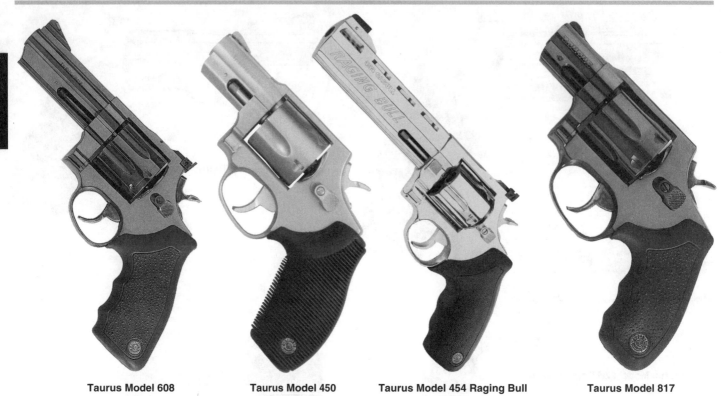

Taurus Model 608   Taurus Model 450   Taurus Model 454 Raging Bull   Taurus Model 817

TAURUS MODEL 608 REVOLVER
Caliber: 357 Mag. 38 Spec., 8-shot. Barrel: 4", 6-1/2", 8-3/8". Weight: 44-57 oz. Length: 9-3/8" overall. Grips: Soft black rubber. Sights: Adjustable. Features: Double action, integral key-lock action. Available in blue or stainless. Introduced 1995. Imported by Taurus International.
Price: . . . . $445.00 to $575.00

TAURUS MODEL 650CIA REVOLVER
Caliber: 357 Magnum, 5-shot. Barrel: 2". Weight: 24.5 oz. Grips: Rubber. Sights: Ramp front, square notch rear. Features: Double-action only, blue or matte stainless steel, integral key-lock, internal hammer. Introduced 2001. From Taurus International.
Price: . . . . $375.00 to $422.00

TAURUS MODEL 651CIA REVOLVER
Caliber: 357 Magnum, 5-shot. Barrel: 2". Weight: 17-24.5 oz. Grips: Rubber. Sights: Fixed. Features: Concealed single action/double action design. Shrouded cockable hammer, blue, matte stainless, Shadow Gray, Total Titanium, integral key-lock.
Price: . . . . $375.00 to $563.00

TAURUS MODEL 450 REVOLVER
Caliber: 45 Colt, 5-shot. Barrel: 2". Weight: 21.2-22.3 oz. Length: 6-5/8" overall. Grips: Rubber. Sights: Ramp front, notch rear. Features: Double action, blue or stainless, ported, integral key-lock. Introduced 1999. Imported by Taurus International.
Price: $470.00
Price: Ultra-Lite (alloy frame) $525.00
Price: Total Titanium, 19.2 oz. $600.00

TAURUS MODEL 444/454/480 RAGING BULL REVOLVERS
Caliber: 44 Mag., 45 LC, 454 Casull, 480 Ruger, 5-shot. Barrel: 5", 6-1/2", 8-3/8". Weight: 53-63 oz. Length: 12" overall (6-1/2" barrel). Grips: Soft black rubber. Sights: Patridge front, adjustable rear. Features: Double action, ventilated rib, ported, integral key-lock. Introduced 1997. Imported by Taurus International.
Price: Blue $785.00
Price: Matte stainless $855.00

TAURUS RAGING BULL MODEL 416
Caliber: 41 Magnum, 6-shot. Barrel: 6-1/2". Weight: 61.9 oz. Grips: Rubber. Sights: Adjustable. Features: Double action, ported, ventilated rib, matte stainless, integral key-lock.
Price: $630.00

TAURUS MODEL 617 REVOLVER
Caliber: 357 Magnum, 7-shot. Barrel: 2". Weight: 28.3 oz. Length: 6-3/4" overall. Grips: Soft black rubber. Sights: Fixed. Features: Double action, blue or matte stainless steel, integral key-lock. Available with porting, concealed hammer. Introduced 1998. Imported by Taurus International.
Price: . . . . $375.00 to $440.00
Price: Total Titanium, 19.9 oz. $600.00

Taurus Model 617ULT Revolver
Similar to Model 617 except aluminum alloy and titanium components, matte stainless finish, integral key-lock action. Weighs 18.5 oz. Available ported or non-ported. Introduced 2001. Imported by Taurus International.
Price: (5-shot cylinder) . . . . $530.00 to $545.00

TAURUS MODEL 817 ULTRA-LITE REVOLVER
Caliber: 38 Spec., 7-shot. Barrel: 2". Weight: 21 oz. Length: 6-1/2" overall. Grips: Soft rubber. Sights: Fixed. Features: Double action, integral key-lock. Introduced 1999. Imported by Taurus International.
Price: Blue $375.00
Price: Blue, ported $395.00
Price: Matte, stainless $420.00
Price: Matte, stainless, ported $440.00

TAURUS MODEL 850CIA REVOLVER
Caliber: 38 Special, 5-shot. Barrel: 2". Weight: 17-24.5 oz. Grips: Rubber. Sights: Ramp front, square notch rear. Features: Double action only, blue or matte stainless steel, rated for +P ammo, integral key-lock, internal hammer. Introduced 2001. From Taurus International.
Price: . . . . $375.00 to $422.00
Price: Total Titanium $563.00

Dan Wesson Firearms
Model 445 Supermag

Taurus Model 941

TAURUS MODEL 851CIA REVOLVER
Caliber: 38 Spec., 5-shot. **Barrel:** 2". **Weight:** 17-24.5 oz. **Grips:** Rubber. **Sights:** Fixed-UL/ULT adjustable. **Features:** Concealed single action/double action design. Shrouded cockable hammer, blue, matte stainless, Total Titanium, blue or stainless UL and ULT, integral key-lock. Rated for +P ammo.
Price: .... **$375.00 to $563.00**

TAURUS MODEL 941 REVOLVER
Caliber: 22 WMR, 8-shot. **Barrel:** 2", 4", 5". **Weight:** 27.5 oz. (4" barrel). **Grips:** Soft black rubber. **Sights:** Serrated ramp front, rear adjustable. **Features:** Double action, integral key-lock. Introduced 1992. Imported by Taurus International.
Price: Blue **$345.00**
Price: Stainless (matte) **$395.00**
Price: Model 941 Ultra Lite, forged aluminum alloy, 2" **$375.00**
Price: As above, stainless **$425.00**

TAURUS MODEL 970/971 TRACKER REVOLVERS
Caliber: 22 LR (Model 970), 22 Magnum (Model 971); 7-shot. **Barrel:** 6". **Weight:** 53.6 oz. **Grips:** Rubber. **Sights:** Adjustable. **Features:** Double barrel, heavy barrel with ventilated rib; matte stainless finish, integral key-lock. Introduced 2001. From Taurus International.
Price: .... **$375.00 to $391.00**

TAURUS MODEL 980/981 SILHOUETTE REVOLVERS
Caliber: 22 LR (Model 980), 22 Magnum (Model 981); 7-shot. **Barrel:** 12". **Weight:** 68 oz. **Grips:** Rubber. **Sights:** Adjustable. **Features:** Double action, heavy barrel with ventilated rib and scope mount, matte stainless finish, integral key-lock. Introduced 2001. From Taurus International.
Price: (Model 980) **$398.00**
Price: (Model 981) **$414.00**

DAN WESSON FIREARMS MODEL 722 SILHOUETTE REVOLVER
Caliber: 22 LR, 6-shot. **Barrel:** 10", vent heavy. **Weight:** 53 oz. **Grips:** Combat style. **Sights:** Patridge-style front, .080" narrow notch rear. **Features:** Single action only. Satin brushed stainless finish. Reintroduced 1997. Made in U.S.A. by Dan Wesson Firearms.
Price: 722 VH10 (vent heavy 10" bbl.) **$888.00**
Price: 722 VH10 SRS1 (Super Ram Silhouette , Bo-Mar sights, front hood, trigger job). **$1,164.00**

DAN WESSON FIREARMS MODEL 3220/73220 TARGET REVOLVER
Caliber: 32-20, 6-shot. **Barrel:** 2.5", 4", 6", 8", 10" standard vent, vent heavy. **Weight:** 47 oz. (6" VH). **Length:** 11.25" overall. **Grips:** Hogue Gripper rubber (walnut, exotic hardwoods optional). **Sights:** Red ramp interchangeable front, fully adjustable rear. **Features:** Bright blue (3220) or stainless (73220). Reintroduced 1997. Made in U.S.A. by Dan Wesson Firearms.
Price: 3220 VH2.5 (blued, 2.5" vent heavy bbl.). **$643.00**
Price: 73220 VH10 (stainless 10" vent heavy bbl.). **$873.00**

DAN WESSON FIREARMS MODEL 40/740 REVOLVERS
Caliber: 357 Maximum, 6-shot. **Barrel:** 4", 6", 8", 10". **Weight:** 72 oz. (8" bbl.). **Length:** 14.3" overall (8" bbl.). **Grips:** Hogue Gripper rubber (walnut or exotic hardwood optional). **Sights:** 1/8" serrated front, fully adjustable rear. **Features:** Blue or stainless steel. Made in U.S.A. by Dan Wesson Firearms.
Price: Blue, 4". **$702.00**
Price: Blue, 6". **$749.00**
Price: Blue, 8". **$795.00**
Price: Blue, 10". **$858.00**
Price: Stainless, 4" **$834.00**
Price: Stainless, 6" **$892.00**
Price: Stainless, 8" slotted **$1,024.00**
Price: Stainless, 10" **$998.00**
Price: 4", 6", 8" Compensated, blue .... **$749.00 to $885.00**
Price: As above, stainless .... **$893.00 to $1,061.00**

Dan Wesson Firearms Model 414/7414 and 445/7445 SuperMag Revolvers
Similar size and weight as Model 40 revolvers. Chambered for 414 SuperMag or 445 SuperMag cartridge. Barrel lengths of 4", 6", 8", 10". Contact maker for complete price list. Reintroduced 1997. Made in the U.S. by Dan Wesson Firearms.
Price: 4", vent heavy, blue or stainless. **$904.00**
Price: 8", vent heavy, blue or stainless. **$1,026.00**
Price: 10", vent heavy, blue or stainless. **$1,103.00**
Price: Compensated models .... **$965.00 to $1,149.00**

DAN WESSON FIREARMS MODEL 22/722 REVOLVERS
Caliber: 22 LR, 22 WMR, 6-shot. **Barrel:** 2-1/2", 4", 6", 8" or 10"; interchangeable. **Weight:** 36 oz. (2-1/2"), 44 oz. (6"). **Length:** 9-1/4" overall (4" barrel). **Grips:** Hogue Gripper rubber (walnut, exotic woods optional). **Sights:** 1/8" serrated, interchangeable front, white outline rear adjustable for windage and elevation. **Features:** Built on the same frame as the Wesson 357; smooth, wide trigger with over-travel adjustment, wide spur hammer, with short double-action travel. Available in blue or stainless steel. Reintroduced 1997. Contact Dan Wesson Firearms for complete price list.
Price: 22 VH2.5/722 VH2.5 (blued or stainless 2-1/2" bbl.) **$551.00**
Price: 22VH10/722 VH10 (blued or stainless 10" bbl.). **$750.00**

Dan Wesson 722M Small Frame Revolver
Similar to Model 22/722 except chambered for 22 WMR. Blued or stainless finish, 2-1/2", 4", 6", 8" or 10" barrels.
Price: Blued or stainless finish .... **$643.00 to $873.00**

DAN WESSON FIREARMS MODEL 15/715 and 32/732 REVOLVERS
Caliber: 32-20, 32 H&R Mag. (Model 32), 357 Mag. (Model 15). **Barrel:** 2-1/2", 4", 6", 8" (M32), 2-1/2", 4", 6", 8", 10" (M15); vent heavy. **Weight:** 36 oz. (2-1/2" barrel). **Length:** 9-1/4" overall (4" barrel). **Grips:** Checkered, interchangeable. **Sights:** 1/8" serrated front, fully adjustable rear. **Features:** New Generation Series. Interchangeable barrels; wide, smooth trigger, wide hammer spur; short double-action travel. Available in blue or stainless. Reintroduced 1997. Made in U.S.A. by Dan Wesson Firearms. Contact maker for full list of models.
Price: Model 15/715, 2-1/2" (blue or stainless). **$551.00**
Price: Model 15/715, 8" (blue or stainless). **$612.00**
Price: Model 15/715, compensated .... **$704.00 to $827.00**
Price: Model 32/732, 4" (blue or stainless). **$674.00**
Price: Model 32/732, 8" (blue or stainless). **$766.00**

HANDGUNS

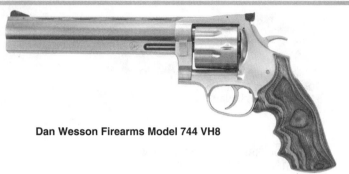

Dan Wesson Firearms Model 744 VH8

**Dan Wesson Firearms
Super Ram Silhouette**

Dan Wesson Firearms Alaskan Guide Special

DAN WESSON FIREARMS MODEL 41/741, 44/744 and 45/745 REVOLVERS

Caliber: 41 Mag., 44 Mag., 45 Colt, 6-shot. **Barrel:** 4", 6", 8", 10"; interchangeable; 4", 6", 8" Compensated. **Weight:** 48 oz. (4"). **Length:** 12" overall (6" bbl.) **Grips:** Smooth. **Sights:** 1/8" serrated front, white outline rear adjustable for windage and elevation. **Features:** Available in blue or stainless steel. Smooth, wide trigger with adjustable over-travel, wide hammer spur. Available in Pistol Pac set also. Reintroduced 1997. Contact Dan Wesson Firearms for complete price list.

Price: 41 Mag., 4", vent heavy (blue or stainless) **$643.00**
Price: 44 Mag., 6", vent heavy (blue or stainless) **$689.00**
Price: 45 Colt, 8", vent heavy (blue or stainless) **$766.00**
Price: Compensated models (all calibers) . . . . **$812.00 to $934.00**

DAN WESSON FIREARMS LARGE FRAME SERIES REVOLVERS

Caliber: 41, 741/41 Magnum; 44, 744/44 Magnum; 45, 745/45 Long Colt; 360, 7360/357; 460, 7460/45. **Barrel:** 2"-10". **Weight:** 49 oz.-69 oz. **Grips:** Standard, Hogue rubber Gripper Grips. **Sights:** Standard front, serrated ramp with color insert. Standard rear, adustable wide notch. Other sight options available. **Features:** Available in blue or stainless steel. Smooth, wide trigger with overtravel, wide hammer spur. Double and single action.

Price: . . . . **$769.00 to $889.00**

DAN WESSON FIREARMS MODEL 360/7360 REVOLVERS

Caliber: 357 Mag. **Barrel:** 4", 6", 8", 10"; vent heavy. **Weight:** 64 oz. (8" barrel). **Grips:** Hogue rubber finger groove. **Sights:** Interchangeable ramp or Patridge front, fully adjustable rear. **Features:** New Generation Large Frame Series. Interchangeable barrels and grips; smooth trigger, wide hammer spur. Blue (360) or stainless (7360). Introduced 1999. Made in U.S.A. by Dan Wesson Firearms.

Price: 4" bbl., blue or stainless **$735.00**
Price: 10" bbl., blue or stainless **$873.00**
Price: Compensated models . . . . **$858.00 to $980.00**

DAN WESSON FIREARMS MODEL 460/7460 REVOLVERS

Caliber: 45 ACP, 45 Auto Rim, 45 Super, 45 Winchester Magnum and 460 Rowland. **Barrel:** 4", 6", 8", 10"; vent heavy. **Weight:** 49 oz. (4" barrel). **Grips:** Hogue rubber finger groove; interchangeable. **Sights:** Interchangeable ramp or Patridge front, fully adjustable rear. **Features:** New Generation Large Frame Series. Shoots five cartridges (45 ACP, 45 Auto Rim, 45 Super, 45 Winchester Magnum and 460 Rowland; six half-moon clips for auto cartridges included). Interchangeable barrels and grips. Available with non-fluted cylinder and Slotted Lightweight barrel shroud. Introduced 1999. Made in U.S.A. by Dan Wesson Firearms.

Price: 4" bbl., blue or stainless **$735.00**
Price: 10" bbl., blue or stainless **$888.00**
Price: Compensated models . . . . **$919.00 to $1,042.00**

DAN WESSON FIREARMS STANDARD SILHOUETTE REVOLVERS

Caliber: 357 SuperMag/Maxi, 41 Mag., 414 SuperMag, 445 SuperMag. **Barrel:** 8", 10". **Weight:** 64 oz. (8" barrel). **Length:** 14.3" overall (8" barrel). **Grips:** Hogue rubber finger groove; interchangeable. **Sights:** Patridge front, fully adjustable rear. **Features:** Interchangeable barrels and grips, fluted or non-fluted cylinder, satin brushed stainless finish. Introduced 1999. Made in U.S.A. by Dan Wesson Firearms.

Price: 357 SuperMag/Maxi, 8" **$1,057.00**
Price: 41 Mag., 10" **$888.00**
Price: 414 SuperMag., 8" **$1,057.00**
Price: 445 SuperMag., 8" **$1,057.00**

Dan Wesson Firearms Super Ram Silhouette Revolver

Similar to Standard Silhouette except has 10 land and groove Laser Coat barrel, Bo-Mar target sights with hooded front, special laser engraving. Fluted or non-fluted cylinder. Introduced 1999. Made in U.S.A. by Dan Wesson Firearms.

Price: 357 SuperMag/Maxi, 414 SuperMag., 445 SuperMag., 8", blue or stainless **$1,364.00**
Price: 41 Magnum, 44 Magnum, 8", blue or stainless **$1,241.00**
Price: 41 Magnum, 44 Magnum, 10", blue or stainless **$1,333.00**

DAN WESSON FIREARMS ALASKAN GUIDE SPECIAL

Caliber: 445 SuperMag, 44 Magnum. **Barrel:** Compensated 4" vent heavy barrel assembly. **Features:** Stainless steel with baked on, non-glare, matte black coating, special laser engraving.

Price: Model 7445 VH4C AGS **$995.00**
Price: Model 744 VH4C AGS **$855.00**

Both classic six-shooters and modern adaptations for hunting and sport.

American Frontier 1871-1872 Open-Top

American Frontier 1851 Mason

Century Model 100

Cimarron 1873 Model P

AMERICAN FRONTIER 1851 NAVY CONVERSION
Caliber: 38, 44. **Barrel:** 5-1/2", 7-1/2", octagon. **Grips:** Varnished walnut, Navy size. **Sights:** Blade front, fixed rear. **Features:** Shoots metallic cartridge ammunition. Non-rebated cylinder; blued steel backstrap and trigger guard; color case-hardened hammer, trigger, ramrod, plunger; no ejector rod assembly. Introduced 1996.
Price: **$795.00**

AMERICAN FRONTIER 1871-1872 OPEN-TOP REVOLVERS
Caliber: 38, 44. **Barrel:** 5-1/2", 7-1/2", 8" round. **Grips:** Varnished walnut. **Sights:** Blade front, fixed rear. **Features:** Reproduction of the early cartridge conversions from percussion. Made for metallic cartridges. High polish blued steel, silver-plated brass backstrap and trigger guard, color case-hardened hammer; straight non-rebated cylinder with naval engagement engraving; stamped with original patent dates. Does not have conversion breechplate.
Price: **$795.00**

AMERICAN FRONTIER RICHARDS 1860 ARMY
Caliber: 38, 44. **Barrel:** 5-1/2", 7-1/2", round. **Grips:** Varnished walnut, Army size. **Sights:** Blade front, fixed rear. **Features:** Shoots metallic cartridge ammunition. Rebated cylinder; available with or without ejector assembly; high-polish blue including backstrap; silver-plated trigger guard; color case-hardened hammer and trigger. Introduced 1996.
Price: **$795.00**

American Frontier 1851 Navy Richards & Mason Conversion
Similar to 1851 Navy Conversion except has Mason ejector assembly. Introduced 1996. Imported from Italy by American Frontier Firearms Mfg.
Price: **$695.00**

CABELA'S MILLENNIUM REVOLVER
Caliber: 45 Colt. **Barrel:** 4-3/4". **Weight:** NA. **Length:** 10" overall. **Grips:** Hardwood. **Sights:** Blade front, hammer notch rear. **Features:** Matte black finish; unpolished brass accents. Introduced 2001. From Cabela's.
Price: **$219.99**

CENTURY GUN DIST. MODEL 100 SINGLE-ACTION
Caliber: 30-30, 375 Win., 444 Marlin, 45-70, 50-70. **Barrel:** 6-1/2" (standard), 8", 10". **Weight:** 6 lbs. (loaded). **Length:** 15" overall (8" bbl.). **Grips:** Smooth walnut. **Sights:** Ramp front, Millett adjustable square notch rear. **Features:** Highly polished high tensile strength manganese bronze frame; blue cylinder and barrel; coil spring trigger mechanism. Contact maker for full price information. Introduced 1975. Made in U.S.A. From Century Gun Dist., Inc.
Price: 6-1/2" barrel, 45-70 . . . . **$2,000.00**

CIMARRON LIGHTNING SA
Caliber: 38 Special. **Barrel:** 3-1/2", 4-3/4", 5-1/2". **Grips:** Checkered walnut. **Sights:** Blade front. **Features:** Replica of the Colt 1877 Lightning DA. Similar to Cimarron Thunderer™, except smaller grip frame to fit smaller hands. Blue finish with color-case hardened frame. Introduced 2001. From Cimarron F.A. Co.
Price: . . . . **$389.00 to $449.00**

CIMARRON MODEL "P" JR.
Caliber: 38 Special. **Barrel:** 3-1/2", 4-3/4", 5-1/2". **Grips:** Checkered walnut. **Sights:** Blade front. **Features:** Styled after 1873 Colt Peacemaker, except 20 percent smaller. Blue finish with color-case hardened frame; Cowboy Comp® action. Introduced 2001. From Cimarron F.A. Co.
Price: . . . . **$389.00 to $449.00**

CIMARRON U.S. CAVALRY MODEL SINGLE-ACTION
Caliber: 45 Colt. **Barrel:** 7-1/2". **Weight:** 42 oz. **Length:** 13-1/2" overall. **Grips:** Walnut. **Sights:** Fixed. **Features:** Has "A.P. Casey" markings; "U.S." plus patent dates on frame, serial number on backstrap, trigger guard, frame and cylinder, "APC" cartouche on left grip; color case-hardened frame and hammer, rest charcoal blue. Exact copy of the original. Imported by Cimarron F.A. Co.
Price: . . . . **$499.00 to $539.00**

Cimarron Rough Rider Artillery Model Single-Action
Similar to U.S. Cavalry model, 5-1/2" barrel, weighs 39 oz., is 11-1/2" overall. U.S. markings and cartouche, case-hardened frame and hammer; 45 Colt only.
Price: . . . . **$499.00 to $539.00**

CIMARRON 1872 OPEN TOP REVOLVER
Caliber: 38, 44 Special, 45 S&W Schofield. **Barrel:** 5-1/2" and 7-1/2". **Grips:** Walnut. **Sights:** Blade front, fixed rear. **Features:** Replica of first cartridge-firing revolver. Blue, charcoal blue, nickel or Original® finish; Navy-style brass or steel Army-style frame. Introduced 2001 by Cimarron F.A. Co.
Price: . . . . **$469.00 to $509.00**

CIMARRON 1873 MODEL P
Caliber: 38 WCF, 357 Mag., 44 WCF, 44 Spec., 45 Colt. **Barrel:** 4-3/4", 5-1/2", 7-1/2". **Weight:** 39 oz. **Length:** 10" overall (4" barrel). **Grips:** Walnut. **Sights:** Blade front, fixed or adjustable rear. **Features:** Uses "old model" blackpowder frame with "Bullseye" ejector or New Model frame. Imported by Cimarron F.A. Co.
Price: . . . . **$469.00 to $509.00**

Colt Cowboy

Colt Single-Action Army

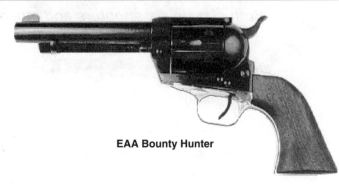

EAA Bounty Hunter

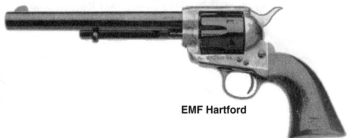

EMF Hartford

Cimarron Bisley Model Single-Action Revolvers

Similar to 1873 Frontier Six Shooter, special grip frame and trigger guard, knurled wide-spur hammer, curved trigger. Available in 357 Mag., 44 WCF, 45 Schofield, 45 Colt. Introduced 1999. Imported by Cimarron F.A. Co.

Price: **$499.00**

Cimarron Flat Top Single-Action Revolvers

Similar to 1873 Frontier Six Shooter, flat top strap with windage-adjustable rear sight, elevation-adjustable front sight. Available in 357 Mag., 44 WCF, 45 Schofield, 45 Colt; 4-3/4", 5-1/2", 7-1/2" barrel. Introduced 1999. Imported by Cimarron F.A. Co.

Price: **$499.00**

Cimarron Bisley Flat Top Revolver

Similar to Flat Top revolver, special grip frame and trigger guard, wide spur hammer, curved trigger. Introduced 1999. Imported by Cimarron F.A. Co.

Price: **$509.00**

CIMARRON THUNDERER REVOLVER

Caliber: 357 Mag., 44 WCF, 45 Colt, 6-shot. **Barrel:** 3-1/2", 4-3/4", 5-1/2", 7-1/2", with ejector. **Weight:** 38 oz. (3-1/2" barrel). **Grips:** Smooth walnut. **Sights:** Blade front, notch rear. **Features:** Thunderer grip; color case-hardened frame with balance blued. Introduced 1993. Imported by Cimarron F.A. Co.

Price: 3-1/2", 4-3/4", smooth grips **$489.00**
Price: As above, checkered grips........................ **$524.00**
Price: 5-1/2", 7-1/2", smooth grips **$529.00**
Price: As above, checkered grips........................ **$564.00**

CIMARRON 1872 OPEN-TOP REVOLVER

Caliber: 38 Spec., 38 Colt, 44 Colt, 44 Russian, 45 Schofield. **Barrel:** 7-1/2". **Grips:** Smooth walnut. **Sights:** Blade front, fixed rear. **Features:** Replica of the original production. Color case-hardened frame, rest blued, including grip frame. Introduced 1999. Imported from Italy by Cimarron F.A. Co.

Price: .... **$469.00 to $509.00**

COLT COWBOY SINGLE-ACTION REVOLVER

Caliber: 45 Colt, 6-shot. **Barrel:** 5-1/2". **Weight:** 42 oz. **Grips:** Black composition, first generation style. **Sights:** Blade front, notch rear. **Features:** Dimensional replica of Colt's original Peacemaker with medium-size color case-hardened frame; transfer bar safety system; half-cock loading. Introduced 1998. Made in U.S.A. by Colt's Mfg. Co.

Price: About **$670.00**

COLT SINGLE-ACTION ARMY REVOLVER

Caliber: 44-40, 45 Colt, 6-shot. **Barrel:** 4-3/4", 5-1/2", 7-1/2". **Weight:** 40 oz. (4-3/4" barrel). **Length:** 10-1/4" overall (4-3/4" barrel). **Grips:** Black Eagle composite. **Sights:** Blade front, notch rear. **Features:** Available in full nickel finish with nickel grip medallions, or Royal Blue with color case-hardened frame, gold grip medallions. Reintroduced 1992.

Price: **$1,938.00**

EAA BOUNTY HUNTER SA REVOLVERS

Caliber: 22 LR/22 WMR, 357 Mag., 44 Mag., 45 Colt, 6-shot. **Barrel:** 4-1/2", 7-1/2". **Weight:** 2.5 lbs. **Length:** 11" overall (4-5/8" barrel). **Grips:** Smooth walnut. **Sights:** Blade front, grooved topstrap rear. **Features:** Transfer bar safety; three position hammer; hammer forged barrel. Introduced 1992. Imported by European American Armory.

Price: Blue or case-hardened........................... **$369.00**
Price: Nickel **$399.00**
Price: 22LR/22WMR, blue **$269.00**
Price: As above, nickel................................. **$299.00**

EMF HARTFORD SINGLE-ACTION REVOLVERS

Caliber: 357 Mag., 32-20, 38-40, 44-40, 44 Spec., 45 Colt. **Barrel:** 4-3/4", 5-1/2", 7-1/2". **Weight:** 45 oz. **Length:** 13" overall (7-1/2" barrel). **Grips:** Smooth walnut. **Sights:** Blade front, fixed rear. **Features:** Identical to the original Colts with inspector cartouche on left grip, original patent dates and U.S. markings. All major parts serial numbered using original Colt-style lettering, numbering. Bullseye ejector head and color case-hardening on frame and hammer. Introduced 1990. From E.M.F.

Price: **$500.00**
Price: Cavalry or Artillery **$390.00**
Price: Nickel plated, add............................... **$125.00**
Price: Casehardened New Model frame **$365.00**

EMF 1894 Bisley Revolver

Similar to the Hartford single-action revolver except has special grip frame and trigger guard, wide spur hammer; available in 38-40 or 45 Colt, 4-3/4", 5-1/2" or 7-1/2" barrel. Introduced 1995. Imported by E.M.F.

Price: Casehardened/blue **$400.00**
Price: Nickel **$525.00**

EMF Hartford Pinkerton Single-Action Revolver

Same as the regular Hartford except has 4" barrel with ejector tube and birds head grip. Calibers: 357 Mag., 45 Colt. Introduced 1997. Imported by E.M.F.

Price: **$375.00**

EMF 1894 Bisley

Freedom Arms Model 83 Premier Grade

EMF 1875 Outlaw

Freedom Arms Model 83 Field Grade

EMF 1890 Police

Freedom Arms Model 83 475 Linebaugh

EMF Hartford Express Single-Action Revolver
  Same as the regular Hartford model except uses grip of the Colt Lightning revolver. Barrel lengths of 4", 4-3/4", 5-1/2". Introduced 1997. Imported by E.M.F.
Price: **$375.00**

EMF 1875 OUTLAW REVOLVER
Caliber: 357 Mag., 44-40, 45 Colt. **Barrel:** 7-1/2". **Weight:** 46 oz. **Length:** 13-1/2" overall. **Grips:** Smooth walnut. **Sights:** Blade front, fixed groove rear. **Features:** Authentic copy of 1875 Remington with firing pin in hammer; color case-hardened frame, blue cylinder, barrel, steel backstrap and brass trigger guard. Also available in nickel, factory engraved. Imported by E.M.F.
Price: All calibers **$575.00**
Price: Nickel **$735.00**

EMF 1890 Police Revolver
  Similar to the 1875 Outlaw except has 5-1/2" barrel, weighs 40 oz., with 12-1/2" overall length. Has lanyard ring in butt. No web under barrel. Calibers 357, 44-40, 45 Colt. Imported by E.M.F.
Price: All calibers **$590.00**
Price: Nickel **$750.00**

FREEDOM ARMS MODEL 83 PREMIER GRADE REVOLVER
Caliber: 357 Mag., 41 Mag., 44 Mag., 454 Casull, 475 Linebaugh, 50 AE, 5-shot. **Barrel:** 4-3/4", 6", 7-1/2", 9" (357 Mag. only), 10". **Weight:** 52.8 oz. **Length:** 13" (7-1/2" bbl.). **Grips:** Impregnated hardwood. **Sights:** Blade front, notch or adjustable rear. **Features:** All stainless steel construction; sliding bar safety system. Lifetime warranty. Made in U.S.A. by Freedom Arms, Inc.
Price: 454 Casull, 475 Linebaugh, 50 AE. **$2,058.00**
Price: 454 Casull, fixed sight **$1,979.00**
Price: 357 Mag., 41 Mag., 44 Mag. **$1,976.00**
Price: 44 Mag., fixed sight **$1,911.00**

Freedom Arms Model 83 Field Grade Revolver
  Model 83 frame. Weighs 52-56 oz. Adjustable rear sight, replaceable front blade, matte finish, Pachmayr grips. All stainless steel. Introduced 1992. Made in U.S.A. by Freedom Arms Inc.
Price: 454 Casull, 475 Linebaugh, 50 AE, adj. sights **$1,591.00**
Price: 454 Casull, fixed sights **$1,553.00**
Price: 357 Mag., 41 Mag., 44 Mag. **$1,527.00**

FREEDOM ARMS MODEL 83 VARIMINT CLASS REVOLVERS
Caliber: 22 LR, 5-shot. **Barrel:** 5-1/8, 7-1/2". **Weight:** 58 oz. (7-1/2" bbl.). **Length:** 11-1/2" (7-1/2" bbl.). **Grips:** Impregnated hardwood. **Sights:** Steel base adjustable "V" notch rear sight and replaceable brass bead front sight. **Features:** Stainless steel, matte finish, manual sliding-bar system, dual firing pins, pre-set trigger stop. One year limited warranty to original owner. Made in U.S.A. by Freedom Arms, Inc.
Price: Varmint Class **$1,828.00**
Price: Extra fitted 22 WMR cylinder **$264.00**

Freedom Arms Model 83 Varmint Class

IAR Model 1873 Six Shooter

Freedom Arms Model 97 Premier Grade

IAR Model 1873 Frontier

Heritage Rough Rider

IAR Model 1873 Frontier Marshal

FREEDOM ARMS MODEL 97 PREMIER GRADE REVOLVER

Caliber: 22 LR, 357 Mag., 41 Mag., 45 Colt, 5-shot. **Barrel:** 4-1/2", 5-1/2", 7-1/2", 10". **Weight:** 37 oz. (45 Colt 5-1/2"). **Length:** 10-3/4" (5-1/2" bbl.). **Grips:** Impregnated hardwood. **Sights:** Adjustable rear, replaceable blade front. **Features:** Stainless steel, brushed finish, automatic transfer bar safety system. Introduced in 1997. Made in U.S.A. by Freedom Arms.

Price: 357 Mag., 41 Mag., 45 Colt **$1,668.00**
Price: 357 Mag., 45 Colt, fixed sight **$1,576.00**
Price: Extra fitted cylinders 38 Special, 45 ACP. **$264.00**
Price: 22 LR with sporting chambers **$1,732.00**
Price: Extra fitted 22 WMR cylinder **$264.00**
Price: Extra fitted 22 LR match grade cylinder **$476.00**
Price: 22 match grade chamber instead of 22 LR sport chamber
. . . . **$214.00**

HERITAGE ROUGH RIDER REVOLVER

Caliber: 22 LR, 22 LR/22 WMR combo, 6-shot. **Barrel:** 2-3/4", 3-1/2", 4-3/4", 6-1/2", 9". **Weight:** 31 to 38 oz. **Length:** NA. **Grips:** Exotic hardwood, laminated wood or mother of pearl; bird's head models offered. **Sights:** Blade front, fixed rear. Adjustable sight on 6-1/2" only. **Features:** Hammer block safety. High polish blue or nickel finish. Introduced 1993. Made in U.S.A. by Heritage Mfg., Inc.

Price: . . . . **$184.95 to $239.95**

IAR MODEL 1873 SIX SHOOTER

Caliber: 22 LR/22 WMR combo. **Barrel:** 5-1/2". **Weight:** 36-1/2" oz. **Length:** 11-3/8" overall. **Grips:** One-piece walnut. **Sights:** Blade front, notch rear. **Features:** A 3/4-scale reproduction. Color case-hardened frame, blued barrel. All-steel construction. Made by Uberti. Imported from Italy by IAR, Inc.

Price: **$360.00**

IAR MODEL 1873 FRONTIER REVOLVER

Caliber: 22 RL, 22 LR/22 WMR. **Barrel:** 4-3/4". **Weight:** 45 oz. **Length:** 10-1/2" overall. **Grips:** One-piece walnut with inspector's cartouche. **Sights:** Blade front, notch rear. **Features:** Color case-hardened frame, blued barrel, black nickel-plated brass trigger guard and backstrap. Bright nickel and engraved versions available. Introduced 1997. Imported from Italy by IAR, Inc.

Price: **$380.00**
Price: Nickel-plated **$425.00**
Price: 22 LR/22WMR combo **$420.00**

IAR MODEL 1873 FRONTIER MARSHAL

Caliber: 357 Mag., 45 Colt. **Barrel:** 4-3/4", 5-1/2, 7-1/2". **Weight:** 39 oz. **Length:** 10-1/2" overall. **Grips:** One-piece walnut. **Sights:** Blade front, notch rear. **Features:** Bright brass trigger guard and backstrap, color case-hardened frame, blued barrel and cylinder. Introduced 1998. Imported from Italy by IAR, Inc.

Price: **$395.00**

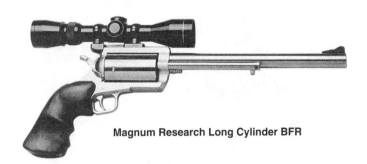

Magnum Research Long Cylinder BFR

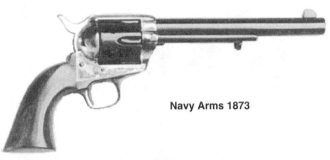

Navy Arms 1873

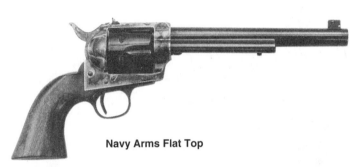

Navy Arms Flat Top

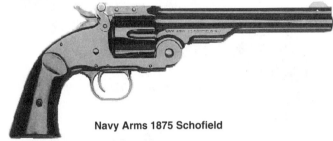

Navy Arms 1875 Schofield

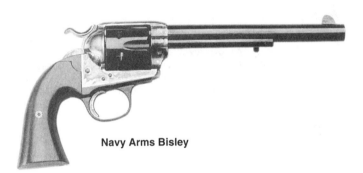

Navy Arms Bisley

Navy Arms New Model Russian

MAGNUM RESEARCH BFR SINGLE-ACTION REVOLVER

(Long cylinder) Caliber: 45/70 Government, 444 Marlin, 45 LC/410, 450 Marlin. **Barrel:** 7.5", 10". **Weight:** 4 lbs., 4.36 lbs. **Length:** 15", 17.5".
(Short cylinder) Caliber: 454 Casull, 22 Hornet, BFR 480/475. **Barrel:** 6.5", 7.5", 10". **Weight:** 3.2 lbs, 3.5 lbs., 4.36 lbs. (10"). **Length:** 12.75 (6"), 13.75", 16.25"
Sights: All have fully adjustable rear, orange blade ramp front. **Features:** Stainless steel construction, all 5-shot (except 45 LC/410 & 22 Hornet are 6-shot). 45 LC/410 with modified choke and wrench, 410 shot shellslug incompatible with 45/70 caliber. Barrels are stress-relieved and cut rifled. Made in U.S.A. From Magnum Research, Inc.
Price: **$999.00**

MAGNUM RESEARCH BFR REVOLVER

Caliber: 22 Hornet, 444 Marlin, 45 LC/410, 450 Marlin, 454 Casull, 45/70, 480 Ruger/475 Linebaugh. **Barrel:** 6-1/2", 7-1/2", 10". **Weight:** 3.2-4.36 lbs. **Length:** 12.75"-17.5". **Grips:** Rubber. **Sights:** Ramp front, adjustable rear. **Features:** Single action, stainless steel construction. Announced 1998. Made in U.S.A. from Magnum Research.
Price: **$999.00**

NAVY ARMS FLAT TOP TARGET MODEL REVOLVER

Caliber: 45 Colt, 6-shot cylinder. **Barrel:** 7-1/2". **Weight:** 40 oz. **Length:** 13-1/4" overall. **Grips:** Smooth walnut. **Sights:** Spring-loaded German silver front, rear adjustable for windage. **Features:** Replica of Colt's Flat Top Frontier target revolver made from 1888 to 1896. Blue with color case-hardened frame. Introduced 1997. Imported by Navy Arms.
Price: **$450.00**

NAVY ARMS BISLEY MODEL SINGLE-ACTION REVOLVER

Caliber: 44-40 or 45 Colt, 6-shot cylinder. **Barrel:** 4-3/4", 5-1/2", 7-1/2". **Weight:** 40 oz. **Length:** 12-1/2" overall (7-1/2" barrel). **Grips:** Smooth walnut. **Sights:** Blade front, notch rear. **Features:** Replica of Colt's Bisley Model. Polished blue finish, color case-hardened frame. Introduced 1997. Imported by Navy Arms.
Price: . . . . **$425.00 to $460.00**

NAVY ARMS 1873 SINGLE-ACTION REVOLVER

Caliber: 357 Mag., 44-40, 45 Colt, 6-shot cylinder. **Barrel:** 4-3/4", 5-1/2", 7-1/2". **Weight:** 36 oz. **Length:** 10-3/4" overall (5-1/2" barrel). **Grips:** Smooth walnut. **Sights:** Blade front, notch rear. **Features:** Blue with color case-hardened frame. Introduced 1991. Imported by Navy Arms.
Price: **$405.00**

NAVY ARMS 1875 SCHOFIELD REVOLVER

Caliber: 44-40, 45 Colt, 6-shot cylinder. **Barrel:** 3-1/2", 5", 7". **Weight:** 39 oz. **Length:** 10-3/4" overall (5" barrel). **Grips:** Smooth walnut. **Sights:** Blade front, notch rear. **Features:** Replica of Smith & Wesson Model 3 Schofield. Single-action, top-break with automatic ejection. Polished blue finish. Introduced 1994. Imported by Navy Arms.
Price: Hideout Model, 3-1/2" barrel **$695.00**
Price: Wells Fargo, 5" barrel. **$695.00**
Price: U.S. Cavalry model, 7" barrel, military markings **$695.00**

NAVY ARMS NEW MODEL RUSSIAN REVOLVER

Caliber: 44 Russian, 6-shot cylinder. **Barrel:** 6-1/2". **Weight:** 40 oz. **Length:** 12" overall. **Grips:** Smooth walnut. **Sights:** Blade front, notch rear. **Features:** Replica of the S&W Model 3 Russian Third Model revolver. Spur trigger guard, polished blue finish. Introduced 1999. Imported by Navy Arms.
Price: **$769.00**

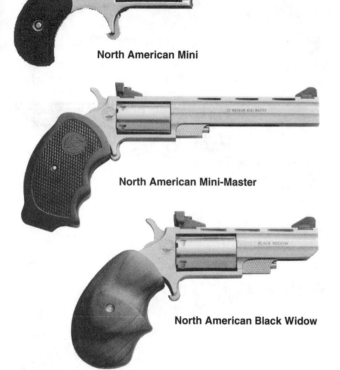

North American Mini

North American Mini-Master

North American Black Widow

Ruger Blackhawk

Ruger KSSMBH-4F

NAVY ARMS 1851 NAVY CONVERSION REVOLVER

Caliber: 38 Spec., 38 Long Colt. **Barrel:** 5-1/2", 7-1/2". **Weight:** 44 oz. **Length:** 14" overall (7-1/2" barrel). **Grips:** Smooth walnut. **Sights:** Bead front, notch rear. **Features:** Replica of Colt's cartridge conversion revolver. Polished blue finish with color case-hardened frame, silver plated trigger guard and backstrap. Introduced 1999. Imported by Navy Arms.
Price: **$165.00**

NAVY ARMS 1860 ARMY CONVERSION REVOLVER

Caliber: 38 Spec., 38 Long Colt. **Barrel:** 5-1/2", 7-1/2". **Weight:** 44 oz. **Length:** 13-1/2" overall (7-1/2" barrel). **Grips:** Smooth walnut. **Sights:** Blade front, notch rear. **Features:** Replica of Colt's conversion revolver. Polished blue finish with color case-hardened frame, full-size 1860 Army grip with blued steel backstrap. Introduced 1999. Imported by Navy Arms.
Price: **$190.00**

NORTH AMERICAN MINI-REVOLVERS

Caliber: 22 Short, 22 LR, 22 WMR, 5-shot. **Barrel:** 1-1/8", 1-5/8". **Weight:** 4 to 6.6 oz. **Length:** 3-5/8" to 6-1/8" overall. **Grips:** Laminated wood. **Sights:** Blade front, notch fixed rear. **Features:** All stainless steel construction. Polished satin and matte finish. Engraved models available. From North American Arms.
Price: 22 Short, 22 LR **$176.00**
Price: 22 WMR, 1-5/8" bbl. **$194.00**
Price: 22 WMR, 1-1/8" or 1-5/8" bbl. with extra 22 LR cylinder .. **$231.00**

NORTH AMERICAN MINI-MASTER

Caliber: 22 LR, 22 WMR, 5-shot cylinder. **Barrel:** 4". **Weight:** 10.7 oz. **Length:** 7.75" overall. **Grips:** Checkered hard black rubber. **Sights:** Blade front, white outline rear adjustable for elevation, or fixed. **Features:** Heavy vent barrel; full-size grips. Non-fluted cylinder. Introduced 1989.
Price: Adjustable sight, 22 WMR or 22 LR **$299.00**
Price: As above with extra WMR/LR cylinder **$336.00**
Price: Fixed sight, 22 WMR or 22 LR **$281.00**
Price: As above with extra WMR/LR cylinder **$318.00**

North American Black Widow Revolver

Similar to Mini-Master, 2" heavy vent barrel. Built on 22 WMR frame. Non-fluted cylinder, black rubber grips. Available with Millett Low Profile fixed sights or Millett sight adjustable for elevation only. Overall length 5-7/8", weighs 8.8 oz. From North American Arms.
Price: Adjustable sight, 22 LR or 22 WMR **$269.00**
Price: As above with extra WMR/LR cylinder **$306.00**
Price: Fixed sight, 22 LR or 22 WMR **$251.00**
Price: As above with extra WMR/LR cylinder **$288.00**

RUGER NEW MODEL BLACKHAWK
AND BLACKHAWK CONVERTIBLE

Caliber: 30 Carbine, 357 Mag./38 Spec., 41 Mag., 45 Colt, 6-shot. **Barrel:** 4-5/8" or 5-1/2", either caliber; 7-1/2" (30 Carbine and 45 Colt). **Weight:** 42 oz. (6-1/2" bbl.). **Length:** 12-1/4" overall (5-1/2" bbl.). **Grips:** American walnut. **Sights:** 1/8" ramp front, micro-click rear adjustable for windage and elevation. **Features:** Ruger transfer bar safety system, independent firing pin, hardened chrome-moly steel frame, music wire springs throughout. Case and lock included.
Price: Blue 30 Carbine, 7-1/2" (BN31) **$435.00**
Price: Blue, 357 Mag., 4-5/8", 6-1/2" (BN34, BN36).......... **$435.00**
Price: As above, stainless (KBN34, KBN36) **$530.00**
Price: Blue, 357 Mag./9mm Convertible, 4-5/8", 6-1/2" (BN34X, BN36X) includes extra cylinder...................... **$489.00**
Price: Blue, 41 Mag., 4-5/8", 6-1/2" (BN41, BN42)............ **$435.00**
Price: Blue, 45 Colt, 4-5/8", 5-1/2", 7-1/2" (BN44, BN455, BN45) **$435.00**
Price: Stainless, 45 Colt, 4-5/8", 7-1/2" (KBN44, KBN45) **$530.00**
Price: Blue, 45 Colt/45 ACP Convertible, 4-5/8", 5-1/2" (BN44X, BN455X) includes extra cylinder **$489.00**

RUGER NEW MODEL SINGLE REVOLVER

Caliber: 32 H&R. **Barrel:** 4-5/8", 6-shot. **Grips:** Black Micarta "birds head", rosewood with color case. **Sights:** Fixed. **Features:** Instruction manual, high impact case, gun lock standard.
Price: Stainless, KSSMBH-4F, birds head **$576.00**
Price: color case, SSMBH-4F, birds head **$576.00**
Price: color case, SSM-4F-S, rosewood **$576.00**

Ruger SSMBH-4F

Ruger Bisley Single-Action

Ruger Super Blackhawk Hunter

Ruger New Bearcat

Ruger Bisley Vaquero

RUGER NEW MODEL SUPER BLACKHAWK

Caliber: 44 Mag., 6-shot. Also fires 44 Spec. **Barrel:** 4-5/8", 5-1/2", 7-1/2", 10-1/2" bull. **Weight:** 48 oz. (7-1/2" bbl.), 51 oz. (10-1/2" bbl.). **Length:** 13-3/8" overall (7-1/2" bbl.). **Grips:** American walnut. **Sights:** 1/8" ramp front, micro-click rear adjustable for windage and elevation. **Features:** Ruger transfer bar safety system, fluted or un-fluted cylinder, steel grip and cylinder frame, round or square back trigger guard, wide serrated trigger, wide spur hammer. With case and lock.

Price: Blue, 4-5/8", 5-1/2", 7-1/2" (S458N, S45N, S47N) **$519.00**
Price: Blue, 10-1/2" bull barrel (S411N) **$529.00**
Price: Stainless, 4-5/8", 5-1/2", 7-1/2" (KS458N, KS45N,
KS47N) **$535.00**
Price: Stainless, 10-1/2" bull barrel (KS411N) **$545.00**

RUGER NEW MODEL SUPER BLACKHAWK HUNTER

Caliber: 44 Mag., 6-shot. **Barrel:** 7-1/2", full-length solid rib, unfluted cylinder. **Weight:** 52 oz. **Length:** 13-5/8". **Grips:** Black laminated wood. **Sights:** Adjustable rear, replaceable front blade. **Features:** Reintroduced Ultimate SA revolver. Includes instruction manual, high-impact case, set 1" medium scope rings, gun lock, ejector rod as standard.
Price: **$639.00**

RUGER VAQUERO SINGLE-ACTION REVOLVER

Caliber: 357 Mag., 44-40, 44 Mag., 45 LC, 6-shot. **Barrel:** 4-5/8", 5-1/2", 7-1/2". **Weight:** 38-41 oz. **Length:** 13-1/8" overall (7-1/2" barrel). **Grips:** Smooth rosewood with Ruger medallion. **Sights:** Blade front, fixed notch rear. **Features:** Uses Ruger's patented transfer bar safety system and loading gate interlock with classic styling. Blued model color case-hardened finish on frame, rest polished and blued. Stainless has high-gloss. Introduced 1993. From Sturm, Ruger & Co.

Price: 357 Mag. BNV34, KBNV34 (4-5/8"),
BNV35, KBNV35 (5-1/2") **$535.00**
Price: 44-40 BNV40, KBNV40 (4-5/8"). BNV405,
KBNV405 (5-1/2"). BNV407, KBNV407 (7-1/2") **$535.00**
Price: 44 Mag., BNV474, KBNV474 (4-5/8"). BNV475,
KBNV475 (5-1/2"). BNV477, KBNV477 (7-1/2") **$535.00**
Price: 45 LC, BN444, KBNV44 (4-5/8"). BNV455,
KBNV455 (5-1/2"). BNV45, KBNV45 (7-1/2") **$535.00**
New!!! Price: 45 LC, BNVBH453, KBNVBH453
3-3/4" with "birds head" grip **$576.00**
Price: 357 Mag., RBNV35 (5-1/2") **$535.00**; KRBNV35 (5-1/2") . **$555.00**
Price: 45 LC, RBNV44 (4-5/8"), RBNV455 (5-1/2") **$535.00**
Price: 45 LC, KRBNV44 (4-5/8"), KRBNV455 (5-1/2"). **$555.00**

Ruger Bisley-Vaquero Single-Action Revolver

Similar to Vaquero, Bisley-style hammer, grip and trigger, available in 357 Magnum, 44 Magnum and 45 LC only, 4-5/8" or 5-1/2" barrel. Smooth rosewood grips with Ruger medallion. Roll-engraved, unfluted cylinder. Introduced 1997. From Sturm, Ruger & Co.
Price: Color case-hardened frame, blue grip frame, barrel and cylinder,
RBNV-475, RBNV-474, 44 Mag. **$535.00**
Price: High-gloss stainless steel, KRBNV-475, KRBNV-474 . . . . **$555.00**
Price: For simulated ivory grips add . . . . **$41.00 to $44.00**

RUGER NEW BEARCAT SINGLE-ACTION

Caliber: 22 LR, 6-shot. **Barrel:** 4". **Weight:** 24 oz. **Length:** 8-7/8" overall. **Grips:** Smooth rosewood with Ruger medallion. **Sights:** Blade front, fixed notch rear. **Features:** Reintroduction of the Ruger Bearcat with slightly lengthened frame, Ruger patented transfer bar safety system. Available in blue only. Introduced 1993. With case and lock. From Sturm, Ruger & Co.
Price: SBC4, blue. **$379.00**
New Price: KSBC-4, ss **$429.00**

RUGER MODEL SINGLE-SIX REVOLVER

Caliber: 32 H&R Magnum. **Barrel:** 4-5/8", 6-shot. **Weight:** 33 oz. **Length:** 10-1/8". **Grips:** Blue, rosewood, stainless, simulated ivory. **Sights:** Blade front, notch rear fixed. **Features:** Transfer bar and loading gate interlock safety, instruction manual, high impact case and gun lock.
Price: **$576.00**
Price: Blue, SSM4FS **$576.00**
Price: SS, KSSM4FSI. **$576.00**

Ruger Super Single-Six

Uberti Cattleman

Uberti 1875 Army

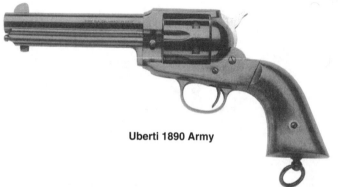

Uberti 1890 Army

RUGER SINGLE-SIX AND SUPER SINGLE-SIX CONVERTIBLE
Caliber: 22 LR, 6-shot; 22 WMR in extra cylinder. **Barrel:** 4-5/8", 5-1/2", 6-1/2", 9-1/2" (6-groove). **Weight:** 35 oz. (6-1/2" bbl.). **Length:** 11-13/16" overall (6-1/2" bbl.). **Grips:** Smooth American walnut. **Sights:** Improved Patridge front on ramp, fully adjustable rear protected by integral frame ribs (super single-six); or fixed sight (single six). **Features:** Ruger transfer bar safety system, loading gate interlock, hardened chrome-moly steel frame, wide trigger, music wire springs throughout, independent firing pin.
Price: 4-5/8", 5-1/2", 6-1/2", 9-1/2" barrel, blue, adjustable sight NR4, NR5, NR6, NR9 . . . . **$389.00**
Price: 5-1/2", 6-1/2" bbl. only, stainless steel, adjustable sight KNR5, KNR6. . . . . **$469.00**
Price: 5-1/2", 6-1/2" barrel, blue fixed sights **$379.00**

Ruger Bisley Small Frame Revolver
Similar to Single-Six, frame is styled after classic Bisley "flat-top." Most mechanical parts are unchanged. Hammer is lower and smoothly curved with deeply checkered spur. Trigger is strongly curved with wide smooth surface. Longer grip frame designed with hand-filling shape, and trigger guard is a large oval. Adjustable dovetail rear sight; front sight base accepts interchangeable square blades of various heights and styles. Un-fluted cylinder and roll engraving. Weighs 41 oz. Chambered for 22 LR, 6-1/2" barrel only. Plastic lockable case. Introduced 1985.
Price: RB-22AW **$422.00**

Ruger Bisley Single-Action Revolver
Similar to standard Blackhawk, hammer is lower with smoothly curved, deeply checkered wide spur. The trigger is strongly curved with wide smooth surface. Longer grip frame has hand-filling shape. Adjustable rear sight, ramp-style front. Unfluted cylinder and roll engraving, adjustable sights. Chambered for 357, 44 Mags. and 45 Colt; 7-1/2" barrel; overall length of 13"; weighs 48 oz. Plastic lockable case. Introduced 1985.
Price: RB-35W, 357Mag, RBD-44W, 44Mag, RB-45W, 45 Colt . . **$535.00**

SMITH & WESSON COMMEMORATIVE MODEL 2000
Caliber: 45 S&W Schofield. **Barrel:** 7". **Features:** 150th Anniversary logo, engraved, gold-plated, walnut grips, blue, original style hammer, trigger, and barrel latch. Wood presentation case. Limited.
Price: . . . . **NA**

TRISTAR/UBERTI REGULATOR REVOLVER
Caliber: 45 Colt. **Barrel:** 4-3/4", 5-1/2", 7-1/2". **Weight:** 32-38 oz. **Length:** 8-1/4" overall (4-3/4" bbl.) **Grips:** One-piece walnut. **Sights:** Blade front, notch rear. **Features:** Uberti replica of 1873 Colt Model "P" revolver. Col-or-case hardened steel frame, brass backstrap and trigger guard, ham-mer-block safety. Imported from Italy by Tristar Sporting Arms.
Price: Regulator **$335.00**
Price: Regulator Deluxe (blued backstrap, trigger guard) **$367.00**

UBERTI 1873 CATTLEMAN SINGLE-ACTION
Caliber: 22 LR/22 WMR, 38 Spec., 357 Mag., 44 Spec., 44-40, 45 Colt/45 ACP, 6-shot. **Barrel:** 4-3/4", 5-1/2", 7-1/2"; 44-40, 45 Colt also with 3", 3-1/2", 4". **Weight:** 38 oz. (5-1/2" bbl.). **Length:** 10-3/4" overall (5-1/2" bbl.). **Grips:** One-piece smooth walnut. **Sights:** Blade front, groove rear; fully adjustable rear available. **Features:** Steel or brass backstrap, trigger guard; color case-hardened frame, blued barrel, cylinder. Imported from It-aly by Uberti U.S.A.
Price: Steel backstrap, trigger guard, fixed sights **$410.00**
Price: Brass backstrap, trigger guard, fixed sights **$359.00**
Price: Bisley model. **$435.00**

Uberti 1873 Buckhorn Single-Action
A slightly larger version of the Cattleman revolver. Available in 44 Mag-num or 44 Magnum/44-40 convertible, otherwise has same specs.
Price: Steel backstrap, trigger guard, fixed sights **$410.00**

UBERTI 1875 SA ARMY OUTLAW REVOLVER
Caliber: 357 Mag., 44-40, 45 Colt, 45 Colt/45 ACP convertible, 6-shot. **Bar-rel:** 5-1/2", 7-1/2". **Weight:** 44 oz. **Length:** 13-3/4" overall. **Grips:** Smooth walnut. **Sights:** Blade front, notch rear. **Features:** Replica of the 1875 Remington S.A. Army revolver. Brass trigger guard, color case-hardened frame, rest blued. Imported by Uberti U.S.A.
Price: **$483.00**
Price: 45 Colt/45 ACP convertible **$525.00**

UBERTI 1890 ARMY OUTLAW REVOLVER
Caliber: 357 Mag., 44-40, 45 Colt, 45 Colt/45 ACP convertible, 6-shot. **Bar-rel:** 5-1/2", 7-1/2". **Weight:** 37 oz. **Length:** 12-1/2" overall. **Grips:** Ameri-can walnut. **Sights:** Blade front, groove rear. **Features:** Replica of the 1890 Remington single-action. Brass trigger guard, rest is blued. Imported by Uberti U.S.A.
Price: **$483.00**

UBERTI NEW MODEL RUSSIAN REVOLVER
Caliber: 44 Russian, 6-shot cylinder. **Barrel:** 6-1/2". **Weight:** 40 oz. **Length:** 12" overall. **Grips:** Smooth walnut. **Sights:** Blade front, notch rear. **Features:** Repica of the S&W Model 3 Russian Third Model revolver. Spur trigger guard, polished blue finish. Introduced 1999. Imported by Uberti USA.
Price: **$800.00**

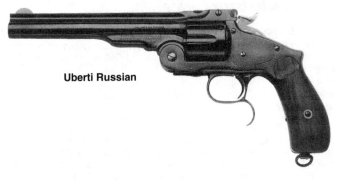

Uberti Russian

Uberti Schofield

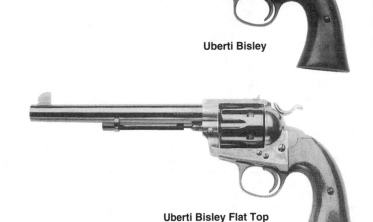

Uberti Bisley

Uberti Bisley Flat Top

HANDGUNS

UBERTI 1875 SCHOFIELD-STYLE BREAK-TOP REVOLVER

Caliber: 44-40, 45 Colt, 6-shot cylinder. **Barrel:** 5", 7". **Weight:** 39 oz. **Length:** 10-3/4" overall (5" barrel). **Grips:** Smooth walnut. **Sights:** Blade front, notch rear. **Features:** Replica of Smith & Wesson Model 3 Schofield. Single-action, top-break with automatic ejection. Polished blue finish. Introduced 1994. Imported by Uberti USA.
Price: **$750.00**

UBERTI BISLEY MODEL SINGLE-ACTION REVOLVER

Caliber: 38-40, 357 Mag., 44 Spec., 44-40 or 45 Colt, 6-shot cylinder. **Barrel:** 4-3/4", 5-1/2", 7-1/2". **Weight:** 40 oz. **Length:** 12-1/2" overall (7-1/2" barrel). **Grips:** Smooth walnut. **Sights:** Blade front, notch rear. **Features:** Replica of Colt's Bisley Model. Polished blue finish, color case-hardened frame. Introduced 1997. Imported by Uberti USA.
Price: **$435.00**

Uberti Bisley Model Flat Top Target Revolver

Similar to standard Bisley model, flat top strap, 7-1/2" barrel only, spring-loaded German silver front sight blade, standing leaf rear sight adjustable for windage. Polished blue finish, color case-hardened frame. Introduced 1998. Imported by Uberti USA.
Price: **$435.00**

U.S. FIRE-ARMS SINGLE ACTION ARMY REVOLVER

Caliber: 44 Russian, 38-40, 44-40, 45 Colt, 6-shot cylinder. **Barrel:** 4-3/4", 5-1/2", 7-1/2", 10". **Weight:** 37 oz. **Length:** NA. **Grips:** Hard rubber. **Sights:** Blade front, notch rear. **Features:** Recreation of original guns; 3" and 4" have no ejector. Available with all-blue, blue with color case-hardening, or full nickel-plate finish. Made in U.S.A. by United States Fire-Arms Mfg. Co.
Price: 4-3/4", blue/cased-colors **$1,250.00**
Price: 7-1/2", carbonal blue/case-colors. **$1,450.00**
Price: 7-1/2" nickel **$1,350.00**

U.S. Fire-Arms Flattop Target Revolver

Similar to Single Action Army, 4-3/4", 5-1/2" or 7-1/2" barrel, two-piece hard rubber stocks, flat top frame, adjustable rear sight. Made in U.S.A. by United States Fire-Arms Mfg. Co.
Price: Dome Blue **$1,175.00**
Price: Armory Blue/bone case **$1,450.00**

U.S. FIRE-ARMS BISLEY MODEL REVOLVER

Caliber: 4 Colt, 6-shot cylinder. **Barrel:** 4-3/4", 5-1/2", 7-1/2", 10". **Weight:** 38 oz. (5-1/2" barrel). **Length:** NA. **Grips:** Two-piece hard rubber. **Sights:** Blade front, notch rear. **Features:** Available in all blue, blue with color case-hardening, or full nickel plate finish. Made in U.S.A. by United States Patent Fire-Arms Mfg. Co.
Price: Dome Blue/Armory Blue, bone case **$1,525.00**
Price: Armory Blue/bone case **$1,852.00**
Price: Nickel **$1,900.00**

U.S. Fire-Arms "China Camp" Cowboy Action Revolver

Similar to Single Action Army revolver, available in Silver Steel finish only. Offered in 4-3/4", 5-1/2", 7-1/2" barrels. Made in U.S.A. by United States Fire-Arms Mfg. Co.
Price: **$1,200.00**

U.S. Fire-Arms "Buntline Special"

Similar to Single Action Army revolver except has 16" barrel, flip-up rear peep sight, 45 Colt only. Bone case frame, Armory Blue or nickel finish. Made in U.S.A. by United States Fire-Arms Mfg. Co.
Price: Cased, deluxe set **$2,895.00**
Price: Nickel/rubber **$2,795.00**

U.S. Fire-Arms Omni-Potent Six Shooter

Similar to Single Action Army revolver, bird's head grip with lanyard ring and hump in backstrap. Offered in 4-3/4", 5-1/2" and 7-1/2" barrels. Made in U.S.A. by United States Fire-Arms Mfg. Co.
Price: Armory Blue/bone case **$1,325.00**
Price: Nickel **$1,375.00**
Price: Snubnose, 2", 3", 4", Armory Blue/case. **$1,325.00**
Price: Snubnose, 2", 3", 4", nickel **$1,375.00**
Price: Target, armory blue/case **$1,365.00**
Price: Target, nickel **$1,500.00**

U.S. FIRE-ARMS NEW RODEO COWBOY ACTION REVOLVER

Caliber: 45 Colt. **Barrel:** 4-3/4", 5-1/2". **Grips:** Rubber. **Features:** Historically correct armory bone case hammer, blue satin finish, transfer bar safety system, correct solid firing pin. Entry level basic cowboy SASS gun for beginner or expert.
Price: **$505.00**

Specially adapted single-shot and multi-barrel arms.

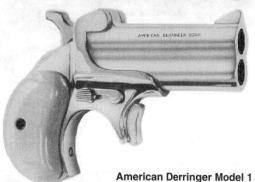

American Derringer Model 1

AMERICAN DERRINGER MODEL 1

Caliber: 22 LR, 22 WMR, 30 Carbine, 30 Luger, 30-30 Win., 32 H&R Mag., 32-20, 380 ACP, 38 Super, 38 Spec., 38 Spec. shotshell, 38 Spec. +P, 9mm Para., 357 Mag., 357 Mag./45/410, 357 Maximum, 10mm, 40 S&W, 41 Mag., 38-40, 44-40 Win., 44 Spec., 44 Mag., 45 Colt, 45 Win. Mag., 45 ACP, 45 Colt/410, 45-70 single shot. **Barrel:** 3". **Weight:** 15-1/2 oz. (38 Spec.). **Length:** 4.82" overall. **Grips:** Rosewood, Zebra wood. **Sights:** Blade front. **Features:** Made of stainless steel with high-polish or satin finish. Two-shot capacity. Manual hammer block safety. Introduced 1980. Available in almost any pistol caliber. Contact the factory for complete list of available calibers and prices. From American Derringer Corp.

Price: 22 LR $320.00
Price: 38 Spec. $320.00
Price: 357 Maximum. $345.00
Price: 357 Mag. $335.00
Price: 9mm, 380 . . . . $320.00
Price: 40 S&W $335.00
Price: 44 Spec. $398.00
Price: 44-40 Win. $398.00
Price: 45 Colt $385.00
Price: 30-30, 45 Win. Mag. $460.00
Price: 41, 44 Mags. $470.00
Price: 45-70, single shot. $387.00
Price: 45 Colt, 410, 2-1/2" $385.00
Price: 45 ACP, 10mm Auto. $340.00

American Derringer Model 4

Similar to the Model 1 except has 4.1" barrel, overall length of 6", and weighs 16-1/2 oz.; chambered for 357 Mag., 357 Maximum, 45-70, 3" 410-bore shotshells or 45 Colt or 44 Mag. Made of stainless steel. Manual hammer block safety. Introduced 1985.

Price: 3" 410/45 Colt. $425.00
Price: 45-70 . . . . $560.00
Price: 44 Mag. with oversize grips $515.00
Price: Alaskan Survival model (45-70 upper barrel, 410 or 45 Colt lower) $475.00

American Derringer Model 6

Similar to the Model 1 except has 6" barrel chambered for 3" 410 shotshells or 22 WMR, 357 Mag., 45 ACP, 45 Colt; rosewood stocks; 8.2" o.a.l. and weighs 21 oz. Shoots either round for each barrel. Manual hammer block safety. Introduced 1986.

Price: 22 WMR $440.00
Price: 357 Mag. $440.00
Price: 45 Colt/410 . . . . $450.00
Price: 45 ACP. $440.00

American Derringer Model 7 Ultra Lightweight

Similar to Model 1 except made of high strength aircraft aluminum. Weighs 7-1/2 oz., 4.82" o.a.l., rosewood stocks. Available in 22 LR, 22 WMR, 32 H&R Mag., 380 ACP, 38 Spec., 44 Spec. Introduced 1986.

Price: 22 LR, WMR. $325.00
Price: 38 Spec. $325.00
Price: 380 ACP. $325.00
Price: 32 H&R Mag/32 S&W Long $325.00
Price: 44 Spec. $565.00

American Derringer Model 10 Lightweight

Similar to the Model 1 except frame is of aluminum, giving weight of 10 oz. Stainless barrels. Available in 38 Spec., 45 Colt or 45 ACP only. Matte gray finish. Introduced 1989.

Price: 45 Colt. $385.00
Price: 45 ACP. $330.00
Price: 38 Spec. $305.00

American Derringer Lady Derringer

Same as the Model 1 except has tuned action, is fitted with scrimshawed synthetic ivory grips; chambered for 32 H&R Mag. and 38 Spec.; 357 Mag., 45 Colt, 45/410. Deluxe Grade is highly polished; Deluxe Engraved is engraved in a pattern similar to that used on 1880s derringers. All come in a French fitted jewelry box. Introduced 1991.

Price: 32 H&R Mag. $375.00
Price: 357 Mag. $405.00
Price: 38 Spec. $360.00
Price: 45 Colt, 45/410 . . . . $435.00

American Derringer Texas Commemorative

A Model 1 Derringer with solid brass frame, stainless steel barrel and rosewood grips. Available in 38 Spec., 44-40 Win., or 45 Colt. Introduced 1987.

Price: 38 Spec. $365.00
Price: 44-40 . . . . $420.00
Price: Brass frame, 45 Colt $450.00

AMERICAN DERRINGER DA 38 MODEL

Caliber: 22 LR, 9mm Para., 38 Spec., 357 Mag., 40 S&W. **Barrel:** 3". **Weight:** 14.5 oz. **Length:** 4.8" overall. **Grips:** Rosewood, walnut or other hardwoods. **Sights:** Fixed. **Features:** Double-action only; two-shots. Manual safety. Made of satin-finished stainless steel and aluminum. Introduced 1989. From American Derringer Corp.

Price: 22 LR $435.00
Price: 38 Spec. $460.00
Price: 9mm Para. $445.00
Price: 357 Mag. $450.00
Price: 40 S&W $475.00

ANSCHUTZ MODEL 64P SPORT/TARGET PISTOL

Caliber: 22 LR, 22 WMR, 5-shot magazine. **Barrel:** 10". **Weight:** 3 lbs., 8 oz. **Length:** 18-1/2" overall. **Stock:** Choate Rynite. **Sights:** None furnished; grooved for scope mounting. **Features:** Right-hand bolt; polished blue finish. Introduced 1998. Imported from Germany by AcuSport.

Price: 22 LR $455.95
Price: 22 WMR $479.95

BOND ARMS DEFENDER DERRINGER

Caliber: 410 Buckshot or slug, 45 Colt/45 Schofield (2.5" chamber), 45 Colt (only), 450 Bond Super/45 ACP/45 Super, 44 Mag./44 Special/44 Russian, 10mm, 40 S&W, 357 SIG, 357 Maximum/357 Mag./38 Special, 357 Mag/38 Special & 38 Long Colt, 38 Short Colt, 9mm Luger (9x19), 32 H&R Mag./38 S&W Long/32 Colt New Police, 22 Mag., 22 LR., 38-40, 44-40. **Barrel:** 3", 3-1/2". **Weight:** 20-21 oz. **Length:** 5"-5-1/2". **Grips:** Exotic woods or animal horn. **Sights:** Blade front, fixed rear. **Features:** Interchangeable barrels, retracting and rebounding firing pins, cross-bolt safety, automatic extractor for rimmed calibers. Stainless steel construction. Right or left hand.

Price: Texas (with TG) 3" bbl. $359.00
Price: Super (with TG) 3" bbl., 450 Bond Super and 45 ACP . . . $359.00
Price: Cowboy (no TG) $359.00
Price: Century 2000 (with TG), Cowboy Century 2000 (no TG), 3-1/2" bbls., 410/45 Colt $379.00
Price: additional calibers available separately

BROWN CLASSIC SINGLE SHOT PISTOL

Caliber: 17 Ackley Hornet through 45-70 Govt. **Barrel:** 15" airgauged match grade. **Weight:** About 3 lbs., 7 oz. **Grips:** Walnut; thumbrest target style. **Sights:** None furnished; drilled and tapped for scope mounting. **Features:** Falling block action gives rigid barrel-receiver mating; hand-fitted and headspaced. Introduced 1998. Made in U.S.A. by E.A. Brown Mfg.

Price: $499.00

Bond Arms Texas Defender

Bond Arms Cowboy Defender

Bond Arms Super Defender

Bond Arms Century 2000 Defender

Comanche Super Single Shot

Davis Big Bore

COMANCHE SUPER SINGLE SHOT PISTOL
Caliber: 45 LC, 410 ga. **Barrel:** 10". **Sights:** Adjustable. **Features:** Blue finish, not available for sale in CA, MA. Distributed by SGS Importers International, Inc.
Price: **$167.95**

DAVIS BIG BORE DERRINGERS
Caliber: 22 WMR, 38 Spec., 9mm Para. **Barrel:** 2.75". **Weight:** 11.5 oz. **Length:** 4.65" overall. **Grips:** Textured black synthetic. **Sights:** Blade front, fixed notch rear. **Features:** Alloy frame, steel-lined barrels, steel breech block. Plunger-type safety with integral hammer block. Chrome or black Teflon finish. Introduced 1992. Made in U.S.A. by Davis Industries.
Price: **$98.00**
Price: 9mm Para. **$104.00**

DAVIS LONG-BORE DERRINGERS
Caliber: 22 WMR, 38 Spec., 9mm Para. **Barrel:** 3.5". **Weight:** 13 oz. **Length:** 5.65" overall. **Grips:** Textured black synthetic. **Sights:** Fixed. **Features:** Chrome or black Teflon finish. Larger than Davis D-Series models. Introduced 1995. Made in U.S.A. by Davis Industries.
Price: **$104.00**
Price: 9mm Para. **$110.00**
Price: Big-Bore models (same calibers, 3/4" shorter barrels). **$98.00**

DAVIS D-SERIES DERRINGERS
Caliber: 22 LR, 22 WMR, 25 ACP, 32 ACP. **Barrel:** 2.4". **Weight:** 9.5 oz. **Length:** 4" overall. **Grips:** Laminated wood or pearl. **Sights:** Blade front, fixed notch rear. **Features:** Choice of black Teflon or chrome finish; spur trigger. Introduced 1986. Made in U.S.A. by Davis Industries.
Price: **$99.50**

DOWNSIZER WSP SINGLE SHOT PISTOL
Caliber: 357 Magnum, 45 ACP. **Barrel:** 2.10". **Weight:** 11 oz. **Length:** 3.25" overall. **Grips:** Black polymer. **Sights:** None. **Features:** Single shot, tip-up barrel. Double action only. Stainless steel construction. Measures .900" thick. Introduced 1997. From Downsizer Corp.
Price: **$499.00**

Davis Long-Bore

IAR Model 1872 Derringer

Downsizer Single Shot

IAR Model 1888 Derringer

Gaucher GN1 Silhouette

Maximum Single Shot

GAUCHER GN1 SILHOUETTE PISTOL

Caliber: 22 LR, single shot. **Barrel:** 10". **Weight:** 2.4 lbs. **Length:** 15.5" overall. **Grips:** European hardwood. **Sights:** Blade front, open adjustable rear. **Features:** Bolt action, adjustable trigger. Introduced 1990. Imported from France by Mandall Shooting Supplies.

Price: About **$525.00**
Price: Model GP Silhouette **$425.00**

IAR MODEL 1872 DERRINGER

Caliber: 22 Short. **Barrel:** 2-3/8". **Weight:** 7 oz. **Length:** 5-1/8" overall. **Grips:** Smooth walnut. **Sights:** Blade front, notch rear. **Features:** Gold or nickel frame with blue barrel. Reintroduced 1996 using original Colt designs and tooling for the Colt Model 4 Derringer. Made in U.S.A. by IAR, Inc.

Price: **$109.00**
Price: Single cased gun **$125.00**
Price: Double cased set **$215.00**

IAR MODEL 1866 DOUBLE DERRINGER

Caliber: 38 Special. **Barrel:** 2-3/4". **Weight:** 16 oz. **Grips:** Smooth walnut. **Sights:** Blade front, notch rear. **Features:** All steel construction. Blue barrel, color case-hardened frame. Uses original designs and tooling for the Uberti New Maverick Derringer. Introduced 1999. Made in U.S.A. by IAR, Inc.

Price: **$395.00**

MAXIMUM SINGLE SHOT PISTOL

Caliber: 22 LR, 22 Hornet, 22 BR, 22 PPC, 223 Rem., 22-250, 6mm BR, 6mm PPC, 243, 250 Savage, 6.5mm-35M, 270 MAX, 270 Win., 7mm TCU, 7mm BR, 7mm-35, 7mm INT-R, 7mm-08, 7mm Rocket, 7mm Super-Mag., 30 Herrett, 30 Carbine, 30-30, 308 Win., 30x39, 32-20, 350 Rem. Mag., 357 Mag., 357 Maximum, 358 Win., 375 H&H, 44 Mag., 454 Casull. **Barrel:** 8-3/4", 10-1/2", 14". **Weight:** 61 oz. (10-1/2" bbl.); 78 oz. (14" bbl.). **Length:** 15", 18-1/2" overall (with 10-1/2" and 14" bbl., respectively). **Grips:** Smooth walnut stocks and forend. Also available with 17" finger groove grip. **Sights:** Ramp front, fully adjustable open rear. **Features:** Falling block action; drilled and tapped for M.O.A. scope mounts; integral grip frame/receiver; adjustable trigger; Douglas barrel (interchangeable). Introduced 1983. Made in U.S.A. by M.O.A. Corp.

Price: Stainless receiver, blue barrel **$799.00**
Price: Stainless receiver, stainless barrel **$883.00**
Price: Extra blued barrel **$254.00**
Price: Extra stainless barrel **$317.00**
Price: Scope mount **$60.00**

RPM XL SINGLE SHOT PISTOL

Caliber: 22 LR through 45-70. **Barrel:** 8", 10-3/4", 12", 14". **Weight:** About 60 oz. **Grips:** Smooth Goncalo Alves with thumb and heel rests. **Sights:** Hooded front with interchangeable post, or Patridge; ISGW rear adjustable for windage and elevation. **Features:** Barrel drilled and tapped for scope mount. Visible cocking indicator. Spring-loaded barrel lock, positive hammer-block safety. Trigger adjustable for weight of pull and over-travel. Contact maker for complete price list. Made in U.S.A. by RPM.

Price: XL Hunter model (action only) **$1,045.00**
Price: Extra barrel, 8" through 10-3/4" **$407.50**
Price: Extra barrel, 12" through 14" **$547.50**
Price: Muzzle brake **$160.00**
Price: Left hand action, add **$50.00**

SAVAGE STRIKER BOLT-ACTION HUNTING HANDGUN

Caliber: 223, 243, 7mm-08, 308, 300 WSM 2-shot mag. **Barrel:** 14". **Weight:** About 5 lbs. **Length:** 22-1/2" overall. **Stock:** Black composite ambidextrous mid-grip; grooved forend; "Dual Pillar" bedding. **Sights:** None furnished; drilled and tapped for scope mounting. **Features:** Short left-hand bolt with right-hand ejection; free-floated barrel; uses Savage Model 110 rifle scope rings/bases. Introduced 1998. Made in U.S.A. by Savage Arms, Inc.

Price: Model 510F (blued barrel and action) **$425.00**
Price: Model 516FSS (stainless barrel and action) **$462.00**

HANDGUNS

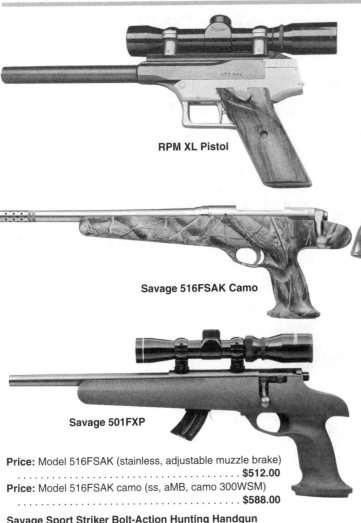

RPM XL Pistol

T/C Encore

Savage 516FSAK Camo

Weatherby Mark V CFP

Savage 501FXP

Price: Model 516FSAK (stainless, adjustable muzzle brake)
. . . . **$512.00**
Price: Model 516FSAK camo (ss, aMB, camo 300WSM)
. . . . **$588.00**

Savage Sport Striker Bolt-Action Hunting Handgun

Similar to Striker, but chambered in 22 LR and 22 WMR. Detachable, 10-shot magazine (5-shot magazine for 22 WMR). Overall length 19", weighs 4 lbs. Ambidextrous fiberglass/graphite composite rear grip. Drilled and tapped, scope mount installed. Introduced 2000. Made in U.S.A. by Savage Arms Inc.

Price: Model 501F (blue finish, 22LR) **$216.00**
New!!! Price: Model 501FXP with soft case, 1.25-4x28 scope . . **$258.00**
Price: Model 502F (blue finish, 22 WMR) **$238.00**

THOMPSON/CENTER ENCORE PISTOL

Caliber: 22-250, 223, 260 Rem., 7mm-08, 243, 308, 270, 30-06, 44 Mag., 454 Casull, 480 Ruger, 444 Marlin single shot, 450 Marlin with muzzle tamer, no sights. **Barrel:** 12", 15", tapered round. **Weight:** NA. **Length:** 21" overall with 12" barrel. **Grips:** American walnut with finger grooves, walnut forend. **Sights:** Blade on ramp front, adjustable rear, or none. **Features:** Interchangeable barrels; action opens by squeezing the trigger guard; drilled and tapped for scope mounting; blue finish. Announced 1996. Made in U.S.A. by Thompson/Center Arms.

Price: **$561.00**
Price: Extra 12" barrels **$250.00**
Price: Extra 15" barrels **$258.00**
Price: 45 Colt/410 barrel, 12" **$274.00**
Price: 45 Colt/410 barrel, 15" **$292.00**

Thompson/Center Stainless Encore Pistol

Similar to blued Encore, made of stainless steel, available with 15" barrel in 223, 22-250, 243 Win., 7mm-08, 308, 30/06 Sprgfld., 45/70 Gov't., 45/410 VR. With black rubber grip and forend. Made in U.S.A. by Thompson/Center Arms.

Price: **$619.00**

Thompson/Center Stainless Super 14

Same as standard Super 14 and Super 16 except made of stainless steel with blued sights. Both models have black Rynite forend and finger-groove, ambidextrous grip with a built-in rubber recoil cushion with sealed-in air pocket. Receiver has different cougar etching. Available in 22 LR Match, .223 Rem., 30-30 Win., 35 Rem. (Super 14), 45 Colt/410. Introduced 1993.

Price: **$578.40**
Price: 45 Colt/410, 14" **$613.94**

Thompson/Center Contender Shooter's Package

Package contains a 14" barrel without iron sights (10" for the 22 LR Match); Weaver-style base and rings; 2.5x-7x Recoil Proof pistol scope; and a soft carrying case. Calibers 22 LR, 223, 7-30 Waters, 30-30. Frame and barrel are blued; grip and forend are black composite. Introduced 1998. Made in U.S.A. by Thompson/Center Arms.

Price: **$735.00**

THOMPSON/CENTER CONTENDER

Caliber: 7mm TCU, 30-30 Win., 22 LR, 22 WMR, 22 Hornet, 223 Rem., 270 Rem., 7-30 Waters, 32-20 Win., 357 Mag., 357 Rem. Max., 44 Mag., 10mm Auto, 445 SuperMag., 45/410, single shot. **Barrel:** 10", bull barrel and vent. rib. **Weight:** 43 oz. (10" bbl.). **Length:** 13-1/4" (10" bbl.). **Stock:** T/C "Competitor Grip." Right or left hand. **Sights:** Under-cut blade ramp front, rear adjustable for windage and elevation. **Features:** Break-open action with automatic safety. Single-action only. Interchangeable bbls., both caliber (rim & centerfire), and length. Drilled and tapped for scope. Engraved frame. See T/C catalog for exact barrel/caliber availability.

Price: Blued (rimfire cals.) **$509.03**
Price: Blued (centerfire cals.) **$509.03**
Price: Extra bbls. **$229.02**
Price: 45/410, internal choke bbl. **$235.11**

Thompson/Center Stainless Contender

Same as standard Contender except made of stainless steel with blued sights, black Rynite forend and ambidextrous finger-groove grip with built-in rubber recoil cushion with sealed-in air pocket. Receiver has different cougar etching. Available with 10" bull barrel in 22 LR, 22 LR Match, 22 Hornet, 223 Rem., 30-30 Win., 357 Mag., 44 Mag., 45 Colt/410. Introduced 1993.

Price: **$566.59**
Price: 45 Colt/410 . . . . **$590.44**
Price: With 22 LR match chamber **$578.40**

UBERTI ROLLING BLOCK TARGET PISTOL

Caliber: 22 LR, 22 WMR, 22 Hornet, 357 Mag., 45 Colt, single shot. **Barrel:** 9-7/8", half-round, half-octagon. **Weight:** 44 oz. **Length:** 14" overall. **Stock:** Walnut grip and forend. **Sights:** Blade front, fully adjustable rear. **Features:** Replica of the 1871 rolling block target pistol. Brass trigger guard, color case-hardened frame, blue barrel. Imported by Uberti U.S.A.

Price: **$410.00**

Both classic arms and recent designs in American-style repeaters for sport and field shooting.

Armalite M15A2

Armalite AR-10A4

Auto-Ordnance 1927 A-1 Thompson

Barrett Model 82A-1

RIFLES

ARMALITE M15A2 CARBINE
Caliber: 223, 7-shot magazine. **Barrel:** 16" heavy chrome lined; 1:9" twist. **Weight:** 7 lbs. **Length:** 35-11/16" overall. **Stock:** Green or black composition. **Sights:** Standard A2. **Features:** Upper and lower receivers have push-type pivot pin; hard coat anodized; A2-style forward assist; M16A2-type raised fence around magazine release button. Made in U.S.A. by ArmaLite, Inc.
Price: Green **$930.00**
Price: Black **$945.00**

ARMALITE AR-10A4 SPECIAL PURPOSE RIFLE
Caliber: 308 Win., 10-shot magazine. **Barrel:** 20" chrome-lined, 1:12" twist. **Weight:** 9.6 lbs. **Length:** 41" overall **Stock:** Green or black composition. **Sights:** Detachable handle, front sight, or scope mount available; comes with international style flattop receiver with Picatinny rail. **Features:** Proprietary recoil check. Forged upper receiver with case deflector. Receivers are hard-coat anodized. Introduced 1995. Made in U.S.A. by ArmaLite, Inc.
Price: Green **$1,378.00**
Price: Black **$1,393.00**

AUTO-ORDNANCE 1927 A-1 THOMPSON
Caliber: 45 ACP. **Barrel:** 16-1/2". **Weight:** 13 lbs. **Length:** About 41" overall (Deluxe). **Stock:** Walnut stock and vertical forend. **Sights:** Blade front, open rear adjustable for windage. **Features:** Recreation of Thompson

Model 1927. Semi-auto only. Deluxe model has finned barrel, adjustable rear sight and compensator; Standard model has plain barrel and military sight. From Auto-Ordnance Corp.
Price: Deluxe **$950.00**
Price: 1927A1C Lightweight model (9-1/2 lbs.) **$950.00**

Auto-Ordnance Thompson M1/M1-C
Similar to the 1927 A-1 except is in the M-1 configuration with side cocking knob, horizontal forend, smooth unfinned barrel, sling swivels on butt and forend. Matte black finish. Introduced 1985.
Price: M1 semi-auto carbine. **$950.00**
Price: M1-C lightweight semi-auto **$925.00**

Auto-Ordnance 1927A1 Commando
Similar to the 1927A1 except has Parkerized finish, black-finish wood butt, pistol grip, horizontal forend. Comes with black nylon sling. Introduced 1998. Made in U.S.A. by Auto-Ordnance Corp.
Price: **$950.00**

BARRETT MODEL 82A-1 SEMI-AUTOMATIC RIFLE
Caliber: 50 BMG, 10-shot detachable box magazine. **Barrel:** 29". **Weight:** 28.5 lbs. **Length:** 57" overall. **Stock:** Composition with energy-absorbing recoil pad. **Sights:** Scope optional. **Features:** Semi-automatic, recoil operated with recoiling barrel. Three-lug locking bolt; muzzle brake. Adjustable bipod. Introduced 1985. Made in U.S.A. by Barrett Firearms.
Price: From. **$7,200.00**

Browning Mark II Safari

Bushmaster M17S

Bushmaster M15 E2S Carbine

BROWNING BAR MARK II SAFARI SEMI-AUTO RIFLE

Caliber: 243, 25-06, 270, 30-06, 308. **Barrel:** 22" round tapered. **Weight:** 7-3/8 lbs. **Length:** 43" overall. **Stock:** French walnut pistol grip stock and forend, hand checkered. **Sights:** Gold bead on hooded ramp front, click adjustable rear, or no sights. **Features:** Has new bolt release lever; removable trigger assembly with larger trigger guard; redesigned gas and buffer systems. Detachable 4-round box magazine. Scroll-engraved receiver is tapped for scope mounting. BOSS barrel vibration modulator and muzzle brake system available only on models without sights. Mark II Safari introduced 1993. Imported from Belgium by Browning.

Price: Safari, with sights **$833.00**
Price: Safari, no sights **$815.00**
Price: Safari, 270 and 30-06, no sights, BOSS **$891.00**

Browning BAR MARK II Lightweight Semi-Auto

Similar to the Mark II Safari except has lighter alloy receiver and 20" barrel. Available in 243, 308, 270, 30-06, 7mm Rem. Mag., 300 Win. Mag., 338 Win. Mag. Weighs 7 lbs., 2 oz.; overall length 41". Has dovetailed, gold bead front sight on hooded ramp, open rear click adjustable for windage and elevation. Introduced 1997. Imported from Belgium by Browning.

Price: 243, 308, 270, 30-06 . . . . **$833.00**
Price: 7mm Rem. Mag., 300 Win. Mag., 338 Win. Mag **$909.00**

Browning BAR Mark II Safari Rifle in magnum calibers

Same as the standard caliber model, except weighs 8-3/8 lbs., 45" overall, 24" bbl., 3-round mag. Cals. 7mm Mag., 300 Win. Mag., 338 Win. Mag. BOSS barrel vibration modulator and muzzle brake system available only on models without sights. Introduced 1993.

Price: Safari, with sights **$909.00**
Price: Safari, no sights **$890.00**
Price: Safari, no sights, BOSS **$967.00**

Browning BAR High-Grade Auto Rifles

Similar to BAR Mark II Safari model except has grayed receiver with big-game scenes framed in gold with select walnut stock and forearm. Furnished with no sights. Introduced 2001.

Price: 270, 30-06 (whitetail and mule deer scenes) **$1,820.00**
Price: 7mm Rem. Mag., 300 Win. Mag. (moose and elk scenes)
. . . . **$1,876.00**

BROWNING BAR STALKER AUTO RIFLES

Caliber: 243, 308, 270, 30-06, 7mm Rem. Mag., 300 Win. Mag., 338 Win. Mag. **Barrel:** 20", 22" and 24". **Weight:** 6 lbs., 12 oz. (243) to 8 lbs., 2 oz. (magnum cals.) **Length:** 41" to 45" overall. **Stock:** Black composite stock and forearm. **Sights:** Hooded front and adjustable rear or none. **Features:** Optional BOSS (no sights); gas-operated action with seven-lug rotary bolt; dual action bars; 3- or 4-shot magazine (depending on caliber). Introduced 2001. Imported by Browning.

Price: BAR Stalker, open sights (243, 308, 270, 30-06) **$809.00**
Price: BAR Stalker, open sights (7mm, 300 Win. Mag.,
338 Win. Mag.) **$883.00**
Price: BAR Stalker, BOSS (7mm, 300 Win. Mag., 338 Win. Mag.) **$941.00**

BUSHMASTER M17S BULLPUP RIFLE

Caliber: 223, 10-shot magazine. **Barrel:** 21.5", chrome lined;1:9" twist. **Weight:** 8.2 lbs. **Length:** 30" overall. **Stock:** Fiberglass-filled nylon. **Sights:** Designed for optics—carrying handle incorporates scope mount rail for Weaver-type rings; also includes 25-meter open iron sights. **Features:** Gas-operated, short-stroke piston system; ambidextrous magazine release. Introduced 1993. Made in U.S.A. by Bushmaster Firearms, Inc./Quality Parts Co.

Price: **$765.00**

BUSHMASTER SHORTY XM15 E2S CARBINE

Caliber: 223,10-shot magazine. **Barrel:** 16", heavy; 1:9" twist. **Weight:** 7.2 lbs. **Length:** 34.75" overall. **Stock:** A2 type; fixed black composition. **Sights:** Fully adjustable M16A2 sight system. **Features:** Patterned after Colt M-16A2. Chrome-lined barrel with manganese phosphate finish. "Shorty" handguards. Has forged aluminum receivers with push-pin. Made in U.S.A. by Bushmaster Firearms Inc.

Price: **$950.00**

Calico Liberty 50

Carbon 15

Colt Match Target Lightweight

Bushmaster XM15 E2S Dissipator Carbine
Similar to the XM15 E2S Shorty carbine except has full-length "Dissipator" handguards. Weighs 7.6 lbs.; 34.75" overall; forged aluminum receivers with push-pin style takedown. Made in U.S.A. by Bushmaster Firearms, Inc.
Price **$965.00**

Bushmaster XM15 E25 AK Shorty Carbine
Similar to the XM15 E2S Shorty except has 14.5" barrel with an AK muzzle brake permanently attached giving 16" barrel length. Weighs 7.3 lbs. Introduced 1999. Made in U.S.A. by Bushmaster Firearms, Inc.
Price: **$975.00**

BUSHMASTER VARMINTER RIFLE
Caliber: 223 Rem., 5-shot. **Barrel:** 24", 1:9" twist, fluted, heavy. **Weight:** 8/3/4 lbs. **Length:** 42-1/4". **Stock:** Rubberized pistol grip. **Sights:** 1/2" scope risers. **Features:** Gas-operated, semi-auto, 2 stage trigger, slotted free floater forend, lockable hard case.
Price: **$1,195.00**

CALICO LIBERTY 50, 100 CARBINES
Caliber: 9mm Para. **Barrel:** 16.1". **Weight:** 7 lbs. **Length:** 34.5" overall. **Stock:** Glass-filled, impact resistant polymer. **Sights:** Adjustable front post, fixed notch and aperture flip rear. **Features:** Helical feed magazine; ambidextrous, rotating sear/striker block safety; static cocking handle; retarded blowback action; aluminum alloy receiver. Introduced 1995. Made in U.S.A. by Calico.
Price: Liberty 50 . . . . **$860.00**
Price: Liberty 100 . . . . **$925.00**

CARBON 15 (TYPE 97) AUTO RIFLE
Caliber: 223. **Barrel:** 16". **Weight:** 3.9 lbs. **Length:** 35" overall. **Stock:** Carbon fiber butt and forend, rubberized pistol grip. **Sights:** None furnished; optics base. **Features:** Carbon fiber upper and lower receivers; stainless steel match-grade barrel; hard-chromed bolt and carrier; quick-detachable compensator. Made in U.S.A. by Professional Ordnance Inc.
Price: . . . . **$1,120.00 to $1,285.00**

COLT MATCH TARGET RIFLE
Caliber: 223 Rem., 5-shot magazine. **Barrel:** 16.1" or 20". **Weight:** 7.1 to 8-1/2 lbs. **Length:** 34-1/2" to 39" overall. **Stock:** Composition stock, grip, forend. **Sights:** Post front, rear adjustable for windage and elevation. **Features:** 5-round detachable box magazine, flash suppressor, sling swivels. Forward bolt assist included. Introduced 1991. Made in U.S.A. by Colt's Manufacturing Co. Inc.
Price: Colt Light Rifle **$779.00**
Price: Match Target HBAR, from **$1,194.00**

DPMS PANTHER ARMS A-15 RIFLES
Caliber: 223 Rem., 7.62x39. **Barrel:** 16" to 24". **Weight:** 7-3/4 to 11-3/4 lbs. **Length:** 34-1/2 to 42-1/4" overall. **Stock:** Black Zytel® composite. **Sights:** Square front post, adjustable A2 rear. **Features:** Steel or stainless steel heavy or bull barrel; hard-coat anodized receiver; aluminum free-float tube handguard; many options. From DPMS Panther Arms.
Price: Panther Bull A-15 (20" stainless bull barrel). **$915.00**
Price: Panther Bull Twenty-Four (24" stainless bull barrel) **$945.00**
Price: Bulldog (20" stainless fluted barrel, flat top receiver) **$1,219.00**
Price: Panther Bull Sweet Sixteen (16" stainless bull barrel) **$885.00**
Price: DCM Panther (20" stainless heavy bbl., n.m. sights) **$1,099.00**
Price: Panther 7.62x39 (20" steel heavy barrel). **$849.00**

DSA SA58 STANDARD
Caliber: 308 Win. **Barrel:** 21" with integrally machined muzzle brake. **Weight:** 8.75 lbs. **Length:** 43". **Stock:** Fiberglass reinforced synthetic handguard. **Sights:** Adjustable post front, adjustable rear peep. **Features:** Gas-operated semi-auto with fully adjustable gas system, high grade steel upper receiver. In variety of camo finishes. Made in U.S.A. by DSA, Inc.
Price: **$1,395.00**

DSA SA58 CARBINE
Caliber: 308 Win., limited 243 and 260. **Barrel:** 16.25" with integrally machined muzzle brake. **Weight:** 8.75 lbs. **Length:** 38.25". **Stock:** Fiberglass reinforced synthetic handguard. **Sights:** Adjustable post front, adjustable rear peep. **Features:** Gas-operated semi-auto with fully adjustable gas system, high grade steel or 416 stainless upper receiver. In variety of camo finishes. Made in U.S.A. by DSA, Inc.
Price: chrome moly bbl. **$1,395.00**
Price: stainless steel bbl. **$1,645.00**

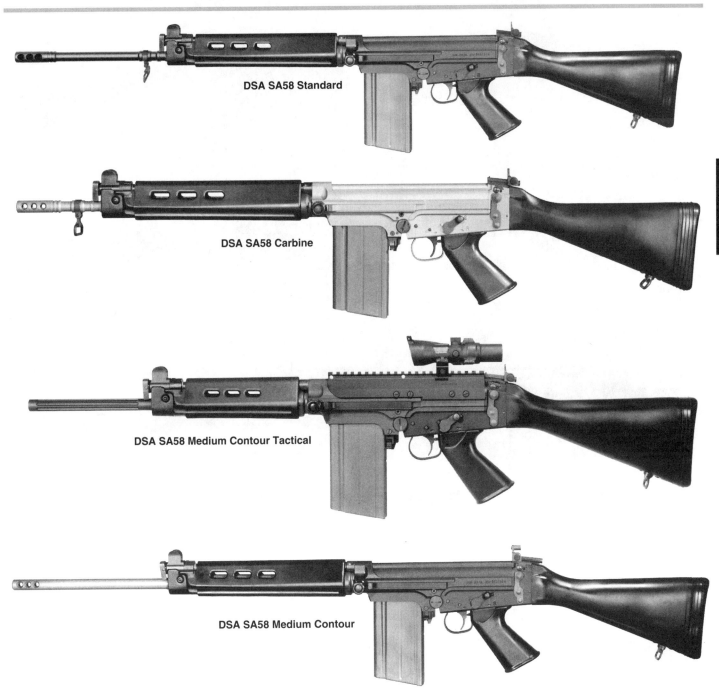

DSA SA58 Standard

DSA SA58 Carbine

DSA SA58 Medium Contour Tactical

DSA SA58 Medium Contour

DSA SA58 MEDIUM CONTOUR TACTICAL
Caliber: 308 Win. **Barrel:** Fluted, 16.25". **Weight:** 8 lbs. **Length:** 38.25". **Stock:** Fiberglass reinforced short synthetic handguard. **Sights:** Adjustable post front, adjustable rear peep. **Features:** Gas-operated semi-auto with fully adjustable gas system, high grade steel upper receiver. In variety of camo finishes. Made in U.S.A. by DSA, Inc.
Price: **$1,475.00**

DSA SA58 MEDIUM CONTOUR
Caliber: 308 Win., limited 243 and 260. **Barrel:** 21" with integrally machined muzzle brake. **Weight:** 9.75 lbs. **Length:** 43". **Stock:** Fiberglass reinforced synthetic handguard. **Sights:** Adjustable post front with match rear peep. **Features:** Gas-operated semi-auto with fully adjustable gas system, high grade steel or 416 stainless upper receiver. In variety of camo finishes. Made in U.S.A. by DSA, Inc.
Price: chrome moly. **$1,475.00**
Price: stainless steel. **$1,525.00**

DSA SA58 21" OR 24" BULL
Caliber: 308 Win. **Barrel:** 21" or 24". **Weight:** 11.1 and 11.5 lbs. **Length:** 41.5" and 44.5". **Stock:** Free floating handguard. **Sights:** Elevation adjustable protected post front, match rear peep. **Features:** Gas-operated semi-auto with fully adjustable gas system, high grade steel or stainless upper receiver. Made in U.S.A. by DSA, Inc.
Price: chrome moly bbl. **$1,745.00**
Price: stainless steel bbl. **$1,795.00**

DSA SA58 T48 TACTICAL
Caliber: 308 Win. **Barrel:** 21" chrome molly. with Browning flashhider. **Weight:** 9.68 lbs. **Length:** 45" overall. **Stock:** Field grade finish wood. **Sights:** Adjustable post front, adjustable rear peep. **Features:** 10- or 20-round fixed magazine with stripper clip top cover. Gas operated semi-auto with fully adjustable gas system. Made in U.S.A. by DSA, Inc.
Price: **$1,575.00**

DSA SA58 Bull

DSA SA58 T48 Replica

DSA SA58 OSW

EAA/Saiga 380

DSA SA58 21" OR 24" BULL

Caliber: 7.62 NATO. **Barrel:** 11" or 13" chrome mollly with muzzle brake. **Weight:** 7.85 lbs. **Length:** 33". **Features:** Gas-operated semi-auto or select fire with fully adjustable short gas system, optional FAL Rail Interface Handguard, SureFire Vertical Foregrip System, EOTech HOLOgraphic Sight and ITC Cheekrest. Made in U.S.A. by DSA, Inc.
Price: **$1,525.00**

EAA/SAIGA SEMI-AUTO RIFLE

Caliber: 7.62x39, 308, 223. **Barrel:** 20.5", 22", 16.3". **Weight:** 7 to 8-1/2 lbs. **Length:** 43". **Stock:** Synthetic or wood. **Sights:** Adjustable, sight base. **Features:** Based on AK Combat rifle by Kalashnikov. Imported from Russia by EAA Corp.
Price: 7.62x39 (syn.). **$239.00**
Price: 308 (syn. or wood) **$429.00**
Price: 223 (syn.) **$389.00**

HECKLER & KOCH SLB 2000 RIFLE

Caliber: 30-06; 2-, 5- and 10-shot magazines. **Barrel:** 19.7". **Weight:** 8 lb. **Length:** 41.3". **Stock:** Oil-finished, checkered walnut. **Sights:** Ramp front, patridge rear. **Features:** Short-stroke, piston-actuated gas operation; modular steel and polymer construction; free-floating barrel; pistol grip angled for natural feel. Introduced 2001. From H&K.
Price: **$1,399.00**

HECKLER & KOCH SL8-1 RIFLE

Caliber: 223; 10-shot magazine. **Barrel:** 17.7". **Weight:** 8.6 lbs. **Length:** 38.6" overall. **Stock:** Polymer thumbhole. **Sights:** Blade front with integral hood; fully adjustable rear diopter. Picatinny rail. **Features:** Based on German military G36 rifle. Uses short-stroke piston-actuated gas operation; almost entirely constructed of carbon fiber-reinforced polymer. Free-floating heavy target barrel. Introduced 2000. From H&K.
Price: **$1,249.00**

CENTERFIRE RIFLES — AUTOLOADERS

Heckler & Koch SLB 2000

Heckler & Koch SL8-1

Heckler & Koch USC

Hi-Point Carbine

HECKLER & KOCH USC CARBINE
Caliber: 45 ACP, 10-shot magazine. **Barrel:** 16". **Weight:** 8.6 lb. **Length:** 35.4" overall. **Stock:** Skeletonized polymer thumbhole. **Sights:** Blade front with integral hood, fully adjustable diopter. **Features:** Based on German UMP submachine gun. Blowback operation; almost entirely constructed of carbon fiber-reinforced polymer. Free-floating heavy target barrel. Introduced 2000. From H&K.
Price: **$1,249.00**

HI-POINT 9MM CARBINE
Caliber: 9mm Para., 40 S&W, 10-shot magazine. **Barrel:** 16-1/2" (17-1/2" for 40 S&W). **Weight:** 4-1/2 lbs. **Length:** 31-1/2" overall. **Stock:** Black polymer. **Sights:** Protected post front, aperture rear. Integral scope mount. **Features:** Grip-mounted magazine release. Black or chrome finish. Sling swivels. Introduced 1996. Made in U.S.A. by MKS Supply, Inc.
Price: Black or chrome, 9mm **$199.00**
Price: 40 S&W **$225.00**

IAI M-333 M1 GARAND
Caliber: 30-06, 8-shot clip. **Barrel:** 24". **Weight:** 9-1/2 lbs. **Length:** 43.6" overall. **Stock:** Hardwood. **Sights:** Blade front, aperture adjustable rear. **Features:** Parkerized finish; gas-operated semi-automatic; remanufactured to military specifications. From IAI.
Price: **$971.75**

IAI M-888 M1 CARBINE SEMI-AUTOMATIC RIFLE
Caliber: 22, 30 Carbine. **Barrel:** 18"-20". **Weight:** 5-1/2 lbs. **Length:** 35"-37" overall. **Stock:** Laminate, walnut or birch. **Sights:** Blade front, adjustable rear. **Features:** Gas-operated, air cooled, manufactured to military specifications. 10/15/30 rnd. mag. scope available. From IAI.
Price: 30 cal. . . . . **$556.00 to $604.00**
Price: 22 cal. . . . . **$567.00 to $654.00**

LES BAER CUSTOM ULTIMATE AR 223 RIFLES
Caliber: 223. **Barrel:** 18", 20", 22", 24". **Weight:** 7-3/4 to 9-3/4 lb. **Length:** NA. **Stock:** Black synthetic. **Sights:** None furnished; Picatinny-style flat top rail for scope mounting. **Features:** Forged receiver; Ultra single-stage trigger (Jewell two-stage trigger optional); titanium firing pin; Versa-Pod bipod; chromed National Match carrier; stainless steel, hand-lapped and cryo-treated barrel; guaranteed to shoot 1/2 or 3/4 MOA, depending on model. Made in U.S.A. by Les Bear Custom Inc.
Price: Super Varmint Model **$1,989.00**
Price: M4 Flattop Model **$2,195.00**
Price: IPSC Action Model **$2,195.00**

LR 300 SR LIGHT SPORT RIFLE
Caliber: 223. **Barrel:** 16-1/4"; 1:9" twist. **Weight:** 7.2 lbs. **Length:** 36" overall (extended stock), 26-1/4" (stock folded). **Stock:** Folding, tubular steel, with thumbhold-type grip. **Sights:** Trijicon post front, Trijicon rear. **Features:** Uses AR-15 type upper and lower receivers; flattop receiver with weaver base. Accepts all AR-15/M-16 magazines. Introduced 1996. Made in U.S.A. from Z-M Weapons.
Price: **$2,550.00**

Remington Model 7400

Ruger Deerfield 99/44 Carbine

Ruger PC4 Carbine

Ruger Ranch Mini 14/5R

OLYMPIC ARMS CAR-97 RIFLES

Caliber: 223, 7-shot; 9mm Para., 45 ACP, 40 S&W, 10mm, 10-shot. **Barrel:** 16". **Weight:** 7 lbs. **Length:** 34.75" overall. **Stock:** A2 stowaway grip, telescoping-look butt. **Sights:** Post front, fully adjustable aperature rear. **Features:** Based on AR-15 rifle. Post-ban version of the CAR-15. Made in U.S.A. by Olympic Arms, Inc.

Price: 223 . . . . **$780.00**
Price: 9mm Para., 45 ACP, 40 S&W, 10mm **$840.00**
Price: PCR Eliminator (223, full-length handguards) **$803.00**

OLYMPIC ARMS PCR-4 RIFLE

Caliber: 223, 10-shot magazine. **Barrel:** 20". **Weight:** 8 lbs., 5 oz. **Length:** 38.25" overall. **Stock:** A2 stowaway grip, trapdoor buttstock. **Sights:** Post front, A1 rear adjustable for windage. **Features:** Based on the AR-15 rifle. Barrel is button rifled with 1:9" twist. No bayonet lug. Introduced 1994. Made in U.S.A. by Olympic Arms, Inc.

Price: **$792.00**

OLYMPIC ARMS PCR-6 RIFLE

Caliber: 7.62x39mm (PCR-6), 10-shot magazine. **Barrel:** 16". **Weight:** 7 lbs. **Length:** 34" overall. **Stock:** A2 stowaway grip, trapdoor buttstock. **Sights:** Post front, A1 rear adjustable for windage. **Features:** Based on the CAR-15. No bayonet lug. Button-cut rifling. Introduced 1994. Made in U.S.A. by Olympic Arms, Inc.

Price: **$845.00**

REMINGTON MODEL 7400 AUTO RIFLE

Caliber: 243 Win., 270 Win., 280 Rem., 308 Win., 30-06, 4-shot magazine. **Barrel:** 22" round tapered. **Weight:** 7-1/2 lbs. **Length:** 42-5/8" overall. **Stock:** Walnut, deluxe cut checkered pistol grip and forend. Satin or high-gloss finish. **Sights:** Gold bead front sight on ramp; step rear sight with windage adjustable. **Features:** Redesigned and improved version of the Model 742. Positive cross-bolt safety. Receiver tapped for scope mount. Introduced 1981.

Price: About **$612.00**
Price: Carbine (18-1/2" bbl., 30-06 only) **$612.00**
Price: With black synthetic stock, matte black metal, rifle or carbine **$509.00**

ROCK RIVER ARMS STANDARD A2 RIFLE

Caliber: 45 ACP. **Barrel:** NA. **Weight:** 8.2 lbs. **Length:** NA. **Stock:** Thermoplastic. **Sights:** Standard AR-15 style sights. **Features:** Two-stage, national match trigger; optional muzzle brake. Made in U.S.A. From River Rock Arms.

Price: **$925.00**

RUGER DEERFIELD 99/44 CARBINE

Caliber: 44 Mag., 4-shot rotary magazine. **Barrel:** 18-1/2". **Weight:** 6-1/4 lbs. **Length:** 36-7/8" overall. **Stock:** Hardwood. **Sights:** Gold bead front, folding adjustable aperture rear. **Features:** Semi-automatic action; dual front-locking lugs lock directly into receiver; integral scope mount; push-button safety; includes 1" rings and gun lock. Introduced 2000. Made in U.S.A. by Sturm, Ruger & Co.

Price: **$675.00**

RUGER PC4, PC9 CARBINES

Caliber: 9mm Para., 40 cal., 10-shot magazine. **Barrel:** 16.25". **Weight:** 6 lbs., 4 oz. **Length:** 34.75" overall. **Stock:** Black high impact synthetic checkered grip and forend. **Sights:** Blade front, open adjustable rear; integral Ruger scope mounts. **Features:** Delayed blowback action; manual push-button cross bolt safety and internal firing pin block safety automatic slide lock. Introduced 1997. Made in U.S.A. by Sturm, Ruger & Co.

Price: PC9, PC4, (9mm, 40 cal.) **$605.00**
Price: PC4GR, PC9GR, (40 auto, 9mm, post sights, ghost ring) **$628.00**

RIFLES

Springfield M1A

Springfield National Match M1A

Springfield Super Match with Camo M1A

RUGER MINI-14/5 AUTOLOADING RIFLE

Caliber: 223 Rem., 5-shot detachable box magazine. **Barrel:** 18-1/2". Rifling twist 1:9". **Weight:** 6.4 lbs. **Length:** 37-1/4" overall. **Stock:** American hardwood, steel reinforced. **Sights:** Ramp front, fully adjustable rear. **Features:** Fixed piston gas-operated, positive primary extraction. New buffer system, redesigned ejector system. Ruger S100RM scope rings included.

Price: Mini-14/5R, Ranch Rifle, blued, scope rings	**$675.00**
Price: K-Mini-14/5R, Ranch Rifle, stainless, scope rings	**$745.00**
Price: Mini-14/5, blued, no scope rings	**$636.00**
Price: K-Mini-14/5, stainless, no scope rings	**$696.00**
Price: K-Mini-14/5P, stainless, synthetic stock	**$696.00**
Price: K-Mini-14/5RP, Ranch Rifle, stainless, synthetic stock	**$745.00**

Ruger Mini Thirty Rifle

Similar to the Mini-14 Ranch Rifle except modified to chamber the 7.62x39 Russian service round. Weight is about 6-7/8 lbs. Has 6-groove barrel with 1:10" twist, Ruger Integral Scope Mount bases and folding peep rear sight. Detachable 5-shot staggered box magazine. Blued finish. Introduced 1987.

Price: Blue, scope rings	**$675.00**
Price: Stainless, scope rings	**$745.00**

SPRINGFIELD, INC. M1A RIFLE

Caliber: 7.62mm NATO (308), 5- or 10-shot box magazine. **Barrel:** 25-1/16" with flash suppressor, 22" without suppressor. **Weight:** 9-3/4 lbs. **Length:** 44-1/4" overall. **Stock:** American walnut with walnut-colored heat-resistant fiberglass handguard. Matching walnut handguard available. Also available with fiberglass stock. **Sights:** Military, square blade front, full click-adjustable aperture rear. **Features:** Commercial equivalent of the U.S. M-14 service rifle with no provision for automatic firing. From Springfield, Inc.

Price: Standard M1A, black fiberglass stock	**$1,569.00**
Price: Standard M1A, black fiberglass stock, stainless	**$1,629.00**
Price: National Match	**$1,995.00**

Price: Super Match (heavy premium barrel), about	**$2,449.00**
Price: M21 Tactical Rifle (adj. cheekpiece), about	**$2,975.00**

STONER SR-15 M-5 RIFLE

Caliber: 223. **Barrel:** 20". **Weight:** 7.6 lbs. **Length:** 38" overall. **Stock:** Black synthetic. **Sights:** Post front, fully adjustable rear (300-meter sight). **Features:** Modular weapon system; two-stage trigger. Black finish. Introduced 1998. Made in U.S.A. by Knight's Mfg.

Price:	**$1,650.00**
Price: M-4 Carbine (16" barrel, 6.8 lbs)	**$1,555.00**

STONER SR-25 CARBINE

Caliber: 7.62 NATO, 10-shot steel magazine. **Barrel:** 16" free-floating **Weight:** 7-3/4 lbs. **Length:** 35.75" overall. **Stock:** Black synthetic. **Sights:** Integral Weaver-style rail. Scope rings, iron sights optional. **Features:** Shortened, non-slip handguard; removable carrying handle. Matte black finish. Introduced 1995. Made in U.S.A. by Knight's Mfg. Co.

Price:	**$3,345.00**

WILKINSON LINDA CARBINE

Caliber: 9mm Para. **Barrel:** 16-3/16". **Weight:** 7 lbs. **Stocks:** Fixed tubular with wood pad. **Sights:** Aperture rear sight. **Features:** Aluminum receiver, pre-ban configuration (limited supplies), vent. barrel shroud, small wooden forearm, 18 or 31 shot mag. Many accessories.

Price:	**$1,800.00**

Linda L2 Limited Edition

Manufactured from the last 600 of the original 2,200 pre-ban Linda Carbines, includes many upgrades and accessories. New 2002.

Price:	**$4,800.00**

WILKINSON TERRY CARBINE

Caliber: 9mm Para. **Barrel:** 16-3/16". **Weight:** 7 lbs. **Stocks:** Black or maple. **Sights:** Adjustable. **Features:** Blowback semi-auto action, 31 shot mag., closed breech.

Price:	**NA**

Both classic arms and recent designs in American-style repeaters for sport and field shooting.

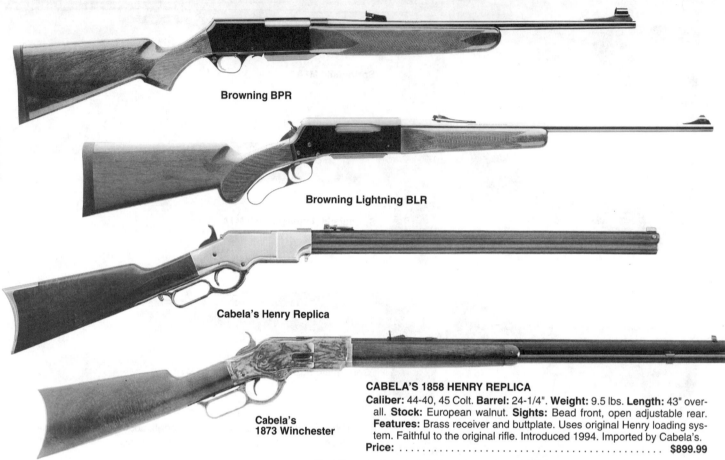

Browning BPR

Browning Lightning BLR

Cabela's Henry Replica

Cabela's 1873 Winchester

BROWNING BPR PUMP RIFLE

Caliber: 243, 308 (short action); 270, 30-06, 7mm Rem. Mag., 300 Win. Mag., 4-shot magazine (3 for magnums). **Barrel:** 22"; 24" for magnum calibers. **Weight:** 7 lbs., 3 oz. **Length:** 43" overall (22" barrel). **Stock:** Select walnut with full pistol grip, high gloss finish. **Sights:** Gold bead on hooded ramp front, open click adjustable rear. **Features:** Slide-action mechanism cams forend down away from the barrel. Seven-lug rotary bolt; cross-bolt safety behind trigger; removable magazine; alloy receiver. Introduced 1997. Imported from Belgium by Browning.

Price: Standard calibers **$718.00**
Price: Magnum calibers **$772.00**

BROWNING LIGHTNING BLR LEVER-ACTION RIFLE

Caliber: 22-250, 243, 7mm-08, 308 Win., 4-shot detachable magazine. **Barrel:** 20" round tapered. **Weight:** 6 lbs., 8 oz. **Length:** 39-1/2" overall. **Stock:** Walnut. Checkered grip and forend, high-gloss finish. **Sights:** Gold bead on ramp front; low profile square notch adjustable rear. **Features:** Wide, grooved trigger; half-cock hammer safety; fold-down hammer. Receiver tapped for scope mount. Recoil pad installed. Introduced 1996. Imported from Japan by Browning.

Price: **$649.00**

Browning Lightning BLR Long Action

Similar to the standard Lightning BLR except has long action to accept 30-06, 270, 7mm Rem. Mag. and 300 Win. Mag. Barrel lengths are 22" for 30-06 and 270, 24" for 7mm Rem. Mag. and 300 Win. Mag. Has six-lug rotary bolt; bolt and receiver are full-length fluted. Fold-down hammer at half-cock. Weighs about 7 lbs., overall length 42-7/8" (22" barrel). Introduced 1996.

Price: **$686.00**

CABELA'S 1858 HENRY REPLICA

Caliber: 44-40, 45 Colt. **Barrel:** 24-1/4". **Weight:** 9.5 lbs. **Length:** 43" overall. **Stock:** European walnut. **Sights:** Bead front, open adjustable rear. **Features:** Brass receiver and buttplate. Uses original Henry loading system. Faithful to the original rifle. Introduced 1994. Imported by Cabela's.
Price: **$899.99**

CABELA'S 1866 WINCHESTER REPLICA

Caliber: 44-40, 45 Colt. **Barrel:** 24-1/4". **Weight:** 9 lbs. **Length:** 43" overall. **Stock:** European walnut. **Sights:** Bead front, open adjustable rear. **Features:** Solid brass receiver, buttplate, forend cap. Octagonal barrel. Faithful to the original Winchester '66 rifle. Introduced 1994. Imported by Cabela's.
Price: **$729.99**

CABELA'S 1873 WINCHESTER REPLICA

Caliber: 44-40, 45 Colt. **Barrel:** 24-1/4", 30". **Weight:** 8.5 lbs. **Length:** 43-1/4" overall. **Stock:** European walnut. **Sights:** Bead front, open adjustable rear; globe front, tang rear. **Features:** Color case-hardened steel receiver. Faithful to the original Model 1873 rifle. Introduced 1994. Imported by Cabela's.
Price: Sporting model, 30" barrel, 44-40, 45 Colt **$899.99**
Price: Sporting model, 24" or 25" barrel **$849.99**

CIMARRON 1860 HENRY REPLICA

Caliber: 44 WCF, 13-shot magazine. **Barrel:** 24-1/4" (rifle), 22" (carbine). **Weight:** 9-1/2 lbs. **Length:** 43" overall (rifle). **Stock:** European walnut. **Sights:** Bead front, open adjustable rear. **Features:** Brass receiver and buttplate. Uses original Henry loading system. Faithful to the original rifle. Introduced 1991. Imported by Cimarron F.A. Co.
Price: **$1,029.00**

CIMARRON 1866 WINCHESTER REPLICAS

Caliber: 22 LR, 22 WMR, 38 Spec., 44 WCF. **Barrel:** 24-1/4" (rifle), 19" (carbine). **Weight:** 9 lbs. **Length:** 43" overall (rifle). **Stock:** European walnut. **Sights:** Bead front, open adjustable rear. **Features:** Solid brass receiver, buttplate, forend cap. Octagonal barrel. Faithful to the original Winchester '66 rifle. Introduced 1991. Imported by Cimarron F.A. Co.
Price: Rifle **$839.00**
Price: Carbine **$829.00**

CENTERFIRE RIFLES — LEVER AND SLIDE

Cimarron 1866 Winchester Replica

Cimarron Long Range 30"

Dixie 1873

IAR 1873
Revolver Carbine

CIMARRON 1873 SHORT RIFLE
Caliber: 357 Mag., 38 Spec., 32 WCF, 38 WCF, 44 Spec., 44 WCF, 45 Colt. **Barrel:** 20" tapered octagon. **Weight:** 7.5 lbs. **Length:** 39" overall. **Stock:** Walnut. **Sights:** Bead front, adjustable semi-buckhorn rear. **Features:** Has half "button" magazine. Original-type markings, including caliber, on barrel and elevator and "Kings" patent. From Cimarron F.A. Co.
Price: . . . . **$949.00 to $999.00**

CIMARRON 1873 LONG RANGE RIFLE
Caliber: 44 WCF, 45 Colt. **Barrel:** 30", octagonal. **Weight:** 8-1/2 lbs. **Length:** 48" overall. **Stock:** Walnut. **Sights:** Blade front, semi-buckhorn ramp rear. Tang sight optional. **Features:** Color case-hardened frame; choice of modern blue-black or charcoal blue for other parts. Barrel marked "Kings Improvement." From Cimarron F.A. Co.
Price: . . . . **$999.00 to $1,199.00**

Cimarron 1873 Sporting Rifle
Similar to the 1873 Short Rifle except has 24" barrel with half-magazine.
Price: . . . . **$949.00 to $999.00**

DIXIE ENGRAVED 1873 RIFLE
Caliber: 44-40, 11-shot magazine. **Barrel:** 20", round. **Weight:** 7-3/4 lbs. **Length:** 39" overall. **Stock:** Walnut. **Sights:** Blade front, adjustable rear. **Features:** Engraved and case-hardened frame. Duplicate of Winchester 1873. Made in Italy. From 21 Gun Works.
Price: **$1,295.00**
Price: Plain, blued carbine **$850.00**

E.M.F. 1860 HENRY RIFLE
Caliber: 44-40 or 45 Colt. **Barrel:** 24.25". **Weight:** About 9 lbs. **Length:** About 43.75" overall. **Stock:** Oil-stained American walnut. **Sights:** Blade front, rear adjustable for elevation. **Features:** Reproduction of the original Henry rifle with brass frame and buttplate, rest blued. From E.M.F.
Price: Brass frame **$850.00**
Price: Steel frame **$950.00**

E.M.F. 1866 YELLOWBOY LEVER ACTIONS
Caliber: 38 Spec., 44-40. **Barrel:** 19" (carbine), 24" (rifle). **Weight:** 9 lbs. **Length:** 43" overall (rifle). **Stock:** European walnut. **Sights:** Bead front, open adjustable rear. **Features:** Solid brass frame, blued barrel, lever, hammer, buttplate. Imported from Italy by E.M.F.

Price: Rifle **$690.00**
Price: Carbine **$675.00**

E.M.F. HARTFORD MODEL 1892 LEVER-ACTION RIFLE
Caliber: 45 Colt. **Barrel:** 24", octagonal. **Weight:** 7-1/2 lbs. **Length:** 43" overall. **Stock:** European walnut. **Sights:** Blade front, open adjustable rear. **Features:** Color case-hardened frame, lever, trigger and hammer with blued barrel, or overall blue finish. Introduced 1998. Imported by E.M.F.
Price: Standard **$590.00**

E.M.F. MODEL 1873 LEVER-ACTION RIFLE
Caliber: 32/20, 357 Mag., 38/40, 44-40, 44 Spec., 45 Colt. **Barrel:** 24". **Weight:** 8 lbs. **Length:** 43-1/4" overall. **Stock:** European walnut. **Sights:** Bead front, rear adjustable for windage and elevation. **Features:** Color case-hardened frame (blue on carbine). Imported by E.M.F.
Price: Rifle **$865.00**
Price: Carbine, 19" barrel **$865.00**

IAR MODEL 1873 REVOLVER CARBINE
Caliber: 357 Mag., 45 Colt. **Barrel:** 18". **Weight:** 4 lbs., 8 oz. **Length:** 34" overall. **Stock:** One-piece walnut. **Sights:** Blade front, notch rear. **Features:** Color case-hardened frame, blue barrel, backstrap and triggerguard. Introduced 1998. Imported from Italy by IAR, Inc.
Price: Standard **$490.00**

MARLIN MODEL 336C LEVER-ACTION CARBINE
Caliber: 30-30 or 35 Rem., 6-shot tubular magazine. **Barrel:** 20" Micro-Groove®. **Weight:** 7 lbs. **Length:** 38-1/2" overall. **Stock:** Checkered American black walnut, capped pistol grip with white line spacers. Mar-Shield® finish; rubber butt pad; swivel studs. **Sights:** Ramp front with Wide-Scan hood, semi-buckhorn folding rear adjustable for windage and elevation. **Features:** Hammer-block safety. Receiver tapped for scope mount, offset hammer spur; top of receiver sandblasted to prevent glare. Includes safety lock.
Price: **$518.00**

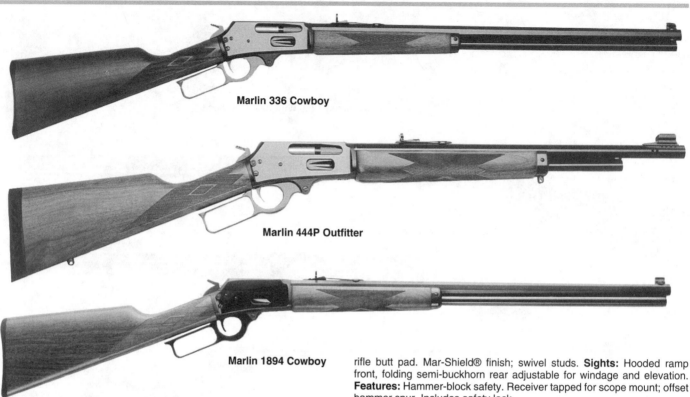

Marlin 336 Cowboy

Marlin 444P Outfitter

Marlin 1894 Cowboy

Marlin Model 336 Cowboy

Similar to the Model 336CS except chambered for 30-30 and 38-55 Win., 24" tapered octagon barrel with deep-cut Ballard-type rifling; straight-grip walnut stock with hard rubber buttplate; blued steel forend cap; weighs 7-1/2 lbs.; 42-1/2" overall. Introduced 1999. Includes safety lock. Made in U.S.A. by Marlin.

Price: **$719.00**

Marlin Model 336A Lever-Action Carbine

Same as the Marlin 336CS except has cut-checkered, walnut-finished hardwood pistol grip stock with swivel studs, 30-30 only, 6-shot. Hammer-block safety. Adjustable rear sight, brass bead front. Includes safety lock.

Price: **$441.00**
Price: With 4x scope and mount. **$487.00**

Marlin Model 336CC Lever-Action Carbine

Same as the Marlin 336A except has Mossy Oak® Break-Up camouflage stock and forearm. 30-30 only, 6-shot; receiver tapped for scope mount or receiver sight. Introduced 2001. Includes safety lock. Made in U.S.A. by Marlin.

Price: **$491.00**

Marlin Model 336SS Lever-Action Carbine

Same as the 336C except receiver, barrel and other major parts are machined from stainless steel. 30-30 only, 6-shot; receiver tapped for scope. Includes safety lock.

Price: **$627.00**

Marlin Model 336W Lever-Action Rifle

Similar to the Model 336CS except has walnut-finished, cut-checkered Maine birch stock; blued steel barrel band has integral sling swivel; no front sight hood; comes with padded nylon sling; hard rubber butt plate. Introduced 1998. Includes safety lock. Made in U.S.A. by Marlin.

Price: **$447.00**
Price: With 4x scope and mount. **$495.00**

MARLIN MODEL 444 LEVER-ACTION SPORTER

Caliber: 444 Marlin, 5-shot tubular magazine. **Barrel:** 22" deep cut Ballard rifling. **Weight:** 7-1/2 lbs. **Length:** 40-1/2" overall. **Stock:** Checkered American black walnut, capped pistol grip with white line spacers, rubber rifle butt pad. Mar-Shield® finish; swivel studs. **Sights:** Hooded ramp front, folding semi-buckhorn rear adjustable for windage and elevation. **Features:** Hammer-block safety. Receiver tapped for scope mount; offset hammer spur. Includes safety lock.

Price: **$618.00**

Marlin Model 444P Outfitter Lever-Action

Similar to the 444SS with deep-cut Ballard-type rifling; weighs 6-3/4 lbs.; overall length 37". Available only in 444 Marlin. Introduced 1999. Includes safety lock. Made in U.S.A. by Marlin.

Price: **$631.00**

MARLIN MODEL 1894 LEVER-ACTION CARBINE

Caliber: 44 Spec./44 Mag., 10-shot tubular magazine. **Barrel:** 20" Ballard-type rifling. **Weight:** 6 lbs. **Length:** 37-1/2" overall. **Stock:** Checkered American black walnut, straight grip and forend. Mar-Shield® finish. Rubber rifle butt pad; swivel studs. **Sights:** Wide-Scan hooded ramp front, semi-buckhorn folding rear adjustable for windage and elevation. **Features:** Hammer-block safety. Receiver tapped for scope mount, offset hammer spur, solid top receiver sand blasted to prevent glare. Includes safety lock.

Price: **$544.00**

Marlin Model 1894C Carbine

Similar to the standard Model 1894S except chambered for 38 Spec./357 Mag. with full-length 9-shot magazine, 18-1/2" barrel, hammer-block safety, hooded front sight. Introduced 1983. Includes safety lock.

Price: **$544.00**

Marlin Model 1894P/1894CP Carbine

Similar to the Model 1894 except has ported 16-1/4" barrel with 8-shot magazine. Overal length 33-1/4", weighs 5-3/4 lbs. Includes safety lock. Made in U.S.A. by Marlin.

Price: Model 1894P (44 Spec./44 Mag.) **$566.00**
New! **Price:** Model 1894CP (38 Spec./357 Mag.). **$566.00**

MARLIN MODEL 1894 COWBOY

Caliber: 357 Mag., 44 Mag., 45 Colt, 10-shot magazine. **Barrel:** 24" tapered octagon, deep cut rifling. **Weight:** 7-1/2 lbs. **Length:** 41-1/2" overall. **Stock:** Straight grip American black walnut, hard rubber buttplate, Mar-Shield® finish. **Sights:** Marble carbine front, adjustable Marble semi-buckhorn rear. **Features:** Squared finger lever; straight grip stock; blued steel forend tip. Designed for Cowboy Shooting events. Introduced 1996. Includes safety lock. Made in U.S.A. by Marlin.

Price: **$802.00**

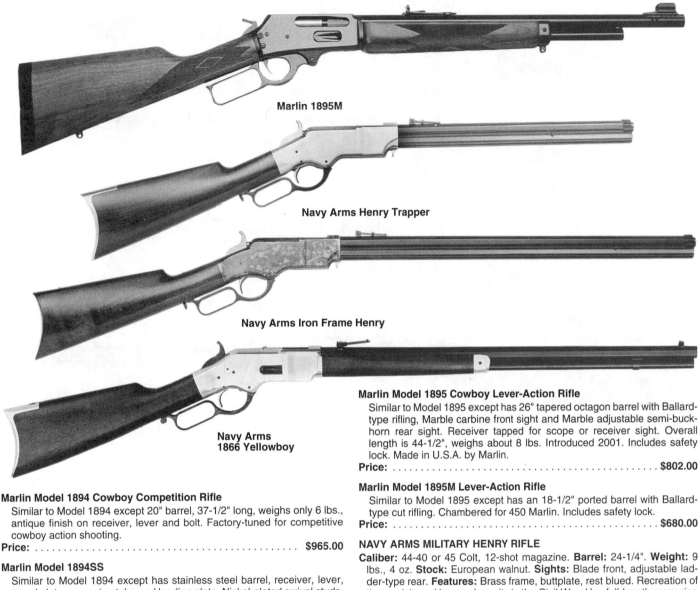

Marlin 1895M

Navy Arms Henry Trapper

Navy Arms Iron Frame Henry

Navy Arms 1866 Yellowboy

EW!

Marlin Model 1894 Cowboy Competition Rifle

Similar to Model 1894 except 20" barrel, 37-1/2" long, weighs only 6 lbs., antique finish on receiver, lever and bolt. Factory-tuned for competitive cowboy action shooting.
Price: **$965.00**

Marlin Model 1894SS

Similar to Model 1894 except has stainless steel barrel, receiver, lever, guard plate, magazine tube and loading plate. Nickel-plated swivel studs.
Price: **$665.00**

MARLIN MODEL 1895 LEVER-ACTION RIFLE

Caliber: 45-70, 4-shot tubular magazine. **Barrel:** 22" round. **Weight:** 7-1/2 lbs. **Length:** 40-1/2" overall. **Stock:** Checkered American black walnut, full pistol grip. Mar-Shield® finish; rubber butt pad; quick detachable swivel studs. **Sights:** Bead front with Wide-Scan hood, semi-buckhorn folding rear adjustable for windage and elevation. **Features:** Hammer-block safety. Solid receiver tapped for scope mounts or receiver sights; offset hammer spur. Includes safety lock.
Price: **$618.00**

Marlin Model 1895G Guide Gun Lever-Action Rifle

Similar to Model 1895 with deep-cut Ballard-type rifling; straight-grip walnut stock. Overall length is 37", weighs 7 lbs. Introduced 1998. Includes safety lock. Made in U.S.A. by Marlin.
Price: **$631.00**

Marlin Model 1895GS Guide Gun

Similar to Model 1895G except receiver, barrel and most metal parts are machined from stainless steel. Chambered for 45-70, 4-shot, 18-1/2" barrel. Overall length is 37", weighs 7 lbs. Introduced 2001. Includes safety lock. Made in U.S.A. by Marlin.
Price: **$744.00**

Marlin Model 1895 Cowboy Lever-Action Rifle

Similar to Model 1895 except has 26" tapered octagon barrel with Ballard-type rifling, Marble carbine front sight and Marble adjustable semi-buckhorn rear sight. Receiver tapped for scope or receiver sight. Overall length is 44-1/2", weighs about 8 lbs. Introduced 2001. Includes safety lock. Made in U.S.A. by Marlin.
Price: **$802.00**

Marlin Model 1895M Lever-Action Rifle

Similar to Model 1895 except has an 18-1/2" ported barrel with Ballard-type cut rifling. Chambered for 450 Marlin. Includes safety lock.
Price: **$680.00**

NAVY ARMS MILITARY HENRY RIFLE

Caliber: 44-40 or 45 Colt, 12-shot magazine. **Barrel:** 24-1/4". **Weight:** 9 lbs., 4 oz. **Stock:** European walnut. **Sights:** Blade front, adjustable ladder-type rear. **Features:** Brass frame, buttplate, rest blued. Recreation of the model used by cavalry units in the Civil War. Has full-length magazine tube, sling swivels; no forend. Imported from Italy by Navy Arms.
Price: **$989.00**

Navy Arms Iron Frame Henry

Similar to the Military Henry Rifle except receiver is blued or color case-hardened steel. Imported by Navy Arms.
Price: **$1,035.00**

NAVY ARMS 1860 HENRY RIFLES

Caliber: 45 Colt. **Barrel:** 24-1/4" octagonal; 1:16" twist. **Weight:** 9.26 lbs. **Length:** 43-3/4" overall. **Stock:** Walnut. **Sights:** Blade front, adjustable folding rear. **Features:** Steel color-case hardened or brass receiver; 13-shot magazine. Introduced 2001. Imported from Uberti by Navy Arms.
Price: (steel color-case hardened receiver) **$984.00**
Price: (brass receiver) **$1,035.00**

NAVY ARMS 1866 YELLOW BOY RIFLE

Caliber: 38 Spec., 44-40, 45 Colt, 12-shot magazine. **Barrel:** 20" or 24", full octagon. **Weight:** 8-1/2 lbs. **Length:** 42-1/2" overall. **Stock:** Walnut. **Sights:** Blade front, adjustable ladder-type rear. **Features:** Brass frame, forend tip, buttplate, blued barrel, lever, hammer. Introduced 1991. Imported from Italy by Navy Arms.
Price: **$761.00**
Price: Carbine, 19" barrel **$746.00**

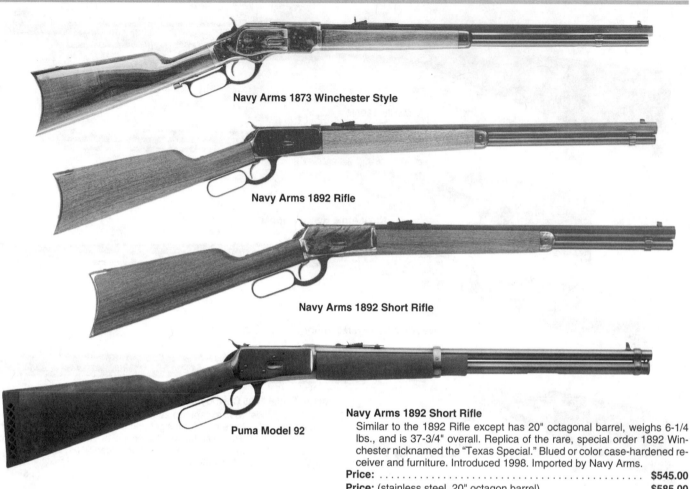

Navy Arms 1873 Winchester Style

Navy Arms 1892 Rifle

Navy Arms 1892 Short Rifle

Puma Model 92

NAVY ARMS 1866 SPORTING YELLOWBOY RIFLES
Caliber: 45 Colt. **Barrel:** 24-1/4" octagonal; 1:16" twist. **Weight:** 8.16 lbs. **Length:** 43-3/4"overall. **Stock:** Walnut. **Sights:** Blade front, adjustable folding rear. **Features:** Brass receiver; blued or white barrel; 13-shot magazine. Introduced 2001. Imported from Uberti by Navy Arms.
Price: (blued barrel) $761.00

NAVY ARMS 1873 WINCHESTER-STYLE RIFLE
Caliber: 357 Mag., 44-40, 45 Colt, 12-shot magazine. **Barrel:** 24-1/4". **Weight:** 8-1/4 lbs. **Length:** 43" overall. **Stock:** European walnut. **Sights:** Blade front, buckhorn rear. **Features:** Color case-hardened frame, rest blued. Full-octagon barrel. Imported by Navy Arms.
Price: $890.00
Price: 1873 Carbine, 19" barrel $869.00
Price: 1873 Sporting Rifle (full oct. bbl., checkered walnut stock
   and forend) $1,005.00
Price: 1873 Border Model, 20" octagon barrel $890.00
Price: 1873 Deluxe Border Model. $1,005.00

NAVY ARMS 1892 RIFLE
Caliber: 357 Mag., 44-40, 45 Colt. **Barrel:** 24-1/4" octagonal. **Weight:** 7 lbs. **Length:** 42" overall. **Stock:** American walnut. **Sights:** Blade front, semi-buckhorn rear. **Features:** Replica of Winchester's early Model 1892 with octagonal barrel, forend cap and crescent buttplate. Blued or color case-hardened receiver. Introduced 1998. Imported by Navy Arms.
Price: $545.00

Navy Arms 1892 Stainless Carbine
Similar to the 1892 Rifle except stainless steel, has 20" round barrel, weighs 5-3/4 lbs., and is 37-1/2" overall. Introduced 1998. Imported by Navy Arms.
Price: $585.00

Navy Arms 1892 Short Rifle
Similar to the 1892 Rifle except has 20" octagonal barrel, weighs 6-1/4 lbs., and is 37-3/4" overall. Replica of the rare, special order 1892 Winchester nicknamed the "Texas Special." Blued or color case-hardened receiver and furniture. Introduced 1998. Imported by Navy Arms.
Price: $545.00
Price: (stainless steel, 20" octagon barrel) $585.00

NAVY ARMS 1892 STAINLESS RIFLE
Caliber: 357 Mag., 44-40, 45 Colt. **Barrel:** 24-1/4" octagonal. **Weight:** 7 lbs. **Length:** 42". **Stock:** American walnut. **Sights:** Brass bead front, semi-buckhorn rear. **Features:** Designed for the Cowboy Action Shooter. Stainless steel barrel, receiver and furniture. Introduced 2000. Imported by Navy Arms.
Price: $585.00

PUMA MODEL 92 RIFLES & CARBINES
Caliber: 38 Spec./357 Mag., 44 Mag., 45 Colt, 454 Casull (20" carbine only). **Barrel:** 20" round, 24"octagonal. **Weight:** 6.1-7.7 lbs. **Stock:** Walnut-stained hardwood. **Sights:** Open, buckhorn front & rear available. **Features:** Blue, case-hardened, stainless steel and brass receivers, matching buttplates. Blued, stainless steel barrels, full-length magazines. Thumb safety on top of both. 454 Casull carbine loads through magazine tube, has rubber recoil pad. 45 Colt brass-framed, saddle-ring rifle and 454 Casull carbine introduced 2002. Imported from Brazil by Legacy Sports International.
Price: . . . . NA

REMINGTON MODEL 7600 PUMP ACTION
Caliber: 243, 270, 30-06, 308. **Barrel:** 22" round tapered. **Weight:** 7--1/2 lbs. **Length:** 42-5/8" overall. **Stock:** Cut-checkered walnut pistol grip and forend, Monte Carlo with full cheekpiece. Satin or high-gloss finish. **Sights:** Gold bead front sight on matted ramp, open step adjustable sporting rear. **Features:** Redesigned and improved version of the Model 760. Detachable 4-shot clip. Cross-bolt safety. Receiver tapped for scope mount. Introduced 1981.
Price: $588.00
Price: Carbine (18-1/2" bbl., 30-06 only) $588.00
Price: With black synthetic stock, matte black metal, rifle or
   carbine $484.00

RIFLES

Remington 7600 Rifle

Ruger Model 96/44

Winchester Model 94 Big Bore

Winchester 94 Traditional

RUGER MODEL 96/44 LEVER-ACTION RIFLE

Caliber: 44 Mag., 4-shot rotary magazine. **Barrel:** 18-1/2". **Weight:** 5-7/8 lbs. **Length:** 37-5/16" overall. **Stock:** American hardwood. **Sights:** Gold bead front, folding leaf rear. **Features:** Solid chrome-moly steel receiver. Manual cross-bolt safety, visible cocking indicator; short-throw lever action; integral scope mount; blued finish; color case-hardened lever. Introduced 1996. Made In U.S. by Sturm, Ruger & Co.
Price: 96/44M, 44 Mag **$499.00**

TRISTAR/UBERTI 1873 SPORTING RIFLE

Caliber: 44-40, 45 Colt. **Barrel:** 24-1/4", 30", octagonal. **Weight:** 8.1 lbs. **Length:** 43-1/4" overall. **Stock:** Walnut. **Sights:** Blade front adjustable for windage, open rear adjustable for elevation. **Features:** Color case-hardened frame, blued barrel, hammer, lever, buttplate, brass elevator. Imported from Italy by Tristar Sporting Arms Ltd.
Price: 24-1/4" barrel **$919.00**
Price: 30" barrel **$964.00**

TRISTAR/UBERTI 1866 SPORTING RIFLE, CARBINE

Caliber: 22 LR, 22 WMR, 38 Spec., 44-40, 45 Colt. **Barrel:** 24-1/4", octagonal. **Weight:** 8.1 lbs. **Length:** 43-1/4" overall. **Stock:** Walnut. **Sights:** Blade front for windage, rear adjustable for elevation. **Features:** Frame, buttplate, forend cap of polished brass, balance charcoal blued. Imported by Tristar Sporting Arms Ltd.
Price: **$775.00**
Price: Yellowboy Carbine (19" round bbl.) **$735.00**

TRISTAR/UBERTI 1860 HENRY RIFLE

Caliber: 44-40, 45 Colt. **Barrel:** 24-1/4", half-octagon. **Weight:** 9.2 lbs. **Length:** 43-3/4" overall. **Stock:** American walnut. **Sights:** Blade front, rear adjustable for elevation. **Features:** Frame, elevator, magazine follower, buttplate are brass, balance blue. Imported by Tristar Sporting Arms Ltd. Arms, Inc.
Price: **$982.00**

TRISTAR/UBERTI 1860 HENRY TRAPPER CARBINE

Similar to the 1860 Henry Rifle except has 18-1/2" barrel, measures 37-3/4" overall, and weighs 8 lbs. Introduced 1999. Imported from Italy by Tristar Sporting Arms Ltd.
Price: Brass frame, blued barrel **$982.00**

VEKTOR H5 SLIDE-ACTION RIFLE

Caliber: 223 Rem., 5-shot magazine. **Barrel:** 18", 22". **Weight:** 9 lbs., 15 oz. **Length:** 42-1/2" overall (22" barrel). **Stock:** Walnut thumbhole. **Sights:** Comes with 1" 4x32 scope with low-light reticle. **Features:** Rotating bolt mechanism. Matte black finish. Introduced 1999. Imported from South Africa by Vektor USA.
Price: **$849.95**

WINCHESTER MODEL 94 TRADITIONAL BIG BORE

Caliber: 444 Marlin, 6-shot magazine. **Barrel:** 20". **Weight:** 6-1/2 lbs. **Length:** 38-5/8" overall. **Stock:** American walnut. Satin finish. **Sights:** Hooded ramp front, semi-buckhorn rear adjustable for windage and elevation. **Features:** All external metal parts have Winchester's deep blue finish. Rifling twist 1:12". Rubber recoil pad fitted to buttstock. Introduced 1983. From U.S. Repeating Arms Co., Inc.
Price: **$465.00**

Winchester Timber Carbine

Similar to the Model 94 Big Bore. Chambered for 444 Marlin; 18" barrel is ported; half-pistol grip stock with butt pad; checkered grip and forend. Introduced 1999. Made in U.S.A. by U.S. Repeating Arms Co., Inc.
Price: **$573.00**

WINCHESTER MODEL 94 TRADITIONAL-CW

Caliber: 30-30 Win., 6-shot; 44 Mag., 11-shot tubular magazine. **Barrel:** 20". **Weight:** 6-1/2 lbs. **Length:** 37-3/4" overall. **Stock:** Straight grip checkered walnut stock and forend. **Sights:** Hooded blade front, semi-buckhorn rear. Drilled and tapped for scope mount. Post front sight on Trapper model. **Features:** Solid frame, forged steel receiver; side ejection, exposed rebounding hammer with automatic trigger-activated transfer bar. Introduced 1984.
Price: 30-30 . . . . **$440.00**
Price: 44 Mag. **$463.00**
Price: Traditional (no checkering, 30-30 only) **$407.00**

RIFLES

CENTERFIRE RIFLES — LEVER AND SLIDE

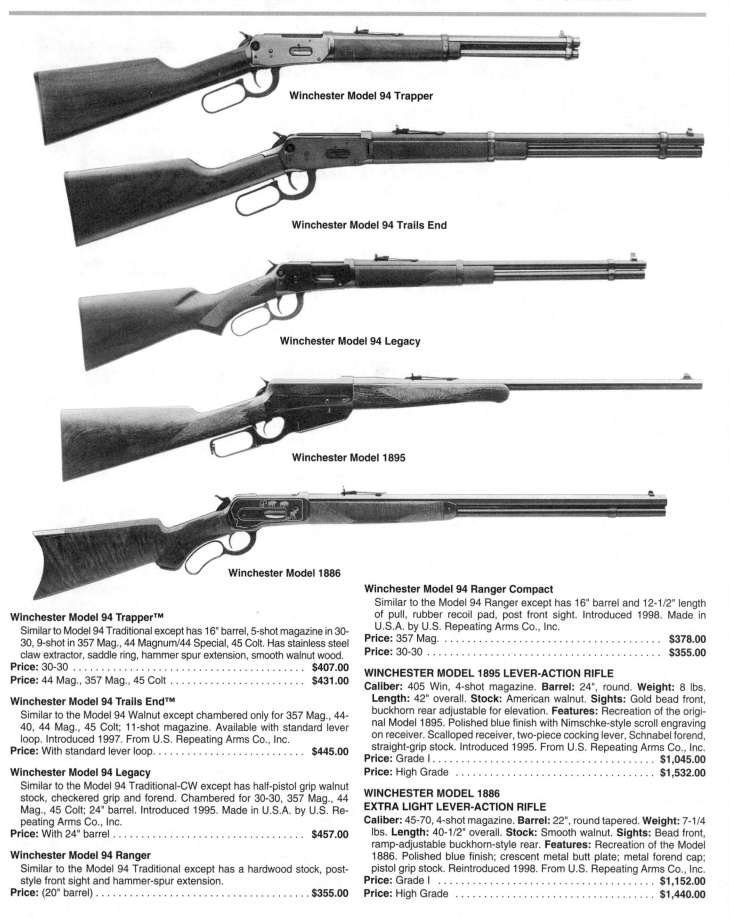

Winchester Model 94 Trapper

Winchester Model 94 Trails End

Winchester Model 94 Legacy

Winchester Model 1895

Winchester Model 1886

Winchester Model 94 Trapper™
Similar to Model 94 Traditional except has 16" barrel, 5-shot magazine in 30-30, 9-shot in 357 Mag., 44 Magnum/44 Special, 45 Colt. Has stainless steel claw extractor, saddle ring, hammer spur extension, smooth walnut wood.
Price: 30-30 . . . . **$407.00**
Price: 44 Mag., 357 Mag., 45 Colt **$431.00**

Winchester Model 94 Trails End™
Similar to the Model 94 Walnut except chambered only for 357 Mag., 44-40, 44 Mag., 45 Colt; 11-shot magazine. Available with standard lever loop. Introduced 1997. From U.S. Repeating Arms Co., Inc.
Price: With standard lever loop. **$445.00**

Winchester Model 94 Legacy
Similar to the Model 94 Traditional-CW except has half-pistol grip walnut stock, checkered grip and forend. Chambered for 30-30, 357 Mag., 44 Mag., 45 Colt; 24" barrel. Introduced 1995. Made in U.S.A. by U.S. Repeating Arms Co., Inc.
Price: With 24" barrel **$457.00**

Winchester Model 94 Ranger
Similar to the Model 94 Traditional except has a hardwood stock, post-style front sight and hammer-spur extension.
Price: (20" barrel) **$355.00**

Winchester Model 94 Ranger Compact
Similar to the Model 94 Ranger except has 16" barrel and 12-1/2" length of pull, rubber recoil pad, post front sight. Introduced 1998. Made in U.S.A. by U.S. Repeating Arms Co., Inc.
Price: 357 Mag. **$378.00**
Price: 30-30 . . . . **$355.00**

WINCHESTER MODEL 1895 LEVER-ACTION RIFLE
Caliber: 405 Win, 4-shot magazine. **Barrel:** 24", round. **Weight:** 8 lbs. **Length:** 42" overall. **Stock:** American walnut. **Sights:** Gold bead front, buckhorn rear adjustable for elevation. **Features:** Recreation of the original Model 1895. Polished blue finish with Nimschke-style scroll engraving on receiver. Scalloped receiver, two-piece cocking lever, Schnabel forend, straight-grip stock. Introduced 1995. From U.S. Repeating Arms Co., Inc.
Price: Grade I **$1,045.00**
Price: High Grade **$1,532.00**

WINCHESTER MODEL 1886
EXTRA LIGHT LEVER-ACTION RIFLE
Caliber: 45-70, 4-shot magazine. **Barrel:** 22", round tapered. **Weight:** 7-1/4 lbs. **Length:** 40-1/2" overall. **Stock:** Smooth walnut. **Sights:** Bead front, ramp-adjustable buckhorn-style rear. **Features:** Recreation of the Model 1886. Polished blue finish; crescent metal butt plate; metal forend cap; pistol grip stock. Reintroduced 1998. From U.S. Repeating Arms Co., Inc.
Price: Grade I **$1,152.00**
Price: High Grade **$1,440.00**

Includes models for a wide variety of sporting and competitive purposes and uses.

Anschutz 1733D

Arnold Arms Alaskan

Arnold Arms Safari

ANSCHUTZ 1743D BOLT-ACTION RIFLE

Caliber: 222 Rem., 3-shot magazine. **Barrel:** 19.7". **Weight:** 6.4 lbs. **Length:** 39" overall. **Stock:** European walnut. **Sights:** Hooded blade front, folding leaf rear. **Features:** Receiver grooved for scope mounting; single stage trigger; claw extractor; sling safety; sling swivels. Imported from Germany by AcuSport Corp.

Price: **$1,588.95**

ANSCHUTZ 1740 MONTE CARLO RIFLE

Caliber: 22 Hornet, 5-shot clip; 222 Rem., 3-shot clip. **Barrel:** 24". **Weight:** 6-1/2 lbs. **Length:** 43.25" overall. **Stock:** Select European walnut. **Sights:** Hooded ramp front, folding leaf rear; drilled and tapped for scope mounting. **Features:** Uses match 54 action. Adjustable single stage trigger. Stock has roll-over Monte Carlo cheekpiece, slim forend with Schnabel tip, Wundhammer palm swell on grip, rosewood gripcap with white diamond insert. Skip-line checkering on grip and forend. Introduced 1997. Imported from Germany by AcuSport Corp.

Price: From **$1,439.00**
Price: Model 1730 Monte Carlo, as above except in
22 Hornet **$1,439.00**

Anschutz 1733D Rifle

Similar to the 1740 Monte Carlo except has full-length, walnut, Mannlicher-style stock with skip-line checkering, rosewood Schnabel tip, and is chambered for 22 Hornet. Weighs 6.4 lbs., overall length 39", barrel length 19.7". Imported from Germany by AcuSport Corp.

Price: **$1,588.95**

ARNOLD ARMS ALASKAN RIFLE

Caliber: 243 to 338 Magnum. **Barrel:** 22" to 26". **Weight:** NA. **Length:** NA. **Stock:** Synthetic; black, woodland or arctic camouflage. **Sights:** Optional; drilled and tapped for scope mounting. **Features:** Uses Apollo, Remington or Winchester action with controlled round feed or push feed; chrome-moly steel or stainless; one-piece bolt, handle, knob; cone head bolt and breech; three-position safety; fully adjustable trigger. Introduced 1996. Made in U.S.A. by Arnold Arms Co.

Price: From **$2,695.00**

Arnold Arms Alaskan Guide Rifle

Similar to the Alaskan rifle except chambered for 257 to 338 Magnum; choice of A-grade English walnut or synthetic stock; three-position safety; scope mount only. Introduced 1996. Made in U.S.A. by Arnold Arms Co.

Price: From **$3,249.00**

Arnold Arms Grand Alaskan Rifle

Similar to the Alaskan rifle except has AAA fancy select or exhibition-grade English walnut; barrel band swivel; comes with iron sights and scope mount; 24" to 26" barrel; 300 Magnum to 458 Win. Mag. Introduced 1996. Made in U.S.A. by Arnold Arms Co.

Price: From **$7,570.00**

Arnold Arms Alaskan Trophy Rifle

Similar to the Alaskan rifle except chambered for 300 Magnum to 458 Win. Mag.; 24" to 26" barrel; black synthetic or laminated stock; comes with barrel band on 375 H&H and larger; scope mount; iron sights. Introduced 1996. Made in U.S.A. by Arnold Arms Co.

Price: From **$3,249.00**

ARNOLD ARMS SAFARI RIFLE

Caliber: 243 to 458 Win. Mag. **Barrel:** 22" to 26". **Weight:** NA. **Length:** NA. **Stock:** Grade A and AA Fancy English walnut. **Sights:** Optional; drilled and tapped for scope mounting. **Features:** Uses Apollo, Remington or Winchester action with controlled or push round feed; one-piece bolt, handle, knob; cone head bolt and breech; three-position safety; fully adjustable trigger; chrome-moly steel in matte blue, polished, or bead blasted stainless. Introduced 1996. Made in U.S.A. by Arnold Arms Co.

Price: From **$6,495.00**

Arnold Arms African Trophy Rifle

Similar to the Safari rifle except has AAA Extra Fancy English walnut stock with wrap-around checkering; matte blue chrome-moly or polished or bead blasted stainless steel; scope mount standard or optional Express sights. Introduced 1996. Made in U.S.A. by Arnold Arms Co.

Price: Blued chrome-moly steel **$6,921.00**
Price: Stainless steel **$6,971.00**

Arnold Arms Grand African Rifle

Similar to the Safari rifle except has Exhibition Grade stock; polished blue chrome-moly steel or bead-blasted or Teflon-coated stainless; barrel band; scope mount, express sights; calibers 338 Magnum to 458 Win. Mag.; 24" to 26" barrel. Introduced 1996. Made in U.S.A. by Arnold Arms Co.

Price: Chrome-moly steel **$8,172.00**
Price: Stainless steel **$8,022.00**

Beretta Mato Deluxe

Barrett Model 95

Beretta Mato Synthetic

Blaser R93 Classic

BARRETT MODEL 95 BOLT-ACTION RIFLE

Caliber: 50 BMG, 5-shot magazine. **Barrel:** 29". **Weight:** 22 lbs. **Length:** 45" overall. **Stock:** Energy-absorbing recoil pad. **Sights:** Scope optional. **Features:** Bolt-action, bullpup design. Disassembles without tools; extendable bipod legs; match-grade barrel; high efficiency muzzle brake. Introduced 1995. Made in U.S.A. by Barrett Firearms Mfg., Inc.

Price: From $4,950.00

BERETTA MATO DELUXE BOLT-ACTION RIFLE

Caliber: 270, 280 Rem., 30-06, 7mm Rem. Mag., 300 Win. Mag., 338 Win. Mag., 375 H&H. **Barrel:** 23.6". **Weight:** 7.9 lbs. **Length:** 44.5" overall. **Stock:** XXX claro walnut with ebony forend tip, hand-rubbed oil finish. **Sights:** Bead on ramp front, open fully adjustable rear; drilled and tapped for scope mounting. **Features:** Mauser-style action with claw extractor; three-position safety; removable box magazine; 375 H&H has muzzle brake. Introduced 1998. From Beretta U.S.A.

Price: $2,470.00
Price: 375 H&H $2,795.00

Beretta Mato Synthetic Bolt-Action Rifle

Similar to the Mato except has fiberglass/Kevlar/carbon fiber stock in classic American style with shadow line cheekpiece, aluminum bedding block and checkering. Introduced 1998. From Beretta U.S.A.

Price: $1,117.00
Price: 375 H&H $1,474.00

BLASER R93 BOLT-ACTION RIFLE

Caliber: 22-250, 243, 6.5x55, 270, 7x57, 7mm-08, 308, 30-06, 257 Wea. Mag., 7mm Rem. Mag., 300 Win. Mag., 300 Wea. Mag., 338 Win Mag., 375 H&H, 416 Rem. Mag. **Barrel:** 22" (standard calibers), 26" (magnum). **Weight:** 7 lbs. **Length:** 40" overall (22" barrel). **Stock:** Two-piece European walnut. **Sights:** None furnished; drilled and tapped for scope mounting. **Features:** Straight pull-back bolt action with thumb-activated safety slide/cocking mechanism; interchangeable barrels and bolt heads. Introduced 1994. Imported from Germany by SIGARMS.

Price: R93 Classic $3,680.00
Price: R93 LX $1,895.00
Price: R93 Synthetic (black synthetic stock) $1,595.00
Price: R93 Safari Synthetic (416 Rem. Mag. only) $1,855.00
Price: R93 Grand Lux $4,915.00
Price: R93 Attaché $5,390.00

BRNO 98 BOLT-ACTION RIFLE

Caliber: 7x64, 243, 270, 308, 30-06, 300 Win. Mag., 9.3x62. **Barrrel:** 23.6". **Weight:** 7.2 lbs. **Length:** 40.9" overall. **Stock:** European walnut. **Sights:** Blade on ramp front, open adjustable rear. **Features:** Uses Mauser 98-type action; polished blue. Announced 1998. Imported from the Czech Republic by Euro-Imports.

Price: Standard calibers $507.00
Price: Magnum calibers $547.00
Price: With set trigger, standard calibers $615.00
Price: As above, magnum calibers $655.00
Price: With full stock, set trigger, standard calibers $703.00
Price: As above, magnum calibers $743.00

RIFLES

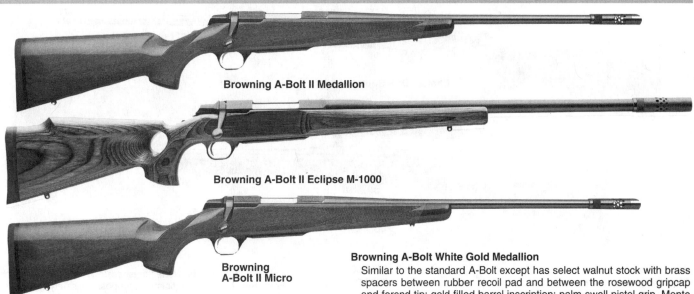

Browning A-Bolt II Medallion

Browning A-Bolt II Eclipse M-1000

Browning A-Bolt II Micro

BROWNING ACERA STRAIGHT-PULL RIFLE
Caliber: 30-06, 300 Win. Mag. **Barrel:** 22"; 24" for magnums. **Weight:** 6 lbs., 9 oz. **Length:** 41-1/4" overall. **Stock:** American walnut with high gloss finish. **Sights:** Blade on ramp front, open adjustable rear. **Features:** Straight-pull action; detachable box magazine; Teflon coated breech-block; drilled and tapped for scope mounting. Introduced 1999. Imported by Browning.
Price: 30-06, no sights $845.00
Price: 300 Win. Mag., no sights $877.00
Price: 30-06 with sights $869.00
Price: 300 Win. Mag., with sights $901.00
Price: 30-06, with BOSS. $901.00
Price: 300 Win. Mag., with BOSS. $933.00

BROWNING A-BOLT RIFLES
Caliber: 223, 22-250, 243, 7mm-08, 308, 25-06, 260, 270, 30-06, 260 Rem., 7mm Rem. Mag., 300 Win. Short Mag., 300 Win. Mag., 338 Win. Mag., 375 H&H Mag. **Barrel:** 22" medium sporter weight with recessed muzzle; 26" on mag. cals. **Weight:** 6-1/2 to 7-1/2 lbs. **Length:** 44-3/4" overall (magnum and standard); 41-3/4" (short action). **Stock:** Classic style American walnut; recoil pad standard on magnum calibers. **Features:** Short-throw (60") fluted bolt, three locking lugs, plunger-type ejector; adjustable trigger is grooved and gold-plated. Hinged floorplate, detachable box magazine (4 rounds std. cals., 3 for magnums). Slide tang safety. BOSS barrel vibration modulator and muzzle brake system not available in 375 H&H. Introduced 1985. Imported from Japan by Browning.
Price: Hunter, no sights $620.00
Price: Hunter, no sights, magnum calibers. $646.00
Price: For BOSS add $80.00

Browning A-Bolt Medallion
Similar to standard A-Bolt except has glossy stock finish, rosewood grip and forend caps, engraved receiver, high-polish blue, no sights.
Price: Short-action calibers. $730.00
Price: Long-action calibers $756.00
Price: Medallion, 375 H&H Mag., open sights $767.00
New! **Price:** 300 Win. Short Magnum $756.00
New! **Price:** 300 Rem. Ultra Mag., 338 Rem. Ultra Mag. $756.00
Price: For BOSS, add. $80.00

Browning A-Bolt Medallion Left-Hand
Same as the Medallion model A-Bolt except has left-hand action and is available in 270, 30-06, 7mm Rem. Mag., 300 Win. Mag. Introduced 1987.
Price: 270, 30-06 (no sights) $758.00
Price: 7mm Mag., 300 Win. Mag. (no sights) $784.00
Price: For BOSS, add. $80.00

Browning A-Bolt White Gold Medallion
Similar to the standard A-Bolt except has select walnut stock with brass spacers between rubber recoil pad and between the rosewood gripcap and forend tip; gold-filled barrel inscription; palm-swell pistol grip, Monte Carlo comb, 22 lpi checkering with double borders; engraved receiver flats. In 270, 30-06, 7mm Rem. Mag. and 300 Win. Mag. Introduced 1988.
Price: 270, 30-06 . . . . $1,046.00
Price: 7mm Rem. Mag, 300 Win. Mag. $1,072.00
Price: For BOSS, add. $76.00

Browning A-Bolt Custom Trophy Rifle
Similar to the A-Bolt Medallion except has select American walnut stock with recessed swivel studs, octagon barrel, skeleton pistol gripcap, gold highlights, shadowline cheekpiece. Calibers 270, 30-06, 7mm Rem. Mag., 300 Win. Mag. Introduced 1998. Imported from Japan by Browning.
Price: $1,360.00

Browning A-Bolt Eclipse Hunter
Similar to the A-Bolt II except has gray/black laminated, thumbhole stock, BOSS barrel vibration modulator and muzzle brake. Available in long and short action with heavy barrel. In 270 Win., 30-06, 7mm Rem. Mag. Introduced 1996. Imported from Japan by Browning.
Price: 270, 30-06, with BOSS. $1,017.00
Price: 7mm Rem. Mag, with BOSS $1,043.00

Browning A-Bolt Eclipse M-1000
Similar to the A-Bolt II Eclipse except has long action and heavy target barrel. Chambered only for 300 Win. Mag. Adjustable trigger, bench-style forend, 3-shot magazine; laminated thumbhold stock; BOSS system standard. Introduced 1997. Imported for Japan by Browning.
Price: $1,048.00

Browning A-Bolt Micro Hunter
Similar to the A-Bolt II Hunter except has 13-5/16" length of pull, 20" barrel, and comes in 260 Rem., 243, 308, 7mm-08, 223, 22-250, 22 Hornet. Weighs 6 lbs., 1 oz. Introduced 1999. Imported by Browning.
Price: (no sights) $614.00

Browning A-Bolt Classic Hunter
Similar to the A-Bolt unter except has low-luster bluing and walnut stock with Monte Carlo comb, pistol grip palm swell, double-border checkering. Available in 270, 30-06, 7mm Rem. Mag., 300 Win. Mag. Introduced 1999. Imported by Browning.
Price: 270, 30-06 . . . . $698.00
Price: 7mm Mag., 300 Mag.. . . . . $724.00

Browning A-Bolt Stainless Stalker
Similar to the Hunter model A-Bolt except receiver and barrel are made of stainless steel; the rest of the exposed metal surfaces are finished with a durable matte silver-gray. Graphite-fiberglass composite textured stock. No sights are furnished. Available in 260, 243, 308, 7mm-08, 270, 280,30-06, 7mm Rem. Mag., 300 WSM, 300 Rem. Ultra Mag., 338 Win. Mag., 338 Rem. Ultra Mag., 375 H&H. Introduced 1987.

Charles Daly Superior

CZ 527

Price: Short-action calibers. **$813.00**
Price: Magnum calibers **$839.00**
New! Price: 300 Win. Short Magnum **$839.00**
New! Price: 300 Rem. Ultra Mag., 338 Rem. Ultra Mag. **$839.00**
Price: For BOSS, add **$80.00**
Price: Left-hand, 270, 30-06 . . . . **$838.00**
Price: Left-hand, 7mm, 300 Win. Mag., 338 Win. Mag. **$864.00**
Price: Left-hand, 375 H&H, with sights. **$864.00**
Price: Left-hand, for BOSS, add. **$80.00**
Price: Carbon-fiber barrel, 22-250 . . . . **$1,750.00**
Price: Carbon-fiber barrel, 300 Win. Mag. **$1,776.00**

Browning A-Bolt Composite Stalker

Similar to the A-Bolt Hunter except has black graphite-fiberglass stock with textured finish. Matte blue finish on all exposed metal surfaces. Available in 223, 22-250, 243, 7mm-08, 308, 30-06, 270, 280, 25-06, 7mm Rem. Mag., 300 WSM, 300 Win. Mag., 338 Win. Mag. BOSS barrel vibration modulator and muzzle brake system offered in all calibers. Introduced 1994.
Price: Standard calibers, no sights. **$639.00**
Price: Magnum calibers, no sights **$665.00**
Price: For BOSS, add. **$77.00**

CARBON ONE BOLT-ACTION RIFLE

Caliber: 22-250 to 375 H&H. **Barrel:** Up to 28". **Weight:** 5-1/2 to 7-1/4 lbs. **Length:** Varies. **Stock:** Synthetic or wood. **Sights:** None furnished. **Features:** Choice of Remington, Browning or Winchester action with free-floated Christensen graphite/epoxy/steel barrel, trigger pull tuned to 3 - 3-1/2 lbs. Made in U.S.A. by Christensen Arms.
Price: Carbon One Hunter Rifle, 6-1/2 to 7 lbs. **$1,499.00**
Price: Carbon One Custom, 5-1/2 to 6-1/2 lbs., Shilen trigger . . **$2,750.00**
Price: Carbon Ranger, 50 BMG, 5-shot repeater **$4,750.00**
Price: Carbon Ranger, 50 BMG, single shot **$3,950.00**

CHARLES DALY SUPERIOR BOLT-ACTION RIFLE

Caliber: 22 Hornet, 5-shot magazine. **Barrel:** 22.6". **Weight:** 6.6 lbs. **Length:** 41.25" overall. **Stock:** Walnut-finished hardwood with Monte Carlo comb and cheekpiece. **Sights:** Ramped blade front, fully adjustable open rear. **Features:** Receiver dovetailed for tip-off scope mount. Introduced 1996. Imported by K.B.I., Inc.
Price: **$364.95**

Charles Daly Empire Grade Rifle

Similar to the Superior except has oil-finished American walnut stock with 18 lpi hand checkering; black hardwood gripcap and forend tip; highly polished barreled action; jewelled bolt; recoil pad; swivel studs. Imported by K.B.I., Inc.
Price: **$469.95**

COLT LIGHT RIFLE BOLT ACTION

Caliber: 243, 7x57, 7mm-08, 308 (short action); 25-06, 270, 280, 7mm Rem., Mag., 30-06, 300 Win. Mag. **Barrel:** 24" **Weight:** 5.4 to 6 lbs.

Stock: Black synthetic. **Sights:** None furnished; low, medium, high scope mounts. **Features:** Matte black finish; three-position safety. Introduced 1999. Made in U.S.A. From Colt's Mfg., Inc.
Price: **$779.00**

COOPER MODEL 21, 38 BOLT-ACTION RIFLES

Caliber: 17 Rem., 17 Mach IV, 17 Javelina, 19-223 Calhoon, 20 VarTag, 22 PPC, Model 21, 6mm PPC, 221 Fireball, 222 Rem., 222 Rem. Mag., 223 Rem., 223 Ackley Imp., 6x45, 6x47, single shot; Model 38—17 Squirrel, 17 HeBee, 17 Ackley Hornet, 22 Hornet, 22 K Hornet, 218 Mashburn Bee, 218 Bee, 22 Squirrel, single shot. **Barrel:** 24" stainless match grade. **Weight:** 6-1/2 to 7-1/4 lbs. **Stock:** AA Claro walnut; 20 l.p.i. checkering. **Sights:** None furnished. **Features:** Uses three front locking lug system. Fully adjustable trigger. Many options available. Contact maker for details. Made in U.S.A. by Cooper Firearms.
Price: Classic **$1,050.00**
Price: Varminter **$995.00**
Price: Varmint Extreme **$1,795.00**
Price: Custom Classic **$1,995.00**
Price: Western Classic **$2,295.00**

COOPER MODEL 22 BOLT-ACTION RIFLE

Caliber: 22-250 Rem., 22-250 AI, 25-06 Rem., 25-06 AI, 243 Win., 243 AI, 220 Swift, 257 Roberts, 257 AI, 7-08, 6mm Rem., 6x284, 6.5x284, 22 BR, 6 BR, 308 Win., 260 Rem. **Barrel:** 24" or 26" stainless or 4140 match grade. **Weight:** 7 to 8 lbs. **Stock:** Claro walnut, hand checkering. **Sights:** None furnished. **Features:** Three front locking lug bolt-action single shot. Fully adjustable trigger. Many options available. Made in U.S.A. by Cooper Firearms.
Price: Varminter **$1,199.00**
Price: Montana Varminter. **$1,495.00**
Price: Varmint Extreme **$1,995.00**
Price: Classic **$1,295.00**
Price: Custom Classic **$2,195.00**
Price: Western Classic **$2,795.00**

CZ 527 LUX BOLT-ACTION RIFLE

Caliber: 22 Hornet, 222 Rem., 223 Rem., detachable 5-shot magazine. **Barrel:** 23-1/2"; standard or heavy barrel. **Weight:** 6 lbs., 1 oz. **Length:** 42-1/2" overall. **Stock:** European walnut with Monte Carlo. **Sights:** Hooded front, open adjustable rear. **Features:** Improved mini-Mauser action with non-rotating claw extractor; single set trigger; grooved receiver. Imported from the Czech Republic by CZ-USA.
Price: **$540.00**
Price: Model FS, full-length stock, cheekpiece. **$607.00**

CZ 527 American Classic Bolt-Action Rifle

Similar to the CZ 527 Lux except has classic-style stock with 18 l.p.i. checkering; free-floating barrel; recessed target crown on barrel. No sights furnished. Introduced 1999. Imported from the Czech Republic by CZ-USA.
Price: 22 Hornet, 222 Rem., 223 Rem. **$540.00**

RIFLES

CZ 550 Lux

CZ 550 American Classic

CZ 550 Magnum

Dakota 76 Classic

CZ 550 LUX BOLT-ACTION RIFLE

Caliber: 22-250, 243, 6.5x55, 7x57, 7x64, 308 Win., 9.3x62, 270 Win., 30-06. **Barrel:** 20.47". **Weight:** 7.5 lbs. **Length:** 44.68" overall. **Stock:** Turkish walnut in Bavarian style or FS (Mannlicher). **Sights:** Hooded front, adjustable rear. **Features:** Improved Mauser-style action with claw extractor, fixed ejector, square bridge dovetailed receiver; single set trigger. Imported from the Czech Republic by CZ-USA.
Price: Lux . . . . **$561.00 to $609.00**
Price: FS (full stock) **$645.00**

CZ 550 American Classic Bolt-Action Rifle

Similar to CZ 550 Lux except has American classic-style stock with 18 l.p.i. checkering; free-floating barrel; recessed target crown. Has 25.6" barrel; weighs 7.48 lbs. No sights furnished. Introduced 1999. Imported from the Czech Republic by CZ-USA.
Price: . . . .**$576.00 to $609.00**

CZ 550 Medium Magnum Bolt-Action Rifle

Similar to the CZ 550 Lux except chambered for the 300 Win. Mag. and 7mm Rem. Mag.; 5-shot magazine. Adjustable iron sights, hammer-forged barrel, single-set trigger, Turkish walnut stock. Weighs 7.5 lbs. Introduced 2001. Imported from the Czech Republic by CZ USA.
Price: **$621.00**

CZ 550 Magnum Bolt-Action Rifle

Similar to CZ 550 Lux except has long action for 300 Win. Mag., 375 H&H, 416 Rigby, 458 Win. Mag. Overall length is 46.45"; barrel length 25"; weighs 9.24 lbs. Hooded front sight, express rear with one standing, two folding leaves. Imported from the Czech Republic by CZ-USA.
Price: 300 Win. Mag. **$717.00**
Price: 375 H&H. **$756.00**
Price: 416 Rigby **$796.00**
Price: 458 Win. Mag. **$744.00**

CZ 700 M1 SNIPER RIFLE

Caliber: 308 Winchester, 10-shot magazine. **Barrel:** 25.6". **Weight:** 11.9 lbs. **Length:** 45" overall. **Stock:** Laminated wood thumbhole with adjustable buttplate and cheekpiece. **Sights:** None furnished; permanently attached Weaver rail for scope mounting. **Features:** 60-degree bolt throw; oversized trigger guard and bolt handle for use with gloves; full-length equipment rail on forend; fully adjustable trigger. Introduced 2001. Imported from the Czech Republic by CZ USA.
Price: **$2,097.00**

DAKOTA 76 TRAVELER TAKEDOWN RIFLE

Caliber: 257 Roberts, 25-06, 7x57, 270, 280, 30-06, 338-06, 35 Whelen (standard length); 7mm Rem. Mag., 300 Win. Mag., 338 Win. Mag., 416 Taylor, 458 Win. Mag. (short magnums); 7mm, 300, 330, 375 Dakota Magnums. **Barrel:** 23". **Weight:** 7-1/2 lbs. **Length:** 43-1/2" overall. **Stock:** Medium fancy-grade walnut in classic style. Checkered grip and forend; solid butt pad. **Sights:** None furnished; drilled and tapped for scope mounts. **Features:** Threadless disassembly—no threads to wear or stretch, no interrupted cuts, and headspace remains constant. Uses modified Model 76 design with many features of the Model 70 Winchester. Left-hand model also available. Introduced 1989. Made in U.S.A. by Dakota Arms, Inc.
Price: Classic **$4,495.00**
Price: Safari **$5,495.00**
Price: Extra barrels. . . . .**$1,650.00 to $1,950.00**

DAKOTA 76 CLASSIC BOLT-ACTION RIFLE

Caliber: 257 Roberts, 270, 280, 30-06, 7mm Rem. Mag., 338 Win. Mag., 300 Win. Mag., 375 H&H, 458 Win. Mag. **Barrel:** 23". **Weight:** 7-1/2 lbs. **Length:** 43-1/2" overall. **Stock:** Medium fancy grade walnut in classic style. Checkered pistol grip and forend; solid butt pad. **Sights:** None furnished; drilled and tapped for scope mounts. **Features:** Has many features of the original Model 70 Winchester. One-piece rail trigger guard assembly; steel gripcap. Model 70-style trigger. Many options available. Left-hand rifle available at same price. Introduced 1988. From Dakota Arms, Inc.
Price: **$3,595.00**

Dakota 76 Safari

Dakota Longbow

Dakota 97 Lightweight Hunter

Dakota Hunter

DAKOTA 76 SAFARI BOLT-ACTION RIFLE
Caliber: 270 Win., 7x57, 280, 30-06, 7mm Dakota, 7mm Rem. Mag., 300 Dakota, 300 Win. Mag., 330 Dakota, 338 Win. Mag., 375 Dakota, 458 Win. Mag., 300 H&H, 375 H&H, 416 Rem. **Barrel:** 23". **Weight:** 8-1/2 lbs. **Length:** 43-1/2" overall. **Stock:** XXX fancy walnut with ebony forend tip; point-pattern with wrap-around forend checkering. **Sights:** Ramp front, standing leaf rear. **Features:** Has many features of the original Model 70 Winchester. Barrel band front swivel, inletted rear. Cheekpiece with shadow line. Steel gripcap. Introduced 1988. From Dakota Arms, Inc.
Price: Wood stock. **$4,595.00**

Dakota African Grade
Similar to 76 Safari except chambered for 338 Lapua Mag., 404 Jeffery, 416 Rigby, 416 Dakota, 450 Dakota, 4-round magazine, select wood, two stock cross-bolts. 24" barrel, weighs 9-10 lbs. Ramp front sight, standing leaf rear. Introduced 1989.
Price: **$4,995.00**

DAKOTA LONGBOW TACTICAL E.R. RIFLE
Caliber: 300 Dakota Magnum, 330 Dakota Magnum, 338 Lapua Magnum. **Barrel:** 28", .950" at muzzle **Weight:** 13.7 lbs. **Length:** 50" to 52" overall. **Stock:** Ambidextrous McMillan A-2 fiberglass, black or olive green color; adjustable cheekpiece and buttplate. **Sights:** None furnished. Comes with Picatinny one-piece optical rail. **Features:** Uses the Dakota 76 action with controlled-round feed; three-position firing pin block safety, claw extractor; Model 70-style trigger. Comes with bipod, case tool kit. Introduced 1997. Made in U.S.A. by Dakota Arms, Inc.
Price: **$4,250.00**

DAKOTA 97 LIGHTWEIGHT HUNTER
Caliber: 22-250 to 330. **Barrel:** 22"-24". **Weight:** 6.1-6.5 lbs. **Length:** 43" overall. **Stock:** Fiberglass. **Sights:** Optional. **Features:** Matte blue finish, black stock. Right-hand action only. Introduced 1998. Made in U.S.A. by Dakota Arms, Inc.
Price: **$1,995.00**

DAKOTA LONG RANGE HUNTER RIFLE
Caliber: 25-06, 257 Roberts, 270 Win., 280 Rem., 7mm Rem. Mag., 7mm Dakota Mag., 30-06, 300 Win. Mag., 300 Dakota Mag., 338 Win. Mag., 330 Dakota Mag., 375 H&H Mag., 375 Dakota Mag. **Barrel:** 24", 26", match-quality; free-floating. **Weight:** 7.7 lbs. **Length:** 45" to 47" overall. **Stock:** H-S Precision black synthetic, with one-piece bedding block system. **Sights:** None furnished. Drilled and tapped for scope mounting. **Features:** Cylindrical machined receiver controlled round feed; Mauser-style extractor; three-position striker blocking safety; fully adjustable match trigger. Right-hand action only. Introduced 1997. Made in U.S.A. by Dakota Arms, Inc.
Price: **$1,995.00**

HARRIS GUNWORKS SIGNATURE CLASSIC SPORTER
Caliber: 22-250, 243, 6mm Rem., 7mm-08, 284, 308 (short action); 25-06, 270, 280 Rem., 30-06, 7mm Rem. Mag., 300 Win. Mag., 300 Wea. (long action); 338 Win. Mag., 340 Wea., 375 H&H (magnum action). **Barrel:** 22", 24", 26". **Weight:** 7 lbs. (short action). **Stock:** Fiberglass in green, beige, brown or black. Recoil pad and 1" swivels installed. Length of pull up to 14-1/4". **Sights:** None furnished. Comes with 1" rings and bases. **Features:** Uses right- or left-hand action with matte black finish. Trigger pull set at 3 lbs. Four-round magazine for standard calibers; three for magnums. Aluminum floorplate. Wood stock optional. Introduced 1987. From Harris Gunworks, Inc.
Price: **$2,700.00**

Harris Gunworks Alaskan

Harris Gunworks Signature Titanium Mountain

Harris Gunworks Signature Super Varminter

Harris Gunworks Talon Safari

Harris Gunworks Signature Classic Stainless Sporter

Similar to Signature Classic Sporter except action is made of stainless steel. Same calibers, in addition to 416 Rem. Mag. Fiberglass stock, right- or left-hand action in natural stainless, glass bead or black chrome sulfide finishes. Introduced 1990. From Harris Gunworks, Inc.

Price: **$2,900.00**

Harris Gunworks Signature Alaskan

Similar to Classic Sporter except match-grade barrel with single leaf rear sight, barrel band front, 1" detachable rings and mounts, steel floorplate, electroless nickel finish. Wood Monte Carlo stock with cheekpiece, palm-swell grip, solid butt pad. Chambered for 270, 280 Rem., 30-06, 7mm Rem. Mag., 300 Win. Mag., 300 Wea., 358 Win., 340 Wea., 375 H&H. Introduced 1989.

Price: **$3,800.00**

Harris Gunworks Signature Titanium Mountain Rifle

Similar to Classic Sporter except action made of titanium alloy, barrel of chrome-moly steel. Stock is graphite reinforced fiberglass. Weight is 5-1/2 lbs. Chambered for 270, 280 Rem., 30-06, 7mm Rem. Mag., 300 Win. Mag. Fiberglass stock optional. Introduced 1989.

Price: **$3,300.00**
Price: With graphite-steel composite light weight barrel. **$3,700.00**

Harris Gunworks Signature Varminter

Similar to Signature Classic Sporter except has heavy contoured barrel, adjustable trigger, field bipod and special hand-bedded fiberglass stock. Chambered for 223, 22-250, 220 Swift, 243, 6mm Rem., 25-06, 7mm-08, 7mm BR, 308, 350 Rem. Mag. Comes with 1" rings and bases. Introduced 1989.

Price: **$2,700.00**

HARRIS GUNWORKS TALON SAFARI RIFLE

Caliber: 300 Win. Mag., 300 Wea. Mag., 300 Phoenix, 338 Win. Mag., 30/378, 338 Lapua, 300 H&H, 340 Wea. Mag., 375 H&H, 404 Jeffery, 416 Rem. Mag., 458 Win. Mag. (Safari Magnum); 378 Wea. Mag., 416 Rigby, 416 Wea. Mag., 460 Wea. Mag. (Safari Super Magnum). **Barrel:** 24". **Weight:** About 9-10 lbs. **Length:** 43" overall. **Stock:** Gunworks fiberglass Safari. **Sights:** Barrel band front ramp, multi-leaf express rear. **Features:** Uses Harris Gunworks Safari action. Has quick detachable 1" scope mounts, positive locking steel floorplate, barrel band sling swivel. Match-grade barrel. Matte black finish standard. Introduced 1989. From Harris Gunworks, Inc.

Price: Talon Safari Magnum. **$3,900.00**
Price: Talon Safari Super Magnum **$4,200.00**

HARRIS GUNWORKS TALON SPORTER RIFLE

Caliber: 22-250, 243, 6mm Rem., 6mm BR, 7mm BR, 7mm-08, 25-06, 270, 280 Rem., 284, 308, 30-06, 350 Rem. Mag. (long action); 7mm Rem. Mag., 7mm STW, 300 Win. Mag., 300 Wea. Mag., 300 H&H, 338 Win. Mag., 340 Wea. Mag., 375 H&H, 416 Rem. Mag. **Barrel:** 24" (standard). **Weight:** About 7-1/2 lbs. **Length:** NA. **Stock:** Choice of walnut or fiberglass. **Sights:** None furnished; comes with rings and bases. Open sights optional. **Features:** Uses pre-'64 Model 70-type action with cone breech, controlled feed, claw extractor and three-position safety. Barrel and action are of stainless steel; chrome-moly optional. Introduced 1991. From Harris Gunworks, Inc.

Price: **$2,900.00**

Howa Lightning

Howa M-1500 Hunter

Howa M-1500 PCS Police Counter Sniper

Howa M-1500 Ultralight

Howa M-1500 Varmint Supreme

HOWA LIGHTNING BOLT-ACTION RIFLE

Caliber: 223, 22-250, 243, 6.5x55, 270, 308, 30-06, 7mm Rem. Mag., 300 Win. Mag., 338 Win. Mag. **Barrel:** 22", 24" magnum calibers. **Weight:** 7-1/2 lbs. **Length:** 42" overall (22" barrel). **Stock:** Black Bell & Carlson Carbelite composite with Monte Carlo comb; checkered grip and forend. **Sights:** None furnished. Drilled and tapped for scope mounting. **Features:** Sliding thumb safety; hinged floorplate; polished blue/black finish. Introduced 1993. From Legacy Sports International.

Price: Blue, standard calibers	$478.00
Price: Blue, magnum calibers	$500.00
Price: Stainless, standard calibers	$565.00
Price: Stainless, magnum calibers	$588.00

Howa M-1500 Hunter Bolt-Action Rifle

Similar to Lightning Model except has walnut-finished hardwood stock. Polished blue finish or stainless steel. Introduced 1999. From Legacy Sports International.

Price: Blue, standard calibers	$500.00
Price: Stainless, standard calibers	$588.00
Price: Blue, magnum calibers	$522.00
Price: Stainless, magnum calibers	$612.00

Howa M-1500 Supreme Rifles

Similar to Howa M-1500 Lightning except stocked with JRS Classic or Thumbhole Sporter laminated wood stocks in Nutmeg (brown/black) or Pepper (gray/black) colors. Barrel 22"; 24" magnum calibers. Weights are JRS stock 8 lbs., THS stock 8.3 lbs. Introduced 2001. Imported from Japan by Legacy Sports International.

Price: Blue, standard calibers, JRS stock	$616.00
Price: Blue, standard calibers, THS stock	$668.00
Price: Blue, magnum calibers, JRS stock	$638.00
Price: Blue, magnum calibers, THS stock	$638.00
Price: Stainless, standard calibers, JRS stock	$720.00
Price: Stainless, standard calibers, THS stock	$771.00
Price: Stainless, magnum calibers, JRS stock	$720.00
Price: Stainless, magnum calibers, THS stock	$742.00

Howa M-1500 Ultralight

Similar to Howa M-1500 Lightning except receiver milled to reduce weight, tapered 22" barrel; 1-10" twist. Chambered for 243 Win. Stocks are black texture-finished hardwood. Weighs 6.4 lbs. Length 40" overall.

Price: Blued	$511.00

Howa M-1500 Varminter and Varminter Supreme Rifles

Similar to M-1500 Lightning except has heavy 24" hammer-forged barrel. Chambered for 223, 22-250, 380. Weighs 9.3 lbs.; overall length 44.5". Introduced 1999. Imported from Japan by Interarms/Howa.

Varminter Supreme has heavy barrel, target crown muzzle. Heavy 24" barrel, laminated wood with raised comb stocks, rollover cheekpiece, vented beavertail forearm; available in 223 Rem., 22-250 Rem., 308 Win. Weighs 9.9 lbs. Introduced 2001. Imported from Japan by Legacy Sports International.

Price: Varminter, blue, polymer stock	$511.00
Price: Varminter, stainless, polymer stock	$612.00
Price: Varminter, blue, wood stock	$533.00
Price: Varminter, stainless, wood stock	$636.00
Price: Varminter Supreme, blued	$668.00
Price: Varminter Supreme, stainless	$771.00

L.A.R. Grizzly

Legacy Sports International M-1500

Legacy Sports International Texas Safari

Legacy Sports International Mauser 98

KIMBER MODEL 84M BOLT-ACTION RIFLE

Caliber: 22-250, 243, 260 Rem., 7mm-08, 308, 5-shot. **Barrel:** 22", 24", 26". **Weight:** 5 lbs., 10 oz. to 10 lbs. **Length:** 41"-45". **Stock:** Claro walnut, checkered with steel grip cap or gray laminate. **Sights:** None; drilled and tapped for bases. **Features:** Mauser claw extractor, two-position wing safety, action bedded on aluminum pillars, free-floated barrel, match-grade trigger set at 4 lbs., matte blue finish. Includes cable lock. Introduced 2001. Made in U.S.A. by Kimber Mfg. Inc.
Price: Classic (243, 260, 7mm-08, 308) $917.00
Price: Varmint (22-250) $1,001.00
Price: Long Master VT $1,122.00

L.A.R. GRIZZLY 50 BIG BOAR RIFLE

Caliber: 50 BMG, single shot. **Barrel:** 36". **Weight:** 30.4 lbs. **Length:** 45.5" overall. **Stock:** Integral. Ventilated rubber recoil pad. **Sights:** None furnished; scope mount. **Features:** Bolt-action bullpup design, thumb and bolt stop safety. All-steel construction. Unsurpassed accuracy and impact. Introduced 1994. Made in U.S.A. by L.A.R. Mfg., Inc.
Price: $2,195.00

LEGACY SPORTS INTERNATIONAL M-1500 CUSTOM RIFLES

Caliber: 300 WSM, 300 Win. Mag.; 3 plus 1 in chamber. **Weight:** 7.6-8.3 lbs. **Length:** 42.5" overall. **Stock:** Black polymer, laminated wood. **Features:** Built on Howa M-1500 stainless steel short-action, 3-position thumb safety, hinged floorplate, drilled and tapped for standard scope mounts. 300 WSM has stainless steel short action, 22 bbl. 300 Win. Mag. has blued long action, 24" bbl. with integral ported muzzle brake by Bill Wiseman. Introduced 2001 by Legacy Sports International.
Price: JRS Classic Pepper stock $995.00
Price: Thumbhole Pepper stock $1,035.00
Price: 300 WSM, polymer stock $895.00
Price: 300 Win. Mag., JRS Nutmeg stock $855.00

LEGACY SPORTS INTERNATIONAL TEXAS SAFARI RIFLES

Caliber: 270 Win., 300 Win. Mag. 270 Win.: 5 plus 1 in chamber; 300 Mag., 3 plus 1 in chamber. **Weight:** 7.8 lbs. **Length:** 42.5" overall; 44.5" in 300 Win. Mag. **Stock:** Brown/black laminated wood. **Features:** Built on Howa M-1500 action customized by Bill Wiseman, College Station, TX; Wiseman-designed 3-position thumb safety and bolt-release, hinged floorplate, drilled and tapped for standard scope mounts. Action glass-bedded, farrel free floated. 300 Win. Mag. has integral muzzle brake. Introduced 2001 by Legacy Sports International.
Price: 270 Win. $1,522.00
Price: 300 Win. Mag. $1,753.00

LEGACY SPORTS INTERNATIONAL MAUSER 98 RIFLE

Caliber: 300 Win. Mag. **Barrel:** 24", 1-10" twist. **Weight:** 8.4 lbs. **Length:** 45" overall. **Stock:** Premium American walnut. **Sights:** None. **Features:** Square-bridge Mauser 98 action dovetailed for ring mounts (scope and rings not included). 3-position thumb safety, hinged floorplate, adjustable trigger. Introduced 2001. Imported from Italy by Legacy Sports International.
Price: $955.00

RIFLES

Magnum Research Tactical

Magnum Lite Sporter

Raptor Bolt-Action

Remington 700 ADL Synthetic

MAGNUM RESEARCH MAGNUM LITE TACTICAL RIFLE

Caliber: 223 Rem., 22-250, 308 Win., 300 Win. Mag., 300 WSM. **Barrel:** 26" Magnum Lite™ graphite. **Weight:** 8.3 lbs. **Length:** NA. **Stock:** H-S Precision™ tactical black synthetic. **Sights:** None furnished; drilled and tapped for scope mount. **Features:** Accurized Remington 700 action; adjustable trigger; adjustable comb height. Tuned to shoot 1/2" MOA or better. Introduced 2001. From Magnum Research Inc.
Price: **$2,400.00**

MOUNTAIN EAGLE MAGNUM LITE RIFLE

Caliber: 22-250, 223 Rem. (Varmint); 280, 30-06 (long action); 7mm Rem. Mag., 300 Win. Mag., (magnum action). **Barrel:** 24", 26", free floating. **Weight:** 7 lbs., 13 oz. **Length:** 44" overall (24" barrel). **Stock:** Kevlar-graphite with aluminum bedding block, high comb, recoil pad, swivel studs; made by H-S Precision. **Sights:** None furnished; accepts any Remington 700-type base. **Features:** Special Sako action with one-piece forged bolt, hinged steel floorplate, lengthened receiver ring; adjustable trigger. Krieger cut-rifled benchrest barrel. Introduced 1996. From Magnum Research, Inc.
Price: Magnum Lite (graphite barrel) **$2,295.00**

NEW ULTRA LIGHT ARMS BOLT-ACTION RIFLES

Caliber: 17 Rem. to 416 Rigby (numerous calibers available). **Barrel:** Douglas, length to order. **Weight:** 4-3/4 to 7-1/2 lbs. **Length:** Varies. **Stock:** Kevlar®/graphite composite, variety of finishes. **Sights:** None furnished; drilled and tapped for scope mount. **Features:** Timney trigger, hand-lapped action, button-rifled barrel, hand-bedded action, recoil pad, sling-swivel studs, optional Jewell Trigger. Made in U.S.A. by New Ultra Light Arms.
Price: Model 20 (short action)............................ **$2,500.00**
Price: Model 24 (long action) **$2,600.00**
Price: Model 28 (magnum action)...................... **$2,900.00**
Price: Model 40 (300 Wea. Mag., 416 Rigby).............. **$2,900.00**
Price: Left-hand models, add **$100.00**

RAPTOR BOLT-ACTION RIFLE

Caliber: 270, 30-06, 243, 25-06, 308; 4-shot magazine. **Barrel:** 22". **Weight:** 7 lbs., 6 oz. **Length:** 42.5" overall. **Stock:** Black synthetic, fiberglass reinforced; checkered grip and forend; vented recoil pad; Monte Carlo cheekpiece. **Sights:** None furnished; drilled and tapped for scope mounts. **Features:** Rust-resistant "Taloncote" treated barreled action; pillar bedded; stainless bolt with three locking lugs; adjustable trigger. Announced 1997. Made in U.S.A. by Raptor Arms Co., Inc.
Price: **$249.00**

REMINGTON MODEL 700 CLASSIC RIFLE

Caliber: 221 Fireball. **Barrel:** 26". **Weight:** About 7-1/4 lbs. **Length:** 44-1/2" overall. **Stock:** American walnut, 20 lpi checkering on pistol grip and forend. Classic styling. Satin finish. **Sights:** None furnished. Receiver drilled and tapped for scope mounting. **Features:** A "classic" version of the BDL with straight comb stock. Fitted with rubber recoil pad. Sling swivel studs installed. Hinged floorplate. Limited production in 2002 only.
Price: **$661.00**

REMINGTON MODEL 700 ADL DELUXE RIFLE

Caliber: 270, 30-06 and 7mm Rem. Mag. **Barrel:** 22" or 24" round tapered. **Weight:** 7-1/4 to 7-1/2 lbs. **Length:** 41-5/8" to 44-1/2" overall. **Stock:** Walnut. Satin-finished pistol grip stock with fine-line cut checkering, Monte Carlo. **Sights:** Gold bead ramp front; removable, step-adjustable rear with windage screw. **Features:** Side safety, receiver tapped for scope mounts.
Price: From.............................. **$559.00 to $585.00**

Remington Model 700 ADL Synthetic

Similar to the 700 ADL except has a fiberglass-reinforced synthetic stock with straight comb, raised cheekpiece, positive checkering, and black rubber butt pad. Metal has matte finish. Available in 22-250, 223, 243, 270, 308, 30-06 with 22" barrel, 300 Win. Mag., 7mm Rem. Mag. with 24" barrel. Introduced 1996.
Price: From.............................. **$484.00 to $511.00**

Remington Model 700 ADL Synthetic Youth

Similar to the Model 700 ADL Synthetic except has 1" shorter stock, 20" barrel. Chambered for 243, 308. Introduced 1998.
Price: **$484.00**

Remington 700 BDL

Remington 700 BDL Left Hand

Remington 700 BDL SS DM

Remington 700 BDL SS DM-B

Remington Model 700 BDL Custom Deluxe Rifle

Same as 700 ADL except chambered for 222, 223 (short action, 24" barrel), 7mm-08, 280, 22-250, 25-06. (short action, 22" barrel), 243, 270, 30-06, skip-line checkering, black forend tip and gripcap with white line spacers. Matted receiver top, quick-release floorplate. Hooded ramp front sight, quick detachable swivels.

Price: **$661.00**

Also available in 17 Rem., 7mm Rem. Mag., 7mm Rem. Ultra Mag., 300 Win. Mag. (long action, 24" barrel); 338 Win. Mag., (long action, 22" barrel); 300 Rem. Ultra Mag. 338 Rem. Ultra Mag. (26" barrel), 375 Rem. Ultra Mag. Overall length 44-1/2", weight about 7-1/2 lbs.

Price: . . . . **$688.00 to $701.00**

Remington Model 700 BDL Left Hand Custom Deluxe

Same as 700 BDL except mirror-image left-hand action, stock. Available in 270, 30-06, 7mm Rem. Mag., 300 Rem. Ultra Mag, 338 Rem. Ultra Mag., 7mm Rem. Ultra Mag.

Price: . . . . **$688.00 to $728.00**

Remington Model 700 BDL DM Rifle

Same as 700 BDL except detachable box magazine (4-shot, standard calibers, 3-shot for magnums). Glossy stock finish, open sights, recoil pad, sling swivels. Available in 270, 30-06, 7mm Rem. Mag., 300 Win. Mag. Introduced 1995.

Price: From . . . . **$728.00 to $755.00**

Remington Model 700 BDL SS Rifle

Similar to 700 BDL rifle except hinged floorplate, 24" standard weight barrel in all calibers; magnum calibers have magnum-contour barrel. No sights supplied, but comes drilled and tapped. Corrosion-resistant follower and fire control, stainless BDL-style barreled action with fine matte finish. Synthetic stock has straight comb and cheekpiece, textured finish, positive checkering, plated swivel studs. Calibers—270, 30-06; magnums—7mm Rem. Mag., 7mm Rem. UltraMag., 375 Rem. Ultra Mag.,

300 Rem. Ultra Mag. (26" barrel) 300 Win. Mag., 338 Win. Mag., 338 Rem. Ultra Mag., 375 H&H. Weighs 7-3/8 - 7-1/2 lbs. Introduced 1993.

Price: From . . . . **$708.00 to $748.00**

Remington Model 700 BDL SS DM Rifle

Same as 700 BDL SS except detachable box magazine. Barrel, receiver and bolt made of #416 stainless steel; black synthetic stock, fine-line engraving. Available in 25-06, 270, 280, 30-06, 7mm Rem. Mag., 300 Win. Mag. Introduced 1995.

Price: From . . . . **$775.00 to $801.00**

Remington Model 700 Custom KS Mountain Rifle

Similar to 700 BDL except custom finished with aramid fiber reinforced resin synthetic stock. Available in left- and right-hand versions. Chambered 270 Win., 280 Rem., 30-06, 7mm Rem. Mag., 7mm STW, 300 Rem. Ultra Mag., 338 Rem. Ultra Mag., 300 Win. Mag., 300 Wea. Mag., 35 Whelen, 338 Win. Mag., 8mm Rem. Mag., 375 H&H, with 24" barrel (except 300 Rem. Ultra Mag., 26"). Weighs 6 lbs., 6 oz. Introduced 1986.

Price: 7mm Rem. Ultra Mag., right-hand **$1,294.00**
Price: 375 Rem. Ultra Mag., left-hand **$1,373.00**

Remington Model 700 LSS Mountain Rifle

Similar to Model 700 Custom KS Mountain Rifle except stainless steel 22" barrel and two-tone laminated stock. Chambered in 260 Rem., 7mm-08, 270 Winchester and 30-06. Overall length 42-1/2", weighs 6-5/8 oz. Introduced 1999.

Price: **$776.00**

Remington Model 700 Safari Grade

Similar to 700 BDL aramid fiber reinforced fiberglass stock, blued carbon steel bbl. and action, or stainless, w/cheekpiece, custom finished and tuned. In 8mm Rem. Mag., 375 H&H, 416 Rem. Mag. or 458 Win. Mag. calibers only with heavy barrel. Right- and left-hand versions.

Price: Safari KS . . . . **$1,497.00-$1,577.00**
Price: Safari KS (stainless right-hand only) **$1,672.00**

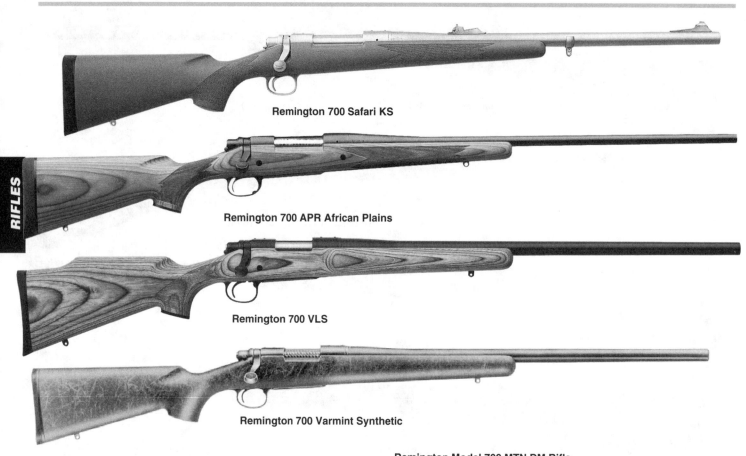

Remington 700 Safari KS

Remington 700 APR African Plains

Remington 700 VLS

Remington 700 Varmint Synthetic

Remington Model 700 AWR Alaskan Wilderness Rifle
Similar to the 700 BDL except has stainless barreled action finishBlack Teflon 24" bbl. 26" Ultra Mag raised cheekpiece, magnum-grade black rubber recoil pad. Chambered for 7mm Rem. Mag., 7mm STW, 300 Rem. Ultra Mag., 300 Win. Mag., 300 Wea. Mag., 338 Rem. Ultra Mag., 338 Win. Mag., 375 H&H. Aramid fiber reinforced fiberglass stock. Introduced 1994.
Price: 7mm Rem. Ultra Mag., 375 Rem. Ultra Mag. **$1,569.00**

Remington Model 700 APR African Plains Rifle
Similar to Model 700 BDL except magnum receiver and specially contoured 26" Custom Shop barrel with satin blued finish, laminated wood stock with raised cheekpiece, satin finish, black butt pad, 20 lpi cut checkering. Chambered for 7mm Rem. Mag., 300 Rem. Ultra Mag., 300 Win. Mag., 300 Wea. Mag., 338 Win. Mag., 338 Rem. Ultra Mag., 375 H&H. Introduced 1994.
Price: 7mm Rem. Ultra Mag., 375 Rem. Ultra Mag. **$1,690.00**

Remington Model 700 EtronX Electronic Ignition Rifle
Similar to Model 700 VS SF except features battery-powered ignition system for near-zero lock time and electronic trigger mechanism. Requires ammunition with EtronX electrically fired primers. Aluminum-bedded 26" heavy, stainless steel, fluted barrel; overall length 45-7/8"; weight 8 lbs., 14 oz. Black, Kevlar-reinforced composite stock. Light-emitting diode display on grip top indicates fire or safe mode, loaded or unloaded chamber, battery condition. Introduced 2000.
Price: 220 Swift, 22-250 or 243 Win. **$1,999.00**

Remington Model 700 LSS Rifle
Similar to 700 BDL except stainless steel barreled action, gray laminated wood stock with Monte Carlo comb and cheekpiece. No sights furnished. Available in 7mm Rem. Mag., 7mm Rem. Ultra Mag., 375 Rem. Ultra Mag., LH 7mm Rem. Ultra Mag., 300 Rem. Ultra Mag., 300 Win. Mag., and 338 Rem. Ultra Mag. in right-hand, and 30-06, 300 Rem. Ultra Mag., 338 Rem. Ultra Mag. in left-hand model. Introduced 1996.
Price: From. . . . . **$803.00 to $843.00**

Remington Model 700 MTN DM Rifle
Similar to 700 BDL except weighs 6-1/2 to 6-5/8 lbs., 22" tapered barrel. Redesigned pistol grip, straight comb, contoured cheekpiece, hand-rubbed oil stock finish, deep cut checkering, hinged floorplate and magazine follower, two-position thumb safety. Chambered for 260 Rem., 270 Win., 7mm-08, 25-06, 280 Rem., 30-06, 4-shot detachable box magazine. Overall length is 41-5/8"-42-1/2". Introduced 1995.
Price: **$728.00**

Remington Model 700 Titanium
Similar to 700 BDL except has titanium receiver, spiral-cut fluted bolt, skeletonized bolt handle and carbon-fiber and aramid fiber reinforced stock with sling swivel studs. Barrel 22"; weighs 5-1/4 lbs. (short action) or 5-1/2 lbs. (long action). Satin stainless finish. 260 Rem., 270 Win., 7mm-08, 30-06, 308 Win. Introduced 2001.
Price: **$1,239.00**

Remington Model 700 VLS Varmint Laminated Stock
Similar to 700 BDL except 26" heavy barrel without sights, brown laminated stock with beavertail forend, gripcap, rubber butt pad. Available in 223 Rem., 22-250, 6mm, 243, 308. Polished blue finish. Introduced 1995.
Price: From. **$705.00**

Remington Model 700 VS Varmint Synthetic Rifles
Similar to 700 BDL Varmint Laminated except composite stock reinforced with aramid fiber reinforced, fiberglass and graphite. Aluminum bedding block that runs full length of receiver. Free-floating 26" barrel. Metal has black matte finish; stock has textured black and gray finish and swivel studs. Available in 223, 22-250, 308. Right- and left-hand. Introduced 1992.
Price: . . . . **$788.00 to $815.00**

Remington Model 700 VS SF Rifle
Similar to Model 700 Varmint Synthetic except satin-finish stainless barreled action with 26" fluted barrel, spherical concave muzzle crown. Chambered for 223, 220 Swift, 22-250. Introduced 1994.
Price: **$949.00**

CENTERFIRE RIFLES — BOLT ACTION

Remington 700 VF SF

Remington 700 Sendero SF

Remington Model Seven

Remington Model Seven LS Mag

Remington Model Seven SS Mag

Remington Model 700 Sendero Rifle
Similar to Model 700 Varmint Synthetic except long action for magnum calibers. 26" heavy varmint barrel with spherical concave crown. Chambered for 25-06, 270, 7mm Rem. Mag., 300 Win. Mag. Introduced 1994.
Price: . . . . **$788.00 to $815.00**

Remington Model 700 Sendero SF Rifle
Similar to 700 Sendero except stainless steel action and 26" fluted stainless barrel. Weighs 8-1/2 lbs. Chambered for 25-06, 7mm Rem. Mag., 7mm STW, 300 Rem. Ultra Mag., 338 Rem. Ultra Mag., 300 Win. Mag., 7mm Rem. Ultra Mag. Introduced 1996.
Price: . . . . **$976.00 to $989.00**

REMINGTON MODEL 700 RMEF
Caliber: 7mm Rem. Ultra Mag. **Barrel:** 26". **Weight:** 7-5/8 lbs. **Length:** 46.5". **Stock:** Synthetic, Realtree hardwood finish. **Sights:** None; drilled and tapped. **Features:** Special Edition (sold one year only), Rocky Mountain Elk Foundation rifle, 416 stainless bolt, varrel, receiver. Portion of proceeds to RMEF.
Price: **$808.00**

REMINGTON MODEL 710 BOLT-ACTION RIFLE
Caliber: 270 Win., 30-06. **Barrel:** 22". **Weight:** 7-1/8 lbs. **Length:** 42-1/2" overall. **Stock:** Gray synthetic. **Sights:** Bushnell Sharpshooter 3-9x scope mounted and bore-sighted. **Features:** Unique action locks bolt directly into barrel; 60-degree bolt throw; 4-shot dual-stack magazine; key-

operated Integrated Security System locks bolt open. Introduced 2001. Made in U.S.A. by Remington Arms Co.
Price: **$425.00**

REMINGTON MODEL SEVEN LSS
Caliber: 22-250, 7mm-08. **Barrel:** 20". **Weight:** 6-1/2 lbs. **Length:** 39-1/4" overall. **Stock:** Brown laminated. Cut checkering. **Features:** Short-action design; silent side safety; free-floated barrel except for single pressure point at forend tip. Stainless barreled action. Introduced 1983.
Price: **$770.00**

Remington Model Seven Custom KS
Similar to Model Seven except gray aramid fiber reinforced stock with 1" black rubber recoil pad and swivel studs. Blued satin carbon steel barreled action. No sights on 223, 260 Rem., 7mm-08, 308; 35 Rem. and 350 Rem. have iron sights.
Price: **$1,294.00**

Remington Model Seven LS
Similar to Model Seven except has satin-finished, brown laminated stock with 20" carbon steel barrel. 223, 243 Win., 7mm-08, 300 Win. Introduced 2000.
Price: **$677.00**
New Price: 7mmRSAUM, 300RSAUM, 22" bbl. **$743.00**

Remington Model Seven SS
Similar to Model Seven except stainless steel barreled action and black synthetic stock, 20" barrel. Chambered for 223, 243, 260 Rem., 7mm-08, 308. Introduced 1994.
Price: **$703.00**
New Price: 7mmRSAUM, 300RSAUM, 22" bbl. **$717.00**

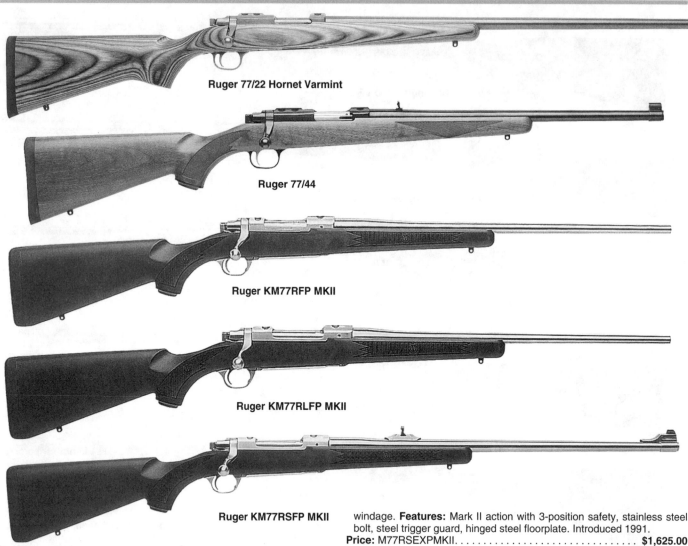

Ruger 77/22 Hornet Varmint

Ruger 77/44

Ruger KM77RFP MKII

Ruger KM77RLFP MKII

Ruger KM77RSFP MKII

Remington Model Seven Custom MS Rifle

Similar to Model Seven except full-length Mannlicher-style stock of laminated wood with straight comb, solid black recoil pad, black steel forend tip, cut checkering, gloss finish. Barrel length 20", weighs 6-3/4 lbs. Available in 222 Rem., 223, 22-250, 243, 6mm Rem., 260 Rem., 7mm-08 Rem., 308, 350 Rem. Mag. Calibers 250 Savage, 257 Roberts, 35 Rem. Polished blue finish. Introduced 1993. From Remington Custom Shop.
Price: From **$1,312.00**

Remington Model Seven Youth Rifle

Similar to Model Seven except hardwood stock, 1" shorter length of pull, chambered for 223, 243, 260 Rem., 7mm-08. Introduced 1993.
Price: **$531.00**

Ruger M77RSI International Carbine

Same as standard Model 77 except 18" barrel, full-length International-style stock, steel forend cap, loop-type steel sling swivels. Integral-base receiver, open sights, Ruger 1" steel rings. Improved front sight. Available in 243, 270, 308, 30-06. Weighs 7 lbs. Length overall is 38-3/8".
Price: M77RSIMKII **$769.00**

RUGER M77 MARK II EXPRESS RIFLE

Caliber: 270, 30-06, 7mm Rem. Mag., 300 Win. Mag., 338 Win. Mag., 375 H&H Magnum, 4-shot (416 Rigby Magnum 3-shot). **Barrel:** 22" (std. calibers) 23" or 24" (Magnum calibers), with integral steel rib; barrel-mounted front swivel stud; hammer forged. **Weight:** 7.5 lbs. 9+ lbs. Magnum. **Length:** 42.125" overall. **Stock:** Circassian walnut with rubber recoil pad, swivel studs. **Sights:** Blade front, V-notch express rear adjustable for

windage. **Features:** Mark II action with 3-position safety, stainless steel bolt, steel trigger guard, hinged steel floorplate. Introduced 1991.
Price: M77RSEXPMKII **$1,625.00**
Price: M77RSMMKII **$1,695.00**

RUGER 77/22 HORNET BOLT-ACTION RIFLE

Caliber: 22 Hornet, 6-shot rotary magazine. **Barrel:** 20". **Weight:** About 6 lbs. **Length:** 39-3/4" overall. **Stock:** Checkered American walnut, black rubber butt pad. **Sights:** Brass bead front, open adjustable rear; also available without sights. **Features:** Same basic features as rimfire model except slightly lengthened receiver. Uses Ruger rotary magazine. Three-position safety. Comes with 1" Ruger scope rings. Introduced 1994.
Price: 77/22RH (rings only) **$589.00**
Price: 77/22RSH (with sights) **$609.00**
Price: K77/22VHZ Varmint, laminated stock, no sights **$625.00**

RUGER M77 MARK II RIFLE

Caliber: 223, 220 Swift, 22-250, 243, 6mm Rem., 257 Roberts, 25-06, 6.5x55 Swedish, 270, 7x57mm, 260 Rem., 280 Rem., 308, 30-06, 7mm Rem. Mag., 7mm Rem. Short Ultra Mag., 300 Rem. Short Ultra Mag., 300 WSM, 300 Win. Mag., 338 Win. Mag., 4-shot magazine. **Barrel:** 20", 22"; 24" (magnums). **Weight:** About 7 lbs. **Length:** 39-3/4" overall. **Stock:** Synthetic American walnut; swivel studs, rubber butt pad. **Sights:** None furnished. Receiver has Ruger integral scope mount base, Ruger 1" rings. Some with iron sights. **Features:** Short action with new trigger, 3-position safety. Steel trigger guard. Left-hand available. Introduced 1989.
Price: M77RMKII (no sights) **$675.00**
Price: M77RSMKII (open sights) **$759.00**
Price: M77LRMKII (left-hand, 270, 30-06, 7mm Rem. Mag.,300 Win. Mag.) **$675.00**
Price: KM77REPMKII (Shorts) **$675.00**

Ruger M77VT Target

Sako TRG-S

Sako 75 Hunter

Ruger M77 Mark II All-Weather and Sporter Model Stainless Rifle

Similar to wood-stock M77 Mark II except all metal parts are stainless steel, has an injection-moulded, glass-fiber-reinforced polymer stock. Laminated wood stock. Chambered for 223, 243, 270, 308, 30-06, 7mm Rem. Mag., 300 Win. Mag., 338 Win. Mag. Fixed-blade-type ejector, 3-position safety, new trigger guard with patented floorplate latch. Integral Scope Base Receiver, 1" Ruger scope rings, built-in sling swivel loops. Introduced 1990.

Price: K77RFPMKII **$675.00**
Price: K77RLFPMKII Ultra-Light, synthetic stock, rings, no sights. **$675.00**
Price: K77LRBBZMKII, left-hand bolt, rings, no sights, laminated
   stock **$729.00**
Price: K77RSFPMKII, synthetic stock, open sights **$759.00**
Price: K77RBZMKII, no sights, laminated wood stock, 223,
   22/250, 243, 270, 280 Rem., 7mm Rem. Mag., 30-06,
   308, 300 Win. Mag., 338 Win. Mag. **$729.00**
Price: K77RSBZMKII, open sights, laminated wood stock, 243,
   270, 7mm Rem. Mag., 30-06, 300 Win. Mag., 338 Win. Mag. . . **$799.00**
Price: KM77RFPMKII (Shorts), M77RMKII. **$675.00**

Ruger M77RL Ultra Light

Similar to standard M77 except weighs 6 lbs., chambered for 223, 243, 308, 270, 30-06, 257 Roberts, barrel tapped for target scope blocks, 20" Ultra Light barrel. Overall length 40". Ruger's steel 1" scope rings supplied. Introduced 1983.

Price: M77RLMKII **$729.00**

Ruger M77 Mark II Compact Rifles

Similar to standard M77 except reduced 16-1/2" barrel, weighs 5-3/4 lbs. Chambered for 223, 243, 260 Rem., 308, and 7mm-08.

Price: M77CR MKII (blued finish, walnut stock) **$649.00**
Price: KM77CRBBZ MkII (stainless finish, black laminated stock). **$699.00**

RUGER M77 MARK II MAGNUM RIFLE

Caliber: 375 H&H, 4-shot magazine; 416 Rigby, 3-shot magazine. **Barrel:** 23", with integral steel rib; hammer forged. **Weight:** 9.25 lbs. (375); 9-3/4 lbs. (416, Rigby). **Length:** 42-3/8" to 44-5/8" overall. **Stock:** Circassian walnut with hand-cut checkering, swivel studs, steel gripcap, rubber butt pad. **Sights:** Ramp front, two leaf express on serrated integral steel rib. Rib also serves as base for front scope ring. **Features:** Uses an enlarged Mark II action with three-position safety, stainless bolt, steel trigger guard and hinged steel floorplate. Controlled feed. Introduced 1989.

Price: M77RSMMKII. **$1,695.00**

RUGER 77/44 BOLT-ACTION RIFLE

Caliber: 44 Magnum, 4-shot magazine. **Barrel:** 18-1/2". **Weight:** 6 lbs. **Length:** 38-1/4" overall. **Stock:** American walnut with rubber butt pad and swivel studs or black polymer (stainless only). **Sights:** Gold bead front, folding leaf rear. Comes with Ruger 1" scope rings. **Features:** Uses same action as the Ruger 77/22. Short bolt stroke; rotary magazine; three-position safety. Introduced 1997. Made in U.S.A. by Sturm, Ruger & Co.

Price: Blue, walnut, 77/44RS **$599.00**
Price: Stainless, polymer, stock, K77/44RS **$599.00**

RUGER M77VT TARGET RIFLE

Caliber: 22-250, 220 Swift, 223, 243, 25-06, 308. **Barrel:** 26" heavy stainless steel with target gray finish. **Weight:** 9-3/4 lbs. **Length:** Approx. 44" overall. **Stock:** Laminated American hardwood with beavertail forend, steel swivel studs; no checkering or gripcap. **Sights:** Integral scope mount bases in receiver. **Features:** Ruger diagonal bedding system. Ruger steel 1" scope rings supplied. Fully adjustable trigger. Steel floorplate and trigger guard. New version introduced 1992.

Price: K77VTMKII. **$819.00**

SAKO TRG-S BOLT-ACTION RIFLE

Caliber: 338 Lapua Mag., 30-378 Weatherby, 3-shot magazine. **Barrel:** 26". **Weight:** 7.75 lbs. **Length:** 45.5" overall. **Stock:** Reinforced polyurethane with Monte Carlo comb. **Sights:** None furnished. **Features:** Resistance-free bolt with 60-degree lift. Recoil pad adjustable for length. Free-floating barrel, detachable magazine, fully adjustable trigger. Matte blue metal. Introduced 1993. Imported from Finland by Beretta USA.

Price: **$882.00**

Sako TRG-42 BOLT-ACTION RIFLE

Similar to TRG-S except 5-shot magazine, fully adjustable stock and competition trigger. Offered in 338 Lapua Mag. and 300 Win. Mag. Imported from Finland by Beretta USA.

Price: **$2,829.00**

SAKO 75 HUNTER BOLT-ACTION RIFLE

Caliber: 17 Rem., 222, 223, 22-250, 243, 7mm-08, 308 Win., 25-06, 270, 280, 30-06; 270 Wea. Mag., 7mm Rem. Mag., 7mm STW, 7mm Wea. Mag., 300 Win. Mag., 300 Wea. Mag., 338 Win. Mag., 340 Wea. Mag., 375 H&H, 416 Rem. Mag. **Barrel:** 22", standard calibers; 24", 26" magnum calibers. **Weight:** About 6 lbs. **Length:** NA. **Stock:** European walnut with matte lacquer finish. **Sights:** None furnished; dovetail scope mount rails. **Features:** New design with three locking lugs and a mechanical ejector, key locks firing pin and bolt, cold hammer-forged barrel is free-floating, 2-position safety, hinged floorplate or detachable magazine that can be loaded from the top, short 70 degree bolt lift. Five action lengths. Introduced 1997. Imported from Finland by Beretta USA.

Price: Standard calibers **$1,129.00**
Price: Magnum Calibers **$1,163.00**

RIFLES

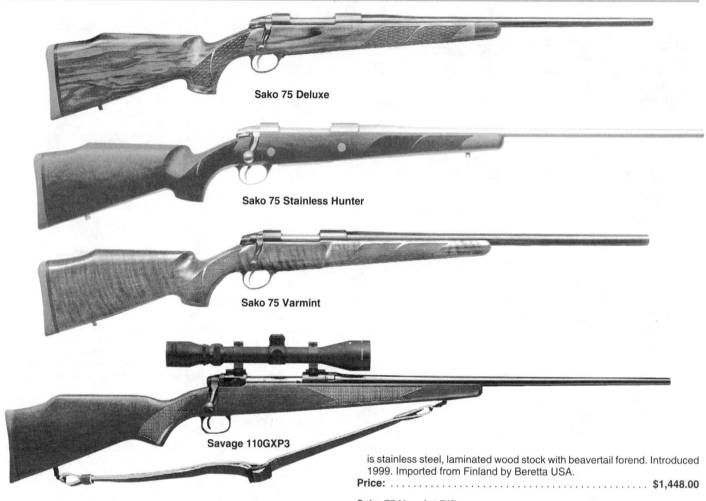

Sako 75 Deluxe

Sako 75 Stainless Hunter

Sako 75 Varmint

Savage 110GXP3

Sako 75 Stainless Synthetic Rifle

Similar to 75 Hunter except all metal is stainless steel, synthetic stock has soft composite panels moulded into forend and pistol grip. Available in 22-250, 243, 308 Win., 25-06, 270, 30-06 with 22" barrel, 7mm Rem. Mag., 7mm STW, 300 Win. Mag., 338 Win. Mag. and 375 H&H Mag. with 24" barrel and 300 Wea. Mag., 300 Rem.Ultra Mag. with 26" barrel. Introduced 1997. Imported from Finland by Beretta USA.

Price: Standard calibers **$1,239.00**
Price: Magnum calibers **$1,274.00**

Sako 75 Deluxe Rifle

Similar to 75 Hunter except select wood rosewood gripcap and forend tip. Available in 17 Rem., 222, 223, 25-06, 243, 7mm-08, 308, 25-06, 270, 280, 30-06; 270 Wea. Mag., 7mm Rem. Mag., 7mm STW, 7mm Wea. Mag., 300 Win. Mag., 300 Wea. Mag., 338 Win. Mag., 340 Wea. Mag., 375 H&H, 416 Rem. Mag. Introduced 1997. Imported from Finland by Beretta USA.

Price: Standard calibers **$1,653.00**
Price: Magnum calibers **$1,688.00**

Sako 75 Hunter Stainless Rifle

Similar to Sako 75 Hunter except all metal is stainless steel. Walnut stock with matte lacquer finish, rubber butt pad. Introduced 1999. Imported from Finland by Beretta USA.

Price: 270, 30-06 . . . . **$1,239.00**
Price: 7mm Rem. Mag., 7mm STW, 300 Win. Mag.,
300 Wea. Mag., 338 Win. Mag. **$1,274.00**

Sako 75 Varmint Stainless Laminated Rifle

Similar to Sako 75 Hunter except chambered only for 222, 223, 22-250, 22 PPC USA, 6mm PPC, heavy 24" barrel with recessed crown, all metal

is stainless steel, laminated wood stock with beavertail forend. Introduced 1999. Imported from Finland by Beretta USA.
Price: **$1,448.00**

Sako 75 Varmint Rifle

Similar to Model 75 Hunter except chambered only for 17 Rem., 222 Rem., 223 Rem., 22-250 Rem., 22 PPC and 6mm PPC, 24" heavy barrel with recessed crown, beavertail forend. Introduced 1998. Imported from Finland by Beretta USA.
Price: **$1,337.00**

SAUER 202 BOLT-ACTION RIFLE

Caliber: Standard—243, 6.5x55, 270 Win., 308 Win., 30-06; magnum—7mm Rem. Mag., 300 Win. Mag., 300 Wea. Mag., 375 H&H. **Barrel:** 23.6" (standard), 26" (magnum). **Weight:** 7.7 lbs. (standard). **Length:** 44.3" overall (23.6" barrel). **Stock:** Select American Claro walnut with high-gloss epoxy finish, rosewood grip and forend caps; 22 lpi checkering. Synthetic also available. **Sights:** None furnished; drilled and tapped for scope mounting. **Features:** Short 60" bolt throw; detachable box magazine; six-lug bolt; quick-change barrel; tapered bore; adjustable two-stage trigger; firing pin cocking indicator. Introduced 1994. Imported from Germany by Sigarms, Inc.

Price: Standard calibers, right-hand **$1,035.00**
Price: Magnum calibers, right-hand **$1,106.00**
Price: Standard calibers, synthetic stock **$985.00**
Price: Magnum calibers, synthetic stock **$1,056.00**

SAVAGE MODEL 10GXP3, 110GXP3 PACKAGE GUNS

Caliber: 223 Rem., 22-250 Rem., 243 Win., 7mm-08 Rem., 308 Win., 300 WSM (10GXP3). 25-06 Rem., 270 Win., 30-06 Spfld., 7mm Rem. Mag., 300 Win. Mag., 300 Rem. Ultra Mag. (110GXP3). **Barrel:** 22" 24", 26". **Weight:** 7.5 lbs. average. **Length:** 43"-47". **Stock:** Walnut Monte Carlo with checkering. **Sights:** 3-9X40mm scope, mounted & bore sighted. **Features:** Blued, free floating and button rifled, internal box magazines, swivel studs, leather sling. Left-hand available.
Price: **$476.00**

CENTERFIRE RIFLES — BOLT ACTION

Savage 111FXP3

Savage 111FCXP3

Savage 11FYXP3

Savage 16FXP3

SAVAGE MODEL 11FXP3, 111FXP3, 111FCXP3 PACKAGE GUNS

Caliber: 223 Rem., 22-250 Rem., 243 Win., 308 Win., 300 WSM (11FXP3). 270 Win., 30-06 Spfld., 25-06 Rem., 7mm Rem. Mag., 300 Win. Mag., 338 Win. Mag., 300 Rem. Ultra Mag. (11FCXPE & 111FXP3). **Barrel:** 22"-26". **Weight:** 6.5 lbs. **Length:** 41"-47". **Stock:** Synthetic checkering, dual pillar bed. **Sights:** 3-9X40mm scope, mounted & bore sighted. **Features:** Blued, free floating and button rifled, Top loading internal box mag (except 111FXCP3 has detachable box mag.). Nylon sling and swivel studs. Some left-hand available.

Price: **$502.00**
Price: Model 111FCXP3 .... **$436.00**
Price: Model 11FYXP3, 243 Win., 12.5" pull **$453.00**

SAVAGE MODEL 16FXP3, 116FXP3 SS ACTION PACKAGE GUNS

Caliber: 223 Rem., 243 Win., 308 Win., 300 WSM, 270 Win., 30-06 Spfld., 7mm Rem. Mag., 300 Win. Mag., 338 Win. Mag., 375 H&H, 7mm S&W, 7mm Rem. Ultra Mag., 300 Rem. Ultra Mag. **Barrel:** 22", 24", 26". **Weight:** 6.75 lbs. average. **Length:** 41"-46". **Stock:** Synthetic checkering, dual pillar bed. **Sights:** 3-9X40mm scope, mounted & bore sighted. **Features:** Free floating and button rifled. Internal box mag., nylon sling and swivel studs.

Price: **$534.00**

SAVAGE MODEL 10FM SIERRA ULTRA LIGHT RIFLE

Caliber: 223, 243, 308. **Barrel:** 20". **Weight:** 6 lbs. **Length:** 41-1/2". **Stock:** "Dual Pillar" bedding in black synthetic stock with silver medallion in grip-cap. **Sights:** None furnished; drilled and tapped for scope mounting. **Features:** True short action. Comes with sling and quick-detachable swivels. Introduced 1998. Made in U.S.A. by Savage Arms, Inc.

Price: **$476.00**

Savage 10FM Sierra Ultra Light

Savage Model 10FP

Savage Model 11F

Savage Hunter 11G

SAVAGE MODEL 10FCM SCOUT ULTRA LIGHT RIFLE

Caliber: 7mm-08 Rem., 308 Win. **Barrel:** 20", 4-shot. **Weight:** 6.25 lbs. **Length:** 39.75" overall. **Stock:** Synthetic checkering, dual pillar bed. **Sights:** Ghost ring rear, gold bead front. **Features:** Blued, detachable box magazine, Savage shooting sling/carry strap. Quick detach swivels.
Price: **$559.00**

SAVAGE MODEL 110FP TACTICAL RIFLE

Caliber: 223, 25-06, 308, 30-06, 300 Win. Mag., 7mm Rem. Mag., 4-shot magazine. **Barrel:** 24", heavy; recessed target muzzle. **Weight:** 8-1/2 lbs. **Length:** 45.5" overall. **Stock:** Black graphite/fiberglass composition; positive checkering. **Sights:** None furnished. Receiver drilled and tapped for scope mounting. **Features:** Pillar-bedded stock. Black matte finish on all metal parts. Double swivel studs on the forend for sling and/or bipod mount. Right or left-hand. Introduced 1990. From Savage Arms, Inc.
Price: Right- or left-hand. **$502.00**

Savage Model 10FP Tactical Rifle

Similar to the Model 110FP except has true short action, chambered for 223, 308; black synthetic stock with "Dual Pillar" bedding. Introduced 1998. Made in U.S.A. by Savage Arms, Inc.
Price: **$502.00**
Price: Model 10FLP (left-hand). **$502.00**
Price: Model 10FPLEI (20"), 10FPLE2 (26") **$511.00**
Price: Model 10FPXP-LE w/Burris 3.5-10X50 scope,
  Harris bipod package **$1,100.00**

SAVAGE MODEL 111 CLASSIC HUNTER RIFLES

Caliber: 223, 22-250, 243, 25-06, 270, 30-06, 308, 7mm Rem. Mag., 7mm-08, 300 Win. Mag., 338 Win. Mag., 300 Rem. Ultra Mag., 7mm WSM, 300 Rem. Ultra Mag., 7mm Rem. Ultra Mag., 270 WSM, 300 Win. Short Mag., 7mm Rem. Short Ultra Mag. (Models 111G, GL, GNS, F, FL, FNS); 270, 30-06, 7mm Rem. Mag., 300 Win. Mag. (Models 111GC, GLC, FAK, FC, FLC). **Barrel:** 22", 24" (magnum calibers). **Weight:** 6.3 to 7 lbs. **Length:** 43.5" overall (22" barrel). **Stock:** Walnut-finished hardwood (M111G, GC); graphite/fiberglass filled composite. **Sights:** Ramp front, open fully adjustable rear; drilled and tapped for scope mounting. **Features:** Three-position top tang safety, double front locking lugs, free-floated button-rifled barrel. Comes with trigger lock, target, ear puffs. Introduced 1994. Made in U.S.A. by Savage Arms, Inc.
Price: Model 111FC (detachable magazine, composite stock,
  right- or left-hand) **$468.00**
Price: Model 111F (top-loading magazine, composite stock,
  right- or left-hand) . . . . **$394.00 to $442.00**
Price: Model 111FNS (as above, no sights, right-hand only) **$434.00**
Price: Model 111G (wood stock, top-loading magazine,
  right- or left-hand) **$418.00**
Price: Model 111GC (as above, detachable magazine),
  right- or left-hand **$433.00**
Price: Model 111GNS (wood stock, top-loading magzine,
  no sights, right-hand only) **$411.00**
Price: Model 111FAK Express (blued, composite stock,
  top loading magazine, Adjustable muzzle brake). . . . . **NA**

Savage Model 11 Hunter Rifles

Similar to the Model 111F except has true short action, chambered for 223, 22-250, 243, 308; black synthetic stock with "Dual Pillar" bedding, positive checkering. Introduced 1998. Made in U.S.A. by Savage Arms, Inc.
Price: Model 11F **$442.00**
Price: Model 11FL (left-hand). **$442.00**
Price: Model 11FNS (right-hand, no sights) **$434.00**
Price: Model 11G (wood stock) **$418.00**
Price: Model 11GL (as above, left-hand) **$418.00**
Price: Model 11GNS (wood stock, no sights). **$411.00**

CENTERFIRE RIFLES — BOLT ACTION

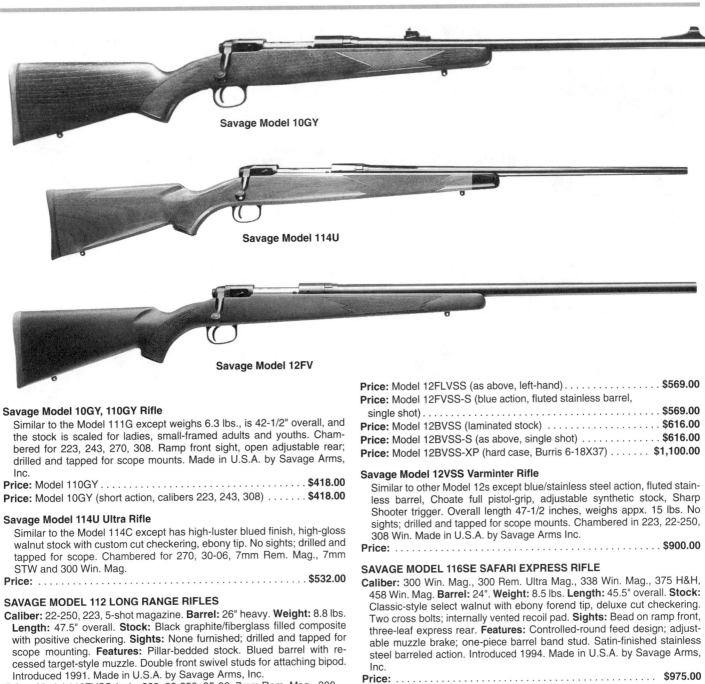

Savage Model 10GY

Savage Model 114U

Savage Model 12FV

Savage Model 10GY, 110GY Rifle

Similar to the Model 111G except weighs 6.3 lbs., is 42-1/2" overall, and the stock is scaled for ladies, small-framed adults and youths. Chambered for 223, 243, 270, 308. Ramp front sight, open adjustable rear; drilled and tapped for scope mounts. Made in U.S.A. by Savage Arms, Inc.

Price: Model 110GY **$418.00**
Price: Model 10GY (short action, calibers 223, 243, 308) **$418.00**

Savage Model 114U Ultra Rifle

Similar to the Model 114C except has high-luster blued finish, high-gloss walnut stock with custom cut checkering, ebony tip. No sights; drilled and tapped for scope. Chambered for 270, 30-06, 7mm Rem. Mag., 7mm STW and 300 Win. Mag.

Price: **$532.00**

SAVAGE MODEL 112 LONG RANGE RIFLES

Caliber: 22-250, 223, 5-shot magazine. **Barrel:** 26" heavy. **Weight:** 8.8 lbs. **Length:** 47.5" overall. **Stock:** Black graphite/fiberglass filled composite with positive checkering. **Sights:** None furnished; drilled and tapped for scope mounting. **Features:** Pillar-bedded stock. Blued barrel with recessed target-style muzzle. Double front swivel studs for attaching bipod. Introduced 1991. Made in U.S.A. by Savage Arms, Inc.

Price: Model 112FVSS (cals. 223, 22-250, 25-06, 7mm Rem. Mag., 300 Win. Mag., stainless barrel, bolt handle, trigger guard), right- or left-hand **$569.00**
Price: Model 112FVSS-S (as above, single shot) **$569.00**
Price: Model 112BVSS (heavy-prone laminated stock with high comb, Wundhammer swell, fluted stainless barrel, bolt handle, trigger guard) **$616.00**
Price: Model 112BVSS-S (as above, single shot) **$616.00**

Savage Model 12 Long Range Rifles

Similar to the Model 112 Long Range except with true short action, chambered for 223, 22-250, 308. Models 12FV, 12FVSS have black synthetic stocks with "Dual Pillar" bedding, positive checkering, swivel studs; model 12BVSS has brown laminated stock with beavertail forend, fluted stainless barrel. Introduced 1998. Made in U.S.A. by Savage Arms, Inc.

Price: Model 12FV (223, 22-250, 243 Win., 308 Win., blue) **$481.00**
Price: Model 12FVSS (blue action, fluted stainless barrel) **$569.00**

Price: Model 12FLVSS (as above, left-hand) **$569.00**
Price: Model 12FVSS-S (blue action, fluted stainless barrel, single shot) **$569.00**
Price: Model 12BVSS (laminated stock) **$616.00**
Price: Model 12BVSS-S (as above, single shot) **$616.00**
Price: Model 12BVSS-XP (hard case, Burris 6-18X37) **$1,100.00**

Savage Model 12VSS Varminter Rifle

Similar to other Model 12s except blue/stainless steel action, fluted stainless barrel, Choate full pistol-grip, adjustable synthetic stock, Sharp Shooter trigger. Overall length 47-1/2 inches, weighs appx. 15 lbs. No sights; drilled and tapped for scope mounts. Chambered in 223, 22-250, 308 Win. Made in U.S.A. by Savage Arms Inc.

Price: **$900.00**

SAVAGE MODEL 116SE SAFARI EXPRESS RIFLE

Caliber: 300 Win. Mag., 300 Rem. Ultra Mag., 338 Win. Mag., 375 H&H, 458 Win. Mag. **Barrel:** 24". **Weight:** 8.5 lbs. **Length:** 45.5" overall. **Stock:** Classic-style select walnut with ebony forend tip, deluxe cut checkering. Two cross bolts; internally vented recoil pad. **Sights:** Bead on ramp front, three-leaf express rear. **Features:** Controlled-round feed design; adjustable muzzle brake; one-piece barrel band stud. Satin-finished stainless steel barreled action. Introduced 1994. Made in U.S.A. by Savage Arms, Inc.

Price: **$975.00**

SAVAGE MODEL 116 WEATHER WARRIORS

Caliber: 375 H&H, 300 Rem. Ultra Mag., 308 Win., 300 Rem. Ultra Mag., 300 WSM, 7mm Rem. Ultra Mag., 7mm Rem. Short Ultra Mag., 7mm S&W, 7mm-08 Rem. **Barrel:** 22", 24" for 7mm Rem. Mag., 300 Win. Mag., 338 Win. Mag. (M116FSS only). **Weight:** 6.25 to 6.5 lbs. **Length:** 41"-47". **Stock:** Graphite/fiberglass filled composite. **Sights:** None furnished; drilled and tapped for scope mounting. **Features:** Stainless steel with matte finish; free-floated barrel; quick-detachable swivel studs; laser-etched bolt; scope bases and rings. Left-hand models available in all models, calibers at same price. Model 116FSS introduced 1991; 116FSAK introduced 1994. Made in U.S.A. by Savage Arms, Inc.

Price: Model 116FSS (top-loading magazine) **$500.00**
Price: Model 116FSAK (top-loading magazine, Savage Adjustable Muzzle Brake system) **$578.00**
Price: Model 16BSS (brown laminate, 24") **$644.00**
Price: Model 116BSS (brown laminate, 26") **$644.00**

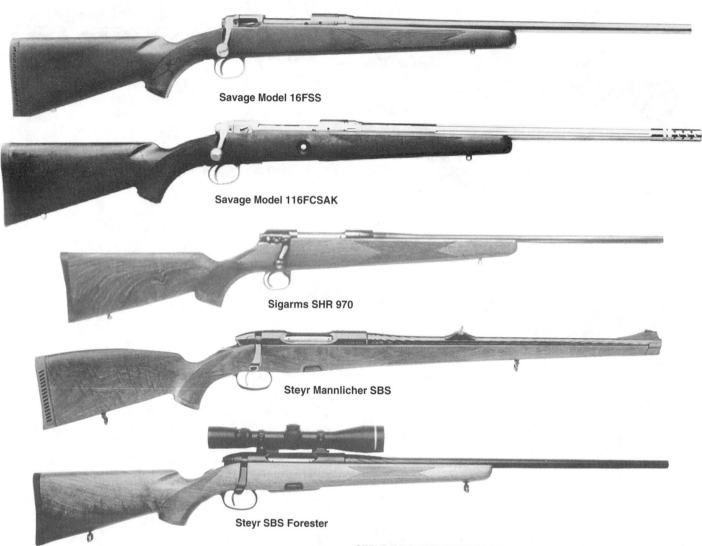

Savage Model 16FSS

Savage Model 116FCSAK

Sigarms SHR 970

Steyr Mannlicher SBS

Steyr SBS Forester

Savage Model 16FSS Rifle

Similar to Model 116FSS except true short action, chambered for 223, 243, 22" free-floated barrel; black graphite/fiberglass stock with "Dual Pillar" bedding. Also left-hand. Introduced 1998. Made in U.S.A. by Savage Arms, Inc.

Price: **$500.00**

SIGARMS SHR 970 SYNTHETIC RIFLE

Caliber: 270, 30-06. **Barrel:** 22". **Weight:** 7.2 lbs. **Length:** 41.9" overall. **Stock:** Textured black fiberglass or walnut. **Sights:** None furnished; drilled and tapped for scope mounting. **Features:** Quick takedown; interchangeable barrels; removable box magazine; cocking indicator; three-position safety. Introduced 1998. Imported by Sigarms, Inc.

Price: Synthetic stock **$499.00**
Price: Walnut stock **$550.00**

STEYR CLASSIC MANNLICHER SBS RIFLE

Caliber: 243, 25-06, 308, 6.5x55, 6.5x57, 270, 7x64 Brenneke, 7mm-08, 7.5x55, 30-06, 9.3x62, 6.5x68, 7mm Rem. Mag., 300 Win. Mag., 8x685, 4-shot magazine. **Barrel:** 23.6" standard; 26" magnum; 20" full stock standard calibers. **Weight:** 7 lbs. **Length:** 40.1" overall. **Stock:** Hand-checkered fancy European oiled walnut with standard forend. **Sights:** Ramp front adjustable for elevation, V-notch rear adjustable for windage. **Features:** Single adjustable trigger; 3-position roller safety with "safe-bolt" setting; drilled and tapped for Steyr factory scope mounts. Introduced 1997. Imported from Austria by GSI, Inc.

Price: Full-stock, standard calibers **$1,749.00**

STEYR SBS FORESTER RIFLE

Caliber: 243, 25-06, 270, 7mm-08, 308 Win., 30-06, 7mm Rem. Mag., 300 Win. Mag. Detachable 4-shot magazine. **Barrel:** 23.6", standard calibers; 25.6", magnum calibers. **Weight:** 7.5 lbs. **Length:** 44.5" overall (23.6" barrel). **Stock:** Oil-finished American walnut with Monte Carlo cheekpiece. Pachmayr 1" swivels. **Sights:** None furnished. Drilled and tapped for Browning A-Bolt mounts. **Features:** Steyr Safe Bolt systems, three-position ambidextrous roller tang safety, for Safe, Loading Fire. Matte finish on barrel and receiver; adjustable trigger. Rotary cold-hammer forged barrel. Introduced 1997. Imported by GSI, Inc.

Price: Standard calibers **$799.00**
Price: Magnum calibers **$829.00**

Steyr SBS Prohunter Rifle

Similar to the SBS Forester except has ABS synthetic stock with adjustable butt spacers, straight comb without cheekpiece, palm swell, Pachmayr 1" swivels. Special 10-round magazine conversion kit available. Introduced 1997. Imported by GSI.

Price Standard calibers **$769.00**
Price Magnum calibers **$799.00**

STEYR SCOUT BOLT-ACTION RIFLE

Caliber: 308 Win., 5-shot magazine. **Barrel:** 19", fluted. **Weight:** NA. **Length:** NA. **Stock:** Gray Zytel. **Sights:** Pop-up front & rear, Leupold M8 2.5x28 IER scope on Picatinny optic rail with Steyr mounts. **Features:** luggage case, scout sling, two stock spacers, two magazines. Introduced 1998. From GSI.

Price: From **$1,969.00**

Steyr SBS Prohunter

Steyr Scout Rifle

Tikka Whitetail Hunter

Tikka Whitetail Hunter Stainless Synthetic

Tikka Varmint

STEYR SSG BOLT-ACTION RIFLE

Caliber: 308 Win., detachable 5-shot rotary magazine. **Barrel:** 26" **Weight:** 8.5 lbs. **Length:** 44.5" overall. **Stock:** Black ABS Cycolac with spacers for length of pull adjustment. **Sights:** Hooded ramp front adjustable for elevation, V-notch rear adjustable for windage. **Features:** Sliding safety; NATO rail for bipod; 1" swivels; Parkerized finish; single or double-set triggers. Imported from Austria by GSI, Inc.

Price: SSG-PI, iron sights. **$1,699.00**
Price: SSG-PII, heavy barrel, no sights **$1,699.00**
Price: SSG-PIIK, 20" heavy barrel, no sights **$1,699.00**
Price: SSG-PIV, 16.75" threaded heavy barrel with flash hider . **$2,659.00**

TIKKA WHITETAIL HUNTER BOLT-ACTION RIFLE

Caliber: 22-250, 223, 243, 7mm-08, 25-06, 270, 308, 30-06, 7mm Rem. Mag., 300 Win. Mag., 338 Win. Mag. **Barrel:** 22-1/2" (std. cals.), 24-1/2" (magnum cals.). **Weight:** 7-1/8 lbs. **Length:** 43" overall (std. cals.). **Stock:** European walnut with Monte Carlo comb, rubber butt pad, checkered grip and forend. **Sights:** None furnished. **Features:** Detachable four-shot magazine (standard calibers), three-shot in magnums. Receiver dovetailed for scope mounting. Reintroduced 1996. Imported from Finland by Beretta USA.

Price: Standard calibers **$615.00**

Price: Magnum calibers **$645.00**
Price: Left-hand **$680.00**
Price: Mag. left-hand **$710.00**

Tikka Continental Varmint Rifle

Similar to the standard Tikka rifle except has 26" heavy barrel, extra-wide forend. Chambered for 17 Rem., 22-250, 223, 308. Reintroduced 1996. Made in Finland by Sako. Imported by Beretta USA.

Price: **$720.00**

Tikka Whitetail Hunter Deluxe Rifle

Similar to the Whitetail Hunter except has select walnut stock with rollover Monte Carlo comb, rosewood grip cap and forend tip. Has adjustable trigger, detachable magazine, free-floating barrel. Same calibers as the Hunter. Introduced 1999. Imported from Finland by Beretta USA.

Price: Standard calibers **$745.00**
Price: Magnum calibers **$775.00**

Tikka Whitetail Hunter Synthetic Rifle

Similar to the Whitetail Hunter except has black synthetic stock; calibers 223, 22-250, 243, 7mm-08, 25-06, 270 Win., 30-06, 7mm Rem. Mag., 300 Win. Mag., 338 Win. Mag. Introduced 1996. Imported from Finland by Beretta USA.

Price: Standard calibers **$615.00**
Price: Magnum calibers **$645.00**

Weatherby Mark V Lazermark

Weatherby Mark V Euromark

Weatherby Mark V Stainless

Tikka Continental Long Range Hunting Rifle

Similar to the Whitetail Hunter except has 26" heavy barrel. Available in 25-06, 270 Win., 7mm Rem. Mag., 300 Win. Mag. Introduced 1996. Imported from Finland by Beretta USA.

Price: 25-06, 270 Win. **$720.00**
Price: 7mm Rem. Mag., 300 Win. Mag. **$750.00**

Tikka Whitetail Hunter Stainless Synthetic

Similar to the Whitetail Hunter except all metal is of stainless steel, and it has a black synthetic stock. Available in 22-250, 223, 243, 7mm-08, 25-06, 270, 308, 30-06, 7mm Rem. Mag., 300 Win. Mag., 338 Win. Mag. Introduced 1997. Imported from Finland by Beretta USA.

Price: Standard calibers **$680.00**
Price: Magnum calibers **$710.00**

VEKTOR BUSHVELD BOLT-ACTION RIFLE

Caliber: 243, 308, 7x57, 7x64 Brenneke, 270 Win., 30-06, 300 Win. Mag., 300 H&H, 9.3x62. **Barrel:** 22"-26". **Weight:** NA. **Length:** NA. **Stock:** Turkish walnut with wrap-around hand checkering. **Sights:** Blade on ramp front, fixed standing leaf rear. **Features:** Combines the best features of the Mauser 98 and Winchester 70 actions. Controlled-round feed; Mauser-type extractor; no cut-away through the bolt locking lug; M70-type three-position safety; Timney-type adjustable trigger. Introduced 1999. Imported from South Africa by Vektor USA.
Price: . . . . **$1,595.00 to $1,695.00**

VEKTOR MODEL 98 BOLT-ACTION RIFLE

Caliber: 243, 308, 7x57, 7x64 Brenneke, 270 Win., 30-06, 300 Win. Mag., 300 H&H, 375 H&H, 9.3x62. **Barrel:** 22"-26". **Weight:** NA. **Length:** NA. **Stock:** Turkish walnut with hand-checkered grip and forend. **Sights:** None furnished; drilled and tapped for scope mounting. **Features:** Bolt has guide rib; non-rotating, long extractor enhances positive feeding; polished blue finish. Updated Mauser 98 action. Introduced 1999. Imported from South Africa by Vektor USA.
Price: . . . . **$1,149.00 to $1,249.00**

WEATHERBY MARK V DELUXE BOLT-ACTION RIFLE

Caliber: All Weatherby calibers plus 22-250, 243, 25-06, 270 Win., 280 Rem., 7mm-08, 30-06, 308 Win. **Barrel:** 24" barrel on standard calibers. **Weight:** 8-1/2 to 10-1/2 lbs. **Length:** 46-5/8" to 46-3/4" overall. **Stock:** Walnut, Monte Carlo with cheekpiece; high luster finish; checkered pistol grip and forend; recoil pad. **Sights:** None furnished. **Features:** Cocking indicator; adjustable trigger; hinged floorplate, thumb safety; quick detachable sling swivels. Made in U.S.A. From Weatherby.

Price: 257, 270, 7mm. 300, 340 Wea. Mags., 26" barrel **$1,767.00**
Price: 416 Wea. Mag. with Accubrake, 28" barrel **$2,079.00**
Price: 460 Wea. Mag. with Accubrake, 28" barrel **$2,443.00**
Price: 24" barrel **$1,715.00**

Weatherby Mark V Lazermark Rifle

Same as Mark V Deluxe except stock has extensive oak leaf pattern laser carving on pistol grip and forend. Introduced 1981.

Price: 257, 270, 7mm Wea. Mag., 300, 340, 26" **$1,923.00**
Price: 378 Wea. Mag., 28" **$2,266.00**
Price: 416 Wea. Mag., 28", Accubrake. **$2,266.00**
Price: 460 Wea. Mag., 28", Accubrake. **$2,661.00**

Weatherby Mark V Sporter Rifle

Same as the Mark V Deluxe without the embellishments. Metal has low-luster blue, stock is Claro walnut with high-gloss epoxy finish, Monte Carlo comb, recoil pad. Introduced 1993.

Price: 270 WCF, 280, 7mm-08, 30-06, 308, Wea. Mags., 26". . **$1,091.00**
Price: 270, 7 mm, 300 Wea. Mag., 338 Win. Mag., 26" **$1,143.00**

Weatherby Mark V Euromark Rifle

Similar to the Mark V Deluxe except has raised-comb Monte Carlo stock with hand-rubbed oil finish, fine-line hand-cut checkering, ebony grip and forend tips. All metal has low-luster blue. Right-hand only. Uses Mark V action. Introduced 1995. Made in U.S.A. From Weatherby.

Price: 257, 270, 7mm, 300, 340 Wea. Mags., 26" barrel **$1,819.00**
Price: 7mm Rem. Mag., 300 Win. Mag., 338 Win. Mag.,
375 H&H, 24" barrel **$1,819.00**
Price: 378 Wea. Mag., 416 Wea. Mag., 28" barrel. **$2,131.00**

Weatherby Mark V Stainless Rifle

Similar to the Mark V Deluxe except made of 410-series stainless steel. Also available in 30-378 Wea. Mag. Has lightweight injection-moulded synthetic stock with raised Monte Carlo comb, checkered grip and forend, custom floorplate release. Right-hand only. Introduced 1995. Made in U.S.A. From Weatherby.

Price: 22-250 Rem., 243 Win., 240 Wby. Mag., 25-06 Rem., 270 Win.,
280 Rem., 7mm-08 Rem., 30-06 Spfld., 308 Win., 24" barrel . **$1,018.00**
Price: 257, 270, 7mm, 300, 340 Wby. Mag., 26" barrel **$1,070.00**
Price: 7mm Rem. Mag., 300 Win. Mag., 338 Win. Mag.,
375 H&H Mag., 24" barrel **$1,070.00**

Weatherby Mark V Synthetic

Weatherby Accumark

Weatherby Mark V SLS Stainless Laminate Sporter

Similar to the Mark V Stainless except all metalwork is 400 series stainless with a corrosion-resistant black oxide bead-blast matte finish. Action is hand-bedded in a laminated stock with a 1" recoil pad. Weighs 8-1/2 lbs. Introduced 1997. Made in U.S.A. From Weatherby.

Price: 257, 270, 7mm, 300, 340 Wea. Mags., 26" barrel **$1,393.00**
Price: 7mm Rem. Mag., 300 Win. Mag., 338 Win. Mag., 24" barrel

.... **$1,393.00**

Weatherby Mark V Eurosport Rifle

Similar to the Mark V Deluxe except has raised-comb Monte Carlo stock with hand-rubbed satin oil finish, low-luster blue metal. No gripcap or forend tip. Right-hand only. Introduced 1995. Made in U.S.A. From Weatherby.

Price: 257, 270, 7mm, 300, 340 Wea. Mags., 26" barrel **$1,143.00**
Price: 7mm Rem. Mag., 300, 338 Win. Mags., 24" barrel **$1,143.00**
Price: 375 H&H, 24" barrel........................... **$1,143.00**

Weatherby Mark V Synthetic

Similar to the Mark V Stainless except made of matte finished blued steel. Injection moulded synthetic stock. Weighs 6-1/2 lbs., 24" barrel. Available in 22-250, 240 Wea. Mag., 243, 25-06, 270, 7mm-08, 280, 30-06, 308. Introduced 1997. Made in U.S.A. From Weatherby.

Price: **$923.00**
Price: 257, 270, 7mm, 300, 340 Wea. Mags., 26" barrel **$975.00**
Price: 7mm STW, 7mm Rem. Mag., 300, 338 Win. Mags **$975.00**
Price: 375 H&H, 24" barrel............................ **$975.00**
Price: 30-378 Wea. Mag., 338-378 Wea 28" barrel.......... **$1,151.00**

WEATHERBY MARK V ACCUMARK RIFLE

Caliber: 257, 270, 7mm, 300, 340 Wea. Mags., 338-378 Wea. Mag., 30-378 Wea. Mag., 7mm STW, 7mm Rem. Mag., 300 Win. Mag. **Barrel:** 26", 28". **Weight:** 8-1/2 lbs. **Length:** 46-5/8" overall. **Stock:** Bell & Carlson with full length aluminum bedding block. **Sights:** None furnished. Drilled and tapped for scope mounting. **Features:** Uses Mark V action with heavy-contour stainless barrel with black oxidized flutes, muzzle diameter of .705". Introduced 1996. Made in U.S.A. From Weatherby.

Price: 26" **$1,507.00**
Price: 30-378 Wea. Mag., 338-378 Wea. Mag., 28", Accubrake. **$1,724.00**
Price: 223, 22-250, 243, 240 Wea. Mag., 25-06, 270, 280 Rem., 7mm-08, 30-06, 308; 24" **$1,455.00**
Price: Accumark Left-Hand 257, 270, 7mm, 300, 340 Wea. Mag., 7mm Rem. Mag., 7mm STW, 300 Win. Mag.......... **$1,559.00**
Price: Accumark Left-Hand 30-378, 333-378 Wea. Mags...... **$1,788.00**

Weatherby Mark V Accumark Ultra Lightweight Rifles

Similar to the Mark V Accumark except weighs 5-3/4 lbs.; 24", 26" fluted barrel with recessed target crown; hand-laminated stock with CNC-machined aluminum bedding plate and faint gray "spider web" finish. Available in 257, 270, 7mm, 300 Wea. Mags., (26"); 243, 240 Wea. Mag., 25-06, 270 Win., 280 Rem., 7mm-08, 7mm Rem. Mag., 30-06, 338-06 A-Square, 308, 300 Win. Mag. (24"). Introduced 1998. Made in U.S.A. by Weatherby.

Price: .... **$1,459.00 to $1,517.00**
Price: Left-hand models **$1,559.00**

Weatherby Mark V SVM/SPM Rifles

Similar to the Mark V Accumark except has 26" fluted (SVM) or 24" fluted Krieger barrel, spiderweb-pattern tan laminated synthetic stock. SVM has a fully adjustable trigger. Chambered for 223, 22-250, 220 Swift (SVM only), 243, 7mm-08 and 308. Made in U.S.A. by Weatherby.

Price: SVM (Super VarmintMaster), repeater or single-shot ... **$1,517.00**
New! **Price:** SPM (Super PredatorMaster) **$1,459.00**

Weatherby Mark V Fibermark Rifles

Similar to other Mark V models except has black Kevlar® and fiberglass composite stock and bead-blast blue or stainless finish. Chambered for 19 standard and magnum calibers. Introduced 1983; reintroduced 2001. Made in U.S.A. by Weatherby.

Price: Fibermark.......................... **$1,070.00 to $1,347.00**
Price: Fibermark Stainless .... **$1,165.00 to $1,390.00**

WEATHERBY MARK V DANGEROUS GAME RIFLE

Caliber: 375 H&H, 375 Wea. Mag., 378 Wea. Mag., 416 Rem. Mag., 416 Wea. Mag., 458 Win. Mag., 460 Wea. Mag. 300 Win. Mag., 300 Wby., Mag., 338 Win. Mag., 340 Wby. Mag., 24" only **Barrel:** 24" or 26". **Weight:** 8-3/4 to 9-1/2 lbs. **Length:** 44-5/8" to 46-5/8" overall. **Stock:** Kevlar® and fiberglass composite. **Sights:** Barrel-band hooded front with large gold bead, adjustable ramp/shallow "V" rear. **Features:** Designed for dangerous-game hunting. Black oxide matte finish on all metalwork; Pachmayr Decelerator™ recoil pad, short-throw Mark V action. Introduced 2001. Made in U.S.A. by Weatherby.

Price: .... **$2,703.00 to $2,935.00**

WEATHERBY MARK V SUPER BIG GAME MASTER DEER RIFLE

Caliber: 240 Wby. Mag., 25-06 Rem., 270 Win., 280 Rem., 30-06 Spfld., 257 Wby. Mag., 270 Wby. Mag., 7mm Rem., Mag., 7mm Wby. Mag., 338-06 A-Square, 300 Win. Mag., 300 Wby. Mag. **Barrel:** 26", target crown. **Weight:** 5-3/4 lbs., (6-3/4 lbs. Magnum). **Stock:** Raised comb Monte Carlo composite. **Features:** Fluted barrel, aluminum bedding block, Pachmayr decelerator, 54-degree bolt lift, adj. trigger.

Price: **$1,459.00**
Price: Magnum...................................... **$1,517.00**

WEATHERBY MARK V ROYAL CUSTOM RIFLE

Caliber: 257, 270, 7mm, 300, 340 all Wby. Mags. Other calibers available upon request. **Barrel:** 26". **Stock:** Monte Carlo hand-checkered claro walnut with high gloss finish. **Features:** Bolt and follower are damascened with checkered knob. Engraced receiver, bolt sleeve and floorplate sport scroll paattern. Animal images on floorplate optional. High glass blue, 24-karat gold and nickel-plating. Made in U.S.A.

Price: **$5,399.00**

Wilderness Explorer

Winchester Model 70 Classic

Winchester Model 70 Classic Stainless

Winchester Model 70 Classic Featherweight

WEATHERBY THREAT RESPONSE RIFLES (TRR) SERIES
Caliber: TRR 223 Rem., 300 Win. TRR Magnum and Magnum Custom 300 Win. Mag., 300 Wby. Mag., 30-378 Wby. Mag., 328-378 Wby. Mag. **Barrel:** 22", 26", target crown. **Stock:** Hand-laminated composite. TTR & TRR Magnum have raised comb Monte Carlo style. TRR Magnum Custom adjustable ergonomic stock. **Features:** Adjustable trigger, aluminum bedding block, beavertail forearms dual tapered, flat-bottomed. "Rocker Arm" lockdown scope mounting. 54 degree bolt. Pachmayr decelerator pad. Made in U.S.A.

Price: TRR	**$1,517.00**
Price: TRR Magnum 300	**$1,569.00**
Price: 30-378, 338-378 with accubrake	**$1,725.00**
Price: TRR Magnum Custom 300	**$2,499.00**
Price: 30-378, 338-378 with accubrake	**$2,649.00**

WILDERNESS EXPLORER MULTI-CALIBER CARBINE
Caliber: 22 Hornet, 218 Bee, 44 Magnum, 50 A.E. (interchangeable). **Barrel:** 18", match grade. **Weight:** 5.5 lbs **Length:** 38-1/2" overall. **Stock:** Synthetic or wood. **Sights:** None furnished; comes with Weaver-style mount on barrel. **Features:** Quick-change barrel and bolt face for caliber switch. Removable box magazine; adjustable trigger with side safety; detachable swivel studs. Introduced 1997. Made in U.S.A. by Phillips & Rogers, Inc.

Price:	**$995.00**

WINCHESTER MODEL 70 CLASSIC SPORTER LT
Caliber: 25-06, 270 Win., 30-06, 7mm STW, 7mm Rem. Mag., 300 Win. Mag., 338 Win. Mag., 3-shot magazine; 5-shot for 25-06, 270 Win., 30-06. **Barrel:** 24", 26" for magnums. **Weight:** 7-3/4 to 8 lbs. **Length:** 46-3/4" overall (26" bbl.). **Stock:** American walnut with cut checkering and satin finish. Classic style with straight comb. **Sights:** None furnished. Drilled and tapped for scope mounting. **Features:** Uses pre-64-type action with controlled round feeding. Three-position safety, stainless steel magazine follower; rubber butt pad; epoxy bedded receiver recoil lug. From U.S. Repeating Arms Co.

Price: 25-06, 270, 30-06	**$699.00**
Price: Other calibers	**$727.00**
Price: Left-hand, 270 or 30-06	**$733.00**
Price: Left-hand, 7mm Rem. Mag or 300 Win. Mag.	**$761.00**

Winchester Model 70 Classic Stainless Rifle
Same as Model 70 Classic Sporter except stainless steel barrel and pre-64-style action with controlled round feeding and matte gray finish, black composite stock impregnated with fiberglass and graphite, contoured rubber recoil pad. No sights (except 375 H&H). Available in 270 Win., 30-06, 7mm STW, 7mm Rem. Mag., 300 Win. Mag., 300 Ultra Mag., 338 Win. Mag., 375 H&H Mag. (24" barrel), 3- or 5-shot magazine. Weighs 7-1/2 lbs. Introduced 1994.

Price: 270, 30-06	**$785.00**
Price: 375 H&H Mag., with sights	**$906.00**
Price: Other calibers	**$813.00**

Winchester Model 70 Classic Featherweight
Same as Model 70 Classic except action bedded in standard-grade walnut stock. Available in 22-250, 243, 6.5x55, 308, 7mm-08, 270 Win., 30-06. Drilled and tapped for scope mounts. Weighs 7 lbs. Introduced 1992.

Price:	**$726.00**

Winchester Model 70 Classic Compact
Similar to Classic Featherweight except scaled down for smaller shooters. 20" barrel, 12-1/2" length of pull. Pre-'64-type action. Available in 243, 308 or 7mm-08. Introduced 1998. Made in U.S.A. by U. S. Repeating Arms Co.

Price:	**$726.00**

CENTERFIRE RIFLES — BOLT ACTION

**Winchester Model 70
Classic Super Grade**

Winchester Model 70 Black Shadow

Similar to Ranger except black composite stock, matte blue barrel and action. Push-feed bolt design; hinged floorplate. Available in 270, 30-06, 7mm Rem. Mag., 300 Win. Mag. Made in U.S.A. by U.S. Repeating Arms Co.
Price: 270, 30-06 . . . . **$512.00**
Price: 7mm Rem. Mag., 300 Win. Mag. **$541.00**

Winchester Model 70 Coyote

Similar to Model 70 Black Shadow except laminated wood stock, 24" medium-heavy stainless steel barrel.
Price: Coyote (223, 22-250 or 243) **$691.00**

WINCHESTER MODEL 70 STEALTH RIFLE

Caliber: 223, 22-250, 308 Win. **Barrel:** 26". **Weight:** 10-3/4 lbs. **Length:** 46" overall. **Stock:** Kevlar/fiberglass/graphite Pillar Plus Accu-Block with full-length aluminum bedding block. **Sights:** None furnished. **Features:** Push-feed bolt design; matte finish. Introduced 1999. Made in U.S.A. by U.S. Repeating Arms Co.
Price: **$785.00**

WINCHESTER MODEL 70 CLASSIC SUPER GRADE

Caliber: 25-06, 270, 30-06, 5-shot magazine; 7mm Rem. Mag., 300 Win. Mag., 338 Win. Mag., 3-shot magazine. **Barrel:** 24", 26" for magnums. **Weight:** 7-3/4 lbs. to 8 lbs. **Length:** 44-1/2" overall (24" bbl.) **Stock:** Walnut with straight comb, sculptured cheekpiece, wrap-around cut checkering, tapered forend, solid rubber butt pad. **Sights:** None furnished; comes with scope bases and rings. **Features:** Controlled round feeding with stainless steel claw extractor, bolt guide rail, three-position safety; all steel bottom metal, hinged floorplate, stainless magazine follower. Introduced 1994. From U.S. Repeating Arms Co.
Price: 25-06, 270, 30-06 . . . . **$995.00**
Price: Other calibers **$1,024.00**

WINCHESTER MODEL 70 CLASSIC SAFARI EXPRESS

Caliber: 375 H&H Mag., 416 Rem. Mag., 458 Win. Mag., 3-shot magazine. **Barrel:** 24". **Weight:** 8-1/4 to 8-1/2 lbs. **Stock:** American walnut with Monte Carlo cheekpiece. Wrap-around checkering and finish. **Sights:** Hooded ramp front, open rear. **Features:** Controlled round feeding. Two steel cross bolts in stock for added strength. Front sling swivel stud mounted on barrel. Contoured rubber butt pad. From U.S. Repeating Arms Co.
Price: **$1,103.00**
Price: Left-hand, 375 H&H only **$1,140.00**

WINCHESTER MODEL 70 WSM RIFLES

Caliber: 300 WSM, 3-shot magazine. **Barrel:** 24". **Weight:** 7-1/4 to 7-3/4 lbs. **Length:** 44" overall. **Stock:** Checkered walnut, black synthetic or laminated wood. **Sights:** None. **Features:** Model 70 designed for the new 300 Winchester Short Magnum cartridge. Short-action receiver, three-position safety, knurled bolt handle. Introduced 2001. From U.S. Repeating Arms Co.
Price: Classic Featherweight WSM (checkered walnut stock and forearm) **$754.00**
Price: Classic Stainless WSM (black syn. stock, stainless steel bbl.) **$813.00**
Price: Classic Laminated WSM (laminated wood stock) **$777.00**

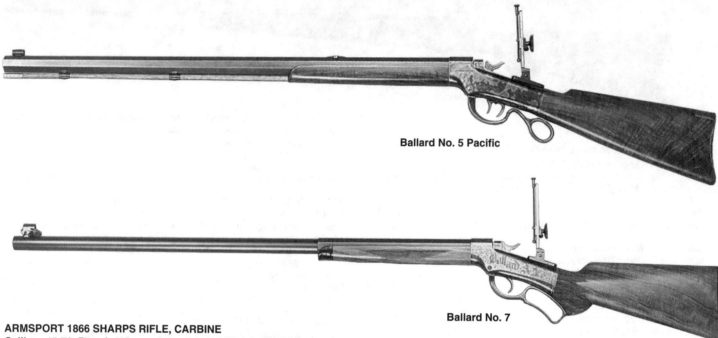

Ballard No. 5 Pacific

Ballard No. 7

ARMSPORT 1866 SHARPS RIFLE, CARBINE
Caliber: 45-70. **Barrel:** 28", round or octagonal. **Weight:** 8.10 lbs. **Length:** 46" overall. **Stock:** Walnut. **Sights:** Blade front, folding adjustable rear. Tang sight set optionally available. **Features:** Replica of the 1866 Sharps. Color case-hardened frame, rest blued. Imported by Armsport.
Price: **$865.00**
Price: With octagonal barrel **$900.00**
Price: Carbine, 22" round barrel **$850.00**

BALLARD NO. 1 3/4 FAR WEST RIFLE
Caliber: 22 LR, 32-40, 38-55, 40-65, 40-70, 45-70, 45-110, 50-70, 50-90. **Barrel:** 30" std. or heavyweight. **Weight:** 10-1/2 lbs. (std.) or 11-3/4 lbs. (heavyweight bbl.) **Length:** NA. **Stock:** Walnut. **Sights:** Blade front, Rocky Mountain rear. **Features:** Single or double-set triggers, S-lever or ring-style lever; color case-hardened finish; hand polished and lapped Badger barrel. Made in U.S.A. by Ballard Rifle & Cartridge Co.
Price: **$2,475.00**

BALLARD NO. 4 PERFECTION RIFLE
Caliber: 22 LR, 32-40, 38-55, 40-65, 40-70, 45-70, 45-90, 45-110, 50-70, 50-90. **Barrel:** 30" or 32" octagon, standard or heavyweight. **Weight:** 10-1/2 lbs. (standard) or 11-3/4 lbs. (heavyweight bbl.). **Length:** NA. **Stock:** Smooth walnut. **Sights:** Blade front, Rocky Mountain rear. **Features:** Rifle or shotgun-style buttstock, straight grip action, single or double-set trigger, "S" or right lever, hand polished and lapped Badger barrel. Made in U.S.A. by Ballard Rifle & Cartridge Co.
Price: **$2,475.00**

BALLARD NO. 5 PACIFIC SINGLE-SHOT RIFLE
Caliber: 32-40, 38-55, 40-65, 40-90, 40-70 SS, 45-70 Govt., 45-110 SS, 50-70 Govt., 50-90 SS. **Barrel:** 30", or 32" octagonal. **Weight:** 10-1/2 lbs. **Length:** NA. **Stock:** High-grade walnut; rifle or shotgun style. **Sights:** Blade front, Rocky Mountain rear. **Features:** Standard or heavy barrel; double-set triggers; under-barrel wiping rod; ring lever. Introduced 1999. Made in U.S.A. by Ballard Rifle & Cartridge Co.
Price: **$2,832.00**

BALLARD NO. 7 LONG RANGE RIFLE
Caliber: 32-40, 38-55, 40-65, 40-70 SS, 45-70 Govt., 45-90, 45-110. **Barrel:** 32", 34" half-octagon. **Weight:** 11-3/4 lbs. **Length:** NA. **Stock:** Walnut; checkered pistol grip shotgun butt, ebony forend cap. **Sights:** Globe front. **Features:** Designed for shooting up to 1000 yards. Standard or heavy barrel; single or double-set trigger; hard rubber or steel buttplate. Introduced 1999. Made in U.S.A. by Ballard Rifle & Cartridge Co.
Price: From **$2,475.00**

BALLARD NO. 8 UNION HILL RIFLE
Caliber: 22 LR, 32-40, 38-55, 40-65 Win., 40-70 SS. **Barrel:** 30" half-octagon. **Weight:** About 10-1/2 lbs. **Length:** NA. **Stock:** Walnut; pistol grip butt with cheekpiece. **Sights:** Globe front. **Features:** Designed for 200-yard offhand shooting. Standard or heavy barrel; double-set triggers; full loop lever; hook Schuetzen buttplate. Introduced 1999. Made in U.S.A. by Ballard Rifle & Cartridge Co.
Price: From **$2,750.00**

BALLARD MODEL 1885 HIGH WALL SINGLE SHOT RIFLE
Caliber: 17 Bee, 22 Hornet, 218 Bee, 219 Don Wasp, 219 Zipper, 22 Hi-Power, 225 Win., 25-20 WCF, 25-35 WCF, 25 Krag, 7mmx57R, 30-30, 30-40 Krag, 303 British, 33 WCF, 348 WCF, 35 WCF, 35-30/30, 9.3x74R, 405 WCF, 50-110 WCF, 500 Express, 577 Express. **Barrel:** Lengths to 34". **Weight:** NA. **Length:** NA. **Stock:** Straight-grain American walnut. **Sights:** buckhorn or flat top rear, blade front. **Features:** Faithful copy of original Model 1885 High Wall; parts interchange with original rifles; variety of options available. Introduced 2000. Made in U.S.A. by Ballard Rifle & Cartridge LLC.
Price: From **$2,255.00**
Price: With single set trigger from **$2,355.00**

BARRETT MODEL 99 SINGLE SHOT RIFLE
Caliber: 50 BMG. **Barrel:** 33". **Weight:** 25 lbs. **Length:** 50.4" overall. **Stock:** Anodized aluminum with energy-absorbing recoil pad. **Sights:** None furnished; integral M1913 scope rail. **Features:** Bolt action; detachable bipod; match-grade barrel with high-efficiency muzzle brake. Introduced 1999. Made in U.S.A. by Barrett Firearms.
Price: From **$3,000.00**

BROWN MODEL 97D SINGLE SHOT RIFLE
Caliber: 17 Ackley Hornet through 45-70 Govt. **Barrel:** Up to 26", air gauged match grade. **Weight:** About 5 lbs., 11 oz. **Stock:** Sporter style with pistol grip, cheekpiece and Schnabel forend. **Sights:** None furnished; drilled and tapped for scope mounting. **Features:** Falling block action gives rigid barrel-receiver matting; polished blue/black finish. Hand-fitted action. Many options. Made in U.S.A. by E. Arthur Brown Co. Inc.
Price: From **$699.00**

RIFLES

Browning Model 1885 Traditional Hunter

Browning Model 1885 Low Wall

Cabela's Sharps

BROWNING MODEL 1885 HIGH WALL SINGLE SHOT RIFLE

Caliber: 22-250, 30-06, 270, 7mm Rem. Mag., 454 Casull, 45-70. **Barrel:** 28". **Weight:** 8 lbs., 12 oz. **Length:** 43-1/2" overall. **Stock:** Walnut with straight grip, Schnabel forend. **Sights:** None furnished; drilled and tapped for scope mounting. **Features:** Replica of J.M. Browning's high-wall falling block rifle. Octagon barrel with recessed muzzle. Imported from Japan by Browning. Introduced 1985.
Price: **$1,027.00**

Browning Model 1885 BPCR Rifle

Similar to the 1885 High Wall rifle except the ejector system and shell deflector have been removed; chambered only for 40-65 and 45-70; color case-hardened full-tang receiver, lever, buttplate and gripcap; matte blue 30" part octagon, part round barrel. The Vernier tang sight has indexed elevation, is screw adjustable windage, and has three peep diameters. The hooded front sight has a built-in spirit level and comes with sight interchangeable inserts. Adjustable trigger. Overall length 46-1/8", weighs about 11 lbs. Introduced 1996. Imported from Japan by Browning.
Price: **$1,766.00**

Browning Model 1885 Low Wall Traditional Hunter

Similar to the Model 1885 Low Wall except chambered for 357 Mag., 44 Mag. and 45 Colt; steel crescent buttplate; 1/16" gold bead front sight, adjustable buckhorn rear, and tang-mounted peep sight with barrel-type elevation adjuster and knob-type windage adjustments. Barrel is drilled and tapped for a Browning scope base. Oil-finished select walnut stock with swivel studs. Introduced 1997. Imported for Japan by Browning.
Price: **$1,289.00**

Browning Model 1885 Low Wall Rifle

Similar to the Model 1885 High Wall except has trimmer receiver, thinner 24" octagonal barrel. Forend is mounted to the receiver. Adjustable trigger. Walnut pistol grip stock, trim Schnabel forend with high-gloss finish. Available in 22 Hornet and 260 Rem. Overall length 39-1/2", weighs 6 lbs., 11 oz. Rifling twist rates: 1:16" (22 Hornet); 1:9" (260). Polished blue finish. Introduced 1995. Imported from Japan by Browning.
Price: **$997.00**

BRNO ZBK 110 SINGLE SHOT RIFLE

Caliber: 222 Rem., 5.6x52R, 22 Hornet, 5.6x50 Mag., 6.5x57R, 7x57R, 8x57JRS. **Barrel:** 23.6". **Weight:** 5.9 lbs. **Length:** 40.1" overall. **Stock:** European walnut. **Sights:** None furnished; drilled and tapped for scope mounting. **Features:** Top tang opening lever; cross-bolt safety; polished blue finish. Announced 1998. Imported from The Czech Republic by Euro-Imports.
Price: Standard calibers **$223.00**
Price: 7x57R, 8x57JRS **$245.00**
Price: Lux model, standard calibers **$311.00**
Price: Lux model, 7x57R, 8x57JRS **$333.00**

CABELA'S SHARPS SPORTING RIFLE

Caliber: 45-70 or 45-120. **Barrel:** 32", tapered octagon. **Weight:** 9 lbs. **Length:** 47-1/4" overall. **Stock:** Checkered walnut. **Sights:** Blade front, open adjustable rear. **Features:** Color case-hardened receiver and hammer, rest blued. Introduced 1995. Imported by Cabela's.
Price: **$849.99**
Price: (Deluxe engraved Sharps) **$1,429.99**
Price: (Heavy target Sharps, 45-70 or 45-120) **$999.99**
Price: (Quigley Sharps, 45-70 or 45-120) **$1,299.99**

CIMARRON BILLY DIXON 1874 SHARPS SPORTING RIFLE

Caliber: 40-90, 45-70. **Barrel:** 32" tapered octagonal. **Weight:** NA. **Length:** NA. **Stock:** European walnut. **Sights:** Blade front, Creedmoor rear. **Features:** Color case-hardened frame, blued barrel. Hand-checkered grip and forend; hand-rubbed oil finish. Introduced 1999. Imported by Cimarron F.A. Co.
Price: **$1,295.00**

CIMARRON QUIGLEY MODEL 1874 SHARPS SPORTING RIFLE

Caliber: 45-70, 45-90, 45-120. **Barrel:** 34" octagonal. **Weight:** NA. **Length:** NA. **Stock:** Checkered walnut. **Sights:** Blade front, adjustable rear. **Features:** Blued finish; double set triggers. From Cimarron F.A. Co.
Price: **$1,495.00**

CIMARRON SILHOUETTE MODEL 1874 SHARPS SPORTING RIFLE

Caliber: 45-70. **Barrel:** 32" octagonal. **Weight:** NA. **Length:** NA. **Stock:** Walnut. **Sights:** Blade front, adjustable rear. **Features:** Pistol-grip stock with shotgun-style butt plate; cut-rifled barrel. From Cimarron F.A. Co.
Price: **$1,095.00**

CIMARRON MODEL 1885 HIGH WALL RIFLE

Caliber: 38-55, 40-65, 45-70, 45-90, 45-120. **Barrel:** 30" octagonal. **Weight:** NA. **Length:** NA. **Stock:** European walnut. **Sights:** Bead front, semi-buckhorn rear. **Features:** Replica of the Winchester 1885 High Wall rifle. Color case-hardened receiver and lever, blued barrel. Curved buttplate. Optional double set triggers. Introduced 1999. Imported by Cimarron F.A. Co.
Price: **$995.00**
Price: With pistol grip **$1,175.99**

Cumberland Mountain Plateau

Dakota Single Shot

Dixie 1874 Sharps Silhouette

H&R Ultra Hunter

CUMBERLAND MOUNTAIN PLATEAU RIFLE

Caliber: 40-65, 45-70. **Barrel:** Up to 32"; round. **Weight:** About 10-1/2 lbs. (32" barrel). **Length:** 48" overall (32" barrel). **Stock:** American walnut. **Sights:** Marble's bead front, Marble's open rear. **Features:** Falling block action with underlever. Blued barrel and receiver. Stock has lacquer finish, crescent buttplate. Introduced 1995. Made in U.S.A. by Cumberland Mountain Arms, Inc.

Price: **$1,085.00**

DAKOTA MODEL 10 SINGLE SHOT RIFLE

Caliber: Most rimmed and rimless commercial calibers. **Barrel:** 23". **Weight:** 6 lbs. **Length:** 39-1/2" overall. **Stock:** Medium fancy grade walnut in classic style. Checkered grip and forend. **Sights:** None furnished. Drilled and tapped for scope mounting. **Features:** Falling block action with under-lever. Top tang safety. Removable trigger plate for conversion to single set trigger. Introduced 1990. Made in U.S.A. by Dakota Arms.

Price: **$3,595.00**
Price: Barreled action **$2,095.00**
Price: Action only **$1,850.00**
Price: Magnum calibers **$3,595.00**
Price: Magnum barreled action. **$2,050.00**
Price: Magnum action only **$1,675.00**

DIXIE 1874 SHARPS BLACKPOWDER SILHOUETTE RIFLE

Caliber: 45-70. **Barrel:** 30"; tapered octagon; blued; 1:18" twist. **Weight:** 10 lbs., 3 oz. **Length:** 47-1/2" overall. **Stock:** Oiled walnut. **Sights:** Blade front, ladder-type hunting rear. **Features:** Replica of the Sharps #1 Sporter. Shotgun-style butt with checkered metal buttplate; color case-hardened receiver, hammer, lever and buttplate. Tang is drilled and tapped for tang sight. Double-set triggers. Meets standards for NRA blackpowder cartridge matches. Introduced 1995. Imported from Italy by Dixie Gun Works.

Price: **$995.00**

Dixie 1874 Sharps Lightweight Hunter/Target Rifle

Same as the Dixie 1874 Sharps Blackpowder Silhouette model except has a straight-grip buttstock with military-style buttplate. Based on the 1874 military model. Introduced 1995. Imported from Italy by Dixie Gun Works.

Price: **$995.00**

E.M.F. 1874 METALLIC CARTRIDGE SHARPS RIFLE

Caliber: 45-70, 45/120. **Barrel:** 28", octagon. **Weight:** 10-3/4 lbs. **Length:** NA. **Stock:** Oiled walnut. **Sights:** Blade front, flip-up open rear. **Features:** Replica of the 1874 Sharps Sporting rifle. Color case-hardened lock; double-set trigger; blue finish. Imported by E.M.F.

Price: From. **$700.00**
Price: With browned finish **$1,000.00**
Price: Military Carbine **$650.00**

HARRINGTON & RICHARDSON ULTRA VARMINT RIFLE

Caliber: 223, 243. **Barrel:** 24", heavy. **Weight:** About 7.5 lbs. **Stock:** Hand-checkered laminated birch with Monte Carlo comb. **Sights:** None furnished. Drilled and tapped for scope mounting. **Features:** Break-open action with side-lever release, positive ejection. Scope mount. Blued receiver and barrel. Swivel studs. Introduced 1993. From H&R 1871, Inc.

Price: **$254.95**

Harrington & Richardson Ultra Hunter Rifle

Similar to Ultra Varmint rifle except chambered for 25-06 with 26" barrel, or 308 Win. with 22" barrel. Stock and forend are of cinnamon-colored laminate; hand-checkered grip and forend. Introduced 1995. Made in U.S.A. by H&R 1871, LLC.

Price: **$268.95**
New! Price: 450 Marlin, 22" barrel **$268.95**

Harrington & Richardson Ultra Comp Rifle

Similar to Ultra Varmint except chambered for 270 or 30-06; compensator to reduce recoil; camo-laminate stock and forend; blued, highly polished frame; scope mount. Made in U.S.A. by H&R 1871, LLC.

Price: **$303.95**

Model 1885 High Wall

Mossberg SSi-One Sporter

Navy Arms 1874 Sharps

RIFLES

HARRIS GUNWORKS ANTIETAM SHARPS RIFLE

Caliber: 40-65, 45-75. **Barrel:** 30", 32", octagon or round, hand-lapped stainless or chrome-moly. **Weight:** 11.25 lbs. **Length:** 47" overall. **Stock:** Choice of straight grip, pistol grip or Creedmoor with Schnabel forend; pewter tip optional. Standard wood is A Fancy; higher grades available. **Sights:** Montana Vintage Arms #111 Low Profile Spirit Level front, #108 mid-range tang rear with windage adjustments. **Features:** Recreation of the 1874 Sharps sidehammer. Action is color case-hardened, barrel satin black. Chrome-moly barrel optionally blued. Optional sights include #112 Spirit Level Globe front with windage, #107 Long Range rear with windage. Introduced 1994. Made in U.S.A. by Harris Gunworks.
Price: **$2,400.00**

KRIEGHOFF HUBERTUS SINGLE-SHOT RIFLE

Caliber: 222, 243, 270, 308, 30-06, 5.6x50R Mag., 5.6x52R, 6x62R Freres, 6.5x57R, 6.5x65R, 7x57R, 7x65R, 8x57JRS, 8x75RS, 7mm Rem. Mag., 300 Win. Mag. **Barrel:** 23-1/2". **Weight:** 6-1/2 lbs. **Length:** NA. **Stock:** High-grade walnut. **Sights:** Blade front, open rear. **Features:** Break-loading with manual cocking lever on top tang; take-down; extractor; Schnabel forearm; many options. Imported from Germany by Krieghoff International Inc.
Price: Hubertus single shot, from **$5,850.00**
Price: Hubertus, magnum calibers **$6,850.00**

MERKEL K-1 MODEL LIGHTWEIGHT STALKING RIFLE

Caliber: 243 Win., 270 Win., 7x57R, 308 Win., 30-06, 7mm Rem. Mag., 300 Win. Mag., 9.3x74R. **Barrel:** 23.6". **Weight:** 5.6 lbs. unscoped. **Stock:** Satin-finished walnut, fluted and checkered; sling-swivel studs. **Sights:** None (scope base furnished). **Features:** Franz Jager single-shot break-open action, cocking/uncocking slide-type safety, matte silver receiver, selectable trigger pull weights, integrated, quick detach 1" or 30mm optic mounts (optic not included). Imported from Germany by GSI.
Price: Standard, simple border engraving **$3,795.00**
Price: Premium, light arabesque scroll. **$3,795.00**
Price: Jagd, fine engraved hunting scenes. **$4,395.00**

MODEL 1885 HIGH WALL RIFLE

Caliber: 30-40 Krag, 32-40, 38-55, 40-65 WCF, 45-70. **Barrel:** 26" (30-40), 28" all others. Douglas Premium #3 tapered octagon. **Stock:** Premium American black walnut. **Sights:** Marble's standard ivory bead front, #66 long blade top rear with reversible notch and elevator. **Features:** Recreation of early octagon top, thick-wall High Wall with Coil spring action. Tang drilled, tapped for High Wall tang sight. Receiver, lever, hammer and breechblock color case-hardened. Introduced 1991. Available from Montana Armory, Inc.
Price: **$1,095.00**

MOSSBERG SSi-ONE SINGLE SHOT RIFLE

Caliber: 223 Rem., 22-250 Rem., 243 Win., 270 Win., 308 Rem., 30-06. **Barrel:** 24". **Weight:** 8 lbs. **Length:** 40". **Stock:** Satin-finished walnut, fluted and checkered; sling-swivel studs. **Sights:** None (scope base furnished). **Features:** Frame accepts interchangeable barrels, including 12-gauge, fully rifled slug barrel and 12 ga., 3-1/2" chambered barrel with Ulti-Full Turkey choke tube. Lever-opening, break-action design; single-stage trigger; ambidextrous, top-tang safety; internal eject/extract selector. Introduced 2000. From Mossberg.
Price: SSi-One Sporter (standard barrel) or 12 ga.,
3-1/2" chamber. **$459.00**
Price: SSi-One Varmint (bull barrel, 22-250 Rem. only;
weighs 10 lbs.) **$480.00**
Price: SSi-One 12-gauge Slug (fully rifled barrel, no sights,
scope base) **$480.00**

NAVY ARMS 1874 SHARPS CAVALRY CARBINE

Caliber: 45-70. **Barrel:** 22". **Weight:** 7 lbs., 12 oz. **Length:** 39" overall. **Stock:** Walnut. **Sights:** Blade front, military ladder-type rear. **Features:** Replica of the 1874 Sharps military carbine. Color case-hardened receiver and furniture. Imported by Navy Arms.
Price: **$1,000.00**

NAVY ARMS 1874 SHARPS BUFFALO RIFLE

Caliber: 45-70, 45-90. **Barrel:** 28" heavy octagon. **Weight:** 10 lbs., 10 oz. **Length:** 46" overall. **Stock:** Walnut; checkered grip and forend. **Sights:** Blade front, ladder rear; tang sight optional. **Features:** Color case-hardened receiver, blued barrel; double-set triggers. Imported by Navy Arms.
Price: **$1,160.00**

Navy Arms Sharps Plains Rifle

Similar to Sharps Buffalo rifle except 45-70 only, 32" medium-weight barrel, weighs 9 lbs., 8 oz., and is 49" overall. Imported by Navy Arms.
Price: **$1,125.00**

Navy Arms 1885 High Wall

Navy Arms 1873 Springfield

Navy Arms #2 Creedmoor

Navy Arms John Bodine

Navy Arms No. 3 Long Range

Navy Arms Sharps Sporting Rifle

Same as the Navy Arms Sharps Plains Rifle except has pistol grip stock. Introduced 1997. Imported by Navy Arms.
Price: 45-70 only. **$1,160.00**

NAVY ARMS 1885 HIGH WALL RIFLE

Caliber: 45-70; others available on special order. **Barrel:** 28" round, 30" octagonal. **Weight:** 9.5 lbs. **Length:** 45-1/2" overall (30" barrel). **Stock:** Walnut. **Sights:** Blade front, vernier tang-mounted peep rear. **Features:** Replica of Winchester's High Wall designed by Browning. Color case-hardened receiver, blued barrel. Introduced 1998. Imported by Navy Arms.
Price: 28", round barrel, target sights **$920.00**
Price: 30" octagonal barrel, target sights **$995.00**

NAVY ARMS 1873 SPRINGFIELD CAVALRY CARBINE

Caliber: 45-70. **Barrel:** 22". **Weight:** 7 lbs. **Length:** 40-1/2" overall. **Stock:** Walnut. **Sights:** Blade front, military ladder rear. **Features:** Blued lockplate and barrel; color case-hardened breechblock; saddle ring with bar. Replica of 7th Cavalry gun. Imported by Navy Arms.
Price: **$930.00**

NAVY ARMS ROLLING BLOCK RIFLE

Caliber: 45-70. **Barrel:** 26", 30". **Stock:** Walnut. **Sights:** Blade front, adjustable rear. **Features:** Reproduction of classic rolling block action. Available with full-octagon or half-octagon-half-round barrel. Color case-hardened action, steel fittings. From Navy Arms.
Price: Buffalo **$825.00**
Price: Special Sporting, 26" half round bbl. **$730.00**

Navy Arms No. 2 Creedmoor Target Rifle

Similar to Navy Arms Rolling Block Buffalo Rifle except 30" tapered octagon barrel, checkered full-pistol grip stock, blade front sight, open adjustable rear sight, Creedmoor tang sight. Imported by Navy Arms.
Price: **$995.00**

NAVY ARMS "JOHN BODINE" ROLLING BLOCK RIFLE

Caliber: 45-70. **Barrel:** 30" heavy octagonal. **Stock:** Walnut. **Sights:** Globe front, "soule" tang rear. **Features:** Double set triggers.
Price: **$1,385.00**

NAVY ARMS SHARPS NO. 3 LONG RANGE RIFLE

Caliber: 45-70, 45-90. **Barrel:** 34" octagon. **Weight:** 10 lbs., 12 oz. **Length:** 51-1/2". **Stock:** Deluxe walnut. **Sights:** Globe target front and match grade rear tang. **Features:** Shotgun buttplate, German silver forend cap, color case hardenend receiver. Imported by Navy Arms.
Price: **$1,885.00**

New England
Firearms Handi-Rifle

New England Firearms Super Light

New England Firearms Survivor

Remington No. 1 Mid-Range

NEW ENGLAND FIREARMS HANDI-RIFLE
Caliber: 22 Hornet, 223, 243, 7x57, 7x64 Brenneke, 30-30, 270, 280 Rem., 308, 30-06, 357 Mag., 44 Mag., 45-70. **Barrel:** 22", 24"; 26" for 280 Rem. **Weight:** 7 lbs. **Stock:** Walnut-finished hardwood; black rubber recoil pad. **Sights:** Ramp front, folding rear (22 Hornet, 30-30, 45-70). Drilled and tapped for scope mount; 223, 243, 270, 280, 30-06 have no open sights, come with scope mounts. **Features:** Break-open action with side-lever release. The 223, 243, 270 and 30-06 have recoil pad and Monte Carlo stock for shooting with scope. Swivel studs on all models. Blue finish. Introduced 1989. From New England Firearms.
Price: **$219.95**
Price: 7x57, 7x64 Brenneke, 24" barrel **$219.95**
Price: 280 Rem., 26" barrel **$219.95**
Price: Synthetic Handi-Rifle (black polymer stock and forend, swivels, recoil pad) **$228.95**
Price: Handi-Rifle Youth (223, 243) **$219.95**

New England Firearms Super Light Rifle
Similar to Handi-Rifle except new barrel taper, shorter 20" barrel with recessed muzzle, special lightweight synthetic stock and forend. No sights furnished on 223 and 243 versions, but have factory-mounted scope base and offset hammer spur; Monte Carlo stock; 22 Hornet has ramp front, fully adjustable open rear. Overall length 36", weight is 5.5 lbs. Introduced 1997. Made in U.S.A. by New England Firearms.
Price: 22 Hornet, 223 Rem. or 243 Win. **$228.95**

NEW ENGLAND FIREARMS SURVIVOR RIFLE
Caliber: 223, 308 Win., single shot. **Barrel:** 22". **Weight:** 6 lbs. **Length:** 36" overall. **Stock:** Black polymer, thumbhole design. **Sights:** None furnished; scope mount provided. **Features:** Receiver drilled and tapped for scope mounting. Stock and forend have storage compartments for ammo, etc.; comes with integral swivels and black nylon sling. Introduced 1996. Made in U.S.A. by New England Firearms.
Price: Blue finish. **$227.95**

REMINGTON NO. 1 ROLLING BLOCK MID-RANGE SPORTER
Caliber: 45-70. **Barrel:** 30" round. **Weight:** 8-3/4 lbs. **Length:** 46-1/2" overall. **Stock:** American walnut with checkered pistol grip and forend. **Sights:** Beaded blade front, adjustable center-notch buckhorn rear. **Features:** Recreation of the original. Polished blue metal finish. Many options available. Introduced 1998. Made in U.S.A. by Remington.
Price: **$1,348.00**

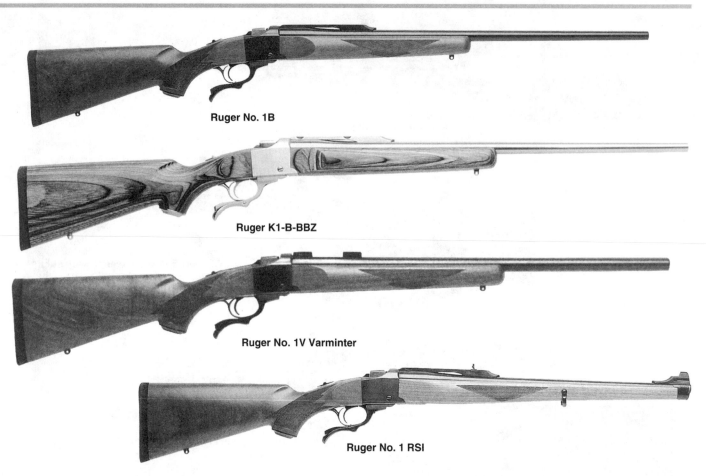

Ruger No. 1B

Ruger K1-B-BBZ

Ruger No. 1V Varminter

Ruger No. 1 RSI

ROSSI SINGLE SHOT CENTERFIRE RIFLE

Caliber: 308 Win., 270 Win., 30-06 Spfld., 223 Rem., 243 Win. **Barrel:** 23".
Weight: 6-6.5 lbs. **Stock:** Monte carlo, exotic woods, walnut finish & swivels with white line space and recoil pad. **Sights:** None, scope rails and hammer extension included. **Features:** Break Open, positive ejection, internal transfer bar mechanism and manual external safety. Trigger block system included.
Price: **$179.95**

ROSSI CENTERFIRE/SHOTGUN "MATCHED PAIRS"

Caliber: 12 ga./223 Rem., full size, 20 ga./223 Rem. full & youth, 12 ga./342 Win. full, 20 ga./243 Win., full & youth, 12 ga./308 Win. full, 20 ga./308 Win. full & youth, 12 ga./30-06 Spfld. full, 20 ga./30-06 Spfld. full, 12 ga./270 Win. full, 20 ga./270 Win. full. **Barrel:** 28"/23 full, 22"/22 youth. **Weight:** 5-7 lbs. **Stock:** Straight, exotic woods, walnut finish and swivels wtih white line space and recoil pad. **Sights:** Bead front shotgun, fully adjustable rifle, drilled and tapped. **Features:** Break Open, positive ejection, internal transfer bar mechanism and manual external safety. Trigger block system included.
Price: **$199.95**

RUGER NO. 1B SINGLE SHOT

Caliber: 218 Bee, 22 Hornet, 220 Swift, 22-250, 223, 243, 6mm Rem., 25-06, 257 Roberts, 270, 280, 30-06, 7mm Rem. Mag., 300 Win. Mag., 308 Win., 338 Win. Mag., 270 Wea., 300 Wea. **Barrel:** 26" round tapered with quarter-rib; with Ruger 1" rings. **Weight:** 8 lbs. **Length:** 42-1/4" overall. **Stock:** Walnut, two-piece, checkered pistol grip and semi-beavertail forend. **Sights:** None, 1" scope rings supplied for integral mounts. **Features:** Under-lever, hammerless falling block design has auto ejector, top tang safety.
Price: 1B... **$850.00**
Price: Barreled action...................................... **$600.00**
Price: K1-B-BBZ Stainless steel, laminated stock 25-06, 7MM mag, 7MM STW, 300 Win Mag., 243 Win., 30-06, 308 Win. **$885.00**

Ruger No. 1A Light Sporter

Similar to the No. 1B Standard Rifle except has lightweight 22" barrel, Alexander Henry-style forend, adjustable folding leaf rear sight on quarter-rib, dovetailed ramp front with gold bead. Calibers 243, 30-06, 270 and 7x57. Weighs about 7-1/4 lbs.
Price: No. 1A **$850.00**
Price: Barreled action...................................... **$600.00**

Ruger No. 1V Varminter

Similar to the No. 1B Standard Rifle except has 24" heavy barrel. Semi-beavertail forend, barrel ribbed for target scope block, with 1" Ruger scope rings. Calibers 22-250, 220 Swift, 223, 25-06, 6mm Rem. Weight about 9 lbs.
Price: No. 1V **$850.00**
Price: Barreled action...................................... **$600.00**
Price: K1-V-BBZ stainless steel, laminated stock 22-250 .... **$885.00**

Ruger No. 1 RSI International

Similar to the No. 1B Standard Rifle except has lightweight 20" barrel, full-length International-style forend with loop sling swivel, adjustable folding leaf rear sight on quarter-rib, ramp front with gold bead. Calibers 243, 30-06, 270 and 7x57. Weight is about 7-1/4 lbs.
Price: No. 1 RSI **$865.00**
Price: Barreled action...................................... **$600.00**

Ruger No. 1H Tropical Rifle

Similar to the No. 1B Standard Rifle except has Alexander Henry forend, adjustable folding leaf rear sight on quarter-rib, ramp front with dovetail gold bead, 24" heavy barrel. Calibers 375 H&H, 416 Rem. Mag., 416 Rigby, and 458 Win. Mag. (weighs about 9 lbs.).
Price: No. 1H **$850.00**
Price: Barreled action...................................... **$600.00**
Price: K1-H-BBZ, S/S, 375 H&H, 416 Rigby **$885.00**

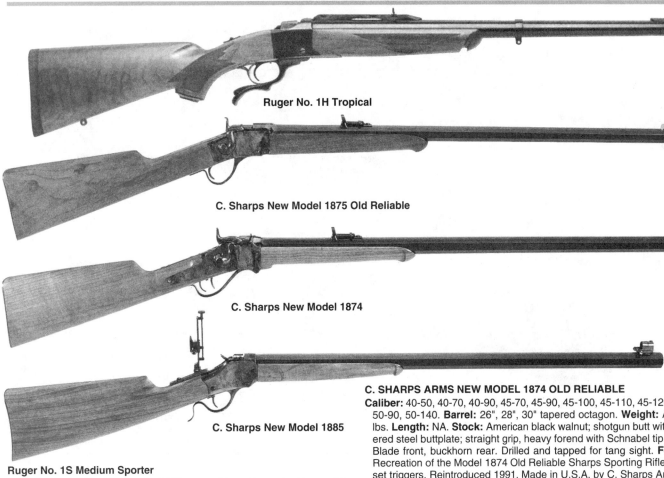

Ruger No. 1H Tropical

C. Sharps New Model 1875 Old Reliable

C. Sharps New Model 1874

C. Sharps New Model 1885

Ruger No. 1S Medium Sporter

Similar to the No. 1B Standard Rifle except has Alexander Henry-style forend, adjustable folding leaf rear sight on quarter-rib, ramp front sight base and dovetail-type gold bead front sight. Calibers 218 Bee, 7mm Rem. Mag., 338 Win. Mag., 300 Win. Mag. with 26" barrel, 45-70 with 22" barrel. Weighs about 7-1/2 lbs. In 45-70.

Price: No. 1S	**$850.00**
Price: Barreled action	**$600.00**
Price: K1-S-BBZ, S/S, 45-70	**$885.00**

C. SHARPS ARMS NEW MODEL 1875 OLD RELIABLE RIFLE

Caliber: 22LR, 32-40 & 38-55 Ballard, 38-56 WCF, 40-65 WCF, 40-90 3-1/4", 40-90 2-5/8", 40-70 2-1/10", 40-70 2-1/4", 40-70 2-1/2", 40-50 1-11/16", 40-50 1-7/8", 45-90, 45-70, 45-100, 45-110, 45-120. Also available on special order only in 50-70, 50-90, 50-140. **Barrel:** 24", 26", 30" (standard), 32", 34" optional. **Weight:** 8-12 lbs. **Stock:** Walnut, straight grip, shotgun butt with checkered steel buttplate. **Sights:** Silver blade front, Rocky Mountain buckhorn rear. **Features:** Recreation of the 1875 Sharps rifle. Production guns will have case colored receiver. Available in Custom Sporting and Target versions upon request. Announced 1986. From C. Sharps Arms Co.
Price: 1875 Sporting Rifle (30" tapered oct. bbl.) **$1,185.00**

C. Sharps Arms 1875 Classic Sharps

Similar to New Model 1875 Sporting Rifle except 26", 28" or 30" full octagon barrel, crescent buttplate with toe plate, Hartford-style forend with cast German silver nose cap. Blade front sight, Rocky Mountain buckhorn rear. Weighs 10 lbs. Introduced 1987. From C. Sharps Arms Co.
Price: **$1,470.00**

C. Sharps Arms New Model 1875 Target & Long Range

Similar to New Model 1875 in all listed calibers except 22 LR; 34" tapered octagon barrel; globe with post front sight, Long Range Vernier tang sight with windage adjustments. Pistol grip stock with cheek rest; checkered steel buttplate. Introduced 1991. From C. Sharps Arms Co.
Price: **$1,549.50**

C. SHARPS ARMS NEW MODEL 1874 OLD RELIABLE

Caliber: 40-50, 40-70, 40-90, 45-70, 45-90, 45-100, 45-110, 45-120, 50-70, 50-90, 50-140. **Barrel:** 26", 28", 30" tapered octagon. **Weight:** About 10 lbs. **Length:** NA. **Stock:** American black walnut; shotgun butt with checkered steel buttplate; straight grip, heavy forend with Schnabel tip. **Sights:** Blade front, buckhorn rear. Drilled and tapped for tang sight. **Features:** Recreation of the Model 1874 Old Reliable Sharps Sporting Rifle. Double set triggers. Reintroduced 1991. Made in U.S.A. by C. Sharps Arms.
Price: **$1,584.00**

C. SHARPS ARMS NEW MODEL 1885 HIGHWALL RIFLE

Caliber: 22 LR, 22 Hornet, 219 Zipper, 25-35 WCF, 32-40 WCF, 38-55 WCF, 40-65, 30-40-Krag, 40-50 ST or BN, 40-70 ST or BN, 40-90 ST or BN, 45-70 2-1/10" ST, 45-90 2-4/10" ST, 45-100 2-6/10" ST, 45-110 2-7/8" ST, 45-120 3-1/4" ST. **Barrel:** 26", 28", 30", tapered full octagon. **Weight:** About 9 lbs., 4 oz. **Length:** 47" overall. **Stock:** Oil-finished American walnut; Schnabel-style forend. **Sights:** Blade front, buckhorn rear. Drilled and tapped for optional tang sight. **Features:** Single trigger; octagonal receiver top; checkered steel buttplate; color case-hardened receiver and buttplate, blued barrel. Many options available. Made in U.S.A. by C. Sharps Arms Co
Price: From **$1,439.00**

C. SHARPS ARMS CUSTOM NEW MODEL 1877 LONG RANGE TARGET RIFLE

Caliber: 44-90 Sharps/Rem., 45-70, 45-90, 45-100 Sharps. **Barrel:** 32", 34" tapered round with Rigby flat. **Weight:** Appx. 10 lbs. **Stock:** Walnut, checkered. Pistol grip/forend. **Sights:** Classic long range with windage. **Features:** Elegant single shot, limited to custom production only.
Price: . . . . **$5,550.00 and up**

NEW!

SHILOH RIFLE CO. SHARPS 1874 LONG RANGE EXPRESS

Caliber: 40-50 BN, 40-70 BN, 40-90 BN, 45-70 ST, 45-90 ST, 45-110 ST, 50-70 ST, 50-90 ST, 38-55, 40-70 ST, 40-90 ST. **Barrel:** 34" tapered octagon. **Weight:** 10-1/2 lbs. **Length:** 51" overall. **Stock:** Oil-finished semi-fancy walnut with pistol grip, shotgun-style butt, traditional cheek rest, Schnabel forend. **Sights:** Globe front, sporting tang rear. **Features:** Recreation of the Model 1874 Sharps rifle. Double set triggers. Made in U.S.A. by Shiloh Rifle Mfg. Co.
Price: **$1,796.00**
Price: Sporting Rifle No. 1 (similar to above except with 30" bbl., blade front, buckhorn rear sight) **$1,706.00**

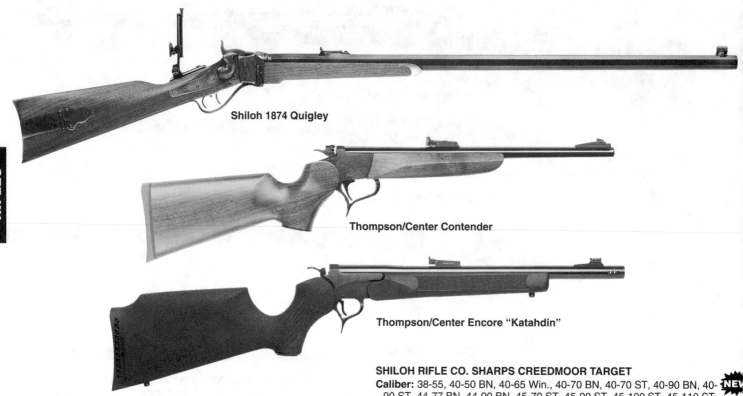

Shiloh 1874 Quigley

Thompson/Center Contender

Thompson/Center Encore "Katahdin"

Price: Sporting Rifle No. 3 (similar to No. 1 except straight-grip stock, standard wood) **$1,504.00**
Price: 1874 Hartford (Hartford collar, pewter tip) **$1,702.00**
Price: 1874 Sporter #1 (30" bbl, blade, buckhorn sights) **$1,706.00**
Price: 1874 Sporter #3 (walnut, shotgun or military stock)..... **$1,504.00**

Shiloh Rifle Co. Sharps 1874 Business Rifle

Similar to No. 3 Rifle with 28" heavy round barrel, military-style buttstock and steel buttplate. Weight about 9-1/2 lbs. Calibers 40-50 BN, 40-70 BN, 40-90 BN, 45-70 ST, 45-90 ST, 50-70 ST, 50-100 ST, 32-40, 38-55, 40-70 ST, 40-90 ST.
Price: **$1,604.00**
Price: 1874 Saddle Rifle (similar to Carbine except has 26" octagon barrel, semi-fancy shotgun butt) **$1,706.00**

SHILOH RIFLE CO. SHARPS 1874 QUIGLEY

Caliber: 45-70, 45-110. **Barrel:** 34" heavy octagon. **Stock:** Military-style with patch box, standard grade American walnut. **Sights:** Semi buckhorn, interchangeable front and midrange vernier tang wight with windage. **Features:** Gold inlay initials, pewter tip, hartford collar, case color or antique finish. Double set triggers.
Price: **$2,860.00**

SHILOH RIFLE CO. SHARPS 1874 SADDLE RIFLE

Caliber: 38-55, 40-50 BN, 40-65 Win., 40-70 BN, 40-70 ST, 40-90 BN, 40-90 ST, 44-77 BN, 44-90 BN, 45-70 ST, 45-90 ST, 45-100 ST, 45-110 ST, 45-120 ST, 50-70 ST, 50-90 ST. **Barrel:** 26" full or h alf octagon. **Stock:** Semi fancy American walnut. Shotgun style with cheekrest. **Sights:** Buckhorn and blade. **Features:** Double set trigger, numerous custom features can be added.
Price: **$1,504.00**

SHILOH RIFLE CO. SHARPS 1874 MONTANA ROUGHRIDER

Caliber: 38-55, 40-50 BN, 40-65 Win., 40-70 BN, 40-70 ST, 40-90 BN, 40-90 ST, 44-77 BN, 44-90 BN, 45-70 ST, 45-90 ST, 45-100 ST, 45-110 ST, 45-120 ST, 50-70 ST, 50-90 ST. **Barrel:** 30" full or half octagon. **Stock:** American walnut in shotgun or military style. **Sights:** Buckhorn and blade. **Features:** Double set triggers, numerous custom features can be added.
Price: **$1,504.00**

SHILOH RIFLE CO. SHARPS CREEDMOOR TARGET

Caliber: 38-55, 40-50 BN, 40-65 Win., 40-70 BN, 40-70 ST, 40-90 BN, 40-90 ST, 44-77 BN, 44-90 BN, 45-70 ST, 45-90 ST, 45-100 ST, 45-110 ST, 45-120 ST, 50-70 ST, 50-90 ST. **Barrel:** 32", half round-half octagon. **Stock:** Extra fancy American walnut. Shotgun style with pistol grip. **Sights:** Customer's choice. **Features:** Single trigger, AA finish on stock, polished barrel and screws, pewter tip.
Price: **$2,442.00**

THOMPSON/CENTER CONTENDER CARBINE

Caliber: 22 LR, 22 Hornet, 223 Rem., 7x30 Waters, 30-30 Win. **Barrel:** 21". **Weight:** 5 lbs., 2 oz. **Length:** 35" overall. **Stock:** Checkered American walnut with rubber butt pad. Also with Rynite stock and forend. **Sights:** Blade front, open adjustable rear. **Features:** Uses the T/C Contender action. Eleven interchangeable barrels available, all with sights, drilled and tapped for scope mounting. Introduced 1985. Offered as a complete Carbine only.
Price: Rifle calibers................................... **$571.38**
Price: Extra barrels, rifle calibers, each **$251.08**

THOMPSON/CENTER ENCORE RIFLE

Caliber: 22-250, 223, 243, 25-06, 270, 7mm-08, 308, 30-06, 7mm Rem. Mag., 300 Win. Mag. **Barrel:** 24", 26". **Weight:** 6 lbs, 12 oz. (24" barrel). **Length:** 38-1/2" (24" barrel). **Stock:** American walnut. Monte Carlo style; Schnabel forend or black composite. **Sights:** Ramp-style white bead front, fully adjustable leaf-type rear. **Features:** Interchangeable barrels; action opens by squeezing trigger guard; drilled and tapped for T/C scope mounts; polished blue finish. Introduced 1996. Made in U.S.A. by Thompson/Center Arms.
Price: **$614.00**
Price: Extra barrels.................................... **$261.00**
Price: With black composite stock and forend **$588.00**

Thompson/Center Stainless Encore Rifle

Similar to blued Encore except stainless steel with blued sights, black composite stock and forend. Available in 22-250, 223, 7mm-08, 30-06, 308. Introduced 1999. Made in U.S.A. by Thompson/Center Arms.
Price: **$657.00**

THOMPSON/CENTER ENCORE "KATAHDIN" CARBINE

Caliber: 45-70 Gov't., 444 Marlin, 450 Marlin. **Barrel:** 18" with muzzle tamer. **Stock:** Composite.
Price: .... **NA**

RIFLES

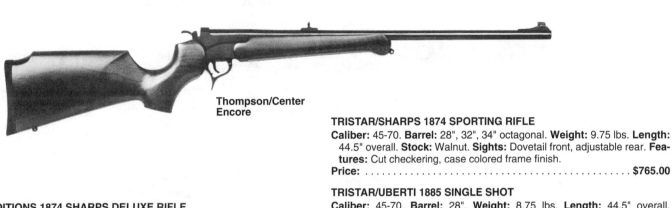

Thompson/Center Encore

TRADITIONS 1874 SHARPS DELUXE RIFLE

Caliber: 45-70. **Barrel:** 32" octagonal; 1:18" twist. **Weight:** 11.67 lbs. **Length:** 48.8" overall. **Stock:** Checkered walnut with German silver nose cap and steel butt plate. **Sights:** Globe front, adjustable creedmore rear with 12 inserts. **Features:** Color-case hardened receiver; double-set triggers. Introduced 2001. Imported from Pedersoli by Traditions.
Price: **$999.00**

Traditions 1874 Sharps Sporting Deluxe Rifle

Similar to Sharps Deluxe but custom silver engraved receiver, European walnut stock and forend, satin finish, set trigger, fully adjustable.
Price: **$1,999.00**

TRADITIONS 1874 SHARPS STANDARD RIFLE

Similar to 1874 Sharps Deluxe Rifle, except has blade front and adjustable buckhorn-style rear sight. Weighs 10.67 pounds. Introduced 2001. Imported from Pedersoli by Traditions.
Price: **$769.00**

TRADITIONS ROLLING BLOCK SPORTING RIFLE

Caliber: 45-70. **Barrel:** 30" octagonal; 1:18" twist. **Weight:** 11.67 lbs. **Length:** 46.7" overall. **Stock:** Walnut. **Sights:** Blade front, adjustable rear. **Features:** Antique silver, color-case hardened receiver, drilled and tapped for tang/globe sights; brass butt plate and trigger guard. Introduced 2001. Imported from Pedersoli by Traditions.
Price: **$769.00**

TRADITIONS ROLLING BLOCK SPORTING RIFLE IN 30-30 WINCHESTER

Caliber: 45-70. **Barrel:** 28" round, blued. **Weight:** 8.25 lbs. **Stock:** Walnut. **Sights:** Fixed front, adjustable rear. **Features:** For hunting like in the Old West. Steel butt plate, trigger guard, barrel band. Classic reproduction.
Price: **$769.00**

TRISTAR/SHARPS 1874 SPORTING RIFLE

Caliber: 45-70. **Barrel:** 28", 32", 34" octagonal. **Weight:** 9.75 lbs. **Length:** 44.5" overall. **Stock:** Walnut. **Sights:** Dovetail front, adjustable rear. **Features:** Cut checkering, case colored frame finish.
Price: **$765.00**

TRISTAR/UBERTI 1885 SINGLE SHOT

Caliber: 45-70. **Barrel:** 28". **Weight:** 8.75 lbs. **Length:** 44.5" overall. **Stock:** European walnut. **Sights:** Bead on blade front, open step-adjustable rear. **Features:** Recreation of the 1885 Winchester. Color case-hardened receiver and lever, blued barrel. Introduced 1998. Imported from Italy by Tristar Sporting Arms Ltd.
Price: **$765.00**

UBERTI BABY ROLLING BLOCK CARBINE

Caliber: 22 LR, 22 WMR, 22 Hornet, 357 Mag., single shot. **Barrel:** 22". **Weight:** 4.8 lbs. **Length:** 35-1/2" overall. **Stock:** Walnut stock and forend. **Sights:** Blade front, fully adjustable open rear. **Features:** Resembles Remington New Model No. 4 carbine. Brass trigger guard and buttplate; color case-hardened frame, blued barrel. Imported by Uberti USA Inc.
Price: **$490.00**
Price: Baby Rolling Block Rifle, 26" bbl. **$590.00**

WESSON & HARRINGTON BUFFALO CLASSIC RIFLE

Caliber: 45-70. **Barrel:** 32" heavy. **Weight:** 9 lbs. **Length:** 52" overall. **Stock:** American black walnut. **Sights:** None furnished; drilled and tapped for peep sight; barrel dovetailed for front sight. **Features:** Color case-hardened Handi-Rifle action with exposed hammer; color case-hardened crescent buttplate; 19th century checkering pattern. Introduced 1995. Made in U.S.A. by H&R 1871, Inc.
Price: About **$349.95**

Wesson & Harrington 38-55 Target Rifle

Similar to the Buffalo Classic rifle except chambered for 38-55 Win., has 28" barrel. The barrel and steel furniture, including steel trigger guard and forend spacer, are highly polished and blued. Color case-hardened receiver and buttplate. Barrel is dovetailed for a front sight, and drilled and tapped for receiver sight or scope mount. Introduced 1998. Made in U.S.A. by H&R 1871, Inc.
Price: **$389.95**

RIFLES

Designs for sporting and utility purposes worldwide.

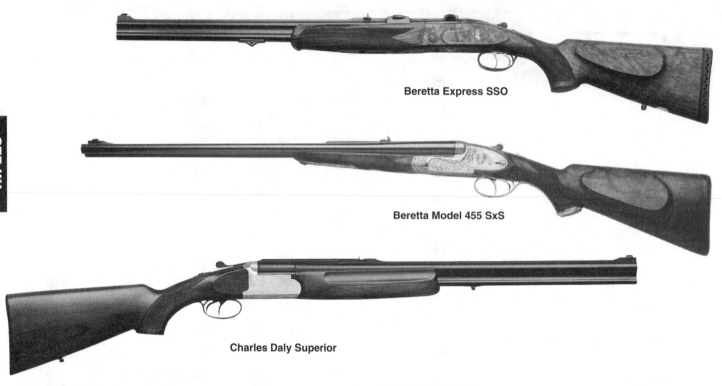

Beretta Express SSO

Beretta Model 455 SxS

Charles Daly Superior

BERETTA EXPRESS SSO O/U DOUBLE RIFLES

Caliber: 375 H&H, 458 Win. Mag., 9.3x74R. **Barrel:** 25.5". **Weight:** 11 lbs. **Stock:** European walnut with hand-checkered grip and forend. **Sights:** Blade front on ramp, open V-notch rear. **Features:** Sidelock action with color case-hardened receiver (gold inlays on SSO6 Gold). Ejectors, double triggers, recoil pad. Introduced 1990. Imported from Italy by Beretta U.S.A.
Price: SSO6 . . . . **$21,000.00**
Price: SSO6 Gold **$23,500.00**

BERETTA MODEL 455 SxS EXPRESS RIFLE

Caliber: 375 H&H, 458 Win. Mag., 470 NE, 500 NE 3", 416 Rigby. **Barrel:** 23-1/2" or 25-1/2". **Weight:** 11 lbs. **Stock:** European walnut with hand-checkered grip and forend. **Sights:** Blade front, folding leaf V-notch rear. **Features:** Sidelock action with easily removable sideplates; color case-hardened finish (455), custom big game or floral motif engraving (455EELL). Double triggers, recoil pad. Introduced 1990. Imported from Italy by Beretta U.S.A.
Price: Model 455 . . . . **$36,000.00**
Price: Model 455EELL **$47,000.00**

BRNO 500 COMBINATION GUNS

Caliber/Gauge: 12 (2-3/4" chamber) over 5.6x52R, 5.6x50R, 222 Rem., 243, 6.x55, 308, 7x57R, 7x65R, 30-06. **Barrel:** 23.6". **Weight:** 7.6 lbs. **Length:** 40.5" overall. **Stock:** European walnut. **Sights:** Bead front, V-notch rear; grooved for scope mounting. **Features:** Boxlock action; double set trigger; blue finish with etched engraving. Announced 1998. Imported from The Czech Republic by Euro-Imports.
Price: **$1,023.00**
Price: O/U double rifle, 7x57R, 7x65R, 8x57JRS **$1,125.00**

BRNO ZH 300 COMBINATION GUN

Caliber/Gauge: 22 Hornet, 5.6x50R Mag., 5.6x52R, 7x57R, 7x65R, 8x57JRS over 12, 16 (2-3/4" chamber). **Barrel:** 23.6". **Weight:** 7.9 lbs. **Length:** 40.5" overall. **Stock:** European walnut. **Sights:** Blade front, open adjustable rear. **Features:** Boxlock action; double triggers; automatic safety. Announced 1998. Imported from The Czech Republic by Euro-Imports.
Price: **$724.00**

BRNO ZH Double Rifles

Similar to ZH 300 combination guns except double rifle barrels. Available in 7x65R, 7x57R and 8x57JRS. Announced 1998. Imported from The Czech Republic by Euro-Imports.
Price: **$1,125.00**

CHARLES DALY SUPERIOR COMBINATION GUN

Caliber/Gauge: 12 ga. over 22 Hornet, 223 Rem., 22-250, 243 Win., 270 Win., 308 Win., 30-06. **Barrel:** 23.5", shotgun choked Imp. Cyl. **Weight:** About 7.5 lbs. **Stock:** Checkered walnut pistol grip buttstock and semi-beavertail forend. **Features:** Silvered, engraved receiver; chrome-moly steel barrels; double triggers; extractors; sling swivels; gold bead front sight. Introduced 1997. Imported from Italy by K.B.I. Inc.
Price: **$1,249.95**

Charles Daly Empire Combination Gun

Same as the Superior grade except has deluxe wood with European-style comb and cheekpiece; slim forend. Introduced 1997. Imported from Italy by K.B.I., Inc.
Price: **$1,789.95**

CZ 584 SOLO COMBINATION GUN

Caliber/Gauge: 7x57R; 12, 2-3/4" chamber. **Barrel:** 24.4". **Weight:** 7.37 lbs. **Length:** 45.25" overall. **Stock:** Circassian walnut. **Sights:** Blade front, open rear adjustable for windage. **Features:** Kersten-style double lump locking system; double-trigger Blitz-type mechanism with drop safety and adjustable set trigger for the rifle barrel; auto safety, dual extractors; receiver dovetailed for scope mounting. Imported from the Czech Republic by CZ-USA.
Price: **$850.00**

CZ 589 STOPPER OVER/UNDER GUN

Caliber: 458 Win. Magnum. **Barrels:** 21.7". **Weight:** 9.3 lbs. **Length:** 37.7" overall. **Stock:** Turkish walnut with sling swivels. **Sights:** Blade front, fixed rear. **Features:** Kersten-style action; Blitz-type double trigger; hammer-forged, blued barrels; satin-nickel, engraved receiver. Introduced 2001. Imported from the Czech Republic by CZ USA.
Price: **$2,999.00**
Price: Fully engraved model **$3,999.00**

DRILLINGS, COMBINATION GUNS, DOUBLE GUNS

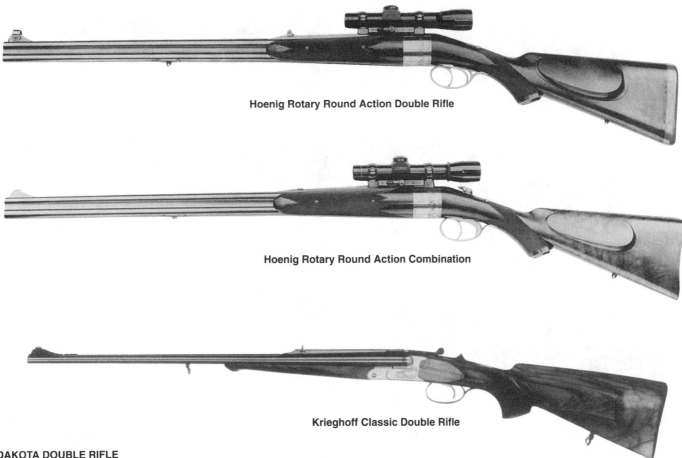

Hoenig Rotary Round Action Double Rifle

Hoenig Rotary Round Action Combination

Krieghoff Classic Double Rifle

DAKOTA DOUBLE RIFLE
Caliber: 470 Nitro Express, 500 Nitro Express. **Barrel:** 25". **Stock:** Exhibition-grade walnut. **Sights:** Express. **Features:** Round action; selective ejectors; recoil pad; Americase. From Dakota Arms Inc.
Price: **$25,000.00**

EAA/BAIKAL IZH-94 COMBINATION GUN
Caliber/Gauge: 12, 3" chamber; 222 Rem., 223, 5.6x50R, 5.6x55E, 7x57R, 7x65R, 7.62x39, 7.62x51, 308, 7.62x53R, 7.62x54R, 30-06. **Barrel:** 24", 26"; imp., mod. and full choke tubes. **Weight:** 7.28 lbs. **Stock:** Walnut; rubber butt pad. **Sights:** Express style. **Features:** Hammer-forged barrels with chrome-lined bores; machined receiver; single-selective or double triggers. Imported by European American Armory.
Price: Blued finish. **$549.00**
New Price: 20 ga./22 LR, 20/22 Mag, 3" **$629.00**

GARBI EXPRESS DOUBLE RIFLE
Caliber: 7x65R, 9.3x74R, 375 H&H. **Barrel:** 24-3/4". **Weight:** 7-3/4 to 8-1/2 lbs. **Length:** 41-1/2" overall. **Stock:** Turkish walnut. **Sights:** Quarter-rib with express sight. **Features:** Side-by-side double; H&H-pattern sidelock ejector with reinforced action, chopper lump barrels of Boehler steel; double triggers; fine scroll and rosette engraving, or full coverage ornamental; coin-finished action. Introduced 1997. Imported from Spain by Wm. Larkin Moore.
Price: **$19,900.00**

HOENIG ROTARY ROUND ACTION DOUBLE RIFLE
Caliber: Most popular calibers from 225 Win. to 9.3x74R. **Barrel:** 22"-26". **Stock:** English Walnut; to customer specs. **Sights:** Swivel hood front with button release (extra bead stored in trap door gripcap), express-style rear on quarter-rib adjustable for windage and elevation; scope mount. **Features:** Round action opens by rotating barrels, pulling forward. Inertia extractor system, rotary safety blocks strikers. single lever quick-detachable scope mount. Simple takedown without removing forend. Introduced 1997. Made in U.S.A. by George Hoenig.
Price: **$24,975.00**

HOENIG ROTARY ROUND ACTION COMBINATION
Caliber: 28 ga. **Barrel:** 26". **Weight:** 7 lbs. **Stock:** English Walnut to customer specs. **Sights:** Front ramp with button release blades. Foldable aperture tang sight windage and elevation adjustable. Quarter rib with scope mount. **Features:** Round action opens by rotating barrels, pulling forward. Inertia extractor; rotary safety blocks strikers. Simple takedown without removing forend. Made in U.S.A. by George Hoenig.
Price: **$24,975.00**

KRIEGHOFF CLASSIC DOUBLE RIFLE
Caliber: 7x65R, 308 Win., 30-06, 8x57 JRS, 8x75RS, 9.3x74R. **Barrel:** 23.5". **Weight:** 7.3 to 8 lbs. **Stock:** High grade European walnut. Standard has conventional rounded cheekpiece, Bavaria has Bavarian-style cheekpiece. **Sights:** Bead front with removable, adjustable wedge (375 H&H and below), standing leaf rear on quarter-rib. **Features:** Boxlock action; double triggers; short opening angle for fast loading; quiet extractors; sliding, self-adjusting wedge for secure bolting; Purdey-style barrel extension; horizontal firing pin placement. Many options available. Introduced 1997. Imported from Germany by Krieghoff International.
Price: With small Arabesque engraving **$7,850.00**
Price: With engraved sideplates. **$9,800.00**
Price: For extra barrels. **$4,500.00**
Price: Extra 20-ga., 28" shotshell barrels **$3,200.00**

Krieghoff Classic Big Five Double Rifle
Similar to the standard Classic excpet available in 375 Flanged Mag. N.E., 500/416 N.E., 470 N.E., 500 N.E. 3". Has hinged front trigger, non-removable muzzle wedge (larger than 375-caliber), Universal Trigger System, Combi Cocking Device, steel trigger guard, specially weighted stock bolt for weight and balance. Many options available. Introduced 1997. Imported from Germany by Krieghoff International.
Price: **$9,450.00**
Price: With engraved sideplates. **$11,400.00**

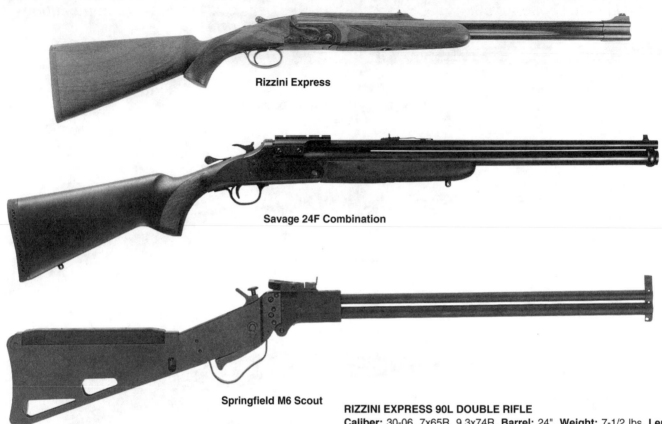

Rizzini Express

Savage 24F Combination

Springfield M6 Scout

LEBEAU - COURALLY EXPRESS RIFLE SxS

Caliber: 7x65R, 8x57JRS, 9.3x74R, 375 H&H, 470 N.E. **Barrel:** 24" to 26". **Weight:** 7-3/4 to 10-1/2 lbs. **Stock:** Fancy French walnut with cheekpiece. **Sights:** Bead on ramp front, standing left express rear on quarter-rib. **Features:** Holland & Holland-type sidelock with automatic ejectors; double triggers. Built to order only. Imported from Belgium by Wm. Larkin Moore.
Price: **$41,000.00**

MERKEL DRILLINGS

Caliber/Gauge: 12, 20, 3" chambers, 16, 2-3/4" chambers; 22 Hornet, 5.6x50R Mag., 5.6x52R, 222 Rem., 243 Win., 6.5x55, 6.5x57R, 7x57R, 7x65R, 308, 30-06, 8x57JRS, 9.3x74R, 375 H&H. **Barrel:** 25.6". **Weight:** 7.9 to 8.4 lbs. depending upon caliber. **Stock:** Oil-finished walnut with pistol grip; cheekpiece on 12-, 16-gauge. **Sights:** Blade front, fixed rear. **Features:** Double barrel locking lug with Greener cross-bolt; scroll-engraved, case-hardened receiver; automatic trigger safety; Blitz action; double triggers. Imported from Germany by GSI.
Price: Model 96K (manually cocked rifle system), from **$7,495.00**
Price: Model 96K Engraved (hunting series on receiver) **$8,595.00**

Merkel Boxlock Double Rifles

Similar to the Model 160 double rifle except with Anson & Deely boxlock action with cocking indicators, double triggers, engraved color case-hardened receiver. Introduced 1995. Imported from Germany by GSI.
Price: Model 140-1, from **$6,695.00**
Price: Model 140-1.1 (engraved silver-gray receiver), from **$7,795.00**

RIZZINI EXPRESS 90L DOUBLE RIFLE

Caliber: 30-06, 7x65R, 9.3x74R. **Barrel:** 24". **Weight:** 7-1/2 lbs. **Length:** 40" overall. **Stock:** Select European walnut with satin oil finish; English-style cheekpiece. **Sights:** Ramp front, quarter-rib with express sight. **Features:** Color case-hardened boxlock action; automatic ejectors; single selective trigger; polished blue barrels. Extra 20-gauge shotshell barrels available. Imported for Italy by Wm. Larkin Moore.
Price: With case **$3,850.00**

SAVAGE 24F PREDATOR O/U COMBINATION GUN

Caliber/Gauge: 22 Hornet, 223, 30-30 over 12 (24F-12) or 22 LR, 22 Hornet, 223, 30-30 over 20-ga. (24F-20); 3" chambers. **Action:** Takedown, low rebounding visible hammer. Single trigger, barrel selector spur on hammer. **Barrel:** 24" separated barrels; 12-ga. has mod. choke tubes, 20-ga. has fixed Mod. choke. **Weight:** 8 lbs. **Length:** 40-1/2" overall. **Stock:** Black Rynite composition. **Sights:** Blade front, rear open adjustable for elevation. **Features:** Introduced 1989.
Price: 24F-12 . . . . **$531.00**
Price: 24F-20 . . . . **$504.00**

SPRINGFIELD, INC. M6 SCOUT RIFLE/SHOTGUN

Caliber/Gauge: 22 LR or 22 Hornet over 410-bore. **Barrel:** 18.25". **Weight:** 4 lbs. **Length:** 32" overall. **Stock:** Folding detachable with storage for 15 22 LR, four 410 shells. **Sights:** Blade front, military aperture for 22; V-notch for 410. **Features:** All-metal construction. Designed for quick disassembly and minimum maintenance. Folds for compact storage. Introduced 1982; reintroduced 1996. Imported from the Czech Republic by Springfield, Inc.
Price: Parkerized **$185.00**
Price: Stainless steel **$219.00**

Designs for hunting, utility and sporting purposes, including training for competition

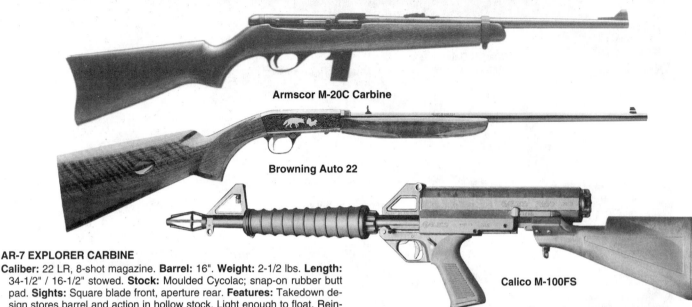

Armscor M-20C Carbine

Browning Auto 22

Calico M-100FS

AR-7 EXPLORER CARBINE

Caliber: 22 LR, 8-shot magazine. **Barrel:** 16". **Weight:** 2-1/2 lbs. **Length:** 34-1/2" / 16-1/2" stowed. **Stock:** Moulded Cycolac; snap-on rubber butt pad. **Sights:** Square blade front, aperture rear. **Features:** Takedown design stores barrel and action in hollow stock. Light enough to float. Reintroduced 1999. From AR-7 Industries, LLC.
Price: Black matte finish $150.00
Price: AR-20 Sporter (tubular stock, barrel shroud) $200.00
New! **Price:** AR-7 camo- or walnut-finish stock $164.95

ARMSCOR MODEL AK22 AUTO RIFLE

Caliber: 22 LR, 10-shot magazine. **Barrel:** 18.5". **Weight:** 7.5 lbs. **Length:** 38" overall. **Stock:** Plain mahogany. **Sights:** Adjustable post front, leaf rear adjustable for elevation. **Features:** Resembles the AK-47. Matte black finish. Introduced 1987. Imported from the Philippines by K.B.I., Inc.
Price: About $219.95

ARMSCOR M-1600 AUTO RIFLE

Caliber: 22 LR, 10-shot magazine. **Barrel:** 18.25". **Weight:** 6.2 lbs. **Length:** 38.5" overall. **Stock:** Black finished mahogany. **Sights:** Post front, aperture rear. **Features:** Resembles Colt AR-15. Matte black finish. Introduced 1987. Imported from the Philippines by K.B.I., Inc.
Price: About $199.95

ARMSCOR M-20C AUTO CARBINE

Caliber: 22 LR, 10-shot magazine. **Barrel:** 18.25". **Weight:** 6.5 lbs. **Length:** 38" overall. **Stock:** Walnut-finished mahogany. **Sights:** Hooded front, rear adjustable for elevation. **Features:** Receiver grooved for scope mounting. Blued finish. Introduced 1990. Imported from the Philippines by K.B.I., Inc.
Price: $154.95

BROWNING BUCK MARK SEMI-AUTO RIFLES

Caliber: 22 LR, 10-shot magazine. **Barrel:** 18" tapered (Sporter) or heavy bull (Target). **Weight:** 4 lbs., 2 oz. (Sporter) or 5 lbs., 4 oz. (Target). **Length:** 34" overall. **Stock:** Walnut stock and forearm with full pistol grip. **Sights:** Hi-Viz adjustable (Sporter). **Features:** A rifle version of the Buck Mark Pistol; straight blowback action; machined aluminum receiver with integral rail scope mount; recessed muzzle crown; manual thumb safety. Introduced 2001. From Browning.
Price: Sporter (adj. sights) $518.00
Price: Target (heavy bbl., no sights)....................... $518.00

BROWNING SEMI-AUTO 22 RIFLE

Caliber: 22 LR, 11-shot. **Barrel:** 19-1/4". **Weight:** 5 lbs., 3 oz. **Length:** 37" overall. **Stock:** Checkered select walnut with pistol grip and semi-beavertail forend. **Sights:** Gold bead front, folding leaf rear. **Features:** Engraved receiver with polished blue finish; cross-bolt safety; tubular magazine in buttstock; easy takedown for carrying or storage. Imported from Japan by Browning.
Price: Grade I $479.00

Browning Semi-Auto 22, Grade VI

Same as the Grade I Auto-22 except available with either grayed or blued receiver with extensive engraving with gold-plated animals: right side pictures a fox and squirrel in a woodland scene; left side shows a beagle chasing a rabbit. On top is a portrait of the beagle. Stock and forend are of high-grade walnut with a double-bordered cut checkering design. Introduced 1987.
Price: Grade VI, blue or gray receiver $1,028.00

BRNO ZKM 611 AUTO RIFLE

Caliber: 22 WMR, 6- or 10-shot magazine. **Barrel:** 20.4". **Weight:** 5.9 lbs. **Length:** 38.9" overall. **Stock:** European walnut. **Sights:** Hooded blade front, open adjustable rear. **Features:** Removable box magazine; polished blue finish; cross-bolt safety; grooved receiver for scope mounting; easy takedown for storage. Imported from The Czech Republic by Euro-Imports.
Price: $475.00

CALICO M-100FS CARBINE

Caliber: 22 LR. **Barrel:** 16.25". **Weight:** 5 lbs. **Length:** 36" overall. **Stock:** Glass-filled, impact-resistant polymer. **Sights:** Adjustable post front, notch rear. **Features:** Has helical-feed magazine; aluminum receiver; ambidextrous safety. Made in U.S.A. by Calico.
Price: $650.00

CHARLES DALY FIELD GRADE AUTO RIFLE

Caliber: 22 LR, 10-shot magazine. **Barrel:** 20-3/4". **Weight:** 6.5 lbs. **Length:** 40-1/2" overall. **Stock:** Walnut-finished hardwood with Monte Carlo. **Sights:** Hooded front, adjustable open rear. **Features:** Receiver grooved for scope mounting; blue finish; shell deflector. Introduced 1998. Imported by K.B.I.
Price: $124.00
Price: Superior Grade (cut checkered stock, fully adjustable sight).. $199.00

Charles Daly Empire Grade Auto Rifle

Similar to the Field Grade except has select California walnut stock with 24 l.p.i. hand checkering, contrasting forend and gripcaps, damascened bolt, high-polish blue. Introduced 1998. Imported by K.B.I.
Price: $369.00

CZ 511 AUTO RIFLE

Caliber: 22 LR, 8-shot magazine. **Barrel:** 22.2". **Weight:** 5.39 lbs. **Length:** 38.6" overall. **Stock:** Walnut with checkered pistol grip. **Sights:** Hooded front, adjustable rear. **Features:** Polished blue finish; detachable magazine; sling swivel studs. Imported from the Czech Republic by CZ-USA.
Price: $351.00

RIFLES

Charles Daly Superior Grade

CZ 511 Auto

Henry U.S. Survival

Marlin Model 60

Marlin Model 60 SSK

Marlin Model 70PSS

HENRY U.S. SURVIVAL RIFLE .22

Caliber: 22 LR, 8-shot magazine. **Barrel:** 16" steel lined. **Weight:** 2.5 lbs. **Stock:** ABS plastic. **Sights:** Blade front on ramp, aperture rear. **Features:** Takedown design stores barrel and action in hollow stock. Light enough to float. Silver, black or camo finish. Comes with two magazines. Introduced 1998. From Henry Repeating Arms Co.

Price: $165.00

MAGTECH MT 7022 AUTO RIFLE

Caliber: 22 LR, 10-shot magazine. **Barrel:** 18". **Weight:** 4.8 lbs. **Length:** 37" overall. **Stock:** Brazilian hardwood. **Sights:** Hooded blade front, fully adjustable open rear. **Features:** Cross-bolt safety; last-shot bolt hold-open; alloy receiver is drilled and tapped for scope mounting. Introduced 1998. Imported from Brazil by Magtech Ammunition Co.

Price: $100.00

MARLIN MODEL 60 AUTO RIFLE

Caliber: 22 LR, 14-shot tubular magazine. **Barrel:** 22" round tapered. **Weight:** About 5-1/2 lbs. **Length:** 40-1/2" overall. **Stock:** Press-checkered, walnut-finished Maine birch with Monte Carlo, full pistol grip; Mar-Shield® finish. **Sights:** Ramp front, open adjustable rear. **Features:** Matted receiver is grooved for scope mount. Manual bolt hold-open; automatic last-shot bolt hold-open.

Price: $181.00
Price: With 4x scope. $188.00

Marlin Model 60SS Self-Loading Rifle

Same as the Model 60 except breech bolt, barrel and outer magazine tube are made of stainless steel; most other parts are either nickel-plated or coated to match the stainless finish. Monte Carlo stock is of black/gray Maine birch laminate, and has nickel-plated swivel studs, rubber butt pad. Introduced 1993.

Price: $290.00
Price: Model 60SSK (black fiberglass-filled stock) $252.00
Price: Model 60SB (walnut-finished birch stock) $231.00
Price: Model 60SB with 4x scope. $244.00

MARLIN 70PSS PAPOOSE STAINLESS RIFLE

Caliber: 22 LR, 7-shot magazine. **Barrel:** 16-1/4" stainless steel, Micro-Groove® rifling. **Weight:** 3-1/4 lbs. **Length:** 35-1/4" overall. **Stock:** Black fiberglass-filled synthetic with abbreviated forend, nickel-plated swivel studs, moulded-in checkering. **Sights:** Ramp front with orange post, cut-away Wide Scan® hood; adjustable open rear. Receiver grooved for scope mounting. **Features:** Takedown barrel; cross-bolt safety; manual bolt hold-open; last shot bolt hold-open; comes with padded carrying case. Introduced 1986. Made in U.S.A. by Marlin.

Price: $297.00

MARLIN MODEL 7000 AUTO RIFLE

Caliber: 22 LR, 10-shot magazine **Barrel:** 18" heavy target with 12-groove Micro-Groove® rifling, recessed muzzle. **Weight:** 5-1/2 lbs. **Length:** 37" overall. **Stock:** Black fiberglass-filled synthetic with Monte Carlo combo, swivel studs, moulded-in checkering. **Sights:** None furnished; comes with ring mounts. **Features:** Automatic last-shot bolt hold-open, manual bolt hold-open; cross-bolt safety; steel charging handle; blue finish, nickel-plated magazine. Introduced 1997. Made in U.S.A. by Marlin Firearms Co.

Price: $245.00

RIFLES

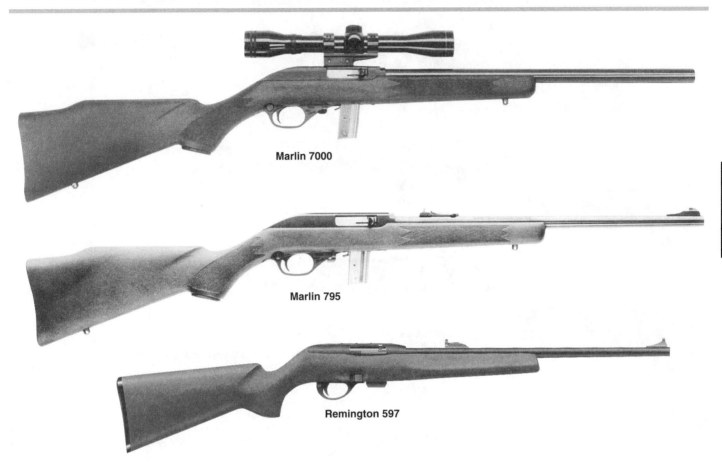

Marlin 7000

Marlin 795

Remington 597

Marlin Model 795 Auto Rifle

Similar to Model 7000 except standard-weight 18" barrel with 16-groove Micro-Groove rifling. Ramp front sight with brass bead, screw adjustable open rear. Receiver grooved for scope mount. Introduced 1997. Made in U.S.A. by Marlin Firearms Co.

Price: **$173.00**

Marlin Model 795SS Auto Rifle

Similar to Model 795 excapt stainless steel barrel. Most other parts nickel-plated. Adjustable folding semi-buckhorn rear sights, ramp front high-visibility post and removeable cutaway wide scan hood.

Price: **$173.00**

REMINGTON MODEL 552 BDL DELUXE SPEEDMASTER RIFLE

Caliber: 22 S (20), L (17) or LR (15) tubular mag. **Barrel:** 21" round tapered. **Weight:** 5-3/4 lbs. **Length:** 40" overall. **Stock:** Walnut. Checkered grip and forend. **Sights:** Big game. **Features:** Positive cross-bolt safety, receiver grooved for tip-off mount.

Price: **$385.00**

REMINGTON 597 AUTO RIFLE

Caliber: 22 LR, 10-shot clip. **Barrel:** 20". **Weight:** 5-1/2 lbs. **Length:** 40" overall. **Stock:** Black synthetic. **Sights:** Big game. **Features:** Matte black finish, nickel-plated bolt. Receiver is grooved and drilled and tapped for scope mounts. Introduced 1997. Made in U.S.A. by Remington.

Price: **$163.00**
Price: Model 597 Magnum, 22 WMR, 8-shot clip **$321.00**
Price: Model 597 LSS (laminated stock, stainless) **$272.00**
Price: Model 597 Magnum LS (laminated stock) **$377.00**
Price: Model 597 SS (22 LR, stainless steel, black synthetic
stock) **$217.00**
New! **Price:** Model 597 LS Heavy Barrel (22 LR, laminated stock) **$265.00**
New! **Price:** Model 597 Magnum LS Heavy Barrel
(22 WMR, lam. stock) **$399.00**

RUGER 10/22 AUTOLOADING CARBINE

Caliber: 22 LR, 10-shot rotary magazine. **Barrel:** 18-1/2" round tapered. **Weight:** 5 lbs. **Length:** 37-1/4" overall. **Stock:** American hardwood with pistol grip and barrel band or synthetic. **Sights:** Brass bead front, folding leaf rear adjustable for elevation. **Features:** Detachable rotary magazine fits flush into stock, cross-bolt safety, receiver tapped and grooved for scope blocks or tip-off mount. Scope base adaptor furnished with each rifle.

Price: Model 10/22 RB (blue) **$239.00**
Price: Model K10/22RB (bright finish stainless barrel) **$279.00**
Price: Model 10/22RPF (blue, synthetic stock) **$239.00**

Ruger 10/22 International Carbine

Similar to the Ruger 10/22 Carbine except has full-length International stock of American hardwood, checkered grip and forend; comes with rubber butt pad, sling swivels. Reintroduced 1994.

Price: Blue (10/22RBI) **$279.00**
Price: Stainless (K10/22RBI) **$299.00**

Ruger 10/22 Deluxe Sporter

Same as 10/22 Carbine except walnut stock with hand checkered pistol grip and forend; straight buttplate, no barrel band, has sling swivels.

Price: Model 10/22 DSP **$299.00**

Ruger 10/22T Target Rifle

Similar to the 10/22 except has 20" heavy, hammer-forged barrel with tight chamber dimensions, improved trigger pull, laminated hardwood stock dimensioned for optical sights. No iron sights supplied. Introduced 1996. Made in U.S.A. by Sturm, Ruger & Co.

Price: 10/22T **$425.00**
Price: K10/22T, stainless steel **$485.00**
New! **Price:** K10/22TNZ, stainless steel 20" bbl. with cut-out pistol-grip
laminated stock. **$649.00**

Ruger 10/22 International

Savage Model 64FV

Thompson/Center 22 LR Classic

Price: Model 64GXP Package Gun includes 4x15 scope and
mounts **$148.00**
Price: Model 64FXP (black stock, 4x15 scope) **$136.00**

Savage Model 64FV Auto Rifle
Similar to the Model 64F except has heavy 21" barrel with recessed
crown; no sights provided—comes with Weaver-style bases. Introduced
1998. Imported from Canada by Savage Arms, Inc.
Price: **$173.00**
New! Price: Model 64FVSS, stainless **$225.00**

THOMPSON/CENTER 22 LR CLASSIC RIFLE
Caliber: 22 LR, 8-shot magazine. **Barrel:** 22" match-grade. **Weight:** 5-1/2
pounds. **Length:** 39-1/2" overall. **Stock:** Satin-finished American walnut
with Monte Carlo-type comb and pistol grip cap, swivel studs. **Sights:**
Ramp-style front and fully adjustable rear, both with fiber optics. **Features:** All-steel receiver drilled and tapped for scope mounting; barrel
threaded to receiver; thumb-operated safety; trigger-guard safety lock included.
Price: T/C 22 LR Classic (blue) **$349.00**

WINCHESTER MODEL 63 AUTO RIFLE
Caliber: 22 LR, 10-shot magazine. **Barrel:** 23". **Weight:** 6-1/4 lbs. **Length:**
39" overall. **Stock:** Walnut. **Sights:** Bead front, open adjustable rear. **Features:** Recreation of the original Model 63. Magazine tube loads through
a port in the buttstock; forward cocking knob at front of forend; easy takedown for cleaning, storage; engraved receiver. Reintroduced 1997. From
U.S. Repeating Arms Co.
Price: Grade I **$678.00**
Price: High grade, select walnut, cut checkering, engraved scenes
with gold accents on receiver (made in 1997 only) **$1,083.00**

Ruger K10/22RPF All-Weather Rifle
Similar to the stainless K10/22/RB except has black composite stock of
thermoplastic polyester resin reinforced with fiberglass; checkered grip
and forend. Brushed satin, natural metal finish with clear hardcoat finish.
Weighs 5 lbs., measures 36-3/4" overall. Introduced 1997. From Sturm,
Ruger & Co.
Price: **$279.00**

RUGER 10/22 MAGNUM AUTOLOADING CARBINE
Caliber: 22 WMR, 9-shot rotary magazine. **Barrel:** 18-1/2". **Weight:** 6 lbs.
Length: 37-1/4" overall. **Stock:** Birch. **Sights:** Gold bead front, folding
rear. **Features:** All-steel receiver has integral Ruger scope bases for the
included 1" rings. Introduced 1999. Made in U.S.A. by Sturm, Ruger & Co.
Price: **$499.00**

SAVAGE MODEL 64G AUTO RIFLE
Caliber: 22 LR, 10-shot magazine. **Barrel:** 20, 21"". **Weight:** 5-1/2 lbs.
Length: 40", 41". **Stock:** Walnut-finished hardwood with Monte Carlo-
type comb, checkered grip and forend. **Sights:** Bead front, open adjust-
able rear. Receiver grooved for scope mounting. **Features:** Thumb-oper-
ated rotating safety. Blue finish. Side ejection, bolt hold-open device.
Introduced 1990. Made in Canada, from Savage Arms.
Price: **$142.00**
New! Price: Model 64FSS, stainless **$171.00**
Price: Model 64F, black synthetic stock **$132.00**

Classic and modern models for sport and utility, including training.

Browning BL-22

Henry Lever-Action 22

Henry Goldenboy 22

Henry Pump-Action 22

Marlin Model 39AS

BROWNING BL-22 LEVER-ACTION RIFLE

Caliber: 22 S (22), L (17) or LR (15), tubular magazine. **Barrel:** 20" round tapered. **Weight:** 5 lbs. **Length:** 36-3/4" overall. **Stock:** Walnut, two-piece straight grip Western style. **Sights:** Bead post front, folding-leaf rear. **Features:** Short throw lever, half-cock safety, receiver grooved for tip-off scope mounts, gold-colored trigger. Imported from Japan by Browning.
Price: Grade I **$415.00**
Price: Grade II (engraved receiver, checkered grip and forend) . **$471.00**
Price: Classic, Grade I (blued trigger, no checkering) **$415.00**
Price: Classic, Grade II (cut checkering, satin wood finish, polished blueing) **$471.00**

HENRY LEVER-ACTION 22

Caliber: 22 Long Rifle (15-shot). **Barrel:** 18-1/4" round. **Weight:** 5-1/2 lbs. **Length:** 34" overall. **Stock:** Walnut. **Sights:** Hooded blade front, open adjustable rear. **Features:** Polished blue finish; full-length tubular magazine; side ejection; receiver grooved for scope mounting. Introduced 1997. Made in U.S.A. by Henry Repeating Arms Co.
Price: **$239.95**
Price: Youth model (33" overall, 11-rounds 22 LR) **$229.95**

HENRY GOLDENBOY 22 LEVER-ACTION RIFLE

Caliber: 22 LR, 22 Magnum, 16-shot. **Barrel:** 20" octagonal. **Weight:** 6.25 lbs. **Length:** 38" overall. **Stock:** American walnut. **Sights:** Blade front, open rear. **Features:** Brasslite receiver, brass buttplate, blued barrel and lever. Introduced 1998. Made in U.S.A. from Henry Repeating Arms Co.
Price: **$379.95**
Price: Magnum **$449.95**

HENRY PUMP-ACTION 22 PUMP RIFLE

Caliber: 22 LR, 15-shot. **Barrel:** 18.25". **Weight:** 5.5 lbs. **Length:** NA. **Stock:** American walnut. **Sights:** Bead on ramp front, open adjustable rear. **Features:** Polished blue finish; receiver groved for scope mount; grooved slide handle; two barrel bands. Introduced 1998. Made in U.S.A. from Henry Repeating Arms Co.
Price: **$249.95**

MARLIN MODEL 39A GOLDEN LEVER-ACTION RIFLE

Caliber: 22, S (26), L (21), LR (19), tubular mag. **Barrel:** 24" Micro-Groove®. **Weight:** 6-1/2 lbs. **Length:** 40" overall. **Stock:** Checkered American black walnut with white line spacers at pistol gripcap and buttplate; Mar-Shield® finish. Swivel studs; rubber butt pad. **Sights:** Bead ramp front with detachable Wide-Scan™ hood, folding rear semi-buckhorn adjustable for windage and elevation. **Features:** Hammer block safety; rebounding hammer. Takedown action, receiver tapped for scope mount (supplied), offset hammer spur, gold-plated steel trigger.
Price: **$540.00**

Marlin Model 1897T

Remington Model 572

Ruger Model 96/22

Winchester 9422 Large Loop

MARLIN MODEL 1897T RIFLE

Caliber: 22, S (21), L (16), LR (14), tubular mag. **Barrel:** 20" tapered octagon. **Weight:** Marble semi-buckhorn rear, Marble front brass beaded. **Features:** Hammer block safety solid top receiver tapped, 2-lever base for 3/4", 7/8" scope ring and " detached, blued, safety lock.

Price: **$732.00**

REMINGTON 572 BDL DELUXE FIELDMASTER PUMP RIFLE

Caliber: 22 S (20), L (17) or LR (15), tubular mag. **Barrel:** 21" round tapered. **Weight:** 5-1/2 lbs. **Length:** 40" overall. **Stock:** Walnut with checkered pistol grip and slide handle. **Sights:** Big game. **Features:** Cross-bolt safety; removing inner magazine tube converts rifle to single shot; receiver grooved for tip-off scope mount.

Price: **$399.00**

RUGER MODEL LEVER-ACTION RIFLE

Caliber: 22 LR, 10 rounds; 22 WMR, 9 rounds; 44 Magnum, 4 rounds. **Barrel:** 18-1/2". **Weight:** 5-1/4 lbs. **Length:** 37-1/4" overall. **Stock:** Hardwood. **Sights:** Gold bead front, folding leaf rear. **Features:** Sliding cross button safety, visible cocking indicator; short-throw lever action. Introduced 1996. Made in U.S.A. by Sturm, Ruger & Co.

Price: 96/22 (22 LR) **$349.00**
Price: 96/22M (22 WMR) **$375.00**
Price: 96/22M (44 Mag.).................................. **$525.00**

TAURUS MODEL 62 PUMP RIFLE

Caliber: 22 LR, 12- or 13-shot. **Barrel:** 16-1/2" or 23" round. **Weight:** 90.4 oz. **Length:** 39" overall. **Stock:** Premium hardwood. **Sights:** Adjustable rear, bead blade front, optional tang. **Features:** Blue, case hardened or stainless, bolt-mounted safety, pump action, manual firing pin block, integral security lock system. Imported from Brazil by Taurus International.

Price: .... **$280.00 to $390.00**

Taurus Model 72 Pump Rifle

Same as Model 62 except chambered in 22 Magnum; 16-1/2" bbl. holds 10 shots, 23" bbl. holds 11 shots. Weighs 108.8 oz. Introduced 2001. Imported from Brazil by Taurus International.

Price: .... **$280.00 to $390.00**

WINCHESTER MODEL 9422 LEVER-ACTION RIFLES

Caliber: 22 LR, 22 WMR, tubular magazine. **Barrel:** 20-1/2". **Weight:** 6-1/4 lbs. **Length:** 37-1/8" overall. **Stock:** American walnut, two-piece, straight grip (Traditional) or semi-pistol grip (Legacy). **Sights:** Hooded ramp front, adjustable semi-buckhorn rear. **Features:** Side ejection, receiver grooved for scope mounting, takedown action. From U.S. Repeating Arms Co.

Price: Traditional, 22 LR 15-shot **$452.00**
Price: Traditional, 22WMR, 11-shot **$472.00**
Price: Legacy, 22 LR 15-shot........................... **$484.00**
Price: Legacy 22 WMR, 11-shot........................ **$505.00**

WINCHESTER MODEL 1886 EXTRA LIGHT GRADE I

Caliber: 45-70, 4-shot magazine. **Barrel:** 22". **Weight:** 7-1.4 lbs. **Length:** 40-1/2" overall. **Sights:** Blade front, buckhorn-style ramp-adjustable rear. **Features:** Round, tapered barrel; shotgun-style steel buttplate; half-magazine. Limited production. Introduced 2000. From U.S. Repeating Arms Co., Inc.

Price: **$1,152.00**
Price: High Grade (extra-fancy, checkered walnut stock, engraved elk and deer scenes) **$1,440.00**

Includes models for a variety of sports, utility and competitive shooting.

Anschutz 1518D Luxus

Anschutz 1710D

Charles Daly Field Grade

ANSCHUTZ 1416D/1516D CLASSIC RIFLES

Caliber: 22 LR (1416D), 5-shot clip; 22 WMR (1516D), 4-shot clip. **Barrel:** 22-1/2". **Weight:** 6 lbs. **Length:** 41" overall. **Stock:** European hardwood with walnut finish; classic style with straight comb, checkered pistol grip and forend. **Sights:** Hooded ramp front, folding leaf rear. **Features:** Uses Match 64 action. Adjustable single stage trigger. Receiver grooved for scope mounting. Imported from Germany by AcuSport Corp.
Price: 1416D, 22 LR **$755.95**
Price: 1516D, 22 WMR **$779.95**
Price: 1416D Classic left-hand **$679.95**

Anschutz 1416D/1516D Walnut Luxus Rifles

Similar to the Classic models except have European walnut stocks with Monte Carlo cheekpiece, slim forend with Schnabel tip, cut checkering on grip and forend. Introduced 1997. Imported from Germany by AcuSport Corp.
Price: 1416D (22 LR) **$755.95**
Price: 1516D (22 WMR) **$779.95**

ANSCHUTZ 1518D LUXUS BOLT-ACTION RIFLE

Caliber: 22 WMR, 4-shot magazine. **Barrel:** 19-3/4". **Weight:** 5-1/2 lbs. **Length:** 37-1/2" overall. **Stock:** European walnut. **Sights:** Blade on ramp front, folding leaf rear. **Features:** Receiver grooved for scope mounting; single stage trigger; skip-line checkering; rosewood forend tip; sling swivels. Imported from Germany by AcuSport Corp.
Price: **$1,186.95**

ANSCHUTZ 1710D CUSTOM RIFLE

Caliber: 22 LR, 5-shot clip. **Barrel:** 24-1/4". **Weight:** 7-3/8 lbs. **Length:** 42-1/2" overall. **Stock:** Select European walnut. **Sights:** Hooded ramp front, folding leaf rear; drilled and tapped for scope mounting. **Features:** Match 54 action with adjustable single-stage trigger; roll-over Monte Carlo cheekpiece, slim forend with Schnabel tip, Wundhammer palm swell on pistol grip, rosewood gripcap with white diamond insert; skip-line checkering on grip and forend. Introduced 1988. Imported from Germany by AcuSport Corp.
Price: **$1,289.95**

CABANAS MASTER BOLT-ACTION RIFLE

Caliber: 177, round ball or pellet; single shot. **Barrel:** 19-1/2". **Weight:** 8 lbs. **Length:** 45-1/2" overall. **Stocks:** Walnut target-type with Monte Carlo. **Sights:** Blade front, fully adjustable rear. **Features:** Fires round ball or pellet with 22-cal. blank cartridge. Bolt action. Imported from Mexico by Mandall Shooting Supplies. Introduced 1984.
Price: **$189.95**
Price: Varmint model (has 21-1/2" barrel, 4-1/2 lbs., 41" overall length, varmint-type stock) **$119.95**

Cabanas Leyre Bolt-Action Rifle

Similar to Master model except 44" overall, has sport/target stock.
Price: **$149.95**
Price: Model R83 (17" barrel, hardwood stock, 40" o.a.l.) **$79.95**
Price: Mini 82 Youth (16-1/2" barrel, 33" overall length, 3-1/2 lbs.) . **$69.95**
Price: Pony Youth (16" barrel, 34" overall length, 3.2 lbs.) **$69.95**

Cabanas Espronceda IV Bolt-Action Rifle

Similar to the Leyre model except has full sporter stock, 18-3/4" barrel, 40" overall length, weighs 5-1/2 lbs.
Price: **$134.95**

CABANAS LASER RIFLE

Caliber: 177. **Barrel:** 19". **Weight:** 6 lbs., 12 oz. **Length:** 42" overall. **Stock:** Target-type thumbhole. **Sights:** Blade front, open fully adjustable rear. **Features:** Fires round ball or pellets with 22 blank cartridge. Imported from Mexico by Mandall Shooting Supplies.
Price: **$159.95**

CHARLES DALY SUPERIOR BOLT-ACTION RIFLE

Caliber: 22 LR, 10-shot magazine. **Barrel:** 22-5/8". **Weight:** 6.7 lbs. **Length:** 41.25" overall. **Stock:** Walnut-finished mahogany. **Sights:** Bead front, rear adjustable for elevation. **Features:** Receiver grooved for scope mounting. Blued finish. Introduced 1998. Imported by K.B.I., Inc.
Price: **$189.95**

Charles Daly Field Grade Rifle

Similar to the Superior except has short walnut-finished hardwood stock for small shooters. Introduced 1998. Imported by K.B.I., Inc.
Price: **$134.95**
Price: Field Youth (17.5" barrel) **$144.95**

Charles Daly Superior Magnum Grade Rifle

Similar to the Superior except chambered for 22 WMR. Has 22.6" barrel, double lug bolt, checkered stock, weighs 6.5 lbs. Introduced 1987.
Price: About **$204.95**

Charles Daly Empire Magnum Grade Rifle

Similar to the Superior Magnum except has oil-finished American walnut stock with 18 lpi hand checkering; black hardwood gripcap and forend tip; highly polished barreled action; jewelled bolt; recoil pad; swivel studs. Imported from the Philippines by K.B.I., Inc.
Price: **$364.95**

RIFLES

Chipmunk Deluxe

CZ 452 American Classic

Henry "Mini" Bolt 22

Charles Daly Empire Grade Rifle

Similar to the Superior except has oil-finished American walnut stock with 18 lpi hand checkering; black hardwood gripcap and forend tip; highly polished barreled action; jewelled bolt; recoil pad; swivel studs. Imported by K.B.I., Inc.

Price: **$329.00**

CHARLES DALY TRUE YOUTH BOLT-ACTION RIFLE

Caliber: 22 LR, single shot. **Barrel:** 16-1/4". **Weight:** About 3 lbs. **Length:** 32" overall. **Stock:** Walnut-finished hardwood. **Sights:** Blade front, adjustable rear. **Features:** Scaled-down stock for small shooters. Blue finish. Introduced 1998. Imported by K.B.I., Inc.

Price: **$154.95**

CHIPMUNK SINGLE SHOT RIFLE

Caliber: 22 LR, 22 WMR, single shot. **Barrel:** 16-1/8". **Weight:** About 2-1/2 lbs. **Length:** 30" overall. **Stocks:** American walnut. **Sights:** Post on ramp front, peep rear adjustable for windage and elevation. **Features:** Drilled and tapped for scope mounting using special Chipmunk base ($13.95). Engraved model also available. Made in U.S.A. Introduced 1982. From Rogue Rifle Co., Inc.

Price: Standard. **$194.25**
Price: Standard 22 WMR **$209.95**
Price: Deluxe (better wood, checkering). **$246.95**
Price: Deluxe 22 WMR. **$262.95**
Price: Laminated stock **$209.95**
Price: Laminated stock, 22 WMR **$225.95**
Price: Bull barrel models of above, add **$16.00**

CHIPMUNK TM (TARGET MODEL)

Caliber: 22 S, L, or LR. **Barrel:** 18" blue. **Weight:** 5 lbs. **Length:** 33". **Stocks:** Walnut with accessory rail. **Sights:** 1/4 minute micrometer adjustable. **Features:** Manually cocking single shot bolt action, blue receiver, adjustable butt plate and butt pad.

Price: **$329.95**

COOPER MODEL 57-M BOLT-ACTION RIFLE

Caliber: 22 LR, 22 WMR, 17 HMR. **Barrel:** 23-3/4" stainless steel or 41-40 match grade. **Weight:** 6.6 lbs. **Stock:** Claro walnut, 22 lpi chand checkering. **Sights:** None furnished. **Features:** Three rear locking lug, repeating bolt-action with 5-shot mag. Fully adjustable trigger. Many options. Made 100% in the U.S.A. by Cooper Firearms of Montana, Inc.

Price: Classic **$1,100.00**
Price: LVT. **$1,295.00**
Price: Custom Classic **$1,895.00**
Price: Western Classic **$2,495.00**

CZ 452 M 2E LUX BOLT-ACTION RIFLE

Caliber: 22 LR, 22 WMR, 5-shot detachable magazine. **Barrel:** 24.8". **Weight:** 6.6 lbs. **Length:** 42.63" overall. **Stock:** Walnut with checkered pistol grip. **Sights:** Hooded front, fully adjustable tangent rear. **Features:** All-steel construction, adjustable trigger, polished blue finish. Imported from the Czech Republic by CZ-USA.

Price: 22 LR **$351.00**
Price: 22 WMR **$378.00**
Price: Synthetic stock, nickel finish, 22 LR. **$344.00**

CZ 452 M 2E Varmint Rifle

Similar to the Lux model except has heavy 20.8" barrel; stock has beavertail forend; weighs 7 lbs.; no sights furnished. Available only in 22 LR. Imported from the Czech Republic by CZ-USA.

Price: **$369.00**

CZ 452 American Classic Bolt-Action Rifle

Similar to the CZ 452 M 2E Lux except has classic-style stock of Circassian walnut; 22.5" free-floating barrel with recessed target crown; receiver dovetail for scope mounting. No open sights furnished. Introduced 1999. Imported from the Czech Republic by CZ-USA.

Price: 22 LR **$351.00**
Price: 22 WMR **$378.00**

DAN WESSON COYOTE CLASSIC BOLT-ACTION RIMFIRE RIFLE

Caliber: 22 LR or 22 WMR. 5-shot magazine (10-shot optional magazine). **Barrel:** 22-3/4". **Weight:** NA. **Length:** NA. **Stock:** Laminated wood or exotic hardwood. **Sights:** Fully adjustable V-notch rear, brass bead ramp front. **Features:** Receiver drilled and tapped for scope mount; checkered pistol grip and fore end with DW medallion end cap; recessed target crown; sling swivel studs. Introduced 2001. From Dan Wesson Firearms.

Price: Coyote Classic, 22 LR or 22 WMR **$219.00**

DAN WESSON COYOTE TARGET BOLT-ACTION RIMFIRE RIFLE

Caliber: 22 LR or 22 WMR, 5-shot magazine (10-shot optional magazine). **Barrel:** 18-3/8" heavy. **Weight:** NA. **Length:** NA. **Stock:** Laminated wood or exotic hardwood. **Sights:** None furnished. **Features:** Receiver drilled and tapped for scope mount; target-crowned muzzle; high comb, smooth pistol grip and rubber butt plate. Introduced 2001. From Dan Wesson Firearms.

Price: Coyote Target, 22 LR or 22 WMR **$259.00**

Kimber 22 Classic

Kimber 22 SVT

Kimber 22 HS

Marlin 17V

Price: Youth $746.00
Price: SVT (Short Varmint Target) $949.00
Price: HS (Hunter Silhouette) $813.00
Price: Super America $1,764.00

Kimber 22 SuperAmerica Bolt-Action Rifle
Similar to 22 Classic except has AAA Claro walnut stock with wrap-around 22 l.p.i. hand-cut checkering, ebony forened tip, beaded cheekpiece. Introduced 1999. Made in U.S.A. by Kimber Mfg., Inc.
Price: $1,764.00

Kimber 22 SVT Bolt-Action Rilfe
Similar to 22 Classic except has 18" stainless steel, fluted bull barrel, gray laminated, high-comb target-style stock with deep pistol grip, high comb, beavertail forend with bipod stud. Weighs 7.5 lbs., overall length 36.5". Matte finish on action. Introduced 1999. Made in U.S.A. by Kimber Mfg., Inc.
Price: $949.00

Kimber 22 HS (Hunter Silhouette) Bolt-Action Rifle
Similar to 22 Classic except 24" medium sporter match-grade barrel with half-fluting; high comb, walnut, Monte Carlo target stock with 18 l.p.i. checkering; matte blue metal finish. Introduced 1999. Made in U.S.A. by Kimber Mfg., Inc.
Price: $814.00

MARLIN MODEL 17V HORNADY MAGNUM
Caliber: 17 Magnum, 7-shot. **Barrel:** 22. **Weight:** 6 lbs., stainless 7 lbs. **Length:** 41". **Stock:** Checkered walnut Monte Carlo SS, laminated black/grey. **Sights:** No sights but receiver grooved. **Features:** Swivel studs, positive thumb safety, red cocking indicator, 1" scope rings, safety lock, SS 1" brushed aluminum scope ring.
Price: $263.00
Price: Bead blasted SS barrel & receiver $392.00

HARRINGTON & RICHARDSON ULTRA HEAVY BARREL 22 MAG RIFLE
Caliber: 22 WMR, single shot. **Barrel:** 22" bull. **Stock:** Cinnamon laminated wood with Monte Carlo cheekpiece. **Sights:** None furnished; scope mount rail included. **Features:** Hand-checkered stock and forend; deep-crown rifling; tuned trigger; trigger locking system; hammer extension. Introduced 2001. From H&R 1871 LLC.
Price: $135.95

HENRY "MINI" BOLT 22 RIFLE
Caliber: 22 LR, single shot. **Barrel:** 16" stainless, 8-groove rifling. **Weight:** 3.25 lbs. **Length:** 30", LOP 11-1/2". **Stock:** Synthetic, pistol grip, wrap-around checkering and beavertail forearm. **Sights:** William Fire sights. **Features:** One piece bolt configuration manually operated safety. Ideal for beginners or ladies.
Price: $169.95

KIMBER 22 BOLT-ACTION RIFLE
Caliber: 22 LR, 5-shot magazine. **Barrel:** 18", 22", 24" match grade; 11-degree target crown. **Weight:** 5-8 lbs. **Length:** 35"-43". **Stock:** Classic Claro walnut, hand-cut checkering, steel gripcap, swivel studs. **Sights:** None, drilled and tapped. **Features:** All-new action with Mauser-style full-length claw extractor, two-position wing safety, match trigger, pillar-bedded action with recoil lug. Introduced 1999. Made in U.S.A. by Kimber Mfg., Inc.
Price: New Classic $1,085.00
Price: Classic $949.00
Price: Hunter $678.00

Marlin Model 15YN "Little Buckaroo"

Marlin Model 880SS

Marlin 880SQ Squirrel

Marlin 25N

Marlin 25MNC

MARLIN MODEL 15YN "LITTLE BUCKAROO"
Caliber: 22 S, L, LR, single shot. **Barrel:** 16-1/4" Micro-Groove®. **Weight:** 4-1/4 lbs. **Length:** 33-1/4" overall. **Stock:** One-piece walnut-finished, press-checkered Maine birch with Monte Carlo; Mar-Shield® finish. **Sights:** Ramp front, adjustable open rear. **Features:** Beginner's rifle with thumb safety, easy-load feed throat, red cocking indicator. Receiver grooved for scope mounting. Introduced 1989.
Price: $204.00
Price: Stainless steel with fire sights $228.00

MARLIN MODEL 880SS BOLT-ACTION RIFLE
Caliber: 22 LR, 7-shot clip magazine. **Barrel:** 22" Micro-Groove®. **Weight:** 6 lbs. **Length:** 41" overall. **Stock:** Black fiberglass-filled synthetic with nickel-plated swivel studs and moulded-in checkering. **Sights:** Ramp front with orange post and cutaway Wide-Scan™ hood, adjustable semi-buckhorn folding rear. **Features:** Stainless steel barrel, receiver, front breech bolt and striker; receiver grooved for scope mounting. Introduced 1994. Made in U.S.A. by Marlin.
Price: $308.00

Marlin Model 81TS Bolt-Action Rifle
Same as Marlin 880SS except blued steel, tubular magazine, holds 17 Long Rifle cartridges. Weighs 6 lbs.
Price: $207.00

Marlin Model 880SQ Squirrel Rifle
Similar to Model 880SS except uses heavy target barrel of Marlin's Model 2000L target rifle. Black synthetic stock with moulded-in checkering, double bedding screws, matte blue finish. Without sights, no dovetail or filler screws; receiver grooved for scope mount. Weighs 7 lbs. Introduced 1996. Made in U.S.A. by Marlin.
Price: $322.00

Marlin Model 25N Bolt-Action Repeater
Similar to Marlin 880, except walnut-finished hardwood stock, adjustable open rear sight, ramp front.
Price: $205.00
Price: With 4x scope and mount. $213.00

Marlin Model 25NC Bolt-Action Repeater
Same as Model 25N except Mossy Oak® Break-Up camouflage stock. Made in U.S.A. by Marlin.
Price: $241.00

Marlin Model 25MN/25MNC Bolt-Action Rifles
Similar to the Model 25N except chambered for 22 WMR. Has 7-shot clip magazine, 22" Micro-Groove® barrel, checkered walnut-finished Maine birch stock. Introduced 1989.
Price: 25MN $235.00
New! **Price:** 25MNC (Mossy Oak® Break-Up camouflage stock). . $272.00

Marlin Model 882 Bolt-Action Rifle
Same as the Marlin 880 except 22 WMR cal. only with 7-shot clip magazine; weight about 6 lbs. Comes with swivel studs.
Price: $314.00
Price: Model 882L (laminated hardwood stock; weighs 6-1/4 lbs.) $333.00

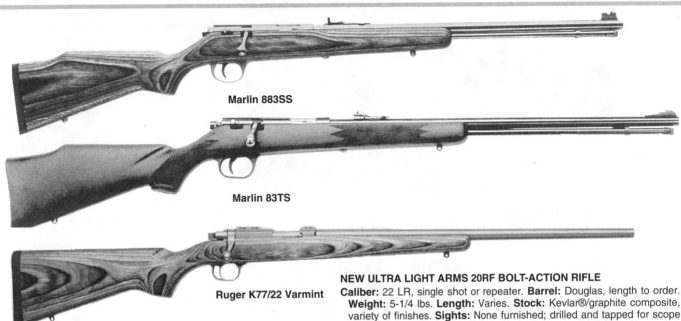

Marlin 883SS

Marlin 83TS

Ruger K77/22 Varmint

Marlin Model 882SS Bolt-Action Rifle

Same as the Marlin Model 882 except has stainless steel front breech bolt, barrel, receiver and bolt knob. All other parts are either stainless steel or nickel-plated. Has black Monte Carlo stock of fiberglass-filled polycarbonate with moulded-in checkering, nickel-plated swivel studs. Introduced 1995. Made in U.S.A. by Marlin Firearms Co.

Price: **$336.00**

Marlin Model 882SSV Bolt-Action Rifle

Similar to the Model 882SS except has selected heavy 22" stainless steel barrel with recessed muzzle, and comes without sights; receiver is grooved for scope mount and 1" ring mounts are included. Weighs 7 lbs. Introduced 1997. Made in U.S.A. by Marlin Firearms Co.

Price: **$330.00**

MARLIN MODEL 883 BOLT-ACTION RIFLE

Caliber: 22 WMR. **Barrel:** 22"; 1:16" twist. **Weight:** 6 lbs. **Length:** 41" overall. **Stock:** Walnut Monte Carlo with sling swivel studs, rubber butt pad. **Sights:** Ramp front with brass bead, removable hood; adjustable semi-buckhorn folding rear. **Features:** Thumb safety, red cocking indicator, receiver grooved for scope mount. Made in U.S.A. by Marlin Firearms Co.

Price: **$328.00**

Marlin Model 883SS Bolt-Action Rifle

Same as the Model 883 except front breech bolt, striker knob, trigger stud, cartridge lifter stud and outer magazine tube are of stainless steel; other parts are nickel-plated. Has two-tone brown laminated Monte Carlo stock with swivel studs, rubber butt pad. Introduced 1993.

Price: **$348.00**

Marlin Model 83TS Bolt-Action Rifle

Same as the Model 883 except has a black Monte Carlo fiberglass-filled synthetic stock with sling swivel studs. Weighs 6 lbs., length 41" overall. Introduced 2001. Made in U.S.A. by Marlin Firearms Co.

Price: **$252.00**

NEW ENGLAND FIREARMS SPORTSTER™
SINGLE-SHOT RIFLES

Caliber: 22 LR, 22 WMR, single-shot. **Barrel:** 20". **Weight:** 5-1/2 lbs. **Length:** 36-1/4" overall. **Stock:** Black polymer. **Sights:** None furnished; scope mount included. **Features:** Break open, side-lever release; automatic ejection; recoil pad; sling swivel studs; trigger locking system. Introduced 2001. Made in U.S.A. by New England Firearms.

Price: **$121.95**

Price: Youth model (20" bbl., 33" overall, weighs 5-1/3 lbs.) **$121.95**

NEW ULTRA LIGHT ARMS 20RF BOLT-ACTION RIFLE

Caliber: 22 LR, single shot or repeater. **Barrel:** Douglas, length to order. **Weight:** 5-1/4 lbs. **Length:** Varies. **Stock:** Kevlar®/graphite composite, variety of finishes. **Sights:** None furnished; drilled and tapped for scope mount. **Features:** Timney trigger, hand-lapped action, button-rifled barrel, hand-bedded action, recoil pad, sling-swivel studs, optional Jewell Trigger. Made in U.S.A. by New Ultra Light Arms.

Price: 20 RF single shot **$800.00**
Price: 20 RF repeater **$850.00**

ROSSI MATCHED PAIR SINGLE-SHOT RIFLE/SHOTGUN

Caliber: 22 LR or 22 Mag. **Barrel:** 18-1/2" or 23". **Weight:** 6 lbs. **Stock:** Hardwood (brown or black finish). **Sights:** Fully adjustable front and rear. **Features:** Break-open breech, transfer-bar manual safety, includes matched 410-, 20- or 12-gauge shotgun barrel with bead front sight. Introduced 2001. Imported by BrazTech/Taurus.

Price: blue **$139.95**
Price: stainless steel **$169.95**

RUGER K77/22 VARMINT RIFLE

Caliber: 22 LR, 10-shot, 22 WMR, 9-shot detachable rotary magazine. **Barrel:** 24", heavy. **Weight:** 6-7/8 lbs. **Length:** 43.25" overall. **Stock:** Laminated hardwood with rubber butt pad, quick-detachable swivel studs. **Sights:** None furnished. Comes with Ruger 1" scope rings. **Features:** Stainless steel or blued finish. Three-position safety, dual extractors. Stock has wide, flat forend. Introduced 1993.

Price: K77/22VBZ, 22 LR **$599.00**
Price: K77/22VMBZ, 22 WMR **$599.00**

RUGER 77/22 RIMFIRE BOLT-ACTION RIFLE

Caliber: 22 LR, 10-shot rotary magazine; 22 WMR, 9-shot rotary magazine. **Barrel:** 20". **Weight:** About 5-3/4 lbs. **Length:** 39-3/4" overall. **Stock:** Checkered American walnut, laminated hardwood, or synthetic stocks, stainless sling swivels. **Sights:** Brass bead front, adjustable folding leaf rear or plain barrel with 1" Ruger rings. **Features:** Mauser-type action uses Ruger's rotary magazine. Three-position safety, simplified bolt stop, patented bolt locking system. Uses the dual-screw barrel attachment system of the 10/22 rifle. Integral scope mounting system with 1" Ruger rings. Blued model introduced 1983. Stainless steel and blued with synthetic stock introduced 1989.

Price: 77/22R (no sights, rings, walnut stock) **$565.00**
Price: 77/22RS (open sights, rings, walnut stock) **$585.00**
Price: K77/22RP (stainless, no sights, rings, synthetic stock) ... **$565.00**
Price: K77/22RSP (stainless, open sights, rings, synthetic stock) . **$585.00**
Price: 77/22RM (22 WMR, blue, walnut stock) **$565.00**
Price: K77/22RSMP (22 WMR, stainless, open sights, rings, synthetic stock) **$585.00**
Price: K77/22RMP (22 WMR, stainless, synthetic stock)........ **$565.00**
Price: 77/22RSM (22 WMR, blue, open sights, rings, walnut stock) **$585.00**
New!! Price: K77/17RM (17 HMR, walnut, no sights, rings) **$565.00**

RIFLES

Ruger 77/22R

Sako Finnfire

Savage Mark II-FXP

SAKO FINNFIRE HUNTER BOLT-ACTION RIFLE

Caliber: 22 LR, 5-shot magazine. **Barrel:** 22". **Weight:** 5.75 lbs. **Length:** 39-1/2" overall. **Stock:** European walnut with checkered grip and forend. **Sights:** Hooded blade front, open adjustable rear. **Features:** Adjustable single-stage trigger; has 50-degree bolt lift. Introduced 1994. Imported from Finland by Beretta USA.

Price: $854.00
Price: Varmint (heavy barrel) $896.00

SAKO FINNFIRE SPORTER RIFLE

Caliber: 22 LR. **Barrel:** 22"; heavy, free-floating. **Stock:** Match style of European walnut; adjustable cheekpiece and buttplate; stippled pistol grip and forend. **Sights:** None furnished; has 11mm integral dovetail scope mount. **Features:** Based on the Sako P94S action with two bolt locking lugs, 50-degree bolt lift and 30mm throw; adjustable trigger. Introduced 1999. Imported from Finland by Beretta USA.

Price: $951.00

SAKO 75 FINNLIGHT

Caliber: 243 Rem., 7mm-08 Rem., 308 Win., 25-06 Rem., 270 Win., 280 Rem, 30-06 Spfld, 6.5x55, 7mm Rem. Mag., 300 Win. Mag. **Barrel:** 20", 22". **Weight:** 6-1/2 lbs. **Stock:** Synthetic. **Sights:** None. **Features:** Bolt-action with 3 locking lugs, mechanical ejector, 2 position safety with bolt handle release, single-stage adjustable trigger, detachable magazine with hinged floor plate, stainless steel action and internal parts. Imported from Finland bu Beretta USA.

Price: From ....$1,239.00 to $1,274.00

SAVAGE MARK I-G BOLT-ACTION RIFLE

Caliber: 22 LR, single shot. **Barrel:** 20-3/4". **Weight:** 5-1/2 lbs. **Length:** 39-1/2" overall. **Stock:** Walnut-finished hardwood with Monte Carlo-type comb, checkered grip and forend. **Sights:** Bead front, open adjustable rear. Receiver grooved for scope mounting. **Features:** Thumb-operated rotating safety. Blue finish. Rifled or smooth bore. Introduced 1990. Made in Canada, from Savage Arms Inc.

Price: Mark I, rifled or smooth bore, right- or left-handed......$135.00
Price: Mark I-GY (Youth), 19" bbl., 37" overall, 5 lbs...........$135.00
New!! Price: Mark I-LY (Youth), 19" bbl., color laminate $166.00
New!! Price: Mark I-Y (Youth), 19" bbl., camo................$167.00
New!! Price: Mark I-GYXP (Youth), with scope $154.00

SAVAGE MARK II-G BOLT-ACTION RIFLE

Caliber: 22 LR, 10-shot magazine. **Barrel:** 20-1/2". **Weight:** 5-1/2 lbs. **Length:** 39-1/2" overall. **Stock:** Walnut-finished hardwood with Monte Carlo-type comb, checkered grip and forend. **Sights:** Bead front, open adjustable rear. Receiver grooved for scope mounting. **Features:** Thumb-operated rotating safety. Blue finish. Introduced 1990. Made in Canada, from Savage Arms, Inc.

Price: Mark II $148.00
New!!! Price: Mark II Camo $167.00
Price: Mark II-GY (youth), 19" barrel, 37" overall, 5 lbs.........$148.00
Price: Mark II-GL, left-hand $148.00
Price: Mark II-GLY (youth) left-hand........................$148.00
Price: Mark II-GXP Package Gun (comes with 4x15 scope), right- or left-handed $155.00
Price: Mark II-FXP (as above with black synthetic stock).......$141.00
Price: Mark II-F (as above, no scope) $135.00
Price: Mark II-FVXP (as above, with scope and rings).........$240.00

Savage Mark II-LV Heavy Barrel Rifle

Similar to Mark II-G except heavy 21" barrel with recessed target-style crown, gray, laminated hardwood stock with cut checkering. No sights furnished, has dovetailed receiver for scope mounting. Overall length is 39-3/4", weight is 6-1/2 lbs. Comes with 10-shot clip magazine. Introduced 1997. Imported from Canada by Savage Arms, Inc.

Price: $235.00
Price: Mark II-FV, with black graphite/polymer stock $205.00

Savage Mark II-FSS Stainless Rifle

Similar to the Mark II-G except has stainless steel barreled action and graphite/polymer filled stock; free-floated barrel. Weighs 5 lbs. Introduced 1997. Imported from Canada by Savage Arms, Inc.

Price: $179.00

Savage Model 93FVSS Magnum Rifle

Similar to Model 93FSS Magnum except 21" heavy barrel with recessed target-style crown, satin-finished stainless barreled action, black graphite/fiberglass stock. Drilled and tapped for scope mounting; comes with Weaver-style bases. Introduced 1998. Imported from Canada by Savage Arms, Inc.

Price: $240.00
New!!! Price: With scope $274.00

Savage Model 93G

Winchester Model 52B

SAVAGE MODEL 93G MAGNUM BOLT-ACTION RIFLE

Caliber: 22 WMR, 5-shot magazine. **Barrel:** 20-3/4". **Weight:** 5-3/4 lbs. **Length:** 39-1/2" overall. **Stock:** Walnut-finished hardwood with Monte Carlo-type comb, checkered grip and forend. **Sights:** Bead front, adjustable open rear. Receiver grooved for scope mount. **Features:** Thumb-operated rotary safety. Blue finish. Introduced 1994. Made in Canada, from Savage Arms.

Price: $173.00

Price: Model 93F (as above with black graphite/fiberglass stock) $166.00

Savage Model 93FSS Magnum Rifle

Similar to Model 93G except stainless steel barreled action and black synthetic stock with positive checkering. Weighs 5-1/2 lbs. Introduced 1997. Imported from Canada by Savage Arms, Inc.

Price: $209.00

SAVAGE MARK 30G STEVENS "FAVORITE"

Caliber: 22 LR, (22WMR - Model 30GM). **Barrel:** 20-1/2". **Weight:** 4.25 lbs. **Length:** 36.75". **Stock:** Walnut, straight grip, Schnabel forend. **Sights:** Adjustable rear, bead post front. **Features:** Lever action falling block, inertia firing pin system, Model 30G half octagonal bbl. Model 30GM full octagonal bbl.

Price: Model 30G $214.00

Price: Model 30GM $251.00

WINCHESTER MODEL 52B BOLT-ACTION RIFLE

Caliber: 22 Long Rifle, 5-shot magazine. **Barrel:** 24". **Weight:** 7 lbs. **Length:** 41-3/4" overall. **Stock:** Walnut with checkered grip and forend. **Sights:** None furnished; grooved receiver and drilled and tapped for scope mounting. **Features:** Has Micro Motion trigger adjustable for pull and over-travel; match chamber; detachable magazine. Reintroduced 1997. From U.S. Repeating Arms Co.

Price: $662.00

WINCHESTER MODEL 1885 LOW WALL RIMFIRE

Caliber: 22 LR, single-shot. **Barrel:** 24-1/2"; half-octagon. **Weight:** 8 lbs. **Length:** 41" overall. **Stock:** Walnut. **Sights:** Blade front, semi-buckhorn rear. **Features:** Drilled and tapped for scope mount or tang sight; target chamber. Limited production. From U.S. Repeating Arms Co.

Price: Grade I (2,400 made) $828.00

Price: High Grade (1,100 made; engraved/gold inlaid squirrel and rabbit) $1,180.00

Includes models for classic American and ISU target competition and other sporting and competitive shooting.

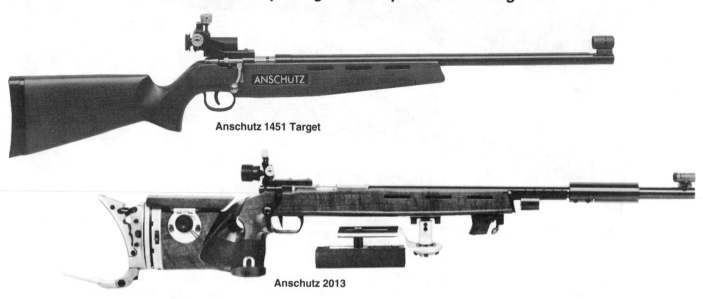

Anschutz 1451 Target

Anschutz 2013

ANSCHUTZ 1451R SPORTER TARGET RIFLE

Caliber: 22 LR, 5-shot magazine. **Barrel:** 22" heavy match. **Weight:** 6.4 lbs. **Length:** 39.75" overall. **Stock:** European hardwood with walnut finish. **Sights:** None furnished. Grooved receiver for scope mounting or Anschutz micrometer rear sight. **Features:** Sliding safety, two-stage trigger. Adjustable buttplate; forend slide rail to accept Anschutz accessories. Imported from Germany by AcuSport Corp.
Price: **$549.00**

ANSCHUTZ 1451 TARGET RIFLE

Caliber: 22 LR. **Barrel:** 22". **Weight:** About 6.5 lbs. **Length:** 40". **Sights:** Optional. Receiver grooved for scope mounting. **Features:** Designed for the beginning junior shooter with adjustable length of pull from 13.25" to 14.25" via removable butt spacers. Two-stage trigger factory set at 2.6 lbs. Introduced 1999. Imported from Germany by Gunsmithing, Inc.
Price: **$347.00**
Price: #6834 Match Sight Set............................ **$227.10**

ANSCHUTZ 1808D-RT SUPER RUNNING TARGET RIFLE

Caliber: 22 LR, single shot. **Barrel:** 32-1/2". **Weight:** 9 lbs. **Length:** 50" overall. **Stock:** European walnut. Heavy beavertail forend; adjustable cheekpiece and buttplate. Stippled grip and forend. **Sights:** None furnished. Grooved for scope mounting. **Features:** Designed for Running Target competition. Nine-way adjustable single-stage trigger, slide safety. Introduced 1991. Imported from Germany by Accuracy International, Gunsmithing, Inc.
Price: Right-hand **$1,364.10**

ANSCHUTZ 1903 MATCH RIFLE

Caliber: 22 LR, single shot. **Barrel:** 25.5", .75" diameter. **Weight:** 10.1 lbs. **Length:** 43.75" overall. **Stock:** Walnut-finished hardwood with adjustable cheekpiece; stippled grip and forend. **Sights:** None furnished. **Features:** Uses Anschutz Match 64 action and #5098 two-stage trigger. A medium weight rifle for intermediate and advanced Junior Match competition. Introduced 1987. Imported from Germany by Accuracy International, Gunsmithing, Inc.
Price: Right-hand **$720.40**
Price: Left-hand **$757.90**

ANSCHUTZ 64-MSR SILHOUETTE RIFLE

Caliber: 22 LR, 5-shot magazine. **Barrel:** 21-1/2", medium heavy; 7/8" diameter. **Weight:** 8 lbs. **Length:** 39.5" overall. **Stock:** Walnut-finished hardwood, silhouette-type. **Sights:** None furnished. **Features:** Uses Match 64 action. Designed for metallic silhouette competition. Stock has stippled checkering, contoured thumb groove with Wundhammer swell.

Two-stage #5098 trigger. Slide safety locks sear and bolt. Introduced 1980. Imported from Germany by AcuSport Corp., Accuracy International, Gunsmithing, Inc.
Price: 64-MSR **$704.30**

ANSCHUTZ 2013 BENCHREST RIFLE

Caliber: 22 LR, single shot. **Barrel:** 19.6". **Weight:** About 10.3 lbs. **Length:** 37.75" to 42.5" overall. **Stock:** Benchrest style of European hardwood. Stock length adjustable via spacers and buttplate. **Sights:** None furnished. Receiver grooved for mounts. **Features:** Uses the Anschutz 2013 target action, #5018 two-stage adjustable target trigger factory set at 3.9 oz. Introduced 1994. Imported from Germany by Accuracy International, Gunsmithing, Inc.
Price: **$1,757.20**

Anschutz 2007 Match Rifle

Uses same action as the Model 2013, but has a lighter barrel. European walnut stock in right-hand, true left-hand or extra-short models. Sights optional. Available with 19.6" barrel with extension tube, or 26", both in stainless or blue. Introduced 1998. Imported from Germany by Gunsmithing, Inc., Accuracy International.
Price: Right-hand, blue, no sights **$1,766.60**
Price: Right-hand, blue, no sights, extra-short stock **$1,756.60**
Price: Left-hand, blue, no sights........................ **$1,856.80**

ANSCHUTZ 1827 BIATHLON RIFLE

Caliber: 22 LR, 5-shot magazine. **Barrel:** 21-1/2". **Weight:** 8-1/2 lbs. with sights. **Length:** 42-1/2" overall. **Stock:** European walnut with cheekpiece, stippled pistol grip and forend. **Sights:** Optional globe front specially designed for Biathlon shooting, micrometer rear with hinged snow cap. **Features:** Uses Super Match 54 action and nine-way adjustable trigger; adjustable wooden buttplate, Biathlon butthook, adjustable hand-stop rail. Introduced 1982. Imported from Germany by Accuracy International, Gunsmithing, Inc.
Price: Right-hand, with sights, about .... **$1,500.50 to $1,555.00**

Anschutz 1827BT Fortner Biathlon Rifle

Similar to the Anschutz 1827 Biathlon rifle except uses Anschutz/Fortner system straight-pull bolt action, blued or stainless steel barrel. Introduced 1982. Imported from Germany by Accuracy International, Gunsmithing, Inc.
Price: Right-hand, with sights................. **$1,908.00 to $2,210.00**
Price: Left-hand, with sights .... **$2,099.20 to $2,395.00**
Price: Right-hand, sights, stainless barrel (Gunsmithing, Inc.).. **$2,045.20**

RIFLES

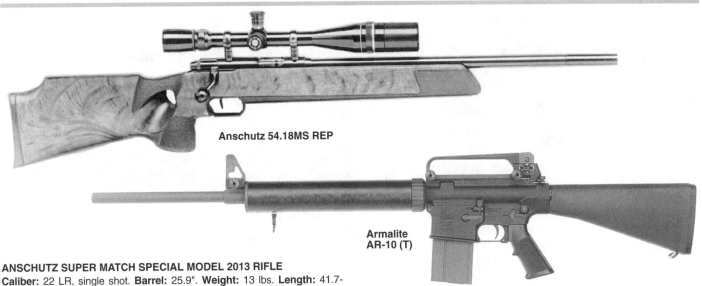

Anschutz 54.18MS REP

Armalite
AR-10 (T)

ANSCHUTZ SUPER MATCH SPECIAL MODEL 2013 RIFLE
Caliber: 22 LR, single shot. **Barrel:** 25.9". **Weight:** 13 lbs. **Length:** 41.7-42.9". **Stock:** A thumbhole version made of European walnut, both the cheekpiece and buttplate are highly adjustable. **Sights:** None furnished. **Features:** Developed by Anschütz for women to shoot in the sport rifle category. Stainless or blue. This top of the line rifle was introduced in 1997.
Price: Right-hand, blue, no sights, walnut **$2,219.30**
Price: Right-hand, stainless, no sights, walnut **$2,345.30**
Price: Left-hand, blue, no sights, walnut **$2,319.50**

ANSCHUTZ 2012 SPORT RIFLE
Caliber: 22 LR, 5-shot magazine. **Barrel:** 22.4" match; detachable muzzle tube. **Weight:** 7.9 lbs. **Length:** 40.9" overall. **Stock:** European walnut, thumbhole design. **Sights:** None furnished. **Features:** Uses Anschutz 54.18 action with two-stage match trigger. Introduced 1997. Imported from Germany by Accuracy International, AcuSport Corp.
Price: . . . . **$1,425.00 to $2,219.95**

ANSCHUTZ 1911 PRONE MATCH RIFLE
Caliber: 22 LR, single shot. **Barrel:** 27-1/4". **Weight:** 11 lbs. **Length:** 46" overall. **Stock:** Walnut-finished European hardwood; American prone-style with adjustable cheekpiece, textured pistol grip, forend with swivel rail and adjustable rubber buttplate. **Sights:** None furnished. Receiver grooved for Anschutz sights (extra). **Features:** Two-stage #5018 trigger adjustable from 2.1 to 8.6 oz. Extremely fast lock time. Stainless or blue barrel. Imported from Germany by Accuracy International, Gunsmithing, Inc.
Price: Right-hand, no sights **$1,714.20**

ANSCHUTZ 1912 SPORT RIFLE
Caliber: 22 LR, single shot. **Barrel:** 25.9". **Weight:** About 11.4 lbs. **Length:** 41.7-42.9". **Stock:** European walnut or aluminum. **Sights:** None furnished. **Features:** Light weight sport rifle version. Still uses the 54 match action like the 1913 but weighs 1.5 pounds less. Stainless or blue barrel. Introduced 1997.
Price: Right-hand, blue, no sights, walnut **$1,789.50**
Price: Right-hand, blue, no sights, aluminum **$2,129.80**
Price: Right-hand, stainless, no sights, walnut **$1,910.30**
Price: Left-hand, blue, no sights, walnut **$1,879.00**

ANSCHUTZ 1913 SUPER MATCH RIFLE
Caliber: 22 LR, single shot. **Barrel:** 27.1". **Weight:** About 14.3 lbs. **Length:** 44.8-46". **Stock:** European walnut, color laminate, or aluminum. **Sights:** None furnished. **Features:** Two-stage #5018 trigger. Extremely fast lock time. Stainless or blue barrel.
Price: Right-hand, blue, no sights, walnut stock **$2,262.90**
Price: Right-hand, blue, no sights, color laminate stock **$2,275.10**
Price: Right-hand, blue, no sights, aluminum stock **$2,262.90**
Price: Left-hand, blue, no sights, walnut stock **$2,382.20**

Anschutz 1913 Super Match Rifle
Same as the Model 1911 except European walnut International-type stock with adjustable cheekpiece, or color laminate, both available with straight or lowered forend, adjustable aluminum hook buttplate, adjustable hand stop, weighs 15.5 lbs., 46" overall. Stainless or blue barrel. Imported from Germany by Accuracy International, Gunsmithing, Inc.
Price: Right-hand, blue, no sights, walnut stock. . . **$2,139.00 to $2,175.00**
Price: Right-hand, blue, no sights, color laminate stock. **$2,199.40**
Price: Right-hand, blue, no sights, walnut, lowered forend **$2,181.80**
Price: Right-hand, blue, no sights, color laminate, lowered forend **$2,242.20**
Price: Left-hand, blue, no sights, walnut stock . . . **$2,233.10 to $2,275.00**

Anschutz 54.18MS REP Deluxe Silhouette Rifle
Same basic action and trigger specifications as the Anschutz 1913 Super Match but with removable 5-shot clip magazine, 22.4" barrel extendable to 30" using optional extension and weight set. Weight id 8.1 lbs. Receiver drilled and tapped for scope mounting. Stock is Thumbhole silhouette version or standard silhouette version, both are European walnut. Introduced 1990. Imported from Germany by Accuracy International, Gunsmithing, Inc.
Price: Thumbhole stock **$1,461.40**
Price: Standard stock **$1,212.10**

Anschutz 1907 Standard Match Rifle
Same action as Model 1913 but with 7/8" diameter 26" barrel (stainless or blue). Length is 44.5" overall, weighs 10.5 lbs. Choice of stock configurations. Vented forend. Designed for prone and position shooting ISU requirements; suitable for NRA matches. Also available with walnut flat-forend stock for benchrest shooting. Imported from Germany by Accuracy International, Gunsmithing, Inc.
Price: Right-hand, blue, no sights, hardwood stock **$1,253.40 to $1,299.00**
Price: Right-hand, blue, no sights, colored laminated stock . . . . **$1,316.10 to $1,375.00**
Price: Right-hand, blue, no sights, walnut stock. **$1,521.10**
Price: Left-hand, blue barrel, no sights, walnut stock. **$1,584.60**

ARMALITE AR-10 (T) RIFLE
Caliber: 308, 10-shot magazine. **Barrel:** 24" target-weight Rock 5R custom. **Weight:** 10.4 lbs. **Length:** 43.5" overall. **Stock:** Green or black compostion; N.M. fiberglass handguard tube. **Sights:** Detachable handle, front sight, or scope mount available. Comes with international-style flat-top receiver with Picatinny rail. **Features:** National Match two-stage trigger. Forged upper receiver. Receivers hard-coat anodized. Introduced 1995. Made in U.S.A. by ArmaLite, Inc.
Price: Green **$2,075.00**
Price: Black **$2,090.00**
Price: AR-10 (T) Carbine, lighter 16" barrel, single stage trigger, weighs 8.8 lbs. Green **$1,970.00**
Price: Black **$1,985.00**

RIFLES

Bushmaster XM15 E2S Target

Bushmaster DCM

Colt Match Target HBAR

ARMALITE M15A4 (T) EAGLE EYE RIFLE

Caliber: 223, 7-shot magazine. **Barrel:** 24" heavy stainless; 1:8" twist. **Weight:** 9.2 lbs. **Length:** 42-3/8" overall. **Stock:** Green or black butt, N.M. fiberglass handguard tube. **Sights:** One-piece international-style flattop receiver with Weaver-type rail, including case deflector. **Features:** Detachable carry handle, front sight and scope mount (30mm or 1") available. Upper and lower receivers have push-type pivot pin, hard coat anodized. Made in U.S.A. by ArmaLite, Inc.

Price: Green **$1,378.00**

Price: Black **$1,393.00**

ARMALITE M15A4 ACTION MASTER RIFLE

Caliber: 223, 7-shot magazine. **Barrel:** 20" heavy stainless; 1:9" twist. **Weight:** 9 lbs. **Length:** 40-1/2" overall. **Stock:** Green or black plastic; N.M. fiberglass handguard tube. **Sights:** One-piece international-style flattop receiver with Weaver-type rail. **Features:** Detachable carry handle, front sight and scope mount available. National Match two-stage trigger group; Picatinny rail; upper and lower receivers have push-type pivot pin; hard coat anodized finish. Made in U.S.A. by ArmaLite, Inc.

Price: **$1,175.00**

BLASER R93 LONG RANGE RIFLE

Caliber: 308 Win., 10-shot detachable box magazine. **Barrel:** 24". **Weight:** 10.4 lbs. **Length:** 44" overall. **Stock:** Aluminum with synthetic lining. **Sights:** None furnished; accepts detachable scope mount. **Features:** Straight-pull bolt action with adjustable trigger; fully adjustable stock; quick takedown; corrosion resistant finish. Introduced 1998. Imported from Germany by Sigarms.

Price: **$2,360.00**

BUSHMASTER XM15 E2S TARGET MODEL RIFLE

Caliber: 223. **Barrel:** 20", 24", 26"; 1:9" twist; heavy. **Weight:** 8.3 lbs. **Length:** 38.25" overall (20" barrel). **Stock:** Black composition; A2 type. **Sights:** Adjustable post front, adjustable aperture rear. **Features:** Patterned after Colt M-16A2. Chrome-lined barrel with manganese phosphate exterior. Forged aluminum receivers with push-pin takedown. Made in U.S.A. by Bushmaster Firearms Co./Quality Parts Co.

Price: 20" match heavy barrel **$965.00**

Bushmaster DCM Competition Rifle

Similar to the XM15 E2S Target Model except has 20" extra-heavy (1" diameter) barrel with 1.8" twist for heavier competition bullets. Weighs about 12 lbs. with balance weights. Has special competition rear sight with interchangeable apertures, extra-fine 1/2- or 1/4-MOA windage and elevation adjustments; specially ground front sight post in choice of three widths. Full-length handguards over free-floater barrel tube. Introduced 1998. Made in U.S.A. by Bushmaster Firearms, Inc.

Price: **$1,495.00**

BUSHMASTER XM15 E2S V-MATCH RIFLE

Caliber: 223. **Barrel:** 20", 24""; 1:9" twist; heavy. **Weight:** 8.1 lbs. **Length:** 38.25" overall (20" barrel). **Stock:** Black composition. A2 type. **Sights:** None furnished; upper receiver has integral scope mount base. **Features:** Chrome-lined .950" heavy barrel with counter-bored crown, manganese phosphate finish, free-floating aluminum handguard, forged aluminum receivers with push-pin takedown, hard anodized mil-spec finish. Competition trigger optional. Made in U.S.A. by Bushmaster Firearms, Inc.

Price: 20" Match heavy barrel **$1,030.00**

Price: 24" Match heavy barrel **$1,040.00**

Price: V-Match Carbine (16" barrel) **$1,015.00**

COLT MATCH TARGET MODEL RIFLE

Caliber: 223 Rem., 8-shot magazine. **Barrel:** 20". **Weight:** 7.5 lbs. **Length:** 39" overall. **Stock:** Composition stock, grip, forend. **Sights:** Post front, aperture rear adjustable for windage and elevation. **Features:** Five-round detachable box magazine, standard-weight barrel, sling swivels. Has forward bolt assist. Military matte black finish. Model introduced 1991.

Price: **$1,144.00**

Price: With compensator **$1,150.00**

Colt Accurized Rifle

Similar to the Colt Match Target Model except has 24" stainless steel heavy barrel with 1.9" rifling, flattop receiver with scope mount and 1" rings, weighs 9.25 lbs. Introduced 1998. Made in U.S.A. by Colt's Mfg. Co., Inc.

Price: **$1,424.00**

Colt Match Target HBAR Rifle

Similar to the Target Model except has heavy barrel, 800-meter rear sight adjustable for windage and elevation. Introduced 1991.

Price: **$1,194.00**

Colt Match Target Competition HBAR Rifle

Similar to the Sporter Target except has flat-top receiver with integral Weaver-type base for scope mounting. Counter-bored muzzle, 1:9" rifling twist. Introduced 1991.

Price: Model R6700 . . . . **$1,199.00**

EAA/IZHMASH URAL 5.1

EAA/IZHMASH Biathlon

EAA/IZHMASH Biathlon Target

Harris Gunworks Long Range

RIFLES

Colt Match Target Competition HBAR II Rifle

Similar to the Match Target Competition HBAR except has 16:1" barrel, weighs 7.1 lbs., overall length 34.5"; 1:9" twist barrel. Introduced 1995.

Price: **$1,172.00**

EAA/HW 660 MATCH RIFLE

Caliber: 22 LR. **Barrel:** 26". **Weight:** 10.7 lbs. **Length:** 45.3" overall. **Stock:** Match-type walnut with adjustable cheekpiece and buttplate. **Sights:** Globe front, match aperture rear. **Features:** Adjustable match trigger; stippled pistol grip and forend; forend accessory rail. Introduced 1991. Imported from Germany by European American Armory.

Price: About **$999.00**
Price: With laminate stock **$1,159.00**

EAA/IZHMASH URAL 5.1 TARGET RIFLE

Caliber: 22 LR. **Barrel:** 26.5". **Weight:** 11.3 lbs. **Length:** 44.5". **Stock:** Wood, international style. **Sights:** Adjustable click rear, hooded front with inserts. **Features:** Forged barrel with rifling, adjustable trigger, aluminum rail for accessories, hooked adjustable butt plate. Adjustable comb, adjustable large palm rest. Hand stippling on grip area.

Price: . . . . **NA**

EAA/Izhmash Biathlon Target Rifle

Similar to URAL with addition of snow covers for barrel and sights, stock holding extra mags, round trigger block. Unique bolt utilizes toggle action. Designed to compete in 40 meter biathlon event. 22 LR, 19.5" bbl.

Price: **$979.00**

EAA/Izhmash Biathalon Bacic Target Rifle

Same action as Biathlon but designed for plinking or fun. Beech stock, heavy barrel with Weaver rail for scope mount. 22 LR, 19.5" bbl.

Price: **$339.00**

HARRIS GUNWORKS NATIONAL MATCH RIFLE

Caliber: 7mm-08, 308, 5-shot magazine. **Barrel:** 24", stainless steel. **Weight:** About 11 lbs. (std. bbl.). **Length:** 43" overall. **Stock:** Fiberglass with adjustable buttplate. **Sights:** Barrel band and Tompkins front; no rear sight furnished. **Features:** Gunworks repeating action with clip slot, Canjar trigger. Match-grade barrel. Available in right-hand only. Fiberglass stock, sight installation, special machining and triggers optional. Introduced 1989. From Harris Gunworks, Inc.

Price: **$3,500.00**

HARRIS GUNWORKS LONG RANGE RIFLE

Caliber: 300 Win. Mag., 7mm Rem. Mag., 300 Phoenix, 338 Lapua, single shot. **Barrel:** 26", stainless steel, match-grade. **Weight:** 14 lbs. **Length:** 46-1/2" overall. **Stock:** Fiberglass with adjustable buttplate and cheekpiece. Adjustable for length of pull, drop, cant and cast-off. **Sights:** Barrel band and Tompkins front; no rear sight furnished. **Features:** Uses Gunworks solid bottom single shot action and Canjar trigger. Barrel twist 1:12". Introduced 1989. From Harris Gunworks, Inc.

Price: **$3,620.00**

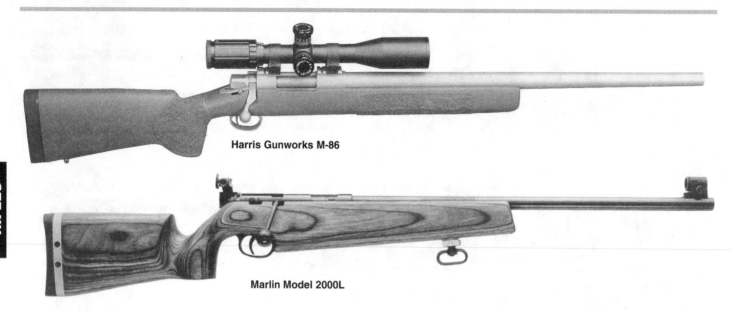

Harris Gunworks M-86

Marlin Model 2000L

HARRIS GUNWORKS M-86 SNIPER RIFLE

Caliber: 308, 30-06, 4-shot magazine; 300 Win. Mag., 3-shot magazine. **Barrel:** 24", Gunworks match-grade in heavy contour. **Weight:** 11-1/4 lbs. (308), 11-1/2 lbs. (30-06, 300). **Length:** 43-1/2 overall. **Stock:** Specially designed McHale fiberglass stock with textured grip and forend, recoil pad. **Sights:** None furnished. **Features:** Uses Gunworks repeating action. Comes with bipod. Matte black finish. Sling swivels. Introduced 1989. From Harris Gunworks, Inc.
Price: **$2,700.00**

HARRIS GUNWORKS M-89 SNIPER RIFLE

Caliber: 308 Win., 5-shot magazine. **Barrel:** 28" (with suppressor). **Weight:** 15 lbs., 4 oz. **Stock:** Fiberglass; adjustable for length; recoil pad. **Sights:** None furnished. Drilled and tapped for scope mounting. **Features:** Uses Gunworks repeating action. Comes with bipod. Introduced 1990. From Harris Gunworks, Inc.
Price: Standard (non-suppressed) **$3,200.00**

HARRIS GUNWORKS
COMBO M-87 SERIES 50-CALIBER RIFLES

Caliber: 50 BMG, single shot. **Barrel:** 29, with muzzle brake. **Weight:** About 21-1/2 lbs. **Length:** 53" overall. **Stock:** Gunworks fiberglass. **Sights:** None furnished. **Features:** Right-handed Gunworks stainless steel receiver, chrome-moly barrel with 1:15" twist. Introduced 1987. From Harris Gunworks, Inc.
Price: **$3,885.00**
Price: M87R 5-shot repeater **$4,000.00**
Price: M-87 (5-shot repeater) "Combo" **$4,300.00**
Price: M-92 Bullpup (shortened M-87 single shot with bullpup stock) **$4,770.00**
Price: M-93 (10-shot repeater with folding stock, detachable magazine)... **$4,150.00**

MARLIN MODEL 2000L TARGET RIFLE

Caliber: 22 LR, single shot. **Barrel:** 22" heavy, Micro-Groove® rifling, match chamber, recessed muzzle. **Weight:** 8 lbs. **Length:** 41" overall. **Stock:** Laminated black/gray with ambidextrous pistol grip. **Sights:** Hooded front with ten aperture inserts, fully adjustable target rear peep. **Features:** Buttplate adjustable for length of pull, height and angle. Aluminum forend rail with stop and quick-detachable swivel. Two-stage target trigger; red cocking indicator. Five-shot adaptor kit available. Introduced 1991. From Marlin.
Price: **$745.00**

OLYMPIC ARMS PCR-SERVICEMATCH RIFLE

Caliber: 223, 10-shot magazine. **Barrel:** 20", broach-cut 416 stainless steel. **Weight:** About 10 lbs. **Length:** 39.5" overall. **Stock:** A2 stowaway grip and trapdoor buttstock. **Sights:** Post front, E2-NM fully adjustable aperture rear. **Features:** Based on the AR-15. Conforms to all DCM standards. Free-floating 1:8.5" or 1:10" barrel; crowned barrel; no bayonet lug. Introduced 1996. Made in U.S.A. by Olympic Arms, Inc.
Price: **$1,062.00**

OLYMPIC ARMS PCR-1 RIFLE

Caliber: 223, 10-shot magazine. **Barrel:** 20", 24"; 416 stainless steel. **Weight:** 10 lbs., 3 oz. **Length:** 38.25" overall with 20" barrel. **Stock:** A2 stowaway grip and trapdoor butt. **Sights:** None supplied; flattop upper receiver, cut-down front sight base. **Features:** Based on the AR-15 rifle. Broach-cut, free-floating barrel with 1:8.5" or 1:10" twist. No bayonet lug. Crowned barrel; fluting available. Introduced 1994. Made in U.S.A. by Olympic Arms, Inc.
Price: **$1,038.00**

Olympic Arms PCR-2, PCR-3 Rifles

Similar to the PCR-1 except has 16" barrel, weighs 8 lbs., 2 oz.; has post front sight, fully adjustable aperture rear. Model PCR-3 has flattop upper receiver, cut-down front sight base. Introduced 1994. Made in U.S.A. by Olympic Arms, Inc.
Price: **$958.00**

REMINGTON 40-XB RANGEMASTER TARGET CENTERFIRE

Caliber: 15 calibers from 220 Swift to 300 Win. Mag. **Barrel:** 27-1/4". **Weight:** 11-1/4 lbs. **Length:** 47" overall. **Stock:** American walnut, laminated thumbhole or Kevlar with high comb and beavertail forend stop. Rubber non-slip buttplate. **Sights:** None. Scope blocks installed. **Features:** Adjustable trigger. Stainless barrel and action. Receiver drilled and tapped for sights.
Price: Standard single shot **$1,612.00**
Price: Repeater **$1,734.00**

REMINGTON 40-XBBR KS

Caliber: Five calibers from 22 BR to 308 Win. **Barrel:** 20" (light varmint class), 24" (heavy varmint class). **Weight:** 7-1/4 lbs. (light varmint class); 12 lbs. (heavy varmint class). **Length:** 38" (20" bbl.), 42" (24" bbl.). **Stock:** Aramid fiber. **Sights:** None. Supplied with scope blocks. **Features:** Un-blued benchrest with stainless steel barrel, trigger adjustable from 1-1/2 lbs. to 3-1/2 lbs. Special 2-oz. trigger extra cost. Scope and mounts extra.
Price: Single shot **$1,848.00**

REMINGTON 40-XCKS TARGET RIFLE

Caliber: 7.62 NATO, 5-shot. **Barrel:** 24", stainless steel. **Weight:** 11 lbs. without sights. **Length:** 43-1/2" overall. **Stock:** Aramid fiber. **Sights:** None furnished. **Features:** Designed to meet the needs of competitive shooters. Stainless steel barrel and action.
Price: **$1,794.00**

Springfield, Inc. M1A Super Match

Springfield, Inc.
M1A/M-21

REMINGTON 40-XR CUSTOM SPORTER

Caliber: 22 LR, 22 WM. **Features:** Model XR-40 Target rifle action with craftsmanship of Model 700 Custom. Many options available.
Price: Single shot **$3,333.00**

SAKO TRG-22 BOLT-ACTION RIFLE

Caliber: 308 Win., 10-shot magazine. **Barrel:** 26". **Weight:** 10-1/4 lbs. **Length:** 45-1/4" overall. **Stock:** Reinforced polyurethane with fully adjustable cheekpiece and buttplate. **Sights:** None furnished. Optional quick-detachable, one-piece scope mount base, 1" or 30mm rings. **Features:** Resistance-free bolt, free-floating heavy stainless barrel, 60-degree bolt lift. Two-stage trigger is adjustable for length, pull, horizontal or vertical pitch. Introduced 2000. Imported from Finland by Beretta USA.
Price: Green **$2,484.00**
Price: Model TRG-42, as above except in 338 Lapua Mag or 300
Win. Mag. **$2,829.00**
Price: Green (new) **$3,243.00**

SPRINGFIELD, INC. M1A SUPER MATCH

Caliber: 308 Win. **Barrel:** 22", heavy Douglas Premium. **Weight:** About 11 lbs. **Length:** 44.31" overall. **Stock:** Heavy walnut competition stock with longer pistol grip, contoured area behind the rear sight, thicker butt and forend, glass bedded. **Sights:** National Match front and rear. **Features:** Has figure-eight-style operating rod guide. Introduced 1987. From Springfield, Inc.
Price: About **$2,479.00**

Springfield, Inc. M1A/M-21 Tactical Model Rifle

Similar to M1A Super Match except special sniper stock with adjustable cheekpiece and rubber recoil pad. Weighs 11.6 lbs. From Springfield, Inc.
Price: **$2,975.00**

SPRINGFIELD, INC. M-1 GARAND AMERICAN COMBAT RIFLES

Caliber: 30-06, 308 Win., 8-shot. **Barrel:** 24". **Weight:** 9.5 lbs. **Length:** 43.6". **Stock:** American walnut. **Sights:** Military square post front, military aperture, MOA adjustable rear. **Features:** Limited production, certificate of authenticity, all new receiver, barrel and stock wtih remaining parts USGI mil-spec. 2-stage military trigger.
Price: About **$2,479.00**

STONER SR-15 MATCH RIFLE

Caliber: 223. **Barrel:** 20". **Weight:** 7.9 lbs. **Length:** 38" overall. **Stock:** Black synthetic. **Sights:** None furnished; flat-top upper receiver for scope mounting. **Features:** Short Picatinny rail, two-stage match trigger. Introduced 1998. Made in U.S.A. by Knight's Mfg.Co.
Price: **$1,650.00**

STONER SR-25 MATCH RIFLE

Caliber: 7.62 NATO, 10-shot steel magazine, 5-shot optional. **Barrel:** 24" heavy match; 1:11.25" twist. **Weight:** 10.75 lbs. **Length:** 44" overall.

Stock: Black synthetic AR-15A2 design. Full floating forend of Mil-spec synthetic attaches to upper receiver at a single point. **Sights:** None furnished. Has integral Weaver-style rail. Rings and iron sights optional. **Features:** Improved AR-15 trigger, AR-15-style seven-lug rotating bolt. Gas block rail mounts detachable front sight. Introduced 1993. Made in U.S.A. by Knight's Mfg. Co.
Price: **$3,345.00**
Price: SR-25 Lightweight Match (20" medium match target
contour barrel, 9.5 lbs., 40" overall) **$3,345.00**

TANNER 50 METER FREE RIFLE

Caliber: 22 LR, single shot. **Barrel:** 27.7". **Weight:** 13.9 lbs. **Length:** 44.4" overall. **Stock:** Seasoned walnut with palm rest, accessory rail, adjustable hook buttplate. **Sights:** Globe front with interchangeable inserts, Tanner micrometer-diopter rear with adjustable aperture. **Features:** Bolt action with externally adjustable set trigger. Supplied with 50-meter test target. Imported from Switzerland by Mandall Shooting Supplies. Introduced 1984.
Price: About **$3,900.00**

TANNER STANDARD UIT RIFLE

Caliber: 308, 7.5mm Swiss, 10-shot. **Barrel:** 25.9". **Weight:** 10.5 lbs. **Length:** 40.6" overall. **Stock:** Match style of seasoned nutwood with accessory rail; coarsely stippled pistol grip; high cheekpiece; vented forend. **Sights:** Globe front with interchangeable inserts, Tanner micrometer-diopter rear with adjustable aperture. **Features:** Two locking lug revolving bolt encloses case head. Trigger adjustable from 1/2 to 6-1/2 lbs., match trigger optional. Comes with 300-meter test target. Imported from Switzerland by Mandall Shooting Supplies. Introduced 1984.
Price: About **$4,700.00**

TANNER 300 METER FREE RIFLE

Caliber: 308 Win., 7.5 Swiss, single shot. **Barrel:** 27.58". **Weight:** 15 lbs. **Length:** 45.3" overall. **Stock:** Seasoned walnut, thumbhole style, with accessory rail, palm rest, adjustable hook butt. **Sights:** Globe front with interchangeable inserts, Tanner-design micrometer-diopter rear with adjustable aperture. **Features:** Three-lug revolving-lock bolt design, adjustable set trigger; short firing pin travel, supplied with 300-meter test target. Imported from Switzerland by Mandall Shooting Supplies. Introduced 1984.
Price: About **$4,900.00**

TIKKA SPORTER RIFLE

Caliber: 223, 22-250, 308, detachable 5-shot magazine. **Barrel:** 23-1/2" heavy. **Weight:** 9 lbs. **Length:** 43-5/8" overall. **Stock:** European walnut with adjustable comb, adjustable buttplate; stippled grip and forend. **Sights:** None furnished; drilled and tapped for scope mounting. **Features:** Buttplate adjustable for distance, angle, height and pitch, adjustable trigger, free-floating barrel. Introduced 1998. Imported from Finland by Beretta USA.
Price: **$950.00**

Includes a wide variety of sporting guns and guns suitable for various competitions.

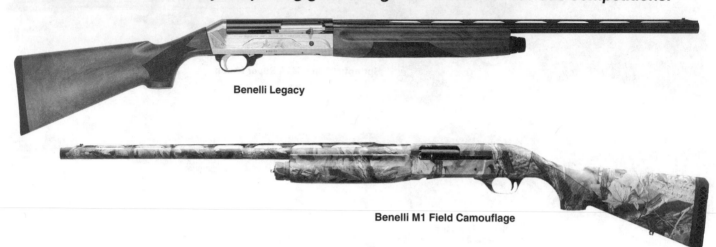

Benelli Legacy

Benelli M1 Field Camouflage

Benelli Super Black Eagle

BENELLI LEGACY SHOTGUN
Gauge: 12, 20, 2-3/4" and 3" chamber. **Barrel:** 24", 26", 28" (Full, Mod., Imp. Cyl., Imp. Mod., cylinder choke tubes). Mid-bead sight. **Weight:** 5.8 to 7.6 lbs. **Length:** 49-5/8" overall (28" barrel). **Stock:** Select European walnut with satin finish. **Features:** Uses the rotating bolt inertia recoil operating system with a two-piece steel/aluminum etched receiver (bright on lower, blue upper). Drop adjustment kit allows the stock to be custom fitted without modifying the stock. Introduced 1998. Imported from Italy by Benelli USA, Corp.
Price: **$1,390.00**

Benelli Sport Shotgun
Similar to the Legacy model except has matte blue receiver, two carbon fiber interchangeable ventilated ribs, adjustable butt pad, adjustable buttstock, and functions with ultra-light target loads. Walnut stock with satin finish. Introduced 1997. Imported from Italy by Benelli U.S.A.
Price: **$1,375.00**

BENELLI M1 FIELD SHOTGUN
Gauge: 12, 20 ga. **Barrel:** 21", 24", 26", 28". **Weight:** 7 lbs., 4 oz. **Stock:** High impact polymer; wood on 26", 28". **Sights:** Red bar. **Features:** Sporting version of the military & police gun. Uses the rotating Montefeltro bolt system. Ventilated rib; blue finish. Comes with set of five choke tubes. Imported from Italy by Benelli U.S.A.
Price: Synthetic stock version. **$970.00**
Price: Wood stock version **$980.00**
Price: 24" rifled barrel, polymer stock. **$1,040.00**
Price: 24" rifled barrel, camo stock **$1,150.00**
Price: Synthetic stock, left-hand version (24", 26", 28" brls.) **$990.00**
Price: Timber HD camo left-hand, 21", 24" barrel **$1,190.00**

Benelli Montefeltro Shotgun
Similar to the M1 Super except has checkered walnut stock with satin finish. Uses the Montefeltro rotating bolt system with a simple inertia recoil design. Full, Imp. Mod., Mod., Imp. Cyl. choke tubes. Weighs 6.8-7.1 lbs. Finish is blue. Introduced 1987.
Price: 24", 26", 28" **$980.00**
Price: Left-hand, 26", 28" **$995.00**

Price: Timber HD Camo, 21", 24" barrel **$1,070.00**
Price: 20 ga., 24", 26" brl. syn. **$970.00**

BENELLI MONTEFELTRO SHOTGUN
Gauge: 12, 20 ga., 2-3/4" and 3" chamber. **Barrel:** 24", 26", 28" with 5 choke tubes. **Stock:** Satin walnut. **Sights:** Red bar. **Features:** L:ight-weight, one-piece receiver. Ideal Upland gun.
Price: 12 ga., 20 ga. **$980.00**
Price: Left-hand 26", 28", 12 ga. **$995.00**
Price: 20 ga. short stock **$1,015.00**

BENELLI SUPER BLACK EAGLE SHOTGUN
Gauge: 12, 3-1/2" chamber. **Barrel:** 24", 26", 28" (Cyl. Imp. Cyl., Mod., Imp. Mod., Full choke tubes). **Weight:** 7 lbs., 5 oz. **Length:** 49-5/8" overall (28" barrel). **Stock:** European walnut with satin finish, or polymer. Adjustable for drop. **Sights:** Red bar front. **Features:** Uses Montefeltro inertia recoil bolt system. Fires all 12 gauge shells from 2-3/4" to 3-1/2" magnums, vent rib. Introduced 1991. Imported from Italy by Benelli U.S.A.
Price: With 26" and 28" barrel, wood stock **$1,275.00**
Price: Timber HD Camo 24", 26", 28" barrel **$1,360.00**
Price: With 24", 26" and 28" barrel, polymer stock. **$1,260.00**
Price: Left-hand, 24", 26", 28", polymer stock **$1,310.00**
Price: Left-hand, 24", 26", 28", camo stock **$1,415.00**

Benelli Super Black Eagle Slug Gun
Similar to the Benelli Super Black Eagle except has 24" rifled barrel with 2-3/4" and 3" chamber, drilled and tapped for scope. Uses the inertia recoil bolt system. Matte-finish receiver. Weight is 7.5 lbs., overall length 45.5". Wood or polymer stocks available. Introduced 1992. Imported from Italy by Benelli U.S.A.
Price: With wood stock. **$1,335.00**
Price: With polymer stock. **$1,320.00**
Price: 24" barrel, Timber HD Camo **$1,450.00**

Benelli Executive Series Shotguns
Similar to the Legacy except has grayed steel lower receiver, hand-engraved and gold inlaid (Grade III), and has highest grade of walnut stock with drop adjustment kit. Barrel lengths 26" or 28"; 2-3/4" and 3" chamber. Special order only. Introduced 1995. Imported from Italy by Benelli U.S.A.
Price: Grade I (engraved game scenes) **$5,200.00**
Price: Grade II (game scenes with scroll engraving) **$5,870.00**
Price: Grade III (full coverage, gold inlays) **$6,800.00**

SHOTGUNS

Beretta Urika Gold Sporting

Beretta Urika Sporting

Beretta Urika Gold Trap

Beretta A391 Xtreme

BERETTA AL391 URIKA AUTO SHOTGUNS

Gauge: 12, 20 gauge; 3" chamber. **Barrel:** 22", 24", 26", 28", 30"; five Mobilchoke choke tubes. **Weight:** 5.95 to 7.28 lbs. **Length:** Varies by model. **Stock:** Walnut, black or camo synthetic; shims, spacers and interchangeable recoil pads allow custom fit. **Features:** Self-compensating gas operation handles full range of loads; recoil reducer in receiver; enlarged trigger guard; reduced-weight receiver, barrel and forend; hard-chromed bore. Introduced 2000. Imported from Italy by Beretta USA.

Price: AL391 Urika (12 ga., 26", 28", 30" barrels) **$984.00**
Price: AL391 Urika (20 ga., 24", 26", 28" barrels) **$984.00**
Price: AL391 Urika Synthetic (12 ga., 24", 26", 28", 30" barrels) **$984.00**
Price: AL391 Urika Camo. (12 ga., Realtree Hardwoods
or Advantage Wetlands) **$1,083.00**

Beretta AL391 Urika Gold and Gold Sporting Auto Shotguns

Similar to AL391 Urika except features deluxe wood, jeweled bolt and carrier, gold-inlaid receiver with black or silver finish. Introduced 2000. Imported from Italy by Beretta USA.

Price: AL391 Urika Gold (12 or 20 ga., black receiver) **$1,213.00**
Price: AL391 Urika Gold (silver, lightweight receiver). **$1,254.00**
Price: AL391 Urika Gold Sporting (12 or 20, black receiver, engraving)
. . . . **$1,254.00**
Price: AL391 Urika Gold Sporting (12 ga., silver receiver, engraving)
. . . . **$1,296.00**

Beretta AL391 Urika Sporting Auto Shotguns

Similar to AL391 Urika except has competition sporting stock with rounded rubber recoil pad, wide ventilated rib with white front and mid-rib beads, satin-black receiver with silver markings. Available in 12 and 20 gauge. Introduced 2000. Imported from Italy by Beretta USA.

Price: AL391 Urika Sporting. **$1,027.00**

Beretta AL391 Urika Trap and Gold Trap Auto Shotguns

Similar to AL391 Urika except in 12 ga. only, has wide ventilated rib with white front and mid-rib beads, Monte Carlo stock and special trap recoil pad. Gold Trap features highly figured walnut stock and forend, gold-filled Beretta logo and signature on receiver. Introduced 2000. Imported from Italy by Beretta USA.

Price: AL391 Urika Trap **$1,027.00**
Price: AL391 Urika Gold Trap **$1,254.00**

Beretta AL391 Urika Parallel Target RL and SL Auto Shotguns

Similar to AL391 Urika except has parallel-comb, Monte Carlo stock with tighter grip radius to reduce trigger reach and stepped ventilated rib. SL model has same features but with 13.5" length of pull stock. Introduced 2000. Imported from Italy by Beretta USA.

Price: AL391 Urika Parallel Target RL **$1,027.00**
Price: AL391 Urika Parallel Target SL **$1,027.00**

Beretta AL391 Urika Youth Shotgun

Similar to AL391 except has a 24" or 26" barrel with 13.5" stock for youth and smaller shooters. Introduced 2000. From Beretta USA.

Price: **$984.00**

Beretta ES100 Auto Shotguns

Similar to the ES100 MWTF model except offered with walnut, black synthetic or camouflage stock and fully rifled slug barrel model. Recoil-operated action. Imported from Italy by Beretta U.S.A.

Price: ES100 Pintail (24", 26" or 28" bbl., black synthetic stock) . . **$725.00**
Price: ES100 Camouflage (28" bbl., Advantage Wetlands camo stock)
. . . . **$766.00**
Price: ES100 Rifled Slug Combo (24" rifled and 28" smoothbore bbls.)
. . . . **$932.00**

BERETTA A391 XTREME 3.5 AUTO SHOTGUNS

Gauge: 12 ga. 3-1/2" chamber. **Barrel:** 24", 26", 28". **Weight:** 7.8 lbs. **Stock:** Synthetic. **Features:** Semi-auto goes with two-lug rotating bolt and self-compensating gas valve, extended tang, cross bolt safety, self-cleaning, with case.

Price: Synthetic **$1,129.00**
Price: Realtree Hardwood HD Camo **$1,241.00**

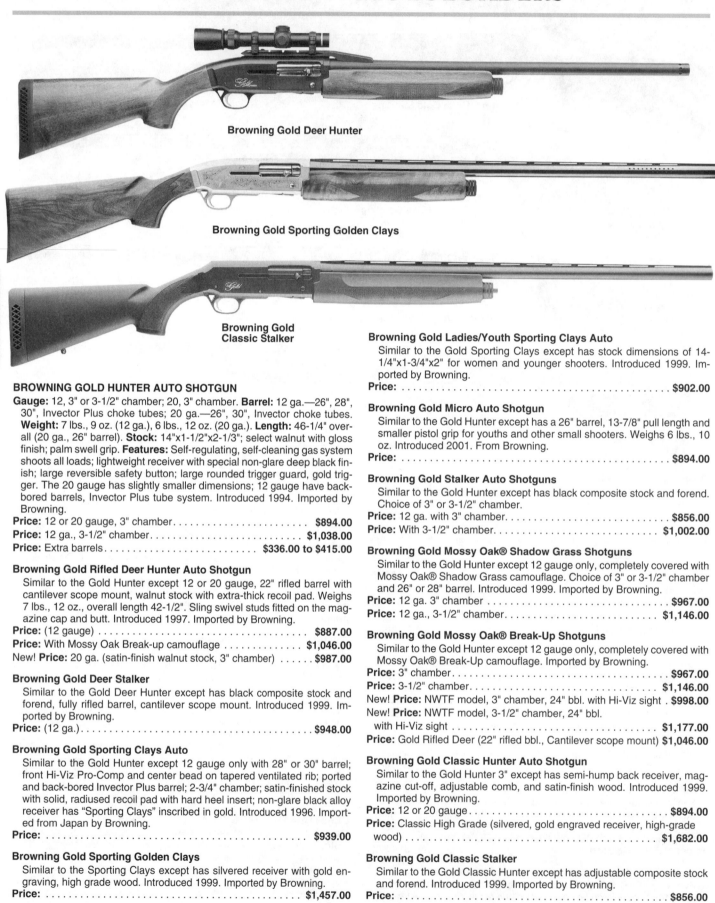

Browning Gold Deer Hunter

Browning Gold Sporting Golden Clays

Browning Gold Classic Stalker

BROWNING GOLD HUNTER AUTO SHOTGUN

Gauge: 12, 3" or 3-1/2" chamber; 20, 3" chamber. **Barrel:** 12 ga.—26", 28", 30", Invector Plus choke tubes; 20 ga.—26", 30", Invector choke tubes. **Weight:** 7 lbs., 9 oz. (12 ga.), 6 lbs., 12 oz. (20 ga.). **Length:** 46-1/4" overall (20 ga., 26" barrel). **Stock:** 14"x1-1/2"x2-1/3"; select walnut with gloss finish; palm swell grip. **Features:** Self-regulating, self-cleaning gas system shoots all loads; lightweight receiver with special non-glare deep black finish; large reversible safety button; large rounded trigger guard, gold trigger. The 20 gauge has slightly smaller dimensions; 12 gauge have back-bored barrels, Invector Plus tube system. Introduced 1994. Imported by Browning.

Price: 12 or 20 gauge, 3" chamber. $894.00
Price: 12 ga., 3-1/2" chamber. $1,038.00
Price: Extra barrels. . . . . $336.00 to $415.00

Browning Gold Rifled Deer Hunter Auto Shotgun

Similar to the Gold Hunter except 12 or 20 gauge, 22" rifled barrel with cantilever scope mount, walnut stock with extra-thick recoil pad. Weighs 7 lbs., 12 oz., overall length 42-1/2". Sling swivel studs fitted on the magazine cap and butt. Introduced 1997. Imported by Browning.

Price: (12 gauge) $887.00
Price: With Mossy Oak Break-up camouflage $1,046.00
New! **Price:** 20 ga. (satin-finish walnut stock, 3" chamber) $987.00

Browning Gold Deer Stalker

Similar to the Gold Deer Hunter except has black composite stock and forend, fully rifled barrel, cantilever scope mount. Introduced 1999. Imported by Browning.

Price: (12 ga.) $948.00

Browning Gold Sporting Clays Auto

Similar to the Gold Hunter except 12 gauge only with 28" or 30" barrel; front Hi-Viz Pro-Comp and center bead on tapered ventilated rib; ported and back-bored Invector Plus barrel; 2-3/4" chamber; satin-finished stock with solid, radiused recoil pad with hard heel insert; non-glare black alloy receiver has "Sporting Clays" inscribed in gold. Introduced 1996. Imported from Japan by Browning.

Price: $939.00

Browning Gold Sporting Golden Clays

Similar to the Sporting Clays except has silvered receiver with gold engraving, high grade wood. Introduced 1999. Imported by Browning.

Price: $1,457.00

Browning Gold Ladies/Youth Sporting Clays Auto

Similar to the Gold Sporting Clays except has stock dimensions of 14-1/4"x1-3/4"x2" for women and younger shooters. Introduced 1999. Imported by Browning.

Price: $902.00

Browning Gold Micro Auto Shotgun

Similar to the Gold Hunter except has a 26" barrel, 13-7/8" pull length and smaller pistol grip for youths and other small shooters. Weighs 6 lbs., 10 oz. Introduced 2001. From Browning.

Price: $894.00

Browning Gold Stalker Auto Shotguns

Similar to the Gold Hunter except has black composite stock and forend. Choice of 3" or 3-1/2" chamber.

Price: 12 ga. with 3" chamber. $856.00
Price: With 3-1/2" chamber. $1,002.00

Browning Gold Mossy Oak® Shadow Grass Shotguns

Similar to the Gold Hunter except 12 gauge only, completely covered with Mossy Oak® Shadow Grass camouflage. Choice of 3" or 3-1/2" chamber and 26" or 28" barrel. Introduced 1999. Imported by Browning.

Price: 12 ga. 3" chamber $967.00
Price: 12 ga., 3-1/2" chamber. $1,146.00

Browning Gold Mossy Oak® Break-Up Shotguns

Similar to the Gold Hunter except 12 gauge only, completely covered with Mossy Oak® Break-Up camouflage. Imported by Browning.

Price: 3" chamber. $967.00
Price: 3-1/2" chamber. $1,146.00
New! **Price:** NWTF model, 3" chamber, 24" bbl. with Hi-Viz sight . $998.00
New! **Price:** NWTF model, 3-1/2" chamber, 24" bbl.
with Hi-Viz sight $1,177.00
Price: Gold Rifled Deer (22" rifled bbl., Cantilever scope mount) $1,046.00

Browning Gold Classic Hunter Auto Shotgun

Similar to the Gold Hunter 3" except has semi-hump back receiver, magazine cut-off, adjustable comb, and satin-finish wood. Introduced 1999. Imported by Browning.

Price: 12 or 20 gauge $894.00
Price: Classic High Grade (silvered, gold engraved receiver, high-grade wood) $1,682.00

Browning Gold Classic Stalker

Similar to the Gold Classic Hunter except has adjustable composite stock and forend. Introduced 1999. Imported by Browning.

Price: $856.00

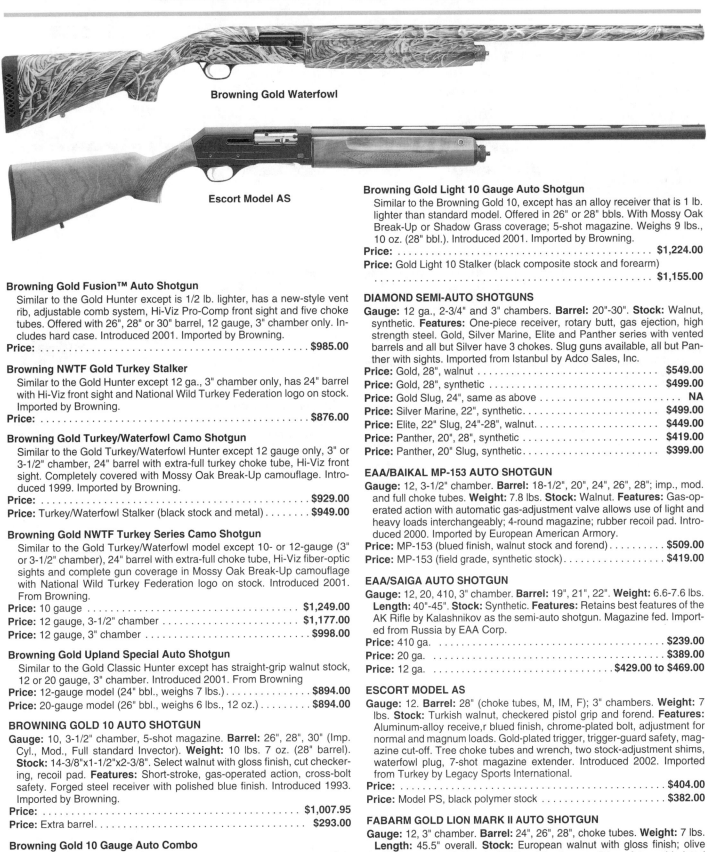

Browning Gold Waterfowl

Escort Model AS

Browning Gold Fusion™ Auto Shotgun

Similar to the Gold Hunter except is 1/2 lb. lighter, has a new-style vent rib, adjustable comb system, Hi-Viz Pro-Comp front sight and five choke tubes. Offered with 26", 28" or 30" barrel, 12 gauge, 3" chamber only. Includes hard case. Introduced 2001. Imported by Browning.
Price: **$985.00**

Browning NWTF Gold Turkey Stalker

Similar to the Gold Hunter except 12 ga., 3" chamber only, has 24" barrel with Hi-Viz front sight and National Wild Turkey Federation logo on stock. Imported by Browning.
Price: **$876.00**

Browning Gold Turkey/Waterfowl Camo Shotgun

Similar to the Gold Turkey/Waterfowl Hunter except 12 gauge only, 3" or 3-1/2" chamber, 24" barrel with extra-full turkey choke tube, Hi-Viz front sight. Completely covered with Mossy Oak Break-Up camouflage. Introduced 1999. Imported by Browning.
Price: **$929.00**
Price: Turkey/Waterfowl Stalker (black stock and metal) **$949.00**

Browning Gold NWTF Turkey Series Camo Shotgun

Similar to the Gold Turkey/Waterfowl model except 10- or 12-gauge (3" or 3-1/2" chamber), 24" barrel with extra-full choke tube, Hi-Viz fiber-optic sights and complete gun coverage in Mossy Oak Break-Up camouflage with National Wild Turkey Federation logo on stock. Introduced 2001. From Browning.
Price: 10 gauge **$1,249.00**
Price: 12 gauge, 3-1/2" chamber **$1,177.00**
Price: 12 gauge, 3" chamber **$998.00**

Browning Gold Upland Special Auto Shotgun

Similar to the Gold Classic Hunter except has straight-grip walnut stock, 12 or 20 gauge, 3" chamber. Introduced 2001. From Browning
Price: 12-gauge model (24" bbl., weighs 7 lbs.) **$894.00**
Price: 20-gauge model (26" bbl., weighs 6 lbs., 12 oz.) **$894.00**

BROWNING GOLD 10 AUTO SHOTGUN

Gauge: 10, 3-1/2" chamber, 5-shot magazine. **Barrel:** 26", 28", 30" (Imp. Cyl., Mod., Full standard Invector). **Weight:** 10 lbs. 7 oz. (28" barrel). **Stock:** 14-3/8"x1-1/2"x2-3/8". Select walnut with gloss finish, cut checkering, recoil pad. **Features:** Short-stroke, gas-operated action, cross-bolt safety. Forged steel receiver with polished blue finish. Introduced 1993. Imported by Browning.
Price: **$1,007.95**
Price: Extra barrel. **$293.00**

Browning Gold 10 Gauge Auto Combo

Similar to the Gold 10 except comes with 24" and 26" barrels with Imp. Cyl., Mod., Full Invector choke tubes. Introduced 1999. Imported by Browning.
Price: **$1,059.00**

Browning Gold Light 10 Gauge Auto Shotgun

Similar to the Browning Gold 10, except has an alloy receiver that is 1 lb. lighter than standard model. Offered in 26" or 28" bbls. With Mossy Oak Break-Up or Shadow Grass coverage; 5-shot magazine. Weighs 9 lbs., 10 oz. (28" bbl.). Introduced 2001. Imported by Browning.
Price: **$1,224.00**
Price: Gold Light 10 Stalker (black composite stock and forearm)
. . . . **$1,155.00**

DIAMOND SEMI-AUTO SHOTGUNS

Gauge: 12 ga., 2-3/4" and 3" chambers. **Barrel:** 20"-30". **Stock:** Walnut, synthetic. **Features:** One-piece receiver, rotary butt, gas ejection, high strength steel. Gold, Silver Marine, Elite and Panther series with vented barrels and all but Silver have 3 chokes. Slug guns available, all but Panther with sights. Imported from Istanbul by Adco Sales, Inc.
Price: Gold, 28", walnut **$549.00**
Price: Gold, 28", synthetic **$499.00**
Price: Gold Slug, 24", same as above . . . . **NA**
Price: Silver Marine, 22", synthetic. **$499.00**
Price: Elite, 22" Slug, 24"-28", walnut **$449.00**
Price: Panther, 20", 28", synthetic **$419.00**
Price: Panther, 20" Slug, synthetic. **$399.00**

EAA/BAIKAL MP-153 AUTO SHOTGUN

Gauge: 12, 3-1/2" chamber. **Barrel:** 18-1/2", 20", 24", 26", 28"; imp., mod. and full choke tubes. **Weight:** 7.8 lbs. **Stock:** Walnut. **Features:** Gas-operated action with automatic gas-adjustment valve allows use of light and heavy loads interchangeably; 4-round magazine; rubber recoil pad. Introduced 2000. Imported by European American Armory.
Price: MP-153 (blued finish, walnut stock and forend) **$509.00**
Price: MP-153 (field grade, synthetic stock) **$419.00**

EAA/SAIGA AUTO SHOTGUN

Gauge: 12, 20, 410, 3" chamber. **Barrel:** 19", 21", 22". **Weight:** 6.6-7.6 lbs. **Length:** 40"-45". **Stock:** Synthetic. **Features:** Retains best features of the AK Rifle by Kalashnikov as the semi-auto shotgun. Magazine fed. Imported from Russia by EAA Corp.
Price: 410 ga. **$239.00**
Price: 20 ga. **$389.00**
Price: 12 ga. . . . . **$429.00 to $469.00**

ESCORT MODEL AS

Gauge: 12. **Barrel:** 28" (choke tubes, M, IM, F); 3" chambers. **Weight:** 7 lbs. **Stock:** Turkish walnut, checkered pistol grip and forend. **Features:** Aluminum-alloy receive,r blued finish, chrome-plated bolt, adjustment for normal and magnum loads. Gold-plated trigger, trigger-guard safety, magazine cut-off. Tree choke tubes and wrench, two stock-adjustment shims, waterfowl plug, 7-shot magazine extender. Introduced 2002. Imported from Turkey by Legacy Sports International.
Price: **$404.00**
Price: Model PS, black polymer stock **$382.00**

FABARM GOLD LION MARK II AUTO SHOTGUN

Gauge: 12, 3" chamber. **Barrel:** 24", 26", 28", choke tubes. **Weight:** 7 lbs. **Length:** 45.5" overall. **Stock:** European walnut with gloss finish; olive wood grip cap. **Features:** TriBore barrel, reversible safety; gold-plated trigger and carrier release button; leather-covered rubber recoil pad. Introduced 1998. Imported from Italy by Heckler & Koch, Inc.
Price: **$849.00**

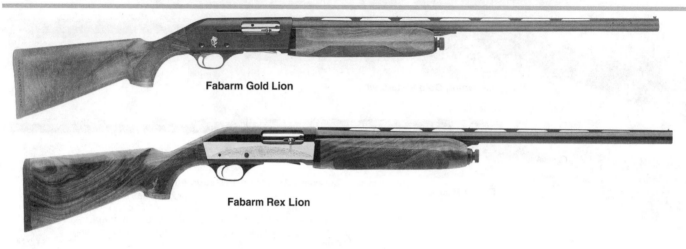

Fabarm Gold Lion

Fabarm Rex Lion

Remington Model 11-87 Premier

Fabarm Camo Lion Auto Shotgun

Similar to Gold Lion except 24", 26" or 28" ported TriBore barrel system with five choke tubes, completely covered with Wetlands camouflage pattern. Red front sight bead and mid-rib bead. Introduced 1999. Imported from Italy by Heckler & Koch, Inc.

Price: **$979.00**

Fabarm Sporting Clays Extra Auto Shotgun

Similar to Gold Lion except 28" TriBore ported barrel with interchangeable colored front-sight beads, mid-rib bead, 10mm channeled vent rib, carbon-fiber finish, oil-finished walnut stock and forend with olive wood grip-cap. Stock dimensions are 14.58"x1.58"x2.44". Distinctive gold-colored receiver logo. Available in 12 gauge only, 3" chamber. Introduced 1999. Imported from Italy by Heckler & Koch, Inc.

Price: **$1,249.00**

FABARM RED LION

Gauge: 12, 3" chamber. **Barrel:** 26", 28", five screw-in chokes. **Weight:** 7-7.2 lbs. **Length:** 46.25"-48.25" overall. **Stock:** Premium walnut, olive grip cap. **Sights:** Red bar. **Features:** TriBore barrel system. Limited edition Gold Lion, black and silver finish receiver with English-style gold inlaid engraving, Fabarm semi-automatic operating system. Blue finish.

Price: **$1,049.00**

FRANCHI 48AL SHOTGUN

Gauge: 20 or 28, 2-3/4" chamber. **Barrel:** 24", 26", 28" (Full, cyl., mod., choke tubes). **Weight:** 5.5 lbs. (20 gauge). **Length:** 44"-48.". **Stock:** 14-1/4"x1-5/8"x2-1/2". Walnut with checkered grip and forend. **Features:** Long recoil-operated action. Chrome-lined bore; cross-bolt safety. Imported from Italy by Benelli U.S.A.

Price: 20 ga. **$715.00**
Price: 28 ga. **$825.00**

Franchi 48AL Deluxe Shotgun

Similar to 48AL but with select walnut stock and forend and high-polish blue finish with gold trigger. Introduced 2000.

Price: (20 gauge, 26" barrel) **$940.00**
Price: (28 gauge, 26" barrel) **$990.00**

Franchi 48AL English

Similar to 48AL Deluxe but with straight grip "English style" stock. 20 ga., 28 ga., 26" bbl, ICMF tubes.

Price: 20 gauge **$940.00**
Price: 28 gauge **$990.00**

Franchi 48AL Short Stock Shotgun

Similar to 48AL but with stock shortened to 12-1/2 " length of pull.

Price: (20 gauge, 26" barrel) **$715.00**

FRANCHI 612 AND 620 SHOTGUNS

Gauge: 12, 20, 3" chamber. **Barrel:** 24", 26", 28", IC, MF tubes. **Weight:** 7 lbs. **Stock:** European walnut, synthetic and Timber HD. **Features:** Alloy frame with matte black finish; gas-operated with Vario System, four-lug rotating bolt. Introduced 1996. Imported from Italy by Benelli U.S.A.

Price: Walnut wood **$750.00**
Price: Camo, Timber HD **$825.00**
Price: Synthetic (black synthetic stock, forend) **$710.00**
Price: 20 ga., 24", 26", 28", walnut **$750.00**
Price: Variopress 620 (Timber HD Camo) **$875.00**

Franchi 612 Defense Shotgun

Similar to 612 except has 18-1/2 ",cylinder-bore barrel with black, synthetic stock. Available in 12 gauge, 3" chamber only. Weighs 6-1/2 lbs. 2-shot magazine extension available. Introduced 2000.

Price: **$635.00**

Franchi 612 Sporting Shotgun

Similar to 612 except has 30" ported barrel to reduce muzzle jump. Available in 12 gauge, 3" chamber only. Introduced 2000.

Price: **$1,045.00**

Franchi 620 Short Stock Shotgun

Similar to 620 but with stock shortened to 12-1/2 "length of pull for smaller shooters. Introduced 2000.

Price: (20 gauge, 26" barrel) **$730.00**

REMINGTON MODEL 11-87 PREMIER SHOTGUN

Gauge: 12, 20, 3" chamber. **Barrel:** 26", 28", 30" Rem Choke tubes. Light Contour barrel. **Weight:** About 7-3/4 lbs. **Length:** 46" overall (26" bbl.). **Stock:** Walnut with satin or high-gloss finish; cut checkering; solid brown buttpad; no white spacers. **Sights:** Bradley-type white-faced front, metal bead middle. **Features:** Pressure compensating gas system allows shooting 2-3/4" or 3" loads interchangeably with no adjustments. Stainless magazine tube; redesigned feed latch, barrel support ring on operating bars; pinned forend. Introduced 1987.

Price: **$765.00**
Price: Left-hand **$819.00**
Price: Premier Cantilever Deer Barrel, sling, swivels, Monte Carlo
stock **$845.00**
Price: 3-1/2" Super Magnum **$852.00**

SHOTGUNS

Remington Model 11-87 SPS Camo

Remington Model 11-87 SPS-T Turkey Camo

**Remington Model 1100
Youth Turkey Camo**

Remington Model 11-87 Special Purpose Magnum

Similar to the 11-87 Premier except has dull stock finish, Parkerized exposed metal surfaces. Bolt and carrier have dull blackened coloring. Comes with 26" or 28" barrel with Rem Chokes, padded Cordura nylon sling and quick detachable swivels. Introduced 1987.

Price: **$765.00**
Price: With synthetic stock and forend (SPS). **$765.00**

Remington Model 11-87 SPS Special Purpose Synthetic Camo

Similar to the 11-87 Special Purpose Magnum except has synthetic stock and all metal (except bolt and trigger guard) and stock covered with Mossy Oak Break-Up camo finish. In 12 gauge only, 26", Rem Choke. Comes with camo sling, swivels. Introduced 1992.

Price: **$879.00**

Remington Model 11-87 SPS-T Turkey Camo

Similar to the 11-87 Special Purpose Magnum except with synthetic stock, 21" vent. rib barrel with Rem Choke tube. Completely covered with Mossy Oak Break-Up Brown camouflage. Bolt body, trigger guard and recoil pad are non-reflective black.

Price: **$879.00**
Price: Model 11-87 SPS-T RS/TG (TruGlo fiber optics sights). ... **$897.00**
Price: Model 11-87 SPS-T Camo CL cantilever **$907.00**

Remington Model 11-87 SPS-T Super Magnum Synthetic Camo

Similar to the 11-87 SPS-T Turkey Camo except has 23" vent rib barrel with Turkey Super full choke tube, chambered for 12 ga., 3-1/2", TruGlo rifle sights. Introduced 2001.

Price: **$935.00**

Remington Model 11-87 SPS-Deer Shotgun

Similar to the 11-87 Special Purpose Camo except has fully-rifled 21" barrel with rifle sights, black non-reflective, synthetic stock and forend, black carrying sling. Introduced 1993.

Price: **$799.00**
Price: With wood stock (Model 11-87 SP Deer Gun) Rem choke, 21" barrel w/rifle sights **$745.00**

Remington Model 11-87 SPS Cantilever Shotgun

Similar to the 11-87 SPS except has fully rifled barrel; synthetic stock with Monte Carlo comb; cantilever scope mount deer barrel. Comes with sling and swivels. Introduced 1994.

Price: **$845.00**

Remington Model 11-87 SP and SPS Super Magnum Shotguns

Similar to Model 11-87 Special Purpose Magnum except has 3-1/2" chamber. Available in flat-finish American walnut or black synthetic stock, 26" or 28" black-matte finished barrel and receiver; imp. cyl., modified and full Rem Choke tubes. Overall length 45-3/4", weighs 8 lbs., 2 oz. Introduced 2000. From Remington Arms Co.

Price: 11-87 SP Super Magnum (walnut stock) **$852.00**
Price: 11-87 SPS Super Magnum (synthetic stock) **$852.00**
Price: 11-87 SPS Super Magnum (camo) **$935.00**

Remington Model 11-87 Upland Special Shotgun

Similar to 11-87 Premier except has 23" ventilated rib barrel with straight-grip, English-style walnut stock. Available in 12 or 20 gauge. Overall length 43-1/2", weighs 7-1/4 lbs. (6-1/2 lbs. in 20 ga.). Comes with imp. cyl., modified and full choke tubes. Introduced 2000.

Price: 12 or 20 gauge **$765.00**

REMINGTON MODEL 1100 SYNTHETIC LT-20

Gauge: 20. **Barrel:** 26" Rem Chokes. **Weight:** 6-3/4 lbs. **Stock:** 14"x1-1/2"x2-1/2". Black synthetic, checkered pistol grip and forend. **Features:** Matted receiver top with scroll work on both sides of receiver.

Price: **$549.00**
Price: Youth Gun LT-20 (21" Rem Choke). **$549.00**

Remington Model 1100 Synthetic

12 gauge, and has black synthetic stock; vent. rib 28" barrel on 12 gauge, both with Mod. Rem Choke tube. Weighs about 7-1/2 lbs. Introduced 1996.

Price: **$549.00**

Remington Model 1100 Youth Synthetic Turkey Camo

Similar to the Model 1100 LT-20 except has 1" shorter stock, 21" vent rib barrel with Full Rem Choke tube; 3" chamber; synthetic stock and forend are covered with RealTree Advantage camo, and barrel and receiver have non-reflective, black matte finish. Introduced 1999.

Price: **$612.00**

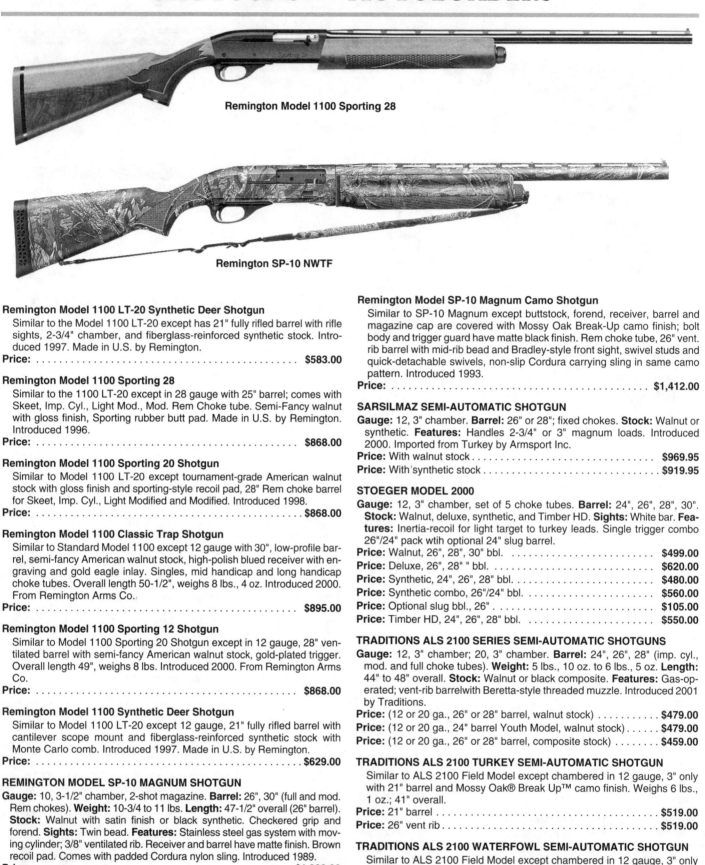

Remington Model 1100 Sporting 28

Remington SP-10 NWTF

Remington Model 1100 LT-20 Synthetic Deer Shotgun

Similar to the Model 1100 LT-20 except has 21" fully rifled barrel with rifle sights, 2-3/4" chamber, and fiberglass-reinforced synthetic stock. Introduced 1997. Made in U.S. by Remington.

Price: **$583.00**

Remington Model 1100 Sporting 28

Similar to the 1100 LT-20 except in 28 gauge with 25" barrel; comes with Skeet, Imp. Cyl., Light Mod., Mod. Rem Choke tube. Semi-Fancy walnut with gloss finish, Sporting rubber butt pad. Made in U.S. by Remington. Introduced 1996.

Price: **$868.00**

Remington Model 1100 Sporting 20 Shotgun

Similar to Model 1100 LT-20 except tournament-grade American walnut stock with gloss finish and sporting-style recoil pad, 28" Rem choke barrel for Skeet, Imp. Cyl., Light Modified and Modified. Introduced 1998.

Price: **$868.00**

Remington Model 1100 Classic Trap Shotgun

Similar to Standard Model 1100 except 12 gauge with 30", low-profile barrel, semi-fancy American walnut stock, high-polish blued receiver with engraving and gold eagle inlay. Singles, mid handicap and long handicap choke tubes. Overall length 50-1/2", weighs 8 lbs., 4 oz. Introduced 2000. From Remington Arms Co.

Price: **$895.00**

Remington Model 1100 Sporting 12 Shotgun

Similar to Model 1100 Sporting 20 Shotgun except in 12 gauge, 28" ventilated barrel with semi-fancy American walnut stock, gold-plated trigger. Overall length 49", weighs 8 lbs. Introduced 2000. From Remington Arms Co.

Price: **$868.00**

Remington Model 1100 Synthetic Deer Shotgun

Similar to Model 1100 LT-20 except 12 gauge, 21" fully rifled barrel with cantilever scope mount and fiberglass-reinforced synthetic stock with Monte Carlo comb. Introduced 1997. Made in U.S. by Remington.

Price: **$629.00**

REMINGTON MODEL SP-10 MAGNUM SHOTGUN

Gauge: 10, 3-1/2" chamber, 2-shot magazine. **Barrel:** 26", 30" (full and mod. Rem chokes). **Weight:** 10-3/4 to 11 lbs. **Length:** 47-1/2" overall (26" barrel). **Stock:** Walnut with satin finish or black synthetic. Checkered grip and forend. **Sights:** Twin bead. **Features:** Stainless steel gas system with moving cylinder; 3/8" ventilated rib. Receiver and barrel have matte finish. Brown recoil pad. Comes with padded Cordura nylon sling. Introduced 1989.

Price: **$1,292.00**
Price: SP-10 Magnum Turkey Camo (26" vent rib barrel, Rem choke tube)
Mossy Oak Break-up **$1,412.00**

Remington Model SP-10 Magnum Camo Shotgun

Similar to SP-10 Magnum except buttstock, forend, receiver, barrel and magazine cap are covered with Mossy Oak Break-Up camo finish; bolt body and trigger guard have matte black finish. Rem choke tube, 26" vent. rib barrel with mid-rib bead and Bradley-style front sight, swivel studs and quick-detachable swivels, non-slip Cordura carrying sling in same camo pattern. Introduced 1993.

Price: **$1,412.00**

SARSILMAZ SEMI-AUTOMATIC SHOTGUN

Gauge: 12, 3" chamber. **Barrel:** 26" or 28"; fixed chokes. **Stock:** Walnut or synthetic. **Features:** Handles 2-3/4" or 3" magnum loads. Introduced 2000. Imported from Turkey by Armsport Inc.

Price: With walnut stock **$969.95**
Price: With synthetic stock **$919.95**

STOEGER MODEL 2000

Gauge: 12, 3" chamber, set of 5 choke tubes. **Barrel:** 24", 26", 28", 30". **Stock:** Walnut, deluxe, synthetic, and Timber HD. **Sights:** White bar. **Features:** Inertia-recoil for light target to turkey leads. Single trigger combo 26"/24" pack wtih optional 24" slug barrel.

Price: Walnut, 26", 28", 30" bbl. **$499.00**
Price: Deluxe, 26", 28" " bbl. **$620.00**
Price: Synthetic, 24", 26", 28" bbl. **$480.00**
Price: Synthetic combo, 26"/24" bbl. **$560.00**
Price: Optional slug bbl., 26" **$105.00**
Price: Timber HD, 24", 26", 28" bbl. **$550.00**

TRADITIONS ALS 2100 SERIES SEMI-AUTOMATIC SHOTGUNS

Gauge: 12, 3" chamber; 20, 3" chamber. **Barrel:** 24", 26", 28" (imp. cyl., mod. and full choke tubes). **Weight:** 5 lbs., 10 oz. to 6 lbs., 5 oz. **Length:** 44" to 48" overall. **Stock:** Walnut or black composite. **Features:** Gas-operated; vent-rib barrelwith Beretta-style threaded muzzle. Introduced 2001 by Traditions.

Price: (12 or 20 ga., 26" or 28" barrel, walnut stock) **$479.00**
Price: (12 or 20 ga., 24" barrel Youth Model, walnut stock) **$479.00**
Price: (12 or 20 ga., 26" or 28" barrel, composite stock) **$459.00**

TRADITIONS ALS 2100 TURKEY SEMI-AUTOMATIC SHOTGUN

Similar to ALS 2100 Field Model except chambered in 12 gauge, 3" only with 21" barrel and Mossy Oak® Break Up™ camo finish. Weighs 6 lbs., 1 oz.; 41" overall.

Price: 21" barrel **$519.00**
Price: 26" vent rib **$519.00**

TRADITIONS ALS 2100 WATERFOWL SEMI-AUTOMATIC SHOTGUN

Similar to ALS 2100 Field Model except chambered in 12 gauge, 3" only with 28" barrel and Advantage® Wetlands™ camo finish. Weighs 6 lbs., 5 oz.; 48" overall.

Price: Comes with steel chokes for 2002 . . . . **$529.00**

Weatherby SAS

TRADITIONS ALS 2100 HUNTER COMBO

Similar to ALS 2100 Field Model except 2 barrels, 28" vent rib and 24" fully rifled deer. Choice TruGlo adj. sights or fixed cantilever mount on rifled barrel. Multi chokes.

Price: Walnut, rifle barrel **$609.00**
Price: Walnut, cantilever **$629.00**
Price: Synthetic **$579.00**

TRISTAR PHANTOM AUTO SHOTGUNS

Gauge: 12, shoots 2-3/4" or 3" interchangeably. **Barrel:** 24", 26", 28" (Imp. Cyl., Mod., Full choke tubes). **Stock:** European walnut or black synthetic. **Features:** Gas-operated action; blued barrel; checkered pistol grip and forend; vent rib barrel. Introduced 1999. Imported by Tristar Sporting Arms Ltd.

Price: . . . . **$381.00 to $499.00**

VERONA MODEL SX400 SEMI AUTO SHOTGUN

Gauge: 12. **Barrel:** 26", 30". **Weight:** 6-1/2 lbs. **Stock:** Walnut, black composite. **Sights:** Red dot. **Features:** Aluminum receivers, gas-operated, 2-3/4" or 3" Magnum shells without adj. or mod., 4 screw-in chokes and wrench included. Sling swivels, gold trigger. Blued barrel. Imported from Italy by B.C. Outdoors.

Price: 401S, 12 ga.. . . . . **$398.40**
Price: 405SDS, 12 ga.. . . . . **$610.00**
Price: 405L, 12 ga. **$331.20**

WEATHERBY SAS AUTO SHOTGUN

Gauge: 12, 2-3/4" or 3" chamber. **Barrel:** 26", 28" (20 ga.); 26", 28", 30" (12 ga.); Briley Multi-Choke tubes. **Weight:** 6-3/4 to 7-3/4 lbs. **Stock:** 14-1/4"x2-1/4"x1-1/2". Claro walnut; black, Shadow Grass or Mossy Oak Break-Up camo synthetic. **Features:** Alloy receiver with matte finish; gold-plated trigger; magazine cut-off. Introduced 1999. Imported by Weatherby.

Price: 12 or 20 ga. (walnut stock). **$945.00**
Price: 12 or 20 ga. (black synthetic stock) **$979.00**
Price: 12 ga. (camo stock) **$1,115.00**

WEATHERBY SAS (SEMI-AUTOMATIC SHOTGUNS)

5 Models: SAS Field, SAS Sporting Clays, SAS Shadow Grass, SAS Break-Up, SAS Synthetic
Gauge: 12 ga. **Barrel:** Vent ribbed, 24"-30". **Stock:** SAS Field and Sporting Clays, walnut. SAS Shadow Grass, Break-Up, Synthetic, composite. **Sights:** SAS Sporting Clays, frass front and mid-point back. SAS Shadow Grass and Break-Up, HiViz front and brass mid. Synthetic has brass front. **Features:** Easy to shoot, load, clean, lightweight, lessened recoil, IMC system includes 3 Briley screw-in choke tubes. Case included.
Price: . . . . **$749.00 to $899.00**

WINCHESTER SUPER X2 AUTO SHOTGUN

Gauge: 12, 3", 3-1/2" chamber. **Barrel:** 24", 26", 28"; Invector Plus choke tubes. **Weight:** 7-1/4 to 7-1/2 lbs. **Stock:** 14-1/4"x1-3/4"x2". Walnut or black synthetic. **Features:** Gas-operated action shoots all loads without adjustment; vent. rib barrels; 4-shot magazine. Introduced 1999. Made in U.S. by U.S. Repeating Arms Co.

Price: Field, walnut or synthetic stock, 3". **$819.00**
Price: Magnum, 3-1/2", synthetic stock, 26" or 28" bbl. **$936.00**
Price: Camo Waterfowl, 3-1/2", Mossy Oak Shadow Grass. . . . **$1,080.00**
New! **Price:** NWTF Turkey, 3-1/2", black synthetic stock, 24" bbl. . **$997.00**
New! **Price:** NWTF Turkey, 3-1/2", Mossy Oak Break-Up camo **$1,080.00**

Winchester Super X2 Sporting Clays Auto Shotgun

Similar to the Super X2 except has two gas pistons (one for target loads, one for heavy 3" loads), adjustable comb system and high-post rib. Back-bored barrel with Invector Plus choke tubes. Offered in 28" and 30" barrels. Introduced 2001. From U.S. Repeating Arms Co.
Price: Super X2 Sporting Clays **$1,206.00**

Winchester Super X2 Field 3" Auto Shotgun

Similar to the Super X2 except has a 3" chamber, walnut stock and forearm and high-profile rib. Back-bored barrel and Invector Plus choke tubes. Introduced 2001. From U.S. Repeating Arms Co.
Price: Super X2 Field 3", 26" or 28" bbl.. . . . . **$819.00**

Includes a wide variety of sporting guns and guns suitable for competitive shooting.

Armscor M-30F Field

Benelli Nova Pump

Benelli Nova Pump Rifled Slug

Browning BPS 10 gauge

ARMSCOR M-30F FIELD PUMP SHOTGUN

Gauge: 12, 3" chamber. **Barrel:** 28" fixed Mod., or with Mod. and Full choke tubes. **Weight:** 7.6 lbs. **Stock:** Walnut-finished hardwood. **Features:** Double action slide bars; blued steel receiver; damascened bolt. Introduced 1996. Imported from the Philippines by K.B.I., Inc.

Price: With fixed choke **$239.00**
Price: With choke tubes **$269.00**

BENELLI NOVA PUMP SHOTGUN

Gauge: 12, 20. **Barrel:** 24", 26", 28". **Stock:** Synthetic, X-tra Brown 12 ga., Timber HD 20 ga. **Sights:** Red bar. **Features:** 2-3/4", 3" chamber (3-2/1" 12 ga. only). Montefeltro rotating bolt design with dual action bars, magazine cut-off, synthetic trigger assembly, 4-shot magazine. Introduced 1999. Imported from Italy by Benelli USA.

Price: Black stock, 12 ga. **$405.00**
Price: X-tra Brown, 12 ga. **$470.00**
Price: Black stock, 20 ga. **$450.00**
Price: Timber HD, 20 ga. **$535.00**

Benelli Nova Pump Slug Gun

Similar to the Nova except has 18.5" barrel with adjustable rifle-type or ghost ring sights; weighs 7.2 lbs.; black synthetic stock. Introduced 1999. Imported from Italy by Benelli USA.

Price: With rifle sights **$355.00**
Price: With ghost-ring sights **$395.00**

Benelli Nova Pump Rifled Slug Gun

Similar to Nova Pump Slug Gun except has 24" barrel and rifled bore; open rifle sights; synthetic stock; weighs 8.1 pounds.

Price: **$575.00**

BROWNING BPS PUMP SHOTGUN

Gauge: 10, 12, 3-1/2" chamber; 12 or 20, 3" chamber (2-3/4" in target guns), 28, 2-3/4" chamber, 5-shot magazine, 410 ga., 3" chamber. **Barrel:** 10 ga.— 24" Buck Special, 28", 30", 32" Invector; 12, 20 ga.—22", 24", 26", 28", 30", 32" (Imp. Cyl., mod. or full). 410 ga.—26" barrel. (Imp. Cyl., mod. and full choke tubes.) Also available with Invector choke tubes, 12 or 20 ga.; Upland Special has 22" barrel with Invector tubes. BPS 3" and 3-1/2" have back-bored barrel. **Weight:** 7 lbs., 8 oz. (28" barrel). **Length:** 48-3/4" overall (28" barrel). **Stock:** 14-1/4"x1-1/2"x2-1/2". Select walnut, semi-beavertail forend, full pistol grip stock. **Features:** All 12 gauge 3" guns except Buck Special and game guns have back-bored barrels with Invector Plus choke tubes. Bottom feeding and ejection, receiver top safety, high post vent. rib. Double action bars eliminate binding. Vent. rib barrels only. All 12 and 20 gauge guns with 3" chamber available with fully engraved receiver flats at no extra cost. Each gauge has its own unique game scene. Introduced 1977. Imported from Japan by Browning.

Price: 10 ga., Hunter, Invector **$552.00**
Price: 12 ga., 3-1/2" Magnum Hunter, Invector Plus **$552.00**
Price: 12 ga., 3-1/2" Magnum Stalker (black syn. stock) **$537.00**
Price: 12, 20 ga., Hunter, Invector Plus **$464.00**
Price: 12 ga. Deer Hunter (22" rifled bbl., cantilever mount) **$568.00**
Price: 28 ga., Hunter, Invector **$495.00**
Price: 410 ga., Hunter, Invector **$495.00**

Browning BPS 10 Gauge Shotguns

Chambered for the 10 gauge, 3-1/2" load. Offered in 24", 26" and 28" barrels. Offered with walnut, black composite (Stalker models) or camouflage stock and forend. Introduced 1999. Imported by Browning.

Price: Hunter (walnut). **$552.00**
Price: Stalker (composite) **$537.00**
Price: Mossy Oak® Shadow Grass or Break-Up Camo. **$617.00**

Browning BPS 10 gauge Camo Pump

Similar to the BPS 10 gauge Hunter except completely covered with Mossy Oak Shadow Grass camouflage. Available with 24", 26", 28" barrel. Introduced 1999. Imported by Browning.

Price: **$602.00**

Browning BPS Waterfowl Camo Pump Shotgun

Similar to the BPS Hunter except completely covered with Mossy Oak Shadow Grass camouflage. Available in 12 gauge, with 24", 26" or 28" barrel, 3" chamber. Introduced 1999. Imported by Browning.

Price: **$514.00**

Fabarm Field Pump

Browning BPS Game Gun Deer Hunter
Similar to the standard BPS except has newly designed receiver/magazine tube/barrel mounting system to eliminate play, heavy 20.5" barrel with rifle-type sights with adjustable rear, solid receiver scope mount, "rifle" stock dimensions for scope or open sights, sling swivel studs. Gloss or matte finished wood with checkering, polished blue metal. Introduced 1992.
Price: **$568.00**

Browning BPS Game Gun Turkey Special
Similar to the standard BPS except has satin-finished walnut stock and dull-finished barrel and receiver. Receiver is drilled and tapped for scope mounting. Rifle-style stock dimensions and swivel studs. Has Extra-Full Turkey choke tube. Introduced 1992.
Price: **$500.00**

Browning BPS Stalker Pump Shotgun
Same gun as the standard BPS except all exposed metal parts have a matte blued finish and the stock has a durable black finish with a black recoil pad. Available in 10 ga. (3-1/2") and 12 ga. with 3" or 3-1/2" chamber, 22", 28", 30" barrel with Invector choke system. Introduced 1987.
Price: 12 ga., 3" chamber, Invector Plus **$448.00**
Price: 10, 12 ga., 3-1/2" chamber. **$537.00**

Browning BPS NWTF Turkey Series Pump Shotgun
Similar to the BPS Stalker except has full coverage Mossy Oak® Break-Up camo finish on synthetic stock, forearm and exposed metal parts. Offered in 10 and 12 gauge, 3" or 3-1/2" chamber; 24" bbl. has extra-full choke tube and Hi-Viz fiber optic sights. Introduced 2001. From Browning.
Price: 10 ga., 3-1/2" chamber. **$637.00**
Price: 12 ga., 3-1/2" chamber. **$637.00**
Price: 12 ga., 3" chamber **$549.00**

Browning BPS Micro Pump Shotgun
Same as BPS Upland Special except 20 ga. only, 22" Invector barrel, stock has pistol grip with recoil pad. Length of pull is 13-1/4"; weighs 6 lbs., 12 oz. Introduced 1986.
Price: **$464.00**

DIAMOND 12 GA. PUMP SHOTGUN
Gauge: 12, 2-3/4" and 3" chambers. **Barrel:** 18"-30". **Weight:** 7 lbs. **Stock:** Walnut, synthetic. **Features:** Aluminum one-piece receiver sculpted for lighter weight. Double locking on fixed bolt. Gold, Elite and Panther series with vented barrels and 3 chokes. All series slug guns available (Gold and Elite with sights). Imported from Istanbul by ADCO Sales.
Price: Gold, 28", walnut **$399.00**
Price: Gold, 28", synthetic **$379.00**
Price: Gold Slug, 24", same as above . . . . **NA**
Price: Silver Mariner 20" Slug, synthetic **$319.00**
Price: Elite, 20"-28", walnut **$359.00**
Price: Elite, 20" Slug, walnut **$359.00**
Price: Panther, 20", 28", synthetic **$239.00**
Price: Panther,18.5" Slug, synthetic. **$209.00**

EAA/BAIKAL MP-133 PUMP SHOTGUN
Gauge: 12, 3-1/2" chamber. **Barrel:** 18-1/2", 20", 24", 26", 28"; imp., mod. and full choke tubes. **Weight:** NA. **Stock:** Walnut; checkered grip and grooved forearm. **Features:** Hammer-forged, chrome-lined barrel with ventilated rib; machined steel parts; dual action bars; trigger-block safety; 4-shot magazine tube; handles 2-3/4" through 3-1/2" shells. Introduced 2000. Imported by European American Armory.
Price: MP-133 (blued finish, walnut stock and forend) **$329.00**

FABARM FIELD PUMP SHOTGUN
Gauge: 12, 3" chamber. **Barrel:** 28" (24" rifled slug barrel available). **Weight:** 76.6 lbs. **Length:** 48.25" overall. **Stock:** Polymer. **Features:** Similar to Fabarm FP6 Pump Shotgun. Alloy receiver; twin action bars; available in black or Mossy Oak Break-Up™ camo finish. Includes cyl., mod. and full choke tubes. Introduced 2001. Imported from Italy by Heckler & Koch Inc.
Price: Matte black finish **$399.00**
Price: Mossy Oak Break-Up™ finish **$469.00**

ITHACA MODEL 37 DELUXE PUMP SHOTGUN
Gauge: 12, 16, 20, 3" chamber. **Barrel:** 26", 28", 30" (12 gauge), 26", 28" (16 and 20 gauge), choke tubes. **Weight:** 7 lbs. **Stock:** Walnut with cut-checkered grip and forend. **Features:** Steel receiver; bottom ejection; brushed blue finish, vent rib barrels. Reintroduced 1996. Made in U.S. by Ithaca Gun Co.
Price: **$618.00**
Price: With straight English-style stock **$618.00**
Price: Model 37 New Classic (ringtail forend, sunburst recoil pad, hand-finished walnut stock, 26" or 28" barrel) **$803.00**

Ithaca Model 37 Waterfowler
Similar to Model 37 Deluxe except in 12 gauge only with 28" barrel, special extended steel shot choke tube system. Complete coverage of Advantage Wetlands or Hardwoods camouflage. Introduced 1999. Made in U.S. by Ithaca Gun Co.
Price: **$595.00**

ITHACA MODEL 37 DEERSLAYER II PUMP SHOTGUN
Gauge: 12, 20, 3" chamber. **Barrel:** 20", 25", fully rifled. **Weight:** 7 lbs. **Stock:** Cut-checkered American walnut with Monte Carlo comb. **Sights:** Rifle-type. **Features:** Integral barrel and receiver. Bottom ejection. Brushed blue finish. Reintroduced 1997. Made in U.S. by Ithaca Gun Co.
Price: **$633.00**
Price: Smooth Bore Deluxe **$582.00**
Price: Rifled Deluxe **$582.00**

ITHACA MODEL 37 DEERSLAYER III PUMP SHOTGUN
Gauge: 12, 20, 2-3/4" and 3" chambers. **Barrel:** 26" free floated. **Weight:** 9 lbs. **Stock:** Monte Carlo laminate. **Sights:** Rifled. **Features:** Barrel length gives increased velocity. Trigger and sear set hand filed and stoned for creep free operation. Weaver-style scope base. Swivel studs. Matte blue.
Price: **$900.00**

ITHACA MODEL 37 RUFFED GROUSE SPECIAL EDITION
Gauge: 20 ga. **Barrel:** 22", 24", interchangeable choke tubes. **Weight:** 5.25 lbs. **Stock:** American black walnut. **Features:** Laser engraved stock wtih line art drawing. Bottom eject. Vent rib and English style. Right- or left-hand thru simple safety change. Aluminum receiver. Made in U.S.A. by Ithaca Gun Co.
Price: **$840.00**

ITHACA ELLETT SPECIAL MODEL 37 TURKEYSLAYER
Gauge: 12 ga., 3" chamber. **Barrel:** 22" ported. **Stock:** Composite. **Sights:** Fully adjustable, TruGlo front and rear. **Features:** Recreated from "Golden Age." Complete camo covering. Drilled and tapped. Extended turkey chokes. Matte metal, Realtree Hardwoods 20/200 or Advantage Timber patterns.
Price: **$654.00**

ITHACA QUAD BORE MODEL 37 TURKEYSLAYER
Gauge: 20 ga. **Barrel:** 22" ported. **Weight:** 6.25 lbs. **Stock:** Black walnut stock and forend. **Sights:** Fully adjustable, TruGlo. **Features:** Sling swivel studs, matte blue, turkey full choke tube, 100% American made.
Price: **$680.00**

SHOTGUNS

Mossberg Model 835 Shadowgrass

Mossberg Model 500 Sporting

Mossberg Model 500
Trophy Slugster

ITHACA MODEL 37 ULTRALIGHT DELUXE
Gauge: 16 ga. 2-3/4" chamber. **Barrel:** 24", 26", 28". **Weight:** 5.25 lbs. **Stock:** Standard deluxe. **Sights:** Raybar. **Features:** Vent rib, drilled and tapped, interchangeable barrel. F, M, IC choke tubes.
Price: Deluxe **$649.00**
Price: Classic/English **$824.00**
Price: Classic/Pistol **$824.00**

ITHACA HOMELAND SECURITY GUNS
Gauge: 12 ga., 2-3/4" and 3" chambers. **Barrel:** 18-1/2" interchangeable. **Weight:** 6.5 lbs. **Stock:** Synthetic deluxe and oil finish. **Sights:** Bead.
Price: Synthetic/Standard **$515.00**
Price: Synthetic/Ported **$546.00**

MOSSBERG MODEL 835 ULTI-MAG PUMP
Gauge: 12, 3-1/2" chamber. **Barrel:** Ported 24" rifled bore, 24", 28", Accu-Mag choke tubes for steel or lead shot. **Weight:** 7-3/4 lbs. **Length:** 48-1/2" overall. **Stock:** 14"x1-1/2"x2-1/2". Dual Comb. Cut-checkered hardwood or camo synthetic; both have recoil pad. **Sights:** White bead front, brass mid-bead; Fiber Optic. **Features:** Shoots 2-3/4", 3" or 3-1/2" shells. Back-bored and ported barrel to reduce recoil, improve patterns. Ambidextrous thumb safety, twin extractors, dual slide bars. Mossberg Cablelock included. Introduced 1988.
Price: 28" vent. rib, hardwood stock **$370.00**
Price: Combo, 24" rifled bore, rifle sights, 24" vent. rib, Accu-Mag Ulti-Full choke tube, Woodlands camo finish **$572.00**
Price: RealTree Camo Turkey, 24" vent. rib, Accu-Mag Extra-Full tube, synthetic stock. **$525.00**
Price: Mossy Oak Camo, 28" vent. rib, Accu-Mag tubes, synthetic stock **$583.00**
Price: OFM Camo, 28" vent. rib, Accu-Mag Mod. tube, synthetic stock **$407.00**

Mossberg Model 835 Synthetic Stock
Similar to the Model 835, except with 28" ported barrel with Accu-Mag Mod. choke tube, Parkerized finish, black synthetic stock and forend. Introduced 1998. Made in U.S. by Mossberg.
Price: **$370.00**

MOSSBERG MODEL 500 SPORTING PUMP
Gauge: 12, 20, 410, 3" chamber. **Barrel:** 18-1/2" to 28" with fixed or Accu-Choke, plain or vent. rib. **Weight:** 6-1/4 lbs. (410), 7-1/4 lbs. (12). **Length:** 48" overall (28" barrel). **Stock:** 14"x1-1/2"x2-1/2". Walnut-stained hard-wood. Cut-checkered grip and forend. **Sights:** White bead front, brass mid-bead; Fiber Optic. **Features:** Ambidextrous thumb safety, twin extractors, disconnecting safety, dual action bars. Quiet Carry forend. Many barrels are ported. Mossberg Cablelock included. From Mossberg.
Price: From about **$301.00**
Price: Sporting Combos (field barrel and Slugster barrel), from. . **$403.00**

Mossberg Model 500 Bantam Pump
Same as the Model 500 Sporting Pump except 12 (new for 2001) or 20 gauge, 22" vent. rib Accu-Choke barrel with choke tube set; has 1" shorter stock, reduced length from pistol grip to trigger, reduced forend reach. Introduced 1992.
Price: **$301.00**
Price: With full Woodlands camouflage finish (20 ga. only) **$384.00**

Mossberg Model 500 Camo Pump
Same as the Model 500 Sporting Pump except 12 gauge only and entire gun is covered with special camouflage finish. Receiver drilled and tapped for scope mounting. Comes with quick detachable swivel studs, swivels, camouflage sling, Mossberg Cablelock.
Price: From about **$370.00**

Mossberg Model 500 Persuader/Cruiser Shotguns
Similar to Mossberg Model 500 except has 18-1/2" or 20" barrel with cyl-inder bore choke, synthetic stock and blue or parkerized finish. Available in 12, 20 and 410 gauge with bead or ghost ring sights, 6- or 8-shot magazines. From Mossberg.
Price: 12 gauge, 20" barrel, 8-shot, bead sight. **$308.00**
Price: 20 or 410 gauge, 18-1/2" barrel, 6-shot, bead sight **$329.00**
Price: 12 gauge, parkerized finish, 6-shot, 18-1/2" barrel, ghost ring sights **$437.00**
Price: Home Security 410 (410 gauge, 18-1/2" barrel with spreader choke) **$335.00**

Mossberg Model 590 Special Purpose Shotguns
Similar to Model 500 except has parkerized or Marinecote finish, 9-shot magazine and black synthetic stock (some models feature Speed Feed. Available in 12 gauge only with 20", cylinder bore barrel. Weighs 7-1/4 lbs. From Mossberg.
Price: Bead sight, heat shield over barrel **$389.00**
Price: Ghost ring sight, Speed Feed stock. **$546.00**

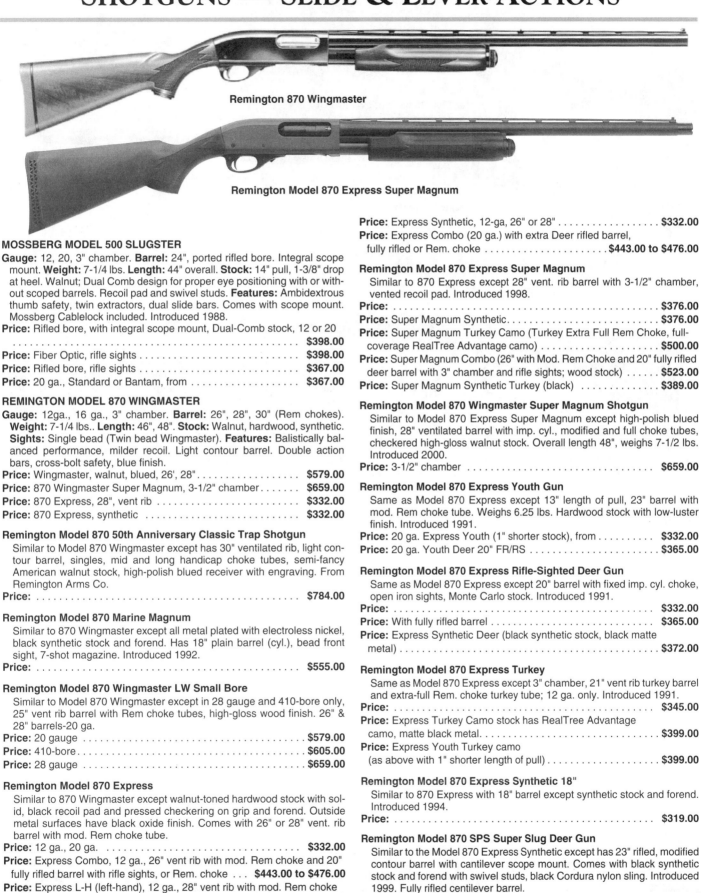

Remington 870 Wingmaster

Remington Model 870 Express Super Magnum

MOSSBERG MODEL 500 SLUGSTER

Gauge: 12, 20, 3" chamber. **Barrel:** 24", ported rifled bore. Integral scope mount. **Weight:** 7-1/4 lbs. **Length:** 44" overall. **Stock:** 14" pull, 1-3/8" drop at heel. Walnut; Dual Comb design for proper eye positioning with or without scoped barrels. Recoil pad and swivel studs. **Features:** Ambidextrous thumb safety, twin extractors, dual slide bars. Comes with scope mount. Mossberg Cablelock included. Introduced 1988.
Price: Rifled bore, with integral scope mount, Dual-Comb stock, 12 or 20
. . . . **$398.00**
Price: Fiber Optic, rifle sights **$398.00**
Price: Rifled bore, rifle sights **$367.00**
Price: 20 ga., Standard or Bantam, from **$367.00**

REMINGTON MODEL 870 WINGMASTER

Gauge: 12ga., 16 ga., 3" chamber. **Barrel:** 26", 28", 30" (Rem chokes). **Weight:** 7-1/4 lbs.. **Length:** 46", 48". **Stock:** Walnut, hardwood, synthetic. **Sights:** Single bead (Twin bead Wingmaster). **Features:** Balistically balanced performance, milder recoil. Light contour barrel. Double action bars, cross-bolt safety, blue finish.
Price: Wingmaster, walnut, blued, 26', 28". **$579.00**
Price: 870 Wingmaster Super Magnum, 3-1/2" chamber. **$659.00**
Price: 870 Express, 28", vent rib **$332.00**
Price: 870 Express, synthetic **$332.00**

Remington Model 870 50th Anniversary Classic Trap Shotgun

Similar to Model 870 Wingmaster except has 30" ventilated rib, light contour barrel, singles, mid and long handicap choke tubes, semi-fancy American walnut stock, high-polish blued receiver with engraving. From Remington Arms Co.
Price: **$784.00**

Remington Model 870 Marine Magnum

Similar to 870 Wingmaster except all metal plated with electroless nickel, black synthetic stock and forend. Has 18" plain barrel (cyl.), bead front sight, 7-shot magazine. Introduced 1992.
Price: **$555.00**

Remington Model 870 Wingmaster LW Small Bore

Similar to Model 870 Wingmaster except in 28 gauge and 410-bore only, 25" vent rib barrel with Rem choke tubes, high-gloss wood finish. 26" & 28" barrels-20 ga.
Price: 20 gauge **$579.00**
Price: 410-bore. **$605.00**
Price: 28 gauge **$659.00**

Remington Model 870 Express

Similar to 870 Wingmaster except walnut-toned hardwood stock with solid, black recoil pad and pressed checkering on grip and forend. Outside metal surfaces have black oxide finish. Comes with 26" or 28" vent. rib barrel with mod. Rem choke tube.
Price: 12 ga., 20 ga. **$332.00**
Price: Express Combo, 12 ga., 26" vent rib with mod. Rem choke and 20" fully rifled barrel with rifle sights, or Rem. choke . . . **$443.00 to $476.00**
Price: Express L-H (left-hand), 12 ga., 28" vent rib with mod. Rem choke tube. **$359.00**

Price: Express Synthetic, 12-ga., 26" or 28" **$332.00**
Price: Express Combo (20 ga.) with extra Deer rifled barrel,
fully rifled or Rem. choke . . . . **$443.00 to $476.00**

Remington Model 870 Express Super Magnum

Similar to 870 Express except 28" vent. rib barrel with 3-1/2" chamber, vented recoil pad. Introduced 1998.
Price: **$376.00**
Price: Super Magnum Synthetic. **$376.00**
Price: Super Magnum Turkey Camo (Turkey Extra Full Rem Choke, full-coverage RealTree Advantage camo) **$500.00**
Price: Super Magnum Combo (26" with Mod. Rem Choke and 20" fully rifled deer barrel with 3" chamber and rifle sights; wood stock) **$523.00**
Price: Super Magnum Synthetic Turkey (black) **$389.00**

Remington Model 870 Wingmaster Super Magnum Shotgun

Similar to Model 870 Express Super Magnum except high-polish blued finish, 28" ventilated barrel with imp. cyl., modified and full choke tubes, checkered high-gloss walnut stock. Overall length 48", weighs 7-1/2 lbs. Introduced 2000.
Price: 3-1/2" chamber **$659.00**

Remington Model 870 Express Youth Gun

Same as Model 870 Express except 13" length of pull, 23" barrel with mod. Rem choke tube. Weighs 6.25 lbs. Hardwood stock with low-luster finish. Introduced 1991.
Price: 20 ga. Express Youth (1" shorter stock), from **$332.00**
Price: 20 ga. Youth Deer 20" FR/RS **$365.00**

Remington Model 870 Express Rifle-Sighted Deer Gun

Same as Model 870 Express except 20" barrel with fixed imp. cyl. choke, open iron sights, Monte Carlo stock. Introduced 1991.
Price: **$332.00**
Price: With fully rifled barrel **$365.00**
Price: Express Synthetic Deer (black synthetic stock, black matte metal) **$372.00**

Remington Model 870 Express Turkey

Same as Model 870 Express except 3" chamber, 21" vent rib turkey barrel and extra-full Rem. choke turkey tube; 12 ga. only. Introduced 1991.
Price: **$345.00**
Price: Express Turkey Camo stock has RealTree Advantage camo, matte black metal. **$399.00**
Price: Express Youth Turkey camo
(as above with 1" shorter length of pull) **$399.00**

Remington Model 870 Express Synthetic 18"

Similar to 870 Express with 18" barrel except synthetic stock and forend. Introduced 1994.
Price: **$319.00**

Remington Model 870 SPS Super Slug Deer Gun

Similar to the Model 870 Express Synthetic except has 23" rifled, modified contour barrel with cantilever scope mount. Comes with black synthetic stock and forend with swivel studs, black Cordura nylon sling. Introduced 1999. Fully rifled centilever barrel.
Price: **$561.00**

Winchester 1300 Black Shadow Field Gun

Winchester NWTF Turkey

Winchester 9410

Remington Model 870 SPS-T Synthetic Camo Shotgun

Chambered for 12 ga., 3" shells, has Mossy Oak Break-Up® synthetic stock and metal treatment, TruGlo fiber optic sights. Introduced 2001.
Price: 20" RS, Rem. choke. **$576.00**

Remington Model 870 SPS Super Magnum Camo

Has synthetic stock and all metal (except bolt and trigger guard) and stock covered with Mossy Oak Break-Up camo finish. In 12 gauge 3-1/2", 26", 28" vent rib, Rem choke. Comes with camo sling, swivels.
Price: **$572.00**

SARSILMAZ PUMP SHOTGUN

Gauge: 12, 3" chamber. **Barrel:** 26" or 28". **Stocks:** Oil-finished hardwood. **Features:** Includes extra pistol-grip stock. Introduced 2000. Imported from Turkey by Armsport Inc.
Price: With pistol-grip stock **$299.95**
Price: With metal stock. **$349.95**

NEW! TRISTAR MODEL 1887

Gauge: 12. **Barrel:** 22". **Weight:** 8.75 lbs. **Length:** 40-1/2". **Stocks:** Walnut. **Features:** Imp. cylinder choke, 5 shell, oil finish. Introduced 2002. Made in Australia. Available through AcuSport Corp.
Price: With pistol-grip stock **$299.95**

WINCHESTER MODEL 1300 WALNUT FIELD PUMP

Gauge: 12, 20, 3" chamber, 5-shot capacity. **Barrel:** 26", 28", vent. rib, with Full, Mod., Imp. Cyl. Winchoke tubes. **Weight:** 6-3/8 lbs. **Length:** 42-5/8" overall. **Stock:** American walnut, with deep cut checkering on pistol grip, traditional ribbed forend; high luster finish. **Sights:** Metal bead front. **Features:** Twin action slide bars; front-locking rotary bolt; roll-engraved receiver; blued, highly polished metal; cross-bolt safety with red indicator. Introduced 1984. From U.S. Repeating Arms Co., Inc.
Price: **$405.00**

Winchester Model 1300 Upland Pump Gun

Similar to Model 1300 Walnut except straight-grip stock, 24" barrel. Introduced 1999. Made in U.S. by U.S. Repeating Arms Co.
Price: **$405.00**

Winchester Model 1300 Black Shadow Field Gun

Similar to Model 1300 Walnut except black composite stock and forend, matte black finish. Has vent rib 26" or 28" barrel, 3" chamber, mod. WinChoke tube. Introduced 1995. From U.S. Repeating Arms Co., Inc.
Price: 12 or 20 gauge. **$343.00**

Winchester Model 1300 Deer Black Shadow Gun

Similar to Model 1300 Black Shadow Turkey Gun except ramp-type front sight, fully adjustable rear, drilled and tapped for scope mounting. Black composite stock and forend, matte black metal. Smoothbore 22" barrel with one imp. cyl. WinChoke tube; 12 gauge only, 3" chamber. Weighs 6-3/4 lbs. Introduced 1994. From U.S. Repeating Arms Co., Inc.
Price: **$341.00**
Price: With rifled barrel. **$366.00**
Price: With cantilever scope mount **$409.00**
Price: Combo (22" rifled and 28" smoothbore bbls.) **$442.00**
Price: Compact (20 ga., 22" rifled barrel, shorter stock). **$409.00**

WINCHESTER MODEL 1300 RANGER PUMP GUN

Gauge: 12, 20, 3" chamber, 5-shot magazine. **Barrel:** 28" vent. rib with Full, Mod., Imp. Cyl. Winchoke tubes. **Weight:** 7 to 7-1/4 lbs. **Length:** 48-5/8" to 50-5/8" overall. **Stock:** Walnut-finished hardwood with ribbed forend. **Sights:** Metal bead front. **Features:** Cross-bolt safety, black rubber recoil pad, twin action slide bars, front-locking rotating bolt. From U.S. Repeating Arms Co., Inc.
Price: Vent. rib barrel, Winchoke **$357.00**
Price: Model 1300 Compact, 24" vent. rib **$356.00**

Winchester Model 1300 Turkey and Universal Hunter Models

Rotary bolt action. Durable Mossy oak break-up finish on 26" VR barrel extra full turkey improved cylinder, modified and full WinChoke tubes included. 3", 12 gauge chamber.
Price: Universal Hunter **$550.00**
Price: Buck and Tom **$525.00**
Price: Short Turkey **$439.00**

WINCHESTER MODEL 9410 LEVER-ACTION SHOTGUN

Gauge: 410, 2-1/2" chamber. **Barrel:** 24" (Cyl. bore). **Weight:** 6-3/4 lbs. **Length:** 42-1/8" overall. **Stock:** Checkered walnut straight-grip; checkered walnut forearm. **Sights:** Adjustable "V" rear, TruGlo® front. **Features:** Model 94 rifle action (smoothbore) chambered for 410 shotgun. Angle Controlled Eject extractor/ejector; 9-shot tubular magazine; 13-1/2" length of pull. Introduced 2001. From U.S. Repeating Arms Co.
Price: 9410 Lever-Action Shotgun **$553.00**
Price: 9410 Packer Shotgun. **$574.00**

Includes a variety of game guns and guns for competitive shooting.

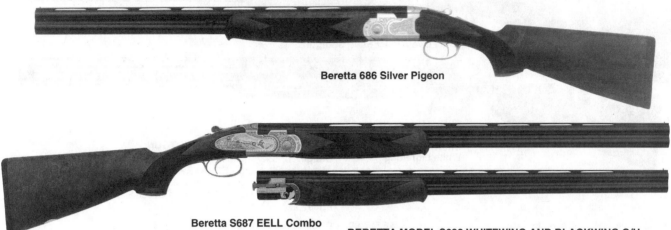

Beretta 686 Silver Pigeon

Beretta S687 EELL Combo

APOLLO TR AND TT SHOTGUNS

Gauge: 12, 20, 410, 3" chambers; 28 2-3/4" chambers. **Barrel:** 26", 28", 30", 32". **Weight:** 6 to 7-1/4 lbs. **Stock:** Oil-finished European walnut. **Features:** Boxlock action, hard-chromed bores, automatic ejectors, single selective trigger, choke tubes (12 and 20 ga. only). Introduced 2000. From Sigarms.
Price: Apollo TR 30 Field (color casehardened side plates). . . . **$2,240.00**
Price: Apollo TR 40 Gold (gold overlays on game scenes) **$2,675.00**
Price: Apollo TT 25 Competition (wide vent. rib with mid-bead). **$1,995.00**

BERETTA DT10 TRIDENT SHOTGUNS

Gauge: 12, 2-3/4", 3" chambers. **Barrel:** 28", 30", 32", 34"; competition-style vent rib; fixed or Optima Choke tubes. **Weight:** 7.9 to 9 lbs. **Stock:** High-grade walnut stock with oil finish; hand-checkered grip and forend, adjustable stocks available. **Features:** Detachable, adjustable trigger group, raised and thickened receiver, forend iron has replaceable nut to guarantee wood-to-metal fit, Optima Bore to improve shot pattern and reduce felt recoil. Introduced 2000. Imported from Italy by Beretta USA.
Price: DT10 Trident Trap (selective, lockable single trigger,
 adjustable stock). **$9,500.00**
Price: DT10 Trident Trap Combo (single and o/u barrels) **$10,790.00**
New! **Price:** DT 10 Trident Trap Bottom Single Combo
 (adj. point of impact rib on single bbl.) **$11,040.00**
Price: DT10 Trident Skeet (skeet stock with rounded recoil
 pad, tapered rib) **$8,030.00**
Price: DT10 Trident Sporting (sporting clays stock with
 rounded recoil pad) **$7,850.00**

BERETTA SERIES 682 GOLD E SKEET, TRAP, SPORTING OVER/UNDERS

Gauge: 12, 2-3/4" chambers. **Barrel:** Skeet—28"; trap—30" and 32", imp. mod. & full and Mobilchoke; trap mono shotguns—32" and 34" Mobilchoke; trap top single guns—32" and 34" full and Mobilchoke; trap combo sets—from 30" O/U, to 32" O/U, 34" top single. **Stock:** Close-grained walnut, hand checkered. **Sights:** White Bradley bead front sight and center bead. **Features:** Receiver has Greystone gunmetal gray finish with gold accents. Trap Monte Carlo stock has deluxe trap recoil pad. Various grades available; contact Beretta USA for details. Imported from Italy by Beretta USA
Price: S682 Gold E Skeet, adjustable stock. **$4,320.00**
Price: S682 Gold E Trap Top Combo. **$5,305.00**
Price: S682 Gold E Trap with adjustable stock **$4,320.00**
Price: S692 Gold E Sporting **$3,850.00**
Price: S687 EELL Diamond Pigeon Skeet **$4,984.00**
Price: S687 EELL Diamond Pigeon Skeet, adjustable stock . . . **$6,050.00**
Price: S687 EELL Diamond Pigeon Sporting **$5,761.00**

BERETTA MODEL S686 WHITEWING AND BLACKWING O/U

Gauge: 12, 3" chambers. **Barrel:** 26", 28", Mobilchoke tubes (Imp. Cyl., Mod., Full). **Weight:** 6.7 lbs. **Length:** 45.7" overall (28" barrels). **Stock:** 14.5"x2.2"x1.4". American walnut, radiused black buttplate. **Features:** Matte chrome finish on receiver, matte blue barrels, hard-chrome bores; low-profile receiver with dual conical locking lugs, single selective trigger, ejectors. Imported from Italy by Beretta U.S.A.
Price: Whitewing **$1,295.00**
Price: Blackwing (Rugged Blue, schnable forend) **$1,398.00**

BERETTA S686 ONYX O/U SHOTGUN

Gauge: 12, 3" chambers. **Barrel:** 28", 30" (Mobilchoke tubes). **Weight:** 7.7 lbs. **Stock:** Checkered American walnut. **Features:** Intended for the beginning Sporting Clays shooter. Has wide, vented 12.5mm target rib, radiused recoil pad. Polished black finish on receiver and barrels. Introduced 1993. Imported from Italy by Beretta U.S.A.
Price: **$1,583.00**
Price: With X-Tra Wood (highly figured) **$1,737.00**

BERETTA S686 SILVER PIGEON O/U SHOTGUN

Gauge: 12, 20, 28, 3" chambers (2-3/4" 28 ga.). **Barrel:** 26", 28". **Weight:** 6.8 lbs. **Stock:** Checkered walnut. **Features:** Interchangeable barrels (20 and 28 ga.), single selective gold-plated trigger, boxlock action, auto safety, schnabel forend.
Price: **$1,917.00**
Price: 20 ga. and 28 ga. **$2,634.00**

BERETTA ULTRALIGHT OVER/UNDER

Gauge: 12, 2-3/4" chambers. **Barrel:** 26", 28", Mobilchoke choke tubes. **Weight:** About 5 lbs., 13 oz. **Stock:** Select American walnut with checkered grip and forend. **Features:** Low-profile aluminum alloy receiver with titanium breech face insert. Electroless nickel receiver with game scene engraving. Single selective trigger; automatic safety. Introduced 1992. Imported from Italy by Beretta U.S.A.
Price: **$1,931.00**

Beretta Ultralight Deluxe Over/Under Shotgun

Similar to the Ultralight except has matte electroless nickel finish receiver with gold game scene engraving; matte oil-finished, select walnut stock and forend. Imported from Italy by Beretta U.S.A.
Price: **$2,323.00**

BERETTA OVER/UNDER FIELD SHOTGUNS

Gauge: 12, 20, 28, and 410 bore, 2-3/4", 3" and 3-1/2" chambers. **Barrel:** 26" and 28" (Mobilchoke tubes). **Stock:** Close-grained walnut. **Features:** Highly-figured, American walnut stocks and forends, and a unique, weather-resistant finish on barrels. Silver designates standard 686, 687 models with silver receivers; 686 Silver Pigeon has enhanced engraving pattern, Schnabel forend; 686 Silver Essential has matte chrome finish; Gold indicates higher grade 686EL, 687EL models with full sideplates; Diamond is for 687EELL models with highest grade wood, engraving. Case provided with Gold and Diamond grades. Imported from Italy by Beretta U.S.A.

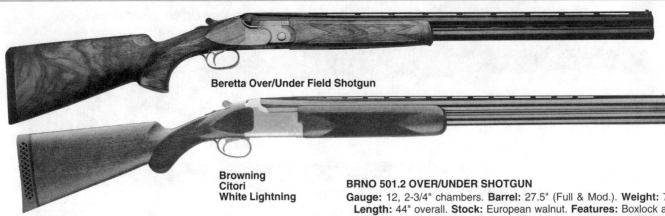

Beretta Over/Under Field Shotgun

Browning
Citori
White Lightning

Price: S686 Silver Pigeon two-bbl. set $2,587.00
Price: S686 Silver Pigeon. $1,817.00
Price: S687 Silver Pigeon II Sporting $2,196.00
Price: Combo 29" and 30" $3,151.00
Price: S687EL Gold Pigeon (gold inlays, sideplates) $4,099.00
Price: S687EL Gold Pigeon, 410, 26"; 28 ga., 28" $4,273.00
Price: S687 EL Gold Pigeon II (deep relief engraving). $4,513.00
Price: S687 EL Gold Pigeon II Sporting (d.r. engraving) $4,554.00

BERETTA MODEL SO5, SO6, SO9 SHOTGUNS
Gauge: 12, 2-3/4" chambers. **Barrel:** To customer specs. **Stock:** To customer specs. **Features:** SO5—Trap, Skeet and Sporting Clays models SO5; SO6—SO6 and SO6 EELL are field models. SO6 has a case-hardened or silver receiver with contour hand engraving. SO6 EELL has hand-engraved receiver in a fine floral or "fine English" pattern or game scene, with bas-relief chisel work and gold inlays. SO6 and SO6 EELL are available with sidelocks removable by hand. Imported from Italy by Beretta U.S.A.
Price: SO5 Trap, Skeet, Sporting $13,000.00
Price: SO6 Trap, Skeet, Sporting $17,500.00
Price: SO6 EELL Field, custom specs $28,000.00
Price: SO9 (12, 20, 28, 410, 26", 28", 30", any choke) $31,000.00

BERETTA SPORTING CLAYS SHOTGUNS
Gauge: 12 and 20, 2-3/4" and 3" chambers. **Barrel:** 28", 30", 32" Mobilchoke. **Stock:** Close-grained walnut. **Features:** Equipped with Beretta Mobilchoke flush-mounted screw-in choke tube system.12 or 20 gauge, 28", 30" Mobilchoke tubes (four, Skeet, Imp. Cyl., Mod., Full). Wide 12.5mm top rib with 2.5mm center groove; 686 Silver Pigeon has silver receiver with scroll engraving; 687 Silver Pigeon Sporting has silver receiver, highly figured walnut; 687 EL Pigeon Sporting has game scene engraving with gold inlaid animals on full sideplate. Introduced 1994. Imported from Italy by Beretta USA.
Price: $2,008.00

Beretta S687EL Gold Pigeon Sporting O/U
Similar to S687 Silver Pigeon Sporting except sideplates with gold inlay game scene, vent side and top ribs, bright orange front sight. Stock and forend are high grade walnut with fine-line checkering. Available in 12 gauge only with 28" or 30" barrels and Mobilchoke tubes. Weighs 6 lbs., 13 oz. Imported from Italy by Beretta USA.
Price: $4,595.00
Price: Combo (28 and 410) $5,244.00

BRNO ZH 300 OVER/UNDER SHOTGUN
Gauge: 12, 2-3/4" chambers. **Barrel:** 26", 27-1/2", 29" (Skeet, Imp. Cyl., Mod., Full). **Weight:** 7 lbs. **Length:** 44.4" overall. **Stock:** European walnut. **Features:** Double triggers; automatic safety; polished blue finish engraved receiver. Announced 1998. Imported from the Czech Republic by Euro-Imports.
Price: ZH 301, field. $594.00
Price: ZH 302, Skeet $608.00
Price: ZH 303, 12 ga. trap $608.00
Price: ZH 321, 16 ga. $595.00

BRNO 501.2 OVER/UNDER SHOTGUN
Gauge: 12, 2-3/4" chambers. **Barrel:** 27.5" (Full & Mod.). **Weight:** 7 lbs. **Length:** 44" overall. **Stock:** European walnut. **Features:** Boxlock action with double triggers, ejectors; automatic safety; hand-cut checkering. Announced 1998. Imported from The Czech Republic by Euro-Imports.
Price: $850.00

BROWNING CITORI O/U SHOTGUNS
Gauge: 12, 20, 28 and 410. **Barrel:** 26", 28" in 28 and 410. Offered with Invector choke tubes. All 12 and 20 gauge models have back-bored barrels and Invector Plus choke system. **Weight:** 6 lbs., 8 oz. (26" 410) to 7 lbs., 13 oz. (30" 12 ga.). **Length:** 43" overall (26" bbl.). **Stock:** Dense walnut, hand checkered, full pistol grip, beavertail forend. Field-type recoil pad on 12 ga. field guns and trap and Skeet models. **Sights:** Medium raised beads, German nickel silver. **Features:** Barrel selector integral with safety, automatic ejectors, three-piece takedown. Imported from Japan by Browning. Contact Browning for complete list of models and prices.
Price: Grade I, Hunter, Invector, 12 and 20 . . . . $1,486.00
Price: Grade I, Lightning, 28 and 410, Invector $1,594.00
Price: Grade III, Lightning, 28 and 410, Invector $2,570.00
Price: Grade VI, 28 and 410 Lightning, Invector $3,780.00
Price: Grade I, Lightning, Invector Plus, 12, 20 . . . . $1,534.00
Price: Grade I, Hunting, 28", 30" only, 3-1/2", Invector Plus . . . $1,489.00
Price: Grade III, Lightning, Invector, 12, 20 . . . . $2,300.00
Price: Grade VI, Lightning, Invector, 12, 20 . . . . $3,510.00
Price: Gran Lightning, 26", 28", Invector, 12, 20 . . . . $2,184.00
Price: Gran Lightning, 28, 410 . . . . $2,302.00
Price: Micro Lightning, 20 ga., 24" bbl., 6 lbs., 4 oz. $1,591.00
Price: White Lightning (silver nitride receiver w/engraving, 12 or 20 ga., 26", 28"). $1,583.00
Price: White Lightning, 28 or 410 gauge $1,654.00
Price: Citori Satin Hunter (12 ga., satin-finished wood, matte-finished barrels and receiver) 3-1/2" chambers $1,535.00

Browning Superlight Citori Over/Under
Similar to the standard Citori except available in 12, 20 with 24", 26" or 28" Invector barrels, 28 or 410 with 26" barrels choked Imp. Cyl. & Mod. or 28" choked Mod. & Full. Has straight grip stock, Schnabel forend tip. Superlight 12 weighs 6 lbs., 9 oz. (26" barrels); Superlight 20, 5 lbs., 12 oz. (26" barrels). Introduced 1982.
Price: Grade I, 28 or 410, Invector $1,666.00
Price: Grade III, Invector, 12 . . . . $2,300.00
Price: Grade VI, Invector, 12 or 20, gray or blue $3,510.00
Price: Grade VI, 28 or 410, Invector, gray or blue $3,780.00
Price: Grade I Invector, 12 or 20 . . . . $1,580.00
Price: Grade I Invector, White Upland Special (24" bbls.), 12 or 20 . . . . $1,583.00
Price: Citori Superlight Feather (12 ga., alloy receiver, 6 lbs. 4 oz.). $1,756.00

Browning Citori XT Trap Over/Under
Similar to the Citori Special Trap except has engraved silver nitride receiver with gold highlights, vented side barrel rib. Available in 12 gauge with 30" or 32" barrels, Invector-Plus choke tubes. Introduced 1999. Imported by Browning.
Price: $1,834.00
Price: With adjustable-comb stock $2,054.00

SHOTGUNS

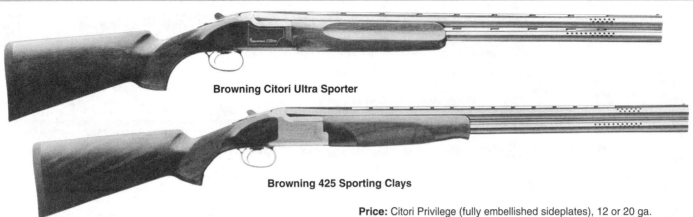

Browning Citori Ultra Sporter

Browning 425 Sporting Clays

SHOTGUNS

Browning Micro Citori Lightning

Similar to the standard Citori 20 ga. Lightning except scaled down for smaller shooter. Comes with 24" Invector Plus back-bored barrels, 13-3/4" length of pull. Weighs about 6 lbs., 3 oz. Introduced 1991.
Price: Grade I **$1,486.00**

Browning Citori Lightning Feather O/U

Similar to the 12 gauge Citori Grade I except has 2-3/4" chambers, rounded pistol grip, Lightning-style forend, and lighweight alloy receiver. Weighs 6 lbs. 15 oz. with 26" barrels (12 ga.); 6 lbs., 2 oz. (20 ga., 26" bbl.). Silvered, engraved receiver. Introduced 1999. Imported by Browning.
Price: 12 or 20 ga., 26" or 28" barrels **$1,693.00**
Price: Lightning Feather Combo (20 and 28 ga. bbls., 27" each) **$2,751.00**

Browning Citori Sporting Hunter

Similar to the Citori Hunting I except has Sporting Clays stock dimensions, a Superposed-style forend, and Sporting Clays butt pad. Available in 12 gauge with 3" chambers, back-bored 26", 28" and 30", all with Invector Plus choke tube system. Introduced 1998. Imported from Japan by Browning.
Price: 12 gauge, 3-1/2" **$1,709.00**
Price: 12, 20 gauge, 3" **$1,607.00**

Browning Citori Ultra XS Skeet

Similar to other Citori Ultra models except features a semi-beavertail forearm with deep finger grooves, ported barrels and triple system. Adjustable comb is optional. Introduced 2000.
Price: 12 ga., 28" or 30" barrel **$2,162.00**
New! Price: 20 ga., 28" or 30" barrel **$2,162.00**
Price: Adjustable comb model, 12 or 20 ga. **$2,380.00**

Browning Citori Ultra XS Trap

Similar to other Citori Ultra models except offered in 12 ga. only with 30" or 32" ported barrel, high-post rib, ventilated side ribs, Triple Trigger System™ and silver nitride receiver. Includes full, modified and imp. cyl. choke tubes. From Browning.
Price: 30" or 32" barrel **$2,022.00**
Price: Adjustable-comb model **$2,265.00**

Browning Citori Ultra XS Sporting

Similar to other Citori Ultra XS models except offered in 12, 20, 28 and 410 gauge. Silver nitride receiver, Schnabel forearm, ventilated side rib. Imported by Browning.
Price: 410 or 28 ga. **$2,268.00**
Price: 12 or 20 ga. **$2,196.00**

Browning Citori Feather XS Shotguns

Similar to the standard Citori except has lightweight alloy receiver, silver nitrade Nitex receiver, Schnabel forearm, ventilated side rib and Hi-Viz Comp fiber optics sight. Available in 12, 20, 28 and 410 gauges. Introduced 2000.
Price: 28" or 30" barrel . . . . **$2,266.00 to $2,338.00**

Browning Citori High Grade Shotguns

Similar to standard Citori except has full sideplates with engraved hunting scenes and gold inlays, high-grade, hand-oiled walnut stock and forearm. Introduced 2000. From Browning.

Price: Citori Privilege (fully embellished sideplates), 12 or 20 ga.
. . . . **$5,376.00**
Price: Citori BG VI Lightning (gold inlays of ducks and pheasants)
. . . . from **$3,340.00**
Price: Citori BG III Superlight (scroll engraving on grayed receiver, gold inlays) **$2,190.00**
Price: Citori 425 Golden Clays (engraving of game bird-clay bird transition, gold accents), 12 or 20 ga. **$3,977.00**

Browning Nitra Citori XS Sporting Clays

Similar to the Citori Grade I except has silver nitride receiver with gold accents, stock dimensions of 14-3/4"x1-1/2"x2-1/4" with satin finish, right-hand palm swell, Schnabel forend. Comes with Modified, Imp. Cyl. and Skeet Invector-Plus choke tubes. Back-bored barrels; vented side ribs. Introduced 1999. Imported by Browning.
Price: 12, 20 ga. **$2,011.00**
Price: 28 ga., 410-bore **$2,077.00**

Browning Special Sporting Clays

Similar to the Citori Ultra Sporter except has full pistol grip stock with palm swell, gloss finish, 28", 30" or 32" barrels with back-bored Invector Plus chokes (ported or non-ported); high post tapered rib. Also available as 28" and 30" two-barrel set. Introduced 1989.
Price: With ported barrels **$1,636.00**
Price: As above, adjustable comb **$1,856.00**

Browning Lightning Sporting Clays

Similar to the Citori Lightning with rounded pistol grip and classic forend. Has high post tapered rib or lower hunting-style rib with 30" back-bored Invector Plus barrels, ported or non-ported, 3" chambers. Gloss stock finish, radiused recoil pad. Has "Lightning Sporting Clays Edition" engraved and gold filled on receiver. Introduced 1989.
Price: Low-rib, ported **$1,691.00**
Price: High-rib, ported **$1,770.00**

BROWNING LIGHT SPORTING 802 ES O/U

Gauge: 12, 2-3/4" chambers. **Barrel:** 28", back-bored Invector Plus. Comes with flush-mounted Imp. Cyl. and Skeet; 2" extended Imp. Cyl. and Mod.; and 4" extended Imp. Cyl. and Mod. tubes. **Weight:** 7 lbs., 5 oz. **Length:** 45" overall. **Stock:** 14-3/8" x 1/8" x 1-9/16" x 1-3/4". Select walnut with radiused solid recoil pad, Schnabel-type forend. **Features:** Trigger adjustable for length of pull; narrow 6.2mm ventilated rib; ventilated barrel side rib; blued receiver. Introduced 1996. Imported from Japan from Browning.
Price: **$2,063.00**

BROWNING 425 SPORTING CLAYS

Gauge: 12, 20, 2-3/4" chambers. **Barrel:** 12 ga.—28", 30", 32" (Invector Plus tubes), back-bored; 20 ga.—28", 30" (Invector Plus tubes). **Weight:** 7 lbs., 13 oz. (12 ga., 28"). **Stock:** 14-13/16" (1/8")x1-7/16"x2-3/16" (12 ga.). Select walnut with gloss finish, cut checkering, Schnabel forend. **Features:** Grayed receiver with engraving, blued barrels. Barrels are ported on 12 gauge guns. Has low 10mm wide vent rib. Comes with three interchangeable trigger shoes to adjust length of pull. Introduced in U.S. 1993. Imported by Browning.
Price: Grade I, 12, 20 ga., Invector Plus **$2,006.00**
Price: Golden Clays, 12, 20 ga., Invector Plus **$3,977.00**

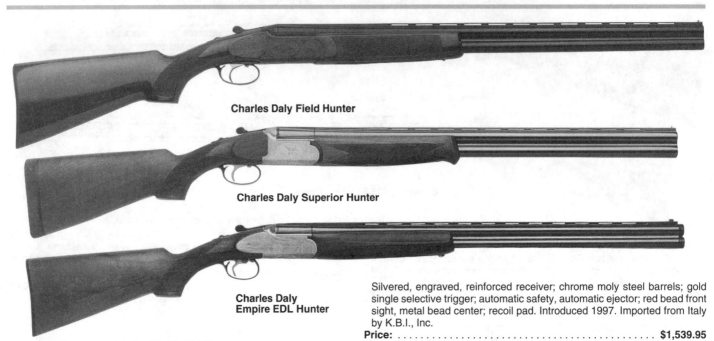

Charles Daly Field Hunter

Charles Daly Superior Hunter

Charles Daly
Empire EDL Hunter

CHARLES DALY SUPERIOR TRAP AE MC

Gauge: 12, 2-3/4" chambers. **Barrel:** 30" choke tubes. **Weight:** About 7 lbs. **Stock:** Checkered walnut; pistol grip, semi-beavertail forend. **Features:** Silver engraved receiver, chrome moly steel barrels; gold single selective trigger; automatic safety, automatic ejectors; red bead front sight, metal bead center; recoil pad. Introduced 1997. Imported from Italy by K.B.I., Inc.
Price: $1,219.00

CHARLES DALY FIELD HUNTER OVER/UNDER SHOTGUN

Gauge: 12, 20, 28 and 410 bore (3" chambers, 28 ga. has 2-3/4"). **Barrel:** 28" Mod & Full, 26" Imp. Cyl. & Mod (410 is Full & Full). **Weight:** About 7 lbs. **Length:** NA. **Stock:** Checkered walnut pistol grip and forend. **Features:** Blued engraved receiver, chrome moly steel barrels; gold single selective trigger; automatic safety; extractors; gold bead front sight. Introduced 1997. Imported from Italy by K.B.I., Inc.
Price: 12 or 20 ga. $749.00
Price: 28 ga. $809.00
Price: 410 bore $849.00

Charles Daly Field Hunter AE Shotgun

Similar to the Field Hunter except 28 gauge and 410-bore only; 26" (Imp. Cyl. & Mod., 28 gauge), 26" (Full & Full, 410); automatic; ejectors. Introduced 1997. Imported from Italy by K.B.I., Inc.
Price: 28 . . . . $889.00
Price: 410 . . . . $929.00

Charles Daly Superior Hunter AE Shotgun

Similar to the Field Hunter AE except has silvered, engraved receiver. Introduced 1997. Imported from Italy by F.B.I., Inc.
Price: 28 ga. $1,059.00
Price: 410 bore $1,099.00

Charles Daly Field Hunter AE-MC

Similar to the Field Hunter except in 12 or 20 only; 26" or 28" barrels with five multichoke tubes; automatic ejectors. Introduced 1997. Imported from Italy by K.B.I., Inc.
Price: 12 or 20 . . . . $979.95

Charles Daly Superior Sporting O/U

Similar to the Field Hunter AE-MC except 28" or 30" barrels; silvered, engraved receiver; five choke tubes; ported barrels; red bead front sight. Introduced 1997. Imported from Italy by K.B.I., Inc.
Price: $1,259.95

CHARLES DALY EMPIRE TRAP AE MC

Gauge: 12, 2-3/4" chambers. **Barrel:** 30" choke tubes. **Weight:** About 7 lbs. **Stock:** Checkered walnut; pistol grip, semi-beavertail forend. **Features:**

Silvered, engraved, reinforced receiver; chrome moly steel barrels; gold single selective trigger; automatic safety, automatic ejector; red bead front sight, metal bead center; recoil pad. Introduced 1997. Imported from Italy by K.B.I., Inc.
Price: $1,539.95

CHARLES DALY DIAMOND REGENT GTX DL HUNTER O/U

Gauge: 12, 20, 410, 3" chambers, 28, 2-3/4" chambers. **Barrel:** 26", 28", 30" (choke tubes), 26" (Imp. Cyl. & Mod. in 28, 26" (Full & Full) in 410. **Weight:** About 7 lbs. **Stock:** Extra select fancy European walnut with 24" hand checkering, hand rubbed oil finish. **Features:** Boss-type action with internal side lumps. Deep cut hand-engraved scrollwork and game scene set in full sideplates. GTX detachable single selective trigger system with coil springs; chrome moly steel barrels; automatic safety; automatic ejectors, white bead front sight, metal bead center sight. Introduced 1997. Imported from Italy by K.B.I., Inc.
Price: 12 or 20 . . . . $22,299.00
Price: 28 . . . . $22,369.00
Price: 410 . . . . $22,419.00
Price: Diamond Regent GTX EDL Hunter (as above with engraved scroll and birds, 10 gold inlays), 12 or 20 . . . . $26,249.00
Price: As above, 28 . . . . $26,499.00
Price: As above, 410 . . . . $26,549.00

CHARLES DALY EMPIRE EDL HUNTER O/U

Gauge: 12, 20, 410, 3" chambers, 28 ga., 2-3/4". **Barrel:** 26", 28" (12, 20, choke tubes), 26" (Imp. Cyl. & Mod., 28 ga.), 26" (Full & Full, 410). **Weight:** About 7 lbs. **Stocks:** Checkered walnut pistol grip buttstock, semi-beavertail forend; recoil pad. **Features:** Silvered, engraved receiver; chrome moly barrels; gold single selective trigger; automatic safety; automatic ejectors; red bead front sight, metal bead middle sight. Introduced 1997. Imported from Italy by K.B.I., Inc.
Price: Empire EDL (dummy sideplates) 12 or 20 . . . . $1,559.95
Price: Empire EDL, 28 . . . . $1,559.95
Price: Empire EDL, 410 . . . . $1,599.95

Charles Daly Empire Sporting O/U

Similar to the Empire EDL Hunter except 12 or 20 gauge only, 28", 30" barrels with choke tubes; ported barrels; special stock dimensions. Introduced 1997. Imported from Italy by K.B.I., Inc.
Price: $1,499.95

CHARLES DALY DIAMOND GTX SPORTING O/U SHOTGUN

Gauge: 12, 20, 3" chambers. **Barrel:** 28", 30" with choke tubes. **Weight:** About 8.5 lbs. **Stock:** Checkered deluxe walnut; Sporting clays dimensions. Pistol grip; semi-beavertail forend; hand rubbed oil finish. **Features:** Chromed, hand-engraved receiver; chrome moly steel barrels; GTX detachable single selective trigger system with coil springs, automatic safety; automatic ejectors; red bead front sight; ported barrels. Introduced 1997. Imported from Italy by K.B.I., Inc.
Price: $5,804.95

SHOTGUNS — OVER/UNDERS

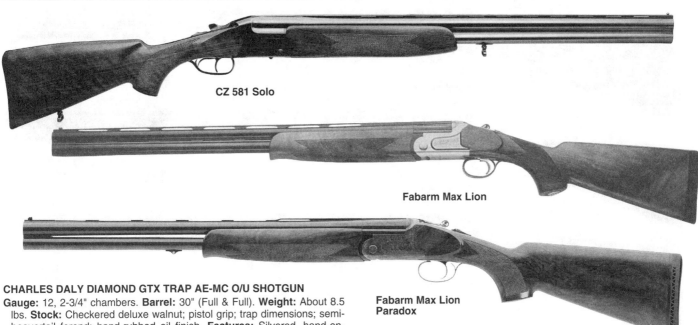

CZ 581 Solo

Fabarm Max Lion

Fabarm Max Lion Paradox

CHARLES DALY DIAMOND GTX TRAP AE-MC O/U SHOTGUN

Gauge: 12, 2-3/4" chambers. **Barrel:** 30" (Full & Full). **Weight:** About 8.5 lbs. **Stock:** Checkered deluxe walnut; pistol grip; trap dimensions; semi-beavertail forend; hand-rubbed oil finish. **Features:** Silvered, hand-engraved receiver; chrome moly steel barrels; GTX detachable single selective trigger system with coil springs, automatic safety, automatic-ejectors, red bead front sight, metal bead middle; recoil pad. Introduced 1997. Imported from Italy by K.B.I., Inc.

Price: $5,804.95

CHARLES DALY DIAMOND GTX DL HUNTER O/U

Gauge: 12, 20, 410, 3" chambers, 28, 2-3/4" chambers. **Barrel:** 26, 28", choke tubes in 12 and 20 ga., 26" (Imp. Cyl. & Mod.), 26" (Full & Full) in 410-bore. **Weight:** About 8.5 lbs. **Stock:** Select fancy European walnut stock, with 24 lpi hand checkering; hand-rubbed oil finish. **Features:** Boss-type action with internal side lugs, hand-engraved scrollwork and game scene. GTX detachable single selective trigger system with coil springs; chrome moly steel barrels, automatic safety, automatic ejectors, red bead front sight, recoil pad. Introduced 1997. Imported from Italy by K.B.I., Inc.

Price: 12 or 20 . . . . $12,399.00
Price: 28 . . . . $12,489.00
Price: 410 . . . . $12,529.00
Price: GTX EDL Hunter (with gold inlays), 12, 20 . . . . $15,999.00
Price: As above, 28 . . . . $16,179.00
Price: As above, 410 . . . . $16,219.00

CZ 581 SOLO OVER/UNDER SHOTGUN

Gauge: 12, 2-3/4" chambers. **Barrel:** 27.6" (Mod. & Full). **Weight:** 7.37 lbs. **Length:** 44.5" overall. **Stock:** Circassian walnut. **Features:** Automatic ejectors; double triggers; Kersten-style double lump locking system. Imported from the Czech Republic by CZ-USA.

Price: $799.00

EAA/BAIKAL MP-233 OVER/UNDER SHOTGUN

Gauge: 12, 3" chambers. **Barrel:** 26", 28", 30"; imp., mod. and full choke tubes. **Weight:** 7.28 lbs. **Stock:** Walnut; checkered forearm and grip. **Features:** Hammer-forged barrels; chrome-lined bores; removable trigger assembly (optional single selective trigger or double trigger); ejectors. Introduced 2000. Imported by European American Armory.

Price: MP-233. . . . . $939.00

EAA/BAIKAL IZH-27 OVER/UNDER SHOTGUN

Gauge: 12 (3" chambers), 16 (2-3/4" chambers), 20 (3" chambers), 28 (2-3/4" chambers), 410 (3"). **Barrel:** 26-1/2", 28-1/2" (imp., mod. and full choke tubes for 12 and 20 gauges; improved cylinder and modified for 16 and 28 gauges; improved modified and full for 410; 16 also offered in mod. and full). **Weight:** NA. **Stock:** Walnut, checkered forearm and grip. Imported by European American Armory.

Price: IZH-27 (12, 16 and 20 gauge) $509.00
Price: IZH-27 (28 and 410 gauge) $569.00

EAA IZH-27 Sporting O/U

Basic IZH-27 with barrel porting, wide vent rib with double sight beads, engraved nickel receiver, checkered walnut stock and forend with palm swell and semi beavertail, 3 screw chokes, SS trigger, selectable ejectors, auto tang safety

Price: 12 ga., 29" bbl. $589.00

FABARM MAX LION OVER/UNDER SHOTGUNS

Gauge: 12, 3" chambers, 20, 3" chambers. **Barrel:** 26", 28", 30" (12 ga.); 26", 28" (20 ga.), choke tubes. **Weight:** 7.4 lbs. **Length:** 47.5" overall (26" barrel). **Stock:** European walnut; leather-covered recoil pad. **Features:** TriBore barrel, boxlock action with single selective trigger, manual safety, automatic ejectors; chrome-lined barrels; adjustable trigger. Silvered, engraved receiver. Comes with locking, fitted luggage case. Introduced 1998. Imported from Italy by Heckler & Koch, Inc.

Price: 12 or 20 . . . . $1,899.00

FABARM ULTRA CAMO MAG LION O/U SHOTGUN

Gauge: 12, 3-1/2" chambers. **Barrel:** 28" (cyl., imp. cyl., mod., imp. mod., full, SS-mod., SS-full choke tubes). **Weight:** 7.9 lbs. **Length:** 50" overall. **Stock:** Camo-colored walnut. **Features:** TriBore barrel, Wetlands Camo finished metal surfaces, single selective trigger, non-auto ejectors, leather-covered recoil pad. Locking hard plastic case. Introduced 1998. Imported from Italy by Heckler & Koch, Inc.

Price: $1,229.00

FABARM MAX LION PARADOX

Gauge: 12, 3" chambers. **Barrel:** 24". **Weight:** 7.6 lbs. **Length:** 44.5" overall. **Stock:** Walnut with special enhancing finish. **Features:** TriBore upper barrel, both wood and receiver are enhanced with special finishes, color-case hardened type finish.

Price: 12 or 20 . . . . $1,199.00

FABARM SILVER LION OVER/UNDER SHOTGUNS

Gauge: 12, 3" chambers, 20, 3" chambers. **Barrel:** 26", 28", 30" (12 ga.); 26", 28" (20 ga.), choke tubes. **Weight:** 7.2 lbs. **Length:** 47.5" overall (26" barrels). **Stock:** Walnut; leather-covered recoil pad. **Features:** TriBore barrel, boxlock action with single selective trigger; silvered receiver with engraving; automatic ejectors. Comes with locking hard plastic case. Introduced 1998. Imported from Italy by Heckler & Koch, Inc.

Price: 12 or 20 . . . . $1,299.00

Fabarm Silver Lion Cub Model O/U

Similar to the Silver Lion except has 12.5" length of pull, is in 20 gauge only (3-1/2" chambers), and comes with 24" TriBore barrel system. Weight is 6 lbs. Introduced 1999. Imported from Italy by Heckler & Koch, Inc.

Price: $1,299.00

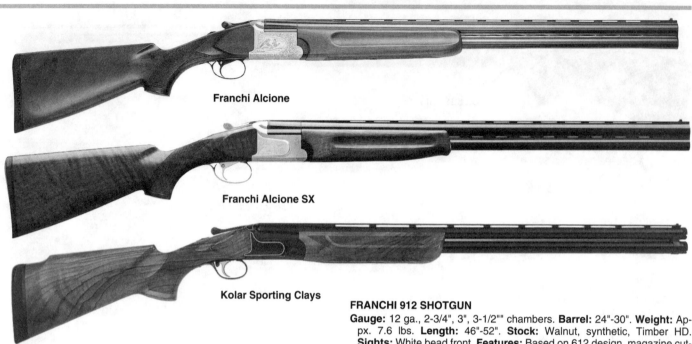

Franchi Alcione

Franchi Alcione SX

Kolar Sporting Clays

FABARM CAMO TURKEY MAG O/U SHOTGUN

Gauge: 12, 3-1/2" chambers. **Barrel:** 20" TriBore (Ultra-Full ported tubes). **Weight:** 7.5 lbs. **Length:** 46" overall. **Stock:** 14.5"x1.5"x2.29". Walnut. **Sights:** Front bar, Picatinny rail scope base. **Features:** Completely covered with Xtra Brown camouflage finish. Unported barrels. Introduced 1999. Imported from Italy by Heckler & Koch, Inc.
Price: **$1,339.00**

FABARM SPORTING CLAYS COMPETITION EXTRA O/U

Gauge: 12, 20, 3" chambers. **Barrel:** 12 ga. has 30", 20 ga. has 28"; ported TriBore barrel system with five tubes. **Weight:** 7 to 7.8 lbs. **Length:** 49.6" overall (20 ga.). **Stock:** 14.50"x1.38"x2.17" (20 ga.); deluxe walnut; leather-covered recoil pad. **Features:** Single selective trigger, auto ejectors; 10mm channeled rib; carbon fiber finish. Introduced 1999. Imported from Italy by Heckler & Koch, Inc.
Price: **$1,749.00**

FRANCHI ALCIONE FIELD OVER/UNDER SHOTGUN

Gauge: 12, 20, 3" chambers. **Barrel:** 26", 28"; IC, M, F tubes. **Weight:** 7.5 lbs. **Length:** 43" overall with 26" barrels. **Stock:** European walnut. **Features:** Boxlock action with ejectors, barrel selector mounted on trigger; silvered, engraved receiver, vent center rib, automatic safety, interchangeable 20 ga. bbls., left-hand available. Imported from Italy by Benelli USA. Hard case included.
Price: **$1,200.00**
Price: (20 gauge barrel set) **$460.00**

Franchi SX O/U Shotgun

NEW! Similar to Alcione Field model with high grade walnut stock and forend. Gold engraved removeable sideplates, interchangeable barrels.
Price: **$1,800.00**

Franchi Alcione Sport SL O/U Shotgun

Similar to Alcione except 2-3/4" chambers, elongated forcing cones and porting for Sporting Clays shooting. 10mm vent rib, tightly curved pistol grip, manual safety, removeable sideplates. Imported from Italy by Benelli USA.
Price: **$1,300.00**

FRANCHI ALCIONE TITANIUM OVER/UNDER SHOTGUN

Gauge: 12, 20, 3" chambers. **Barrel:** 26", 28"; IC, M, F tubes. **Weight:** 6.8 lbs. **Length:** 43", 45". **Stock:** Select walnut. **Sights:** Front/mid. **Features:** Receiver (titanium inserts) made of aluminum alloy. 7mm vent rib. Fast locking triggers. Left-hand available.
Price: **$1,425.00**

FRANCHI 912 SHOTGUN

Gauge: 12 ga., 2-3/4", 3", 3-1/2"" chambers. **Barrel:** 24"-30". **Weight:** Appx. 7.6 lbs. **Length:** 46"-52". **Stock:** Walnut, synthetic, Timber HD. **Sights:** White bead front. **Features:** Based on 612 design, magazine cut-off, stepped vent rib, dual-recoil-reduction system.
Price: Satin walnut **$1,000.00**
Price: Synthetic **$940.00**
Price: Timber HD **$1,050.00**

FRANCHI VELOCE OVER/UNDER SHOTGUN

Gauge: 20, 28. **Barrel:** 26", 28"; IC, M, F tubes. **Weight:** 5.5-5.8 lbs. **Length:** 43"-45". **Stock:** High grade walnut. **Features:** Aluminum receiver with steel reinforcement scaled to 20 gauge for light weight. Pistol grip stock wtih slip recoil pad. Imported by Benelli USA. Hard case included.
Price: **$1,425.00**
Price: 28 ga. **$1,500.00**

Franchi Veloce English Over/Under Shotgun

Similar to Veloce standard model with straight grip "English" style stock. Available with 26" barrels in 20 and 28 gauge. Hard case included.
Price: **$1,425.00**
Price: 28 ga. **$1,500.00**

HOENIG ROTARY ROUND ACTION GAME GUN

Gauge: 28. **Barrel:** 26", 28", solid tapered rib. **Weight:** 6 lbs. **Stock:** English walnut. **Features:** Round action opens by rotating barrels, pulling forward. Inertia extractor, rotary safety blocks strikers. Simple takedown without removing forend. Elegance and class of guns of yesteryear. Made in U.S.A. by George Hoenig.
Price: **$19,980.00**

KIMBER AUGUSTA SHOTGUN

NEW Premium over/under, Boss type action. 12 ga. only. Tri-alloy barrel with choke tubes. Backbored 736. Long forcing cones. HiViz sight with center bead on vent ribl. Available with many features. Custom dimensions available. Imported from Italy by Kimber Mfg., Inc.
Price: **$5,000.00**

KOLAR SPORTING CLAYS O/U SHOTGUN

Gauge: 12, 2-3/4" chambers. **Barrel:** 30", 32"; extended choke tubes. **Stock:** 14-5/8"x2-1/2"x1-7/8"x1-3/8". French walnut. **Features:** Single selective trigger, detachable, adjustable for length; overbored barrels with long forcing cones; flat tramline rib; matte blue finish. Made in U.S. by Kolar.
Price: Standard. **$7,250.00**
Price: Elite **$10,245.00**
Price: Elite Gold **$12,245.00**
Price: Legend **$13,245.00**
Price: Custom Gold **$24,750.00**

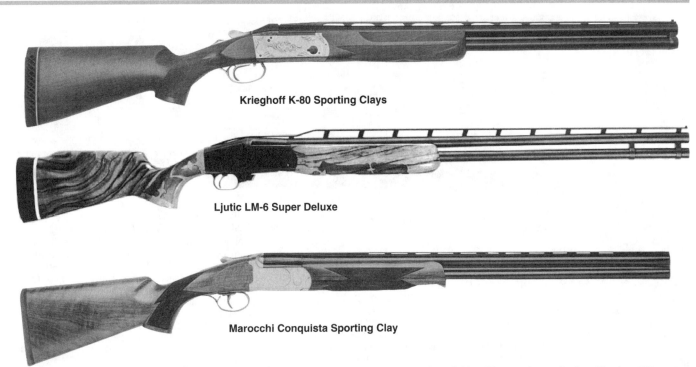

Krieghoff K-80 Sporting Clays

Ljutic LM-6 Super Deluxe

Marocchi Conquista Sporting Clay

Kolar AAA Competition Trap Over/Under Shotgun

Similar to the Sporting Clays gun except has 32" O/U /34" Unsingle or 30" O/U /34" Unsingle barrels as an over/under, unsingle, or combination set. Stock dimensions are 14-1/2"x2-1/2"x1-1/2"; American or French walnut; step parallel rib standard. Contact maker for full listings. Made in U.S. by Kolar.

Price: Over/under, choke tubes, Standard $7,025.00
Price: Unsingle, choke tubes, Standard $7,775.00
Price: Combo (30"/34", 32"/34"), Standard. $10,170.00

Kolar AAA Competition Skeet Over/Under Shotgun

Similar to the Sporting Clays gun except has 28" or 30" barrels with Kolar-ite AAA sub gauge tubes; stock of American or French walnut with matte finish; flat tramline rib; under barrel adjustable for point of impact. Many options available. Contact maker for complete listing. Made in U.S. by Kolar.

Price: Standard, choke tubes $8,645.00
Price: Standard, choke tubes, two-barrel set $10,710.00

KRIEGHOFF K-80 SPORTING CLAYS O/U

Gauge: 12. **Barrel:** 28", 30" or 32" with choke tubes. **Weight:** About 8 lbs. **Stock:** #3 Sporting stock designed for gun-down shooting. **Features:** Standard receiver with satin nickel finish and classic scroll engraving. Selective mechanical trigger adjustable for position. Choice of tapered flat or 8mm parallel flat barrel rib. Free-floating barrels. Aluminum case. Imported from Germany by Krieghoff International, Inc.

Price: Standard grade with five choke tubes, from $8,150.00

KRIEGHOFF K-80 SKEET SHOTGUN

Gauge: 12, 2-3/4" chambers. **Barrel:** 28", 30", (Skeet & Skeet), optional choke tubes). **Weight:** About 7-3/4 lbs. **Stock:** American Skeet or straight Skeet stocks, with palm-swell grips. Walnut. **Features:** Satin gray receiver finish. Selective mechanical trigger adjustable for position. Choice of ventilated 8mm parallel flat rib or ventilated 8-12mm tapered flat rib. Introduced 1980. Imported from Germany by Krieghoff International, Inc.

Price: Standard, Skeet chokes. $6,900.00
Price: Skeet Special (28" or 30", tapered flat rib,
Skeet & Skeet choke tubes) $7,575.00

KRIEGHOFF K-80 O/U TRAP SHOTGUN

Gauge: 12, 2-3/4" chambers. **Barrel:** 30", 32" (Imp. Mod. & Full or choke tubes). **Weight:** About 8-1/2 lbs. **Stock:** Four stock dimensions or

adjustable stock available; all have palm swell grips. Checkered European walnut. **Features:** Satin nickel receiver. Selective mechanical trigger, adjustable for position. Ventilated step rib. Introduced 1980. Imported from Germany by Krieghoff International, Inc.

Price: K-80 O/U (30", 32", Imp. Mod. & Full), from $7,375.00
Price: K-80 Unsingle (32", 34", Full), Standard, from $7,950.00
Price: K-80 Combo (two-barrel set), Standard, from $10,475.00

Krieghoff K-20 O/U Shotguns

Similar to the K-80 except built on a 20-gauge frame. Designed for skeet, sporting clays and field use. Offered in 20, 28 and 410 gauge, 28" and 30" barrels. Imported from Germany by Krieghoff International Inc.

Price: K-20, 20 gauge, from $8,150.00
Price: K-20, 28 gauge, from $8,425.00
Price: K-20, 410 gauge, from $8,425.00

LEBEAU - COURALLY BOSS-VEREES O/U

Gauge: 12, 20, 2-3/4" chambers. **Barrel:** 25" to 32". **Weight:** To customer specifications. **Stock:** Exhibition-quality French walnut. **Features:** Boss-type sidelock with automatic ejectors; single or double triggers; chopper lump barrels. A custom gun built to customer specifications. Imported from Belgium by Wm. Larkin Moore.

Price: From. $70,000.00

LJUTIC LM-6 SUPER DELUXE O/U SHOTGUN

Gauge: 12. **Barrel:** 28" to 34", choked to customer specs for live birds, trap, International Trap. **Weight:** To customer specs. **Stock:** To customer specs. Oil finish, hand checkered. **Features:** Custom-made gun. Hollow-milled rib, pull or release trigger, pushbutton opener in front of trigger guard. From Ljutic Industries.

Price: Super Deluxe LM-6 O/U. $17,995.00
Price: Over/Under Combo (interchangeable single barrel, two trigger guards, one for single trigger, one for doubles) $24,995.00
Price: Extra over/under barrel sets, 29"-32" $5,995.00

LUGER CLASSIC O/U SHOTGUNS

Gauge: 12, 3" and 3-1/2" chambers. **Barrel:** 26", 28", 30"; imp. cyl. mod. and full choke tubes. **Weight:** 7-1/2 lbs. **Length:** 45" overall (28" barrel) **Stock:** Select-grade European walnut, hand-checkered grip and forend. **Features:** Gold, single selective trigger; automatic ejectors. Introduced 2000.

Price: Classic (26", 28" or 30" barrel; 3-1/2" chambers). $919.00
Price: Classic Sporting (30" barrel; 3" chambers) $964.00

SHOTGUNS — OVER/UNDERS

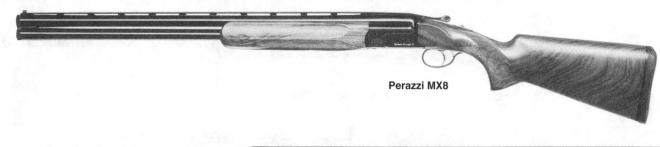

Perazzi MX8

Perazzi Sporting Classic

MAROCCHI CONQUISTA SPORTING CLAYS O/U SHOTGUNS

Gauge: 12, 2-3/4" chambers. **Barrel:** 28", 30", 32" (ContreChoke tubes); 10mm concave vent rib. **Weight:** About 8 lbs. **Stock:** 14-1/2"-14-7/8"x2-3/16"x1-7/16"; American walnut with checkered grip and forend; Sporting Clays butt pad. **Sights:** 16mm luminescent front. **Features:** Lower monoblock and frame profile. Fast lock time. Ergonomically-shaped trigger adjustable for pull length. Automatic selective ejectors. Coin-finished receiver, blued barrels. Five choke tubes, hard case. Available as true left-hand model—opening lever operates from left to right; stock has left-hand cast. Introduced 1994. Imported from Italy by Precision Sales International.

Price: Grade I, right-hand $1,490.00
Price: Grade I, left-hand $1,615.00
Price: Grade II, right-hand $1,828.00
Price: Grade II, left-hand $2,180.00
Price: Grade III, right-hand, from $3,093.00
Price: Grade III, left-hand, from $3,093.00

Marocchi Conquista Trap Over/Under Shotgun

Similar to Conquista Sporting Clays model except 30" or 32" barrels choked Full & Full, stock dimensions of 14-1/2"-14-7/8"x1-11/16"x1-9/32"; weighs about 8-1/4 lbs. Introduced 1994. Imported from Italy by Precision Sales International.

Price: Grade I, right-hand $1,490.00
Price: Grade II, right-hand $1,828.00
Price: Grade III, right-hand, from $3,093.00

Marocchi Conquista Skeet Over/Under Shotgun

Similar to Conquista Sporting Clays except 28" (Skeet & Skeet) barrels, stock dimensions of 14-3/8"-14-3/4"x2-3/16"x1-1/2". Weighs about 7-3/4 lbs. Introduced 1994. Imported from Italy by Precision Sales International.

Price: Grade I, right-hand $1,490.00
Price: Grade II, right-hand $1,828.00
Price: Grade III, right-hand, from $3,093.00

MAROCCHI MODEL 99 SPORTING TRAP AND SKEET

Gauge: 12, 2-3/4", 3" chambers. **Barrel:** 28", 30", 32". **Stock:** French walnut. **Features:** Boss Locking system, screw-in chokes, low recoil, lightweight monoblock barrels and ribs. Imported from Italy by Precision Sales International.

Price: Grade I $2,350.00
Price: Grade II $2,870.00
Price: Grade II Gold $3,025.00
Price: Grade III $3,275.00
Price: Grade III Gold $3,450.00
Price: Blackgold $4,150.00
Price: Lodestar $5,125.00
Price: Brittania $5,125.00
Price: Diana $6,350.00

MAROCCHI CONQUISTA USA
MODEL 92 SPORTING CLAYS O/U SHOTGUN

Gauge: 12, 3" chambers. **Barrel:** 30"; back-bored, ported (ContreChoke Plus tubes); 10 mm concave ventilated top rib, ventilated middle rib. **Weight:** 8 lbs. 2 oz. **Stock:** 14-1/4"-14-5/8"x 2-1/8"x1-3/8"; American walnut with checkered grip and forend; Sporting Clays butt pad. **Features:** Low profile frame; fast lock time; automatic selective ejectors; blued receiver and barrels. Comes with three choke tubes. Ergonomically shaped trigger adjustable for pull length without tools. Barrels are back-bored and ported. Introduced 1996. Imported from Italy by Precision Sales International.

Price: $1,490.00

MERKEL MODEL 2001EL O/U SHOTGUN

Gauge: 12, 20, 3" chambers, 28, 2-3/4" chambers. **Barrel:** 12—28"; 20, 28 ga.—26-3/4". **Weight:** About 7 lbs. (12 ga.). **Stock:** Oil-finished walnut; English or pistol grip. **Features:** Self-cocking Blitz boxlock action with cocking indicators; Kersten double cross-bolt lock; silver-grayed receiver with engraved hunting scenes; coil spring ejectors; single selective or double triggers. Imported from Germany by GSI, Inc.

Price: 12, 20 . . . . $7,295.00
Price: 28 ga. $7,295.00
Price: Model 2000EL (scroll engraving, 12, 20 or 28) $5,795.00

Merkel Model 303EL O/U Shotgun

Similar to Model 2001 EL except Holland & Holland-style sidelock action with cocking indicators; English-style Arabesque engraving. Available in 12, 20, 28 gauge. Imported from Germany by GSI, Inc.

Price: $19,995.00

Merkel Model 2002 EL O/U Shotgun

Similar to Model 2001 EL except dummy sideplates, Arabesque engraving with hunting scenes; 12, 20, 28 gauge. Imported from Germany by GSI, Inc.

Price: $10,995.00

PERAZZI MX8 OVER/UNDER SHOTGUNS

Gauge: 12, 2-3/4" chambers. **Barrel:** 28-3/8" (Imp. Mod. & Extra Full), 29-1/2" (choke tubes). **Weight:** 7 lbs., 12 oz. **Stock:** Special specifications. **Features:** Has single selective trigger; flat 7/16"x5/16" vent. rib. Many options available. Imported from Italy by Perazzi U.S.A., Inc.

Price: Sporting $9,980.00
Price: Trap Double Trap (removable trigger group) $9,010.00
Price: Skeet $9,010.00
Price: SC3 grade (variety of engraving patterns) . . . . . Starting at **$15,300**
Price: SCO grade (more intricate engraving, gold inlays)
. . . . Starting at **$26,000**

PERAZZI MX12 HUNTING OVER/UNDER

Gauge: 12, 2-3/4" chambers. **Barrel:** 26-3/4", 27-1/2", 28-3/8", 29-1/2" (Mod. & Full); choke tubes available in 27-5/8", 29-1/2" only (MX12C). **Weight:** 7 lbs., 4 oz. **Stock:** To customer specs; Interchangeable. **Features:** Single selective trigger; coil springs used in action; Schnabel forend tip. Imported from Italy by Perazzi U.S.A., Inc.

Price: From $9,010.00
Price: MX12C (with choke tubes), from $9,460.00

Perazzi MX8 Special Combo Single Barrel

Perazzi MX28

Piotti Boss

Rizzini S790 Emel

Perazzi MX20 Hunting Over/Under

Similar to the MX12 except 20 ga. frame size. Non-removable trigger group. Available in 20, 28, 410 with 2-3/4" or 3" chambers. 26" standard, and choked Mod. & Full. Weight is 6 lbs., 6 oz.
Price: From **$9,010.00**
Price: MX20C (as above, 20 ga. only, choke tubes), from **$9,460.00**

PERAZZI MX8/MX8 SPECIAL TRAP, SKEET

Gauge: 12, 2-3/4" chambers. **Barrel:** Trap—29-1/2" (Imp. Mod. & Extra Full), 31-1/2" (Full & Extra Full). Choke tubes optional. Skeet—27-5/8" (Skeet & Skeet). **Weight:** About 8-1/2 lbs. (Trap); 7 lbs., 15 oz. (Skeet). **Stock:** Interchangeable and custom made to customer specs. **Features:** Has detachable and interchangeable trigger group with flat V springs. Flat 7/16" ventilated rib. Many options available. Imported from Italy by Perazzi U.S.A., Inc.
Price: From **$8,840.00**
Price: MX8 Special (adj. four-position trigger), from **$9,350.00**
Price: MX8 Special Combo (o/u and single barrel sets), from . **$12,340.00**

Perazzi MX8 Special Skeet Over/Under

Similar to the MX8 Skeet except has adjustable four-position trigger, Skeet stock dimensions.
Price: From **$9,350.00**

Perazzi MX8/20 Over/Under Shotgun

Similar to the MX8 except has smaller frame and has a removable trigger mechanism. Available in trap, Skeet, sporting or game models with fixed chokes or choke tubes. Stock is made to customer specifications. Introduced 1993.
Price: From **$9,790.00**

PERAZZI MX10 OVER/UNDER SHOTGUN

Gauge: 12, 2-3/4" chambers. **Barrel:** 29.5", 31.5" (fixed chokes). **Weight:** NA. **Stock:** Walnut; cheekpiece adjustable for elevation and cast. **Features:** Adjustable rib; vent. side rib. Externally selective trigger. Available in single barrel, combo, over/under trap, Skeet, pigeon and sporting models. Introduced 1993. Imported from Italy by Perazzi U.S.A., Inc.
Price: From **$11,030.00**

PERAZZI MX28, MX410 GAME O/U SHOTGUNS

Gauge: 28, 2-3/4" chambers, 410, 3" chambers. **Barrel:** 26" (Imp. Cyl. & Full). **Weight:** NA. **Stock:** To customer specifications. **Features:** Made on scaled-down frames proportioned to the gauge. Introduced 1993. Imported from Italy by Perazzi U.S.A., Inc.
Price: From **$17,670.00**

PIOTTI BOSS OVER/UNDER SHOTGUN

Gauge: 12, 20. **Barrel:** 26" to 32", chokes as specified. **Weight:** 6.5 to 8 lbs. **Stock:** Dimensions to customer specs. Best quality figured walnut. **Features:** Essentially a custom-made gun with many options. Introduced 1993. Imported from Italy by Wm. Larkin Moore.
Price: From **$35,780.00**

REMINGTON MODEL 332 O/U SHOTGUN

Gauge: 12, 3" chambers. **Barrel:** 26", 28", 30". **Weight:** 7.75 lbs. **Length:** 42"-47" **Stock:** Satin-finished American walnut. **Sights:** Twin bead. **Features:** Light-contour, vent rib, Rem chock barrel, blued, traditional M-32 experience with M-300 Ideal performance, standard auto ejectors, set trigger. Proven boxlock action.
Price: **$1,532.00**

RIZZINI S790 EMEL OVER/UNDER SHOTGUN

Gauge: 20, 28, 410. **Barrel:** 26", 27.5" (Imp. Cyl. & Imp. Mod.). **Weight:** About 6 lbs. **Stock:** 14"x1-1/2"x2-1/8". Extra-fancy select walnut. **Features:** Boxlock action with profuse engraving; automatic ejectors; single selective trigger; silvered receiver. Comes with Nizzoli leather case. Introduced 1996. Imported from Italy by Wm. Larkin Moore & Co.
Price: From **$8,200.00**

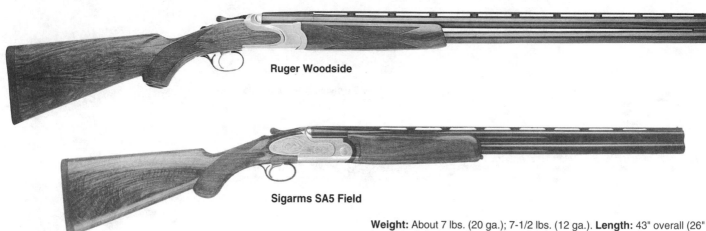

Ruger Woodside

Sigarms SA5 Field

Rizzini S792 EMEL Over/Under Shotgun
Similar to S790 EMEL except dummy sideplates with extensive engraving coverage. Nizzoli leather case. Introduced 1996. Imported from Italy by Wm. Larkin Moore & Co.
Price: From **$7,900.00**

RIZZINI UPLAND EL OVER/UNDER SHOTGUN
Gauge: 12, 16, 20, 28, 410. **Barrel:** 26", 27-1/2", Mod. & Full, Imp. Cyl. & Imp. Mod. choke tubes. **Weight:** About 6.6 lbs. **Stock:** 14-1/2"x1-1/2"x2-1/4". **Features:** Boxlock action; single selective trigger; ejectors; profuse engraving on silvered receiver. Comes with fitted case. Introduced 1996. Imported from Italy by Wm. Larkin Moore & Co.
Price: From **$2,750.00**

Rizzini Artemis Over/Under Shotgun
Same as Upland EL model except dummy sideplates with extensive game scene engraving. Fancy European walnut stock. Fitted case. Introduced 1996. Imported from Italy by Wm. Larkin Moore & Co.
Price: From **$1,800.00**

RIZZINI S782 EMEL OVER/UNDER SHOTGUN
Gauge: 12, 2-3/4" chambers. **Barrel:** 26", 27.5" (Imp. Cyl. & Imp. Mod.). **Weight:** About 6.75 lbs. **Stock:** 14-1/2"x1-1/2"x2-1/4". Extra fancy select walnut. **Features:** Boxlock action with dummy sideplates, extensive engraving with gold inlaid game birds, silvered receiver, automatic ejectors, single selective trigger. Nizzoli leather case. Introduced 1996. Imported from Italy by Wm. Larkin Moore & Co.
Price: From **$9,900.00**

ROTTWEIL PARAGON OVER/UNDER
Gauge: 12, 2-3/4" chambers. **Barrel:** 28", 30", five choke tubes. **Weight:** 7 lbs. **Stock:** 14-1/2"x1-1/2"x2-1/2"; European walnut. **Features:** Boxlock action. Detachable trigger assembly; ejectors can be deactivated; convertible top lever for right- or left-hand use; trigger adjustable for position. Imported from Germany by Dynamit Nobel-RWS, Inc.
Price: **$5,995.00**

RUGER WOODSIDE OVER/UNDER SHOTGUN
Gauge: 12, 3" chambers. **Barrel:** 26", 28", 30" (Full, Mod., Imp. Cyl. and two Skeet tubes). **Weight:** 7-1/2 to 8 lbs. **Stock:** 14-1/8"x1-1/2"x2-1/2". Select Circassian walnut; pistol grip or straight English grip. **Features:** Newly patented Ruger cocking mechanism for easier, smoother opening. Buttstock extends forward into action as two side panels. Single selective mechanical trigger, selective automatic ejectors; serrated free-floating rib; back-bored barrels with stainless steel choke tubes. Blued barrels, stainless steel receiver. Engraved action available. Introduced 1995. Made in U.S. by Sturm, Ruger & Co.
Price: **$1,889.00**
Price: Woodside Sporting Clays (30" barrels) **$1,889.00**

RUGER RED LABEL O/U SHOTGUN
Gauge: 12, 20, 3" chambers; 28 2-3/4" chambers. **Barrel:** 26", 28" (Skeet [two], Imp. Cyl., Full, Mod. screw-in choke tubes). Proved for steel shot.

Weight: About 7 lbs. (20 ga.); 7-1/2 lbs. (12 ga.). **Length:** 43" overall (26" barrels). **Stock:** 14"x1-1/2"x2-1/2". Straight grain American walnut or black synthetic. Checkered pistol grip and forend, rubber butt pad. **Features:** Stainless steel receiver. Single selective mechanical trigger, selective automatic ejectors; serrated free-floating vent. rib. Comes with two Skeet, one Imp. Cyl., one Mod., one Full choke tube and wrench. Made in U.S. by Sturm, Ruger & Co.
Price: Red Label with pistol grip stock **$1,489.00**
Price: English Field with straight-grip stock **$1,489.00**
Price: All-Weather Red Label with black synthetic stock **$1,489.00**
Price: Factory engraved All-Weather models . . . . **$1,650.00 to $1,725.00**

Ruger Engraved Red Label O/U Shotguns
Similar to Red Label except scroll engraved receiver with 24-carat gold game bird (pheasant in 12 gauge, grouse in 20 gauge, woodcock in 28 gauge, duck on All-Weather 12 gauge). Introduced 2000.
Price: Engraved Red Label (12 gauge, 30" barrel). **$1,725.00**
Price: Engraved Red Label (12, 20 and 28 gauge in 26" and 28" barrels) **$1,650.00**
Price: Engraved Red Label, All-Weather (synthetic stock, 12 gauge only; 26" and 28" brls.) **$1,650.00**
Price: Engraved Red Label, All-Weather (synthetic stock, 12 gauge only, 30" barrel) **$1,650.00**

Ruger Sporting Clays O/U Shotgun
Similar to Red Label except 30" back-bored barrels, stainless steel choke tubes. Weighs 7.75 lbs., overall length 47". Stock dimensions of 14-1/8"x1-1/2"x2-1/2". Free-floating serrated vent rib with brass front and mid-rib beads. No barrel side spacers. Comes with two Skeet, one imp. cyl., one mod. + full choke tubes. 12 ga. introduced 1992. 20 ga. introduced 1994.
Price: 12 or 20 . . . . **$1,545.00**
Price: All-Weather with black synthetic stock **$1,545.00**

SARSILMAZ OVER/UNDER SHOTGUN
Gauge: 12, 3" chambers. **Barrel:** 26", 28"; fixed chokes or choke tubes. **Weight:** NA. **Length:** NA. **Stock:** Oil-finished hardwood. **Features:** Double or single selective trigger, wide ventilated rib, chrome-plated parts, blued finish. Introduced 2000. Imported from Turkey by Armsport Inc.
Price: Double triggers; mod. and full or imp. cyl. and mod. fixed chokes **$499.95**
Price: Single selective trigger; imp. cyl. and mod. or mod. and full fixed chokes **$575.00**
Price: Single selective trigger; five choke tubes and wrench **$695.00**

SIGARMS SA5 OVER/UNDER SHOTGUN
Gauge: 12, 20, 3" chamber. **Barrel:** 26-1/2", 27" (Full, Imp. Mod., Mod., Imp. Cyl., Cyl. choke tubes). **Weight:** 6.9 lbs. (12 gauge), 5.9 lbs. (20 gauge). **Stock:** 14-1/2" x 1-1/2" x 2-1/2". Select grade walnut; checkered 20 l.p.i. at grip and forend. **Features:** Single selective trigger; automatic ejectors; hand-engraved detachable sideplated; matte nickel receiver, rest blued; tapered bolt lock-up. Introduced 1997. Imported by Sigarms, Inc.
Price: Field, 12 gauge **$2,670.00**
Price: Sporting Clays **$2,800.00**
Price: Field 20 gauge **$2,670.00**

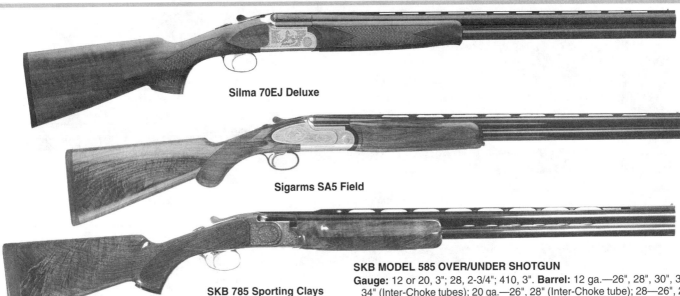

Silma 70EJ Deluxe

Sigarms SA5 Field

SKB 785 Sporting Clays

SILMA MODEL 70EJ DELUXE

Gauge: 12 (3-1/2" chambers), 20, 410 (3" chambers), 28 (2-3/4" chambers). **Barrel:** 28" (12 and 20 gauge, fixed and tubed, 28 and 410 fixed), 26" (12 and 20 fixed). **Weight:** 7.6 lbs 12 gauge, 6.9 lbs, 20, 28 and 410. **Stock:** Checkered select European walnut, pistol grip, solid rubber recoil pad. **Features:** Monobloc construction, chrome-moly blued steel barrels, raised vent rib, automatic safety and ejectors, single mechanical gold-plated trigger, bead front sight. Brushed, engraved receiver. Introduced 2002. Imported from Italy by Legacy sports International.
Price: 12, 20 multichokes (IC, M, F) $817.00
Price: 28, 410 multichokes (IC, M, F), fixed (M&F) $950.00

Silma Model 70 EJ Superlight

Similar to Silma 70EJ Deluxe except 12 gauge, 3" chambers, alloy receiver, weighs 5.6 lbs.
Price: 12, 20 multichokes (IC, M, F) $735.00
Price: 12, 20 fixed chokes (M&F) $657.00

Silma Model 70 EJ Standard

Similar to Silma 70EJ Deluxe except 12 and 20 gauge only, standard walnut stock, light engraving, silver-plated trigger.
Price: 12 multichokes (IC, M, F) $995.00

SKB MODEL 785 OVER/UNDER SHOTGUN

Gauge: 12, 20, 3"; 28, 2-3/4"; 410, 3". **Barrel:** 26", 28", 30", 32" (Inter-Choke tubes). **Weight:** 6 lbs., 10 oz. to 8 lbs. **Stock:** 14-1/8"x1-1/2"x2-3/16" (Field). Hand-checkered American black walnut with high-gloss finish; semi-beavertail forend. Target stocks available in standard or Monte Carlo styles. **Sights:** Metal bead front (Field), target style on Skeet, trap, Sporting Clays models. **Features:** Boxlock action with Greener-style cross bolt; single selective chrome-plated trigger, chrome-plated selective ejectors; manual safety. Chrome-plated, over-size, back-bored barrels with lengthened forcing cones. Introduced 1995. Imported from Japan by G.U. Inc.
Price: Field, 12 or 20 .... $2,119.00
Price: Field, 28 or 410 .... $2,199.00
Price: Field set, 12 and 20 .... $3,079.00
Price: Field set, 20 and 28 or 28 and 410. .... $3,179.00
Price: Sporting Clays, 12 or 20. .... $2,269.00
Price: Sporting Clays, 28 .... $2,349.00
Price: Sporting Clays set, 12 and 20 .... $3,249.00
Price: Skeet, 12 or 20. .... $2,199.00
Price: Skeet, 28 or 410. .... $2,239.00
Price: Skeet, three-barrel set, 20, 28, 410 .... $4,439.00
Price: Trap, standard or Monte Carlo. $2,199.00
Price: Trap combo, standard or Monte Carlo. $3,079.00

SKB MODEL 585 OVER/UNDER SHOTGUN

Gauge: 12 or 20, 3"; 28, 2-3/4"; 410, 3". **Barrel:** 12 ga.—26", 28", 30", 32", 34" (Inter-Choke tubes); 20 ga.—26", 28" (Inter-Choke tube); 28—26", 28" (Inter-Choke tubes); 410—26", 28" (Inter-Choke tubes). Ventilated side ribs. **Weight:** 6.6 to 8.5 lbs. **Length:** 43" to 51-3/8" overall. **Stock:** 14-1/8"x1-1/2"x2-3/16". Hand checkered walnut with high-gloss finish. Target stocks available in standard and Monte Carlo. **Sights:** Metal bead front (field), target style on Skeet, trap, Sporting Clays. **Features:** Boxlock action; silver nitride finish with Field or Target pattern engraving; manual safety, automatic ejectors, single selective trigger. All 12 gauge barrels are back-bored, have lengthened forcing cones and longer choke tube system. Sporting Clays models in 12 gauge with 28" or 30" barrels available with optional 3/8" step-up target-style rib, matte finish, nickel center bead, white front bead. Introduced 1992. Imported from Japan by G.U., Inc.
Price: Field $1,499.00
Price: Two-barrel Field Set, 12 & 20 .... $2,399.00
Price: Two-barrel Field Set, 20 & 28 or 28 & 410. ... $2,469.00
Price: Trap, Skeet. $1,619.00
Price: Two-barrel trap combo. $2,419.00
Price: Sporting Clays model .... $1,679.00 to $1,729.00
Price: Skeet Set (20, 28, 410) $3,779.00

SKB Model 585 Gold Package

Similar to Model 585 Field except gold-plated trigger, two gold-plated game inlays, Schnabel forend. Silver or blue receiver. Introduced 1998. Imported from Japan by G.U. Inc.
Price: 12, 20 ga. $1,689.00
Price: 28, 410 .... $1,749.00

SKB Model 505 Shotguns

Similar to Model 585 except blued receiver, standard bore diameter, standard Inter-Choke system on 12, 20, 28, different receiver engraving. Imported from Japan by G.U. Inc.
Price: Field, 12 (26", 28"), 20 (26", 28") $1,189.00
Price: Sporting Clays, 12 (28", 30") $1,299.00

STOEGER CONDOR SPECIAL

Gauge: 12, 20, 2-3/4" 3" chambers. **Barrel:** 26", 28". **Weight:** 7.7 lbs. **Sights:** Brass bead. **Features:** IC and M screw-in choke trubes with each gun. Oil finished hardwood with pistol grip and forend. Auto safety, single trigger, automatic extractors.
Price: $430.00
Price: With choke tubes $390.00
Price: Supreme Deluxe w/SS and red bar sights $490.00

TRADITIONS CLASSIC SERIES O/U SHOTGUNS

Gauge: 12, 3"; 20, 3"; 16, 2-3/4"; 28, 2-3/4"; 410, 3". **Barrel:** 26" and 28". **Weight:** 6 lbs., 5 oz. to 7 lbs., 6 oz. **Length:** 43" to 45" overall. **Stock:** Walnut. **Features:** Single-selective trigger; chrome-lined barrels with screw-in choke tubes; extractors (Field Hunter and Field I models) or automatic ejectors (Field II and Field III models); rubber butt pad; top tang safety. Imported from Fausti of Italy by Traditions.

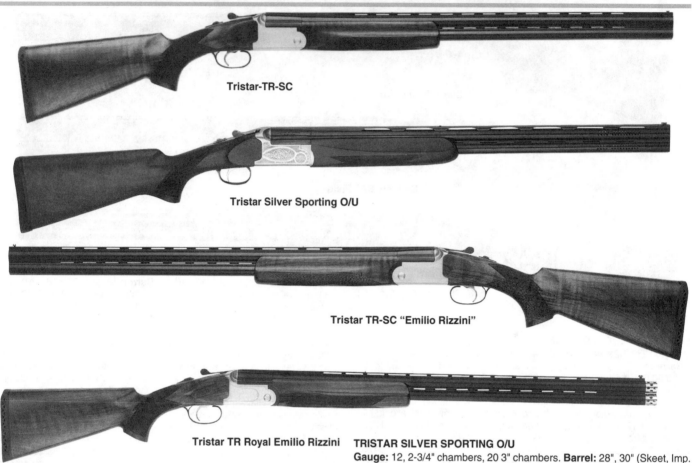

Tristar-TR-SC

Tristar Silver Sporting O/U

Tristar TR-SC "Emilio Rizzini"

Tristar TR Royal Emilio Rizzini

Price: (Field Hunter — blued receiver; 12 or 20 ga.; 26" bbl. has I.C. and mod. tubes, 28" has mod. and full tubes) **$669.00**
Price: (Field I — blued receiver; 12, 20, 28 or 410 ga.; fixed chokes [26" has I.C. and mod., 28" has mod. and full]) **$619.00**
Price: (Field II — coin-finish receiver; 12, 16, 20, 28 or 410 ga.; gold trigger; choke tubes) **$789.00**
Price: (Field III — coin-finish receiver; gold engraving and trigger; 12 ga.; 26" or 28" bbl.; choke tubes) **$999.00**
Price: (Upland II — blued receiver; 12 or 20 ga.; English-style straight walnut stock; choke tubes) **$839.00**
Price: (Upland III — blued receiver, gold engraving; 20 ga.; high-grade pistol grip walnut stock; choke tubes) **$1,059.00**
Price: (Upland III — blued, gold engraved receiver, 12 ga. Round pistol grip stock, choke tubes) **$1,059.00**
Price: (Sporting Clay II — silver receiver; 12 ga.; ported barrels with skeet, i.c., mod. and full extended tubes) **$959.00**
Price: (Sporting Clay III — engraved receivers, 12 and 20 ga., walnut stock, vent rib, extended choke tubes) **$1,189.00**

TRADITIONS MAG 350 SERIES O/U SHOTGUNS
Gauge: 12, 3-1/2". **Barrels:** 24", 26" and 28". **Weight:** 7 lbs. to 7 lbs., 4 oz. **Length:** 41" to 45" overall. **Stock:** Walnut or composite with Mossy Oak® Break-Up™ or Advantage® Wetlands ™ camouflage. **Features:** Black matte, engraved receiver; vent rib; automatic ejectors; single-selective trigger; three screw-in choke tubes; rubber recoil pad; top tang safety. Imported from Fausti of Italy by Traditions.
Price: (Mag Hunter II — 28" black matte barrels, walnut stock, includes I.C., Mod. and Full tubes) **$799.00**
Price: (Turkey II — 24" or 26" camo barrels, Break-Up camo stock, includes Mod., Full and X-Full tubes) **$889.00**
Price: (Waterfowl II — 28" camo barrels, Advantage Wetlands camo stock, includes I.C., Mod. and Full tubes) **$899.00**

TRISTAR SILVER SPORTING O/U
Gauge: 12, 2-3/4" chambers, 20 3" chambers. **Barrel:** 28", 30" (Skeet, Imp. Cyl., Mod., Full choke tubes). **Weight:** 7-3/8 lbs. **Length:** 45-1/2" overall. **Stock:** 14-3/8"x1-1/2"x2-3/8". Figured walnut, cut checkering; Sporting Clays quick-mount buttpad. **Sights:** Target bead front. **Features:** Boxlock action with single selective trigger; automatic selective ejectors; special broadway channeled rib; vented barrel rib; chrome bores. Chrome-nickel finish on frame, with engraving. Introduced 1990. Imported from Italy by Tristar Sporting Arms Ltd.
Price: **$765.00**

Tristar Silver II Shotgun
Similar to the Silver I except 26" barrel (Imp. Cyl., Mod., Full choke tubes, 12 and 20 ga.), 28" (Imp. Cyl., Mod., Full choke tubes, 12 ga. only), 26" (Imp. Cyl. & Mod. fixed chokes, 28 and 410), automatic selective ejectors. Weight is about 6 lbs., 15 oz. (12 ga., 26").
Price: **$566.00**

TRISTAR TR-SC "EMILIO RIZZINI" OVER/UNDER
Gauge: 12, 20, 3" chambers. **Barrel:** 28", 30" (Imp. Cyl., Mod., Full choke tubes). **Weight:** 7-1/2 lbs. **Length:** 46" overall (28" barrel). **Stock:** 1-1/2"x2-3/8"x14-3/8". Semi-fancy walnut; pistol grip with palm swell; semi-beavertail forend; black Sporting Clays recoil pad. **Features:** Silvered boxlock action with Four Locks locking system, auto ejectors, single selective (inertia) trigger, auto safety. Hard chrome bores. Vent. 10mm rib with target-style front and mid-rib beads. Introduced 1998. Imported from Italy by Tristar Sporting Arms, Ltd.
Price: Sporting Clay model **$996.00**
Price: 20 ga. **$1,073.00**

Tristar TR-Royal "Emilio Rizzin"i Over/Under
Similar to the TR-SC except has special parallel stock dimensions (1-1/2"x1-5/8"x14-3/8") to give low felt recoil; Rhino ported, extended choke tubes; solid barrel spacer; has "TR-Royal" gold engraved on the silvered receiver. Available in 12 gauge (28", 30") 20 and 28 gauge (28" only). Introduced 1999. Imported from Italy by Tristar Sporting Arms, Ltd.
Price: 12 ga. **$1,340.00**
Price: 20, 28 ga. **$1,258.00**

SHOTGUNS — OVER/UNDERS

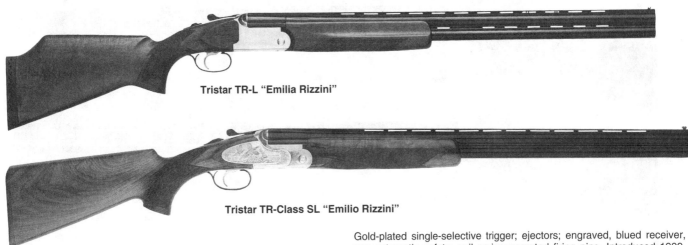

Tristar TR-L "Emilia Rizzini"

Tristar TR-Class SL "Emilio Rizzini"

Tristar TR-L "Emilio Rizzini" Over/Under
Similar to the TR-SC except has stock dimensions designed for female shooters (1-1/2" x 3" x 13-1/2"). Standard grade walnut. Introduced 1998. Imported from Italy by Tristar Sporting Arms, Ltd.
Price: **$1,014.00**

TRISTAR TR-I, II "EMILIO RIZZINI" OVER/UNDERS
Gauge: 12, 20, 3" chambers (TR-I); 12, 16, 20, 28, 410 3" chambers. **Barrel:** 12 ga., 26" (Imp. Cyl. & Mod.), 28" (Mod. & Full); 20 ga., 26" (Imp. Cyl. & Mod.), fixed chokes. **Weight:** 7-1/2 lbs. **Stock:** 1-1/2"x2-3/8"x14-3/8". Walnut with palm swell pistol grip, hand checkering, semi-beavertail forend, black recoil pad. **Features:** Boxlock action with blued finish, Four Locks locking system, gold single selective (inertia) trigger system, automatic safety, extractors. Introduced 1998. Imported from Italy by Tristar Sporting Arms, Ltd.
Price: TR-I **$748.00**
Price: TR-II (automatic ejectors, choke tubes) 12, 16 ga. **$879.00**
Price: 20, 28 ga., 410 . . . . **$924.00**

Tristar TR-Mag "Emilio Rizzini" Over/Under
Similar to TR-I, 3-1/2" chambers; choke tubes; 24" or 28" barrels with three choke tubes; extractors; auto safety. Matte blue finish on all metal, non-reflective wood finish. Introduced 1998. Imported from Italy by Tristar Sporting Arms, Ltd.
Price: **$764.00**
Price: Mossy Oak® Break-Up camo. **$942.00**
Price: Mossy Oak® Shadow Grass camo **$942.00**
Price: 10 ga., Mossy Oak® camo patterns **$1,132.10**

TRISTAR TR-CLASS SL EMILIO RIZZINI O/U
Gauge: 12, 2-3/4" chambers. **Barrel:** 28", 30". **Weight:** 7-3/4 lbs. **Stock:** Fancy walnut, hand checkering, semi-beavertail forend, black recoil pad, gloss finish. **Features:** Boxlock action with silvered, engraved sideplates; Four Lock locking system; automatic ejectors; hard chrome bores; vent tapered 7mm rib with target-style front bead. hand-fitted gun. Introduced 1999. Imported from Italy by Tristar Sporting Arms, Ltd.
Price: **$1,775.00**

TRISTAR WS/OU 12 SHOTGUN
Gauge: 12, 3-1/2" chambers. **Barrel:** 28" or 30" (imp. cyl., mod., full choke tubes). **Weight:** 6 lbs., 15 oz. **Length:** 46" overall. **Stock:** 14-1/8"x1-1/8"x2-3/8". European walnut with cut checkering, black vented recoil pad, matte finish. **Features:** Boxlock action with single selective trigger, automatic selective ejectors; chrome bores. Matte metal finish. Imported by Tristar Sporting Arms Ltd.
Price: **$610.00**

VERONA LX501 HUNTING O/U SHOTGUNS
Gauge: 12, 20, 28, 410 (2-3/4", 3" chambers). **Barrel:** 28"; 12, 20 ga. have Interchoke tubes, 28 ga. and 410 have fixed Full & Mod. **Weight:** 6-7 lbs. **Stock:** Matte-finished walnut with machine-cut checkering. **Features:**

Gold-plated single-selective trigger; ejectors; engraved, blued receiver, non-automatic safety; coil spring-operated firing pins. Introduced 1999. Imported from Italy by B.C. Outdoors.
Price: 12 and 20 ga. **$720.00**
Price: 28 ga. and 410 . . . . **$755.00**
Price: Combos 20/28, 28/410 . . . . **$1,470.00**

Verona LX692 Gold Hunting Over/Under Shotguns
Similar to Verona LX501 except engraved, silvered receiver with false sideplates showing gold-inlaid bird hunting scenes on three sides; Schnabel forend tip; hand-cut checkering; black rubber butt pad. Available in 12 and 20 gauge only, five InterChoke tubes. Introduced 1999. Imported from Italy by B.C. Outdoors.
Price: **$1,295.00**
New!!! Price: LX692G Combo 28/410 . . . . **$2,192.40**

Verona LX680 Sporting Over/Under Shotguns
Similar to Verona LX501 except engraved, silvered receiver; ventilated middle rib; beavertail forend; hand-cut checkering; available in 12 or 20 gauge only with 2-3/4" chambers. Introduced 1999. Imported from Italy by B.C. Outdoors.
Price: **$1,020.00**

Verona LX680 Skeet/Sporting, Trap O/U Shotguns
Similar to Verona LX501 except Skeet or trap stock dimensions; beavertail forend, palm swell on pistol grip; ventilated center barrel rib. Introduced 1999. Imported from Italy by B.C. Outdoors.
Price: **$1,130.00**
Price: Gold Competition (false sideplates with gold-inlaid hunting scenes) **$1,500.00**

Verona LX692 Gold Sporting Over/Under Shotguns
Similar to Verona LX680 except false sideplates have gold-inlaid bird hunting scenes on three sides; red high-visibility front sight. Introduced 1999. Imported from Italy by B.C. Outdoors.
Price: **$1,365.00**

VERONA LX680 COMPETITION TRAP
Gauge: 12. **Barrel:** 30" O/U, 32" single bbl. **Weight:** 8-3/8 lbs. combo, 7 lbs. single. **Stock:** Walnut. **Sights:** White front, mid-rib bead. **Features:** Interchangeable barrels switch from O/U to single configurations. 5 Briley chokes in combo, 4 in single bbl. extended forcing cones, parted barrels 32" with raised rib. By B.C. Outdoors.
Price: Trap Single **$1,581.00**
Price: Trap Combo **$2,382.00**

VERONA LX702 GOLD TRAP COMBO
Gauge: 20/28, 2-3/4"chamber. **Barrel:** 30". **Weight:** 7 lbs. **Stock:** Turkish walnut with beavertail forearm. **Sights:** White front bead. **Features:** 2-barrel competition gun. Color case-hardened side plates and receiver with gold inlaid pheasant. Ventilated rib between barrels. 5 interchokes. Imported from Italy by B.C. Outdoors.
Price: Combo **$2,246.40**
Price: 20 ga. **$1,662.00**

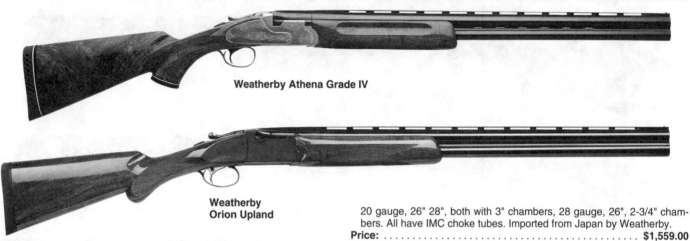

Weatherby Athena Grade IV

Weatherby
Orion Upland

WEATHERBY ATHENA GRADE IV O/U SHOTGUNS

Gauge: 12, 20, 3" chambers. Action: Boxlock (simulated sidelock) top lever break-open. Selective auto ejectors, single selective trigger (selector inside trigger guard). **Barrel:** 26", 28", IMC Multi-Choke tubes. **Weight:** 12 ga., 7-3/8 lbs.; 20 ga. 6-7/8 lbs. **Stock:** American walnut, checkered pistol grip and forend (14-1/4"x1-1/2"x2-1/2"). **Features:** Inertia trigger. Top tang safety, Greener cross bolt, fully engraved receiver, recoil pad installed. IMC models furnished with three interchangeable flush-fitting choke tubes. Imported from Japan by Weatherby. Introduced 1982.
Price: 12 ga., IMC, 26", 28" **$2,499.00**
Price: 20 ga., IMC, 26", 28" **$2,499.00**

Weatherby Athena Grade V Classic Field O/U

Similar to Athena Grade IV except rounded pistol grip, slender forend, oil-finished Claro walnut stock with fine-line checkering, Old English recoil pad. Sideplate receiver has rose and scroll engraving. Available in 12 gauge, 26", 28", 20 gauge, 26", 28", all with 3" chambers. Introduced 1993.
Price: **$2,919.00**

Weatherby Athena III Classic Field O/U

Has Grade III Claro walnut with oil finish, rounded pistol grip, slender forend; silver nitride/gray receiver has rose and scroll engraving with gold-overlay upland game scenes. Introduced 1999. Imported from Japan by Weatherby.
Price: 12, 20, 28 ga. **$2,089.00**

WEATHERBY ORION GRADE III FIELD O/U SHOTGUNS

Gauge: 12, 20, 3" chambers. **Barrel:** 26", 28", IMC Multi-Choke tubes. **Weight:** 6-1/2 to 9 lbs. **Stock:** 14-1/4"x1-1/2"x2-1/2". American walnut, checkered grip and forend. Rubber recoil pad. **Features:** Selective automatic ejectors, single selective inertia trigger. Top tang safety, Greener cross bolt. Has silver-gray receiver with engraving and gold duck/pheasant. Imported from Japan by Weatherby.
Price: Orion III, Field, 12, IMC, 26", 28" **$1,879.00**
Price: Orion III, Field, 20, IMC, 26", 28" **$1,879.00**

Weatherby Orion Grade III Classic Field O/U

Similar to Orion III Field except stock has rounded pistol grip, satin oil finish, slender forend, Old English recoil pad. Introduced 1993. Imported from Japan by Weatherby.
Price: **$1,879.00**

Weatherby Orion III English Field O/U

Similar to Orion III Classic Field except straight grip English-style stock. Available in 12 gauge (28"), 20 gauge (26", 28") with IMC Multi-Choke tubes. Silver/gray nitride receiver engraved and gold-plate overlay. Introduced 1997. Imported from Japan by Weatherby.
Price: **$1,959.00**

Weatherby Orion Grade II Classic Field O/U

Similar to Orion III Classic Field except stock has high-gloss finish, and bird on receiver is not gold. Available in 12 gauge, 26", 28", 30" barrels,

20 gauge, 26" 28", both with 3" chambers, 28 gauge, 26", 2-3/4" chambers. All have IMC choke tubes. Imported from Japan by Weatherby.
Price: **$1,559.00**

Weatherby Orion Grade I Field O/U

Similar to Orion Grade III Field except blued receiver with engraving, and the bird is not gold. Available in 12 gauge, 26", 28", 30", 20 gauge, 20", 28", both with 3" chambers and IMC choke tubes. Imported from Japan by Weatherby.
Price: **$1,509.00**

Weatherby Orion Upland O/U

Similar to Orion Grade I. Plain blued receiver, gold W on trigger guard; rounded pistol grip, slender forend of Claro walnut with high-gloss finish; black butt pad. Available in 12 and 20 gauge with 26" and 28" barrels. Introduced 1999. Imported from Japan by Weatherby.
Price: **$1,249.00**

WEATHERBY ORION SSC OVER/UNDER SHOTGUN

Gauge: 12, 3" chambers. **Barrel:** 28", 30", 32" (Skeet, SC1, Imp. Cyl., SC2, Mod. IMC choke tubes). **Weight:** About 8 lbs. **Stock:** 14-3/4"x2-1/4"x1-1/2". Claro walnut with satin oil finish; Schnabel forend tip; Sporter-style pistol grip; Pachmayr Decelerator recoil pad. **Features:** Designed for Sporting Clays competition. Has lengthened forcing cones and back-boring; ported barrels with 12mm grooved rib with mid-bead sight; mechanical trigger is adjustable for length of pull. Introduced 1998. Imported from Japan by Weatherby.
Price: SSC (Super Sporting Clays) **$1,979.00**

Weatherby Orion Grade II Classic Sporting O/U

Similar to Orion II Classic Field except 12 gauge only with (3" chambers), 28", 30" barrels with Skeet, SC1, SC2 imp. cyl., mod. chokes. Weighs 7.5-8 lbs. Competition center vent rib; middle barrel and enlarged front beads. Rounded grip; high gloss stock. Radiused heel recoil pad. Receiver finished in silver nitride with acid-etched, gold-plate clay pigeon monogram. Barrels have lengthened forcing cones. Introduced 1993. Imported by Weatherby.
Price: **$1,719.00**

Weatherby Orion Grade II Sporting

Similar to the Orion II Classic Sporting except has traditional pistol grip with diamond inlay, and standard full-size forend. Available in 12 gauge only, 28", 30" barrels with Skeet, Imp. Cyl., SC2, Mod. Has lengthened forcing cones, back-boring, stepped competition rib, radius heel recoil pad, hand-engraved, silver/nitride receiver. Introduced 1992. Imported by Weatherby.
Price: **$1,719.00**

WINCHESTER SUPREME O/U SHOTGUNS

Gauge: 12, 2-3/4", 3" chambers. **Barrel:** 28", 30", Invector Plus choke tubes. **Weight:** 7 lbs. 6 oz. to 7 lbs. 12. oz. **Length:** 45" overall (28" barrel). **Stock:** Checkered walnut stock. **Features:** Chrome-plated chambers; back-bored barrels; tang barrel selector/safety; deep-blued finish. Introduced 2000. From U.S. Repeating Arms. Co.
Price: Supreme Field (26" or 28" barrel, 6mm ventilated rib) . . **$1,383.00**
Price: Supreme Sporting (28" or 30" barrel, 10mm rib,
adj. trigger) **$1,551.00**

Variety of models for utility and sporting use, including some competitive shooting.

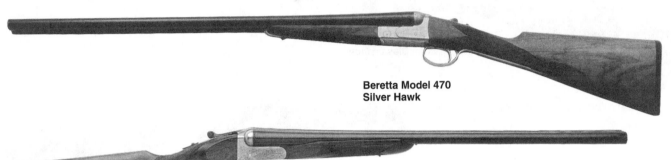

Beretta Model 470 Silver Hawk

Charles Daly Field Hunter

ARRIETA SIDELOCK DOUBLE SHOTGUNS

Gauge: 12, 16, 20, 28, 410. **Barrel:** Length and chokes to customer specs. **Weight:** To customer specs. **Stock:** To customer specs. Straight English with checkered butt (standard), or pistol grip. Select European walnut with oil finish. **Features:** Essentially custom gun with myriad options. H&H pattern hand-detachable sidelocks, selective automatic ejectors, double triggers (hinged front) standard. Some have self-opening action. Finish and engraving to customer specs. Imported from Spain by Wingshooting Adventures.

Price: Model 557, auto ejectors, from $3,250.00
Price: Model 570, auto ejectors, from $3,950.00
Price: Model 578, auto ejectors, from $4,350.00
Price: Model 600 Imperial, self-opening, from $6,050.00
Price: Model 601 Imperial Tiro, self-opening, from $6,950.00
Price: Model 801, from $9,135.00
Price: Model 802, from $9,135.00
Price: Model 803, from $6,930.00
Price: Model 871, auto ejectors, from $5,060.00
Price: Model 872, self-opening, from $12,375.00
Price: Model 873, self-opening, from $8,200.00
Price: Model 874, self-opening, from $9,250.00
Price: Model 875, self-opening, from $14,900.00

BERETTA MODEL 470 SILVER HAWK SHOTGUN

Gauge: 12, 20, 3" chambers. **Barrel:** 26" (Imp. Cyl. & Imp. Mod.), 28" (Mod. & Full). **Weight:** 5.9 lbs. (20 gauge). **Stock:** Select European walnut, straight English grip. **Features:** Boxlock action with single selective trigger; selector provides automatic ejection or extraction; silver-chrome action and forend iron with fine engraving; top lever highlighted with gold inlaid hawk's head. ABS case. Imported from Italy by Beretta U.S.A.

Price: 12 ga. $3,630.00
Price: 20 ga. $3,755.00

CHARLES DALY SUPERIOR HUNTER DOUBLE SHOTGUN

Gauge: 12, 20, 3" chambers, 28, 2-3/4" chambers. **Barrel:** 28" (Mod. & Full) 26" (Imp. Cyl. & Mod.). **Weight:** About 7 lbs. **Stock:** Checkered walnut pistol grip buttstock, splinter forend. **Features:** Silvered, engraved receiver; chrome-lined barrels; gold single trigger; automatic safety; extractors; gold bead front sight. Introduced 1997. Imported from Italy by K.B.I., Inc.

Price: $2,596.95
Price: 28 ga., 26" $2,726.95
New!!! Price: 470 EL $5,980.95

Charles Daly Empire Hunter Double Shotgun

Similar to Superior Hunter except deluxe wood, game scene engraving, automatic ejectors. Introduced 1997. Imported from Italy by K.B.I., Inc.

Price: 12 or 20 . . . . $1,595.95

CHARLES DALY DIAMOND REGENT DL DOUBLE SHOTGUN

Gauge: 12, 20, 410, 3" chambers, 28, 2-3/4" chambers. **Barrel:** 28" (Mod. & Full), 26" (Imp. Cyl. & Mod.), 26" (Full & Full, 410). **Weight:** About 5-7 lbs. **Stock:** Special select fancy European walnut, English-style butt, splinter forend; hand-checkered; hand-rubbed oil finish. **Features:** Drop-forged action with gas escape valves; demiblock barrels of chrome-nickel steel with concave rib; selective automatic-ejectors; hand-detachable, double-safety H&H sidelocks with demi-relief hand engraving; H&H pattern easy-opening feature; hinged trigger; coin finished action. Introduced 1997. Imported from Spain by K.B.I., Inc.

Price: 12 or 20 . . . . $19,999.00
Price: 28 . . . . $20,499.00
Price: 410 . . . . $20,499.00

CHARLES DALY FIELD HUNTER DOUBLE SHOTGUN

Gauge: 10, 12, 20, 28, 410 (3" chambers; 28 has 2-3/4"). **Barrel:** 32" (Mod. & Mod.), 28, 30" (Mod. & Full), 26" (Imp. Cyl. & Mod.) 410 (Full & Full). **Weight:** 6 lbs. to 11.4 lbs. **Stock:** Checkered walnut pistol grip and forend. **Features:** Silvered, engraved receiver; gold single selective trigger in 10-, 12, and 20 ga.; double triggers in 28 and 410; automatic safety; extractors; gold bead front sight. Introduced 1997. Imported from Spain by K.B.I., Inc.

Price: 10 ga. $984.95
Price: 12 or 20 ga. $809.95
Price: 28 ga. $854.95
Price: 410-bore $854.95
Price: As above, 12 or 20 AE. MC $939.95

CHARLES DALY DIAMOND DL DOUBLE SHOTGUN

Gauge: 12, 20, 410, 3" chambers, 28, 2-3/4" chambers. **Barrel:** 28" (Mod. & Full), 26" (Imp. Cyl. & Mod.), 26" (Full & Full, 410). **Weight:** About 5-7 lbs. **Stock:** Select fancy European walnut, English-style butt, beavertail forend; hand-checkered, hand-rubbed oil finish. **Features:** Drop-forged action with gas escape valves; demiblock barrels with concave rib; selective automatic ejectors; hand-detachable double safety sidelocks with hand-engraved rose and scrollwork. Hinged front trigger. Color case-hardened receiver. Introduced 1997. Imported from Spain by K.B.I., Inc.

Price: 12 or 20 . . . . $6,959.95
Price: 28 . . . . $7,274.95
Price: 410 . . . . $7,274.95

DAKOTA PREMIER GRADE SHOTGUNS

Gauge: 12, 16, 20, 28, 410. **Barrel:** 27". **Weight:** NA. **Length:** NA. **Stock:** Exhibition-grade English walnut, hand-rubbed oil finish with straight grip and splinter forend. **Features:** French grey finish; 50 percent coverage engraving; double triggers; selective ejectors. Finished to customer specifications. Made in U.S. by Dakota Arms.

Price: 12, 16, 20 gauge $13,950.00
Price: 28 and 410 gauge $15,345.00

Dakota The Dakota Legend Shotguns

Similar to Premier Grade except has special selection English walnut, full-coverage scroll engraving, oak and leather case. Made in U.S. by Dakota Arms.

Price: 12, 16, 20 gauge $18,000.00
Price: 28 and 410 gauge $19,800.00

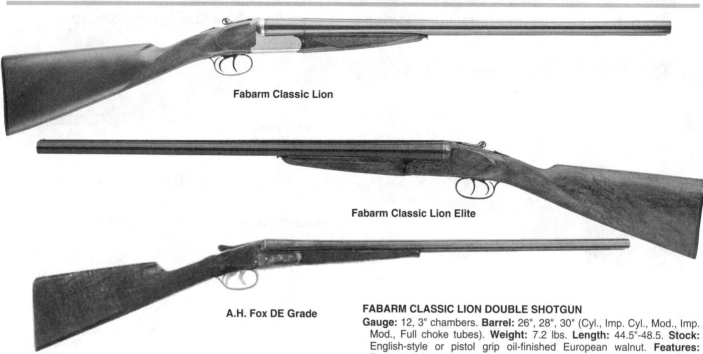

Fabarm Classic Lion

Fabarm Classic Lion Elite

A.H. Fox DE Grade

EAA/BAIKAL BOUNTY HUNTER IZH-43K SHOTGUN

Gauge: 12 (2-3/4", 3" chambers), 20 (3" chambers), 28 (2-3/4" chambers), 410 (3" chambers). **Barrel:** 18-1/2", 20", 24", 26", 28", three choke tubes. **Weight:** 7.28 lbs. Overall **length:** NA. **Stock:** Walnut, checkered forearm and grip. **Features:** Machined receiver; hammer-forged barrels with chrome-line bores; external hammers; double triggers (single, selective trigger available); rifle barrel inserts optional. Imported by European American Armory.
Price: . . . .$379.00 to $429.00

EAA/BAIKAL IZH-43 BOUNTY HUNTER SHOTGUNS

Gauge: 12 (2-3/4", 3" chambers), 16 (2-3/4" chambers), 20 (2-3/4" and 3" chambers). **Barrel:** 20", 24", 26", 28"; imp., mod. and full choke tubes. **Stock:** Hardwood or walnut; checkered forend and grip. **Features:** Hammer forged barrel; internal hammers; extractors; engraved receiver; automatic tang safety; non-glare rib. Imported by European American Armory.
Price: IZH-43 Bounty Hunter (12 gauge, 2-3/4" chambers, 20" brl., dbl. triggers, hardwood stock) $299.00
Price: IZH-43 Bounty Hunter (12 or 20 gauge, 2-3/4" chambers, 20" brl., dbl. triggers, walnut stock). $359.00

EAA/BAIKAL MP-213 SHOTGUN

Gauge: 12, 3" chambers. **Barrel:** 24", 26", 28"; imp., mod. and full choke tubes. **Weight:** 7.28 lbs. **Stock:** Walnut, checkered forearm and grip; rubber butt pad. **Features:** Hammer-forged barrels; chrome-lined bores; machined receiver; double trigger (each trigger fires both barrels independently); ejectors. Introduced 2000. Imported by European American Armory.
Price: IZH-213 . . . . $939.00

EAA/BAIKAL BOUNTY HUNTER MP-213 COACH GUN

Gauge: 12, 2-3/4" chambers. **Barrel:** 20", imp., mod. and full choke tubes. **Weight:** 7 lbs. **Stock:** Walnut, checkered forend and grip. **Features:** Selective double trigger with removable assembly (single trigger and varied pull weights available); ejectors; engraved receiver. Imported by European American Armory.
Price: MP-213. . . . . $939.00

E.M.F. HARTFORD MODEL COWBOY SHOTGUN

Gauge: 12. **Barrel:** 20". **Weight:** NA. **Length:** NA. **Stock:** Checkered walnut. **Sights:** Center bead. **Features:** Exposed hammers; color-case hardened receiver; blued barrel. Introduced 2001. Imported from Spain by E.M.F. Co. Inc.
Price: $625.00

FABARM CLASSIC LION DOUBLE SHOTGUN

Gauge: 12, 3" chambers. **Barrel:** 26", 28", 30" (Cyl., Imp. Cyl., Mod., Imp. Mod., Full choke tubes). **Weight:** 7.2 lbs. **Length:** 44.5"-48.5. **Stock:** English-style or pistol grip oil-finished European walnut. **Features:** Boxlock action with double triggers, automatic ejectors, automatic safety. Introduced 1998. Imported from Italy by Heckler & Koch, Inc.
Price: Grade I $1,499.00
Price: Grade II $2,249.00
New!!! Price: Elite (color-case hardened type finish, 44.5"). . . . $1,599.00

A.H. FOX SIDE-BY-SIDE SHOTGUNS

Gauge: 16, 20, 28, 410. **Barrel:** Length and chokes to customer specifications. Rust-blued Chromox or Krupp steel. **Weight:** 5-1/2 to 6-3/4 lbs. **Stock:** Dimensions to customer specifications. Hand-checkered Turkish Circassian walnut with hand-rubbed oil finish. Straight, semi or full pistol grip; splinter, Schnabel or beavertail forend; traditional pad, hard rubber buttplate or skeleton butt. **Features:** Boxlock action with automatic ejectors; double or Fox single selective trigger. Scalloped, rebated and color case-hardened receiver; hand finished and hand-engraved. Grades differ in engraving, inlays, grade of wood, amount of hand finishing. Add $1,500 for 28 or 410-bore. Introduced 1993. Made in U.S. by Connecticut Shotgun Mfg.
Price: CE Grade $11,000.00
Price: XE Grade $12,500.00
Price: DE Grade $15,000.00
Price: FE Grade $20,000.00
Price: Exhibition Grade. $30,000.00
Price: 28/410 CE Grade $12,500.00
Price: 28/410 XE Grade $14,000.00
Price: 28/410 DE Grade $16,500.00
Price: 28/410 FE Grade $21,500.00
Price: 28/410 Exhibition Grade. $30,000.00

GARBI MODEL 100 DOUBLE

Gauge: 12, 16, 20, 28. **Barrel:** 26", 28", choked to customer specs. **Weight:** 5-1/2 to 7-1/2 lbs. **Stock:** 14-1/2"x2-1/4"x1-1/2". European walnut. Straight grip, checkered butt, classic forend. **Features:** Sidelock action, automatic ejectors, double triggers standard. Color case-hardened action, coin finish optional. Single trigger; beavertail forend, etc. optional. Five other models are available. Imported from Spain by Wm. Larkin Moore.
Price: From. $4,000.00

Garbi Model 200 Side-by-Side

Similar to the Garbi Model 100 except has heavy-duty locks, magnum proofed. Very fine Continental-style floral and scroll engraving, well figured walnut stock. Other mechanical features remain the same. Imported from Spain by Wm. Larkin Moore.
Price: $8,700.00

SHOTGUNS

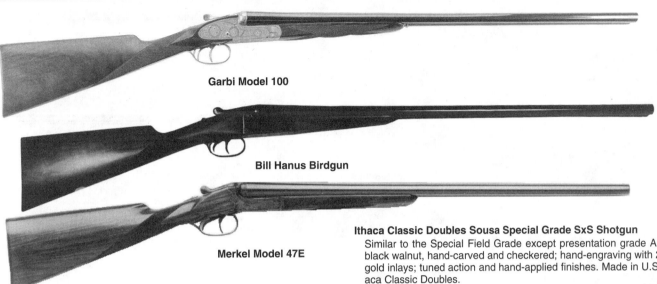

Garbi Model 100

Bill Hanus Birdgun

Merkel Model 47E

Garbi Model 101 Side-by-Side

Similar to the Garbi Model 100 except is hand engraved with scroll engraving, select walnut stock. Better overall quality than the Model 100. Imported from Spain by Wm. Larkin Moore.
Price: From **$5,150.00**

Garbi Model 103A, B Side-by-Side

Similar to the Garbi Model 100 except has Purdey-type fine scroll and rosette engraving. Better overall quality than the Model 101. Model 103B has nickel-chrome steel barrels, H&H-type easy opening mechanism; other mechanical details remain the same. Imported from Spain by Wm. Larkin Moore.
Price: Model 103A, from **$6,600.00**
Price: Model 103B, from **$9,100.00**

BILL HANUS BIRDGUN

Gauge: 16, 20, 28. **Barrel:** 27", 20 and 28 ga.; 28", 16 ga. (Skeet 1 & Skeet 2). **Weight:** 5 lbs., 4 oz. to 6 lbs., 4 oz. **Stock:** 14-3/8"x1-1/2"x2-3/8", with 1/4" cast-off. Select walnut. **Features:** Boxlock action with ejectors; splinter forend, straight English grip; checkered butt; English leather-covered handguard included. Made by AYA. Introduced 1998. Imported from Spain by Bill Hanus Birdguns.
Price: **$2,295.00**
Price: Single-selective trigger, add **$350.00**

ITHACA CLASSIC DOUBLES SPECIAL FIELD GRADE SxS

Gauge: 20, 28, 2-3/4" chambers, 410, 3". **Barrel:** 26", 28", 30", fixed chokes. **Weight:** 5 lbs., 14 oz. (20 gauge). **Stock:** 14-1/2"x2-1/4"x1-3/8". High-grade American black walnut, hand-rubbed oil finish; splinter or beavertail forend, straight or pistol grip. **Features:** Double triggers, ejectors; color case-hardened, engraved action body with matted top surfaces. Introduced 1999. Made in U.S. by Ithaca Classic Doubles.
Price: From **$3,150.00**

Ithaca Classic Doubles Grade 4E Classic SxS Shotgun

Similar to Special Field Grade except gold-plated triggers, jeweled barrel flats and hand-turned locks. Feather crotch and flame-grained black walnut hand-checkered 28 lpi with fleur de lis pattern. Action body engraved with three game scenes and bank note scroll, color case-hardened. Introduced 1999. Made in U.S. by Ithaca Classic Doubles.
Price: From **$4,900.00**

Ithaca Classic Doubles Grade 7E Classic SxS Shotgun

Similar to Special Field Grade except engraved with bank note scroll and flat 24k gold game scenes: gold setter and gold pointer on opposite action sides, American bald eagle inlaid on bottom plate. Hand-timed, polished, jeweled ejectors and locks. Exhibition grade American black walnut stock and forend with eight-panel fleur de lis borders. Introduced 1999. Made in U.S. by Ithaca Classic Doubles.
Price: From **$9,700.00**

Ithaca Classic Doubles Sousa Special Grade SxS Shotgun

Similar to the Special Field Grade except presentation grade American black walnut, hand-carved and checkered; hand-engraving with 24-karat gold inlays; tuned action and hand-applied finishes. Made in U.S. by Ithaca Classic Doubles.
Price: From **$14,900.00**

LEBEAU - COURALLY BOXLOCK SxS SHOTGUN

Gauge: 12, 16, 20, 28, 410-bore. **Barrel:** 25" to 32". **Weight:** To customer specifications. **Stock:** French walnut. **Features:** Anson & Deely-type action with automatic ejectors; single or double triggers. Essentially a custom gun built to customer specifications. Imported from Belgium by Wm. Larkin Moore.
Price: From **$21,000.00**

LEBEAU - COURALLY SIDELOCK SxS SHOTGUN

Gauge: 12, 16, 20, 28, 410-bore. **Barrel:** 25" to 32". **Weight:** To customer specifications. **Stock:** Fancy French walnut. **Features:** Holland & Holland-type action with automatic ejectors; single or double triggers. Essentially a custom gun built to customer specifications. Imported from Belgium by Wm. Larkin Moore.
Price: From **$43,000.00**

MERKEL MODEL 47E, 147E SIDE-BY-SIDE SHOTGUNS

Gauge: 12, 3" chambers, 16, 2-3/4" chambers, 20, 3" chambers. **Barrel:** 12, 16 ga.—28"; 20 ga.—26-3/4" (Imp. Cyl. & Mod., Mod. & Full). **Weight:** About 6-3/4 lbs. (12 ga.). **Stock:** Oil-finished walnut; straight English or pistol grip. **Features:** Anson & Deeley-type boxlock action with single selective or double triggers, automatic safety, cocking indicators. Color case-hardened receiver with standard Arabesque engraving. Imported from Germany by GSI.
Price: Model 47E (H&H ejectors) **$3,295.00**
Price: Model 147E (as above with ejectors) **$3,995.00**

Merkel Model 47SL, 147SL Side-by-Sides

Similar to Model 122 except H&H style sidelock action with cocking indicators, ejectors. Silver-grayed receiver and sideplates have Arabesque engraving, engraved border and screws (Model 47S), or fine hunting scene engraving (Model 147S). Imported from Germany by GSI.
Price: Model 47SL **$5,995.00**
Price: Model 147SL **$7,995.00**
Price: Model 247SL (English-style engraving, large scrolls) . . . **$7,995.00**
Price: Model 447SL (English-style engraving, small scrolls) . . . **$9,995.00**

Merkel Model 280EL and 360EL Shotguns

Similar to Model 47E except smaller frame. Greener cross bolt with double under-barrel locking lugs, fine engraved hunting scenes on silver-grayed receiver, luxury-grade wood, Anson and Deely box-lock action. H&H ejectors, single-selective or double triggers. Introduced 2000. From Merkel.
Price: Model 280EL (28 gauge, 28" barrel, imp. cyl. and
mod. chokes) 4 mod. chokes) **$5,795.00**
Price: Model 360EL (410 gauge, 28" barrel, mod. and
full chokes) **$5,795.00**
Price: Model 280/360EL two-barrel set (28 and 410 gauge
as above) **$8,295.00**

SHOTGUNS

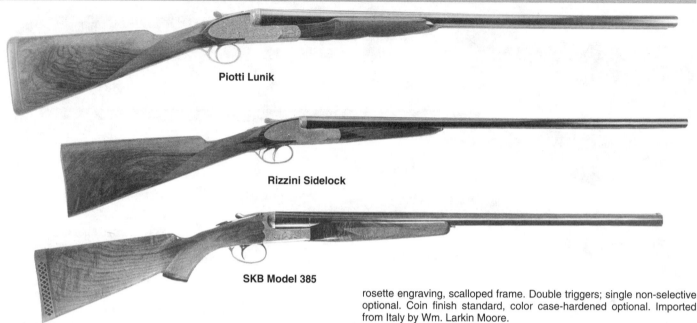

Piotti Lunik

Rizzini Sidelock

SKB Model 385

Merkel Model 280SL and 360SL Shotguns

Similar to Model 280EL and 360EL except has sidelock action, double triggers, English-style Arabesque engraving. Introduced 2000. From Merkel.
Price: Model 280SL (28 gauge, 28" barrel, imp. cyl. and
mod. chokes) **$8,495.00**
Price: Model 360SL (410 gauge, 28" barrel, mod. and
full chokes) **$8,495.00**
Price: Model 280/360SL two-barrel set **$11,995.00**

PIOTTI KING NO. 1 SIDE-BY-SIDE

Gauge: 12, 16, 20, 28, 410. **Barrel:** 25" to 30" (12 ga.), 25" to 28" (16, 20, 28, 410). To customer specs. Chokes as specified. **Weight:** 6-1/2 lbs. to 8 lbs. (12 ga. to customer specs.). **Stock:** Dimensions to customer specs. Finely figured walnut; straight grip with checkered butt with classic splinter forend and hand-rubbed oil finish standard. Pistol grip, beavertail forend. **Features:** Holland & Holland pattern sidelock action, automatic ejectors. Double trigger; non-selective single trigger optional. Coin finish standard; color case-hardened optional. Top rib; level, file-cut; concave, ventilated optional. Very fine, full coverage scroll engraving with small floral bouquets. Imported from Italy by Wm. Larkin Moore.
Price: From **$20,900.00**

Piotti King Extra Side-by-Side

Similar to the Piotti King No. 1 except with upgraded engraving. Choice of any type of engraving, including bulino game scene engraving and game scene engraving with gold inlays. Engraved and signed by a master engraver. Other mechanical specifications remain the same. Imported from Italy by Wm. Larkin Moore.
Price: From **$25,900.00**

Piotti Lunik Side-by-Side

Similar to the Piotti King No. 1 in overall quality. Has Renaissance-style large scroll engraving in relief. Best quality Holland & Holland-pattern sidelock ejector double with chopper lump (demi-bloc) barrels. Other mechanical specifications remain the same. Imported from Italy by Wm. Larkin Moore.
Price: From **$21,900.00**

PIOTTI PIUMA SIDE-BY-SIDE

Gauge: 12, 16, 20, 28, 410. **Barrel:** 25" to 30" (12 ga.), 25" to 28" (16, 20, 28, 410). **Weight:** 5-1/2 to 6-1/4 lbs. (20 ga.). **Stock:** Dimensions to customer specs. Straight grip stock with walnut checkered butt, classic splinter forend, hand-rubbed oil finish are standard; pistol grip, beavertail forend, satin luster finish optional. **Features:** Anson & Deeley boxlock ejector double with chopper lump barrels. Level, file-cut rib, light scroll and

rosette engraving, scalloped frame. Double triggers; single non-selective optional. Coin finish standard, color case-hardened optional. Imported from Italy by Wm. Larkin Moore.
Price: From **$13,400.00**

RIZZINI SIDELOCK SIDE-BY-SIDE

Gauge: 12, 16, 20, 28, 410. **Barrel:** 25" to 30" (12, 16, 20 ga.), 25" to 28" (28, 410). To customer specs. Chokes as specified. **Weight:** 6-1/2 lbs. to 8 lbs. (12 ga. to customer specs). **Stock:** Dimensions to customer specs. Finely figured walnut; straight grip with checkered butt with classic splinter forend and hand-rubbed oil finish standard. Pistol grip, beavertail forend. **Features:** Sidelock action, auto ejectors. Double triggers or non-selective single trigger standard. Coin finish standard. Imported from Italy by Wm. Larkin Moore.
Price: 12, 20 ga., from **$52,000.00**
Price: 28, 410 bore, from **$60,000.00**

RUGER GOLD LABEL SIDE-BY-SIDE SHOTGUN

Gauge: 12, 3" chambers. **Barrel:** 28" with skeet tubes. **Weight:** 6-1/2 lbs. **Length:** 45". **Stock:** American walnut straight or pistol grip. **Sights:** Gold bead front, full length rib, serrated top. **Features:** Spring-assisted break-open, SS trigger, auto eject. 5 interchangeable screw-in choke tubes, combination safety/barrel selector with auto safety reset.
Price: **$1,950.00**

SKB MODEL 385 SIDE-BY-SIDE

Gauge: 12, 20, 3" chambers; 28, 2-3/4" chambers. **Barrel:** 26" (Imp. Cyl., Mod., Skeet choke tubes). **Weight:** 6-3/4 lbs. **Length:** 42-1/2" overall. **Stock:** 14-1/8"x1-1/2"x2-1/2" American walnut with straight or pistol grip stock, semi-beavertail forend. **Features:** Boxlock action. Silver nitrided receiver with engraving; solid barrel rib; single selective trigger, selective automatic ejectors, automatic safety. Introduced 1996. Imported from Japan by G.U. Inc.
Price: **$2,049.00**
Price: Field Set, 20, 28 ga., 26" or 28", English or pistol grip . . . **$2,929.00**

SKB Model 385 Sporting Clays

Similar to the Field Model 385 except 12 gauge only; 28" barrel with choke tubes; raised ventilated rib with metal middle bead and white front. Stock dimensions 14-1/4"x1-7/16"x1-7/8". Introduced 1998. Imported from Japan by G.U. Inc.
Price: **$2,159.00**
Price: Sporting Clays set, 20, 28 ga. **$3,059.00**

SKB Model 485 Side-by-Side

Similar to the Model 385 except has dummy sideplates, raised ventilated rib with metal middle bead and white front, extensive upland game scene engraving, semi-fancy American walnut English or pistol grip stock. Imported from Japan by G.U. Inc.
Price: **$2,769.00**
Price: Field set, 20, 28 ga., 26" **$2,769.00**

Stoeger Silverado Coach

Tristar
Model 411

STOEGER/IGA UPLANDER SIDE-BY-SIDE SHOTGUN
Gauge: 16, 28, 2-3/4 chambers. 12, 20, 410, 3" chambers. **Barrel:** 26", 28". **Weight:** 7.3 lbs. **Sights:** Brass bead. **Features:** Double trigger, IC, M fixed choke tubes with gun.
Price: $325.00
Price: With screw-in chokes $345.00
Price: Upland Special $365.00
Price: Upland Supreme with SST, red bar sights $435.00

Stoeger/IGA English Stock Side-by-Side
Similar to Uplander except in 410 or 20 ga. only with 24" barrels, straight English stock and beavertail forend. Automatic safety, extractors, double triggers. Introduced 1996. Imported from Brazil by Stoeger.
Price: 410 ga (mod. and mod. chokes). $325.00
Price: 20 ga (imp. cyl and mod. choke tubes) $345.00

Stoeger Upland Short Stock Side-by-Side
Similar to English stock, only 13" length of pull. Excellent for ladies and youth. 20 ga., IC, M fixed, 410 M, F. Rubber recoil.
Price: $325.00

STOEGER SILVERADO COACH SIDE-BY-SIDE
Gauge: 12, 20, 410, 2-3/4", 3" chambers. **Barrel:** 20". **Weight:** 6-1/2 lbs. **Stock:** Brown hardwood, classic beavertail forend. **Sights:** Brass bead. **Features:** IC & M fixed chokes, tang auto safety, auto extractors, black plastic butt plate. 12 ga. and 20 ga. also with English style stock.
Price: $365.00

STOEGER UPLANDER SHOTGUN
Gauge: 12, 20, 410 (3" chambers); 28 (2-3/4" chambers). **Barrel:** 24", 26", 28". **Weight:** 6-3/4 lbs. **Length:** 40" to 44" overall. **Stock:** Brazilian hardwood; checkered grip and forearm. **Features:** Automatic safety; extractors; handles steel shot. Introduced 1997. Imported from Brazil by Stoeger.
Price: With chokes tubes $325.00

Stoeger Uplander Supreme Shotgun
Similar to Uplander except American walnut soft black rubber recoil pad, gloss finish. Choke tubes and 3" chambers standard 12, 20 gauge; 28 gauge has 26", 3" chokes, fixed IC and Mod. Single selective gold plated triggers; extractors. Introduced 1997. Imported from Brazil by Stoeger.
Price: 12, 20 . . . . $435.00

TRADITIONS ELITE SERIES SIDE-BY-SIDE SHOTGUNS
Gauge: 12, 3"; 20, 3"; 28, 2-3/4"; 410, 3". **Barrel:** 26". **Weight:** 5 lbs., 12 oz. to 6-1/2 lbs. **Length:** 43" overall. **Stock:** Walnut. **Features:** Chrome-lined barrels; fixed chokes (Elite Field III ST, Field I DT and Field I ST) or choke tubes (Elite Hunter ST); extractors (Hunter ST and Field I models) or automatic ejectors (Field III ST); top tang safety. Imported from Fausti of Italy by Traditions.
Price: (Elite Field I DT — 12, 20, 28 or 410 ga.; I.C. and Mod. fixed chokes [F and F on 410]; double triggers) . . . . $789.00 to $869.00

Price: (Elite Field I ST — 12, 20, 28 or 410 ga.; same as DT but with single trigger) . . . . $919.00 to $999.00
Price: (Elite Field III ST — 28 or 410 ga.; gold-engraved receiver; high-grade walnut stock) $2,009.00
Price: (Elite Hunter ST — 12 or 20 ga.; blued receiver; I.C. and Mod. choke tubes) $999.00

TRISTAR ROTA MODEL 411 SIDE-BY-SIDE
Gauge: 12, 16, 20, 410, 3" chambers; 28, 2-3/4". **Barrel:** 12 ga., 26", 28"; 16, 20, 28 ga., 410-bore, 26"; 12 and 20 ga. have three choke tubes, 16, 28 (Imp. Cyl. & Mod.), 410 (Mod. & Full) fixed chokes. **Weight:** 6-1/2 to 7-1/4 lbs. **Stock:** 14-3/8" l.o.p. Standard walnut with pistol grip, splinter-style forend; hand checkered. **Features:** Engraved, color case-hardened boxlock action; double triggers, extractors; solid barrel rib. Introduced 1998. Imported from Italy by Tristar Sporting Arms, Ltd.
Price: $849.00

Tristar Rota Model 411D Side-by-Side
Similar to Model 411 except automatic ejectors, straight English-style stock, single trigger. Solid barrel rib with matted surface; chrome bores; color case-hardened frame; splinter forend. Introduced 1999. Imported from Italy by Tristar Sporting Arms, Ltd.
Price: $1,110.00

Tristar Rota Model 411R Coach Gun Side-by-Side
Similar to Model 411 except in 12 or 20 gauge only with 20" barrels and fixed chokes (Cyl. & Cyl.). Double triggers, extractors, choke tubes. Introduced 1999. Imported from Italy by Tristar Sporting Arms, Ltd.
Price: $745.00

Tristar Rota Model 411F Side-by-Side
Similar to Model 411 except silver, engraved receiver, ejectors, IC, M and F choke tubes, English-style stock, single gold trigger, cut checkering. Imported from Italy by Tristar Sporting Arms Ltd.
Price: $1,602.00

TRISTAR DERBY CLASSIC SIDE-BY-SIDE
Gauge: 12. **Barrel:** 28" Mod. & Full fixed chokes. **Features:** Sidelock action, engraved, double trigger, auto ejectors, English straight stock. Maide in Eruope for Tristar Sporting Arms Ltd.
Price: $1,059.00

WEATHERBY ATHENA SIDE-BY-SIDE
Gauge: 12, 20. **Barrel:** 26", 28". **Stock:** Turkish walnut, straight grip. **Sights:** Brass bead front. **Features:** Barrel selector independent of cross-bolt safety. Integral multi-choke system, interchangeable screw-in Briley choke tubes (excepting 410 bored IC & Mod.). Receivers engraved with rose and scroll.
Price: $1,549.00

WEATHERBY ORION SIDE-BY-SIDE
Gauge: 12, 20, 28, 410. **Barrel:** 26", 28". **Stock:** Turkish walnut, half round pistol grip. **Sights:** Brass bead front. **Features:** Barrel selector independent of crossbolt safety. Integral multi-choke system, interchangeable screw-in Briley choke tubes (excepting 410 bored IC & Mod.). Receivers engraved with rose and scroll.
Price: $1,099.00

SHOTGUNS

Variety of designs for utility and sporting purposes, as well as for competitive shooting.

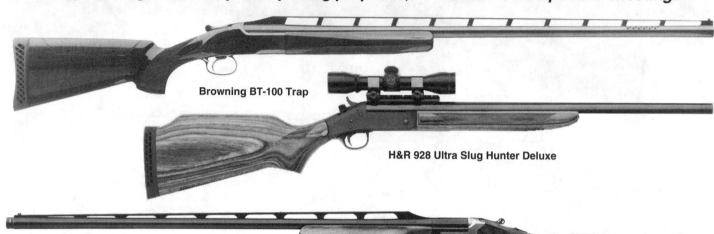

Browning BT-100 Trap

H&R 928 Ultra Slug Hunter Deluxe

Fabarm Monotrap

BERETTA DT 10 TRIDENT TRAP TOP SINGLE SHOTGUN

Gauge: 12, 3" chamber. **Barrel:** 34"; five Optima Choke tubes (full, full, imp. modified, mod. and imp. cyl.). **Weight:** 8.8 lbs. **Stock:** High-grade walnut; adjustable. **Features:** Detachable, adjustable trigger group; Optima Bore for improved shot pattern and reduced recoil; slim Optima Choke tubes; raised and thickened receiver for long life. Introduced 2000. Imported from Italy by Beretta USA.
Price: **$9,450.00**

BRNO ZBK 100 SINGLE BARREL SHOTGUN

Gauge: 12 or 20. **Barrel:** 27.5". **Weight:** 5.5 lbs. **Length:** 44" overall. **Stock:** Beech. **Features:** Polished blue finish; sling swivels. Announced 1998. Imported from The Czech Republic by Euro-Imports.
Price: **$185.00**

BROWNING BT-99 TRAP SHOTGUN

Gauge: 12, 2-3/4" chamber. **Barrel:** 32" or 34"; Invector choke system (full choke tube only included); High Post Rib; back-bored. **Weight:** 8 lbs., 10 oz. (34" bbl.). **Length:** 50-1/2" overall (34" bbl.). **Stock:** Conventional or adjustable-comb. **Features:** Re-introduction of the BT-99 Trap Shotgun. Full beavertail forearm; checkered walnut stock; ejector; rubber butt pad. Re-introduced 2001. Imported by Browning.
Price: Conventional stock, 32" or 34" barrel **$1,216.00**
Price: Adj.-comb stock, 32" or 34" barrel **$1,449.00**

BROWNING BT-100 TRAP SHOTGUN

Gauge: 12, 2-3/4" chamber. **Barrel:** 32", 34" (Invector Plus); back-bored; also with fixed Full choke. **Weight:** 8 lbs., 10 oz. (34" bbl.). **Length:** 48-1/2" overall (32" barrel). **Stock:** 14-3/8"x1-9/16"x1-7/16x2" (Monte Carlo); 14-3/8"x1-3/4"x1-1/4"x2-1/8" (thumbhole). Walnut with high gloss finish; cut checkering. Wedge-shaped forend with finger groove. **Features:** Available in stainless steel or blue. Has drop-out trigger adjustable for weight of pull from 3-1/2 to 5-1/2 lbs., and for three length positions; Ejector-Selector allows ejection or extraction of shells. Available with adjustable comb stock and thumbhole style. Introduced 1995. Imported from Japan by Browning.
Price: Grade I, blue, Monte Carlo, Invector Plus **$2,222.00**
Price: Grade I, blue, adj. comb, Invector Plus **$2,455.00**
Price: Stainless steel, Monte Carlo, Invector Plus **$2,688.00**
Price: Stainless steel, adj. comb, Invector Plus **$2,923.00**

CHIPMUNK 410 YOUTH SHOTGUN

Gauge: 410. **Barrel:** 18-1/4" tapered, blue. **Weight:** 3.25 lbs. **Length:** 33". **Stock:** Walnut. **Features:** Manually cocking single shot bolt, blued receiver.
Price: **$225.95**

EAA/BAIKAL IZH-18 SINGLE BARREL SHOTGUN

Gauge: 12 (2-3/4" and 3" chambers), 20 (2-3/4" and 3"), 16 (2-3/4"), 410 (3"). **Barrel:** 26-1/2", 28-1/2"; modified or full choke (12 and 20 gauge); full only (16 gauge), improved cylinder (20 gauge) and full or improved modified (410). **Stock:** Walnut-stained hardwood; rubber recoil pad. **Features:** Hammer-forged steel barrel; machined receiver; cross-block safety; cocking lever with external cocking indicator; optional automatic ejector, screw-in chokes and rifle barrel. Imported by European American Armory.
Price: IZH-18 (12, 16, 20 or 410) **$95.00**
Price: IZH-18 (20 gauge with imp. cyl. or 410 with imp. mod.). . . . **$109.00**

EAA/BAIKAL IZH-18MAX SINGLE BARREL SHOTGUN

Gauge: 12, 3"; 20, 3"; 410, 3". **Barrel:** 24" (410), 26" (410 or 20 ga.) or 28" (12 ga.). **Weight:** 6.4 to 6.6 lbs. **Stock:** Walnut. **Features:** Polished nickel receiver; ventilated rib; I.C., Mod. and Full choke tubes; titanium-coated trigger; internal hammer; selectable ejector/extractor; rubber butt pad; decocking system. Imported by European American Armory.
Price: (12 or 20 ga., choke tubes) **$169.00**
Price: (410 ga., full choke only) **$189.00**
New!!! Price: Sporting, 12 ga., ported, Monte Carlo stock **$219.00**

FABARM MONOTRAP SHOTGUN

Caliber: 12; 2-3/4" chamber. **Barrel:** 30", 34". **Weight:** 6.7 to 6.9 lbs. **Length:** 48.5" overall (30" bbl.) **Stock:** Walnut; adjustable comb competition-style. **Sights:** Red front sight bar, mid-rib bead. **Features:** Built on 20-gauge receiver for quick handling. Silver receiver with blued barrel; special trap rib (micrometer adjustable); includes three choke tubes (M, IM, F). Introduced 2000.
Price: **$1,799.00**

HARRINGTON & RICHARDSON NWTF SHOTGUNS

Gauge: 12, 3-1/2" chamber, fixed full choke; 20, 3" chamber, fixed modified choke. **Barrel:** 24" (12 ga.) or 22" (20 ga.) **Weight:** 5 to 6 lbs. **Stock:** Straight-grip camo laminate with recoil pad and sling swivel studs. **Sights:** Bead front. **Features:** Break-open single-shot action with side lever release; hand-checkered stock and forearm; includes trigger lock. Purchase supports National Wild Turkey Federation; NWTF logo on receiver.
Price: 12 ga.. . . . . **$176.95**
Price: 20 ga. youth gun (12-1/2" length of pull, weighs 5 lbs.) **$169.95**

HARRINGTON & RICHARDSON SB2-980 ULTRA SLUG

Gauge: 12, 20, 3" chamber. **Barrel:** 22" (20 ga. Youth) 24", fully rifled. **Weight:** 9 lbs. **Length:** NA. **Stock:** Walnut-stained hardwood. **Sights:** None furnished; comes with scope mount. **Features:** Uses the H&R 10 gauge action with heavy-wall barrel. Monte Carlo stock has sling swivels; comes with black nylon sling. Introduced 1995. Made in U.S. by H&R 1871, LLC.
Price: **$209.95**

SHOTGUNS

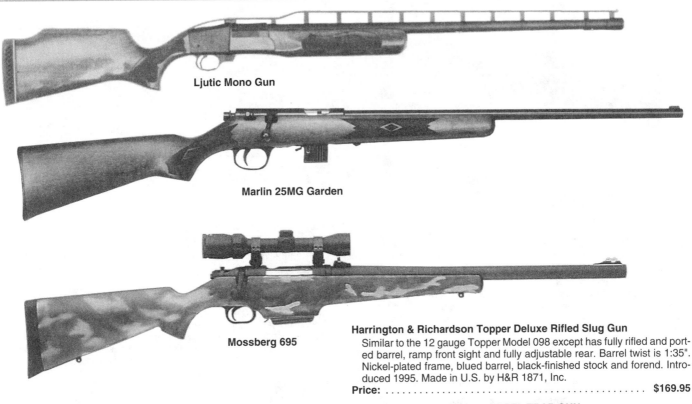

Ljutic Mono Gun

Marlin 25MG Garden

Mossberg 695

Harrington & Richardson Model 928 Ultra Slug Hunter Deluxe

Similar to the SB2-980 Ultra Slug except uses 12 gauge action and 12 gauge barrel blank bored to 20 gauge, then fully rifled with 1:35" twist. Has hand-checkered camo laminate Monte Carlo stock and forend. Comes with Weaver-style scope base, offset hammer extension, ventilated recoil pad, sling swivels and nylon sling. Introduced 1997. Made in U.S. by H&R 1871 LLC.

Price: **$255.95**

HARRINGTON & RICHARDSON TAMER SHOTGUN

Gauge: 410, 3" chamber. **Barrel:** 20" (Full). **Weight:** 5-6 lbs. **Length:** 33" overall. **Stock:** Thumbhole grip of high density black polymer. **Features:** Uses H&R Topper action with matte electroless nickel finish. Stock holds four spare shotshells. Introduced 1994. From H&R 1871, LLC.

Price: **$124.95**

HARRINGTON & RICHARDSON TOPPER MODEL 098

Gauge: 12, 16, 20, 28 (2-3/4"), 410, 3" chamber. **Barrel:** 12 ga.—28" (Mod., Full); 16 ga.— 28" (Mod.); 20 ga.—26" (Mod.); 28 ga.—26" (Mod.); 410 bore—26" (Full). **Weight:** 5-6 lbs. **Stock:** Black-finish hardwood with full pistol grip; semi-beavertail forend. **Sights:** Gold bead front. **Features:** Break-open action with side-lever release, automatic ejector. Satin nickel frame, blued barrel. Reintroduced 1992. From H&R 1871, LLC.

Price: **$116.95**
Price: Topper Junior 098 (as above except 22" barrel, 20 ga. (Mod.), 410-bore (Full), 12-1/2" length of pull) **$122.95**

Harrington & Richardson Topper Deluxe Model 098

Similar to the standard Topper 098 except 12 gauge only with 3-1/2" chamber, 28" barrel with choke tube (comes with Mod. tube, others optional). Satin nickel frame, blued barrel, black-finished wood. Introduced 1992. From H&R 1871, LLC.

Price: **$136.95**

Harrington & Richardson Topper Junior Classic Shotgun

Similar to the Topper Junior 098 except available in 20 gauge (3", Mod.), 410-bore (Full) with 3" chamber; 28 gauge, 2-3/4" chamber (Mod.); all have 22" barrel. Stock is American black walnut with cut-checkered pistol grip and forend. Ventilated rubber recoil pad with white line spacers. Blued barrel, blued frame. Introduced 1992. From H&R 1871, LLC.

Price: **$150.95**

Harrington & Richardson Topper Deluxe Rifled Slug Gun

Similar to the 12 gauge Topper Model 098 except has fully rifled and ported barrel, ramp front sight and fully adjustable rear. Barrel twist is 1:35". Nickel-plated frame, blued barrel, black-finished stock and forend. Introduced 1995. Made in U.S. by H&R 1871, Inc.

Price: **$169.95**

KRIEGHOFF K-80 SINGLE BARREL TRAP GUN

Gauge: 12, 2-3/4" chamber. **Barrel:** 32" or 34" Unsingle. Fixed Full or choke tubes. **Weight:** About 8-3/4 lbs. **Stock:** Four stock dimensions or adjustable stock available. All hand-checkered European walnut. **Features:** Satin nickel finish. Selective mechanical trigger adjustable for finger position. Tapered step vent. rib. Adjustable point of impact.

Price: Standard grade full Unsingle, from. **$7,950.00**

KRIEGHOFF KX-5 TRAP GUN

Gauge: 12, 2-3/4" chamber. **Barrel:** 34"; choke tubes. **Weight:** About 8-1/2 lbs. **Stock:** Factory adjustable stock. European walnut. **Features:** Ventilated tapered step rib. Adjustable position trigger, optional release trigger. fully adjustable rib shooter to adjust point of impact from 50%/50% to nearly 90%/10%. Satin gray electroless nickel receiver. Fitted aluminum case. Imported from Germany by Krieghoff International, Inc.

Price: **$4,200.00**

LJUTIC MONO GUN SINGLE BARREL

Gauge: 12 only. **Barrel:** 34", choked to customer specs; hollow-milled rib, 35-1/2" sight plane. **Weight:** Approx. 9 lbs. **Stock:** To customer specs. Oil finish, hand checkered. **Features:** Totally custom made. Pull or release trigger; removable trigger guard contains trigger and hammer mechanism; Ljutic pushbutton opener on front of trigger guard. From Ljutic Industries.

Price: With standard, medium or Olympic rib, custom 32"-34" bbls., and fixed choke. **$5,795.00**
Price: As above with screw-in choke barrel **$6,095.00**
Price: Stainless steel mono gun........................ **$6,795.00**

Ljutic LTX PRO 3 Deluxe Mono Gun

Deluxe light weight version of the Mono Gun with high quality wood, upgrade checkering, special rib height, screw in chokes, ported and cased.

Price: **$8,995.00**
Price: Stainless steel model **$9,995.00**

MARLIN MODEL 25MG GARDEN GUN SHOTGUN

Gauge: 22 WMR shotshell, 7-shot magazine. **Barrel:** 22" smoothbore. **Weight:** 6 lbs. **Length:** 41" overall. **Stock:** Press-checkered hardwood. **Sights:** High-visibility bead front. **Features:** Bolt action; thumb safety; red cocking indicator. Introduced 1999. Made in U.S. by Marlin.

Price: **$245.00**

SHOTGUNS

New England
Firearms
Camo Turkey

Ruger KTS-1234-BRE

MOSSBERG MODEL 695 SLUGSTER

Gauge: 12, 3" chamber. **Barrel:** 22"; fully rifled, ported. **Weight:** 7-1/2 lbs. **Stock:** Black synthetic, with swivel studs and rubber recoil pad. **Sights:** Blade front, folding rifle-style leaf rear; Fiber Optic. Comes with Weaver-style scope bases. **Features:** Matte metal finish; rotating thumb safety; detachable 2-shot magazine. Mossberg Cablelock. Made in U.S. by Mossberg. Introduced 1996.

Price: **$345.00**
Price: With Fiber Optic rifle sights **$367.00**
Price: With woodlands camo stock, Fiber Optic sights. **$397.00**

MOSSBERG SSi-ONE 12 GAUGE SLUG SHOTGUN

Gauge: 12, 3" chamber. **Barrel:** 24", fully rifled. **Weight:** 8 pounds. **Length:** 40" overall. **Stock:** Walnut, fluted and cut checkered; sling-swivel studs; drilled and tapped for scope base. **Sights:** None (scope base supplied). **Features:** Frame accepts interchangeable rifle barrels (see Mossberg SSi-One rifle listing); lever-opening, break-action design; ambidextrous, top-tang safety; internal eject/extract selector. Introduced 2000. From Mossberg.

Price: **$480.00**

Mossberg SSi-One Turkey Shotgun

Similar to SSi-One 12 gauge Slug Shotgun, but chambered for 12 ga., 3-1/2" loads. Includes Accu-Mag Turkey Tube. Introduced 2001. From Mossberg.

Price: **$459.00**

NEW ENGLAND FIREARMS CAMO TURKEY SHOTGUNS

Gauge: 10, 3-1/2 "; 12, 20, 3" chamber. **Barrel:** 24"; extra-full, screw-in choke tube (10 ga.); fixed full choke (12, 20). **Weight:** NA. **Stock:** American hardwood, green and black camouflage finish with sling swivels and ventilated recoil pad. **Sights:** Bead front. **Features:** Matte metal finish; stock counterweight to reduce recoil; patented transfer bar system for hammer-down safety; includes camo sling and trigger lock. Accepts other factory-fitted barrels. Introduced 2000. From New England Firearms.

Price: 10, 12 ga. **$205.95**
Price: 20 ga. youth model (22" bbl.) **$128.95**

NEW ENGLAND FIREARMS TRACKER SLUG GUN

Gauge: 12, 20, 3" chamber. **Barrel:** 24" (Cyl.). **Weight:** 5-1/4 lbs. **Length:** 40" overall. **Stock:** Walnut-finished hardwood with full pistol grip, recoil pad. **Sights:** Blade front, fully adjustable rifle-type rear. **Features:** Break-open action with side-lever release; blued barrel, color case-hardened frame. Introduced 1992. From New England Firearms.

Price: Tracker **$142.95**
Price: Tracker II (as above except fully rifled bore) **$150.95**

NEW ENGLAND FIREARMS SPECIAL PURPOSE SHOTGUNS

Gauge: 10, 3-1/2" chamber. **Barrel:** 28" (Full), 32" (Mod.). **Weight:** 9.5 lbs. **Length:** 44" overall (28" barrel). **Stock:** American hardwood with walnut or matte camo finish; ventilated rubber recoil pad. **Sights:** Bead front. **Features:** Break-open action with side-lever release; ejector. Matte finish on metal. Introduced 1992. From New England Firearms.

Price: Walnut-finish wood sling and swivels. **$168.95**
Price: Camo finish, sling and swivels **$183.95**
Price: Camo finish, 32", sling and swivels **$197.95**
Price: Black matte finish, 24", Turkey Full choke tube, sling and swivels. **$199.95**

NEW ENGLAND FIREARMS SURVIVOR

Gauge: 12, 20, 410/45 Colt, 3" chamber. **Barrel:** 22" (Mod.); 20" (410/45 Colt, rifled barrel, choke tube). **Weight:** 6 lbs. **Length:** 36 overall. **Stock:** Black polymer with thumbhole/pistol grip, sling swivels; beavertail forend. **Sights:** Bead front. **Features:** Buttplate removes to expose storage for extra ammunition; forend also holds extra ammunition. Black or nickel finish. Introduced 1993. From New England Firearms.

Price: Black **$129.95**
Price: Nickel **$150.95**
Price: 410/45 Colt, black **$164.95**
Price: 410/45 Colt, nickel **$178.95**

NEW ENGLAND FIREARMS STANDARD PARDNER

Gauge: 12, 20, 410, 3" chamber; 16, 28, 2-3/4" chamber. **Barrel:** 12 ga.—28" (Full, Mod.), 32" (Full); 16 ga.—28" (Full), 32" (Full); 20 ga.—26" (Full, Mod.); 28 ga.—26" (Mod.); 410-bore—26" (Full). **Weight:** 5-6 lbs. **Length:** 43" overall (28" barrel). **Stock:** Walnut-finished hardwood with full pistol grip. **Sights:** Bead front. **Features:** Transfer bar ignition; break-open action with side-lever release. Introduced 1987. From New England Firearms.

Price: **$106.95**
Price: Youth model (12, 20, 28 ga., 410, 22" barrel, recoil pad). . **$114.95**
Price: 12 ga., 32" (Full). **$119.95**

ROSSI SINGLE-SHOT SHOTGUN

Gauge: 12, 20, 2-3/4" chamber; 410, 3" chamber. **Barrel:** 28" full, 22"Youth. **Weight:** 5 lbs. **Stock:** Stained hardwood. **Sights:** Bead. **Features:** Break-open, positive ejection, internal transfer bar, trigger block.

Price: **$101.00**

ROSSI MATCHED PAIR SINGLE-SHOT SHOTGUN/RIFLE

Gauge: 410, 20 or 12. **Barrel:** 22" (18.5"Youth), 28" (23"full). **Weight:** 4-6 lbs **Stock:** Hardwood (brown or black finish). **Sights:** Bead front. **Features:** Break-open internal transfer bar manual external safety; blued or stainless steel finish; sling-swivel studs; includes matched 22 LR or 22 Mag. barrel with fully adjustable front and rear sight. Trigger block system. Introduced 2001. Imported by BrazTech/Taurus.

Price: Blue **$139.95**
Price: Stainless steel **$169.95**

RUGER KTS-1234-BRE TRAP MODEL
SINGLE-BARREL SHOTGUN

Gauge: 12, 2-3/4" chamber. **Barrel:** 34". **Weight:** 9 lbs. **Length:** 50 -1/2" overall. **Stock:** Select walnut checkered; adjustable pull length 13 -15". **Features:** Fully adjustable rib for pattern position; adjustable stock comb cast for right- or left-handed shooters; straight grooves the length of barrel to keep wad from rotating for pattern improvement. Full and modified choke tubes supplied. Gold inlaid eagle and Ruger name on receiver. Introduced 2000. From Sturm Ruger & Co.

Price: **$2,850.00**

Savage 210 F Master Shot Slug Gun

Stoeger 2002 Single-Shot

Tar-Hunt Mountaineer

SAVAGE MODEL 210F MASTER SHOT SLUG GUN

Gauge: 12, 3" chamber; 2-shot magazine. **Barrel:** 24" 1:35" rifling twist. **Weight:** 7-1/2 lbs. **Length:** 43.5" overall. **Stock:** Glass-filled polymer with positive checkering. **Features:** Based on the Savage Model 110 action; 60 bolt lift; controlled round feed; comes with scope mount. Introduced 1996. Made in U.S. by Savage Arms.
Price: $416.00

STOEGER 2002 SINGLE-SHOT SHOTGUN

Gauge: 12, 20, 410, 2-3/4", 3" chambers. **Barrel:** 26", 28". **Weight:** 5.4 lbs **Sights:** Brass bead. **Features:** 410 ga. full fixed choke tubes, rest M, screw-in. 410 ga. 24"bbl available (lop 13"). 12 ga. hardwood pistol-grip stock and forend. 20 ga. 26" bbl., hardwood forend.
Price: Blue $90.00

TAR-HUNT RSG-12 PROFESSIONAL RIFLED SLUG GUN

Gauge: 12, 2-3/4" chamber, 1-shot magazine. **Barrel:** 21-1/2"; fully rifled, with muzzle brake. **Weight:** 7-3/4 lbs. **Length:** 41-1/2" overall. **Stock:** Matte black McMillan fiberglass with Pachmayr Decelerator pad. **Sights:** None furnished; comes with Leupold windage or Weaver bases. **Features:** Uses rifle-style action with two locking lugs; two-position safety; Shaw barrel; single-stage, trigger; muzzle brake. Many options available. Right- and left-hand models at same prices. Introduced 1991. Made in U.S. by Tar-Hunt Custom Rifles, Inc.
Price: Professional model, right- or left-hand, Elite 16 ga. $1,885.00
Price: Millennium/10th Anniversary models (limited to 25 guns): NP-3 nickel/Teflon metal finish, black McMillan
Fibergrain stock, Jewell adj. trigger $2,300.00

TAR-HUNT RSG-20 MOUNTAINEER SLUG GUN

Similar to the RSG-12 Professional except chambered for 20 gauge (2-3/4") shells; 21" Shaw rifled barrel, with muzzle brake; two-lug bolt; one-shot blind magazine; matte black finish; McMillan fiberglass stock with Pachmayr Decelerator pad; receiver drilled and tapped for Rem. 700 bases. Weighs 6-1/2 lbs. Introduced 1997. Made in U.S. by Tar-Hunt Custom Rifles, Inc.
Price: $1,695.00

THOMPSON/CENTER ENCORE RIFLED SLUG GUN

Gauge: 20, 3" chamber. **Barrel:** 26", fully rifled. **Weight:** About 7 pounds. **Length:** 40-1/2" overall. **Stock:** Walnut with walnut forearm. **Sights:** Steel, click-adjustable rear and ramp-style front, both with fiber optics. **Features:** Encore system features a variety of rifle, shotgun and muzzle-loading rifle barrels interchangeable with the same frame. Break-open design operates by pulling up and back on trigger guard spur. Composite stock and forearm available. Introduced 2000.
Price: $612.48

THOMPSON/CENTER ENCORE TURKEY GUN

Gauge: 12 ga. **Barrel:** 24". **Features:** Blued, high definition Adv. Timber camo.
Price: $726.00

WESSON & HARRINGTON LONG TOM CLASSIC SHOTGUN

Gauge: 12, 3" chamber. **Barrel:** 32", (Full). **Weight:** 7-1/2 lbs. **Length:** 46" overall. **Stock:** 14"x1-3/4"x2-5/8". American black walnut with hand-checkered grip and forend. **Features:** Color case-hardened receiver and crescent steel buttplate, blued barrel. Receiver engraved with the National Wild Turkey Federation logo. Introduced 1998. Made in U.S. by H&R 1871, Inc.
Price: $349.95

Designs for utility, suitable for and adaptable to competitions and other sporting purposes.

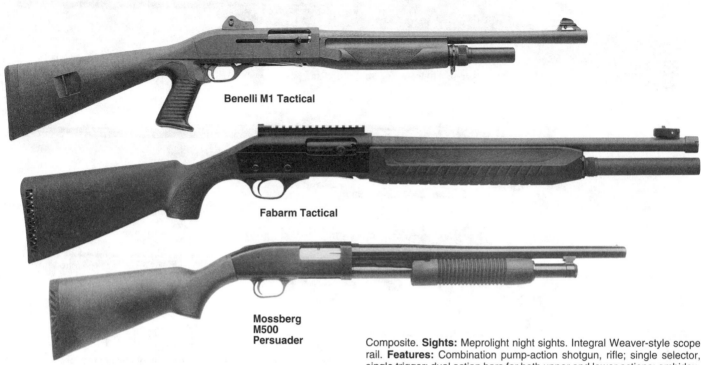

Benelli M1 Tactical

Fabarm Tactical

Mossberg
M500
Persuader

BENELLI M3 CONVERTIBLE SHOTGUN

Gauge: 12, 2-3/4", 3" chambers, 5-shot magazine. **Barrel:** 19-3/4" (Cyl.). **Weight:** 7 lbs., 4oz. **Length:** 41" overall. **Stock:** High-impact polymer with sling loop in side of butt; rubberized pistol grip on stock. **Sights:** Open rifle, fully adjustable. Ghost ring and rifle type. **Features:** Combination pump/auto action. Alloy receiver with inertia recoil rotating locking lug bolt; matte finish; automatic shell release lever. Introduced 1989. Imported by Benelli USA. Price with pistol grip, open rifle sights.

Price: With standard stock, open rifle sights. **$1,110.00**
Price: With ghost ring sight system, standard stock **$1,155.00**
Price: With ghost ring sights, pistol grip stock **$1,170.00**

BENELLI M1 TACTICAL SHOTGUN

Gauge: 12, 2-3/4", 3" chambers, 5-shot magazine. **Barrel:** 18.5" IC, M, F choke tubes. **Weight:** 6.7 lbs. **Length:** 39.75" overall. **Stock:** Black polymer. **Sights:** Rifle type with ghost ring system, tritium night sights optional. **Features:** Semi-auto intertia recoil action. Cross-bolt safety; bolt release button; matte-finish metal. Introduced 1993. Imported from Italy by Benelli USA.

Price: With rifle sights, standard stock **$935.00**
Price: With ghost ring rifle sights, standard stock **$1,000.00**
Price: With ghost ring sights, pistol grip stock **$1,015.00**
Price: With rifle sights, pistol grip stock **$950.00**

Benelli M1 Practical

Similar to M1 Field Shotgun, Picatinny receiver rail for scope mounting, nine-round magazine, 26" compensated barrel and ghost ring sights. Designed for IPSC competition.

Price: **$1,255.00**

BERETTA MODEL 1201FP GHOST RING AUTO SHOTGUN

Gauge: 12, 3" chamber. **Barrel:** 18" (Cyl.). **Weight:** 6.3 lbs. **Stock:** Special strengthened technopolymer, matte black finish. **Stock:** Fixed rifle type. **Features:** Has 5-shot magazine. Adjustable Ghost Ring rear sight, tritium front. Introduced 1988. Imported from Italy by Beretta U.S.A.

Price: **$890.00**

CROSSFIRE SHOTGUN/RIFLE

Gauge/Caliber: 12, 2-3/4" **Chamber:** 4-shot/223 Rem. (5-shot). **Barrel:** 20" (shotgun), 18" (rifle). **Weight:** About 8.6 lbs. **Length:** 40" overall. **Stock:**

Composite. **Sights:** Meprolight night sights. Integral Weaver-style scope rail. **Features:** Combination pump-action shotgun, rifle; single selector; single trigger; dual action bars for both upper and lower actions; ambidextrous selector and safety. Introduced 1997. Made in U.S. From Hesco.

Price: About **$1,895.00**
Price: With camo finish. **$1,995.00**

FABARM FP6 PUMP SHOTGUN

Gauge: 12, 3" chamber. **Barrel:** 20" (Cyl.); accepts choke tubes. **Weight:** 6.6 lbs. **Length:** 41.25" overall. **Stock:** Black polymer with textured grip, grooved slide handle. **Sights:** Blade front. **Features:** Twin action bars; anodized finish; free carrier for smooth reloading. Introduced 1998. Imported from Italy by Heckler & Koch, Inc.

Price: (Carbon fiber finish) **$499.00**
Price: With flip-up front sight, Picatinny rail with rear sight, oversize safety button **$499.00**

FABARM TACTICAL SEMI-AUTOMATIC SHOTGUN

Gauge: 12, 3" chamber. **Barrel:** 20". **Weight:** 6.6 lbs. **Length:** 41.2" overall. **Stock:** Polymer or folding. **Sights:** Ghost ring (tritium night sights optional). **Features:** Gas operated; matte receiver; twin forged action bars; oversized bolt handle and safety button; Picatinny rail; includes cylinder bore choke tube. Introduced 2001. Imported from Italy by Heckler & Koch Inc.

Price: **$999.00**

MOSSBERG MODEL 500 PERSUADER SECURITY SHOTGUNS

Gauge: 12, 20, 410, 3" chamber. **Barrel:** 18-1/2", 20" (Cyl.). **Weight:** 7 lbs. **Stock:** Walnut-finished hardwood or black synthetic. **Sights:** Metal bead front. **Features:** Available in 6- or 8-shot models. Top-mounted safety, double action slide bars, swivel studs, rubber recoil pad. Blue, Parkerized, Marinecote finishes. Mossberg Cablelock included. From Mossberg.

Price: 12 or 20 ga., 18-1/2", blue, wood or synthetic stock, 6-shot **$342.00**
Price: Cruiser, 12 or 20 ga., 18-1/2", blue, pistol grip, heat shield **$347.00**
Price: As above, 410-bore **$335.00**

Mossberg Model 500, 590 Mariner Pump

Similar to the Model 500 or 590 Security except all metal parts finished with Marinecote metal finish to resist rust and corrosion. Synthetic field stock; pistol grip kit included. Mossberg Cablelock included.

Price: 6-shot, 18-1/2" barrel **$510.00**
Price: 9-shot, 20" barrel **$541.00**

Tactical Response TR-870

Winchester Model 1300 Defender

Mossberg Model HS410 Shotgun

Similar to the Model 500 Security pump except chambered for 20 gauge or 410 with 3" chamber; has pistol grip forend, thick recoil pad, muzzle brake and has special spreader choke on the 18.5" barrel. Overall length is 37.5", weight is 6.25 lbs. Blue finish; synthetic field stock. Mossberg Cablelock and video included. Introduced 1990.

Price: HS 410 .... **$345.00**

Mossberg Model 500, 590 Ghost-Ring Shotguns

Similar to the Model 500 Security except has adjustable blade front, adjustable Ghost-Ring rear sight with protective "ears." Model 500 has 18.5" (Cyl.) barrel, 6-shot capacity; Model 590 has 20" (Cyl.) barrel, 9-shot capacity. Both have synthetic field stock. Mossberg Cablelock included. Introduced 1990. From Mossberg.

Price: 500 parkerized **$454.00**
Price: 590 parkerized **$463.00**
Price: Parkerized Speedfeed stock .... **$568.00 to $634.00**

MOSSBERG MODEL 590 SHOTGUN

Gauge: 12, 3" chamber. **Barrel:** 20" (Cyl.). **Weight:** 7-1/4 lbs. **Stock:** Synthetic field or Speedfeed. **Sights:** Metal bead front. **Features:** Top-mounted safety, double slide action bars. Comes with heat shield, bayonet lug, swivel studs, rubber recoil pad. Blue, Parkerized or Marinecote finish. Mossberg Cablelock included. From Mossberg.

Price: Blue, synthetic stock............................. **$406.00**
Price: Parkerized, synthetic stock....................... **$527.00**
Price: Parkerized, Speedfeed stock **$568.00**

Mossberg 590DA Double-Action Pump Shotgun

Similar to Model 590 except trigger requires a long stroke for each shot, duplicating the trigger pull of double-action-only pistols and revolvers. Available in 12 gauge only with black synthetic stock and parkerized finish with 14" (law enforcement only), 18-1/2 "and 20" barrels. Six-shot magazine tube (nine-shot for 20" barrel). Front bead or ghost ring sights. Weighs 7 pounds (18 1/2" barrel). Introduced 2000. From Mossberg.

Price: Bead sight, 6-shot magazine **$510.00**
Price: Ghost ring sights, 6-shot magazine **$558.00**
Price: Bead sight, 9-shot magazine **$541.00**
Price: Ghost ring sights, 9-shot magazine **$597.00**

TACTICAL RESPONSE TR-870 STANDARD MODEL SHOTGUN

Gauge: 12, 3" chamber, 7-shot magazine. **Barrel:** 18" (Cyl.). **Weight:** 9 lbs. **Length:** 38" overall. **Stock:** Fiberglass-filled polypropolene with non-snag recoil absorbing butt pad. Nylon tactical forend houses flashlight. **Sights:** Trak-Lock ghost ring sight system. Front sight has tritium insert. **Features:** Highly modified Remington 870P with Parkerized finish. Comes with nylon three-way adjustable sling, high visibility non-binding follower, high performance magazine spring, Jumbo Head safety, and Side Saddle extended 6-shot shell carrier on left side of receiver. Introduced 1991. From Scattergun Technologies, Inc.

Price: Standard model **$815.00**
Price: FBI model................................... **$770.00**
Price: Patrol model................................ **$595.00**
Price: Border Patrol model.......................... **$605.00**
Price: K-9 model (Rem. 11-87 action) **$995.00**
Price: Urban Sniper, Rem. 11-87 action............... **$1,290.00**
Price: Louis Awerbuck model........................ **$705.00**
Price: Practical Turkey model........................ **$725.00**
Price: Expert model **$1,350.00**
Price: Professional model........................... **$815.00**
Price: Entry model **$840.00**
Price: Compact model **$635.00**
Price: SWAT model **$1,195.00**

TRISTAR PHANTOM HP AUTO SHOTGUN

Gauge: 12, 3" chamber. **Barrel:** 19"; threaded for external choke tubes. **Stock:** Black synthetic. **Sights:** Bead front. **Features:** Gas-operated action; blue/black finish; five-shot extended magazine tube. Imported by Tristar Sporting Arms Ltd.

Price: .... **NA**

WINCHESTER MODEL 1300 DEFENDER PUMP GUNS

Gauge: 12, 20, 3" chamber, 5- or 8-shot capacity. **Barrel:** 18" (Cyl.). **Weight:** 6-3/4 lbs. **Length:** 38-5/8" overall. **Stock:** Walnut-finished hardwood stock and ribbed forend, synthetic or pistol grip. **Sights:** Metal bead front or TRUGLO® fiber-optic. **Features:** Cross-bolt safety, front-locking rotary bolt, twin action slide bars. Black rubber butt pad. From U.S. Repeating Arms Co.

Price: 8-Shot (black synthetic stock, TRUGLO® sight) **$326.00**
Price: 8-Shot Pistol Grip (pistol grip synthetic stock) **$326.00**

Winchester Model 1300 Stainless Marine Pump Gun

Same as the Defender 8-Shot except has bright chrome finish, stainless steel barrel, bead front sight. Phosphate coated receiver for corrosion resistance.

Price: **$518.00**

Winchester Model 1300 Camp Defender®

Same as the Defender 8-Shot except has hardwood stock and forearm, fully adjustable open sights and 22" barrel with WinChoke® choke tube system (cylinder choke tube included). Weighs 6-7/8 lbs. Introduced 2001. From U.S. Repeating Arms Co.

Price: Camp Defender®................................ **$373.00**

SHOTGUNS

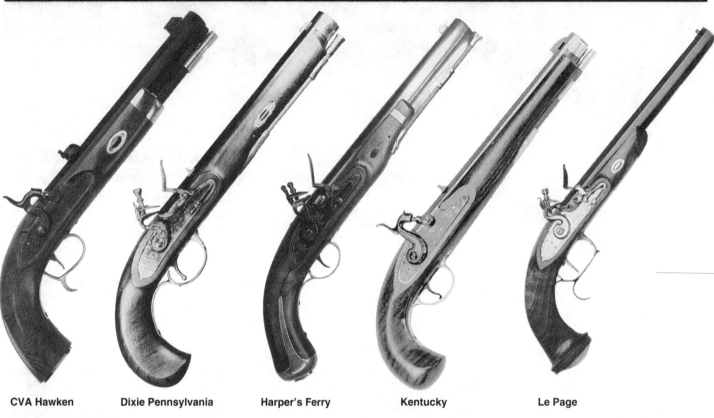

CVA Hawken   Dixie Pennsylvania   Harper's Ferry   Kentucky   Le Page

BLACKPOWDER (side tab)

CVA HAWKEN PISTOL
Caliber: 50. **Barrel:** 9-3/4"; 15/16" flats. **Weight:** 50 oz. **Length:** 16-1/2" overall. **Stocks:** Select hardwood. **Sights:** Beaded blade front, fully adjustable open rear. **Features:** Color case-hardened lock, polished brass wedge plate, instep, ramrod thimble, trigger guard, grip cap. Imported by CVA.
Price: $167.95
Price: Kit $127.95

DIXIE PENNSYLVANIA PISTOL
Caliber: 44 (.430" round ball). **Barrel:** 10", (7/8" octagon). **Weight:** 2-1/2 labs. **Stocks:** Walnut-stained hardwood. **Sights:** Blade front, open rear drift-adjustable for windage; brass. **Features:** Available in flint only. Brass trigger guard, thimbles, instep, wedge plates; high-luster blue barrel. Imported from Italy by Dixie Gun Works.
Price: Finished $215.00
Price: Kit $195.00

FRENCH-STYLE DUELING PISTOL
Caliber: 44. **Barrel:** 10". **Weight:** 35 oz. **Length:** 15-3/4" overall. **Stocks:** Carved walnut. **Sights:** Fixed. **Features:** Comes with velvet-lined case and accessories. Imported by Mandall Shooting Supplies.
Price: $295.00

HARPER'S FERRY 1806 PISTOL
Caliber: 58 (.570" round ball). **Barrel:** 10". **Weight:** 40 oz. **Length:** 16" overall. **Stocks:** Walnut. **Sights:** Fixed. **Features:** Case-hardened lock, brass-mounted browned barrel. Replica of the first U.S. Gov't.-made flintlock pistol. Imported by Navy Arms, Dixie Gun Works.
Price: .... $275.00 to $405.00
Price: Kit (Dixie) $249.00

KENTUCKY FLINTLOCK PISTOL
Caliber: 44, 45. **Barrel:** 10-1/8". **Weight:** 32 oz. **Length:** 15-1/2" overall. **Stocks:** Walnut. **Sights:** Fixed. **Features:** Specifications, including caliber, weight and length may vary with importer. Case-hardened lock, blued barrel; available also as brass barrel flint Model 1821. Imported by Navy Arms, The Armoury.
Price: .... $145.00 to $235.00

Price: In kit form, from .... $90.00 to $112.00
Price: Single cased set (Navy Arms) $360.00
Price: Double cased set (Navy Arms) $590.00

Kentucky Percussion Pistol
Similar to flint version but percussion lock. Imported by The Armoury, Navy Arms, CVA (50-cal.).
Price: .... $129.95 to $225.00
Price: Blued steel barrel (CVA) $167.95
Price: Kit form (CVA) $119.95
Price: Steel barrel (Armoury) $179.00
Price: Single cased set (Navy Arms) $355.00
Price: Double cased set (Navy Arms) $600.00

LE PAGE PERCUSSION DUELING PISTOL
Caliber: 44. **Barrel:** 10", rifled. **Weight:** 40 oz. **Length:** 16" overall. **Stocks:** Walnut, fluted butt. **Sights:** Blade front, notch rear. **Features:** Double-set triggers. Blued barrel; trigger guard and buttcap are polished silver. Imported by Dixie Gun Works.
Price: $395.00

LYMAN PLAINS PISTOL
Caliber: 50 or 54. **Barrel:** 8"; 1:30" twist, both calibers. **Weight:** 50 oz. **Length:** 15" overall. **Stocks:** Walnut half-stock. **Sights:** Blade front, square notch rear adjustable for windage. **Features:** Polished brass trigger guard and ramrod tip, color case-hardened coil spring lock, spring-loaded trigger, stainless steel nipple, blackened iron furniture. Hooked patent breech, detachable belt hook. Introduced 1981. From Lyman Products.
Price: Finished $244.95
Price: Kit $189.95

PEDERSOLI MANG TARGET PISTOL
Caliber: 38. **Barrel:** 10.5", octagonal; 1:15" twist. **Weight:** 2.5 lbs. **Length:** 17.25" overall. **Stocks:** Walnut with fluted grip. **Sights:** Blade front, open rear adjustable for windage. **Features:** Browned barrel, polished breech plug, rest color case-hardened. Imported from Italy by Dixie Gun Works.
Price: $825.00

Lyman Plains Pistol   Pedersoli Mang   Queen Anne   Thompson/Center Encore   Traditions Pioneer   Traditions William Parker

QUEEN ANNE FLINTLOCK PISTOL
Caliber: 50 (.490" round ball). **Barrel:** 7-1/2", smoothbore. **Stocks:** Walnut. **Sights:** None. **Features:** Browned steel barrel, fluted brass trigger guard, brass mask on butt. Lockplate left in the white. Made by Pedersoli in Italy. Introduced 1983. Imported by Dixie Gun Works.
Price: **$225.00**
Price: Kit **$175.00**

THOMPSON/CENTER ENCORE 209x50 MAGNUM PISTOL
Caliber: 50. **Barrel:** 15"; 1:20" twist. **Weight:** About 4 lbs. Grips: American walnut grip and forend. **Sights:** Click-adjustable, steel rear, ramp front. **Features:** Uses 209 shotgun primer for closed-breech ignition; accepts charges up to 110 grains of FFg black powder or two, 50-grain Pyrodex pellets. Introduced 2000.
Price: **$310.00**

TRADITIONS BUCKHUNTER PRO IN-LINE PISTOL
Caliber: 50. **Barrel:** 9-1/2", round. **Weight:** 48 oz. **Length:** 14" overall. **Stocks:** Smooth walnut or black epoxy-coated hardwood grip and forend. **Sights:** Beaded blade front, folding adjustable rear. **Features:** Thumb safety; removable stainless steel breech plug; adjustable trigger, barrel drilled and tapped for scope mounting. From Traditions.
Price: With walnut grip **$229.00**
Price: Nickel with black grip **$239.00**
Price: With walnut grip and 12-1/2" barrel **$239.00**
Price: Nickel with black grip, muzzle brake and 14-3/4" fluted barrel. **$289.00**
Price: 45 cal. nickel w/bl. grip, muzzlebrake and 14-3/4" fluted bbl.
. . . . **$289.00**

TRADITIONS KENTUCKY PISTOL
Caliber: 50. **Barrel:** 10"; octagon with 7/8" flats; 1:20" twist. **Weight:** 40 oz. **Length:** 15" overall. **Stocks:** Stained beech. **Sights:** Blade front, fixed rear. **Features:** Birds-head grip; brass thimbles; color case-hardened lock. Percussion only. Introduced 1995. From Traditions.
Price: Finished **$139.00**
Price: Kit. **$109.00**

TRADITIONS PIONEER PISTOL
Caliber: 45. **Barrel:** 9-5/8"; 13/16" flats, 1:16" twist. **Weight:** 31 oz. **Length:** 15" overall. **Stocks:** Beech. **Sights:** Blade front, fixed rear. **Features:** V-type mainspring. Single trigger. German silver furniture, blackened hardware. From Traditions.

Traditions Buckhunter Pro

Price: **$139.00**
Price: Kit. **$119.00**

TRADITIONS TRAPPER PISTOL
Caliber: 50. **Barrel:** 9-3/4"; 7/8" flats; 1:20" twist. **Weight:** 2-3/4 lbs. **Length:** 16" overall. **Stocks:** Beech. **Sights:** Blade front, adjustable rear. **Features:** Double-set triggers; brass buttcap, trigger guard, wedge plate, forend tip, thimble. From Traditions.
Price: Percussion **$189.00**
Price: Flintlock **$209.00**
Price: Kit **$149.00**

TRADITIONS VEST-POCKET DERRINGER
Caliber: 31. **Barrel:** 2-1/4"; brass. **Weight:** 8 oz. **Length:** 4-3/4" overall. **Stocks:** Simulated ivory. **Sights:** Beed front. **Features:** Replica of riverboat gamblers' derringer; authentic spur trigger. From Traditions.
Price: **$109.00**

TRADITIONS WILLIAM PARKER PISTOL
Caliber: 50. **Barrel:** 10-3/8"; 15/16" flats; polished steel. **Weight:** 37 oz. **Length:** 17-1/2" overall. **Stocks:** Walnut with checkered grip. **Sights:** Brass blade front, fixed rear. **Features:** Replica dueling pistol with 1:20" twist, hooked breech. Brass wedge plate, trigger guard, cap guard; separate ramrod. Double-set triggers. Polished steel barrel, lock. Imported by Traditions.
Price: **$269.00**

BLACKPOWDER

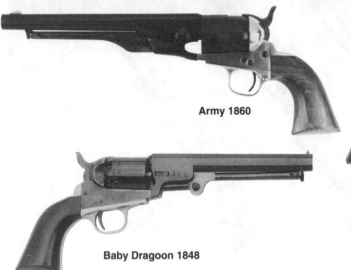

Army 1860

Colt 1860 Army

Baby Dragoon 1848

ARMY 1860 PERCUSSION REVOLVER

Caliber: 44, 6-shot. **Barrel:** 8". **Weight:** 40 oz. **Length:** 13-5/8" overall. **Stocks:** Walnut. **Sights:** Fixed. **Features:** Engraved Navy scene on cylinder; brass trigger guard; case-hardened frame, loading lever and hammer. Some importers supply pistol cut for detachable shoulder stock, have accessory stock available. Imported by Cabela's (1860 Lawman), E.M.F., Navy Arms, The Armoury, Cimarron, Dixie Gun Works (half-fluted cylinder, not roll engraved), Euroarms of America (brass or steel model), Armsport, Traditions (brass or steel) Uberti U.S.A. Inc., United States Patent Fire-Arms.

Price: About **$190.00**
Price: Hartford model, steel frame, German silver trim,
    cartouches (E.M.F.) **$215.00**
Price: Single cased set (Navy Arms) **$300.00**
Price: Double cased set (Navy Arms). **$490.00**
Price: 1861 Navy: Same as Army except 36-cal., 7-1/2" bbl., weighs 41 oz., cut for shoulder stock; round cylinder (fluted available), from Cabela's, CVA (brass frame, 44-cal.), United States Patent Fire-Arms
 . . . . **$99.95 to $385.00**
Price: Steel frame kit (E.M.F., Euroarms). . . . . **$125.00 to $216.25**
Price: Colt Army Police, fluted cyl., 5-1/2", 36-cal. (Cabela's) . . . **$124.95**
Price: With nickeled frame, barrel and backstrap, gold-tone fluted cylinder, trigger and hammer, simulated ivory grips (Traditions) **$199.00**

BABY DRAGOON 1848, 1849 POCKET, WELLS FARGO

Caliber: 31. **Barrel:** 3", 4", 5", 6"; seven-groove; RH twist. **Weight:** About 21 oz. **Stocks:** Varnished walnut. **Sights:** Brass pin front, hammer notch rear. **Features:** No loading lever on Baby Dragoon or Wells Fargo models. Unfluted cylinder with stagecoach holdup scene; cupped cylinder pin; no grease grooves; one safety pin on cylinder and slot in hammer face; straight (flat) mainspring. From Armsport, Cimarron F.A. Co., Dixie Gun Works, Uberti U.S.A. Inc.

Price: 6" barrel, with loading lever (Dixie Gun Works) **$254.95**
Price: 4" (Uberti USA Inc.) **$335.00**

COLT 1860 ARMY PERCUSSION REVOLVER

Caliber: 44. **Barrel:** 8", 7-groove, left-hand twist. **Weight:** 42 oz. **Stocks:** One-piece walnut. **Sights:** German silver front sight, hammer notch rear. **Features:** Steel backstrap cut for shoulder stock; brass trigger guard. Cylinder has Navy scene. Color case-hardened frame, hammer, loading lever. Reproduction of original gun with all original markings. From Colt Blackpowder Arms Co.

Price: **$190.00**

COLT 1848 BABY DRAGOON REVOLVER

Caliber: 31, 5-shot. **Barrel:** 4". **Weight:** About 21 oz. **Stocks:** Smooth walnut. **Sights:** Brass pin front, hammer notch rear. **Features:** Color case-hardened frame; no loading lever; square-back trigger guard; round bolt cuts; octagonal barrel; engraved cylinder scene. Imported by Colt Blackpowder Arms Co.

Price: **$429.95**

Colt 1860 "Cavalry Model" Percussion Revolver

Similar to the 1860 Army except has fluted cylinder. Color case-hardened frame, hammer, loading lever and plunger; blued barrel, backstrap and cylinder, brass trigger guard. Has four-screw frame cut for optional shoulder stock. From Colt Blackpowder Arms Co.

Price: **$399.95**

COLT 1851 NAVY PERCUSSION REVOLVER

Caliber: 36. **Barrel:** 7-1/2", octagonal; 7-groove left-hand twist. **Weight:** 40-1/2 oz. **Stocks:** One-piece oiled American walnut. **Sights:** Brass pin front, hammer notch rear. **Features:** Faithful reproduction of the original gun. Color case-hardened frame, loading lever, plunger, hammer and latch. Blue cylinder, trigger, barrel, screws, wedge. Silver-plated brass backstrap and square-back trigger guard. From Colt Blackpowder Arms Co.

Price: **$449.95**

COLT 1861 NAVY PERCUSSION REVOLVER

Caliber: 36. **Barrel:** 7-1/2". **Weight:** 42 oz. **Length:** 13-1/8" overall. **Stocks:** One-piece walnut. **Sights:** Blade front, hammer notch rear. **Features:** Color case-hardened frame, loading lever, plunger; blued barrel, backstrap, trigger guard; roll-engraved cylinder and barrel. From Colt Blackpowder Arms Co.

Price: **$449.95**

COLT 1849 POCKET DRAGOON REVOLVER

Caliber: 31. **Barrel:** 4". **Weight:** 24 oz. **Length:** 9-1/2" overall. **Stocks:** One-piece walnut. **Sights:** Fixed. Brass pin front, hammer notch rear. **Features:** Color case-hardened frame. No loading lever. Unfluted cylinder with engraved scene. Exact reproduction of original. From Colt Blackpowder Arms Co.

Price: **$429.95**

COLT 1862 POCKET POLICE "TRAPPER MODEL" REVOLVER

Caliber: 36. **Barrel:** 3-1/2". **Weight:** 20 oz. **Length:** 8-1/2" overall. **Stocks:** One-piece walnut. **Sights:** Blade front, hammer notch rear. **Features:** Has separate 4-5/8" brass ramrod. Color case-hardened frame and hammer; silver-plated backstrap and trigger guard; blued semi-fluted cylinder, blued barrel. From Colt Blackpowder Arms Co., Navy Arms.

Price: (Colt Blackpowder Arms) **$429.95**
Price: "New" Pocket Police, Navy Arms **$315.00**

COLT THIRD MODEL DRAGOON

Caliber: 44. **Barrel:** 7-1/2". **Weight:** 66 oz. **Length:** 13-3/4" overall. **Stocks:** One-piece walnut. **Sights:** Blade front, hammer notch rear. **Features:** Color case-hardened frame, hammer, lever and plunger; round trigger guard; flat mainspring; hammer roller; rectangular bolt cuts. From Colt Blackpowder Arms Co.

Price: Three-screw frame with brass grip straps **$499.95**
Price: First Dragoon (oval bolt cuts in cylinder, square-back
    trigger guard) **$499.95**
Price: Second Dragoon (rectangular bolt cuts in cylinder,
    square-back trigger guard) **$499.95**

BLACKPOWDER

BLACKPOWDER REVOLVERS

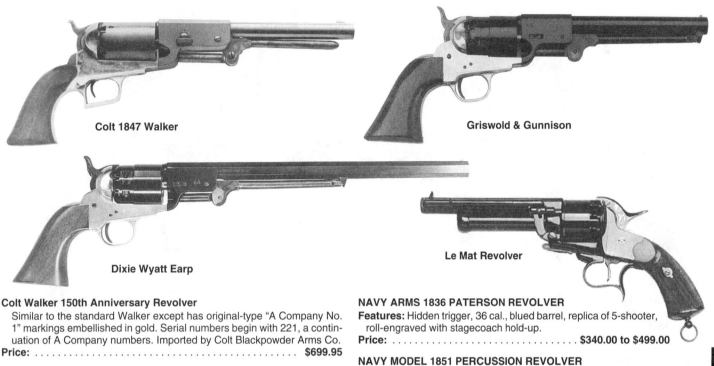

Colt 1847 Walker

Griswold & Gunnison

Dixie Wyatt Earp

Le Mat Revolver

Colt Walker 150th Anniversary Revolver
Similar to the standard Walker except has original-type "A Company No. 1" markings embellished in gold. Serial numbers begin with 221, a continuation of A Company numbers. Imported by Colt Blackpowder Arms Co.
Price: **$699.95**

COLT 1847 WALKER PERCUSSION REVOLVER
Caliber: 44. **Barrel:** 9", 7-groove; right-hand twist. **Weight:** 73 oz. **Stocks:** One-piece walnut. **Sights:** German silver front sight, hammer notch rear. **Features:** Made in U.S. Faithful reproduction of the original gun, including markings. Color case-hardened frame, hammer, loading lever and plunger. Blue steel backstrap, brass square-back trigger guard. Blue barrel, cylinder, trigger and wedge. From Colt Blackpowder Arms Co.
Price: **$499.95**

DIXIE WYATT EARP REVOLVER
Caliber: 44. **Barrel:** 12", octagon. **Weight:** 46 oz. **Length:** 18" overall. **Stocks:** Two-piece walnut. **Sights:** Fixed. **Features:** Highly polished brass frame, backstrap and trigger guard; blued barrel and cylinder; case-hardened hammer, trigger and loading lever. Navy-size shoulder stock ($45) will fit with minor fitting. From Dixie Gun Works.
Price: **$150.00**
Price: Double cased set **$365.00**

LE MAT REVOLVER
Caliber: 44/65. **Barrel:** 6-3/4" (revolver); 4-7/8" (single shot). **Weight:** 3 lbs., 7 oz. **Stocks:** Hand-checkered walnut. **Sights:** Post front, hammer notch rear. **Features:** Exact reproduction with all-steel construction; 44-cal. 9-shot cylinder, 65-cal. single barrel; color case-hardened hammer with selector; spur trigger guard; ring at butt; lever-type barrel release. From Navy Arms.
Price: Cavalry model (lanyard ring, spur trigger guard) **$595.00**
Price: Army model (round trigger guard, pin-type barrel release) **$595.00**
Price: Naval-style (thumb selector on hammer) **$595.00**

NAVY 1851 PERCUSSION REVOLVER
Caliber: 44, 6-shot. **Barrel:** 7-1/2". **Weight:** 45 oz. **Length:** 13" overall. **Stocks:** Walnut finish. **Sights:** Fixed. **Features:** 44-caliber version of the 1851 Navy. Imported by The Armoury, Armsport, Traditions.
Price: Brass **$139.00**
Price: Steel **$169.00**

NAVY ARMS NEW MODEL POCKET REVOLVER
Caliber: 31, 5-shot. **Barrel:** 3-1/2", octagon. **Weight:** 15 oz. **Length:** 7-3/4". **Stocks:** Two-piece walnut. **Sights:** Fixed. **Features:** Replica of the Remington New Model Pocket. Available with polisehd brass frame or nickel plated finish. Introduced 2000. Imported by Navy Arms.
Price: **$300.00**

NAVY ARMS 1836 PATERSON REVOLVER
Features: Hidden trigger, 36 cal., blued barrel, replica of 5-shooter, roll-engraved with stagecoach hold-up.
Price: . . . . **$340.00 to $499.00**

NAVY MODEL 1851 PERCUSSION REVOLVER
Caliber: 36, 44, 6-shot. **Barrel:** 7-1/2". **Weight:** 44 oz. **Length:** 13" overall. **Stocks:** Walnut finish. **Sights:** Post front, hammer notch rear. **Features:** Brass backstrap and trigger guard; some have 1st Model squareback trigger guard, engraved cylinder with navy battle scene; case-hardened frame, hammer, loading lever. Imported by The Armoury, Cabela's, Cimarron F.A. Co., Navy Arms, E.M.F., Dixie Gun Works, Euroarms of America, Armsport, CVA (44-cal. only), Traditions (44 only), Uberti U.S.A. Inc., United States Patent Fire-Arms.
Price: Brass frame . . . . **$99.95 to $385.00**
Price: Steel frame . . . . **$130.00 to $285.00**
Price: Kit form . . . . **$110.00 to $123.95**
Price: Engraved model (Dixie Gun Works) **$159.95**
Price: Single cased set, steel frame (Navy Arms) **$280.00**
Price: Double cased set, steel frame (Navy Arms) **$455.00**
Price: Confederate Navy (Cabela's) **$89.99**
Price: Hartford model, steel frame, German silver trim, cartouche (E.M.F.) **$190.00**

NEW MODEL 1858 ARMY PERCUSSION REVOLVER
Caliber: 36 or 44, 6-shot. **Barrel:** 6-1/2" or 8". **Weight:** 38 oz. **Length:** 13-1/2" overall. **Stocks:** Walnut. **Sights:** Blade front, groove-in-frame rear. **Features:** Replica of Remington Model 1858. Also available from some importers as Army Model Belt Revolver in 36-cal., a shortened and lightened version of the 44. Target Model (Uberti U.S.A. Inc., Navy Arms) has fully adjustable target rear sight, target front, 36 or 44. Imported by Cabela's, Cimarron F.A. Co., CVA (as 1858 Army, brass frame, 44 only), Dixie Gun Works, Navy Arms, The Armoury, E.M.F., Euroarms of America (engraved, stainless and plain), Armsport, Traditions (44 only), Uberti U.S.A. Inc.
Price: Steel frame, about . . . . **$99.95 to $280.00**
Price: Steel frame kit (Euroarms, Navy Arms) . . . . . . **$115.95 to $150.00**
Price: Single cased set (Navy Arms) **$290.00**
Price: Double cased set (Navy Arms) **$480.00**
Price: Stainless steel Model 1858 (Euroarms, Uberti U.S.A. Inc., Cabela's, Navy Arms, Armsport, Traditions) . . . . **$169.95 to $380.00**
Price: Target Model, adjustable rear sight (Cabela's, Euroarms, Uberti U.S.A. Inc., Stone Mountain Arms) . . . . **$95.95 to $399.00**
Price: Brass frame (CVA, Cabela's, Traditions, Navy Arms) . . . . **$79.95 to $159.95**
Price: As above, kit (Dixie Gun Works, Navy Arms) . . **$145.00 to $188.95**

BLACKPOWDER

BLACKPOWDER

Uberti 1858

North American Companion

Ruger Old Army

Rogers & Spencer

Pocket Police 1862

Price: Buffalo model, 44-cal. (Cabela's) **$119.99**
Price: Hartford model, steel frame, German silver trim,
   cartouche (E.M.F.) **$215.00**

NORTH AMERICAN COMPANION PERCUSSION REVOLVER

Caliber: 22. **Barrel:** 1-1/8". **Weight:** 5.1 oz. **Length:** 4-5/10" overall. **Stocks:** Laminated wood. **Sights:** Blade front, notch fixed rear. **Features:** All stainless steel construction. Uses standard #11 percussion caps. Comes with bullets, powder measure, bullet seater, leather clip holster, gun rug. Long Rifle or Magnum frame size. Introduced 1996. Made in U.S. by North American Arms.
Price: Long Rifle frame **$191.00**

North American Magnum Companion Percussion Revolver

Similar to the Companion except has larger frame. Weighs 7.2 oz., has 1-5/8" barrel, measures 5-7/16" overall. Comes with bullets, powder measure, bullet seater, leather clip holster, gun rag. Introduced 1996. Made in U.S. by North American Arms.
Price: **$209.00**

POCKET POLICE 1862 PERCUSSION REVOLVER

Caliber: 36, 5-shot. **Barrel:** 4-1/2", 5-1/2", 6-1/2", 7-1/2". **Weight:** 26 oz. **Length:** 12" overall (6-1/2" bbl.). **Stocks:** Walnut. **Sights:** Fixed. **Features:** Round tapered barrel; half-fluted and rebated cylinder; case-hardened frame, loading lever and hammer; silver or brass trigger guard and backstrap. Imported by Dixie Gun Works, Navy Arms (5-1/2" only), Uberti U.S.A. Inc. (5-1/2", 6-1/2" only), United States Patent Fire-Arms and Cimarron F.A. Co.
Price: About . . . . **$139.95 to $335.00**
Price: Single cased set with accessories (Navy Arms) **$365.00**
Price: Hartford model, steel frame, German silver trim,
   cartouche (E.M.F.) **$215.00**

ROGERS & SPENCER PERCUSSION REVOLVER

Caliber: 44. **Barrel:** 7-1/2". **Weight:** 47 oz. **Length:** 13-3/4" overall. **Stocks:** Walnut. **Sights:** Cone front, integral groove in frame for rear. **Features:** Accurate reproduction of a Civil War design. Solid frame; extra large nipple cut-out on rear of cylinder; loading lever and cylinder easily removed for cleaning. From Dixie Gun Works, Euroarms of America (standard blue, engraved, burnished, target models), Navy Arms.
Price: . . . . **$160.00 to $299.95**
Price: Nickel-plated. **$215.00**
Price: Engraved (Euroarms) **$287.00**

Price: Kit version . . . . **$245.00 to $252.00**
Price: Target version (Euroarms) . . . . **$239.00 to $270.00**
Price: Burnished London Gray (Euroarms) . . . . **$245.00 to $270.00**

RUGER OLD ARMY PERCUSSION REVOLVER

Caliber: 45, 6-shot. Uses .457" dia. lead bullets or 454 conical. **Barrel:** 7-1/2" (6-groove; 1:16" twist). **Weight:** 2-7/8 lbs. **Length:** 13-1/2" overall. **Stocks:** Rosewood. **Sights:** Ramp front, rear adjustable for windage and elevation; or fixed (groove). **Features:** Stainless steel; standard size nipples, chrome-moly steel cylinder and frame, same lockwork as original Super Blackhawk. Also stainless steel. Includes hard case and lock. Made in USA. From Sturm, Ruger & Co.
Price: Stainless steel (Model KBP-7) **$535.00**
Price: Blued steel (Model BP-7) **$499.00**
Price: Blued steel, fixed sight (BP-7F) **$499.00**
Price: Stainless steel, fixed sight (KBP-7F) **$535.00**

SHERIFF MODEL 1851 PERCUSSION REVOLVER

Caliber: 36, 44, 6-shot. **Barrel:** 5". **Weight:** 40 oz. **Length:** 10-1/2" overall. **Stocks:** Walnut. **Sights:** Fixed. **Features:** Brass backstrap and trigger guard; engraved navy scene; case-hardened frame, hammer, loading lever. Imported by E.M.F.
Price: Steel frame **$169.95**
Price: Brass frame **$140.00**

SPILLER & BURR REVOLVER

Caliber: 36 (.375" round ball). **Barrel:** 7", octagon. **Weight:** 2-1/2 lbs. **Length:** 12-1/2" overall. **Stocks:** Two-piece walnut. **Sights:** Fixed. **Features:** Reproduction of the C.S.A. revolver. Brass frame and trigger guard. Also available as a kit. From Dixie Gun Works, Navy Arms.
Price: **$145.00**
Price: Kit form (Dixie) **$149.95**
Price: Single cased set (Navy Arms) **$270.00**
Price: Double cased set (Navy Arms) **$430.00**

TEXAS PATERSON 1836 REVOLVER

Caliber: 36 (.375" round ball). **Barrel:** 7-1/2". **Weight:** 42 oz. **Stocks:** One-piece walnut. **Sights:** Fixed. **Features:** Copy of Sam Colt's first commercially-made revolving pistol. Has no loading lever but comes with loading tool. From Cimarron F.A. Co., Dixie Gun Works, Navy Arms, Uberti U.S.A. Inc.
Price: About . . . . **$310.00 to $395.00**
Price: With loading lever (Uberti U.S.A. Inc.) **$450.00**
Price: Engraved (Navy Arms) **$485.00**

BLACKPOWDER REVOLVERS

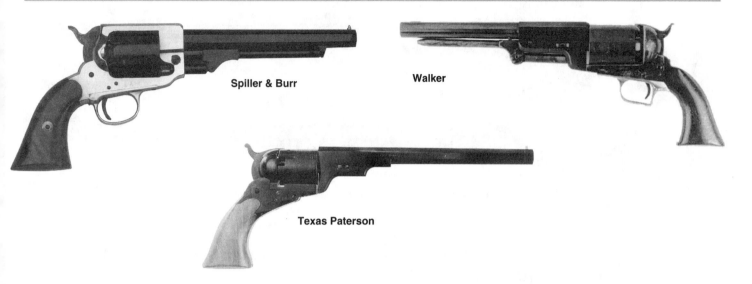

Spiller & Burr

Walker

Texas Paterson

Uberti 1861 Navy Percussion Revolver
Similar to Colt 1851 Navy except has round 7-1/2" barrel, rounded trigger guard, German silver blade front sight, "creeping" loading lever. Available with fluted or round cylinder. Imported by Uberti U.S.A. Inc.
Price: Steel backstrap, trigger guard, cut for stock **$265.00**

1ST U.S. MODEL DRAGOON
Caliber: 44. **Barrel:** 7-1/2", part round, part octagon. **Weight:** 64 oz. **Stocks:** One-piece walnut. **Sights:** German silver blade front, hammer notch rear. **Features:** First model has oval bolt cuts in cylinder, square-back flared trigger guard, V-type mainspring, short trigger. Ranger and Indian scene roll-engraved on cylinder. Color case-hardened frame, loading lever, plunger and hammer; blue barrel, cylinder, trigger and wedge. Available with old-time charcoal blue or standard blue-black finish. Polished brass backstrap and trigger guard. From Cimarron F.A. Co., Dixie Gunworks, Uberti U.S.A. Inc., United States Patent Fire-Arms, Navy Arms.
Price: . . . . **$295.00 to $435.00**

2nd U.S. Model Dragoon Revolver
Similar to the 1st Model except distinguished by rectangular bolt cuts in the cylinder. From Cimarron F.A. Co., Uberti U.S.A. Inc., United States Patent Fire-Arms, Navy Arms, Dixie Gunworks.
Price: . . . . **$295.00 to $435.00**

3rd U.S. Model Dragoon Revolver
Similar to the 2nd Model except for oval trigger guard, long trigger, modifications to the loading lever and latch. Imported by Cimarron F.A. Co., Uberti U.S.A. Inc., United States Patent Fire-Arms, Dixie Gunworks.
Price: Military model (frame cut for shoulder stock,
steel backstrap) . . . . **$295.00 to $435.00**
Price: Civilian (brass backstrap, trigger guard). . . . . . **$295.00 to $325.00**

1862 POCKET NAVY PERCUSSION REVOLVER
Caliber: 36, 5-shot. **Barrel:** 5-1/2", 6-1/2", octagonal, 7-groove, LH twist. **Weight:** 27 oz. (5-1/2" barrel). **Length:** 10-1/2" overall (5-1/2" bbl.).

Stocks: One-piece varnished walnut. **Sights:** Brass pin front, hammer notch rear. **Features:** Rebated cylinder, hinged loading lever, brass or silver-plated backstrap and trigger guard, color-cased frame, hammer, loading lever, plunger and latch, rest blued. Has original-type markings. From Cimarron F.A. Co., Uberti U.S.A. Inc., Dixie Gunworks.
Price: With brass backstrap, trigger guard . . . . **$260.00 to $310.00**

1861 Navy Percussion Revolver
Similar to Colt 1851 Navy except has round 7-1/2" barrel, rounded trigger guard, German silver blade front sight, "creeping" loading lever. Fluted or round cylinder. Imported by Cimarron F.A. Co., Uberti U.S.A. Inc., Dixie Gunworks.
Price: Steel backstrap, trigger guard, cut for stock. . . **$255.00 to $300.00**

U.S. PATENT FIRE-ARMS 1862 POCKET NAVY
Caliber: 36. **Barrel:** 4-1/2", 5-1/2", 6-1/2". **Weight:** 27 oz. (5-1/2" barrel). **Length:** 10-1/2" overall (5-1/2" barrel). **Stocks:** Smooth walnut. **Sights:** Brass pin front, hammer notch rear. **Features:** Blued barrel and cylinder, color case-hardened frame, hammer, lever; silver-plated backstrap and trigger guard. Imported from Italy; available from United States Patent Fire-Arms Mfg. Co.
Price: **$335.00**

WALKER 1847 PERCUSSION REVOLVER
Caliber: 44, 6-shot. **Barrel:** 9". **Weight:** 84 oz. **Length:** 15-1/2" overall. **Stocks:** Walnut. **Sights:** Fixed. **Features:** Case-hardened frame, loading lever and hammer; iron backstrap; brass trigger guard; engraved cylinder. Imported by Cabela's, Cimarron F.A. Co., Navy Arms, Dixie Gun Works, Uberti U.S.A. Inc., E.M.F., Cimarron, Traditions, United States Patent Fire-Arms.
Price: About . . . . **$225.00 to $445.00**
Price: Single cased set (Navy Arms) **$405.00**
Price: Deluxe Walker with French fitted case (Navy Arms) **$540.00**
Price: Hartford model, steel frame, German silver trim,
cartouche (E.M.F.) **$295.00**

Austin & Halleck 420 LR In-Line

Austin & Halleck 320 LR In-Line

Austin & Halleck Mountain

Cabela's Blue Ridge

ARMOURY R140 HAWKEN RIFLE

Caliber: 45, 50 or 54. **Barrel:** 29". **Weight:** 8-3/4 to 9 lbs. **Length:** 45-3/4" overall. **Stock:** Walnut, with cheekpiece. **Sights:** Dovetail front, fully adjustable rear. **Features:** Octagon barrel, removable breech plug; double set triggers; blued barrel, brass stock fittings, color case-hardened percussion lock. From Armsport, The Armoury.
Price: . . . . $225.00 to $245.00

AUSTIN & HALLECK MODEL 420 LR IN-LINE RIFLE

Caliber: 50. **Barrel:** 26", 1" octagon to 3/4" round; 1:28" twist. **Weight:** 7-7/8 lbs. **Length:** 47-1/2" overall. **Stock:** Lightly figured maple in Classic or Monte Carlo style. **Sights:** Ramp front, fully adjustable rear. **Features:** Blue or electroless nickel finish; in-line percussion action with removable weather shroud; Timney adjustable target trigger with sear block safety. Introduced 1998. Made in U.S. by Austin & Halleck.
Price: Blue $459.00
Price: Stainless steel $549.00
Price: Blue, hand-select highly figured stock $775.00
Price: Blue, exhibition-grade Monte Carlo stock. $1,322.00
Price: Stainless steel, exhibition-grade Monte Carlo stock. $1,422.00

Austin & Halleck Model 320 LR In-Line Rifle

Similar to the Model 420 LR except has black resin synthetic stock with checkered grip and forend. Introduced 1998. Made in U.S. by Austin & Halleck.
Price: Blue $380.00
Price: Stainless steel $447.00

AUSTIN & HALLECK MOUNTAIN RIFLE

Caliber: 50. **Barrel:** 32"; 1:28" or 1:66" twist; 1" flats. **Weight:** 7-1/2 lbs. **Length:** 49" overall. **Stock:** Curly maple. **Sights:** Silver blade front, buckhorn rear. **Features:** Available in percussion or flintlock; double throw adjustable set triggers; rust brown finish. Made in U.S. by Austin & Halleck.

Price: Flintlock $539.00
Price: Percussion $578.00
Price: Percussion, fancy wood $592.00
Price: Percussion, select wood $660.00

BOSTONIAN PERCUSSION RIFLE

Caliber: 45. **Barrel:** 30", octagonal. **Weight:** 7-1/4 lbs. **Length:** 46" overall. **Stock:** Walnut. **Sights:** Blade front, fixed notch rear. **Features:** Color case-hardened lock, brass trigger guard, buttplate, patchbox. Imported from Italy by E.M.F.
Price: $285.00

CABELA'S TRADITIONAL HAWKEN

Caliber: 50, 54. **Barrel:** 29". **Weight:** About 9 lbs. **Stock:** Walnut. **Sights:** Blade front, open adjustable rear. **Features:** Flintlock or percussion. Adjustable double-set triggers. Polished brass furniture, color case-hardened lock. Imported by Cabela's.
Price: Percussion, right-hand $189.99
Price: Percussion, left-hand $199.99
Price: Flintlock, right-hand $224.99

Cabela's Sporterized Hawken Hunter Rifle

Similar to the Traditional Hawken except has more modern stock style with rubber recoil pad, blued furniture, sling swivels. Percussion only, in 50- or 54-caliber.
Price: Carbine or rifle, right-hand $219.99

CABELA'S BLUE RIDGE RIFLE

Caliber: 32, 36, 45, 50. **Barrel:** 39", octagonal. **Weight:** About 7-3/4 lbs. **Length:** 55" overall. **Stock:** American black walnut. **Sights:** Blade front, rear drift adjustable for windage. **Features:** Color case-hardened lockplate and cock/hammer, brass trigger guard and buttplate, double set, double-phased triggers. From Cabela's.
Price: Percussion $379.99
Price: Flintlock $399.99

BLACKPOWDER MUSKETS & RIFLES

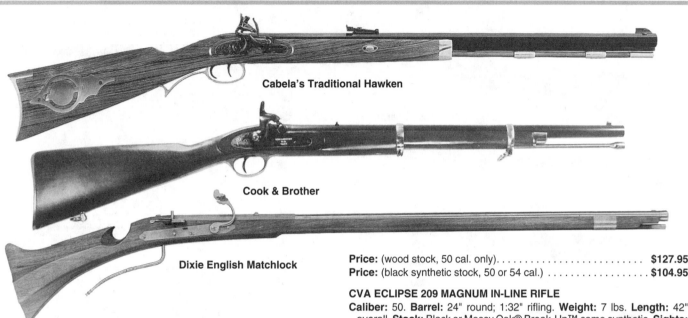

Cabela's Traditional Hawken

Cook & Brother

Dixie English Matchlock

CABELA'S KODIAK EXPRESS DOUBLE RIFLE

Caliber: 50, 54, 58, 72. **Barrel:** Length n/a; 1:48" twist. **Weight:** 9.3 lbs. **Length:** 45-1/4" overall. **Stock:** European walnut, oil finish. **Sights:** Fully adjustable double folding-leaf rear, ramp front. **Features:** Percussion. Barrels regulated to point of aim at 75 yards; polished and engraved lock, top tang and trigger guard. From Cabela's.
Price: 50, 54, 58 calibers $649.99
Price: 72 caliber $679.99

COLT MODEL 1861 MUSKET

Caliber: 58. **Barrel:** 40". **Weight:** 9 lbs., 3 oz. **Length:** 56" overall. **Stock:** Oil-finished walnut. **Sight:** Blade front, adjustable folding leaf rear. **Features:** Made to original specifications and has authentic Civil War Colt markings. Bright-finished metal, blued nipple and rear sight. Bayonet and accessories available. From Colt Blackpowder Arms Co.
Price: $799.95

COOK & BROTHER CONFEDERATE CARBINE

Caliber: 58. **Barrel:** 24". **Weight:** 7-1/2 lbs. **Length:** 40-1/2" overall. **Stock:** Select walnut. **Features:** Recreation of the 1861 New Orleans-made artillery carbine. Color case-hardened lock, browned barrel. Buttplate, trigger guard, barrel bands, sling swivels and nosecap of polished brass. From Euroarms of America.
Price: $447.00
Price: Cook & Brother rifle (33" barrel) $480.00

CUMBERLAND MOUNTAIN BLACKPOWDER RIFLE

Caliber: 50. **Barrel:** 26", round. **Weight:** 9-1/2 lbs. **Length:** 43" overall. **Stock:** American walnut. **Sights:** Bead front, open rear adjustable for windage. **Features:** Falling block action fires with shotshell primer. Blued receiver and barrel. Introduced 1993. Made in U.S. by Cumberland Mountain Arms, Inc.
Price: $931.50

CVA YOUTH HUNTER RIFLE

Caliber: 50. **Barrel:** 24"; 1:48" twist, octagonal. **Weight:** 5-1/2 lbs. **Length:** 38" overall. **Stock:** Stained hardwood. **Sights:** Bead front, Williams adjustable rear. **Features:** Oversize trigger guard; wooden ramrod. Introduced 1999. From CVA.
Price: $135.95

CVA BOBCAT RIFLE

Caliber: 50 or 54. **Barrel:** 26"; 1:48" twist. **Weight:** 6-1/2 lbs. **Length:** 42" overall. **Stock:** Dura-Grip synthetic or wood. **Sights:** Blade front, open rear. **Features:** Oversize trigger guard; wood ramrod; matte black finish. Introduced 1995. From CVA.

Price: (wood stock, 50 cal. only) $127.95
Price: (black synthetic stock, 50 or 54 cal.) $104.95

CVA ECLIPSE 209 MAGNUM IN-LINE RIFLE

Caliber: 50. **Barrel:** 24" round; 1:32" rifling. **Weight:** 7 lbs. **Length:** 42" overall. **Stock:** Black or Mossy Oak® Break-Up™ camo synthetic. **Sights:** Illuminator Fiber Optic Sight System; drilled and tapped for scope mounting. **Features:** In-line action uses modern trigger with automatic safety; stainless percussion bolt; swivel studs. Three-way ignition system (No. 11, musket or No. 209 shotgun primers). From CVA.
Price: Blue, black stock $159.95
Price: Blue, Break-Up™ camo stock $189.95

CVA Stag Horn 209 Magnum Rifle

Similar to the Eclipse except has light-gathering Solar Sights, manual safety, black synthetic stock and ramrod. Weighs 6 lbs. From CVA.
Price: 50 cal. $129.95

CVA MOUNTAIN RIFLE

Caliber: 50. **Barrel:** 32"; 1:66" rifling. **Weight:** 8-1/2 lbs. **Length:** NA. **Stock:** American hard maple. **Sights:** Blade front, buckhorn rear. **Features:** Browned steel furniture; German silver wedge plates; patchbox. Made in U.S. From CVA.
Price: $399.95

CVA ST. LOUIS HAWKEN RIFLE

Caliber: 50, 54. **Barrel:** 28", octagon; 15/16" across flats; 1:48" twist. **Weight:** 8 lbs. **Length:** 44" overall. **Stock:** Select hardwood. **Sights:** Beaded blade front, fully adjustable open rear. **Features:** Fully adjustable double-set triggers; synthetic ramrod (kits have wood); brass patchbox, wedge plates, nosecap, thimbles, trigger guard and buttplate; blued barrel; color case-hardened, engraved lockplate. V-type mainspring. Button breech. Introduced 1981. From CVA.
Price: St. Louis Hawken, finished (50- , 54-cal.) $229.95
Price: Left-hand, percussion. $274.95
Price: Flintlock, 50-cal. only $274.95
Price: Percussion kit (50-cal., blued, wood ramrod) $191.95

CVA HunterBolt 209 Magnum Rifle

Similar to the Firebolt except has 24" barrel and black or Mossy Oak® Break-Up™ synthetic stock. Three-way ignition system. Weighs 6 lbs. From CVA.
Price: 45 or 50 cal. . . . . $199.95 to $254.95

CVA FIREBOLT MUSKETMAG BOLT-ACTION IN-LINE RIFLES

Caliber: 45 or 50. **Barrel:** 26". **Weight:** 7 lbs. **Length:** 44". **Stock:** Rubber-coated black or Mossy Oak® Break-Up™ camo synthetic. **Sights:** CVA Illuminator Fiber Optic Sight System. **Features:** Bolt-action, in-line ignition system handles up to 150 grains blackpowder or Pyrodex; Nickel or matte blue barrel; removable breech plug; trigger-block safety. Introduced 1997. Three-way ignition system. From CVA.
Price: Nickel finish, black stock, 50 cal. $279.95
Price: Nickel finish, black stock, 45 cal. $289.95

BLACKPOWDER MUSKETS & RIFLES

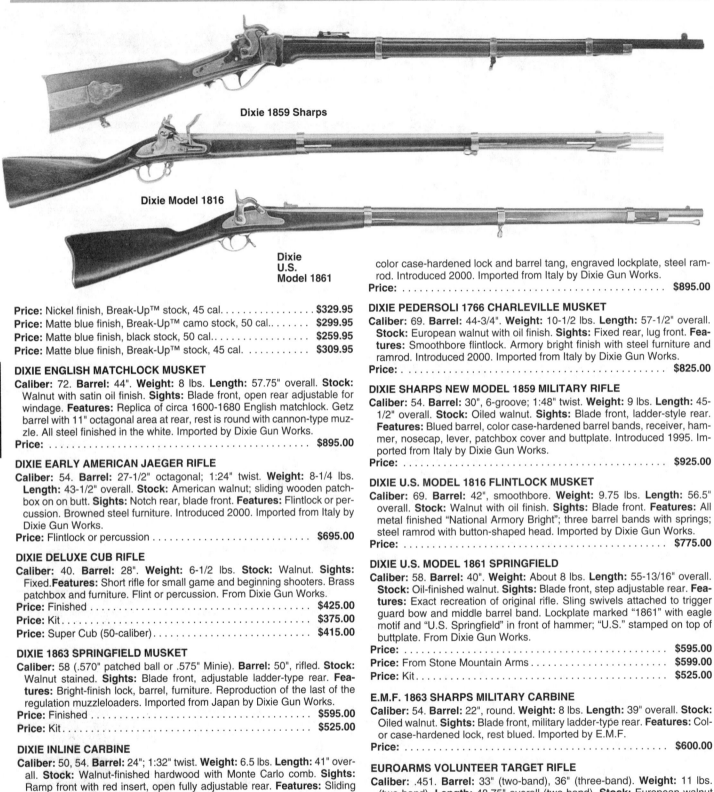

Dixie 1859 Sharps

Dixie Model 1816

Dixie U.S. Model 1861

Price: Nickel finish, Break-Up™ stock, 45 cal. $329.95
Price: Matte blue finish, Break-Up™ camo stock, 50 cal. $299.95
Price: Matte blue finish, black stock, 50 cal. $259.95
Price: Matte blue finish, Break-Up™ stock, 45 cal. $309.95

DIXIE ENGLISH MATCHLOCK MUSKET
Caliber: 72. **Barrel:** 44". **Weight:** 8 lbs. **Length:** 57.75" overall. **Stock:** Walnut with satin oil finish. **Sights:** Blade front, open rear adjustable for windage. **Features:** Replica of circa 1600-1680 English matchlock. Getz barrel with 11" octagonal area at rear, rest is round with cannon-type muzzle. All steel finished in the white. Imported by Dixie Gun Works.
Price: $895.00

DIXIE EARLY AMERICAN JAEGER RIFLE
Caliber: 54. **Barrel:** 27-1/2" octagonal; 1:24" twist. **Weight:** 8-1/4 lbs. **Length:** 43-1/2" overall. **Stock:** American walnut; sliding wooden patchbox on on butt. **Sights:** Notch rear, blade front. **Features:** Flintlock or percussion. Browned steel furniture. Introduced 2000. Imported from Italy by Dixie Gun Works.
Price: Flintlock or percussion $695.00

DIXIE DELUXE CUB RIFLE
Caliber: 40. **Barrel:** 28". **Weight:** 6-1/2 lbs. **Stock:** Walnut. **Sights:** Fixed.**Features:** Short rifle for small game and beginning shooters. Brass patchbox and furniture. Flint or percussion. From Dixie Gun Works.
Price: Finished $425.00
Price: Kit $375.00
Price: Super Cub (50-caliber) $415.00

DIXIE 1863 SPRINGFIELD MUSKET
Caliber: 58 (.570" patched ball or .575" Minie). **Barrel:** 50", rifled. **Stock:** Walnut stained. **Sights:** Blade front, adjustable ladder-type rear. **Features:** Bright-finish lock, barrel, furniture. Reproduction of the last of the regulation muzzleloaders. Imported from Japan by Dixie Gun Works.
Price: Finished $595.00
Price: Kit $525.00

DIXIE INLINE CARBINE
Caliber: 50, 54. **Barrel:** 24"; 1:32" twist. **Weight:** 6.5 lbs. **Length:** 41" overall. **Stock:** Walnut-finished hardwood with Monte Carlo comb. **Sights:** Ramp front with red insert, open fully adjustable rear. **Features:** Sliding "bolt" fully encloses cap and nipple. Fully adjustable trigger, automatic safety. Aluminum ramrod. Imported from Italy by Dixie Gun Works.
Price: $349.95

DIXIE PEDERSOLI 1857 MAUSER RIFLE
Caliber: 54. **Barrel:** 39-3/8". **Weight:** N/A. **Length:** 52" overall. **Stock:** European walnut with oil finish, sling swivels. **Sights:** Fully adjustable rear, lug front. **Features:** Percussion (musket caps). Armory bright finish with color case-hardened lock and barrel tang, engraved lockplate, steel ramrod. Introduced 2000. Imported from Italy by Dixie Gun Works.
Price: $895.00

DIXIE PEDERSOLI 1766 CHARLEVILLE MUSKET
Caliber: 69. **Barrel:** 44-3/4". **Weight:** 10-1/2 lbs. **Length:** 57-1/2" overall. **Stock:** European walnut with oil finish. **Sights:** Fixed rear, lug front. **Features:** Smoothbore flintlock. Armory bright finish with steel furniture and ramrod. Introduced 2000. Imported from Italy by Dixie Gun Works.
Price: $825.00

DIXIE SHARPS NEW MODEL 1859 MILITARY RIFLE
Caliber: 54. **Barrel:** 30", 6-groove; 1:48" twist. **Weight:** 9 lbs. **Length:** 45-1/2" overall. **Stock:** Oiled walnut. **Sights:** Blade front, ladder-style rear. **Features:** Blued barrel, color case-hardened barrel bands, receiver, hammer, nosecap, lever, patchbox cover and buttplate. Introduced 1995. Imported from Italy by Dixie Gun Works.
Price: $925.00

DIXIE U.S. MODEL 1816 FLINTLOCK MUSKET
Caliber: 69. **Barrel:** 42", smoothbore. **Weight:** 9.75 lbs. **Length:** 56.5" overall. **Stock:** Walnut with oil finish. **Sights:** Blade front. **Features:** All metal finished "National Armory Bright"; three barrel bands with springs; steel ramrod with button-shaped head. Imported by Dixie Gun Works.
Price: $775.00

DIXIE U.S. MODEL 1861 SPRINGFIELD
Caliber: 58. **Barrel:** 40". **Weight:** About 8 lbs. **Length:** 55-13/16" overall. **Stock:** Oil-finished walnut. **Sights:** Blade front, step adjustable rear. **Features:** Exact recreation of original rifle. Sling swivels attached to trigger guard bow and middle barrel band. Lockplate marked "1861" with eagle motif and "U.S. Springfield" in front of hammer; "U.S." stamped on top of buttplate. From Dixie Gun Works.
Price: $595.00
Price: From Stone Mountain Arms $599.00
Price: Kit $525.00

E.M.F. 1863 SHARPS MILITARY CARBINE
Caliber: 54. **Barrel:** 22", round. **Weight:** 8 lbs. **Length:** 39" overall. **Stock:** Oiled walnut. **Sights:** Blade front, military ladder-type rear. **Features:** Color case-hardened lock, rest blued. Imported by E.M.F.
Price: $600.00

EUROARMS VOLUNTEER TARGET RIFLE
Caliber: .451. **Barrel:** 33" (two-band), 36" (three-band). **Weight:** 11 lbs. (two-band). **Length:** 48.75" overall (two-band). **Stock:** European walnut with checkered wrist and forend. **Sights:** Hooded bead front, adjustable rear with interchangeable leaves. **Features:** Alexander Henry-type rifling with 1:20" twist. Color case-hardened hammer and lockplate, brass trigger guard and nosecap, rest blued. Imported by Euroarms of America, Dixie Gun Works.
Price: Two-band . . . . $720.00 to $750.00
Price: Three-band . . . . $773.00 to $795.00

BLACKPOWDER

BLACKPOWDER MUSKETS & RIFLES

Euroarms Volunteer

Euroarms 1861

Gonic Model 93 Thumbhole

Harper's Ferry 1803

J.P. Murray

EUROARMS 1861 SPRINGFIELD RIFLE
Caliber: 58. **Barrel:** 40". **Weight:** About 10 lbs. **Length:** 55.5" overall. **Stock:** European walnut. **Sights:** Blade front, three-leaf military rear. **Features:** Reproduction of the original three-band rifle. Lockplate marked "1861" with eagle and "U.S. Springfield." Metal left in the white. Imported by Euroarms of America.
Price: **$530.00**

GONIC MODEL 93 M/L RIFLE
Caliber: 45, 50. **Barrel:** 26"; 1:24" twist. **Weight:** 6-1/2 to 7 lbs. **Length:** 43" overall. **Stock:** American hardwood with black finish. **Sights:** Adjustable or aperture rear, hooded post front. **Features:** Adjustable trigger with side safety; unbreakable ram rod; comes with A. Z. scope bases installed. Introduced 1993. Made in U.S. by Gonic Arms, Inc.
Price: Model 93 Standard (blued barrel). **$720.00**
Price: Model 93 Standard (stainless brl., 50 cal. only) **$782.00**

Gonic Model 93 Deluxe M/L Rifle
Similar to the Model 93 except has classic-style walnut or gray laminated wood stock. Introduced 1998. Made in U.S. by Gonic Arms, Inc.
Price: Blue barrel, sights, scope base, choice of stock **$902.00**
Price: Stainless barrel, sights, scope base, choice of stock
(50 cal. only). **$964.00**

Gonic Model 93 Mountain Thumbhole M/L Rifles
Similar to the Model 93 except has high-grade walnut or gray laminate stock with extensive hand-checkered panels, Monte Carlo cheekpiece and beavertail forend; integral muzzle brake. Introduced 1998. Made in U.S. by Gonic Arms, Inc.
Price: Blue or stainless. **$2,700.00**

HARPER'S FERRY 1803 FLINTLOCK RIFLE
Caliber: 54 or 58. **Barrel:** 35". **Weight:** 9 lbs. **Length:** 59-1/2" overall. **Stock:** Walnut with cheekpiece. **Sights:** Brass blade front, fixed steel rear. **Features:** Brass trigger guard, sideplate, buttplate; steel patchbox. Imported by Euroarms of America, Navy Arms (54-cal. only), Cabela's, and Dixie Gun Works.
Price: . . . . **$495.95 to $729.00**
Price: 54-cal. (Navy Arms) **$625.00**
Price: 54-caliber (Cabela's) **$599.99**
Price: 54-caliber (Dixie Gun Works) **$645.00**

HAWKEN RIFLE
Caliber: 45, 50, 54 or 58. **Barrel:** 28", blued, 6-groove rifling. **Weight:** 8-3/4 lbs. **Length:** 44" overall. **Stock:** Walnut with cheekpiece. **Sights:** Blade front, fully adjustable rear. **Features:** Coil mainspring, double-set triggers, polished brass furniture. From Armsport and E.M.F.
Price: . . . . **$220.00 to $345.00**

J.P. MURRAY 1862-1864 CAVALRY CARBINE
Caliber: 58 (.577" Minie). **Barrel:** 23". **Weight:** 7 lbs., 9 oz. **Length:** 39" overall. **Stock:** Walnut. **Sights:** Blade front, rear drift adjustable for windage. **Features:** Browned barrel, color case-hardened lock, blued swivel and band springs, polished brass buttplate, trigger guard, barrel bands. From Euroarms of America.
Price: . . . . **$405.00 to $453.00**

J.P. HENRY TRADE RIFLE
Caliber: 54. **Barrel:** 34"; 1" flats. **Weight:** 8-1/2 lbs. **Length:** 45" overall. **Stock:** Premium curly maple. **Sights:** Silver blade front, fixed buckhorn rear. **Features:** Brass buttplate, side plate, trigger guard and nosecap; browned barrel and lock; L&R Large English percussion lock; single trigger. Made in U.S. by J.P. Gunstocks, Inc.
Price: **$965.50**

BLACKPOWDER

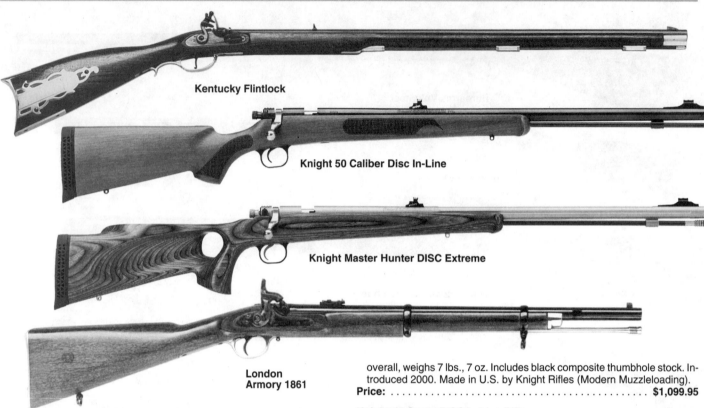

Kentucky Flintlock

Knight 50 Caliber Disc In-Line

Knight Master Hunter DISC Extreme

London Armory 1861

KENTUCKIAN RIFLE

Caliber: 44. **Barrel:** 35". **Weight:** 7 lbs. (Rifle), 5-1/2 lbs. (Carbine). **Length:** 51" overall (Rifle), 43" (Carbine). **Stock:** Walnut stain. **Sights:** Brass blade front, steel V-ramp rear. **Features:** Octagon barrel, case-hardened and engraved lockplates. Brass furniture. Imported by Dixie Gun Works.

Price: Flintlock **$269.95**
Price: Percussion **$259.95**

KENTUCKY FLINTLOCK RIFLE

Caliber: 44, 45, or 50. **Barrel:** 35". **Weight:** 7 lbs. **Length:** 50" overall. **Stock:** Walnut stained, brass fittings. **Sights:** Fixed. **Features:** Available in carbine model also, 28" bbl. Some variations in detail, finish. Kits also available from some importers. Imported by The Armoury.

Price: About .... **$217.95 to $345.00**

Kentucky Percussion Rifle

Similar to flintlock except percussion lock. Finish and features vary with importer. Imported by The Armoury and CVA.

Price: About **$259.95**
Price: 45- or 50-cal. (Navy Arms) **$425.00**
Price: Kit, 50-cal. (CVA) **$189.95**

KNIGHT 50 CALIBER DISC IN-LINE RIFLE

Caliber: 50. **Barrel:** 24", 26". **Weight:** 7 lbs., 14 oz. **Length:** 43" overall (24" barrel). **Stock:** Checkered synthetic with palm swell grip, rubber recoil pad, swivel studs; black, Advantage or Mossy Oak Break-Up camouflage. **Sights:** Bead on ramp front, fully adjustable open rear. **Features:** Bolt-action in-line system uses #209 shotshell primer for ignition; primer is held in plastic drop-in Primer Disc. Available in blued or stainless steel. Made in U.S. by Knight Rifles (Modern Muzzleloading).

Price: .... **$459.95 to $615.95**

Knight Master Hunter II DISC In-Line Rifle

Similar to Knight 50 caliber DISC rifle except features premier, wood laminated two-tone stock, gold-plated trigger and engraved trigger guard, jeweled bolt and fluted, air-gauged Green Mountain 26" barrel. Length 45"

overall, weighs 7 lbs., 7 oz. Includes black composite thumbhole stock. Introduced 2000. Made in U.S. by Knight Rifles (Modern Muzzleloading).

Price: **$1,099.95**

Knight 45 Super DISC In-Line Rifle

Similar to 50 caliber DISC rifle except in 45 caliber to fire saboted bullets and up to 150 grains of blackpowder or equivalent at up to 2,600 fps. Fluted 26" Green Mountain barrel in blue or stainless finish; thumbhole or standard synthetic stock in black, Advantage Timber HD or Mossy Oak Break-Up camouflage. Weighs 8 lbs., 3 oz. Made in U.S. by Knight Rifles (Modern Muzzleloading).

Price: .... **NA**

KNIGHT MUZZLELOADER DISC EXTREME

Caliber: 45 fluted, 50. **Barrel:** 26". **Stock:** Stainless steel laminate, blued walnut, black composite thumbhole with blued or SS. **Sights:** Fully adjustable metallic. **Features:** New full plastic jacket ignition system.

Price: 50 SS laminate **$639.95**
Price: 45 SS laminate **$699.95**
Price: 50 blue walnut **$569.95**
Price: 45 blue walnut **$639.95**

Knight Master Hunter DISC Extreme

Similar to DISC Extreme except fluted barrel, two-tone laminated thumbhole Monte Carlo-style stock, black composite thumbhole field stock included. Jeweled bolt, adjustable premium trigger.

Price: 50 .... **$949.95**
Price: 45 .... **$999.95**

KNIGHT AMERICAN KNIGHT M/L RIFLE

Caliber: 50. **Barrel:** 22"; 1:28" twist. **Weight:** 6 lbs. **Length:** 41" overall. **Stock:** Black composite. **Sights:** Bead on ramp front, open fully adjustable rear. **Features:** Double safety system; one-piece removable hammer assembly; drilled and tapped for scope mounting. Introduced 1998. Made in U.S. by Knight Rifles.

Price: **$199.95**

KNIGHT WOLVERINE 209

Caliber: 50. **Barrel:** 22". **Stock:** HD stock with SS barrel, break-up stock blued, black composite thumbhole with stainless steel, standard black composite with blued or SS. **Sights:** Metallic with fiber optic. **Features:** Double safety system, adjustable match grade trigger, left-hand model available. Full plastic jacket ignition system.

Price: Starting at **$274.95**

BLACKPOWDER

Lyman Trade

Lyman Deerstalker

Lyman Great Plains

Price: 50- or 54-cal., percussion **$304.95**
Price: 50- or 54-cal., flintlock **$349.95**
Price: 50- or 54-cal., percussion, left-hand **$329.95**
Price: 50-cal., new 54 cal., flintlock, left-hand **$359.95**
Price: Stainless steel **$394.95**

LONDON ARMORY 2-BAND 1858 ENFIELD
Caliber: .577" Minie, .575" round ball. **Barrel:** 33". **Weight:** 10 lbs. **Length:** 49" overall. **Stock:** Walnut. **Sights:** Folding leaf rear adjustable for elevation. **Features:** Blued barrel, color case-hardened lock and hammer, polished brass buttplate, trigger guard, nosecap. From Navy Arms, Euroarms of America, Dixie Gun Works.
Price: . . . . **$385.00 to $600.00**

LONDON ARMORY 1861 ENFIELD MUSKETOON
Caliber: 58, Minie ball. **Barrel:** 24", round. **Weight:** 7 - 7-1/2 lbs. **Length:** 40-1/2" overall. **Stock:** Walnut, with sling swivels. **Sights:** Blade front, graduated military-leaf rear. **Features:** Brass trigger guard, nosecap, buttplate; blued barrel, bands, lockplate, swivels. Imported by Euroarms of America, Navy Arms.
Price: . . . . **$300.00 to $515.00**
Price: Kit . . . . **$365.00 to $373.00**

LONDON ARMORY 3-BAND 1853 ENFIELD
Caliber: 58 (.577" Minie, .575" round ball, .580" maxi ball). **Barrel:** 39". **Weight:** 9-1/2 lbs. **Length:** 54" overall. **Stock:** European walnut. **Sights:** Inverted "V" front, traditional Enfield folding ladder rear. **Features:** Recreation of the famed London Armory Company Pattern 1853 Enfield Musket. One-piece walnut stock, brass buttplate, trigger guard and nosecap. Lockplate marked "London Armoury Co." and with a British crown. Blued Baddeley barrel bands. From Dixie Gun Works, Euroarms of America, Navy Arms.
Price: About . . . . **$350.00 to $645.00**
Price: Assembled kit (Dixie, Euroarms of America) . . **$425.00 to $431.00**

LYMAN TRADE RIFLE
Caliber: 50, 54. **Barrel:** 28" octagon;1:48" twist. **Weight:** 8-3/4 lbs. **Length:** 45" overall. **Stock:** European walnut. **Sights:** Blade front, open rear adjustable for windage or optional fixed sights. **Features:** Fast twist rifling for conical bullets. Polished brass furniture with blue steel parts, stainless steel nipple. Hook breech, single trigger, coil spring percussion lock. Steel barrel rib and ramrod ferrules. Introduced 1980. From Lyman.
Price: Percussion **$314.95**
Price: Flintlock **$339.95**

LYMAN DEERSTALKER RIFLE
Caliber: 50, 54. **Barrel:** 24", octagonal; 1:48" rifling. **Weight:** 7-1/2 lbs. **Stock:** Walnut with black rubber buttpad. **Sights:** Lyman #37MA beaded front, fully adjustable fold-down Lyman #16A rear. **Features:** Stock has less drop for quick sighting. All metal parts are blackened, with color case-hardened lock; single trigger. Comes with sling and swivels. Available in flint or percussion. Introduced 1990. From Lyman.

LYMAN GREAT PLAINS RIFLE
Caliber: 50- or 54-cal. **Barrel:** 32"; 1:60" twist. **Weight:** 9 lbs. **Stock:** Walnut. **Sights:** Steel blade front, buckhorn rear adjustable for windage and elevation and fixed notch primitive sight included. **Features:** Blued steel furniture. Stainless steel nipple. Coil spring lock, Hawken-style trigger guard and double-set triggers. Round thimbles recessed and sweated into rib. Steel wedge plates and toe plate. Introduced 1979. From Lyman.
Price: Percussion **$469.95**
Price: Flintlock **$494.95**
Price: Percussion kit **$359.95**
Price: Flintlock kit **$384.95**
Price: Left-hand percussion **$474.95**
Price: Left-hand flintlock **$499.95**

Lyman Great Plains Hunter Rifle
Similar to Great Plains model except 1:32" twist shallow-groove barrel and comes drilled and tapped for Lyman 57GPR peep sight.
Price: . . . . **$469.95 to $494.95**

MARKESBERY KM BLACK BEAR M/L RIFLE
Caliber: 36, 45, 50, 54. **Barrel:** 24"; 1:26" twist. **Weight:** 6-1/2 lbs. **Length:** 38-1/2" overall. **Stock:** Two-piece American hardwood, walnut, black laminate, green laminate, black composition, X-Tra or Mossy Oak Break-Up camouflage. **Sights:** Bead front, open fully adjustable rear. **Features:** Interchangeable barrels; exposed hammer; Outer-Line Magnum ignition system uses small rifle primer or standard No. 11 cap and nipple. Blue, black matte, or stainless. Made in U.S. by Markesbery Muzzle Loaders.
Price: American hardwood walnut, blue finish **$437.63**
Price: American hardwood walnut, stainless **$447.09**
Price: Black laminate, blue finish **$460.67**
Price: Camouflage stock, blue finish **$556.46**
Price: Black composite, blue finish **$532.65**

MARKESBERY KM COLORADO ROCKY MOUNTAIN M/L RIFLE
Caliber: 36, 45, 50, 54. **Barrel:** 24"; 1:26" twist. **Weight:** 6-1/2 lbs. **Length:** 38-1/2" overall. **Stock:** American hardwood walnut, green or black laminate. **Sights:** Firesight bead on ramp front, fully adjustable open rear. **Features:** Replicates Reed/Watson rifle of 1851. Straight grip stock with or without two barrel bands, rubber recoil pad, large-spur hammer. Made in U.S. by Markesbery Muzzle Loaders, Inc.
Price: American hardwood walnut, blue finish **$447.00**
Price: Black or green laminate, blue finish **$447.00**
Price: American hardwood walnut, stainless **$457.00**
Price: Black or green laminate, stainless **$457.34**

Markesbery KM Colorado

Mississippi 1841

Navy Arms 1763

Markesbery KM Brown Bear M/L Rifle

Similar to KM Black Bear except one-piece thumbhole stock with Monte Carlo comb. Stock in Crotch Walnut composite, green or black laminate, black composite or X-Tra or Mossy Oak Break-Up camouflage. Contact maker for complete price listing. Made in U.S. by Markesbery Muzzle Loaders, Inc.

Price: Black composite, blue finish........................ **$515.00**
Price: Crotch Walnut composite, stainless.................. **$525.00**
Price: Green laminate, stainless........................ **$552.00**

Markesbery KM Grizzly Bear M/L Rifle

Similar to KM Black Bear except thumbhole buttstock with Monte Carlo comb. Stock in Crotch Walnut composite, green or black laminate, black composite or X-Tra or Mossy Oak Break-Up camouflage. Contact maker for complete price listing. Made in U.S. by Markesbery Muzzle Loaders, Inc.

Price: Black composite, blue finish........................ **$575.00**
Price: Crotch Walnut composite, stainless.................. **$515.00**
Price: Camouflage composite, blue finish **$557.00**

Markesbery KM Polar Bear M/L Rifle

Similar to KM Black Bear except one-piece stock with Monte Carlo comb. Stock in American Hardwood walnut, green or black laminate, black composite, or X-Tra or Mossy Oak Break-Up camouflage. Interchangeable barrel system, Outer-Line ignition system, cross-bolt double safety. Available in 36, 45, 50, 54 caliber. Contact maker for full price listing. Made in U.S. by Markesbery Muzzle Loaders, Inc.

Price: American Hardwood walnut , blue finish **$447.00**
Price: Black composite, blue finish........................ **$536.63**
Price: Black laminate, blue finish **$447.00**
Price: Camouflage, stainless **$480.00**

MDM BUCKWACKA IN-LINE RIFLES

Caliber: 45, 50. **Barrel:** 23", 25". **Weight:** 7 to 7-3/4 lbs. **Stock:** Black, walnut, laminated and camouflage finishes. **Sights:** Williams Fire Sight blade front, Williams fully adjustable rear with ghost-ring peep aperture. **Features:** Break-open action; Incinerating Ignition System incorporates 209 shotshell primer directly into breech plug; 50-caliber models handle up to 150 grains of Pyrodex; synthetic ramrod; transfer bar safety; stainless or blued finish. Made in U.S. by Millennium Designed Muzzleloaders Ltd.

Price: 50 cal., blued finish............................. **$309.95**
Price: 50 cal., stainless............................... **$339.95**
Price: Camouflage stock........................ **$359.95 to $389.95**

MDM M2K In-Line Rifle

Similar to Buckwacka except adjustable trigger and double-safety mechanism designed to prevent misfires. Made in U.S. by Millennium Designed Muzzleloaders Ltd.

Price: .... **$529.00 to $549.00**

Mississippi 1841 Percussion Rifle

Similar to Zouave rifle but patterned after U.S. Model 1841. Imported by Dixie Gun Works, Euroarms of America, Navy Arms.

Price: About .... **$430.00 to $495.00**

NAVY ARMS 1763 CHARLEVILLE

Caliber: 69. **Barrel:** 44-5/8". **Weight:** 8 lbs., 12 oz. **Length:** 59-3/8" overall. **Stock:** Walnut. **Sights:** Brass blade front. **Features:** Replica of French musket used by American troops during the Revolution. Imported by Navy Arms.

Price: **$1,020.00**

NAVY ARMS PARKER-HALE VOLUNTEER RIFLE

Caliber: .451. **Barrel:** 32". **Weight:** 9-1/2 lbs. **Length:** 49" overall. **Stock:** Walnut, checkered wrist and forend. **Sights:** Globe front, adjustable ladder-type rear. **Features:** Recreation of the type of gun issued to volunteer regiments during the 1860s. Rigby-pattern rifling, patent breech, detented lock. Stock is glass bedded for accuracy. Imported by Navy Arms.

Price: **$905.00**

NAVY ARMS 1859 SHARPS CAVALRY CARBINE

Caliber: 54. **Barrel:** 22". **Weight:** 7-3/4 lbs. **Length:** 39" overall. **Stock:** Walnut. **Sights:** Blade front, military ladder-type rear. **Features:** Color case-hardened action, blued barrel. Has saddle ring. Introduced 1991. Imported from Navy Arms.

Price: **$1,000.00**

NAVY ARMS BERDAN 1859 SHARPS RIFLE

Caliber: 54. **Barrel:** 30". **Weight:** 8 lbs., 8 oz. **Length:** 46-3/4" overall. **Stock:** Walnut. **Sights:** Blade front, folding military ladder-type rear. **Features:** Replica of the Union sniper rifle used by Berdan's 1st and 2nd Sharpshooter regiments. Color case-hardened receiver, patchbox, furniture. Double-set triggers. Imported by Navy Arms.

Price: **$1,165.00**
Price: 1859 Sharps Infantry Rifle (three-band)............. **$1,100.00**

NAVY ARMS PARKER-HALE WHITWORTH MILITARY TARGET RIFLE

Caliber: 45. **Barrel:** 36". **Weight:** 9-1/4 lbs. **Length:** 52-1/2" overall. **Stock:** Walnut. Checkered at wrist and forend. **Sights:** Hooded post front, open step-adjustable rear. **Features:** Faithful reproduction of Whitworth rifle, only bored for 45-cal. Trigger has detented lock, capable of being adjusted very finely without risk of the sear nose catching on the half-cock bent and damaging both parts. Introduced 1978. Imported by Navy Arms.

Price: **$930.00**

BLACKPOWDER MUSKETS & RIFLES

Navy Arms 1859 Sharps

Navy Arms Berdan

Navy Arms Whitworth

Navy Arms Smith Carbine

NAVY ARMS SMITH CARBINE
Caliber: 50. **Barrel:** 21-1/2". **Weight:** 7-3/4 lbs. **Length:** 39" overall. **Stock:** American walnut. **Sights:** Brass blade front, folding ladder-type rear. **Features:** Replica of breech-loading Civil War carbine. Color case-hardened receiver, rest blued. Cavalry model has saddle ring and bar, Artillery model has sling swivels. Imported by Navy Arms.
Price: Cavalry model $645.00
Price: Artillery model. $645.00

NAVY ARMS 1863 C.S. RICHMOND RIFLE
Caliber: 58. **Barrel:** 40". **Weight:** 10 lbs. **Length:** NA. **Stocks:** Walnut. **Sights:** Blade front, adjustable rear. **Features:** Copy of three-band rifle musket made at Richmond Armory for the Confederacy. All steel polished bright. Imported by Navy Arms.
Price: $590.00

NAVY ARMS 1861 SPRINGFIELD RIFLE
Caliber: 58. **Barrel:** 40" **Weight:** 10 lbs., 4 oz. **Length:** 56" overall. **Stock:** Walnut. **Sights:** Blade front, military leaf rear. **Features:** Steel barrel, lock and all furniture have polished bright finish. Has 1855-style hammer. Imported by Navy Arms.
Price: $590.00

NAVY ARMS 1863 SPRINGFIELD
Caliber: 58, uses .575 Minie. **Barrel:** 40", rifled. **Weight:** 9-1/2 lbs. **Length:** 56" overall. **Stock:** Walnut. **Sights:** Open rear adjustable for elevation. **Features:** Full-size, three-band musket. Polished bright metal, including lock. From Navy Arms.
Price: Finished rifle. $590.00

NAVY ARMS 1873 SHARPS "QUIGLEY"
Caliber: 45/70. **Barrel:** 34" heavy octagonal. **Stock:** Walnut. **Features:** Case-hardened receiver and military patchbox. Exact reproduction from *"Quigley Down Under."*
Price: $1,390.00

NAVY ARMS 1873 SHARPS NO. 2 CREEDMOOR RIFLE
Caliber: 45/70. **Barrel:** 30" tapered round. **Stock:** Walnut. **Sights:** Front globe, "soule" tang rear. **Features:** Nickel receiver and action. Lightweight sporting rifle.
Price: $1,300.00

OCTOBER COUNTRY GREAT AMERICAN SPORTING RIFLE
Caliber: 62, 66, 69, 72. **Barrel:** 28" or 36"; tapered octagon 1-1/4" to 1"; 1:104" twist. **Weight:** 9 lbs. (28" bbl.) **Length:** 48" overall. **Stock:** Walnut (optional maple with ebony nosecap). **Sights:** Silver blade front, adjustable shallow "V" rear (optional three-blade express or A.O. ghost ring). **Features:** Hooked, patent Manton-style breech plug, iron furniture, bedded barrel, blue finish. Made in U.S. by October Country Muzzleloading Inc.
Price: $1,695.00

OCTOBER COUNTRY LIGHT AMERICAN SPORTING RIFLE
Caliber: 62. **Barrel:** 28" or 36"; tapered octagon 1-1/8" to 1"; 1:104" twist. **Weight:** 8 lbs. **Length:** 48" overall. **Stock:** Walnut (optional maple with ebony nosecap). **Sights:** Blade front, adjustable shallow "V" rear (optional three-blade express or A.O. ghost ring). **Features:** English-style hooked breach with side bar; L&R lock; iron furniture; bedded barrel; hot blue finish. Made in U.S. by October Country Muzzleloading Inc.
Price: $1,595.00

OCTOBER COUNTRY HEAVY RIFLE
Caliber: 8 bore or 4 bore. **Barrel:** 30"; tapered octagon 1-1/2" to 1-1/4" (8 bore) or 1-3/4" to 1-1/2" (4 bore); 1:144" twist. **Weight:** 14 lbs. (8 bore) or 18 lbs. (4 bore). **Length:** 50" overall. **Stock:** Checkered English walnut. **Sights:** Blade front, three-blade express rear. **Features:** English-style hooked breech; L&R lock; iron furniture; bedded barrel; hot blue finish. Made in U.S. by October Country Muzzleloading Inc.
Price: $2,995.00

OCTOBER COUNTRY DOUBLE RIFLE
Caliber: 8 bore. **Barrel:** 30" round; 1:144" twist. **Weight:** 14 lbs. **Length:** 50". **Stock:** Checkered English walnut. **Sights:** Blade front, three-blade express rear. **Features:** English-style hooked breech; L& R lock; iron furniture; bedded barrel; hot blue finish. Made in U.S. by October Country Muzzleloaders Inc.
Price: $4,995.00

PACIFIC RIFLE MODEL 1837 ZEPHYR
Caliber: 62. **Barrel:** 30", tapered octagon. **Weight:** 7-3/4 lbs. **Length:** NA. **Stock:** Oil-finished fancy walnut. **Sights:** German silver blade front, semi-buckhorn rear. Options available. **Features:** Improved underhammer action. First production rifle to offer Forsyth rifle, with narrow lands and shallow rifling with 1:144" pitch for high-velocity round balls. Metal finish is slow rust brown with nitre blue accents. Optional sights, finishes and integral muzzle brake available. Introduced 1995. Made in U.S. by Pacific Rifle Co.
Price: From $995.00

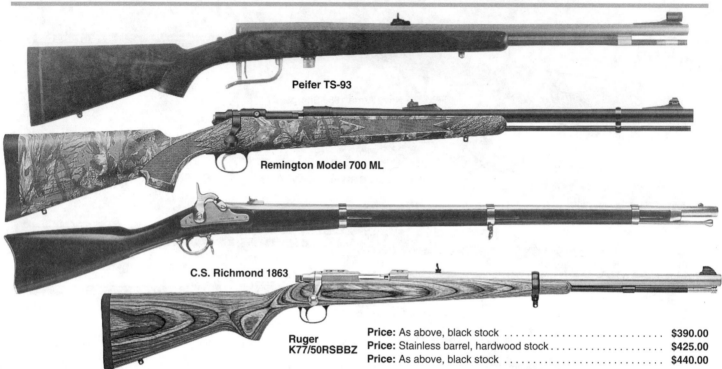

Peifer TS-93

Remington Model 700 ML

C.S. Richmond 1863

Ruger K77/50RSBBZ

Pacific Rifle Big Bore, African Rifles

Similar to the 1837 Zephyr except in 72-caliber and 8-bore. The 72-caliber is available in standard form with 28" barrel, or as the African with flat buttplate, checkered upgraded wood; weight is 9 lbs. The 8-bore African has dual-cap ignition, 24" barrel, weighs 12 lbs., checkered English walnut, engraving, gold inlays. Introduced 1998. Made in U.S. by Pacific Rifle Co.

Price: 72-caliber, from **$1,150.00**
Price: 8-bore from. **$2,500.00**

PEIFER MODEL TS-93 RIFLE

Caliber: 45, 50. **Barrel:** 24" Douglas premium; 1:20" twist in 45; 1:28" in 50. **Weight:** 7 lbs. **Length:** 43-1/4" overall. **Stock:** Bell & Carlson solid composite, with recoil pad, swivel studs. **Sights:** Williams bead front on ramp, fully adjustable open rear. Drilled and tapped for Weaver scope mounts with dovetail for rear peep. **Features:** In-line ignition uses #209 shotshell primer; extremely fast lock time; fully enclosed breech; adjustable trigger; automatic safety; removable primer holder. Blue or stainless. Made in U.S. by Peifer Rifle Co. Introduced 1996.

Price: Blue, black stock **$730.00**
Price: Blue, wood or camouflage composite stock, or stainless
with black composite stock. **$803.00**
Price: Stainless, wood or camouflage composite stock **$876.00**

PRAIRIE RIVER ARMS PRA CLASSIC RIFLE

Caliber: 50, 54. **Barrel:** 26"; 1:28" twist. **Weight:** 7-1/2 lbs. **Length:** 40-1/2" overall. **Stock:** Hardwood or black all-weather. **Sights:** Blade front, open adjustable rear. **Features:** Patented internal percussion ignition system. Drilled and tapped for scope mount. Introduced 1995. Made in U.S. by Prairie River Arms, Ltd.

Price: 4140 alloy barrel, hardwood stock **$375.00**
Price: As above, stainless barrel **$425.00**
Price: 4140 alloy barrel, black all-weather stock **$390.00**
Price: As above, stainless barrel **$440.00**

PRAIRIE RIVER ARMS PRA BULLPUP RIFLE

Caliber: 50, 54. **Barrel:** 28"; 1:28" twist. **Weight:** 7-1/2 lbs. **Length:** 31-1/2" overall. **Stock:** Hardwood or black all-weather. **Sights:** Blade front, open adjustable rear. **Features:** Bullpup design thumbhole stock. Patented internal percussion ignition system. Left-hand model available. Dovetailed for scope mount. Introduced 1995. Made in U.S. by Prairie River Arms, Ltd.

Price: 4140 alloy barrel, hardwood stock **$375.00**

Price: As above, black stock **$390.00**
Price: Stainless barrel, hardwood stock **$425.00**
Price: As above, black stock **$440.00**

REMINGTON MODEL 700 ML, MLS RIFLES

Caliber: 50, new 45 (MLS Magnum).**Barrel:** 24"; 1:28" twist. **Weight:** 7-3/4 lbs. **Length:** 42"-44-1/2" overall. **Stock:** Black fiberglass-reinforced synthetic with checkered grip and forend; magnum-style buttpad. **Sights:** Ramped bead front, open fully adjustable rear. Drilled and tapped for scope mounts. **Features:** Uses the Remington 700 bolt action, stock design, safety and trigger mechanisms; removable stainless steel breech plug, No. 11 nipple; solid aluminum ramrod. Comes with cleaning tools and accessories.

Price: ML, blued, 50-caliber only **$415.00**
Price: MLS, stainless, 45 Magnum, 50-caliber. **$533.00**
Price: MLS, stainless, Mossy Oak Break-Up camo stock **$569.00**

C.S. RICHMOND 1863 MUSKET

Caliber: 58. **Barrel:** 40". **Weight:** 11 lbs. **Length:** 56-1/4" overall. **Stock:** European walnut with oil finish. **Sights:** Blade front, adjustable folding leaf rear. **Features:** Reproduction of the three-band Civil War musket. Sling swivels attached to trigger guard and middle barrel band. Lockplate marked "1863" and "C.S. Richmond." All metal left in white. Brass buttplate and forend cap. Imported by Euroarms of America, Navy Arms, and Dixie Gun Works.

Price: Euroarms **$530.00**
Price: Dixie Gun Works **$525.00**

RUGER 77/50 IN-LINE PERCUSSION RIFLE

Caliber: 50. **Barrel:** 22"; 1:28" twist. **Weight:** 6-1/2 lbs. **Length:** 41-1/2" overall. **Stock:** Birch with rubber buttpad and swivel studs. **Sights:** Gold bead front, folding leaf rear. Comes with Ruger scope mounts. **Features:** Shares design features with Ruger 77/22 rifle. Stainless steel bolt and nipple/breech plug; uses #11 caps, three-position safety, blued steel ramrod. Introduced 1997. Made in U.S. by Sturm, Ruger & Co.

Price: 77/50RS **$434.00**
Price: 77/50RSO Officer's (straight-grip checkered walnut stock,
blued) **$555.00**
Price: K77/50RSBBZ (stainless steel, black laminated stock) **$601.00**
Price: K77/50RSP All-Weather (stainless steel, synthetic stock) . . **$580.00**

SAVAGE MODEL 10ML MUZZLELOADER RIFLE SERIES

Caliber: 50. **Barrel:** 24", 1:24 twist, blue or stainless. **Weight:** 7.75 lbs. **Stock:** Black synthetic, Realtree Hardwood JD Camo, brown laminate. **Sights:** Green adjustable rear, Red FiberOptic front. **Features:** XP Models scoped, no sights, smokeless powder, "easy to prime", #209 primer ignition. Removeable breech plut and vent liner.

BLACKPOWDER MUSKETS & RIFLES

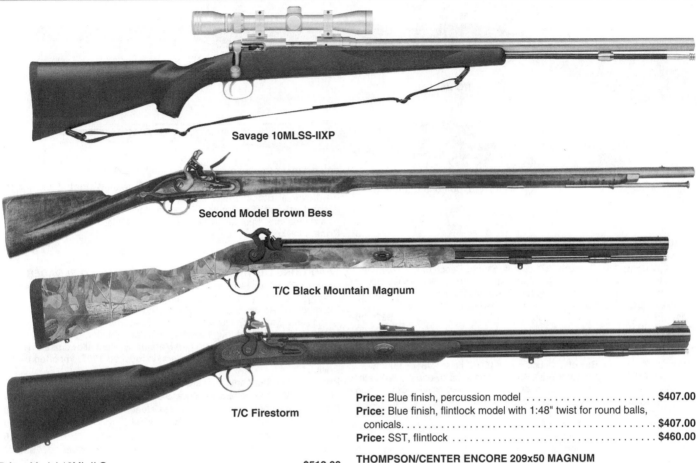

Savage 10MLSS-IIXP

Second Model Brown Bess

T/C Black Mountain Magnum

T/C Firestorm

Price: Model 10ML-II Camo **$512.00**
Price: Model 10MLSS-II Camo **$567.00**
Price: Model 10MLBSS-II **$602.00**
Price: Model 10ML-IIXP **$512.00**
Price: Model 10MLSS-IIXP **$567.00**

SECOND MODEL BROWN BESS MUSKET

Caliber: 75, uses .735" round ball. **Barrel:** 42", smoothbore. **Weight:** 9-1/2 lbs. **Length:** 59" overall. **Stock:** Walnut (Navy); walnut-stained hardwood (Dixie). **Sights:** Fixed. **Features:** Polished barrel and lock with brass trigger guard and buttplate. Bayonet and scabbard available. From Navy Arms, Dixie Gun Works, Cabela's.
Price: Finished . . . . **$475.00 to $850.00**
Price: Kit (Dixie Gun Works, Navy Arms) . . . . **$575.00 to $625.00**
Price: Carbine (Navy Arms) **$835.00**
Price: Dixie Gun Works **$725.00**

THOMPSON/CENTER BLACK MOUNTAIN MAGNUM RIFLE

Caliber: 50, 54. **Barrel:** 26"; 1:28" twist. **Weight:** 7 lbs. **Length:** 4-3/4" overall. **Stock:** American Walnut or black composite. **Sights:** Ramp front with Tru-Glo fiber optic inseat, click adjustable open rear with Tru-Glo fiber optic inserts. **Features:** Side lock percussion with breeech designed for Pyrodex Pellets, loose blackpowder and Pyrodex. blued steel. Uses QLA muzzle system. Introduced 1999. Made in U.S. by Thompson/Center Arms.
Price: Blue, walnut stock, 50 . . . . **$427.00**

THOMPSON/CENTER FIRE STORM RIFLE

Caliber: 50. **Barrel:** 26"; 1:28" twist. **Weight:** 7 lbs. **Length:** 41-3/4" overall. **Stock:** Black synthetic with rubber recoil pad, swivel studs. **Sights:** Click-adjustable steel rear and ramp-style front, both with fiber optic inserts. **Features:** Side hammer lock is the first designed for up to three 50-grain Pyrodex pellets; patented Pyrodex Pyramid breech directs ignition fire 360 degrees around base of pellet; uses 209 shotgun primers; Quick Load Accurizor Muzzle System; aluminum ramrod. Introduced 2000. Made in U.S. by Thomson/Center Arms.

Price: Blue finish, percussion model **$407.00**
Price: Blue finish, flintlock model with 1:48" twist for round balls, conicals. **$407.00**
Price: SST, flintlock **$460.00**

THOMPSON/CENTER ENCORE 209x50 MAGNUM

Caliber: 50. **Barrel:** 26"; interchangeable with centerfire calibers. **Weight:** 7 lbs. **Length:** 40-1/2" overall. **Stock:** American walnut butt and forend, or black composite. **Sights:** Tru-Glo Fiber Optic front, Tru-Glo Fiber Optic rear. **Features:** Blue or stainless steel. Uses the stock, frame and forend of the Encore centerfire pistol; break-open design using trigger guard spur; stainless steel universal breech plug; uses #209 shotshell primers. Introduced 1998. Made in U.S. by Thompson/Center Arms.
Price: Stainless wtih camo stock **$724.00**
Price: Blue, walnut stock and forend **$497.00**
Price: Blue, composite stock and forend **$476.00**
Price: Stainless, composite stock and forend. **$537.00**

THOMPSON/CENTER BLACK DIAMOND RIFLE

Caliber: 50. **Barrel:** 22-1/2" with QLA; 1:28" twist. **Weight:** 6 lbs., 9 oz. **Length:** 41-1/2" overall. **Stock:** Black Rynite with moulded-in checkering and grip cap, or walnut. **Sights:** Tru-Glo Fiber Optic ramp-style front, Tru-Glo Fiber Optic open rear. **Features:** In-line ignition system for musket cap, No. 11 cap, or 209 shotshell primer; removable universal breech plug; stainless steel construction. Introduced 1998. Made in U.S. by Thompson/Center Arms.
Price: With composite stock, blued **$317.00**
Price: With walnut stock **$385.00**
Price: 50 cal. Omega . . . . **$405.60 to $516.99**
Price: Black Diamond XR . . . . **$ 330.75 to $428.94**
Price: Black Diamond XR 45 Super . . . . **$345.50 to $392.06**
Price: Encore 209X45 Super . . . . **$ 636.95 to $687.18**

THOMPSON/CENTER HAWKEN RIFLE

Caliber: 45, 50 or 54. **Barrel:** 28" octagon, hooked breech. **Stock:** American walnut. **Sights:** Blade front, rear adjustable for windage and elevation. **Features:** Solid brass furniture, double-set triggers, button rifled barrel, coil-type mainspring. From Thompson/Center Arms.
Price: Percussion model (45-, 50- or 54-cal.) **$529.00**
Price: Flintlock model (50-cal.) **$552.00**

BLACKPOWDER

BLACKPOWDER MUSKETS & RIFLES

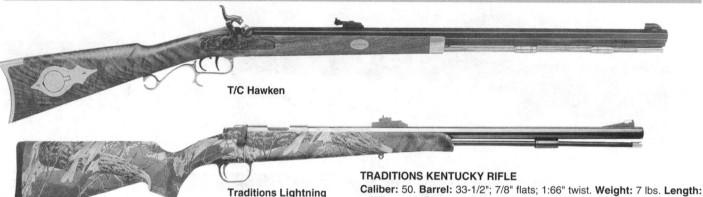

T/C Hawken

Traditions Lightning

TRADITIONS BUCKSKINNER CARBINE

Caliber: 50. **Barrel:** 21"; 15/16" flats, half octagon, half round; 1:20" or 1:66" twist. **Weight:** 6 lbs. **Length:** 37" overall. **Stock:** Beech or black laminated. **Sights:** Beaded blade front, fiber optic open rear click adjustable for windage and elevation or fiber optics. **Features:** Uses V-type mainspring, single trigger. Non-glare hardware; sling swivels. From Traditions.
Price: Flintlock **$229.00**
Price: Flintlock, laminated stock **$299.00**

TRADITIONS DEERHUNTER RIFLE SERIES

Caliber: 32, 50 or 54. **Barrel:** 24", octagonal; 15/16" flats; 1:48" or 1:66" twist. **Weight:** 6 lbs. **Length:** 40" overall. **Stock:** Stained hardwood or All-Weather composite with rubber buttpad, sling swivels. **Sights:** Lite Optic blade front, adjustable rear fiber optics. **Features:** Flint or percussion with color case-hardened lock. Hooked breech, oversized trigger guard, blackened furniture, PVC ramrod. All-Weather has composite stock and C-Nickel barrel. Drilled and tapped for scope mounting. Imported by Traditions, Inc.
Price: Percussion, 50; blued barrel; 1:48" twist **$169.00**
Price: Flintlock, 50-caliber only; 1:48" twist **$189.00**
Price: Flintlock, All-Weather, 50-cal.. . . . . **$179.00**
New! **Price:** Flintlock, left-handed hardwood, 50-cal. **$189.00**
Price: Percussion, All-Weather, 50 or 54 cal.. . . . . **$159.00**
Price: Percussion; 32 cal.. . . . . **$179.00**

TRADITIONS E-BOLT 209 BOLT-ACTION RIFLES

Caliber: 45, 50. **Barrel:** 22" blued or C-Nickel finish, 1:20 and 1:28" twist. **Weight:** 6 lbs., 7 oz. **Length:** 41" overall. **Stock:** Black or Advantage Timber® composite. **Sights:** Lite Optic blade front, adjustable rear. **Features:** Thumb safety; quick-release bolt; covered breech; one-piece breech plug takes 209 shotshell primers; accepts 150 grains of Pyrodex pellets, receiver drilled and tapped for scope, sling swivel studs and rubber butt pad. Introduced 2001. From Traditions.
Price: Black composite stock with 22" blued barrel **$169.00**
Price: Black composite stock with 22" C-Nickel barrel **$179.00**
Price: Advantage Timber® stock with 22" C-Nickel barrel **$229.00**
Price: Redi-Pak with black stock/blued barrel and powder flask,
capper, ball starter, other supplies **$219.00**
Price: Redi-Pak with Advantage Timber® stock/C-Nickel barrel
and powder flask, capper, ball starter, other supplies **$279.00**
Price: Blue, Mossy Oak break-up **$219.00**
Price: 4X32 fixed scope **$219.00**
Price: Scoped w/Redi-Pak **$269.00**

TRADITIONS HAWKEN WOODSMAN RIFLE

Caliber: 50 and 54. **Barrel:** 28"; 15/16" flats. **Weight:** 7 lbs., 11 oz. **Length:** 44-1/2" overall. **Stock:** Walnut-stained hardwood. **Sights:** Beaded blade front, hunting-style open rear adjustable for windage and elevation. **Features:** Percussion only. Brass patchbox and furniture. Double triggers. From Traditions.
Price: 50 or 54 . . . . **$239.00**
Price: 50-cal., left-hand. **$249.00**
Price: 50-caliber, flintlock **$269.00**

TRADITIONS KENTUCKY RIFLE

Caliber: 50. **Barrel:** 33-1/2"; 7/8" flats; 1:66" twist. **Weight:** 7 lbs. **Length:** 49" overall. **Stock:** Beech; inletted toe plate. **Sights:** Blade front, fixed rear. **Features:** Full-length, two-piece stock; brass furniture; color case-hardened lock. Introduced 1995. From Traditions.
Price: Finished **$229.00**
Price: Kit. **$179.00**

TRADITIONS LIGHTNING MAG BOLT-ACTION MUZZLELOADER

Caliber: 50, 54. **Barrel:** 24" round; blued, stainless, C-Nickel or Ultra Coat. **Weight:** 6-1/2 to 7 lbs. 10 oz. **Length:** 43" overall. **Stock:** All-Weather composite, Advantage, or Break-Up camouflage. **Sights:** Fiber Optic blade front, fully adjustable open rear. **Features:** Field-removable stainless steel bolt; silent thumb safety; adjustable trigger; drilled and tapped for scope mounting. Lightning Fire Magnum System allows use of No. 11, musket caps or 209 shotgun primers. Introduced 1997. Imported by Traditions.
Price: All-Weather composite stock, blue finish **$199.00**
Price: All-Weather composite stock, blue finish, muzzle brake . . **$229.00**
Price: All-Weather composite, stainless steel **$279.00**
Price: Camouflage composite, stainless steel **$309.00**
Price: Camouflage composite **$229.00**
Price: Composite, with muzzle brake, stainless, fluted barrel . . . **$329.00**
Price: Walnut finish, synthetic stock. **$239.00**

TRADITIONS LIGHTNING 45 LD BOLT-ACTION RIFLES

Similar to Lightning Mag. but chambered for 45, 50 caliber with 26"fluted blued or C-Nickel barrel, 1:20", 1:28" twist. Black, synthetic break-up or Advantage Timber stock, fiber optic blade front, adjustable rear sights. Accepts 150 grains of Pyrodex. Weighs 7 lbs., 2 oz. Overal length 45". Introduced 2001. From Traditions.
Price: (black stock with blued barrel) **$229.00**
Price: (black stock with C-Nickel barrel). **$239.00**
Price: (Advantage Timber® stock with C-Nickel barrel) **$289.00**

TRADITIONS LIGHTNING LIGHTWEIGHT MAGNUM BOLT-ACTION RIFLES

Similar to Lightning Mag except features 22" lightweight, fluted barrel and Spider Web-pattern black composite stock. Overall length 41", weighs 6 lb., 5 oz. Introduced 2000. From Traditions.
Price: Blued finish. **$219.00**
Price: C-Nickel finish. **$229.00**
Price: Nickel, camo stock **$259.00**

TRADITIONS PANTHER SIDELOCK RIFLE

Similar to Deerhunter rifle, but has blade front and windage-adjustable-only rear sight, black composite stock.
Price: **$119.00**

TRADITIONS PA PELLET FLINTLOCK

Caliber: 50. **Barrel:** 26", blued, nickel. **Weight:** 7 lbs. **Stock:** Hardwood, synthetic and synthetic break-up. **Sights:** FO. **Features:** Removeable breech plug, left-hand model wtih hardwood stock. 1:48" twist.
Price: Hardwood, blued **$249.00**
Price: Hardwood left, blued **$269.00**
Price: Synthetic, blued **$229.00**
Price: Synthetic, nickel. **$239.00**
Price: Synthetic/Break-up, nickel **$269.00**

BLACKPOWDER

BLACKPOWDER MUSKETS & RIFLES

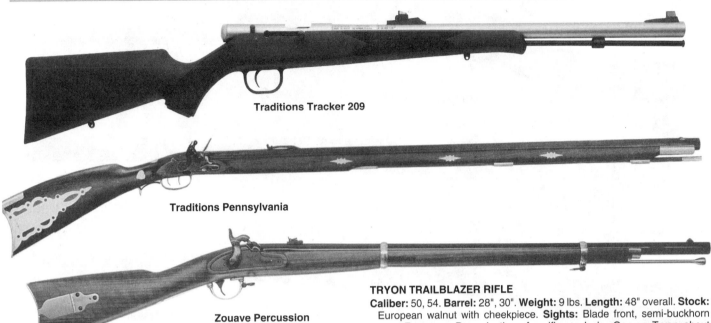

Traditions Tracker 209

Traditions Pennsylvania

Zouave Percussion

TRADITIONS PENNSYLVANIA RIFLE
Caliber: 50. **Barrel:** 40-1/4"; 7/8" flats; 1:66" twist, octagon. **Weight:** 9 lbs. **Length:** 57-1/2" overall. **Stock:** Walnut. **Sights:** Blade front, adjustable rear. **Features:** Brass patchbox and ornamentation. Double-set triggers. From Traditions.
Price: Flintlock **$479.00**
Price: Percussion **$469.00**

TRADITIONS SHENANDOAH RIFLE
Caliber: 36, 50. **Barrel:** 33-1/2" octagon; 1:66" twist. **Weight:** 7 lbs., 3 oz. **Length:** 49-1/2" overall. **Stock:** Walnut. **Sights:** Blade front, buckhorn rear. **Features:** V-type mainspring; double-set trigger; solid brass buttplate, patchbox, nosecap, thimbles, trigger guard. Introduced 1996. From Traditions.
Price: Flintlock **$369.00**
Price: Percussion **$349.00**
Price: 36 cal. Flintlock, 1:48"twist **$399.00**
Price: 36 cal. Percussion, 1:48"twist **$389.00**

TRADITIONS TENNESSEE RIFLE
Caliber: 50. **Barrel:** 24", octagon; 15/16" flats; 1:66" twist. **Weight:** 6 lbs. **Length:** 40-1/2" overall. **Stock:** Stained beech. **Sights:** Blade front, fixed rear. **Features:** One-piece stock has inletted brass furniture, cheekpiece; double-set trigger; V-type mainspring. Flint or percussion. Introduced 1995. From Traditions.
Price: Flintlock **$299.00**
Price: Percussion **$279.00**

TRADITIONS TRACKER 209 IN-LINE RIFLES
Caliber: 45, 50. **Barrel:** 22" blued or C-Nickel finish; 1:28" twist, 50 cal. 1:20" 45 cal. **Weight:** 6 lbs., 4 oz. **Length:** 41" overall. **Stock:** Black, Advantage Timber® composite, synthetic. **Sights:** Lite Optic blade front, adjustable rear. **Features:** Thumb safety; adjustable trigger; rubber butt pad and sling swivel studs; takes 150 grains of Pyrodex pellets; one-piece breech system takes 209 shotshell primers. Drilled and tapped for scope. Introduced 2001. From Traditions.
Price: (Black composite or synthetic stock, 22" blued barrel) **$119.00**
Price: (Black composite or synthetic stock, 22" C-Nickel barrel) . . **$129.00**
Price: (Advantage Timber® stock, 22" C-Nickel barrel) **$179.00**
Price: (Redi-Pak, black stock and blued barrel, powder flask, capper, ball starter, other accessories) **$169.00**
Price: (Redi-Pak, synthetic stock and blued barrel, with scope) . . . **$229.00**

TRYON TRAILBLAZER RIFLE
Caliber: 50, 54. **Barrel:** 28", 30". **Weight:** 9 lbs. **Length:** 48" overall. **Stock:** European walnut with cheekpiece. **Sights:** Blade front, semi-buckhorn rear. **Features:** Reproduction of a rifle made by George Tryon about 1820. Double-set triggers, back action lock, hooked breech with long tang. From Armsport.
Price: About **$825.00**

WHITE MODEL 97 WHITETAIL HUNTER RIFLE
Caliber: 45, 50. **Barrel:** 22", 1:24" twist (50 cal.). **Weight:** 7.6 lbs. **Length:** 39-7/8" overall. **Stock:** Black laminated or black composite with swivel studs. **Sights:** TruGlo fully adjustable, steel rear with white diamond, red bead front with high-visibility inserts. **Features:** In-line ignition with Flash-Fire one-piece nipple and breech plug that uses standard or magnum No. 11 caps, fully adjustable trigger, double safety system, aluminum ramrod; drilled and tapped for scope. Hard gun case. Introduced 1997. Made in U.S.A. by Split Fire Sporting Goods.
Price: Laminated wood stock **$549.95**
Price: Black composite stock **$499.95**

White Model 98 Elite Hunter Rifle
Caliber: 45, 50. **Barrel:** 24", 1:24" twist (50 cal). **Weight:** 8.2 lbs. **Length:** 43-1/4" overall. **Stock:** Black laminate wtih swivel studs. **Sights:** TruGlo fully adjustable, steel rear with white diamond, red bead front with high-visibility inserts. **Features:** In-line ignition with FlashFire one-piece nipple and breech plug that uses standard or magnum No. 11 caps, fully adjustable trigger, double safety system, aluminum ramrod, drilled and taped for scope, hard gun case. Introduced 1998. Made in U.S.A. by Split Fire Sporting Goods.
Price: Laminate wood stock **$649.95**

WHITE MODEL 2000 BLACKTAIL HUNTER RIFLE
Caliber: 50. **Barrel:** 22", 1:24" twist (50 cal.). **Weight:** 7.6 lbs. **Length:** 39-7/8" overall. **Stock:** Black laminated with swivel studs with laser engraved deer or elk scene. **Sights:** TruGlo fully adjustable, steel rear with white diamond, red bead front with high-visibility inserts. **Features:** Teflon finished barrel, in-line ignition with FlashFire one-piece nipple and breech plug that uses standard or magnum No. 11 caps, fully adjustable trigger, double safety system, aluminum ramrod, drilled and tapped for scope. Hard gun case. Introduced 2000. Made in U.S.A. by Split Fire Sporting Goods.
Price: Laminate wood stock, deer scene **$649.95**
Price: Laminate wood stock, elk **$649.95**

ZOUAVE PERCUSSION RIFLE
Caliber: 58, 59. **Barrel:** 32-1/2". **Weight:** 9-1/2 lbs. **Length:** 48-1/2" overall. **Stock:** Walnut finish, brass patchbox and buttplate. **Sights:** Fixed front, rear adjustable for elevation. **Features:** Color case-hardened lockplate, blued barrel. From Navy Arms, Dixie Gun Works, E.M.F., Cabela's.
Price: About . . . . **$325.00 to $465.00**

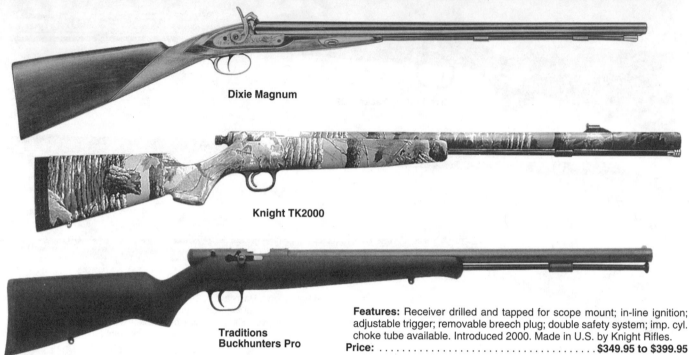

Dixie Magnum

Knight TK2000

Traditions Buckhunters Pro

CABELA'S BLACKPOWDER SHOTGUNS

Gauge: 10, 12, 20. **Barrel:** 10-ga., 30"; 12-ga., 28-1/2" (Extra-Full, Mod., Imp. Cyl. choke tubes); 20-ga., 27-1/2" (Imp. Cyl. & Mod. fixed chokes). **Weight:** 6-1/2 to 7 lbs. **Length:** 45" overall (28-1/2" barrel). **Stock:** American walnut with checkered grip; 12- and 20-gauge have straight stock, 10-gauge has pistol grip. **Features:** Blued barrels, engraved, color case-hardened locks and hammers, brass ramrod tip. From Cabela's.
Price: 10-gauge $499.99
Price: 12-gauge $449.99
Price: 20-gauge $429.99

CVA TRAPPER PERCUSSION SHOTGUN

Gauge: 12. **Barrel:** 28". **Weight:** 6 lbs. **Length:** 46" overall. **Stock:** English-style checkered straight grip of walnut-finished hardwood. **Sights:** Brass bead front. **Features:** Single-blued barrel; color case-hardened lockplate and hammer; screw adjustable sear engagements, V-type mainspring; brass wedge plates; color case-hardened and engraved trigger guard and tang. From CVA.
Price: Finished $287.95

DIXIE MAGNUM PERCUSSION SHOTGUN

Gauge: 10, 12, 20. **Barrel:** 30" (Imp. Cyl. & Mod.) in 10-gauge; 28" in 12-gauge. **Weight:** 6-1/4 lbs. **Length:** 45" overall. **Stock:** Hand-checkered walnut, 14" pull. **Features:** Double triggers; light hand engraving; case-hardened locks in 12-gauge, polished steel in 10-gauge; sling swivels. From Dixie Gun Works.
Price: Upland $449.00
Price: 12-ga. kit $375.00
Price: 20-ga. $495.00
Price: 10-ga. $495.00
Price: 10-ga. kit $395.00

KNIGHT TK2000 MUZZLELOADING SHOTGUN (209)

Gauge: 12. **Barrel:** 26", extra-full choke tube. **Weight:** 7 lbs., 9 oz. **Length:** 45" overall. **Stock:** Synthetic black or Advantage Timber HD; recoil pad; swivel studs. **Sights:** Fully adjustable rear, blade front with fiber optics.
Features: Receiver drilled and tapped for scope mount; in-line ignition; adjustable trigger; removable breech plug; double safety system; imp. cyl. choke tube available. Introduced 2000. Made in U.S. by Knight Rifles.
Price: . . . . $349.95 to $399.95

KNIGHT VERSATILE TK2002

Gauge: 12. **Stock:** Black composite, blued, Advantage Timber HD finish. Both with sling swivel studs installed. **Sights:** Adjustable metallic TruGol fiber optic. **Features:** Full plastic jacket ignition system, screw-on choke tubes, load without removing choke tubes, incredible shot density with jug-chocked barrel design. Improved cylinder and modified choke tubes available.
Price: . . . . $349.95 to $399.95

NAVY ARMS STEEL SHOT MAGNUM SHOTGUN

Gauge: 10. **Barrel:** 28" (Cyl. & Cyl.). **Weight:** 7 lbs., 9 oz. **Length:** 45-1/2" overall. **Stock:** Walnut, with cheekpiece. **Features:** Designed specifically for steel shot. Engraved, polished locks; sling swivels; blued barrels. Imported by Navy Arms.
Price: $605.00

NAVY ARMS T&T SHOTGUN

Gauge: 12. **Barrel:** 28" (Full & Full). **Weight:** 7-1/2 lbs. **Stock:** Walnut. **Sights:** Bead front. **Features:** Color case-hardened locks, double triggers, blued steel furniture. From Navy Arms.
Price: $580.00

TRADITIONS BUCKHUNTER PRO SHOTGUN

Gauge: 12. **Barrel:** 24", choke tube. **Weight:** 6 lbs., 4 oz. **Length:** 43" overall. **Stock:** Composite matte black, Break-Up or Advantage camouflage. **Features:** In-line action with removable stainless steel breech plug; thumb safety; adjustable trigger; rubber buttpad. Introduced 1996. From Traditions.
Price: $248.00
Price: With Advantage, Shadow Branch, or Break-Up
camouflage stock $292.00

THOMPSON/CENTER BLACK MOUNTAIN MAGNUM SHOTGUN

Gauge: 12. **Barrel:** 27" screw-in Turkey choke tube. **Weight:** 7 lbs. **Length:** 41-3/4" overall. **Stock:** Black composite. **Sights:** Bead front. **Features:** Sidelock percussion action. Polished blue finish. Introduced in 1999. Made in U.S. by Thompson/Center Arms.
Price: $362.00

BLACKPOWDER

Benjamin Sheridan CO2

BRNO-Tau-CO$_2$ Match

Beeman/FWB P30

BEEMAN P1 MAGNUM AIR PISTOL
Caliber: 177, 5mm, single shot. **Barrel:** 8.4". **Weight:** 2.5 lbs. **Length:** 11" overall. **Power:** Top lever cocking; spring-piston. **Stocks:** Checkered walnut. **Sights:** Blade front, square notch rear with click micrometer adjustments for windage and elevation. Grooved for scope mounting. **Features:** Dual power for 177 and 20-cal.: low setting gives 350-400 fps; high setting 500-600 fps. Rearward expanding mainspring simulates firearm recoil. All Colt 45 auto grips fit gun. Dry-firing feature for practice. Optional wooden shoulder stock. Introduced 1985. Imported by Beeman.
Price: 177, 5mm **$415.00**

Beeman P2 Match Air Pistol
Similar to the Beeman P1 Magnum except shoots only 177 pellets; completely recoilless single-stroke pnuematic action. Weighs 2.2 lbs. Choice of thumbrest match grips or standard style. Introduced 1990.
Price: 177, 5mm, standard grip **$385.00**
Price: 177, match grip **$455.00**

BEEMAN P3 AIR PISTOL
Caliber: 177 pellet, single shot. **Barrel:** N/A. **Weight:** 1.7 lbs. **Length:** 9.6" overall. **Power:** Single-stroke pneumatic; overlever barrel cocking. **Grips:** Reinforced polymer. **Sights:** Adjustable rear, blade front. **Features:** Velocity 410 fps. Polymer frame; automatic safety; two-stage trigger; built-in muzzle brake. Introduced 1999 by Beeman.
Price: **$159.00**

BEEMAN/FEINWERKBAU 65 MKII AIR PISTOL
Caliber: 177, single shot. **Barrel:** 6.1", removable bbl. wgt. available. **Weight:** 42 oz. **Length:** 13.3" overall. **Power:** Spring, sidelever cocking. **Stocks:** Walnut, stippled thumbrest; adjustable or fixed. **Sights:** Front, interchangeable post element system, open rear, click adjustable for windage and elevation and for sighting notch width. Scope mount available. **Features:** New shorter barrel for better balance and control. Cocking effort 9 lbs. Two-stage trigger, four adjustments. Quiet firing, 525 fps. Programs instantly for recoil or recoilless operation. Permanently lubricated. Steel piston ring. Imported by Beeman.
Price: Right-hand **$1,070.00**

BEEMAN/FEINWERKBAU 103 PISTOL
Caliber: 177, single shot. **Barrel:** 10.1", 12-groove rifling. **Weight:** 2.5 lbs. **Length:** 16.5" overall. **Power:** Single-stroke pneumatic, underlever cocking. **Stocks:** Stippled walnut with adjustable palm shelf. **Sights:** Blade front, open rear adjustable for windage and elevation. Notch size adjustable for width. Interchangeable front blades. **Features:** Velocity 510 fps. Fully adjustable trigger. Cocking effort of 2 lbs. Imported by Beeman.
Price: Right-hand **$1,195.00**
Price: Left-hand **$1,235.00**

BEEMAN/FWB P30 MATCH AIR PISTOL
Caliber: 177, single shot. **Barrel:** 10-5/16", with muzzlebrake. **Weight:** 2.4 lbs. **Length:** 16.5" overall. **Power:** Pre-charged pneumatic. **Stocks:** Stippled walnut; adjustable match type. **Sights:** Undercut blade front, fully adjustable match rear. **Features:** Velocity to 525 fps; up to 200 shots per CO2 cartridge. Fully adjustable trigger; built-in muzzlebrake. Introduced 1995. Imported from Germany by Beeman.
Price: Right-hand **$1,275.00**
Price: Left-hand **$1,350.00**

BEEMAN/FWB C55 CO2 RAPID FIRE PISTOL
Caliber: 177, single shot or 5-shot magazine. **Barrel:** 7.3". **Weight:** 2.5 lbs. **Length:** 15" overall. **Power:** Special CO2 cylinder. **Stocks:** Anatomical, adjustable. **Sights:** Interchangeable front, fully adjustable open micro-click rear with adjustable notch size. **Features:** Velocity 510 fps. Has 11.75" sight radius. Built-in muzzlebrake. Introduced 1993. Imported by Beeman Precision Airguns.
Price: Right-hand **$1,460.00**
Price: Left-hand **$1,520.00**

BEEMAN HW70A AIR PISTOL
Caliber: 177, single shot. **Barrel:** 6-1/4", rifled. **Weight:** 38 oz. **Length:** 12-3/4" overall. **Power:** Spring, barrel cocking. **Stocks:** Plastic, with thumbrest. **Sights:** Hooded post front, square notch rear adjustable for windage and elevation. Comes with scope base. **Features:** Adjustable trigger, 31-lb. cocking effort, 440 fps MV; automatic barrel safety. Imported by Beeman.
Price: **$185.00**
Price: HW70S, black grip, silver finish **$210.00**

BEEMAN/WEBLEY TEMPEST AIR PISTOL
Caliber: 177, 22, single shot. **Barrel:** 6-7/8". **Weight:** 32 oz. **Length:** 8.9" overall. **Power:** Spring-piston, break barrel. **Stocks:** Checkered black plastic with thumbrest. **Sights:** Blade front, adjustable rear. **Features:** Velocity to 500 fps (177), 400 fps (22). Aluminum frame; black epoxy finish; manual safety. Imported from England by Beeman.
Price: **$180.00**

Beeman/Webley Hurricane Air Pistol
Similar to the Tempest except has extended frame in the rear for a click-adjustable rear sight; hooded front sight; comes with scope mount. Imported from England by Beeman.
Price: **$225.00**

BENJAMIN SHERIDAN CO2 PELLET PISTOLS
Caliber: 177, 20, 22, single shot. **Barrel:** 6-3/8", rifled brass. **Weight:** 29 oz. **Length:** 9.8" overall. **Power:** 12-gram CO2 cylinder. **Stocks:** Walnut. **Sights:** High ramp front, fully adjustable notch rear. **Features:** Velocity to 500 fps. Turn-bolt action with cross-bolt safety. Gives about 40 shots per CO2 cylinder. Black or nickel finish. Made in U.S. by Benjamin Sheridan Co.
Price: Black finish, EB17 (177), EB20 (20), about **$115.23**

BENJAMIN SHERIDAN PNEUMATIC PELLET PISTOLS
Caliber: 177, 20, 22, single shot. **Barrel:** 9-3/8", rifled brass. **Weight:** 38 oz. **Length:** 13-1/8" overall. **Power:** Underlever pnuematic, hand pumped. **Stocks:** Walnut stocks and pump handle. **Sights:** High ramp front, fully adjustable notch rear. **Features:** Velocity to 525 fps (variable). Bolt action with cross-bolt safety. Choice of black or nickel finish. Made in U.S. by Benjamin Sheridan Co.
Price: Black finish, HB17 (177), HB20 (20), HB22 (22), about **$129.50**

BERETTA 92 FS/CO2 AIR PISTOLS
Caliber: 177 pellet, 8-shot magazine. **Barrel:** 4.9". **Weight:** 44.4 oz. **Length:** 8.2" (10.2" with compensator). **Power:** CO2 cartridge. **Grips:** Plastic or wood. **Sights:** Adjustable rear, blade front. **Features:** Velocity 375 fps. Replica of Beretta 92 FS pistol. Single- and double-action trigger; ambidextrous safety; black or nickel-plated finish. Made by Umarex for Beretta USA.
Price: . . . . **$200.00 to $465.00**

BRNO TAU-7 CO2 MATCH PISTOL
Caliber: 177. **Barrel:** 10.24". **Weight:** 37 oz. **Length:** 15.75" overall. **Power:** 12.5-gram CO2 cartridge. **Stocks:** Stippled hardwood with adjustable palm rest. **Sights:** Blade front, open fully adjustable rear. **Features:** Comes with extra seals and counterweight. Blue finish. Imported by Great Lakes Airguns.
Price: About **$299.50**

BSA 240 MAGNUM AIR PISTOL
Caliber: 177, 22, single shot. **Barrel:** 6". **Weight:** 2 lbs. **Length:** 9" overall. **Power:** Spring-air, top-lever cocking. **Stocks:** Walnut. **Sights:** Blade front, micrometer adjustable rear. **Features:** Velocity 510 fps (177), 420 fps (22); crossbolt safety. Combat autoloader styling. Imported from U.K. by Precision Sales International, Inc.
Price: **$259.99**

COLT GOVERNMENT 1911 A1 AIR PISTOL
Caliber: 177, 8-shot cylinder magazine. **Barrel:** 5", rifled. **Weight:** 38 oz. **Length:** 8-1/2" overall. **Power:** CO2 cylinder. **Stocks:** Checkered black plastic or smooth wood. **Sights:** Post front, adjustable rear. **Features:** Velocity to 393 fps. Quick-loading cylinder magazine; single and double action; black or silver finish. Introduced 1998. Imported by Colt's Mfg. Co., Inc.
Price: Black finish **$199.00**
Price: Silver finish **$209.00**

AIRGUNS

Crosman Model 1377

Daisy/Power Line 717

CROSMAN BLACK VENOM PISTOL
Caliber: 177 pellets, BB, 17-shot magazine; darts, single shot. **Barrel:** 4.75" smoothbore. **Weight:** 16 oz. **Length:** 10.8" overall. **Power:** Spring. **Stocks:** Checkered. **Sights:** Blade front, adjustable rear. **Features:** Velocity to 270 fps (BBs), 250 fps (pellets). Spring-fed magazine; cross-bolt safety. Introduced 1996. Made in U.S. by Crosman Corp.
Price: About $20.00

CROSMAN BLACK FANG PISTOL
Caliber: 177 BB, 17-shot magazine. **Barrel:** 4.75" smoothbore. **Weight:** 10 oz. **Length:** 10.8" overall. **Power:** Spring. **Stocks:** Checkered. **Sights:** Blade front, fixed notch rear. **Features:** Velocity to 250 fps. Spring-fed magazine; cross-bolt safety. Introduced 1996. Made in U.S. by Crosman Corp.
Price: About $16.00

CROSMAN MODEL 1377 AIR PISTOLS
Caliber: 177 (M1377), single shot. **Barrel:** 8", rifled steel. **Weight:** 39 oz. **Length:** 13-5/8". **Power:** Hand pumped. **Sights:** Blade front, rear adjustable for windage and elevation. **Features:** Bolt action moulded plastic grip, hand size pump forearm. Cross-bolt safety. From Crosman.
Price: About $60.00

CROSMAN AUTO AIR II PISTOL
Caliber: BB, 17-shot magazine, 177 pellet, single shot. **Barrel:** 8-5/8" steel, smoothbore. **Weight:** 13 oz. **Length:** 10-3/4" overall. **Power:** CO2 Powerlet. **Stocks:** Grooved plastic. **Sights:** Blade front, adjustable rear; highlighted system. **Features:** Velocity to 480 fps (BBs), 430 fps (pellets). Semi-automatic action with BBs, single shot with pellets. Black. Introduced 1991. From Crosman.
Price: About $38.00

CROSMAN MODEL 357 SERIES AIR PISTOL
Caliber: 177 10-shot pellet clips. **Barrel:** 4" (Model 3574W), 6" (Model 3576W). **Weight:** 32 oz. (6"). **Length:** 11-3/8" overall (357-6). **Power:** CO2 Powerlet. **Stocks:** Grip, wrap-around style. **Sights:** Ramp front, fully adjustable rear. **Features:** Average 430 fps (Model 3574W). Break-open barrel for easy loading. Single or double action. Vent. rib barrel. Wide, smooth trigger. Black finish. From Crosman.
Price: 4" or 6", about $65.00

CROSMAN MODEL 1008 REPEAT AIR
Caliber: 177, 8-shot pellet clip. **Barrel:** 4.25", rifled steel. **Weight:** 17 oz. **Length:** 8.625" overall. **Power:** CO2 Powerlet. **Stocks:** Checkered black plastic. **Sights:** Post front, adjustable rear. **Features:** Velocity about 430 fps. Break-open barrel for easy loading; single or double semi-automatic action; two 8-shot clips included. Optional carrying case available. Introduced 1992. From Crosman.
Price: About $60.00
Price: With case, about $70.00
Price: Model 1008SB (silver and black finish), about $60.00

DAISY MODEL 2003 PELLET PISTOL
Caliber: 177 pellet, 35-shot clip. **Barrel:** Rifled steel. **Weight:** 2.2 lbs. **Length:** 11.7" overall. **Power:** CO2. **Stocks:** Checkered plastic. **Sights:** Blade front, open rear. **Features:** Velocity to 400 fps. Crossbolt trigger-block safety. Made in U.S. by Daisy Mfg. Co.
Price: About $67.95

DAISY MODEL 454 AIR PISTOL
Caliber: 177 BB, 20-shot clip. **Barrel:** Smoothbore steel. **Weight:** 1.6 lbs. **Length:** 10.4" overall. **Power:** CO2. **Stocks:** Moulded black, ribbed composition. **Sights:** Blade front, fixed rear. **Features:** Velocity to 420 fps. Semi-automatic action; cross-bolt safety; black finish. Introduced 1998. Made in U.S. by Dairy Mfg. Co.
Price: $61.95

DAISY/POWERLINE 717 PELLET PISTOL
Caliber: 177, single shot. **Barrel:** 9.61". **Weight:** 2.25 lbs. **Length:** 13-1/2" overall. **Stocks:** Moulded wood-grain plastic, with thumbrest. **Sights:** Blade and ramp front, micro-adjustable notch rear. **Features:** Single pump pneumatic pistol. Rifled steel barrel. Cross-bolt trigger block. Muzzle velocity 385 fps. From Daisy Mfg. Co. Introduced 1979.
Price: About $71.95

Daisy/PowerLine 747 Pistol
Similar to the 717 pistol except has a 12-groove rifled steel barrel by Lothar Walther, and adjustable trigger pull weight. Velocity of 360 fps. Manual cross-bolt safety.
Price: About $140.00

DAISY/POWERLINE 1140 PELLET PISTOL
Caliber: 177, single shot. **Barrel:** Rifled steel. **Weight:** 1.3 lbs. **Length:** 11.7" overall. **Power:** Single-stroke barrel cocking. **Stocks:** Checkered resin. **Sights:** Hooded post front, open adjustable rear. **Features:** Velocity to 325 fps. Made of black lightweight engineering resin. Introduced 1995. From Daisy.
Price: About $38.95

DAISY/POWERLINE 44 REVOLVER
Caliber: 177 pellets, 6-shot. **Barrel:** 6", rifled steel; interchangeable 4" and 8". **Weight:** 2.7 lbs. **Length:** 13.1" overall. **Power:** CO2. **Stocks:** Moulded plastic with checkering. **Sights:** Blade on ramp front, fully adjustable notch rear. **Features:** Velocity up to 400 fps. Replica of 44 Magnum revolver. Has swingout cylinder and interchangeable barrels. Introduced 1987. From Daisy Mfg. Co.
Price: $59.95

DAISY/POWERLINE 1270 CO2 AIR PISTOL
Caliber: BB, 60-shot magazine. **Barrel:** Smoothbore steel. **Weight:** 17 oz. **Length:** 11.1" overall. **Power:** CO2 pump action. **Stocks:** Moulded black polymer. **Sights:** Blade on ramp front, adjustable rear. **Features:** Velocity to 420 fps. Crossbolt trigger block safety; plated finish. Introduced 1997. Made in U.S. by Daisy Mfg. Co.
Price: About $39.95

EAA/BAIKAL IZH-46 TARGET AIR PISTOL
Caliber: 177, single shot. **Barrel:** 11.02". **Weight:** 2.87 lbs. **Length:** 16.54" overall. **Power:** Underlever single-stroke pneumatic. **Grips:** Adjustable wooden target. **Sights:** Micrometer fully adjustable rear, blade front. **Features:** Velocity about 420 fps. Hammer-forged, rifled barrel. Imported from Russia by European American Armory.
Price: $319.00

EAA/BAIKAL MP-654K AIR PISTOL
Caliber: 177 BB, detachable 13-shot magazine. **Barrel:** 3.75". **Weight:** 1.6 lbs. **Length:** 6.34". **Power:** CO2 cartridge. **Grips:** Black checkered plastic. **Sights:** Notch rear, blade front. **Features:** Velocity about 380 fps. Double-action trigger; slide safety; metal slide and frame. Replica of Makarov pistol. Imported from Russia by European American Armory.
Price: $119.00

EAA/BAIKAL MP-651K AIR PISTOL/RIFLE
Caliber: 177 pellet (8-shot magazine); 177 BB (23-shot). **Barrel:** 5.9" (17.25" with rifle attachment). **Weight:** 1.54 lbs. (3.3 lbs. with rifle attachment). **Length:** 9.4" (31.3" with rifle attachment) **Power:** CO2 cartridge, semi-automatic. **Stock:** Plastic. **Sights:** Notch rear/blade front (pistol); periscopic sighting system (rifle). **Features:** Velocity 328 fps. Unique pistol/rifle combination allows the pistol to be inserted into the rifle shell. Imported from Russia by European American Armory.
Price: $99.00

"GAT" AIR PISTOL
Caliber: 177, single shot. **Barrel:** 7-1/2" cocked, 9-1/2" extended. **Weight:** 22 oz. **Power:** Spring-piston. **Stocks:** Cast checkered metal. **Sights:** Fixed. **Features:** Shoots pellets, corks or darts. Matte black finish. Imported from England by Stone Enterprises, Inc.
Price: $24.95

HAMMERLI 480 MATCH AIR PISTOL
Caliber: 177, single shot. **Barrel:** 9.8". **Weight:** 37 oz. **Length:** 16.5" overall. **Power:** Air or CO2. **Stocks:** Walnut with 7-degree rake adjustment. Stippled grip area. **Sights:** Undercut blade front, fully adjustable open match rear. **Features:** Underbarrel cannister charges with air or CO2 for power supply; gives 320 shots per filling. Trigger adjustable for position. Introduced 1994. Imported from Switzerland by Hammerli Pistols U.S.A.
Price: $1,391.00

Hammerli 480K2 Match Air Pistol
Similar to 480 except short, detachable aluminum air cylinder for use only with compressed ai, can be filled while on gun or off; special adjustable barrel weights. Muzzle velocity of 470 fps, gives about 180 shots. Stippled black composition grip with adjustable palm shelf and rake angle. Case and cylinder. Introduced 1996. Imported from Switzerland by SIGARMS, Inc.
Price: $1,218.00

AIRGUNS

Morini Sam K-11

HAMMERLI AP40 AIR PISTOL
Caliber: 177. **Barrel:** 10". **Stocks:** Adjustable orthopaedic. **Sights:** Fully adjustable micrometer. **Features:** Sleek, light, well balanced and accurate. Imported from Switzerland by Nygord Precision Products.
Price: $985.00

MARKSMAN 1010 REPEATER PISTOL
Caliber: 177, 18-shot BB repeater. **Barrel:** 2-1/2", smoothbore. **Weight:** 24 oz. **Length:** 8-1/4" overall. **Power:** Spring. **Features:** Velocity to 200 fps. Thumb safety. Black finish. Uses BBs, darts, bolts or pellets. Repeats with BBs only. From Marksman Products.
Price: Matte black finish $26.00
Price: Model 2000 (as above except silver-chrome finish). $27.00

MARKSMAN 2005 LASERHAWK SPECIAL EDITION AIR PISTOL
Caliber: 177, 24-shot magazine. **Barrel:** 3.8", smoothbore. **Weight:** 22 oz. **Length:** 10.3" overall. **Power:** Spring-air. **Stocks:** Checkered. **Sights:** Fixed fiber optic front sight. **Features:** Velocity to 300 fps with Hyper-Velocity pellets. Square trigger guard with skeletonized trigger; extended barrel for greater velocity and accuracy. Shoots BBs, pellets, darts or bolts. Made in the U.S. From Marksman Products.
Price: $32.00

MORINI 162E MATCH AIR PISTOL
Caliber: 177, single shot. **Barrel:** 9.4". **Weight:** 32 oz. **Length:** 16.1" overall. **Power:** Scuba air. **Stocks:** Adjustable match type. **Sights:** Interchangeable blade front, fully adjustable match-type rear. **Features:** Power mechanism shuts down when pressure drops to a pre-set level. Adjustable electronic trigger. Introduced 1995. Imported from Switzerland by Nygord Precision Products.
Price: $995.00
Price: 162M mechanical trigger $975.00

MORINI SAM K-11 AIR PISTOL
Caliber: 177. **Barrel:** 10". **Weight:** 38 oz. **Stocks:** Fully adjustable. **Sights:** Fully adjustable. **Features:** Improved trigger, more angle adjustment on grip. Sophisticated counter balance system. Deluxe aluminum case, two cylinders and manometer. Imported from Switzerland by Nygord Precision Products.
Price: $995.00

PARDINI K58 MATCH AIR PISTOL
Caliber: 177, single shot. **Barrel:** 9". **Weight:** 37.7 oz. **Length:** 15.5" overall. **Power:** Pre-charged compressed air; single-stroke cocking. **Stocks:** Adjustable match type; stippled walnut. **Sights:** Interchangeable post front, fully adjustable match rear. **Features:** Fully adjustable trigger. Short version K-2 available. Imported from Italy by Nygord Precision Products.
Price: $750.00
Price: K2 model, precharged air pistol, introduced in 1998 .... $895.00

RWS 9B/9N AIR PISTOLS
Caliber: 177, single shot. **Grips:** Plastic with thumbrest. **Sights:** Adjustable. **Features:** Spring-piston powered; 550 fps. Black or nickel finish. Introduced 2001. Imported from Germany by Dynamit Nobel-RWS.
Price: 9B. $169.00
Price: 9N $185.00

RWS C-225 AIR PISTOLS
Caliber: 177, 8-shot rotary magazine. **Barrel:** 4", 6". **Power:** CO2. **Stocks:** Checkered black plastic. **Sights:** Post front, rear adjustable for windage. **Features:** Velocity to 385 fps. Semi-automatic fire; decocking lever. Imported from Germany by Dynamit Nobel-RWS.
Price: 4", blue. $210.00
Price: 4", nickel. $220.00
Price: 6", blue. $220.00

STEYR LP 5CP MATCH AIR PISTOL
Caliber: 177, 5-shot magazine. **Weight:** 40.7 oz. **Length:** 15.2" overall. **Power:** Pre-charged air cylinder. **Stocks:** Adjustable match type. **Sights:** Interchangeable blade front, fully adjustable match rear. **Features:** Adjustable sight radius; fully adjustable trigger. Barrel compensator. One-shot magazine available. Introduced 1995. Imported from Austria by Nygord Precision Products.
Price: $1,150.00

STEYR LP10P MATCH PISTOL
Caliber: 177, single shot. **Barrel:** 9". **Weight:** 38.7 oz. **Length:** 15.3" overall. **Power:** Scuba air. **Stocks:** Fully adjustable Morini match, palm shelf, stippled walnut. **Sights:** Interchangeable blade in 4mm, 4.5mm or 5mm widths, fully adjustable open rear, interchangeable 3.5mm or 4mm leaves. **Features:** Velocity about 500 fps. Adjustable trigger, adjustable sight radius from 12.4" to 13.2". With compensator. New "aborber" eliminates recoil. Imported from Austria by Nygord Precision Products.
Price: $1,125.00

TECH FORCE SS2 OLYMPIC COMPETITION AIR PISTOL
Caliber: 177 pellet, single shot. **Barrel:** 7.4". **Weight:** 2.8 lbs. **Length:** 16.5" overall. **Power:** Spring piston, sidelever. **Grips:** Hardwood. **Sights:** Extended adjustable rear, blade front accepts inserts. **Features:** Velocity 520 fps. Recoilless design; adjustments allow duplication of a firearm's feel. Match-grade, adjustable trigger; includes carrying case. Imported from China by Compasseco Inc.
Price: $295.00

TECH FORCE 35 AIR PISTOL
Caliber: 177 pellet, single shot. **Weight:** 2.86 lbs. **Length:** 14.9" overall. **Power:** Spring piston, underlever. **Grips:** Hardwood. **Sights:** Micrometer adjustable rear, blade front. **Features:** Velocity 400 fps. Grooved for scope mount; trigger safety. Imported from China by Compasseco Inc.
Price: $49.95

Tech Force 8 Air Pistol
Similar to Tech Force 35, but with break-barrel action, ambidextrous polymer grips. From Compasseco Inc.
Price: $59.95

Tech Force S2-1 Air Pistol
Similar to Tech Force 8, more basic grips and sights for plinking. From Compasseco Inc.
Price: $29.95

WALTHER CP88 PELLET PISTOL
Caliber: 177, 8-shot rotary magazine. **Barrel:** 4", 6". **Weight:** 37 oz. (4" barrel) **Length:** 7" (4" barrel). **Power:** CO2. **Stocks:** Checkered plastic. **Sights:** Blade front, fully adjustable rear. **Features:** Faithfully replicates size, weight and trigger pull of the 9mm Walther P88 compact pistol. Has SA/DA trigger mechanism; ambidextrous safety, levers. Comes with two magazines, 500 pellets, one CO2 cartridge. Introduced 1997. Imported from Germany by Interarms.
Price: Blue $179.00
Price: Nickel $189.00

WALTHER LP20I MATCH PISTOL
Caliber: 177, single shot. **Barrel:** 8.66". **Weight:** NA. **Length:** 15.1" overall. **Power:** Scuba air. **Stocks:** Orthopaedic target type. **Sights:** Undercut blade front, open match rear fully adjustable for windage and elevation. **Features:** Adjustable velocity; matte finish. Introduced 1995. Imported from Germany by Nygord Precision Products.
Price: $1,095.00

Walther CP88 Competition Pellet Pistol
Similar to the standard CP88 except has 6" match-grade barrel, muzzle weight, wood or plastic stocks. Weighs 41 oz., has overall length of 9". Introduced 1997. Imported from Germany by Interarms.
Price: Blue, plastic grips. $170.00
Price: Nickel, plastic grips $195.00
Price: Blue, wood grips $205.00
Price: Nickel, wood grips $232.00

WALTHER CP99 AIR PISTOL
Caliber: 177 pellet, 8-shot rotary magazine. **Barrel:** 3". **Weight:** 26 oz. **Length:** 7.1" overall. **Power:** CO2 cartridge. **Grip:** Polymer. **Sights:** Drift-adjustable rear, blade front. **Features:** Velocity 320 fps. Replica of Walther P99 pistol. Trigger allows single and double action; ambidextrous magazine release; interchangeable backstraps to fit variety of hand sizes. Introduced 2000. From Walther USA.
Price: .... NA

WALTHER PPK/S AIR PISTOL
Caliber: 177 BB. **Barrel:** N/A. **Weight:** 20 oz. **Length:** 6.3" overall. **Power:** CO2 cartridge. **Grip:** Plastic. **Sights:** Fixed rear, blade front. **Features:** Replica of Walther PPK pistol. Blow back system moves slide when fired; trigger allows single and double action. Introduced 2000. From Walther USA.
Price: .... NA

AIRGUNS

AirForce Talon

AIRFORCE TALON AIR RIFLE

Caliber: 22, single-shot. **Barrel:** 18". **Weight:** 5.5 lbs. **Length:** 32.6". **Power:** Precharged pneumatic. **Sights:** Intended for scope use, fiber optic open sights optional. **Features:** Lothar Walther match barrel, adjustable power levels from 400-1000 FPS, operates on high pressure air from scuba tank or hand pump. Wide variety of accessories easily attach to multiple dovetail mounting rails. Manufactured in the U.S.A. by AirForce Airguns.
Price: About $419.95

AIRFORCE TALON SS AIR RIFLE

Caliber: 177, 22, single-shot. **Barrel:** 12". **Weight:** 5.25 lbs. **Length:** 32.75". **Power:** Precharged pneumatic. **Sights:** Intended for scope use, fiber optic open sights optional. **Features:** Lothar Walther match barrel, adjustable power levels from 400-1000 FPS. Chamber in front of barrel strips away air turbulence, protects muzzle and reduces firing report. Operates on high pressure air from scuba tank or hand pump. Wide variety of accessories easily attach to multiple dovetail mounting rails. Manufactured in the U.S.A. by AirForce Airguns.
Price: About $419.95

AIRROW MODEL A-8SRB STEALTH AIR GUN

Caliber: 177, 22, 25, 9-shot. **Barrel:** 20"; rifled. **Weight:** 6 lbs. **Length:** 34" overall. **Power:** CO2 or compressed air; variable power. **Stock:** Telescoping CAR-15-type. **Sights:** Variable 3.5-10x scope. **Features:** Velocity 1100 fps in all calibers. Pneumatic air trigger. All aircraft aluminum and stainless steel construction. Mil-spec materials and finishes. Introduced 1992. From Swivel Machine Works, Inc.
Price: About $2,299.00

AIRROW MODEL A-8S1P STEALTH AIR GUN

Caliber: #2512 16" arrow. **Barrel:** 16". **Weight:** 4.4 lbs. **Length:** 30.1" overall. **Power:** CO2 or compressed air; variable power. **Stock:** Telescoping CAR-15-type. **Sights:** Scope rings only. 7 oz. rechargeable cylinder and valve. **Features:** Velocity to 650 fps with 260-grain arrow. Pneumatic air trigger. Broadhead guard. All aircraft aluminum and stainless steel construction. Mil-spec materials and finishes. A-8S Models perform to 2,000 PSIG above or below water levels. Waterproof case. Introduced 1991. From Swivel Machine Works, Inc.
Price: About $1,699.00

ARS/KING HUNTING MASTER AIR RIFLE

Caliber: 22, 5-shot repeater. **Barrel:** 22-3/4". **Weight:** 7-3/4 lbs. **Length:** 42" overall. **Power:** Pre-compressed air from 3000 psi diving tank. **Stock:** Indonesian walnut with checkered grip and forend; rubber buttpad. **Sights:** Blade front, fully adjustable open rear. Receiver grooved for scope mounting. **Features:** Velocity over 1000 fps with 32-grain pellet. High and low power switch for hunting or target velocities. Side lever cocks action and inserts pellet. Rotary magazine. Imported from Korea by Air Rifle Specialists.
Price: $580.00
Price: Hunting Master 900 (9mm, limited production) $1,000.00

ARS/Magnum 6 Air Rifle

Similar to King Hunting Master except 6-shot repeater with 23-3/4" barrel, weighs 8-1/4 lbs. Stock is walnut-stained hardwood with checkered grip and forend; rubber buttpad. Velocity of 1000+ fps with 32-grain pellet. Imported from Korea by Air Rifle Specialists.
Price: $500.00

ARS HUNTING MASTER AR6 AIR RIFLE

Caliber: 22, 6-shot repeater. **Barrel:** 25-1/2". **Weight:** 7 lbs. **Length:** 41-1/4" overall. **Power:** Pre-compressed air from 3000 psi diving tank. **Stock:** Indonesian walnut with checkered grip; rubber buttpad. **Sights:** Blade front, adjustable peep rear. **Features:** Velocity over 1000 fps with 32-grain pellet. Receiver grooved for scope mounting. Has 6-shot rotary magazine. Imported by Air Rifle Specialists.
Price: $580.00

ARS/CAREER 707 AIR RIFLE

Caliber: 22, 6-shot repeater. **Barrel:** 23". **Weight:** 7.75 lbs. **Length:** 40.5" overall. **Power:** Pre-compressed air; variable power. **Stock:** Indonesian walnut with checkered grip, gloss finish. **Sights:** Hooded post front with interchangeable inserts, fully adjustable diopter rear. **Features:** Velocity to 1000 fps. Lever-action with straight feed magazine; pressure gauge in lower front air reservoir; scope mounting rail included. Introduced 1996. Imported from the Philippines by Air Rifle Specialists.
Price: $580.00

ARS/FARCO FP SURVIVAL AIR RIFLE

Caliber: 22, 25, single shot. **Barrel:** 22-3/4". **Weight:** 5-3/4 lbs. **Length:** 42-3/4" overall. **Power:** Multi-pump foot pump. **Stock:** Philippine hardwood. **Sights:** Blade front, fixed rear. **Features:** Velocity to 850 fps (22 or 25). Receiver grooved for scope mounting. Imported from the Philippines by Air Rifle Specialists.
Price: $295.00

ARS/FARCO CO2 AIR SHOTGUN

Caliber: 51 (28-gauge). **Barrel:** 30". **Weight:** 7 lbs. **Length:** 48-1/2" overall. **Power:** 10-oz. refillable CO2 tank. **Stock:** Hardwood. **Sights:** Blade front, fixed rear. **Features:** Gives over 100 ft. lbs. energy for taking small game. Imported from the Philippines by Air Rifle Specialists.
Price: $460.00

ARS/Farco CO2 Stainless Steel Air Rifle

Similar to ARS/Farco CO2 shotgun except in 22- or 25-caliber, 21-1/2" barrel; weighs 6-3/4 lbs., 42-1/2". Philippine hardwood stock, stippled grip and forend, blade front sight, adjustable rear, grooved for scope mount. Uses 10-oz. refillable CO2 cylinder. Stainless steel. Imported from Philippines by Air Rifle Specialists.
Price: Including CO2 cylinder $460.00

ARS/QB77 DELUXE AIR RIFLE

Caliber: 177, 22, single shot. **Barrel:** 21-1/2". **Weight:** 5-1/2 lbs. **Length:** 40" overall. **Power:** Two 12-oz. CO2 cylinders. **Stock:** Walnut-stained hardwood. **Sights:** Blade front, adjustable rear. **Features:** Velocity to 625 fps (22), 725 fps (177). Receiver grooved for scope mounting. Comes with bulk-fill valve. Imported by Air Rifle Specialists.
Price: $195.00

ANSCHUTZ 2002 MATCH AIR RIFLE

Caliber: 177, single shot. **Barrel:** 25.2". **Weight:** 10.4 lbs. **Length:** 44.5" overall. **Stock:** European walnut, blonde hardwood or colored laminated hardwood; stippled grip and forend. Also available with flat-forend walnut stock for benchrest shooting and aluminum. **Sights:** Optional sight set #6834. **Features:** Muzzle velocity 575 fps. Balance, weight match the 1907 ISU smallbore rifle. Uses #5021 match trigger. Recoil and vibration free. Fully adjustable cheekpiece and buttplate; accessory rail under forend. Available in Pneumatic and Compressed Air versions. Introduced 1988. Imported from Germany by Gunsmithing, Inc., Accuracy International, Champion's Choice.
Price: Right-hand, blonde hardwood stock, with sights $1,275.00
Price: Right-hand, walnut stock $1,275.00
Price: Right-hand, color laminate stock $1,300.00
Price: Right-hand, aluminum stock, butt plate $1,495.00
Price: Left-hand, color laminate stock $1,595.00
Price: Model 2002D-RT Running Target, right-hand, no sights $1,248.90
Price: #6834 Sight Set $227.10

BEEMAN BEARCUB AIR RIFLE

Caliber: 177, single shot. **Barrel:** 13". **Weight:** 7.2 lbs. **Length:** 37.8" overall. **Power:** Spring-piston, barrel cocking. **Stock:** Stained hardwood. **Sights:** Hooded post front, open fully adjustable rear. **Features:** Velocity to 915 fps. Polished blue finish; receiver dovetailed for scope mounting. Imported from England by Beeman Precision Airguns.
Price: $325.00

BEEMAN CROW MAGNUM AIR RIFLE

Caliber: 20, 22, 25, single shot. **Barrel:** 16"; 10-groove rifling. **Weight:** 8.5 lbs. **Length:** 46" overall. **Power:** Gas-spring; adjustable power to 32 foot pounds muzzle energy. Barrel-cocking. **Stock:** Classic-style hardwood; hand checkered. **Sights:** For scope use only; built-in base and 1" rings included. **Features:** Adjustable two-stage trigger. Automatic safety. Available in 22-caliber on special order. Introduced 1992. Imported by Beeman.
Price: $1,220.00

BEEMAN KODIAK AIR RIFLE

Caliber: 25, single shot. **Barrel:** 17.6". **Weight:** 9 lbs. **Length:** 45.6" overall. **Power:** Spring-piston, barrel cocking. **Stock:** Stained hardwood. **Sights:** Blade front, open fully adjustable rear. **Features:** Velocity to 820 fps. Up to 30 foot pounds muzzle energy. Introduced 1993. Imported by Beeman.
Price: $625.00

BEEMAN MAKO AIR RIFLE
Caliber: 177, single shot. **Barrel:** 20", with compensator. **Weight:** 7.3 lbs. **Length:** 38.5" overall. **Power:** Pre-charged pneumatic. **Stock:** Stained beech; Monte Carlo cheekpiece; checkered grip. **Sights:** None furnished. **Features:** Velocity to 930 fps. Gives over 50 shots per charge. Manual safety; brass trigger blade; vented rubber butt pad. Requires scuba tank for air. Introduced 1994. Imported from England by Beeman.
Price: **$1,000.00**
Price: Mako FT (thumbhole stock) **$1,350.00**

BEEMAN R1 AIR RIFLE
Caliber: 177, 20 or 22, single shot. **Barrel:** 19.6", 12-groove rifling. **Weight:** 8.5 lbs. **Length:** 45.2" overall. **Power:** Spring-piston, barrel cocking. **Stock:** Walnut-stained beech; cut-checkered pistol grip; Monte Carlo comb and cheekpiece; rubber buttpad. **Sights:** Tunnel front with interchangeable inserts, open rear click-adjustable for windage and elevation. Grooved for scope mounting. **Features:** Velocity of 940-1000 fps (177), 860 fps (20), 800 fps (22). Non-drying nylon piston and breech seals. Adjustable metal trigger. Milled steel safety. Right- or left-hand stock. Adjustable cheekpiece and buttplate at extra cost. Custom and Super Laser versions available. Imported by Beeman.
Price: Right-hand, 177, 20, 22 .... **$540.00**
Price: Left-hand, 177, 20, 22 .... **$575.00**

BEEMAN R6 AIR RIFLE
Caliber: 177, single shot. **Barrel:** NA. **Weight:** 7.1 lbs. **Length:** 41.8" overall. **Power:** Spring-piston, barrel cocking. **Stock:** Stained hardwood. **Sights:** Tunnel post front, open fully adjustable rear. **Features:** Velocity to 815 fps. Two-stage Rekord adjustable trigger; receiver dovetailed for scope mounting; automatic safety. Introduced 1996. Imported from Germany by Beeman Precision Airguns.
Price: **$285.00**

BEEMAN R1 LASER MK II AIR RIFLE
Caliber: 177, 20, 22, 25, single shot. **Barrel:** 16.1" or 19.6". **Weight:** 8.4 lbs. **Length:** 41.7" overall. **Power:** Spring-piston, barrel cocking. **Stock:** Laminated wood with high cheekpiece, ventilated recoil pad. **Sights:** Tunnel front with interchangeable inserts, open adjustable rear; receiver grooved for scope mounting. **Features:** Velocity to 1150 fps (177). Special powerplant components. Built from the Beeman R1 rifle by Beeman.
Price: **$895.00**

BEEMAN R7 AIR RIFLE
Caliber: 177, 20, single shot. **Barrel:** 17". **Weight:** 6.1 lbs. **Length:** 40.2" overall. **Power:** Spring piston. **Stock:** Stained beech. **Sights:** Hooded front, fully adjustable micrometer click open rear. **Features:** Velocity to 700 fps (177), 620 fps (20). Receiver grooved for scope mounting; double-jointed cocking lever; fully adjustable trigger; checkered grip. Imported by Beeman.
Price: **$280.00**

BEEMAN R9 AIR RIFLE
Caliber: 177, 20, single shot. **Barrel:** NA. **Weight:** 7.3 lbs. **Length:** 43" overall. **Power:** Spring-piston, barrel cocking. **Stock:** Stained hardwood. **Sights:** Tunnel post front, fully adjustable open rear. **Features:** Velocity to 1000 fps (177), 800 fps (20). Adjustable Rekord trigger; automatic safety; receiver dovetailed for scope mounting. Introduced 1996. Imported from Germany by Beeman Precision Airguns.
Price: **$320.00**

Beeman R9 Deluxe Air Rifle
Same as the R9 except has an extended forend stock, checkered pistol grip, grip cap, carved Monte Carlo cheekpiece. Globe front sight with inserts. Introduced 1997. Imported by Beeman.
Price: **$370.00**

BEEMAN R11 AIR RIFLE
Caliber: 177, single shot. **Barrel:** 19.6". **Weight:** 8.8 lbs. **Length:** 47" overall. **Power:** Spring-piston, barrel cocking. **Stock:** Walnut-stained beech; adjustable buttplate and cheekpiece. **Sights:** None furnished. Has dovetail for scope mounting. **Features:** Velocity 910-940 fps. All-steel barrel sleeve. Imported by Beeman.
Price: **$530.00**

BEEMAN SUPER 12 AIR RIFLE
Caliber: 22, 25, 12-shot magazine. **Barrel:** 19", 12-groove rifling. **Weight:** 7.8 lbs. **Length:** 41.7" overall. **Power:** Pre-charged pneumatic; external air reservoir. **Stock:** European walnut. **Sights:** None furnished; drilled and tapped for scope mounting; scope mount included. **Features:** Velocity to 850 fps (25-caliber). Adjustable power setting gives 30-70 shots per 400 cc air bottle. Requires scuba tank for air. Introduced 1995. Imported by Beeman.
Price: **$1,675.00**

BEEMAN S1 MAGNUM AIR RIFLE
Caliber: 177, single shot. **Barrel:** 19". **Weight:** 7.1 lbs. **Length:** 45.5" overall. **Power:** Spring-piston, barrel cocking. **Stock:** Stained beech with Monte Carlo cheekpiece; checkered grip. **Sights:** Hooded post front, fully adjustable micrometer click rear. **Features:** Velocity to 900 fps. Automatic safety; receiver grooved for scope mounting; two-stage adjustable trigger; curved rubber buttpad. Introduced 1995. Imported by Beeman.
Price: **$210.00**

BEEMAN RX-1 GAS-SPRING MAGNUM AIR RIFLE
Caliber: 177, 20, 22, 25, single shot. **Barrel:** 19.6", 12-groove rifling. **Weight:** 8.8 lbs. **Power:** Gas-spring piston air; single stroke barrel cocking. **Stock:** Walnut-finished hardwood, hand checkered, with cheekpiece. Adjustable cheekpiece and buttplate. **Sights:** Tunnel front, click-adjustable rear. **Features:** Velocity adjustable to about 1200 fps. Uses special sealed chamber of air as a mainspring. Gas-spring cannot take a set. Introduced 1990. Imported by Beeman.
Price: 177, 20, 22 or 25 regular, right-hand **$590.00**
Price: 177, 20, 22, 25, left-hand **$625.00**

BEEMAN R1 CARBINE
Caliber: 177, 20, 22, 25, single shot. **Barrel:** 16.1". **Weight:** 8.6 lbs. **Length:** 41.7" overall. **Power:** Spring-piston, barrel cocking. **Stock:** Stained beech; Monte Carlo comb and checkpiece; cut checkered pistol grip; rubber buttpad. **Sights:** Tunnel front with interchangeable inserts, open adjustable rear; receiver grooved for scope mounting. **Features:** Velocity up to 1000 fps (177). Non-drying nylon piston and breech seals. Adjustable metal trigger. Machined steel receiver end cap and safety. Right- or left-hand stock. Imported by Beeman.
Price: 177, 20, 22, 25, right-hand **$540.00**
Price: As above, left-hand **$575.00**
Price: R1-AW (synthetic stock, nickel plating) **$650.00**

BEEMAN/FEINWERKBAU 300-S SERIES MATCH RIFLE
Caliber: 177, single shot. **Barrel:** 19.9", fixed solid with receiver. **Weight:** Approx. 10 lbs. with optional bbl. sleeve. **Length:** 42.8" overall. **Power:** Spring-piston, single stroke sidelever. **Stock:** Match model—walnut, deep forend, adjustable buttplate. **Sights:** Globe front with interchangeable inserts. Click micro. adjustable match aperture rear. Front and rear sights move as a single unit. **Features:** Recoilless, vibration free. Five-way adjustable match trigger. Grooved for scope mounts. Permanent lubrication, steel piston ring. Cocking effort 9 lbs. Optional 10-oz. barrel sleeve. Available from Beeman.
Price: Right-hand **$1,235.00**
Price: Left-hand **$1,370.00**

BEEMAN/FEINWERKBAU 603 AIR RIFLE
Caliber: 177, single shot. **Barrel:** 16.6". **Weight:** 10.8 lbs. **Length:** 43" overall. **Power:** Single stroke pneumatic. **Stock:** Special laminated hardwoods and hard rubber for stability. Multi-colored stock also available. **Sights:** Tunnel front with interchangeable inserts, click micrometer match aperture rear. **Features:** Velocity to 570 fps. Recoilless action; double supported barrel; special, short rifled area frees pellet form barrel faster so shooter's motion has minimum effect on accuracy. Fully adjustable match trigger with separately adjustable trigger and trigger slack weight. Trigger and sights blocked when loading latch is open. Introduced 1997. Imported by Beeman.
Price: Right-hand **$1,625.00**
Price: Left-hand **$1,775.00**

BEEMAN/FEINWERKBAU 300-S MINI-MATCH
Caliber: 177, single shot. **Barrel:** 17-1/8". **Weight:** 8.8 lbs. **Length:** 40" overall. **Power:** Spring-piston, single stroke sidelever cocking. **Stock:** Walnut. Stippled grip, adjustable buttplate. Scaled-down for youthful or slightly built shooters. **Sights:** Globe front with interchangeable inserts, micro. adjustable rear. Front and rear sights move as a single unit. **Features:** Recoilless, vibration free. Grooved for scope mounts. Steel piston ring. Cocking effort about 9-1/2 lbs. Barrel sleeve optional. Left-hand model available. Introduced 1978. Imported by Beeman.
Price: Right-hand **$1,270.00**
Price: Left-hand **$1,370.00**

BEEMAN/FEINWERKBAU P70 AIR RIFLE
Caliber: 177, single shot. **Barrel:** 16.6". **Weight:** 10.6 lbs. **Length:** 42.6" overall. **Power:** Precharged pneumatic. **Stock:** Laminated hardwoods and hard rubber for stability. Multi-colored stock also available. **Sights:** Tunnel front with interchangeable inserts, click micrometer match aperture rear. **Features:** Velocity to 570 fps. Recoilless action; double supported barrel; special short rifled area frees pellet from barrel faster so shooter's motion has minimum effect on accuracy. Fully adjustable match trigger with separately adjustable trigger and trigger slack weight. Trigger and sights blocked when loading latch is open. Introduced 1997. Imported by Beeman.
Price: P70, pre-charged, right-hand **$1,545.00**
Price: P70, pre-charged, left-hand **$1,640.00**
Price: P70, pre-charged, right-hand, multi **$1,645.00**
Price: P70, pre-charged, left-hand, multi **$1,745.00**

BEEMAN/HW 97 AIR RIFLE
Caliber: 177, 20, single shot. **Barrel:** 17.75". **Weight:** 9.2 lbs. **Length:** 44.1" overall. **Power:** Spring-piston, underlever cocking. **Stock:** Walnut-stained beech; rubber buttpad. **Sights:** None. Receiver grooved for scope mounting. **Features:** Velocity 830 fps (177). Fixed barrel with fully opening, direct loading breech. Adjustable trigger. Introduced 1994. Imported by Beeman Precision Airguns.
Price: Right-hand only **$530.00**

BENJAMIN SHERIDAN PNEUMATIC (PUMP-UP) AIR RIFLES
Caliber: 177 or 22, single shot. **Barrel:** 19-3/8", rifled brass. **Weight:** 5-1/2 lbs. **Length:** 36-1/4" overall. **Power:** Underlever pneumatic, hand pumped. **Stock:** American walnut stock and forend. **Sights:** High ramp front, fully adjustable notch rear. **Features:** Variable velocity to 800 fps. Bolt action with ambidextrous push-pull safety. Black or nickel finish. Introduced 1991. Made in the U.S. by Benjamin Sheridan Co.
Price: Black finish, Model 397 (177), Model 392 (22), about **$140.00**
Price: Nickel finish, Model S397 (177), Model S392 (22), about **$150.00**

AIRGUNS

**BRNO TAU-200
Sporter**

BENJAMIN SHERIDAN AIR RIFLE
Caliber: 177 single-shot. **Barrel:** 19-3/8", rifled brass. **Weight:** 5 lbs. **Length:** 36-1/2" overall. **Power** 12-gram CO_2 cylinder. **Stocks:** American walnut with buttplate. **Sights:** High ramp front, fully adjustable notch rear. **Features:** Velocity to 680 fps (177). Bolt action with ambidextrous push-pull safety. Gives about 40 shots per cylinder. Black finish. Introduced 1991. Made in the U.S. by Benjamin Sheridan Co.
Price: Black finish, Model G397 (177) **$140.00**

BRNO TAU-200 AIR RIFLE
Caliber: 177, single shot. **Barrel:** 19", rifled. **Weight:** 7-1/2 lbs. **Length:** 42" overall. **Power:** 6-oz. CO_2 cartridge. **Stock:** Wood match style with adjustable comb and buttplate. **Sights:** Globe front with interchangeable inserts, fully adjustable open rear. **Features:** Adjustable trigger. Comes with extra seals, large CO_2 bottle, counterweight. Introduced 1993. Imported by Great Lakes Airguns. Available in Standard Universal, Deluxe Universal, International and Target Sporter versions.
Price: Standard Universal (ambidex. stock with buttstock extender,
adj. cheekpiece).. . . . . **$349.50**
Price: Deluxe Universal (as above but with micro-adj. aperture sight) **$449.50**
Price: International (like Deluxe Universal but with right- or
left-hand stock) **$454.50**
Price: Target Sporter (like Std. Universal with 4X scope, no sights) **$412.50**

BSA MAGNUM SUPERSTAR™ MK2 MAGNUM AIR RIFLE, CARBINE
Caliber: 177, 22, 25, single shot. **Barrel:** 18-1/2". **Weight:** 8 lbs., 8 oz. **Length:** 43" overall. **Power:** Spring-air, underlever cocking. **Stock:** Oil-finished hardwood; Monte Carlo with cheekpiece, checkered at grip; recoil pad. **Sights:** Ramp front, micrometer adjustable rear. Maxi-Grip scope rail. **Features:** Velocity 950 fps (177), 750 fps (22), 600 fps (25). Patented rotating breech design. Maxi-Grip scope rail protects optics from recoil; automatic anti-beartrap plus manual safety. Imported from U.K. by Precision Sales International, Inc.
Price: **$349.95**
Price: MKII Carbine (14" barrel, 39-1/2" overall) **$349.95**

BSA MAGNUM SUPERSPORT™ AIR RIFLE
Caliber: 177, 22, 25, single shot. **Barrel:** 18-1/2". **Weight:** 6 lbs., 8 oz. **Length:** 41" overall. **Power:** Spring-air, barrel cocking. **Stock:** Oil-finished hardwood; Monte Carlo with cheekpiece, recoil pad. **Sights:** Ramp front, micrometer adjustable rear. Maxi-Grip scope rail. **Features:** Velocity 950 fps (177), 750 fps (22), 600 fps (25). Patented Maxi-Grip scope rail protects optics from recoil; automatic anti-beartrap plus manual tang safety. Muzzle brake standard. Imported for U.K. by Precision Sales International, Inc.
Price: **$194.95**
Price: Carbine, 14" barrel, muzzle brake **$214.95**

BSA MAGNUM GOLDSTAR MAGNUM AIR RIFLE
Caliber: 177, 22, 10-shot repeater. **Barrel:** 17-1/2". **Weight:** 8 lbs., 8 oz. **Length:** 42.5" overall. **Power:** Spring-air, underlever cocking. **Stock:** Oil-finished hardwood; Monte Carlo with cheekpiece, checkered at grip; recoil pad. **Sights:** Ramp front, micrometer adjustable rear; comes with Maxi-Grip scope rail. **Features:** Velocity 950 fps (177), 750 fps (22). Patented 10-shot indexing magazine; Maxi-Grip scope rail protects optics from recoil; automatic anti-beartrap plus manual safety; muzzlebrake standard. Imported from U.K. by Precision Sales International, Inc.
Price: **$499.95**

BSA MAGNUM SUPERTEN AIR RIFLE
Caliber: 177, 22 10-shot repeater. **Barrel:** 17-1/2". **Weight:** 7 lbs., 8 oz. **Length:** 37" overall. **Power:** Precharged pneumatic via buddy bottle. **Stock:** Oil-finished hardwood; Monte Carlo with cheekpiece, cut checkering at grip; adjustable recoil pad. **Sights:** No sights; intended for scope use. **Features:** Velocity 1000+ fps (177), 1000+ fps (22). Patented 10-shot indexing magazine, bolt-action loading. Left-hand version also available. Imported from U.K. by Precision Sales International, Inc.
Price: **$599.95**

BSA METEOR MK6 AIR RIFLE
Caliber: 177, 22, single shot. **Barrel:** 18-1/2". **Weight:** 6 lbs. **Length:** 41" overall. **Power:** Spring-air, barrel cocking. **Stock:** Oil-finished hardwood. **Sights:** Ramp

front, micrometer adjustable rear. **Features:** Velocity 650 fps (177), 500 fps (22). Automatic anti-beartrap; manual tang safety. Receiver grooved for scope mounting. Imported from U.K. by Precision Sales International, Inc.
Price: Rifle **$144.95**
Price: Carbine **$164.95**

CROSMAN CHALLENGER 2000 AIR RIFLE
Caliber: 177, single shot. **Barrel:** N/A. **Weight:** 6.95 lbs. **Power:** CO_2 Powerlet. **Length:** 36 1/4" overall. **Stock:** Black synthetic with adjustable buttplate and cheekpiece.**Sights:** Hooded front, micrometer-adjustable aperture rear. **Features:** Up to 485 fps. Two-stage trigger; accessory rail on forearm. Designed for competition shooting. Introduced 2001. Made in U.S. by Crosman Corp.
Price: **$299.00**

CROSMAN MODEL 66 POWERMASTER
Caliber: 177 (single shot pellet) or BB, 200-shot reservoir. **Barrel:** 20", rifled steel. **Weight:** 3 lbs. **Length:** 38-1/2" overall. **Power:** Pneumatic; hand pumped. **Stock:** Wood-grained ABS plastic; checkered pistol grip and forend. **Sights:** Ramp front, fully adjustable open rear. **Features:** Velocity about 645 fps. Bolt action, cross-bolt safety. Introduced 1983. From Crosman.
Price: About **$60.00**
Price: Model 664X (as above, with 4x scope) **$70.00**
Price: Model 664SB (as above with silver and black finish), about **$75.00**
Price: Model 664GT (black and gold finish, 4x scope) about **$73.00**

CROSMAN MODEL 760 PUMPMASTER
Caliber: 177 pellets (single shot) or BB (200-shot reservoir). **Barrel:** 19-1/2", rifled steel. **Weight:** 2 lbs., 12 oz. **Length:** 33.5" overall. **Power:** Pneumatic, hand pumped. **Stock:** Walnut-finished ABS plastic stock and forend. **Features:** Velocity to 590 fps (BBs, 10 pumps). Short stroke, power determined by number of strokes. Post front sight and adjustable rear sight. Cross-bolt safety. Introduced 1966. From Crosman.
Price: About **$40.00**
Price: Model 760SB (silver and black finish), about **$55.00**

CROSMAN MODEL 795 SPRING MASTER RIFLE
Caliber: 177, single shot. **Barrel:** Rifled steel. **Weight:** 4 lbs., 8 oz. **Length:** 42" overall. **Power:** Spring-piston. **Stock:** Black synthetic. **Sights:** Hooded front, fully adjustable rear. **Features:** Velocity about 550 fps. Introduced 1995. From Crosman.
Price: About **$90.00**

CROSMAN MODEL 1077 REPEATAIR RIFLE
Caliber: 177 pellets, 12-shot clip. **Barrel:** 20.3", rifled steel. **Weight:** 3 lbs., 11 oz. **Length:** 38.8" overall. **Power:** CO_2 Powerlet. **Stock:** Textured synthetic or American walnut. **Sights:** Blade front, fully adjustable rear. **Features:** Velocity 590 fps. Removable 12-shot clip. True semi-automatic action. Introduced 1993. From Crosman.
Price: About **$75.00**
Price: 1077W (walnut stock). **$110.00**

CROSMAN 2260 AIR RIFLE
Caliber: 22, single shot. **Barrel:** 24". **Weight:** 4 lbs., 12 oz. **Length:** 39.75" overall. **Power:** CO_2 Powerlet. **Stock:** Hardwood. **Sights:** Blade front, adjustable rear open or peep. **Features:** About 600 fps. Made in U.S. by Crosman Corp.
Price: . . . . **NA**

CROSMAN MODEL 2289 RIFLE
Caliber: .22, single shot. **Barrel:** 14.625", rifled steel. **Weight:** 3 lbs. 3 oz. **Length:** 31" overall. **Power:** Hand pumped, pneumatic. **Stock:** Composition, skeletal type. **Sights:** Blade front, rear adjustable for windage and elevation. **Features:** Velocity to 575 fps. Detachable stock. Metal parts blued. From Crosman.
Price: About **$73.00**

CROSMAN MODEL 2100 CLASSIC AIR RIFLE
Caliber: 177 pellets (single shot), or BB (200-shot BB reservoir). **Barrel:** 21", rifled. **Weight:** 4 lbs., 13 oz. **Length:** 39-3/4" overall. **Power:** Pump-up, pneumatic. **Stock:** Wood-grained checkered ABS plastic. **Features:** Three pumps give about 450 fps, 10 pumps about 755 fps (BBs). Cross-bolt safety; concealed reservoir holds over 200 BBs. From Crosman.
Price: About **$75.00**
Price: Model 2104GT (black and gold finish, 4x scope), about **$95.00**
Price: Model 2100W (walnut stock, pellets only), about **$120.00**

AIRGUNS

Crosman 1077W

CROSMAN MODEL 2200 MAGNUM AIR RIFLE
Caliber: 22, single shot. **Barrel:** 19", rifled steel. **Weight:** 4 lbs., 12 oz. **Length:** 39" overall. **Stock:** Full-size, wood-grained ABS plastic with checkered grip and forend or American walnut. **Sights:** Ramp front, open step-adjustable rear. **Features:** Variable pump power—three pumps give 395 fps, six pumps 530 fps, 10 pumps 595 fps (average). Full-size adult air rifle. Has white line spacers at pistol grip and buttplate. Introduced 1978. From Crosman.
Price: About **$75.00**
Price: 2200W, about **$120.00**

DAISY MODEL 840
Caliber: 177 pellet single shot; or BB 350-shot. **Barrel:** 19", smoothbore, steel. **Weight:** 2.7 lbs. **Length:** 36.8" overall. **Power:** Pneumatic, single pump. **Stock:** Moulded wood-grain stock and forend. **Sights:** Ramp front, open, adjustable rear. **Features:** Muzzle velocity 335 fps (BB), 300 fps (pellet). Steel buttplate; straight pull bolt action; cross-bolt safety. Forend forms pump lever. Introduced 1978. From Daisy Mfg. Co.
Price: About **$32.95**

DAISY/POWERLINE 853
Caliber: 177 pellets. **Barrel:** 20.9"; 12-groove rifling, high-grade solid steel by Lothar Waltherô, precision crowned; bore size for precision match pellets. **Weight:** 5.08 lbs. **Length:** 38.9" overall. **Power:** Single-pump pneumatic. **Stock:** Full-length, select American hardwood, stained and finished; black buttplate with white spacers. **Sights:** Globe front with four aperture inserts; precision micrometer adjustable rear peep sight mounted on a standard 3/8" dovetail receiver mount. **Features:** Single shot. From Daisy Mfg. Co.
Price: About **$225.00**

DAISY/POWERLINE 856 PUMP-UP AIRGUN
Caliber: 177 pellets (single shot) or BB (100-shot reservoir). **Barrel:** Rifled steel with shroud. **Weight:** 2.7 lbs. **Length:** 37.4" overall. **Power:** Pneumatic pump-up. **Stock:** Moulded wood-grain with Monte Carlo cheekpiece. **Sights:** Ramp front, open rear adjustable for elevation. **Features:** Velocity from 315 fps (two pumps) to 650 fps (10 pumps). Shoots BBs or pellets. Heavy die-cast metal receiver. Cross-bolt trigger-block safety. Introduced 1984. From Daisy Mfg. Co.
Price: **$39.95**

DAISY MODEL 990 DUAL-POWER AIR RIFLE
Caliber: 177 pellets (single shot) or BB (100-shot magazine). **Barrel:** Rifled steel. **Weight:** 4.1 lbs. **Length:** 37.4" overall. **Power:** Pneumatic pump-up and 12-gram CO2. **Stock:** Moulded woodgrain. **Sights:** Ramp and blade front, adjustable open rear. **Features:** Velocity to 650 fps (BB), 630 fps (pellet). Choice of pump or CO2 power. Shoots BBs or pellets. Heavy die-cast receiver dovetailed for scope mount. Cross-bolt trigger block safety. Introduced 1993. From Daisy Mfg. Co.
Price: About **$58.95**

DAISY 1938 RED RYDER 60th ANNIVERSARY CLASSIC
Caliber: BB, 650-shot repeating action. **Barrel:** Smoothbore steel with shroud. **Weight:** 2.2 lbs. **Length:** 35.4" overall. **Stock:** Walnut stock burned with Red Ryder lariat signature. **Sights:** Post front, adjustable V-slot rear. **Features:** Walnut forend. Saddle ring with leather thong. Lever cocking. Gravity feed. Controlled velocity. One of Daisy's most popular guns. From Daisy Mfg. Co.
Price: About **$39.95**

DAISY/POWERLINE 1170 PELLET RIFLE
Caliber: 177, single shot. **Barrel:** Rifled steel. **Weight:** 5.5 lbs. **Length:** 42.5" overall. **Power:** Spring-air, barrel cocking. **Stock:** Hardwood. **Sights:** Hooded post front, micrometer adjustable open rear. **Features:** Velocity to 800 fps. Monte Carlo comb. Introduced 1995. From Daisy Mfg. Co.
Price: About **$129.95**
Price: Model 131 (velocity to 600 fps) **$117.95**
Price: Model 1150 (black copolymer stock, velocity to 600 fps). **$77.95**

DAISY/POWERLINE EAGLE 7856 PUMP-UP AIRGUN
Caliber: 177 (pellets), BB, 100-shot BB magazine. **Barrel:** Rifled steel with shroud. **Weight:** 3.3 lbs. **Length:** 37.4" overall. **Power:** Pneumatic pump-up. **Stock:** Moulded wood-grain plastic. **Sights:** Ramp and blade front, open rear adjustable for elevation. **Features:** Velocity from 315 fps (two pumps) to 650 fps (10 pumps). Finger grooved forend. Cross-bolt trigger-block safety. Introduced 1985. From Daisy Mfg. Co.
Price: With 4x scope, about **$49.95**

DAISY/POWERLINE 880
Caliber: 177 pellet or BB, 50-shot BB magazine, single shot for pellets. **Barrel:** Rifled steel. **Weight:** 3.7 lbs. **Length:** 37.6" overall. **Power:** Multi-pump pneumatic. **Stock:** Moulded wood grain; Monte Carlo comb. **Sights:** Hooded front, adjustable rear. **Features:** Velocity to 685 fps. (BB). Variable power (velocity and range) increase with pump strokes; resin receiver with dovetail scope mount. Introduced 1997. Made in U.S. by Daisy Mfg. Co.
Price: About **$50.95**
Price: Model 4880 with Glo-Point fiber optic sight **$57.95**

DAISY/POWERLINE 1000 AIR RIFLE
Caliber: 177, single shot. **Barrel:** NA. **Weight:** 6.15 lbs. **Length:** 43" overall. **Power:** Spring-air, barrel cocking. **Stock:** Stained hardwood. **Sights:** Hooded blade front on ramp, fully adjustable micrometer rear. **Features:** Velocity to 1000 fps. Blued finish; trigger block safety. Introduced 1997. From Daisy Mfg. Co.
Price: About **$208.95**

DAISY/YOUTHLINE MODEL 105 AIR RIFLE
Caliber: BB, 400-shot magazine. **Barrel:** 13-1/2". **Weight:** 1.6 lbs. **Length:** 29.8" overall. **Power:** Spring. **Stock:** Moulded woodgrain. **Sights:** Blade on ramp front, fixed rear. **Features:** Velocity to 275 fps. Blue finish. Cross-bolt trigger block safety. Made in U.S. by Daisy Mfg. Co.
Price: **$28.95**

DAISY/YOUTHLINE MODEL 95 AIR RIFLE
Caliber: BB, 700-shot magazine. **Barrel:** 18". **Weight:** 2.4 lbs. **Length:** 35.2" overall. **Power:** Spring. **Stock:** Stained hardwood. **Sights:** Blade on ramp front, open adjustable rear. **Features:** Velocity to 325 fps. Cross-bolt trigger block safety. Made in U.S. by Daisy Mfg. Co.
Price: **$38.95**

EAA/BAIKAL IZH-32BK AIR RIFLE
Caliber: 177 pellet, single shot. **Barrel:** 11.68". **Weight:** 12.13 lbs. **Length:** 47.24" overall. **Power:** Single-stroke pneumatic. **Stock:** Walnut with full pistol grip, adjustable cheek piece and butt plate. **Sights:** None; integral rail for scope mount. **Features:** Velocity 541 fps. Side-cocking mechanism; hammer-forged, rifled barrel; five-way adjustable trigger. Designed for 10-meter running target competition. Introduced 2000. Imported from Russia by European American Armory.
Price: **$1,099.00**

EAA/BAIKAL IZH-61 AIR RIFLE
Caliber: 177 pellet, 5-shot magazine. **Barrel:** 17.75". **Weight:** 6.39 lbs. **Length:** 30.98" overall. **Power:** Spring piston, side-cocking lever. **Stock:** Black plastic. **Sights:** Adjustable rear, fully hooded front. **Features:** Velocity 490 fps. Futuristic design with adjustable stock. Imported from Russia by European American Armory.
Price: **$99.00**

EAA/BAIKAL MP-512 AIR RIFLE
Caliber: 177 or 22 pellet, single shot. **Barrel:** 17.7". **Weight:** 6.17 lbs. **Length:** 41.34" overall. **Power:** Spring-piston, single stroke. **Stock:** Black synthetic. **Sights:** Adjustable rear, hooded front. **Features:** Velocity 490 fps. Hammer-forged, rifled barrel; automatic safety; scope mount rail. Introduced 2000. Imported from Russia by European American Armory.
Price: 177 caliber **$50.00**
Price: 22 caliber **$63.00**

EAA/BAIKAL MP-532 AIR RIFLE
Caliber: 177 pellet, single shot. **Barrel:** 15.75". **Weight:** 9.26 lbs. **Length:** 46.06" overall. **Power:** Single-stroke pneumatic. **Stock:** One- or two-piece competition-style stock with adjustable butt pad, pistol grip. **Sights:** Fully adjustable rear, hooded front. **Features:** Velocity 460 fps. Five-way adjustable trigger. Introduced 2000. Imported from Russia by European American Armory.
Price: **$599.00**

HAMMERLI AR 50 AIR RIFLE
Caliber: 177. **Barrel:** 19.8". **Weight:** 10 lbs. **Length:** 43.2" overall. **Power:** Compressed air. **Stock:** Anatomically-shaped universal and right-hand; match style; multi-colored laminated wood. **Sights:** Interchangeable element tunnel front, fully adjustable Hammerli peep rear. **Features:** Vibration-free firing release; fully adjustable match trigger and trigger stop; stainless air tank, built-in pressure gauge. Gives 270 shots per filling. Introduced 1998. Imported from Switzerland by Sigarms, Inc.
Price: . . . . **$1,062.50 to $1,400.00**

HAMMERLI MODEL 450 MATCH AIR RIFLE
Caliber: 177, single shot. **Barrel:** 19.5". **Weight:** 9.8 lbs. **Length:** 43.3" overall. **Power:** Pneumatic. **Stock:** Match style with stippled grip, rubber buttpad. Beach or walnut. **Sights:** Match tunnel front, Hammerli diopter rear. **Features:** Velocity about 560 fps. Removable sights; forend sling rail; adjustable trigger; adjustable comb. Introduced 1994. Imported from Switzerland by Sigarms, Inc.
Price: Beech stock **$1,355.00**
Price: Walnut stock **$1,395.00**

AIRGUNS

MARKSMAN BB BUDDY AIR RIFLE

Caliber: 177, 20-shot magazine. **Barrel:** 10.5" smoothbore. **Weight:** 1.6 lbs. **Length:** 33" overall. **Power:** Spring-air. **Stock:** Moulded composition. **Sights:** Blade on ramp front, adjustable V-slot rear. **Features:** Velocity 275 fps. Positive feed; automatic safety. Youth-sized lightweight design. Introduced 1998. Made in U.S. From Marksman Products.

Price: $27.95

MARKSMAN 1798 COMPETITION TRAINER AIR RIFLE

Caliber: 177, single shot. **Barrel:** 15", rifled. **Weight:** 4.7 lbs. **Power:** Spring-air, barrel cocking. **Stock:** Synthetic. **Sights:** Laserhawk fiber optic front, match-style diopter rear. **Features:** Velocity about 495 fps. Automatic safety. Introduced 1998. Made in U.S. From Marksman Products.

Price: $70.00

MARKSMAN 1745 BB REPEATER AIR RIFLE

Caliber: 177 BB or pellet, 18-shot BB reservoir. **Barrel:** 15-1/2", rifled. **Weight:** 4.75 lbs. **Length:** 36" overall. **Power:** Spring-air. **Stock:** Moulded composition with ambidextrous Monte Carlo cheekpiece and rubber recoil pad. **Sights:** Hooded front, adjustable rear. **Features:** Velocity about 450 fps. Break-barrel action; automatic safety. Uses BBs, pellets, darts or bolts. Introduced 1997. Made in the U.S. From Marksman Products.

Price: $58.00
Price: Model 1745S (same as above except comes with #1804 4x20 scope) . $73.00

MARKSMAN 1790 BIATHLON TRAINER

Caliber: 177, single shot. **Barrel:** 15", rifled. **Weight:** 4.7 lbs. **Power:** Spring-air, barrel cocking. **Stock:** Synthetic. **Sights:** Hooded front, match-style diopter rear. **Features:** Velocity of 450 fps. Endorsed by the U.S. Shooting Team. Introduced 1989. From Marksman Products.

Price: $70.00

MARKSMAN 2015 LASERHAWK™ BB REPEATER AIR RIFLE

Caliber: 177 BB, 20-shot magazine. **Barrel:** 10.5" smoothbore. **Weight:** 1.6 lbs. **Length:** Adjustable to 33", 34" or 35" overall. **Power:** Spring-air. **Stock:** Moulded composition. **Sights:** Fixed fiber optic front sight, adjustable elevation V-slot rear. **Features:** Velocity about 275 fps. Positive feed; automatic safety. Adjustable stock. Introduced 1997. Made in the U.S. From Marksman Products.

Price: $33.00

RWS/DIANA MODEL 24 AIR RIFLE

Caliber: 177, 22, single shot. **Barrel:** 17", rifled. **Weight:** 6 lbs. **Length:** 42" overall. **Power:** Spring-air, barrel cocking. **Stock:** Beech. **Sights:** Hooded front, adjustable rear. **Features:** Velocity of 700 fps (177). Easy cocking effort; blue finish. Imported from Germany by Dynamit Nobel-RWS, Inc.

Price: 24, 24C $225.00

RWS/Diana Model 34 Air Rifle

Similar to the Model 24 except has 19" barrel, weighs 7.5 lbs. Gives velocity of 1000 fps (177), 800 fps (22). Adjustable trigger, synthetic seals. Comes with scope rail.

Price: 177 or 22 . . . . $395.00
Price: Model 34N (nickel-plated metal, black epoxy-coated wood stock) . . . $365.00
Price: Model 34BC (matte black metal, black stock, 4x32 scope, mounts) . . $395.00

RWS/DIANA MODEL 36 AIR RIFLE

Caliber: 177, 22, single shot. **Barrel:** 19", rifled. **Weight:** 8 lbs. **Length:** 45" overall. **Power:** Spring-air, barrel cocking. **Stock:** Beech. **Sights:** Hooded front (interchangeable inserts available), adjustable rear. **Features:** Velocity of 1000 fps (177-cal.). Comes with scope mount; two-stage adjustable trigger. Imported from Germany by Dynamit Nobel-RWS, Inc.

Price: 36, 36C $429.00

RWS/DIANA MODEL 52 AIR RIFLE

Caliber: 177, 22, single shot. **Barrel:** 17", rifled. **Weight:** 8-1/2 lbs. **Length:** 43" overall. **Power:** Spring-air, sidelever cocking. **Stock:** Beech, with Monte Carlo, cheekpiece, checkered grip and forend. **Sights:** Ramp front, adjustable rear. **Features:** Velocity of 1100 fps (177). Blue finish. Solid rubber buttpad. Imported from Germany by Dynamit Nobel-RWS, Inc.

Price: $575.00
Price: Model 48B (as above except matte black metal, black stock) $535.00
Price: Model 48 (same as Model 52 except no Monte Carlo, cheekpiece or checkering) $520.00

RWS/DIANA MODEL 45 AIR RIFLE

Caliber: 177, single shot. **Weight:** 8 lbs. **Length:** 45" overall. **Power:** Spring-air, barrel cocking. **Stock:** Walnut-finished hardwood with rubber recoil pad. **Sights:** Globe front with interchangeable inserts, micro. click open rear with four-way blade. **Features:** Velocity of 820 fps. Dovetail base for either micrometer peep sight or scope mounting. Automatic safety. Imported from Germany by Dynamit Nobel-RWS, Inc.

Price: $350.00

RWS/DIANA MODEL 46 AIR RIFLE

Caliber: 177, 22, single shot. **Barrel:** 18". **Weight:** 8.2 lbs. **Length:** 45" overall. **Stock:** Hardwood Monte Carlo. **Sights:** Blade front, adjustable rear. **Features:** Underlever cocking spring-air (950 fps in 177, 780 fps in 22); extended scope rail, automatic safety, rubber buttpad, adjustable trigger. Imported from Germany by Dynamit Nobel-RWS Inc.

Price: $515.00

RWS/DIANA MODEL 54 AIR RIFLE

Caliber: 177, 22, single shot. **Barrel:** 17". **Weight:** 9 lbs. **Length:** 43" overall. **Power:** Spring-air, sidelever cocking. **Stock:** Walnut with Monte Carlo cheekpiece, checkered grip and forend. **Sights:** Ramp front, fully adjustable rear. **Features:** Velocity to 1000 fps (177), 900 fps (22). Totally recoilless system; floating action absorbs recoil. Imported from Germany by Dynamit Nobel-RWS, Inc.

Price: $795.00

RWS/DIANA MODEL 93/94 AIR RIFLES

Caliber: 177, 22, single shot. **Barrel:** N/A. **Weight:** N/A. **Length:** N/A. **Stock:** Beechwood; Monte Carlo. **Sights:** Hooded front, fully adjustable rear. **Features:** Break-barrel, spring-air; receiver grooved for scope; adjustable trigger; lifetime warranty. Imported from Spain by Dynamit Nobel-RWS Inc.

Price: Model 93 (manual safety, 850 fps in 177) $180.00
Price: Model 94 (auto safety, 1,000 fps in 177) $240.00

RWS/DIANA MODEL 350 MAGNUM AIR RIFLE

Caliber: 177, single shot. **Barrel:** 19-1/2". **Weight:** 8 lbs. **Length:** 48". **Stock:** Beechwood; Monte Carlo. **Sights:** Hooded front, fully adjustable rear. **Features:** Break-barrel, spring-air; 1,250 fps. Imported from Germany by Dynamit Nobel-RWS Inc.

Price: Model 350 . . . . $525.00

RWS/DIANA MODEL 707/EXCALIBRE AIR RIFLES

Caliber: 22, 25, 9mm, 8-shot lever-action repeater or side-loading single shot. **Barrel:** 23". **Weight:** 7 to 9 1/4 lbs. **Length:** 40" to 42" overall. **Stock:** Checkered walnut. **Sights:** Hooded post front, fully adjustable rear (Excalibre has no sights, integral scope grooves). **Features:** Pre-charged pneumatic stores compressed air from SCUBA tank or optional hand pump in reservoir for 18 to 30 shots at full power (adjustable power to 1,200 fps in 22 cal.); pressure gauge; adjustable trigger (9mm and Excalibre). Imported from Germany by Dynamit Nobel-RWS Inc.

Price: 707 (22, 25, 9 mm) $730.00
Price: 707 Carbine (22) $730.00

TECH FORCE BS4 OLYMPIC COMPETITION AIR RIFLE

Caliber: 177 pellet, single shot. **Barrel:** N/A. **Weight:** 10.8 lbs. **Length:** 43.3" overall. **Power:** Spring piston, sidelever action. **Stock:** Wood with semi-pistol grip, adjustable butt plate. **Sights:** Micro-adjustable competition rear, hooded front. **Features:** Velocity 640 fps. Recoilless action; adjustable trigger. Includes carrying case. Imported from China by Compasseco Inc.

Price: $595.00
Price: Optional diopter rear sight $79.95

TECH FORCE 6 AIR RIFLE

Caliber: 177 pellet, single shot. **Barrel:** 14". **Weight:** 6 lbs. **Length:** 35.5" overall. **Power:** Sspring piston, sidelever action. **Stock:** Paratrooper-style folding, full pistol grip. **Sights:** Adjustable rear, hooded front. **Features:** Velocity 800 fps. All-metal construction; grooved for scope mounting. Imported from China by Compasseco Inc.

Price: $69.95

Tech Force 51 Air Rifle

Similar to Tech Force 6, but with break-barrel cocking mechanism and folding stock fitted with recoil pad. Overall length, 36". Weighs 6 lbs. From Compasseco Inc.

Price: $69.95

TECH FORCE 25 AIR RIFLE

Caliber: 177, 22 pellet; single shot. **Barrel:** N/A. **Weight:** 7.5 lbs. **Length:** 46.2" overall. **Power:** Spring piston, break-action barrel. **Stock:** Oil-finished wood; Monte Carlo stock with recoil pad. **Sights:** Adjustable rear, hooded front with insert. **Features:** Velocity 1,000 fps (177); grooved receiver and scope stop for scope mounting; adjustable trigger; trigger safety. Imported from China by Compasseco Inc.

Price:177 or 22 caliber $125.00
Price: Includes rifle and Tech Force 96 red dot point sight $164.95

TECH FORCE 36 AIR RIFLE

Caliber: 177 pellet, single shot. **Barrel:** N/A. **Weight:** 7.4 lbs. **Length:** 43" overall. **Power:** Spring piston, underlever cocking. **Stock:** Monte Carlo hardwood stock; recoil pad. **Sights:** Adjustable rear, hooded front. **Features:** Velocity 900 fps; grooved receiver and scope stop for scope mounting; auto-reset safety. Imported from China by Compasseco Inc.

Price: $89.95

WHISCOMBE JW SERIES AIR RIFLES

Caliber: 177, 20, 22, 25, single shot. **Barrel:** 15", Lothar Walther. Polygonal rifling. **Weight:** 9 lbs., 8 oz. **Length:** 39" overall. **Power:** Dual spring-piston, multi-stroke; underlever cocking. **Stock:** Walnut with adjustable buttplate and cheekpiece. **Sights:** None furnished; grooved scope rail. **Features:** Velocity 660-1000 (JW80) fps (22-caliber, fixed barrel) depending upon model. Interchangeable barrels; automatic safety; muzzle weight; semi-floating action; twin opposed pistons with counter-wound springs; adjustable trigger. All models include H.O.T. System (Harmonic Optimization Tunable System). Introduced 1995. Imported from England by Pelaire Products.

Price: JW50, MKII fixed barrel only $2,085.00
Price: JW65, MKII. $2,085.00
Price: JW80, MKII. $2,195.00

AIRGUNS

CH4D Heavyduty Champion

Frame: Cast iron
Frame Type: O-frame
Die Thread: 7/8-14 or 1-14
Avg. Rounds Per Hour: NA
Ram Stroke: 3-1/4"
Weight: 26 lbs.
Features: 1.185" diameter ram with 16 square inches of bearing surface; ram drilled to allow passage of spent primers; solid steel handle; toggle that slightly breaks over the top dead center. Includes universal primer arm with large and small punches. From CH Tool & Die/4D Custom Die.
Price: **$220.00**

CH4D No. 444 4-Station "H" Press

Frame: Aluminum alloy
Frame Type: H-frame
Die Thread: 7/8-14
Avg. Rounds Per Hour: 200
Ram Stroke: 3-3/4"
Weight: 12 lbs.
Features: Two 7/8" solid steel shaft "H" supports; platen rides on permanently lubed bronze bushings; loads smallest pistol to largest magnum rifle cases and has strength to full-length resize. Includes four rams, large and small primer arm and primer catcher. From CH Tool & Die/4D Custom Die, Co.
Price: **$195.00**

CH4D No. 444-X Pistol Champ

Frame: Aluminum alloy
Frame Type: H-frame
Die Thread: 7/8-14
Avg. Rounds Per Hour: 200
Ram Stroke: 3-3/4"
Weight: 12 lbs.
Features: Tungsten carbide sizing die; Speed Seater seating die with tapered entrance to automatically align bullet on case mouth; automatic primer feed for large or small primers; push-button powder measure with easily changed bushings for 215 powder/load combinations; taper crimp die. Conversion kit for caliber changeover available. From CH Tool & Die/4D Custom Die, Co.
Price: . . . . **$292.00-$316.50**

FORSTER Co-Ax Press B-2

Frame: Cast iron
Frame Type: Modified O-frame
Die Thread: 7/8-14
Avg. Rounds Per Hour: 120
Ram Stroke: 4"
Weight: 18 lbs.
Features: Snap in/snap out die change; spent primer catcher with drop tube threaded into carrier below shellholder; automatic, handle-activated, cammed shellholder with opposing spring-loaded jaws to contact extractor groove; floating guide rods for alignment and reduced friction; no torque on the head due to design of linkage and pivots; shellholder jaws that float with die permitting case to center in the die; right- or left-hand operation; priming device for seating to factory specifications. "S" shellholder jaws included. From Forster Products.
Price: **$298.00**
Price: Extra shellholder jaws **$26.00**

HOLLYWOOD Senior Press

Frame: Ductile iron
Frame Type: O-frame
Die Thread: 7/8-14
Avg. Rounds Per Hour: 50-100
Ram Stroke: 6-1/2"
Weight: 50 lbs.
Features: Leverage and bearing surfaces ample for reloading cartridges or swaging bullets. Precision ground one-piece 2-1/2" pillar with base; operating handle of 3/4" steel and 15" long; 5/8" steel tie-down rod fro added strength when swaging; heavy steel toggle and camming arms held by 1/2" steel pins in reamed holes. The 1-1/2" steel die bushing takes standard threaded dies; removed, it allows use of Hollywood shotshell dies. From Hollywood Engineering.
Price: **$500.00**

HOLLYWOOD Senior Turret Press

Frame: Ductile iron
Frame Type: H-frame
Die Thread: 7/8-14
Avg. Rounds Per Hour: 50-100
Ram Stroke: 6-1/2"
Weight: 50 lbs.
Features: Same features as Senior press except has three-position turret head; holes in turret may be tapped 1-1/2" or 7/8" or four of each. Height, 15". Comes complete with one turret indexing handle; one 1-1/2" to 7/8" die hole bushing; one 5/8" tie down bar for swaging. From Hollywood Engineering.
Price: **$600.00**

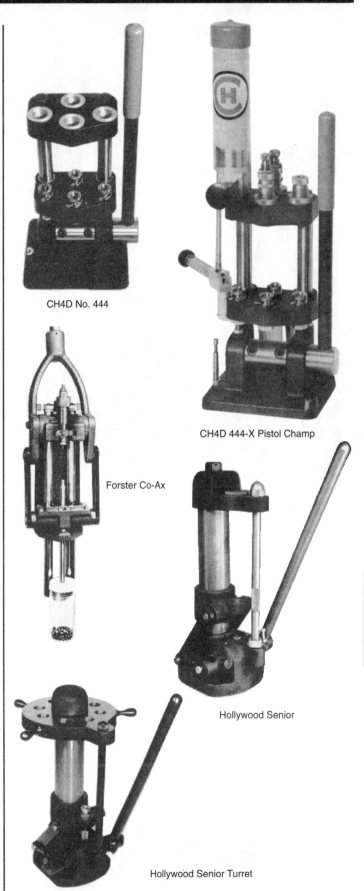

CH4D No. 444

CH4D 444-X Pistol Champ

Forster Co-Ax

Hollywood Senior

Hollywood Senior Turret

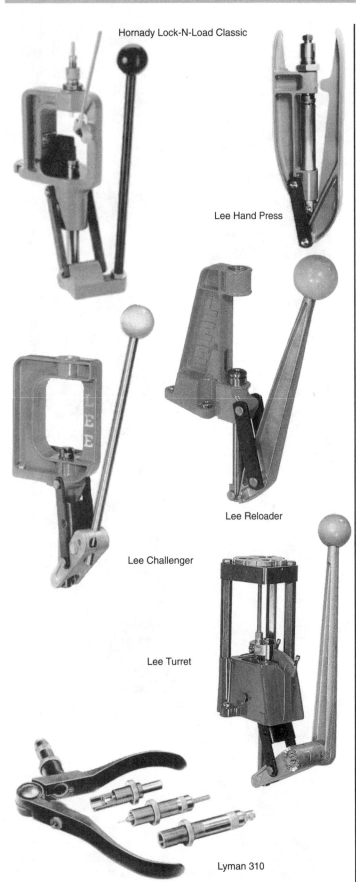

Hornady Lock-N-Load Classic

Lee Hand Press

Lee Reloader

Lee Challenger

Lee Turret

Lyman 310

HORNADY Lock-N-Load Classic

Frame: Die cast heat-treated aluminum alloy
Frame Type: O-frame
Die Thread: 7/8-14
Avg. Rounds Per Hour: NA
Ram Stroke: 3-5/8"
Weight: 14 lbs.

Features: Features Lock-N-Load bushing system that allows instant die changeovers. Solid steel linkage arms that rotate on steel pins; 30° angled frame design for improved visibility and accessibility; primer arm automatically moves in and out of ram for primer pickup and solid seating; two primer arms for large and small primers; long offset handle for increased leverage and unobstructed reloading; lifetime warranty. Comes as a package with primer catcher, PPS automatic primer feed and three Lock-N-Load die bushings. Dies and shellholder available separately or as a kit with primer catcher, positive priming system, automatic primer feed, three die bushings and reloading accessories. From Hornady Mfg. Co.
Price: Press and Three Die Bushings $99.95
Price: Classic Reloading Kit. $259.95

LEE Hand Press

Frame: ASTM 380 aluminum
Frame Type: NA
Die Thread: 7/8-14
Avg. Rounds Per Hour: 100
Ram Stroke: 3-1/4"
Weight: 1 lb., 8 oz.

Features: Small and lightweight for portability; compound linkage for handling up to 375 H&H and case forming. Dies and shellholder not included. From Lee Precision, Inc.
Price: $22.98

LEE Challenger Press

Frame: ASTM 380 aluminum
Frame Type: O-frame
Die Thread: 7/8-14
Avg. Rounds Per Hour: 100
Ram Stroke: 3-1/2"
Weight: 4 lbs., 1 oz.

Features: Larger than average opening with 30° offset for maximum hand clearance; steel connecting pins; spent primer catcher; handle adjustable for start and stop positions; handle repositions for left- or right-hand use; shortened handle travel to prevent springing the frame from alignment. Dies and shellholders not included. From Lee Precision, Inc.
Price: $45.00

LEE Loader

Kit consists of reloading dies to be used with mallet or soft hammer. Neck sizes only. Comes with powder charge cup. From Lee Precision, Inc.
Price: $19.98

LEE Reloader Press

Frame: ASTM 380 aluminum
Frame Type: C-frame
Die Thread: 7/8-14
Avg. Rounds Per Hour: 100
Ram Stroke: 3"
Weight: 1 lb., 12 oz.

Features: Balanced lever to prevent pinching fingers; unlimited hand clearance; left- or right-hand use. Dies and shellholders not included. From Lee Precision, Inc.
Price: $24.98

LEE Turret Press

Frame: ASTM 380 aluminum
Frame Type: O-frame
Die Thread: 7/8-14
Avg. Rounds Per Hour: 300
Ram Stroke: 3"
Weight: 7 lbs., 2 oz.

Features: Replaceable turret lifts out by rotating 30°; T-primer arm reverses for large or small primers; built-in primer catcher; adjustable handle for right- or left-hand use or changing angle of down stroke; accessory mounting hole for Lee Auto-Disk powder measure. Optional Auto-Index rotates die turret to next station for semi-progressive use. Safety override prevents overstressing should turret not turn. From Lee Precision, Inc.
Price: $69.98
Price: With Auto-Index $83.98
Price: Four-Hole Turret with Auto-Index $85.98

LYMAN 310 Tool

Frame: Stainless steel
Frame Type: NA
Die Thread: 7/8-14
Avg. Rounds Per Hour: NA
Ram Stroke: NA
Weight: 10 oz.

Features: Compact, portable reloading tool for pistol or rifle cartridges. Adapter allows loading rimmed or rimless cases. Die set includes neck resizing/decapping die, primer seating chamber; neck expanding die; bullet seating die; and case head adapter. From Lyman Products Corp.
Price: Dies $45.00
Price: Handles $47.50
Price: Carrying pouch. $9.95

ACCESSORIES

LYMAN AccuPress

Frame: Die cast
Frame Type: C-frame
Die Thread: 7/8-14
Avg. Rounds Per Hour: 75
Ram Stroke: 3.4"
Weight: 4 lbs.
Features: Reversible, contoured handle for bench mount or hand-held use; for rifle or pistol; compound leverage; Delta frame design. Accepts all standard powder measures. From Lyman Products Corp.
Price: $34.95

LYMAN Crusher II

Frame: Cast iron
Frame Type: O-frame
Die Thread: 7/8-14
Avg. Rounds Per Hour: 75
Ram Stroke: 3-7/8"
Weight: 19 lbs.
Features: Reloads both pistol and rifle cartridges; 1" diameter ram; 4-1/2" press opening for loading magnum cartridges; direct torque design; right- or left-hand use. New base design with 14 square inches of flat mounting surface with three bolt holes. Comes with priming arm and primer catcher. Dies and shellholders not included. From Lyman Products Corp.
Price: $116.50

LYMAN T-Mag II

Frame: Cast iron with silver metalflake powder finish
Frame Type: Turret
Die Thread: 7/8-14
Avg. Rounds Per Hour: 125
Ram Stroke: 3-13/16"
Weight: 18 lbs.
Features: Reengineered and upgraded with new turret system for ease of indexing and tool-free turret removal for caliber changeover; new flat machined base for bench mounting; new nickel-plated non-rust handle and links; and new silver hammertone powder coat finish for durability. Right- or left-hand operation; handles all rifle or pistol dies. Comes with priming arm and primer catcher. Dies and shellholders not included. From Lyman Products Corp.
Price: $164.95
Price: Extra turret $37.50

PONSNESS/WARREN Metal-Matic P-200

Frame: Die cast aluminum
Frame Type: Unconventional
Die Thread: 7/8-14
Avg. Rounds Per Hour: 200+
Weight: 18 lbs.
Features: Designed for straight-wall cartridges; die head with 10 tapped holes for holding dies and accessories for two calibers at one time; removable spent primer box; pivoting arm moves case from station to station. Comes with large and small primer tool. Optional accessories include primer feed, extra die head, primer speed feeder, powder measure extension and dust cover. Dies, powder measure and shellholder not included. From Ponsness/Warren.
Price: $215.00
Price: Extra die head $44.95
Price: Powder measure extension $29.95
Price: Primer feed $44.95
Price: Primer speed feed $14.50
Price: Dust cover $21.95

RCBS Partner

Frame: Aluminum
Frame Type: O-frame
Die Thread: 7/8-14
Avg. Rounds Per Hour: 50-60
Ram Stroke: 3-5/8"
Weight: 5 lbs.
Features: Designed for the beginning reloader. Comes with primer arm equipped with interchangeable primer plugs and sleeves for seating large and small primers. Shellholder and dies not included. Available in kit form (see Metallic Presses—Accessories). From RCBS.
Price: $61.95

RCBS AmmoMaster Single

Frame: Aluminum base; cast iron top plate connected by three steel posts.
Frame Type: NA
Die Thread: 1-1/4"-12 bushing; 7/8-14 threads
Avg. Rounds Per Hour: 50-60
Ram Stroke: 5-1/4"
Weight: 19 lbs.
Features: Single-stage press convertible to progressive. Will form cases or swage bullets. Case detection system to disengage powder measure when no case is present in powder charging station; five-station shellplate; Uniflow Powder measure with clear powder measure adaptor to make bridged powders visible and correctable. 50-cal. conversion kit allows reloading 50 BMG. Kit includes top plate to accommodate either 1-3/8" x 12 or 1-1/2" x 12 reloading dies. Piggyback die plate for quick caliber change-overs available. Reloading dies not included. From RCBS.
Price: $206.95

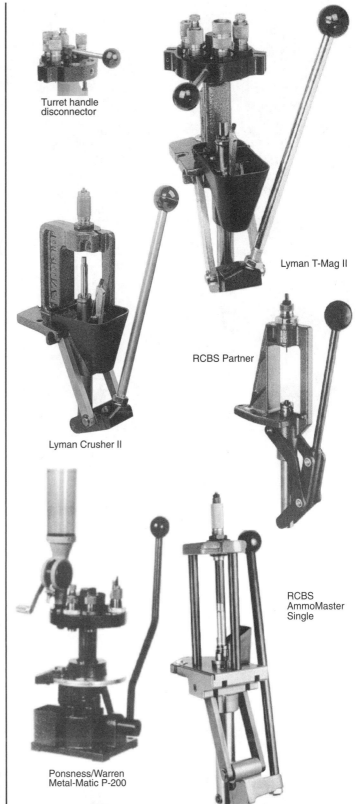

Turret handle disconnector

Lyman T-Mag II

RCBS Partner

Lyman Crusher II

RCBS AmmoMaster Single

Ponsness/Warren Metal-Matic P-200

Price: 50 conversion kit $96.95
Price: Piggyback/AmmoMaster die plate $25.95
Price: Piggyback/AmmoMaster shellplate $25.95
Price: Press cover $10.95

ACCESSORIES

RCBS Reloader Special-5

RCBS Rock Chucker

Redding Model 25

Redding Boss

Rock Crusher

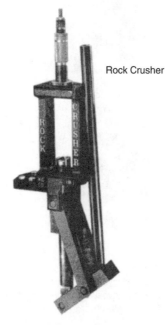

Redding Ultramag

RCBS Reloader Special-5

Frame: Aluminum
Frame Type: 30˚ offset O-frame
Die Thread: 1-1/4"-12 bushing; 7/8-14 threads
Avg. Rounds Per Hour: 50-60
Ram Stroke: 3-1/16"
Weight: 7.5 lbs.
Features: Single-stage press convertible to progressive with RCBS Piggyback II. Primes cases during resizing operation. Will accept RCBS shotshell dies. From RCBS.
Price:... $112.95

RCBS Rock Chucker

Frame: Cast iron
Frame Type: O-frame
Die Thread: 1-1/4"-12 bushing; 7/8-14 threads
Avg. Rounds Per Hour: 50-60
Ram Stroke: 3-1/16"
Weight: 17 lbs.
Features: Designed for heavy-duty reloading, case forming and bullet swaging. Provides 4" of ram-bearing surface to support 1" ram and ensure alignment; ductile-iron toggle blocks; hardened steel pins. Comes standard with Universal Primer Arm and primer catcher. Can be converted from single-stage to progressive with Piggyback II conversion unit. From RCBS.
Price:... $141.95

REDDING Turret Press

Frame: Cast iron
Frame Type: Turret
Die Thread: 7/8-14
Avg. Rounds Per Hour: NA
Ram Stroke: 3.4"
Weight: 23 lbs., 2 oz.
Features: Strength to reload pistol and magnum rifle, case form and bullet swage; linkage pins heat-treated, precision ground and in double shear; hollow ram to collect spent primers; removable turret head for caliber changes; progressive linkage for increased power as ram nears die; slight frame tilt for comfortable operation; rear turret support for stability and precise alignment; six-station turret head; priming arm for both large and small primers. Also available in kit form with shellholder, primer catcher and one die set. From Redding Reloading Equipment.
Price:... $298.50
Price: Kit $336.00

REDDING Boss

Frame: Cast iron
Frame Type: O-frame
Die Thread: 7/8-14
Avg. Rounds Per Hour: NA
Ram Stroke: 3.4"
Weight: 11 lbs., 8 oz.
Features: 36˚ frame offset for visibility and accessibility; primer arm positioned at bottom ram travel; positive ram travel stop machined to hit exactly top-dead-center. Also available in kit form with shellholder and set of Redding A dies. From Redding Reloading Equipment.
Price:... $135.00
Price: Kit $172.00

REDDING Ultramag

Frame: Cast iron
Frame Type: Non-conventional
Die Thread: 7/8-14
Avg. Rounds Per Hour: NA
Ram Stroke: 4-1/8"
Weight: 23 lbs., 6 oz.
Features: Unique compound leverage system connected to top of press for tons of ram pressure; large 4-3/4" frame opening for loading outsized cartridges; hollow ram for spent primers. Kit available with shellholder and one set Redding A dies. From Redding Reloading Equipment.
Price:... $298.50
Price: Kit $336.00

ROCK CRUSHER Press

Frame: Cast iron
Frame Type: O-frame
Die Thread: 2-3/4"-12 with bushing reduced to 1-1/2"-12
Avg. Rounds Per Hour: 50
Ram Stroke: 6"
Weight: 67 lbs.
Features: Designed to load and form ammunition from 50 BMG up to 23x115 Soviet. Frame opening of 8-1/2"x3-1/2"; 1-1/2"x12"; bushing can be removed and bushings of any size substituted; ram pressure can exceed 10,000 lbs. with normal body weight; 40mm diameter ram. Angle block for bench mounting and reduction bushing for RCBS dies available. Accessories for Rock Crusher include powder measure, dies, shellholder, bullet puller, priming tool, case gauge and other accessories found elsewhere in this catalog. From The Old Western Scrounger.
Price:... $795.00
Price: Angle block $57.95
Price: Reduction bushing $21.00
Price: Shellholder $47.25
Price: Priming tool, 50 BMG, 20 Lahti $65.10

METALLIC CARTRIDGE PRESSES

PROGRESSIVE PRESSES

CORBIN BENCHREST S-PRESS

Frame: All steel
Frame Type: O-Frame
Die Thread: 7/8-14 and
T-slot adapter
Avg. Rounds Per Hour: NA
Ram Stroke: 4'
Weight: 22 lbs.
Features: Roller bearing linkage, removeable head, right- or left-hand mount.
Price: **$269.50**

DILLON AT 500

Frame: Aluminum alloy
Frame Type: NA
Die Thread: 7/8-14
Avg. Rounds Per Hour: 200-300
Ram Stroke: 3-7/8"
Weight: NA
Features: Four stations; removable tool head to hold dies in alignment and allow caliber changes without die adjustment; manual indexing; capacity to be upgraded to progressive RL 550B. Comes with universal shellplate to accept 223, 22-250, 243, 30-06, 9mm, 38/357, 40 S&W, 45 ACP. Dies not included. From Dillon Precision Products.
Price: **$193.95**

DILLON RL 550B

Frame: Aluminum alloy
Frame Type: NA
Die Thread: 7/8-14
Avg. Rounds Per Hour: 500-600
Ram Stroke: 3-7/8"
Weight: 25 lbs.
Features: Four stations; removable tool head to hold dies in alignment and allow caliber changes without die adjustment; auto priming system that emits audible warning when primer tube is low; a 100-primer capacity magazine contained in DOM steel tube for protection; new auto powder measure system with simple mechanical connection between measure and loading platform for positive powder bar return; a separate station for crimping with star-indexing system; 220 ejected-round capacity bin; 3/4-lb. capacity powder measure. Height above bench, 35"; requires 3/4" bench overhang. Will reload 120 different rifle and pistol calibers. Comes with one caliber conversion kit. Dies not included. From Dillon Precision Products, Inc.
Price: **$325.95**

DILLON RL 1050

Frame: Ductile iron
Frame Type: Platform type
Die Thread: 7/8-14
Avg. Rounds Per Hour: 1000-1200
Ram Stroke: 2-5/16"
Weight: 62 lbs.
Features: Eight stations; auto case feed; primer pocket swager for military cartridge cases; auto indexing; removable tool head; auto prime system with 100-primer capacity; low primer supply alarm; positive powder bar return; auto powder measure; 515 ejected round bin capacity; 500-600 case feed capacity; 3/4-lb. capacity powder measure. Loads all pistol rounds as well as 30 M1 Carbine, 223, and 7.62x39 rifle rounds. Height above the bench, 43". Dies not included. From Dillon Precision Products, Inc.
Price: **$1,199.95**

DILLON Super 1050

Similar to RL1050, but has lengthened frame and short-stroke crank to accommodate long calibers.
Price: **$1,299.95**

DILLON Square Deal B

Frame: Zinc alloy
Frame Type: NA
Die Thread: None
(unique Dillon design)
Avg. Rounds Per Hour: 400-500
Ram Stroke: 2-5/16"
Weight: 17 lbs.
Features: Four stations; auto indexing; removable tool head; auto prime system with 100-primer capacity; low primer supply alarm; auto powder measure; positive powder bar return; 170 ejected round capacity bin; 3/4-lb. capacity powder measure. Height above the bench, 34". Comes complete with factory adjusted carbide die set. From Dillon Precision Products, Inc.
Price: **$252.95**

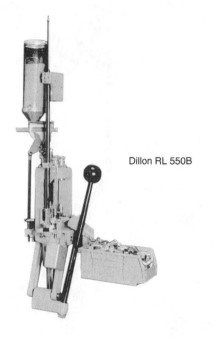

Dillon RL 550B

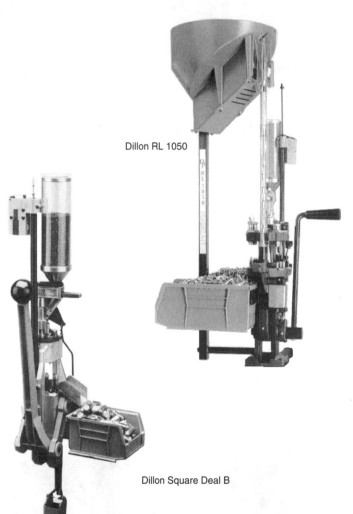

Dillon RL 1050

Dillon Square Deal B

ACCESSORIES

Hornady Lock-N-Load AP

Dillon XL 650

Lee Pro 1000

Lee Load-Master

DILLON XL 650

Frame: Aluminum alloy
Frame Type: NA
Die Thread: 7/8-14
Avg. Rounds Per Hour: 800-1000
Ram Stroke: 4-9/16"
Weight: 46 lbs.
Features: Five stations; auto indexing; auto case feed; removable tool head; auto prime system with 100-primer capacity; low primer supply alarm; auto powder measure; positive powder bar return; 220 ejected round capacity bin; 3/4-lb. capacity powder measure. 500-600 case feed capacity with optional auto case feed. Loads all pistol/rifle calibers less than 3-1/2" in length. Height above the bench, 44"; 3/4" bench overhang required. From Dillon Precision Products, Inc.
Price: Less dies.. **$443.95**

HORNADY Lock-N-Load AP

Frame: Die cast heat-treated aluminum alloy
Frame Type: O-frame
Die Thread: 7/8-14
Avg. Rounds Per Hour: NA
Ram Stroke: 3-3/4"
Weight: 26 lbs.
Features: Features Lock-N-Load bushing system that allows instant die changeovers; five-station die platform with option of seating and crimping separately or adding taper-crimp die; auto prime with large and small primer tubes with 100-primer capacity and protective housing; brass kicker to eject loaded rounds into 80-round capacity cartridge catcher; offset operating handle for leverage and unobstructed operation; 2" diameter ram driven by heavy-duty cast linkage arms rotating on steel pins. Comes with five Lock-N-Load die bushings, shellplate, deluxe powder measure, auto powder drop, and auto primer feed and shut-off, brass kicker and primer catcher. Lifetime warranty. From Hornady Mfg. Co.
Price: **$367.65**

LEE Load-Master

Frame: ASTM 380 aluminum
Frame Type: O-frame
Die Thread: 7/8-14
Avg. Rounds Per Hour: 600
Ram Stroke: 3-1/4"
Weight: 8 lbs., 4 oz.
Features: Available in kit form only. A 1-3/4" diameter hard chrome ram for handling largest magnum cases; loads rifle or pistol rounds; five station press to factory crimp and post size; auto indexing with wedge lock mechanism to hold one ton; auto priming; removable turrets; four-tube case feeder with optional case collator and bullet feeder (late 1995); loaded round ejector with chute to optional loaded round catcher; quick change shellplate; primer catcher. Dies and shellholder for one caliber included. From Lee Precision, Inc.
Price: Rifle **$320.00**
Price: Pistol **$330.00**
Price: Extra turret **$10.98**
Price: Adjustable charge bar **$9.98**

LEE Pro 1000

Frame: ASTM 380 aluminum and steel
Frame Type: O-frame
Die Thread: 7/8-14
Avg. Rounds Per Hour: 600
Ram Stroke: 3-1/4"
Weight: 8 lbs., 7 oz.
Features: Optional transparent large/small or rifle case feeder; deluxe auto-disk case-activated powder measure; case sensor for primer feed. Comes complete with carbide die set (steel dies for rifle) for one caliber. Optional accessories include: case feeder for large/small pistol cases or rifle cases; shell plate carrier with auto prime, case ejector, auto-index and spare parts; case collator for case feeder. From Lee Precision, Inc.
Price: **$199.98**

PONSNESS/WARREN Metallic II

Frame: Die cast aluminum
Frame Type: H-frame
Die Thread: 7/8-14
Avg. Rounds Per Hour: 150+
Ram Stroke: NA
Weight: 32 lbs.
Features: Die head with five tapped 7/8-14 holes for dies, powder measure or other accessories; pivoting die arm moves case from station to station; depriming tube for removal of spent primers; auto primer feed; interchangeable die head. Optional accessories include additional die heads, powder measure extension tube to accommodate any standard powder measure, primer speed feeder to feed press primer tube without disassembly. Comes with small and large primer seating tools. Dies, powder measure and shellholder not included. From Ponsness/Warren.
Price: **$375.00**
Price: Extra die head **$56.95**
Price: Primer speed feeder **$14.50**
Price: Powder measure extension **$29.95**
Price: Dust cover **$27.95**

ACCESSORIES

METALLIC CARTRIDGE PRESSES

RCBS AmmoMaster-Auto

Frame: Aluminum base; cast iron top plate connected by three steel posts
Frame Type: NA

Die Thread: 1-1/4-12 bushing; 7/8-14 threads
Avg. Rounds Per Hour: 400-500
Ram Stroke: 5-1/4"
Weight: 19 lbs.

Features: Progressive press convertible to single-stage. Features include: 1-1/2" solid ram; automatic indexing, priming, powder charging and loaded round ejection. Case detection system disengages powder measure when no case is present in powder charging station. Comes with five-station shellplate and Uniflow powder measure with clear powder measure adaptor to make bridged powders visible and correctable. Piggyback die plate for quick caliber change-over available. Reloading dies not included. From RCBS.
Price: $394.95
Price: Piggyback/AmmoMaster die plate $22.95
Price: Piggyback/AmmoMaster shellplate $27.95
Price: Press cover $10.95

RCBS Pro 2000™

Frame: Cast iron
Frame Type: H-Frame
Die Thread: 7/8 x 14

Avg. Rounds Per Hour: NA
Ram Stroke: NA
Weight: NA

Features: Five-station manual indexing; full-length sizing; removable die plate; fast caliber conversion. Uses APS Priming System. From RCBS.
Price: $468.95

STAR Universal Pistol Press

Frame: Cast iron with aluminum base
Frame Type: Unconventional
Die Thread: 11/16-24 or 7/8-14

Avg. Rounds Per Hour: 300
Ram Stroke: NA
Weight: 27 lbs.

Features: Four or five-station press depending on need to taper crimp; handles all popular handgun calibers from 32 Long to 45 Colt. Comes completely assembled and adjusted with carbide dies (except 30 Carbine) and shellholder to load one caliber. Prices slightly higher for 9mm and 30 Carbine. From Star Machine Works.
Price: With taper crimp $1,055.00
Price: Without taper crimp $1,025.00
Price: Extra tool head, taper crimp $425.00
Price: Extra tool head, w/o taper crimp $395.00

RCBS AmmoMaster

Fully-automated Star Universal

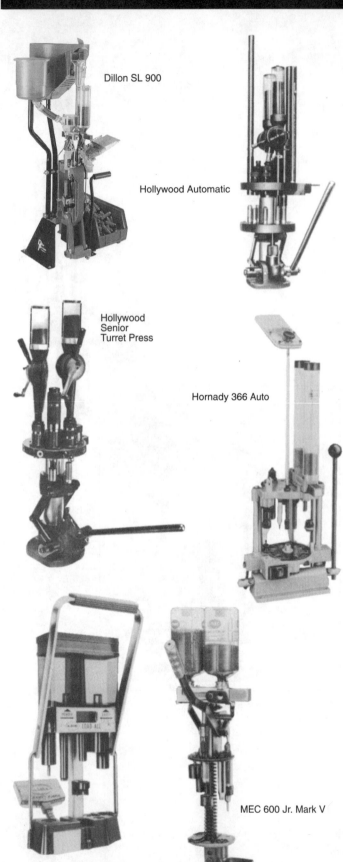

Dillon SL 900

Hollywood Automatic

Hollywood Senior Turret Press

Hornady 366 Auto

MEC 600 Jr. Mark V

Lee Load-All II

DILLON SL 900

Press Type: Progressive
Avg. Rounds Per Hour: 700-900
Weight: 51 lbs.
Features: 12-ga. only; factory adjusted to load AA hulls; extra large 25-pound capacity shot hopper; fully-adjustable case-activated shot system; hardened steel starter crimp die; dual-action final crimp and taper die; tilt-out wad guide; auto prime; auto index; strong mount machine stand. From Dillon Precision Products.
Price: **$819.95**

HOLLYWOOD Automatic Shotshell Press

Press Type: Progressive
Avg. Rounds Per Hour: 1,800
Weight: 100 lbs.
Features: Ductile iron frame; fully automated press with shell pickup and ejector; comes completely set up for one gauge; one starter crimp; one finish crimp; wad guide for plastic wads; decap and powder dispenser unit; one wrench for inside die lock screw; one medium and one large spanner wrench for spanner nuts; one shellholder; powder and shot measures. Available for 10, 12, 20, 28 or 410. From Hollywood Engineering.
Price: **$3,600.00**

HOLLYWOOD Senior Turret Press

Press Type: Turret
Avg. Rounds Per Hour: 200
Weight: 50 lbs.
Features: Multi-stage press constructed of ductile iron comes completely equipped to reload one gauge; one starter crimp; one finish crimp; wad guide for plastic wads; decap and powder dispenser unit; one wrench for inside die lock screw; one medium and one large spanner wrench for spanner nuts; one shellholder; powder and shot measures. Available for 10, 12, 16, 20, 28 or 410. From Hollywood Engineering.
Price: Press only **$700.00**
Price: Dies **$195.00**

HORNADY 366 Auto

Press Type: Progressive
Avg. Rounds Per Hour: NA
Weight: 25 lbs.
Features: Heavy-duty die cast and machined steel body and components; auto primer feed system; large capacity shot and powder tubes; adjustable for right- or left-hand use; automatic charge bar with shutoff; swing-out wad guide; primer catcher at base of press; interchangeable shot and powder bushings; life-time warranty. Available for 12, 20, 28 2-3/4 and 410 2-1/2. From Hornady Mfg. Co.
Price: **$434.95**
Price: Die set, 12, 20, 28 . . . . **$196.86**
Price: Magnum conversion dies, 12, 20 . . . . **$43.25**

LEE Load-All II

Press Type: Single stage
Avg. Rounds Per Hour: 100
Weight: 3 lbs., 3 oz.
Features: Loads steel or lead shot; built-in primer catcher at base with door in front for emptying; recesses at each station for shell positioning; optional primer feed. Comes with safety charge bar with 24 shot and powder bushings. Available for 12-, 16- or 20-gauge. From Lee Precision, Inc.
Price: **$49.98**

MEC 600 Jr. Mark V

Press Type: Single stage
Avg. Rounds Per Hour: 200
Weight: 10 lbs.
Features: Spindex crimp starter for shell alignment during crimping; a cam-action crimp die; Pro-Check to keep charge bar properly positioned; adjustable for three shells. Available in 10, 12, 16, 20, 28 gauges and 410 bore. Die set not included. From Mayville Engineering Company, Inc.
Price: **$84.95**
Price: Die set **$59.38**

MEC 650

Press Type: Progressive
Avg. Rounds Per Hour: 400
Weight: NA
Features: Six-station press; does not resize except as separate operation; auto primer feed standard; three crimping stations for starting, closing and tapering crimp. Die sets not available. Available in 12, 16, 20, 28 and 410. From Mayville Engineering Company, Inc.
Price: $179.95

MEC 8567 Grabber

Press Type: Progressive
Avg. Rounds Per Hour: 400
Weight: 15 lbs.
Features: Ten-station press; auto primer feed; auto-cycle charging; three-stage crimp; power ring resizer returns base to factory specs; resizes high and low base shells; optional kits to reload three shells and steel shot. Available in 12, 16, 20, 28 gauge and 410 bore. From Mayville Engineering Company, Inc.
Price: $239.95
Price: 3" kit, 12-ga. $60.00
Price: 3" kit, 20-ga. $16.95
Price: Steel shot kit. $22.95

MEC 9000 Grabber

Press Type: Progressive
Avg. Rounds Per Hour: 400
Weight: 18 lbs.
Features: All same features as the MEC Grabber, but with auto-indexing and auto-eject. Finished shells automatically ejected from shell carrier to drop chute for boxing. Available in 12, 16, 20, 28 and 410. From Mayville Engineering Company, Inc.
Price: $269.95
Price: 3" kit, 12-ga. $60.00
Price: 3" kit, 20-ga. $16.95
Price: Steel shot kit. $22.95

MEC 9000 Hustler

Press Type: Progressive
Avg. Rounds Per Hour: 400
Weight: 23 lbs.
Features: Same features as 9000G with addition of foot pedal-operated hydraulic system for complete automation. Operates on standard 110V household current. Comes with bushing-type charge bar and three bushings. Available in 12, 16, 20, 28 gauge and 410 bore. From Mayville Engineering Company, Inc.
Price: $669.95
Price: Steel shot kit. $22.95

MEC Sizemaster

Press Type: Single stage
Avg. Rounds Per Hour: 150
Weight: 13 lbs.
Features: Power ring eight-fingered collet resizer returns base to factory specs; handles brass or steel, high or low base heads; auto primer feed; adjustable for three shells. Available in 10, 12, 16, 20, 28 gauges and 410 bore. From Mayville Engineering Company, Inc.
Price: $129.95
Price: Die set, 12, 16, 20, 28, 410 .... $88.67
Price: Die set, 10-ga. $104.06
Price: Steel shot kit. $12.95
Price: Steel shot kit, 12-ga. 3-1/2" $70.27

MEC Steelmaster

Press Type: Single stage
Avg. Rounds Per Hour: 150
Weight: 13 lbs.
Features: Same features as Sizemaster except can load steel shot. Press is available for 3-1/2" 10-ga. and 12-ga. 2-3/4",3" or 3-1/2". For loading lead shot, die sets available in 10, 12, 16, 20, 28 and 410. From Mayville Engineering Company, Inc.
Price: $139.95
Price: 12 ga. 3-1/2" $154.95

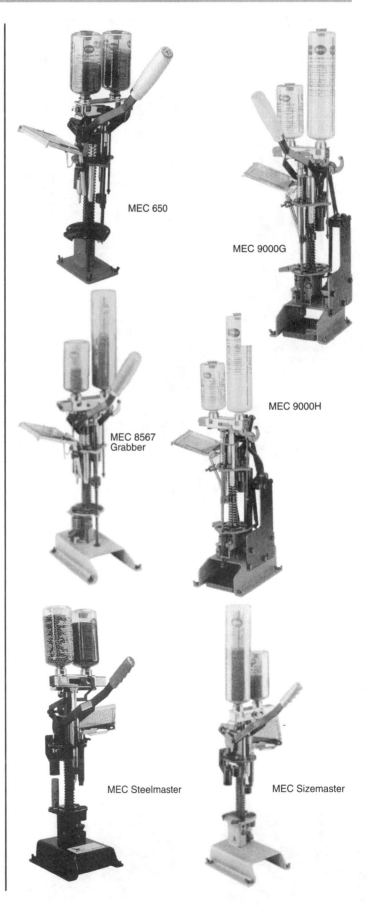

MEC 650

MEC 9000G

MEC 8567 Grabber

MEC 9000H

MEC Steelmaster

MEC Sizemaster

SHOTSHELL RELOADING PRESSES

Ponsness/Warren
Hydro-Multispeed

Ponsness/Warren
Du-O-Matic 375C

Ponsness/Warren
L/S-1000

Ponsness/Warren
Platinum 2000

Ponsness/Warren
Size-O-Matic
900 Elite

PONSNESS/WARREN Du-O-Matic 375C

Press Type: Progressive
Avg. Rounds Per Hour: NA
Weight: 31 lbs.
Features: Steel or lead shot reloader; large shot and powder reservoirs; bushing access plug for dropping in shot buffer or buckshot; positive lock charging ring to prevent accidental flow of powder; double-post construction for greater leverage; removable spent primer box; spring-loaded ball check for centering size die at each station; tip-out wad guide; two-gauge capacity tool head. Available in 10 (extra charge), 12, 16, 20, 28 and 410 with case lengths of 2-1/2, 2-3/4, 3 and 3-1/2 inches. From Ponsness/ Warren.
  Price: 12-, 20-, and 28-ga., 2-3/4" and 410, 2-1/2" **$289.00**
  Price: 12-ga. 3-1/2"; 3" 12, 20, 410. . . . .**$305.00**
  Price: 12, 20 2-3/4". **$383.95**
  Price: 10-ga. press. **$315.00**

PONSNESS/WARREN Hydro-Multispeed

Hydraulic system developed for the Ponsness/Warren L/S-1000. Also usable for the 950, 900 and 800 series presses. Three reloading speed settings operated with variable foot pedal control. Features stop/reverse at any station; automatic shutdown with pedal control release; fully adjustable hydraulic cylinder rod to prevent racking or bending of machine; quick disconnect hoses for ease of installation. Comes preassembled with step-by-step instructions. From Ponsness/Warren.
  Price: **$879.00**
  Price: Cylinder kit. **$399.95**

PONSNESS/WARREN L/S-1000

Frame: Die cast aluminum
Avg. Rounds Per Hour: NA
Weight: 55 lbs.
Features: Fully progressive press to reload steel, bismuth or lead shot. Equipped with new Uni-Drop shot measuring and dispensing system which allows the use of all makes of shot in any size. Shells automatically resized and deprimed with new Auto-Size and De-Primer system. Loaded rounds drop out of shellholders when completed. Each shell pre-crimped and final crimped with Tru-Crimp system. Available in 10-gauge 3-1/2 or 12-gauge 2-3/4" and 3". 12-gauge 3-1/2" conversion kit also available. 20-gauge 2-3/4 and 3 special order only. From Ponsness/Warren.
  Price: 12 ga. **$849.00**
  Price: 10 ga. **$895.00**
  Price: Conversion kit **$199.00**

PONSNESS/WARREN Size-O-Matic 900 Elite

Press Type: Progressive
Avg. Rounds Per Hour: 500-800
Weight: 49 lbs.
Features: Progressive eight-station press; frame of die cast aluminum; center post design index system ensures positive indexing; timing factory set, drilled and pinned. Automatic features include index, deprime, reprime, powder and shot drop, crimp start, tapered final crimp, finished shell ejection. Available in 12, 20, 28 and 410. 16-ga. special order. Kit includes the new shellholders, seating port, resize/primer knockout assembly and new crimp assembly. From Ponsness/Warren.
  Price: **$749.00**
  Price: Conversion tooling, 12, 20, 28, 410. . . . .**$189.00**

PONSNESS/WARREN Platinum 2000

Press Type: Progressive
Avg. Rounds Per Hour: 500-800
Weight: 52 lbs.
Features: Progressive eight-station press is similar to the 900 and 950 except has die removal system that allows removal of any die component during the reloading cycle. Comes standard with 25-lb. shot tube, 19" powder tube, brass adjustable priming feed allows adjustment of primer seating depth. From Ponsness/Warren.
  Price **$889.00**

Maker and Model	Magn.	Field at 100 Yds. (feet)	Eye Relief (in.)	Length (in.)	Tube Dia. (in.)	W & E Adjustments	Weight (ozs.)	Price	Other Data
ADCO									[1]Multi-Color Dot system changes from red to green. [2]For airguns, paint-ball, rimfires. Uses common lithium water battery. [3]Comes with standard dovetail mount. [4].75" dovetail mount; poly body; adj. intensity diode. [5]10 MOA dot; black or nickel. [6]Square format; with mount battery. From ADCO Sales.
Magnum 50 mm[5]	0	—	—	4.1	45 mm	Int.	6.8	$269.00	
MIRAGE Ranger 1"	0	—	—	5.2	1	Int.	3.9	159.00	
MIRAGE Ranger 30mm	0	—	—	5.5	30mm	Int.	5	159.00	
MIRAGE Competitor	0	—	—	5.5	30mm	Int.	5.5	229.00	
IMP Sight[2]	0	—	—	4.5	—	Int.	1.3	17.95	
Square Shooter 2[3]	0	—	—	5	—	Int.	5	99.00	
MIRAGE Eclipse[1]	0	—	—	5.5	30mm	Int.	5.5	229.00	
Champ Red Dot	0	—	—	4.5	—	Int.	2	33.95	
Vantage 1"	0	—	—	3.9	1	Int.	3.9	129.00	
Vantage 30mm	0	—	—	4.2	30mm	Int.	4.9	132.00	
Vision 2000[6]	0	60	—	4.7	—	Int.	6.2	79.00	
e-dot ESB[1]	0	—	—	4.12	1	Int.	3.7	139.00	
e-dot E1B	0	—	—	4.12	1	Int.	3.7	119.00	
e-dot ECB	0	—	—	3.8	30mm	Int.	6.4	119.00	
e-dot E30B	0	—	—	4.3	30mm	Int.	4.6	119.00	
AIMPOINT									Illuminates red dot in field of view. Noparallax (dot does not need to be centered). Unlimited field of view and eye relief. On/off, adj. intensity. Dot covers 3" @100 yds. [1]Comes with 30mm rings, battery, lense cloth. [2]Requires 1" rings. Black finish. AP Comp avail. in black, blue, SS, camo. [3]Black finish (AP 5000-B) ; avail. with regular 3-min. or 10-min. Mag Dot as B2 or S2. [4]Band pass reflection coating for compatibility with night vision equipment; U.S. Army contract model; with anti-reflex coated lenses (Comp ML), $359.00. From Aimpoint U.S.A.
Comp	0	—	—	4.6	30mm	Int.	4.3	331.00	
Comp M[4]	0	—	—	5	30mm	Int.	6.1	409.00	
Series 5000[3]	0	—	—	6	30mm	Int.	6	297.00	
Series 3000 Universal[2]	0	—	—	6.25	1	Int.	6	232.00	
Series 5000/2x[1]	2	—	—	7	30mm	Int.	9	388.00	
ARMSON O.E.G.									Shown red dot aiming point. No batteries needed. Standard model fits 1" ring mounts (not incl.). Other O.E.G. models for shotguns and rifles can be special ordered. [1]Daylight Only Sight with .375" dovetail mount for 22s. Does not contain tritium. From Trijicon, Inc.
Standard	0	—	—	5.125	1	Int.	4.3	202.00	
22 DOS[1]	0	—	—	3.75	—	Int.	3	127.00	
22 Day/Night	0	—	—	3.75	—	Int.	3	169.00	
M16/AR-15	0	—	—	5.125	—	Int.	5.5	226.00	
ARTEMIS 2000									Click-stop windage and elevation adjustments; constantly centered reticle; rubber eyepiece ring; nitrogen filled. Imported from the Czech Republic by CZ-USA.
4x32	4	34.4	3.15	10.7	1	Int.	17.5	215.00	
6x42	6	23	3.15	13.7	1	Int.	17.5	317.00	
7x50	7	18.7	3.15	13.9	1	Int.	17.5	329.00	
1.5-6x42	1.5-6	40-12.8	2.95	12.4	30mm	Int.	19.4	522.00	
2-8x42	2-8	31-9.5	2.95	13.1	30mm	Int.	21.1	525.00	
3-9x42	3-9	24.6-8.5	2.95	12.4	30mm	Int.	19.4	466.00	
3-12x50	3-12	20.6-6.2	2.95	14	30mm	Int.	22.9	574.00	
BEC									Black matte finish. Multi-coated lenses; 1/4-MOA click adjustments (1/2-MOA on EL4x25, AR4x22WA); fog and water-proof. [1]For AR-15;bullet drop compensator; q.d. mount. [2]Rubber armored. Imported by BEC Inc. Partial listing shown. Contact BEC for complete details. [3]All Goldlabel scopes feature lighted reticles and finger-adjustable windage and elevation adjustments. [4]Bullet-drop compensator system for Mini-14 and AR-15 rifles.
EuroLux									
EL2510x56	2.5-10	39.4-11.5	3.25-2	15.1	30mm	Int.	25.4	249.90	
EL39x42	3-9	34.1-13.2	3.5-3	12.3	30mm	Int.	17.7	99.80	
EL28x36	2-8	44.9-11.5	3.8-3	12.2	30mm	Int.	15.9	149.50	
ELA39x40RB[2]	3-9	39-13	3	12.7	30mm	Int.	14.3	95.95	
EL6x42	6	21	3	12.6	30mm	Int.	14.8	69.00	
EL4x42	4	29	3	12.6	30mm	Int.	14.8	59.60	
EL4x36	4	29	3	12	30mm	Int.	14	49.90	
EL4x25	4	26	3	7	30mm	Int.	7.6	37.00	
AR4x22WA[1]	4	24	3	7	34mm	Int.	13.6	109.97	
Goldlabel[3]									
GLI 624x50	6-24	16-4	3.5-3	15.3	1	Int.	22.5	139.00	
GLI 416x50	4-16	25-6	3.5-3	13.5	1	Int.	21.8	135.00	
GLI 39x40R[2]	3-9	39-13	3.5-3	12.7	28mm	Int.	18.5	99.00	
GLC 5x42BD[4]	5	24	3.5	8.7	1	Int.	16.5	79.00	
BEEMAN									All scopes have 5 point reticle, all glass fully coated lenses. [1]Parallel adjustable. [2]Reticle lighted by ambient light. [3]Available with lighted Electro-Dot reticle. Imported by Beeman.
Rifle Scopes									
5045[1]	4-12	26.9-9	3	13.2	1	Int.	15	275.00	
5046[1]	6-24	18-4.5	3	16.9	1	Int.	20.2	395.00	
5050[1]	4	26	3.5	11.7	1	Int.	11	80.00	
5055[1]	3-9	38-13	3.5	10.75	1	Int.	11.2	90.00	
5060[1]	4-12	30-10	3	12.5	1	Int.	16.2	210.00	
5065[1]	6-18	17-6	3	14.7	1	Int.	17.3	265.00	
5066RL[2]	2-7	58-15	3	11.4	1	Int.	17	380.00	
5047L[2]	4	25	3.5	7	1	Int.	13.7	NA	
Pistol Scopes									
5021	2	19	10-24	9.1	1	Int.	7.4	85.50	
5020	1.5	14	11-16	8.3	.75	Int.	3.6	NA	
BSA									[1]Waterproof, fogproof; multi-coated lenses; finger-adjustable knobs. [2]Waterproof, fogproof; matte black finish. [3]With 4" sunshade; target knobs; 1/8-MOA click adjustments. [4]Adjustable for parallax; with sunshades; target knobs, 1/8-MOA adjustments. Imported by BSA. [5]Illuminated reticle model; also available in 3-10x, 3.5-10x, and 3-9x. [6]Red dot sights also available in 42mm and 50mm versions. [7]Includes Universal Bow Mount. [8]Five other models offered. From BSA.
Catseye[1]									
CE1545x32	1.5-4.5	78-23	4	11.25	1	Int.	12	91.95	
CE310x44	3-10	39-12	3.25	12.75	1	Int.	16	151.95	
CE3510x50	3.5-10	30-10.5	3.25	13.25	1	Int.	17.25	171.95	
CE416x50	4-16	25-6	3	15.25	1	Int.	22	191.95	
CE624x50	6-24	16-3	3	16	1	Int.	23	222.95	
CE1545x32IR	1.5-4.5	78-23	5	11.25	1	Int.	12	121.95	
Deer Hunter[2]									
DH25x20	2.5	72	6	7.5	1	Int.	7.5	59.95	
DH4x32	4	32	3	12	1	Int.	12.5	49.95	
DH39x32	3-9	39-13	3	12	1	Int.	11	69.95	
DH39x40	3-9	39-13	3	13	1	Int.	12.1	89.95	

Maker and Model	Magn.	Field at 100 Yds. (feet)	Eye Relief (in.)	Length (in.)	Tube Dia. (in.)	W & E Adjustments	Weight (ozs.)	Price	Other Data
DH39x50	3-9	41-15	3	12.75	1	Int.	13	109.95	
DH2510x44	2.5-10	42-12	3	13	1	Int.	12.5	99.95	
DH1545x32	1.5-4.5	78-23	5	11.25	1	Int.	12	79.95	
Contender[3]									
CT24x40TS	24	6	3	15	1	Int.	18	129.95	
CT36x40TS	36	3	3	15.25	1	Int.	19	139.95	
CT312x40TS	3-12	28-7	3	13	1	Int.	17.5	119.95	
CT416x40TS	4-16	21-5	3	13.5	1	Int.	18	129.95	
CT624x40TS	6-24	16-4	3	15.5	1	Int.	20	144.95	
CT832x40TS	8-32	11-3	3	15.5	1	Int.	20	169.95	
CT24x50TS	24	6	3	15	1	Int.	22	149.95	
CT36x50TS	36	3	3	15.25	1	Int.	23	159.95	
CT312x50TS	3-12	28-7	3	13.75	1	Int.	21	129.95	
CT416x50TS	4-16	21-5	3	15.25	1	Int.	22	149.95	
CT624x50TS	6-24	16-4	3	16	1	Int.	23	169.95	
CT832x50TS	8-32	11-3	3	16.5	1	Int.	24	189.95	
Pistol									
P52x20	2	N/A	N/A	N/A	N/A	Int.	N/A	79.95	
P54x28	4	N/A	N/A	N/A	N/A	Int.	N/A	89.95	
Platinum[4]									
PT24x44TS	24	4.5	3	16.25	1	Int.	17.9	189.55	
PT36x44TS	36	3	3	14.9	1	Int.	17.9	199.95	
PT624x44TS	6-24	15-4.5	3	15.25	1	Int.	18.5	219.95	
PT832x44TS	8-32	11-3.5	3	17.25	1	Int.	19.5	239.95	
PT1050x60TS	10-50	7-2	3	18	1	Int.	22	399.95	
.22 Special									
S25x20WR	2.5	58	3	8	1	Int.	7	39.95	
S4x32WR	4	26	3	10.75	1	Int.	9	49.95	
Air Rifle									
AR4x32	4	33	3	13	1	Int.	14	69.95	
AR27x32	2-7	48	3	12.25	1	Int.	14	79.95	
AR312x44	3-12	36	3	12.25	1	Int.	15	109.95	
Red Dot									
RD30[6]	0	—	—	3.8	30mm	Int.	5	59.95	
PB30[6]	0	—	—	3.8	30mm	Int.	4.5	79.95	
Bow30[7]	0	—	—	N/A	30mm	Int.	5	89.95	
BIgCat[8]	3.5-10	30-11	5	9.7	1	Int.	16.8	219.95	

BURRIS

Mr. T Black Diamond Titanium									
2.5-10x50[A]	2.5-10	4.25-4.75		13.6	30mm	Int.	29	2,129.00	
Black Diamond									
3-12x50[3,4,6]	3.2-11.9	34-12	3.5-4	13.8	30mm	Int.	25	880.00	
6-24x50	6-24	18-6	3.5-4	16.2	30mm	Int.	25	954.00	
Fullfield & Fullfield II									
2.5x[9]	2.5	55	3.5-3.75	10.25	1	Int.	9	308.00	
4x[1,2,3]	3.75	36	3.5-3.75	11.25	1	Int.	11.5	314.00	
6x[1,3]	5.8	23	3.5-3.75	13	1	Int.	12	343.00	
1.75-5x[1,2,9,10]	1.7-4.6	66-25	3.5-3.75	10.875	1	Int.	13	374.00	
2-7x[1,2,3]	2.5-6.8	47-18	3.5-3.75	12	1	Int.	14	399.00	
3-9x40[1,2,3,10]	3.3-8.7	38-15	3.5-3.75	12.625	1	Int.	15	356.00	
3-9x50	3-9	35-15	3.5-3.75	13	1	Int.	18	427.00	
3.5-10x50mm[3,5,10]	3.7-9.7	29.5-11	3.5-3.75	14	1	Int.	19	496.00	
4-12x[1,4,8,11]	4.4-11.8	27-10	3.5-3.75	15	1	Int.	18	500.00	
6-18x[1,3,4,6,7,8]	6.5-17.6	16.7	3.5-3.75	15.8	1	Int.	18.5	527.00	
Compact Scopes									
1x XER[3]	1	51	4.5-20	8.8	1	Int.	7.9	290.00	
4x[4,5]	3.6	24	3.75-5	8.25	1	Int.	7.8	270.00	
6x[1,4]	5.5	17	3.75-5	9	1	Int.	8.2	287.00	
6x HBR[1,5,8]	6	13	4.5	11.25	1	Int.	13	451.00	
1-4x XER[3]	1-3.8	53-15	4.25-30	8.8	1	Int.	10.3	377.00	
3-9x[4,5]	3.6-8.8	25-11	3.75-5	12.625	1	Int.	11.5	368.00	
4-12x[1,4,6]	4.5-11.6	19-8	3.75-4	15	1	Int.	15	500.00	
Signature Series									
1.5-6x[2,3,5,9,10]	1.7-5.8	70-20	3.5-4	10.8	1	Int.	13	484.00	
6x[3]	6	20	3.5-4	12.125	1	Int.	14	413.00	
2-8x[3,5,11]	2.1-7.7	53-17	3.5-4	11.75	1	Int.	14	558.00	
3-9x[3,5,10,13]	3.3-8.8	36-14	3.5-4	12.875	1	Int.	15.5	571.00	
2.50-10x[3,5,10]	2.7-9.5	37-10.5	3.5-4	14	1	Int.	19	635.00	
3-12x[3,10]	3.3-11.7	34-9	3.5-4	14.25	1	Int.	21	691.00	
4-16x[1,3,5,6,8,10]	4.3-15.7	33-9	3.5-4	15.4	1	Int.	23.7	723.00	
6-24x[1,3,5,6,8,10,13]	6.6-23.8	17-6	3.5-4	16	1	Int.	22.7	742.00	
8-32x[8,10,12]	8.6-31.4	13-3.8	3.5-4	17	1	Int.	24	798.00	
Speeddot 135[13]									
Red Dot	1	—	—	4.85	35mm	Int.	5	291.00	
Handgun									
1.50-4x LER[1,5,10]	1.6-3.	16-11	11-25	10.25	1	Int.	11	363.00	
2-7x LER[3,4,5,10]	2-6.5	21-7	7-27	9.5	1	Int.	12.6	401.00	
3-9x LER[4,5,10]	3.4-8.4	12-5	22-14	11	1	Int.	14	453.00	
2x LER[4,5,6]	1.7	21	10-24	8.75	1	Int.	6.8	265.00	
4x LER[1,4,5,6,10]	3.7	11	10-22	9.625	1	Int.	9	296.00	
10x LER[1,4,6]	9.5	4	8-12	13.5	1	Int.	14	460.00	
Scout Scope									
1xXER[3,9]	1.5	32	4-24	9	1	Int.	7.0	290.00	
2.75x[3,9]	2.7	15	7-14	9.375	1	Int.	7.0	319.00	

[A]Available in Carbon Black, Titanium Gray and Autumn Gold finishes. **Black Diamond & Fullfield:** All scopes avail. with Plex reticle. Steel-on-steel click adjustments. [1]Dot reticle on some models. [2]Post crosshair reticle extra. [3]Matte satin finish. [4]Available with parallax adjustment (standard on 10x, 12x, 4-12x, 6-12x, 6-18x, 6x HBR and 3-12x Signature). [5]Silver matte finish extra. [6]Target knobs extra, standard on silhouette models. LER and XER with P.A., 6x HBR. [7]Sunshade avail. [8]Avail. with Fine Plex reticle. [9]Available with Heavy Plex reticle. [10]Available with Posi-Lock. [11]Available with Peep Plex reticle. [12]Also avail. for rimfires, airguns. [13]Selected models available with camo finish.
Signature Series: LER=Long Eye Relief; IER=Intermediate Eye Relief; XER=Extra Eye Relief.
Speeddot 135: [13]Waterproof, fogproof, coated lenses, 11 brightness settings; 3-MOA or 11-MOA dot size; includes Weaver-style rings and battery.
Partial listing shown. Contact Burris for complete details.

Plex

Fine Plex

Heavy Plex & Electro-Dot Plex

Peep Plex

Ballistic Mil-Dot

Target Dot

Mil-Dot

Maker and Model	Magn.	Field at 100 Yds. (feet)	Eye Relief (in.)	Length (in.)	Tube Dia. (in.)	W & E Adjustments	Weight (ozs.)	Price	Other Data
BUSHNELL (Bausch & Lomb Elite rifle scopes now sold under Bushnell brand)									
Elite 4200 RainGuard									
42-6244M[1]	6-24	18-6	3	16.9	1	Int.	20.2	729.95	
42-2104G[2]	2.5-10	41.5-10.8	3	13.5	1	Int.	16	642.95	
42-2151M[6, 9]	2.5-10	40.3-10.8	3.3	14.3	1	Int.	18	798.95	
42-1636M[3]	1.5-6	61.8-16.1	3	12.8	1	Int.	15.4	608.95	
42-4164M[5, 6]	4-16	26-7	3.5	18.6	1	Int.	18.6	645.95	
42-4165M[5]	4-16	26-7	3	15.6	1	Int.	22	834.95	
42-8324M	8-32	14-3.75	3.3	18	1	Int.	22	802.95	
Elite 3200 RainGuard									
32-5155M	5-15	21-7	3	15.9	1	Int.	19	528.95	
32-4124A[1]	4-12	26.9-9	3	13.2	1	Int.	15	469.95	
32-1040M	10	11	3.5	11.7	1	Int.	15.5	319.95	
32-3940G[4]	3-9	33.8-11.5	3	12.6	1	Int.	13	319.95	
32-2732M	2-7	44.6-12.7	3	11.6	1	Int.	12	303.95	
32-3950G[6]	3-9	31.5-10.5	3	15.7	1	Int.	19	382.95	
32-3955E	3-9	31.5-10.5	3	15.6	30mm	Int.	22	640.95	
Elite 3200 Handgun RainGuard									
32-2632M[7]	2-6	10-4	20	9	1	Int.	10	444.95	
32-2632G	2-6	10-4	20	9	1	Int.	10	444.95	
Trophy									
73-0134	1	68	Unlimited	5.5	1	Int.	6	136.95	
73-1500[1]	1.75-5	68-23	3.5	10.8	1	Int.	12.3	177.95	
73-4124[1]	4-12	32-11	3	12.5	1	Int.	16.1	300.95	
73-3940[2]	3-9	42-14	3	11.7	1	Int.	13.2	159.95	
73-6184[7]	6-18	17.3-6	3	14.8	1	Int.	17.9	378.95	
Turkey & Brush									
73-1421[11]	1.75-4	73-30	3.5	10.8	32mm	Int.	10.9	171.95	
HOLOsight Model[8]	1	—	—	6	—	Int.	8.7	444.95	
Trophy Handgun									
73-0232[2]	2	20	9-26	8.7	1	Int.	7.7	218.95	
73-2632[3]	2-6	21-7	9-26	9.1	1	Int.	10.9	287.95	
Banner									
71-1545	1.5-4.5	67-23	3.5	10.5	1	Int.	10.5	116.95	
71-3944[9]	3-9	36-13	4	11.5	1	Int.	12.5	125.95	
71-3950[10]	3-9	26-10	3	16	1	Int.	19	186.95	
71-4124[7]	4-12	29-11	3	12	1	Int.	15	157.95	
71-4228	4	26.5	3	11.75	1	Int.	10	81.95	
71-6185[10]	6-18	17-6	3	16	1	Int.	18	209.95	
Sportsman									
72-0004	4	31	4	11.7	1	Int.	11.2	98.95	
72-0038	3-9	37-14	3.5	12	1	Int.	6	79.95	
72-0039	3-9	38-13	3.5	10.75	1	Int.	11.2	116.95	
72-0412[7]	4-12	27-9	3.2	13.1	1	Int.	14.6	141.95	
72-1393[6]	3-9	35-12	3.5	11.75	1	Int.	10	68.95	
72-1545	1.5-4.5	69-24	3	10.7	1	Int.	8.6	86.95	
72-1548[11]	1.5-4.5	71-25	3.5	10.4	1	Int.	11.8	104.95	
72-1403	4	29	4	11.75	1	Int.	9.2	57.95	
72-3940M	3-9	42-14	3	12.7	1	Int.	12.5	95.95	
22 Rimfire									
76-2239	3-9	40-13	3	11.75	1	Int.	11.2	61.95	
76-2243	4	30	3	11.5	1	Int.	10	52.95	
EUROPTIK SUPREME									
4x36K	4	39	3.5	11.6	26mm	Int.	14	795.00	
6x42K	6	21	3.5	13	26mm	Int.	15	875.00	
8x56K	8	18	3.5	14.4	26mm	Int.	20	925.00	
1.5-6x42K	1.5-6	61.7-23	3.5	12.6	30mm	Int.	17	1,095.00	
2-8x42K	2-8	52-17	3.5	13.3	30mm	Int.	17	1,150.00	
2.5-10x56K	2.5-10	40-13.6	3.5	15	30mm	Int.	21	1,295.00	
3-12x56 Super	3-12	10.8-34.7	3.5-2.5	15.2	30mm	Int.	24	1,495.00	
4-16x56 Super	4-16	9.8-3.9	3.1	18	30mm	Int.	26	1,575.00	
3-9x40 Micro	3-9	3.2-12.1	2.7	13	1	Int.	14	1,450.00	
2.5-10x46 Micro	2.5-10	13.7-33.4	2.7	14	30mm	Int.	20	1,395.00	
4-16x56 EDP[1]	4-16	22.3-7.5	3.1	18	30mm	Int.	29	1,995.00	
7-12x50 Target	7-12	8.8-5.5	3.5	15	30mm	Int.	21	1,495.00	
KAHLES									
4x36	4	34.5	3.15	11.2	1	Int.	12.7	555.00	
6x42	6	23	3.15	12.4	1	Int.	14.4	694.00	
8x50[1]	8	17.3	3.15	13	1	Int.	16.5	749.00	
1.1-4x24	1.1-4	108-31.8	3.5	10.8	30mm	Int.	12.7	722.00	
1.5-6x42[1]	1.5-6	72-21.3	3.5	12.0	30mm	Int.	15.8	832.00	
2.5-10x50[1]	2.5-10	43.5-12.9	3.5	12.8	30mm	Int.	15.8	1,353.00	
3-9x42	3-9	43-16	3.5	12	1	Int.	13	621.06	
3-9x42AH	3-9	43-15	3.5	12.36	1	Int.	12.7	665.00	
3-12x56[1]	3-12	30-11	3.5	15.4	30mm	Int.	18	1,377.72	

(Bushnell Elite)
[1]Adj. objective, sunshade; with 1/4-MOA dot or Mil Dot reticle. [2]Also in matte and silver finish. [3]Only in matte finish. [4]Also in matte and silver finish. [5]Adjustable objective. [6]50mm objective; also in matte finish. [7]Also in silver finish. [8]40mm. [9]Ill. dot reticle. **Partial listings shown. Contact Bushnell Performance Optics for details.**

(Bushnell)
[1]Wide Angle. [2]Also silver finish. [3]Also silver finish. [4]Matte finish. [5]Also silver finish. [7]Adj. obj. [8]Variable intensity; fits Weaver-style base. [9]Blackpowder scope; extended eye relief, Circle-X reticle. [10]50mm objective. [11]With Circle-X reticle, matte finish. [12]Matte finish, adjustable objective.

HOLOSIGHT RETICLE

Standard

SCOPE RETICLES

Multi

Euro

Circle-X

[1]Military scope with adjustable parallax. Fixed powers have 26mm tubes, variables have 30mm tubes. Some models avail. with steel tubes. All lenses multi-coated. Dust and water tight. From Europtik.

Aluminum tube. Multi-coated, waterproof. [1]Also available with illuminated reticle. Imported from Austria by Swarovski Optik.

No. 4A

No. 7A

Plex

Illuminated No. 4N

Illuminated Plex N

TD Smith

ACCESSORIES

Maker and Model	Magn.	Field at 100 Yds. (feet)	Eye Relief (in.)	Length (in.)	Tube Dia. (in.)	W & E Adjustments	Weight (ozs.)	Price	Other Data
KILHAM									
Hutson Handgunner II	1.7	8	—	5.5	.875	Int.	5.1	119.95	Unlimited eye relief; internal click adjustments; crosshair reticle. Fits Thompson/Center rail mounts, for S&W K, N, Ruger Blackhawk, Super, Super Single-Six, Contender.
Hutson Handgunner	3	8	10-12	6	.875	Int.	5.3	119.95	
LEICA									
Ultravid 1.75-6x32	1.75-6	47-18	4.8-3.7	11.25	30mm	Int.	14	749.00	Aluminum tube with hard anodized matte black finish with titanium
Ultravid 3.5-10x42	3.5-10	29.5-10.7	4.6-3.6	12.62	30mm	Int.	16	849.00	accents; finger-adjustable windage and elevation with 1/4-MOA clicks.
Ultravid 4.5-14x42	4.5-14	20.5-7.4	5-3.7	12.28	30mm	Int.	18	949.00	Made in U.S. From Leica.

Leicaplex Standard   Leica Dot   Standard Dot   Crosshair   Euro   Post & Plex

Maker and Model	Magn.	Field at 100 Yds. (feet)	Eye Relief (in.)	Length (in.)	Tube Dia. (in.)	W & E Adjustments	Weight (ozs.)	Price	Other Data
LEUPOLD									
Vari-X III 3.5x10 Tactical	3.5-10	29.5-10.7	3.6-4.6	12.5	1	Int.	13.5	801.80	Constantly centered reticles, choice of Duplex, tapered CPC, Leupold
M8-2X EER[1]	1.7	21.2	12-24	7.9	1	Int.	6	312.50	Dot, Crosshair and Dot. CPC and Dot reticles extra. [1]2x and 4x scopes
M8-2X EER Silver[1]	1.7	21.2	12-24	7.9	1	Int.	6	337.50	have from 12"-24" of eye relief and are suitable for handguns, top ejection
M8-2.5x28 IER Scout	2.3	22	9.3	10.1	1	Int.	7.5	408.90	arms and muzzleloaders. [2]3x9 Compact, 6x Compact, 12x, 3x9, and
M8-4X EER[1]	3.7	9	12-24	8.4	1	Int.	7	425.00	6.5x20 come with adjustable objective. Sunshade available for all adjust-
M8-4X EER Silver[1]	3.7	9	12-24	8.4	1	Int.	7	425.00	able objective scopes, **$23.20-$41.10**. [3]Long Range scopes have side
Vari-X 2.5-8 EER	2.5-8	13-4.3	11.7-12	9.7	1	Int.	10.9	608.90	focus parallax adjustment, additional windage and elevation travel. Partial
M8-4X Compact	3.6	25.5	4.5	9.2	1	Int.	7.5	382.10	listing shown. **Contact Leupold for complete details.**
Vari-X 2-7x Compact	2.5-6.6	41.7-16.5	5-3.7	9.9	1	Int.	8.5	478.60	*Models available with illuminated reticle for additional cost.
Vari-X 3-9x Compact	3.2-8.6	34-13.5	4-3	11-11.3	1	Int.	11	519.60	
M8-4X	4	24	4	10.7	1	Int.	9.3	385.70	
M8-6x36mm	5.9	17.7	4.3	11.4	1	Int.	10	410.70	
M8-6x 42mm	6	17	4.5	12	1	Int.	11.3	510.70	
*M8-6x42 A.O. Tactical	6	17	4.2	12.1	1	Int.	11.3	628.60	
M8-12x A.O. Varmint	11.6	9.1	4.2	13	1	Int.	13.5	571.40	
Vari-X 3-9x Compact EFR A.O.	3.8-8.6	34-13.5	4-3	11	1	Int.	11	550.00	
*Vari-X-III 1.5-5x20	1.5-4.5	66-23	5.3-3.7	9.4	1	Int.	9.5	635.70	
Vari-X-III 1.75-6x32	1.9-5.6	47-18	4.8-3.7	9.8	1	Int.	11	683.90	
Vari-X-III 2.5x8	2.6-7.8	37-13.5	4.7-3.7	11.3	1	Int.	11.5	678.60	
Vari-X-III 3.5-10x40 Long Range M3[4]	3.9-9.7	29.8-11	4-3.5	13.5	30mm	Int.	19.5	1,157.10	
Vari-X-III 3.5-10x50	3.3-9.7	29.5-10.7	4.6-3.6	12.4	1	Int.	13	796.40	
Vari-X-III 4.5-14x40 A.O.	4.7-13.7	20.8-7.4	5-3.7	12.4	1	Int.	14.5	780.40	
*Vari-X-III 4.5-14x50 A.O.	4.7-13.7	20.8-7.4	5-3.7	12.4	1	Int.	14.5	903.60	
Vari-X III 4.5-14x 50 Long Range Tactical[4]	4.9-14.3	19-6	5-3.7	12.1	30mm	Int.	17.5	1,082.10	
Vari-X-III 6.5-20 A.O.	6.5-19.2	14.2-5.5	5.3-3.6	14.2	1	Int.	17.5	823.20	
Vari-X-III 6.5x20xTarget EFR A.O.	6.5-19.2	—	5.3-3.6	14.2	1	Int.	16.5	919.60	
Vari-X-III 6.5-20x 50 Long Range Target[4]	6.8-19.2	14.7-5.4	4.9-3.7	14.3	30mm	Int.	19	1,166.10	
Vari-X-III 8.5-25x40 A.O. Target	8.5-25	10.86-4.2	5.3	14.3	1	Int.	17.5	900.00	
Vari-X-III 8.5-25x 50 Long Range Target[4]	8.3-24.2	11.4-4.3	4.4-3.6	14.3	30mm	Int.	19	1,260.70	
Mark 4 M1-10x40	10	11.1	3.6	13.125	30mm	Int.	21	1,807.10	
Mark 4 M1-16x40	16	6.6	4.1	12.875	30mm	Int.	22	1,807.10	
Mark 4 M3-10x40	10	11.1	3.6	13.125	30mm	Int.	21	1,807.10	
Vari-X-III 6.5x20[2] A.O.	6.5-19.2	14.2-5.5	5.3-3.6	14.2	1	Int.	16	823.20	
LPS 1.5-6x42	1.5-6	58.7-15.7	4	11.2	30mm	Int.	16	1,476.80	
LPS 2.5-10x45	2.6-9.8	37.2	4.5-3.8	—	1	Int.	17.2	1,480.00	
LPS 3.5-14x52 A.O.	3.5-14	28-7.2	4	13.1	30mm	Int.	22	1,569.60	
Rimfire									
Vari-X 2-7x RF Special	3.6	25.5	4.5	9.2	1	Int.	7.5	478.60	
Shotgun									
M8 4x33	3.7	9	12-24	8.4	1	Int.	6	410.70	
LYMAN									
Super TargetSpot[1]	10, 12, 15, 20, 25, 30	5.5	2	24.3	.75	Int.	27.5	685.00	Made under license from Lyman to Lyman's orig. specs. Blue steel. Three-point suspension rear mount with .25-min. click adj. Data listed for 20x model. [1]Price appx. Made in U.S. by Parsons Optical Mfg. Co.
McMILLAN									
Vision Master 2.5-10x	2.5-10	14.2-4.4	4.3-3.3	13.3	30mm	Int.	17	1,250.00	42mm obj. lens; .25-MOA clicks; nitrogen filled, fogproof, waterproof; etched duplex-type reticle. [1]Tactical Scope with external adj. knobs, military reticle; 60+ min. adj.
Vision Master Model 1[1]	2.5-10	14.2-4.4	4.3-3.3	13.3	30mm	Int.	17	1,250.00	
MEOPTA									
Artemis									
4x32A[1]	4	34	3.15	11	1	Int.	14.7	194.00	Steel tubes are waterproof, dustproof, and shockproof; nitrogen fille.d Anti-reflective coatings, protective rubber eye piece, clear caps. Made in Czech Replublic by Meopta. [1]Range finder reticles available. Partial listing shown.
6x42A[1]	6	23	3.15	13.6	1	Int.	18.2	267.00	
7x50A[1]	7	18	3.15	14.1	1	Int.	19	278.00	

Duplex   CPC   Post & Duplex

Leupold Dot   Dot

German #1   German #2   Turkey Reticle

3/4-Mil. Dot   Crosshair

Maker and Model	Magn.	Field at 100 Yds. (feet)	Eye Relief (in.)	Length (in.)	Tube Dia. (in.)	W & E Adjustments	Weight (ozs.)	Price	Other Data
MEPROLIGHT									
Meprolight Reflex Sights 14-21 5.5 MOA 1x30[1]	1	—	—	4.4	30mm	Int.	5.2	335.00	[1]Also available with 4.2 MOA dot. Uses tritium and fiber optics-no batteries required. From Hesco, Inc.
MILLETT									
Buck 3-9x44	3-9	38-14	3.25-4	13	1	Int.	16.2	549.00	[1]3-MOA dot. [2]5-MOA dot. [3]3-, 5-, 8-, 10-MOA dots. [4]10-MOA dot. All
SP-1 Compact[1] Red Dot	1	36.65	—	4.1	1	Int.	3.2	149.95	have click adjustments; waterproof; shockproof; 11 dot intensity settings.
SP-2 Compact[2] Red Dot	1	58	—	4.5	30mm	Int.	4.3	149.95	All avail. in matte/black or silver finish. From Millett Sights.
MultiDot SP[3]	1	50	—	4.8	30mm	Int.	5.3	289.95	
30mm Wide View[4]	1	60	—	5.5	30mm	Int.	5	289.95	
MIRADOR									
RXW 4x40[1]	4	37	3.8	12.4	1	Int.	12	179.95	[1]Wide angle scope. Multi-coated objective lens. Nitrogen filled; water-
RXW 1.5-5x20[1]	1.5-5	46-17.4	4.3	11.1	1	Int.	10	188.95	proof; shockproof. From Mirador Optical Corp.
RXW 3-9x40	3-9	43-14.5	3.1	12.9	1	Int.	13.4	251.95	
NIGHTFORCE									
2.5-10x50	2.5-10	31.4-9.4	3.3	13.9	30mm	Int.	28	847.87	Lighted reticles with eleven intensity levels. Most scopes have choice of
3.5-15x56	3.5-15	24.5-6.9	3	15.8	30mm	Int.	32	507.78	reticles. From Lightforce U.S.A.
5.5-22x56	5.5-22	15.7-4.4	3	19.4	30mm	Int.	38.5	965.53	
8-32x56	8-32	9.4-3.1	3	16.6	30mm	Int.	36	997.90	
12-42x56	12-42	6.7-2.3	3	17	30mm	Int.	36	1,053.64	
NIKON									
Monarch UCC									Super multi-coated lenses and blackening of all internal metal parts
4x40[2]	4	26.7	3.5	11.7	1	Int.	11.7	229.99	for maximum light gathering capability; positive .25-MOA; fogproof;
1.5-4.5x20[3]	1.5-4.5	67.8-22.5	3.7-3.2	10.1	1	Int.	9.5	239.99	waterproof; shockproof; luster and matte finish. [1]Also available in matte
2-7x32	2-7	46.7-13.7	3.9-3.3	11.3	1	Int.	11.3	259.99	silver finish. [2]Available in silver matte finish. [3]Available with TurkeyPro
3-9x40[1]	3-9	33.8-11.3	3.6-3.2	12.5	1	Int.	12.5	299.99	or Nikoplex reticle. [4]Silver Shadow finish; black matte $296.95. Partial
3.5-10x50	3.5-10	25.5-8.9	3.9-3.8	13.7	1	Int.	15.5	429.99	listing shown. From Nikon, Inc.
4-12x40 A.O.	4-12	25.7-8.6	3.6-3.2	14	1	Int.	16.6	369.99	
6.5-20x44	6.5-19.4	16.2-5.4	3.5-3.1	14.8	1	Int.	19.6	459.99	
2x20 EER	2	22	26.4	8.1	1	Int.	6.3	169.99	
Buckmasters									
4x40	4	30.4	3.3	12.7	1	Int.	11.8	159.99	
3-9x40[4]	3.3-8.6	33.8-11.3	3.5-3.4	12.7	1	Int.	13.4	209.99	
3-9x50	3.3-8.6	33.8-11.3	3.5-3.4	12.9	1	Int.	18.2	299.99	
NORINCO									
N2520	2.5	44.1	4	—	1	Int.	—	52.28	Partial listing shown. Some with Ruby Lens coating, blue/black and matte
N420	4	29.3	3.7	—	1	Int.	—	52.70	finish. Imported by Nic Max, Inc.
N640	6	20	3.1	—	1	Int.	—	67.88	
N154520	1.5-4.5	63.9-23.6	4.1-3.2	—	1	Int.	—	80.14	
N251042	2.5-10	27-11	3.5-2.8	—	1	Int.	—	206.60	
N3956	3-9	35.1-6.3	3.7-2.6	—	1	Int.	—	231.88	
N31256	3-12	26-10	3.5-2.8	—	1	Int.	—	290.92	
NC2836M	2-8	50.8-14.8	3.6-2.7	—	1	Int.	—	255.60	
PARSONS									
Parsons Long Scope	6	10	2	28-34+	.75	Ext.	13	475.00-525.00	Adj. for parallax, focus. Micrometer rear mount with .25-min. click adjust-ments. Price is approximate. Made in U.S. by Parsons Optical Mfg. Co.
PENTAX									
Lightseeker 1.75-6x[1]	1.75-6	71-20	3.5-4	10.8	1	Int.	13	546.00	[1]Glossy finish; Matte finish, Heavy Plex or Penta-Plex, $546.00.
Lightseeker 2-8x[2]	2-8	53-17	3.5-4	11.7	1	Int.	14	594.00	[2]Glossy finish; Matte finish, $594.00. [3]Glossy finish; Matte finish,
Lightseeker 3-9x [3, 4, 10, 11]	3-9	36-14	3.5-4	12.7	1	Int.	15	594.00	$628.00; Heavy Plex, add $20.00. [4]Matte finish; Mil-Dot, $798.00.
Lightseeker 3.5-10x[5]	3.5-10	29.5-11	3.5-4	14	1	Int.	19.5	630.00	[5]Glossy finish; Matte finish, $652.00; Heavy Plex add $10.00. [6]Glossy
Lightseeker 4-16x[6, 9]	4-16	33-9	3.5-4	15.4	1	Int.	22.7	888.00	finish; Matte finish, $816.00; with Heavy Plex, $830.00; with Mil-Dot,
Lightseeker 6-24x [7, 12]	6-24	18-5.5	3.5-4	16	1	Int.	23.7	1,028.00	$978.00. [7]Matte finish; with Mil-Dot, $1,018.00. [8]Matte finish, with Mil-Dot, $1098.00. [9]Lightseeker II, Matte finish, $844.00. [10]Lightseeker II,
Lightseeker 8.5-32x[8]	8.5-32	13-3.8	3.5-4	17.2	1	Int.	24	968.00	Glossy finish, $636.00. [11]Lightseeker II, Matte finish, $660.00.
Shotgun									[12]Lightseeker II, Matte finish, $878.00. [13]Matte finish; Advantage finish,
Lightseeker 2.5x[13]	2.5	55	3.5-4	10	1	Int.	9	398.00	Break-up Mossy Oak finish, Treestand Mossy Oak finish, $364.00.
Lightseeker Zero-X SG Plus	0	51	4.5-15	8.9	1	Int.	7.9	372.00	From Pentax Corp.
Lightseeker Zero-X/V Still-Target	0-4	53.8-15	3.5-7	8.9	1	Int.	10.3	476.00	
Lightseeker Zero X/V	0-4	53.8-15	3.5-7	8.9	1	Int.	10.3	454.00	

Heavy Plex **Fine Plex** **Penta-Plex**

Deepwoods Plex **Comp-Plex** **Mil-dot**

Maker and Model	Magn.	Field at 100 Yds. (feet)	Eye Relief (in.)	Length (in.)	Tube Dia. (in.)	W & E Adjustments	Weight (ozs.)	Price	Other Data
RWS									
300	4	36	3.5	11.75	1	Int.	13.2	170.00	
400[1]	2-7	55-16	3.5	11.75	1	Int.	13.2	190.00	
450	3-9	43-14	3.5	12	1	Int.	14.3	215.00	
500	4	36	3.5	12.25	1	Int.	13.9	225.00	
550	2-7	55-16	3.5	12.75	1	Int.	14.3	235.00	
600	3-9	43-14	3.5	13	1	Int.	16.5	260.00	

ACCESSORIES

Maker and Model	Magn.	Field at 100 Yds. (feet)	Eye Relief (in.)	Length (in.)	Tube Dia. (in.)	W & E Adjustments	Weight (ozs.)	Price	Other Data
SCHMIDT & BENDER									
Fixed									
4x36	4	30	3.25	11	1	Int.	14	684.00	All scopes have 30-yr. warranty, click adjustments, centered reticles, rotation indicators. [1]Glass reticle; aluminum. Available in aluminum with mounting rail. [2]Aluminum only. [3]Aluminum tube. Choice of two bullet drop compensators, choice of two sunshades, two range finding reticles. From Schmidt & Bender, Inc. [4]Parallax adjustment in third turret; extremely fine crosshairs. [5]Available with illuminated reticle that glows red; third turret houses on/off switch, dimmer and battery. [6]4-16x50/Long Range. [7]Also with Long Eye Relief. From Schmidt & Bender, Inc. Available with illuminated crosshairs and parallax adjustment.
6x42	6	21	3.25	13	1	Int.	17	751.00	
8x56	8	16.5	3.25	14	1	Int.	22	864.00	
10x42	10	10.5	3.25	13	1	Int.	18	859.00	
Variables									
1.25-4x20[5]	1.25-4	96-16	3.75	10	30mm	Int.	15.5	895.00	
1.5-6x42[1,5]	1.5-6	60-19.5	3.70	12	30mm	Int.	19.7	1,012.00	
2.5-10x56[1,5]	2.5-10	37.5-12	3.90	14	30mm	Int.	24.6	1,251.00	
3-12x42[2]	3-12	34.5-11.5	3.90	13.5	30mm	Int.	19	1,161.00	
3-12x50[1,5]	3-12	33.3-12.6	3.90	13.5	30mm	Int.	22.9	1,224.00	
4-16x50 Varmint[4,6]	4-16	22.5-7.5	3.90	14	30mm	Int.	26	1,372.00	
Police/Marksman II									
3-12x50[7]	3-12	33.3-12.6	3.74	13.9	34mm	Int.	18.5	1,430.00	

No 1 (fixed) No. 1 variable No. 2 No. 3 No. 4 No. 6 No. 7 No. 8 No. 8 Dot No. 9

Maker and Model	Magn.	Field at 100 Yds. (feet)	Eye Relief (in.)	Length (in.)	Tube Dia. (in.)	W & E Adjustments	Weight (ozs.)	Price	Other Data
SHEPHERD									
310-PI[1]	3-10	41.5-15	3-3.5	12.8	1	Int.	17	549.00	[1]Also avail. as 310-P1, 310-P2, 310-P3, 310-PIA, 310-PE1, 310-P22, 310-P22 Mag., 310-PE, **$549.00**. All have patented Dual Reticle system with range finder bullet drop compensation; multi-coated lenses, waterproof, shock-proof, nitrogen filled, matte finish. From Shepherd Scope, Ltd.
6x18x40 Varminter	6-18	5.5 (16x)	3-3.5	16.25	40mm	Int.	20.8	625.00	
SIGHTRON									
Variables									
SII 1.56x42	1.5-6	50-15	3.8-4	11.69	1	Int.	15.35	287.95	[1]Adjustable objective. [2]3MOA dot; also with 5 or 10 MOA dot. [3]Variable 3, 5, 10 MOA dot; black finish; also stainless. [4]Satin black; also stainless. Electronic Red Dot scopes come with ring mount, front and rear extension tubes, polarizing filter, battery, haze filter caps, wrench. Rifle, pistol, shotgun scopes have aluminum tubes, Exac Trak adjustments. Lifetime warranty. From Sightron, Inc. [5]3" sun shade. [6]Mil Dot or Plex reticle. [7]Dot or Plex reticle. [8]Double Diamond reticle.
SII 2.58x42	2.5-8	36-12	3.6-4.2	11.89	1	Int.	12.82	261.95	
SII 39x42[4,6,7]	3-9	34-12	3.6-4.2	12.00	1	Int.	13.22	274.95	
SII 312x42[6]	3-12	32-9	3.6-4.2	11.89	1	Int.	12.99	311.95	
SII 3.510x42	3.5-10	32-11	3.6	11.89	1	Int.	13.16	324.95	
SII 4.514x42[1]	4.5-14	22-7.9	3.6	13.88	1	Int.	16.07	371.95	
Target									
SII 24x44	24	4.1	4.33	13.30	1	Int.	15.87	341.95	
SII 416x42[1,4,5,6,7]	4-16	26-7	3.6	13.62	1	Int.	16	371.95	
SII 624-42[1,4,5,7]	6-24	16-5	3.6	14.6	1	Int.	18.7	393.95	
SII1040x42	10-40	8.9-4	3.6	16.1	1	Int.	19	563.95	
Compact									
SII 4x32	4	25	4.5	9.69	1	Int.	9.34	205.95	
SII2.5-10x32	2.5-10	41-10.5	3.75-3.5	10.9	1	Int.	10.39	260.95	
Shotgun									
SII 2.5x20SG	2.5	41	4.3	10.28	1	Int.	8.46	194.95	
Pistol									
SII 1x28P[4]	1	30	9-24	9.49	1	Int.	8.46	212.95	
SII 2x28P[4]	2	16-10	9-24	9.49	1	Int.	8.28	212.95	
SIMMONS									
AETEC									
2100[8]	2.8-10	44-14	5	11.9	1	Int.	15.5	234.99	[1]Matte; also polished finish. [2]Silver; also black matte or polished. [3]Black matte finish. [4]Granite finish. [5]Camouflage. [6]Black polish. [7]With ring mounts. [8]Silver; black polish avail. [9]Black or silver matte. [10]50mm obj.; black matte. [11]Black or silver matte. [12]275-yd. parallax; black or silver matte. [13]TV view. [14]Adj. obj. [15]Silver matte. [16]Adj. objective; 4" sunshade; black matte. [17]Octagon body; rings included; black matte or silver finish. [18]Black matte finish; also available in silver. [19]Smart reticle. [20]Target turrets. [21]With dovetail rings. [23]With 3V lithium battery, extension tube, polarizing filter, Weaver rings. **Only selected models shown.** Contact Simmons Outdoor Corp. for complete details.
2104[16]	3.8-12	33-11	4	13.5	1	Int.	20	259.99	
44Mag									
M-1044[3]	3-10	34-10.5	3	12.75	1	Int.	15.5	179.99	
M-1045[3]	4-12	29.5-9.5	3	13.2	1	Int.	18.25	278.99	
M-1047[3]	6.5-20	14-.5	2.6-3.4	12.8	1	Int.	19.5	224.99	
1048[3,20] (3)	6.5-20	16-5.5	2.6-3.4	14.5	1	Int.	20	259.99	
M-1050DM[3,19]	3.8-12	26-9	3	13.08	1	Int.	16.75	269.99	
8-Point									
4-12x40mmAO[3]	4-12	29-10	3-2 7/8	13.5	1	Int.	15.75	129.99	
4x32mm[3]	4	28.75	3	11.625	1	Int.	14.25	44.99	
3-9x32mm[3]	3-9	37.5-13	3-2 7/8	11.875	1	Int.	11.5	60.99	
3-9x40mm[18]	3-9	37-13	3-2 7/8	12.25	1	Int.	12.25	84.99-94.99	
3-9x50mm[3]	3-9	32-11.75	3-2 7/8	13	1	Int.	15.25	97.99	
Prohunter									
7700	2-7	53-16.25	3	11.5	1	Int.	12.5	124.99	
7710[2]	3-9	36-13	3	12.6	1	Int.	13.5	139.99	
7716	4-12	26-9	3	12.6	1	Int.	16.75	159.99	
7721	6-18	18.5-6	3	13.75	1	Int.	16	179.99	
7740[3]	6	21.75	3	12.5	1	Int.	12	120.99	
Prohunter Handgun									
7732[18]	2	22	9-17	8.75	1	Int.	7	139.99	
7738[18]	4	15	11.8-17.6	8.5	1	Int.	8	149.99	
Whitetail Classic									
WTC 11[4]	1.5-5	75-23	3.4-3.2	9.3	1	Int.	9.7	184.99	
WTC 12[4]	2.5-8	45-14	3.2-3	11.3	1	Int.	13	199.99	
WTC 13[4]	3.5-10	30-10.5	3.2-3	12.4	1	Int.	13.5	209.99	
WTC 15[4]	3.5-10	29.5-11.5	3.2	12.75	1	Int.	13.5	289.99	
WTC 45[4]	4.5-14	22.5-8.6	3.2	13.2	1	Int.	14	265.99	
Whitetail Expedition									
1.5-6x32mm[3]	1.5-6	72-19	3	11.16	1	Int.	15	289.99	

Truplex™ Smart ProDiamond® Crossbow

Maker and Model	Magn.	Field at 100 Yds. (feet)	Eye Relief (in.)	Length (in.)	Tube Dia. (in.)	W & E Adjustments	Weight (ozs.)	Price	Other Data
3-9x42mm[3]	3-9	40-13.5	3	13.2	1	Int.	17.5	309.99	
4-12x42mm[3]	4-12	29-9.6	3	13.46	1	Int.	21.25	334.99	
6-18x42mm[3]	6-18	18.3-6.5	3	15.35	1	Int.	22.5	364.99	
Pro50									
880[10]	4-12	27-9	3.5	13.2	1	Int.	18.25	219.99	
8810[10]	6-18	17-5.8	3.6	13.2	1	Int.	18.25	239.99	
Shotgun									
21004	4	16	5.5	8.8	1	Int.	9.1	84.99	
21005	2.5	24	6	7.4	1	Int.	7	59.99	
7789D	2	31	5.5	8.8	1	Int.	8.75	99.99	
7790D	4	17	5.5	8.5	1	Int.	8.75	114.99	
7791D	1.5-5	76-23.5	3.4	9.5	1	Int.	10.75	138.99	
Rimfire									
1031[18]	4	23.5	3	7.25	1	Int.	8.25	79.99	
1022[7]	4	29.5	3	11.75	1	Int.	11	69.99	
1022T	3-9	42-14	3.5	11.5	1	Int.	12	166.99	
1039[18]	3-9	38-13	3.3-2.9	11.6	1	Int.	13	84.99	
Blackpowder									
BP0420M[17]	4	19.5	4	7.5	1	Int.	8.3	114.99	
BP2732M[12]	2-7	57.7-16.6	3	11.6	1	Int.	12.4	135.99	
Red Dot									
51004[21]	1	—	—	4.8	25mm	Int.	4.7	59.99	
51112[22]	1	—	—	5.25	30mm	Int.	6	99.99	
Pro Air Gun									
21608 A.O.	4	25	3.5	12	1	Int.	11.3	109.99	
21613 A.O.	4-12	25-9	3.1-2.9	13.1	1	Int.	15.8	199.99	
21619 A.O.	6-18	18-7	2.9-2.7	13.8	1	Int.	18.2	209.99	

SPRINGFIELD ARMORY

Maker and Model	Magn.	Field at 100 Yds. (feet)	Eye Relief (in.)	Length (in.)	Tube Dia. (in.)	W & E Adjustments	Weight (ozs.)	Price
6x40 Government Model 7.62mm[1]	6	—	3.5	13	1	Int.	14.7	379.00
4-14x70 Tactical Government Model[2]	4-14	—	3.5	14.25	1	Int.	15.8	395.00
4-14x56 1st Gen. Government Model[3]	4-14	—	3.5	14.75	30mm	Int.	23	480.00
10x56 Mil Dot Government Model[4]	10	—	3.5	14.75	30mm	Int.	28	672.00
6-20x56 Mil Dot Government Model	6-20	—	3.5	18.25	30mm	Int.	33	783.00

[1]Range finding reticle with automatic bullet drop compensator for 308 match ammo to 700 yds. [2]Range finding reticle with automatic bullet drop compensator for 223 match ammo to 700 yds. [3]Also avail. as 2nd Gen. with target knobs and adj. obj., $549.00; as 3rd Gen. with illuminated reticle, $749.00; as Mil Dot model with illuminated Target Tracking reticle, target knobs, adj. obj., $698.00. [4]Unlimited range finding, target knobs, adj. obj., illuminated Target Tracking green reticle. All scopes have matte black finish, internal bubble level, 1/4-MOA clicks. From Springfield, Inc.

STEINER

Maker and Model	Magn.	Field at 100 Yds. (feet)	Eye Relief (in.)	Length (in.)	Tube Dia. (in.)	W & E Adjustments	Weight (ozs.)	Price
Hunting Z								
1.5-5x20[1]	1.5-5	32-12	4.3	9.6	30mm	Int.	11.7	1,399.00
2.5-8x36[1]	2.5-8	40-15	4	11.6	30mm	Int.	13.4	1,599.00
3.5-10x50[1]	3.5-10	77-25	4	12.4	30mm	Int.	16.9	1,799.00

Waterproof, fogproof, nitrogen filled. [1]Heavy-Duplex, Duplex or European #4 reticle. Aluminum tubes; matte black finish. From Pioneer Research.

SWAROVSKI OPTIK

Maker and Model	Magn.	Field at 100 Yds. (feet)	Eye Relief (in.)	Length (in.)	Tube Dia. (in.)	W & E Adjustments	Weight (ozs.)	Price
PF Series								
8x50[1, 3]	8	17	3.15	13.9	30mm	Int.	21.5	987.78
8x56[1, 3]	8	17	3.15	14.29	30mm	Int.	24	1,054.44
PH Series								
1.25-4x24[1]	1.25-4	98.4-31.2	3.15	10.63	30mm	Int.	16.2	1,087.78
1.5-6x42[1]	1.5-6	65.4-21	3.15	12.99	30mm	Int.	20.8	1,221.11
2.5-10x42[1, 2]	2.5-10	39.6-12.6	3.15	13.23	30mm	Int.	19.8	1,376.67
3-12x50[1]	3-12	33-10.5	3.15	14.33	30mm	Int.	22.4	1,421.11
4-16x50	4-16	30-8.5	3.15	14.22	30mm	Int.	22.3	1,476.67
6-24x50	6-24	18.6-5.4	3.15	15.4	30mm	Int.	23.6	1,687.78
A-Line Series								
3-9x36AV[4]	3-9	39-13.5	3.35	11.8	1	Int.	11.7	743.33
3-10x42AV[4]	3-10	33-11.7	3.35	12.44	1	Int.	12.7	821.11
4-12x50AV[4]	4-12	29.1-9.9	3.35	13.5	1	Int.	13.9	843.33

[1]Aluminum tubes; special order for steel. [2]Also with 56mm obj., $1,398.89. [3]Also available with illuminated reticle. [4]Aluminum only. Partial listing shown. Imported from Austria by Swarovski Optik.

No. 1 No. 1A No. 2

No. 4 No. 4A No. 7A

Plex No. 24

SWIFT

Maker and Model	Magn.	Field at 100 Yds. (feet)	Eye Relief (in.)	Length (in.)	Tube Dia. (in.)	W & E Adjustments	Weight (ozs.)	Price
600 4x15	4	17	2.8	10.6	.75	Int.	3.5	15.00
601 3-7x20	3-7	25-12	3-2.9	11	.75	Int.	5.6	35.00
650 4x32	4	26	4	12	1	Int.	9.1	75.00
653 4x40WA[1]	4	35	4	12.2	1	Int.	12.6	125.00
654 3-9x32	3-9	35-12	3.4-2.9	12	1	Int.	9.8	125.00
656 3-9x40WA[1]	3-9	40-14	3.4-2.8	12.6	1	Int.	12.3	140.00
657 6x40	6	28	4	12.6	1	Int.	10.4	125.00
658 2-7x40WA[3]	2-7	55-18	3.3-3	11.6	1	Int.	12.5	160.00
659 3.5-10x44WA	3.5-10	34-12	3-2.8	12.8	1	Int.	13.5	230.00
665 1.5-4.5x21	1.5-4.5	69-24.5	3.5-3	10.9	1	Int.	9.6	125.00
665M 1.5-4.5x21	1.5-4.5	69-24.5	3.5-3	10.9	1	Int.	9.6	125.00
666M Shotgun 1x20	1	113	3.2	7.5	1	Int.	9.6	130.00

All Swift scopes, with the exception of the 4x15, have Quadraplex reticles and are fogproof and waterproof. The 4x15 has crosshair reticle and is non-waterproof. [1]Available in regular matte black or silver finish. [2]Comes with ring mounts, wrench, lens caps, extension tubes, filter, battery. [3]Regular and matte black finish. [4]Speed Focus scopes. Partial listing shown. From Swift Instruments.

ACCESSORIES

SCOPES / HUNTING, TARGET & VARMINT

Maker and Model	Magn.	Field at 100 Yds. (feet)	Eye Relief (in.)	Length (in.)	Tube Dia. (in.)	W & E Adjustments	Weight (ozs.)	Price	Other Data
667 Fire-Fly[2]	1	40	—	5.4	30mm	Int.	5	220.00	
668M 4x32	4	25	4	10	1	Int.	8.9	120.00	
669M 6-18x44	6-18	18-6.5	2.8	14.5	1	Int.	17.6	220.00	
680M	3.9	43-14	4	18	40mm	Int.	17.5	399.95	
681M	1.5-6	56-13	4	11.8	40mm	Int.	17.5	399.95	
682M	4-12	33-11	4	15.4	50mm	Int.	21.7	499.95	
683M	2-7	55-17	3.3	11.6	32mm	Int.	10.6	499.95	
Premier[4]									
649R 4-12x50WA[3]	4-12	29.5-9.5	3.2-3	13.8	1	Int.	17.8	245.00	
671M 3-9x50WA	3-9	35-12	3.24-3.12	15.5	1	Int.	18.2	250.00	
672M 6-18x50WA	6-18	19.4-6.7	3.25-3	15.8	1	Int.	20.9	260.00	
673M 2.5-10x50WA	2.5-10	33-9	4-3.5	11.8	30mm	Int.	18.9	295.00	
674M 3-5x40WA	3-9	40-14.2	3.6-2.9	12	1	Int.	13.1	170.00	
676 4-12x40WA[1]	4-12	29.3-10.5	3.15-2.9	12.4	1	Int.	15.4	180.00	
Pistol									
679M 1.25-4x28	1.25-4	23-9	23-15	9.3	1	Int.	8.2	250.00	
Pistol Scopes									
661 4x32	4	90	10-22	9.2	1	Int.	9.5	130.00	
663 2x20[1]	2	18.3	9-21	7.2	1	Int.	8.4	130.00	

THOMPSON/CENTER RECOIL PROOF SERIES

Pistol Scopes									[1]Black finish; silver optional. [2]Black; lighted reticle. From Thompson/Center Arms.
8315[2]	2.5-7	15-5	8-21, 8-11	9.25	1	Int.	9.2	343.00	
8326[4]	2.5-7	15-5	8-21, 8-11	9.25	1	Int.	10.5	408.00	
Muzzleloader Scopes									
8658	1	60	3.8	9.125	1	Int.	10.2	145.00	
8662	4	16	3	8.8	1	Int.	9.1	139.00	

TRIJICON

ReflexII 1x24	1	—	—	4.25	—	Int.	4.2	425.00	[1]Advanced Combat Optical Gunsight for AR-15, M16, with integral mount. Other mounts available. All models feature tritium and fiber optics dual lighting system that requires no batteries. From Trijicon, Inc.
TA44 1.5x16[1]	1.5	43.8	2.4	5.34	—	Int.	5.31	895.00	
TA45 1.5x24[1]	1.5	28.9	3.6	5.76	—	Int.	5.92	895.00	
TA47 2x20[1]	2	33.1	2.1	5.3	—	Int.	5.82	895.00	
TA50 3x24[1]	3	28.9	1.4	5	—	Int.	5.89	895.00	
TA11 3.5x35[1]	3.5	28.9	2.4	8	—	Int.	14	1,295.00	
TA01 4x32[1]	4	36.8	1.5	5.8	—	Int.	9.9	950.00	
Variable AccuPoint									
3-9x40	3-9	33.8-11.3	3.6-3.2	12.2	1	Int.	12.8	720.00	
1.25-4x24	1.25-4	61.6-20.5	4.8-3.4	10.2	1	Int.	11.4	700.00	

ULTRA DOT

Micro-Dot Scopes[1]									[1]Brightness-adjustable fiber optic red dot reticle. Waterproof, nitrogen-filled one-piece tube. Tinted see-through lens covers and battery included. [2]Parallax adjustable. [3]Ultra Dot sights include rings, battery, polarized filter, and 5-year warranty. All models available in black or satin finish. [4]Illuminated red dot has eleven brightness settings. Shock-proof aluminum tube. From Ultra Dot Distribution.
1.5-4.5x20 Rifle	1.5-4.5	80-26	3	9.8	1	Int.	10.5	297.00	
2-7x32	2-7	54-18	3	11	1	Int.	12.1	308.00	
3-9x40	3-9	40-14	3	12.2	1	Int.	13.3	327.00	
4x-12x56[2]	4-12	30-10	3	14.3	1	Int.	18.3	417.00	
Ultra-Dot Sights[3]									
Ultra-Dot 25[4]	1	—	—	5.1	1	Int.	3.9	159.00	
Ultra-Dot 30[4]	1	—	—	5.1	30mm	Int.	4	179.00	

UNERTL

1" Target	6, 8, 10	16-10	2	21.5	.75	Ext.	21	675.00	[1]Dural .25-MOA click mounts. Hard coated lenses. Non-rotating objective lens focusing. [2].25-MOA click mounts. [3]With target mounts. [4]With calibrated head. [5]Same as 1" Target but without objective lens focusing. [6]With new Posa mounts. [7]Range focus unit near rear of tube. Price is with Posa or standard mounts. Magnum clamp. From Unertl.
1.25: Target[1]	8, 10, 12, 14	12-16	2	25	.75	Ext.	21	466.00	
1.5" Target	10, 12, 14, 16, 18, 20	11.5-3.2	2.25	25.5	.75	Ext.	31	752.50	
2" Target[2]	10, 12, 14, 16, 18, 24, 30, 32, 36,	8	2.25	26.25	1	Ext.	44	918.50	
Varmint, 1.25"[3]	6, 8, 10, 12, 8, 10, 12,	1-7	2.50	19.50	.875	Ext.	26	466.00	
Ultra Varmint, 2"[4]	15	12.6-7	2.25	24	1	Ext.	34	918.50	
Small Game[5]	3, 4, 6	25-17	2.25	18	.75	Ext.	16	284.00	
Programmer 200[7]	10, 12, 14, 16, 18, 20, 24, 30, 36	11.3-4	—	26.5	1	Ext.	45	1,290.00	
BV-20[8]	2	8	4.4	17.875	1	Ext.	21.25	595.00	
Tube Sight	—	—	—	17	—	Ext.	—	262.50	

U.S. OPTICS

SN-1/TAR Fixed Power System									Prices shown are estimates; scopes built to order; choice of reticles; choice of front or rear focal plane; extra-heavy MIL-SPEC construction; extra-long turrets; individual w&e rebound springs; up to 100mm dia. objectives; up to 50mm tubes; all lenses multi-coated. Other magnifications available. [1]Modular components allow a variety of fixed or variable magnifications, night vision, etc. Made in U.S. by U.S. Optics.
16.2x	15	8.6	4.3	16.5	30mm	Int.	27	1,700.00	
22.4x	20	5.8	3.8	18	30mm	Int.	29	1,800.00	
26x	24	5	3.4	18	30mm	Int.	31	1,900.00	
31x	30	4.6	3.5	18	30mm	Int.	32	2,100.00	
37x	36	4	3.6	18	30mm	Int.	32	2,300.00	
48x	50	3	3.8	18	30mm	Int.	32	2,500.00	
Variables									
SN-2	4-22	26.8-5.8	5.4-3.8	18	30mm	Int.	24	1,762.00	
SN-3	1.6-8	—	4.4-4.8	18.4	30mm	Int.	36	1,435.00	
SN-4	1-4	116-31.2	4.6-4.9	18	30mm	Int.	35	1,065.00	
Fixed Power									
SN-6	8, 10, 17, 22	14-8.5	3.8-4.8	9.2	30mm	Int.	18	1,195.00	
SN-8 Modular[1]	4, 10, 20, 40	32	3.3	7.5	30mm	Int.	11.1	890.00-4,000.00	

Maker and Model	Magn.	Field at 100 Yds. (feet)	Eye Relief (in.)	Length (in.)	Tube Dia. (in.)	W & E Adjustments	Weight (ozs.)	Price	Other Data
WEAVER									
Riflescopes									¹Gloss black, ²Matte black, ³Silver, ⁴Satin, ⁵Silver and black (slightly higher in price). ⁶Field of view measured at 18" eye relief..25 MOA click adjustments, except T-Series which vary from .125 to .25 clicks. One-piece tubes with multi-coated lenses. All scopes are shock-proof, water-proof, and fogproof. Dual-X reticle available in all except V24 which has a fine X-hair and ot; T-Series in which certain models are available in fine X-hair and dots; Qwik-Point red dot scopes which are available in fixed 4 or 12 MOA, or variable 4-8-12 MOA. V16 also available with fine X-hair, dot or Dual-X reticle. T-Series scopes have Micro-Trac® adjustments. From Weaver Products.
K2.5¹	2.5	35	3.7	9.5	1	Int.	7.3	**179.99**	
K4¹⁻²	3.7	26.5	3.3	11.3	1	Int.	10	**194.99**	
K6¹	5.7	18.5	3.3	11.4	1	Int.	10	**194.99**	
KT15¹	14.6	7.5	3.2	12.9	1	Int.	14.7	**374.99**	
V3¹⁻²	1.1-2.8	88-32	3.9-3.7	9.2	1	Int.	8.5	**299.99**	
V9¹⁻²	2.8-8.7	33-11	3.5-3.4	12.1	1	Int.	11.1	**249.99- 299.99**	
V9x50¹⁻²	3-9	29.4-9.9	3.6-3	13.1	1	Int.	14.5	**319.99**	
V10¹⁻²⁻³	2.2-9.6	38.5-9.5	3.4-3.3	12.2	1	Int.	11.2	**259.99- 269.99**	
V10-50¹⁻²⁻³	2.3-9.7	40.2-9.2	2.9-2.8	13.75	1	Int.	15.2	**365.99**	
V16 MDX²⁻³	3.8-15.5	26.8-6.8	3.1	13.9	1	Int.	16.5	**434.99**	
V16 MFC²⁻³	3.8-15.5	26.8-6.8	3.1	13.9	1	Int.	16.5	**434.99**	
V16 MDT²⁻³	3.8-15.5	26.8-6.8	3.1	13.9	1	Int.	16.5	**434.99**	
V24 Varmint²	6-24	15.3-4	3.15	14.3	1	Int.	17.5	**509.99**	
Handgun									
H2¹⁻³	2	21	4-29	8.5	1	Int.	6.7	**212.99- 224.99**	
H4¹⁻³	4	18	11.5-18	8.5	1	Int.	6.7	**234.99**	
VH4¹⁻³	1.5-4	13.6-5.8	11-17	8.6	1	Int.	8.1	**289.99**	
VH8¹⁻²⁻³	2.5-8	8.5-3.7	12.16	9.3	1	Int.	8.3	**299.99**	
Rimfire									
R4²⁻³	3.9	29	3.9	9.7	1	Int.	8.8	**159.99**	
RV7²	2.5-7	37-13	3.7-3.3	10.75	1	Int.	10.7	**184.99- 189.99**	
Grand Slam									
6-20x40mm Varminter Reticle²	6-20X	16.5-5.25	2.75-3	14.48	1	Int.	17.75	**499.99**	
6-20x40mm Fine Crosshairs with a Dot²	6-20X	16.5-5.25	2.75-3	14.48	1	Int.	17.75	**499.99**	
1.5-5x32mm²	1.5-5X	71-21	3.25	10.5	1	Int.	10.5	**429.99**	
4.75x40mm²	4.75X	14.75	3.25	11	1	Int.	10.75	**359.99**	
3-10x40mm²	3-10X	35-11.33	3.5-3	12.08	1	Int.	12.08	**379.99**	
3.5-10x50mm²	3.5-10X	30.5-10.8	3.5-3	12.96	1	Int.	16.25	**459.99**	
4.5-14x40mm	4.5-14X	22.5-10.5	3.5-3	14.48	1	Int.	17.5	**499.99**	
T-Series									
T-6⁴	614	14	3.58	12.75	1	Int.	14.9	**424.95**	
T-36³⁻⁴	36	3	3	15.1	1	Int.	16.7	**794.99**	
ZEISS									
ZM/Z									¹Also avail. with illuminated reticle. ²Illuminated Vari-point reticle. Black matte finish. All scopes have .25-min. click-stop adjustments. Choice of Z-Plex or fine crosshair reticles. Rubber armored objective bell, rubber eyepiece ring. Lenses have T-Star coating for highest light transmission. VM/V scopes avail. with rail mount. Partial listing shown. From Carl Zeiss Optical, Inc.
6x42MC	6	22.9	3.2	12.7	1	Int.	13.4	**749.00**	
8x56MC	8	18	3.2	13.8	1	Int.	17.6	**829.00**	
1.25-4x24MC	1.25-4	105-33	3.2	11.46	30mm	Int.	17.3	**779.00**	
1.5-6x42MC	1.5-6	65.5-22.9	3.2	12.4	30mm	Int.	18.5	**899.00**	
2.5-10x48MC¹	2.5-10	33-11.7	3.2	14.5	30mm	Int.	24	**1,029.00**	
3-12x56MC¹	3-12	27.6-9.9	3.2	15.3	30mm	Int.	25.8	**1,099.00**	
Conquest									
3-9x36MC	3-9	34-11	4	13.15	1	Int.	15	**499.00**	
VM/V									
1.1-4x24 VariPoint T²	1.1-4	120-34	3.5	11.8	30mm	Int.	15.8	**1,799.00**	
1.5-6x42T*	1.5-6	65.5-22.9	3.2	12.4	30mm	Int.	18.5	**1,349.00**	
2.5-10x50T*¹	2.5-10	47.1-13	3.5	12.5	30mm	Int.	16.25	**1,549.00**	
3-12x56T*	3-12	37.5-10.5	3.5	13.5	30mm	Int.	19.5	**1,599.00**	
3-9x42T*	3-9	42-15	3.74	13.3	1	Int.	15.3	**1,249.00**	
5-15x42T*	5-15	25.7-8.5	3.74	13.3	1	Int.	15.4	**1,499.00**	

Hunting scopes in general are furnished with a choice of reticle—crosshairs, post with crosshairs, tapered or blunt post, or dot crosshairs, etc. The great majority of target and varmint scopes have medium or fine crosshairs but post or dot reticles may be ordered. W—Windage E—Elevation MOA—Minute of Angle or 1" (approx.) at 100 yards.

ACCESSORIES

LASER SIGHTS

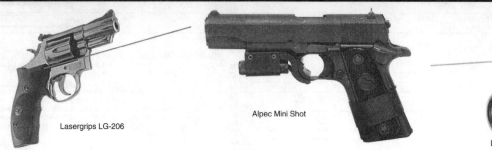

Lasergrips LG-206

Alpec Mini Shot

Laser Devices ULS 2001 with TLS 8R light

Maker and Model	Wavelength (nm)	Beam Color	Lens	Operating Temp. (degrees F.)	Weight (ozs.)	Price	Other Data
ALPEC							[1]Range 1000 yards. [2]Range 300 yards. Mini Shot II range 500 yards, output 650mm, **$129.95**. [3]Range 300 yards; Laser Shot II 500 yards; Super Laser Shot 1000 yards. Black or stainless finish aluminum; removable pressure or push-button switch. Mounts for most handguns, many rifles and shotguns. From Alpec Team, Inc.
Power Shot[1]	635	Red	Glass	NA	2.5	$199.95	
Mini Shot[2]	670	Red	Glass	NA	2.5	99.95	
Laser Shot[3]	670	Red	Glass	NA	3.0	99.95	
BEAMSHOT							[1]Black or silver finish; adj. for windage and elevation; 300-yd. range; also M1000/S (500-yd. range), M1000/u (800-yd.). [2]Black finish; 300-, 500-, 800-yd. models. All come with removable touch pad switch, 5" cable. Mounts to fit virtually any firearm. From Quarton USA Co.
1000[1]	670	Red	Glass	—	3.8	NA	
3000[2]	635/670	Red	Glass	—	2	NA	
1001/u	635	Red	Glass	—	3.8	NA	
780	780	Red	Glass	—	3.8	NA	
BSA							[1]Comes with mounts for 22/air rifle and Weaver-style bases.
LS650[1]	N/A	Red	N/A	N/A	N/A	49.95	
LASERAIM							[1]Red dot/laser combo; 300-yd. range: LA3xHD Hotdot has 500-yd. range **$249.00**; 4 MOA dot size, laser gives 2" dot size at 100 yds. [2]30mm obj. lens: 4 MOA dot at 100 yds: fits Weaver base. [3]300-yd range; 2" dot at 100 yds.; rechargeable Nicad battery [4]1.5-mile range; 1" dot at 100 yds.; 20+ hrs. batt. life. [5]1.5-mile range; 1" dot at 100 yds; rechargeable Nicad battery (comes with in-field charger); [6]Black or satin finish. With mount, **$169.00**. [7]Laser projects 2" dot at 100 yds.: with rotary switch; with Hotdot **$237.00**; with Hotdot touch switch **$357.00**. [8]For Glock 17-27; G1 Hotdot **$299.00**; price installed. [10]Fits std. Weaver base, no rings required; 6-MOA dot; seven brightness settings. All have w&e adj.; black or satin silver finish. From Laseraim Technologies, Inc.
LA10 Hotdot[4]	—	—	—	—	NA	199.00	
Lasers							
MA-35RB Mini Aimer[7]	—	—	—	—	1.0	129.00	
G1 Laser[8]	—	—	—	—	2.0	229.00	
LASER DEVICES							[1]For S&W P99 semi-auto pistols; also BA-2, 5 oz., **$339.00**. [2]For revolvers. [3]For HK, Walther P99. [4]For semi-autos. [5]For rifles; also FA-4/ULS, 2.5 oz., **$325.00**. [6]For HK sub guns. [7]For military rifles. [8]For shotguns. [9]For SIG-Pro pistol. [10]Universal, semi-autos. All avail. with Magnum Power Point (650nM) or daytime-visible Super Power Point (632nM) diode. Infrared diodes avail. for law enforcement. From Laser Devices, Inc.
BA-1[1]	632	Red	Glass	—	2.4	372.00	
BA-3[2]	632	Red	Glass	—	3.3	332.50	
BA-5[3]	632	Red	Glass	—	3.2	372.00	
Duty-Grade[4]	632	Red	Glass	—	3.5	372.00	
FA-4[5]	632	Red	Glass	—	2.6	358.00	
LasTac[1]	632	Red	Glass	—	5.5	298.00 to 477.00	
MP-5[6]	632	Red	Glass	—	2.2	495.00	
MR-2[7]	632	Red	Glass	—	6.3	485.00	
SA-2[8]	632	Red	Glass	—	3.0	360.00	
SIG-Pro[9]	632	Red	Glass	—	2.6	372.00	
ULS-2001[10]	632	Red	Glass	—	4.5	210.95	
Universal AR-2A	632	Red	Glass	—	4.5	445.00	
LASERGRIPS							Replaces existing grips with built-in laser high in the right grip panel. Integrated pressure sensitive pad in grip activates the laser. Also has master on/off switch. [1]For Colt 1911/Commander. [2]For all Glock models. Option on/off switch. Requires factory installation. [3]For S&W K, L, N frames, round or square butt (LG-207); [4]For Taurus small-frame revolvers. [5]For Ruger SP-101. [6]For SIG Sauer P226. From Crimson Trace Corp. [7]For Beretta 92/96. [8]For Ruger MK II. [9]For S&W J-frame. [10]For Sig Sauer P228/229. [11]For Colt 1911 full size, wraparound. [12]For Beretta 92/96, wraparound. [13]For Colt 1911 compact, wraparound. [14]For S&W J-frame, rubber.
LG-201[1]	633	Red-Orange	Glass	NA	—	299.00	
LG-206[3]	633	Red-Orange	Glass	NA	—	229.00	
LG-085[4]	633	Red-Orange	Glass	NA	—	229.00	
LG-101[5]	633	Red-Orange	Glass	NA	—	229.00	
LG-226[6]	633	Red-Orange	Glass	NA	—	229.00	
GLS-630[2]	633	Red-Orange	Glass	NA	—	595.00	
LG202[7]	633	Red-Orange	Glass	NA	—	299.00	
LG203[8]	633	Red-Orange	Glass	NA	—	299.00	
LG205[9]	633	Red-Orange	Glass	NA	—	299.00	
LG229[10]	633	Red-Orange	Glass	NA	—	299.00	
LG301[11]	633	Red-Orange	Glass	NA	—	329.00	
LG302[12]	633	Red-Orange	Glass	NA	—	329.00	
LG304[13]	633	Red-Orange	Glass	NA	—	329.00	
LG305[14]	633	Red-Orange	Glass	NA	—	299.00	
LASERLYTE							[1]Dot/circle or dot/crosshair projection; black or stainless. [2]Also 635/645mm model. From TacStar Laserlyte.
LLX-0006-140/090[1]	635/645	Red	—	—	1.4	159.95	
WPL-0004-140/090[2]	670	Red	—	—	1.2	109.95	
TPL-0004-140/090[2]	670	Red	—	—	1.2	109.95	
T7S-0004-140[2]	670	Red	—	—	0.8	109.95	
LASERMAX							Replaces the recoil spring guide rod; includes a customized takedown lever that serves as the laser's instant on/off switch. For Glock, Smith & Wesson, Sigarms, Beretta and select Taurus models. Installs in most pistols without gunsmithing. Battery life 1/2 hour to 2 hours in continuous use. From LaserMax.
LMS-1000 Internal Guide Rod	635	Red-Orange	Glass	40-120	.25	389.00	
NIGHT STALKER							Waterproof; LCD panel displays power remaining; programmable blink rate; constant or memory on. From Wilcox Industries Corp.
S0 Smart	635	Red	NA	NA	2.46	515.00	

SCOPE RINGS & BASES

Maker, Model, Type	Adjust.	Scopes	Price
AIMTECH			
Handguns			
AMT Auto Mag II .22 Mag.	No	Weaver rail	$56.99
Astra .44 Mag Revolver	No	Weaver rail	63.25
Beretta/Taurus 92/99	No	Weaver rail	63.25
Browning Buckmark/Challenger II	No	Weaver rail	56.99
Browning Hi-Power	No	Weaver rail	63.25
Glock 17, 17L, 19, 23, 24 etc. no rail	No	Weaver rail	63.25
Glock 20, 21 no rail	No	Weaver rail	63.25
Glock 9mm and .40 with access. rail	No	Weaver rail	74.95
Govt. 45 Auto/.38 Super	No	Weaver rail	63.25
Hi-Standard (Mitchell version) 107	No	Weaver rail	63.25
H&K USP 9mm/40 rail mount	No	Weaver rail	74.95
Rossi 85/851/951 Revolvers	No	Weaver rail	63.25
Ruger Mk I, Mk II	No	Weaver rail	49.95
Ruger P85/P89	No	Weaver rail	63.25
S&W K, L, N frames	No	Weaver rail	63.25
S&W K, L, N with tapped top strap*	No	Weaver rail	69.95
S&W Model 41 Target 22	No	Weaver rail	63.25
S&W Model 52 Target 38	No	Weaver rail	63.25
S&W Model 99 Walther frame rail mount	No	Weaver rail	74.95
S&W 2nd Gen. 59/459/659 etc.	No	Weaver rail	56.99
S&W 3rd Gen. full size 5906 etc.	No	Weaver rail	69.95
S&W 422, 622, 2206	No	Weaver rail	56.99
S&W 645/745	No	Weaver rail	56.99
S&W Sigma	No	Weaver rail	64.95
Taurus PT908	No	Weaver rail	63.25
Taurus 44 6.5" bbl.	No	Weaver rail	69.95
Walther 99	No	Weaver rail	74.95
Shotguns			
Benelli M-1 Super 90	No	Weaver rail	44.95
Benelli Montefeltro	No	Weaver rail	44.95
Benelli Nova	No	Weaver rail	69.95
Benelli Super Black Eagle	No	Weaver rail	49.95
Browning A-5 12-ga.	No	Weaver rail	40.95
Browning BPS 12-ga.	No	Weaver rail	40.95
Browning Gold Hunter 12-ga.	No	Weaver rail	44.95
Browning Gold Hunter 20-ga.	No	Weaver rail	49.95
Browning Gold Hunter 10-ga.	No	Weaver rail	49.95
Beretta 303 12-ga.	No	Weaver rail	44.95
Beretta 390 12-ga.	No	Weaver rail	44.95
Beretta Pintail	No	Weaver rail	44.95
H&K Fabarms Gold/SilverLion	no	Weaver rail	49.95
Ithaca 37/87 12-ga.	No	Weaver rail	40.95
Ithaca 37/87 20-ga.	No	Weaver rail	40.95
Mossberg 500/Maverick 12-ga.	No	Weaver rail	40.95
Mossberg 500/Maverick 20-ga.	No	Weaver rail	40.95
Mossberg 835 3.5" Ulti-Mag	No	Weaver rail	40.95
Mossberg 5500/9200	No	Weaver rail	40.95
Remington 1100/1187 12-ga.	No	Weaver rail	40.95
Remington 1100/1187 12-ga. LH	No	Weaver rail	40.95
Remington 1100/1187 20-ga.	No	Weaver rail	40.95
Remington 1100/1187 20-ga. LH	No	Weaver rail	40.95
Remington 870 12-ga.	No	Weaver rail	40.95
Remington 870 12-ga. LH	No	Weaver rail	40.95
Remington 870 20-ga.	No	Weaver rail	40.95
Remington 870 20-ga. LH	No	Weaver rail	40.95
Remington 870 Express Magnum	No	Weaver rail	40.95
Remington SP-10 10-ga.	No	Weaver rail	49.95
Winchester 1300 12-ga.	No	Weaver rail	40.95
Winchester 1400 12-ga.	No	Weaver rail	40.95
Winchester Super X2	No	Weaver rail	44.95
Rifles			
AR-15/M16	No	Weaver rail	21.95
Browning A-Bolt	No	Weaver rail	21.95
Browning BAR	No	Weaver rail	21.95
Browning BLR	No	Weaver rail	21.95
CVA Apollo	No	Weaver rail	21.95
Marlin 336	No	Weaver rail	21.95
Mauser Mark X	No	Weaver rail	21.95
Modern Muzzleloading	No	Weaver rail	21.95
Remington 700 Short Action	No	Weaver rail	21.95
Remington 700 Long Action	No	Weaver rail	21.95
Remington 7400/7600	No	Weaver rail	21.95
Ruger 10/22	No	Weaver rail	21.95
Ruger Mini 14 Scout Rail**	No	Weaver rail	89.50
Savage 110, 111, 113, 114, 115, 116	No	Weaver rail	21.95
Thompson Center Thunderhawk	No	Weaver rail	21.95
Traditions Buckhunter	No	Weaver rail	21.95
White W Series	No	Weaver rail	21.95
White G Series	No	Weaver rail	21.95
White WG Series	No	Weaver rail	21.95
Winchester Model 70	No	Weaver rail	21.95
Winchester 94 AE	No	Weaver rail	21.95

Maker, Model, Type	Adjust.	Scopes	Price
AIMTECH (cont.)			

All mounts no-gunsmithing, iron sight usable. Rifle mounts are solid see-through bases. All mounts accommodate standard Weaver-style rings of all makers. From Aimtech division, L&S Technologies, Inc. *3-blade sight mount combination. **Replacement handguard and mounting rail.

Maker, Model, Type	Adjust.	Scopes	Price
A.R.M.S.			
M16A1,A2,AR-15	No	Weaver rail	$59.95
Multibase	No	Weaver rail	59.95
#19 ACOG Throw Lever Mt.	No	Weaver rail	150.00
#19 Weaver/STANAG Throw Lever Rail	No	Weaver rail	140.00
STANAG Rings	No	30mm	75.00
Throw Lever Rings	No	Weaver rail	99.00
Ring Inserts	No	1", 30mm	29.00
#22M68 Aimpoint Comp Ring Throw Lever	No	Weaver rail	99.00
#38 Std. Swan Sleeve[1]	No	—	180.00
#39 A2 Plus Mod. Mt.	No	#39T rail	125.00

[1]Avail. in three lengths. From A.R.M.S., Inc.

Maker, Model, Type	Adjust.	Scopes	Price
ARMSON			
AR-15[1]	No	1"	45.00
Mini-14[2]	No	1"	66.00
H&K[3]	No	1"	82.00

[1]Fastens with one nut. [2]Models 181, 182, 183, 184, etc. [3]Claw mount. From Trijicon, Inc.

Maker, Model, Type	Adjust.	Scopes	Price
ARMSPORT			
100 Series [1]	No	1" rings, Low, med., high	10.75
104 22-cal.	No	1"	10.75
201 See-Thru	No	1"	13.00
1-Piece Base[2]	No	—	5.50
2-Piece Base[2]	No	—	2.75

[1]Weaver-type ring. [2]Weaver-type base; most popular rifles. Made in U.S. From Armsport.

Maker, Model, Type	Adjust.	Scopes	Price
AO			
AO/Lever Scout Scope	No	Weaver rail	50.00

No gunsmithing required for lever-action rifles with 8" Weaver-style rails; surrounds barrel shank; 6" long; low profile. AO Sight Systems Inc.

Maker, Model, Type	Adjust.	Scopes	Price
B-SQUARE			
Pistols (centerfire)			
Beretta 92, 96/Taurus 99	No	Weaver rail	69.95
Colt M1911	E only	Weaver rail	69.95
Desert Eagle	No	Weaver rail	69.95
Glock	No	Weaver rail	69.95
H&K USP, 9mm and 40 S&W	No	Weaver rail	69.95
Ruger P85/89	E only	Weaver rail	69.95
SIG Sauer P226	E only	Weaver rail	69.95
Pistols (rimfire)			
Browning Buck Mark	No	Weaver rail	32.95
Colt 22	No	Weaver rail	49.95
Ruger Mk I/II, bull or taper	No	Weaver rail	32.95-49.95
Smith & Wesson 41, 2206	No	Weaver rail	36.95-49.95
Revolvers			
Colt Anaconda/Python	No	Weaver rail	35.95-74.95
Ruger Single-Six	No	Weaver rail	64.95
Ruger GP-100	No	Weaver rail	64.95
Ruger Blackhawk, Super	No	Weaver rail	64.95
Ruger Redhawk, Super	No	Weaver rail	64.95
Smith & Wesson K, L, N	No	Weaver rail	36.95-74.95
Taurus 66, 669, 607, 608	No	Weaver rail	64.95
Rifles (sporting)			
Browning BAR, A-Bolt	No	Weaver rail	45.90
Marlin MR7	No	Weaver rail	45.90
Mauser 98 Large Ring	No	Weaver rail	45.90
Mauser 91/93/95/96 Small Ring	No	Weaver rail	45.90
Remington 700, 740, 742, 760	No	Weaver rail	45.90
Remington 7400, 7600	No	Weaver rail	45.90
Remington Seven	No	Weaver rail	45.90
Rossi 62, 59 and 92	No	Weaver rail	44.95
Ruger Mini-14	W&E	Weaver rail	66.95
Ruger 96/22	No	Weaver rail	45.90
Ruger M77 (short and long)	No	Weaver rail	62.95
Ruger 10/22 (reg. and See-Thru)	No	Weaver rail	45.90
Savage 110-116, 10-16	No	Weaver rail	45.90
Modern Military (rings incl.)			
AK-47/MAC 90	No	Weaver rail	49.95
Colt AR-15	No	Weaver rail	66.95-81.95
FN/FAL/LAR (See-Thru rings)	No	Weaver rail	81.95

SCOPE RINGS & BASES

Maker, Model, Type	Adjust.	Scopes	Price
B-SQUARE (cont.)			
Classic Military (rings incl.)			
FN 49	No	Weaver rail	72.95
Hakim	No	Weaver rail	72.95
Mauser 38, 94, 96, 98	E only	Weaver rail	72.95
Mosin-Nagant (all)	E only	Weaver rail	72.95
Air Rifles			
RWS, Diana, BSA, Gamo	W&E	11mm rail	49.95-59.95
Weihrauch, Anschutz, Beeman, Webley	W&E	11mm rail	59.95-69.95
Shotguns/Slug Guns			
Benelli Super 90 (See-Thru)	No	Weaver rail	53.95
Browning BPS, A-5 9 (See-Thru)	No	Weaver rail	53.95
Browning Gold 10/12/20-ga. (See-Thru)	No	Weaver rail	53.95
Ithaca 37, 87	No	Weaver rail	53.95
Mossberg 500/Mav. 88	No	Weaver rail	53.95
Mossberg 835/Mav. 91	No	Weaver rail	53.95
Remington 870/1100/11-87	No	Weaver rail	53.95
Remington SP10	No	Weaver rail	53.95
Winchester 1200-1500	No	Weaver rail	53.95

Prices shown for anodized black finish; add $10 for stainless finish. Partial listing of mounts shown here. Contact B-Square for complete listing and details.

Maker, Model, Type	Adjust.	Scopes	Price
BEEMAN			
Two-Piece, Med.	No	1"	31.50
Deluxe Two-Piece, High	No	1"	33.00
Deluxe Two-Piece	No	30mm	41.00
Deluxe One-Piece	No	1"	50.00
Dampa Mount	No	1"	120.00

All grooved receivers and scope bases on all known air rifles and 22-cal. rimfire rifles (1/2" to 5/8"—6mm to 15mm).

Maker, Model, Type	Adjust.	Scopes	Price
BOCK			
Swing ALK[1]	W&E	1", 26mm, 30mm	349.00
Safari KEMEL[2]	W&E	1", 26mm, 30mm	149.00
Claw KEMKA[3]	W&E	1", 26mm, 30mm	224.00
ProHunter Fixed[4]	No	1", 26mm, 30mm	95.00

[1]Q.D.: pivots right for removal. For Steyr-Mannlicher, Win. 70, Rem. 700, Mauser 98, Dakota, Sako, Sauer 80, 90. Magnum has extra-wide rings, same price. [2]Heavy-duty claw-type reversible for front or rear removal. For Steyr-Mannlicher rifles. [3]True claw mount for bolt-action rifles. Also in extended model. For Steyr-Mannlicher, Win. 70, Rem. 700. Also avail. as Gunsmith Bases—bases not drilled or contoured—same price. [4]Extra-wide rings. Imported from Germany by GSI, Inc.

Maker, Model, Type	Adjust.	Scopes	Price
BSA			
AA Airguns	Yes	Super Ten, 240 Magnum, Maxi gripped scope rail equipped air rifles	59.99 (adj). 29.99 (fixed)

Maker, Model, Type	Adjust.	Scopes	Price
BURRIS			
Supreme (SU) One-Piece (T)[1]	W only	1" split rings, 3 heights	1-piece base - 23.00-27.00
Trumount (TU) Two-Piece (T)	W only	1" split rings, 3 heights	2-piece base - 21.00-30.00
Trumount (TU) Two-Piece Ext.	W only	1" split rings	26.00
Browning 22-cal. Auto Mount[2]	No	1" split rings	20.00
1" 22-cal. Ring Mounts[3]	No	1" split rings	1"rings - 24.00-41.00
L.E.R. (LU) Mount Bases[4]	W only	1" split rings	24.00-52.00
L.E.R. No Drill-No Tap Bases[4,7,8]	W only	1" split rings	48.00-52.00
Extension Rings[5]	No	1" scopes	28.00-46.00
Ruger Ring Mount[6,9]	W only	1" split rings	50.00-68.00
Std. 1" Rings[9]	—	Low, medium, high heights	29.00-43.00
Zee Rings[9]	—	Fit Weaver bases; medium and high heights	29.00-44.00
Signature Rings	No	30mm split rings	68.00
Rimfire/Airgun Rings	W only	1" split rings, med. & high	24.00-41.00
Double Dovetail (DD) Bases	No	30mm Signature	23.00-26.00

[1]Most popular rifles. Universal rings, mounts fit Burris, Universal, Redfield, Leupold and Browning bases. Comparable prices. [2]Browning Standard 22 Auto rifle. [3]Grooved receivers. [4]Universal dovetail; accepts Burris, Universal, Redfield, Leupold rings. For Dan Wesson, S&W, Virginian, Ruger Blackhawk, Win. 94. [5]Medium standard front, extension rear, per pair. Low standard front, extension rear per pair. [6]Compact scopes, scopes with 2" bell for M77R. [7]Selected rings and bases available with matte Safari or silver finish. [8]For S&W K, L, N frames, Colt Python, Dan Wesson with 6" or longer barrels. [9]Also in 30mm.

Maker, Model, Type	Adjust.	Scopes	Price
CATCO			
Enfield Drop-In	No	1"	39.95

Uses Weaver-style rings (not incl.). No gunsmithing required. See-Thru design. From CATCO.

Maker, Model, Type	Adjust.	Scopes	Price
CLEAR VIEW			
Universal Rings, Mod. 101[1]	No	1" split rings	21.95
Standard Model[2]	No	1" split rings	21.95
Broad View[3]	No	1"	21.95
22 Model[4]	No	3/4", 7/8", 1"	13.95
SM-94 Winchester[5]	No	1" split rings	23.95
94 EJ[6]	No	1" split rings	21.95

[1]Most rifles by using Weaver-type base; allows use of iron sights. [2]Most popular rifles; allows use of iron sights. [3]Most popular rifles; low profile, wide field of view. [4]22 rifles with grooved receiver. [5]Side mount. [6]For Win. A.E. From Clear View Mfg.

Maker, Model, Type	Adjust.	Scopes	Price
CONETROL			
Huntur[1] (inc. AQD)	W only	1", split rings, 3 heights	99.96
Gunnur[2] (inc. AQD)	W only	1", split rings, 3 heights	119.88
Custom[3] (inc. AQD)	W only	1", split rings, 3 heights	149.88
One-Piece Side Mount Base[4]	W only	1", 26.5mm solid or split rings, 3 heights	NA
DapTar Bases[5]	W only	1", 26.5mm solid or split rings, 3 heights	NA
Pistol Bases, 2-or 3-ring[6]	W only		NA
Fluted Bases[7]	W only	Standard Conetrol rings	149.88
Metric Rings[8]	W only	26mm, 26.5mm, 30mm	99.96-149.88

[1]All popular rifles, including metric-drilled foreign guns. Price shown for base, two rings. Matte finish. [2]Gunnur grade has mirror-finished rings to match scopes. Satin-finish base to match guns. Price shown for base, two rings. [3]Custom grade has mirror-finished rings and mirror-finished, streamlined base. Price shown for base, two rings. [4]Win. 94, Krag, older split-bridge Mannlicher-Schoenauer, Mini-14, etc. Prices same as above. [5]For all popular guns with integral mounting provision, including Sako. BSA Ithacagun, Ruger, Tikka, H&K, BRNO—$39.96-$59.94—and many others. Also for grooved-receiver rimfires and air rifles. Prices same as above. [6]For XP-100, T/C Contender, Colt SAA, Ruger Blackhawk, S&W and others. [7]Sculptured two-piece bases as found on fine custom rifles. Price shown is for base alone. Also available unfinished—$99.96, or finished but unblued—$119.88. [8]26mm, 26.5mm, and 30mm rings made in projectionless style, in three heights. Three-ring mount for T/C Contender and other pistols in Conetrol's three grades. Any Conetrol mount available in stainless or Teflon for double regular cost of grade.

Maker, Model, Type	Adjust.	Scopes	Price
CUSTOM QUALITY			
Custom See-Thru	No	Up to 44mm	29.95
Dovetail 101-1 See-Thru	No	1"	29.95
Removable Rings	No	1"	29.95
Solid Dovetail	No	1", 30mm vertically split	29.95
Dovetail 22 See-Thru	No	1"	29.95

Mounts for many popular rifles. From Custom Quality Products, Inc.

Maker, Model, Type	Adjust.	Scopes	Price
EAW			
Quick-Loc Mount	W&E	1", 26mm	253.00
	W&E	30mm	271.00
Magnum Fixed Mount	W&E	1", 26mm	198.00
	W&E	30mm	215.00

Fit most popular rifles. Avail. in 4 heights, 4 extensions. Reliable return to zero. Stress-free mounting. Imported by New England Custom Gun Svc.

Maker, Model, Type	Adjust.	Scopes	Price
EXCEL INDUSTRIES, INC.			
Titanium Weaver-Style Rings	No	1" and 30mm, low and high	179.00
Steel Weaver-Style Rings	No	1" and 30mm, low and high	149.00
Flashlight Mounts - Titanium and Steel	No	1" and 30mm, low and high	89.50/75.00

Maker, Model, Type	Adjust.	Scopes	Price
GENTRY			
Feather-Light Rings and Bases	No	1", 30mm	90.00-125.00

Bases for Rem. Seven, 700, Mauser 98, Browning A-Bolt, Weatherby Mk. V, Win. 70, HVA, Dakota. Two-piece base for Rem. Seven, chrome moly or stainless. Rings in matte or regular blue, or stainless gray; four heights. From David Gentry.

Maker, Model, Type	Adjust.	Scopes	Price
GRIFFIN & HOWE			
Topmount[1]	No	1", 30mm	625.00
Sidemount[2]	No	1", 30mm	255.00
Garand Mount[3]	No	1"	255.00

[1]Quick-detachable, double-lever mount with 1" rings, installed; with 30mm rings $875.00. [2]Quick-detachable, double-lever mount with 1" rings; with 30mm rings $375.00; installed, 1" rings $405.00; installed, 30mm rings $525.00. [3]Price installed, with 1" rings $405.00. From Griffin & Howe.

Maker, Model, Type	Adjust.	Scopes	Price
G. G. & G.			
Remington 700 Rail	No	Weaver base	135.00
Sniper Grade Rings	No	30mm	159.95
M16/AR15 F.I.R.E. Std.[1]	No	Weaver rail	75.00

Maker, Model, Type	Adjust.	Scopes	Price
G. G. & G. (cont.)			
M16/AR15 F.I.R.E. Scout	No	Weaver rail	82.95
Aimpoint Standard Ring	No	—	164.95
Aimpoint Cantilever Ring	No	Weaver rail	212.00

[1]For M16/A3, AR15 flat top receivers; also in extended length. [2]For Aimpoint 5000 and Comp; quick detachable; spare battery compartment. [3]Low profile; quick release. From G. G. & G.

Maker, Model, Type	Adjust.	Scopes	Price
IRONSIGHTER			
Ironsighter See-Through Mounts[1]	No	1" split rings	29.40-64.20
Ironsighter S-94	No	1" split rings	45.28
Ironsighter AR-15/M-16[8]	No	1", 30mm	70.10
Ironsighter 22-Cal.Rimfire[2]	No	1"	18.45
Model #570[9]	No	1" split rings	29.40
Model #573[9]	No	30mm split rings	45.28
Model #727[3]	No	.875" split rings	18.45
Blackpowder Mount[7]	No	1"	34.20-78.25

[1]Most popular rifles. Rings have oval holes to permit use of iron sights. [2]For 1" dia. scopes. [3]For .875 dia. scopes. [4]For 1" dia. extended eye relief scopes. [6]732—Ruger 77/22 R&RS, No. 1, Ranch Rifle; 778 fits Ruger 77R, RS. Both 733, 778 fits Ruger Integral bases. [7/8]Fits most popular blackpowder rifles; two-piece (CVA, Knight, Marlin and Austin & Halleck) and one-piece integral (T/C). [8]Model 716 with 1" #540 rings; Model 717 with 30mm #530 rings. [9]Fits Weaver-style bases. Some models in stainless finish. From Ironsighter Co.

Maker, Model, Type	Adjust.	Scopes	Price
K MOUNT By KENPATABLE			
Shotgun Mount	No	1", laser or red dot device	49.95
SKS[1]	No	1"	39.95

Wrap-around design; no gunsmithing required. Models for Browning BPS, A-5 (Sweet 16, 20, Rem. 870/1100 (LTW, and L.H.), S&W 916, Mossberg 500, Ithaca 37 & 51 12-ga., S&W 1000/3000, Win. 1400. [1]Requires simple modification to gun. From KenPatable Ent.

Maker, Model, Type	Adjust.	Scopes	Price
KRIS MOUNTS			
Side-Saddle[1]	No	1",26mm split rings	12.98
Two-Piece (T)[2]	No	1", 26mm split rings	8.98
One Piece (T)[3]	No	1", 26mm split rings	12.98

[1]One-piece mount for Win. 94. [2]Most popular rifles and Ruger. [3]Blackhawk revolver. Mounts have oval hole to permit use of iron sights.

Maker, Model, Type	Adjust.	Scopes	Price
KWIK-SITE			
KS-See-Thru[1]	No	1"	27.95-57.95
AA-22 See-Thru[2]	No	1"	21.95
KS-W94[3]	No	1"	42.95
KS-WEV (Weaver-style rings)	No	1"	19.95
KS-WEV-HIGH	No	1"	19.95
KS-T22 1"[4]	No	1"	17.95
KS-FL Flashlite[5]	No	Mini or C cell flashlight	37.95
KS-T88[6]	No	1"	21.95
KS-T89	No	30mm	21.95
KSN 22 See-Thru	No	1", 7/8"	17.95
KSN-T22	No	1", 7/8"	17.95
KSN-M-16 See-Thru (for M16 + AR-15)	No	1"	49.95
KS-202[1]	No	1"	27.97
KS-203	No	30mm	42.95
KSBP[7]	No	Integral	76.95
KSB Base Set	—		5.95
Combo Bases & Rings	No	1"	21.95

Bases interchangeable with Weaver bases. [1]Most rifles. Allows use of iron sights. [2]22-cal. rifles with grooved receivers. Allows use of iron sights. [3]Model 94, 94 Big Bore. No drilling or tapping. Also in adjustable model $57.95. [4]Non-See-Thru model for grooved receivers. [5]Allows C-cell or, Mini Mag Lites to be mounted atop See-Thru mounts. [6]Fits any Redfield, Tasco, Weaver or Universal-style Kwik-Site dovetail base. [7]Blackpowder mount with integral rings and sights. [8]Shotgun side mount. Bright blue, black matte or satin finish. Standard, high heights.

Maker, Model, Type	Adjust.	Scopes	Price
LASER AIM	No	Laser Aim	19.99-69.00

Mounts Laser Aim above or below barrel. Avail. for most popular handguns, rifles, shotguns, including militaries. From Laser Aim Technologies, Inc.

Maker, Model, Type	Adjust.	Scopes	Price
LEUPOLD			
STD Bases[1]	W only	One- or two-piece bases	24.60
STD Rings[2]	—	1" super low, low, medium, high	32.40
DD RBH Handgun Mounts[2]	No	—	59.40
Dual Dovetail Bases[3]	No	—	24.60
Dual Dovetail Rings[8]	—	1", low, med, high	32.40
Ring Mounts[4,5,6]	No	7/8", 1"	81.00
22 Rimfire[9]	No	7/8", 1"	60.00
Gunmaker Base[7]	W only	1"	16.50
Quick Release Rings	—	1", low, med., high	33.00-71.00
Quick Release Bases[9]	No	1", one- or two-piece	71.40

[1]Base and two rings; Casull, Ruger, S&W, T/C; add $5.00 for silver finish. [2]Rem. 700, Win. 70-type actions. For Ruger No. 1, 77, 77/22; interchangeable with Ruger units. For dovetailed rimfire rifles. Sako; high, medium, low.[7] Must be drilled, tapped for each action. [8]13mm dovetail receiver. [9]BSA Monarch, Rem. 40x, 700, 721, 725, Ruger M77, S&W 1500, Weatherby Mark V, Vanguard, Win. M70.

Maker, Model, Type	Adjust.	Scopes	Price
MARLIN			
One-Piece QD (T)	No	1" split rings	10.10

Most Marlin lever actions.

Maker, Model, Type	Adjust.	Scopes	Price
MILLETT			
Black Onyx Smooth	—	1", low, medium, high	31.15
Chaparral Engraved	—	engraved	46.15
One-Piece Bases[6]	Yes	1"	23.95
Universal Two-Piece Bases			
700 Series	W only	Two-piece bases	25.15
FN Series	W only	Two-piece bases	25.15
70 Series	W only	1", two-piece bases	25.15
Angle-Loc Rings[2]	W only	1", low, medium, high	32.20-47.20
Ruger 77 Rings[3]	—	1"	47.20
Shotgun Rings[4]	—	1"	28.29
Handgun Bases, Rings[5]	—	1"	34.60-69.15
30mm Rings[7]	—	30mm	37.75-42.95
Extension Rings[8]	—	1"	35.65
See-Thru Mounts[9]	No	1"	27.95-32.95
Shotgun Mounts[10]	No	1"	49.95
Timber Mount	No	1"	78.00

BRNO, Rem. 40x, 700, 722, 725, 7400 Ruger 77 (round top), Marlin, Weatherby, FN Mauser, FN Brownings, Colt 57, Interarms Mark X, Parker-Hale, Savage 110, Sako (round receiver), many others. [1]Fits Win. M70 70XTR, 670, Browning BBR, BAR, BLR, A-Bolt, Rem. 7400/7600, Four, Six, Marlin 336, Win. 94 A. E., Sav. 110. [2]To fit Weaver-type bases. [3]Engraved. Smooth $34.60. [4]For Rem. 870, 1100; smooth. [5]Two- and three-ring sets for Colt Python, Trooper, Diamondback, Peacekeeper, Dan Wesson, Ruger Redhawk, Super Redhawk. [6]Turn-in bases and Weaver-style for most popular rifles and T/C Contender, XP-100 pistols. [7]Both Weaver and turn-in styles; three heights. [8]Med. or high; ext. front—std. rear, ext. rear—std. front, ext. front—ext. rear. [9]Many popular rifles, Knight MK-85, T/C Hawken, Renegade, Mossberg 500 Slugster, 835 slug. [10]For Rem. 879/1100, Win. 1200, 1300/1400, 1500, Mossberg 500. Some models available in nickel at extra cost. [11]For T/C Hawken and Renegade; See-Thru with adj. open sight inside. From Millett Sights.

Maker, Model, Type	Adjust.	Scopes	Price
MMC			
AK[1]	No	—	39.95
FN FAL/LAR[2]	No	—	59.95

[1]Fits all AK derivative receivers; Weaver-style base; low-profile scope position. [2]Fits all FAL versions; Weaver-style base. From MMC.

Maker, Model, Type	Adjust.	Scopes	Price
RAM-LINE			
Mini-14 Mount	Yes	1"	24.97

No drilling or tapping. Uses std. dovetail rings. Has built-in shell deflector. Made of solid black polymer. From Ram-Line, Inc.

Maker, Model, Type	Adjust.	Scopes	Price
REDFIELD			
JR-SR (T)[1]. One/two-piece bases.	W only	3/4", 1", 26mm, 30mm	JR-15.99-46.99 SR-15.99-33.49
Ring (T)[2]	No	3/4" and 1"	27.95-29.95
Widefield See-Thru Mounts	No	1"	15.95
Ruger Rings[4]	No	1", med., high	30.49-36.49
Ruger 30mm[5]	No	1"	37.99-40.99
Midline Ext. Rings	No	1"	24.95

[1]Low, med. & high, split rings. Reversible extension front rings for 1". 2-piece bases for Sako. Colt Sauer bases $39.95. Med. Top Access JR rings nickel-plated. $28.95. SR two-piece ABN mount nickel-plated. $22.95. [2]Split rings for grooved 22s; 30mm, black matte $42.95. [3]Used with MP scopes for; S&W K, L or N frame, XP-100, T/C Contender, Ruger receivers. [4]For Ruger Model 77 rifles, medium and high; medium only for M77/22. [5]For Model 77. Also in matte finish $45.95. [6]Aluminun 22 groove mount $14.95; base and medium rings $18.95. [7]Fits American or Weaver-style base. Non-Gunsmithing mount system. For many popular shotguns, rifles, handguns and blackpowder rifles. Uses existing screw holes.

Maker, Model, Type	Adjust.	Scopes	Price
S&K			
Insta-Mount (T) Bases and Rings[1]	W only	Uses S&K rings only	47.00-117.00
Conventional Rings and Bases[2]	W only	1" split rings	From 65.00
Sculptured Bases, Rings[2]	W only	1", 26mm, 30mm	From 65.00
Smooth Contoured Rings[3]	Yes	1", 26mm, 30mm	90.00-120.00

[1]1903, A3, M1 Carbine, Lee Enfield #1. Mk.III, #4, #5, M1917, M98 Mauser, AR-15, AR-180, M-14, M-1, Ger. K-43, Mini-14, M1-A, Krag, AKM, Win. 94, SKS Type 56, Daewoo, H&K. [2]Most popular rifles already drilled and tapped and Sako, Tikka dovetails. [3]No projections; weigh 1/2-oz. each; matte or gloss finish. Horizontally and vertically split rings; matte or high gloss.

Maker, Model, Type	Adjust.	Scopes	Price
SAKO			
QD Dovetail	W only	1"	70.00-155.00

Sako, or any rifle using Sako action, 3 heights available. Stoeger, importer.

Maker, Model, Type	Adjust.	Scopes	Price
SPRINGFIELD, INC.			
M1A Third Generation	No	1" or 30mm	123.00
M1A Standard	NO	1" or 30mm	77.00
M6 Scout Mount	No	—	29.00

Weaver-style bases. From Springfield, Inc.

SCOPE RINGS & BASES

Maker, Model, Type	Adjust.	Scopes	Price
TALBOT			
QD Bases	No	—	180.00-190.00
Rings	No	1", 30mm	50.00-70.00
Blue or stainless steel; standard or extended bases; rings in three heights. For most popular rifles. From Talbot QD Mounts.			
TASCO			
World Class			
Aluminum Ringsets	Yes	1", 30mm	12.00-17.00
See-Thru	No	1"	19.00
Shotgun Bases	Yes	—	34.00
From Tasco.			
THOMPSON/CENTER			
Duo-Ring Mount[1]	No	1"	61.99-62.99
Weaver-Style Bases	No	—	10.28-33.36
Weaver-Style Rings[3]	No	1"	27.74-42.13
Weaver-Style See-Thru Rings[4]	No	1"	27.74
[1]Attaches directly to T/C Contender bbl., no drilling/tapping; also for T/C M/L rifles, needs base adapter; blue or stainless. [3]Medium and high; blue or silver finish. [4]For T.C FireHawk, ThunderHawk; blue; silver $29.80. From Thompson/Center.			
UNERTL			
1/4 Click[1]	Yes	3/4", 1" target scopes	Per set 186.00
[1]Unertl target or varmint scopes. Posa or standard mounts, less bases. From Unertl.			
WARNE			
Premier Series (all steel)			
T.P.A. (Permanently Attached)	No	1", 4 heights	87.75
		30mm, 2 heights	98.55
Premier Series Rings fit Premier Series Bases			
Premier Series (all-steel Q.D. rings)			
Premier Series (all steel)	No	1", 4 heights	131.25
Quick detachable lever		26mm, 2 heights	129.95
		30mm, 3 heights	142.00
BRNO 19mm	No	1", 3 heights	125.00
		30mm, 2 heights	136.70
BRNO 16mm		1", 2 heights	125.00
Ruger	No	1", 4 heights	125.00
		30mm, 3 heights	136.70
Ruger M77	No	1", 3 heights	125.00
		30mm, 3 heights	136.70
Sako Medium & Long Action	No	1", 4 heights	125.00
		30mm, 3 heights	136.70
Sako Short Action	No	1", 3 heights	125.00
All-Steel One-Piece Base, ea.			38.50
All-Steel Two-Piece Base, ea.			14.00
Maxima Series (fits all Weaver-style bases)			
Permanently Attached[1]	No	1", 3 heights	25.50
		30mm, 3 heights	36.00
Adjustable Double Lever[2]	No	1", 3 heights	72.60
		30mm, 3 heights	80.75
Thumb Knob	No	1", 3 heights	59.95
		30mm, 3 heights	68.25
Stainless-Steel Two-Piece Base, ea.			15.25
Vertically split rings with dovetail clamp, precise return to zero. Fit most popular rifles, handguns. Regular blue, matte blue, silver finish. [1]All-Steel, non-Q.D. rings. [2]All-steel, Q.D. rings. From Warne Mfg. Co.			
WEAVER			
Detachable Mounts			
Top Mount	No	7/8", 1", 30mm, 33mm	24.95-38.95
Side Mount	No	1", 1" long	14.95-34.95
Tip-Off Rings	No	7/8", 1"	24.95-32.95
Pivot Mounts	No	1"	38.95
Complete Mount Systems			
Pistol	No	1"	75.00-105.00
Rifle	No	1"	32.95
SKS Mount System	No	1"	49.95
Pro-View (no base required)	No	1"	13.95-15.95
Converta-Mount, 12-ga. (Rem. 870, Moss. 500)	No	1", 30mm	74.95

Maker, Model, Type	Adjust.	Scopes	Price
WEAVER (cont.)			
See-Thru Mounts			
Detachable	No	1"	27.00-32.00
System (no base required)	No	1"	15.00-35.00
Tip-Off	No	1"	15.00
Nearly all modern rifles, pistols, and shotguns. Detachable rings in standard, See-Thru, and extension styles, in Low, Medium, High or X-High heights; gloss (blued), silver and matte finishes to match scopes. Extension rings are only available in 1" High style and See-Thru X-tensions only in gloss finish. Tip-Off rings only for 3/8" grooved receivers or 3/8"grooved adaptor bases; no base required. See-Thru & Pro-View mounts for most modern big bore rifles, some in silver. No Drill & Tap Pistol systems in gloss or silver for: Colt Python, Trooper, 357, Officer's Model; Ruger Single-Six, Security-Six (gloss finish only), Blackhawk, Super Blackhawk, Blackhawk SRM 357, Redhawk, Mini-14 Series (not Ranch), Ruger 22 Auto Pistols, Mark II; Smith & Wesson I- and current K-frames with adj. rear sights. Converta-Mount Systems in Standard and See-Under for: Mossberg 500 (12- and 20-ga.); Remington 870, 11-87 (12- and 20-ga. lightweight); Winchester 1200, 1300, 1400, 1500. Converta Brackets, Bases, Rings also avail. for Beretta A303 and A390; Browning A-5, BPS Pump; Ithaca 37, 87. From Weaver.			
WEIGAND			
Browning Buck Mark[1]	No	—	29.95
Colt 22 Automatic[1]	No	—	19.95
Integra Mounts[2]	No	—	39.95-69.00
S&W Revolver[3]	No	—	29.95
Ruger 10/22[4]	No	—	14.95-39.95
Ruger Revolver[5]	No	—	29.95
Taurus Revolver[4]	No	—	29.95-65.00
T/C Encore Monster Mount	No	—	69.00
T/C Contender Monster Mount	No	—	69.00
Lightweight Rings	No	1", 30mm	29.95-39.95
1911, P-9 Scopemounts			
SM3[6]	No	Weaver rail	99.95
SRS 1911-2[7]	No	30mm	59.95
APCMNT[8]	No	—	69.95
[1]No gunsmithing. [2] S&W K, L, N frames; Taurus vent rib models; Colt Anaconda/Python; Ruger Redhawk; Ruger 10/22. [3]K, L, N frames. [4]Three models. [5] Redhawk, Blackhawk, GP-100. [6]3rd Gen.; drill and tap; without slots $59.95. [7]Ringless design, silver only. [8]For Aimpoint Comp. Red Dot scope, silver only. From Weigand Combat Handguns, Inc.			
WIDEVIEW			
Premium 94 Angle Eject and side mount	No	1"	18.70
Premium See-Thru	No	1"	18.70
22 Premium See-Thru	No	3/4", 1"	13.60
Universal Ring Angle Cut	No	1"	18.70
Universal Ring Straight Cut	No	1"	18.70
Solid Mounts			
Lo Ring Solid[1]	No	1"	13.60
Hi Ring Solid[1]	No	1"	13.60
SR Rings	—	1", 30mm	13.60
22 Grooved Receiver	No	1"	13.60
Blackpowder Mounts[2]	No	1"	18.70-37.40
High, extra-high ring mounts with base	No	up to 60mm	18.70
Desert Eagle Pistol Mount	No	1", 30mm	34.95-44.95
[1]For Weaver-type base. Models for many popular rifles. Low ring, high ring and grooved receiver types. [2]No drilling, tapping, for T/C Renegade, Hawken, CVA, Knight Traditions guns. From Wideview Scope Mount Corp.			
WILLIAMS			
Side Mount with HCO Rings[1]	No	1", split or extension rings	74.35
Side Mount, Offset Rings[2]	No	Same	61.45
Sight-Thru Mounts[3]	No	1", 7/8" sleeves	19.50
Streamline Mounts	No	1" (bases form rings)	26.50
[1]Most rifles, Br. S.M.L.E. (round rec.) $14.41 extra. [2]Most rifles including Win. 94 Big Bore. [3]Many modern rifles, including CVA Apollo, others with 1" octagon barrels.			
YORK			
M-1 Garand	Yes	1"	39.95
Centers scope over the action. No drilling, tapping or gunsmithing. Uses standard dovetail rings. From York M-1 Conversions.			
NOTES			
(S)—Side Mount; (T)—Top Mount; 22mm=.866"; 25.4mm=1.024"; 26.5mm=1.045"; 30mm=1.81".			

ACCESSORIES

ACCESSORIES

METALLIC SIGHTS

Sporting Leaf and Open Sights

AUTOMATIC DRILLING REAR SIGHT Most German and Austrian drillings have this kind of rear sight. When rifle barrel is selected, the rear sight automatically comes to the upright position. Base length 2.165", width .472", folding leaf height .315". From New England Custom Gun Service.
Price: $48.50

CLASSIC MARBLE/WILLIAMS STYLE FULLY ADJUSTABLE REAR SPORTING SIGHTS Screw-on attachment. Dovetailed graduated windage and elevation adjustment. Elevation and windage lock with set screws. Available in steel or lightweight alloy construction. From Sarco, Inc.
Price: $13.50

ERA MASTERPIECE ADJUSTABLE REAR SIGHTS Precision-machined, all-steel, polished and blued. Attaches with 8-36 socket head screw. Use small screwdriver to adjust windage and elevation. Available for various barrel widths. From New England Custom Gun Service.
Price: $82.00

ERA CLASSIC ADJUSTABLE REAR SIGHT Similar to the Masterpiece unit except windage is adjusted by pushing sight sideways, then locking it with a reliable clamp. Precision machined all steel construction, polished, with 6-48 fastening screw and Allen wrench. Shallow "V" and "U" notch. Length 2.170", width .550". From New England Custom Gun Service.
Price: $55.00

ERA EXPRESS SIGHTS A wide variety of open sights and bases for custom installation. Partial listing shown. From New England Custom Gun Service.
Price: One-leaf express $66.00
Price: Two-leaf express $71.50
Price: Three-leaf express $77.00
Price: Bases for above $27.50
Price: Standing rear sight, straight $13.25
Price: Base for above $16.50

ERA PROFESSIONAL EXPRESS SIGHTS Standing or folding leaf sights are securely locked to the base with the ERA Magnum Clamp, but can be loosened for sighting in. Base can be attached with two socket-head cap screws or soldered. Finished and blued. Barrel diameters from .600" to .930". From New England Custom Gun Service.
Price: Standing leaf $54.00
Price: One-leaf express $96.00
Price: Two-leaf express $101.00
Price: Three-leaf express $120.00

ERA MASTERPIECE REAR SIGHT Adjustable for windage and elevation, and adjusted and locked with a small screwdriver. Comes with 8-36 socket-head cap screw and wrench. Barrel diameters from .600" to .930".
Price: $75.00

G.G. & G. SAME PLANE APERTURE M-16/AR-15 A2-style dual aperture rear sight with both large and small apertures centered on the same plane.
Price: $45.00

LYMAN No.16 Middle sight for barrel dovetail slot mounting. Folds flat when scope or peep sight is used. Sight notch plate adjustable for elevation. White triangle for quick aiming. Designed to fit 3/8" dovetail slots. Three heights: A-.400" to.500", B-.345" to .445", C-.500" to .600". A slot blank designed to fill dovetail notch when sight is removed is available
Price: $5.00
Price: $13.25

MARBLE FALSE BASE #76, #77, #78 New screw-on base for most rifles replaces factory base. 3/8" dovetail slot permits installation of any folding rear sight. Can be had in sweat-on models also.
Price: $8.00

MARBLE FOLDING LEAF Flattop or semi-buckhorn style. Folds down when scope or peep sights are used. Reversible plate gives choice of "U" or "V" notch. Adjustable for elevation.
Price: $16.00
Price: Also available with both windage and elevation adjustment $18.00

MARBLE SPORTING REAR With white enamel diamond, gives choice of two "U" and two "V" notches or different sizes. Adjustment in height by means of double step elevator and sliding notch piece. For all rifles; screw or dovetail installation.
Price: $16.00 to $17.00

MARBLE #20 UNIVERSAL New screw or sweat-on base. Both have .100" elevation adjustment. In five base sizes. Three styles of U-notch, square notch, peep. Adjustable for windage and elevation.
Price: Screw-on $23.00
Price: Sweat-on $21.00

MILLETT SPORTING & BLACKPOWDER RIFLE Open click adjustable rear fits 3/8" dovetail cut in barrel. Choice of white outline, target black or open express V rear blades. Also available is a replacement screw-on sight with express V, .562" hole centers. Dovetail fronts in white or blaze orange in seven heights (.157"-.540").
Price: Dovetail or screw-on rear $55.60
Price: Front sight $12.34

MILLETT SCOPE-SITE Open, adjustable or fixed rear sights dovetail into a base integral with the top scope-mounting ring. Blaze orange front ramp sight is integral with the front ring half. Rear sights have white outline aperture. Provides fast, short-radius, Patridge-type open sights on the top of the scope. Can be used with all Millett rings, Weaver-style bases, Ruger 77 (also fits Redhawk), Ruger Ranch Rifle, No. 1, No. 3, Rem. 870, 1100; Burris, Leupold and Redfield bases.
Price: Scope-Site top only, windage only $31.15
Price: As above, fully adjustable $66.10
Price: Scope-Site Hi-Turret, fully adjustable, low, medium, high $66.10

RUGER WINDAGE ADJUSTABLE FOLDING REAR SIGHT Fits all Ruger rifles produced with standard folding rear sights. Available in low (.480"), medium (.503") and high (.638") heights. From Sturm, Ruger & Co., Inc.
Price: $18.00

TRIJICON 3-DOT NIGHT SIGHTS Self-luminous and machined from steel. Available for the M16/AR-15, H&K rifles. Front and rear sets and front only.
Price: $52.00-$84.00

WHITWORTH STYLE ENGLISH 3 LEAF EXPRESS SIGHTS Folding leafs marked in 100, 200 and 300 yard increments. Slide assembly is dovetailed in base. Available in four different styles: 3 folding leaves, flat bottom; 1 fixed, 2 folding leaves, flat bottom; 3 folding leaves, round bottom; 1 fixed, 2 folding leaves, round bottom. Available from Sarco, Inc.
Price: $49.95

WICHITA MULTI RANGE SIGHT SYSTEM Designed for silhouette shooting. System allows you to adjust the rear sight to four repeatable range settings, once it is pre-set. Sight clicks to any of the settings by turning a serrated wheel. Front sight is adjustable for weather and light conditions with one adjustment. Specify gun when ordering.
Price: Rear sight $120.00
Price: Front sight $90.00

WILLIAMS DOVETAIL OPEN SIGHT (WDOS) Open rear sight with windage and elevation adjustment. Furnished "U" notch or choice of blades. Slips into dovetail and locks with gib lock. Heights from .281" to .531".
Price: With blade $17.95
Price: Less blade $11.05
Price: Rear sight blades, each $6.29

WILLIAMS GUIDE OPEN SIGHT (WGOS) Open rear sight with windage and elevation adjustment. Bases to fit most military and commercial barrels. Choice of square "U" or "V" notch blade, 3/16", 1/4", 5/16", or 3/8" high.
Price: Less blade $17.95 to $19.50
Price: Extra blades, each $6.90

WILLIAMS WGOS OCTAGON Open rear sight for 1" octagonal barrels. Installs with two 6-48 screws and uses same hole spacing as most T/C muzzleloading rifles. Four heights, choice of square, U, V, or B blade.
Price: $21.99

WILLIAMS WSKS,WAK47 Replaces original military-type rear sight. Adjustable for windage and elevation. No drilling or tapping. Peep aperture or open. For SKS carbines, AK-47-style rifles.
Price: Aperture $25.95
Price: Open $24.00

WILLIAMS WM–96 Fits Mauser 96-type military rifles. Replaces original rear sight with open blade or aperture. Fully adjustable for windage and elevation. No drilling or tapping.
Price: Aperture $25.95
Price: Open $24.00

WILLIAMS FIRE RIFLE SETS Replacement front and rear fiber optic sights. Red bead front, two green elements in the fully-adjustable rear. Made of CNC-machined metal.
Price: For Ruger 10/22 $35.95
Price: For most Marlin and Win. (3/8" dovetail) $29.95
Price: For Remington (newer style sight base) $24.95

Aperture and Micrometer Receiver Sights

A2 REAR SIGHT KIT Featuring an exclusive numbered windage knob. For .223 AR-style rifles. From ArmaLite, Inc.
Price: $55.00

AO GHOST RING HUNTING SIGHT Fully adjustable for windage and elevation. Available for most rifles, including blackpowder guns. Minimum gunsmithing required for most installations; matches most mounting holes. From AO Sight Systems, Inc.
Price: $90.00

AO AR-15/M-16 APERTURE Drop-in replacement of factory sights. Both apertures are on the same plane. Large ghost ring has .230" inside diameter; small ghost ring has .100" inside diameter. From AO Sight Systems, Inc.
Price: $30.00

AO BACKUP GHOST RING SIGHTS Mounts to scope base and retains zero when reinstalled in the field. Affords same elevation/windage adjustability as AO Hunting Ghost Rings. Included are both .191" and .230" apertures and test posts. Available for Ruger, Sako, Remington 700 and other rifles. From AO Sight Systems, Inc.
Price: $65.00

AO Ghost Ring

AO TACTICAL SIGHTS For HK UMP/USC/G36/SL8/MP5. The Big Dot Tritium or standard dot tritium is mated with a large .300" diameter rear ghost ring. The "same plane" rear aperture flips from the .300" to a .230" diameter ghost ring. From AO Sight Systems, Inc.
Price: $90 to $120.00

BEEMAN/FEINWERKBAU 5454 MATCH APERTURE SIGHT Small size, new-design sight uses constant-pressure flat springs to eliminate point of impact shifts.
Price: $350.00

BEEMAN SPORT APERTURE SIGHT Positive click micrometer adjustments. Standard units with flush surface screwdriver adjustments. Deluxe version has target knobs. For air rifles with grooved receivers.
Price: Standard $40.00
Price: Deluxe $50.00

METALLIC SIGHTS

DPMS NATIONAL MATCH Replaces the standard A2 rear sight on M16/AR-15 rifles. Has 1/4-minute windage and 1/2-minute elevation adjustments. Includes both a .052" and .200" diameter aperture.
Price:..$92.99

ENFIELD No. 4 TARGET/MATCH SIGHT Originally manufactured by Parker-Hale, has adjustments up to 1,300 meters. Micrometer click adjustments for windage. Adjustable aperture disc has six different openings from .030" to .053". From Sarco, Inc.
Price:..$49.95

ERA RUGER PEEP SIGHT Made for Ruger M-77 and No. 1 rifles, it is furnished with .093" and .125" opening apertures. Can be installed on a standard Ruger rear mount base or quarter rib. Tightening the aperture disk will lock the elevation setting in place. From New England Custom Gun Service.
Price:..$80.00

EAW RECEIVER SIGHT A fully adjustable aperture sight that locks securely into the EAW quick-detachable scope mount rear base. Made by New England Custom Gun Service.
Price:..$95.00

ERA SEE-THRU Contains fiber optic center dot. Fits standard 3/8" American dovetails. Locks in place with set screw. Ideal for use on moving targets. Width 19.5mm. Available in low (.346", medium .425" and high .504" models. From New England Custom Gun Service.
Price:..$27.50

G. G.& G. MAD IRIS Multiple Aperture Device is a four sight, rotating aperture disk with small and large apertures on the same plane. Mounts on M-16/AR-15 flattop receiver. Fully adjustable.
Price:..$141.95
Price: A2 IRIS, two apertures, full windage adjustments........$124.95

KNIGHT'S ARMAMENT 600 METER FOLDING REAR SIGHT Click adjustable from 200 to 600 meters with clearly visible range markings. Intermediate clicks allows for precise zero at known ranges. Allows use of optical scopes by folding don. Mounts on rear of upper receiver rail on SR-25 and similar rifles. From Knight's Armament Co.
Price:..$181.00

KNIGHT'S ARMAMENT FOLDING 300M SIGHT Mounts on flat-top upper receivers on SR-25 and similar rifles. May be used as a back-up iron sight for a scoped rifle/carbine or a primary sight. Peep insert may be removed to expose the 5mm diameter ghost ring aperture. From Knight's Armament Co.
Price:..$144.00

Lyman No. 57

LYMAN NO. 2 TANG SIGHT Designed for the Winchester Model 94. Has high index marks on aperture post; comes with both .093" quick sighting aperture, and .040" large disk aperture, and replacement mounting screws.
Price:..$76.00
Price: For Marlin lever actions.$76.00

LYMAN No. 57 1/4-minute clicks. Stayset knobs. Quick-release slide, adjustable zero scales. Made for almost all modern rifles.
Price:..$67.50
Price: No. 57SME, 57SMET (for White Systems Model 91 and Whitetail rifles)..$62.50

LYMAN 57GPR Designed especially for the Lyman Great Plains Rifle. Mounts directly onto the tang of the rifle and has 1/4-minute micrometer click adjustments.
Price:..$62.50

LYMAN No. 66 Fits close to the rear of flat-sided receivers, furnished with Stayset knobs. Quick-release slide, 1/4-min. adjustments. For most lever or slide action or flat-sided automatic rifles.
Price:..$67.50
Price: No. 66MK (for all current versions of the Knight MK-85 in-line rifle with flat-sided receiver)...$67.50
Price: No. 66 SKS fits Russian and Chinese SKS rifles; large and small apertures...$67.50
Price: No. 66 WB for Model 1886 Winchester lever actions........$67.50

LYMAN No. 66U Light weight, designed for most modern shotguns with a flat-sided, round-top receiver. 1/4-minute clicks. Requires drilling, tapping. Not for Browning A-5, Rem. M11.
Price:..$71.50

LYMAN 90MJT RECEIVER SIGHT Mounts on standard Lyman and Williams FP bases. Has 1/4-minute audible micrometer click adjustments, target knobs with direction indicators. Adjustable zero scales, quick-release slide. Large 7/8" diameter aperture disk.
Price: Right- or left-hand.......................................$74.95

LYMAN RECEIVER SIGHT Audible-click adjustments for windage and elevation, coin-slotted "stayset" knobs and two interchangeable apertures. For Mauser, Springfield, Sako, T/C Hawken, Rem. 700, Win. 70, Savage 110, SKS, Win. 94, Marlin 336 and 1894.
Price:..$53.99

LYMAN 1886 #2 TANG SIGHT Fits the Winchester 1886 lever action rifle and replicas thereof not containing a tang safety. Has height index marks on the aperture post and an .800" maximum elevation adjustment. Included is a .093" x 1/2" quick-sighting aperture and .040 x 5/8" target disk.
Price:..$76.00

MARBLE PEEP TANG SIGHT All-steel construction. Micrometer-like click adjustments for windage and elevation. For most popular old and new lever-action rifles.
Price:..$125.00

MILLETT PEEP RIFLE SIGHTS Fully adjustable, heat-treated nickel steel peep aperture receiver sight for the Mini-14. Has fine windage and elevation adjustments; replaces original.
Price: Rear sight, Mini-14.......................................$49.00
Price: Front sight, Mini-14......................................$18.75
Price: Front and rear combo with hood.............................$64.00

NECG PEEP SIGHT FOR WEAVER SCOPE MOUNT BASES Attaches to Weaver scope mount base. Windage adjusts with included Allen wrenches, elevation with a small screwdriver. Furnished with two apertures (.093" and .125" diameter hole) and two interchangeable elevation slides for high or low sight line. From New England Custom Gun Service.
Price:..$80.00

T/C HUNTING STYLE TANG PEEP SIGHT Compact, all steel construction, with locking windage and elevation adjustments. For use with "bead style" and fiber optic front sights. Models available to fit all traditional T/C muzzleloading rifles. From Thompson/Center Arms.
Price:..$56.70

T/C CONTENDER CARBINE PEEP SIGHT All-steel, low profile, click-adjustable unit mounting on the pre-drilled tapped scope mount holes on the T/C Contender Carbine. From Thompson/Center Arms.
Price:..$55.05

WILLIAMS APERTURE SIGHT Made to fit SKS rifles.
Price:..$23.49

WILLIAMS FIRE SIGHT PEEP SETS Combines the Fire Sight front bead with Williams fully adjustable metallic peep rear.
Price: For SKS...$39.95
Price: For Ruger 10/22...$39.95
Price: For Marlin or Winchester lever actions.....................$73.95

WILLIAMS FP Internal click adjustments. Positive locks. For virtually all rifles, T/C Contender, Heckler & Koch HK-91, Ruger Mini-14, plus Win., Rem., and Ithaca shotguns.
Price: From..$57.99
Price: With Target Knobs...$71.20
Price: With Square Notched Blade.................................$63.03
Price: With Target Knobs & Square Notched Blade....................$74.45
Price: FP-GR (for dovetail-grooved receivers, .22s and air guns)...$59.95
Price: FP-94BBSE (for Win. 94 Big Bore A.E.; uses top rear scope mount holes)...$59.95

WILLIAMS TARGET FP Similar to the FP series but developed for most bolt-action rimfire rifles. Target FP High adjustable from 1.250" to 1.750" above centerline of bore; Target FP Low adjustable from .750" to 1.250". Attaching bases for Rem. 540X, 541-S, 580, 581, 582 (#540); Rem. 510, 511, 512, 513-T, 521-T (#510); Win. 75 (#75); Savage/Anschutz 64 and Mark 12 (#64). Some rifles require drilling, tapping.
Price: High or Low...............................$73.90 to $77.15
Price: Base only...$13.30
Price: FP-T/C Scout rifle, from...................................$59.95
Price: FP-94BBSE (for Win. 94 Big Bore A.E.; uses top rear scope mount holes)...$59.95

WILLIAMS 5-D SIGHT Low cost sight for shotguns, 22s and more popular big game rifles. Adjustment for windage and elevation. Fits most guns without drilling and tapping. Also for British SMLE, Winchester M94 Side Eject.
Price: From..$34.50
Price: With Shotgun Aperture.....................................$34.50

WILLIAMS 5D RECEIVER SIGHT Alloy construction and similar design to the FP model except designed to fit Win. 94, Marlin 336, Marlin 1895, Mauser 98.
Price:..$34.50

WILLIAMS GUIDE (WGRS) Receiver sight for 30 M1 Carbine, M1903A3 Springfield, Savage 24s, Savage-Anschutz and Weatherby XXII. Utilizes military dovetail; no drilling. Double-dovetail windage adjustment, sliding dovetail adjustment for elevation.
Price:....................................$32.80 to $45.95

Vernier Tang Sights

BALLARD TANG SIGHTS Available in variety of models including short & long staff hunter, Pacific & Montana, custom units allowing windage & elevation adjustments. Uses 8x40 base screws with screw spacing of 1.120". From Axtell Rifle Co.
Price:....................................$175.00 to $325.00

LYMAN TANG SIGHT Made for Win. 94, 1886, Marlin 30, 336 and 1895.
Price:....................................$59.99-$64.99

MARLIN TANG SIGHTS Available in short and long staff hunter models using 8x40 base screws and screw spacing of 1.120". From Axtell Rifle Co.
Price:....................................$170.00 to $180.00

PEDERSOLI CREEDMORE Adjustable for windage and elevation, fits Traditions by Pedersoli rifles and other brands.
Price:..$99.00

REMINGTON TANG SIGHTS Available in short-range hunter and vernier, mid- and long-range vernier and custom models with windage and elevation adjustments. Uses 10x28 base screws, with screw spacing of 1.940". Eye disk has .052" hole with 10x40 thread. From Axtell Rifle Co.
Price:....................................$175.00 to $325.00

SHARPS TANG SIGHTS Reproduction tang sights as manufactured for various Sharps rifles through the years 1859 –1878. Wide variety of models available including Standard Issue Sporting Peep, Hartford Transition Mid and Long Range, and Custom Express Sights. From Axtell Rifle Co.
Price:....................................$150.00 to $340.00

ACCESSORIES

STEVENS CUSTOM Available in thin base short and long staff hunter, mid and long range sporting vernier, custom mid and long range (custom models allow windage and elevation adjustments) models. Uses 5x40 base screws with screw spacing of 1.485". From Axtell Rifle Co.
Price: .... **$170.00 to $325.00**
WINCHESTER & BROWNING TANG SIGHTS Available in variety of models, including thin & thick base short & long staff hunter, mid & long range sporting vernier and custom units. Screw spacing of 2.180" on all models. From Axtell Rifle Co.
Price: .... **$170.00 to $325.00**

Globe Target Front Sights

AXTELL CUSTOM GLOBE Designed similar to the original Winchester #35 sight, it contains five inserts. Also available with spirit level. From Axtell Rifle Co.
Price: .... **$125.00 to $175.00**
BALLARD FRONT SIGHTS Available in windgauge with spirit level, globe with clip, and globe with spirit level (all with five inserts) and beach combination with gold plated rocker models. Dovetail of .375" for all. From Axtell Rifle Co.
Price: .... **$125.00 to $240.00**
LYMAN 20 MJT TARGET FRONT Has 7/8 diameter, one-piece steel globe with 3/8" dovetail base. Height is .700" from bottom of dovetail to center of aperture; height on 20 LJT is .750". Comes with seven Anschutz-size steel inserts—two posts and five apertures .126" through .177".
Price: 20 MJT or 20 LJT **$33.75**
LYMAN No. 17A TARGET Includes seven interchangeable inserts: four apertures, one transparent amber and two posts .50" and .100" in width.
Price: **$28.25**
Price: Insert set. **$13.25**

Lyman No. 17A Target

LYMAN 17AEU Similar to the Lyman 17A except has a special dovetail design to mount easily onto European muzzleloaders such as CVA, Traditions and Investarm. All steel, comes with eight inserts.
Price: **$26.00**
LYMAN No. 93 MATCH Has 7/8 diameter, fits any rifle with a standard dovetail mounting block. Comes with seven target inserts and accepts most Anschutz accessories. Hooked locking bolt and nut allows quick removal, installation. Base available in .860" (European) and .562" (American) hole spacing.
Price: **$45.00**
MAYNARD FRONT SIGHTS Custom globe with five inserts and clip. Also available with spirit level bracket and windgauge styles. From Axtell Rifle Co.
Price: .... **$125.00 to $240.00**
PEDERSOLI GLOBE A tunnel front sight with 12 interchangeable inserts for high precision target shooting. Fits Traditions by Pedersoli and other rifles.
Price: **$59.00**
REMINGTON FRONT SIGHTS Available in windgauge with spirit level, custom globe with clip and custom globe with spirit level (all with five inserts) and beach combination with gold plated rocker models. Dovetail .460". From Axtell Rifle Co.
Price: .... **$125.00 to $250.00**
SHARPS FRONT SIGHTS Original-style globe with non-moveable post and pinhead. Also available with windgauge and spirit level. From Axtell Rifle Co.
Price: .... **$100.00 to $265.00**
WILLIAMS TARGET GLOBE FRONT Adapts to many rifles. Mounts to the base with a knurled locking screw. Height is .545" from center, not including base. Comes with inserts.
Price: **$42.00**
Price: Dovetail base (low) .220" **$17.50**
Price: Dovetail base (high) .465" **$17.50**
Price: Screw-on base, .300" height, .300" radius **$15.90**
Price: Screw-on base, .450" height, .350" radius **$15.90**
Price: Screw-on base, .215" height, .400" radius **$15.90**
WINCHESTER & BROWNING FRONT SIGHTS Available in windgauge with spirit level, globe with clip, globe with spirit level (all with five inserts) and beach combination with gold plated rocker models. From Axtell Rifle Co.
Price: .... **$125.00 to $240.00**

Front Sights

AO TACTICAL SIGHTS Three types of drop-in replacement front posts – round top or square top night sight posts in standard and Big Dot sizes, or white stripe posts in .080 and .100 widths. For AR15 and M16 rifles. From AO Sight Systems, Inc.
Price: .... **$30.00 to $90.00**
AO RIFLE TEST POSTS Allows easy establishment of correct front post height. Provides dovetail post with .050" segments to allow shooter to "shoot-n-snip", watching point-of-impact walk into point of aim. Available for 3/8" standard dovetail, Ruger-style or Mauser. From AO Sight Systems, Inc.
Price: **$5.00**
AR-10 DETACHABLE FRONT SIGHT Allows use of the iron rear sight, but are removable for use of telescopic sights with no obstruction to the sight line, For AR-style rifles. From ArmaLite, Inc.
Price: .... **$50.00 to $70.00**

ASHLEY AR-15/M-16 FRONT SIGHTS Drop-in replacement sight post. Double faced so it can be rotated 180 degrees for 2.5 MOA elevation adjustment. Available in .080" width with .030" white stripe, or .100" with .040" stripe. From Ashley Outdoors, Inc.
Price: **$30.00**
Price: Tritium Dot Express. **$60.00**
BUSHMASTER FLIP-UP FRONT SIGHT Made for V Match AR-style rifles, this sight unit slips over milled front sight bases and clamps around barrel. Locks with the push of a button. For use with flip-up style rear sights or the A3 removable carry handle. From Bushmaster Firearms.
Price: **$99.95**
BUSHMASTER A2 COMPETITION FRONT SIGHT POST Surface ground on three sides for optimum visual clarity. Available in three widths: .052"; .062"; and .072". From Bushmaster Firearms.
Price: **$12.95**
CLASSIC STREAMLINED FRONT SPORTER RAMP SIGHT Comes with blade and sight cover. Serrated and contoured ramp. Screw-on attachment. Slide-on sight cover is easily detachable. Gold bead. From Sarco, inc.
Price: **$13.50**
ERA BEADS FOR RUGER RIFLES White bead and fiber optic front sights that replace the standard sights on M-77 and No. 1 Ruger rifles. Using 3/32" beads, they are available in heights of .330", .350", .375", .415" and .435". From New England Custom Gun Service.
Price: .... **$16.00 to $24.00**
ERA FRONT SIGHTS European-type front sights inserted from the front. Various heights available. From New England Custom Gun Service.
Price: 1/16" silver bead. **$11.50**
Price: 3/32" silver bead. **$16.00**
Price: Sourdough bead. **$14.50**
Price: Tritium night sight. **$44.00**
Price: Folding night sight with ivory bead. **$39.50**
KNIGHT'S ARMAMENT FRONT STANDING/FOLDING SIGHT Mounts to the SR-25 rifle barrel gas block's MilStd top rail. Available in folding sight model. From Knight's Armament Co.
Price: .... **$145.00 to $175.00**
KNIGHT'S ARMAMENT CARRYING HANDLE SIGHT Rear sight and carry handle for the SR-25 rifle. Has fixed range and adjustable windage. From Knight's Armament Co.
Price: **$181.15**
KNIGHT'S ARMAMENT Mk II FOLDING FRONT SIGHT For the SR-25 rifle. Requires modified handguard. From Knight's Armament Co.
Price: **$175.00**
KNIGHT'S ARMAMENT FOR FREE-FLOATING RAS Mounts to free-floating SR-25 and SR-15 RAS (rail adapter system) rifle forends. Adjustable for elevation. Made of aluminum. From Knight's Armament Co.
Price: **$155.25**

Knight's Armament

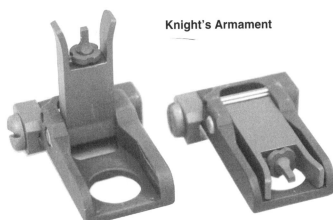

KNS PRECISION SYSTEMS SIGHT Screws into front base. Hooded for light consistency; precision machined with fine wire crosshairs measuring .010-inches thick. Aperture measures .240-inches diameter. Standard and duplex reticles. Available for AK-47, MAK-90, AR-15, M16, FN-FAL, H&K 91, 93, 94, MP5, SP89, L1A1, M1 Garand.
Price: **$25.99**
LYMAN HUNTING SIGHTS Made with gold or white beads 1/16" to 3/32" wide and in varying heights for most military and commercial rifles. Dovetail bases.
Price: **$8.95**
MARBLE STANDARD Ivory, red, or gold bead. For all American-made rifles, 1/16" wide bead with semi-flat face that does not reflect light. Specify type of rifle when ordering.
Price: **$10.00**
MARBLE CONTOURED Has 3/8" dovetail base, .090" deep, is 5/8" long. Uses standard 1/16" or 3/32" bead, ivory, red, or gold. Specify rifle type.
Price: **$11.50**
NATIONAL MATCH FRONT SIGHT POST Has .050" blade. For AR-style rifle. From ArmaLite, Inc.
Price: **$12.00**

METALLIC SIGHTS

T/C FIBER OPTIC FRONT MUZZLELOADER SIGHT Ramp-style steel with fiber optic bead for all tradition cap locks, both octagonal and round barrels with dovetail, and most T/C rifles. From Thompson/Center Arms.
Price: ... **$16.95 to $21.30**

TRIJICON NIGHT SIGHT Self-luminous tritium gas-filled front sight for the M16/AR-15 series.
Price: ... **$52.00**

WILLIAMS STREAMLINED HOODLESS RAMP Available in 3/16", 5/16", 3/8", and 7/16" models.
Price: Less blade ... **$15.49**

WILLAMS SHORTY RAMPS Available in 1/8", 3/16", 9/32" and 3/8" models.
Price: Less blade ... **$15.49**

WILLIAMS GOLD BEAD Available in .312", .343", and .406" high models all with 3/32" bead.
Price: ... **$8.49**

WILLIAMS RISER BLOCKS For adding .250" height to front sights when using a receiver sight. Two widths available: .250" for Williams Streamlined Ramp or .340" on all standard ramps having this base width. Uses standard 3/8" dovetail.
Price: ... **$5.46**

WILLIAMS AR-15 FIRESIGHT Fiber optic unit attaches to any standard AR-15-style front sight assembly. Machined from aircraft-strength aluminum. Adjustable for elevation. Green-colored light-gathering fiber optics. From Williams Gun Sight Co.
Price: ... **NA**

Ramp Sights

ERA MASTERPIECE Banded ramps; 21 sizes; hand-detachable beads and hood; beads inserted from the front. Various heights available. From New England Custom Gun Service.
Price: Banded ramp ... **$54.00**
Price: Hood ... **$10.50**
Price: 1/16" silver bead ... **$11.50**
Price: 3/32" silver bead ... **$16.00**
Price: Sourdough bead ... **$14.50**
Price: Tritium night sight ... **$47.00**
Price: Folding night sight with ivory bead ... **$39.50**

HOLLAND & HOLLAND STYLE FRONT SIGHT RAMPS Banded and screw-on models in the Holland & Holland-style night sight. Flips forward to expose a .0781" silver bead. Flip back for use of the .150" diameter ivory bead for poor light or close-up hunting. Band thickness .040", overall length 3.350", band length 1.180". From New England Custom Gun Service.
Price: ... **$90.00 to $115.00**

LYMAN NO. 18 SCREW-ON RAMP Used with 8-40 screws but may also be brazed on. Heights from .10" to .350". Ramp without sight.
Price: ... **$13.75**

MARBLE FRONT RAMPS Available in polished or dull matte finish or serrated style. Standard 3/8x.090" dovetail slot. Made for MR-width (.340") front sights. Can be used as screw-on or sweat-on. Heights: .100", .150", .300".
Price: Polished or matte ... **$14.00**
Price: Serrated ... **$10.00**

NECG UNIVERSAL FRONT SIGHTS Available in five ramp heights and three front sight heights. Sights can be adjusted up or down .030" with an Allen wrench. Slips into place and then locks into position with a set screw. Six different front sight shapes are offered, including extra large and fiber optic. All hoods except the extra low ramp slide on from the rear and click in place. Extra low ramp has spring-loaded balls to lock hood. Choose from three hood sizes. From New England Custom Gun Service.
Price: ... **$25.50**

T/C TARGET SIGHT FOR OCTAGON BARREL MUZZLELOADERS A precision rear sight with click adjustments (via knurled knobs) for windage and elevation. Available for 15/16-inch and 1-inch octagon barrels with a screw hole spacing of .836-inch between centers. From Thompson/Center Arms.
Price: ... **$55.05**

T/C FIBER OPTIC MUZZLELOADER SIGHT Click adjustable for windage and elevation. Steel construction fitted with Tru-Glo™ fiber optics. Models available for most T/C muzzleloading rifles. Fits others with 1-inch and 15/16-inch octagon barrels with a hole spacing of .836-inch between screws. From Thompson/Center Arms.
Price: ... **$35.90**

T/C ENCORE FIBER OPTIC SIGHT SETS Click-adjustable, steel rear sight and ramp-style front sight, both fitted with Tru-Glo™ fiber optics. Specifically-designed for the T/C Encore pistol series. From Thompson/Center Arms.
Price: ... **$49.35**

T/C ENCORE TARGET REAR SIGHT Precision, steel construction with click adjustments (via knurled knobs) for windage and elevation. Models available with low, medium and high blades. From Thompson/Center Arms.
Price: ... **$54.00**

WILLIAMS SHORTY RAMP Companion to "Streamlined" ramp, about 1/2" shorter. Screw-on or sweat-on. It is furnished in 1/8", 3/16", 9/32", and 3/8" heights without hood only. Also for shotguns.
Price: ... **$15.90**
Price: With dovetail lock ... **$18.55**

WILLIAMS STREAMLINED RAMP Available in screw-on or sweat-on models. Furnished in 9/16", 7/16", 3/8", 5/16", 3/16" heights.
Price: ... **$17.35**
Price: Sight hood ... **$3.95**

WILLIAMS STREAMLINED FRONT SIGHTS Narrow (.250" width) for Williams Streamlined ramps and others with 1/4 " top width; medium (.340" width) for all standard factory ramps. Available with white, gold or fluorescent beads, 1/16" or 3/32".
Price: ... **$8.93 to $9.25**

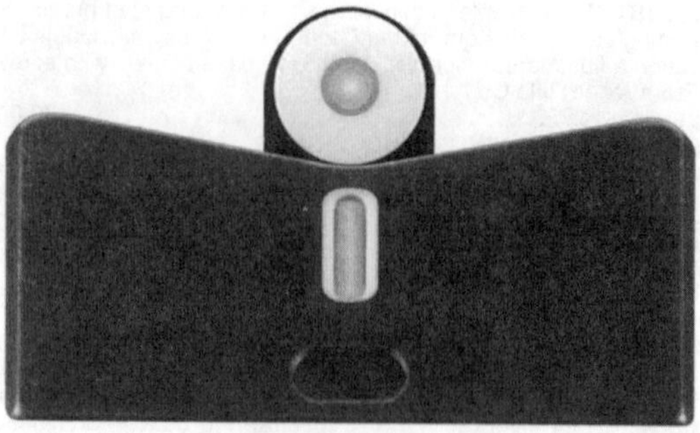

AO Express

Handgun Sights

AO EXPRESS SIGHTS Low-profile, snag-free express-type sights. Shallow V rear with white vertical line, white dot front. All-steel, matte black finish. Rear is available in different heights. Made for most pistols, many with double set-screws. From AO Sight Systems, Inc.
Price: Standard Set, front and rear ... **$60.00**
Price: Big Dot Set, front and rear ... **$60.00**
Price: Tritium Set, Standard or Big Dot ... **$90.00**
Price: 24/7 Pro Express, Std. or Big Dot Tritium ... **$120.00**

BO-MAR DELUXE BMCS Gives 3/8" windage and elevation adjustment at 50 yards on Colt Gov't 45; sight radius under 7". For GM and Commander models only. Uses existing dovetail slot. Has shield-type rear blade.
Price: ... **$65.95**
Price: BMCS-2 (for GM and 9mm) ... **$68.95**
Price: Flat bottom ... **$65.95**
Price: BMGC (for Colt Gold Cup), angled serrated blade, rear ... **$68.95**
Price: BMGC front sight ... **$12.95**
Price: BMCZ-75 (for CZ-75,TZ-75, P-9 and most clones). Works with factory front ... **$68.95**

BO-MAR FRONT SIGHTS Dovetail style for S&W 4506, 4516, 1076; undercut style (.250", .280", 5/16" high); Fast Draw style (.210", .250", .230" high).
Price: ... **$12.95**

BO-MAR BMU XP-100/T/C CONTENDER No gunsmithing required; has .080" notch.
Price: ... **$77.00**

BO-MAR BMML For muzzleloaders; has .062" notch, flat bottom.
Price: ... **$65.95**
Price: With 3/8" dovetail ... **$65.95**

BO-MAR RUGER "P" ADJUSTABLE SIGHT Replaces factory front and rear sights.
Price: Rear sight ... **$65.95**
Price: Front sight ... **$12.00**

BO-MAR BMR Fully adjustable rear sight for Ruger MKI, MKII Bull barrel autos.
Price: Rear ... **$65.95**
Price: Undercut front sight ... **$12.00**

BO-MAR GLOCK Fully adjustable, all-steel replacement sights. Sight fits factory dovetail. Longer sight radius. Uses Novak Glock .275" high, .135" wide front, or similar.
Price: Rear sight ... **$68.95**
Price: Front sight ... **$20.95**

BO-MAR LOW PROFILE RIB & ACCURACY TUNER Streamlined rib with front and rear sights; 7 1/8" sight radius. Brings sight line closer to the bore than standard or extended sight and ramp. Weight 5 oz. Made for Colt Gov't 45, Super 38, and Gold Cup 45 and 38.
Price: ... **$140.00**

BO-MAR COMBAT RIB For S&W Model 19 revolver with 4" barrel. Sight radius 5 3/4", weight 5 1/2 oz.
Price: ... **$127.00**

BO-MAR WINGED RIB For S&W 4" and 6" length barrels—K-38, M10, HB 14 and 19. Weight for the 6" model is about 7 1/4 oz.
Price: ... **$140.00**

BO-MAR COVER-UP RIB Adjustable rear sight, winged front guards. Fits right over revolver's original front sight. For S&W 4" M-10HB, M-13, M-58, M-64 & 65, Ruger 4" models SDA-34, SDA-84, SS-34, SS-84, GF-34, GF-84.
Price: ... **$130.00**

CHIP MCCORMICK "DROP-IN" A low mount sight that fits any 1911-style slide with a standard military-type dovetail sight cut (60x.290"). Dovetail front sights also available. From Chip McCormick Corp.
Price: ... **$47.95**

CHIP MCCORMICK FIXED SIGHTS Same sight picture (.110" rear - .110" front) that's become the standard for pro combat shooters. Low mount design with rounded edges. For 1911-style pistols. May require slide machining for installation. From Chip McCormick Corp.
Price: ... **$24.95**

C-MORE SIGHTS Replacement front sight blades offered in two types and five styles. Made of Du Pont Acetal, they come in a set of five high-contrast colors: blue, green, pink, red and yellow. Easy to install. Patridge style for Colt Python (all barrels), Ruger Super Blackhawk (7 1/2"), Ruger Blackhawk (4 5/8"); ramp style for Python (all barrels), Blackhawk (4 5/8"), Super Blackhawk (7 1/2" and 10 1/2"). From C-More Systems.
Price: Per set ... **$19.95**

METALLIC SIGHTS

Heinie Slant Pro

G.G. & G. GHOST RINGS Replaces the factory rear sight without gunsmithing. Black phosphate finish. Available for Colt M1911 and Commander, Beretta M92F, Glock, S&W, SIG Sauer.
Price: $65.00

HEINIE SLANT PRO Made with a slight forward slant, the unique design of these rear sights is snag free for unimpeded draw from concealment. The combination of the slant and the rear serrations virtually eliminates glare. Made for most popular handguns. From Heinie Specialty Products.
Price: ....**$50.35 to $122.80**

HEINIE STRAIGHT EIGHT SIGHTS Consists of one tritium dot in the front sight and a slightly smaller Tritium dot in the rear sight. When aligned correctly, an elongated 'eight' is created. The Tritium dots are green in color. Designed with the belief that the human eye can correct vertical alignment faster than horizontal. Available for most popular handguns. From Heinie Specialty Products.
Price: ....**$104.95 to $122.80**

HEINIE CROSS DOVETAIL FRONT SIGHTS Made in a variety of heights, the standard dovetail is 60 degrees x .305" x .062" with a .002 taper. From Heinie Specialty Products.
Price: ....**$20.95 to $47.20**

JP GHOST RING Replacement bead front, ghost ring rear for Glock and M1911 pistols. From JP Enterprises.
Price: $79.95
Price: Bo-Mar replacement leaf with JP dovetail front bead. $99.95

LES BAER CUSTOM ADJUSTABLE LOW MOUNT REAR SIGHT Considered one of the top adjustable sights in the world for target shooting with 1911-style pistols. Available with Tritium inserts. From Les Baer Custom.
Price: ....$49.00 (standard); $99.00 (tritium)

LES BAER DELUXE FIXED COMBAT SIGHT A tactical-style sight with a very low profile. Incorporates a no-snag design and has serrations on sides. For 1911-style pistols. Available with Tritium inserts for night shooting. From Les Baer Custom.
Price: ....$26.00 (standard); $67.00 (with Tritium)

LES BAER DOVETAIL FRONT SIGHT Blank dovetail sight machined from bar stock. Can be contoured to many different configurations to meet user's needs. Available with Tritium insert. From Les Baer Custom.
Price: ....$17.00 (standard); $47.00 (with Tritium insert)

LES BAER FIBER OPTIC FRONT SIGHT Dovetail .330x65 degrees, .125" wide post, .185" high, .060" diameter. Red and green fiber optic. From Les Baer Custom.
Price: $24.00

LES BAER PPC-STYLE ADJUSTABLE REAR SIGHT Made for use with custom built 1911-style pistols, allows the user to preset three elevation adjustments for PPC-style shooting. Milling required for installation. Made from 4140 steel. From Les Baer Custom.
Price: $120.00

LES BAER DOVETAIL FRONT SIGHT WITH TRITIUM INSERT This fully contoured and finished front sight comes ready for gunsmith installation. From Les Baer Custom.
Price: $47.00

MMC TACTICAL ADJUSTABLE SIGHTS Low-profile, snag free design. Twenty-two click positions for elevation, drift adjustable for windage. Machined from 4140 steel and heat treated to 40 RC. Tritium and non-tritium. Ten different configurations and colors. Three different finishes. For 1911s, all Glock, HK USP, S&W, Browning Hi-Power.
Price: Sight set, tritium. $144.92
Price: Sight set, white outline or white dot. $99.90
Price: Sight set, black. $93.90

MEPROLIGHT TRITIUM NIGHT SIGHTS Replacement sight assemblies for use in low-light conditions. Available for rifles, shotguns, handguns and bows. TRU-DOT models carry a 12-year warranty on the useable illumination, while non-TRU-DOT have a 5-year warranty. Contact Hesco, Inc. for complete list of available models.
Price: Kahr K9, K40, fixed, TRU-DOT. $100.00
Price: Ruger P85, P89, P94, adjustable, TRU-DOT. $156.00
Price: Ruger Mini-14R sights. $140.00
Price: SIG Sauer P220, P225, P226, P228, adjustable, TRU-DOT. $156.00
Price: Smith&Wesson autos, fixed or adjustable, TRU-DOT. $100.00
Price: Taurus PT92, PT100, adjustable, TRU-DOT. $156.00
Price: Walther P-99, fixed, TRU-DOT. $100.00
Price: Shotgun bead. $32.00
Price: Beretta M92, Cougar, Brigadier, fixed, TRU-DOT. $100.00
Price: Browning Hi-Power, adjustable, TRU-DOT. $156.00
Price: Colt M1911 Govt., adjustable, TRU-DOT. $156.00

MILLETT SERIES 100 REAR SIGHTS All-steel highly visible, click adjustable. Blades in white outline, target black, silhouette, 3-dot, and tritium bars. Fit most popular revolvers and autos.
Price: ....**$49.30 to $80.00**

MILLETT BAR-DOT-BAR TRITIUM NIGHT SIGHTS Replacement front and rear combos fit most automatics. Horizontal tritium bars on rear, dot front sight.
Price: $145.00

MILLETT BAR/DOT Made with orange or white bar or dot for increased visibility. Available for Beretta 84, 85, 92S, 92SB, Browning, Colt Python & Trooper, Ruger GP 100, P85, Redhawk, Security Six.
Price: ....**$14.99 to $24.99**

MILLETT 3-DOT SYSTEM SIGHTS The 3-Dot System sights use a single white dot on the front blade and two dots flanking the rear notch. Fronts available in Dual-Crimp and Wide Stake-On styles, as well as special applications. Adjustable rear sight available for most popular auto pistols and revolvers including Browning Hi-Power, Colt 1911 Government and Ruger P85.
Price: Front, from. $16.00
Price: Adjustable rear. $55.60

MILLETT REVOLVER FRONT SIGHTS All-steel replacement front sights with either white or orange bar. Easy to install. For Ruger GP-100, Redhawk, Security-Six, Police-Six, Speed-Six, Colt Trooper, Diamondback, King Cobra, Peacemaker, Python, Dan Wesson 22 and 15-2.
Price: ....**$13.60 to $16.00**

MILLETT DUAL-CRIMP FRONT SIGHT Replacement front sight for automatic pistols. Dual-Crimp uses an all-steel two-point hollow rivet system. Available in eight heights and four styles. Has a skirted base that covers the front sight pad. Easily installed with the Millett Installation Tool Set. Available in Blaze Orange Bar, White Bar, Serrated Ramp, Plain Post. Available in heights of .185", .200", .225", .275", .312", .340" and .410".
Price: $16.00

MILLETT STAKE-ON FRONT SIGHT Replacement front sight for automatic pistols. Stake-On sights have skirted base that covers the front sight pad. Easily installed with the Millet Installation Tool Set. Available in seven heights and four styles—Blaze Orange Bar, White Bar, Serrated Ramp, Plain Post. Available for Glock 17L and 24, others.
Price: $16.00

MILLETT ADJUSTABLE TARGET Positive light-deflection serration and slant to eliminate glare and sharp edge sight notch. Audible "click" adjustments. For AMT Hardballer, Beretta 84, 85, 92S, 92SB, Browning Hi-Power, Colt 1911 Government and Gold Cup, Colt revolvers, Dan Wesson 15, 41, 44, Ruger revolvers, Glock 17, 17L, 19, 20, 21, 22, 23.
Price: $44.99

MILLETT ADJUSTABLE WHITE OUTLINE Similar to the Target sight, except has a white outline on the blade to increase visibility. Available for the same handguns as the Target model, plus BRNO CZ-75/TZ-75/TA-90 without pin on front sight, and Ruger P85.
Price: ....**$44.99 to $49.99**

OMEGA OUTLINE SIGHT BLADES Replacement rear sight blades for Colt and Ruger single action guns and the Interarms Virginian Dragoon. Standard Outline available in gold or white notch outline on blue metal. From Omega Sales, Inc.
Price: $8.95

OMEGA MAVERICK SIGHT BLADES Replacement "peep-sight" blades for Colt, Ruger SAs, Virginian Dragoon. Three models available—No. 1, Plain; No. 2, Single Bar; No. 3, Double Bar Rangefinder. From Omega Sales, Inc.
Price: Each. $6.95

ONE RAGGED HOLE Replacement rear sight ghost ring sight for Ruger handguns. Fits Blackhawks, Redhawks, Super Blackhawks, GP series and Mk. II target pistols with adjustable sights. From One Ragged Hole, Tallahassee, Florida.
Price: .... NA

PACHMAYR ACCU-SET Low-profile, fully adjustable rear sight to be used with existing front sight. Available with target, white outline or 3-dot blade. Blue finish. Uses factory dovetail and locking screw. For Browning, Colt, Glock, SIG Sauer, S&W and Ruger autos. From Pachmayr.
Price: $59.98

Pachmayr Accu-Set

P-T TRITIUM NIGHT SIGHTS Self-luminous tritium sights for most popular handguns, Colt AR-15, H&K rifles and shotguns. Replacement handgun sight sets available in 3-Dot style (green/green, green/yellow, green/orange) with bold outlines around inserts; Bar-Dot available in green/green with or without white outline rear sight. Functional life exceeds 15 years. From Innovative Weaponry, Inc.
Price: Handgun sight sets. $99.95
Price: Rifle sight sets. $99.95
Price: Rifle, front only. $49.95
Price: Shotgun, front only. $49.95

TRIJICON NIGHT SIGHTS Three-dot night sight system uses tritium lamps in the front and rear sights. Tritium "lamps" are mounted in silicone rubber inside a metal cylinder. A polished crystal sapphire provides protection and clarity. Inlaid white outlines provide 3-dot aiming in daylight also. Available for most popular handguns including Glock 17, 19, 20, 21, 23, 24, 25, 26, 29, 30, H&K USP, Ruger SIG P220, P225, 226, Colt 1911. Front and rear sets available. From Trijicon, Inc.
Price: ....**$80.00 to $299.00**

TRIJICON 3-DOT Self-luminous front iron night sight for the Ruger SP101.
Price: $39.99

WICHITA SERIES 70/80 SIGHT Provides click windage and elevation adjustments with precise repeatability of settings. Sight blade is grooved and angled back at the top to reduce glare. Available in Low Mount Combat or Low Mount Target styles for Colt 45s and their copies, S&W 645, Hi-Power, CZ 75 and others.
Price: Rear sight, target or combat. $75.00
Price: Front sight, Patridge or ramp. $15.00

METALLIC SIGHTS

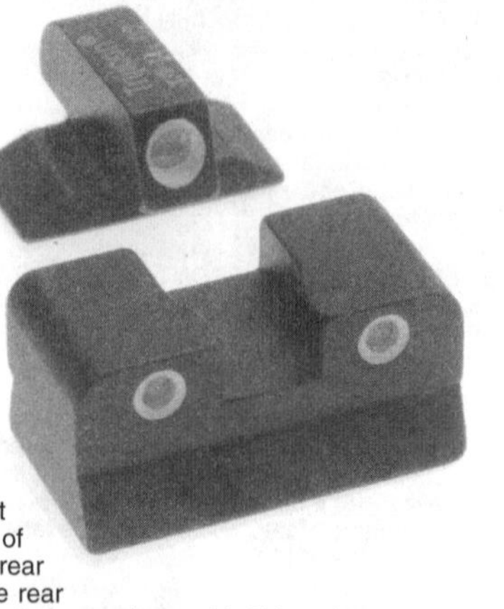

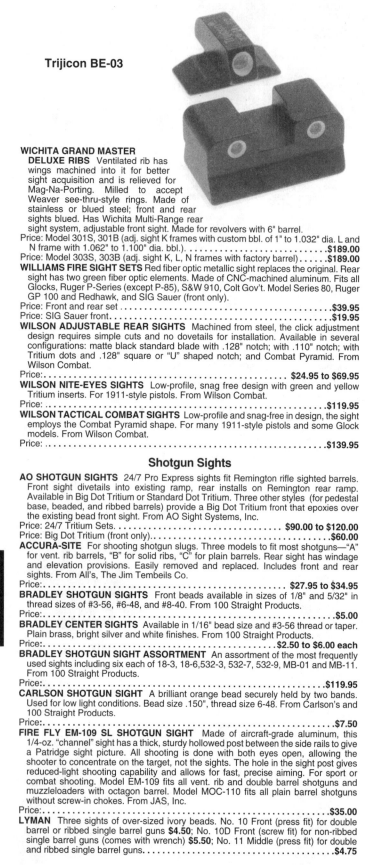

Trijicon BE-03

WICHITA GRAND MASTER DELUXE RIBS Ventilated rib has wings machined into it for better sight acquisition and is relieved for Mag-Na-Porting. Milled to accept Weaver see-thru-style rings. Made of stainless or blued steel; front and rear sights blued. Has Wichita Multi-Range rear sight system, adjustable front sight. Made for revolvers with 6" barrel.
Price: Model 301S, 301B (adj. sight K frames with custom bbl. of 1" to 1.032" dia. L and N frame with 1.062" to 1.100" dia. bbl.). **$189.00**
Price: Model 303S, 303B (adj. sight K, L, N frames with factory barrel) **$189.00**

WILLIAMS FIRE SIGHT SETS Red fiber optic metallic sight replaces the original. Rear sight has two green fiber optic elements. Made of CNC-machined aluminum. Fits all Glocks, Ruger P-Series (except P-85), S&W 910, Colt Gov't. Model Series 80, Ruger GP 100 and Redhawk, and SIG Sauer (front only).
Price: Front and rear set **$39.95**
Price: SIG Sauer front. **$19.95**

WILSON ADJUSTABLE REAR SIGHTS Machined from steel, the click adjustment design requires simple cuts and no dovetails for installation. Available in several configurations: matte black standard blade with .128" notch; with .110" notch; with Tritium dots and .128" square or "U" shaped notch; and Combat Pyramid. From Wilson Combat.
Price: . . . . **$24.95 to $69.95**

WILSON NITE-EYES SIGHTS Low-profile, snag free design with green and yellow Tritium inserts. For 1911-style pistols. From Wilson Combat.
Price: **$119.95**

WILSON TACTICAL COMBAT SIGHTS Low-profile and snag-free in design, the sight employs the Combat Pyramid shape. For many 1911-style pistols and some Glock models. From Wilson Combat.
Price: **$139.95**

Shotgun Sights

AO SHOTGUN SIGHTS 24/7 Pro Express sights fit Remington rifle sighted barrels. Front sight divetails into existing ramp, rear installs on Remington rear ramp. Available in Big Dot Tritium or Standard Dot Tritium. Three other styles (for pedestal base, beaded, and ribbed barrels) provide a Big Dot Tritium front that epoxies over the existing bead front sight. From AO Sight Systems, Inc.
Price: 24/7 Tritium Sets. . . . . **$90.00 to $120.00**
Price: Big Dot Tritium (front only). **$60.00**

ACCURA-SITE For shooting shotgun slugs. Three models to fit most shotguns—"A" for vent. rib barrels, "B" for solid ribs, "C" for plain barrels. Rear sight has windage and elevation provisions. Easily removed and replaced. Includes front and rear sights. From All's, The Jim Tembeils Co.
Price: . . . . **$27.95 to $34.95**

BRADLEY SHOTGUN SIGHTS Front beads available in sizes of 1/8" and 5/32" in thread sizes of #3-56, #6-48, and #8-40. From 100 Straight Products.
Price: **$5.00**

BRADLEY CENTER SIGHTS Available in 1/16" bead size and #3-56 thread or taper. Plain brass, bright silver and white finishes. From 100 Straight Products.
Price: . . . . **$2.50 to $6.00 each**

BRADLEY SHOTGUN SIGHT ASSORTMENT An assortment of the most frequently used sights including six each of 18-3, 18-6,532-3, 532-7, 532-9, MB-01 and MB-11. From 100 Straight Products.
Price: **$119.95**

CARLSON SHOTGUN SIGHT A brilliant orange bead securely held by two bands. Used for low light conditions. Bead size .150", thread size 6-48. From Carlson's and 100 Straight Products.
Price: **$7.50**

FIRE FLY EM-109 SL SHOTGUN SIGHT Made of aircraft-grade aluminum, this 1/4-oz. "channel" sight has a thick, sturdy hollowed post between the side rails to give a Patridge sight picture. All shooting is done with both eyes open, allowing the shooter to concentrate on the target, not the sights. The hole in the sight post gives reduced-light shooting capability and allows for fast, precise aiming. For sport or combat shooting. Model EM-109 fits all vent. rib and double barrel shotguns and muzzleloaders with octagon barrel. Model MOC-110 fits all plain barrel shotguns without screw-in chokes. From JAS, Inc.
Price: **$35.00**

LYMAN Three sights of over-sized ivory beads. No. 10 Front (press fit) for double barrel or ribbed single barrel guns **$4.50**; No. 10D Front (screw fit) for non-ribbed single barrel guns (comes with wrench) **$5.50**; No. 11 Middle (press fit) for double and ribbed single barrel guns. **$4.75**

MMC M&P COMBAT SHOTGUN SIGHT SET A durable, protected ghost ring aperture, combat sight made of steel. Fully adjustable for windage and elevation.
Price: M&P Sight Set (front and rear). **$73.45**
Price: As above, installed. **$83.95**

MMC TACTICAL GHOST RING SIGHT Click adjustable for elevation with 30 MOA total adjustment in 3 MOA increments. Click windage adjustment. Machined from 4140 steel, heat-treated to 40 RC. Front sight available in banded tactical or serrated ramp. Front and rear sights available with or without tritium. Available in three different finishes.
Price: Rear Ghost Ring with tritium. **$119.95**
Price: Rear Ghost Ring without tritium. **$99.95**
Price: Front Banded Tactical with tritium. **$59.95**
Price: Front Banded Tactical without tritium. **$39.95**
Price: Front serrated ramp. **$24.95**

MARBLE SHOTGUN BEAD SIGHTS No. 214—Ivory front bead, 11/64", tapered shank **$4.40**; No. 223—Ivory rear bead, .080", tapered shank **$4.40**; No. 217— Ivory front bead, 11/64", threaded shank **$4.75**; No. 223-T—Ivory rear bead, .080 , threaded shank **$5.95.** Reamers, taps and wrenches available from Marble Arms.

MEPROLIGHT Ghost ring sight set for Benelli tactical shotguns. From MEPROLIGHT, Inc.
Price: **$100.00**

MILLETT SHURSHOT SHOTGUN SIGHT A sight system for shotguns with ventilated rib. Rear sight attaches to the rib, front sight replaces the front bead. Front has an orange face, rear has two orange bars. For 870, 1100 or other models.
Price: Rear. **$13.15**
Price: Adjustable front and rear set. **$31.00**
Price: Front. **$12.95**

NECG IVORY SHOTGUN BEAD Genuine ivory shotgun beads with 6-48 thread. Available in heights of .157" and .197". From New England Custom Gun Service.
Price: **$9.00**

POLY-CHOKE Replacement front shotgun sights in four styles—Xpert, Poly Bead, Xpert Mid Rib sights, and Bev-L-Block. Xpert Front available in 3x56, 6x48 thread, 3/32" or 5/32" shank length, gold, ivory **$4.70;** or Sun Spot orange bead **$5.95**; Poly Bead is standard replacement 1/8" bead, 6x48 **$2.95;** Xpert Mid Rib in tapered carrier (ivory only) **$5.95,** or 3x56 threaded shank (gold only) **$2.95;** Hi and Lo Blok sights with 6x48 thread, gold or ivory **$5.25**. From Marble Arms.

SLUG SIGHTS Made of non-marring black nylon, front and rear sights stretch over and lock onto barrel. Sights are low profile with blaze orange front blade. Adjustable for windage and elevation. For plain-barrel (non-ribbed) guns in 12-, 16- and 20-gauge, and for shotguns with 5/16" and 3/8" ventilated ribs. From Innovision Ent.
Price: **$11.95**

TRIJICON 3-DOT NIGHT SIGHTS Self-luminous and machined from steel. Available for Remington 870, 1100, 1187.
Price: . . . . **$75.00 to $175.00**

WILLIAMS GUIDE BEAD SIGHT Fits all shotguns, 1/8" ivory, red or gold bead. Screws into existing sight hole. Various thread sizes and shank lengths.
Price: **$4.77**

WILLIAMS SLUGGER SIGHTS Removable aluminum sights attach to the shotgun rib. High profile front, fully adjustable rear. Fits 1/4", 5/16" or 3/8" (special) ribs.
Price: **$34.95**

WILLIAMS FIRE SIGHTS Fiber optic light gathering front sights in red or yellow, glow with natural light. Fit 1/4", 5/16" or 3/8" vent. ribs, most popular shotguns.
Price: **$13.95**

WILLIAMS SIGHT KITS Contains over 36 beads to fit any shotgun (with drills and taps).
Price: **$102.99**

Sight Attachments

MERIT ADJUSTABLE APERTURES Eleven clicks give 12 different apertures. No. 3 Disc and Master, primarily target types, 0.22" to .125"; No. 4, 1/2" dia. hunting type, .025" to .155". Available for all popular sights. The Master, with flexible rubber light shield, is particularly adapted to extension, scope height, and tang sights. All models have internal click springs; are hand fitted to minimum tolerance.
Price: No. 3 Master Disk. **$66.00**
Price: No. 3 Target Disc (Plain Face). **$56.00**
Price: No. 4 Hunting Disc. **$48.00**

MERIT LENS DISC Similar to Merit Iris Shutter (Model 3 or Master) but incorporates provision for mounting prescription lens integrally. Lens may be obtained locally from your optician. Sight disc is 7/16" wide (Model 3), or 3/4" wide (Master).
Price: No. 3 Target Lens Disk. **$68.00**
Price: No. 3 Master Lens Disk. **$78.00**

MERIT OPTICAL ATTACHMENT For iron sight shooting with handgun or rifle. Instantly attached by rubber suction cup to prescription or shooting glasses. Swings aside. Aperture adjustable from .020" to .156".
Price: **$65.00**

WILLIAMS APERTURES Standard thread, fits most sights. Regular series 3/8" to 1/2" O.D., .050" to .125" hole. "Twilight" series has white reflector ring.
Price: Regular series. **$4.97**
Price: Twilight series. **$6.79**
Price: Wide open 5/16" aperture for shotguns fits 5-D or Foolproof sights (specify model). **$8.77**

ACCESSORIES

Swift M700T Scout

BAUSCH & LOMB DISCOVERER 15x to 60x zoom, 60mm objective. Constant focus throughout range. Field at 1000 yds. 38 ft (60x), 150 ft. (15x). Comes with lens caps. Length 17 1/2"; weight 48.5 oz.
Price: **$391.95**

BAUSCH & LOMB ELITE 15x to 45x zoom, 60mm objective. Field of view at 1000 yds., 125-65 ft. Length is 12.2"; weight, 26.5 oz. Waterproof, armored. Tripod mount. Comes with black case.
Price: **$766.95**

BAUSCH & LOMB ELITE ZOOM 20x-60x, 70mm objective. Roof prism. Field at 1000 yds. 90-50 ft. Length is 16"; weight 40 oz. Waterproof, armored. Tripod mount. Comes with black case.
Price: **$921.95**

BAUSCH & LOMB 80MM ELITE 20x-60x zoom, 80mm objective. Field of view at 1000 yds. 98-50 ft. (zoom). Weight 51 oz. (20x, 30x), 54 oz. (zoom); length 17". Interchangeable bayonet-style eyepieces. Built-in peep sight.
Price: With EDPrime Glass **$1,276.95**

BUSHNELL TROPHY 63mm objective, 20x-60x zoom. Field at 1000 yds. 90ft. (20x), 45 ft. (60x). Length 12.7"; weight 20 oz. Black rubber armored, waterproof. Case included.
Price: **$421.95**

BUSHNELL COMPACT TROPHY 50mm objective, 20x-50x zoom. Field at 1000 yds. 92 ft. (20x), 52 ft. (50x). Length 12.2"; weight 17 oz. Black rubber armored, waterproof. Case included.
Price: **$337.95**

BUSHNELL SENTRY 16-32 zoom, 50mm objective. Field at 1000 yds. 140-65 ft. Length 8.7", weight 21.5 oz. Black rubber armored. Built-in peep sight. Comes with tripod and hardcase.
Price: **$205.95**

BUSHNELL SPACEMASTER 20x-45x zoom. Long eye relief. Rubber armored, prismatic. 60mm objective. Field at 1000 yds. 90-58 ft. Minimum focus 20 ft. Length 12.7"; weight 43 oz.
Price: With tripod, carrying case and 20x-45x LER eyepiece. **$560.95**

BUSHNELL SPORTVIEW 12x-36x zoom, 50mm objective. Field at 100 yds. 160 ft. (12x), 90 ft. (36x). Length 14.6"; weight 25 oz.
Price: With tripod and carrying case **$159.95**

BUSHNELL XTRA-WIDE® 15-45x zoom, 60mm objective. Field at 1000 yds. 160-87 ft. Length 13"; weight 35 oz.
Price: **$640.95**

HERMES 1 70mm objective, 16x, 25x, 40x. Field at 1000 meters 160 ft. (16x), 75ft. (40x). Length 12.2"; weight 33 oz. From CZ-USA.
Price: Body **$359.00**
Price: 25x eyepiece **$86.00**
Price: 40x eyepiece **$128.00**

KOWA TS-500 SERIES Offset 45° or straight body. Comes with 20-40x zoom eyepiece or 20x fixed eyepiece. 50mm obj. Field of view at 1000 yds.: 171 ft. (20x fixed), 132-74 ft. (20-40x zoom). Length 8.9-10.4", weight 13.4-14.8 oz.
Price: TS-501 (offset 45° body w/20x fixed eyepiece) **$258.00**
Price: TS-502 (straight body w/20x fixed eyepiece) **$231.00**
Price: TS-501Z (offset 45° body w/20-40x zoom eyepiece) **$321.00**
Price: TS-502Z (straight body w/20-40x zoom eyepiece) **$290.00**

KOWA TS-610 SERIES Offset 45° or straight body. Available with fluroite lens. Sunshade. 60mm obj. Field of view at 1000 yds.: 177 ft. (20xW), 154 ft. (22xW), 102 ft. (25x), 92 ft. (25xLER), 62 ft. (40x), 102-56 ft. (20-60x zoom). Length 11.2"; weight 27 oz. Note: Eyepieces for TSN 7mm series, TSN-660 series, and TS-610 series are interchangeable.
Price: TS-611 body (45° offset) **$530.00**
Price: TS-612 body (straight) **$489.00**
Price: TS-614 body (straight, fluorite lens) **$1,010.00**
Price: TSE-Z2M (20-60x zoom eyepiece) **$231.00**
Price: TSE-17HB (25x long eye relief eyepiece) **$240.00**
Price: TSE-15WM (27x wide angle eyepiece) **$182.00**
Price: TSE-21WB (20x wide angle high-grade eyepiece) .. **$230.00**
Price: TSE-10PM (40x eyepiece) **$108.00**

Price: TSE-16PM (25x eyepiece) **$108.00**
Price: TSN-DA1 (digital photo adapter) **$105.00**
Price: Adapter rings for DA1 .... **$43.00**
Price: TSN-PA2 (800mm photo adapter) **$269.00**
Price: TSN-PA4 (1200mm photo adapter) **$330.00**
Price: Camera mounts (for use with photo adapter) **$30.00**

KOWA TSN-660 SERIES Offset 45° or straight body. Fully waterproof. Available with fluorite lens. Sunshade and rotating tripod mount. 66mm obj., field of view at 1000 yds.: 177 ft. (20x@), 154 ft. (27xW), 131 ft. (30xW), 102 ft. (25x), 92 ft. (25xLER), 62 ft. (40x), 108-79 ft. (20-40x Multi-Coated Zoom), 102-56 ft. (20-60x Zoom), 98-62 ft. (20-60x High Grade Zoom). Length 12.3"; weight 34.9-36.7 oz. Note: Eyepieces for TSN 77mm Series, TSN-660 Series, and TSN610 Series are interchangeable.
Price: TSN-661 body (45° offset) **$660.00**
Price: TSN-662 body (straight) **$610.00**
Price: TSN-663 body (45° offset, fluorite lens) **$1,070.00**
Price: TSN-664 body (straight, fluorite lens) **$1,010.00**
Price: TSE-Z2M (20-60x zoom eyepiece) **$231.00**
Price: TSE-Z4 (20-60x high-grade zoom eyepiece) **$378.00**
Price: TSE-Z6 (20-40x multi-coated zoom eyepiece) **$250.00**
Price: TSE-17HB (25x long eye relief eyepiece) **$240.00**
Price: TSE-14W (30x wide angle eyepiece) **$288.00**
Price: TSE-21WB (20x wide angle eyepiece) **$230.00**
Price: TSE-15PM (27x wide angle eyepiece) **$182.00**
Price: TSE-10PM (40x eyepiece) **$108.00**
Price: TSE-16PM (25x eyepiece) **$108.00**
Price: TSNE5B (77x eyepiece) **$235.00**
Price: TSNE7B (60x eyepiece) **$230.00**
Price: TSN-DA1 (digital photo adapter) **$105.00**
Price: Adapter rings for DA1 .... **$43.00**
Price: TSN-PA2 (800mm photo adapter) **$269.00**
Price: TSN-PA4 (1200mm photo adapter) **$330.00**
Price: Camera mounts (for use with photo adapter) **$30.00**

KOWA TSN-820 SERIES Offset 45 or straight body. Fully waterproof. Available with fluorite lens. Sunshade and rotating tripod mount. 82mm obj., field of view at 1000 yds.: 75 ft (27xLER, 50xW), 126 ft. (32xW), 115-58 ft. (20-60xZoom). Length 15"; weight 49.4-52.2 oz.
Price: TSN-821M body (45° offset) **$850.00**
Price: TSN-822M body (straight) **$770.00**
Price: TSN-823M body (45° offset, fluorite lens) **$1,850.00**
Price: TSN-824M body (straight, fluorite lens) **$1,730.00**
Price: TSE-Z7 (20-60x zoom eyepiece) **$433.00**
Price: TSE-9W (50x wide angle eyepiece) **$345.00**
Price: TSE-14WB (32x wide angle eyepiece) **$366.00**
Price: TSE-17HC (27x long eye relief eyepiece) **$248.00**
Price: TSN-Da1 (digital photo adapter) **$105.00**
Price: Adapter rings for DA1 .... **$43.00**
Price: TSN-PA2C (850mm photo adapter) **$300.00**
Price: Camera mounts (for use with photo adapter) **$30.00**

LEUPOLD 12-40x60 VARIABLE 60mm objective, 12-40x. Field at 100 yds. 17.5-5.3 ft.; eye relief 1.2" (20x). Overall length 11.5", weight 32 oz. Rubber armored.
Price: **$1,217.90**

LEUPOLD 25x50 COMPACT 50mm objective, 25x. Field at 100 yds. 8.3 ft.; eye relief 1"; length overall 9.4"; weight 20.5 oz.
Price: Armored model **$848.20**
Price: Packer Tripod **$96.40**

MEOPTA HA 70 (Hermes I) Spotting scope 70mm objective, 16x, 25xWA, 40x, 50x or 20-45x. Length 12.2"; weight 32.5 oz.
Price: .... **NA**

MIRADOR TTB SERIES Draw tube armored spotting scopes. Available with 75mm or 80mm objective. Zoom model (28x-62x, 80mm) is 11 7/8" (closed), weighs 50 oz. Field at 1000 yds. 70-42 ft. Comes with lens covers.
Price: 28-62x80mm **$1,133.95**
Price: 32x80mm **$971.95**
Price: 26-58x75mm **$989.95**
Price: 30x75mm **$827.95**

MIRADOR SSD SPOTTING SCOPES 60mm objective, 15x, 20x, 22x, 25x, 40x, 60x, 20-60x; field at 1000 yds. 37 ft.; length 10 1/4"; weight 33 oz.
Price: 25x **$575.95**
Price: 22x Wide Angle **$593.95**
Price: 20-60x Zoom **$746.95**
Price: As above, with tripod, case..................... **$944.95**

MIRADOR SIA SPOTTING SCOPES Similar to the SSD scopes except with 45° eyepiece. Length 12 1/4"; weight 39 oz.
Price: 25x **$809.95**
Price: 22x Wide Angle **$827.95**
Price: 20-60x Zoom **$980.95**

MIRADOR SSR SPOTTING SCOPES 50mm or 60mm objective. Similar to SSD except rubber armored in black or camouflage. Length 11 1/8"; weight 31 oz.
Price: Black, 20x **$521.95**
Price: Black, 18x Wide Angle **$539.95**
Price: Black, 16-48x Zoom **$692.95**
Price: Black, 20x, 60mm, EER **$692.95**
Price: Black, 22x Wide Angle, 60mm **$701.95**
Price: Black, 20-60x Zoom **$854.95**

MIRADOR SSF FIELD SCOPES Fixed or variable power, choice of 50mm, 60mm, 75mm objective lens. Length 9 3/4"; weight 20 oz. (15-32x50).
Price: 20x50mm **$359.95**

ACCESSORIES

SPOTTING SCOPES

Price: 25x60mm **$440.95**
Price: 30x75mm **$584.95**
Price: 15-32x50mm Zoom **$548.95**
Price: 18-40x60mm Zoom **$629.95**
Price: 22-47x75mm Zoom **$773.95**

MIRADOR SRA MULTI ANGLE SCOPES Similar to SSF Series except eyepiece head rotates for viewing from any angle.
Price: 20x50mm **$503.95**
Price: 25x60mm **$647.95**
Price: 30x75mm **$764.95**
Price: 15-32x50mm Zoom **$692.95**
Price: 18-40x60mm Zoom **$836.95**
Price: 22-47x75mm Zoom **$953.95**

MIRADOR SIB FIELD SCOPES Short-tube, 45° scopes with porro prism design. 50mm and 60mm objective. Length 10 1/4"; weight 18.5 oz. (15-32x50mm); field at 1000 yds. 129-81 ft.
Price: 20x50mm **$386.95**
Price: 25x60mm **$449.95**
Price: 15-32x50mm Zoom **$575.95**
Price: 18-40x60mm Zoom **$638.95**

NIKON FIELDSCOPES 60mm and 78mm lens. Field at 1000 yds. 105 ft. (60mm, 20x), 126 ft. (78mm, 25x). Length 12.8" (straight 60mm), 12.6" (straight 78mm); weight 34.5-47.5 oz. Eyepieces available separately.
Price: 60mm straight body **$499.99**
Price: 60mm angled body **$519.99**
Price: 60mm straight ED body **$779.99**
Price: 60mm angled ED body **$849.99**
Price: 78mm straight ED body **$899.99**
Price: 78mm angled ED body **$999.99**
Price: Eyepieces (15x to 60x) . . . . . . **$146.95** to **$324.95**
Price: 20-45x eyepiece (25-56x for 78mm) **$320.55**

NIKON SPOTTING SCOPE 60mm objective, 20x fixed power or 15-45x zoom. Field at 1000 yds. 145 ft. (20x). Gray rubber armored. Straight or angled eyepiece. Weighs 44.2 oz., length 12.1" (20x).
Price: 20x60 fixed (with eyepiece) **$290.95**
Price: 15-45x zoom (with case, tripod, eyepiece) **$578.95**

PENTAX PF-80ED spotting scope 80mm objective lens available in 18x, 24x, 36x, 48x, 72x and 20-60x. Length 15.6", weight 11.9 to 19.2 oz.
Price: **$1,320.00**

SIGHTRON SII 2050X63 63mm objective lens, 20x-50x zoom. Field at 1000 yds 91.9 ft. (20x), 52.5 ft. (50x). Length 14"; weight 30.8 oz. Black rubber finish. Also available with 80mm objective lens.
Price: 63mm or 80mm **$339.95**

SIMMONS 1280 50mm objective, 15-45x zoom. Black matte finish. Ocular focus. Peep finder sight. Waterproof. FOV 95-51 ft. @ 1000 yards. Wgt. 33.5 oz., length 12".
Price: With tripod **$267.99**

SIMMONS 1281 60mm objective, 20-60x zoom. Black matte finish. Ocular focus. Peep finder sight. Waterproof. FOV 78-43 ft. @ 1000 yards. Wgt. 34.5 oz. Length 12".
Price: With tripod **$295.99**

SIMMONS 77206 PROHUNTER 50mm objectives, 25x fixed power. Field at 1000 yds. 113 ft.; length 10.25"; weighs 33.25 oz. Black rubber armored.
Price: With tripod case **$160.60**

SIMMONS 41200 REDLINE 50mm objective, 15x-45x zoom. Field at 1000 yds. 104-41 ft.; length 16.75"; weighs 32.75 oz.
Price: With hard case and tripod **$99.99**
Price: 20-60x, Model 41201 . . . . . . **$129.99**

STEINER FIELD TELESCOPE 24x, 80mm objective. Field at 1000 yds. 105 ft. Weight 44 oz. Tripod mounts. Rubber armored.
Price: **$1,299.00**

SWAROVSKI CT EXTENDIBLE SCOPES 75mm or 85mm objective, 20-60x zoom, or fixed 15x, 22x, 30x, 32x eyepieces. Field at 1000 yds. 135 ft. (15x), 99 ft. (32x); 99 ft. (20x), 5.2 ft. (60x) for zoom. Length 12.4" (closed), 17.2" (open) for the CT75; 9.7"/17.2" for CT85. Weight 40.6 oz. (CT75), 49.4 oz. (CT85). Green rubber armored.
Price: CT75 body **$765.56**
Price: CT85 body **$1,094.44**
Price: 20-60x eyepiece **$343.33**
Price: 15x, 22x eyepiece **$232.22**
Price: 30x eyepiece **$265.55**

SWAROVSKI AT-80/ST-80 SPOTTING SCOPES 80mm objective, 20-60x zoom, or fixed 15x, 22x, 30x, 32x eyepieces. Field at 1000 yds. 135 ft. (15x), 99 ft. (32x); 99 ft. (20x), 52.5 ft. (60x) for zoom. Length 16" (AT-80), 15.6" (ST-80); weight 51.8 oz. Available with HD (high density) glass.
Price: AT-80 (angled) body **$1,094.44**
Price: ST-80 (straight) body **$1,094.44**
Price: With HD glass **$1,555.00**
Price: 20-60x eyepiece **$343.33**
Price: 15x, 22x eyepiece **$232.22**
Price: 30x eyepiece **$265.55**

SWIFT LYNX M836 15x-45x zoom, 60mm objective. Weight 7 lbs., length 14". Has 45° eyepiece, sunshade.
Price: **$315.00**

SWIFT NIGHTHAWK M849U 80mm objective, 20x-60x zoom, or fixed 19, 25x, 31x, 50x, 75x eyepieces. Has rubber armored body, 1.8x optical finder, retractable lens hood, 45° eyepiece. Field at 1000 yds. 60 ft. (28x), 41 ft. (75x). Length 13.4 oz.; weight 39 oz.
Price: Body only **$870.00**
Price: 20-68x eyepiece **$370.00**
Price: Fixed eyepieces . . . . . . **$130.00** to **$240.00**
Price: Model 849 (straight) body **$795.00**

SWIFT NIGHTHAWK M850U 65mm objective, 16x-48x zoom, or fixed 19x, 20x, 25x, 40x, 60x eyepieces. Rubber armored with a 1.8x optical finder, retractable lens hood. Field at 1000 yds. 83 ft. (22x), 52 ft. (60x). Length 12.3"; weight 30 oz. Has 45° eyepiece.
Price: Body only **$650.00**
Price: 16x-48x eyepiece **$370.00**
Price: Fixed eyepieces . . . . . . **$130.00** to **$240.00**
Price: Model 850 (straight) body **$575.00**

SWIFT LEOPARD M837 50mm objective, 25x. Length 9 11/16" to 10 1/2". Weight with tripod 28 oz. Rubber armored. Comes with tripod.
Price: **$160.00**

SWIFT TELEMASTER M841 60mm objective. 15x to 60x variable power. Field at 1000 yds. 160 feet (15x) to 40 feet (60x). Weight 3.25 lbs.; length 18" overall.
Price: **$399.50**

SWIFT PANTHER M844 15x-45x zoom or 22x WA, 15x, 20x, 40x. 60mm objective. Field at 1000 yds. 141 ft. (15x), 68 ft. (40x), 95-58 ft. (20x-45x).
Price: Body only **$380.00**
Price: 15x-45x zoom eyepiece **$120.00**
Price: 20x-45x zoom (long eye relief) eyepiece **$140.00**
Price: 15x, 20x, 40x eyepiece **$65.00**
Price: 22x WA eyepiece **$80.00**

SWIFT M700T 12x-36x, 50mm objective. Field of view at 100 yds. 16 ft. (12x), 9 ft. (36x). Length 14"; weight with tripod 3.22 lbs.
Price: **$225.00**

SWIFT SEARCHER M839 60mm objective, 20x, 40x. Field at 1000 yds. 118 ft. (30x), 59 ft. (40x). Length 12.6"; weight 3 lbs. Rotating eyepiece head for straight or 45° viewing.
Price: **$580.00**
Price: 30x, 50x eyepieces, each **$67.00**

TASCO 29TZBWP WATERPROOF SPOTTER 60mm objective lens, 20x-60x zoom. Field at 100 yds. 7 ft., 4 in. to 3 ft., 8 in. Black rubber armored. Comes with tripod, hard case.
Price: **$356.50**

TASCO WC28TZ WORLD CLASS SPOTTING SCOPE 50mm objective, 12-36x zoom. Field at 100 yds. World Class. 13-3.8 ft. Comes with tripod and case.
Price: **$220.00**

TASCO CW5001 COMPACT ZOOM 50mm objective, 12x-36x zoom. Field at 100 yds. 16 ft., 9 in. Includes photo adapter tube, tripod with panhead lever, case.
Price: **$280.00**

TASCO 3700WP WATERPROOF SPOTTER 50mm objective, 18x-36x zoom. Field at 100 yds. 12ft., 6 in. to 7 ft., 9 in. Black rubber armored. Comes with tripod, hard case.
Price: **$288.60**

TASCO 3700, 3701 SPOTTING SCOPE 50mm objective. 18x-36x zoom. Field at 100 yds. 12 ft., 6 in. to 7 ft., 9 in. Black rubber armored.
Price: Model 3700 (black, with tripod, case) **$237.00**
Price: Model 3701 (as above, brown camo) **$237.00**

TASCO 21EB ZOOM 50mm objective lens, 15x-45x zoom. Field at 100 yds. 11 ft. (15x). Weight 22 oz.; length 18.3" overall. Comes with panhead lever tripod.
Price: **$119.00**

TASCO 22EB ZOOM 60mm objective lens, 20x-60x zoom. Field at 100 yds. 7 ft., 2 in. (20x). Weight 28 oz.; length 21.5" overall. Comes with micro-adjustable tripod.
Price: **$183.00**

UNERTL "FORTY-FIVE" 54mm objective. 20x (single fixed power). Field at 100 yds. 10',10"; eye relief 1"; focusing range infinity to 33 ft. Weight about 32 oz.; overall length 15 3/4". With lens covers.
Price: With multi-layer lens coating **$662.00**
Price: With mono-layer magnesium coating **$572.00**

UNERTL STRAIGHT PRISMATIC 63.5mm objective, 24x. Field at 100 yds., 7 ft. Relative brightness, 6.96. Eye relief 1/2". Weight 40 oz.; length closed 19". Push-pull and screw-focus eyepiece. 16x and 32x eyepieces **$125.00** each.
Price: **$515.00**

UNERTL 20x STRAIGHT PRISMATIC 54mm objective, 20x. Field at 100 yds. 8.5 ft. Relative brightness 6.1. Eye relief 1/2". Weight 36 oz.; length closed 13 1/2". Complete with lens covers.
Price: **$477.00**

UNERTL TEAM SCOPE 100mm objective. 15x, 24x, 32x eyepieces. Field at 100 yds. 13 to 7.5 ft. Relative brightness, 39.06 to 9.79. Eye relief 2" to 1 1/2". Weight 13 lbs.; length 29 7/8" overall. Metal tripod, yoke and wood carrying case furnished (total weight 80 lbs.).
Price: **$2,810.00**

WEAVER 20x50 50mm objective. Field of view 124 ft. at 100 yds. Eye relief .85"; weighs 21 oz.; overall length 10". Waterproof, armored.
Price: **$368.99**

WEAVER 15-40x60 ZOOM 60mm objective. 15x-40x zoom. Field at 100 yds. 119 ft. (15x), 66 ft. (60x). Overall length 12.5", weighs 26 oz. Waterproof, armored.
Price: **$551.99**

Briley Screw-In Chokes

Installation of these choke tubes requires that all traces of the original choking be removed, the barrel threaded internally with square threads and then the tubes are custom fitted to the specific barrel diameter. The tubes are thin and, therefore, made of stainless steel. Cost of installation for single-barrel guns (pumps, autos), lead shot, 12-gauge **$149.00**, 20-gauge **$159.00**; steel shot **$179.00** and **$189.00**, all with three chokes; un-single target guns run **$219.00**; over/unders and side-by-sides, lead shot, 12-gauge, **$369.00**, 20-gauge **$389.00**; steel shot **$469.00** and **$489.00**, all with five chokes. For 10-gauge auto or pump with two steel shot chokes, **$189.00**; over/unders, side-by-sides with three steel shot chokes, **$349.00**. For 16-gauge auto or pump, three lead shot chokes, **$179.00**; over/unders, side-by-sides with five lead shot chokes, **$449.00**. The 28 and 410-bore run **$179.00** for autos and pumps with three lead shot chokes, **$449.00** for over/unders and side-by-sides with five lead shot chokes.

Cutts Compensator

The Cutts Compensator is one of the oldest variable choke devices available. Manufactured by Lyman Gunsight Corporation, it is available with a steel body. A series of vents allows gas to escape upward and downward. For the 12-ga. Comp body, six fixed-choke tubes are available: the Spreader—popular with Skeet shooters; Improved Cylinder; Modified; Full; Superfull, and Magnum Full. Full, Modified and Spreader tubes are available for 12 or 20. Cutts Compensator, complete with wrench, adaptor and any single tube **$87.50**. All single choke tubes **$26.00** each. No factory installation available.

Dayson Automatic Brake System

This system fits most single barrel shotguns threaded for choke tubes, and cuts away 30 grooves on the exterior of a standard one-piece wad as it exits the muzzle. This slows the wad, allowing shot and wad to separate faster, reducing shot distortion and tightening patterns. The A.B.S. Choke Tube is claimed to reduce recoil by about 25 percent, and with the Muzzle Brake up to 60 percent. Ventilated Choke Tubes available from .685" to .725", in .005" increments. Model I Ventilated Choke Tube for use with A.B.S. Muzzle Brake, **$49.95**; for use without Muzzle Brake, **$52.95**; A.B.S. Muzzle Brake, from **$69.95**. Contact Dayson Arms for more data.

Gentry Quiet Muzzle Brake

Developed by gunmaker David Gentry, the "Quiet Muzzle Brake" is said to reduce recoil by up to 85 percent with no loss of accuracy or velocity. There is no increase in noise level because the noise and gases are directed away from the shooter. The barrel is threaded for installation and the unit is blued to match the barrel finish. Price, installed, is **$150.00**. Add **$15.00** for stainless steel, **$45.00** for knurled cap to protect threads. Shipping extra.

JP Muzzle Brake

JP Muzzle Brake

Designed for single shot handguns, AR-15, Ruger Mini-14, Ruger Mini Thirty and other sporting rifles, the JP Muzzle Brake redirects high pressure gases against a large frontal surface which applies forward thrust to the gun. All gases are directed up, rearward and to the sides. Priced at **$79.95** (AR-15 or sporting rifles), **$89.95** (bull barrel and SKS, AK models), **$89.95** (Ruger Minis), Dual Chamber model **$79.95.** From JP Enterprises, Inc.

KDF Slim Line Muzzle Brake

This threaded muzzle brake has 30 pressure ports that direct combustion gases in all directions to reduce felt recoil up to a claimed 80 percent without affecting accuracy or ballistics. It is said to reduce felt recoil of a 30-06 to that of a 243. Price, installed, is **$179.00**. From KDF, Inc.

Laseraim

Simple, no-gunsmithing compensator reduces felt recoil and muzzle flip by up to 30 percent. Machined from single piece of Stainless Steel (Beretta/Taurus

model made of aircraft aluminum). In black and polished finish. For Colt Government/Commander and Beretta/Taurus full-size pistols. Weighs 1 ounce. **$49.00**. From Laseraim Arms Inc.

Mag-Na-Port

Electrical Discharge Machining works on any firearm except those having non-conductive shrouded barrels. EDM is a metal erosion technique using carbon electrodes that control the area to be processed. The Mag-Na-Port venting process utilizes small trapezoidal openings to direct powder gases upward and outward to reduce recoil. No effect is had on bluing or nickeling outside the Mag-Na-Port area so no refinishing is needed. Rifle-style porting on single shot or large caliber handguns with barrels 7 1/2" or longer is **$110.00**; Dual Trapezoidal porting on most handguns with minimum barrel length of 3", **$100.00**; standard revolver porting, **$78.50**; porting through the slide and barrel for semi-autos, **$115.00**; traditional rifle porting, **$125.00**. Prices do not include shipping, handling and insurance. From Mag-Na-Port International.

Mag-Na-Brake

A screw-on brake under 2" long with progressive integrated exhaust chambers to neutralize expanding gases. Gases dissipate with an opposite twist to prevent the brake from unscrewing, and with a 5-degree forward angle to minimize sound pressure level. Available in blue, satin blue, bright or satin stainless. Standard and Light Contour installation cost **$179.00** for bolt-action rifles, many single action and single shot handguns. A knurled thread protector supplied at extra cost. Also available in Varmint style with exhaust chambers covering 220 degrees for prone-position shooters. From Mag-Na-Port International.

Poly-Choke

Marble Arms Corp., manufacturer of the Poly-Choke adjustable shotgun choke, now offers two models in 12-, 16-, 20-, and 28-gauge—the Ventilated and Standard style chokes. Each provides nine choke settings including Xtra-Full and Slug. The Ventilated model reduces 20 percent of a shotgun's recoil, the company claims, and is priced at **$135.00**. The Standard Model is **$125.00**. Postage not included. Contact Marble Arms for more data.

Pro-port

A compound ellipsoid muzzle venting process similar to Mag-Na-Porting, only exclusively applied to shotguns. Like Mag-Na-Porting, this system reduces felt recoil, muzzle jump, and shooter fatigue. Very helpful for trap doubles shooters. Pro-Port is a patented process and installation is available in both the U.S. and Canada. Cost for the Pro-Port process is **$129.50** for over/unders (both barrels); **$99.50** for only the top or bottom barrel; and **$78.50** for single-barrel shotguns. Optional pigeon porting costs **$25.00** extra per barrel. Prices do not include shipping and handling. From Pro-port Ltd.

Que Industries Adjustable Muzzle Brake

The Que Brake allows for fine-tuning of a rifle's accuracy by rotating the brake to one of 100 indexed stops. Mounts in minutes without barrel modification with heat-activated tensioning ring. The slotted exhaust ports reduce recoil by venting gases sideways, away from rifle. **$189.50**. From Que Industries.

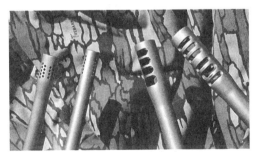

SSK Arrestor muzzle brakes

SSK Arrestor Brake

This is a true muzzle brake with an expansion chamber. It takes up about 1" of barrel and reduces velocity accordingly. Some Arrestors are added to a barrel, increasing its length. Said to reduce the felt recoil of a 458 to that approaching a 30-06. Can be set up to give zero muzzle rise in any caliber, and can be added to most guns. For handgun or rifle. Prices start at **$95.00**. Contact SSK Industries for full data.

Periodical Publications

AAFTA News (M)
5911 Cherokee Ave., Tampa, FL 33604. Official newsletter of the American Airgun Field Target Assn.

Action Pursuit Games Magazine (M)
CFW Enterprises, Inc., 4201 W. Vanowen Pl., Burbank, CA 91505 818-845-2656. $4.99 single copy U.S., $5.50 Canada. Editor: Dan Reeves. World's leading magazine of paintball sports.

Air Gunner Magazine
4 The Courtyard, Denmark St., Wokingham, Berkshire RG11 2AZ, England/011-44-734-771677. $U.S. $44 for 1 yr. Leading monthly airgun magazine in U.K.

Airgun Ads
Box 33, Hamilton, MT 59840/406-363-3805; Fax: 406-363-4117. $35 1 yr. (for first mailing; $20 for second mailing; $35 for Canada and foreign orders.) Monthly tabloid with extensive For Sale and Wanted airgun listings.

The Airgun Letter
Gapp, Inc., 4614 Woodland Rd., Ellicott City, MD 21042-6329/410-730-5496; Fax: 410-730-9544; e-mail: staff@airgnltr.net; http://www.airgunletter.com. $21 U.S., $24 Canada, $27 Mexico and $33 other foreign orders, 1 yr. Monthly newsletter for airgun users and collectors.

Airgun World
4 The Courtyard, Denmark St., Wokingham, Berkshire RG40 2AZ, England/011-44-734-771677. Call for subscription rates. Oldest monthly airgun magazine in the U.K., now a sister publication to Air Gunner.

Alaska Magazine
Morris Communications, 735 Broad Street, Augusta, GA 30901/706-722-6060. Hunting, Fishing and Life on the Last Frontier articles of Alaska and western Canada.

American Firearms Industry
Nat'l. Assn. of Federally Licensed Firearms Dealers, 2455 E. Sunrise Blvd., Suite 916, Ft. Lauderdale, FL 33304. $35.00 yr. For firearms retailers, distributors and manufacturers.

American Guardian
NRA, 11250 Waples Mill Rd., Fairfax, VA 22030. Publications division. $15.00 1 yr. Magazine features personal protection; home-self-defense; family recreation shooting; women's issues; etc.

American Gunsmith
Belvoir Publications, Inc., 75 Holly Hill Lane, Greenwich, CT 06836-2626/203-661-6111. $49.00 (12 issues). Technical journal of firearms repair and maintenance.

American Handgunner*
Publisher's Development Corp., 591 Camino de la Reina, Suite 200, San Diego, CA 92108/800-537-3006 $16.95 yr. Articles for handgun enthusiasts, competitors, police and hunters.

American Hunter (M)
National Rifle Assn., 11250 Waples Mill Rd., Fairfax, VA 22030 (Same address for both.) Publications Div. $35.00 yr. Wide scope of hunting articles.

American Rifleman (M)
National Rifle Assn., 11250 Waples Mill Rd., Fairfax, VA 22030 (Same address for both). Publications Div. $35.00 yr. Firearms articles of all kinds.

American Survival Guide
McMullen Angus Publishing, Inc., 774 S. Placentia Ave., Placentia, CA 92670-6846. 12 issues $19.95/714-572-2255; FAX: 714-572-1864.

Armes & Tir*
c/o FABECO, 38, rue de Trévise 75009 Paris, France. Articles for hunters, collectors, and shooters. French text.

Arms Collecting (Q)
Museum Restoration Service, P.O. Box 70, Alexandria Bay, NY 13607-0070. $22.00 yr.; $62.00 3 yrs.; $112.00 5 yrs.

Australian Shooter (formerly Australian Shooters Journal)
Sporting Shooters' Assn. of Australia, Inc., P.O. Box 2066, Kent Town SA 5071, Australia. $60.00 yr. locally; $65.00 yr. overseas surface mail. Hunting and shooting articles.

The Backwoodsman Magazine
P.O. Box 627, Westcliffe, CO 81252. $16.00 for 6 issues per yr.; $30.00 for 2 yrs.; sample copy $2.75. Subjects include muzzle-loading, woodslore, primitive survival, trapping, homesteading, blackpowder cartridge guns, 19th century how-to.

Black Powder Cartridge News (Q)
SPG, Inc., P.O. Box 761, Livingston, MT 59047/Phone/Fax: 406-222-8416. $17 yr. (4 issues) ($6 extra 1st class mailing). For the blackpowder cartridge enthusiast.

Blackpowder Hunting (M)
Intl. Blackpowder Hunting Assn., P.O. Box 1180Z, Glenrock, WY 82637/307-436-9817. $20.00 1 yr., $36.00 2 yrs. How-to and where-to features by experts on hunting; shooting; ballistics; traditional and modern blackpowder rifles, shotguns, pistols and cartridges.

Black Powder Times
P.O. Box 234, Lake Stevens, WA 98258. $20.00 yr.; add $5 per year for Canada, $10 per year other foreign. Tabloid newspaper for blackpowder activities; test reports.

Blade Magazine
Krause Publications, 700 East State St., Iola, WI 54990-0001. $25.98 for 12 issues. Foreign price (including Canada-Mexico) $50.00. A magazine for all enthusiasts of handmade, factory and antique knives.

Caliber
GFI-Verlag, Theodor-Heuss Ring 62, 50668 K"ln, Germany. For hunters, target shooters and reloaders.

The Caller (Q) (M)
National Wild Turkey Federation, P.O. Box 530, Edgefield, SC 29824. Tabloid newspaper for members; 4 issues per yr. (membership fee $25.00)

Cartridge Journal (M)
Robert Mellichamp, 907 Shirkmere, Houston, TX 77008/713-869-0558. Dues $12 for U.S. and Canadian members (includes the newsletter); 6 issues.

The Cast Bullet*(M)
Official journal of The Cast Bullet Assn. Director of Membership, 203 E. 2nd St., Muscatine, IA 52761. Annual membership dues $14, includes 6 issues.

COLTELLI, che Passione (Q)
Casella postale N.519, 20101 Milano, Italy/Fax:02-48402857. $15 1 yr., $27 2 yrs. Covers all types of knives—collecting, combat, historical. Italian text.

Combat Handguns*
Harris Publications, Inc., 1115 Broadway, New York, NY 10010.

Deer & Deer Hunting Magazine
Krause Publications, 700 E. State St., Iola, WI 54990-0001. $19.95 yr. (9 issues). For the serious deer hunter. Website: www.krause.com

The Derringer Peanut (M)
The National Association of Derringer Collectors, P.O. Box 20572, San Jose, CA 95160. A newsletter dedicated to developing the best derringer information. Write for details.

Deutsches Waffen Journal
Journal-Verlag Schwend GmbH, Postfach 100340, D-74503 Schwäbisch Hall, Germany/0791-404-500; FAX:0791-404-505 and 404-424. DM102 p. yr. (interior); DM125.30 (abroad), postage included. Antique and modern arms and equipment. German text.

Double Gun Journal
P.O. Box 550, East Jordan, MI 49727/800-447-1658. $35 for 4 issues.

Ducks Unlimited, Inc. (M)
1 Waterfowl Way, Memphis, TN 38120

The Engraver (M) (Q)
P.O. Box 4365, Estes Park, CO 80517/970-586-2388; Fax: 970-586-0394. Mike Dubber, editor. The journal of firearms engraving.

The Field
King's Reach Tower, Stamford St., London SE1 9LS England. £36.40 U.K. 1 yr.; 49.90 (overseas, surface mail) yr.; £82.00 (overseas, air mail) yr. Hunting and shooting articles, and all country sports.

Field & Stream
Time4 Media, Two Park Ave., New York, NY 10016/212-779-5000. Monthly shooting column. Articles on hunting and fishing.

Field Tests
Belvoir Publications, Inc., 75 Holly Hill Lane; P.O. Box 2626, Greenwich, CT 06836-2626/203-661-6111; 800-829-3361 (subscription line). U.S. & Canada $29 1 yr., $58 2 yrs.; all other countries $45 1 yr., $90 2 yrs. (air).

Fur-Fish-Game
A.R. Harding Pub. Co., 2878 E. Main St., Columbus, OH 43209. $15.95 yr. Practical guidance regarding trapping, fishing and hunting.

The Gottlieb-Tartaro Report
Second Amendment Foundation, James Madison Bldg., 12500 NE 10th Pl., Bellevue, WA 98005/206-454-7012;Fax:206-451-3959. $30 for 12 issues. An insiders guide for gun owners.

Gray's Sporting Journal
Gray's Sporting Journal, P.O. Box 1207, Augusta, GA 30903. $36.95 per yr. for 6 issues. Hunting and fishing journals. Expeditions and Guides Book (Annual Travel Guide).

Gun List†
700 E. State St., Iola, WI 54990. $36.98 yr. (26 issues); $65.98 2 yrs. (52 issues). Indexed market publication for firearms collectors and active shooters; guns, supplies and services. Website: www.krause.com

Gun News Digest (Q)
Second Amendment Fdn., P.O. Box 488, Station C, Buffalo, NY 14209/716-885-6408;Fax:716-884-4471. $10 U.S.; $20 foreign.

The Gun Report
World Wide Gun Report, Inc., Box 38, Aledo, IL 61231-0038. $33.00 yr. For the antique and collectable gun dealer and collector.

Gunmaker (M) (Q)
ACGG, P.O. Box 812, Burlington, IA 52601-0812. The journal of custom gunmaking.

The Gunrunner
Div. of Kexco Publ. Co. Ltd., Box 565G, Lethbridge, Alb., Canada T1J 3Z4. $23.00 yr., sample $2.00. Monthly newspaper, listing everything from antiques to artillery.

Gun Show Calendar (Q)
700 E. State St., Iola, WI 54990. $14.95 yr. (4 issues). Gun shows listed; chronologically and by state. Website: www.krause.com

Gun Tests
11 Commerce Blvd., Palm Coast, FL 32142. The consumer resource for the serious shooter. Write for information.

Gun Trade News
Bruce Publishing Ltd., P.O. Box 82, Wantage, Ozon OX12 7A8, England/44-1-235-771770; Fax: 44-1-235-771848. Britain's only "trade only" magazine exclusive to the gun trade.

Gun Week†
Second Amendment Foundation, P.O. Box 488, Station C, Buffalo, NY 14209. $35.00 yr. U.S. and possessions; $45.00 yr. other countries. Tabloid paper on guns, hunting, shooting and collecting (36 issues).

Gun World
Y-Visionary Publishing, LP 265 South Anita Drive, Ste. 120, Orange, CA 92868. $21.97 yr.; $34.97 2 yrs. For the hunting, reloading and shooting enthusiast.

Guns & Ammo
Primedia, 6420 Wilshire Blvd., Los Angeles, CA 90048/213-782-2780. $23.94 yr. Guns, shooting, and technical articles.

Guns
Publishers Development Corporation, P.O. Box 85201, San Diego, CA 92138/800-537-3006. $19.95 yr. In-depth articles on a wide range of guns, shooting equipment and related accessories for gun collectors, hunters and shooters.

Guns Review
Ravenhill Publishing Co. Ltd., Box 35, Standard House, Bonhill St., London EC 2A 4DA, England. £20.00 sterling (approx. U.S. $38 USA & Canada) yr. For collectors and shooters.

H.A.C.S. Newsletter (M)
Harry Moon, Pres., P.O. Box 50117, South Slope RPO, Burnaby BC, V5J 5G3, Canada/604-438-0950; Fax:604-277-3646. $25 p. yr. U.S. and Canada. Official newsletter of The Historical Arms Collectors of B.C. (Canada).

Handgunner*
Richard A.J. Munday, Seychelles house, Brightlingsen, Essex CO7 ONN, England/012063-305201. £18.00 (sterling).

Handguns
Primedia, 6420 Wilshire Blvd., Los Angeles, CA 90048/323-782-2868. $23/94 yr. For the handgunning and shooting enthusiast.

Handloader*
Wolfe Publishing Co., 2626 Stearman Road, Ste. A, Prescott, AZ 86301/520-445-7810;Fax:520-778-5124. $22.00 yr. The journal of ammunition reloading.

INSIGHTS*
NRA, 11250 Waples Mill Rd., Fairfax, VA 22030. Editor, John E. Robbins. $15.00 yr., which includes NRA junior membership; $10.00 for adult subscriptions (12 issues). Plenty of details for the young hunter and target shooter; emphasizes gun safety, marksmanship training, hunting skills.

International Arms & Militaria Collector (Q)
Arms & Militaria Press, P.O. Box 80, Labrador, Qld. 4215, Australia. A$39.50 yr. (U.S. & Canada), 2 yrs. A$77.50; A$37.50 (others), 1 yr., 2 yrs. $73.50 all air express mail; surface mail is less. Editor: Ian D. Skennerton.

International Shooting Sport*/UIT Journal
International Shooting Union (UIT), Bavariaring 21, D-80336 Munich, Germany. Europe: (Deutsche Mark) DM44.00 yr., 2 yrs. DM83.00; outside Europe: DM50.00 yr., 2 yrs. DM95.00 (air mail postage included.) For international sport shooting.

Internationales Waffen-Magazin
Habegger-Verlag Zürich, Postfach 9230, CH-8036 Zürich, Switzerland. SF 105.00 (approx. U.S. $73.00) surface mail for 10 issues. Modern and antique arms, self-defense. German text; English summary of contents.

The Journal of the Arms & Armour Society (M)
A. Dove, P.O. Box 10232, London, SW19 2ZD England. £15.00 surface mail; £20.00 airmail sterling only yr. Articles for the historian and collector.

Journal of the Historical Breechloading Smallarms Assn.
Published annually. P.O. Box 12778, London, SE1 6XB, England. $21.00 yr. Articles for the collector plus mailings of short articles on specific arms, reprints, newsletters, etc.

Knife World
Knife World Publications, P.O. Box 3395, Knoxville, TN 37927. $15.00 yr.; $25.00 2 yrs. Published monthly for knife enthusiasts and collectors. Articles on custom and factory knives; other knife-related interests, monthly column on knife identification, military knives.

Man At Arms*
P.O. Box 460, Lincoln, RI 02865. $27.00 yr., $52.00 2 yrs. plus $8.00 for foreign subscribers. The N.R.A. magazine of arms collecting-investing, with excellent articles for the collector of antique arms and militaria.

The Mannlicher Collector (Q)(M)
Mannlicher Collectors Assn., Inc., P.O. Box 7144, Salem Oregon 97303. $20/ yr. subscription included in membership.

---

*Published bi-monthly
† Published weekly
‡Published three times per month. All others are published monthly.

M=Membership requirements; write for details.
Q=Published Quarterly.

REFERENCE

PERIODICAL PUBLICATIONS

MAN/MAGNUM
S.A. Man (Pty) Ltd., P.O. Box 35204, Northway, Durban 4065, Republic of South Africa. SA Rand 200.00 for 12 issues. Africa's only publication on hunting, shooting, firearms, bushcraft, knives, etc.

The Marlin Collector (M)
R.W. Paterson, 407 Lincoln Bldg., 44 Main St., Champaign, IL 61820.

Muzzle Blasts (M)
National Muzzle Loading Rifle Assn., P.O. Box 67, Friendship, IN 47021/812-667-5131. $35.00 yr. annual membership. For the blackpowder shooter.

Muzzleloader Magazine*
Scurlock Publishing Co., Inc., Dept. Gun, Route 5, Box 347-M, Texarkana, TX 75501. $18.00 U.S.; $22.50 U.S./yr. for foreign subscribers. The publication for blackpowder shooters.

National Defense (M)*
American Defense Preparedness Assn., Two Colonial Place, Suite 400, 2101 Wilson Blvd., Arlington, VA 22201-3061/703-522-1820; FAX: 703-522-1885. $35.00 yr. Articles on both military and civil defense field, including weapons, materials technology, management.

National Knife Magazine (M)
Natl. Knife Coll. Assn., 7201 Shallowford Rd., P.O. Box 21070, Chattanooga, TN 37424-0070. Membership $35 yr.; $65.00 International yr.

National Rifle Assn. Journal (British) (Q)
Natl. Rifle Assn. (BR.), Bisley Camp, Brookwood, Woking, Surrey, England. GU24, OPB. £24.00 Sterling including postage.

National Wildlife*
Natl. Wildlife Fed., 1400 16th St. NW, Washington, DC 20036, $16.00 yr. (6 issues); International Wildlife, 6 issues, $16.00 yr. Both, $22.00 yr., includes all membership benefits. Write attn.: Membership Services Dept., for more information.

New Zealand GUNS*
Waitekauri Publishing, P.O. 45, Waikino 3060, New Zealand. $NZ90.00 (6 issues) yr. Covers the hunting and firearms scene in New Zealand.

New Zealand Wildlife (Q)
New Zealand Deerstalkers Assoc., Inc., P.O. Box 6514, Wellington, N.Z. $30.00 (N.Z.). Hunting, shooting and firearms/game research articles.

North American Hunter* (M)
P.O. Box 3401, Minnetonka, MN 55343/612-936-9333; e-mail: huntingclub@pclink.com. $18.00 yr. (7 issues). Articles on all types of North American hunting.

Outdoor Life
Time4 Media, Two Park Ave., New York, NY 10016. $16.95/yr. Extensive coverage of hunting and shooting. Shooting column by Jim Carmichel.

La Passion des Courteaux (Q)
Phenix Editions, 25 rue Mademoiselle, 75015 Paris, France. French text.

Paintball Games International Magazine
Aceville Publications, Castle House, 97 High St., Colchester, Essex, England CO1 1TH/011-44-206-564840. Write for subscription rates. Leading magazine in the U.K. covering competitive paintball activities.

Paintball News
PBN Publishing, P.O. Box 1608, 24 Henniker St., Hillsboro, NH 03244/603-464-6080. $35 U.S. 1 yr. Bi-weekly. Newspaper covering the sport of paintball, new product reviews and industry features.

Paintball Sports (Q)
Paintball Publications, Inc., 540 Main St., Mount Kisco, NY 10549/941-241-7400. $24.75 U.S. 1 yr., $32.75 foreign. Covering the competitive paintball scene.

Performance Shooter
Belvoir Publications, Inc., 75 Holly Hill Lane, Greenwich, CT 06836-2626/203-661-6111. $45.00 yr. (12 issues). Techniques and technology for improved rifle and pistol accuracy.

Petersen's HUNTING Magazine
Primedia, 6420 Wilshire Blvd., Los Angeles, CA 90048. $19.94 yr.; Canada $29.34 yr.; foreign countries $29.94 yr. Hunting articles for all game; test reports.

P.I. Magazine
America's Private Investigation Journal, 755 Bronx Dr., Toledo, OH 43609. Chuck Klein, firearms editor with column about handguns.

Pirsch
BLV Verlagsgesellschaft mbH, Postfach 400320, 80703 Munich, Germany/089-12704-0;Fax:089-12705-354. German text.

Point Blank
Citizens Committee for the Right to Keep and Bear Arms (sent to contributors), Liberty Park, 12500 NE 10th Pl., Bellevue, WA 98005

POINTBLANK (M)
Natl. Firearms Assn., Box 4384 Stn. C, Calgary, AB T2T 5N2, Canada. Official publication of the NFA.

The Police Marksman*
6000 E. Shirley Lane, Montgomery, AL 36117. $17.95 yr. For law enforcement personnel.

Police Times (M)
3801 Biscayne Blvd., Miami, FL 33137/305-573-0070.

Popular Mechanics
Hearst Corp., 224 W. 57th St., New York, NY 10019. Firearms, camping, outdoor oriented articles.

Precision Shooting
Precision Shooting, Inc., 222 McKee St., Manchester, CT 06040. $37.00 yr. U.S. Journal of the International Benchrest Shooters, and target shooting in general. Also considerable coverage of varmint shooting, as well as big bore, small bore, schuetzen, lead bullet, wildcats and precision reloading.

Rifle*
Wolfe Publishing Co., 2626 Stearman Road, Ste. A, Prescott, AZ 86301/520-445-7810; Fax: 520-778-5124. $19.00 yr. The sporting firearms journal.

Rifle's Hunting Annual
Wolfe Publishing Co., 2626 Stearman Road, Ste. A, Prescott, AZ 86301/520-445-7810; Fax: 520-778-5124. $4.99 Annual. Dedicated to the finest pursuit of the hunt.

Rod & Rifle Magazine
Lithographic Serv. Ltd., P.O. Box 38-138, Wellington, New Zealand. $50.00 yr. (6 issues). Hunting, shooting and fishing articles.

Safari* (M)
Safari Magazine, 4800 W. Gates Pass Rd., Tucson, AZ 85745/602-620-1220. $55.00 (6 times). The journal of big game hunting, published by Safari Club International. Also publish Safari Times, a monthly newspaper, included in price of $55.00 national membership.

Second Amendment Reporter
Second Amendment Foundation, James Madison Bldg., 12500 NE 10th Pl., Bellevue, WA 98005. $15.00 yr. (non-contributors).

Shoot! Magazine*
Shoot! Magazine Corp., 1770 West State Stret PMB 340, Boise ID 83702/208-368-9920; Fax: 208-338-8428. Website: www.shootmagazine.com $32.95 (6 times/yr.). Articles of interest to the cowboy action shooter, or others interested the Western-era firearms and ammunition.

Shooter's News
23146 Lorain Rd., Box 349, North Olmsted, OH 44070/216-979-5258;Fax:216-979-5259. $29 U.S. 1 yr., $54 2 yrs.; $52 foreign surface. A journal dedicated to precision riflery.

Shooting Industry
Publisher's Dev. Corp., 591 Camino de la Reina, Suite 200, San Diego, CA 92108. $50.00 yr. To the trade. $25.00.

Shooting Sports USA
National Rifle Assn. of America, 11250 Waples Mill Road, Fairfax, VA 22030. Annual subscriptions for NRA members are $5 for classified shooters and $10 for non-classified shooters. Non-NRA member subscriptions are $15. Covering events, techniques and personalities in competitive shooting.

Shooting Sportsman*
P.O. Box 11282, Des Moines, IA 50340/800-666-4955 (for subscriptions). Editorial: P.O. Box 1357, Camden, ME 04843. $19.95 for six issues. The magazine of wingshooting and fine guns.

The Shooting Times & Country Magazine (England)†
IPC Magazines Ltd., King's Reach Tower, Stamford St, 1 London SE1 9LS, England/0171-261-6180;Fax:0171-261-7179. £65 (approx. $98.00) yr.; £79 yr. overseas (52 issues). Game shooting, wild fowling, hunting, game fishing and firearms articles. Britain's best selling field sports magazine.

Shooting Times
Primedia, 2 News Plaza, P.O. Box 1790, Peoria, IL 61656/309-682-6626. $16.97 yr. Guns, shooting, reloading; articles on every gun activity.

The Shotgun News‡
Primedia, 2 News Plaza, P.O. Box 1790, Peoria, IL 61656/800-495-8362. $28.95 yr.; foreign subscription call for rates. Sample copy $4.00. Gun ads of all kinds.

SHOT Business
National Shooting Sports Foundation, Flintlock Ridge Office Center, 11 Mile Hill Rd., Newtown, CT 06470-2359/203-426-1320; FAX: 203-426-1087. For the shooting, hunting and outdoor trade retailer.

Shotgun Sports
P.O. Box 6810, Auburn, CA 95604/916-889-2220; FAX:916-889-9106. $31.00 yr. Trapshooting how-to's, shotshell reloading, shotgun patterning, shotgun tests and evaluations, Sporting Clays action, waterfowl/upland hunting. Call 1-800-676-8920 for a free sample copy.

The Single Shot Exhange Magazine
PO box 1055, York SC 29745/803-628-5326 phone/fax. $31.50/yr., monthly. Articles of interest to the blackpowder cartridge shooter and antique arms collector.
Single Shot Rifle Journal* (M)
Editor John Campbell, PO Box 595, Bloomfield Hills, MI 48303/248-458-8415. Email: jcampbel@dmbb.com Annual dues $35 for 6 issues. Journal of the American Single Shot Rifle Assn.

The Sixgunner (M)
Handgun Hunters International, P.O. Box 357, MAG, Bloomingdale, OH 43910

The Skeet Shooting Review
National Skeet Shooting Assn., 5931 Roft Rd., San Antonio, TX 78253. $20.00 yr. (Assn. membership includes mag.) Competition results, personality profiles of top Skeet shooters, how-to articles, technical, reloading information.

Soldier of Fortune
Subscription Dept., P.O. Box 348, Mt. Morris, IL 61054. $29.95 yr.; $39.95 Canada; $50.95 foreign.

Sporting Clays Magazine
Patch Communications, 5211 South Washington Ave., Titusville, FL 32780/407-268-5010; FAX: 407-267-7216. $29.95 yr. (12 issues). Official publication of the National Sporting Clays Association.

Sporting Goods Business
Miller Freeman, Inc., One Penn Plaza, 10th Fl., New York, NY 10119-0004. Trade journal.

Sporting Goods Dealer
Two Park Ave., New York, NY 10016. $100.00 yr. Sporting goods trade journal.

Sporting Gun
Bretton Court, Bretton, Peterborough PE3 8DZ, England. £27.00 (approx. U.S. $36.00), airmail £35.50 yr. For the game and clay enthusiasts.

The Squirrel Hunter
P.O. Box 368, Chireno, TX 75937. $14.00 yr. Articles about squirrel hunting.

Stott's Creek Calendar
Stott's Creek Printers, 2526 S 475 W, Morgantown, IN 46160/317-878-5489. 1 yr (3 issues) $11.50; 2 yrs. (6 issues) $20.00. Lists all gun shows everywhere in convenient calendar form; call for information.

Super Outdoors
2695 Aiken Road, Shelbyville, KY 40065/502-722-9463; 800-404-6064; Fax: 502-722-8093. Mark Edwards, publisher. Contact for details.

TACARMI
Via E. De Amicis, 25; 20123 Milano, Italy. $100.00 yr. approx. Antique and modern guns. (Italian text.)

Territorial Dispatch—1800s Historical Publication (M)
National Assn. of Buckskinners, 4701 Marion St., Suite 324, Livestock Exchange Bldg., Denver, CO 80216. Michael A. Nester & Barbara Wyckoff, editors. 303-297-9671.

Trap & Field
1000 Waterway Blvd., Indianapolis, IN 46202. $25.00 yr. Official publ. Amateur Trapshooting Assn. Scores, averages, trapshooting articles.

Turkey Call* (M)
Natl. Wild Turkey Federation, Inc., P.O. Box 530, Edgefield, SC 29824. $25.00 with membership (6 issues per yr.)

Turkey & Turkey Hunting*
Krause Publications, 700 E. State St., Iola, WI 54990-0001. $13.95 (6 issue p. yr.). Magazine with leading-edge articles on all aspects of wild turkey behavior, biology and the successful ways to hunt better with that info. Learn the proper techniques to calling, the right equipment, and more.

The Accurate Rifle
Precisions Shooting, Inc., 222 Mckee Street, Manchester CT 06040. $37 yr. Dedicated to the rifle accuracy enthusiast.

The U.S. Handgunner* (M)
U.S. Revolver Assn., 40 Larchmont Ave., Taunton, MA 02780. $10.00 yr. General handgun and competition articles. Bi-monthly sent to members.

U.S. Airgun Magazine
P.O. Box 2021, Benton, AR 72018/800-247-4867; Fax: 501-316-8549. 10 issues a yr. Cover the sport from hunting, 10-meter, field target and collecting. Write for details.

The Varmint Hunter Magazine (Q)
The Varmint Hunters Assn., Box 759, Pierre, SD 57501/800-528-4868. $24.00 yr.

Waffenmarkt-Intern
GFI-Verlag, Theodor-Heuss Ring 62, 50668 K"In, Germany. Only for gunsmiths, licensed firearms dealers and their suppliers in Germany, Austria and Switzerland.

Wild Sheep (M) (Q)
Foundation for North American Wild Sheep, 720 Allen Ave., Cody, WY 82414. Website: http://iigi.com/os/non/fnaws/fnaws.htm; e-mail: fnaws@wyoming.com. Official journal of the foundation.

Wisconsin Outdoor Journal
Krause Publications, 700 E. State St., Iola, WI 54990-0001. $17.97 yr. (8 issues). For Wisconsin's avid hunters and fishermen, with features from all over that state with regional reports, legislative updates, etc. Website: www.krause.com

Women & Guns
P.O. Box 488, Sta. C, Buffalo, NY 14209. $24.00 yr. U.S.; $72.00 foreign (12 issues). Only magazine edited by and for women gun owners.

World War II*
Cowles History Group, 741 Miller Dr. SE, Suite D-2, Leesburg, VA 20175-8920. Annual subscriptions $19.95 U.S.; $25.95 Canada; 43.95 foreign. The title says it—WWII; good articles, ads, etc.

---

*Published bi-monthly
† Published weekly
‡Published three times per month. All others are published monthly.

M=Membership requirements; write for details.
Q=Published Quarterly.

REFERENCE

THE ARMS LIBRARY

FOR COLLECTOR ◆ HUNTER ◆ SHOOTER ◆ OUTDOORSMAN

IMPORTANT NOTICE TO BOOK BUYERS

Books listed here may be bought from Ray Riling Arms Books Co., 6844 Gorsten St., P.O. Box 18925, Philadelphia, PA 19119, Phone 215/438-2456; FAX: 215-438-5395. E-Mail: sales@rayrilingarmsbooks.com. Joe Riling is the researcher and compiler of "The Arms Library" and a seller of gun books for over 32 years. The Riling stock includes books classic and modern, many hard-to-find items, and many not obtainable elsewhere. These pages list a portion of the current stock. They offer prompt, complete service, with delayed shipments occurring only on out-of-print or out-of-stock books.

Visit our web site at **www.rayrilingarmsbooks.com** and order all of your favorite titles on line from our secure site.

NOTICE FOR ALL CUSTOMERS: Remittance in U.S. funds must accompany all orders. For your convenience we now accept VISA, MasterCard & American Express. For shipments in the U.S. add $7.00 for the 1st book and $2.00 for each additional book for postage and insurance. Mini-mum order $10.00. International Orders add $13.00 for the 1st book and $5.00 for each additional book. All International orders are shipped at the buyer's risk unless an additional $5 for insurance is included. USPS does not offer insurance to all countries unless shipped Air-Mail please e-mail or call for pricing.

Payments in excess of order or for "Backorders" are credited or fully re-funded at request. Books "As-Ordered" are not returnable except by permis-sion and a handling charge on these of 10% or $2.00 per book which ever is greater is deducted from refund or credit. Only Pennsylvania customers must include current sales tax.

A full variety of arms books also available from Rutgers Book Center, 127 Raritan Ave., Highland Park, NJ 08904/908-545-4344; FAX: 908-545-6686 or I.D.S.A. Books, 1324 Stratford Drive, Piqua, OH 45356/937-773-4203; FAX: 937-778-1922.

BALLISTICS AND HANDLOADING

ABC's of Reloading, 6th Edition, by C. Rodney James and the editors of Hand-loader's Digest, DBI Books, a division of Krause Publications, Iola, WI, 1997. 288 pp., illus. Paper covers. $21.95

The definitive guide to every facet of cartridge and shotshell reloading.

Accurate Arms Loading Guide Number 2, by Accurate Arms. McEwen, TN: Accu-rate Arms Company, Inc., 2000. Paper Covers. $18.95

Includes new data on smokeless powders XMR4064 and XMP5744 as well as a special section on Cowboy Action Shooting. The new manual includes 50 new pages of data. An appendix includes nominal rotor charge weights, bullet diameters.

The American Cartridge, by Charles Suydam, Borden Publishing Co. Alhambra, CA, 1986. 184 pp., illus. $24.95

An illustrated study of the rimfire cartridge in the United States.

Ammo and Ballistics, by Robert W. Forker, Safari Press, Inc., Huntington Beach, CA., 1999. 252 pp., illustrated. Paper covers. $18.95

Ballistic data on 125 calibers and 1,400 loads out to 500 yards.

Ammunition: Grenades and Projectile Munitions, by Ian V. Hogg, Stackpole Books, Mechanicsburg, PA, 1998. 144 pp., illus. $22.95

Concise guide to modern ammunition. International coverage with detailed specifications and illustrations.

Barnes Reloading Manual #2, Barnes Bullets, American Fork, UT, 1999. 668 pp., illus. $24.95

Features data and trajectories on the new weight X, XBT and Solids in calibers from .22 to .50 BMG.

Big Bore Rifles And Cartridges, Wolfe Publishing Co., Prescott, AZ, 1991. Paper covers. $26.00

This book covers cartridges from 8mm to .600 Nitro with loading tables.

Black Powder Guide, 2nd Edition, by George C. Nonte, Jr., Stoeger Publishing Co., So. Hackensack, NJ, 1991. 288 pp., illus. Paper covers. $14.95

How-to instructions for selection, repair and maintenance of muzzleloaders, making your own bullets, restoring and refinishing, shooting techniques.

Blackpowder Loading Manual, 3rd Edition, by Sam Fadala, DBI Books, a division of Krause Publications, Iola, WI, 1995. 368 pp., illus. Paper covers. $20.95

Revised and expanded edition of this landmark blackpowder loading book. Covers hundreds of loads for most of the popular blackpowder rifles, handguns and shotguns.

Cartridges of the World, 9th Edition, by Frank Barnes, Krause Publications, Iola, WI, 2000. 512 pp., illus. Paper covers. $27.95

Completely revised edition of the general purpose reference work for which collectors, police, scientists and laymen reach first for answers to cartridge identification questions.

Cartridge Reloading Tools of the Past, by R.H. Chamberlain and Tom Quigley, Tom Quigley, Castle Rock, WA, 1998. 167 pp., illustrated. Paper covers. $25.00

A detailed treatment of the extensive Winchester and Ideal line of handloading tools and bullet molds, plus Remington, Marlin, Ballard, Browning, Maynard, and many others.

Cast Bullets for the Black Powder Rifle, by Paul A. Matthews, Wolfe Publishing Co., Prescott, AZ, 1996. 133 pp., illus. Paper covers. $22.50

The tools and techniques used to make your cast bullet shooting a success.

Complete Blackpowder Handbook, 3rd Edition, by Sam Fadala, DBI Books, a di-vision of Krause Publications, Iola, WI, 1997. 400 pp., illus. Paper covers. $21.95

Expanded and completely rewritten edition of the definitive book on the subject of blackpowder.

Complete Reloading Guide, by Robert & John Traister, Stoeger Publishing Co., Wayne, NJ, 1997. 608 pp., illus. Paper covers. $34.95

Perhaps the finest, most comprehensive work ever published on the subject of reloading.

Complete Reloading Manual, One Book / One Caliber. California: Load Books USA, 2000. $7.95 Each

Containing unabridged information from U. S. Bullet and Powder Makers. With thousands of proven and tested loads, plus dozens of various bullet designs and different powders. Spiral bound. Available in all Calibers.

Early Loading Tools & Bullet Molds, Pioneer Press, 1988. 88 pages, illustrated. Softcover. $7.50

European Sporting Cartridges: Volume 1, by Brad Dixon, Seattle, WA: Armory Publications, 1997. 1st edition. 250 pp., Illus. $60.00

Photographs and drawings of over 550 centerfire cartridge case types in 1,300 illustrations produced in Germany and Austria from 1875-1995.

European Sporting Cartridges: Volume 2, by Brad Dixon, Seattle, WA: Armory Publications, 2000. 1st edition. 240 pages. $60.00

An illustrated history of centerfire hunting and target cartridges produced in Czechoslovakia, Switzerland, Norway, Sweden, Finland, Russia, Italy, Denmark, Belguim from 1875 to 1998. Adds 50 specimens to volume 1, Germany-Austria. Also, illustrates 40 small arms magazine experiments during the late 19th Century, and includes the English-Language export ammunition catalogue of Kovo (Povaszke Strojarne), Prague, Czeck. from the 1930's.

Game Loads and Practical Ballistics for the American Hunter, by Bob Hagel, Wolfe Publishing Co., Prescott, AZ, 1992. 310 pp., illus. $27.90

Hagel's knowledge gained as a hunter, guide and gun enthusiast is gathered in this informative text.

German 7.9MM Military Ammunition 1888-1945, by Daniel Kent, Ann Arbor, MI: Kent, 1990. 153 pp., plus appendix. illus., b&w photos. $35.00

Handbook for Shooters and Reloaders, by P.O. Ackley, Salt Lake City, UT, 1998, (Vol. I), 567 pp., illus. Includes a separate exterior ballistics chart. $21.95 (Vol. II), a new printing with specific new material. 495 pp., illus. $20.95

Handgun Muzzle Flash Tests: How Police Cartridges Compare, by Robert Olsen, Paladin Press, Boulder, CO.Fully illustrated. 133 pages. Softcover. $20.00

Tests dozens of pistols and revolvers for the brightness of muzzle flash, a critical factor in the safety of law enforcement personnel.

Handgun Stopping Power; The Definitive Study, by Marshall & Sandow. Boulder, CO: Paladin Press, 1992. 240 pages. $45.00

Offers accurate predictions of the stopping power of specific loads in calibers from .380 Auto to .45 ACP, as well as such specialty rounds as the Glaser Safety Slug, Federal Hydra-Shok, MagSafe, etc. This is the definitive methodology for predicting the stopping power of handgun loads, the first to take into account what really happens when a bullet meets a man.

Handloader's Digest, 17th Edition, edited by Bob Bell. DBI Books, a division of Krause Publications, Iola, WI, 1997. 480 pp., illustrated. Paper covers. $27.95

Top writers in the field contribute helpful information on techniques and components. Greatly expanded and fully indexed catalog of all currently available tools, accessories and components for metallic, blackpowder cartridge, shotgun reloading and swaging.

Handloader's Manual of Cartridge Conversions, by John J. Donnelly, Stoeger Publishing Co., So. Hackensack, NJ, 1986. Unpaginated. $39.95

From 14 Jones to 70-150 Winchester in English and American cartridges, and from 4.85 U.K. to 15.2x28R Gevelot in metric cartridges. Over 900 cartridges described in detail.

Hatcher's Notebook, by S. Julian Hatcher, Stackpole Books, Harrisburg, PA, 1992. 488 pp., illus. $39.95

A reference work for shooters, gunsmiths, ballisticians, historians, hunters and collectors.

REFERENCE

History and Development of Small Arms Ammunition; Volume 2 Centerfire: Primitive, and Martial Long Arms. by George A. Hoyem. Oceanside, CA: Armory Publications, 1991. 303 pages, illustrated. $60.00
Covers the blackpowder military centerfire rifle, carbine, machine gun and volley gun ammunition used in 28 nations and dominions, together with the firearms that chambered them.

History and Development of Small Arms Ammunition; Volume 4, American Military Rifle Cartridges. Oceanside, CA: Armory Publications, 1998. 244pp., illus. $60.00
Carries on what Vol. 2 began with American military rifle cartridges. Now the sporting rifle cartridges are at last organized by their originators-235 individual case types designed by eight makers of single shot rifles and four of magazine rifles from .50-140 Winchester Express to .22-15-60 Stevens. plus experimentals from .70-150 to .32-80. American Civil War enthusiasts and European collectors will find over 150 primitives in Appendix A to add to those in Volumes One and Two. There are 16 pages in full color of 54 box labels for Sharps, Remington and Ballard cartridges. There are large photographs with descriptions of 15 Maynard, Sharps, Winchester, Browning, Freund, Remington-Hepburn, Farrow and other single shot rifles, some of them rare one of a kind specimens.

Hodgdon Powder Data Manual #27, Hodgdon Powder Co., Shawnee Mission, KS, 1999. 800 pp. $27.95
Reloading data for rifle and pistol loads.

Hodgdon Shotshell Data Manual, Hodgdon Powder Co., Shawnee Mission, KS, 1999. 208 pp. $19.95
Contains hundreds of loads for lead shot, buck shot, slugs, bismuth shot and steel shot plus articles on ballistics, patterning, special reloads and much more.

Home Guide to Cartridge Conversions, by Maj. George C. Nonte Jr., The Gun Room Press, Highland Park, NJ, 1976. 404 pp., illus. $24.95
Revised and updated version of Nonte's definitive work on the alteration of cartridge cases for use in guns for which they were not intended.

Hornady Handbook of Cartridge Reloading, 5th Edition, Vol. I and II, Edited by Larry Steadman, Hornady Mfg. Co., Grand Island, NE, 2000., illus. $49.95
2 Volumes; Volume 1, 773 pp.; Volume 2, 717 pp. New edition of this famous reloading handbook covers rifle and handgun reloading data and ballistic tables. Latest loads, ballistic information, etc.

How-To's for the Black Powder Cartridge Rifle Shooter, by Paul A. Matthews, Wolfe Publishing Co., Prescott, AZ, 1995. 45 pp. Paper covers. $22.50
Covers lube recipes, good bore cleaners and over-powder wads. Tips include compressing powder charges, combating wind resistance, improving ignition and much more.

The Illustrated Reference of Cartridge Dimensions, edited by Dave Scovill, Wolfe Publishing Co., Prescott, AZ, 1994. 343 pp., illus. Paper covers. $19.00
A comprehensive volume with over 300 cartridges. Standard and metric dimensions have been taken from SAAMI drawings and/or fired cartridges.

Kynock, by Dale J. Hedlund, Armory Publications, Seattle, WA, 2000. 130 pages, illus. 9" x 12" with four color dust jacket. $59.95
A comprehensive review of Kynoch shotgun cartridges covering over 50 brand names and case types, and over 250 Kynoch shotgun cartridge headstamps. Additional information on Kynoch metallic ammunition including the identity of the mysterious .434 Seelun.

Lee Modern Reloading, by Richard Lee, 350 pp. of charts and data and 85 illustrations. 512 pp. $24.95
Bullet casting, lubricating and author's formula for calculating proper charges for cast bullets. Includes virtually all current load data published by the powder suppliers. Exclusive source of volume measured loads.

Loading the Black Powder Rifle Cartridge, by Paul A Matthews, Wolfe Publishing Co., Prescott, AZ, 1993. 121 pp., illus. Paper covers. $22.50
Author Matthews brings the blackpowder cartridge shooter valuable information on the basics, including cartridge care, lubes and moulds, powder charges and developing and testing loads in his usual authoritative style.

Loading the Peacemaker—Colt's Model P, by Dave Scovill, Wolfe Publishing Co., Prescott, AZ, 1996. 227 pp., illus. $24.95
A comprehensive work about the history, maintenance and repair of the most famous revolver ever made, including the most extensive load data ever published.

Lyman Cast Bullet Handbook, 3rd Edition, edited by C. Kenneth Ramage, Lyman Publications, Middlefield, CT, 1980. 416 pp., illus. Paper covers. $19.95
Information on more than 5000 tested cast bullet loads and 19 pages of trajectory and wind drift tables for cast bullets.

Lyman Black Powder Handbook, edited by C. Kenneth Ramage, Lyman Products for Shooters, Middlefield, CT, 1975. 239 pp., illus. Paper covers. $14.95
Comprehensive load information for the modern blackpowder shooter.

Lyman Pistol & Revolver Handbook, 2nd Edition, edited by Thomas J. Griffin, Lyman Products Co., Middlefield, CT, 1996. 287 pp., illus. Paper covers. $18.95
The most up-to-date loading data available including the hottest new calibers, like 40 S&W, 9x21, 9mm Makarov, 9x25 Dillon and 454 Casull.

Lyman Reloading Handbook No. 47, edited by Edward A. Matunas, Lyman Publications, Middlefield, CT, 1992. 480 pp., illus. Paper covers. $24.95
A comprehensive reloading manual complete with "How to Reload" information. Expanded data section with all the newest rifle and pistol calibers.

Lyman Shotshell Handbook, 4th Edition, edited by Edward A. Matunas, Lyman Products Co., Middlefield, CT, 1996. 330 pp., illus. Paper covers. $24.95
Has 9000 loads, including slugs and buckshot, plus feature articles and a full color I.D. section.

Lyman's Guide to Big Game Cartridges & Rifles, by Edward Matunas, Lyman Publishing Corporation, Middlefield, CT, 1994. 287 pp. Paper covers. $17.95
A selection guide to cartridges and rifles for big game—antelope to elephant.

Making Loading Dies and Bullet Molds, by Harold Hoffman, H & P Publishing, San Angelo, TX, 1993. 230 pp., illus. Paper covers. $24.95
A good book for learning tool and die making.

Metallic Cartridge Reloading, 3rd Edition, by M.L. McPherson, DBI Books, a division of Krause Publications, Iola, WI., 1996. 352 pp., illus. Paper covers. $21.95
A true reloading manual with over 10,000 loads for all popular metallic cartridges and a wealth of invaluable technical data provided by a recognized expert.

Military Rifle and Machine Gun Cartridges, by Jean Huon, Alexandria, VA: Ironside International, 1995. 1st edition. 378 pages, over 1,000 photos. $34.95
Superb reference text.

Modern Combat Ammunition, by Duncan Long, Paladin Press, Boulder, CO, 1997, soft cover, photos, illus., 216 pp. $34.00
Now, Paladin's leading weapons author presents his exhaustive evaluation of the stopping power of modern rifle, pistol, shotgun and machine gun rounds based on actual case studies of shooting incidents. He looks at the hot new cartridges that promise to dominate well into the next century .40 S&W, 10mm auto, sub-sonic 9mm's - as well as the trusted standbys. Find out how to make your own exotic tracers, fléchette and sabot rounds, caseless ammo and fragmenting bullets.

Modern Exterior Ballistics, by Robert L. McCoy, Schiffer Publishing Co., Atglen, PA, 1999. 128 pp. $95.00
Advanced students of exterior ballistics and flight dynamics will find this comprehensive textbook on the subject a useful addition to their libraries.

Modern Handloading, by Maj. Geo. C. Nonte, Winchester Press, Piscataway, NJ, 1972. 416 pp., illus. $15.00
Covers all aspects of metallic and shotshell ammunition loading, plus more loads than any book in print.

Modern Reloading, by Richard Lee, Inland Press, 1996. 510 pp., illus. $24.98
The how-to's of rifle, pistol and shotgun reloading plus load data for rifle and pistol calibers.

Modern Sporting Rifle Cartridges, by Wayne van Zwoll, Stoeger Publishing Co., Wayne, NJ, 1998. 310 pp., illustrated. Paper covers. $21.95
Illustrated with hundreds of photos and backed up by dozens of tables and schematic drawings, this four-part book tells the story of how rifle bullets and cartridges were developed and, in some cases, discarded.

Modern Practical Ballistics, by Art Pejsa, Pejsa Ballistics, Minneapolis, MN, 1990. 150 pp., illus. $29.95
Covers all aspects of ballistics and new, simplified methods. Clear examples illustrate new, easy but very accurate formulas.

Mr. Single Shot's Cartridge Handbook, by Frank de Haas, Mark de Haas, Orange City, IA, 1996. 116 pp., illus. Paper covers. $21.50
This book covers most of the cartridges, both commercial and wildcat, that the author has known and used.

Nick Harvey's Practical Reloading Manual, by Nick Harvey, Australian Print Group, Maryborough, Victoria, Australia, 1995. 235 pp., illus. Paper covers. $24.95
Contains data for rifle and handgun including many popular wildcat and improved cartridges. Tools, powders, components and techniques for assembling optimum reloads with particular application to North America.

Nosler Reloading Manual #4, edited by Gail Root, Nosler Bullets, Inc., Bend, OR, 1996. 516 pp., illus. $26.99
Combines information on their Ballistic Tip, Partition and Handgun bullets with traditional powders and new powders never before used, plus trajectory information from 100 to 500 yards.

The Paper Jacket, by Paul Matthews, Wolfe Publishing Co., Prescott, AZ, 1991. Paper covers. $13.50
Up-to-date and accurate information about paper-patched bullets.

Reloading Tools, Sights and Telescopes for S/S Rifles, by Gerald O. Kelver, Brighton, CO, 1982. 163 pp., illus. Softcover. $15.00
A listing of most of the famous makers of reloading tools, sights and telescopes with a brief description of the products they manufactured.

Reloading for Shotgunners, 4th Edition, by Kurt D. Fackler and M.L. McPherson, DBI Books, a division of Krause Publications, Iola, WI, 1997. 320 pp., illus. Paper covers. $19.95
Expanded reloading tables with over 11,000 loads. Bushing charts for every major press and component maker. All new presentation on all aspects of shotshell reloading by two of the top experts in the field.

The Rimfire Cartridge in the United States and Canada, Illustrated history of rimfire cartridges, manufacturers, and the products made from 1857-1984. by John L. Barber, Thomas Publications, Gettysburg, PA 2000. 1st edition. Profusely illustrated. 221 pages. $50.00
The author has written an encyclopedia of rimfire cartridges from the .22 to the massive 1.00 in. Gatling. Fourteen chapters, six appendices and an excellent bibliography make up a reference volume that all cartridge collectors should acquire.

Sierra 50th Anniversary, 4th Edition Rifle Manual, edited by Ken Ramage, Sierra Bullets, Santa Fe Springs, CA, 1997. 800 pp., illus. $26.99
New cartridge introductions, etc.

Sierra 50th Anniversary, 4th Edition Handgun Manual, edited by Ken Ramage, Sierra Bullets, Santa Fe, CA, 1997. 700 pp., illus. $21.99
Histories, reloading recommendations, bullets, powders and sections on the reloading process, etc.

Sixgun Cartridges and Loads, by Elmer Keith, The Gun Room Press, Highland Park, NJ, 1986. 151 pp., illus. $24.95
A manual covering the selection, uses and loading of the most suitable and popular revolver cartridges. Originally published in 1936. Reprint.

REFERENCE

Speer Reloading Manual No. 13, edited by members of the Speer research staff, Omark Industries, Lewiston, ID, 1999. 621 pp., illustrated. $24.95
With thirteen new sections containing the latest technical information and reloading trends for both novice and expert in this latest edition. More than 9,300 loads are listed, including new propellant powders from Accurate Arms, Alliant, Hodgdon and Vihtavuori.

Street Stoppers, The Latest Handgun Stopping Power Street Results, by Marshall & Lanow. Boulder, CO, Paladin Press, 1996. 374 pages, illus. Softcover. $42.95
Street Stoppers is the long-awaited sequel to Handgun Stopping Power. It provides the latest results of real-life shootings in all of the major handgun calibers, plus more than 25 thought-provoking chapters that are vital to anyone interested in firearms, would ballistics, and combat shooting. This book also covers the street results of the hottest new caliber to hit the shooting world in years, the .40 Smith & Wesson. Updated street results of the latest exotic ammunition including Remington Golden Saber and CCI-Speer Gold Dot, plus the venerable offerings from MagSafe, Glaser, Cor-Bon and others. A fascinating look at the development of Hydra-Shok ammunition is included.

Understanding Ballistics, Revised 2nd Edition by Robert A. Rinker, Mulberry House Publishing Co., Corydon, IN, 2000. 430 pp., illus Paper covers. New, Revised and Expanded. 2nd Edition. $24.95
Explains basic to advanced firearm ballistics in understandable terms.

Why Not Load Your Own?, by Col. T. Whelen, Gun Room Press, Highland Park, NJ 1996, 4th ed., rev. 237 pp., illus. $20.00
A basic reference on handloading, describing each step, materials and equipment. Includes loads for popular cartridges.

Wildcat Cartridges Volumes 1 & 2 Combination, by the editors of Handloaders magazine, Wolfe Publishing Co., Prescott, AZ, 1997. 350 pp., illus. Paper covers. $39.95
A profile of the most popular information on wildcat cartridges that appeared in the Handloader magazine.

COLLECTORS

A Glossary of the Construction, Decoration and Use of Arms and Armor in All Countries and in All Times. By George Cameron Stone., Dover Publishing, New York 1999. Softcover. $39.95
An exhaustive study of arms and armor in all countries through recorded history - from the stone age up to the second world war. With over 4500 Black & White Illustrations. This Dover edition is an unabridged republication of the work originally published in 1934 by the Southworth Press, Portland MA. A new Introduction has been specially prepared for this edition.

Accoutrements of the United States Infantry, Riflemen, and Dragoons 1834-1839. by R.T. Huntington, Historical Arms Series No. 20. Canada: Museum Restoration. 58 pp. illus. Softcover. $8.95
Although the 1841 edition of the U.S. Ordnance Manual provides ample information on the equipment that was in use during the 1840s, it is evident that the patterns of equipment that it describes were not introduced until 1838 or 1839. This guide is intended to fill this gap in our knowledge by providing an overview of what we now know about the accoutrements that were issued to the regular infantryman, rifleman, and dragoon, in the 1830's with excursions into earlier and later years.

Age of the Gunfighter; Men and Weapons on the Frontier 1840-1900, by Joseph G. Rosa, University of Oklahoma Press, Norman, OK, 1999. 192 pp., illustrated. Paper covers. $21.95
Stories of gunfighters and their encounters and detailed descriptions of virtually every firearm used in the old West.

Air Guns, by Eldon G. Wolff, Duckett's Publishing Co., Tempe, AZ, 1997. 204 pp., illus Paper covers. $35.00
Historical reference covering many makers, European and American guns, canes and more.

Allied and Enemy Aircraft: May 1918; Not to be Taken from the Front Lines, Historical Arms Series No. 27. Canada: Museum Restoration. Softcover. $8.95
The basis for this title is a very rare identification manual published by the French government in 1918 that illustrated 60 aircraft with three or more views: French, English American, German, Italian, and Belgian, which might have been seen over the trenches ofFrance. Each is describe in a text translated from the original French. This is probably the most complete collection of illustrations of WW1 aircraft which has survived.

American Beauty; The Prewar Colt National Match Government Model Pistol, by Timothy J. Mullin, Collector Grade Publications, Cobourg, Ontario, Canada. 72 pp., illustrated. $34.95
Includes over 150 serial numbers, and 20 spectacular color photos of factory engraved guns and other authenticated upgrades, including rare "double-carved" ivory grips.

The American Military Saddle, 1776-1945, by R. Stephen Dorsey & Kenneth L. McPheeters, Collector's Library, Eugene, OR, 1999. 400 pp., illustrated. $59.95
The most complete coverage of the subject ever writeen on the American Military Saddle. Nearly 1000 actual photos and official drawings, from the major public and private collections in the U.S. and Great Britain.

American Police Collectibles; Dark Lanterns and Other Curious Devices, by Matthew G. Forte, Turn of the Century Publishers, Upper Montclair, NJ, 1999. 248 pp., illustrated. $24.95
For collectors of police memorabilia (handcuffs, police dark lanterns, mechanical and chain nippers, rattles, billy clubs and nightsticks) and police historians.

Ammunition; Small Arms, Grenades, and Projected Munitions, by Greenhill Publishing. 144 pp., Illustrated. $22.95 The best concise guide to modern ammunition available today. Covers ammo for small arms, grenades, and projected munitions. 144 pp., Illustrated. As NEW – Hardcover.

Antique Guns, the Collector's Guide, 2nd Edition, edited by John Traister, Stoeger Publishing Co., So. Hackensack, NJ, 1994. 320 pp., illus. Paper covers. $19.95
Covers a vast spectrum of pre-1900 firearms: those manufactured by U.S. gunmakers as well as Canadian, French, German, Belgian, Spanish and other foreign firms.

Arming the Glorious Cause; Weapons of the Second War for Independence, by James B. Whisker, Daniel D. Hartzler and Larry W. Tantz, Old Bedford Village Press, Bedford, PA., 1998. 175 pp., illustrated. $45.00
A photographic study of Confederate weapons.

Arms & Accoutrements of the Mounted Police 1873-1973, by Roger F. Phillips and Donald J. Klancher, Museum Restoration Service, Ont., Canada, 1982. 224 pp., illus. $49.95
A definitive history of the revolvers, rifles, machine guns, cannons, ammunition, swords, etc. used by the NWMP, the RNWMP and the RCMP during the first 100 years of the Force.

Arms and Armor In Antiquity and The Middle Ages. By Charles Boutell, Combined Books Inc., PA 1996. 296 pp., w/ b/w illus. Also a descriptive Notice of Modern Weapons. Translated from the French of M.P. Lacombe, and with a preface, notes, and one additional chapter on Arms and Armour in England. $14.95

Arms and Armor in the Art Institute of Chicago. By Waltler J. Karcheski, Bulfinch, New York 1999. 128 pp., 103 color photos, 12 black & white illustrations. $50.00
The George F. Harding Collection of arms and armor is the most visited installation at the Art Institute of Chicago - a testament to the enduring appeal of swords, muskets and the other paraphernalia of medieval and early modern war. Organized both chronologically and by type of weapon, this book captures the best of this astonishing collection in 115 striking photographs - most in color - accompanied by illuminating text. Here are intricately filigreed breastplates and ivory-handled crossbows, samurai katana and Toledo-steel scimitars, elaborately decorated maces and beautifully carved flintlocks - a treat for anyone who has ever been beguiled by arms, armor and the age of chivalry.

Arms and Armor in Colonial America 1526-1783. by Harold Peterson, Dover Publishing, New York, 2000. 350 pages with over 300 illustrations, index, bibliography & appendix. Softcover. $29.95
Over 200 years of firearms, ammunition, equipment & edged weapons.

Arms and Armor: The Cleveland Museum of Art. By Stephen N. Fliegel, Abrams, New York, 1998. 172 color photos, 17 halftones. 181 pages. $49.50
Intense look at the culture of the warrior and hunter, with an intriguing discussion of the decorative arts found on weapons and armor, set against the background of political and social history. Also provides information on the evolution of armor, together with manufacture and decoration, and weapons as technology and art.

Arms and Equipment of the Civil War, by Jack Coggins, Barnes & Noble, Rockleight, N.J., 1999. 160 pp., illustrated. $12.98
This unique encyclopedia provides a new perspective on the war. It provides lively explanations of how ingenious new weapons spelled victory or defeat for both sides. Aided by more than 500 illustrations and on-the-scene comments by Union and Confederate soldiers.

Arms Makers of Colonial America, by James B. Whisker, Selinsgrove, PA:, 1992: Susquehanna University Press. 1st edition. 217 pages, illustrated. $45.00
A comprehensively documented historial survey of the broad spectrum of arms makers in America who were active before 1783.

Arms Makers of Maryland, by Daniel D. Hartzler, George Shumway, York, PA, 1975. 200 pp., illus. $50.00
A thorough study of the gunsmiths of Maryland who worked during the late 18th and early 19th centuries.

Arms Makers of Pennsylvania, by James B. Whisker, Selinsgrove, PA, Susquehanna Univ. Press, 1990. 1st edition. 218 pages, illustrated in black and white and color. $45.00
Concentrates primarily on the cottage industry gunsmiths & gun makers who worked in the Keystone State from it's early years through 1900.

Arms Makers of Western Pennsylvania, by James B. Whisker, Old Bedford Village Press. 1st edition. This deluxe hard bound edition has 176 pages, $45.00
Printed on fine coated paper, with many large photographs, and detailed text describing the period, lives, tools, and artistry of the Arms Makers of Western Pennsylvania.

Arsenal Of Freedom: The Springfield Armory 1890-1948, by Lt. Col. William Brophy, Andrew Mowbray, Inc., Lincoln, RI,1997. 20 pgs. of photos. 400 pages. As new - Softcover. $29.95
A year by year account drawn from offical records. Packed with reports, charts, tables, line drawings, and 20 page photo section.

Artistic Ingredients of the Longrifle, by George Shumway Publisher, 1989 102 pp., with 94 illus. $20.00
After a brief review of Pennsylvania-German folk art and architecture, to establish the artistic enviroment in which the longrifle was made, the author demonstrates that the sophisticated rococo decoration on the many of the finer longrifles is comparable to the best rococo work of Philadelphia cabinet makers and silversmiths.

The Art of Gun Engraving, by Claude Gaier and Pietro Sabatti, Knickerbocker Press, N.Y. 1999. 160 pp., illustrated. $34.95
The richness and detail lavished on early firearms represents a craftmanship nearly vanished. Beginning with crossbows in the 100's, hunting scenes, portraits, or mythological themes are intricately depicted within a few square inches of etched metal. The full-color photos contained herein recaptures this lost art with exquisite detail.

THE ARMS LIBRARY

Astra Automatic Pistols, by Leonardo M. Antaris, FIRAC Publishing Co., Sterling, CO, 1989. 248 pp., illus. $55.00
   Charts, tables, serial ranges, etc. The definitive work on Astra pistols.

Basic Documents on U.S. Martial Arms, commentary by Col. B. R. Lewis, reissue by Ray Riling, Phila., PA, 1956 and 1960. *Rifle Musket Model 1855.*
   The first issue rifle of musket caliber, a muzzle loader equipped with the Maynard Primer, 32 pp. *Rifle Musket Model 1863.* The typical Union muzzle-loader of the Civil War, 26 pp. *Breech-Loading Rifle Musket Model 1866.* The first of our 50-caliber breechloading rifles, 12 pp. *Remington Navy Rifle Model 1870.* A commercial type breech-loader made at Springfield, 16 pp. *Lee Straight Pull Navy Rifle Model 1895.* A magazine cartridge arm of 6mm caliber. 23 pp. *Breech-Loading Arms* (five models) 27 pp. *Ward-Burton Rifle Musket 1871-*16 pp. Each $10.00.

Battle Weapons of the American Revolution, by George C. Neuman, Scurlock Publishing Co., Texarkana, TX, 2001. 400 pp. Illus. Softcovers. $34.95
   The most extensive photographic collection of Revolutionary War weapons ever in one volume. More than 1,600 photos of over 500 muskets, rifles, swords, bayonets, knives and other arms used by both sides in America's War for Independence.

The Bedford County Rifle and Its Makers, by George Shumway. 40pp. illustrated, Softcover. $10.00
   The authors study of the graceful and distinctive muzzle-loading rifles made in Bedford County, Pennsylvania. Stands as a milestone on the long path to the understanding of America's longrifles.

Behold the Longrifle Again, by James B. Whisker, Old Bedford Village Press, Bedford, PA, 1997. 176 pp., illus. $45.00
   Excellent reference work for the collector profusely illustrated with photographs of some of the finest Kentucky rifles showing front and back profiles and overall view.

The Belgian Rattlesnake; The Lewis Automatic Machine Gun, by William M. Easterly, Collector Grade Publications, Cobourg, Ontario, Canada, 1998. 584 pp., illustrated. $79.95
   The most complete account ever published on the life and times of Colonel Isaac Newton Lewis and his crowning invention, the Lewis Automatic machine gun.

Beretta Automatic Pistols, by J.B. Wood, Stackpole Books, Harrisburg, PA, 1985. 192 pp., illus. $24.95
   Only English-language book devoted to the Beretta line. Includes all important models.

The Big Guns, Civil War Siege, Seacoast, and Naval Cannon, by Edwin Olmstead, Wayne E. Stark, and Spencer C. Tucker, Museum Restoration Service, Bloomfield, Ontario, Canada, 1997. 360 pp., illustrated. $80.00
   This book is designed to identify and record the heavy guns available to both sides by the end of the Civil War.

Birmingham Gunmakers, by Douglas Tate, Safari Press, Inc., Huntington Beach, CA, 1997. 300 pp., illus. $50.00
   An invaluable work for anybody interested in the fine sporting arms crafted in this famous British gunmakers' city.

Blue Book of Gun Values, 22nd Edition, edited by S.P. Fjestad, Blue Book Publications, Inc. Minneapolis, MN 2001. $34.95
   This new 22nd Edition simply contains more firearms values and information than any other single publication. Expanded to over 1,600 pages featuring over 100,000 firearms prices, the new Blue Book of Gun Values also contains over million words of text – no other book is even close! Most of the information contained in this publication is simply not available anywhere else, for any price!

Blue Book of Modern Black Powder Values, by Dennis Adler, Blue Book Publications, Inc. Minneapolis, MN 2000. 200 pp., illustrated. 41 color photos. Softcover. $14.95
   This new title contains more up-to-date black powder values and related information than any other single publication. With 120 pages, this new book will keep you up to date on modern black powder models and prices, including most makes & models introduced this year!.

The Blunderbuss 1500-1900, by James D. Forman, Historical Arms Series No. 32. Canada: Museum Restoration, 1994. An excellent and authoritative booklet giving tons of information on the Blunderbuss, a very neglected subject. 40 pages, illustrated. Softcover. $8.95

Boarders Away I: With Steel-Edged Weapons & Polearms, by William Gilkerson, Andrew Mowbray, Inc. Publishers, Lincoln, RI, 1993. 331 pages. $48.00
   Contains the essential 24 page chapter 'War at Sea' which sets the historical and practical context for the arms discussed. Includeds chapters on, Early Naval Weapons, Boarding Axes, Cutlasses, Officers Fighting Swords and Dirks, and weapons at hand of Random Mayhem.

Boarders Away, Volume II: Firearms of the Age of Fighting Sail, by William Gilkerson, Andrew Mowbray, Inc. Publishers, Lincoln, RI, 1993. 331 pp., illus. $65.00
   Covers the pistols, muskets, combustibles and small cannon used aboard American and European fighting ships, 1626-1826.

The Book of Colt Firearms, by R. L. Wilson, Blue Book Publications, Inc, Minneapolis, MN, 1993. 616 pp., illus. $158.00
   A complete Colt library in a single volume. In over 1,250.000 words, over 1,250 black and white and 67 color photographs, this mammoth work tells the Colt story from 1832 throught the present.

Boothroyd's Revised Directory Of British Gunmakers, by Geoffrey Boothroyd, Long Beach, CA: Safari Press, 2000. Revised edition. 412pp, photos. $39.95
   Over a 30 year period Geoffrey Boothroyd has accumulated information on just about every sporting gun maker that ever has existed in the British Isles from 1850 onward. In this magnificent reference work he has placed all the gun makers he has found over the years (over 1000 entries) in an alphabetical listing with as much information as he has been able to unearth. One of the best reference sources on all British makers (including Wales, Scotland and Ireland)

in which you can find data on the most obscure as well as the most famous. Contains starting date of the business, addresses, proprietors, what they made and how long they operated with other interesting details for the collector of fine British guns.

Boston's Gun Bible, by Boston T. Party, Ignacio, CO: Javelin Press, August 2000. Expanded Edition.Softcover. $28.00
   This mammoth guide for gun owners everywhere is a completely updated and expanded edition (more than 500 new pages!) of Boston T. Party's classic Boston on Guns and Courage. Pulling no punches, Boston gives new advice on which shoulder weapons and handguns to buy and why before exploring such topics as why you should consider not getting a concealed carry permit, what guns and gear will likely be outlawed next, how to spend within your budget, why you should go to a quality defensive shooting academy now, which guns and gadgets are inferior and why, how to stay off illegal government gun registration lists, how to spot an undercover agent trying to entrap law-abiding gun owners and much more.

Breech-Loading Carbines of the United States Civil War Period, by Brig. Gen. John Pitman, Armory Publications, Tacoma, WA, 1987. 94 pp., illus. $29.95
   The first in a series of previously unpublished manuscripts originated by the late Brigadier General John Putnam. Exploded drawings showing parts actual size follow each sectioned illustration.

The Breech-Loading Single-Shot Rifle, by Major Ned H. Roberts and Kenneth L. Waters, Wolfe Publishing Co., Prescott, AZ, 1995. 333 pp., illus. $28.50
   A comprehensive and complete history of the evolution of the Schutzen and single-shot rifle.

The Bren Gun Saga, by Thomas B. Dugelby, Collector Grade Publications, Cobourg, Ontario, Canada, 1999, revised and expanded edition. 406 pp., illustrated. $65.95
   A modern, definitive book on the Bren in this revised expanded edition, which in terms of numbers of pages and illustrations is nearly twice the size of the original.

British Board of Ordnance Small Arms Contractors 1689-1840, by De Witt Bailey, Rhyl, England: W. S. Curtis, 2000. 150 pp. $18.00
   Thirty years of research in the Archives of the Ordnance Board in London has identified more than 600 of these suppliers. The names of many can be found marking the regulation firearms of the period. In the study, the contractors are identified both alphabetically and under a combination of their date period together with their specialist trade.

The British Enfield Rifles, Volume 1, The SMLE Mk I and Mk III Rifles, by Charles R. Stratton, North Cape Pub. Tustin, CA, 1997. 150 pp., illus. Paper covers. $16.95
   A systematic and thorough examination on a part-by-part basis of the famous British battle rifle that endured for nearly 70 years as the British Army's number one battle rifle.

British Enfield Rifles, Volume 2, No.4 and No.5 Rifles, by Charles R. Stratton, North Cape Publications, Tustin, CA, 1999. 150 pp., illustrated. Paper covers. $16.95
   The historical background for the development of both rifles describing each variation and an explanation of all the "marks", "numbers" and codes found on most parts.

British Enfield Rifles, Volume 4, The Pattern 1914 and U. S. Model 1917 Rifles, by Charles R. Stratton, North Cape Publications, Tustin, CA, 2000. Paper covers. $16.95
   One of the lease know American and British collectible military rifles is analyzed on a part by part basis. All markings and codes, refurbishment procedures and WW 2 upgrade are included as are the varios sniper rifle versions.

The British Falling Block Breechloading Rifle from 1865, by Jonathan Kirton, Tom Rowe Books, Maynardsville, TN, 2nd edition, 1997. 380 pp., illus. $70.00
   Expanded 2nd edition of a comprehensive work on the British falling block rifle.

British Gun Engraving, by Douglas Tate, Safari Press, Inc., Huntington Beach, CA, 1999. 240 pp., illustrated. Limited, signed and numbered edition, in a slipcase. $80.00
   A historic and photographic record of the last two centuries.

British Service Rifles and Carbines 1888-1900, by Alan M. Petrillo, Excaliber Publications, Latham, NY, 1994. 72 pp., illus, Paper covers. $11.95
   A complete review of the Lee-Metford and Lee-Enfield rifles and carbines.

British Single Shot Rifles, Volume 1, Alexander Henry, by Wal Winfer, Tom Rowe, Maynardsville, TN, 1998, 200 pp., illus. $50.00
   Detailed Study of the single shot rifles made by Henry. Illustrated with hundreds of photographs and drawings.

British Single Shot Rifles Volume 2, George Gibbs, by Wal Winfer, Tom Rowe, Maynardsville, TN, 1998. 177 pp., illus. $50.00
   Detailed study of the Farquharson as made by Gibbs. Hundreds of photos.

British Single Shot Rifles, Volume 3, Jeffery, by Wal Winfer, Rowe Publications, Rochester, N.Y., 1999. 260 pp., illustrated. $60.00
   The Farquharsen as made by Jeffery and his competitors, Holland & Holland, Bland, Westley, Manton, etc. Large section on the development of nitro cartridges including the .600.

British Single Shot Rifles, Vol. 4; Westley Richards, by Wal Winfer, Rowe Publications, Rochester, N.Y., 2000. 265 pages, illustrated, photos. $60.00
   In his 4th volume Winfer covers a detailed study of the Westley Richards single shot rifles, including Monkey Tails, Improved Martini, 1872,1873, 1878,1881, 1897 Falling Blocks. He also covers Westley Richards Cartridges, History and Reloading information.

British Small Arms Ammunition, 1864-1938 (Other than .303 inch), by Peter Labbett, Armory Publications, Seattle, WA. 1993, 358 pages, illus. Four-color dust jacket. $79.00

A study of British military rifle, handgun, machine gun, and aiming tube ammunition through 1 inch from 1864 to 1938. Photo-illustrated including the firearms that chambered the cartridges.

The British Soldier's Firearms from Smoothbore to Rifled Arms, 1850-1864, by Dr. C.H. Roads, R&R Books, Livonia, NY, 1994. 332 pp., illus. $49.00

A reprint of the classic text covering the development of British military hand and shoulder firearms in the crucial years between 1850 and 1864.

British Sporting Guns & Rifles, compiled by George Hoyem, Armory Publications, Coeur d'Alene, ID, 1997. 1024 pp., illus. In two volumes. $250.00

Eighteen old sporting firearms trade catalogs and a rare book reproduced with their color covers in a limited, signed and numbered edition.

Browning Dates of Manufacture, compiled by George Madis, Art and Reference House, Brownsboro, TX, 1989. 48 pp. $10.00

Gives the date codes and product codes for all models from 1824 to the present.

Browning Sporting Arms of Distinction 1903-1992, by Matt Eastman, Matt Eastman Publications, Fitzgerald, GA, 1995. 450 pp., illus. $49.95

The most recognized publication on Browning sporting arms; covers all models.

Buffalo Bill's Wild West: An American Legend, by R.L. Wilson and Greg Martine, Random House, N.Y., 1999. 3,167 pp., illustrated. $60.00

Over 225 color plates and 160 black-and-white illustrations, with in-depth text and captions, the colorful arms, posters, photos, costumes, saddles, accoutrement are brought to life.

Bullard Arms, by G. Scott Jamieson, The Boston Mills Press, Ontario, Canada, 1989. 244 pp., illus. $35.00

The story of a mechanical genius whose rifles and cartridges were the equal to any made in America in the 1880s.

Burning Powder, compiled by Major D.B. Wesson, Wolfe Publishing Company, Prescott, AZ, 1992. 110 pp. Soft cover. $10.95

A rare booklet from 1932 for Smith & Wesson collectors.

The Burnside Breech Loading Carbines, by Edward A. Hull, Andrew Mowbray, Inc., Lincoln, RI, 1986. 95 pp., illus. $16.00

No. 1 in the "Man at Arms Monograph Series." A model-by-model historical/technical examination of one of the most widely used cavalry weapons of the American Civil War based upon important and previously unpublished research.

Camouflage Uniforms of European and NATO Armies; 1945 to the Present, by J. F. Borsarello, Atglen, PA: Schiffer Publications. Over 290 color and b/w photographs, 120 pages. Softcover. $29.95

This full-color book covers nearly all of the NATO, and other European armies' camouflaged uniforms, and not only shows and explains the many patterns, but also their efficacy of design. Described and illustrated are the variety of materials tested in over forty different armies, and includes the history of obsolete trial tests from 1945 to the present time. More than two hundred patterns have been manufactured since World War II using various landscapes and seasonal colors for their look. The Vietnam and Gulf Wars, African or South American events, as well as recent Yugoslavian independence wars have been used as experimental terrains to test a variety of patterns. This book provides a superb reference for the historian, reenactor, designer, and modeler.

Camouflage Uniforms of the Waffen-SS A Photographic Reference, by Michael Beaver, Schiffer Publishing, Atglen, PA. Over 1,000 color and b/w photographs and illustrations, 296 pages. $69.95

Finally a book that unveils the shroud of mystery surrounding Waffen-SS camouflage clothing. Illustrated here, both in full color and in contemporary black and white photographs, this unparalleled look at Waffen-SS combat troops and their camouflage clothing will benefit both the historian and collector.

Canadian Gunsmiths from 1608: A Checklist of Tradesmen, by John Belton, Historical Arms Series No. 29. Canada: Museum Restoration, 1992. 40 pp., 17 illustrations. Softcover. $8.95

This Checklist is a greatly expanded version of HAS No. 14, listing the names, occupation, location, and dates of more than 1,500 men and women who worked as gunmakers, gunsmiths, armorers, gun merchants, gun patent holders, and a few other gun related trades. A collection of contemporary gunsmiths' letterhead have been provided to add color and depth to the study.

Cap Guns, by James Dundas, Schiffer Publishing, Atglen, PA, 1996. 160 pp., illus. Paper covers. $29.95

Over 600 full-color photos of cap guns and gun accessories with a current value guide.

Carbines of the Civil War, by John D. McAulay, Pioneer Press, Union City, TN, 1981. 123 pp., illus. Paper covers. $12.95

A guide for the student and collector of the colorful arms used by the Federal cavalry.

Carbines of the U.S. Cavalry 1861-1905, by John D. McAulay, Andrew Mowbray Publishers, Lincoln, RI, 1996. $35.00

Covers the crucial use of carbines from the beginning of the Civil War to the end of the cavalry carbine era in 1905.

Cartridge Carbines of the British Army, by Alan M. Petrillo, Excalibur Publications, Latham, NY, 1998. 72 pp., illustrated. Paper covers. $11.95

Begins with the Snider-Enfield which was the first regulation cartridge carbine introduced in 1866 and ends with the .303 caliber No.5, Mark 1 Enfield.

Cartridge Catalogues, compiled by George Hoyem, Armory Publications, Coeur d'Alene, ID., 1997. 504 pp., illus. $125.00

Fourteen old ammunition makers' and designers' catalogs reproduced with their color covers in a limited, signed and numbered edition. Completely revised edition of the general purpose reference work for which collectors, police,

scientists and laymen reach first for answers to cartridge identification questions. Available October, 1996.

Cartridge Reloading Tools of the Past, by R.H. Chamberlain and Tom Quigley, Tom Quigley, Castle Rock, WA, 1998. 167 pp., illustrated. Paper covers. $25.00

A detailed treatment of the extensive Winchester and Ideal lines of handloading tools and bulletmolds plus Remington, Marlin, Ballard, Browning and many others.

Cartridges for Collectors, by Fred Datig, Pioneer Press, Union City, TN, 1999. In three volumes of 176 pp. each. Vol.1 (Centerfire); Vol.2 (Rimfire and Misc.) types; Vol.3 (Additional Rimfire, Centerfire, and Plastic.). All illustrations are shown in full-scale drawings. Volume 1, softcover only, $19.95. Volumes 2 & 3, Hardcover $19.95

Civil War Arms Makers and Their Contracts, edited by Stuart C. Mowbray and Jennifer Heroux, Andrew Mowbray Publishing, Lincoln, RI, 1998. 595 pp. $39.50

A facsimile reprint of the Report by the Commissioner of Ordnance and Ordnance Stores, 1862.

Civil War Arms Purchases and Deliveries, edited by Stuart C. Mowbray, Andrew Mowbray Publishing, Lincoln, RI, 1998. 300pp., illus. $39.50

A facsimile reprint of the master list of Civil War weapons purchases and deliveries including Small Arms, Cannon, Ordnance and Projectiles.

Civil War Breech Loading Rifles, by John D. McAulay, Andrew Mowbray, Inc., Lincoln, RI, 1991. 144 pp., illus. Paper covers. $15.00

All the major breech-loading rifles of the Civil War and most, if not all, of the obscure types are detailed, illustrated and set in their historical context.

Civil War Cartridge Boxes of the Union Infantryman, by Paul Johnson, Andrew Mowbray, Inc., Lincoln, RI, 1998. 352 pp., illustrated. $45.00

There were four patterns of infantry cartridge boxes used by Union forces during the Civil War. The author describes the development and subsequent pattern changes to these cartridge boxes.

Civil War Commanders, by Dean Thomas, Thomas Publications, Gettysburg, PA. 1998. 72 pages, illustrated, photos. Paper Covers. $9.95

138 photographs and capsule biographies of Union and Confederate officers. A convenient personalities reference guide.

Civil War Firearms, by Joseph G. Bilby, Combined Books, Conshohocken, PA, 1996. 252 pp., illus. $34.95

A unique work combining background data on each firearm including its battlefield use, and a guide to collecting and firing surviving relics and modern reproductions.

Civil War Guns, by William B. Edwards, Thomas Publications, Gettysburg, PA, 1997. 444 pp., illus. $40.00

The complete story of Federal and Confederate small arms; design, manufacture, identifications, procurement issue, employment, effectiveness, and postwar disposal by the recognized expert.

Civil War Infantryman: In Camp, On the March, And in Battle, by Dean Thomas, Thomas Publications, Gettysburg, PA. 1998. 72 pages, illustrated, Softcovers. $12.95

Uses first-hand accounts to shed some light on the "common soldier" of the Civil War from enlistment to muster-out, including camp, marching, rations, equipment, fighting, and more.

Civil War Pistols, by John D. McAulay, Andrew Mowbray Inc., Lincoln, RI, 1992. 166 pp., illus. $38.50

A survey of the handguns used during the American Civil War.

Civil War Sharps Carbines and Rifles, by Earl J. Coates and John D. McAulay, Thomas Publications, Gettysburg, PA, 1996. 108 pp., illus. Paper covers. $12.95

Traces the history and development of the firearms including short histories of specific serial numbers and the soldiers who received them.

Civil War Small Arms of the U.S. Navy and Marine Corps, by John D. McAulay, Mowbray Publishing, Lincoln, RI, 1999. 186 pp., illustrated. $39.00

The first reliable and comprehensive guide to the firearms and edged weapons of the Civil War Navy and Marine Corps.

The W.F. Cody Buffalo Bill Collector's Guide with Values, by James W. Wojtowicz, Collector Books, Paducah, KY, 1998. 271 pp., illustrated. $24.95

A profusion of colorful collectibles including lithographs, programs, photographs, books, medals, sheet music, guns, etc. and today's values.

Col. Burton's Spiller & Burr Revolver, by Matthew W. Norman, Mercer University Press, Macon, GA, 1997. 152 pp., illus. $22.95

A remarkable archival research project on the arm together with a comprehensive story of the establishment and running of the factory.

Collector's Guide to Colt .45 Service Pistols Models of 1911 and 1911A1, Enlarged and revised edition. Clawson Publications, Fort Wayne, IN, 1998. 130 pp., illustrated. $45.00

From 1911 to the end of production in 1945 with complete military identification including all contractors.

A Collector's Guide to United States Combat Shotguns, by Bruce N. Canfield, Andrew Mowbray Inc., Lincoln, RI, 1992. 184 pp., illus. Paper covers. $24.00

This book provides full coverage of combat shotguns, from the earliest examples right up to the Gulf War and beyond.

A Collector's Guide to Winchester in the Service, by Bruce N. Canfield, Andrew Mowbray, Inc., Lincoln, RI, 1991. 192 pp., illus. Paper covers. $22.00

The firearms produced by Winchester for the national defense. From Hotchkiss to the M14, each firearm is examined and illustrated.

A Collector's Guide to the '03 Springfield, by Bruce N. Canfield, Andrew Mowbray Inc., Lincoln, RI, 1989. 160 pp., illus. Paper covers. $22.00

A comprehensive guide follows the '03 through its unparalleled tenure of service. Covers all of the interesting variations, modifications and accessories of this highly collectible military rifle.

Collector's Illustrated Encyclopedia of the American Revolution, by George C. Neumann and Frank J. Kravic, Rebel Publishing Co., Inc., Texarkana, TX, 1989. 286 pp., illus. $36.95
A showcase of more than 2,300 artifacts made, worn, and used by those who fought in the War for Independence.

Colonial Frontier Guns, by T.M. Hamilton, Pioneer Press, Union City, TN, 1988. 176 pp., illus. Paper covers. $17.50
A complete study of early flint muskets of this country.

Colt: An American Legend, by R.L. Wilson, Artabras, New York, 1997. 406 pages, fully illustrated, most in color. $60.00
A reprint of the commemorative album celebrates 150 years of the guns of Samuel Colt and the manufacturing empire he built, with expert discussion of every model ever produced, the innovations of each model and variants, updated model and serial number charts and magnificent photographic showcases of the weapons.

The Colt Armory, by Ellsworth Grant, Man-at-Arms Bookshelf, Lincoln, RI, 1996. 232 pp., illus. $35.00
A history of Colt's Manufacturing Company.

Colt Blackpowder Reproductions & Replica: A Collector's and Shooter's Guide, by Dennis Miller, Blue Book Publications, Minneapolis, MN, 1999. 288 pp., illustrated. Paper covers. $29.95
The first book on this important subject, and a must for the investor, collector, and shooter.

Colt Heritage, by R.L. Wilson, Simon & Schuster, 1979. 358 pp., illus. $75.00
The official history of Colt firearms 1836 to the present.

Colt Memorabilia Price Guide, by John Ogle, Krause Publications, Iola, WI, 1998. 256 pp., illus. Paper covers. $29.95
The first book ever compiled about the vast array of non-gun merchandise produced by Sam Colt's companies, and other companies using the Colt name.

The Colt Model 1905 Automatic Pistol, by John Potocki, Andrew Mowbray Publishing, Lincoln, RI, 1998. 191 pp., illus. $28.00
Covers all aspects of the Colt Model 1905 Automatic Pistol, from its invention by the legendary John Browning to its numerous production variations.

Colt Peacemaker British Model, by Keith Cochran, Cochran Publishing Co., Rapid City, SD, 1989. 160 pp., illus. $35.00
Covers those revolvers Colt squeezed in while completing a large order of revolvers for the U.S. Cavalry in early 1874, to those magnificent cased target revolvers used in the pistol competitions at Bisley Commons in the 1890s.

Colt Peacemaker Encyclopedia, by Keith Cochran, Keith Cochran, Rapid City, SD, 1986. 434 pp., illus. $65.00
A must book for the Peacemaker collector.

Colt Peacemaker Encyclopedia, Volume 2, by Keith Cochran, Cochran Publishing Co., SD, 1992. 416 pp., illus. $60.00
Included in this volume are extensive notes on engraved, inscribed, historical and noted revolvers, as well as those revolvers used by outlaws, lawmen, movie and television stars.

Colt Percussion Accoutrements 1834-1873, by Robin Rapley, Robin Rapley, Newport Beach, CA, 1994. 432 pp., illus. Paper covers. $39.95
The complete collector's guide to the identification of Colt percussion accoutrements; including Colt conversions and their values.

Colt Pocket Hammerless Pistols, by Dr. John W. Brunner, Phillips Publications, Williamstown, NJ, 1998. 212 pp., illustrated. $59.95
You will never again have to question a .25, .32 or .380 with this well illustrated, definitive reference guide at hand.

Colt Revolvers and the Tower of London, by Joseph G. Rosa, Royal Armouries of the Tower of London, London, England, 1988. 72 pp., illus. Soft covers. $15.00
Details the story of Colt in London through the early cartridge period.

Colt Rifles and Muskets from 1847-1870, by Herbert Houze, Krause Publications, Iola, WI, 1996. 192 pp., illus. $34.95
Discover previously unknown Colt models along with an extensive list of production figures for all models.

Colt's SAA Post War Models, by George Garton, The Gun Room Press, Highland Park, NJ, 1995. 166 pp., illus. $39.95
Complete facts on the post-war Single Action Army revolvers. Information on calibers, production numbers and variations taken from factory records.

Colt Single Action Army Revolvers: The Legend, the Romance and the Rivals, by "Doc" O'Meara, Krause Publications, Iola, WI, 2000. 160 pp., illustrated with 250 photos in b&w and a 16 page color section. $34.95
Production figures, serial numbers by year, and rarities.

Colt Single Action Army Revolvers and Alterations, by C. Kenneth Moore, Mowbray Publishers, Lincoln, RI, 1999. 112 pp., illustrated. $35.00
A comprehensive history of the revolvers that collectors call "Artillery Models." These are the most historical of all S.A.A. Colts, and this new book covers all the details.

Colt Single Action Army Revolvers and the London Agency, by C. Kenneth Moore, Andrew Mowbray Publishers, Lincoln, RI, 1990. 144 pp., illus. $35.00
Drawing on vast documentary sources, this work chronicles the relationship between the London Agency and the Hartford home office.

The Colt U.S. General Officers' Pistols, by Horace Greeley IV, Andrew Mowbray Inc., Lincoln, RI, 1990. 199 pp., illus. $38.00
These unique weapons, issued as a badge of rank to General Officers in the U.S. Army from WWII onward, remain highly personal artifacts of the military leaders who carried them. Includes serial numbers and dates of issue.

Colts from the William M. Locke Collection, by Frank Sellers, Andrew Mowbray Publishers, Lincoln, RI, 1996. 192 pp., illus. $55.00
This important book illustrates all of the famous Locke Colts, with captions by arms authority Frank Sellers.

Colt's Dates of Manufacture 1837-1978, by R.L. Wilson, published by Maurie Albert, Coburg, Australia; N.A. distributor I.D.S.A. Books, Hamilton, OH, 1983. 61 pp. $6.00
An invaluable pocket guide to the dates of manufacture of Colt firearms up to 1978.

Colt's 100th Anniversary Firearms Manual 1836-1936: A Century of Achievement, Wolfe Publishing Co., Prescott, AZ, 1992. 100 pp., illus. Paper covers. $12.95
Originally published by the Colt Patent Firearms Co., this booklet covers the history, manufacturing procedures and the guns of the first 100 years of the genius of Samuel Colt.

Colt's Pocket '49: Its Evolution Including the Baby Dragoon and Wells Fargo, by Robert Jordan and Darrow Watt, privately printed, Loma Mar, CA 2000. 304 pages, with 984 color photos, illus. Beautifully bound in a deep blue leather like case. $125.00
Detailed information on all models and covers engaving, cases, accoutrements, holsters, fakes, and much more. Included is a summary booklet containing information such as serial numbers, production ranges & identifing photos. This book is a masterpiece on its subject.

Complete Guide to all United States Military Medals 1939 to Present, by Colonel Frank C. Foster, Medals of America Press, Fountain Inn, SC, 2000. 121 pp,.illustrated, photos. $29.95
Complete criteria for every Army, Navy, Marines, Air Force, Coast Guard, and Merchant Marine awards since 1939. All decorations, service medals, and ribbons shown in full-color and accompanied by dates and campaigns as well as detailed descriptions on proper wear and display.

Complete Guide to the M1 Garand and the M1 Carbine, by Bruce N. Canfield, 2nd printing, Andrew Mowbray Inc., Lincoln, RI, 1999. 296 pp., illus. $39.50
Expanded and updated coverage of both the M1 Garand and the M1 Carbine, with more than twice as much information as the author's previous book on this topic.

The Complete Guide to U.S. Infantry Weapons of the First War, by Bruce Canfield, Andrew Mowbray, Publisher, Lincoln, RI, 2000. 304 pp., illus. $39.95
The definitive study of the U.S. Infantry weapons used in WW1.

The Complete Guide to U.S. Infantry Weapons of World War Two, by Bruce Canfield, Andrew Mowbray, Publisher, Lincoln, RI, 1995. 303 pp., illus. $39.95
A definitive work on the weapons used by the United States Armed Forces in WWII.

A Concise Guide to the Artillery at Gettysburg, by Gregory Coco, Thomas Publications, Gettysburg, PA, 1998. 96 pp., illus. Paper Covers. $10.00
Coco's tenth book on Gettysburg is a beginner's guide to artillery and its use at the battle. It covers the artillery batteries describing the types of cannons, shells, fuses, etc.using interesting narrative and human interest stories.

Cooey Firearms, Made in Canada 1919-1979, by John A. Belton, Museum Restoration, Canada, 1998. 36pp., with 46 illus. Paper Covers. $8.95
More than 6 million rifles and at least 67 models, were made by this small Canadian riflemaker. They have been identified from the first 'Cooey Canuck' through the last variations made by the 'Winchester-Cooey'. Each is descibed and most are illustrated in this first book on The Cooey.

Cowboy Collectibles and Western Memorabilia, by Bob Bell and Edward Vebell, Schiffer Publishing, Atglen, PA, 1992. 160 pp., illus. Paper covers. $29.95
The exciting era of the cowboy and the wild west collectibles including rifles, pistols, gun rigs, etc.

Cowboy Culture: The Last Frontier of American Antiques, by Michael Friedman, Schiffer Publishing, Ltd., West Chester, PA, 1992. 300 pp., illustrated.
Covers the artful aspects of the old west, the antiques and collectibles. Illustrated with clear color plates of over 1,000 items such as spurs, boots, guns, saddles etc.

Cowboy and Gunfighter Collectible, by Bill Mackin, Mountain Press Publishing Co., Missoula, MT, 1995. 178 pp., illus. Paper covers. $25.00
A photographic encyclopedia with price guide and makers' index.

Cowboys and the Trappings of the Old West, by William Manns and Elizabeth Clair Flood, Zon International Publishing Co., Santa Fe, NM, 1997, 1st edition. 224 pp., illustrated. $45.00
A pictorial celebration of the cowboys dress and trappings.

Cowboy Hero Cap Pistols, by Rudy D'Angelo, Antique Trader Books, Dubuque, IA, 1998. 196 pp., illus. Paper covers. $34.95
Aimed at collectors of cap pistols created and named for famous film and television cowboy heros, this in-depth guide hits all the marks. Current values are given.

Custom Firearms Engraving, by Tom Turpin, Krause Publications, Iola, WI, 1999. 208 pp., illustrated. $49.95
Over 200 four-color photos with more than 75 master engravers profiled. Engravers Directory with addresses in the U.S. and abroad.

The Decorations, Medals, Ribbons, Badges and Insignia of the United States Army; World War 2 to Present, by Col. Frank C. Foster, Medals of America Press, Fountain Inn, SC. 2001. 145 pages, illustrated. $29.95
The most complete guide to United States Army medals, ribbons, rank, insignia nad patches from WWII to the present day. Each medal and insignia shown in full color. Includes listing of respective criteria and campaigns.

The Decorations, Medals, Ribbons, Badges and Insignia of the United States Navy; World War 2 to Present, by James G. Thompson, Medals of America Press, Fountain Inn, SC. 2000. 123 pages, illustrated. $29.95
The most complete guide to United States Army medals, ribbons, rank, insignia nad patches from WWII to the present day. Each medal and insignia shown in full color. Includes listing of respective criteria and campaigns.

The Derringer in America, Volume 1, The Percussion Period, by R.L. Wilson and L.D. Eberhart, Andrew Mowbray Inc., Lincoln, RI, 1985. 271 pp., illus. $48.00
A long awaited book on the American percussion derringer.

THE ARMS LIBRARY

The Derringer in America, Volume 2, The Cartridge Period, by L.D. Eberhart and R.L. Wilson, Andrew Mowbray Inc., Publishers, Lincoln, RI, 1993. 284 pp., illus. $65.00
Comprehensive coverage of cartridge deringers organized alphabetically by maker. Includes all types of deringers known by the authors to have been offered to the American market.

The Devil's Paintbrush: Sir Hiram Maxim's Gun, by Dolf Goldsmith, 3rd Edition, expanded and revised, Collector Grade Publications, Toronto, Canada, 2000. 384 pp., illus. $79.95
The classic work on the world's first true automatic machine gun.

Dr. Josephus Requa Civil War Dentist and the Billinghurst-Requa Volley Gun, by John M. Hyson, Jr., & Margaret Requa DeFrancisco, Museum Restoration Service, Bloomfield, Ont., Canada, 1999. 36 pp., illus. Paper covers. $8.95
The story of the inventor of the first practical rapid-fire gun to be used during the American Civil War.

The Duck Stamp Story, by Eric Jay Dolin and Bob Dumaine, Krause Publications, Iola, WI, 2000. 208 pp., illustrated with color throughout. Paper covers. $29.95; Hardbound. $49.95.
Detailed information on the value and rarity of every federal duck stamp. Outstanding art and illustrations.

The Dutch Luger (Parabellum) A Complete History, by Bas J. Martens and Guus de Vries, Ironside International Publishers, Inc., Alexandria, VA, 1995. 268 pp., illus. $79.95
The history of the Luger in the Netherlands. An extensive description of the Dutch pistol and trials and the different models of the Luger in the Dutch service.

The Eagle on U.S. Firearms, by John W. Jordan, Pioneer Press, Union City, TN, 1992. 140 pp., illus. Paper covers. $17.50.
Stylized eagles have been stamped on government owned or manufactured firearms in the U.S. since the beginning of our country. This book lists and illustrates these various eagles in an informative and refreshing manner.

Encyclopedia of Rifles & Handguns; A Comprehensive Guide to Firearms, edited by Sean Connolly, Chartwell Books, Inc., Edison, NJ., 1996. 160 pp., illustrated. $26.00.
A lavishly illustrated book providing a comprehensive history of military and civilian personal firepower.

Eprouvettes: A Comprehensive Study of Early Devices for the Testing of Gunpowder, by R.T.W. Kempers, Royal Armouries Museum, Leeds, England, 1999. 352 pp., illustrated with 240 black & white and 28 color plates. $125.00.
The first comprehensive study of eprouvettes ever attempted in a single volume.

European Firearms in Swedish Castles, by Kaa Wennberg, Bohuslaningens Boktryckeri AB, Uddevalla, Sweden, 1986. 156 pp., illus. $50.00.
The famous collection of Count Keller, the Ettersburg Castle collection, and others. English text.

European Sporting Cartridges, Part 1, by W.B. Dixon, Armory Publications, Inc., Coeur d'Alene, ID, 1997. 250 pp., illus. $63.00
Photographs and drawings of over 550 centerfire cartridge case types in 1,300 illustrations produced in German and Austria from 1875 to 1995.

European Sporting Cartridges, Part 2, by W.B. Dixon, Armory Publications, Inc., Coeur d'Alene, ID, 2000. 240 pp., illus. $63.00
An illustrated history of centerfire hunting and target cartridges produced in Czechoslovakia, Switzerland, Norway, Sweden, Finland, Russia, Italy, Denmark, Belguim from 1875 to 1998. Adds 50 specimens to volume 1 (Germany-Austria). Also, illustrates 40 small arms magazine experiments during the late 19th Century, and includes the English-Language export ammunition catalogue of Kovo (Povazske Strojarne), Prague, Czeck. from the, 1930's.

Fifteen Years in the Hawken Lode, by John D. Baird, The Gun Room Press, Highland Park, NJ, 1976. 120 pp., illus. $24.95.
A collection of thoughts and observations gained from many years of intensive study of the guns from the shop of the Hawken brothers.

'51 Colt Navies, by Nathan L. Swayze, The Gun Room Press, Highland Park, NJ, 1993. 243 pp., illus. $59.95.
The Model 1851 Colt Navy, its variations and markings.

Fighting Iron, by Art Gogan, Andrew Mowbray, Inc., Lincoln, R.I., 1999. 176 pp., illustrated. $28.00.
It doesn't matter whether you collect guns, swords, bayonets or accountrement—sooner or later you realize that it all comes down to the metal. If you don't understand the metal you don't understand your collection.

Fine Colts, The Dr. Joseph A. Murphy Collection, by R.L. Wilson, Sheffield Marketing Associates, Inc., Doylestown, PA, 1999. 258 pp., illustrated. Limited edition signed and numbered.
This lavish new work covers exquisite, deluxe and rare Colt arms from Paterson and other percussion revolvers to the cartridge period and up through modern times.

Firearms, by Derek Avery, Desert Publications, El Dorado, AR, 1999. 95 pp., illustrated. $9.95.
The firearms included in this book are by necessity only a selection, but nevertheless one that represents the best and most famous weapons seen since the Second World War.

Firearms and Tackle Memorabilia, by John Delph, Schiffer Publishing, Ltd., West Chester, PA, 1991. 124 pp., illus. $39.95.
A collector's guide to signs and posters, calendars, trade cards, boxes, envelopes, and other highly sought after memorabilia. With a value guide.

Firearms of the American West 1803-1865, Volume 1, by Louis A. Garavaglia and Charles Worman, University of Colorado Press, Niwot, CO, 1998. 402 pp., illustrated. $59.95.
Traces the development and uses of firearms on the frontier during this period.

Firearms of the American West 1866-1894, by Louis A. Garavaglia and Charles G. Worman, University of Colorado Press, Niwot, CO, 1998. 416 pp., illus. $59.95.
A monumental work that offers both technical information on all of the important firearms used in the West during this period and a highly entertaining history of how they were used, who used them, and why.

Firearms from Europe, by David Noe, Larry W. Yantz, Dr. James B. Whisker, Rowe Publications, Rochester, N.Y., 1999. 192 pp., illustrated. $45.00.
A history and description of firearms imported during the American Civil War by the United States of America and the Confederate States of America.

Firepower from Abroad, by Wiley Sword, Andrew Mowbray Publishing, Lincoln, R.I., 2000. 120 pp., illustrated. $23.00.
The Confederate Enfield and the LeMat revolver and how they reached the Confederate market.

Flayderman's Guide to Antique American Firearms and Their Values, 7th Edition, edited by Norm Flayderman, DBI books, a division of Krause Publications, Iola, WI, 1998. 656 pp., illus. Paper covers. $32.95.
A completely updated and new edition with more than 3,600 models and variants extensively described with all marks and specifications necessary for quick identification.

The FN-FAL Rifle, et al, by Duncan Long, Paladin Press, Boulder, CO, 1999. 144 pp., illustrated. Paper covers. $18.95.
Detailed descriptions of the basic models produced by Fabrique Nationale and the myriad variants that evolved as a result of the firearms universal acceptance.

The .45-70 Springfield, by Joe Poyer and Craig Riesch, North Cape Publications, Tustin, CA, 1996. 150 pp., illus. Paper covers. $16.95.
A revised and expanded second edition of a best-selling reference work organized by serial number and date of production to aid the collector in identifying popular "Trapdoor" rifles and carbines.

The French 1935 Pistols, by Eugene Medlin and Colin Doane, Eugene Medlin, El Paso, TX, 1995. 172 pp., illus. Paper covers. $25.95.
The development and identification of successive models, fakes and variants, holsters and accessories, and serial numbers by dates of production.

Freund & Bro. Pioneer Gunmakers to the West, by F.J. Pablo Balentine, Graphic Publishers, Newport Beach, CA, 1997. 380 pp., illustrated $69.95.
The story of Frank W. and George Freund, skilled German gunsmiths who plied their trade on the Western American frontier during the final three decades of the nineteenth century.

From the Kingdom of Lilliput: The Miniature Firearms of David Kucer, by K. Corey Keeble and **The Making of Miniatures,** by David Kucer, Museum Restoration Service, Ontario, Canada, 1994. 51 pp., illus, $25.00.
An overview of the subject of miniatures in general combined with an outline by the artist himself on the way he makes a miniature firearm.

Frontier Pistols and Revolvers, by Dominique Venner, Book Sales Inc., Edison, N.J., 1998. 144 pp., illus. $19.95.
Colt, Smith & Wesson, Remington and other early-brand revolvers which tamed the American frontier are shown amid vintage photographs, etchings and paintings to evoke the wild West.

The Fusil de Tulole in New France, 1691-1741, by Russel Bouchard, Museum Restorations Service, Bloomfield, Ontario, Canada, 1997. 36 pp., illus. Paper covers. $8.95
The development of the company and the identification of their arms.

Game Guns & Rifles: Percussion to Hammerless Ejector in Britain, by Richard Akehurst, Trafalgar Square, N. Pomfret, VT, 1993. 192 pp., illus. $39.95.
Long considered a classic this important reprint covers the period of British gunmaking between 1830-1900.

The Gas Trap Garand, by Billy Pyle, Collector Grade Publications, Cobourg, Ontario, Canada, 1999 316 pp., illustrated. $59.95.
The in-depth story of the rarest Garands of them all, the initial 80 Model Shop rifles made under the personal supervision of John Garand himself in 1934 and 1935, and the first 50,000 plus production "gas trap" M1's manufactured at Springfield Armory between August, 1937 and August, 1940.

George Schreyer, Sr. and Jr., Gunmakers of Hanover, Pennsylvania, by George Shumway, George Shumway Publishers, York, PA, 1990. 160pp., illus. $50.00.
This monograph is a detailed photographic study of almost all known surviving long rifles and smoothbore guns made by highly regarded gunsmiths George Schreyer, Sr. and Jr.

The German Assault Rifle 1935-1945, by Peter R. Senich, Paladin Press, Boulder, CO, 1987. 328 pp., illus. $60.00.
A complete review of machine carbines, machine pistols and assault rifles employed by Hitler's Wehrmacht during WWII.

The German K98k Rifle, 1934-1945: The Backbone of the Wehrmacht, by Richard D. Law, Collector Grade Publications, Toronto, Canada, 1993. 336 pp., illus. $69.95.
The most comprehensive study ever published on the 14,000,000 bolt-action K98k rifles produced in Germany between 1934 and 1945.

German Machine Guns, by Daniel D. Musgrave, revised edition, Ironside International Publishers, Inc. Alexandria, VA, 1992. 586 pp., 650 illus. $49.95.
The most definitive book ever written on German machineguns. Covers the introduction and development of machineguns in Germany from 1899 to the rearmament period after WWII.

German Military Rifles and Machine Pistols, 1871-1945, by Hans Dieter Gotz, Schiffer Publishing Co., West Chester, PA, 1990. 245 pp., illus. $35.00.
This book portrays in words and pictures the development of the modern German weapons and their ammunition including the scarcely known experimental types.

The German MP40 Maschinenpistole, by Frank Iannamico, Moose Lake Publishing, Harmony, ME, 1999. 185 pp., illustrated. Paper covers. $19.95.
The history, development and use of this famous gun of World War 2.

German 7.9mm Military Ammunition, by Daniel W. Kent, Daniel W. Kent, Ann Arbor, MI, 1991. 244 pp., illus. $35.00.

The long-awaited revised edition of a classic among books devoted to ammunition.

The Golden Age of Remington, by Robert W.D. Ball, Krause publications, Iola, WI, 1995. 194 pp., illus. $29.95.

For Remington collectors or firearms historians, this book provides a pictorial history of Remington through World War I. Includes value guide.

The Government Models, by William H.D. Goddard, Andrew Mowbray Publishing, Lincoln, RI, 1998. 296 pp., illustrated. $58.50.

The most authoritative source on the development of the Colt model of 1911.

Grasshoppers and Butterflies, by Adrian B. Caruana, Museum Restoration Service, Alexandria, Bay, N.Y., 1999. 32 pp., illustrated. Paper covers. $8.95.

No.39 in the Historical Arms Series. The light 3 pounders of Pattison and Townsend.

The Greener Story, by Graham Greener, Quiller Press, London, England, 2000. 256 pp., illustrated with 32 pages of color photos. $64.50.

W.W. Greener, his family history, inventions, guns, patents, and more.

A Guide to American Trade Catalogs 1744-1900, by Lawrence B. Romaine, Dover Publications, New York, NY. 422 pp., illus. Paper covers. $12.95

A Guide to Ballard Breechloaders, by George J. Layman, Pioneer Press, Union City, TN, 1997. 261 pp., illus. Paper covers. $19.95

Documents the saga of this fine rifle from the first models made by Ball & Williams of Worchester, to its production by the Marlin Firearms Co, to the cessation of 19th century manufacture in 1891, and finally to the modern reproductions made in the 1990's.

A Guide to the Maynard Breechloader, by George J. Layman, George J. Layman, Ayer, MA, 1993. 125 pp., illus. Paper covers. $11.95.

The first book dedicated entirely to the Maynard family of breech-loading firearms. Coverage of the arms is given from the 1850s through the 1880s.

A Guide to U. S. Army Dress Helmets 1872-1904, by Kasal and Moore, North Cape Publications, 2000. 88 pp., illus. Paper covers. $15.95

This thorough study provides a complete description of the Model 1872 & 1881 dress helmets worn by the U.S. Army. Including all componets from bodies to plates to plumes & shoulder cords and tells how to differentiate the originals from reproductions. Extensively illustrated with photographs, '8 pages in full color' of complete helmets and their components.

Gun Collecting, by Geoffrey Boothroyd, Sportsman's Press, London, 1989. 208 pp., illus. $29.95.

The most comprehensive list of 19th century British gunmakers and gunsmiths ever published.

Gunmakers of London 1350-1850, by Howard L. Blackmore, George Shumway Publisher, York, PA, 1986. 222 pp., illus. $35.00.

A listing of all the known workmen of gun making in the first 500 years, plus a history of the guilds, cutlers, armourers, founders, blacksmiths, etc. 260 gunmarks are illustrated.

Gunmakers of London Supplement 1350-1850, by Howard L. Blackmore, Museum Restoration Service, Alexandria Bay, NY, 1999. 156 pp., illustrated. $60.00.

Begins with an introductory chapter on "foreighn" gunmakers followed by records of all the new information found about previously unidentified armourers, gunmakers and gunsmiths.

The Guns that Won the West: Firearms of the American Frontier, 1865-1898, by John Walter, Stackpole Books, Inc., Mechanicsburg, PA.,1999. 256 pp., illustrated. $34.95.

Here is the story of the wide range of firearms from pistols to rifles used by plainsmen and settlers, gamblers, native Americans and the U.S. Army.

Gunsmiths of Illinois, by Curtis L. Johnson, George Shumway Publishers, York, PA, 1995. 160 pp., illus. $50.00.

Genealogical information is provided for nearly one thousand gunsmiths. Contains hundreds of illustrations of rifles and other guns, of handmade origin, from Illinois.

The Gunsmiths of Manhattan, 1625-1900: A Checklist of Tradesmen, by Michael H. Lewis, Museum Restoration Service, Bloomfield, Ont., Canada, 1991. 40 pp., illus. Paper covers. $8.95.

This listing of more than 700 men in the arms trade in New York City prior to about the end of the 19th century will provide a guide for identification and further research.

The Guns of Dagenham: Lanchester, Patchett, Sterling, by Peter Laidler and David Howroyd, Collector Grade Publications, Inc., Cobourg, Ont., Canada, 1995. 310 pp., illus. $39.95.

An in-depth history of the small arms made by the Sterling Company of Dagenham, Essex, England, from 1940 until Sterling was purchased by British Aerospace in 1989 and closed.

Guns of the Western Indian War, by R. Stephen Dorsey, Collector's Library, Eugene, OR, 1997. 220 pp., illus. Paper covers. $30.00.

The full story of the guns and ammunition that made western history in the turbulent period of 1865-1890.

Gun Powder Cans & Kegs, by Ted & David Bacyk and Tom Rowe, Rowe Publications, Rochester, NY, 1999. 150 pp., illus. $65.00.

The first book devoted to powder tins and kegs. All cans and kegs in full color. With a price guide and rarity scale.

The Guns of Remington: Historic Firearms Spanning Two Centuries, compiled by Howard M. Madaus, Biplane Productions, Publisher, in cooperation with Buffalo Bill Historical Center, Cody, WY, 1998. 352 pp., illustrated with over 800 color photos. $79.95.

A complete catalog of the firearms in the exhibition, "It Never Failed Me: The Arms & Art of Remington Arms Company" at the Buffalo Bill Historical Center, Cody, Wyoming.

Gun Tools, Their History and Identification by James B. Shaffer, Lee A. Rutledge and R. Stephen Dorsey, Collector's Library, Eugene, OR, 1992. 375 pp., illus. $30.00.

Written history of foreign and domestic gun tools from the flintlock period to WWII.

Gun Tools, Their History and Identifications, Volume 2, by Stephen Dorsey and James B. Shaffer, Collectors' Library, Eugene, OR, 1997. 396 pp., illus. Paper covers. $30.00.

Gun tools from the Royal Armouries Museum in England, Pattern Room, Royal Ordnance Reference Collection in Nottingham and from major private collections.

Gunsmiths of the Carolinas 1660-1870, by Daniel D. Hartzler and James B. Whisker, Old Bedford Village Press, Bedford, PA, 1998. 176 pp., illustrated. $40.00.

This deluxe hard bound edition of 176 pages is printed on fine coated paper, with about 90 pages of large photographs of fine longrifles from the Carolinas, and about 90 pages of detailed research on the gunsmiths who created the highly prized and highly collectable longrifles. Dedicated to serious students of original Kentucky rifles, who may seldom encounter fine longrifles from the Carolinas.

Gunsmiths of Maryland, by Daniel D. Hartzler and James B. Whisker, Old Bedford Village Press, Bedford, PA, 1998. 208 pp., illustrated. $45.00.

Covers firelock Colonial period through the breech-loading patent models. Featuring longrifles.

Gunsmiths of Virginia, by Daniel D. Hartzler and James B. Whisker, Old Bedford Village Press, Bedford, PA, 1992. 206 pp., illustrated. $45.00.

A photographic study of American longrifles.

Gunsmiths of West Virginia, by Daniel D. Hartzler and James B. Whisker, Old Bedford Village Press, Bedford, PA, 1998. 176 pp., illustrated. $40.00.

A photographic study of American longrifles.

Gunsmiths of York County, Pennsylvania, by Daniel D. Hartzler and James B. Whisker, Old Bedford Village Press, Bedford, PA, 1998. 160 pp., illustrated. $40.00.

160 pages of photographs and research notes on the longrifles and gunsmiths of York County, Pennsylvania. Many longrifle collectors and gun builders have noticed that York County style rifles tend to be more formal in artistic decoration than some other schools of style. Patriotic themes, and folk art were popular design elements.

Hall's Military Breechloaders, by Peter A. Schmidt, Andrew Mowbray Publishers, Lincoln, RI, 1996. 232 pp., illus. $55.00.

The whole story behind these bold and innovative firearms.

The Handgun, by Geoffrey Boothroyd, David and Charles, North Pomfret, VT, 1989. 566 pp., illus. $60.00.

Every chapter deals with an important period in handgun history from the 14th century to the present.

Handgun of Military Rifle Marks 1866-1950, by Richard A. Hoffman and Noel P. Schott, Mapleleaf Militaria Publishing, St. Louis, MO, 1999, second edition. 60 pp., illustrated. Paper covers. $20.00.

An illustrated guide to identifying military rifle and marks.

Handguns & Rifles: The Finest Weapons from Around the World, by Ian Hogg, Random House Value Publishing, Inc., N.Y., 1999. 128 pp., illustrated. $18.98.

The serious gun collector will welcome this fully illustrated examination of international handguns and rifles. Each entry covers the history of the weapon, what purpose it serves, and its advantages and disadvantages.

The Hawken Rifle: Its Place in History, by Charles E. Hanson, Jr., The Fur Press, Chadron, NE, 1979. 104 pp., illus. Paper covers. $15.00.

A definitive work on this famous rifle.

Hawken Rifles, The Mountain Man's Choice, by John D. Baird, The Gun Room Press, Highland Park, NJ, 1976. 95 pp., illus. $29.95.

Covers the rifles developed for the Western fur trade. Numerous specimens are described and shown in photographs.

High Standard: A Collector's Guide to the Hamden & Hartford Target Pistols, by Tom Dance, Andrew Mowbray, Inc., Lincoln, RI, 1991. 192 pp., illus. Paper covers. $24.00.

From Citation to Supermatic, all of the production models and specials made from 1951 to 1984 are covered according to model number or series.

Historic Pistols: The American Martial Flintlock 1760-1845, by Samuel E. Smith & Edwin W. Bitter, The Gun Room Press, Highland Park, NJ, 1986. 353 pp., illus. $45.00.

Covers over 70 makers and 163 models of American martial arms.

Historical Hartford Hardware, by William W. Dalrymple, Colt Collector Press, Rapid City, SD, 1976. 42 pp., illus. Paper covers. $10.00.

Historically associated Colt revolvers.

The History and Development of Small Arms Ammunition, Volume 2, by George A. Hoyem, Armory Publications, Oceanside, CA, 1991. 303 pp., illus. $65.00.

Covers the blackpowder military centerfire rifle, carbine, machine gun and volley gun ammunition used in 28 nations and dominions, together with the firearms that chambered them.

The History and Development of Small Arms Ammunition, Volume 4, by George A. Hoyem, Armory Publications, Seattle, WA, 1998. 200 pp., illustrated $65.00.

A comprehensive book on American black powder and early smokeless rifle cartridges.

The History of Colt Firearms, by Dean Boorman, Lyons Press, New York, NY, 2001. 144 pp., illus. $29.95

Discover the fascinating story of the world's most famous revolver, complete with more than 150 stunning full-color photographs.

History of Modern U.S. Military Small Arms Ammunition. Volume 1, 1880-1939, revised by F.W. Hackley, W.H. Woodin and E.L. Scranton, Thomas Publications, Gettysburg, PA, 1998. 328 pp., illus. $49.95.

This revised edition incorporates all publicly available information concerning military small arms ammunition for the period 1880 through 1939 in a single volume.

History of Modern U.S. Military Small Arms Ammunition. Volume 2, 1940-1945 by F.W. Hackley, W.H. Woodin and E.L. Scranton. Gun Room Press, Highland Park, NJ. 300 + pages, illustrated. $39.95

Based on decades of original research conducted at the National Archives, numerous military, public and private museums and libraries, as well as individual collections, this edition incorporates all publicly available information concerning military small arms ammunition for the period 1940 through 1945.

The History of Winchester Rifles, by Dean Boorman, Lyons Press, New York, NY, 2001. 144 pp., illus. $29.95.

A captivating and wonderfully photographed history of one of the most legendary names in gun lore. 150 full-color photos.

The History of Winchester Firearms 1866-1992, sixth edition, updated, expanded, and revised by Thomas Henshaw, New Win Publishing, Clinton, NJ, 1993. 280 pp., illus. $27.95.

This classic is the standard reference for all collectors and others seeking the facts about any Winchester firearm, old or new.

History of Winchester Repeating Arms Company, by Herbert G. Houze, Krause Publications, Iola, WI, 1994. 800 pp., illus. $50.00.

The complete Winchester history from 1856-1981.

Honour Bound: The Chauchat Machine Rifle, by Gerard Demaison and Yves Buffetaut, Collector Grade Publications, Inc., Cobourg, Ont., Canada, 1995. $39.95.

The story of the CSRG (Chauchat) machine rifle, the most manufactured automatic weapon of World War One.

Hopkins & Allen Revolvers & Pistols, by Charles E. Carder, Avil Onze Publishing, Delphos, OH, 1998, illustrated. Paper covers. $24.95.

Covers over 165 photos, graphics and patent drawings.

How to Buy and Sell Used Guns, by John Traister, Stoeger Publishing Co., So. Hackensack, NJ, 1984. 192 pp., illus. Paper covers. $10.95.

A new guide to buying and selling guns.

Hunting Weapons From the Middle Ages to the Twentieth Century, by Howard L. Blackmore, Dover Publications, Meneola, NY, 2000. 480 pp., illustrated. Paper covers. $16.95.

Dealing mainly with the different classes of weapons used in sport—swords, spears, crossbows, guns, and rifles—from the Middle Ages until the present day.

Identification Manual on the .303 British Service Cartridge, No. 1-Ball Ammunition, by B.A. Temple, I.D.S.A. Books, Piqua, OH, 1986. 84 pp., 57 illus. $12.50

Identification Manual on the .303 British Service Cartridge, No. 2-Blank Ammunition, by B.A. Temple, I.D.S.A. Books, Piqua, OH, 1986. 95 pp., 59 illus. $12.50

Identification Manual on the .303 British Service Cartridge, No. 3-Special Purpose Ammunition, by B.A. Temple, I.D.S.A. Books, Piqua, OH, 1987. 82 pp., 49 illus. $12.50

Identification Manual on the .303 British Service Cartridge, No. 4-Dummy Cartridges Henry 1869-c.1900, by B.A. Temple, I.D.S.A. Books, Piqua, OH, 1988. 84 pp., 70 illus. $12.50

Identification Manual on the .303 British Service Cartridge, No. 5-Dummy Cartridges (2), by B.A. Temple, I.D.S.A. Books, Piqua, OH, 1994. 78 pp. $12.50

The Illustrated Book of Guns, by David Miller, Salamander Books, N.Y., N.Y., 2000. 304 pp., illustrated in color. $34.95.

An illustrated directory of over 1,000 military and sporting firearms.

The Illustrated Encyclopedia of Civil War Collectibles, by Chuck Lawliss, Henry Holt and Co., New York, NY, 1997. 316 pp., illus. Paper covers. $22.95.

A comprehensive guide to Union and Confederate arms, equipment, uniforms, and other memorabilia.

Illustrations of United States Military Arms 1776-1903 and Their Inspector's Marks, compiled by Turner Kirkland, Pioneer Press, Union City, TN, 1988. 37 pp., illus. Paper covers. $7.00.

Reprinted from the 1949 Bannerman catalog. Valuable information for both the advanced and beginning collector.

Indian War Cartridge Pouches, Boxes and Carbine Boots, by R. Stephen Dorsey, Collector's Library, Eugene, OR, 1993. 156 pp., illus. Paper Covers. $20.00.

The key reference work to the cartridge pouches, boxes, carbine sockets and boots of the Indian War period 1865-1890.

An Introduction to the Civil War Small Arms, by Earl J. Coates and Dean S. Thomas, Thomas Publishing Co., Gettysburg, PA, 1990. 96 pp., illus. Paper covers. $10.00.

The small arms carried by the individual soldier during the Civil War.

Japanese Rifles of World War Two, by Duncan O. McCollum, Excalibur Publications, Latham, NY, 1996. 64 pp., illus. Paper covers. $18.95.

A sweeping view of the rifles and carbines that made up Japan's arsenal during the conflict.

Kalashnikov Arms, compiled by Alexei Nedelin, Design Military Parade, Ltd., Moscow, Russia, 1997. 240 pp., illus. $49.95.

Weapons versions stored in the St. Petersburg Military Historical Museum of Artillery, Engineer Troops and Communications and in the Izhmash JSC.

Kalashnikov "Machine Pistols, Assault Rifles, and Machine Guns, 1945 to the Present," by John Walter, Paladin Press, Boulder, CO, 1999, hardcover, photos, illus., 146 pp. $22.95

This exhaustive work published by Greenhill Military Manuals features a gun-by-gun directory of Kalashnikov variants. Technical specifications and illustrations are provided throughout, along with details of sights, bayonets, markings and ammunition. A must for the serious collector and historian.

The Kentucky Pistol, by Roy Chandler and James Whisker, Old Bedford Village Press, Bedford, PA, 1997. 225 pp., illus. $60.00

A photographic study of Kentucky pistols from famous collections.

The Kentucky Rifle, by Captain John G.W. Dillin, George Shumway Publisher, York, PA, 1993. 221 pp., illus. $50.00.

This well-known book was the first attempt to tell the story of the American longrifle. This edition retains the original text and illustrations with supplemental footnotes provided by Dr. George Shumway.

Know Your Broomhandle Mausers, by R.J. Berger, Blacksmith Corp., Southport, CT, 1985. 96 pp., illus. Paper covers. $12.95.

An interesting story on the big Mauser pistol and its variations.

Krag Rifles, by William S. Brophy, The Gun Room Press, Highland Park, NJ, 1980. 200 pp., illus. $35.00.

The first comprehensive work detailing the evolution and various models, both military and civilian.

The Krieghoff Parabellum, by Randall Gibson, Midland, TX, 1988. 279 pp., illus. $40.00.

A comprehensive text pertaining to the Lugers manufactured by H. Krieghoff Waffenfabrik.

Las Pistolas Espanolas Tipo "Mauser," by Artemio Mortera Perez, Quiron Ediciones, Valladolid, Spain, 1998. 71 pp., illustrated. Paper covers. $34.95.

This book covers in detail Spanish machine pistols and C96 copies made in Spain. Covers all Astra "Mauser" pistol series and the complete line of Beistegui C96 type pistols. Spanish text.

Law Enforcement Memorabilia Price and Identification Guide, by Monty McCord, DBI Books a division of Krause Publications, Inc. Iola, WI, 1999. 208 pp., illustrated. Paper covers. $19.95.

An invaluable reference to the growing wave of law enforcement collectors. Hundreds of items are covered from miniature vehicles to clothes, patches, and restraints.

Legendary Sporting Guns, by Eric Joly, Abbeville Press, New York, N.Y., 1999. 228 pp., illustrated. $65.00.

A survey of hunting through the ages and relates how many different types of firearms were created and refined for use afield.

Legends and Reality of the AK, by Val Shilin and Charlie Cutshaw, Paladen Press, Boulder, CO, 2000. 192 pp., illustrated. Paper covers. $35.00.

A behind-the-scenes look at history, design and impact of the Kalashnikov family of weapons.

LeMat, the Man, the Gun, by Valmore J. Forgett and Alain F. and Marie-Antoinette Serpette, Navy Arms Co., Ridgefield, NJ, 1996. 218 pp., illus. $49.95.

The first definitive study of the Confederate revolvers invention, development and delivery by Francois Alexandre LeMat.

Les Pistolets Automatiques Francaise 1890-1990, by Jean Huon, Combined Books, Inc., Conshohocken, PA, 1997. 160 pp., illus. French text. $34.95

French automatic pistols from the earliest experiments through the World Wars and Indo-China to modern security forces.

Levine's Guide to Knives And Their Values, 4th Edition, by Bernard Levine, DBI Books, a division of Krause Publications, Iola, WI, 1997. 512 pp., illus. Paper covers. $27.95

All the basic tools for identifying, valuing and collecting folding and fixed blade knives.

The Light 6-Pounder Battalion Gun of 1776, by Adrian Caruana, Museum Restoration Service, Bloomfield, Ontario, Canada, 2001. 76 pp., illus. Paper covers. $8.95

The London Gun Trade, 1850-1920, by Joyce E. Gooding, Museum Restoration Service, Bloomfield, Ontario, Canada, 2001. 48 pp., illus. Paper covers. $8.95

Names, dates and locations of London gunmakers working between 1850 and 1920 are listed. Compiled from the original Kelly's Post Office Directories of the City of London.

The London Gunmakers and the English Duelling Pistol, 1770-1830, by Keith R. Dill, Museum Restoration Service, Bloomfield, Ontario, Canada, 1997. 36 pp., illus. Paper covers. $8.95

Ten gunmakers made London one of the major gunmaking centers of the world. This book examines how the design and construction of their pistols contributed to that reputation and how these characteristics may be used to date flintlock arms.

Longrifles of North Carolina, by John Bivens, George Shumway Publisher, York, PA, 1988. 256 pp., illus. $50.00.

Covers art and evolution of the rifle, immigration and trade movements. Committee of Safety gunsmiths, characteristics of the North Carolina rifle.

Longrifles of Pennsylvania, Volume 1, Jefferson, Clarion & Elk Counties, by Russel H. Harringer, George Shumway Publisher, York, PA, 1984. 200 pp., illus. $50.00.

First in series that will treat in great detail the longrifles and gunsmiths of Pennsylvania.

The Luger Handbook, by Aarron Davis, Krause Publications, Iola, WI, 1997. 112 pp., illus. Paper covers. $9.95.

Quick reference to classify Luger models and variations with complete details including proofmarks.

Lugers at Random, by Charles Kenyon, Jr., Handgun Press, Glenview, IL, 1990. 420 pp., illus. $59.95.

A new printing of this classic, comprehensive reference for all Luger collectors.

The Luger Story, by John Walter, Stackpole Books, Mechanicsburg, PA, 2001. 256 pp., illus. Paper Covers $29.95.

The standard history of the world's most famous handgun.

M1 Carbine, by Larry Ruth, Gun room Press, Highland Park, NJ, 1987. 291 pp., illus. Paper $19.95.

The origin, development, manufacture and use of this famous carbine of World War II.

The M1 Carbine: Owner's Guide, by Scott A. Duff, Scott A. Duff, Export, PA, 1997. 126 pp., illus. Paper covers. $19.95.

This book answers the questions M1 owners most often ask concerning maintenance activities not encounted by military users.

The M1 Garand: Owner's Guide, by Scott A. Duff, Scott A. Duff, Export, PA, 1998. 132 pp., illus. Paper covers. $19.95.

This book answers the questions M1 owners most often ask concerning maintenance activities not encounted by military users.

The M1 Garand Serial Numbers and Data Sheets, by Scott A. Duff, Export, PA, 1995. 101 pp., illus. Paper covers. $11.95.

Provides the reader with serial numbers related to dates of manufacture and a large sampling of data sheets to aid in identification or restoration.

The M1 Garand 1936 to 1957, by Joe Poyer and Craig Riesch, North Cape Publications, Tustin, CA, 1996. 216 pp., illus. Paper covers. $19.95.

Describes the entire range of M1 Garand production in text and quick-scan charts.

The M1 Garand: Post World War, by Scott A. Duff, Scott A. Duff, Export, PA, 1990. 139 pp., illus. Soft covers. $19.95.

A detailed account of the activities at Springfield Armory through this period. International Harvester, H&R, Korean War production and quantities delivered. Serial numbers.

The M1 Garand: World War 2, by Scott A. Duff, Scott A. Duff, Export, PA, 1993. 210 pp., illus. Paper covers. $39.95.

The most comprehensive study available to the collector and historian on the M1 Garand of World War II.

Maine Made Guns and Their Makers, by Dwight B. Demeritt Jr., Maine State Museum, Augusta, ME, 1998. 209 pp., illustrated. $55.00.

An authoritative, biographical study of Maine gunsmiths.

Marlin Firearms: A History of the Guns and the Company That Made Them, by Lt. Col. William S. Brophy, USAR, Ret., Stackpole Books, Harrisburg, PA, 1989. 672 pp., illus. $75.00.

The definitive book on the Marlin Firearms Co. and their products.

Martini-Henry .450 Rifles & Carbines, by Dennis Lewis, Excalibur Publications, Latham, NY, 1996. 72 pp., illus. Paper covers. $11.95.

The stories of the rifles and carbines that were the mainstay of the British soldier through the Victorian wars.

Mauser Bolt Rifles, by Ludwig Olson, F. Brownell & Son, Inc., Montezuma, IA, 1999. 364 pp., illus. $59.95.

The most complete, detailed, authoritative and comprehensive work ever done on Mauser bolt rifles. Completely revised deluxe 3rd edition.

Mauser Military Rifles of the World, 2nd Edition, by Robert Ball, Krause Publications, Iola, WI, 2000. 304 pp., illustrated with 1,000 b&w photos and a 48 page color section. $44.95.

This 2nd edition brings more than 100 new photos of these historic rifles and the wars in which they were carried.

Mauser Smallbores Sporting, Target and Training Rifles, by Jon Speed, Collector Grade Publications, Cobourg, Ontario, Canada 1998. 349 pp., illustrated. $67.50.

A history of all the smallbore sporting, target and training rifles produced by the legendary Mauser-Werke of Obendorf Am Neckar.

Military Holsters of World War 2, by Eugene J. Bender, Rowe Publications, Rochester, NY, 1998. 200 pp., illustrated. $45.00.

A revised edition with a new price guide of the most definitive book on this subject.

Military Pistols of Japan, by Fred L. Honeycutt, Jr., Julin Books, Palm Beach Gardens, FL, 1997. 168 pp., illus. $42.00.

Covers every aspect of military pistol production in Japan through WWII.

The Military Remington Rolling Block Rifle, by George Layman, Pioneer Press, TN, 1998. 146 pp., illus. Paper covers. $24.95.

A standard reference for those with an interest in the Remington rolling block family of firearms.

Military Rifles of Japan, 5th Edition, by F.L. Honeycutt, Julin Books, Lake Park, FL, 1999. 208 pp., illus. $42.00.

A new revised and updated edition. Includes the early Murata-period markings, etc.

Military Small Arms Data Book, by Ian V. Hogg, Stackpole Books, Mechanicsburg, PA, 1999. $44.95. 336 pp., illustrated.

Data on more than 1,500 weapons. Covers a vast range of weapons from pistols to anti-tank rifles. Essential data, 1870-2000, in one volume.

Modern Beretta Firearms, by Gene Gangarosa, Jr., Stoeger Publishing Co., So. Hackensack, NJ, 1994. 288 pp., illus. Paper covers. $16.95.

Traces all models of modern Beretta pistols, rifles, machine guns and combat shotguns.

Modern Gun Values, The Gun Digest Book of, 10th Edition, by the Editors of Gun Digest, DBI Books, a division of Krause Publications, Iola, WI., 1996. 560 pp. illus. Paper covers. $21.95.

Greatly updated and expanded edition describing and valuing over 7,000 firearms manufactured from 1900 to 1996. The standard for valuing modern firearms.

Modern Gun Identification & Value Guide, 13th Edition, by Russell and Steve Quertermous, Collector Books, Paducah, KY, 1998. 504 pp., illus. Paper covers. $14.95.

Features current values for over 2,500 models of rifles, shotguns and handguns, with over 1,800 illustrations.

More Single Shot Rifles, by James C. Grant, The Gun Room Press, Highland Park, NJ, 1976. 324 pp., illus. $35.00.

Details the guns made by Frank Wesson, Milt Farrow, Holden, Borchardt, Stevens, Remington, Winchester, Ballard and Peabody-Martini.

Mortimer, the Gunmakers, 1753-1923, by H. Lee Munson, Andrew Mowbray Inc., Lincoln, RI, 1992. 320 pp., illus. $65.00.

Seen through a single, dominant, English gunmaking dynasty this fascinating study provides a window into the classical era of firearms artistry.

The Mosin-Nagant Rifle, by Terence W. Lapin, North Cape Publications, Tustin, CA, 1998. 30 pp., illustrated. Paper covers. $19.95.

The first ever complete book on the Mosin-Nagant rifle written in English. Covers every variation.

The Navy Luger, by Joachim Gortz and John Walter, Handgun Press, Glenview, IL, 1988. 128 pp., illus. $24.95.

The 9mm Pistole 1904 and the Imperial German Navy. A concise illustrated history.

The New World of Russian Small Arms and Ammunition, by Charlie Cutshaw, Paladin Press, Boulder, CO, 1998. 160 pp., illustrated. $42.95.

Detailed descriptions, specifications and first-class illustrations of the AN-94, PSS silent pistol, Bizon SMG, Saifa-12 tactical shotgun, the GP-25 grenade launcher and more cutting edge Russian weapons.

The Number 5 Jungle Carbine, by Alan M. Petrillo, Excalibur Publications, Latham, NY, 1994. 32 pp., illus. Paper covers. $7.95.

A comprehensive treatment of the rifle that collectors have come to call the "Jungle Carbine"—the Lee-Enfield Number 5, Mark 1.

The '03 Era: When Smokeless Revolutionized U.S. Riflery, by Clark S. Campbell, Collector Grade Publications, Inc., Ontario, Canada, 1994. 334 pp., illus. $44.50.

A much-expanded version of Campbell's The '03 Springfields, representing forty years of in-depth research into "all things '03."

Observations on Colt's Second Contract, November 2, 1847, by G. Maxwell Longfield and David T. Basnett, Museum Restoration Service, Bloomfield, Ontario, Canada, 1997. 36 pp., illus. Paper covers. $6.95.

This study traces the history and the construction of the Second Model Colt Dragoon supplied in 1848 to the U.S. Cavalry.

Official Guide to Gunmarks, 3rd Edition, by Robert H. Balderson, House of Collectibles, New York, NY, 1996. 367 pp., illus. Paper covers. $15.00.

Identifies manufacturers' marks that appear on American and foreign pistols, rifles and shotguns.

Official Price Guide to Gun Collecting, by R.L. Wilson, Ballantine/House of Collectibles, New York, NY, 1998. 450 pp., illus. Paper covers. $21.50.

Covers more than 30,000 prices from Colt revolvers to Winchester rifles and shotguns to German Lugers and British sporting rifles and game guns.

Official Price Guide to Military Collectibles, 6th Edition, by Richard J. Austin, Random House, Inc., New York, NY, 1998. 200 pp., illus. Paper cover. $20.00.

Covers weapons and other collectibles from wars of the distant and recent past. More than 4,000 prices are listed. Illustrated with 400 black & white photos plus a full-color insert.

The Official Soviet SVD Manual, by Major James F. Gebhardt (Ret.) Paladin Press, Boulder, CO, 1999. 112 pp., illustrated. Paper covers. $15.00.

Operating instructions for the 7.62mm Dragunov, the first Russian rifle developed from scratch specifically for sniping.

Old Gunsights: A Collector's Guide, 1850 to 2000, by Nicholas Stroebel, Krause Publications, Iola, WI, 1998. 320 pp., illus. Paper covers. $29.95

An in-depth and comprehensive examination of old gunsights and the rifles on which they were used to get accurate feel for prices in this expanding market.

Old Rifle scopes, by Nicholas Stroebel, Krause Publications, Iola, WI, 2000. 400 pp., illustrated. Paper covers. $31.95.

This comprehensive collector's guide takes aim at more than 120 scope makers and 60 mount makers and features photos and current market values for 300 scopes and mounts manufactured from 1950-1985.

The P-08 Parabellum Luger Automatic Pistol, edited by J. David McFarland, Desert Publications, Cornville, AZ, 1982. 20 pp., illus. Paper covers. $11.95.

Covers every facet of the Luger, plus a listing of all known Luger models.

Packing Iron, by Richard C. Rattenbury, Zon International Publishing, Millwood, NY, 1993. 216 pp., illus. $45.00.

The best book yet produced on pistol holsters and rifle scabbards. Over 300 variations of holster and scabbards are illustrated in large, clear plates.

Parabellum: A Technical History of Swiss Lugers, by Vittorio Bobba, Priuli & Verlucca, Editori, Torino, Italy, 1996. Italian and English text. Illustrated. $100.00.

Patents for Inventions, Class 119 (Small Arms), 1855-1930. British Patent Office, Armory Publications, Oceanside, CA, 1993. 7 volume set. $250.00.

Contains 7980 abridged patent descriptions and their sectioned line drawings, plus a 37-page alphabetical index of the patentees.

Pattern Dates for British Ordnance Small Arms, 1718-1783, by DeWitt Bailey, Thomas Publications, Gettysburg, PA, 1997. 116 pp., illus. Paper covers. $20.00

The weapons discussed in this work are those carried by troops sent to North America between 1737 and 1783, or shipped to them as replacement arms while in America.

The Pitman Notes on U.S. Martial Small Arms and Ammunition, 1776-1933, Volume 2, Revolvers and Automatic Pistols, by Brig. Gen. John Pitman, Thomas Publications, Gettysburg, PA, 1990. 192 pp., illus. $29.95.

A most important primary source of information on United States military small arms and ammunition.

The Plains Rifle, by Charles Hanson, Gun Room Press, Highland Park, NJ, 1989. 169 pp., illus. $35.00.

All rifles that were made with the plainsman in mind, including pistols.

REFERENCE

THE ARMS LIBRARY

Powder and Ball Small Arms, by Martin Pegler, Windrow & Green, London, 1998. 128 pp., illus. $39.95.

Part of the new "Live Firing Classic Weapons" series featuring full color photos of experienced shooters dressed in authentic costumes handling, loading and firing historic weapons.

The Powder Flask Book, by Ray Riling, R&R Books, Livonia, NY, 1993. 514 pp., illus. $69.95.

The complete book on flasks of the 19th century. Exactly scaled pictures of 1,600 flasks are illustrated.

Proud Promise: French Autoloading Rifles, 1898-1979, by Jean Huon, Collector Grade Publications, Inc., Cobourg, Ont., Canada, 1995. 216 pp., illus. $39.95.

The author has finally set the record straight about the importance of French contributions to modern arms design.

E. C. Prudhomme's Gun Engraving Review, by E. C. Prudhomme, R&R Books, Livonia, NY, 1994. 164 pp., illus. $60.00.

As a source for engravers and collectors, this book is an indispensable guide to styles and techniques of the world's foremost engravers.

Purdey Gun and Rifle Makers: The Definitive History, by Donald Dallas, Quiller Press, London, 2000. 245 pp., illus. Color throughout. $100.00

A limited edition of 3,000 copies. Signed and Numbered. With a PURDEY book plate.

Reloading Tools, Sights and Telescopes for Single Shot Rifles, by Gerald O. Kelver, Brighton, CO, 1982. 163 pp., illus. Paper covers. $13.95.

A listing of most of the famous makers of reloading tools, sights and telescopes with a brief description of the products they manufactured.

The Remington-Lee Rifle, by Eugene F. Myszkowski, Excalibur Publications, Latham, NY, 1995. 100 pp., illus. Paper covers. $22.50.

Features detailed descriptions, including serial number ranges, of each model from the first Lee Magazine Rifle produced for the U.S. Navy to the last Remington-Lee Small Bores shipped to the Cuban Rural Guard.

Revolvers of the British Services 1854-1954, by W.H.J. Chamberlain and A.W.F. Taylerson, Museum Restoration Service, Ottawa, Canada, 1989. 80 pp., illus. $27.50.

Covers the types issued among many of the United Kingdom's naval, land or air services.

Rhode Island Arms Makers & Gunsmiths, by William O. Archibald, Andrew Mowbray, Inc., Lincoln, RI, 1990. 108 pp., illus. $16.50.

A serious and informative study of an important area of American arms making.

Rifles of the World, by Oliver Achard, Chartwell Books, Inc., Edison, NJ, 141 pp., illus. $24.95.

A unique insight into the world of long guns, not just rifles, but also shotguns, carbines and all the usual multi-barreled guns that once were so popular with European hunters, especially in Germany and Austria.

The Rock Island '03, by C.S. Ferris, C.S. Ferris, Arvada, CO, 1993. 58 pp., illus. Paper covers. $12.50.

A monograph of interest to the collector or historian concentrating on the U.S. M1903 rifle made by the less publicized of our two producing facilities.

Round Ball to Rimfire, Vol. 1, by Dean Thomas, Thomas Publications, Gettysburg, PA, 1997. 144 pp., illus. $40.00.

The first of a two-volume set of the most complete history and guide for all small arms ammunition used in the Civil War. The information includes data from research and development to the arsenals that created it.

Ruger and his Guns, by R.L. Wilson, Simon & Schuster, New York, NY, 1996. 358 pp., illus. $65.00.

A history of the man, the company and their firearms.

Russell M. Catron and His Pistols, by Warren H. Buxton, Ucross Books, Los Alamos, NM, 1998. 224 pp., illustrated. Paper covers. $49.50.

An unknown American firearms inventor and manufacturer of the mid twentieth century. Military, commerical, ammunition.

The SAFN-49 and The FAL, by Joe Poyer and Dr. Richard Feirman, North Cape Publications, Tustin, CA, 1998. 160 pp., illus. Paper covers. $14.95.

The first complete overview of the SAFN-49 battle rifle, from its pre-World War 2 beginnings to its military service in countries as diverse as the Belgian Congo and Argentina. The FAL was "light" version of the SAFN-49 and it became the Free World's most adopted battle rifle.

Sam Colt's Own Record 1847, by John Parsons, Wolfe Publishing Co., Prescott, AZ, 1992. 167 pp., illus. $24.50.

Chronologically presented, the correspondence published here completes the account of the manufacture, in 1847, of the Walker Model Colt revolver.

J. P. Sauer & Sohn, Sauer "Dein Waffenkamerad" Volume 2, by Cate & Krause, Walsworth Publishing, Chattanooga, TN, 2000. 440 pp., illus. $79.00.

A historical study of Sauer automatic pistols. This new volume includes a great deal of new knowledge that has surfaced about the firm J.P. Sauer. You will find new photos, documentation, serial number ranges and historial facts which will expand the knowledge and interest in the oldest and best of the German firearms companies.

Scottish Firearms, by Claude Blair and Robert Woosnam-Savage, Museum Restoration Service, Bloomfield, Ont., Canada, 1995. 52 pp., illus. Paper covers. $8.95.

This revision of the first book devoted entirely to Scottish firearms is supplemented by a register of surviving Scottish long guns.

The Scottish Pistol, by Martin Kelvin. Fairleigh Dickinson University Press, Dist. By Associated University Presses, Cranbury, NJ, 1997. 256 pp., illus. $49.50.

The Scottish pistol, its history, manufacture and design.

Sharps Firearms, by Frank Seller, Frank M. Seller, Denver, CO, 1998. 358 pp., illus. $55.00.

Traces the development of Sharps firearms with full range of guns made including all martial variations.

Simeon North: First Official Pistol Maker of the United States, by S. North and R. North, The Gun Room Press, Highland Park, NJ, 1972. 207 pp., illus. $15.95.

Reprint of the rare first edition.

The SKS Carbine, by Steve Kehaya and Joe Poyer, North Cape Publications, Tustin, CA, 1997. 150 pp., illus. Paper covers. $16.95.

The first comprehensive examination of a major historical firearm used through the Vietnam conflict to the diamond fields of Angola.

The SKS Type 45 Carbines, by Duncan Long, Desert Publications, El Dorado, AZ, 1992. 110 pp., illus. Paper covers. $19.95.

Covers the history and practical aspects of operating, maintaining and modifying this abundantly available rifle.

Smith & Wesson 1857-1945, by Robert J. Neal and Roy G. Jinks, R&R Books, Livonia, NY, 1996. 434 pp., illus. $50.00.

The bible for all existing and aspiring Smith & Wesson collectors.

Sniper Variations of the German K98k Rifle, by Richard D. Law, Collector Grade Publications, Ontario, Canada, 1997. 240 pp., illus. $47.50.

Volume 2 of "Backbone of the Wehrmacht" the author's in-depth study of the German K98k rifle. This volume concentrates on the telescopic-sighted rifle of choice for most German snipers during World War 2.

Southern Derringers of the Mississippi Valley, by Turner Kirkland, Pioneer Press, Tenn., 1971. 80 pp., illus., paper covers. $4.00.

A guide for the collector, and a much-needed study.

Soviet Russian Postwar Military Pistols and Cartridges, by Fred A. Datig, Handgun Press, Glenview, IL, 1988. 152 pp., illus. $29.95.

Thoroughly researched, this definitive sourcebook covers the development and adoption of the Makarov, Stechkin and the new PSM pistols. Also included in this source book is coverage on Russian clandestine weapons and pistol cartridges.

Soviet Russian Tokarev "TT" Pistols and Cartridges 1929-1953, by Fred Datig, Graphic Publishers, Santa Ana, CA, 1993. 168 pp., illus. $39.95.

Details of rare arms and their accessories are shown in hundreds of photos. It also contains a complete bibliography and index.

Soviet Small-Arms and Ammunition, by David Bolotin, Handgun Press, Glenview, IL, 1996. 264 pp., illus. $49.95.

An authoritative and complete book on Soviet small arms.

Sporting Collectibles, by Jim and Vivian Karsnitz, Schiffer Publishing Ltd., West Chester, PA, 1992. 160 pp., illus. Paper covers. $29.95.

The fascinating world of hunting related collectibles presented in an informative text.

The Springfield 1903 Rifles, by Lt. Col. William S. Brophy, USAR, Ret., Stackpole Books Inc., Harrisburg, PA, 1985. 608 pp., illus. $75.00.

The illustrated, documented story of the design, development, and production of all the models, appendages, and accessories.

Springfield Armory Shoulder Weapons 1795-1968, by Robert W.D. Ball, Antique Trader Books, Dubuque, IA, 1998. 264 pp., illus. $34.95.

This book documents the 255 basic models of rifles, including test and trial rifles, produced by the Springfield Armory. It features the entire history of rifles and carbines manufactured at the Armory, the development of each weapon with specific operating characteristics and procedures.

Springfield Model 1903 Service Rifle Production and Alteration, 1905-1910, by C.S. Ferris and John Beard, Arvada, CO, 1995. 66 pp., illus. Paper covers. $12.50.

A highly recommended work for any serious student of the Springfield Model 1903 rifle.

Springfield Shoulder Arms 1795-1865, by Claud E. Fuller, S. & S. Firearms, Glendale, NY, 1996. 76 pp., illus. Paper covers. $17.95.

Exact reprint of the scarce 1930 edition of one of the most definitive works on Springfield flintlock and percussion muskets ever published.

Standard Catalog of Firearms, 11th Edition, by Ned Schwing, Krause Publications, Iola, WI, 2001. 1328 Pages, illustrated. 6,000+ b&w photos plus a 16-page color section. Paper covers. $32.95.

This is the largest, most comprehensive and best-selling firearm book of all time! And this year's edition is a blockbuster for both shooters and firearm collectors. More than 12,000 firearms are listed and priced in up to six grades of condition. That's almost 80,000 prices! Gun enthusiasts will love the new full-color section of photos highlighting the finest firearms sold at auction this past year —including the new record for an American historical firearm: $684,000!

Standard Catalog of Winchester, 1st Edition, edited by David D. Kowalski, Krause Publications, Iola, WI, 2000. 704 pp., illustrated with 2,000 B&W photos and 75 color photos. Paper covers. $39.95.

This book identifies and values more than 5,000 collectibles, including firearms, cartridges shotshells, fishing tackle, sporting goods and tools manufactured by Winchester Repeating Arms Co.

Steel Canvas: The Art of American Arms, by R.L. Wilson, Random House, NY, 1995, 384 pp., illus. $65.00.

Presented here for the first time is the breathtaking panorama of America's extraordinary engravers and embellishers of arms, from the 1700s to modern times.

Stevens Pistols & Pocket Rifles, by K.L. Cope, Museum Restoration Service, Alexandria Bay, NY, 1992. 114 pp., illus. $24.50.

This is the story of the guns and the man who designed them and the company which he founded to make them.

A Study of Colt Conversions and Other Percussion Revolvers, by R. Bruce McDowell, Krause Publications, Iola, WI, 1997. 464 pp., illus. $39.95.

The ultimate reference detailing Colt revolvers that have been converted from percussion to cartridge.

The Sumptuous Flaske, by Herbert G. Houze, Andrew Mowbray, Inc., Lincoln, RI, 1989. 158 pp., illus. Soft covers. $35.00.

Catalog of a recent show at the Buffalo Bill Historical Center bringing together some of the finest European and American powder flasks of the 16th to 19th centuries.

The Swedish Mauser Rifles, by Steve Kehaya and Joe Poyer, North Cape Publications, Tustin, CA, 1999. 267 pp., illustrated. Paper covers. $19.95.

Every known variation of the Swedish Mauser carbine and rifle is described including all match and target rifles and all sniper fersions. Includes serial number and production data.

Televisions Cowboys, Gunfighters & Cap Pistols, by Rudy A. D'Angelo, Antique Trader Books, Norfolk, VA, 1999. 287 pp., illustrated in color and black and white. Paper covers. $31.95.

Over 850 beautifully photographed color and black and white images of cap guns, actors, and the characters they portrayed in the "Golden Age of TV Westerns." With accurate descriptions and current values.

Thompson: The American Legend, by Tracie L. Hill, Collector Grade Publications, Ontario, Canada, 1996. 584 pp., illus. $85.00.

The story of the first American submachine gun. All models are featured and discussed.

Toys That Shoot and Other Neat Stuff, by James Dundas, Schiffer Books, Atglen, PA, 1999. 112 pp., illustrated. Paper covers. $24.95.

Shooting toys from the twentieth century, especially 1920's to 1960's, in over 420 color photographs of BB guns, cap shooters, marble shooters, squirt guns and more. Complete with a price guide.

The Trapdoor Springfield, by M.D. Waite and B.D. Ernst, The Gun Room Press, Highland Park, NJ, 1983. 250 pp., illus. $39.95.

The first comprehensive book on the famous standard military rifle of the 1873-92 period.

Treasures of the Moscow Kremlin: Arsenal of the Russian Tsars, A Royal Armories and the Moscow Kremlin exhibition. HM Tower of London 13, June 1998 to 11 September, 1998. BAS Printers, Over Wallop, Hampshire, England. xxii plus 192 pp. over 180 color illustrations. Text in English and Russian. $65.00.

For this exchibition catalog each of the 94 objects on display are photographed and described in detail to provide a most informative record of this important exhibition.

U.S. Breech-Loading Rifles and Carbines, Cal. 45, by Gen. John Pitman, Thomas Publications, Gettysburg, PA, 1992. 192 pp., illus. $29.95.

The third volume in the Pitman Notes on U.S. Martial Small Arms and Ammunition, 1776-1933. This book centers on the "Trapdoor Springfield" models.

U.S. Handguns of World War 2: The Secondary Pistols and Revolvers, by Charles W. Pate, Andrew Mowbray, Inc., Lincoln, RI, 1998. 515 pp., illus. $39.00.

This indispensable new book covers all of the American military handguns of World War 2 except for the M1911A1 Colt automatic.

United States Martial Flintlocks, by Robert M. Reilly, Mowbray Publishing Co., Lincoln, RI, 1997. 264 pp., illus. $40.00.

A comprehensive history of American flintlock longarms and handguns (mostly military) c. 1775 to c. 1840.

U.S. Martial Single Shot Pistols, by Daniel D. Hartzler and James B. Whisker, Old Bedford Village Pess, Bedford, PA, 1998. 128 pp., illus. $45.00.

A photographic chronicle of military and semi-martial pistols supplied to the U.S. Government and the several States.

U.S. Military Arms Dates of Manufacture from 1795, by George Madis, David Madis, Dallas, TX, 1989. 64 pp. Soft covers. $6.00.

Lists all U.S. military arms of collector interest alphabetically, covering about 250 models.

U.S. Military Small Arms 1816-1865, by Robert M. Reilly, The Gun Room Press, Highland Park, NJ, 1983. 270 pp., illus. $39.95.

Covers every known type of primary and secondary martial firearms used by Federal forces.

U.S. M1 Carbines: Wartime Production, by Craig Riesch, North Cape Publications, Tustin, CA, 1994. 72 pp., illus. Paper covers. $16.95.

Presents only verifiable and accurate information. Each part of the M1 Carbine is discussed fully in its own section; including markings and finishes.

U.S. Naval Handguns, 1808-1911, by Fredrick R. Winter, Andrew Mowbray Publishers, Lincoln, RI, 1990. 128 pp., illus. $26.00.

The story of U.S. Naval Handguns spans an entire century—included are sections on each of the important naval handguns within the period.

Walther: A German Legend, by Manfred Kersten, Safari Press, Inc., Huntington Beach, CA, 2000. 400 pp., illustrated. $85.00.

This comprehensive book covers, in rich detail, all aspects of the company and its guns, including an illustrious and rich history, the WW2 years, all the pistols (models 1 through 9), the P-38, P-88, the long guns, .22 rifles, centerfires, Wehrmacht guns, and even a gun that could shoot around a corner.

Walther Pistols: Models 1 Through P99, Factory Variations and Copies, by Dieter H. Marschall, Ucross Books, Los Alamos, NM. 2000. 140 pages, with 140 b & w illustrations, index. Paper Covers. $19.95.

This is the English translation, revised and updated, of the highly successful and widely acclaimed German language edition. This book provides the collector with a reference guide and overview of the entire line of the Walther military, police, and self-defense pistols from the very first to the very latest. Models 1-9, PP, PPK, MP, AP, HP, P.38, P1, P4, P38K, P5, P88, P99 and the Manurhin models. Variations, where issued, serial ranges, calibers, marks, proofs, logos, and design aspects in an astonishing quantity and variety are crammed into this very well researched and highly regarded work.

The Walther Handgun Story: A Collector's and Shooter's Guide, by Gene Gangarosa, Steiger Publications, 1999. 300., illustrated. Paper covers. $21.95.

Covers the entire history of the Walther empire. Illustrated with over 250 photos.

Walther P-38 Pistol, by Maj. George Nonte, Desert Publications, Cornville, AZ, 1982. 100 pp., illus. Paper covers. $11.95.

Complete volume on one of the most famous handguns to come out of WWII. All models covered.

Walther Models PP & PPK, 1929-1945 – Volume 1, by James L. Rankin, Coral Gables, FL, 1974. 142 pp., illus. $40.00.

Complete coverage on the subject as to finish, proofmarks and Nazi Party inscriptions.

Walther Volume II, Engraved, Presentation and Standard Models, by James L. Rankin, J.L. Rankin, Coral Gables, FL, 1977. 112 pp., illus. $40.00.

The new Walther book on embellished versions and standard models. Has 88 photographs, including many color plates.

Walther, Volume III, 1908-1980, by James L. Rankin, Coral Gables, FL, 1981. 226 pp., illus. $40.00.

Covers all models of Walther handguns from 1908 to date, includes holsters, grips and magazines.

Winchester: An American Legend, by R.L. Wilson, Random House, New York, NY, 1991. 403 pp., illus. $65.00.

The official history of Winchester firearms from 1849 to the present.

Winchester Bolt Action Military & Sporting Rifles 1877 to 1937, by Herbert G. Houze, Andrew Mowbray Publishing, Lincoln, RI, 1998. 295 pp., illus. $45.00.

Winchester was the first American arms maker to commercially manufacture a bolt action repeating rifle, and this book tells the exciting story of these Winchester bolt actions.

The Winchester Book, by George Madis, David Madis Gun Book Distributor, Dallas, TX, 1986. 650 pp., illus. $49.50.

A new, revised 25th anniversary edition of this classic book on Winchester firearms. Complete serial ranges have been added.

Winchester Dates of Manufacture 1849-1984, by George Madis, Art & Reference House, Brownsboro, TX, 1984. 59 pp. illus. $9.95.

A most useful work, compiled from records of the Winchester factory.

Winchester Engraving, by R.L. Wilson, Beinfeld Books, Springs, CA, 1989. 500 pp., illus. $135.00.

A classic reference work of value to all arms collectors.

The Winchester Handbook, by George Madis, Art & Reference House, Lancaster, TX, 1982. 287 pp., illus. $24.95.

The complete line of Winchester guns, with dates of manufacture, serial numbers, etc.

The Winchester-Lee Rifle, by Eugene Myszkowski, Excalibur Publications, Tucson, AZ 2000. 96 pp., illustrated. Paper Covers. $22.95

The development of the Lee Straight Pull, the cartridge and the approval for military use. Covers details of the inventor and memorabilia of Winchester-Lee related material.

Winchester Lever Action Repeating Firearms, Vol. 1, The Models of 1866, 1873 and 1876, by Arthur Pirkle, North Cape Publications, Tustin, CA, 1995. 112 pp., illus. Paper covers. $19.95.

Complete, part-by-part description, including dimensions, finishes, markings and variations throughout the production run of these fine, collectible guns.

Winchester Lever Action Repeating Rifles, Vol. 2, The Models of 1886 and 1892, by Arthur Pirkle, North Cape Publications, Tustin, CA, 1996. 150 pp., illus. Paper covers. $19.95.

Describes each model on a part-by-part basis by serial number range complete with finishes, markings and changes.

Winchester Lever Action Repeating Rifles, Volume 3, The Model of 1894, by Arthur Pirkle, North Cape Publications, Tustin, CA, 1998. 150 pp., illus. Paper covers. $19.95.

The first book ever to provide a detailed description of the Model 1894 rifle and carbine.

The Winchester Lever Legacy, by Clyde "Snooky" Williamson, Buffalo Press, Zachary, LA, 1988. 664 pp., illustrated. $75.00

A book on reloading for the different calibers of the Winchester lever action rifle.

The Winchester Model 94: The First 100 Years, by Robert C. Renneberg, Krause Publications, Iola, WI, 1991. 208 pp., illus. $34.95.

Covers the design and evolution from the early years up to the many different editions that exist today.

Winchester Rarities, by Webster, Krause Publications, Iola, WI, 2000. 208 pp., with over 800 color photos, illus. $49.95.

This book details the rarest of the rare; the one-of-a-kind items and the advertising pieces from years gone by. With nearly 800 full color photos and detailed pricing provided by experts in the field, this book gives collectors and enthusiasts everything they need.

Winchester Shotguns and Shotshells, by Ronald W. Stadt, Krause Publications, Iola, WI, 1995. 256 pp., illus. $34.95.

The definitive book on collectible Winchester shotguns and shotshells manufactured through 1961.

The Winchester Single-Shot- Volume 1; A History and Analysis, by John Campbell, Andrew Mowbray, Inc., Lincoln RI, 1995. 272 pp., illus. $55.00.

Covers every important aspect of this highly-collectible firearm.

The Winchester Single-Shot- Volume 2; Old Secrets and New Discoveries, by John Campbell, Andrew Mowbray, Inc., Lincoln RI, 2000. 280 pp., illus. $55.00.

An exciting follow-up to the classic first volume.

REFERENCE

Winchester Slide-Action Rifles, Volume 1: Model 1890 & 1906, by Ned Schwing, Krause Publications, Iola, WI, 1992. 352 pp., illus. $39.95.

First book length treatment of models 1890 & 1906 with over 50 charts and tables showing significant new information about caliber style and rarity.

Winchester Slide-Action Rifles, Volume 2: Model 61 & Model 62, by Ned Schwing, Krause Publications, Iola, WI, 1993. 256 pp., illus. $34.95.

A complete historic look into the Model 61 and the Model 62. These favorite slide-action guns receive a thorough presentation which takes you to the factory to explore receivers, barrels, markings, stocks, stampings and engraving in complete detail.

Winchester's North West Mounted Police Carbines and other Model 1876 Data, by Lewis E. Yearout, The author, Great Falls, MT, 1999. 224 pp., illustrated. Paper covers. $38.00

An impressive accumulation of the facts on the Model 1876, with particular empasis on those purchased for the North West Mounted Police.

Worldwide Webley and the Harrington and Richardson Connection, by Stephen Cuthbertson, Ballista Publishing and Distributing Ltd., Gabriola Island, Canada, 1999. 259 pp., illus. $50.00

A masterpiece of scholarship. Over 350 photographs plus 75 original documents, patent drawings, and advertisements accompany the text.

EDGED WEAPONS

101 Patented Knife Designs, by Will Hannah, Krause Publications, Iola, WI, 1998. 380 pp., illustrated. Paper covers. $49.95.

Spans 130 years of specs and designs. Indexed by patent number, name, and date with complete descriptions, detailed drawings. Actual reproductions of U.S. Patent Office's approved application.

The American Eagle Pommel Sword: The Early Years 1794-1830, by Andrew Mowbray, Manrat Arms Publications, Lincoln, RI, 1997. 244 pp., illus. $65.00.

The standard guide to the most popular style of American sword.

American Knives; The First History and Collector's Guide, by Harold L. Peterson, The Gun Room Press, Highland Park, NJ, 1980. 178 pp., illus. $24.95.

A reprint of this 1958 classic. Covers all types of American knives.

American Military Bayonets of the 20th Century, by Gary M. Cunningham, Scott A. Duff Publications, Export, PA, 1997. 116 pp., illus. Paper covers. $19.95.

A guide for collectors, including notes on makers, markings, finishes, variations, scabbards, and production data.

American Premium Guide to Knives and Razors, 5th edition, by Jim Sargent, Krause Publications, Iola, WI, 1999. 496 pp., illustrated. Paper covers. $24.95.

Updates current values for thousands of the most popular and collectible pocket knives and razors.

American Primitive Knives 1770-1870, by G.B. Minnes, Museum Restoration Service, Ottawa, Canada, 1983. 112 pp., illus. $24.95.

Origins of the knives, outstanding specimens, structural details, etc.

American Socket Bayonets and Scabbards, by Robert M. Reilly, 2nd printing, Andrew Mowbray, Inc., Lincoln, RI, 1998. 208 pp., illustrated. $45.00.

Full coverage of the socket bayonet in America, from Colonial times through the post-Civil War.

The American Sword, 1775-1945, by Harold L. Peterson, Ray Riling Arms Books, Co., Phila., PA, 2001. 286 pp. plus 60 pp. of illus. $49.95.

1977 reprint of a survey of swords worn by U.S. uniformed forces, plus the rare "American Silver Mounted Swords, (1700-1815)."

American Swords and Makers Marks; A Photographic Guide for Collectors, by Donald Furr, Paragon Agency, Orange, CA, 1999. 253 pp., illus. $64.95

An indepth guide for collectors and dealers of American swords. This new reference book contains over 525 photos of Silverhilts, Cavalry sabres, Eaglehead, Presentation swords, Regalia, Militia, Enlisted & Officers swords of both the U.S. & Confederacy. 8 page color section. Profusely illus & price guide.

American Swords and Sword Makers, by Richard H. Bezdek, Paladin Press, Boulder, CO, 1994. 648 pp., illus. $79.95.

The long-awaited definitive reference volume to American swords, sword makers and sword dealers from Colonial times to the present.

American Swords & Sword Makers Volume 2, by Richard H. Bezdek, Paladin Press, Boulder, CO, 1999. 376 pp., illus. $69.95.

More than 400 stunning photographs of rare, unusual and one-of-a-kind swords from the top collections in the country

American Swords from the Philip Medicus Collection, edited by Stuart C. Mowbray, with photographs and an introduction by Norm Flayderman, Andrew Mowbray Publishers, Lincoln, RI, 1998. 272 pp., with 604 swords illustrated. $55.00.

Covers all areas of American sword collecting.

The Ames Sword Company, 1829-1935, by John D. Hamilton, Andrew Mowbray Publisher, Lincoln, RI, 1995. 255 pp., illus. $45.00.

An exhaustively researched and comprehensive history of America's foremost sword manufacturer and arms supplier during the Civil War.

Antlers & Iron II, by Krause Publications, Iola, WI, 1999. 40 Pages, illustrated with a 100 photos. Paper covers. $12.00.

Lays out actual plans so you can build your mountain man folding knife using ordinary hand tools. Step-by-step instructions, with photos, for layout, design, antler slotting and springs.

The Art of Throwing Weapons, by James W. Madden, Paladin Press, Boulder, CO, 1993. 102 pp., illus. $14.00.

This comprehensive manual covers everything from the history and development of the five most common throwing weapons--spears, knives, tomahawks, shurikens and boomerangs--to their selection or manufacture, grip, distances, throwing motions and advanced combat methods.

Battle Blades: A Professional's Guide to Combat Fighting Knives, by Greg Walker; Foreword by Al Mar, Paladin Press, Boulder, CO, 1993. 168 pp., illus. $40.95.

The author evaluates daggers, Bowies, switchblades and utility blades according to their design, performance, reliability and cost.

The Bayonet in New France, 1665-1760, by Erik Goldstein, Museum Restoration Service, Bloomfield, Ontario, Canada, 1997. 36 pp., illus. Paper covers. $8.95.

Traces bayonets from the recently developed plug bayonet, through the regulation socket bayonets which saw service in North America.

Bayonets, Knives & Scabbards; United States Army Weapons Report 1917 Thru 1945, edited by Frank Trzaska, Knife Books, Deptford, NJ, 1999. 80 pp., illustrated. Paper covers. $15.95.

Follows the United States edged weapons from the close of World War 1 through the end of World War 2. Manufacturers involved, dates, numbers produced, problems encountered, and production data.

The Book of the Sword, by Richard F. Burton, Dover Publications, New York, NY, 1987. 199 pp., illus. Paper covers. $12.95.

Traces the swords origin from its birth as a charged and sharpened stick through diverse stages of development.

Borders Away, Volume 1: With Steel, by William Gilkerson, Andrew Mowbray, Inc., Lincoln, RI, 1991. 184 pp., illus. $48.00.

A comprehensive study of naval armament under fighting sail. This first voume covers axes, pikes and fighting blades in use between 1626-1826.

Borders Away, Volume 2: Firearms of the Age of Fighting Sail, by William Gilkerson, Andrew Mowbray, Inc., Lincoln, RI, 1999. 331 pp., illus. $65.00.

Completing a two volume set, this impressive work covers the pistols, muskets, combustibles, and small cannon once employed aboard American and European fightng ships. 200 photos, 16 color plates.

Bowies, Big Knives, and the Best of Battle Blades, by Bill Bagwell, Paladin Press, Boulder, CO. 2001. 184 pp., illus. Paper covers. $30.00

This book binds the timeless observations and invaluable advice of master bladesmith and blade combat expert Bill Bagwell under one cover for the first time. As the outspoken author of Soldier of Fortune's "Battle Blades" column from 1984 to 1988, Bagwell was considered both outrageous and revolutionary in his advocacy of carrying fighting knives as long as 10 inches and his firm belief that the Bowie was the most effective and efficient fighting knife ever developed. Here, you'llfind all of Bagwell's classic SOF columns, plus all-new material linking his early insights with his latest conclusions. Must reading for serious knife fans.

British & Commonwealth Bayonets, by Ian D. Skennerton and Robert Richardson, I.D.S.A. Books, Piqua, OH, 1986. 404 pp., 1300 illus. $40.00.

British and Commonwealth Military Knives, by Ron Flook, Airlife, Shrewsbury, 1999. 256 pp., illus. 49.95

First major reference on Knives issued to British & Commonwealth Forces from 1850 to the present. Over 500 Knives illustrated and described .

Civil War Knives, by Marc Newman, Paladin Press, Boulder, CO, 1999. 120 pp., illustrated. $44.95.

The author delves into the blade designs used at Gettysburg, Vicksburg, Antitam, Chancellorsville, and Bull Run. Photos of rare and common examples of cut-down swords, poignards, ornate clip-point knives, exquisite presentation knives and more.

Collecting the Edged Weapons of Imperial Germany, by Thomas M. Johnson and Thomas T. Wittmann, Johnson Reference Books, Fredericksburg, VA, 1989. 363 pp., illus. $39.50

An in-depth study of the many ornate military, civilian, and government daggers and swords of the Imperial era.

Collecting Indian Knives, 1st Edition, by Lar Hothem, Krause Publications, Iola, WI, 1992. 152 pp., illustrated. Paper covers. $14.95.

Maps the sharp-edged weapons and ceremonial knives used and crafted by Native Americans from every region. Historic photos and accurate values help you complete your quest for a definitive guide on identification.

Collecting Indian Knives, 2nd Edition, by Lar Hothem, Krause Publications, Iola, WI, 2000. 176 pp., illustrated. Paper covers. $19.95.

Expanded and updated with new photos and information, this 2nd edition will be a must have for anyone who collects or wants to learn about chipped Indian artifacts in the knife family. With an emphasis on prehistoric times, the book is loaded with photos, values and identification guidelines to help identify blades as to general time-period and, in many cases, help date sites where such artifacts are found. Includes information about different regional materials and basic styles, how knives were made and for what they were probably used.

Collector's Guide to Ames U.S. Contract Military Edged Weapons: 1832-1906, by Ron G. Hickox, Pioneer Press, Union City, IN, 1993. 70 pp., illus. Paper covers. $17.50.

While this book deals primarily with edged weapons made by the Ames Manufacturing Company, this guide refers to other manufactureres of United States swords.

A Collector's Guide to Swords, Daggers & Cutlasses, by Gerald Weland, Chartwell Press, London, 1999. 128 pp., illustrated in color. $24.95

An informative overview of edged weapons from medieval through 19th century. Explains the military and technological background and distinguishing features of the most sought-after pieces. Includes lists of leading museums and weapons collections plus a comprehensive bibliography and index.

Collector's Handbook of World War 2 German Daggers, by LtC. Thomas M. Johnson, Johnson Reference Books, Fredericksburg, VA, 2nd edition, 1991. 252 pp., illus. Paper covers. $25.00.

Concise pocket reference guide to Third Reich daggers and accoutrements in a convenient format. With value guide.

Collins Machetes and Bowies 1845-1965, by Daniel E. Henry, Krause Publications, Iola, WI, 1996. 232 pp., illus. Paper covers. $19.95.

A comprehensive history of Collins machetes and bowies including more than 1200 blade instruments and accessories.

The Complete Bladesmith: Forging Your Way to Perfection, by Jim Hrisoulas, Paladin Press, Boulder, CO, 1987. 192 pp., illus. $42.95.

Novice as well as experienced bladesmith will benefit from this definitive guide to smithing world-class blades.

The Complete Book of Pocketknife Repair, by Ben Kelly, Jr., Krause Publications, Iola, WI, 1995. 130 pp., illus. Paper covers. $10.95.

Everything you need to know about repairing knives can be found in this step-by-step guide to knife repair.

Confederate Edged Weapons, by W.A. Albaugh, R&R Books, Lavonia, NY, 1994. 198 pp., illus. $40.00.

The master reference to edged weapons of the Confederate forces. Features precise line drawings and an extensive text.

The Connoisseur's Book of Japanese Swords, by Nagayama, Kodauska International, Tokyo, Japan, 1997. 348pp., illustrated. $69.95

Translated by Kenji Mishina. A comprehensive guide to the appreciation and appraisal of the blades of Japanese swords. The most informative guide to the blades of Japanese swords ever to appear in English.

Daggers and Bayonets a History, by Logan Thompson, Paladin Press, Boulder, CO, 1999. 128 pp., illustrated. $40.00.

This authoritative history of military daggers and bayonets examines all patterns of daggers in detail, from the utilitarian Saxon scamasax used at Hastings to lavishly decorated Cinquedas, Landsknecht and Holbein daggers of the late high Renaissance.

Daggers and Fighting Knives of the Western World: From the Stone Age till 1900, by Harold Peterson, Dover Publishing, Mineola, NY, 2001. 96 pages, plus 32 pages of matte stock. Over 100 illustrations. Softcover. $9.95

The only full-scale reference book devoted entirely to the subject of fighting knives: flint knives, daggers of all sorts, scramasaxes, hauswehren, dirks and more. 108 plates, bibliography and Index.

Eickhorn Edged Weapons Exports, Vol. 1: Latin America, by A.M. de Quesada, Jr. and Ron G. Hicock, Pioneer Press, Union City, TN, 1996. 120 pp., illus. Paper covers. $15.00.

This research studies the various Eickhorn edged weapons and accessories manufactured for various countries outside of Germany.

Encyclopedia of Native American Bows, Arrows & Quivers, Volume 1, by Steve Allely and Jim Hamm, The Lyons Press, N.Y., 1999. 137 pp., illustrated. $29.95.

Beautifully detailed full-page pen-and-ink drawings give dimensions, decorations, and construction details on more than a hundred historic bows, scores of arrows, and more than a dozen quivers from over thirty tribes.

Exploring the Dress Daggers of the German Army, by Thomas T. Wittmann, Johnson Reference Books, Fredericksburg, VA, 1995. 350 pp., illus. $59.95.

The first in-depth analysis of the dress daggers worn by the German Army.

Exploring the Dress Daggers of the German Luftwaffe, by Thomas T. Wittmann, Johnson Reference Books, Fredericksburg, VA, 1998. 350 pp., illus. $59.95.

Examines the dress daggers and swords of the German Luftwaffe. The designs covered include the long DLV patterns, the Glider Pilot designs of the NSFK and DLV, 1st and 2nd model Luftwaffe patterns, the Luftwaffe sword and the General OFficer Dengen. Many are pictured for the first time in color.

Exploring The Dress Daggers Of The German Navy, by Thomas T. Wittmann, Johnson Reference Books, Fredericksburg, VA, 2000. 560 pp., illus. $79.95.

Explores the dress daggers and swords of the Imperial, Weimar, and Third Reich eras, from 1844-1945. Provides detailed information, as well as many superb black and white and color photographs of individual edged weapons. Many are pictured for the first time in full color.

The First Commando Knives, by Prof. Kelly Yeaton and Col. Rex Applegate, Phillips Publications, Williamstown, NJ, 1996. 115 pp., illus. Paper covers. $12.95.

Here is the full story of the Shanghai origins of the world's best known dagger.

German Clamshells and Other Bayonets, by G. Walker and R.J. Weinard, Johnson Reference Books, Fredericksburg, VA, 1994. 157 pp., illus. $22.95.

Includes unusual bayonets, many of which are shown for the first time. Current market values are listed.

German Military Fighting Knives 1914-1945, by Gordon A. Hughes, Johnson Reference Books, Fredericksburg, VA, 1994. 64 pp., illus. Paper covers. $24.50.

Documents the different types of German military fighting knives used during WWI and WWII. Makers' proofmarks are shown as well as details of blade inscriptions, etc.

German Swords and Sword Makers: Edged Weapons Makers from the 14th to the 20th Centuries, by Richard H. Bezdek, Paladin Press, Boulder, CO, 2000. 248 pp., illustrated. $59.95.

This book contains the most informations ever published on German swords and edged weapons makers from the Middle Ages to the present.

A Guide to Military Dress Daggers, Volume 1, by Kurt Glemser, Johnson Reference Books, Fredericksburg, VA, 1991. 160 pp., illus. Softcover. $26.50.

Very informative guide to dress daggers of foreign countries, to include an excellent chapter on DDR daggers. There is also a section on reproduction Third Reich period daggers. Provides, for the first time, identification of many of the war-time foreign dress daggers. There is also a section on Damascus blades. Good photographic work. Mr. Glemser is certainly to be congratulated on this book on such a neglected area of militaria.

A Guide to Military Dress Daggers, Volume 2, by Kurt Glemser, Johnson Reference Books, Fredericksburg, VA, 1993. 160 pp., illus. $32.50.

As in the first volume, reproduction daggers are covered in depth (Third Reich, East German, Italian, Polish and Hungarian). American Navy dirks are featured for the first time. Bulgarian Youth daggers, Croatioan daggers and Imperial German Navy dagger scabbards all have chapters devoted to them. Continues research initiated in Volume I on such subjects as dress daggers, Solingen export daggers, East German daggers and Damascus Smith Max Dinger.

A Guide to Military Dress Daggers, Volume 3, by Kurt Glemser, Johnson Reference Books, Fredericksburg, VA, 1996. 260 pp., illus. $39.50.

Includes studies of Swedish daggers, Italian Cadet daggers, Rumanian daggers, Austrian daggers, Dress daggers of the Kingdom of Yugoslavia, Czechoslovakian daggers, Paul Dinger Damastschmied, Swiss Army daggers, Polish daggers (1952-1994), and Hungarian Presentation daggers.

A Guide to Military Dress Daggers, Volume 4, by Kurt Glemser, Johnson Reference Books, Fredericksburg, VA, 2001. 252 pp., illus. $49.50.

Several chapters dealing with presentation daggers to include a previously unknown series of East German daggers. Other chapters cover: Daggers in wear; Czech & Slovak daggers; Turkish daggers; swiss Army daggers; Solingen Export daggers; Miniature daggers, Youth knives.

The Halberd and other European Polearms 1300-1650, by George Snook, Museum Restoration Service, Bloomfield, Ontario, Canada, 1998. 40 pp., illus. Paper covers. $8.95.

A comprehensive introduction to the history, use, and identification of the staff weapons of Europe.

The Hand Forged Knife, Krause Publications, Iola, WI. 136 pp., illus., $12.95.

Explains the techniques for forging, hardening and tempering knives and other stainless steel tools.

Historic American Swords, by Howard R. Crouch, SCS Publications, 2000. 174 pp., photos, illus. $39.95

Includes a history of each sword, sword types and terminology, the role of the U.S. Ordnance Department, makers- U.S. and Confederate, A nomenclature of the sword, details of design, production and use.

How to Make Folding Knives, by Ron Lake, Frank Centofante and Wayne Clay, Krause Publications, Iola, WI, 1995. 193 pp., illus. Paper covers. $13.95.

With step-by-step instructions, learn how to make your own folding knife from three top custom makers.

How to Make Knives, by Richard W. Barney and Robert W. Loveless, Krause Publications, Iola, WI, 1995. 182 pp., illus. Paper covers. $13.95.

Complete instructions from two premier knife makers on making high-quality, handmade knives.

How to Make Multi-Blade Folding Knives, by Eugene Shadley & Terry Davis, Krause Publications, Iola, WI, 1997. 192 pp., illus. Paper covers. $19.95.

This step-by-step instructional guide teaches knifemakers how to craft these complex folding knives.

How to Make a Tactical Folder, by Bob Tetzuola, Krause Publications, Iola, WI, 2000. 160 pp., illustrated. Paper covers. $16.95.

Step-by-step instructions and outstanding photography guide the knifemaker from start to finish.

The Modern Swordsman, by Fred Hutchinson, Paladin Press, Boulder, CO, 1999. 80 pp., illustrated. Paper covers. $22.00

Realistic training for serious self-defense.

The Wonder of Knifemaking, by Wayne Goddard, Krause Publications, Iola, WI, 2000. 160 pp., illustrated with 150 b&w photos and a 16 page color section. Paper covers. $19.95.

Tips for Knifemakers of all skill levels. Heat treating and steel selection.

KA-BAR: The Next Generation of the Ultimate Fighting Knife, by Greg Walker, Paladin Press, Boulder, CO, 2001. 88 pp., illus. Soft covers. $16.00.

The KA-BAR Fighting/Utility Knife is the most widely recognized and popular combat knife ever to be produced in the United States. Since its introduction on 23 November 1942, the KA-BAR has performed brilliantly on the battlefields of Europe, the South Pacific, Korea, Southeast Asia, Central America and the Middle East, earning its moniker as the "ultimate fighting knife." In this book, Greg Walker gives readers an inside view of the exacting design criteria, cutting-edge materials, extensivefactory tests and exhaustive real-life field tests that went into the historic redesign of the blade, handguard, handle, pommel, and sheath of the ultimate fighting knife of the future. The new knife excelled at these rigorous tests, earning the right tobe called a KA-BAR.

Knife and Tomahawk Throwing: The Art of the Experts, by Harry K. McEvoy, Charles E. Tuttle, Rutland, VT, 1989. 150 pp., illus. Soft covers. $8.95.

The first book to employ side-by-side the fascinating art and science of knives and tomahawks.

Knife Talk, The Art and Science of Knifemaking, by Ed. Fowler, Krause Publications, Iola, WI, 1998. 158 pp., illus. Paper covers. $14.95.

Valuable how-to advice on knife design and construction plus 20 years of memorable articles from the pages of "Blade" Magazine.

Knifemakers of Old San Francisco, by Bernard Levine, 2nd edition, Paladin Press, Boulder, CO, 1998. 150 pp., illus. $39.95.

The definitive history of the knives and knife-makers of 19th century San Francisco.

Knifemaking, The Gun Digest Book of, by Jack Lewis and Roger Combs, DBI Books, a division of Krause Publications, Iola, WI, 1989. 256 pp., illus. Paper covers. $16.95.

All the ins and outs from the world of knifemaking in a brand new book.

Knives, 5th Edition, The Gun Digest Book of, edited by Jack Lewis and Roger Combs, DBI Books, a division of Krause Publications, Iola, WI, 1997. 256 pp., illus. Paper covers. $19.95.

Covers practically every aspect of the knife world.

THE ARMS LIBRARY

Knives 2002, 22st Annual Edition, edited by Joe Kertzman, Krause Publications, Iola, WI, 2001. 320 pp., illustrated. Paper covers. $22.95.

More than 1,200 photos and listings of new knives plus articles from top writers in the field.

Les Baionnettes Reglementaires Francises de 1840 a 1918 'The Bayonets; Military Issue 1840-1918, by French Assoc.of Bayonet Collectors, 2000. 77 pp. illus. $24.95

Profusely illustrated. By far the most comprehenive guide to French military bayonets done for this period. Includes hundreds of illustrations. 77 large 8 1/4 x ll 1/2 inch pages. French Text. Color photos are magnificant!

Living on the Edge; Logos of the Loveless Legend, by Al Williams, Krause Publications, Iola, WI, 1995. 128 pp.,illustrated with full color. $19.95

Also included is an original 32-page section written entirely in the Japanese language for his Japanese customers and fans who have an insatiable appetite for everything Loveless.

The Master Bladesmith: Advanced Studies in Steel, by Jim Hrisoulas, Paladin Press, Boulder, CO, 1990. 296 pp., illus. $49.95.

The author reveals the forging secrets that for centuries have been protected by guilds.

Medieval Swordsmanship, Illustrated Methods and Techniques, by John Clements, Paladin Press, Boulder, CO, 1998. 344 pp., illustrated. $40.00.

The most comprehensive and historically accurate view ever written of the lost fighting arts of Medieval knights.

Military Knives: A Reference Book, by Frank Trzaska (editor), Knife Books, Deptford, NJ, 2001. 255 pp., illustrated. Softcover. $17.95

A collection of your favorite Military Knive articles fron the pages of Knife World Magazine. 67 articles ranging from the Indian Wars to the present day modern military knives.

Modern Combat Blades, by Duncan Long, Paladin Press, Boulder, CO, 1993. 128 pp., illus. $30.00.

Long discusses the pros and cons of bowies, bayonets, commando daggers, kukris, switchblades, butterfly knives, belt-buckle blades and many more.

On Damascus Steel, by Dr. Leo S. Figiel, Atlantis Arts Press, Atlantis, FL, 1991. 145 pp., illus. $65.00.

The historic, technical and artistic aspects of Oriental and mechanical Damascus. Persian and Indian sword blades, from 1600-1800, which have never been published, are illustrated.

The Pattern-Welded Blade: Artistry in Iron, by Jim Hrisoulas, Paladin Press, Boulder, CO, 1994. 120 pp., illus. $44.95.

Reveals the secrets of this craft—from the welding of the starting billet to the final assembly of the complete blade.

Randall Made Knives, by Robert L. Gaddis, Paladin Press, Boulder, CO, 2000. 292 pp., illus. $59.95.

Plots the designs of all 24 of Randall's unique knives. This step-by-step book, seven years in the making, is worth every penny and moment of your time.

The Razor Anthology, by Krause Publications, Iola, WI. 1998. 246 pp., illustrated. Paper covers. $14.95.

Razor Anthology is a cut above the rest. Razor aficionados will find this collection of articles about razors both informative and interesting.

Razor Edge, by John Juranitch, Krause Publications, Iola, WI. 1998. 132 pp., illustrated. Paper covers. $15.00.

Reveals step-by-step instructions for sharpening everything from arrowheads, to blades, to fish hooks.

Renaissance Swordsmanship, by John Clements, Paladin Press, Boulder, CO, 1997. 152 pp., illus. Paper covers. $25.00.

The illustrated use of rapiers and cut-and-thrust swords.

Rice's Trowel Bayonet, reprinted by Ray Riling Arms Books, Co., Phila., PA, 1968. 8 pp., illus. Paper covers. $3.00.

A facsimile reprint of a rare circular originally published by the U.S. government in 1875 for the information of U.S. troops.

The Scottish Dirk, by James D. Forman, Museum Restoration Service, Bloomfield, Ont., Canada, 1991. 60 pp., illus. Paper covers. $8.95.

More than 100 dirks are illustrated with a text that sets the dirk and Sgian Dubh in their socio-historic content following design changes through more than 300 years of evolution.

Scottish Swords from the Battlefield at Culloden, by Lord Archibald Campbell, The Mowbray Co., Providence, RI, 1973. 63 pp., illus. $15.00.

A modern reprint of an exceedingly rare 1894 privately printed edition.

Seitengewehr: History of the German Bayonet, 1919-1945, by George T. Wheeler, Johnson Reference Books, Fredericksburg, VA, 2000. 320 pp., illus. $44.95.

Provides complete information on Weimar and Third Reich bayonets, as well astheir accompanying knots and frogs. Illustrates re-issued German and foreign bayonets utilized by both the Reichswehr and the Wehrmacht, and details the progression ofnewly manufactured bayonets produced after Hitler's rise to power. Photos illustrate rarely seen bayonets worn by the Polizei, Reichsbahn, Postschutz, Hitler Jugend, and other civil and political organiztions. German modified bayonets from other countries are pictured and described. Book contains an up-to-date price guide including current valuations of various Imperial, Weimar, and Third Reich bayonets.

Silver Mounted Swords: The Lattimer Family Collection; Featuring Silver Hilts Through the Golden Age, by Daniel Hartzler, Rowe Publications, New York, 2000. 300 pages, with over 1000 illustrations and 1350 photo's. Oversize 9x12.

The Worlds Largest Silver Hilt Collection. $75.00

Small Arms Identification Series, No. 6-British Service Sword & Lance Patterns, by Ian Skennerton, I.D.S.A. Books, Piqua, OH, 1994. 48 pp. $9.50.

Small Arms Series, No. 2. The British Spike Bayonet, by Ian Skennerton, I.D.S.A. Books, Piqua, OH, 1982. 32 pp., 30 illus. $9.00.

The Socket in the British Army 1667-1783, by Erik Goldstein, Andrew Mowbray, Inc., Lincoln, RI, 2001. 136 pp., illus. $23.00.

The spectacle of English "redcoats" on the attack, relentlessly descending upon enemy lines with fixed bayonets, is one of the most chilling images from European history and the American Revolution. The bayonets covered in this book stood side by side with the famous "Brown Bess" as symbols of English military power throughout the world. Drawing upon new information from archaeological digs and archival records, the author explains how to identify each type of bayonet and shows which bayonets were used where and with which guns. No student of military history or weapons development can afford to do without this useful new book.

Socket Bayonets of the Great Powers, by Robert W. Shuey, Excalibur Publications, Tucson, AZ, 2000 96 pp., illus. Paper covers $22.95

With 175 illustrations the author brings together in one place, many of the standard socket arrnagements used by some of the " Great Powers". With an illustrated glossary of blade shape and socket design.

Spyderco Story: The New Shape of Sharp, by Kenneth T. Delavigne, Paladin Press, Boulder, CO, 1998. 312 pp., illus. $69.95.

Discover the history and inner workings of the company whose design innovations have redefined the shape of the modern folding knife and taken high-performance cutting to a new level.

Standard Knife Collectors Guide, 3rd Edition, by Roy Ritchie, Krause Publications, Iola, WI. 1999. 688 pp, 28 page color section., illustrated. Paper covers. $12.95.

Tap into the latest knife history developments with this updated guide accurately reflects current values for collector pocket-and fixed-blade knives.

Swords and Sword Makers of the War of 1812, by Richard Bezdek, Paladin Press, Boulder, CO, 1997. 104 pp., illus. $49.95.

The complete history of the men and companies that made swords during and before the war. Includes examples of cavalry and artillery sabers.

Swords from Public Collections in the Commonwealth of Pennsylvania, edited by Bruce S. Bazelon, Andrew Mowbray Inc., Lincoln, RI, 1987. 127 pp., illus. Paper covers. $12.00.

Contains new information regarding swordmakers of the Philadelphia area.

Swords And Sabers of the Armory at Springfield, by Burton A. Kellerstedt, Burton A. Kellerstedt, New Britain, CT, 1998. 121 pp, illus. Softcover. $29.95

The basic and most important reference for it's subject, and one that is unlikely to be surpassed for comprehensiveness and accuracy.

Swords and Blades of the American Revolution, by George C. Neumann, Rebel Publishing Co., Inc., Texarkana, TX, 1991. 288 pp., illus. $36.95.

The encyclopedia of bladed weapons—swords, bayonets, spontoons, halberds, pikes, knives, daggers, axes—used by both sides, on land and sea, in America's struggle for independence.

Swords of Imperial Japan, 1868-1945, by Jim Dawson, Published by the Author. 160 Pages, illustrated with 263 b&w photos. Paper covers. $29.95.

Details the military, civilian, diplomatic and civil, police and colonial swords and the post-Samurai era as well as the swords of Manchukuo, the Japanese independent territory.

Tactical Folding Knife; A Study of the Anatomy and Construction of the Liner-Locked Folder, by Terzuola, Krause Publications, Iola, WI. 2000. 160 Pages, 200 b&w photos, illustrated. Paper covers. $16.00

Step-by-step instructions and outstanding photography guide the knifemaker from start to finish. Knifemaker Bob Terzuola has been called the father of the tactical folding knife. This book details everything from the basic definition of a tactical folder to the final polishing as the knife is finished.

U.S. Military Knives, Bayonets and Machetes Price Guide, 4th ed. by Frank Trzaska (editor), Knife Books, Deptford, NJ, 2001. 80 pp., illustrated. Softcover. $7.95

This volume follows in the tradition of the previous three versions of using major works on the subject as a reference to keep the price low to you.

Wayne Goddard's $50 Knife Shop, by Wayne Goddard, Krause Publications, Iola, WI. 2000. 160 Pages, illus. Soft covers. $19.95

This new book expands on information from Goddard's popular column in Blade magazine to show knifemakers of all skill levels how to create helpful gadgets and supply their shop on a shoestring.

Wonder of Knifemaking, by Wayne Goddard, Krause Publications, Iola, WI. 2000. 160 Pages, illus. Soft covers. $19.95

Master bladesmith Wayne Goddard draws on his decades of experience to answer questions of knifemakers at all levels. As a columnist for Blade magazine, Goddard has been answering real questions from real knifemakers for the past eight years. Now, all the details are compiled in one place as a handy reference for every knifemaker, amateur or professional.

The Working Folding Knife, by Steven Dick, Stoeger Publishing Co., Wayne, NJ, 1998. 280 pp., illus. Paper covers. $21.95

From the classic American Barlow to exotic folders like the spanish Navaja this book has it all.

GENERAL

Action Shooting: Cowboy Style, by John Taffin, Krause Publications, Iola, WI, 1999. 320 pp., illustrated. $39.95.

Details on the guns and ammunition. Explanations of the rules used for many events. The essential cowboy wardrobe.

Advanced Muzzleloader's Guide, by Toby Bridges, Stoeger Publishing Co., So. Hackensack, NJ, 1985. 256 pp., illus. Paper covers. $14.95.

The complete guide to muzzle-loading rifles, pistols and shotguns—flintlock and percussion.

THE ARMS LIBRARY

Aids to Musketry for Officers & NCOs, by Capt. B.J. Friend, Excalibur Publications, Latham, NY, 1996. 40 pp., illus. Paper covers. $7.95.
A facsimile edition of a pre-WWI British manual filled with useful information for training the common soldier.

Air Gun Digest, 3rd Edition, by J.I. Galan, DBI Books, a division of Krause Publications, Iola, WI, 1995. 258 pp., illus. Paper covers. $19.95
Everything from A to Z on air gun history, trends and technology.

American and Imported Arms, Ammunition and Shooting Accessories, Catalog No. 18 of the Shooter's Bible, Stoeger, Inc., reprinted by Fayette Arsenal, Fayetteville, NC, 1988. 142 pp., illus. Paper covers. $10.95.
A facsimile reprint of the 1932 Stoeger's Shooter's Bible.

America's Great Gunmakers, by Wayne van Zwoll, Stoeger Publishing Co., So. Hackensack, NJ, 1992. 288 pp., illus. Paper covers. $16.95.
This book traces in great detail the evolution of guns and ammunition in America and the men who formed the companies that produced them.

Ammunition: Small Arms, Grenades and Projected Munitions, by Ian V. Hogg, Greenhill Books, London, England, 1998. 144 pp., illustrated. $22.95.
The best concise guide to modern ammunition. Wide-ranging and international coverage. Detailed specifications and illustrations.

Armed and Female, by Paxton Quigley, E.P. Dutton, New York, NY, 1989. 237 pp., illus. $16.95.
The first complete book on one of the hottest subjects in the media today, the arming of the American woman.

Arming the Glorious Cause: Weapons of the Second War for Independence, by James B. Whisker, Daniel D. Hartzler and Larry W. Yantz, R & R Books, Livonia, NY, 1998. 175 pp., illustrated. $45.00.
A photographic study of Confederate weapons.

Arms and Armour in Antiquity and the Middle Ages, by Charles Boutell, Stackpole Books, Mechanicsburg, PA, 1996. 352 pp., illus. $22.95.
Detailed descriptions of arms and armor, the development of tactics and the outcome of specific battles.

Arms & Armor in the Art Institute of Chicago, by Walter J. Karcheski, Jr., Bulfinch Press, Boston, MA, 1995. 128 pp., illus. $35.00.
Now, for the first time, the Art Institute of Chicago's arms and armor collection is presented in the visual delight of 103 color illustrations.

Arms for the Nation: Springfield Longarms, edited by David C. Clark, Scott A. Duff, Export, PA, 1994. 73 pp., illus. Paper covers. $9.95.
A brief history of the Springfield Armory and the arms made there.

Arsenal of Freedom, The Springfield Armory, 1890-1948: A Year-by-Year Account Drawn from Official Records, compiled and edited by Lt. Col. William S. Brophy, USAR Ret., Andrew Mowbray, Inc., Lincoln, RI, 1991. 400 pp., illus. Soft covers. $29.95.
A "must buy" for all students of American military weapons, equipment and accoutrements.

Assault Pistols, Rifles and Submachine Guns, by Duncan Long, Paladin Press, Boulder, CO, 1997, 8 1/2 x 11, soft cover, photos, illus. 152 pp. $21.95
This book offers up-to-date, practical information on how to operate and field-strip modern military, police and civilian combat weapons. Covers new developments and trends such as the use of fiber optics, liquid-recoil systems and lessening of barrel length are covered. Troubleshooting procedures, ballistic tables and a list of manufacturers and distributors are also included.

Assault Weapons, 5th Edition, The Gun Digest Book of, edited by Jack Lewis and David E. Steele, DBI Books, a division of Krause Publications, Iola, WI, 2000. 256 pp., illustrated. Paper covers. $21.95.
This is the latest word on true assault weaponry in use today by international military and law enforcement organizations.

The Belgian Rattlesnake: The Lewis Automatic Machine Gun, by William M. Easterly, Collector Grade Publications, Inc., Cobourg, Ont. Canada, 1998. 542 pp., illus. $79.95.
A social and technical biography of the Lewis automatic machine gun and its inventors.

The Big Guns: Civil War Siege, Seacoast, and Naval Cannon, by Edwin Olmstead, Wayne E. Stark and Spencer C. Tucker, Museum Restoration Service, Bloomfield, Ontario, Canada, 1997. 360 pp., illus. $80.00.
This book is designed to identify and record the heavy guns available to both sides during the Civil War.

Blackpowder Loading Manual, 3rd Edition, by Sam Fadala, DBI Books, a division of Krause Publications, Iola, WI, 1995. 368 pp., illus. Paper covers. $20.95.
Revised and expanded edition of this landmark blackpowder loading book. Covers hundreds of loads for most of the popular blackpowder rifles, handguns and shotguns.

Bolt Action Rifles, 3rd Edition, by Frank de Haas, DBI Books, a division of Krause Publications, Iola, WI, 1995. 528 pp., illus. Paper covers. $24.95.
A revised edition of the most definitive work on all major bolt-action rifle designs.

The Book of the Crossbow, by Sir Ralph Payne-Gallwey, Dover Publications, Mineola, NY, 1996. 416 pp., illus. Paper covers. $14.95.
Unabridged republication of the scarce 1907 London edition of the book on one of the most devastating hand weapons of the Middle Ages.

Bows and Arrows of the Native Americans, by Jim Hamm, Lyons & Burford Publishers, New York, NY, 1991. 156 pp., illus. $19.95.
A complete step-by-step guide to wooden bows, sinew-backed bows, composite bows, strings, arrows and quivers.

British Small Arms of World War 2, by Ian D. Skennerton, I.D.S.A. Books, Piqua, OH, 1988. 110 pp., 37 illus. $25.00.

"Carbine," the Story of David Marshall Williams, by Ross E. Beard, Jr. Phillips Publications, Williamstown, NJ, 1999. 225 pp., illus. $29.95.
The story of the firearms genius, David Marshall "Carbine" Williams. From prison to the pinnacles of fame, the tale of this North Carolinian is inspiring. The author details many of Williams' firearms inventions and developments.

Combat Handgunnery, 4th Edition, The Gun Digest Book of, by Chuck Taylor, DBI Books, a division of Krause Publications, Iola, WI, 1997. 256 pp., illus. Paper covers. $18.95.
This edition looks at real world combat handgunnery from three different perspectives—military, police and civilian.

The Complete Blackpowder Handbook, 3rd Edition, by Sam Fadala, DBI Books, a division of Krause Publications, Iola, WI, 1997. 400 pp., illus. Paper covers. $21.95.
Expanded and completely rewritten edition of the definitive book on the subject of blackpowder.

The Complete Guide to Game Care and Cookery, 3rd Edition, by Sam Fadala, DBI Books, a division of Krause Publications, Iola, WI, 1994. 320 pp., illus. Paper covers. $18.95.
Over 500 photos illustrating the care of wild game in the field and at home with a separate recipe section providing over 400 tested recipes.

The Complete .50-caliber Sniper Course, by Dean Michaelis, Paladin Press, Boulder, CO, 2000. 576 pp, illustrated, $60.00
The history from German Mauser T-Gewehr of World War 1 to the Soviet PTRD and beyond. Includes the author's Program of Instruction for Special Operations Hard-Target Interdiction Course.

Complete Guide to Guns & Shooting, by John Malloy, DBI Books, a division of Krause Publications, Iola, WI, 1995. 256 pp., illus. Paper covers. $18.95.
What every shooter and gun owner should know about firearms, ammunition, shooting techniques, safety, collecting and much more.

Cowboy Action Shooting, by Charly Gullett, Wolfe Publishing Co., Prescott, AZ, 1995. 400 pp., illus. Paper covers. $24.50.
The fast growing of the shooting sports is comprehensively covered in this text—the guns, loads, tactics and the fun and flavor of this Old West era competition.

Crossbows, edited by Roger Combs, DBI Books, a division of Krause Publications, Iola, WI, 1986. 192 pp., illus. Paper covers. $15.95.
Complete, up-to-date coverage of the hottest bow going—and the most controversial.

Custom Firearms Engraving, by Tom Turpin, Krause Publications, Iola, WI, 1999. 208 pp., illustrated. $49.95.
Provides a broad and comprehensive look at the world of firearms engraving. The exquisite styles of more than 75 master engravers are shown on beautiful examples of handguns, rifles, shotguns, and other firearms, as well as knives.

Dead On, by Tony Noblitt and Warren Gabrilska, Paladin Press, Boulder, CO, 1998. 176 pp., illustrated. Paper covers. $22.00
The long-range marksman's guide to extreme accuracy.

Death from Above: The German FG42 Paratrooper Rifle, by Thomas B. Dugelby and R. Blake Stevens, Collector Grade Publications, Toronto, Canada, 1990. 147 pp., illus. $39.95.
The first comprehensive study of all seven models of the FG42.

Early American Flintlocks, by Daniel D. Hartzler and James B. Whisker, Bedford Valley Press, Bedford, PA 2000. 192 pp., Illustrated.
Covers early Colonial Guns, New England Guns, Pennsylvania Guns and Souther Guns.

Encyclopedia of Modern Firearms, Vol. 1, compiled and publ. by Bob Brownell, Montezuma, IA, 1959. 1057 pp. plus index, illus. $70.00. Dist. By Bob Brownell, Montezuma, IA 50171.
Massive accumulation of basic information of nearly all modern arms pertaining to "parts and assembly." Replete with arms photographs, exploded drawings, manufacturers' lists of parts, etc.

Encyclopedia of Native American Bows, Arrows and Quivers, by Steve Allely and Jim Hamm, The Lyons Press, N.Y., 1999. 160 pp., illustrated. $29.95.
A landmark book for anyone interested in archery history, or Native Americans.

The Exercise of Armes, by Jacob de Gheyn, edited and with an introduction by Bas Kist, Dover Publications, Inc., Mineola, NY, 1999. 144 pp., illustrated. Paper covers. $12.95.
Republications of all 117 engravings from the 1607 classic military manual. A meticulously accurate portrait of uniforms and weapons of the 17th century Netherlands.

Exploded Long Gun Drawings, The Gun Digest Book of, edited by Harold A. Murtz, DBI Books, a division of Krause Publications, Iola, WI, 512 pp., illus. Paper covers. $20.95.
Containing almost 500 rifle and shotgun exploded drawings.

Fighting Iron; A Metals Handbook for Arms Collectors, by Art Gogan, Mowbray Publishers, Inc., Lincoln, RI, 1999. 176 pp., illustrated. $28.00.
A guide that is easy to use, explains things in simple English and covers all of the different historical periods that we are interested in.

The Fighting Submachine Gun, Machine Pistol, and Shotgun, a Hands-On Evaluation, by Timothy J. Mullin, Paladin Press, Boulder, CO, 1999. 224 pp., illustrated. Paper covers. $35.00.
An invaluable reference for military, police and civilian shooters who may someday need to know how a specific weapon actually performs when the targets are shooting back and the margin of errors is measured in lives lost.

Fireworks: A Gunsight Anthology, by Jeff Cooper, Paladin Press, Boulder, CO, 1998. 192 pp., illus. Paper covers. $27.00
A collection of wild, hilarious, shocking and always meaningful tales from the remarkable life of an American firearms legend.

Frank Pachmayr: The Story of America's Master Gunsmith and his Guns, by John Lachuk, Safari Press, Huntington Beach, CA, 1996. 254 pp., illus. First edition, limited, signed and slipcased. $85.00; Second printing trade edition. $50.00.

The colorful and historically significant biography of Frank A. Pachmayr, America's own gunsmith emeritus.

From a Stranger's Doorstep to the Kremlin Gate, by Mikhail Kalashnikov, Ironside International Publishers, Inc., Alexandria, VA, 1999. 460 pp., illustrated. $34.95.

A biography of the most influential rifle designer of the 20th century. His AK-47 assault rifle has become the most widely used (and copied) assault rifle of this century.

The Frontier Rifleman, by H.B. LaCrosse Jr., Pioneer Press, Union City, TN, 1989. 183 pp., illus. Soft covers. $17.50.

The Frontier rifleman's clothing and equipment during the era of the American Revolution, 1760-1800.

The Gatling Gun: 19th Century Machine Gun to 21st Century Vulcan, by Joseph Berk, Paladin Press, Boulder, CO, 1991. 136 pp., illus. $34.95.

Here is the fascinating on-going story of a truly timeless weapon, from its beginnings during the Civil War to its current role as a state-of-the-art modern combat system.

German Artillery of World War Two, by Ian V. Hogg, Stackpole Books, Mechanicsburg, PA, 1997. 304 pp., illus. $44.95.

Complete details of German artillery use in WWII.

Grand Old Lady of No Man's Land: The Vickers Machine Gun, by Dolf L. Goldsmith, Collector Grade Publications, Cobourg, Canada, 1994. 600 pp., illus. $79.95.

Goldsmith brings his years of experience as a U.S. Army armourer, machine gun collector and shooter to bear on the Vickers, in a book sure to become a classic in its field.

The Grenade Recognition Manual, Volume 1, U.S. Grenades & Accessories, by Darryl W. Lynn, Service Publications, Ottawa, Canada, 1998. 112 pp., illus. Paper covers. $29.95.

This new book examines the hand grenades of the United States beginning with the hand grenades of the U.S. Civil War and continues through to the present.

The Grenade Recognition Manual, Vol. 2, British and Commonwealth Grenades and Accessories, by Darryl W. Lynn, Printed by the Author, Ottawa, Canada, 2001. 201 pp., illustrated with over 200 photos and drawings. Paper covers. $29.95.

Covers British, Australian, and Canadian Grenades. It has the complete British Numbered series, most of the L series as well as the Australian and Canadian grenades in use. Also covers Launchers, fuzes and lighters, launching cartridges, fillings, and markings.

Gun Digest Treasury, 7th Edition, edited by Harold A. Murtz, DBI Books, a division of Krause Publications, Iola, WI, 1994. 320 pp., illus. Paper covers. $17.95.

A collection of some of the most interesting articles which have appeared in Gun Digest over its first 45 years.

Gun Digest 2002, 56th Edition, edited by Ken Ramage, DBI Books a division of Krause Publications, Iola, WI, 2001. 544 pp., illustrated. Paper covers. $24.95.

This all new 56th edition continues the editorial excellence, quality, content and comprehensive cataloguing that firearms enthusiasts have come to know and expect. The most read gun book in the world for the last half century.

Gun Engraving, by C. Austyn, Safari Press Publication, Huntington Beach, CA, 1998. 128 pp., plus 24 pages of color photos. $50.00.

A well-illustrated book on fine English and European gun engravers. Includes a fantastic pictorial section that lists types of engravings and prices.

Gun Notes, Volume 1, by Elmer Keith, Safari Press, Huntington Beach, CA, 1995. 219 pp., illustrated Limited Edition, Slipcased. $75.00

A collection of Elmer Keith's most interesting columns and feature stories that appeared in "Guns & Ammo" magazine from 1961 to the late 1970's.

Gun Notes, Volume 2, by Elmer Keith, Safari Press, Huntington Beach, CA, 1997. 292 pp., illus. Limited 1st edition, numbered and signed by Keith's son. Slipcased. $75.00. Trade edition. $35.00.

Covers articles from Keith's monthly column in "Guns & Ammo" magazine during the period from 1971 through Keith's passing in 1982.

Gun Talk, edited by Dave Moreton, Winchester Press, Piscataway, NJ, 1973. 256 pp., illus. $9.95.

A treasury of original writing by the top gun writers and editors in America. Practical advice about every aspect of the shooting sports.

The Gun That Made the Twenties Roar, by Wm. J. Helmer, rev. and enlarged by George C. Nonte, Jr., The Gun Room Press, Highland Park, NJ, 1977. Over 300 pp., illus. $24.95.

Historical account of John T. Thompson and his invention, the infamous "Tommy Gun."

Gun Trader's Guide, 23rd Edition, published by Stoeger Publishing Co., Wayne, NJ, 1999. 592 pp., illus. Paper covers. $23.95.

Complete specifications and current prices for used guns. Prices of over 5,000 handguns, rifles and shotguns both foreign and domestic.

Gun Writers of Yesteryear, compiled by James Foral, Wolfe Publishing Co., Prescott, AZ, 1993. 449 pp. illus. $35.00.

Here, from the pre-American rifleman days of 1898-1920, are collected some 80 articles by 34 writers from eight magazines.

The Gunfighter, Man or Myth? by Joseph G. Rosa, Oklahoma Press, Norman, OK, 1969. 229 pp., illus. (including weapons). Paper covers. $14.95.

A well-documented work on gunfights and gunfighters of the West and elsewhere. Great treat for all gunfighter buffs.

Gunfitting: The Quest for Perfection, by Michael Yardley, Safari Press, Huntington Beach, CA, 1995. 128 pp., illus. $24.95.

The author, a very experienced shooting instructor, examines gun stocks and gunfitting in depth.

Guns Illustrated 2002, 3rd Edition, edited by Ken Ramage, DBI Books a division of Krause Publications, Iola, WI, 1999. 352 pp., illustrated. Paper covers. $22.95.

Highly informative, technical articles on a wide range of shooting topics by some of the top writers in the industry. A catalog section lists more than 3,000 firearms currently manufactured in or imported to the U.S.

Guns & Shooting: A Selected Bibliography, by Ray Riling, Ray Riling Arms Books Co., Phila., PA, 1982. 434 pp., illus. Limited, numbered edition. $75.

A limited edition of this superb bibliographical work, the only modern listing of books devoted to guns and shooting.

Guns, Bullets, and Gunfighters, by Jim Cirillo, Paladin Press, Boulder, CO, 1996. 119 pp., illus. Paper covers. $16.00.

Lessons and tales from a modern-day gunfighter.

Guns, Loads, and Hunting Tips, by Bob Hagel, Wolfe Publishing Co., Prescott, AZ, 1986. 509 pp., illus. $19.95.

A large hardcover book packed with shooting, hunting and handloading wisdom.

Handgun Digest, 3rd Edition, edited by Chris Christian, DBI Books, a division of Krause Publications, Iola, WI, 1995. 256 pp., illus. Paper covers. $18.95.

Full coverage of all aspects of handguns and handgunning from a highly readable and knowledgeable author.

Hidden in Plain Sight, "A Practical Guide to Concealed Handgun Carry" (Revised 2nd Edition), by Trey Bloodworth and Mike Raley, Paladin Press, Boulder, CO, 1997, 5 1/2 x 8 1/2, softcover, photos, 176 pp. $20.00

Concerned with how to comfortably, discreetly and safely exercise the privileges granted by a CCW permit? This invaluable guide offers the latest advice on what to look for when choosing a CCW, how to dress for comfortable, effective concealed carry, traditional and more unconventional carry modes, accessory holsters, customized clothing and accessories, accessibility data based on draw-time comparisons and new holsters on the market. Includes 40 new manufacturer listings.

HK Assault Rifle Systems, by Duncan Long, Paladin Press, Boulder, CO, 1995. 110 pp., illus. Paper covers. $27.95.

The little known history behind this fascinating family of weapons tracing its beginnings from the ashes of World War Two to the present time.

The Hunter's Table, by Terry Libby/Recipes of Chef Richard Blondin, Countrysport Press, Selma, AL, 1999. 230 pp. $30.00.

The Countrysport book of wild game guisine.

I Remember Skeeter, compiled by Sally Jim Skelton, Wolfe Publishing Co., Prescott, AZ, 1998. 401 pp., illus. Paper covers. $19.95.

A collection of some of the beloved storyteller's famous works interspersed with anecdotes and tales from the people who knew best.

In The Line of Fire, "A Working Cop's Guide to Pistol Craft", by Michael E. Conti, Paladin Press, Boulder, CO, 1997, soft cover, photos, illus., 184 pp. $30.00

As a working cop, you want to end your patrol in the same condition you began: alive and uninjured. Improve your odds by reading and mastering the information in this book on pistol selection, stopping power, combat reloading, stoppages, carrying devices, stances, grips and Conti's "secrets" to accurate shooting.

Joe Rychertinik Reflects on Guns, Hunting, and Days Gone By, by Joe Rychertinik, Precision Shooting, Inc., Manchester, CT, 1999. 281 pp., illustrated. Paper covers. $16.95.

Thirty articles by a master story-teller.

Kill or Get Killed, by Col. Rex Applegate, Paladin Press, Boulder, CO, 1996. 400 pp., illus. $39.95.

The best and longest-selling book on close combat in history.

Larrey: Surgeon to Napoleon's Imperial Guard, by Robert G. Richardson, Quiller Press, London, 2000. 269 pp., illus. B & W photos, maps and drawings. $23.95

Not a book for the squeamish, but one full of interest, splendidly researched, bringing both the character of the Napoleonic wars and Larrey himself vividly to life. Authenticity of detail is preserved throughout.

The Long-Range War: Sniping in Vietnam, by Peter R. Senich, Paladin Press, Boulder, CO, 1994. 280 pp., illus. $49.95.

The most complete report on Vietnam-era sniping ever documented.

Manual for H&R Reising Submachine Gun and Semi-Auto Rifle, edited by George P. Dillman, Desert Publications, El Dorado, AZ, 1994. 81 pp., illus. Paper covers. $12.95.

A reprint of the Harrington & Richardson 1943 factory manual and the rare military manual on the H&R submachine gun and semi-auto rifle.

The Manufacture of Gunflints, by Sydney B.J. Skertchly, facsimile reprint with new introduction by Seymour de Lotbiniere, Museum Restoration Service, Ontario, Canada, 1984. 90 pp., illus. $24.50.

Limited edition reprinting of the very scarce London edition of 1879.

Master Tips, by J. Winokur, Potshot Press, Pacific Palisades, CA, 1985. 96 pp., illus. Paper covers. $11.95.

Basics of practical shooting.

The Military and Police Sniper, by Mike R. Lau, Precision Shooting, Inc., Manchester, CT, 1998. 352 pp., illustrated. Paper covers. $44.95.

Advanced precision shooting for combat and law enforcement.

Military Rifle & Machine Gun Cartridges, by Jean Huon, Paladin Press, Boulder, CO, 1990. 392 pp., illus. $34.95.

Describes the primary types of military cartridges and their principal loadings, as well as their characteristics, origin and use.

Military Small Arms of the 20th Century, 7th Edition, by Ian V. Hogg and John Weeks, DBI Books, a division of Krause Publications, Iola, WI, 2000. 416 pp., illustrated. Paper covers. $24.95.

Cover small arms of 46 countries. Over 800 photographs and illustrations.

THE ARMS LIBRARY

Modern Custom Guns, Walnut, Steel, and Uncommon Artistry, by Tom Turpin, Krause Publications, Iola, WI, 1997. 206 pp., illus. $49.95.
From exquisite engraving to breathtaking exotic woods, the mystique of today's custom guns is expertly detailed in word and awe-inspiring color photos of rifles, shotguns and handguns.

Modern Guns Identification & Values, 13th Edition, by Russell & Steve Quertermous, Collector Books, Paducah, KY, 1999. 516 pp., illus. Paper covers. $12.95.
A standard reference for over 20 years. Over 1,800 illustrations of over 2,500 models with their current values.

Modern Law Enforcement Weapons & Tactics, 2nd Edition, by Tom Ferguson, DBI Books, a division of Krause Publications, Iola, WI, 1991. 256 pp., illus. Paper covers. $18.95.
An in-depth look at the weapons and equipment used by law enforcement agencies of today.

Modern Machine Guns, by John Walter, Stackpole Books, Inc. Mechanicsburg, PA, 2000. 144 pp., with 146 illustrations. $22.95.
A compact and authoritative guide to post-war machine-guns. A gun-by-gun directory identifying individual variants and types including detailed evaluations and technical data.

Modern Sporting Guns, by Christopher Austyn, Safari Press, Huntington Beach, CA, 1994. 128 pp., illus. $40.00.
A discussion of the "best" English guns; round action, over-and-under, boxlocks, hammer guns, bolt action and double rifles as well as accessories.

The More Complete Cannoneer, by M.C. Switlik, Museum & Collectors Specialties Co., Monroe, MI, 1990. 199 pp., illus. $19.95.
Compiled agreeably to the regulations for the U.S. War Department, 1861, and containing current observations on the use of antique cannons.

The MP-40 Machine Gun, Desert Publications, El Dorado, AZ, 1995. 32 pp., illus. Paper covers. $11.95.
A reprint of the hard-to-find operating and maintenance manual for one of the most famous machine guns of World War II.

Naval Percussion Locks and Primers, by Lt. J. A. Dahlgren, Museum Restoration Service, Bloomfield, Canada, 1996. 140 pp., illus.
First published as an Ordnance Memoranda in 1853, this is the finest existing study of percussion locks and primers origin and development.

The Official Soviet AKM Manual, translated by Maj. James F. Gebhardt (Ret.), Paladin Press, Boulder, CO, 1999. 120 pp., illustrated. Paper covers. $18.00.
This official military manual, available in English for the first time, was originally published by the Soviet Ministry of Defence. Covers the history, function, maintenance, assembly and disassembly, etc. of the 7.62mm AKM assault rifle.

The One-Round War: U.S.M.C. Scout-Snipers in Vietnam, by Peter Senich, Paladin Press, Boulder, CO, 1996. 384 pp., illus. Paper covers $59.95.
Sniping in Vietnam focusing specifically on the Marine Corps program.

Pin Shooting: A Complete Guide, by Mitchell A. Ota, Wolfe Publishing Co., Prescott, AZ, 1992. 145 pp., illus. Paper covers. $14.95.
Traces the sport from its humble origins to today's thoroughly enjoyable social event, including the mammoth eight-day Second Chance Pin Shoot in Michigan.

Powder and Ball Small Arms, by Martin Pegler, Windrow & Greene Publishing, London, 1998. 128 pp., illustrated with 200 color photos. $39.95.
Part of the new "Live Firing Classic Weapons" series. Full-color photos of experienced shooters dressed in authentic costumes handling, loading and firing historic weapons.

Principles of Personal Defense, by Jeff Cooper, Paladin Press, Boulder, CO, 1999. 56 pp., illustrated. Paper covers. $14.00.
This revised edition of Jeff Cooper's classic on personal defense offers great new illustrations and a new preface while retaining the timeliness theory of individual defense behavior presented in the original book.

E.C. Prudhomme, Master Gun Engraver, A Retrospective Exhibition: 1946-1973, intro. by John T. Amber, The R. W. Norton Art Gallery, Shreveport, LA, 1973. 32 pp., illus. Paper covers. $9.95.
Examples of master gun engravings by Jack Prudhomme.

The Quotable Hunter, edited by Jay Cassell and Peter Fiduccia, The lyons Press, N.Y., 1999. 224 pp., illustrated. $20.00.
This collection of more than three hundred memorable quotes from hunters through the ages captures the essence of the sport, with all its joys idiosyncrasies, and challenges.

A Rifleman Went to War, by H. W. McBride, Lancer Militaria, Mt. Ida, AR, 1987. 398 pp., illus. $29.95.
The classic account of practical marksmanship on the battlefields of World War I.

Sharpshooting for Sport and War, by W.W. Greener, Wolfe Publishing Co., Prescott, AZ, 1995. 192 pp., illus. $30.00.
This classic reprint explores the *first* expanding bullet; service rifles; shooting positions; trajectories; recoil; external ballistics; and other valuable information.

The Shooter's Bible 2002, No. 93, edited by William S. Jarrett, Stoeger Publishing Co., Wayne, NJ, 2001. 576 pp., illustrated. Paper covers. $23.95.
Over 3,000 firearms currently offered by major American and foreign gunmakers. Represented are handguns, rifles, shotguns and black powder arms with complete specifications and retail prices.

Shooting To Live, by Capt. W. E. Fairbairn & Capt. E. A. Sykes, Paladin Press, Boulder, CO, 1997, 4 1/2 x 7, soft cover, illus., 112 pp. $14.00
Shooting to Live is the product of Fairbairn's and Sykes' practical experience with the handgun. Hundreds of incidents provided the basis for the first true book on life-or-death shootouts with the pistol. Shooting to Live teaches all concepts, considerations and applications of combat pistol craft.

Shooting Sixguns of the Old West, by Mike Venturino, MLV Enterprises, Livingston, MT, 1997. 221 pp., illus. Paper covers. $26.50.
A comprehensive look at the guns of the early West: Colts, Smith & Wesson and Remingtons, plus blackpowder and reloading specs.

Sniper Training, FM 23-10, Reprint of the U.S. Army field manual of August, 1994, Paladin Press, Boulder, CO, 1995. 352pp., illus. Paper covers. $30.00
The most up-to-date U.S. military sniping information and doctrine.

Sniping in France, by Major H. Hesketh-Prichard, Lancer Militaria, Mt. Ida, AR, 1993. 224 pp., illus. $24.95.
The author was a well-known British adventurer and big game hunter. He was called upon in the early days of "The Great War" to develop a program to offset an initial German advantage in sniping. How the British forces came to overcome this advantage.

Special Warfare: Special Weapons, by Kevin Dockery, Emperor's Press, Chicago, IL, 1997. 192 pp., illus. $29.95.
The arms and equipment of the UDT and SEALS from 1943 to the present.

Sporting Collectibles, by Dr. Stephen R. Irwin, Stoeger Publishing Co., Wayne, NJ, 1997. 256 pp., illus. Paper covers. $19.95.
A must book for serious collectors and admirers of sporting collectibles.

The Sporting Craftsmen: A Complete Guide to Contemporary Makers of Custom-Built Sporting Equipment, by Art Carter, Countrysport Press, Traverse City, MI, 1994. 240 pp., illus. $35.00.
Profiles leading makers of centerfire rifles; muzzleloading rifles; bamboo fly rods; fly reels; flies; waterfowl calls; decoys; handmade knives; and traditional longbows and recurves.

Sporting Rifle Takedown & Reassembly Guide, 2nd Edition, by J.B. Wood, DBI Books, a division of Krause Publications, Iola, WI, 1997. 480 pp., illus. $19.95.
An updated edition of the reference guide for anyone who wants to properly care for their sporting rifle. (Available September 1997)

2001 Standard Catalog of Firearms, the Collector's Price & Reference Guide, 11th Edition, by Ned Schwing, Krause Publications, Iola, WI, 2000. 1,248 pp., illus. Paper covers. $32.95.
Packed with more than 80,000 real world prices with more than 5,000 photos. Easy to use master index listing every firearm model.

The Street Smart Gun Book, by John Farnam, Police Bookshelf, Concord, NH, 1986. 45 pp., illus. Paper covers. $11.95.
Weapon selection, defensive shooting techniques, and gunfight-winning tactics from one of the world's leading authorities.

Stress Fire, Vol. 1: Stress Fighting for Police, by Massad Ayoob, Police Bookshelf, Concord, NH, 1984. 149 pp., illus. Paper covers. $9.95.
Gunfighting for police, advanced tactics and techniques.

Survival Guns, by Mel Tappan, Desert Publications, El Dorado, AZ, 1993. 456 pp., illus. Paper covers. $21.95.
Discusses in a frank and forthright manner which handguns, rifles and shotguns to buy for personal defense and securing food, and the ones to avoid.

The Tactical Advantage, by Gabriel Suarez, Paladin Press, Boulder, CO, 1998. 216 pp., illustrated. Paper covers. $22.00.
Learn combat tactics that have been tested in the world's toughest schools.

Tactical Marksman, by Dave M. Lauch, Paladin Press, Boulder, CO, 1996. 165 pp., illus. Paper covers. $35.00.
A complete training manual for police and practical shooters.

Thompson Guns 1921-1945, Anubis Press, Houston, TX, 1980. 215 pp., illus. Paper covers. $15.95.
Facsimile reprinting of five complete manuals on the Thompson submachine gun.

To Ride, Shoot Straight, and Speak the Truth, by Jeff Cooper, Paladin Press, Boulder, CO, 1997, 5 1/2 x 8 1/2, soft-cover, illus., 384 pp. $32.00
Combat mind-set, proper sighting, tactical residential architecture, nuclear war - these are some of the many subjects explored by Jeff Cooper in this illustrated anthology. The author discusses various arms, fighting skills and the importance of knowing how to defend oneself, and one's honor, in our rapidly changing world.

Trailriders Guide to Cowboy Action Shooting, by James W. Barnard, Pioneer Press, Union City, TN, 1998. 134 pp., plus 91 photos, drawings and charts. Paper covers. $24.95.
Covers the complete spectrum of this shooting discipline, from how to dress to authentic leather goods, which guns are legal, calibers, loads and ballistics.

The Ultimate Sniper, by Major John L. Plaster, Paladin Press, Boulder, CO, 1994. 464 pp., illus. Paper covers. $42.95.
An advanced training manual for military and police snipers.

Unrepentant Sinner, by Col. Charles Askins, Paladin Press, Boulder, CO, 2000. 322 pp., illustrated. $29.95.
The autobiography of Colonel Charles Askins.

U.S. Marine Corp Rifle and Pistol Marksmanship, 1935, reprinting of a government publication, Lancer Militaria, Mt. Ida, AR, 1991. 99 pp., illus. Paper covers. $11.95.
The old corps method of precision shooting.

U.S. Marine Corps Scout/Sniper Training Manual, Lancer Militaria, Mt. Ida, AR, 1989. Soft covers. $19.95.
Reprint of the original sniper training manual used by the Marksmanship Training Unit of the Marine Corps Development and Education Command in Quantico, Virginia.

U.S. Marine Corps Scout-Sniper, World War II and Korea, by Peter R. Senich, Paladin Press, Boulder, CO, 1994. 236 pp., illus. $44.95.
The most thorough and accurate account ever printed on the training, equipment and combat experiences of the U.S. Marine Corps Scout-Snipers.

U.S. Marine Corps Sniping, Lancer Militaria, Mt. Ida, AR, 1989. Irregular pagination. Soft covers. $17.95.

A reprint of the official Marine Corps FMFM1-3B.

Weapons of the Waffen-SS, by Bruce Quarrie, Sterling Publishing Co., Inc., 1991. 168 pp., illus. $24.95.

An in-depth look at the weapons that made Hitler's Waffen-SS the fearsome fighting machine it was.

Weatherby: The Man, The Gun, The Legend, by Grits and Tom Gresham, Cane River Publishing Co., Natchitoches, LA, 1992. 290 pp., illus. $24.95.

A fascinating look at the life of the man who changed the course of firearms development in America.

The Winchester Era, by David Madis, Art & Reference House, Brownsville, TX, 1984. 100 pp., illus. $19.95.

Story of the Winchester company, management, employees, etc.

Winchester Repeating Arms Company by Herbert Houze, Krause Publications, Iola, WI. 512 pp., illus. $50.00.

With British Snipers to the Reich, by Capt. C. Shore, Lander Militaria, Mt. Ida, AR, 1988. 420 pp., illus. $29.95.

One of the greatest books ever written on the art of combat sniping.

The World's Machine Pistols and Submachine Guns - Vol. 2a 1964 to 1980, by Nelson & Musgrave, Ironside International, Alexandria, VA, 2000. 673 pages, illustrated. $59.95

Containing data, history and photographs of over 200 weapons. With a special section covering shoulder stocked automatic pistols, 100 additional photos.

The World's Submachine Guns - Vol. 1 1918 to 1963, by Nelson & Musgrave, Ironside International, Alexandria, VA, 2001. 673 pages, illustrated. $59.95.

A revised edition covering much new material that has come to light since the book was originally printed in 1963.

The World's Sniping Rifles, by Ian V. Hogg, Paladin Press, Boulder, CO, 1998. 144 pp., illustrated. $22.95.

A detailed manual with descriptions and illustrations of more than 50 high-precision rifles from 14 countries and a complete analysis of sights and systems.

GUNSMITHING

Accurizing the Factory Rifle, by M.L. McPherson, Precision Shooting, Inc., Manchester, CT, 1999. 335 pp., illustrated. Paper covers. $44.95.

A long-awaiting book, which bridges the gap between the rudimentary (mounting sling swivels, scope blocks and that general level of accomplishment) and the advanced (precision chambering, barrel fluting, and that general level of accomplishment) books that are currently available today.

Advanced Rebarreling of the Sporting Rifle, by Willis H. Fowler, Jr., Willis H. Fowler, Jr., Anchorage, AK, 1994. 127 pp., illus. Paper covers. $32.50.

A manual outlining a superior method of fitting barrels and doing chamber work on the sporting rifle.

The Art of Engraving, by James B. Meek, F. Brownell & Son, Montezuma, IA, 1973. 196 pp., illus. $38.95.

A complete, authoritative, imaginative and detailed study in training for gun engraving. The first book of its kind—and a great one.

Artistry in Arms, The R. W. Norton Gallery, Shreveport, LA, 1970. 42 pp., illus. Paper covers. $9.95.

The art of gunsmithing and engraving.

Barrels & Actions, by Harold Hoffman, H&P Publishers, San Angelo, TX, 1990. 309 pp., illus. Spiral bound. $29.95.

A manual on barrel making.

Black Powder Hobby Gunsmithing, by Sam Fadala and Dale Storey, DBI Books, a division of Krause Publications, Iola, WI., 1994. 256 pp., illus. Paper covers. $18.95.

A how-to guide for gunsmithing blackpowder pistols, rifles and shotguns from two men at the top of their respective fields.

Checkering and Carving of Gun Stocks, by Monte Kennedy, Stackpole Books, Harrisburg, PA, 1962. 175 pp., illus. $39.95.

Revised, enlarged cloth-bound edition of a much sought-after, dependable work.

The Complete Metal Finishing Book, by Harold Hoffman, H&P Publishers, San Angelo, TX, 1992. 364 pp., illus. Paper covers. $29.95.

Instructions for the different metal finishing operations that the normal craftsman or shop will use. Primarily firearm related.

Exploded Handgun Drawings, The Gun Digest Book of, edited by Harold A. Murtz, DBI Books, a division of Krause Publications, Iola, WI. 1992. 512 pp., illus. Paper covers. $20.95.

Exploded or isometric drawings for 494 of the most popular handguns.

Exploded Long Gun Drawings, The Gun Digest Book of, edited by Harold A. Murtz, DBI Books, a division of Krause Publications, Iola, WI. 512 pp., illus. Paper covers. $20.95.

Containing almost 500 rifle and shotgun exploded drawings. An invaluable aid to both professionals and hobbyists.

The Finishing of Gun Stocks, by Harold Hoffman, H&P Publishers, San Angelo, TX, 1994. 98 pp., illus. Paper covers. $17.95.

Covers different types of finishing methods and finishes.

Firearms Assembly/Disassembly, Part I: Automatic Pistols, 2ⁿᵈ Revised Edition, The Gun Digest Book of, by J.B. Wood, DBI Books, a division of Krause Publications, Iola, WI, 1999. 480 pp., illus. Paper covers. $24.95.

Covers 58 popular autoloading pistols plus nearly 200 variants of those models integrated into the text and completely cross-referenced in the index.

Firearms Assembly/Disassembly Part II: Revolvers, Revised Edition, The Gun Digest Book of, by J.B. Wood, DBI Books, a division of Krause Publications, Iola, WI, 1990. 480 pp., illus. Paper covers. $19.95.

Covers 49 popular revolvers plus 130 variants. The most comprehensive and professional presentation available to either hobbyist or gunsmith.

Firearms Assembly/Disassembly Part III: Rimfire Rifles, Revised Edition, The Gun Digest Book of, by J. B. Wood, DBI Books, a division of Krause Publications, Iola, WI., 1994. 480 pp., illus. Paper covers. $19.95.

Greatly expanded edition covering 65 popular rimfire rifles plus over 100 variants all completely cross-referenced in the index.

Firearms Assembly/Disassembly Part IV: Centerfire Rifles, Revised Edition, The Gun Digest Book of, by J.B. Wood, DBI Books, a division of Krause Publications, Iola, WI, 1991. 480 pp., illus. Paper covers. $19.95.

Covers 54 popular centerfire rifles plus 300 variants. The most comprehensive and professional presentation available to either hobbyist or gunsmith.

Firearms Assembly/Disassembly, Part V: Shotguns, Revised Edition, The Gun Digest Book of, by J.B. Wood, DBI Books, a division of Krause Publications, Iola, WI, 1992. 480 pp., illus. Paper covers. $19.95.

Covers 46 popular shotguns plus over 250 variants with step-by-step instructions on how to dismantle and reassemble each. The most comprehensive and professional presentation available to either hobbyist or gunsmith.

Firearms Assembly/Disassembly Part VI: Law Enforcement Weapons, The Gun Digest Book of, by J.B. Wood, DBI Books, a division of Krause Publications, Iola, WI, 1981. 288 pp., illus. Paper covers. $16.95.

Step-by-step instructions on how to completely dismantle and reassemble the most commonly used firearms found in law enforcement arsenals.

Firearms Assembly 3: The NRA Guide to Rifle and Shotguns, NRA Books, Wash., DC, 1980. 264 pp., illus. Paper covers. $13.95.

Text and illustrations explaining the takedown of 125 rifles and shotguns, domestic and foreign.

Firearms Assembly 4: The NRA Guide to Pistols and Revolvers, NRA Books, Wash., DC, 1980. 253 pp., illus. Paper covers. $13.95.

Text and illustrations explaining the takedown of 124 pistol and revolver models, domestic and foreign.

Firearms Bluing and Browning, By R.H. Angier, Stackpole Books, Harrisburg, PA. 151 pp., illus. $19.95.

A world master gunsmith reveals his secrets of building, repairing and renewing a gun, quite literally, lock, stock and barrel. A useful, concise text on chemical coloring methods for the gunsmith and mechanic.

Firearms Disassembly—With Exploded Views, by John A. Karns & John E. Traister, Stoeger Publishing Co., S. Hackensack, NJ, 1995. 320 pp., illus. Paper covers. $19.95.

Provides the do's and don'ts of firearms disassembly. Enables owners and gunsmiths to disassemble firearms in a professional manner.

Guns and Gunmaking Tools of Southern Appalachia, by John Rice Irwin, Schiffer Publishing Ltd., 1983. 118 pp., illus. Paper covers. $9.95.

The story of the Kentucky rifle.

Gunsmithing: Pistols & Revolvers, by Patrick Sweeney, DBI Books, a division of Krause Publications, Iola, WI, 1998. 352 pp., illus. Paper covers. $24.95.

Do-it-Yourself projects, diagnosis and repair for pistols and revolvers.

Gunsmithing: Rifles, by Patrick Sweeney, Krause Publications, Iola, WI, 1999. 352 pp., illustrated. Paper covers. $24.95.

Tips for lever-action rifles. Building a custom Ruger 10/22. Building a better hunting rifle.

Gunsmithing Tips and Projects, a collection of the best articles from the *Handloader* and *Rifle* magazines, by various authors, Wolfe Publishing Co., Prescott, AZ, 1992. 443 pp., illus. Paper covers. $25.00.

Includes such subjects as shop, stocks, actions, tuning, triggers, barrels, customizing, etc.

Gunsmith Kinks, by F.R. (Bob) Brownell, F. Brownell & Son, Montezuma, IA, 1st ed., 1969. 496 pp., well illus. $22.98.

A widely useful accumulation of shop kinks, short cuts, techniques and pertinent comments by practicing gunsmiths from all over the world.

Gunsmith Kinks 2, by Bob Brownell, F. Brownell & Son, Publishers, Montezuma, IA, 1983. 496 pp., illus. $22.95.

A collection of gunsmithing knowledge, shop kinks, new and old techniques, shortcuts and general know-how straight from those who do them best—the gunsmiths.

Gunsmith Kinks 3, edited by Frank Brownell, Brownells Inc., Montezuma, IA, 1993. 504 pp., illus. $24.95.

Tricks, knacks and "kinks" by professional gunsmiths and gun tinkerers. Hundreds of valuable ideas are given in this volume.

Gunsmith Kinks 4, edited by Frank Brownell, Brownells Inc., Montezuma, IA, 2001. 564 pp., illus. $27.75

332 detailed illustrations. 560+ pages with 706 separate subject headings and over 5000 cross-indexed entries. An incredible gold mine of information.

Gunsmithing, by Roy F. Dunlap, Stackpole Books, Harrisburg, PA, 1990. 742 pp., illus. $34.95.

A manual of firearm design, construction, alteration and remodeling. For amateur and professional gunsmiths and users of modern firearms.

Gunsmithing at Home: Lock, Stock and Barrel, by John Traister, Stoeger Publishing Co., Wayne, NJ, 1997. 320 pp., illus. Paper covers. $19.95.

A complete step-by-step fully illustrated guide to the art of gunsmithing.

The Gunsmith's Manual, by J.P. Stelle and Wm. B. Harrison, The Gun Room Press, Highland Park, NJ, 1982. 376 pp., illus. $19.95.

For the gunsmith in all branches of the trade.

THE ARMS LIBRARY

Home Gunsmithing the Colt Single Action Revolvers, by Loren W. Smith, Ray Riling Arms Books, Co., Phila., PA, 2001. 119 pp., illus. $29.95.

Affords the Colt Single Action owner detailed, pertinent information on the operating and servicing of this famous and historic handgun.

How to Convert Military Rifles, Williams Gun Sight Co., Davision, MI, new and enlarged seventh edition, 1997. 76 pp., illus. Paper covers. $13.95.

This latest edition updated the changes that have occured over the past thirty years. Tips, instructions and illustratons on how to convert popular military rifles as the Enfield, Mauser 96 nad SKS just to name a few are presented.

Mauser M98 & M96, by R.A. Walsh, Wolfe Publishing Co., Prescott, AR, 1998. 123 pp., illustrated. Paper covers. $32.50.

How to build your own favorite custom Mauser rifle from two of the best bolt action rifle designs ever produced—the military Mauser Model 1898 and Model 1896 bolt rifles.

Mr. Single Shot's Gunsmithing-Idea-Book, by Frank de Haas, Mark de Haas, Orange City, IA, 1996. 168 pp., illus. Paper covers. $21.50.

Offers easy to follow, step-by-step instructions for a wide variety of gunsmithing procedures all reinforced by plenty of photos.

Pistolsmithing, by George C. Nonte, Jr., Stackpole Books, Harrisburg, PA, 1974. 560 pp., illus. $34.95.

A single source reference to handgun maintenance, repair, and modification at home, unequaled in value.

Practical Gunsmithing, by the editors of American Gunsmith, DBI Books, a division of Krause Publications, Iola, WI, 1996. 256 pp., illus. Paper covers. $19.95.

A book intended primarily for home gunsmithing, but one that will be extremely helpful to professionals as well.

Professional Stockmaking, by D. Wesbrook, Wolfe Publishing Co., Prescott AZ, 1995. 308 pp., illus. $54.00.

A step-by-step how-to with complete photographic support for every detail of the art of working wood into riflestocks.

Recreating the American Longrifle, by William Buchele, et al, George Shumway Publisher, York, Pa, 5th edition, 1999. 175 pp., illustrated. $40.00.

Includes full size plans for building a Kentucky rifle.

Riflesmithing, The Gun Digest Book of, by Jack Mitchell, DBI Books, a division of Krause Publications, Iola, WI, 1982. 256 pp., illus. Paper covers. $16.95.

The art and science of rifle gunsmithing. Covers tools, techniques, designs, finishing wood and metal, custom alterations.

Shotgun Gunsmithing, The Gun Digest Book of, by Ralph Walker, DBI Books, a division of Krause Publications, Iola, WI, 1983. 256 pp., illus. Paper covers. $16.95.

The principles and practices of repairing, individualizing and accurizing modern shotguns by one of the world's premier shotgun gunsmiths.

Sporting Rifle Take Down & Reassembly Guide, 2nd Edition, by J.B. Wood, Krause Publications, Iola, WI, 1997. 480 pp., illus. Paper covers. $19.95.

Hunters and shooting enthusiasts must have this reference featuring 52 of the most popular and widely used sporting centerfire and rimfire rifles.

The Story of Pope's Barrels, by Ray M. Smith, R&R Books, Livonia, NY, 1993. 203 pp., illus. $39.00.

A reissue of a 1960 book whose author knew Pope personally. It will be of special interest to Schuetzen rifle fans, since Pope's greatest days were at the height of the Schuetzen-era before WWI.

Survival Gunsmithing, by J.B. Wood, Desert Publications, Cornville, AZ, 1986. 92 pp., illus. Paper covers. $11.95.

A guide to repair and maintenance of the most popular rifles, shotguns and handguns.

The Tactical 1911, by Dave Lauck, Paladin Press, Boulder, CO, 1998. 137 pp., illus. Paper covers. $20.00.

Here is the only book you will ever need to teach you how to select, modify, employ and maintain your Colt.

HANDGUNS

Advanced Master Handgunning, by Charles Stephens, Paladin Press, Boulder, CO., 1994. 72 pp., illus. Paper covers. $14.00.

Secrets and surefire techniques for winning handgun competitions.

American Beauty: The Prewar Colt National Match Government Model Pistol, by Timothy Mullin, Collector Grade Publications, Canada, 1999. 72 pp., 69 illus. $34.95

69 illustrations, 20 in full color photos of factory engraved guns and other authenticated upgrades, including rare 'double-carved' ivory grips.

Axis Pistols: WORLD WAR TWO 50 YEARS COMMEMORATIVE ISSUE, by Jan C. Stills, Walsworth Publishing, 1989. 360 pages, illus. $59.95

The Ayoob Files: The Book, by Massad Ayoob, Police Bookshelf, Concord, NH, 1995. 223 pp., illus. Paper covers. $14.95.

The best of Massad Ayoob's acclaimed series in American Handgunner magazine.

Big Bore Sixguns, by John Taffin, Krause Publications, Iola, WI, 1997. 336 pp., illus. $39.95.

The author takes aim on the entire range of big bores from .357 Magnums to .500 Maximums, single actions and cap-and-ball sixguns to custom touches for big bores..

The Browning High Power Automatic Pistol (Expanded Edition), by Blake R. Stevens, Collector Grade Publications, Canada, 1996. 310 pages, with 313 illus. $49.95

An in-depth chronicle of seventy years of High Power history, from John M Browning's original 16-shot prototypes to the present. Profusely illustrated with rare original photos and drawings from the FN Archive to describe virtually every sporting and military version of the High Power. The numerous modifications made to the basic design over the years are, for the first time, accurately arranged in chronological order, thus permitting the dating of any High Power to within a few years of its production. Full details on the WWII Canadian-made Inglis Browning High Power pistol. The Expanded Edition contains 30 new pages on the interesting Argentine full-auto High Power, the latest FN 'MK3' and BDA9 pistols, plus FN's revolutionary P90 5.7x28mm Personal Defence Weapon, and more!

Browning Hi-Power Pistols, Desert Publications, Cornville, AZ, 1982. 20 pp., illus. Paper covers. $11.95.

Covers all facets of the various military and civilian models of the Browning Hi-Power pistol.

Canadian Military Handguns 1855-1985, by Clive M. Law, Museum Restoration Service, Bloomfield, Ont. Canada, 1994. 130pp., illus. $40.00.

A long-awaited and important history for arms historians and pistol collectors.

The Colt .45 Auto Pistol, compiled from U.S. War Dept. Technical Manuals, and reprinted by Desert Publications, Cornville, AZ, 1978. 80 pp., illus. Paper covers. $11.95.

Covers every facet of this famous pistol from mechanical training, manual of arms, disassembly, repair and replacement of parts.

Colt Automatic Pistols, by Donald B. Bady, Pioneer Press, Union City, TN, 1999. 368 pp., illustrated. Softcover. $19.95.

A revised and enlarged edition of a key work on a fascinating subject. Complete information on every Colt automatic pistol.

Combat Handgunnery, 4th Edition, by Chuck Taylor, DBI Books, a division of Krause Publications, Iola, WI, 1997. 256 pp., illus. Paper covers. $18.95.

This all-new edition looks at real world combat handgunnery from three different perspectives—military, police and civilian. Available, October, 1996.

Combat Revolvers, by Duncan Long, Paladin Press, Boulder, CO, 1999, 8 1/2 x 11, soft cover, 115 photos, 152 pp. $21.95

This is an uncompromising look at modern combat revolvers. All the major foreign and domestic guns are covered: the Colt Python, S&W Model 29, Ruger GP 100 and hundreds more. Know the gun that you may one day stake your life on.

The Complete Book of Combat Handgunning, by Chuck Taylor, Desert Publications, Cornville, AZ, 1982. 168 pp., illus. Paper covers. $20.00.

Covers virtually every aspect of combat handgunning.

Complete Guide to Compact Handguns, by Gene Gangarosa, Jr., Stoeger Publishing Co., Wayne, NJ, 1997. 228 pp., illus. Paper covers. $22.95.

Includes hundreds of compact firearms, along with text results conducted by the author.

Complete Guide to Service Handguns, by Gene Gangarosa, Jr., Stoeger Publishing Co., Wayne, NJ, 1998. 320 pp., illus. Paper covers. $22.95.

The author explores the revolvers and pistols that are used around the globe by military, law enforcement and civilians.

The Custom Government Model Pistol, by Layne Simpson, Wolfe Publishing Co., Prescott, AZ, 1994. 639 pp., illus. Paper covers. $24.50.

The book about one of the world's greatest firearms and the things pistolsmiths do to make it even greater.

The CZ-75 Family: The Ultimate Combat Handgun, by J.M. Ramos, Paladin Press, Boulder, CO, 1990. 100 pp., illus. Soft covers. $25.00.

An in-depth discussion of the early-and-late model CZ-75s, as well as the many newest additions to the Czech pistol family.

Encyclopedia of Pistols & Revolvers, by A.E. Hartnik, Knickerbocker Press, New York, NY, 1997. 272 pp., illus. $19.95.

A comprehensive encyclopedia specially written for collectors and owners of pistols and revolvers.

Experiments of a Handgunner, by Walter Roper, Wolfe Publishing Co., Prescott, AZ, 1989. 202 pp., illus. $37.00.

A limited edition reprint. A listing of experiments with functioning parts of handguns, with targets, stocks, rests, handloading, etc.

The Farnam Method of Defensive Handgunning, by John S. Farnam, Police Bookshelf, 1999. 191 pp., illus. Paper covers. $25.00

A book intended to not only educate the new shooter, but also to serve as a guide and textbook for his and his instructor's training courses.

Fast and Fancy Revolver Shooting, by Ed. McGivern, Anniversary Edition, Winchester Press, Piscataway, NJ, 1984. 484 pp., illus. $18.95.

A fascinating volume, packed with handgun lore and solid information by the acknowledged dean of revolver shooters.

.45 ACP Super Guns, by J.M. Ramos, Paladin Press, Boulder, CO, 1991. 144 pp., illus. Paper covers. $24.00.

Modified .45 automatic pistols for competition, hunting and personal defense.

The .45, The Gun Digest Book of, by Dean A. Grennell, DBI Books, a division of Krause Publications, Iola, WI, 1989. 256 pp., illus. Paper covers. $17.95.

Definitive work on one of America's favorite calibers.

Glock: The New Wave in Combat Handguns, by Peter Alan Kasler, Paladin Press, Boulder, CO, 1993. 304 pp., illus. $27.00.

Kasler debunks the myths that surround what is the most innovative handgun to be introduced in some time.

Glock's Handguns, by Duncan Long, Desert Publications, El Dorado, AR, 1996. 180 pp., illus. Paper covers. $18.95.

An outstanding volume on one of the world's newest and most successful firearms of the century.

Hand Cannons: The World's Most Powerful Handguns, by Duncan Long, Paladin Press, Boulder, CO, 1995. 208 pp., illus. Paper covers. $22.00.

Long describes and evaluates each powerful gun according to their features.

THE ARMS LIBRARY

The Handgun, by Geoffrey Boothroyd, Safari Press, Inc., Huntington Beach, CA, 1999. 566 pp., illustrated. $50.00.

A very detailed history of the handgun. Now revised and a completely new chapter written to take account of developments since the 1970 edition.

Handguns 2002, 13th Edition, edited by Ken Ramage, DBI Books a division of Krause Publications, Iola, WI, 1999. 352 pp., illustrated. Paper covers. $22.95.

Top writers in the handgun industry give you a complete report on new handgun developments, testfire reports on the newest introductions and previews on what's ahead.

Handgun Digest, 3rd Edition, edited by Chris Christian, DBI Books, a division of Krause Publications, Iola, WI, 1995. 256 pp., illus. Paper covers. $18.95.

Full coverage of all aspects of handguns and handgunning from a highly readable and knowledgeable author.

Handgun Reloading, The Gun Digest Book of, by Dean A. Grennell and Wiley M. Clapp, DBI Books, a division of Krause Publications, Iola, WI, 1987. 256 pp., illus. Paper covers. $16.95.

Detailed discussions of all aspects of reloading for handguns, from basic to complex. New loading data.

Handgun Stopping Power "The Definitive Study", by Evan P. Marshall & Edwin J. Sanow, Paladin Press, Boulder, CO, 1997, soft cover, photos, 240 pp. $45.00

Dramatic first-hand accounts of the results of handgun rounds fired into criminals by cops, storeowners, cabbies and others are the heart and soul of this long-awaited book. This is the definitive methodology for predicting the stopping power of handgun loads, the first to take into account what really happens when a bullet meets a man.

Heckler & Koch's Handguns, by Duncan Long, Desert Publications, El Dorado, AR, 1996. 142 pp., illus. Paper covers. $19.95.

Traces the history and the evolution of H&K's pistols from the company's beginning at the end of WWII to the present.

Hidden in Plain Sight, by Trey Bloodworth & Mike Raley, Professional Press, Chapel Hill, NC, 1995. Paper covers. $19.95.

A practical guide to concealed handgun carry.

High Standard Automatic Pistols 1932-1950, by Charles E. Petty, The Gunroom Press, Highland Park, NJ, 1989. 124 pp., illus. $19.95.

A definitive source of information for the collector of High Standard arms.

Hi-Standard Pistols and Revolvers, 1951-1984, by James Spacek, James Spacek, Chesire, CT, 1998. 128 pp., illustrated. Paper covers. $12.50.

Technical details, marketing features and instruction/parts manual of every model High Standard pistol and revolver made between 1951 and 1984. Most accurate serial number information available.

The Hi-Standard Pistol Guide, by Burr Leyson, Duckett's Sporting Books, Tempe AZ, 1995. 128 pp., illus. Paper covers. $22.00.

Complete information on selection, care and repair, ammunition, parts, and accessories.

How to Become a Master Handgunner: The Mechanics of X-Count Shooting, by Charles Stephens, Paladin Press, Boulder, CO, 1993. 64 pp., illus. Paper covers. $14.00.

Offers a simple formula for success to the handgunner who strives to master the technique of shooting accurately.

Hunting for Handgunners, by Larry Kelly and J.D. Jones, DBI Books, a division of Krause Publications, Iola, WI, 1990. 256 pp., illus. Paper covers. $16.95.

Covers the entire spectrum of hunting with handguns in an amusing, easy-flowing manner that combines entertainment with solid information.

Illustrated Encyclopedia of Handguns, by A.B. Zhuk, Stackpole Books, Mechanicsburg, PA, 1994. 256 pp., illus. Cloth cover, $49.95

Identifies more than 2,000 military and commercial pistols and revolvers with details of more than 100 popular handgun cartridges.

The Inglis Diamond: The Canadian High Power Pistol, by Clive M. Law, Collector Grade Publications, Canada, 2001. 312 pp., illustrated. $49.95

This definitive work on Canada's first and indeed only mass produced handgun, in production for a very brief span of time and consequently made in relatively few numbers, the venerable Inglis-made Browning High Power covers the pistol's initial history, the story of Chinese and British adoption, use post-war by Holland, Australia, Greece, Belgium, New Zealand, Peru, Brasil and other countries. All new information on the famous light-weights and the Inglis Diamond variations. Completely researched through official archives in a dozen countries. Many of the bewildering variety of markings have never been satisfactorily explained until now. Also included are many photos of holsters and accessories.

Instinct Combat Shooting, by Chuck Klein, The Goose Creek, IN, 1989. 49 pp., illus. Paper covers. $12.00.

Defensive handgunning for police.

Know Your Czechoslovakian Pistols, by R.J. Berger, Blacksmith Corp., Chino Valley, AZ, 1989. 96 pp., illus. Soft covers. $12.95.

A comprehensive reference which presents the fascinating story of Czech pistols.

Know Your 45 Auto Pistols—Models 1911 & A1, by E.J. Hoffschmidt, Blacksmith Corp., Southport, CT, 1974. 58 pp., illus. Paper covers. $12.95.

A concise history of the gun with a wide variety of types and copies.

Know Your Walther P38 Pistols, by E.J. Hoffschmidt, Blacksmith Corp., Southport, CT, 1974. 77 pp., illus. Paper covers. $12.95.

Covers the Walther models Armee, M.P., H.P., P.38—history and variations.

Know Your Walther PP & PPK Pistols, by E.J. Hoffschmidt, Blacksmith Corp., Southport, CT, 1975. 87 pp., illus. Paper covers. $12.95.

A concise history of the guns with a guide to the variety and types.

La Connaissance du Luger, Tome 1, by Gerard Henrotin, H & L Publishing, Belguim, 1996. 144 pages, illustrated. $45.00.

(The Knowledge of Luger, Volume 1, translated.) B&W and Color photo's. French text.

The Luger Handbook, by Aarron Davis, Krause Publications, Iola, WI, 1997. 112 pp., illus. Paper covers. $9.95.

Now you can identify any of the legendary Luger variations using a simple decision tree. Each model and variation includes pricing information, proof marks and detailed attributes in a handy, user-friendly format. Plus, it's fully indexed. Instantly identify that Luger!

Lugers of Ralph Shattuck, by Ralph Shattuck, Peoria, AZ, 2000. 49 pages, illus. Hardcover. $29.95.

49 pages, illustrated with maps and full color photos of here to now never before shown photos of some of the rarest lugers ever. Written by one of the world's renowned collectors. A MUST have book for any Luger collector.

Lugers at Random (Revised Format Edition), by Charles Kenyon, Jr., Handgun Press, Glenview, IL, 2000. 420 pp., illus. $59.95.

A new printing of this classic, comprehensive reference for all Luger collectors.

The Luger Story, by John Walter, Stackpole Books, Mechanicsburg, PA, 2001. 256 pp., illus. Paper Covers. $29.95.

The standard history of the world's most famous handgun.

The Mauser Self-Loading Pistol, by Belford & Dunlap, Borden Publ. Co., Alhambra, CA. Over 200 pp., 300 illus., large format. $29.95.

The long-awaited book on the "Broom Handles," covering their inception in 1894 to the end of production. Complete and in detail: pocket pistols, Chinese and Spanish copies, etc.

9mm Handguns, 2nd Edition, The Gun Digest Book of, edited by Steve Comus, DBI Books, a division of Krause Publications, Iola, WI, 1993. 256 pp., illus. Paper covers. $18.95.

Covers the 9mm cartridge and the guns that have been made for it in greater depth than any other work available.

9mm Parabellum; The History & Development of the World's 9mm Pistols & Ammunition, by Klaus-Peter Konig and Martin Hugo, Schiffer Publishing Ltd., Atglen, PA, 1993. 304 pp., illus. $39.95.

Detailed history of 9mm weapons from Belgium, Italy, Germany, Israel, France, USA, Czechoslovakia, Hungary, Poland, Brazil, Finland and Spain.

The Official 9mm Markarov Pistol Manual, translated into English by Major James Gebhardt, U.S. Army (Ret.), Desert Publications, El Dorado, AR, 1996. 84 pp., illus. Paper covers. $12.95.

The information found in this book will be of enormous benefit and interest to the owner or a prospective owner of one of these pistols.

The Official Soviet 7.62mm Handgun Manual, by Translation by Maj. James F. Gebhardt Ret.), Paladin Press, Boulder, CO, 1997, soft cover, illus., 104 pp. $20.00

This Soviet military manual, now available in English for the first time, covers instructions for use and maintenance of two side arms, the Nagant 7.62mm revolver, used by the Russian tsarist armed forces and later the Soviet armed forces, and the Tokarev7.62mm semi-auto pistol, which replaced the Nagant.

P-38 Automatic Pistol, by Gene Gangarosa, Jr., Stoeger Publishing Co., S. Hackensack, NJ, 1993. 272 pp., illus. Paper covers. $16.95

This book traces the origins and development of the P-38, including the momentous political forces of the World War II era that caused its near demise and, later, its rebirth.

The P-38 Pistol: The Walther Pistols, 1930-1945. Volume 1. by Warren Buxton, Ucross Books, Los Alamos, MN 1999. $68.50

A limited run reprint of this scarce and sought-after work on the P-38 Pistol. 328 pp. with 160 illustrations.

The P-38 Pistol: The Contract Pistols, 1940-1945. Volume 2. by Warren Buxton, Ucross Books, Los Alamos, MN 1999. 256 pp. with 237 illustrations. $68.50

The P-38 Pistol: Postwar Distributions, 1945-1990. Volume 3. by Warren Buxton, Ucross Books, Los Alamos, MN 1999. $68.50

Plus an addendum to Volumes 1 & 2. 272 pp. with 342 illustrations.

PARABELLUM - A Technical History of Swiss Lugers, by V. Bobba, Italy.1998. 224pp, profuse color photos, large format. $100.00.

The is the most beautifully illustrated and well-documented book on the Swiss Lugers yet produced. This splendidly produced book features magnificent images while giving an incredible amount of detail on the Swiss Luger. In-depth coverage of key issues include: the production process, pistol accessories, charts with serial numbers, production figures, variations, markings, patent drawings, etc. Covers the Swiss Luger story from 1894 when the first Bergmann-Schmeisser models were tested till the commercial model 1965. Shows every imaginable production variation in amazing detail and full color! A must for all Luger collectors. This work has been produced in an extremely attractive package using quality materials throughout and housed in a protective slipcase.

Pistols and Revolvers, by Jean-Noel Mouret, Barns and Noble, Rockleigh, N.J., 1999. 141 pp., illustrated. $12.98.

Here in glorious display is the master guidebook to flintlocks, minatures, the Sig P-210 limited edition, the Springfield Trophy Master with Aimpoint 5000 telescopic sight, every major classic and contemporary handgun, complete with their technical data.

Report of Board on Tests of Revolvers and Automatic Pistols, From the Annual Report of the Chief of Ordnance, 1907. Reprinted by J.C. Tillinghast, Marlow, NH, 1969. 34 pp., 7 plates, paper covers. $9.95.

A comparison of handguns, including Luger, Savage, Colt, Webley-Fosbery and other makes.

THE ARMS LIBRARY

Ruger Automatic Pistols and Single Action Revolvers, by Hugo A. Lueders, edited by Don Findley, Blacksmith Corp., Chino Valley, AZ, 1993. 79 pp., illus. Paper covers. $14.95.

The definitive work on Ruger automatic pistols and single action revolvers.

The Ruger "P" Family of Handguns, by Duncan Long, Desert Publications, El Dorado, AZ, 1993. 128 pp., illus. Paper covers. $14.95.

A full-fledged documentary on a remarkable series of Sturm Ruger handguns.

The Ruger .22 Automatic Pistol, Standard/Mark I/Mark II Series, by Duncan Long, Paladin Press, Boulder, CO, 1989. 168 pp., illus. Paper covers. $16.00.

The definitive book about the pistol that has served more than 1 million owners so well.

The Semiautomatic Pistols in Police Service and Self Defense, by Massad Ayoob, Police Bookshelf, Concord, NH, 1990. 25 pp., illus. Soft covers. $9.95.

First quantitative, documented look at actual police experience with 9mm and 45 police service automatics.

The Sharpshooter—How to Stand and Shoot Handgun Metallic Silhouettes, by Charles Stephens, Yucca Tree Press, Las Cruces, NM, 1993. 86 pp., illus. Paper covers. $10.00.

A narration of some of the author's early experiences in silhouette shooting, plus how-to information.

Shooting Colt Single Actions, by Mike Venturino, Livingston, MT, 1997. 205 pp., illus. Paper covers. $25.00

A definitive work on the famous Colt SAA and the ammunition it shoots.

Sig/Sauer Handguns, by Duncan Long, Desert Publications, El Dorado, AZ, 1995. 150 pp., illus. Paper covers. $16.95.

The history of Sig/Sauer handguns, including Sig, Sig-Hammerli and Sig/Sauer variants.

Sixgun Cartridges and Loads, by Elmer Keith, reprint edition by The Gun Room Press, Highland Park, NJ, 1984. 151 pp., illus. $24.95.

A manual covering the selection, use and loading of the most suitable and popular revolver cartridges.

Sixguns, by Elmer Keith, Wolfe Publishing Company, Prescott, AZ, 1992. 336 pp. Paper covers. $29.95. Hardcover $35.00

The history, selection, repair, care, loading, and use of this historic frontiersman's friend—the one-hand firearm.

Smith & Wesson's Automatics, by Larry Combs, Desert Publications, El Dorado, AZ, 1994. 143 pp., illus. Paper covers. $19.95.

A must for every S&W auto owner or prospective owner.

Spanish Handguns: The History of Spanish Pistols and Revolvers, by Gene Gangarosa, Jr., Stoeger Publishing Co., Accokeek, MD, 2001. 320 pp., illustrated. B & W photos. Paper covers. $21.95

Street Stoppers: The Latest Handgun Stopping Power Street Results, by Evan P. Marshall & Edwin J. Sandow, Paladin Press, Boulder, CO, 1997. 392 pp., illus. Paper covers. $42.95.

Compilation of the results of real-life shooting incidents involving every major handgun caliber.

The Tactical 1911, by Dave Lauck, Paladin Press, Boulder, CO, 1999. 152 pp., illustrated. Paper covers. $22.00.

The cop's and SWAT operator's guide to employment and maintenance.

The Tactical Pistol, by Gabriel Suarez with a foreword by Jeff Cooper, Paladin Press, Boulder, CO, 1996. 216 pp., illus. Paper covers. $25.00.

Advanced gunfighting concepts and techniques.

The Thompson/Center Contender Pistol, by Charles Tephens, Paladin Press, Boulder, CO, 1997. 58 pp., illus. Paper covers. $14.00.

How to tune and time, load and shoot accurately with the Contender pistol.

The .380 Enfield No. 2 Revolver, by Mark Stamps and Ian Skennerton, I.D.S.A. Books, Piqua, OH, 1993. 124 pp., 80 illus. Paper covers. $19.95.

The Truth AboUt Handguns, by Duane Thomas, Paladin Press, Boulder, CO, 1997. 136 pp., illus. Paper covers. $18.00.

Exploding the myths, hype, and misinformation about handguns.

Walther Pistols: Models 1 Through P99, Factory Variations and Copies, by Dieter H. Marschall, Ucross Books, Los Alamos, NM. 2000. 140 pages, with 140 b & w illustrations, index. Paper Covers. $19.95.

This is the English translation, revised and updated, of the highly successful and widely acclaimed German language edition. This book provides the collector with a reference guide and overview of the entire line of the Walther military, police, and self-defense pistols from the very first to the very latest. Models 1-9, PP, PPK, MP, AP, HP, P.38, P1, P4, P38K, P5, P88, P99 and the Manurhin models. Variations, where issued, serial ranges, calibers, marks, proofs, logos, and design aspects in an astonishing quantity and variety are crammed into this very well researched and highly regarded work.

U.S. Handguns of World War 2, The Secondary Pistols and Revolvers, by Charles W. Pate, Mowbray Publishers, Lincoln, RI, 1997. 368 pp., illus. $39.00.

This indispensable new book covers all of the American military handguns of W.W.2 except for the M1911A1.

HUNTING

NORTH AMERICA

Advanced Black Powder Hunting, by Toby Bridges, Stoeger Publishing Co., Wayne, NJ, 1998. 288 pp., illus. Paper covers. $21.95.

The first modern day publication to be filled from cover to cover with guns, loads, projectiles, accessories and the techniques to get the most from today's front loading guns.

Advanced Strategies for Trophy Whitetails, by David Morris, Safari Press, Inc., Huntington Beach, CA, 1999. 399 pp., illustrated. $29.95.

This book is a must-have for any serious trophy hunter.

After the Hunt With Lovett Williams, by Lovett Williams, Krause Publications, Iola, WI, 1996. 256 pp., illus. Paper covers. $15.95.

The author carefully instructs you on how to prepare your trophy turkey for a trip to the taxidermist. Plus help on planning a grand slam hunt.

Aggressive Whitetail Hunting, by Greg Miller, Krause Publications, Iola, WI, 1995. 208 pp., illus. Paper covers. $14.95.

Learn how to hunt trophy bucks in public forests, private farmlands and exclusive hunting grounds from one of America's foremost hunters.

All About Bears, by Duncan Gilchrist, Stoneydale Press Publishing Co., Stevensville, MT, 1989. 176 pp., illus. $19.95.

Covers all kinds of bears—black, grizzly, Alaskan brown, polar and leans on a lifetime of hunting and guiding experiences to explore proper hunting techniques.

American Duck Shooting, by George Bird Grinnell, Stackpole Books, Harrisburg, PA, 1991. 640 pp., illus. Paper covers. $19.95.

First published in 1901 at the height of the author's career. Describes 50 species of waterfowl, and discusses hunting methods common at the turn of the century.

American Hunting and Fishing Books, 1800-1970, Volume 1, by Morris Heller, Nimrod and Piscator Press, Mesilla, NM, 1997. 220 pp., illus. A limited, numbered edition. $125.00.

An up-to-date, profusely illustrated, annotated bibliography on American hunting and fishing books and booklets.

The American Wild Turkey, Hunting Tactics and Techniques, by John McDaniel, The Lyons Press, New York, NY, 2000. 240 pp., illustrated. $29.95.

Loaded with turkey hunting anectdotes gleaned from a lifetime of experience.

American Wingshooting: A Twentieth Century Pictorial Saga, by Ben O. Williams, Willow Creek Press, Minocqua, WI, 2000. 160 pp., illustrated with 180 color photographs. $35.00.

A beautifully photographed celebration of upland bird hunting now and how as it once existed.

The Art of Super-Accurate Hunting with Scoped Rifles, by Don Judd, Wolfe Publishing Co., Prescott, AZ, 1996. 99 pp., illus. Paper covers. $14.95.

The philosophy of super-accurate hunting and the rewards of making your shot a trophy.

As I Look Back; Musings of a Birdhunter, by Robert Branen, Safari Press, Inc., Huntington Beach, CA, 1999. Limited, signed and numbered edition. $60.00.

The author shares his recollections of bird hunting around the world.

Autumn Passages, Compiled by the editors of Ducks Unlimited Magazine, Willow Creek Press, Minocqua, WI, 1997. 320 pp. $27.50.

An exceptional collection of duck hunting stories.

Awesome Antlers of North America, by Odie Sudbeck, HTW Publications, Seneca, KS, 1993. 150 pp., illus. $35.00.

500 world-class bucks in color and black and white. This book starts up where the Boone & Crockett recordbook leaves off.

Backtracking, by I.T. Taylor, Safari Press, Inc., Huntington Beach, CA, 1998. 201 pp., illustrated. $24.95.

Reminiscences of a hunter's life in rural America.

Bare November Days, by George Bird Evans et al, Countrysport Press, Traverse City, MI, 1992. 136 pp., illus. $39.50.

A new, original anthology, a tribute to ruffed grouse, king of upland birds.

Bear Attacks, by K. Etling, Safari Press, Long Beach, CA, 1998. 574 pp., illus. In 2 volumes. $75.00.

Classic tales of dangerous North American bears.

The Bear Hunter's Century, by Paul Schullery, Stackpole Books, Harrisburg, PA, 1989. 240 pp., illus. $19.95.

Thrilling tales of the bygone days of wilderness hunting.

The Best of Babcock, by Havilah Babcock, selected and with an introduction by Hugh Grey, The Gunnerman Press, Auburn Hills, MI, 1985. 262 pp., illus. $19.95.

A treasury of memorable pieces, 21 of which have never before appeared in book form.

The Best of Nash Buckingham, by Nash Buckingham, selected, edited and annotated by George Bird Evans, Winchester Press, Piscataway, NJ, 1973. 320 pp., illus. $35.00.

Thirty pieces that represent the very cream of Nash's output on his whole range of outdoor interests—upland shooting, duck hunting, even fishing.

Better on a Rising Tide, by Tom Kelly, Lyons & Burford Publishers, New York, NY, 1995. 184 pp. $22.95.

Tales of wild turkeys, turkey hunting and Southern folk.

Big Bucks the Benoit Way, by Bryce Towsley, Krause Publications Iola, WI, 1998. 208 pp., illus. $24.95.

Secrets from America's first family of whitetail hunting.

Big December Canvasbacks, by Worth Mathewson, Sand Lake Press, Amity, OR, 1997. 171 pp., illus. By David Hagenbaumer. Limited, signed and numbered edition. $29.95.

Duck hunting stories.

Big Game Hunting, by Duncan Gilchrist, Outdoor Expeditions, books and videos, Corvallis, MT, 1999. 192 pp., illustrated. $14.95

Designed to be a warehouse of hunting information covering the major North American big game species.

Big Woods, by William Faulkner, wilderness adventures, Gallatin Gateway, MT, 1998. 208 pp., illus. Slipcased. $60.00.

A collection of Faulkner's best hunting stories that belongs in the library of every sportsman.

THE ARMS LIBRARY

Birdhunter, by Richard S. Grozik, Safari Press, Huntington Beach, CA, 1998. 180 pp., illus. Limited, numbered and signed edition. Slipcased. $60.00.
An entertaining salute to the closeness between man and his dog, man and his gun, and man and the great outdoors.

Bird Dog Days, Wingshooting Ways, by Archibald Rutledge, edited by Jim Casada, Wilderness Adventure Press, Gallatin Gateway, MT, 1998. 200 pp., illus. $35.00.
One of the most popular and enduring outdoor writers of this century, the poet laureate of South Carolina.

Birds on the Horizon, by Stuart Williams, Countrysport Press, Traverse City, MI, 1993. 288 pp., illus. $49.50.
Wingshooting adventures around the world.

Blacktail Trophy Tactics, by Boyd Iverson, Stoneydale Press, Stevensville, MI, 1992. 166 pp., illus. Paper covers. $14.95.
A comprehensive analysis of blacktail deer habits, describing a deer's and man's use of scents, still hunting, tree techniques, etc.

Boone & Crockett Club's 23rd Big Game Awards, 1995-1997, Boone & Crockett Club, Missoula, MT, 1999. 600 pp., illustrated with black & white photographs plus a 16 page color section. $39.95.
A complete listing of the 3,511 trophies accepted in the 23rd Awards Entry Period.

Bowhunter's Handbook, Expert Strategies and Techniques, by M.R. James with Fred Asbell, Dave Holt, Dwight Schuh & Dave Samuel, DBI Books, a division of Krause Publications, Iola, WI, 1997. 256 pp., illus. Paper covers. $19.95.
Tips from the top on taking your bowhunting skills to the next level.

The Buffalo Harvest, by Frank Mayer as told to Charles Roth, Pioneer Press, Union City, TN, 1995. 96 pp., illus. Paper covers. $8.50.
The story of a hide hunter during his buffalo hunting days on the plains.

Bugling for Elk, by Dwight Schuh, Stoneydale Press Publishing Co., Stevensville, MT, 1983. 162 pp., illus. $18.95.
A complete guide to early season elk hunting.

Call of the Quail: A Tribute to the Gentleman Game Bird, by Michael McIntosh, et al., Countrysport Press, Traverse City, MI, 1990. 175 pp., illus. $35.00.
A new anthology on quail hunting.

Calling All Elk, by Jim Zumbo, Cody, WY, 1989. 169 pp., illus. Paper covers. $14.95.
The only book on the subject of elk hunting that covers every aspect of elk vocalization.

Campfires and Game Trails: Hunting North American Big Game, by Craig Boddington, Winchester Press, Piscataway, NJ, 1985. 295 pp., illus. $23.95.
How to hunt North America's big game species.

Come October, by Gene Hill et al, Countrysport Press, Inc., Traverse City, MI, 1991. 176 pp., illus. $39.50.
A new and all-original anthology on the woodcock and woodcock hunting.

The Complete Book of Grouse Hunting, by Frank Woolner, The Lyons Press, New York, NY, 2000. 192 pp., illustrated Paper covers. $24.95.
The history, habits, and habitat of one of America's great game birds—and the methods used to hunt it.

The Complete Book of Mule Deer Hunting, by Walt Prothero, The Lyons Press, New York, NY, 2000. 192 pp., illustrated. Paper covers. $24.95.
Field-tested practical advice on how to bag the trophy buck of a lifetime.

The Complete Book of Wild Turkey Hunting, by John Trout Jr., The Lyons Press, New York, NY, 2000. 192 pp., illustrated. Paper covers. $24.95.
An illustrated guide to hunting for one of America's most popular game birds.

The Complete Book of Woodcock Hunting, by Frank Woolner, The Lyons Press, New York, NY, 2000. 192 pp., illustrated. Paper covers. $24.95.
A thorough, practical guide to the American woodcock and to woodcock hunting.

The Complete Guide to Bird Dog Training, by John R. Falk, Lyons & Burford, New York, NY, 1994. 288 pp., illus. $22.95.
The latest on live-game field training techniques using released quail and recall pens. A new chapter on the services available for entering field trials and other bird dog competitions.

The Complete Guide to Game Care & Cookery, 3rd Edition, by Sam Fadala, DBI Books, a division of Krause Publications, Iola, WI, 1994. 320 pp., illus. Paper covers. $18.95.
Over 500 photos illustrating the care of wild game in the field and at home with a separate recipe section providing over 400 tested recipes.

The Complete Smoothbore Hunter, by Brook Elliot, Winchester Press, Piscataway, NJ, 1986. 240 pp., illus. $16.95.
Advice and information on guns and gunning for all varieties of game.

The Complete Venison Cookbook from Field to Table, by Jim & Ann Casada, Krause Publications, Iola, WI, 1996. 208 pp., Comb-bound. $12.95.
More than 200 kitchen tested recipes make this book the answer to a table full of hungry hunters or guests.

Coveys and Singles: The Handbook of Quail Hunting, by Robert Gooch, A.S. Barnes, San Diego, CA, 1981. 196 pp., illus. $11.95.
The story of the quail in North America.

Coyote Hunting, by Phil Simonski, Stoneydale Press, Stevensville, MT, 1994. 126 pp., illus. Paper covers. $12.95.
Probably the most thorough "How-to-do-it" book on coyote hunting ever written.

Dabblers & Divers: A Duck Hunter's Book, compiled by the editors of Ducks Unlimited Magazine, Willow Creek Press, Minocqua, WI, 1997. 160 pp., illus. $39.95.
A word-and-photographic portrayal of waterfowl hunter's singular intimacy with, and passion for, watery haunts and wildfowl.

Dancers in the Sunset Sky, by Robert F. Jones, The Lyons Press, New York, NY, 1997. 192 pp., illus. $22.95.
The musings of a bird hunter.

Deer & Deer Hunting, by Al Hofacker, Krause Publications, Iola, WI, 1993. 208 pp., illus. $34.95.
Coffee-table volume packed full of how-to-information that will guide hunts for years to come.

Deer and Deer Hunting: The Serious Hunter's Guide, by Dr. Robert Wegner, Stackpole Books, Harrisburg, PA, 1984. 384 pp., illus. Paper covers. $18.95.
In-depth information from the editor of "Deer & Deer Hunting" magazine. Major bibliography of English language books on deer and deer hunting from 1838-1984.

Deer and Deer Hunting Book 2, by Dr. Robert Wegner, Stackpole Books, Harrisburg, PA, 1987. 400 pp., illus. Paper covers. $18.95.
Strategies and tactics for the advanced hunter.

Deer and Deer Hunting, Book 3, by Dr. Robert Wegner, Stackpole Books, Harrisburg, PA, 1990. 368 pp., illus. $18.95.
This comprehensive volume covers natural history, deer hunting lore, profiles of deer hunters, and discussion of important issues facing deer hunters today.

The Deer Hunters: The Tactics, Lore, Legacy and Allure of American Deer Hunting, Edited by Patrick Durkin, Krause Publications, Iola, WI, 1997. 208 pp., illus. $29.95.
More than twenty years of research from America's top whitetail hunters, researchers, and photographers have gone in to the making of this book.

Deer Hunting, by R. Smith, Stackpole Books, Harrisburg, PA, 1978. 224 pp., illus. Paper covers. $14.95.
A professional guide leads the hunt for North America's most popular big game animal.

Doves and Dove Shooting, by Byron W. Dalrymple, New Win Publishing, Inc., Hampton, NJ, 1992. 256 pp., illus. $17.95.
The author reveals in this classic book his penchant for observing, hunting, and photographing this elegantly fashioned bird.

Dove Hunting, by Charley Dickey, Galahad Books, NY, 1976. 112 pp., illus. $10.00.
This indispensable guide for hunters deals with equipment, techniques, types of dove shooting, hunting dogs, etc.

Dreaming the Lion, by Thomas McIntyre, Countrysport Press, Traverse City, MI, 1994. 309 pp., illus. $35.00.
Reflections on hunting, fishing and a search for the wild. Twenty-three stories by *Sports Afield* editor, Tom McIntyre.

Duck Decoys and How to Rig Them, by Ralf Coykendall, revised by Ralf Coykendall, Jr., Nick Lyons Books, New York, NY, 1990. 137 pp., illus. Paper covers. $14.95.
Sage and practical advice on the art of decoying ducks and geese.

The Duck Hunter's Handbook, by Bob Hinman, revised, expanded, updated edition, Winchester Press, Piscataway, NJ, 1985. 288 pp., illus. $15.95.
The duck hunting book that has it all.

Eastern Upland Shooting, by Dr. Charles C. Norris, Countrysport Press, Traverse City, MI, 1990. 424 pp., illus. $49.00.
A new printing of this 1946 classic with a new, original Foreword by the author's friend and hunting companion, renowned author George Bird Evans.

Elk and Elk Hunting, by Hart Wixom, Stackpole Books, Harrisburg, PA, 1986. 288 pp., illus. $34.95.
Your practical guide to fundamentals and fine points of elk hunting.

Elk Hunting in the Northern Rockies, by Ed. Wolff, Stoneydale Press, Stevensville, MT, 1984. 162 pp., illus. $18.95.
Helpful information about hunting the premier elk country of the northern Rocky Mountain states—Wyoming, Montana and Idaho.

Elk Hunting with the Experts, by Bob Robb, Stoneydale Press, Stevensville, MT, 1992. 176 pp., illus. Paper covers. $15.95.
A complete guide to elk hunting in North America by America's top elk hunting expert.

Elk Rifles, Cartridges and Hunting Tactics, by Wayne van Zwoll, Larsen's Outdoor Publishing, Lakeland, FL, 1992. 414 pp., illus. $24.95.
The definitive work on which rifles and cartridges are proper for hunting elk plus the tactics for hunting them.

Encyclopedia of Deer, by G. Kenneth Whitehead, Safari Press, Huntington, CA, 1993. 704 pp., illus. $130.00.
This massive tome will be the reference work on deer for well into the next century.

A Fall of Woodcock, by Tom Huggler, Countrysport Press, Selman, AL, 1997. 256 pp., illus. $39.00.
A book devoted to the woodcock and to those who await his return to their favorite converts each autumn.

Firelight, by Burton L. Spiller, Gunnerman Press, Auburn Hills, MI, 1990. 196 pp., illus. $19.95.
Enjoyable tales of the outdoors and stalwart companions.

Following the Flight, by Charles S. Potter, Countrysport Books, Selma, AL, 1999. 130 pp., illustrated. $25.00.
The great waterfowl passage and the experiences of a young man who has lived their migration come to life in the pages of this book.

Fresh Looks at Deer Hunting, by Byron W. Dalrymple, New Win Publishing, Inc., Hampton, NJ, 1993. 288 pp., illus. $24.95.
Tips and techniques abound throughout the pages of this latest work by Mr. Dalrymple whose name is synonymous with hunting proficiency.

From the Peace to the Fraser, by Prentis N. Gray, Boone and Crockett Club, Missoula, MT, 1995. 400 pp., illus. $49.95.
Newly discovered North American hunting and exploration journals from 1900 to 1930.

Fur Trapping In North America, by Steven Geary, Winchester Press, Piscataway, NJ, 1985. 160 pp., illus. Paper covers. $19.95.
A comprehensive guide to techniques and equipment, together with fascinating facts about fur bearers.

Getting the Most Out of Modern Waterfowling, by John O. Cartier, St. Martin's Press, NY, 1974. 396 pp., illus. $29.95.
The most comprehensive, up-to-date book on waterfowling imaginable.

Getting a Stand, by Miles Gilbert, Pioneer Press, Union City, TN, 1993. 204 pp., illus. Paper covers. $13.95.
An anthology of 18 short personal experiences by buffalo hunters of the late 1800s, specifically from 1870-1882.

The Gordon MacQuarrie Sporting Treasury. Introduction and commentary by Zack Taylor. Countrysport Press, Selman, AL, 1999. $29.50.
Hunting and fishing masterpieces you can read over and over.

Gordon MacQuarrie Trilogy: Stories of the Old Duck Hunters, by Gordon MacQuarrie, Willow Creek Press, Minocqua, WI, 1994. $49.00.
A slip-cased three volume set of masterpieces by one of America's finest outdoor writers.

The Grand Passage: A Chronicle of North American Waterfowling, by Gene Hill, et al., Countrysport Press, Traverse City, MI, 1990. 175 pp., illus. $35.00.
A new original anthology by renowned sporting authors on our world of waterfowling.

Greatest Elk; The Complete Historical and Illustrated Record of North America's Biggest Elk, by R. Selner, Safari Press, Huntington Beach, CA, 2000. 209 pages, profuse color illus. $39.95
Here is the book all elk hunters have been waiting for! This oversized book holds the stories and statistics of the biggest bulls ever killed in North America. Stunning, full-color photographs highlight over 40 world-class heads, including the old world records!

Grouse and Woodcock, A Gunner's Guide, by Don Johnson, Krause Publications, Iola, WI, 1995. 256 pp., illus. Paper covers. $14.95.
Find out what you need in guns, ammo, equipment, dogs and terrain.

Grouse of North America, by Tom Huggler, NorthWord Press, Inc., Minocqua, WI, 1990. 160 pp., illus. $29.95.
A cross-continental hunting guide.

Grouse Hunter's Guide, by Dennis Walrod, Stackpole Books, Harrisburg, PA, 1985. 192 pp., illus. $19.95.
Solid facts, observations, and insights on how to hunt the ruffed grouse.

Gunning for Sea Ducks, by George Howard Gillelan, Tidewater Publishers, Centreville, MD, 1988. 144 pp., illus. $14.95.
A book that introduces you to a practically untouched arena of waterfowling.

Heartland Trophy Whitetails, by Odie Sudbeck, HTW Publications, Seneca, KS, 1992. 130 pp., illus. $34.95.
A completely revised and expanded edition which includes over 500 photos of Boone & Crockett class whitetail, major mulies and unusual racks.

The Heck with Moose Hunting, by Jim Zumbo, Wapiti Valley Publishing Co., Cody, WY, 1996. 199 pp., illus. $17.95.
Jim's hunts around the continent including encounters with moose, caribou, sheep, antelope and mountain goats.

High Pressure Elk Hunting, by Mike Lapinski, Stoneydale Press Publishing Co., Stevensville, MT, 1996. 192 pp., illus. $19.95.
The secrets of hunting educated elk revealed.

Hill Country, by Gene Hill, Countrysport Press, Traverse City, MI, 1996. 180 pp., illus. $25.00.
Stories about hunting, fishing, dogs and guns.

Home from the Hill, by Fred Webb, Safari Press, Huntington Beach, CA, 1997. 283 pp., illus. Limited edition, signed and numbered. In a slipcase. $50.00.
The story of a big-game guide in the Canadian wilderness.

Horns in the High Country, by Andy Russell, Alfred A. Knopf, NY, 1973. 259 pp., illus. Paper covers. $12.95.
A many-sided view of wild sheep and their natural world.

How to Hunt, by Dave Bowring, Winchester Press, Piscataway, NJ, 1982. 208 pp., illus. Hardcover $15.00.
A basic guide to hunting big game, small game, upland birds, and waterfowl.

Hunt Alaska Now: Self-Guiding for Trophy Moose & Caribou, by Dennis W. Confer, Wily Ventures, Anchorage, AK, 1997. 309 pp., illus. Paper covers. $26.95.
How to plan affordable, successfull, safe hunts you can do yourself.

The Hunters and the Hunted, by George Laycock, Outdoor Life Books, New York, NY, 1990. 280 pp., illus. $34.95.
The pursuit of game in America from Indian times to the present.

A Hunter's Fireside Book, by Gene Hill, Winchester Press, Piscataway, NJ, 1972. 192 pp., illus. $17.95.
An outdoor book that will appeal to every person who spends time in the field—or who wishes he could.

A Hunter's Road, by Jim Fergus, Henry Holt & Co., NY, 1992. 290 pp. $22.50
A journey with gun and dog across the American uplands.

Hunt High for Rocky Mountain Goats, Bighorn Sheep, Chamois & Tahr, by Duncan Gilchrist, Stoneydale Press, Stevensville, MT, 1992. 192 pp., illus. Paper covers. $19.95.
The source book for hunting mountain goats.

The Hunter's Shooting Guide, by Jack O'Connor, Outdoor Life Books, New York, NY, 1982. 176 pp., illus. Paper covers. $9.95.
A classic covering rifles, cartridges, shooting techniques for shotguns/rifles/handguns.

The Hunter's World, by Charles F. Waterman, Winchester Press, Piscataway, NJ, 1983. 250 pp., illus. $29.95.
A classic. One of the most beautiful hunting books that has ever been produced.

Hunting Adventure of Me and Joe, by Walt Prothero, Safari Press, Huntington Beach, CA, 1995. 220 pp., illus. $22.50.
A collection of the author's best and favorite stories.

Hunting America's Game Animals and Birds, by Robert Elman and George Peper, Winchester Press, Piscataway, NJ, 1975. 368 pp., illus. $16.95.
A how-to, where-to, when-to guide—by 40 top experts—covering the continent's big, small, upland game and waterfowl.

Hunting Ducks and Geese, by Steven Smith, Stackpole Books, Harrisburg, PA, 1984. 160 pp., illus. $19.95.
Hard facts, good bets, and serious advice from a duck hunter you can trust.

Hunting for Handgunners, by Larry Kelly and J.D. Jones, DBI Books, a division of Krause Publications, Iola, WI, 1990. 256 pp., illus. Soft covers. $16.95.
A definitive work on an increasingly popular sport.

Hunting in Many Lands, edited by Theodore Roosevelt and George Bird Grinnell, et al., Boone & Crockett Club, Dumphries, VA, 1990. 447 pp., illus. $40.00.
A limited edition reprinting of the original Boone & Crockett Club 1895 printing.

Hunting Mature Bucks, by Larry L. Weishuhn, Krause Publications, Iola, WI, 1995. 256 pp., illus. $14.95.
One of North America's top white-tailed deer authorities shares his expertise on hunting those big, smart and elusive bucks.

Hunting Open-Country Mule Deer, by Dwight Schuh, Sage Press, Nampa, ID, 1989. 180 pp., illus. $18.95.
A guide taking Western bucks with rifle and bow.

Hunting Predators for Hides and Profits, by Wilf E. Pyle, Stoeger Publishing Co., So. Hackensack, NJ, 1985. 224 pp., illus. Paper covers. $11.95.
The author takes the hunter through every step of the hunting/marketing process.

Hunting the American Wild Turkey, by Dave Harbour, Stackpole Books, Harrisburg, PA, 1975. 256 pp., illus. $24.95.
The techniques and tactics of hunting North America's largest, and most popular, woodland game bird.

Hunting the Rockies, Home of the Giants, by Kirk Darner, Marceline, MO, 1996. 291 pp., illus. $25.00.
Understand how and where to hunt Western game in the Rockies.

Hunting the Sun, by Ted Nelson Lundrigan, Countrysport Press, Selma, AL, 1997. 240 pp., illus. $30.00.
One of the best books on grouse and woodcock ever published.

Hunting Trips in North America, by F.C. Selous, Wolfe Publishing Co., Prescott, AZ, 1988. 395 pp., illus. $52.00.
A limited edition reprint. Coverage of caribou, moose and other big game hunting in virgin wilds.

Hunting Trophy Deer, by John Wootters, The Lyons Press, New York, NY, 1997. 272 pp., illus. $24.95.
A revised edition of the definitive manual for identifying, scouting, and successfully hunting a deer of a lifetime.

Hunting Trophy Whitetails, by David Morris, Stoneydale Press, Stevensville, MT, 1993. 483 pp., illus. $29.95.
This is one of the best whitetail books published in the last two decades. The author is the former editor of *North American Whitetail* magazine.

Hunting Upland Birds, by Charles F. Waterman, Countrysport Press, Selma, AL, 1997. 220 pp., illus. $30.00.
Originally published a quarter of a century ago, this classic has been newly updated with the latest information for today's wingshooter.

Hunting Western Deer, by Jim and Wes Brown, Stoneydale Press, Stevensville, MT, 1994. 174 pp., illus. Paper covers. $14.95.
A pair of expert Oregon hunters provide insight into hunting mule deer and blacktail deer in the western states.

Hunting Wild Turkeys in the West, by John Higley, Stoneydale Press, Stevensville, MT, 1992. 154 pp., illus. Paper covers. $12.95.
Covers the basics of calling, locating and hunting turkeys in the western states.

Hunting with the Twenty-two, by Charles Singer Landis, R&R Books, Livonia, NY, 1994. 429 pp., illus. $35.00.
A miscellany of articles touching on the hunting and shooting of small game.

I Don't Want to Shoot an Elephant, by Havilah Babcock, The Gunnerman Press, Auburn Hills, MI, 1985. 184 pp., illus. $19.95.
Eighteen delightful stories that will enthrall the upland gunner for many pleasureable hours.

In Search of the Buffalo, by Charles G. Anderson, Pioneer Press, Union City, TN, 1996. 144 pp., illus. Paper covers. $13.95.
The primary study of the life of J. Wright Mooar, one of the few hunters fortunate enough to kill a white buffalo.

In Search of the Wild Turkey, by Bob Gooch, Great Lakes Living Press, Ltd., Waukegan, IL, 1978. 182 pp., illus. $9.95.
A state-by-state guide to wild turkey hot spots, with tips on gear and methods for bagging your bird.

In the Turkey Woods, by Jerome B. Robinson, The Lyons Press, N.Y., 1998. 207 pp., illustrated. $24.95.
Practical expert advice on all aspects of turkey hunting—from calls to decoys to guns.

Indian Hunts and Indian Hunters of the Old West, by Dr. Frank C. Hibben, Safari Press, Long Beach, CA, 1989. 228 pp., illus. $24.95.
Tales of some of the most famous American Indian hunters of the Old West as told to the author by an old Navajo hunter.

THE ARMS LIBRARY

Jack O'Connor's Gun Book, by Jack O'Connor, Wolfe Publishing Company, Prescott, AZ, 1992. 208 pp. Hardcover. $26.00.
Jack O'Connor imparts a cross-section of his knowledge on guns and hunting. Brings back some of his writings that have here-to-fore been lost.

Jaybirds Go to Hell on Friday, by Havilah Babcock, The Gunnerman Press, Auburn Hills, MI, 1985. 149 pp., illus. $19.95.
Sixteen jewels that reestablish the lost art of good old-fashioned yarn telling.

Last Casts and Stolen Hunts, edited by Jim Casada and Chuck Wechsler, Countrysport Press, Traverse City, MI, 1994. 270 pp., illus. $29.95.
The world's best hunting and fishing stories by writers such as Zane Grey, Jim Corbett, Jack O'Connor, Archibald Rutledge and others.

A Listening Walk...and Other Stories, by Gene Hill, Winchester Press, Piscataway, NJ, 1985. 208 pp., illus. $17.95.
Vintage Hill. Over 60 stories.

Longbows in the Far North, by E. Donnall Thomas, Jr. Stackpole Books, Mechanicsburg, PA, 1994. 200 pp., illus. $18.95.
An archer's adventures in Alaska and Siberia.

Mammoth Monarchs of North America, by Odie Sudbeck, HTW Publications, Seneca, KA, 1995. 288 pp., illus. $35.00.
This book reveals eye-opening big buck secrets.

Matching the Gun to the Game, by Clair Rees, Winchester Press, Piscataway, NJ, 1982. 272 pp., illus. $17.95.
Covers selection and use of handguns, blackpowder firearms for hunting, matching rifle type to the hunter, calibers for multiple use, tailoring factory loads to the game.

Measuring and Scoring North American Big Game Trophies, 2nd Edition, by Wm. H. Nesbitt and Philip L. Wright, The Boone & Crockett Club, Missoula, MT, 1999. 150 pp., illustrated. $34.95.
The definitive manual for anyone wanting to learn the Club's world-famous big game measuring system.

Meditation on Hunting, by Jose Ortego y Gasset, Wilderness Adventures Press, Bozeman, MT, 1996. 140 pp., illus. In a slipcase. $60.00.
The classic work on the philosophy of hunting.

Montana—Land of Giant Rams, by Duncan Gilchrist, Stoneydale Press Publishing Co., Stevensville, MT, 1990. 208 pp., illus. $19.95.
Latest information on Montana bighorn sheep and why so many Montana bighorn rams are growing to trophy size.

Montana—Land of Giant Rams, Volume 2, by Duncan Gilchrist, Outdoor Expeditions and Books, Corvallis, MT, 1992. 208 pp., illus. $34.95.
The reader will find stories of how many of the top-scoring trophies were taken.

Montana—Land of Giant Rams, Volume 3, by Duncan Gilchrist, Outdoor Expeditions, books and videos, Corvallis, MT, 1999. 224 pp., illus. Paper covers. $19.95.
All new sheep information including over 70 photos. Learn about how Montana became the "Land of Giant Rams" and what the prospects of the future as we enter a new millenium.

More Grouse Feathers, by Burton L. Spiller, Crown Publ., NY, 1972. 238 pp., illus. $25.00.
Facsimile of the original Derrydale Press issue of 1938. Guns and dogs, the habits and shooting of grouse, woodcock, ducks, etc. Illus. by Lynn Bogue Hunt.

More Tracks: 78 Years of Mountains, People & Happiness, by Howard Copenhaver, Stoneydale Press, Stevensville, MT, 1992. 150 pp., illus. $18.95.
A collection of stories by one of the back country's best storytellers about the people who shared with Howard his great adventure in the high places and wild Montana country.

Moss, Mallards and Mules, by Robert Brister, Countrysport Books, Selma, AL, 1998. 216 pp., illustrated by David Maass. $30.00.
Twenty-seven short stories on hunting and fishing on the Gulf Coast.

Mostly Huntin', by Bill Jordan, Everett Publishing Co., Bossier City, LA, 1987. 254 pp., illus. $21.95.
Jordan's hunting adventures in North America, Africa, Australia, South America and Mexico.

Mostly Tailfeathers, by Gene Hill, Winchester Press, Piscataway, NJ, 1975. 192 pp., illus. $17.95.
An interesting, general book about bird hunting.

"Mr. Buck": The Autobiography of Nash Buckingham, by Nash Buckingham, Countrysport Press, Traverse City, MI, 1990. 288 pp., illus. $40.00.
A lifetime of shooting, hunting, dogs, guns, and Nash's reflections on the sporting life, along with previously unknown pictures and stories written especially for this book.

Mule Deer: Hunting Today's Trophies, by Tom Carpenter and Jim Van Norman, Krause Publications, Iola, WI, 1998. 256 pp., illustrated. Paper covers. $19.95.
A tribute to both the deer and the people who hunt them. Includes info on where to look for big deer, prime mule deer habitat and effective weapons for the hunt.

Murry Burnham's Hunting Secrets, by Murry Burnham with Russell Tinsley, Winchester Press, Piscataway, NJ, 1984. 244 pp., illus. $17.95.
One of the great hunters of our time gives the reasons for his success in the field.

My Health is Better in November, by Havilah Babcock, University of S. Carolina Press, Columbia, SC, 1985. 284 pp., illus. $24.95.
Adventures in the field set in the plantation country and backwater streams of SC.

North American Big Game Animals, by Byron W. Dalrymple and Erwin Bauer, Outdoor Life Books/Stackpole Books, Harrisburg, PA, 1985. 258 pp., illus. $29.95.
Complete illustrated natural histories. Habitat, movements, breeding, birth and development, signs, and hunting.

North American Elk: Ecology and Management, edited by Jack Ward Thomas and Dale E. Toweill, Stackpole Books, Harrisburg, PA, 1982. 576 pp., illus. $39.95.
The definitive, exhaustive, classic work on the North American elk.

The North American Waterfowler, by Paul S. Bernsen, Superior Publ. Co., Seattle, WA, 1972. 206 pp. Paper covers. $9.95.
The complete inside and outside story of duck and goose shooting. Big and colorful, illustrations by Les Kouba.

Of Bears and Man, by Mike Cramond, University of Oklahoma Press, Norman, OK, 1986. 433 pp., illus. $29.95.
The author's lifetime association with bears of North America. Interviews with survivors of bear attacks.

The Old Man and the Boy, by Robert Ruark, Henry Holt & Co., New York, NY, 303 pp., illus. $24.95.
A timeless classic, telling the story of a remarkable friendship between a young boy and his grandfather as they hunt and fish together.

The Old Man's Boy Grows Older, by Robert Ruark, Henry Holt & Co., Inc., New York, NY, 1993. 300 pp., illus. $24.95.
The heartwarming sequel to the best-selling *The Old Man and the Boy*.

Old Wildfowling Tales, Volume 2, edited by Worth Mathewson, Sand Lake Press, Amity, OR, 1996. 240 pp. $21.95.
A collection of duck and geese hunting stories based around accounts from the past.

One Man, One Rifle, One Land; Hunting all Species of Big Game in North America, by J.Y. Jones, Safari Press, Huntington Beach, CA, 2000. 400 pp., illustrated. $59.95.
Journey with J.Y. Jones as he hunts each of the big-game animals of North America—from the polar bear of the high Artic to the jaguar of the low-lands of Mexico—with just one rifle.

161 Waterfowling Secrets, edited by Matt Young, Willow Creek Press, Minocqua, WI, 1997. 78 pp., Paper covers. $10.95.
Time-honored, field-tested waterfowling tips and advice.

The Only Good Bear is a Dead Bear, by Jeanette Hortick Prodgers, Falcon Press, Helena, MT, 1986. 204 pp. Paper covers. $12.50.
A collection of the West's best bear stories.

Outdoor Pastimes of an American Hunter, by Theodore Roosevelt, Stackpole Books, Mechanicsburg, PA, 1994. 480 pp., illus. Paper covers. $18.95.
Stories of hunting big game in the West and notes about animals pursued and observed.

The Outlaw Gunner, by Harry M. Walsh, Tidewater Publishers, Cambridge, MD, 1973. 178 pp., illus. $22.95.
A colorful story of market gunning in both its legal and illegal phases.

Passing a Good Time, by Gene Hill, Countrysport Press, Traverse City, MI, 1996. 200 pp., illus. $25.00.
Filled with insights and observations of guns, dogs and fly rods that make Gene Hill a master essayist.

Pear Flat Philosophies, by Larry Weishuhn, Safari Press, Huntington Beach, CA, 1995. 234 pp., illus. $24.95.
The author describes his more lighthearted adventures and funny anecdotes while out hunting.

Pheasant Days, by Chris Dorsey, Voyageur Press, Stillwater, MN, 1992. 233 pp., illus. $24.95.
The definitive resource on ringnecks. Includes everything from basic hunting techniques to the life cycle of the bird.

Pheasant Hunter's Harvest, by Steve Grooms, Lyons & Burford Publishers, New York, NY, 1990. 180 pp. $22.95.
A celebration of pheasant, pheasant dogs and pheasant hunting. Practical advice from a passionate hunter.

Pheasant Tales, by Gene Hill et al, Countrysport Press, Traverse City, MI, 1996. 202 pp., illus. $39.00.
Charley Waterman, Michael McIntosh and Phil Bourjaily join the author to tell some of the stories that illustrate why the pheasant is America's favorite game bird.

Pheasants of the Mind, by Datus Proper, Wilderness Adventures Press, Bozeman, MT, 1994. 154 pp., illus. $25.00.
No single title sums up the life of the solitary pheasant hunter like this masterful work.

Portraits of Elk Hunting, by Jim Zumbo, Safari Press, Huntington Beach, CA, 2001. 222 pp. illustrated. $39.95
Zumbo has captured in photos as well as in words the essence, charisma, and wonderful components of elk hunting: back-country wilderness camps, sweaty guides, happy hunters, favorite companions, elk woods, and, of course, the majestic elk. Join Zumbo in the uniqueness of the pursuit of the magnificent and noble elk.

Predator Calling with Gerry Blair, by Gerry Blair, Krause Publications, Iola, WI, 1996. 208 pp., illus. Paper covers. $14.95.
Time-tested secrets lure predators closer to your camera or gun.

Proven Whitetail Tactics, by Greg Miller, Krause Publications, Iola, WI, 1997. 224 pp., illus. Paper covers. $19.95.
Proven tactics for scouting, calling and still-hunting whitetail.

Quail Hunting in America, by Tom Huggler, Stackpole Books, Harrisburg, PA, 1987. 288 pp., illus. $22.95.
Tactics for finding and taking bobwhite, valleys, Gambel's Mountain, scaled-blue, and Mearn's quail by season and habitat.

Quest for Dall Rams, by Duncan Gilchrist, Duncan Gilchrist Outdoor Expeditions and Books, Corvallis, MT, 1997. 224 pp., illus. Limited numbered edition. $34.95.
The most complete book of Dall sheep ever written. Covers information on Alaska and provinces with Dall sheep and explains hunting techniques, equipment, etc.

THE ARMS LIBRARY

Quest for Giant Bighorns, by Duncan Gilchrist, Outdoor Expeditions and Books, Corvallis, MT, 1994. 224 pp., illus. Paper covers. $19.95.
How some of the most successful sheep hunters hunt and how some of the best bighorns were taken.

Radical Elk Hunting Strategies, by Mike Lapinski, Stoneydale Press Publishing Co., Stevensville, MT, 1988. 161 pp., illus. $18.95.
Secrets of calling elk in close.

Rattling, Calling & Decoying Whitetails, by Gary Clancy, Edited by Patrick Durkin, Krause Publications, Iola, WI, 2000. 208 pp., illustrated. Paper covers. $19.95.
How to consistently coax big bucks into range.

Records of North American Big Game 11th Edition, with hunting chapters by Craig Boddington, Tom McIntyre and Jim Zumbo, The Boone and Crockett Club, Missoula, MT, 1999. 700 pp., featuring a 32 page color section. $49.95.
Listing over 17,150, of the top trophy big game animals ever recorded. Over 4,000 new listings are featured in this latest edition.

Records of North American Big Game 1932, by Prentis N. Grey, Boone and Crockett Club, Dumfries, VA, 1988. 178 pp., illus. $79.95.
A reprint of the book that started the Club's record keeping for native North American big game.

Records of North American Caribou and Moose, Craig Boddington et al, The Boone & Crockett Club, Missoula, MT, 1997. 250 pp., illus. $24.95.
More than 1,800 caribou listings and more than 1,500 moose listings, organized by the state or Canadian province where they were taken.

Records of North American Elk and Mule Deer, 2nd Edition, edited by Jack and Susan Reneau, Boone & Crockett Club, Missoula, MT, 1996. 360 pp., illus. Paper cover, $18.95; hardcover, $24.95.
Updated and expanded edition featuring more than 150 trophy, field and historical photos of the finest elk and mule deer trophies ever recorded.

Records of North American Sheep, Rocky Mountain Goats and Pronghorn edited by Jack and Susan Reneau, Boone & Crockett Club, Missoula, MT, 1996. 400 pp., illus. Paper cover, $18.95; hardcover, $24.95.
The first B&C Club records book featuring all 3941 accepted wild sheep, Rocky Mountain goats and pronghorn trophies.

Return of Royalty; Wild Sheep of North America, by Dr. Dale E. Toweill and Dr. Valerius Geist, Boone and Crockett Club, Missoula, MT, 1999. 224 pp., illustrated. $59.95.
A celebration of the return of the wild sheep to many of its historical ranges.

The Rifles, the Cartridges, and the Game, by Clay Harvey, Stackpole Books, Harrisburg, PA, 1991. 254 pp., illus. $32.95.
Engaging reading combines with exciting photos to present the hunt with an intense level of awareness and respect.

Ringneck; A Tribute to Pheasants and Pheasant Hunting, by Steve Grooms, Russ Sewell and Dave Nomsen, The Lyons Press, New York, NY, 2000. 120 pp., illustrated. $40.00.
A glorious full-color coffee-table tribute to the pheasant and those who hunt them.

Ringneck! Pheasants & Pheasant Hunting, by Ted Janes, Crown Publ., NY, 1975. 120 pp., illus. $15.95.
A thorough study of one of our more popular game birds.

Rub-Line Secrets, by Greg Miller, edited by Patrick Durkin, Krause Publications, Iola, WI, 1999. 208 pp., illustrated. Paper covers. $19.95.
Based on nearly 30 years experience. Proven tactics for finding, analyzing and hunting big bucks' rub-lines.

Ruffed Grouse, edited by Sally Atwater and Judith Schnell, Stackpole Books, Harrisburg, PA, 1989. 370 pp., illus. $59.95.
Everything you ever wanted to know about the ruffed grouse. More than 25 wildlife professionals provided in-depth information on every aspect of this popular game bird's life. Lavishly illustrated with over 300 full-color photos.

The Russell Annabel Adventure Series, by Russell Annabel, Safari Press, Huntington Beach, CA: Vol. 2, Adventure is My Business, 1951-1955. $35.00, Vol. 3, Adventure is in My Blood, 1957-1964. $35.00, Vol. 4, High Road to Adventure, 1964-1970. $35.00, Vol. 5, The Way We Were, 1970-1979. $35.00.
A complete collection of previously unpublished magazine articles in book form by this gifted outdoor writer.

The Season, by Tom Kelly, Lyons & Burford, New York, NY, 1997. 160 pp., illus. $22.95.
The delight and challenges of a turkey hunter's Spring season.

Secret Strategies from North America's Top Whitetail Hunters, compiled by Nick Sisley, Krause Publications, Iola, WI, 1995. 256 pp., illus. Paper covers. $14.95.
Bow and gun hunters share their success stories.

Secrets of the Turkey Pros, by Glenn Sapir, North American Hunting Club, Minnetonka, MN, 1999. 176 pp., illustrated. $19.95.
This work written by a seasoned turkey hunter draws on the collective knowledge and experience on some of the most renowned names in the world of wild turkey.

Sheep Hunting in Alaska—The Dall Sheep Hunter's Guide, by Tony Russ, Outdoor Expeditions and Books, Corvallis, MT, 1994. 160 pp., illus. Paper covers. $19.95.
A how-to guide for the Dall sheep hunter.

Shorebirds: The Birds, The Hunters, The Decoys, by John M. Levinson & Somers G. Headley, Tidewater Publishers, Centreville, MD, 1991. 160 pp., illus. $49.95.
A thorough study of shorebirds and the decoys used to hunt them. Photographs of more than 200 of the decoys created by prominent carvers are shown.

Shots at Big Game, by Craig Boddington, Stackpole Books, Harrisburg, PA, 1989. 198 pp., illus. $24.95.
How to shoot a rifle accurately under hunting conditions.

Some Bears Kill!: True-Life Tales of Terror, by Larry Kanuit, Safari Press, Huntington Beach, CA, 1997. 313 pp., illus. $24.95.
A collection of 38 stories as told by the victims, and in the case of fatality, recounted by the author from institutional records, episodes involve all three species of North American bears.

Southern Deer & Deer Hunting, by Larry Weishuhn and Bill Bynum, Krause Publications, Iola, WI, 1995. 256 pp., illus. Paper covers. $14.95.
Mount a trophy southern whitetail on your wall with this firsthand account of stalking big bucks below the Mason-Dixon line.

Spring Gobbler Fever, by Michael Hanback, Krause Publications, Iola, WI, 1996. 256 pp., illus. Paper covers. $15.95.
Your complete guide to spring turkey hunting.

Spirit of the Wilderness, Compiled by Theodore J. Holsten, Jr., Susan C. Reneau and Jack Reneau, the Boone & Crockett Club, Missoula, MT, 1997 300 pp., illus. $29.95.
Stalking wild sheep, tracking a trophy cougar, hiking the back country of British Columbia, fishing for striped bass and coming face-to-face with a grizzly bear are some of the adventures found in this book.

Stand Hunting for Whitetails, by Richard P. Smith, Krause Publications, Iola, WI, 1996. 256 pp., illus. Paper covers. $14.95.
The author explains the tricks and strategies for successful stand hunting.

The Sultan of Spring: A Hunter's Odyssey Through the World of the Wild Turkey, by Bob Saile, The Lyons Press, New York, NY, 1998. 176 pp., illus. $22.95.
A literary salute to the magic and mysticism of spring turkey hunting.

Taking Big Bucks, by Ed Wolff, Stoneydale Press, Stevensville, MT, 1987. 169 pp., illus. $18.95.
Solving the whitetail riddle.

Taking More Birds, by Dan Carlisle and Dolph Adams, Lyons & Burford Publishers, New York, NY, 1993. 160 pp., illus. Paper covers. $15.95.
A practical handbook for success at Sporting Clays and wing shooting.

Tales of Quails 'n Such, by Havilah Babcock, University of S. Carolina Press, Columbia, SC, 1985. 237 pp. $19.95.
A group of hunting stories, told in informal style, on field experiences in the South in quest of small game.

Tears and Laughter, by Gene Hill, Countrysport Press, Traverse City, MI, 1996. 176 pp., illus. $25.00.
In twenty-six stories, Gene Hill explores the ancient and honored bond between man and dog.

Tenth Legion, by Tom Kelly, the Lyons Press, New York, NY, 1998. 128 pp., illus. $21.95.
The classic work on that frustrating, yet wonderful sport of turkey hunting.

They Left Their Tracks, by Howard Coperhaver, Stoneydale Press Publishing Co., Stevensville, MT, 1990. 190 pp., illus. $18.95.
Recollections of 60 years as an outfitter in the Bob Marshall Wilderness.

Timberdoodle, by Frank Woolner, Nick Lyons Books, N. Y., NY, 1987. 168 pp., illus. $18.95.
The classic guide to woodcock and woodcock hunting.

Timberdoodle Tales: Adventures of a Minnesota Woodcock Hunter, by T. Waters, Safari Press, Huntington Beach, CA, 1997. 220 pp., illus. $35.00.
The life history and hunt of the American woodcock by the author. A fresh appreciation of this captivating bird and the ethics of its hunt.

To Heck with Moose Hunting, by Jim Zumbo, Wapiti Publishing Co., Cody, WY, 1996. 199 pp., illus. $17.95.
Jim's hunts around the continent and even an African adventure.

Trail and Campfire, edited by George Bird Grinnel and Theodore Roosevelt, The Boone and Crockett Club, Dumfries, VA, 1989. 357 pp., illus. $39.50.
Reprint of the Boone and Crockett Club's 3rd book published in 1897.

Trailing a Bear, by Robert S. Munger, The Munger Foundation, Albion, MI, 1997. 352 pp., illus. Paper covers. $19.95.
An exciting and humorous account of hunting with legendary archer Fred Bear.

The Trickiest Thing in Feathers, by Corey Ford; compiled and edited by Laurie Morrow and illustrated by Christopher Smith, Wilderness Adventures, Gallatin Gateway, MT, 1998. 208 pp., illus. $29.95.
Here is a collection of Corey Ford's best wing-shooting stories, many of them previously unpublished.

Trophy Mule Deer: Finding & Evaluating Your Trophy, by Lance Stapleton, Outdoor Experiences Unlimited, Salem, OR, 1993. 290 pp., illus. Paper covers. $24.95.
The most comprehensive reference book on mule deer.

Turkey Hunter's Digest, Revised Edition, by Dwain Bland, DBI Books, a division of Krause Publications, Iola, WI, 1994. 256 pp., illus. Paper covers. $17.95.
A no-nonsense approach to hunting all five sub-species of the North American wild turkey that make up the Royal Grand Slam.

The Upland Equation: A Modern Bird-Hunter's Code, by Charles Fergus, Lyons & Burford Publishers, New York, NY, 1996. 86 pp. $18.00
A book that deserves space in every sportsman's library. Observations based on firsthand experience.

Upland Tales, by Worth Mathewson (Ed.), Sand Lake Press, Amity, OR, 1996. 271 pp., illus. $29.95.
A collection of articles on grouse, snipe and quail.

A Varmint Hunter's Odyssey, by Steve Hanson with a guest chapter by Mike Johnson, Precision Shooting, Inc. Manchester, CT, 1999. 279 pp., illustrated. Paper covers. $37.95.
A new classic by a writer who eats, drinks and sleeps varmint hunting and varmint rifles.

Varmint and Small Game Rifles and Cartridges, by various authors, Wolfe Publishing Co., Prescott, AZ, 1993. 228 pp., illus. Paper covers. $26.00.
This is a collection of reprints of articles originally appearing in Wolfe's *Rifle* and *Handloader* magazines from 1966 through 1990.

Waterfowler's World, by Bill Buckley, Ducks Unlimited, Inc., Memphis, TN, 1999. 192 pp., illustrated in color. $37.50.
An unprecedented pictorial book on waterfowl and waterfowlers.

Waterfowling Horizons: Shooting Ducks and Geese in the 21st Century, by Chris and Jason Smith, Wilderness Adventures, Gallatin Gateway, MT, 1998. 320 pp., illus. $49.95.
A compendium of the very latest in everything for the duck and goose hunter today.

Waterfowling These Past 50 Years, Especially Brant, by David Hagerbaumer, Sand Lake Press, Amity, OR, 1999. 182 pp., illustrated. $35.00.
This is the compilation of David Hagerbaumer's experiences as a waterfowler since the end of WW2.

Wegner's Bibliography on Dear and Deer Hunting, by Robert Wegner, St. Hubert's Press, Deforest, WI, 1993. 333 pp., 16 full-page illustrations. $45.00.
A comprehensive annotated compilation of books in English pertaining to deer and their hunting 1413-1991.

Western Hunting Guide, by Mike Lapinski, Stoneydale Press Publishing Co., Stevensville, MT, 1989. 168 pp., illus. $18.95.
A complete where-to-go and how-to-do-it guide to Western hunting.

When the Duck Were Plenty, by Ed Muderlak, Safari Press, Inc., Huntington Beach, CA, 2000. 300 pp., illustrated. Limited edition, numbered, signed, slipcased. $49.95.
The golden age of waterfowling and duck hunting from 1840 till 1920. An anthology.

Whispering Wings of Autumn, by Gene Hill and Steve Smith, Wilderness Adventures Press, Bozeman, MT, 1994. 150 pp., illus. $29.00.
Hill and Smith, masters of hunting literature, treat the reader to the best stories of grouse and woodcock hunting.

Whitetail: Behavior Through the Seasons, by Charles J. Alsheimer, Krause Publications, Iola, WI, 1996. 208 pp., illus. $34.95.
In-depth coverage of whitetail behavior presented through striking portraits of the whitetail in every season.

Whitetail: The Ultimate Challenge, by Charles J. Alsheimer, Krause Publications, Iola, WI, 1995. 228 pp., illus. Paper covers. $14.95.
Learn deer hunting's most intriguing secrets—fooling deer using decoys, scents and calls—from America's premier authority.

Whitetails by the Moon, by Charles J. Alsheimer, edited by Patrick Durkin, Krause Publications, Iola, WI, 1999. 208 pp., illustrated. Paper covers. $19.95.
Predict peak times to hunt whitetails. Learn what triggers the rut.

Wildfowler's Season, by Chris Dorsey, Lyons & Burford Publishers, New York, NY, 1998. 224 pp., illus. $37.95.
Modern methods for a classic sport.

Wildfowling Tales, by William C. Hazelton, Wilderness Adventures Press, Belgrade, MT, 1999. 117 pp., illustrated with etchings by Brett Smith. In a slipcase. $50.00.
Tales from the great ducking resorts of the Continent.

Wildfowling Tales 1888-1913, Volume One, edited by Worth Mathewson, Sand Lake Press, Amity, OR, 1998. 186 pp., illustrated by David Hagerbaumer. $22.50.
A collection of some of the best accounts from our literary heritage.

Windward Crossings: A Treasury of Original Waterfowling Tales, by Chuck Petrie et al, Willow Creek Press, Minocqua, WI, 1999. 144 pp., 48 color art and etching reproductions. $35.00.
An illustrated, modern anthology of previously unpublished waterfowl hunting (fiction and creative non fiction) stories by America's finest outdoor journalists.

Wings of Thunder: New Grouse Hunting Revisited, by Steven Mulak, Countrysport Books, Selma, AL, 1998. 168 pp. illustrated. $30.00.
The author examines every aspect of New England grouse hunting as it is today - the bird and its habits, the hunter and his dog, guns and loads, shooting and hunting techniques, practice on clay targets, clothing and equipment.

Wings for the Heart, by Jerry A. Lewis, West River Press, Corvallis, MT, 1991. 324 pp., illus. Paper covers. $14.95.
A delightful book on hunting Montana's upland birds and waterfowl.

Wisconsin Hunting, by Brian Lovett, Krause Publications, Iola, WI, 1997. 208 pp., illus. Paper covers. $16.95.
A comprehensive guide to Wisconsin's public hunting lands.

The Woodchuck Hunter, by Paul C. Estey, R&R Books, Livonia, NY, 1994. 135 pp., illus. $25.00.
This book contains information on woodchuck equipment, the rifle, telescopic sights and includes interesting stories.

Woodcock Shooting, by Steve Smith, Stackpole Books, Inc., Harrisburg, PA, 1988. 142 pp., illus. $16.95.
A definitive book on woodcock hunting and the characteristics of a good woodcock dog.

World Record Whitetails, by Gordon Whittington, Safari Press, Inc., Huntington Beach, CA, 1998. 246 pp. with over 100 photos in color and black-and-white. $32.95.
The first and only complete chronicle of all the bucks that have ever held the title "World record whitetail."

The Working Retrievers, Tom Quinn, The Lyons Press, New York, NY, 1998. 257 pp., illus. $40.00.
The author covers every aspect of the training of dogs for hunting and field trials - from the beginning to the most advanced levels - for Labradors, Chesapeakes, Goldens and others.

World Record Whitetails, by Gordon Whittington, Safari Press Books, Inc., Huntington Beach, CA, 1998. 246 pp., illustrated. $39.95.
The first and only complete chronicle of all the bucks that have ever held the title "World Record Whitetail." Covers the greatest trophies ever recorded in their categories, typical, non-typical, gun, bow, and muzzleloader.

AFRICA/ASIA/ELSEWHERE

A Hunter's Wanderings in Africa, by Frederick Courteney Selous, Wolfe Publishing Co., Prescott, Arizona, 1986. 504 pp., illustrated plus folding map. $29.95.
A reprinting of the 1920 London edition. A narrative of nine years spent amongst the game of the far interior of South Africa.

The Adventurous Life of a Vagabond Hunter, by Sten Cedergren, Safari Press, Inc., Huntington Beach, CA, 2000. 300 pp., illustrated. Limited edition, numbered, signed, and slipcased. $70.00.
An unusual story in the safari business by a remarkable character.

Africa's Greatest Hunter; The Lost Writings of Frederick C. Selous, edited by Dr. james A. Casada, Safari Press, Huntington Beach, CA, 1999. $50.00.
All the stories in this volume relate to the continent that fascinated Selous his entire life. With many previously unpublished photos.

African Adventures, by J.F. Burger, Safari Press, Huntington Beach, CA, 1993. 222 pp., illus. $35.00.
The reader shares adventures on the trail of the lion, the elephant and buffalo.

The African Adventures: A Return to the Silent Places, by Peter Hathaway Capstick, St. Martin's Press, New York, NY, 1992. 220 pp., illus. $22.95.
This book brings to life four turn-of-the-century adventurers and the savage frontier they braved. Frederick Selous, Constatine "Iodine" Ionides, Johnny Boyes and Jim Sutherland.

African Camp-fire Nights, by J.E. Burger, Safari Press, Huntington Beach, CA, 1993. 192 pp., illus. $32.50.
In this book the author writes of the men who made hunting their life's profession.

African Game Trails, by Theodore Roosevelt, Peter Capstick, Series Editor, St. Martin's Press, New York, NY 1988. 583 pp., illustrated. $24.95.
The famed safari of the noted sportsman, conservationist, and President.

African Hunter, by James Mellon, Safari Press, Huntington Beach, CA, 1996. 522 pp., illus. Paper Covers, $75.00.
Regarded as the most comprehensive title ever published on African hunting.

African Hunting and Adventure, by William Charles Baldwin, Books of Zimbabwe, Bulawayo, 1981. 451 pp., illus. $75.00.
Facsimile reprint of the scarce 1863 London edition. African hunting and adventure from Natal to the Zambezi.

African Jungle Memories, by J.F. Burger, Safari Press, Huntington Beach, CA, 1993. 192 pp., illus. $32.50.
A book of reminiscences in which the reader is taken on many exciting adventures on the trail of the buffalo, lion, elephant and leopard.

African Rifles & Cartridges, by John Taylor, The Gun Room Press, Highland Park, NJ, 1977. 431 pp., illus. $35.00.
Experiences and opinions of a professional ivory hunter in Africa describing his knowledge of numerous arms and cartridges for big game. A reprint.

African Safaris, by Major G.H. Anderson, Safari Press, Long Beach, CA, 1997. 173 pp., illus. $35.00.
A reprinting of one of the rarest books on African hunting, with a foreword by Tony Sanchez.

African Twilight, by Robert F. Jones, Wilderness Adventure Press, Bozeman, MT, 1994. 208 pp., illus. $36.00.
Details the hunt, danger and changing face of Africa over a span of three decades.

A Man Called Lion: The Life and Times of John Howard "Pondoro" Taylor, by P.H. Capstick, Safari Press, Huntington Beach, CA, 1994. 240 pp., illus. $24.95.
With the help of Brian Marsh, an old Taylor acquaintance, Peter Capstick has accumulated over ten years of research into the life of this mysterious man.

An Annotated Bibliography of African Big Game Hunting Books, 1785 to 1950, by Kenneth P. Czech, Land's Edge Press, St. Cloud, MN 2000. $50.00
This bibliography features over 600 big game hunting titles describing the regions the authors hunted, species of game bagged, and physical descriptions of the books (pages, maps, plates, bindings, etc.) It also features a suite of 16 colored plates depicting decorated bindings from some of the books. Limited to 700 numbered, signed copies.

Argali: High-Mountain Hunting, by Ricardo Medem, Safari Press, Huntington Beach, CA, 1995. 304 pp., illus. Limited, signed edition. $150.00.
Medem describes hunting seven different countries in the pursuit of sheep and other mountain game.

Baron in Africa; The Remarkable Adventures of Werner von Alvensleben, by Brian Marsh, Safari Press, Huntington Beach, CA, 2001. 288 pp., illus. $35.00
Follow his career as he hunts lion, goes after large kudu, kills a full-grown buffalo with a spear, and hunts for elephant and ivory in some of the densest brush in Africa. The adventure and the experience were what counted to this fascinating character, not the money or fame; indeed, in the end he left Mozambique with barely more than the clothes on his back. This is a must-read adventure story on one of the most interesting characters to have come out of Africa after World War II. Foreword by Ian Player.

The Big Five; Hunting Adventures in Today's Africa, by Dr. S. Lloyd Newberry, Safari Press, Huntington Beach, CA, 2001. 214 pp., illus. Limited edition, numbered, signed and slipcased. $70.00.
Many books have been written about the old Africa and its fabled Big Five, but almost nothing exits in print that describes hunting the Big Five as its exists today.

THE ARMS LIBRARY

Big Game and Big Game Rifles, by John "Pondoro" Taylor, Safari Press, Huntington Beach, CA, 1999. 215 pp., illus. $24.95.

Covers rifles and calibers for elephant, rhino, hippo, buffalo, and lion.

Big Game Hunting Around the World, by Bert Klineburger and Vernon W. Hurst, Exposition Press, Jericho, NY, 1969. 376 pp., illus. $30.00.

The first book that takes you on a safari all over the world.

Big Game Hunting in North-Eastern Rhodesia, by Owen Letcher, St. Martin's Press, New York, NY, 1986. 272 pp., illus. $24.95.

A classic reprint and one of the very few books to concentrate on this fascinating area, a region that today is still very much safari country.

Big Game Shooting in Cooch Behar, the Duars and Assam, by The Maharajah of Cooch Behar, Wolfe Publishing Co., Prescott, AZ, 1993. 461 pp., illus. $49.50.

A reprinting of the book that has become legendary. This is the Maharajah's personal diary of killing 365 tigers.

Buffalo, Elephant, and Bongo, by Dr. Reinald von Meurers, Safari Press, Huntington Beach, CA, 1999. Limited edition signed and in a slipcase. $75.00.

Alone in the Savannas and Rain Forests of the Cameroon.

Campfire Lies of a Canadian Guide, by Fred Webb, Safari Press, Inc., Huntington Beach, CA, 2000. 250 pp., illustrated. Limited edition, numbered, signed and slipcased. $50.00.

Forty years in the life of a guide in the North Country.

Cottar: The Exception was the Rule, by Pat Cottar, Trophy Room Books, Agoura, CA, 1999. 350 pp., illustrated. Limited, numbered and signed edition. $135.00

The remarkable big game hunting stories of one of Kenya's most remarkable pioneers.

A Country Boy in Africa, by George Hoffman, Trophy Room Books, Agoura, CA, 1998. 267 pp., illustrated with over 100 photos. Limited, numbered edition signed by the author. $85.00

In addition to the author's long and successful hunting career, he is known for developing a most effective big game cartridge, the .416 Hoffman.

Death and Double Rifles, by Mark Sullivan, Nitro Express Safaris, Phoenix, AZ, 2000. 295 pages, illus. $85.00

Sullivan has captured every thrilling detail of hunting dangerous game in this lavishly illustrated book. Full of color pictures of African hunts & rifles.

Death in a Lonely Land, by Peter Capstick, St. Martin's Press, New York, NY, 1990. 284 pp., illus. $22.95

Twenty-three stories of hunting as only the master can tell them.

Death in the Dark Continent, by Peter Capstick, St. Martin's Press, New York, NY, 1983. 238 pp., illus. $22.95

A book that brings to life the suspense, fear and exhilaration of stalking ferocious killers under primitive, savage conditions, with the ever present threat of death.

Death in the Long Grass, by Peter Hathaway Capstick, St. Martin's Press, New York, NY, 1977. 297 pp., illus. $22.95

A big game master's adventures in the African bush.

Death in the Silent Places, by Peter Capstick, St. Martin's Press, New York, NY, 1981. 243 pp., illus. $23.95

The author recalls the extraordinary careers of legendary hunters such as Corbett, Karamojo Bell, Stigand and others.

Duck Hunting in Australia, by Dick Eussen, Australia Outdoor Publishers Pty Ltd., Victoria, Australia, 1994. 106 pp., illus. Paper covers. $17.95

Covers the many aspects of duck hunting from hides to hunting methods.

East Africa and its Big Game, by Captain Sir John C. Willowghby, Wolfe Publishing Co., Prescott, AZ, 1990. 312 pp., illus. $52.00

A deluxe limited edition reprint of the very scarce 1889 edition of a narrative of a sporting trip from Zanzibar to the borders of the Masai.

Elephant Hunting in East Equatorial Africa, by A. Neumann, St. Martin's Press, New York, NY, 1994. 455 pp., illus. $26.95

This is a reprint of one of the rarest elephant hunting titles ever.

Elephants of Africa, by Dr. Anthony Hall-Martin, New Holland Publishers, London, England, 1987. 120 pp., illus. $45.00

A superbly illustrated overview of the African elephant with reproductions of paintings by the internationally acclaimed wildlife artist Paul Bosman.

Encounters with Lions, by Jan Hemsing, Trophy Room books, Agoura, CA, 1995. 302 pp., illus. $75.00

Some stories fierce, fatal, frightening and even humorous of when man and lion meet.

Fourteen Years in the African Bush, by A. Marsh, Safari Press Publication, Huntington Beach, CA, 1998. 312 pp., illus. Limited signed, numbered, slipcased. $70.00

An account of a Kenyan game warden. A graphic and well-written story.

From Sailor to Professional Hunter: The Autobiography of John Northcote, Trophy Room Books, Agoura, CA, 1997. 400 pp., illus. Limited edition, signed and numbered. $125.00

Only a handfull of men can boast of having a fifty-year professional hunting career throughout Africa as John Northcote has had.

Gone are the Days; Jungle Hunting for Tiger and other Game in India and Nepal 1953-1969, by Peter Byrne, Safari Press, Inc., Huntington Beach, CA, 2001. 225 pp., illus. Limited signed, numbered, slipcased. $70.00

Great Hunters: Their Trophy Rooms and Collections, Volume 1, compiled and published by Safari Press, Inc., Huntington Beach, CA, 1997. 172 pp., illustrated in color. $60.00

A rare glimpse into the trophy rooms of top international hunters. A few of these trophy rooms are museums.

Great Hunters: Their Trophy Rooms & Collections, Volume 2, compiled and published by Safari Press, Inc., Huntington Beach, CA, 1998. 224 pp., illustrated with 260 full-color photographs. $60.00

Volume two of the world's finest, best produced series of books on trophy rooms and game collections. 46 sportsmen sharing sights you'll never forget on this guided tour.

Great Hunters: Their Trophy Rooms & Collections, Volume 3, compiled and published by Safari Press, Inc., Huntington Beach, CA, 2000. 204 pp., illustrated with 260 full-color photographs. $60.00

At last, the long-awaited third volume in the best photographic series ever published of trophy room collections is finally available. Unbelievable as it may sound, this book tops all previous volumes. Besides some of the greatest North American trophy rooms ever seen, an extra effort was made to include European collections. Believe it or not, volume 3 includes the Sandringham Castle big-game collection, home of Queen Elizabeth II! Also included is the complete Don Cox African and Asian collection as displayed at his alma mater. This stupendous gallery contains the trophy collections of Prince D' Arenberg, Umberto D'Entreves, George and Edward Keller, Paul Roberts, Joe Bishop, and James Clark to name but a few. Whether it be castles, palaces, mansions, or museums, the finest of the finest in trophy room designs and collection unequaled anywhere will be found in this book. As before, each trophy room is accompanied by an informative text explaining the collection and giving you insights into the hunters who went to such great efforts to create their trophy rooms. All professionally photographed in the highest quality possible.

Heart of an African Hunter, by Peter F. Flack, Safari Press, Inc., Huntington Beach, CA, 1999. Limited, numbered, slipcased edition. $70.00

Stories on the Big Five and Tiny Ten.

Horned Death, by John F. Burger, Safari Press, Huntington Beach, CA, 1992. 343 pp.illus. $35.00

The classic work on hunting the African buffalo.

Horn of the Hunter, by Robert Ruark, Safari Press, Long Beach, CA, 1987. 315 pp., illus. $35.00

Ruark's most sought-after title on African hunting, here in reprint.

Horned Giants, by Capt. John Brandt, Safari Press, Inc., Huntington Beach, CA, 1999. 288 pp., illustrated. Limited edition, numbered, signed and slipcased. $80.00

Hunting Eurasian wild cattle.

Hunter, by J.A. Hunter, Safari Press Publications, Huntington Beach, CA, 1999. 263 pp., illus. $24.95

Hunter's best known book on African big-game hunting. Internationally recognized as being one of the all-time African hunting classics.

A Hunter's Africa, by Gordon Cundill, Trophy Room Books, Agoura, CA, 1998. 298 pp., over 125 photographic illustrations. Limited numbered edition signed by the author. $125.00

A good look by the author at the African safari experience - elephant, lion, spiral-horned antelope, firearms, people and events, as well as the clients that make it worthwhile.

A Hunter's Wanderings in Africa, by Frederick Courteney Selous, Wolfe Publishing Co., Prescott, Arizona, 1986. 504 pp., illustrated plus folding map. $29.95

A reprinting of the 1920 London edition. A narrative of nine years spent amongst the game of the far interior of South Africa.

Hunter's Tracks, by J.A. Hunter, Safari Press Publications, Huntington Beach, CA, 1999. 240 pp., illustrated. $24.95

This is the exciting story of John Hunter's efforts to capture the shady headman of a gang of ivory poachers and smugglers. The story is interwoven with the tale of one of East Africa's most grandiose safaris taken with an Indian maharaja.

Hunting Adventures Worldwide, by Jack Atcheson, Jack Atcheson & Sons, Butte, MT, 1995. 256 pp., illus. $29.95

The author chronicles the richest adventures of a lifetime spent in quest of big game across the world – including Africa, North America and Asia.

Hunting in Ethiopia, An Anthology, by Tony Sanchez-Arino, Safari Press, Huntington Beach, CA, 1996. 350 pp., illus. Limited, signed and numbered edition. $135.00

The finest selection of hunting stories ever compiled on hunting in this great game country.

The Hunting Instinct, by Phillip D. Rowter, Safari Press, Inc., Huntington Beach, CA, 1999. Limited edition signed and numbered and in a slipcase. $50.00

Safari chronicles from the Republic of South Africa and Namibia 1990-1998.

Hunting in Kenya, by Tony Sanchez-Arino, Safari Press, Inc., Huntington Beach, CA, 2000. 350 pp., illustrated. Limited, signed and numbered edition in a slipcase. $135.00

The finest selection of hunting stories ever compiled on hunting in this great game country make up this anthology.

Hunting in Many Lands, by Theodore Roosevelt and George Bird Grinnel, The Boone and Crockett Club, Dumfries, VA, 1987. 447 pp., illus. $40.00

Limited edition reprint of this 1895 classic work on hunting in Africa, India, Mongolia, etc.

Hunting in the Sudan, An Anthology, compiled by Tony Sanchez-Arino, Safari Press, Huntington Beach, CA, 1992. 350 pp., illus. Limited, signed and numbered edition in a slipcase. $125.00

The finest selection of hunting stories ever compiled on hunting in this great game country.

Hunting, Settling and Remembering, by Philip H. Percival, Trophy Room Books, Agoura, CA, 1997. 230 pp., illus. Limited, numbered and signed edition. $85.00

If Philip Percival is to come alive again, it will be through this, the first edition of his easy, intricate and magical book illustrated with some of the best historical big game hunting photos ever taken.

THE ARMS LIBRARY

Hunting the Dangerous Game of Africa, by John Kingsley-Heath, Sycamore Island Books, Boulder, CO, 1998. 477 pp., illustrated. $95.00

Written by one of the most respected, successful, and ethical P.H.'s to trek the sunlit plains of Botswana, Kenya, Uganda, Tanganyika, Somaliland, Eritrea, Ethiopia, and Mozambique. Filled with some of the most gripping and terrifying tales ever to come out of Africa.

In the Salt, by Lou Hallamore, Trophy Room Books, Agoura, CA, 1999. 227 pp., illustrated in black & white and full color. Limited, numbered and signed edition. $125.00

A book about people, animals and the big game hunt, about being outwitted and out maneuvered. It is about knowing that sooner or later your luck will change and your trophy will be "in the salt."

International Hunter 1945-1999, Hunting's Greatest Era, by Bert klineburger, Sportsmen on Film, Kerrville, TX, 1999. 400 pp., illustrated. A limited, numbered and signed edition. $125.00

The most important book of the greatest hunting era by the world's preeminent International hunter.

Jaguar Hunting in the Mato Grosso and Bolivia, by T. Almedia, Safari Press, Long Beach, CA, 1989. 256 pp., illus. $35.00

Not since Sacha Siemel has there been a book on jaguar hunting like this one.

Jim Corbett, Master of the Jungle, by Tim Werling, Safari Press, Huntington Beach, CA, 1998. 215 pp., illus. $30.00

A biography of India's most famous hunter of man-eating tigers and leopards.

King of the Wa-Kikuyu, by John Boyes, St. Martin Press, New York, NY, 1993. 240 pp., illus. $19.95

In the 19th and 20th centuries, Africa drew to it a large number of great hunters, explorers, adventurers and rogues. Many have become legendary, but John Boyes (1874-1951) was the most legendary of them all.

Last Horizons: Hunting, Fishing and Shooting on Five Continents, by Peter Capstick, St. Martin's Press, New York, NY, 1989. 288 pp., illus. $19.95

The first in a two volume collection of hunting, fishing and shooting tales from the selected pages of The American Hunter, Guns & Ammo and Outdoor Life.

Last of the Few: Forty-Two Years of African Hunting, by Tony Sanchez-Arino, Safari Press, Huntington Beach, CA, 1996. 250 pp., illus. $39.95

The story of the author's career with all the highlights that come from pursuing the unusual and dangerous animals that are native to Africa.

Last of the Ivory Hunters, by John Taylor, Safari Press, Long Beach, CA, 1990. 354 pp., illus. $29.95

Reprint of the classic book "Pondoro" by one of the most famous elephant hunters of all time.

Legends of the Field: More Early Hunters in Africa, by W.R. Foran, Trophy Room Press, Agoura, CA, 1997. 319 pp., illus. Limited edition. $100.00

This book contains the biographies of some very famous hunters: William Cotton Oswell, F.C. Selous, Sir Samuel Baker, Arthur Neumann, Jim Sutherland, W.D.M. Bell and others.

The Lost Classics, by Robert Ruark, Safari Press, Huntington Beach, CA, 1996. 260 pp., illus. $35.00

The magazine stories that Ruark wrote in the 1950s and 1960s finally in print in book form.

The Lost Wilderness; True Accounts of Hunters and Animals in East Africa, by Mohamed Ismail & Alice Pianfetti, Safari Press, Inc., Huntington Beach, CA, 2000. 216 pp, photos, illustrated. Limited edition signed and numbered and slipcased. $60.00

The Magic of Big Games, by Terry Wieland, Countrysport Books, Selma, AL, 1998. 200 pp., illus. $39.00

Original essays on hunting big game around the world.

Mahonhboh, by Ron Thomson, Hartbeesport, South Africa, 1997. 312 pp., illustrated. Limited signed and numbered edition. $50.00

Elephants and elephant hunting in South Central Africa.

The Man-Eaters of Tsavo, by Lt. Colonel J.H. Patterson, Peter Capstick, series editor, St. Martin's Press, New York, NY, 1986, 5th printing. 346 pp., illus. $22.95

The classic man-eating story of the lions that halted construction of a railway line and reportedly killed one hundred people, told by the man who risked his life to successfully shoot them.

McElroy Hunts Asia, by C.J. McElroy, Safari Press, Inc., Huntington Beach, CA, 1989. 272 pp., illustrated. $50.00

From the founder of SCI comes a book on hunting the great continent of Asia for big game: tiger, bear, sheep and ibex. Includes the story of the all-time record Altai Argali as well as several markhor hunts in Pakistan.

Memoirs of an African Hunter, by Terry Irwin, Safari Press Publications, Huntington Beach, CA, 1998. 421 pp., illustrated. Limited numbered, signed and slipcased. $125.00

A narrative of a professional hunter's experiences in Africa.

Memoirs of a Sheep Hunter, by Rashid Jamsheed, Safari Press, Inc., Huntington Beach, CA, 1996. 330 pp., illustrated. $70.00

The author reveals his exciting accounts of obtaining world-record heads from his native Iran, and his eventual move to the U.S. where he procured a grand-slam of North American sheep.

Months of the Sun; Forty Years of Elephant Hunting in the Zambezi Valley, by Ian Nyschens, Safari Press, Huntington Beach, CA, 1998. 420 pp., illus. $60.00

The author has shot equally as many elephants as Walter Bell, and under much more difficult circumstances. His book will rank, or surpass, the best elephant-ivory hunting books published this century.

Mundjamba: The Life Story of an African Hunter, by Hugo Seia, Trophy Room Books, Agoura, CA, 1996. 400 pp., illus. Limited, numbered and signed by the author. $125.00

An autobiography of one of the most respected and appreciated professional African hunters.

My Last Kambaku, by Leo Kroger, Safari Press, Huntington Beach, CA, 1997. 272 pp., illus. Limited edition signed and numbered and slipcased. $60.00

One of the most engaging hunting memoirs ever published.

The Nature of the Game, by Ben Hoskyns, Quiller Press, Ltd., London, England, 1994. 160 pp., illus. $37.50

The first complete guide to British, European and North American game.

On Target, by Christian Le Noel, Trophy Room Books, Agoura, CA, 1999. 275 pp., illustrated. Limited, numbered and signed edition. $85.00

History and hunting in Central Africa.

One Long Safari, by Peter Hay, Trophy Room Books, Agoura, CA, 1998. 350 pp., with over 200 photographic illustrations and 7 maps. Limited numbered edition signed by the author. $100.00

Contains hunts for leopards, sitatunga, hippo, rhino, snakes and, of course, the general African big game bag.

Optics for the Hunter, by John Barsness, Safari Press, Inc., Huntington Beach, CA, 1999. 236 pp., illustrated. $24.95

An evaluation of binoculars, scopes, range finders, spotting scopes for use in the field.

Out in the Midday Shade, by William York, Safari Press, Inc., Huntington Beach, CA, 1999. Limited, signed and numbered edition in a slipcase. $70.00

Memoirs of an African Hunter 1949-1968.

The Path of a Hunter, by Gilles Tre-Hardy, Trophy Room Books, Agoura, CA, 1997. 318 pp., illus. Limited Edition, signed and numbered. $85.00

A most unusual hunting autobiography with much about elephant hunting in Africa.

The Perfect Shot; Shot Placement for African Big Game, by Kevin "Doctari" Robertson, Safari Press, Inc., Huntington Beach, CA, 1999. 230 pp., illustrated. $65.00

The most comprehensive work ever undertaken to show the anatomical features for all classes of African game. Includes caliber and bullet selection, rifle selection, trophy handling.

Peter Capstick's Africa: A Return to the Long Grass, by Peter Hathaway Capstick, St. Martin's Press, N. Y., NY, 1987. 213 pp., illus. $35.00

A first-person adventure in which the author returns to the long grass for his own dangerous and very personal excursion.

Pondoro, by John Taylor, Safari Press, Inc., Huntington Beach, CA, 1999. 354 pp., illustrated. $29.95

The author is considered one of the best storytellers in the hunting book world, and Pondoro is highly entertaining. A classic African big-game hunting title.

The Quotable Hunter, by Jay Cassell and Peter Fiduccia, The Lyons Press, N.Y., 1999. 288 pp., illustrated. $20.00

This collection of more than three hundred quotes from hunters through the ages captures the essence of the sport, with all its joys, idosyncrasies, and challenges.

The Recollections of an Elephant Hunter 1864-1875, by William Finaughty, Books of Zimbabwe, Bulawayo, Zimbabwe, 1980. 244 pp., illus. $85.00

Reprint of the scarce 1916 privately published edition. The early game hunting exploits of William Finaughty in Matabeleland and Nashonaland.

Records of Big Game, XXV (25th) Edition, Rowland Ward, distributed by Safari Press, Inc., Huntington Beach, CA, 1999. 1,000 pp., illustrated. Limited edition. $150.00

Covers big game records of Africa, Asia, Europe, and the America's.

Robert Ruark's Africa, by Robert Ruark, edited by Michael McIntosh, Countrysport Press, Selma, AL, 1999. 256 pp illustrated with 19 original etchings by Bruce Langton. $32.00

These previously uncollected works of Robert Ruark make this a classic big-game hunting book.

Safari: A Chronicle of Adventure, by Bartle Bull, Viking/Penguin, London, England, 1989. 383 pp., illus. $40.00

The thrilling history of the African safari, highlighting some of Africa's best-known personalities.

Safari: A Dangerous Affair, by Walt Prothero, Safari Press, Huntington Beach, CA, 2000. 275 pp., illustrated. Limited edition, numbered, signed and slipcased. $60.00

True accounts of hunters and animals of Africa.

Safari Rifles: Double, Magazine Rifles and Cartridges for African Hunting, by Craig Boddington, Safari Press, Huntington Beach, CA, 1990. 416 pp., illus. $37.50

A wealth of knowledge on the safari rifle. Historical and present double-rifle makers, ballistics for the large bores, and much, much more.

Safari: The Last Adventure, by Peter Capstick, St. Martin's Press, New York, NY, 1984. 291 pp., illus. $22.95

A modern comprehensive guide to the African Safari.

Safari Guide - A Guide To Planning Your Hunting Safari, by Richard Conrad, Safari Press, Huntington Beach, CA, 314pp, photos, illustrated. $29.95

Dozens of books have been published in the last decade on tales of African hunting. But few, if any, give a comprehensive country-by-country and animal-by-animal comparison or a guide on how to plan your (first) safari.

Sands of Silence, by Peter H. Capstick, Saint Martin's Press, New York, NY, 1991. 224 pp., illus. $35.00

Join the author on safari in Namibia for his latest big-game hunting adventures.

THE ARMS LIBRARY

Shoot Straight And Stay Alive: A Lifetime of Hunting Experiences, by Fred Bartlett, Safari Press, Huntington Beach, CA, 2000. 256 pp., illus. $35.00
Bartlett grew up on a remote farm in Kenya where he started hunting at an early age. After serving in WWII, he returned to Kenya to farm. After a few years, he decided to join the Kenya Game Department as a game control officer, which required him to shoot buffalo and elephant at very close range. He had a fine reputation as a buffalo hunter and was considered to be one of the quickest shots with a double rifle.

Solo Safari, by T. Cacek, Safari Press, Huntington Beach, CA, 1995. 270 pp., illus. $30.00
Here is the story of Terry Cacek who hunted elephant, buffalo, leopard and plains game in Zimbabwe and Botswana on his own.

Spiral-Horn Dreams, by Terry Wieland, Trophy Room Books, Agoura, CA, 1996. 362 pp., illus. Limited, numbered and signed by the author. $85.00
Everyone who goes to hunt in Africa is looking for something; this is for those who go to hunt the spiral-horned antelope—the bongo, myala, mountain nyala, greater and lesser kudu, etc.

Sport Hunting on Six Continents, by Ken Wilson, Sportsmen of Film, Kerrville, TX, 1999. 300 pp., illustrated. $69.95
Hunting around the world....from Alaska to Australia...from the Americas, to Africa, Asia, and Europe.

Tales of the African Frontier, by J.A. Hunter, Safari Press Publications, Huntington Beach, CA, 1999. 308 pp., illus. $24.95
The early days of East Africa is the subject of this powerful John Hunter book.

Trophy Hunter in Africa, by Elgin Gates, Safari Press, Huntington Beach, CA, 1994. 315 pp., illus. $40.00
This is the story of one man's adventure in Africa's wildlife paradise.

Uganda Safaris, by Brian Herne, Winchester Press, Piscataway, NJ, 1979. 236 pp., illus. $24.95
The chronicle of a professional hunter's adventures in Africa.

Under the African Sun, by Dr. Frank Hibben, Safari Press, Inc., Huntington Beach, CA, 1999. Limited edition signed, numbered and in a slipcase. $85.00
Forty-eight years of hunting the African continent.

Under the Shadow of Man Eaters, by Jerry Jaleel, The Jim Corbett Foundation, Edmonton, Alberta, Canada, 1997. 152 pp., illus. A limited, numbered and signed edition. Paper covers. $35.00
The life and legend of Jim Corbett of Kumaon.

Use Enough Gun, by Robert Ruark, Safari Press, Huntington Beach, CA, 1997. 333 pp., illus. $35.00
Robert Ruark on big game hunting.

Warrior: The Legend of Col. Richard Meinertzhagen, by Peter H. Capstick, St. Martins Press, New York, NY, 1998. 320 pp., illus. $23.95
A stirring and vivid biography of the famous British colonial officer Richard Meinertzhagen, whose exploits earned him fame and notoriety as one of the most daring and ruthless men to serve during the glory days of the British Empire.

The Waterfowler's World, by Bill Buckley, Willow Creek Press, Minocqua, WI, 1999. 176 pp., 225 color photographs. $37.50
Waterfowl hunting from Canadian prairies, across the U.S. heartland, to the wilds of Mexico, from the Atlantic to the Pacific coasts and the Gulf of Mexico.

Where Lions Roar: Ten More Years of African Hunting, by Craig Boddington, Safari Press, Huntington Beach, CA, 1997. 250 pp $35.00
The story of Boddington's hunts in the Dark Continent during the last ten years.

White Hunter, by J.A. Hunter, Safari Press Publications, Huntington Beach, CA, 1999. 282 pp., illustrated. $24.95
This book is a seldom-seen account of John Hunter's adventures in pre-WW2 Africa.

A White Hunters Life, by Angus MacLagan, an African Heritage Book, published by Amwell Press, Clinton, NJ, 1983. 283 pp., illus. Limited, signed, and numbered deluxe edition, in slipcase. $100.00
True to life, a sometimes harsh yet intriguing story.

Wild Sports of Southern Africa, by William Cornwallis Harris, New Holland Press, London, England, 1987. 376 pp., illus. $36.00
Originally published in 1863, describes the author's travels in Southern Africa.

Wind, Dust and Snow, by Robert M. Anderson, Safari Press, Inc., Huntington Beach, CA, 1997. 240 pp., illustrated. $65.00
A complete chronology of modern exploratory and pioneering Asian sheep-hunting expeditions from 1960 until 1996, with wonderful background history and previously untold stories.

With a Gun in Good Country, by Ian Manning, Trophy Room Books, Agoura, CA, 1996. Limited, numbered and signed by the author. $85.00
A book written about that splendid period before the poaching onslaught which almost closed Zambia and continues to the granting of her independence. It then goes on to recount Manning's experiences in Botswana, Congo, and briefly in South Africa.

RIFLES

The Accurate Rifle, by Warren Page, Claymore Publishing, Ohio, 1997. 254 pages, illustrated. Revised edition. Paper Covers. $17.95
Provides hunters & shooter alike with detailed practical information on the whole range of subjects affecting rifle accuracy, he explains techniques in ammo, sights & shooting methods. With a 1996 equipment update from Dave Brennan.

The Accurate Varmint Rifle, by Boyd Mace, Precision Shooting, Inc., Whitehall, NY, 1991. 184 pp., illus. $15.00
A long overdue and long needed work on what factors go into the selection of components and for the subsequent assembly of...the accurate varmint rifle.

The AK-47 Assault Rifle, Desert Publications, Cornville, AZ, 1981. 150 pp., illus. Paper covers. $13.95
Complete and practical technical information on the only weapon in history to be produced in an estimated 30,000,000 units.

American Hunting Rifles: Their Application in the Field for Practical Shooting, by Craig Boddington, Safari Press, Huntington Beach, CA, 1996. 446 pp., illus. First edition, limited, signed and slipcased. $85.00. Second printing trade edition. $35.00
Covers all the hunting rifles and calibers that are needed for North America's diverse game.

The AR-15/M16, A Practical Guide, by Duncan Long. Paladin Press, Boulder, CO, 1985. 168 pp., illus. Paper covers. $22.00
The definitive book on the rifle that has been the inspiration for so many modern assault rifles.

The Art of Shooting With the Rifle, by Col. Sir H. St. John Halford, Excalibur Publications, Latham, NY, 1996. 96 pp., illus. Paper covers. $12.95
A facsimile edition of the 1888 book by a respected rifleman providing a wealth of detailed information.

The Art of the Rifle, by Jeff Cooper, Paladin Press, Boulder, CO, 1997. 104 pp., illus. $29.95
Everything you need to know about the rifle whether you use it for security, meat or target shooting.

Australian Military Rifles & Bayonets, 200 Years of, by Ian Skennerton, I.D.S.A. Books, Piqua, OH, 1988. 124 pp., 198 illus. Paper covers. $19.50

Australian Service Machine Guns, 100 Years of, by Ian Skennerton, I.D.S.A. Books, Piqua, OH, 1989. 122 pp., 150 illus. Paper covers. $19.50

The Big Game Rifle, by Jack O'Connor, Safari Press, Huntington Beach, CA, 1994. 370 pp., illus. $37.50
An outstanding description of every detail of construction, purpose and use of the big game rifle.

Big Game Rifles and Cartridges, by Elmer Keith, reprint edition by The Gun Room Press, Highland Park, NJ, 1984. 161 pp., illus. $17.95
Reprint of Elmer Keith's first book, a most original and accurate work on big game rifles and cartridges.

Black Magic: The Ultra Accurate AR-15, by John Feamster, Precision Shooting, Manchester, CT, 1998. 300 pp., illustrated. $29.95
The author has compiled his experiences pushing the accuracy envelope of the AR-15 to its maximum potential. A wealth of advice on AR-15 loads, modifications and accessories for everything from NRA Highpower and Service Rifle competitions to benchrest and varmint shooting.

The Black Rifle, M16 Retrospective, R. Blake Stevens and Edward C. Ezell, Collector Grade Publications, Toronto, Canada, 1987. 400 pp., illus. $59.95
The complete story of the M16 rifle and its development.

Bolt Action Rifles, 3rd Edition, by Frank de Haas, DBI Books, a division of Krause Publications, Iola, WI, 1995. 528 pp., illus. Paper covers. $24.95
A revised edition of the most definitive work on all major bolt-action rifle designs.

The Book of the Garand, by Maj. Gen. J.S. Hatcher, The Gun Room Press, Highland Park, NJ, 1977. 292 pp., illus. $26.95
A new printing of the standard reference work on the U.S. Army M1 rifle.

The Book of the Twenty-Two: The All American Caliber, by Sam Fadala, Stoeger Publishing Co., So. Hackensack, NJ, 1989. 288 pp., illus. Soft covers. $16.95
The All American Caliber from BB caps up to the powerful 226 Barnes. It's about ammo history, plinking, target shooting, and the quest for the one-hole group.

British Military Martini, Treatise on the, Vol. 1, by B.A. Temple and Ian Skennerton, I.D.S.A. Books, Piqua, OH, 1983. 256 pp., 114 illus. $40.00

British Military Martini, Treatise on the, Vol. 2, by B.A. Temple and Ian Skennerton, I.D.S.A. Books, Piqua, OH, 1989. 213 pp., 135 illus. $40.00

British .22RF Training Rifles, by Dennis Lewis and Robert Washburn, Excalibur Publications, Latham, NY, 1993. 64 pp., illus. Paper covers. $10.95
The story of Britain's training rifles from the early Aiming Tube models to the post-WWII trainers.

Classic Sporting Rifles, by Christopher Austyn, Safari Press, Huntington Beach, CA, 1997. 128 pp., illus. $50.00
As the head of the gun department at Christie's Auction House the author examines the "best" rifles built over the last 150 years.

The Complete AR15/M16 Sourcebook, by Duncan Long, Paladin Press, Boulder, CO, 1993. 232 pp., illus. Paper covers. $35.00
The latest development of the AR15/M16 and the many spin-offs now available, selective-fire conversion systems for the 1990s, the vast selection of new accessories.

The Competitive AR15: The Mouse That Roared, by Glenn Zediker, Zediker Publishing, Oxford, MS, 1999. 286 pp., illustrated. Paper covers. $29.95
A thorough and detailed study of the newest precision rifle sensation.

Complete Book of U.S. Sniping, by Peter R. Senich, Paladin Press, Boulder, CO, 1997, 8 1/2 x 11, hardcover, photos, 288 pp. $52.95
Trace American sniping materiel from its infancy to today's sophisticated systems with this volume, compiled from Senich's early books, Limited War Sniping and The Pictorial History of U.S. Sniping. Almost 400 photos, plus information gleaned from official documents and military archives, pack this informative work.

Complete Guide To The M1 Garand and The M1 Carbine, by Bruce Canfield, Andrew Mowbray, Inc., Lincoln, RI, 1999. 296 pp., illustrated. $39.50
Covers all of the manufacturers of components, parts, variations and markings. Learn which parts are proper for which guns. The total story behind these guns, from their invention through WWII, Korea, Vietnam and beyond! 300+ photos show you features, markings, overall views and action shots. Thirty-three tables and charts give instant reference to serial numbers, markings, dates of issue and

proper configurations. Special sections on Sniper guns, National Match Rifles, exotic variations, and more!

The Complete M1 Garand, by Jim Thompson, Paladin Press, Boulder, CO, 1998. 160 pp., illustrated. Paper cover. $25.00

A guide for the shooter and collector, heavily illustrated.

Exploded Long Gun Drawings, The Gun Digest Book of, edited by Harold A. Murtz, DBI Books, a division of Krause Publications, Iola, WI, 512 pp., illus. Paper covers. $20.95

Containing almost 500 rifle and shotgun exploded drawings. An invaluable aid to both professionals and hobbyists.

The FAL Rifle, by R. Blake Stevens and Jean van Rutten, Collector Grade Publications, Cobourg, Canada, 1993. 848 pp., illus. $129.95

Originally published in three volumes, this classic edition covers North American, UK and Commonwealth and the metric FAL's.

The Fighting Rifle, by Chuck Taylor, Paladin Press, Boulder, CO, 1983. 184 pp., illus. Paper covers. $25.00

The difference between assault and battle rifles and auto and light machine guns.

Firearms Assembly/Disassembly Part III: Rimfire Rifles, Revised Edition, The Gun Digest Book of, by J. B. Wood, DBI Books, a division of Krause Publications, Iola, WI., 1994. 480 pp., illus. Paper covers. $19.95

Covers 65 popular rimfires plus over 100 variants, all cross-referenced in the index.

Firearms Assembly/Disassembly Part IV: Centerfire Rifles, Revised Edition, The Gun Digest Book of, by J.B. Wood, DBI Books, a division of Krause Publications, Iola, WI, 1991. 480 pp., illus. Paper covers. $19.95

Covers 54 popular centerfire rifles plus 300 variants. The most comprehensive and professional presentation available to either hobbyist or gunsmith.

The FN-FAL Rifle, et al, by Duncan Long, Delta Press, El Dorado, AR, 1998. 148 pp., illustrated. Paper covers. $18.95

A comprehensive study of one of the classic assault weapons of all times. Detailed descriptions of the basic models plus the myriad of variants that evolved as a result of its universal acceptance.

Forty Years with the .45-70, second edition, revised and expanded, by Paul A. Matthews, Wolfe Publishing Co., Prescott, AZ, 1997. 184 pp., illus. Paper covers. $14.95

This book is pure gun lore-lore of the .45-70. It not only contains a history of the cartridge, but also years of the author's personal experiences.

F.N.-F.A.L. Auto Rifles, Desert Publications, Cornville, AZ, 1981. 130 pp., illus. Paper covers. $16.95

A definitive study of one of the free world's finest combat rifles.

German Sniper 1914-1945, by Peter R. Senich, Paladin Press, Boulder, CO, 1997 8 1/2 x 11, hardcover, photos, 468 pp. $69.95

The complete story of Germany's sniping arms development through both World Wars. Presents more than 600 photos of Mauser 98's, Selbstladegewehr 41s and 43s, optical sights by Goerz, Zeiss, etc., plus German snipers in action. An exceptional hardcover collector's edition for serious military historians everywhere.

Hints and Advice on Rifle-Shooting, by Private R. McVittie with new introductory material by W.S. Curtis, W.S. Curtis Publishers, Ltd., Clwyd, England, 1993. 32 pp. Paper covers. $10.00

A reprint of the original 1886 London edition.

How-To's for the Black Powder Cartridge Rifle Shooter, by Paul A. Matthews, Wolfe Publishing Co., Prescott, AZ, 1996. 136 pp., illus. Paper covers. $22.50

Practices and procedures used in the reloading and shooting of blackpowder cartridges.

Hunting with the .22, by C.S. Landis, R&R Books, Livonia, NY, 1995. 429 pp., illus. $35.00

A reprinting of the classical work on .22 rifles.

The Hunting Rifle, by Townsend Whelen, Wolfe Publishing Co., Prescott, Arizona, 1984. 463 pp., illustrated. $24.95

A thoroughly dependable coverage on the materiel and marksmanhip with relation to the sportsman's rifle for big game.

Illustrated Handbook of Rifle Shooting, by A.L. Russell, Museum Restoration Service, Alexandria Bay, NY, 1992. 194 pp., illus. $24.50

A new printing of the 1869 edition by one of the leading military marksman of the day.

Know Your M1 Garand, by E. J. Hoffschmidt, Blacksmith Corp., Southport, CT, 1975, 84 pp., illus. Paper covers. $15.95

Facts about America's most famous infantry weapon. Covers test and experimental models, Japanese and Italian copies, National Match models.

Know Your Ruger 10/22 Carbine, by William E. Workman, Blacksmith Corp., Chino Valley, AZ, 1991. 96 pp., illus. Paper covers. $12.95

The story and facts about the most popular 22 autoloader ever made.

The Lee Enfield No. 1 Rifles, by Alan M. Petrillo, Excaliber Publications, Latham, NY, 1992. 64 pp., illus. Paper covers. $10.95

Highlights the SMLE rifles from the Mark 1-VI.

The Lee Enfield Number 4 Rifles, by Alan M. Petrillo, Excalibur Publications, Latham, NY, 1992. 64 pp., illus. Paper covers. $10.95

A pocket-sized, bare-bones reference devoted entirely to the .303 World War II and Korean War vintage service rifle.

Legendary Sporting Rifles, by Sam Fadala, Stoeger Publishing Co., So. Hackensack, NJ, 1992. 288 pp., illus. Paper covers. $16.95

Covers a vast span of time and technology beginning with the Kentucky Long-rifle.

The Li'l M1 .30 Cal. Carbine, by Duncan Long, Desert Publications, El Dorado, AZ, 1995. 203 pp., illus. Paper covers. $14.95

Traces the history of this little giant from its original creation.

Make It Accurate: Get the Maximum Performance from Your Hunting Rifle, by Craig Boddington, Safari Press Publications, Huntington Beach, CA, 1999. 224 pp., illustrated. $24.95

Tips on how to select the rifle, cartridge, and scope best suited to your needs. A must-have for any hunter who wants to improve his shot.

Mauser Smallbore Sporting, Target and Training Rifles, by Jon Speed, Collector Grade Publications, Inc., Cobourg, Ont., Canada, 1998. 372 pp., illustrated. $67.50

The history of all the smallbore sporting, target and training rifles produced by the legendary Mauser-Werke of Obendorf am Neckar.

Mauser: Original-Oberndorf Sporting Rifles, by Jon Speed, Collector Grade Publications, Inc., Cobourg, Ont., Canada, 1997. 508 pp., illustrated. $89.95

The most exhaustive study ever published of the design origins and manufacturing history of the original Oberndorf Mauser Sporter.

M14/M14A1 Rifles and Rifle Markmanship, Desert Publications, El Dorado, AZ, 1995. 236 pp., illus. Paper covers. $18.95

Contains a detailed description of the M14 and M14A1 rifles and their general characteristics, procedures for disassembly and assembly, operating and functioning of the rifles, etc.

The M14 Owner's Guide and Match Conditioning Instructions, by Scott A. Duff and John M. Miller, Scott A. Duff Publications, Export, PA, 1996. 180 pp., illus. Paper covers. $19.95

Traces the history and development from the T44 through the adoption and production of the M14 rifle.

The M-14 Rifle, facsimile reprint of FM 23-8, Desert Publications, Cornville, AZ, 50 pp., illus. Paper $11.95

Well illustrated and informative reprint covering the M-14 and M-14E2.

The M14-Type Rifle: A Shooter's and Collector's Guide, by Joe Poyer, North Cape Publications, Tustin, CA, 1997. 82 pp., illus. Paper covers. $18.95

Covers the history and development, commercial copies, cleaning and maintenance instructions, and targeting and shooting.

The M16/AR15 Rifle, by Joe Poyer, North Cape Publications, Tustin, CA, 1998. 150 pp., illustrated. Paper covers. $19.95

From its inception as the first American assault battle rifle to the firing lines of the National Matches, the M16/AR15 rifle in all its various models and guises has made a significant impact on the American rifleman.

Military Bolt Action Rifles, 1841-1918, by Donald B. Webster, Museum Restoration Service, Alexander Bay, NY, 1993. 150 pp., illus. $34.50

A photographic survey of the principal rifles and carbines of the European and Asiatic powers of the last half of the 19th century and the first years of the 20th century.

The Mini-14, by Duncan Long, Paladin Press, Boulder, CO, 1987. 120 pp., illus. Paper covers. $17.00

History of the Mini-14, the factory-produced models, specifications, accessories, suppliers, and much more.

Mr. Single Shot's Book of Rifle Plans, by Frank de Haas, Mark de Haas, Orange City, IA, 1996. 85 pp., illus. Paper covers. $22.50

Contains complete and detailed drawings, plans and instructions on how to build four different and unique breech-loading single shot rifles of the author's own proven design.

M1 Carbine Owner's Manual, M1, M2 & M3 .30 Caliber Carbines, Firepower Publications, Cornville, AZ, 1984. 102 pp., illus. Paper covers. $16.95

The complete book for the owner of an M1 Carbine.

The M1 Garand Serial Numbers & Data Sheets, by Scott A. Duff, Scott A. Duff, Export, PA, 1995. 101 pp. Paper covers. $11.95

This pocket reference book includes serial number tables and data sheets on the Springfield Armory, Gas Trap Rifles, Gas Port Rifles, Winchester Repeating Arms, International Harvester and H&R Arms Co. and more.

The M1 Garand: Post World War, by Scott A. Duff, Scott A. Duff, Export, PA, 1990. 139 pp., illus. Soft covers. $19.95

A detailed account of the activities at Springfield Armory through this period. International Harvester, H&R, Korean War production and quantities delivered. Serial numbers.

The M1 Garand: World War 2, by Scott A. Duff, Scott A. Duff, Export, PA, 1993. 210 pp., illus. Paper covers. $39.95

The most comprehensive study available to the collector and historian on the M1 Garand of World War II.

Modern Sniper Rifles, by Duncan Long, Paladin Press, Boulder, CO, 1997, 8 1/2 x 11, soft cover, photos, illus., 120 pp. $20.00

Noted weapons expert Duncan Long describes the .22 LR, single-shot, bolt-action, semiautomatic and large-caliber rifles that can be used for sniping purposes, including the U.S. M21, Ruger Mini-14, AUG and HK-94SG1. These and other models are evaluated on the basis of their features, accuracy, reliability and handiness in the field. The author also looks at the best scopes, ammunition and accessories.

More Single Shot Rifles and Actions, by Frank de Haas, Mark de Haas, Orange City, IA, 1996. 146 pp., illus. Paper covers. $22.50

Covers 45 different single shot rifles. Includes the history plus photos, drawings and personal comments.

The Muzzle-Loading Rifle...Then and Now, by Walter M. Cline, National Muzzle Loading Rifle Association, Friendship, IN, 1991. 161 pp., illus. $32.00

This extensive compilation of the muzzleloading rifle exhibits accumulative preserved data concerning the development of the "hallowed old arms of the Southern highlands."

THE ARMS LIBRARY

The No. 4 (T) Sniper Rifle: An Armourer's Perspective, by Peter Laidler with Ian Skennerton, I.D.S.A. Books, Piqua, OH, 1993. 125 pp., 75 illus. Paper covers. $19.95

Notes on Rifle-Shooting, by Henry William Heaton, reprinted with a new introduction by W.S. Curtis, W.S. Curtis Publishers, Ltd., Clwyd, England, 1993. 89 pp. $19.95
A reprint of the 1864 London edition. Captain Heaton was one of the great rifle shots from the earliest days of the Volunteer Movement.

The Official SKS Manual, Translation by Major James F. Gebhardt (Ret.), Paladin Press, Boulder, CO, 1997. 96 pp., illus. Paper covers. $16.00
This Soviet military manual covering the widely distributed SKS is now available in English.

The Pennsylvania Rifle, by Samuel E. Dyke, Sutter House, Lititz, PA, 1975. 61 pp., illus. Paper covers. $10.00
History and development, from the hunting rifle of the Germans who settled the area. Contains a full listing of all known Lancaster, PA, gunsmiths from 1729 through 1815.

Police Rifles, by Richard Fairburn, Paladin Press, Boulder, CO, 1994. 248 pp., illus. Paper covers. $35.00
Selecting the right rifle for street patrol and special tactical situations.

The Poor Man's Sniper Rifle, by D. Boone, Paladin Press, Boulder, CO, 1995. 152 pp., illus. Paper covers. $18.95
Here is a complete plan for converting readily available surplus military rifles to high-performance sniper weapons.

A Potpourri of Single Shot Rifles and Actions, by Frank de Haas, Mark de Haas, Ridgeway, MO, 1993. 153 pp., illus. Paper covers. $22.50
The author's 6th book on non-bolt-action single shots. Covers more than 40 single-shot rifles in historical and technical detail.

Precision Shooting with the M1 Garand, by Roy Baumgardner, Precision Shooting, Inc., Manchester, CT, 1999. 142 pp., illustrated. Paper covers. $12.95
Starts off with the ever popular ten-article series on accurinzing the M1 that originally appeared in Precision Shooting in the 1993-95 era. There follows nine more Baumgardner authored articles on the M1 Garand and finally a 1999 updating chapter.

Purdey Gun and Rifle Makers: The Definitive History, by Donald Dallas, Quiller Press, London, 2000. 245 pp., illus. Color throughout. $100.00
A limited edition of 3,000 copies. Signed and Numbered. With a PURDEY book plate.

The Remington 700, by John F. Lacy, Taylor Publishing Co., Dallas, TX, 1990. 208 pp., illus. $44.95
Covers the different models, limited editions, chamberings, proofmarks, serial numbers, military models, and much more.

The Revolving Rifles, by Edsall James, Pioneer Press, Union City, TN, 1975. 23 pp., illus. Paper covers. $5.00
Valuable information on revolving cylinder rifles, from the earliest matchlock forms to the latest models of Colt and Remington.

Rifle Guide, by Sam Fadala, Stoeger Publishing Co., S. Hackensack, NJ, 1993. 288 pp., illus. Paper covers. $16.95
This comprehensive, fact-filled book beckons to both the seasoned rifleman as well as the novice shooter.

The Rifle: Its Development for Big-Game Hunting, by S.R. Truesdell, Safari Press, Huntington Beach, CA, 1992. 274 pp., illus. Paper covers. $35.00
The full story of the development of the big-game rifle from 1834-1946.

Riflesmithing, The Gun Digest Book of, by Jack Mitchell, DBI Books, a division of Krause Publications, Iola, WI, 1982. 256 pp., illus. Paper covers. $16.95
Covers tools, techniques, designs, finishing wood and metal, custom alterations.

Rifles of the World, 2nd Edition, edited by John Walter, DBI Books, a division of Krause Publications, Iola, WI, 1998. 384 pp., illus. $24.95
The definitive guide to the world's centerfire and rimfire rifles.

Ned H. Roberts and the Schuetzen Rifle, edited by Gerald O. Kelver, Brighton, CO, 1982. 99 pp., illus. $13.95
A compilation of the writings of Major Ned H. Roberts which appeared in various gun magazines.

Schuetzen Rifles, History and Loading, by Gerald O. Kelver, Gerald O. Kelver, Publisher, Brighton, CO, 1972. Illus. $13.95
Reference work on these rifles, their bullets, loading, telescopic sights, accuracy, etc. A limited, numbered ed.

Shooting the Blackpowder Cartridge Rifle, by Paul A. Matthews, Wolfe Publishing Co., Prescott, AZ, 1994. 129 pp., illus. Paper covers. $22.50
A general discourse on shooting the blackpowder cartridge rifle and the procedure required to make a particular rifle perform.

Shooting Lever Guns of the Old West, by Mike Venturino, MLV Enterprises, Livingston, MT, 1999. 300 pp., illustrated. Paper covers. $27.95
Shooting the lever action type repeating rifles of our American west.

Single Shot Rifles and Actions, by Frank de Haas, Orange City, IA, 1990. 352 pp., illus. Soft covers. $27.00
The definitive book on over 60 single shot rifles and actions.

Sixty Years of Rifles, by Paul A. Matthews, Wolfe Publishing Co., Prescott, AZ, 1991. 224 pp., illus. $19.50
About rifles and the author's experience and love affair with shooting and hunting.

S.L.R.—Australia's F.N. F.A.L. by Ian Skennerton and David Balmer, I.D.S.A. Books, Piqua, OH, 1989. 124 pp., 100 illus. Paper covers. $19.50

Small Arms Identification Series, No. 2—.303 Rifle, No. 4 Marks I, & I*, Marks 1/2, 1/3 & 2, by Ian Skennerton, I.D.S.A. Books, Piqua, OH, 1994. 48 pp. $9.50

Small Arms Identification Series, No. 3—9mm Austen Mk I & 9mm Owen Mk I Sub-Machine Guns, by Ian Skennerton, I.D.S.A. Books, Piqua, OH, 1994. 48 pp. $9.50

Small Arms Identification Series, No. 4—.303 Rifle, No. 5 Mk I, by Ian Skennerton, I.D.S.A. Books, Piqua, OH, 1994. 48 pp. $9.50

Small Arms Identification Series, No. 5—.303-in. Bren Light Machine Gun, by Ian Skennerton, I.D.S.A. Books, Piqua, OH, 1994. 48 pp. $9.50

Small Arms Series, No. 1 DeLisle's Commando Carbine, by Ian Skennerton, I.D.S.A. Books, Piqua, OH, 1981. 32 pp., 24 illus. $9.00

Small Arms Identification Series, No. 1—.303 Rifle, No. 1 S.M.L.E. Marks III and III*, by Ian Skennerton, I.D.S.A. Books, Piqua, OH, 1981. 48 pp. $9.50

Sporting Rifle Takedown & Reassembly Guide, 2nd Edition, by J.B. Wood, DBI Books, a division of Krause Publications, Iola, WI, 1997. 480 pp., illus. $19.95
An updated edition of the reference guide for anyone who wants to properly care for their sporting rifle. (Available September 1997)

The Springfield Rifle M1903, M1903A1, M1903A3, M1903A4, Desert Publications, Cornville, AZ, 1982. 100 pp., illus. Paper covers. $12.00
Covers every aspect of disassembly and assembly, inspection, repair and maintenance.

Still More Single Shot Rifles, by James J. Grant, Pioneer Press, Union City, TN, 1995. 211 pp., illus. Paper covers. $29.95
This is Volume Four in a series of Single-Shot Rifles by America's foremost authority. It gives more in-depth information on those single-shot rifles which were presented in the first three books.

The Sturm, Ruger 10/22 Rifle and .44 Magnum Carbine, by Duncan Long, Paladin Press, Boulder, CO, 1988. 108 pp., illus. Paper covers. $15.00
An in-depth look at both weapons detailing the elegant simplicity of the Ruger design. Offers specifications, troubleshooting procedures and ammunition recommendations.

The Tactical Rifle, by Gabriel Suarez, Paladin Press, Boulder, CO, 1999. 264 pp., illustrated. Paper covers. $25.00
The precision tool for urban police operations.

Target Rifle in Australia, by J.E. Corcoran, R&R, Livonia, NY, 1996. 160 pp., illus. $40.00
A most interesting study of the evolution of these rifles from 1860 - 1900. British rifles from the percussion period through the early smokeless era are discussed.

To the Dreams of Youth: The .22 Caliber Single Shot Winchester Rifle, by Herbert Houze, Krause Publications, Iola, WI, 1993. 192 pp., illus. $34.95
A thorougly researched history of the 22-caliber Winchester single shot rifle, including interesting photographs.

The Ultimate in Rifle Accuracy, by Glenn Newick, Stoeger Publishing Co., Wayne, N.J., 1999. 205 pp., illustrated. Paper covers. $11.95
This handbook contains the information you need to extract the best performance from your rifle.

U.S. Marine Corps AR15/M16 A2 Manual, reprinted by Desert Publications, El Dorado, AZ, 1993. 262 pp., illus. Paper covers. $16.95
A reprint of TM05538C-23&P/2, August, 1987. The A-2 manual for the Colt AR15/M16.

U.S. Rifle M14—From John Garand to the M21, by R. Blake Stevens, Collector Grade Publications, Inc., Toronto, Canada, revised second edition, 1991. 350 pp., illus. $49.50
A classic, in-depth examination of the development, manufacture and fielding of the last wood-and-metal ("lock, stock, and barrel") battle rifle to be issued to U.S. troops.

War Baby!: The U.S. Caliber 30 Carbine, Volume I, by Larry Ruth, Collector Grade Publications, Toronto, Canada, 1992. 512 pp., illus. $69.95
Volume 1 of the in-depth story of the phenomenally popular U.S. caliber 30 carbine. Concentrates on design and production of the military 30 carbine during World War II.

War Baby Comes Home: The U.S. Caliber 30 Carbine, Volume 2, by Larry Ruth, Collector Grade Publications, Toronto, Canada, 1993. 386 pp., illus. $49.95
The triumphant competion of Larry Ruth's two-volume in-depth series on the most popular U.S. military small arm in history.

The Winchester Model 52, Perfection in Design, by Herbert G. Houze, Krause Publications, Iola, WI, 1997. 192 pp., illus. $34.95
This book covers the complete story of this technically superior gun.

The Winchester Model 94: The First 100 Years, by Robert C. Renneberg, Krause Publications, Iola, WI, 1991. 208 pp., illus. $34.95
Covers the design and evolution from the early years up to today.

Winchester Slide-Action Rifles, Volume I: Model 1890 and Model 1906 by Ned Schwing, Krause Publications, Iola, WI. 352 pp., illus. $39.95
Traces the history through word and picture in this chronolgy of the Model 1890 and 1906.

Winchester Slide-Action Rifles, Volume II: Model 61 & Model 62 by Ned Schwing, Krause Publications, Iola, WI. 256 pp., illus. $34.95
Historical look complete with markings, stampings and engraving.

SHOTGUNS

Advanced Combat Shotgun: The Stress Fire Concept, by Massad Ayoob, Police Bookshelf, Concord, NH, 1993. 197 pp., illus. Paper covers. $9.95
Advanced combat shotgun fighting for police.

THE ARMS LIBRARY

Best Guns, by Michael McIntosh, Countrysport Press, Selma, AL, 1999, revised edition. 418 pp. $39.00
Combines the best shotguns ever made in America with information on British and Continental makers.

The Better Shot, by Ken Davies, Quiller Press, London, England, 1992. 136 pp., illus. $39.95
Step-by-step shotgun technique with Holland and Holland.

The Big Shots; Edwardian Shooting Parties, by Jonathan Ruffer, Quiller Press, London, England, 1997 160pp. B & W illus. $24.95
A book about Edwardian shooting parties, now a former pastime and enjoyed by the selected few, who recall the hunting of pheasants. Foreword by HRH The Prince of Wales.

The British Shotgun, Volume 1, 1850-1870, by I.M. Crudington and D.J. Baker, Barrie & Jenkins, London, England, 1979. 256 pp., illus. $65.00
An attempt to trace, as accurately as is now possible, the evolution of the shotgun during its formative years in Great Britain.

Boothroyd on British Shotguns, by Geoffrey Boothroyd, Sand Lake Press, Amity, OR, 1996. 221 pp., illus. plus a 32 page reproduction of the 1914 Webley & Scott catalog. A limited, numbered edition. $34.95
Based on articles by the author that appeared in the British Publication *Shooting Times & Country Magazine.*

Boss & Co. Builders of the Best Guns Only, by Donald Dallas, Quiller Press, London, 1995. 262 pp., illustrated. $79.95
Large four colour plates, b/w photos, bibliography. The definitive history authorized by Boss & Co.

The British Over-and-Under Shotgun, by Geoffrey and Susan Boothroyd, Sand Lake Press, Amity, OR, 1996. 137 pp., illus. $34.95
Historical outline of the development of the O/U shotgun with individual chapters devoted to the twenty-two British makers.

The Browning Superposed: John M. Browning's Last Legacy, by Ned Schwing, Krause Publications, Iola, WI, 1996. 496 pp., illus. $49.95
An exclusive story of the man, the company and the best-selling over-and-under shotgun in North America.

Clay Target Handbook, by Jerry Meyer, Lyons & Buford, Publisher, New York, NY, 1993. 182 pp., illus. $22.95
Contains in-depth, how-to-do-it information on trap, skeet, sporting clays, international trap, international skeet and clay target games played around the country.

Clay Target Shooting, by Paul Bentley, A&C Black, London, England, 1987. 144 pp., illus. $25.00
Practical book on clay target shooting written by a very successful international competitor, providing valuable professional advice and instruction for shooters of all disciplines.

Cogswell & Harrison; Two Centuries of Gunmaking, by G. Cooley & J. Newton, Safari Press, Long Beach, CA, 2000. 128pp, 30 color photos, 100 b&w photos. $39.95
The authors have gathered a wealth of fascinating historical and technical material that will make the book indispensable, not only to many thousands of "Coggie" owners worldwide, but also to anyone interested in the general history of British gunmaking.

A Collector's Guide to United States Combat Shotguns, by Bruce N. Canfield, Andrew Mowbray Inc., Publishers, Lincoln, RI, 1993. 184 pp., illus. Paper covers. $24.00
Full coverage of the combat shotgun, from the earliest examples to the Gulf War and beyond.

Combat Shotgun and Submachine Gun, "A Special Weapons Analysis" by Chuck Taylor, Paladin Press, Boulder, CO, 1997, soft cover, photos, 176 pp. $25.00
From one of America's top shooting instructors comes an analysis of two controversial, misunderstood and misemployed small arms. Hundreds of photos detail field-testing of both, basic and advanced training drills, tactical rules, gun accessories and modifications. Loading procedures, carrying and fighting positions and malfunction clearance drills are included to promote weapon effectiveness.

Cradock on Shotguns, by Chris Cradock, Banford Press, London, England, 1989. 200 pp., illus. $45.00
A definitive work on the shotgun by a British expert on shotguns.

The Defensive Shotgun, by Louis Awerbuck, S.W.A.T. Publications, Cornville, AZ, 1989. 77 pp., illus. Soft covers. $14.95
Cuts through the myths concerning the shotgun and its attendant ballistic effects.

The Double Shotgun, by Don Zutz, Winchester Press, Piscataway, NJ, 1985. 304 pp., illus. $22.95
Revised, updated, expanded edition of the history and development of the world's classic sporting firearms.

The Ducks Unlimited Guide to Shotgunning, by Don Zutz, Willow Creek Press, Minocqua, WI, 2000. 166 pg. Illustrated. $24.50
This book covers everything from the grand old guns of yesterday to todays best shotguns and loads, from the basic shotgun fit and function to expert advice on ballistics, chocks, and shooting techniques.

Finding the Extra Target, by Coach John R. Linn & Stephen A. Blumenthal, Shotgun Sports, Inc., Auburn, CA, 1989. 126 pp., illus. Paper covers. $14.95
The ultimate training guide for all the clay target sports.

Fine Gunmaking: Double Shotguns, by Steven Dodd Hughes, Krause Publications Iola, WI, 1998. 167 pp., illustrated. $34.95
An in-depth look at the creation of fine shotguns.

Firearms Assembly/Disassembly, Part V: Shotguns, Revised Edition, The Gun Digest Book of, by J.B. Wood, DBI Books, a division of Krause Publications, Iola, WI, 1992. 480 pp., illus. Paper covers. $19.95
Covers 46 popular shotguns plus over 250 variants. The most comprehensive and professional presentation available to either hobbyist or gunsmith.

A.H. Fox "The Finest Gun in the World", revised and enlarged edition, by Michael McIntosh, Countrysport, Inc., New Albany, OH, 1995. 408 pp., illus. $49.00
The first detailed history of one of America's finest shotguns.

Game Shooting, by Robert Churchill, Countrysport Press, Selma, AL, 1998. 258 pp., illus. $30.00
The basis for every shotgun instructional technique devised and the foundation for all wingshooting and the game of sporting clays.

The Golden Age of Shotgunning, by Bob Hinman, Wolfe Publishing Co., Inc., Prescott, AZ, 1982. $22.50
A valuable history of the late 1800s detailing that fabulous period of development in shotguns, shotshells and shotgunning.

The Greener Story, by Graham Greener, Safari Press, Long Beach, CA, 2000. 231pp, color and b&w illustrations. $69.95
The history of the Greener Gunmakers and their guns

Grand Old Shotguns, by Don Zutz, Shotgun Sports Magazine, Auburn, CA, 1995. 136 pp., illus. Paper covers. $19.95
A study of the great smoothbores, their history and how and why they were discontinued. Find out the most sought-after and which were the best shooters.

Gun Digest Book of Sporting Clays, 2nd Edition, edited by Harold A. Murtz, Krause Publications, Iola, WI, 1999. 256 pp., illus. Paper covers. $21.95
A concise Gun Digest book that covers guns, ammo, chokes, targets and course layouts so you'll stay a step ahead.

The Gun Review Book, by Michael McIntosh, Countrysport Press, Selman, AL, 1999. Paper covers. $19.95
Compiled here for the first time are McIntosh's popular gun reviews from *Shooting Sportsman; The Magazine of Wingshooting* and *Fine Shotguns.* The author traces the history of gunmakes, then examines, analyzes, and critique the fine shotguns of England, Continental Europe and the United States.

Hartman on Skeet, by Barney Hartman, Stackpole Books, Harrisburg, PA, 1973. 143 pp., illus. $19.95
A definitive book on Skeet shooting by a pro.

The Heyday of the Shotgun, by David Baker, Safari Press, Inc., Huntington Beach, CA, 2000. 160 pp., illustrated. $39.95
The art of the gunmaker at the turn of the last century when British craftsmen brought forth the finest guns ever made.

The Italian Gun, by Steve Smith & Laurie Morrow, wilderness Adventures, Gallatin Gateway, MT, 1997. 325 pp., illus. $49.95
The first book ever written entirely in English for American enthusiasts who own, aspire to own, or simply admire Italian guns.

The Ithaca Featherlight Repeater; the Best Gun Going, by Walter C. Snyder, Southern Pines, NC, 1998. 300 pp., illus. $89.95
Describes the complete history of each model of the legendary Ithaca Model 37 and Model 87 Repeaters from their conception in 1930 throught 1997.

The Ithaca Gun Company from the Beginning, by Walter C. Snyder, Cook & Uline Publishing Co., Southern Pines, NC, 2nd Edition, 1999. 384 pp., illustrated in color and black and white. $90.00
The entire family of Ithaca Gun Company products is described along with new historical information and the serial number/date of manufacturing listing has been improved.

L.C. Smith Shotguns, by Lt. Col. William S. Brophy, The Gun Room Press, Highland Park, NJ, 1979. 244 pp., illus. $35.00
The first work on this very important American gun and manufacturing company.

The Little Trapshooting Book, by Frank Little, Shotgun Sports Magazine, Auburn, CA, 1994. 168 pp., illus. Paper covers. $19.95
Packed with know-how from one of the greatest trapshooters of all time.

Lock, Stock, and Barrel, by C. Adams & R. Braden, Safari Press, Huntington Beach, CA, 1996. 254 pp., illus. $24.95
The process of making a best grade English gun from a lump of steel and a walnut tree trunk to the ultimate product plus practical advise on consistent field shooting with a double gun.

Mental Training for the Shotgun Sports, by Michael J. Keyes, Shotgun Sports, Auburn, CA, 1996. 160 pp., illus. Paper covers. $24.95
The most comprehensive book ever published on what it takes to shoot winning scores at trap, Skeet and Sporting Clays.

The Model 12, 1912-1964, by Dave Riffle, Dave Riffle, Ft. Meyers, FL, 1995. 274 pp., illus. $49.95
The story of the greatest hammerless repeating shotgun ever built.

More Shotguns and Shooting, by Michael McIntosh, Countrysport Books, Selma, AL, 1998. 256 pp., illustrated. $30.00
From specifics of shotguns to shooting your way out of a slump, it's McIntosh at his best.

Mossberg: More Gun for the Money, by Victor & Cheryl Havlin, Blue Book Publications, Minneapolis, MN, 1995. 204 pages, illustrated. $24.95
The History of O.F. Mossberg & Sons, Inc.

Mossberg's Shotguns, by Duncan Long, Delta Press, El Dorado, AR, 2000. 120 pp., illustrated. $24.95
This book contains a brief history of the company and it's founder, full coverage of the pump and semiautomatic shotguns, rare products and a care and maintenance section.

The Mysteries of Shotgun Patterns, by George G. Oberfell and Charles E. Thompson, Oklahoma State University Press, Stillwater, OK, 1982. 164 pp., illus. Paper covers. $25.00

Shotgun ballistics for the hunter in non-technical language.

The Parker Gun, by Larry Baer, Gun Room Press, Highland Park, NJ, 1993. 195 pages, illustrated with B & W and Color photos. $35.00

Covers in detail, production of all models on this classic gun. Many fine specimens from great collections are illustrated.

Parker Guns "The Old Reliable", by Ed Muderiak, Safari Press, Inc., Huntington Beach, CA, 1997. 325 pp., illus. $40.00

A look at the small beginnings, the golden years, and the ultimate decline of the most famous of all American shotgun manufacturers.

The Parker Story; Volumes 1 & 2, by Bill Mullins, "etal". The Double Gun Journal, East Jordan, MI, 2000. 1,025 pages of text and 1,500 color and monochrome illustrations. Hardbound in a gold-embossed cover. $295.00

The most complete and attractive "last word" on America's preeminent double gun maker. Includes tables showing the number of guns made by gauge, barrel length and special features for each grade.

Positive Shooting, by Michael Yardley, Safari Press, Huntington Beach, CA, 1995. 160 pp., illus. $30.00

This book will provide the shooter with a sound foundation from which to develop an effective, personal technique that can dramatically improve shooting performance.

Purdey Gun and Rifle Makers: The Definitive History, by Donald Dallas, Quiller Press, London 2000. 245 pages, illus. $100.00

245 Colour plates, b/w photos, ills, bibliography. The definitive history. A limited edition of 3,000 copies. Signed and Numbered. With a PURDEY book plate.

Recognizing Side by Side Shotguns, by Charles Carder, Anvil Onze Publishing, 2000. 25 pp., illus. Paper Covers. $5.95

A graphic description of the visible features of side by side breech loading shotguns.

Reloading for Shotgunners, 4th Edition, by Kurt D. Fackler and M.L. McPherson, DBI Books, a division of Krause Publications, Iola, WI, 1997. 320 pp., illus. Paper covers. $19.95

Expanded reloading tables with over 11,000 loads. Bushing charts for every major press and component maker. All new presentation on all aspects of shotshell reloading by two of the top experts in the field. (Available October 1997.)

Remington Double Shotguns, by Charles G. Semer, Denver, CO, 1997. 617 pp., illus. $60.00

This book deals with the entire production and all grades of double shotguns made by Remington during the period of their production 1873-1910.

75 Years with the Shotgun, by C.T. (Buck) Buckman, Valley Publ., Fresno, CA, 1974. 141 pp., illus. $10.00

An expert hunter and trapshooter shares experiences of a lifetime.

The Shotgun in Combat, by Tony Lesce, Desert Publications, Cornville, AZ, 1979. 148 pp., illus. Paper covers. $14.00

A history of the shotgun and its use in combat.

Shotgun Digest, 4th Edition, edited by Jack Lewis, DBI Books, a division of Krause Publications, Iola, WI, 1993. 256 pp., illus. Paper covers. $17.95

A look at what's happening with shotguns and shotgunning today.

The Shotgun Encyclopedia, by John Taylor, Safari Press, Inc., Huntington Beach, CA, 2000. 260 pp., illustrated. $34.95

A comprehensive reference work on all aspects of shotguns and shotgun shooting.

Shotgun Gunsmithing, The Gun Digest Book of, by Ralph Walker, DBI Books, a division of Krause Publications, Iola, WI, 1983. 256 pp., illus. Paper covers. $16.95

The principles and practices of repairing, individualizing and accurizing modern shotguns by one of the world's premier shotgun gunsmiths.

The Shotgun: History and Development, by Geoffrey Boothroyd, Safari Press, Huntington Beach, CA, 1995. 240 pp., illus. $35.00

The first volume in a series that traces the development of the British shotgun from the 17th century onward.

The Shotgun Handbook, by Mike George, The Croswood Press, London, England, 1999. 128 pp., illus. $35.00

For all shotgun enthusiasts, this detailed guide ranges from design and selection of a gun to adjustment, cleaning, and maintenance.

Shotgun Stuff, by Don Zutz, Shotgun Sports, Inc., Auburn, CA, 1991. 172 pp., illus. Paper covers. $19.95

This book gives shotgunners all the "stuff" they need to achieve better performance and get more enjoyment from their favorite smoothbore.

Shotgunner's Notebook: The Advice and Reflections of a Wingshooter, by Gene Hill, Countrysport Press, Traverse City, MI, 1990. 192 pp., illus. $25.00

Covers the shooting, the guns and the miscellany of the sport.

Shotgunning: The Art and the Science, by Bob Brister, Winchester Press, Piscataway, NJ, 1976. 321 pp., illus. $18.95

Hundreds of specific tips and truly novel techniques to improve the field and target shooting of every shotgunner.

Shotgunning Trends in Transition, by Don Zutz, Wolfe Publishing Co., Prescott, AZ, 1990. 314 pp., illus. $29.50

This book updates American shotgunning from post WWII to present.

Shotguns and Cartridges for Game and Clays, by Gough Thomas, edited by Nigel Brown, A & C Black, Ltd., Cambs, England, 1989. 256 pp., illus. Soft covers. $24.95

Gough Thomas' well-known and respected book for game and clay pigeon shooters in a thoroughly up-dated edition.

Shotguns and Gunsmiths: The Vintage Years, by Geoffrey Boothroyd, Safari Press, Huntington Beach, CA, 1995. 240 pp., illus. $35.00

A fascinating insight into the lives and skilled work of gunsmiths who helped develop the British shotgun during the Victorian and Edwardian eras.

Shotguns and Shooting, by Michael McIntosh, Countrysport Press, New Albany, OH, 1995. 258 pp., illus. $30.00

The art of guns and gunmaking, this book is a celebration no lover of fine doubles should miss.

Shotguns for Wingshooting, by John Barsness, DBI Books, a division of Krause Publications, Inc., Iola, WI, 1999. 208 pp., illustrated. $49.95

Detailed information on all styles of shotgun. How to select the correct ammunition for specific hunting applications.

Side by Sides of the World for Y2K, by Charles Carder, Anvil Onze Publishing, 2000. 221 pp., illus. Paper Covers. $25.95

This book lists more than 1600 names & features side by sides shotguns from all over the world, in alphabetical order. 500 + illustrations.

Sidelocks & Boxlocks, by Geoffrey Boothroyd, Sand Lake Press, Amity, OR, 1991. 271 pp., illus. $24.95

The story of the classic British shotgun.

Spanish Best: The Fine Shotguns of Spain, by Terry Wieland, Countrysport, Inc., Traverse City, MI, 1994. 264 pp., illus. $45.00

A practical source of information for owners of Spanish shotguns and a guide for those considering buying a used shotgun.

The Sporting Clay Handbook, by Jerry Meyer, Lyons and Burford Publishers, New York, NY, 1990. 140 pp., illus. Soft covers. $17.95

Introduction to the fastest growing, and most exciting, gun game in America.

Streetsweepers, "The Complete Book of Combat Shotguns", by Duncan Long, Paladin Press, Boulder, CO,1997, soft cover, 63 photos, illus., appendices, 160 pp. $24.95

Streetsweepers is the newest, most comprehensive book out on combat shotguns, covering single- and double-barreled, slide-action, semi-auto and rotary cylinder shotguns, plus a chapter on grenade launchers you can mount on your weapon and info about shotgun models not yet on the market. Noted gun writer Duncan Long also advises on which ammo to use, accessories and combat shotgun tactics.

The Tactical Shotgun, by Gabriel Suzrez, Paladin Press, Boulder, CO, 1996. 232 pp., illus. Paper covers. $25.00

The best techniques and tactics for employing the shotgun in personal combat.

Taking More Birds, by Dan Carlisle & Dolph Adams, Lyons & Burford, New York, NY, 1993. 120 pp., illus. $19.95

A practical guide to greater success at sporting clays and wing shooting.

Tip Up Shotguns from Hopkins and Allen, by Charles Carder, Anvil Onze Publishing, 2000. 81 pp., illus. Paper Covers. $13.95

All the descriptive material and graphics used in this book have been reproduced from original Hopkins & Allen Arms Company catalogs, except the patent drawings.

Trap & Skeet Shooting, 3rd Edition, by Chris Christian, DBI Books, a division of Krause Publications, Iola, WI, 1994. 288 pp., illus. Paper covers. $17.95

A detailed look at the contemporary world of Trap, Skeet and Sporting Clays.

Trapshooting is a Game of Opposites, by Dick Bennett, Shotgun Sports, Inc., Auburn, CA, 1996. 129 pp., illus. Paper covers. $19.95

Discover everything you need to know about shooting trap like the pros.

Turkey Hunter's Digest, Revised Edition, by Dwain Bland, DBI Books, a division of Krause Publications, Iola, WI, 1994. 256 pp., illus. Paper covers. $17.95

Presents no-nonsense approach to hunting all five sub-species of the North American wild turkey.

U.S. Shotguns, All Types, reprint of TM9-285, Desert Publications, Cornville, AZ, 1987. 257 pp., illus. Paper covers. $9.95

Covers operation, assembly and disassembly of nine shotguns used by the U.S. armed forces.

U.S. Winchester Trench and Riot Guns and Other U.S. Military Combat Shotguns, by Joe Poyer, North Cape Publications, Tustin, CA, 1992. 124 pp., illus. Paper covers. $15.95

A detailed history of the use of military shotguns, and the acquisition procedures used by the U.S. Army's Ordnance Department in both World Wars.

The Winchester Model Twelve, by George Madis, David Madis, Dallas, TX, 1984. 176 pp., illus. $24.95

A definitive work on this famous American shotgun.

The Winchester Model 42, by Ned Schwing, Krause Pub., Iola, WI, 1990. 160 pp., illus. $34.95

Behind-the-scenes story of the model 42's invention and its early development. Production totals and manufacturing dates; reference work.

Winchester Shotguns and Shotshells, by Ron Stadt, Krause Pub., Iola, WI. 288 pp., illus. $34.95

Must-have for Winchester collectors of shotguns manufactured through 1961.

Winchester's Finest, the Model 21, by Ned Schwing, Krause Publications, Iola, WI, 1990. 360 pp., illus. $49.95

The classic beauty and the interesting history of the Model 21 Winchester shotgun.

The World's Fighting Shotguns, by Thomas F. Swearengen, T.B.N. Enterprises, Alexandria, VA, 1979. 500 pp., illus. $39.95

The complete military and police reference work from the shotgun's inception to date, with up-to-date developments.

REFERENCE

ARMS ASSOCIATIONS

UNITED STATES

ALABAMA
Alabama Gun Collectors Assn.
Secretary, P.O. Box 70965, Tuscaloosa, AL 35407

ALASKA
Alaska Gun Collectors Assn., Inc.
C.W. Floyd, Pres., 5240 Little Tree, Anchorage, AK 99507

ARIZONA
Arizona Arms Assn.
Don DeBusk, President, 4837 Bryce Ave., Glendale, AZ 85301

CALIFORNIA
California Cartridge Collectors Assn.
Rick Montgomery, 1729 Christina, Stockton, CA 95204/209-463-7216 evs.
California Waterfowl Assn.
4630 Northgate Blvd., #150, Sacramento, CA 95834
Greater Calif. Arms & Collectors Assn.
Donald L. Bullock, 8291 Carburton St., Long Beach, CA 90808-3302
Los Angeles Gun Ctg. Collectors Assn.
F.H. Ruffra, 20810 Amie Ave., Apt. #9, Torrance, CA 90503
Stock Gun Players Assn.
6038 Appian Way, Long Beach, CA, 90803

COLORADO
Colorado Gun Collectors Assn.
L.E.(Bud) Greenwald, 2553 S. Quitman St., Denver, CO 80219/303-935-3850
Rocky Mountain Cartridge Collectors Assn.
John Roth, P.O. Box 757, Conifer, CO 80433

CONNECTICUT
Ye Connecticut Gun Guild, Inc.
Dick Fraser, P.O. Box 425, Windsor, CT 06095

FLORIDA
Unified Sportsmen of Florida
P.O. Box 6565, Tallahassee, FL 32314

GEORGIA
Georgia Arms Collectors Assn., Inc.
Michael Kindberg, President, P.O. Box 277, Alpharetta, GA 30239-0277

ILLINOIS
Illinois State Rifle Assn.
P.O. Box 637, Chatsworth, IL 60921
Mississippi Valley Gun & Cartridge Coll. Assn.
Bob Filbert, P.O. Box 61, Port Byron, IL 61275/309-523-2593
Sauk Trail Gun Collectors
Gordell M. Matson, P.O. Box 1113, Milan, IL 61264
Wabash Valley Gun Collectors Assn., Inc.
Roger L. Dorsett, 2601 Willow Rd., Urbana, IL 61801/217-384-7302

INDIANA
Indiana State Rifle & Pistol Assn.
Thos. Glancy, P.O. Box 552, Chesterton, IN 46304
Southern Indiana Gun Collectors Assn., Inc.
Sheila McClary, 309 W. Monroe St., Boonville, IN 47601/812-897-3742

IOWA
Beaver Creek Plainsmen Inc.
Steve Murphy, Secy., P.O. Box 298, Bondurant, IA 50035
Central States Gun Collectors Assn.
Dennis Greischar, Box 841, Mason City, IA 50402-0841

KANSAS
Kansas Cartridge Collectors Assn.
Bob Linder, Box 84, Plainville, KS 67663

KENTUCKY
Kentuckiana Arms Collectors Assn.
Charles Billips, President, Box 1776, Louisville, KY 40201
Kentucky Gun Collectors Assn., Inc.
Ruth Johnson, Box 64, Owensboro, KY 42302/502-729-4197

LOUISIANA
Washitaw River Renegades
Sandra Rushing, P.O. Box 256, Main St., Grayson, LA 71435

MARYLAND
Baltimore Antique Arms Assn.
Mr. Cillo, 1034 Main St., Darlington, MD 21304

MASSACHUSETTS
Bay Colony Weapons Collectors, Inc.
John Brandt, Box 111, Hingham, MA 02043
Massachusetts Arms Collectors
Bruce E. Skinner, P.O. Box 31, No. Carver, MA 02355/508-866-5259

MICHIGAN
Association for the Study and Research of .22 Caliber Rimfire Cartridges
George Kass, 4512 Nakoma Dr., Okemos, MI 48864

MINNESOTA
Sioux Empire Cartridge Collectors Assn.
Bob Cameron, 14597 Glendale Ave. SE, Prior Lake, MN 55372

MISSISSIPPI
Mississippi Gun Collectors Assn.
Jack E. Swinney, P.O. Box 16323, Hattiesburg, MS 39402

MISSOURI
Greater St. Louis Cartridge Collectors Assn.
Don MacChesney, 634 Scottsdale Rd., Kirkwood, MO 63122-1109
Mineral Belt Gun Collectors Assn.
D.F. Saunders, 1110 Cleveland Ave., Monett, MO 65708
Missouri Valley Arms Collectors Assn., Inc.
L.P Brammer II, Membership Secy., P.O. Box 33033, Kansas City, MO 64114

MONTANA
Montana Arms Collectors Assn.
Dean E. Yearout, Sr., Exec. Secy., 1516 21st Ave. S., Great Falls, MT 59405
Weapons Collectors Society of Montana
R.G. Schipf, Ex. Secy., 3100 Bancroft St., Missoula, MT 59801/406-728-2995

NEBRASKA
Nebraska Cartridge Collectors Club
Gary Muckel, P.O. Box 84442, Lincoln, NE 68501

NEW HAMPSHIRE
New Hampshire Arms Collectors, Inc.
James Stamatelos, Secy., P.O. Box 5, Cambridge, MA 02139

NEW JERSEY
Englishtown Benchrest Shooters Assn.
Michael Toth, 64 Cooke Ave., Carteret, NJ 07008
Jersey Shore Antique Arms Collectors
Joe Sisia, P.O. Box 100, Bayville, NJ 08721-0100
New Jersey Arms Collectors Club, Inc.
Angus Laidlaw, Vice President, 230 Valley Rd., Montclair, NJ 07042/201-746-0939; e-mail: acclaidlaw@juno.com

NEW YORK
Iroquois Arms Collectors Assn.
Bonnie Robinson, Show Secy., P.O. Box 142, Ransomville, NY 14131/716-791-4096
Mid-State Arms Coll. & Shooters Club
Jack Ackerman, 24 S. Mountain Terr., Binghamton, NY 13903

NORTH CAROLINA
North Carolina Gun Collectors Assn.
Jerry Ledford, 3231-7th St. Dr. NE, Hickory, NC 28601

OHIO
Ohio Gun Collectors Assn.
P.O. Box 9007, Maumee, OH 43537-9007/419-897-0861; Fax:419-897-0860
Shotshell Historical and Collectors Society
Madeline Bruemmer, 3886 Dawley Rd., Ravenna, OH 44266
The Stark Gun Collectors, Inc.
William I. Gann, 5666 Waynesburg Dr., Waynesburg, OH 44688

OREGON
Oregon Arms Collectors Assn., Inc.
Phil Bailey, P.O. Box 13000-A, Portland, OR 97213-0017/503-281-6864; off.:503-281-0918
Oregon Cartridge Collectors Assn.
Boyd Northrup, P.O. Box 285, Rhododendron, OR 97049

PENNSYLVANIA
Presque Isle Gun Collectors Assn.
James Welch, 156 E. 37 St., Erie, PA 16504

SOUTH CAROLINA
Belton Gun Club, Inc.
Attn. Secretary, P.O. Box 126, Belton, SC 29627/864-369-6767

Gun Owners of South Carolina
Membership Div.: William Strozier, Secretary, P.O. Box 70, Johns Island, SC 29457-0070/803-762-3240; Fax:803-795-0711; e-mail:76053.222@compuserve.com

SOUTH DAKOTA
Dakota Territory Gun Coll. Assn., Inc.
Curt Carter, Castlewood, SD 57223

TENNESSEE
Smoky Mountain Gun Coll. Assn., Inc.
Hugh W. Yabro, President, P.O. Box 23225, Knoxville, TN 37933

Tennessee Gun Collectors Assn., Inc.
M.H. Parks, 3556 Pleasant Valley Rd., Nashville, TN 37204-3419

TEXAS
Houston Gun Collectors Assn., Inc.
P.O. Box 741429, Houston, TX 77274-1429
Texas Gun Collectors Assn.
Bob Eder, Pres., P.O. Box 12067, El Paso, TX 79913/915-584-8183
Texas State Rifle Assn.
1131 Rockingham Dr., Suite 101, Richardson, TX 75080-4326

VIRGINIA
Virginia Gun Collectors Assn., Inc.
Addison Hurst, Secy., 38802 Charlestown Height, Waterford, VA 20197/540-882-3543

WASHINGTON
Association of Cartridge Collectors on the Pacific Northwest
Robert Jardin, 14214 Meadowlark Drive KPN, Gig Harbor, WA 98329
Washington Arms Collectors, Inc.
Joyce Boss, P.O. Box 389, Renton, WA, 98057-0389/206-255-8410

WISCONSIN
Great Lakes Arms Collectors Assn., Inc.
Edward C. Warnke, 2913 Woodridge Lane, Waukesha, WI 53188
Wisconsin Gun Collectors Assn., Inc.
Lulita Zellmer, P.O. Box 181, Sussex, WI 53089

WYOMING
Wyoming Weapons Collectors
P.O. Box 284, Laramie, WY 82073/307-745-4652 or 745-9530

NATIONAL ORGANIZATIONS

Amateur Trapshooting Assn.
David D. Bopp, Exec. Director, 601 W. National Rd., Vandalia, OH 45377/937-898-4638; Fax:937-898-5472
American Airgun Field Target Assn.
5911 Cherokee Ave., Tampa, FL 33604
American Coon Hunters Assn.
Opal Johnston, P.O. Cadet, Route 1, Box 492, Old Mines, MO 63630
American Custom Gunmakers Guild
Jan Billeb, Exec. Director, 22 Vista View Drive, Cody, WY 82414-9606 (307) 587-4297 (phone/fax). Email: acgg@acgg.org Website: www.acgg.org
American Defense Preparedness Assn.
Two Colonial Place, 2101 Wilson Blvd., Suite 400, Arlington, VA 22201-3061
American Paintball League
P.O. Box 3561, Johnson City, TN 37602/800-541-9169
American Pistolsmiths Guild
Alex B. Hamilton, Pres., 1449 Blue Crest Lane, San Antonio, TX 78232/210-494-3063
American Police Pistol & Rifle Assn.
3801 Biscayne Blvd., Miami, FL 33137

American Single Shot Rifle Assn.
Charles Kriegel, Secy., 1346C Whispering Woods Drive, West Carrollton OH 45449/937-866-9064. Website: www.assra.com
American Society of Arms Collectors
George E. Weatherly, P.O. Box 2567, Waxahachie, TX 75165
American Tactical Shooting Assn.(A.T.S.A.)
c/o Skip Gochenour, 2600 N. Third St., Harrisburg, PA 17110/717-233-0402; Fax:717-233-5340
Association of Firearm and Tool Mark Examiners
Lannie G. Emanuel, Secy., Southwest Institute of Forensic Sciences, P.O. Box 35728, Dallas, TX 75235/214-920-5979; Fax:214-920-5928; Membership Secy., Ann D. Jones, VA Div. of Forensic Science, P.O. Box 999, Richmond, VA 23208/804-786-4706; Fax:804-371-8328
Boone & Crockett Club
250 Station Dr., Missoula, MT 59801-2753
Browning Collectors Assn.
Secretary:Scherrie L. Brennac, 2749 Keith Dr., Villa Ridge, MO 63089/314-742-0571
The Cast Bullet Assn., Inc.
Ralland J. Fortier, Editor, 4103 Foxcraft Dr., Traverse City, MI 49684
Citizens Committee for the Right to Keep and Bear Arms
Natl. Hq., Liberty Park, 12500 NE Tenth Pl., Bellevue, WA 98005
Colt Collectors Assn.
25000 Highland Way, Los Gatos, CA 95030/408-353-2658.
Ducks Unlimited, Inc.
Natl. Headquarters, One Waterfowl Way, Memphis, TN 38120/901-758-3937
Fifty Caliber Shooters Assn.
PO Box 111, Monroe UT 84754-0111
Firearms Coalition/Neal Knox Associates
Box 6537, Silver Spring, MD 20906/301-871-3006
Firearms Engravers Guild of America
Rex C. Pedersen, Secy., 511 N. Rath Ave., Lundington, MI 49431/616-845-7695(Phone and Fax)
Foundation for North American Wild Sheep
720 Allen Ave., Cody, WY 82414-3402/web site: http://iigi.com/os/non/fnaws/fnaws.htm; e-mail: fnaws@wyoming.com
Freedom Arms Collectors Assn.
P.O. Box 160302, Miami, FL 33116-0302
Garand Collectors Assn.
P.O. Box 181, Richmond, KY 40475
Glock Shooting Sports Foundation
PO Box 309, Smyrna GA 30081 770-432-1202 Website: www.gssfonline.com
Golden Eagle Collectors Assn. (G.E.C.A.)
Chris Showler, 11144 Slate Creek Rd., Grass Valley, CA 95945
Gun Owners of America
8001 Forbes Place, Suite 102, Springfield, VA 22151/703-321-8585

ARMS ASSOCIATION

Handgun Hunters International
J.D. Jones, Director, P.O. Box 357 MAG, Bloomingdale, OH 43910
Harrington & Richardson Gun Coll. Assn.
George L. Cardet, 330 S.W. 27th Ave., Suite 603, Miami, FL 33135
High Standard Collectors' Assn.
John J. Stimson, Jr., Pres., 540 W. 92nd St., Indianapolis, IN 46260 Website: www.highstandard.org
Hopkins & Allen Arms & Memorabilia Society (HAAMS)
P.O. Box 187, 1309 Pamela Circle, Delphos, OH 45833
International Ammunition Association, Inc.
C.R. Punnett, Secy., 8 Hillock Lane, Chadds Ford, PA 19317/610-358-1285;Fax:610-358-1560
International Benchrest Shooters
Joan Borden, RR1, Box 250BB, Springville, PA 18844/717-965-2366
International Blackpowder Hunting Assn.
P.O. Box 1180, Glenrock, WY 82637/307-436-9817
IHMSA (Intl. Handgun Metallic Silhouette Assn.)
PO Box 368, Burlington, IA 52601 Website: www.ihmsa.org
International Society of Mauser Arms Collectors
Michael Kindberg, Pres., P.O. Box 277, Alpharetta, GA 30239-0277
Jews for the Preservation of Firearms Ownership (JPFO) 501(c)(3)
2872 S. Wentworth Ave., Milwaukee, WI 53207/414-769-0760; Fax:414-483-8435
The Mannlicher Collectors Assn.
Membership Office: P.O. Box1249, The Dalles, Oregon 97058
Marlin Firearms Collectors Assn., Ltd.
Dick Paterson, Secy., 407 Lincoln Bldg., 44 Main St., Champaign, IL 61820
Merwin Hulbert Association,
2503 Kentwood Ct., High Point, NC 27265
Miniature Arms Collectors/Makers Society, Ltd.
Ralph Koebbeman, Pres., 4910 Kilburn Ave., Rockford, IL 61101/815-964-2569
M1 Carbine Collectors Assn. (M1-CCA)
623 Apaloosa Ln., Gardnerville, NV 89410-7840
National Association of Buckskinners (NAB)
Territorial Dispatch—1800s Historical Publication, 4701 Marion St., Suite 324, Livestock Exchange Bldg., Denver, CO 80216/303-297-9671
The National Association of Derringer Collectors
P.O. Box 20572, San Jose, CA 95160
National Assn. of Federally Licensed Firearms Dealers
Andrew Molchan, 2455 E. Sunrise, Ft. Lauderdale, FL 33304
National Association to Keep and Bear Arms
P.O. Box 78336, Seattle, WA 98178

National Automatic Pistol Collectors Assn.
Tom Knox, P.O. Box 15738, Tower Grove Station, St. Louis, MO 63163
National Bench Rest Shooters Assn., Inc.
Pat Ferrell, 2835 Guilford Lane, Oklahoma City, OK 73120-4404/405-842-9585; Fax: 405-842-9575
National Muzzle Loading Rifle Assn.
Box 67, Friendship, IN 47021 / 812-667-5131. Website: www.nmlra@nmlra.org
National Professional Paintball League (NPPL)
540 Main St., Mount Kisco, NY 10549/914-241-7400
National Reloading Manufacturers Assn.
One Centerpointe Dr., Suite 300, Lake Oswego, OR 97035
National Rifle Assn. of America
11250 Waples Mill Rd., Fairfax, VA 22030 / 703-267-1000. Website: www.nra.org
National Shooting Sports Foundation, Inc.
Robert T. Delfay, President, Flintlock Ridge Office Center, 11 Mile Hill Rd., Newtown, CT 06470-2359/203-426-1320; FAX: 203-426-1087
National Skeet Shooting Assn.
Dan Snyuder, Director, 5931 Roft Road, San Antonio, TX 78253-9261/800-877-5338. Website: nssa-nsca.com
National Sporting Clays Association
Ann Myers, Director, 5931 Roft Road, San Antonio, TX 78253-9261/800-877-5338. Website: nssa-nsca.com
National Wild Turkey Federation, Inc.
P.O. Box 530, 770 Augusta Rd., Edgefield, SC 29824
North American Hunting Club
P.O. Box 3401, Minnetonka, MN 55343/612-936-9333; Fax: 612-936-9755
North American Paintball Referees Association (NAPRA)
584 Cestaric Dr., Milpitas, CA 95035
North-South Skirmish Assn., Inc.
Stevan F. Meserve, Exec. Secretary, 507 N. Brighton Court, Sterling, VA 20164-3919
Old West Shooter's Association 712 James Street, Hazel TX 76020 817-444-2049
Remington Society of America
Gordon Fosburg, Secretary, 11900 North Brinton Road, Lake, MI 48623
Rocky Mountain Elk Foundation
P.O. Box 8249, Missoula, MT 59807-8249/406-523-4500;Fax: 406-523-4581
Website: www.rmef.org
Ruger Collector's Assn., Inc.
P.O. Box 240, Greens Farms, CT 06436
Safari Club International
4800 W. Gates Pass Rd., Tucson, AZ 85745/520-620-1220
Sako Collectors Assn., Inc.
Jim Lutes, 202 N. Locust, Whitewater, KS 67154
Second Amendment Foundation
James Madison Building, 12500 NE 10th Pl., Bellevue, WA 98005

Single Action Shooting Society (SASS)
23255-A La Palma Avenue, Yorba Linda, CA 92887/714-694-1800; FAX: 714-694-1815/email: sasseot@aol.com Website: www.sassnet.com
Smith & Wesson Collectors Assn.
Cally Pletl, Admin. Asst.,PO Box 444, Afton, NY 13730
The Society of American Bayonet Collectors
P.O. Box 234, East Islip, NY 11730-0234
Southern California Schuetzen Society
Dean Lillard, 34657 Ave. E., Yucaipa, CA 92399
Sporting Arms and Ammunition Manufacturers' Institute (SAAMI)
Flintlock Ridge Office Center, 11 Mile Hill Rd., Newtown, CT 06470-2359/203-426-4358; FAX: 203-426-1087
Sporting Clays of America (SCA)
Ron L. Blosser, Pres., 9257 Buckeye Rd., Sugar Grove, OH 43155-9632/614-746-8334; Fax: 614-746-8605
Steel Challenge 23234 Via Barra, Valencia CA 91355 Website: www.steelchallenge.com
The Thompson/Center Assn.
Joe Wright, President, Box 792, Northboro, MA 01532/508-845-6960
U.S. Practical Shooting Assn./IPSC
Dave Thomas, P.O. Box 811, Sedro Woolley, WA 98284/360-855-2245 Website: www.uspsa.org
U.S. Revolver Assn.
Brian J. Barer, 40 Larchmont Ave., Taunton, MA 02780/508-824-4836
U.S.A. Shooting
U.S. Olympic Shooting Center, One Olympic Plaza, Colorado Springs, CO 80909/719-578-4670. Website: wwwusashooting.org
The Varmint Hunters Assn., Inc.
Box 759, Pierre, SD 57501/Member Services 800-528-4868
Weatherby Collectors Assn., Inc.
P.O. Box 478, Pacific, MO 63069 Website: www.weatherbycollectors.com Email: WCAsecretary@aol.com
The Wildcatters
P.O. Box 170, Greenville, WI 54942
Winchester Arms Collectors Assn.
P.O. Box 230, Brownsboro, TX 75756/903-852-4027
The Women's Shooting Sports Foundation (WSSF)
4620 Edison Avenue, Ste. C, Colorado Springs, CO 80915/719-638-1299; FAX: 719-638-1271/email: wssf@worldnet.att.net

ARGENTINA

Asociacion Argentina de Coleccionistas de Armes y Municiones
Castilla de Correos No. 28, Succursal I B, 1401 Buenos Aires, Republica Argentina

AUSTRALIA

Antique & Historical Arms Collectors of Australia
P.O. Box 5654, GCMC Queensland 9726, Australia
The Arms Collector's Guild of Queensland Inc.
Ian Skennerton, P.O. Box 433, Ashmore City 4214, Queensland, Australia
Australian Cartridge Collectors Assn., Inc.
Bob Bennett, 126 Landscape Dr., E. Doncaster 3109, Victoria, Australia
Sporting Shooters Assn. of Australia, Inc.
P.O. Box 2066, Kent Town, SA 5071, Australia

CANADA

ALBERTA
Canadian Historical Arms Society
P.O. Box 901, Edmonton, Alb., Canada T5J 2L8
National Firearms Assn.
Natl. Hq: P.O. Box 1779, Edmonton, Alb., Canada T5J 2P1

BRITISH COLUMBIA
The Historical Arms Collectors of B.C. (Canada)
Harry Moon, Pres., P.O. Box 50117, South Slope RPO, Burnaby, BC V5J 5G3, Canada/604-438-0950; Fax:604-277-3646

ONTARIO
Association of Canadian Cartridge Collectors
Monica Wright, RR 1, Millgrove, ON, LOR IVO, Canada
Tri-County Antique Arms Fair
P.O. Box 122, RR #1, North Lancaster, Ont., Canada K0C 1Z0

EUROPE

BELGIUM
European Cartridge Research Assn.
Graham Irving, 21 Rue Schaltin, 4900 Spa, Belgium/32.87.77.43.40; Fax:32.87.77.27.51

CZECHOSLOVAKIA
Spolecnost Pro Studium Naboju (Czech Cartridge Research Assn.)
JUDr. Jaroslav Bubak, Pod Homolko 1439, 26601 Beroun 2, Czech Republic

DENMARK
Aquila Dansk Jagtpatron Historic Forening (Danish Historical Cartridge Collectors Club)
Steen Elgaard Møller, Ulriksdalsvej 7, 4840 Nr. Alslev, Denmark 10045-53846218;Fax:00455384 6209

ENGLAND
Arms and Armour Society
Hon. Secretary A. Dove, P.O. Box 10232, London, 5W19 2ZD, England
Dutch Paintball Federation
Aceville Publ., Castle House 97 High Street, Colchester, Essex C01 1TH, England/011-44-206-564840
European Paintball Sports Foundation
c/o Aceville Publ., Castle House 97 High St., Colchester, Essex, C01 1TH, England

Historical Breechloading Smallarms Assn.
D.J. Penn M.A., Secy., P.O. Box 12778, London SE1 6BX, England. Journal and newsletter are $23 a yr., including airmail.
National Rifle Assn.
(Great Britain) Bisley Camp, Brookwood, Woking Surrey GU24 0PB, England/01483.797777; Fax: 014730686275
United Kingdom Cartridge Club
Ian Southgate, 20 Millfield, Elmley Castle, Nr. Pershore, Worcestershire, WR10 3HR, England

FRANCE
STAC-Western Co.
3 Ave. Paul Doumer (N.311); 78360 Montesson, France/01.30.53-43-65; Fax: 01.30.53.19.10

GERMANY
Bund Deutscher Sportschützen e.v. (BDS)
Borsigallee 10, 53125 Bonn 1, Germany
Deutscher Schützenbund
Lahnstrasse 120, 65195 Wiesbaden, Germany

SPAIN
Asociacion Espanola de Coleccionistas de Cartuchos (A.E.C.C.)
Secretary: Apdo. Correos No. 1086, 2880-Alcala de Henares (Madrid), Spain. President: Apdo. Correos No. 682, 50080 Zaragoza, Spain

SWEDEN
Scandinavian Ammunition Research Assn.
c/o Morten Stoen, Annerudstubben 3, N-1383 Asker, Norway

NEW ZEALAND
New Zealand Cartridge Collectors Club
Terry Castle, 70 Tiraumea Dr., Pakuranga, Auckland, New Zealand
New Zealand Deerstalkers Assn.
P.O. Box 6514 TE ARO, Wellington, New Zealand

SOUTH AFRICA
Historical Firearms Soc. of South Africa
P.O. Box 145, 7725 Newlands, Republic of South Africa
Republic of South Africa Cartridge Collectors Assn.
Arno Klee, 20 Eugene St., Malanshof Randburg, Gauteng 2194, Republic of South Africa
S.A.A.C.A. (Southern Africa Arms and Ammunition Assn.)
Gauteng office: P.O. Box 7597, Weltevreden Park, 1715, Republic of South Africa/011-679-1151; Fax: 011-679-1131; e-mail: saaaca@iafrica.com. Kwa-Zulu Natal office: P.O. Box 4065, Northway, Kwazulu-Natal 4065, Republic of South Africa
SAGA (S.A. Gunowners' Assn.)
P.O. Box 35203, Northway, Kwazulu-Natal 4065, Republic of South Africa

The **Product Directory** contains 80 product categories. The **Manufacturer's Directory** alphabetically lists the manufacturers with their addresses, phone numbers, FAX numbers and Internet addresses, if available.

DIRECTORY OF THE ARMS TRADE INDEX

DIRECTORY

AMMUNITION COMPONENTS, SHOTSHELL

A.W. Peterson Gun Shop, Inc.
Ballistic Product, Inc.
Blount, Inc., Sporting Equipment Div.
CCI Ammunition
Cheddite France S.A.
Claybuster Wads & Harvester Bullets
Garcia National Gun Traders, Inc.
Peterson Gun Shop, Inc., A.W.
Precision Reloading, Inc.
Ravell Ltd.
Tar-Hunt Custom Rifles, Inc.
Tar-Hunt Custom Rifles, Inc.
The A.W. Peterson Gun Shop, Inc.
Vitt/Boos

AMMUNITION COMPONENTS-- BULLETS, POWDER, PRIMERS, CASES

3-D Ammunition & Bullets
A.W. Peterson Gun Shop, Inc.
Acadian Ballistic Specialties
Accuracy Unlimited
Accurate Arms Co., Inc.
Action Bullets & Alloy Inc
ADCO Sales, Inc.
Alaska Bullet Works, Inc.
Alliant Techsystems Smokeless
   Powder Group
Allred Bullet Co.
Alpha LaFranck Enterprises
American Products, Inc.
Arizona Ammunition, Inc.
Armfield Custom Bullets
A-Square Company, Inc.
Atlantic Rose, Inc.
Baer's Hollows
Ballard Rifle & Cartridge Co., LLC
Barnes
Barnes Bullets, Inc.
Beartooth Bullets
Bell Reloading, Inc.
Berger Bullets Ltd.
Berry's Mfg., Inc.
Big Bore Bullets of Alaska
Big Bore Express
Bitterroot Bullet Co.
Black Belt Bullets
   (See Big Bore Express)
Black Hills Shooters Supply
Black Powder Products
Blount, Inc., Sporting Equipment Div.
Blue Mountain Bullets
Brenneke KG, Wilhelm
Briese Bullet Co., Inc.
Brown Co, E. Arthur
Brown Dog Ent.
BRP, Inc. High Performance Cast
   Bullets
Buck Stix--SOS Products Co.
Buckeye Custom Bullets
Buckskin Bullet Co.
Buffalo Arms Co.
Buffalo Bullet Co., Inc..
Buffalo Rock Shooters Supply
Bullseye Bullets
Bull-X, Inc.
Butler Enterprises
Cambos Outdoorsman
Canyon Cartridge Corp.
Cascade Bullet Co., Inc.
Cast Performance Bullet Company
Casull Arms Corp.
CCI Ammunition
Champion's Choice, Inc.
Cheddite France S.A.
CheVron Bullets
Chuck's Gun Shop
Clean Shot Technologies
Colorado Sutlers Arsenal
   (See Cumberland States
Competitor Corp. Inc.
Cook Engineering Service
Cor-Bon Bullet & Ammo Co.
Cumberland States Arsenal
Cummings Bullets
Curtis Cast Bullets

Curtis Gun Shop
   (See Curtis Cast Bullets)
Custom Bullets by Hoffman
D&J Bullet Co. & Custom Gun Shop,
   Inc.
Dakota Arms, Inc.
Davide Pedersoli and Co.
DKT, Inc.
Dohring Bullets
Eichelberger Bullets, Wm.
Eldorado Cartridge Corp
   (See PMC/Eldorado
Federal Cartridge Co.
Fiocchi of America Inc.
Fish Mfg. Gunsmith Sptg. Co.,
   Marshall
Forkin, Ben (See Belt MTN Arms)
Forkin Arms
Fowler Bullets
Fowler, Bob
   (See Black Powder Products)
Foy Custom Bullets
Freedom Arms, Inc.
Garcia National Gun Traders, Inc.
Gehmann, Walter
   (See Huntington Die Specialties)
GOEX Inc.
Golden Bear Bullets
Gotz Bullets
Grayback Wildcats
Green Mountain Rifle Barrel Co., Inc.
Grier's Hard Cast Bullets
GTB
Gun City
Hammets VLD Bullets
Hardin Specialty Dist.
Harris Enterprises
Harrison Bullets
Hart & Son, Inc.
Hawk Laboratories, Inc.
   (See Hawk, Inc.)
Hawk, Inc.
Haydon Shooters Supply, Russ
Heidenstrom Bullets
Hercules, Inc.
   (See Alliant Techsystems,
   Smokeless)
Hi-Performance Ammunition
   Company
Hirtenberger Aktiengesellschaft
Hobson Precision Mfg. Co.
Hodgdon Powder Co.
Hornady Mfg. Co.
HT Bullets
Hunters Supply, Inc.
Impact Case Co.
Imperial Magnum Corp.
IMR Powder Co.
Intercontinental Distributors, Ltd.
J&D Components
J&L Superior Bullets
   (See Huntington Die Special)
J.R. Williams Bullet Co.
James Calhoon Mfg.
James Calhoon Varmint Bullets
Jensen Bullets
Jensen's Firearms Academy
Jericho Tool & Die Co., Inc.
Jester Bullets
JLK Bullets
JRP Custom Bullets
Ka Pu Kapili
Kaswer Custom, Inc.
Keith's Bullets
Keng's Firearms Specialty, Inc. / US
   Tactical Systems
Ken's Kustom Kartridges
Kent Cartridge Mfg. Co. Ltd.
KLA Enterprises
Knight Rifles
Knight Rifles
   (See Modern Muzzle Loading, Inc.)
Lapua Ltd.
Lawrence Brand Shot
   (See Precision Reloading)
Legend Products Corp.
Liberty Shooting Supplies
Lightning Performance Innovations,
   Inc.
Lindsley Arms Cartridge Co.
Littleton, J. F.
Lomont Precision Bullets

Loweth, Richard H.R.
Lyman Products Corp.
Magnus Bullets
Maine Custom Bullets
Maionchi-L.M.I.
Marchmon Bullets
Markesbery Muzzle Loaders, Inc.
MarMik, Inc.
MAST Technology
McMurdo, Lynn
   (See Specialty Gunsmithing)
Meister Bullets
   (See Gander Mountain)
Men-Metallwerk Elisenheutte GmbH
Merkuria Ltd.
Michael's Antiques
Mitchell Bullets, R.F.
MI-TE Bullets
Montana Precision Swaging
Mountain State Muzzleloading
   Supplies, Inc.
Mulhern, Rick
Murmur Corp.
Nagel's Custom Bullets
National Bullet Co.
Naval Ordnance Works
Necromancer Industries, Inc.
North American Shooting Systems
North Devon Firearms Services
Northern Precision Custom Swaged
   Bullets
Nosler, Inc.
OK Weber,Inc.
Oklahoma Ammunition Co.
Old Wagon Bullets
Old Western Scrounger,Inc.
Oregon Trail Bullet Company
Pacific Cartridge, Inc.
Pacific Rifle Co.
Page Custom Bullets
Pease Accuracy
Penn Bullets
Peterson Gun Shop, Inc., A.W.
Petro-Explo Inc.
Phillippi Custom Bullets, Justin
Pinetree Bullets
PMC / Eldorado Cartridge Corp.
Polywad, Inc.
Power Plus Enterprises, Inc.
Precision Delta Corp.
Precision Munitions, Inc.
Prescott Projectile Co.
Price Bullets, Patrick W.
PRL Bullets, c/o Blackburn Enterprises
Professional Hunter Supplies
   (See Star Custom Bull)
Proofmark Corp.
R.I.S. Co., Inc.
Rainier Ballistics Corp.
Ramon B. Gonzalez Guns
Ravell Ltd.
Redwood Bullet Works
Reloading Specialties, Inc.
Remington Arms Co., Inc.
Rhino
Robinson H.V. Bullets
Rubright Bullets
Russ Haydon Shooters' Supply
SAECO
   (See Redding Reloading Equipment)
Scharch Mfg., Inc.
Schneider Bullets
Schroeder Bullets
Schumakers Gun Shop
Scot Powder
Seebeck Assoc., R.E.
Shappy Bullets
Sharps Arms Co., Inc., C.
Shilen, Inc.
Sierra Bullets
SOS Products Co.
   (See Buck Stix-SOS Products Co.)
Southern Ammunition Co., Inc.
Specialty Gunsmithing
Speer Bullets
Spencer's Custom Guns
Stanley Bullets
Star Ammunition, Inc.
Star Custom Bullets
Starke Bullet Company
Starline, Inc.
Stewart's Gunsmithing

Swift Bullet Co.
T.F.C. S.p.A.
Taracorp Industries, Inc.
TCCI
TCSR
The A.W. Peterson Gun Shop, Inc.
The Ordnance Works
Thompson Bullet Lube Co.
Thompson Precision
TMI Products
   (See Haselbauer Products, Jerry)
Traditions Performance Firearms
Trico Plastics
True Flight Bullet Co.
Tucson Mold, Inc.
Unmussig Bullets, D. L.
USAC
Vann Custom Bullets
Vihtavuori Oy/Kaltron-Pettibone
Vincent's Shop
Viper Bullet and Brass Works
Vom Hoffe
   (See Old Western Scrounger, Inc.,
   The)
Warren Muzzleloading Co., Inc.
Watson Trophy Match Bullets
Weatherby, Inc.
Western Nevada West Coast Bullets
Widener's Reloading & Shooting
   Supply, Inc.
Winchester Div. Olin Corp.
Winkle Bullets
Woodleigh
   (See Huntington Die Specialties)
Worthy Products, Inc.
Wyant Bullets
Wyoming Custom Bullets
Zero Ammunition Co., Inc.

AMMUNITION, COMMERCIAL

"Su-Press-On",Inc.
3-D Ammunition & Bullets
3-Ten Corp.
A.W. Peterson Gun Shop, Inc.
Ace Custom 45's, Inc.
Ad Hominem
Air Arms
American Ammunition
Arizona Ammunition, Inc.
Arms Corporation of the Philippines
Arundel Arms & Ammunition, Inc., A.
A-Square Company, Inc.
Atlantic Rose, Inc.
Badger Shooters Supply, Inc.
Ballistic Product, Inc.
Ben William's Gun Shop
Benjamin/Sheridan Co., Crossman
Big Bear Arms & Sporting Goods, Inc.
Black Hills Ammunition, Inc.
Blammo Ammo
Blount, Inc., Sporting Equipment Div.
Brenneke KG, Wilhelm
Buffalo Bullet Co., Inc..
Bull-X, Inc.
Cabela's
Cambos Outdoorsman
Casull Arms Corp.
CBC
Champion's Choice, Inc.
Cor-Bon Bullet & Ammo Co.
Crosman Airguns
Cubic Shot Shell Co., Inc.
Cumberland States Arsenal
Daisy Mfg. Co.
Dead Eye's Sport Center
Delta Arms Ltd.
Delta Frangible Ammunition LLC
Diana
   (See U.S. Importer - Dynamit Nobel-
   RWS, Inc.
Dynamit Nobel-RWS, Inc.
Effebi SNC-Dr. Franco Beretta
Eley Ltd.
Elite Ammunition
Estate Cartridge, Inc.
Federal Cartridge Co.
Fiocchi of America Inc.
Fish Mfg. Gunsmith Sptg. Co.,
   Marshall
Garcia National Gun Traders, Inc.
Garrett Cartridges Inc.

Garthwaite Pistolsmith, Inc., Jim
Gibbs Rifle Co., Inc.
Gil Hebard Guns Inc.
Glaser Safety Slug, Inc.
GOEX Inc.
Goodwin's Gun Shop
Gun Accessories
   (See Glaser Safety Slug, Inc.)
Gun City
Hansen & Co.
   (See Hansen Cartridge Co.)
Hart & Son, Inc.
Hi-Performance Ammunition
   Company
Hirtenberger Aktiengesellschaft
Hornady Mfg. Co.
Hunters Supply, Inc.
IMX, LLC
Intercontinental Distributors, Ltd.
Ion Industries, Inc
Keng's Firearms Specialty, Inc. / US
   Tactical Systems
Kent Cartridge America, Inc
Kent Cartridge Mfg. Co. Ltd.
Knight Rifles
Lapua Ltd.
Lethal Force Institute
   (See Police Bookshelf)
Lock's Philadelphia Gun Exchange
Magnum Research, Inc.
MagSafe Ammo Co.
Magtech Ammunition Co. Inc.
Maionchi-L.M.I.
Mandall Shooting Supplies Inc.
Markell,Inc.
McBros Rifle Co.
Men-Metallwerk Elisenhuette GmbH
Mullins Ammunition
New England Ammunition Co.
Oklahoma Ammunition Co.
Omark Industries,Div. of Blount,Inc.
Outdoor Sports Headquarters, Inc.
P.S.M.G. Gun Co.
Pacific Cartridge, Inc.
Paragon Sales & Services, Inc.
Parker & Sons Shooting Supply
Peterson Gun Shop, Inc., A.W.
PMC / Eldorado Cartridge Corp.
Police Bookshelf
Polywad, Inc.
Pony Express Reloaders
Precision Delta Corp.
Pro Load Ammunition, Inc.
R.E.I.
Ravell Ltd.
Remington Arms Co., Inc.
Rucker Dist. Inc.
RWS
   (See US Importer-Dynamit Nobel-
   RWS, Inc.)
Sellier & Bellot, USA Inc
Southern Ammunition Co., Inc.
Speer Bullets
SSK Industries
TCCI
The A.W. Peterson Gun Shop, Inc.
The BulletMakers Workshop
The Gun Room Press
The Gun Works
Thompson Bullet Lube Co.
USAC
Valor Corp.
VAM Distribution Co LLC
Victory USA
Vihtavuori Oy/Kaltron-Pettibone
Visible Impact Targets
Voere-KGH m.b.H.
Vom Hoffe
   (See Old Western Scrounger, Inc.,
   The)
Weatherby, Inc.
Westley Richards & Co.
Whitestone Lumber Corp.
Widener's Reloading & Shooting
   Supply, Inc.
Wilhelm Brenneke KG
Winchester Div. Olin Corp.
Zero Ammunition Co., Inc.

AMMUNITION, CUSTOM

3-D Ammunition & Bullets
3-Ten Corp.

PRODUCT & SERVICE DIRECTORY

A.W. Peterson Gun Shop, Inc.
Accuracy Unlimited
AFSCO Ammunition
Allred Bullet Co.
American Derringer Corp.
American Products, Inc.
Arizona Ammunition, Inc.
Arms Corporation of the Philippines
Atlantic Rose, Inc.
Ballard Rifle & Cartridge Co., LLC
Bear Arms
Belding's Custom Gun Shop
Berger Bullets Ltd.
Big Bore Bullets of Alaska
Black Hills Ammunition, Inc.
Blue Mountain Bullets
Brynin, Milton
Buckskin Bullet Co.
CBC
CFVentures
Cubic Shot Shell Co., Inc.
Custom Tackle and Ammo
Dakota Arms, Inc.
Dead Eye's Sport Center
Delta Frangible Ammunition LLC
DKT, Inc.
Elite Ammunition
Estate Cartridge, Inc.
GDL Enterprises
GOEX Inc.
Gonzalez Guns, Ramon B
Grayback Wildcats
Hirtenberger Aktiengesellschaft
Hobson Precision Mfg. Co.
Hoelscher, Virgil
Horizons Unlimited
Hornady Mfg. Co.
Hunters Supply, Inc.
IMX, LLC
James Calhoon Mfg.
James Calhoon Varmint Bullets
Jensen Bullets
Jensen's Custom Ammunition
Jensen's Firearms Academy
Kaswer Custom, Inc.
Keeler, R. H.
Kent Cartridge Mfg. Co. Ltd.
L E Jurras & Assoc.
L.A.R. Mfg., Inc.
Lethal Force Institute
    (See Police Bookshelf)
Lindsley Arms Cartridge Co.
Linebaugh Custom Sixguns
Loch Leven Industries / Convert-A-Pell
MagSafe Ammo Co.
MAST Technology
McBros Rifle Co.
McMurdo, Lynn
    (See Specialty Gunsmithing)
Men-Metallwerk Elisenhuette GmbH
Milstor Corp.
Mullins Ammunition
Oklahoma Ammunition Co.
Old Western Scrounger,Inc.
P.S.M.G. Gun Co.
Peterson Gun Shop, Inc., A.W.
Phillippi Custom Bullets, Justin
Police Bookshelf
Power Plus Enterprises, Inc.
Precision Delta Corp.
Precision Munitions, Inc.
Professional Hunter Supplies
    (See Star Custom Bull)
R.E.I.
Ramon B. Gonzalez Guns
Sandia Die & Cartridge Co.
SOS Products Co.
    (See Buck Stix-SOS Products Co.)
Specialty Gunsmithing
Spencer's Custom Guns
SSK Industries
Star Custom Bullets
State Arms Gun Co.
Stewart's Gunsmithing
The A.W. Peterson Gun Shop, Inc.
The BulletMakers Workshop
The Country Armourer
Unmussig Bullets, D. L.
Vitt/Boos
Vom Hoffe
    (See Old Western Scrounger, Inc.,
    The)

Vulpes Ventures, Inc. Fox Cartridge
    Division
Warren Muzzleloading Co., Inc.
Weaver Arms Corp. Gun Shop
Worthy Products, Inc.
Zero Ammunition Co., Inc.

AMMUNITION, FOREIGN
A.W. Peterson Gun Shop, Inc.
Ad Hominem
AFSCO Ammunition
Armscorp USA, Inc.
Atlantic Rose, Inc.
B & P America
Beeman Precision Airguns
Cape Outfitters
CBC
Cheddite France S.A.
Cubic Shot Shell Co., Inc.
Dead Eye's Sport Center
Diana
    (See U.S. Importer - Dynamit Nobel-
    RWS, Inc.)
DKT, Inc.
Dynamit Nobel-RWS, Inc.
E. Arthur Brown Co.
Fiocchi of America Inc.
First Inc., Jack
Gamebore Division, Polywad Inc
Gibbs Rifle Co., Inc.
GOEX Inc.
Goodwin's Gun Shop
Gunsmithing, Inc.
Hansen & Co.
    (See Hansen Cartridge Co.)
Heidenstrom Bullets
Hirtenberger Aktiengesellschaft
Hornady Mfg. Co.
IMX, LLC
Intrac Arms International
K.B.I. Inc
MagSafe Ammo Co.
Maionchi-L.M.I.
Mandall Shooting Supplies Inc.
Marksman Products
MAST Technology
Merkuria Ltd.
Mullins Ammunition
Navy Arms Company
Oklahoma Ammunition Co.
Old Western Scrounger,Inc.
P.S.M.G. Gun Co.
Paragon Sales & Services, Inc.
Peterson Gun Shop, Inc., A.W.
Petro-Explo Inc.
Precision Delta Corp.
R.E.T. Enterprises
Ramon B. Gonzalez Guns
RWS
    (See US Importer-Dynamit Nobel-
    RWS, Inc.)
Samco Global Arms, Inc.
Sentinel Arms
Southern Ammunition Co., Inc.
Speer Bullets
Stratco, Inc.
T.F.C. S.p.A.
The A.W. Peterson Gun Shop, Inc.
The BulletMakers Workshop
The Paul Co.
Victory Ammunition
Vihtavuori Oy/Kaltron-Pettibone
Vom Hoffe
    (See Old Western Scrounger, Inc.,
    The)

ANTIQUE ARMS DEALER
Ackerman & Co.
Ad Hominem
Antique American Firearms
Antique Arms Co.
Aplan Antiques & Art, James O.
Armoury, Inc., The
Arundel Arms & Ammunition, Inc., A.
Ballard Rifle & Cartridge Co., LLC
Bear Mountain Gun & Tool
Bob's Tactical Indoor Shooting Range
    & Gun Shop
British Antiques
Buckskin Machine Works, A. Hunkeler
Buffalo Arms Co.
Cape Outfitters

Carlson, Douglas R, Antique American
    Firearms
CBC-BRAZIL
Chadick's Ltd.
Chambers Flintlocks Ltd., Jim
Champlin Firearms, Inc.
Chuck's Gun Shop
Clements' Custom Leathercraft, Chas
Cole's Gun Works
D&D Gunsmiths, Ltd.
David R. Chicoine
Dixie Gun Works
Dixie Gun Works
Dixon Muzzleloading Shop, Inc.
Duffy, Charles E
    (See Guns Antique & Modern DBA)
Ed's Gun House
Enguix Import-Export
Fagan & Co.Inc
Fish Mfg. Gunsmith Sptg. Co.,
    Marshall
Flayderman & Co., Inc.
Frielich Police Equipment
Fulmer's Antique Firearms, Chet
Getz Barrel Co.
Glass, Herb
Goergen's Gun Shop, Inc.
Golden Age Arms Co.
Goodwin's Gun Shop
Gun Hunter Books
    (See Gun Hunter Trading Co)
Gun Hunter Trading Co.
Guns Antique & Modern DBA / Charles
    E. Duffy
Hallowell & Co.
Hammans, Charles E.
HandCrafts Unltd
    (See Clements' Custom Leather)
Handgun Press
Hansen & Co.
    (See Hansen Cartridge Co.)
Hunkeler, A
    (See Buckskin Machine Works)
Imperial Miniature Armory
James Wayne Firearms for Collectors
    and Investors
Kelley's
Knight's Mfg. Co.
Ledbetter Airguns, Riley
LeFever Arms Co., Inc.
Lever Arms Service Ltd.
Lock's Philadelphia Gun Exchange
Log Cabin Sport Shop
Logdewood Mfg.
Mandall Shooting Supplies Inc.
Martin's Gun Shop
Michael's Antiques
Montana Outfitters, Lewis E. Yearout
Muzzleloaders Etcetera, Inc.
Navy Arms Company
New England Arms Co.
Peter Dyson & Son Ltd.
Pony Express Sport Shop
Powder Horn Ltd.
Ravell Ltd.
Reno, Wayne
Retting, Inc., Martin B
Robert Valade Engraving
Rutgers Book Center
Samco Global Arms, Inc.
Sarco, Inc.
Scott Fine Guns Inc., Thad
Shootin' Shack, Inc.
Sportsmen's Exchange & Western
    Gun Traders, Inc.
Steves House of Guns
Stott's Creek Armory, Inc.
The Gun Room
The Gun Room Press
The Gun Shop
The Gun Works
Turnbull Restoration, Doug
Vic's Gun Refinishing
Vintage Arms, Inc.
Wallace, Terry
Westley Richards & Co.
Wild West Guns
William Fagan & Co.
Winchester Consultants
Winchester Sutler, Inc., The
Wood, Frank (See Classic Guns, Inc.)

Yearout, Lewis E.
    (See Montana Outfitters)

APPRAISER - GUNS, ETC.
A.W. Peterson Gun Shop, Inc.
Ackerman & Co.
Antique Arms Co.
Armoury, Inc., The
Arundel Arms & Ammunition, Inc., A.
Barta's Gunsmithing
Beitzinger, George
Blue Book Publications, Inc.
Bob Rogers Gunsmithing
Bob's Tactical Indoor Shooting Range
    & Gun Shop
British Antiques
Bullet N Press
Butterfield's
Cannon's
Cape Outfitters
Chadick's Ltd.
Champlin Firearms, Inc.
Christie's East
Chuilli, Stephen
Clark Firearms Engraving
Clements' Custom Leathercraft, Chas
Cole's Gun Works
Colonial Arms, Inc.
Colonial Repair
Corry, John
Custom Tackle and Ammo
D&D Gunsmiths, Ltd.
David R. Chicoine
DGR Custom Rifles
Dixie Gun Works
Dixon Muzzleloading Shop, Inc.
Duane's Gun Repair
    (See DGR Custom Rifles)
Ed's Gun House
Eversull Co., Inc.
Fagan & Co.Inc
Ferris Firearms
Fish Mfg. Gunsmith Sptg. Co.,
    Marshall
Flayderman & Co., Inc.
Forty Five Ranch Enterprises
Francotte & Cie S.A. Auguste
Frontier Arms Co.,Inc.
Gene's Custom Guns
George E. Mathews & Son, Inc.
Gerald Pettinger Books, see Pettinger
    Books
Getz Barrel Co.
Gillmann, Edwin
Gilmore Sports Concepts
Goergen's Gun Shop, Inc.
Golden Age Arms Co.
Gonzalez Guns, Ramon B
Goodwin's Gun Shop
Griffin & Howe, Inc.
Groenewold, John
Gun City
Gun Hunter Books
    (See Gun Hunter Trading Co)
Gun Hunter Trading Co.
Guncraft Books
    (See Guncraft Sports Inc.)
Guncraft Sports Inc.
Guns
Gunsmithing, Inc.
Hallowell & Co.
Hammans, Charles E.
HandCrafts Unltd
    (See Clements' Custom Leather)
Handgun Press
Hank's Gun Shop
Hansen & Co.
    (See Hansen Cartridge Co.)
Hughes, Steven Dodd
Irwin, Campbell H.
Island Pond Gun Shop
Ithaca Classic Doubles
Jackalope Gun Shop
James Wayne Firearms for Collectors
    and Investors
Jensen's Custom Ammunition
Kelley's
L.L. Bean, Inc.
Lampert, Ron
LaRocca Gun Works
Ledbetter Airguns, Riley

LeFever Arms Co., Inc.
Lock's Philadelphia Gun Exchange
Log Cabin Sport Shop
Logdewood Mfg.
Lomont Precision Bullets
Long, George F.
Mahony, Philip Bruce
Mandall Shooting Supplies Inc.
Martin's Gun Shop
Mathews & Son, Inc., George E.
McCann Industries
McCann's Machine & Gun Shop
Mercer Custom Guns
Montana Outfitters, Lewis E. Yearout
Muzzleloaders Etcetera, Inc.
Navy Arms Company
New England Arms Co.
Nitex Gun Shop
Pasadena Gun Center
Pentheny de Pentheny
Peterson Gun Shop, Inc., A.W.
Pettinger Books, Gerald
Pony Express Sport Shop
Powder Horn Ltd.
R.A. Wells Custom Gunsmith
R.E.T. Enterprises
Ramon B. Gonzalez Guns
Retting, Inc., Martin B
River Road Sporting Clays
Robert Valade Engraving
Rutgers Book Center
Scott Fine Guns Inc., Thad
Shootin' Shack, Inc.
Spencer Reblue Service
Sportsmen's Exchange & Western
    Gun Traders, Inc.
Stott's Creek Armory, Inc.
Stratco, Inc.
Ten-Ring Precision, Inc.
The A.W. Peterson Gun Shop, Inc.
The Gun Room Press
The Gun Shop
The Gun Shop
The Gun Works
The Orvis Co.
The Swampfire Shop
    (See Peterson Gun Shop, Inc.)
Thurston Sports, Inc.
Valade Engraving, Robert
Vic's Gun Refinishing
Walker Arms Co., Inc.
Wallace, Terry
Wasmundt, Jim
Weber & Markin Custom Gunsmiths
Werth, T. W.
Whildin & Sons Ltd, E.H.
Whitestone Lumber Corp.
Wichita Arms, Inc.
Wild West Guns
William Fagan & Co.
Williams Shootin' Iron Service, The
    Lynx-Line
Winchester Consultants
Winchester Sutler, Inc., The
Wood, Frank (See Classic Guns, Inc.)
Yearout, Lewis E.
    (See Montana Outfitters)

AUCTIONEER - GUNS, ETC.
"Little John's" Antique Arms
Buck Stix--SOS Products Co.
Butterfield's
Christie's East
Fagan & Co.Inc
Sotheby's

BOOKS & MANUALS (PUBLISHERS & DEALERS)
"Su-Press-On",Inc.
Alpha 1 Drop Zone
American Handgunner Magazine
Armory Publications
Arms & Armour Press
Ballistic Product, Inc.
Ballistic Product, Inc.
Barnes Bullets, Inc.
Bauska Barrels
Beartooth Bullets
Beeman Precision Airguns
Blacksmith Corp.

Blacktail Mountain Books
Blue Book Publications, Inc.
Blue Ridge Machinery & Tools, Inc.
Boone's Custom Ivory Grips, Inc.
Brown Co, E. Arthur
Brownells, Inc.
Bullet N Press
C. Sharps Arms Co. Inc./Montana
  Armory
Calibre Press, Inc.
Cape Outfitters
Cheyenne Pioneer Products
Colonial Repair
Colorado Sutlers Arsenal
  (See Cumberland States)
Corbin Mfg. & Supply, Inc.
Cumberland States Arsenal
DBI Books Division of Krause
  Publications
Dixon Muzzleloading Shop, Inc.
Executive Protection Institute
Flores Publications Inc, J
  (See Action Direct Inc.)
Galati International
Gerald Pettinger Books, see Pettinger
  Books
Golden Age Arms Co.
Gun City
Gun List (See Krause Publications)
Guncraft Books
  (See Guncraft Sports Inc.)
Guncraft Sports Inc.
Gunnerman Books
GUNS Magazine
Gunsmithing, Inc.
H&P Publishing
Handgun Press
Harris Publications
Hawk Laboratories, Inc.
  (See Hawk, Inc.)
Hawk, Inc.
Heritage / VSP Gun Books
Hodgdon Powder Co.
Home Shop Machinist The Village
  Press Publications
Hornady Mfg. Co.
Hungry Horse Books
Huntington Die Specialties
I.D.S.A. Books
Info-Arm
Ironside International Publishers, Inc.
Jantz Supply
Kelley's
King & Co.
Koval Knives
Krause Publications, Inc.
L.B.T.
Lapua Ltd.
Lethal Force Institute
  (See Police Bookshelf)
Lyman Products Corp.
Madis Books
Magma Engineering Co.
Mandall Shooting Supplies Inc.
MarMik, Inc.
Montana Armory, Inc
  (See C. Sharps Arms Co. Inc.)
Mountain South
Mountain State Muzzleloading
  Supplies, Inc.
Mulberry House Publishing
Navy Arms Company
OK Weber,Inc.
Outdoor Sports Headquarters, Inc.
Paintball Games International
  Magazine Aceville
Pejsa Ballistics
Petersen Publishing Co.
  (See Emap USA)
Pettinger Books, Gerald
PFRB Co.
Police Bookshelf
Precision Shooting, Inc.
Professional Hunter Supplies
  (See Star Custom Bull)
Ravell Ltd.
Ray Riling Arms Books Co.
Remington Double Shotguns
Russ Haydon Shooters' Supply
Rutgers Book Center
S&S Firearms
Safari Press, Inc.

Sanders Gun and Machine Shop
Saunders Gun & Machine Shop
Scharch Mfg., Inc.
Scharch Mfg., Inc.
Semmer, Charles
  (See Remington Double Shotguns)
Sharps Arms Co., Inc., C.
Shotgun Sports Magazine, dba
  Shootin' Accessories Ltd.
Sierra Bullets
Speer Bullets
SPG LLC
Stackpole Books
Star Custom Bullets
Stewart Game Calls, Inc., Johnny
Stoeger Industries
Stoeger Publishing Co.
  (See Stoeger Industries)
Swift Bullet Co.
The A.W. Peterson Gun Shop, Inc.
The Gun Parts Corp.
The Gun Room Press
The Gun Works
The NgraveR Co.
Thomas, Charles C.
Track of the Wolf, Inc.
Trafalgar Square
Trotman, Ken
Tru-Balance Knife Co.
Vega Tool Co.
Vintage Industries, Inc.
VSP Publishers
  (See Heritage/VSP Gun Books)
W.E. Brownell Checkering Tools
WAMCO--New Mexico
Wells Creek Knife & Gun Works
Wilderness Sound Products Ltd.
Williams Gun Sight Co.
Wolfe Publishing Co.
Wolf's Western Traders

BULLET CASTING, ACCESSORIES

Ballisti-Cast, Inc.
Buffalo Arms Co.
Bullet Metals
Cast Performance Bullet Company
CFVentures
Cooper-Woodward
Davide Pedersoli and Co.
Ferguson, Bill
Lee Precision, Inc.
Lithi Bee Bullet Lube
Lyman Products Corp.
Magma Engineering Co.
Ox-Yoke Originals, Inc.
Rapine Bullet Mould Mfg. Co.
SPG LLC
The A.W. Peterson Gun Shop, Inc.
The Gun Works
The Hanned Line
United States Products Co.

BULLET CASTING, FURNACES & POTS

Ballisti-Cast, Inc.
Buffalo Arms Co.
Bullet Metals
Ferguson, Bill
GAR
Lee Precision, Inc.
Lyman Products Corp.
Magma Engineering Co.
Rapine Bullet Mould Mfg. Co.
The A.W. Peterson Gun Shop, Inc.
The Gun Works
Thompson Bullet Lube Co.

BULLET CASTING, LEAD

Action Bullets & Alloy Inc
Ames Metal Products
Belltown Ltd.
Buckskin Bullet Co.
Buffalo Arms Co.
Bullet Metals
Bullseye Bullets
Hunters Supply, Inc.
Jericho Tool & Die Co., Inc.
Lee Precision, Inc.
Lithi Bee Bullet Lube
Magma Engineering Co.
Montana Precision Swaging

Ox-Yoke Originals, Inc.
Penn Bullets
Proofmark Corp.
SPG LLC
Splitfire Sporting Goods, L.L.C.
The A.W. Peterson Gun Shop, Inc.
The Gun Works
Walters Wads

BULLET PULLERS

Battenfeld Technologies
Davide Pedersoli and Co.
Hollywood Engineering
Royal Arms Gunstocks
The A.W. Peterson Gun Shop, Inc.
The Gun Works

BULLET TOOLS

Brynin, Milton
Camdex, Inc.
Corbin Mfg. & Supply, Inc.
Cumberland Arms
Eagan, Donald V.
Holland's Gunsmithing
Hollywood Engineering
Lee Precision, Inc.
Necromancer Industries, Inc.
Niemi Engineering, W. B.
North Devon Firearms Services
Rorschach Precision Products
Sport Flite Manufacturing Co.
The A.W. Peterson Gun Shop, Inc.
The Hanned Line
WTA Manufacturing

BULLET, CASE & DIE LUBRICANTS

Beartooth Bullets
Bonanza (See Forster Products)
Brown Co, E. Arthur
Buckskin Bullet Co.
Buffalo Arms Co.
Camp-Cap Products
CFVentures
Cooper-Woodward
CVA
E-Z-Way Systems
Ferguson, Bill
Forster Products
GAR
Guardsman Products
Heidenstrom Bullets
Hollywood Engineering
Hornady Mfg. Co.
Imperial (See E-Z-Way Systems)
Knoell, Doug
L.B.T.
Le Clear Industries
  (See E-Z-Way Systems)
Lee Precision, Inc.
Lithi Bee Bullet Lube
MI-TE Bullets
Paco's
  (See Small Custom Mould & Bullet
  Co)
RCBS Div. of Blount
Reardon Products
Rooster Laboratories
Shay's Gunsmithing
Small Custom Mould & Bullet Co.
Tamarack Products, Inc.
Uncle Mike's
  (See Michaels of Oregon Co.)
Warren Muzzleloading Co., Inc.
Widener's Reloading & Shooting
  Supply, Inc.
Young Country Arms

CARTRIDGES FOR COLLECTORS

"Gramps" Antiques
Ackerman & Co.
Ad Hominem
Armory Publications
British Antiques
Cameron's
Campbell, Dick
Cartridge Transfer Group,
  Pete de Coux
Cherry Creek State Park Shooting
  Center
Cole's Gun Works
Colonial Repair

Cubic Shot Shell Co., Inc.
de Coux, Pete
  (See Cartridge Transfer Group)
Duane's Gun Repair
  (See DGR Custom Rifles)
Ed's Gun House
Ed's Gun House
Enguix Import-Export
Epps, Ellwood/Isabella (See Gramps)
First Inc., Jack
Fitz Pistol Grip Co.
Forty Five Ranch Enterprises
Goergen's Gun Shop, Inc.
Goodwin's Gun Shop
Grayback Wildcats
Gun City
Gun Hunter Books
  (See Gun Hunter Trading Co)
Gun Hunter Trading Co.
Kelley's
Liberty Shooting Supplies
Mandall Shooting Supplies Inc.
MAST Technology
Michael's Antiques
Montana Outfitters, Lewis E. Yearout
Pasadena Gun Center
Samco Global Arms, Inc.
SOS Products Co.
  (See Buck Stix-SOS Products Co.)
Stone Enterprises Ltd.
The Country Armourer
The Gun Parts Corp.
The Gun Room Press
Vom Hoffe
  (See Old Western Scrounger, Inc.,
  The)
Ward & Van Valkenburg
Winchester Consultants
Yearout, Lewis E.
  (See Montana Outfitters)

CASE & AMMUNITION PROCESSORS, INSPECTORS, BOXERS

Ammo Load, Inc.
Ben's Machines
Hafner World Wide, Inc.
Scharch Mfg., Inc.
The A.W. Peterson Gun Shop, Inc.

CASE CLEANERS & POLISHING MEDIA

3-D Ammunition & Bullets
Battenfeld Technologies
Belltown Ltd.
Buffalo Arms Co.
Chem-Pak Inc.
G96 Products Co., Inc.
Lee Precision, Inc.
Penn Bullets
The A.W. Peterson Gun Shop, Inc.
The Gun Works
Tru-Square Metal Products Inc.
VibraShine, Inc.

CASE PREPARATION TOOLS

Battenfeld Technologies
CONKKO
Dewey Mfg. Co., Inc., J.
High Precision
Hoehn Sales, Inc.
K&M Services
Lee Precision, Inc.
Match Prep--Doyle Gracey
Plum City Ballistic Range
RCBS Div. of Blount
Russ Haydon Shooters' Supply
Sinclair International, Inc.
Stoney Point Products, Inc.
The A.W. Peterson Gun Shop, Inc.

CASE TRIMMERS, TRIM DIES & ACCESSORIES

Buffalo Arms Co.
Fremont Tool Works
Goodwin's Gun Shop
Hollywood Engineering
K&M Services
Lyman Products Corp.
Match Prep--Doyle Gracey
OK Weber,Inc.

Ozark Gun Works
Redding Reloading Equipment
The A.W. Peterson Gun Shop, Inc.
Time Precision

CASE TUMBLERS, VIBRATORS, MEDIA & ACCESSORIES

4-D Custom Die Co.
Battenfeld Technologies
Berry's Mfg., Inc.
Dillon Precision Products, Inc.
Goodwin's Gun Shop
Penn Bullets
Raytech Div. of Lyman Products Corp.
The A.W. Peterson Gun Shop, Inc.
Tru-Square Metal Products Inc.
VibraShine, Inc.

CASES, CABINETS, RACKS & SAFES - GUN

All Rite Products, Inc.
Allen Co., Bob
Allen Co., Inc.
Allen Sportswear, Bob
  (See Allen Co., Bob)
Alumna Sport by Dee Zee
American Display Co.
American Security Products Co.
Americase
Art Jewel Enterprises Ltd.
Ashby Turkey Calls
Bagmaster Mfg., Inc.
Barramundi Corp.
Berry's Mfg., Inc.
Big Sky Racks, Inc.
Big Spring Enterprises "Bore Stores"
Bill's Custom Cases
Bison Studios
Black Sheep Brand
Brauer Bros.
Brown, H. R.
  (See Silhouette Leathers)
Browning Arms Co.
Bushmaster Hunting & Fishing
Cannon Safe, Inc.
Chipmunk (See Oregon Arms, Inc.)
Cobalt Mfg., Inc.
CONKKO
Connecticut Shotgun Mfg. Co.
D&L Industries (See D.J. Marketing)
D.J. Marketing
Dara-Nes, Inc.
  (See Nesci Enterprises, Inc.)
Deepeeka Exports Pvt. Ltd.
Doskocil Mfg. Co., Inc.
DTM International, Inc.
Elk River, Inc.
EMF Co., Inc.
English, Inc., A.G.
Enhanced Presentations, Inc.
Eversull Co., Inc.
Fort Knox Security Products
Freedom Arms, Inc.
Frontier Safe Co.
Galati International
GALCO International Ltd.
Gun-Ho Sports Cases
Hall Plastics, Inc., John
Hastings Barrels
Homak
Hoppe's Div. Penguin Industries, Inc.
Hugger Hooks Co.
Hunter Co., Inc.
Hydrosorbent Products
Impact Case Co.
Johanssons Vapentillbehor, Bert
Johnston Bros.
  (See C&T Corp. TA Johnson
  Brothers)
Kalispel Case Line
Kane Products, Inc.
KK Air International
  (See Impact Case Co.)
Knock on Wood Antiques
Kolpin Mfg., Inc.
Lakewood Products LLC
Liberty Safe
Mandall Shooting Supplies Inc.
Marsh, Mike
McWelco Products
Morton Booth Co.

DIRECTORY

MPC
MTM Molded Products Co., Inc.
Nalpak
Necessary Concepts, Inc.
Nesci Enterprises Inc.
Oregon Arms, Inc.
  (See Rogue Rifle Co., Inc.)
Outa-Site Gun Carriers
Pflumm Mfg. Co.
Poburka, Philip (See Bison Studios)
Powell & Son (Gunmakers) Ltd.,
  William
Prototech Industries, Inc.
Quality Arms, Inc.
Rogue Rifle Co., Inc.
Schulz Industries
Southern Security
Sportsman's Communicators
Sun Welding Safe Co.
Sweet Home, Inc.
Talmage, William G.
The Outdoor Connection,Inc.
The Surecase Co.
Tinks & Ben Lee Hunting Products
  (See Wellington)
Trulock Tool
Universal Sports
W. Waller & Son, Inc.
Whitestone Lumber Corp.
Wilson Case, Inc.
Woodstream
Zanotti Armor, Inc.
Ziegel Engineering

CHOKE DEVICES, RECOIL ABSORBERS & RECOIL PADS

3-Ten Corp.
Action Products, Inc.
Allen Co., Bob
Allen Sportswear, Bob
  (See Allen Co., Bob)
Answer Products Co.
Arms Ingenuity Co.
Baer Custom, Inc, Les
Baker, Stan
Bansner's Ultimate Rifles, LLC
Bartlett Engineering
Battenfeld Technologies
Briley Mfg. Inc.
Brooks Tactical Systems
Brownells, Inc.
B-Square Company, Inc.
Buffer Technologies
Bull Mountain Rifle Co.
C&H Research
Cation
Chicasaw Gun Works
Clearview Products
Colonial Arms, Inc.
Connecticut Shotgun Mfg. Co.
CRR, Inc./Marble's Inc.
Danuser Machine Co.
Dina Arms Corporation
Gentry Custom Gunmaker, David
Goodwin's Gun Shop
Graybill's Gun Shop
Gruning Precision Inc
Guns
Harry Lawson Co.
Hastings Barrels
Hogue Grips
Holland's Gunsmithing
I.N.C. Inc (See Kickeez I.N.C., Inc.)
J.P. Enterprises Inc.
Jackalope Gun Shop
Jenkins Recoil Pads, Inc.
KDF, Inc.
Kickeez I.N.C., Inc.
Lawson Co., Harry
London Guns Ltd.
Lyman Products Corp.
Mag-Na-Port International, Inc.
Mandall Shooting Supplies Inc.
Marble Arms
  (See CRR, Inc./Marble's Inc.)
Menck, Gunsmith Inc., T.W.
Middlebrooks Custom Shop
Morrow, Bud
Nelson/Weather-Rite, Inc.
Oakland Custom Arms,Inc.
One Of A Kind

Original Box, Inc.
P.S.M.G. Gun Co.
Palsa Outdoor Products
Parker & Sons Shooting Supply
Pro-Port Ltd.
Que Industries, Inc.
Shotguns Unlimited
Simmons Gun Repair, Inc.
Sound Technology
Spencer's Custom Guns
Stone Enterprises Ltd.
The A.W. Peterson Gun Shop, Inc.
Truglo, Inc
Trulock Tool
Uncle Mike's
  (See Michaels of Oregon Co.)
Universal Sports
Virgin Valley Custom Guns
Vortek Products, Inc.
Williams Gun Sight Co.
Wilsom Combat
Wise Guns, Dale

CHRONOGRAPHS & PRESSURE TOOLS

Air Rifle Specialists
Brown Co, E. Arthur
C.W. Erickson's L.L.C.
Canons Delcour
Clearview Products
Competition Electronics, Inc.
Custom Chronograph, Inc.
D&H Precision Tooling
Hege Jagd-u. Sporthandels GmbH
Hutton Rifle Ranch
Kent Cartridge Mfg. Co. Ltd.
Mac-1 Airgun Distributors
Oehler Research,Inc.
P.A.C.T., Inc.
Romain's Custom Guns, Inc.
Savage Arms, Inc.
Shooting Chrony, Inc.
Spencer's Custom Guns
Stratco, Inc.
Tepeco

CLEANERS & DEGREASERS

Belltown Ltd.
Camp-Cap Products
G96 Products Co., Inc.
Goodwin's Gun Shop
Hafner World Wide, Inc.
Half Moon Rifle Shop
Kleen-Bore,Inc.
LEM Gun Specialties Inc. The Lewis
  Lead Remover
Modern Muzzleloading, Inc
Northern Precision Custom Swaged
  Bullets
Parker & Sons Shooting Supply
Perazone-Gunsmith, Brian
PrOlixrr Lubricants
R&S Industries Corp.
Sheffield Knifemakers Supply, Inc.
Shooter's Choice Gun Care
Sierra Specialty Prod. Co.
The A.W. Peterson Gun Shop, Inc.
The Gun Works
United States Products Co.

CLEANING & REFINISHING SUPPLIES

AC Dyna-tite Corp.
Alpha 1 Drop Zone
American Gas & Chemical Co., Ltd
Answer Products Co.
Armite Laboratories
Atlantic Mills, Inc.
Atsko/Sno-Seal, Inc.
Barnes Bullets, Inc.
Battenfeld Technologies
Beeman Precision Airguns
Belltown Ltd.
Bill's Gun Repair
Birchwood Casey
Blount, Inc., Sporting Equipment Div.
Blount/Outers
Blue and Gray Products Inc
  (See Ox-Yoke Originals)
Break-Free, Inc.
Bridgers Best

Brown Co, E. Arthur
Brownells, Inc.
C.S. Van Gorden & Son, Inc.
Cambos Outdoorsman
Cambos Outdoorsman
Camp-Cap Products
Chem-Pak Inc.
CONKKO
Connecticut Shotgun Mfg. Co.
Creedmoor Sports, Inc.
CRR, Inc./Marble's Inc.
Custom Products
  (See Jones Custom Products)
Cylinder & Slide, Inc., William R.
  Laughridge
D&H Prods. Co., Inc.
Dara-Nes, Inc.
  (See Nesci Enterprises, Inc.)
Decker Shooting Products
Deepeeka Exports Pvt. Ltd.
Desert Mountain Mfg.
Dewey Mfg. Co., Inc., J.
Du-Lite Corp.
Dykstra, Doug
E&L Mfg., Inc.
Eezox, Inc.
Ekol Leather Care
Faith Associates
Felk Oil Gun Lube
Flitz International Ltd.
Fluoramics, Inc.
Frontier Products Co.
G96 Products Co., Inc.
Golden Age Arms Co.
Guardsman Products
Gunsmithing, Inc.
Hafner World Wide, Inc.
Half Moon Rifle Shop
Heatbath Corp.
Hoppe's Div. Penguin Industries, Inc.
Hornady Mfg. Co.
Hydrosorbent Products
Iosso Products
James Calhoon Varmint Bullets
Jantz Supply
Jantz Supply
Johnston Bros.
  (See C&T Corp. TA Johnson
  Brothers)
Jonad Corp.
K&M Industries, Inc.
Kellogg's Professional Products
Kent Cartridge Mfg. Co. Ltd.
Kesselring Gun Shop
Kleen-Bore,Inc.
Knight Rifles
Laurel Mountain Forge
Lee Supplies, Mark
LEM Gun Specialties Inc. The Lewis
  Lead Remover
List Precision Engineering
LPS Laboratories, Inc.
Lyman Products Corp.
Mac-1 Airgun Distributors
Mandall Shooting Supplies Inc.
Marble Arms
  (See CRR, Inc./Marble's Inc.)
Mark Lee Supplies
Micro Sight Co.
Minute Man High Tech Industries
Mountain State Muzzleloading
  Supplies, Inc.
Mountain View Sports, Inc.
MTM Molded Products Co., Inc.
Muscle Products Corp.
Nesci Enterprises Inc.
Northern Precision Custom Swaged
  Bullets
Now Products, Inc.
October Country Muzzleloading
Old World Oil Products
Omark Industries,Div. of Blount,Inc.
Original Mink Oil, Inc.
Otis Technology, Inc.
Outers Laboratories Div. of Blount,
  Inc. Sporting
Ox-Yoke Originals, Inc.
Parker & Sons Shooting Supply
Parker Gun Finishes
Pendleton Royal, c/o Swingler
  Buckland Ltd.
Perazone-Gunsmith, Brian

Pete Rickard, Inc.
Peter Dyson & Son Ltd.
Precision Airgun Sales, Inc.
PrOlixrr Lubricants
Pro-Shot Products, Inc.
R&S Industries Corp.
Radiator Specialty Co.
Rickard, Inc., Pete
Rooster Laboratories
Russ Haydon Shooters' Supply
Rusty Duck Premium Gun Care
  Products
Saunders Gun & Machine Shop
Schumakers Gun Shop
Sheffield Knifemakers Supply, Inc.
Shiloh Creek
Shooter's Choice Gun Care
Shotgun Sports Magazine, dba
  Shootin' Accessories Ltd.
Silencio/Safety Direct
Sinclair International, Inc.
Sno-Seal, Inc. (See Atsko/Sno-Seal)
Southern Bloomer Mfg. Co.
Spencer's Custom Guns
Splitfire Sporting Goods, L.L.C.
Starr Trading Co., Jedediah
Stoney Point Products, Inc.
Svon Corp.
T.F.C. S.p.A.
TDP Industries, Inc.
Tetra Gun Lubricants (See FTI, Inc.)
Texas Platers Supply Co.
The A.W. Peterson Gun Shop, Inc.
The Dutchman's Firearms, Inc.
The Gun Works
The Lewis Lead Remover
  (See LEM Gun Specialties)
The Paul Co.
Track of the Wolf, Inc.
United States Products Co.
Van Gorden & Son Inc., C. S.
Venco Industries, Inc.
  (See Shooter's Choice)
VibraShine, Inc.
Volquartsen Custom Ltd.
Vom Hoffe
  (See Old Western Scrounger, Inc.,
  The)
Warren Muzzleloading Co., Inc.
Watson Trophy Match Bullets
WD-40 Co.
Wick, David E.
Willow Bend
Wolf's Western Traders
Young Country Arms

COMPUTER SOFTWARE - BALLISTICS

Action Target, Inc.
AmBr Software Group Ltd.
Arms Software
Arms, Programming Solutions
  (See Arms Software)
Barnes Bullets, Inc.
Canons Delcour
Corbin Mfg. & Supply, Inc.
Data Tech Software Systems
Hodgdon Powder Co.
J.I.T. Ltd.
Jensen Bullets
Kent Cartridge Mfg. Co. Ltd.
Maionchi-L.M.I.
Oehler Research,Inc.
Outdoor Sports Headquarters, Inc.
P.A.C.T., Inc.
Pejsa Ballistics
Powley Computer
  (See Hutton Rifle Ranch)
RCBS Div. of Blount
Sierra Bullets
The Ballistic Program Co., Inc.
The Country Armourer
Tioga Engineering Co., Inc.
Vancini, Carl (See Bestload, Inc.)
W. Square Enterprises

CUSTOM GUNSMITH

A&W Repair
A.A. Arms, Inc.
Acadian Ballistic Specialties
Accuracy Unlimited
Ace Custom 45's, Inc.

Acra-Bond Laminates
Adair Custom Shop, Bill
Ahlman Guns
Al Lind Custom Guns
Aldis Gunsmithing & Shooting Supply
Alpha Gunsmith Division
Alpha Precision, Inc.
Alpine Indoor Shooting Range
Amrine's Gun Shop
Answer Products Co.
Antique Arms Co.
Armament Gunsmithing Co., Inc.
Arms Craft Gunsmithing
Arms Ingenuity Co.
Armscorp USA, Inc.
Arnold Arms Co., Inc.
Artistry in Wood
Art's Gun & Sport Shop, Inc.
Arundel Arms & Ammunition, Inc., A.
Autauga Arms, Inc.
Baelder, Harry
Baer Custom, Inc, Les
Bain & Davis, Inc.
Bansner's Ultimate Rifles, LLC
Barnes Bullets, Inc.
Baron Technology
Barta's Gunsmithing
Bear Arms
Bear Mountain Gun & Tool
Beaver Lodge (See Fellowes, Ted)
Behlert Precision, Inc.
Beitzinger, George
Belding's Custom Gun Shop
Ben William's Gun Shop
Bengtson Arms Co., L.
Biesen, Al
Biesen, Roger
Bill Adair Custom Shop
Billings Gunsmiths Inc.
BlackStar AccuMax Barrels
BlackStar Barrel Accurizing
  (See BlackStar AccuMax
Bob Rogers Gunsmithing
Bond Custom Firearms
Borden Ridges Rimrock Stocks
Borovnik KG, Ludwig
Bowen Classic Arms Corp.
Brace, Larry D.
Briese Bullet Co., Inc.
Briganti, A.J.
Briley Mfg. Inc.
Broad Creek Rifle Works, Ltd.
Brockman's Custom Gunsmithing
Broken Gun Ranch
Brown Precision, Inc.
Brown Products, Inc., Ed
Buchsenmachermeister
Buckhorn Gun Works
Buckskin Machine Works, A. Hunkeler
Budin, Dave
Bull Mountain Rifle Co.
Bullberry Barrel Works, Ltd.
Burkhart Gunsmithing, Don
Cache La Poudre Rifleworks
Cambos Outdoorsman
Cambos Outdoorsman
Cannon's
Carolina Precision Rifles
Carter's Gun Shop
Caywood, Shane J.
CBC-BRAZIL
Chambers Flintlocks Ltd., Jim
Chicasaw Gun Works
Chuck's Gun Shop
Chuilli, Stephen
Clark Custom Guns, Inc.
Clark Firearms Engraving
Classic Arms Company
Classic Arms Corp.
Clearview Products
Cleland's Outdoor World, Inc
Cloward's Gun Shop
Coffin, Charles H.
Cogar's Gunsmithing
Cole's Gun Works
Colonial Arms, Inc.
Colonial Repair
Colorado Gunsmithing Academy
Colorado School of Trades
Colt's Mfg. Co., Inc.
Conrad, C. A.
Corkys Gun Clinic

PRODUCT & SERVICE DIRECTORY

Cox, Ed. C.
Craig Custom Ltd., Research & Development
Cullity Restoration
Curtis Custom Shop
Custom Gun Products
Custom Gun Stocks
Custom Single Shot Rifles
Cylinder & Slide, Inc., William R. Laughridge
D&D Gunsmiths, Ltd.
D&J Bullet Co. & Custom Gun Shop, Inc.
Dangler, Homer L.
D'Arcy Echols & Co.
Darlington Gun Works, Inc.
Dave's Gun Shop
David Miller Co.
David R. Chicoine
David W. Schwartz Custom Guns
Davis, Don
Delorge, Ed
Del-Sports, Inc.
DGR Custom Rifles
DGS, Inc., Dale A. Storey
Dilliott Gunsmithing, Inc.
Donnelly, C. P.
Duane A. Hobbie Gunsmithing
Duane's Gun Repair
　(See DGR Custom Rifles)
Duffy, Charles E
　(See Guns Antique & Modern DBA)
Duncan's Gun Works, Inc.
E. Arthur Brown Co.
Eckelman Gunsmithing
Ed Brown Products, Inc.
Eggleston, Jere D.
Entre'prise Arms, Inc.
Erhardt, Dennis
Eversull Co., Inc.
Evolution Gun Works Inc.
Eyster Heritage Gunsmiths, Inc., Ken
F.I., Inc. - High Standard Mfg. Co.
Ferris Firearms
Fish Mfg. Gunsmith Sptg. Co., Marshall
Fisher, Jerry A.
Fisher Custom Firearms
Fleming Firearms
Flynn's Custom Guns
Forkin, Ben (See Belt MTN Arms)
Forkin Arms
Forster, Kathy
　(See Custom Checkering)
Forster, Larry L.
Forthofer's Gunsmithing & Knifemaking
Francesca, Inc.
Francotte & Cie S.A. Auguste
Fred F. Wells / Wells Sport Store
Frontier Arms Co.,Inc.
Fullmer, Geo. M.
G.G. & G.
Galaxy Imports Ltd., Inc.
Gary Reeder Custom Guns
Gator Guns & Repair
Genecco Gun Works
Gene's Custom Guns
Gentry Custom Gunmaker, David
George E. Mathews & Son, Inc.
Gillmann, Edwin
Gilman-Mayfield, Inc.
Gilmore Sports Concepts
Giron, Robert E.
Goens, Dale W.
Gonic Arms/North American Arm
Gonzalez Guns, Ramon B
Goodling's Gunsmithing
Goodwin's Gun Shop
Grace, Charles E.
Grayback Wildcats
Graybill's Gun Shop
Green, Roger M.
Greg Gunsmithing Repair
GrE-Tan Rifles
Griffin & Howe, Inc.
Griffin & Howe, Inc.
Gruning Precision Inc
Guncraft Books
　(See Guncraft Sports Inc.)
Guncraft Sports Inc.
Guncraft Sports, Inc.

Guns
Guns Antique & Modern DBA / Charles E. Duffy
Gunsite Custom Shop
Gunsite Gunsmithy
　(See Gunsite Custom Shop)
Gunsite Training Center
Gunsmithing Ltd.
Hagn Rifles & Actions, Martin
Hamilton, Alex B
　(See Ten-Ring Precision, Inc)
Hammans, Charles E.
Hammond Custom Guns Ltd.
Hank's Gun Shop
Hanson's Gun Center, Dick
Hanus Birdguns Bill
Harris Gunworks
Harry Lawson Co.
Hart & Son, Inc.
Hart Rifle Barrels,Inc.
Hartmann & Weiss GmbH
Harwood, Jack O.
Hawken Shop, The
　(See Dayton Traister)
Hecht, Hubert J, Waffen-Hecht
Heilmann, Stephen
Heinie Specialty Products
Hensley, Gunmaker, Darwin
High Bridge Arms, Inc
High Performance International
High Precision
Highline Machine Co.
Hill, Loring F.
Hiptmayer, Armurier
Hiptmayer, Klaus
Hoag, James W.
Hodgson, Richard
Hoehn Sales, Inc.
Hoelscher, Virgil
Hoenig & Rodman
Hofer Jagdwaffen, P.
Holland's Gunsmithing
Hollis Gun Shop
Huebner, Corey O.
Hughes, Steven Dodd
Hunkeler, A
　(See Buckskin Machine Works)
Imperial Magnum Corp.
Irwin, Campbell H.
Island Pond Gun Shop
Israel Arms International, Inc.
Ivanoff, Thomas G
　(See Tom's Gun Repair)
J&S Heat Treat
J.J. Roberts / Engraver
Jack Dever Co.
Jackalope Gun Shop
James Calhoon Mfg.
Jamison's Forge Works
Jarrett Rifles, Inc.
Jarvis, Inc.
Jay McCament Custom Gunmaker
Jeffredo Gunsight
Jensen's Custom Ammunition
Jim Norman Custom Gunstocks
Jim's Gun Shop (See Spradlin's)
Jim's Precision, Jim Ketchum
John Norrell Arms
Jones Custom Products, Neil A.
Juenke, Vern
K. Eversull Co., Inc.
KDF, Inc.
Keith's Custom Gunstocks
Ken Eyster Heritage Gunsmiths, Inc.
Ken Starnes Gunmaker
Ken's Gun Specialties
Ketchum, Jim (See Jim's Precision)
Kilham & Co.
King's Gun Works
KLA Enterprises
Klein Custom Guns, Don
Kleinendorst, K. W.
Knippel, Richard
KOGOT
Korzinek Riflesmith, J.
KSN Industries Ltd
　(See U.S. Importer-Israel Arms)
L E Jurras & Assoc.
LaFrance Specialties
Lampert, Ron
LaRocca Gun Works
Larry Lyons Gunworks

Lathrop's, Inc.
Laughridge, William R
　(See Cylinder & Slide Inc)
Lawson Co., Harry
Lazzeroni Arms Co.
LeFever Arms Co., Inc.
Lind Custom Guns, Al
Linebaugh Custom Sixguns
List Precision Engineering
Lock's Philadelphia Gun Exchange
Lone Star Rifle Company
Long, George F.
Mag-Na-Port International, Inc.
Mahony, Philip Bruce
Mahony, Philip Bruce
Mahovsky's Metalife
Makinson, Nicholas
Mandall Shooting Supplies Inc.
Marent, Rudolf
Martin's Gun Shop
Martz, John V.
Mathews & Son, Inc., George E.
Mazur Restoration, Pete
McCann's Muzzle-Gun Works
McCluskey Precision Rifles
McGowen Rifle Barrels
McKinney, R.P.
　(See Schuetzen Gun Co.)
McMillan Rifle Barrels
MCS, Inc.
Mercer Custom Guns
Michael's Antiques
Mid-America Recreation, Inc.
Middlebrooks Custom Shop
Miller Arms, Inc.
Miller Custom
Mills Jr., Hugh B.
Moeller, Steve
Monell Custom Guns
Montgomery Community College
Morrison Custom Rifles, J. W.
Morrow, Bud
Mo's Competitor Supplies
　(See MCS Inc)
Mowrey's Guns & Gunsmithing
Mullis Guncraft
Muzzleloaders Etcetera, Inc.
NCP Products, Inc.
Neil A. Jones Custom Products
Nelson's Custom Guns, Inc.
Nettestad Gun Works
New England Arms Co.
New England Custom Gun Service
Newman Gunshop
Nicholson Custom
Nickels, Paul R.
Nicklas, Ted
Nitex Gun Shop
North American Shooting Systems
Nu-Line Guns,Inc.
Oakland Custom Arms,Inc.
Old World Gunsmithing
Olson, Vic
Ottmar, Maurice
Ox-Yoke Originals, Inc.
Ozark Gun Works
P.S.M.G. Gun Co.
Pac-Nor Barreling
Pagel Gun Works, Inc.
Parker & Sons Shooting Supply
Parker Gun Finishes
Pasadena Gun Center
Paterson Gunsmithing
Paulsen Gunstocks
Peacemaker Specialists
PEM's Mfg. Co.
Pence Precision Barrels
Pennsylvania Gunsmith School
Penrod Precision
Pentheny de Pentheny
Performance Specialists
Pete Mazur Restoration
Peter Dyson & Son Ltd.
Peterson Gun Shop, Inc., A.W.
Piquette's Custom Engraving
Plum City Ballistic Range
Powell & Son (Gunmakers) Ltd., William
Power Custom, Inc.
Professional Hunter Supplies
　(See Star Custom Bull)
Quality Custom Firearms

Quality Firearms of Idaho, Inc.
R&J Gun Shop
R.A. Wells Custom Gunsmith
Ramon B. Gonzalez Guns
Ray's Gunsmith Shop
Renfrew Guns & Supplies
Ridgetop Sporting Goods
Ries, Chuck
Rifles, Inc.
Rigby & Co., John
River Road Sporting Clays
RMS Custom Gunsmithing
Robert Valade Engraving
Robinson, Don
Rocky Mountain Arms, Inc.
Romain's Custom Guns, Inc.
Ron Frank Custom Classic Arms
Ruger's Custom Guns
Rupert's Gun Shop
Ryan, Chad L.
Sanders Custom Gun Service
Savage Arms, Inc.
Schiffman, Mike
Schumakers Gun Shop
Score High Gunsmithing
Scott McDougall & Associates
Sharp Shooter Supply
Shaw, Inc., E. R.
　(See Small Arms Mfg. Co.)
Shay's Gunsmithing
Shockley, Harold H.
Shooters Supply
Shootin' Shack, Inc.
Shooting Specialties
　(See Titus, Daniel)
Shotguns Unlimited
Silver Ridge Gun Shop
　(See Goodwin, Fred)
Simmons Gun Repair, Inc.
Singletary, Kent
Siskiyou Gun Works
　(See Donnelly, C. P.)
Skeoch, Brian R.
Sklany's Machine Shop
Slezak, Jerome F.
Small Arms Mfg. Co.
Small Arms Specialists
Smith, Art
Snapp's Gunshop
Sound Technology
Speiser, Fred D.
Spencer Reblue Service
Spencer's Custom Guns
Splitfire Sporting Goods, L.L.C.
Sportsmen's Exchange & Western Gun Traders, Inc.
Springfield, Inc.
SSK Industries
Star Custom Bullets
Steelman's Gun Shop
Steffens, Ron
Stiles Custom Guns
Storey, Dale A. (See DGS Inc.)
Stott's Creek Armory, Inc.
Sturgeon Valley Sporters
Sullivan, David S .
　(See Westwind Rifles Inc.)
Swann, D. J.
Swenson's 45 Shop, A. D.
Swift River Gunworks
Szweda, Robert
　(See RMS Custom Gunsmithing)
Taconic Firearms Ltd., Perry Lane
Talmage, William G.
Tank's Rifle Shop
Tar-Hunt Custom Rifles, Inc.
Tarnhelm Supply Co., Inc.
Taylor & Robbins
Ten-Ring Precision, Inc.
Terry K. Kopp Professional Gunsmithing
The A.W. Peterson Gun Shop, Inc.
The Competitive Pistol Shop
The Custom Shop
The Gun Shop
The Gun Works
The Orvis Co.
The Robar Co.'s, Inc.
The Swampfire Shop
　(See Peterson Gun Shop, Inc.)
Theis, Terry

Thompson, Randall
　(See Highline Machine Co.)
Thurston Sports, Inc.
Time Precision
Tom's Gun Repair, Thomas G. Ivanoff
Tom's Gunshop
Trevallion Gunstocks
Trulock Tool
Tucker, James C.
Turnbull Restoration, Doug
Unmussig Bullets, D. L.
Upper Missouri Trading Co.
Valade Engraving, Robert
Van Horn, Gil
Van Patten, J. W.
Van's Gunsmith Service
Vest, John
Vic's Gun Refinishing
Vintage Arms, Inc.
Virgin Valley Custom Guns
Volquartsen Custom Ltd.
Walker Arms Co., Inc.
Wallace, Terry
Wasmundt, Jim
Wayne E. Schwartz Custom Guns
Weatherby, Inc.
Weaver Arms Corp. Gun Shop
Weber & Markin Custom Gunsmiths
Weems, Cecil
Weigand Combat Handguns, Inc.
Werth, T. W.
Wessinger Custom Guns & Engraving
Western Design
　(See Alpha Gunsmith Division)
Westley Richards & Co.
Westwind Rifles, Inc., David S. Sullivan
White Barn Wor
White Shooting Systems, Inc.
　(See White Muzzleload)
Wichita Arms, Inc.
Wiebe, Duane
Wild West Guns
Wild West Guns
Williams Gun Sight Co.
Williams Shootin' Iron Service, The Lynx-Line
Williamson Precision Gunsmithing
Wilsom Combat
Winter, Robert M.
Wise Guns, Dale
Wiseman and Co., Bill
Wood, Frank (See Classic Guns, Inc.)
Working Guns
Wright's Gunstock Blanks
Yankee Gunsmith
Zeeryp, Russ
Custom Metalsmith
A&W Repair
Ackerman & Co.
Ahlman Guns
Alaskan Silversmith, The
Aldis Gunsmithing & Shooting Supply
Alpha Precision, Inc.
Amrine's Gun Shop
Answer Products Co.
Antique Arms Co.
Arnold Arms Co., Inc.
Artistry in Wood
Baer Custom, Inc, Les
Baron Technology
Bear Mountain Gun & Tool
Behlert Precision, Inc.
Beitzinger, George
Bengtson Arms Co., L.
Biesen, Al
Bill Adair Custom Shop
Billings Gunsmiths Inc.
Billingsley & Brownell
Bob Rogers Gunsmithing
Bone Engraving, Ralph
Bowen Classic Arms Corp.
Brace, Larry D.
Briganti, A.J.
Broad Creek Rifle Works, Ltd.
Brown Precision, Inc.
Buckhorn Gun Works
Bull Mountain Rifle Co.
Bullberry Barrel Works, Ltd.
Burkhart Gunsmithing, Don
Carter's Gun Shop
Caywood, Shane J.

DIRECTORY

57TH EDITION, 2003 • 527

PRODUCT & SERVICE DIRECTORY

Checkmate Refinishing
Cleland's Outdoor World, Inc
Colonial Repair
Colorado Gunsmithing Academy
Craftguard
Crandall Tool & Machine Co.
Cullity Restoration
Custom Gun Products
Custom Single Shot Rifles
D&D Gunsmiths, Ltd.
D&H Precision Tooling
D'Arcy Echols & Co.
Dave's Gun Shop
Delorge, Ed
DGS, Inc., Dale A. Storey
Dietz Gun Shop & Range, Inc.
Dilliott Gunsmithing, Inc.
Duane's Gun Repair
  (See DGR Custom Rifles)
Duncan's Gun Works, Inc.
Erhardt, Dennis
Eversull Co., Inc.
Eyster Heritage Gunsmiths, Inc., Ken
Ferris Firearms
Fisher, Jerry A.
Forster, Larry L.
Forthofer's Gunsmithing &
  Knifemaking
Francesca, Inc.
Fred F. Wells / Wells Sport Store
Fullmer, Geo. M.
Genecco Gun Works
Gentry Custom Gunmaker, David
Grace, Charles E.
Grayback Wildcats
Graybill's Gun Shop
Green, Roger M.
Griffin & Howe, Inc.
Guns
Gunsmithing Ltd.
Hagn Rifles & Actions, Martin
Hamilton, Alex B
  (See Ten-Ring Precision, Inc)
Harry Lawson Co.
Hartmann & Weiss GmbH
Harwood, Jack O.
Hecht, Hubert J, Waffen-Hecht
Heilmann, Stephen
Highline Machine Co.
Hiptmayer, Armurier
Hiptmayer, Klaus
Hoag, James W.
Hoelscher, Virgil
Holland's Gunsmithing
Hollis Gun Shop
Island Pond Gun Shop
Ivanoff, Thomas G
  (See Tom's Gun Repair)
J J Roberts Firearm Engraver
J&S Heat Treat
J.J. Roberts / Engraver
Jamison's Forge Works
Jay McCament Custom Gunmaker
Jeffredo Gunsight
KDF, Inc.
Ken Eyster Heritage Gunsmiths, Inc.
Ken Starnes Gunmaker
Ken's Gun Specialties
Kilham & Co.
Klein Custom Guns, Don
Kleinendorst, K. W.
Knippel, Richard
Lampert, Ron
Larry Lyons Gunworks
Lawson Co., Harry
List Precision Engineering
Mahovsky's Metalife
Makinson, Nicholas
Mazur Restoration, Pete
McCann Industries
McCann's Machine & Gun Shop
Mid-America Recreation, Inc.
Miller Arms, Inc.
Montgomery Community College
Morrison Custom Rifles, J. W.
Morrow, Bud
Mullis Guncraft
Nelson's Custom Guns, Inc.
Nettestad Gun Works
New England Custom Gun Service
Nicholson Custom
Nitex Gun Shop

Noreen, Peter H.
Nu-Line Guns,Inc.
Oakland Custom Arms,Inc.
Olson, Vic
Ozark Gun Works
P.S.M.G. Gun Co.
Pagel Gun Works, Inc.
Parker & Sons Shooting Supply
Parker Gun Finishes
Pasadena Gun Center
Penrod Precision
Pete Mazur Restoration
Precision Specialties
Quality Custom Firearms
R.A. Wells Custom Gunsmith
Rice, Keith
  (See White Rock Tool & Die)
Rifles, Inc.
River Road Sporting Clays
Robert Valade Engraving
Rocky Mountain Arms, Inc.
Romain's Custom Guns, Inc.
Ron Frank Custom Classic Arms
Sanders Custom Gun Service
Score High Gunsmithing
Simmons Gun Repair, Inc.
Singletary, Kent
Skeoch, Brian R.
Sklany's Machine Shop
Small Arms Specialists
Smith, Art
Smith, Sharmon
Snapp's Gunshop
Spencer Reblue Service
Spencer's Custom Guns
Sportsmen's Exchange & Western
  Gun Traders, Inc.
Steffens, Ron
Stiles Custom Guns
Storey, Dale A. (See DGS Inc.)
Taylor & Robbins
Ten-Ring Precision, Inc.
The A.W. Peterson Gun Shop, Inc.
The Custom Shop
The Gun Shop
The Robar Co.'s, Inc.
Thompson, Randall
  (See Highline Machine Co.)
Tom's Gun Repair, Thomas G. Ivanoff
Turnbull Restoration, Doug
Valade Engraving, Robert
Van Horn, Gil
Van Patten, J. W.
Waldron, Herman
Wallace, Terry
Weber & Markin Custom Gunsmiths
Werth, T. W.
Wessinger Custom Guns & Engraving
White Rock Tool & Die
Wiebe, Duane
Wild West Guns
Wild West Guns
Williams Shootin' Iron Service, The
  Lynx-Line
Williamson Precision Gunsmithing
Winter, Robert M.
Wise Guns, Dale
Wood, Frank (See Classic Guns, Inc.)
Wright's Gunstock Blanks
Zufall, Joseph F.

Decoys
Ad Hominem
Baekgaard Ltd.
Belding's Custom Gun Shop
Boyds' Gunstock Industries, Inc.
Carry-Lite, Inc.
Farm Form Decoys, Inc.
Feather, Flex Decoys
Flambeau Products Corp.
G&H Decoys,Inc.
Herter's Manufacturing Inc.
Hiti-Schuch, Atelier Wilma
Klingler Woodcarving
L.L. Bean, Inc.
Molin Industries, Tru-Nord Division
Murphy, R.R. Co., Inc.
North Wind Decoy Co.
Original Deer Formula Co., The.
Quack Decoy & Sporting Clays
Russ Trading Post
Sports Innovations Inc.
Tanglefree Industries

The A.W. Peterson Gun Shop, Inc.
Woods Wise Products

DIE ACCESSORIES, METALLIC
High Precision
King & Co.
MarMik, Inc.
Rapine Bullet Mould Mfg. Co.
Redding Reloading Equipment
Sport Flite Manufacturing Co.
The A.W. Peterson Gun Shop, Inc.
Wolf's Western Traders

DIES, METALLIC
4-D Custom Die Co.
Dakota Arms, Inc.
Dillon Precision Products, Inc.
Dixie Gun Works
Fremont Tool Works
Goodwin's Gun Shop
Gruning Precision Inc
Jones Custom Products, Neil A.
King & Co.
Lee Precision, Inc.
Montana Precision Swaging
Neil A. Jones Custom Products
Ozark Gun Works
Rapine Bullet Mould Mfg. Co.
RCBS Div. of Blount
Redding Reloading Equipment
Romain's Custom Guns, Inc.
Sport Flite Manufacturing Co.
The A.W. Peterson Gun Shop, Inc.
Vega Tool Co.
Wolf's Western Traders

DIES, SHOTSHELL
Goodwin's Gun Shop
Lee Precision, Inc.
MEC, Inc.
The A.W. Peterson Gun Shop, Inc.

DIES, SWAGE
4-D Custom Die Co.
Bullet Swaging Supply Inc.
Goodwin's Gun Shop
Hollywood Engineering
Sport Flite Manufacturing Co.
The A.W. Peterson Gun Shop, Inc.

ENGRAVER, ENGRAVING TOOLS
Ackerman & Co.
Adair Custom Shop, Bill
Ahlman Guns
Alaskan Silversmith, The
Alfano, Sam
Allard, Gary/Creek Side Metal &
  Woodcrafters
Allen Firearm Engraving
Altamont Co.
American Pioneer Video
Baron Technology
Barraclough, John K.
Bates Engraving, Billy
Bill Adair Custom Shop
Billy Bates Engraving
Blair Engraving, Jim
Bleile, C. Roger
Boessler, Erich
Bone Engraving, Ralph
Brooker, Dennis
Buchsenmachermeister
Churchill, Winston G.
Clark Firearms Engraving
Collings, Ronald
Creek Side Metal & Woodcrafters
Cullity Restoration
Cupp, Alana, Custom Engraver
Custom Single Shot Rifles
Dayton Traister
Delorge, Ed
Dolbare, Elizabeth
Drain, Mark
Dremel Mfg. Co.
Dubber, Michael W.
Engraving Artistry
Evans Engraving, Robert
Eversull Co., Inc.
Eyster Heritage Gunsmiths, Inc., Ken
Firearms & Metal Engraving
Firearms Engraver's Guild of America

Flannery Engraving Co., Jeff W
Forty Five Ranch Enterprises
Fountain Products
Francotte & Cie S.A. Auguste
Frank Knives
Fred F. Wells / Wells Sport Store
French, Artistic Engraving, J. R.
Gary Reeder Custom Guns
Gene's Custom Guns
Glimm's Custom Gun Engraving
Golden Age Arms Co.
Gournet Artistic Engraving
Grant, Howard V.
Griffin & Howe, Inc.
GRS / Glendo Corp.
Guns
Gurney, F. R.
Gwinnell, Bryson J.
Hale, Engraver, Peter
Half Moon Rifle Shop
Hands Engraving, Barry Lee
Harris Gunworks
Harris Hand Engraving, Paul A.
Harwood, Jack O.
Hawken Shop, The
  (See Dayton Traister)
Hiptmayer, Armurier
Hiptmayer, Heidemarie
Hofer Jagdwaffen, P.
Ingle, Ralph W.
J J Roberts Firearm Engraver
J.J. Roberts / Engraver
Jantz Supply
Jeff W. Flannery Engraving Co.
Jim Blair Engraving
John J. Adams & Son Engravers
Kamyk Engraving Co., Steve
Kane, Edward
Kehr, Roger
Kelly, Lance
Ken Eyster Heritage Gunsmiths, Inc.
Kenneth W. Warren Engraver
Klingler Woodcarving
Knippel, Richard
Koevenig's Engraving Service
Larry Lyons Gunworks
LeFever Arms Co., Inc.
Leibowitz, Leonard
Lindsay, Steve
Little Trees Ramble
  (See Scott Pilkington)
McCombs, Leo
McDonald, Dennis
McKenzie, Lynton
Mele, Frank
Metals Hand Engraver/European Hand
  Engraving
Mid-America Recreation, Inc.
Mittermeier, Inc., Frank
Montgomery Community College
Nelson, Gary K.
New Orleans Jewelers Supply Co.
Oker's Engraving
Pedersen, C. R.
Pedersen, Rex C.
Peter Hale/Engraver
Pilgrim Pewter,Inc.
  (See Bell Originals Inc. Sid)
Pilkington, Scott
  (See Little Trees Ramble)
Piquette's Custom Engraving
Potts, Wayne E.
Quality Custom Firearms
Rabeno, Martin
Ralph Bone Engraving
Reed, Dave
Reno, Wayne
Riggs, Jim
Robert Evans Engraving
Robert Valade Engraving
Rohner, Hans
Rohner, John
Rosser, Bob
Rundell's Gun Shop
Runge, Robert P.
Sam Welch Gun Engraving
Sampson, Roger
Schiffman, Mike
Sheffield Knifemakers Supply, Inc.
Sherwood, George
Singletary, Kent
Smith, Mark A.

Smith, Ron
Smokey Valley Rifles
Steve Kamyk Engraver
Swanson, Mark
The Gun Room
The NgraveR Co.
Theis, Terry
Thiewes, George W.
Thirion Gun Engraving, Denise
Valade Engraving, Robert
Viramontez Engraving
Vorhes, David
W.E. Brownell Checkering Tools
Wagoner, Vernon G.
Wallace, Terry
Warenski, Julie
Weber & Markin Custom Gunsmiths
Wells, Rachel
Wessinger Custom Guns & Engraving
Winchester Consultants
Ziegel Engineering

GAME CALLS
Adventure Game Calls
African Import Co.
Arkansas Mallard Duck Calls
Ashby Turkey Calls
Bostick Wildlife Calls, Inc.
Cedar Hill Game Calls, Inc.
Crit'R Call
  (See Rocky Mountain Wildlife
  Products)
Custom Calls
D&H Prods. Co., Inc.
D-Boone Ent., Inc.
Deepeeka Exports Pvt. Ltd.
Dr. O's Products Ltd.
Duck Call Specialists
Faulhaber Wildlocker
Faulk's Game Call Co., Inc.
Fibron Products, Inc.
Glynn Scobey Duck & Goose Calls
Goodwin's Gun Shop
Green Head Game Call Co.
Hally Caller
Haydel's Game Calls, Inc.
Herter's Manufacturing Inc.
Hunter's Specialties Inc.
Keowee Game Calls
Kingyon, Paul L. (See Custom Calls)
Knight & Hale Game Calls
Lohman Mfg. Co., Inc.
Mallardtone Game Calls
Moss Double Tone, Inc.
Mountain Hollow Game Calls
Oakman Turkey Calls
Original Deer Formula Co., The.
Outdoor Sports Headquarters, Inc.
Pete Rickard, Inc.
Philip S. Olt Co.
Primos, Inc.
Protektor Model
Quaker Boy, Inc.
Rickard, Inc., Pete
Rocky Mountain Wildlife Products
Russ Trading Post
Sceery Game Calls
Sports Innovations Inc.
Stanley Scruggs' Game Calls
Stewart Game Calls, Inc., Johnny
Sure-Shot Game Calls, Inc.
Tanglefree Industries
The A.W. Peterson Gun Shop, Inc.
Tinks & Ben Lee Hunting Products
  (See Wellington)
Tink's Safariland Hunting Corp.
Wellington Outdoors
Wilderness Sound Products Ltd.
Woods Wise Products
Wyant's Outdoor Products, Inc.

GAUGES, CALIPERS & MICROMETERS
Blue Ridge Machinery & Tools, Inc.
Goodwin's Gun Shop
Gruning Precision Inc
K&M Services
King & Co.
Starrett Co., L. S.
Stoney Point Products, Inc.

GUN PARTS, U.S. & FOREIGN

"Su-Press-On",Inc.
A.A. Arms, Inc.
Ahlman Guns
Amherst Arms
Antique Arms Co.
Armscorp USA, Inc.
Aro-Tek Ltd.
Auto-Ordnance Corp.
B.A.C.
Badger Shooters Supply, Inc.
Bar-Sto Precision Machine
Bear Mountain Gun & Tool
Billings Gunsmiths Inc.
Bill's Gun Repair
Bob's Gun Shop
Briese Bullet Co., Inc.
British Antiques
Brown Products, Inc., Ed
Brownells, Inc.
Bryan & Assoc.
Buffer Technologies
Cambos Outdoorsman
Cambos Outdoorsman
Cape Outfitters
Caspian Arms, Ltd.
CBC-BRAZIL
Chicasaw Gun Works
Ciener Inc., Jonathan Arthur
Cole's Gun Works
Colonial Arms, Inc.
Colonial Repair
Colt's Mfg. Co., Inc.
Cryo-Accurizing
Custom Riflestocks, Inc., Michael M.
    Kokolus
Cylinder & Slide, Inc., William R.
    Laughridge
Delta Arms Ltd.
Dewey Mfg. Co., Inc., J.
DGR Custom Rifles
Dibble, Derek A.
Duane's Gun Repair
    (See DGR Custom Rifles)
Duffy, Charles E
    (See Guns Antique & Modern DBA)
E.A.A. Corp.
Elliott Inc., G. W.
EMF Co., Inc.
Enguix Import-Export
Entre'prise Arms, Inc.
European American Armory Corp (See
    E.A.A. Corp)
Evolution Gun Works Inc.
F.I., Inc. - High Standard Mfg. Co.
Faloon Industries, Inc.
Federal Arms Corp. of America
Fleming Firearms
Forrest Inc., Tom
Gentry Custom Gunmaker, David
Glimm's Custom Gun Engraving
Goodwin's Gun Shop
Granite Mountain Arms, Inc
Greider Precision
Groenewold, John
Gun Hunter Books
    (See Gun Hunter Trading Co)
Gun Hunter Trading Co.
Guns Antique & Modern DBA / Charles
    E. Duffy
Gunsmithing, Inc.
Hastings Barrels
Hawken Shop, The
    (See Dayton Traister)
High Performance International
I.S.S.
Irwin, Campbell H.
Jamison's Forge Works
Jonathan Arthur Ciener, Inc.
K.K. Arms Co.
Kimber of America, Inc.
Knight's Mfg. Co.
Krico Deutschland GmbH
Lampert, Ron
LaPrade
Laughridge, William R
    (See Cylinder & Slide Inc)
Leapers, Inc.
List Precision Engineering
Lodewick, Walter H.

Logdewood Mfg.
Long, George F.
Mandall Shooting Supplies Inc.
Markell,Inc.
Martin's Gun Shop
McCormick Corp., Chip
MCS, Inc.
Merkuria Ltd.
Mid-America Recreation, Inc.
Morrow, Bud
Mo's Competitor Supplies
    (See MCS Inc)
North Star West
Northwest Arms
Nu-Line Guns,Inc.
Nygord Precision Products, Inc.
Olympic Arms Inc.
P.S.M.G. Gun Co.
Pacific Armament Corp
Parts & Surplus
Pennsylvania Gun Parts Inc
Performance Specialists
Peter Dyson & Son Ltd.
Peterson Gun Shop, Inc., A.W.
Quality Firearms of Idaho, Inc.
Ranch Products
Randco UK
Raptor Arms Co., Inc.
Ravell Ltd.
Retting, Inc., Martin B
Romain's Custom Guns, Inc.
Ruger (See Sturm, Ruger & Co., Inc.)
S&S Firearms
Sabatti S.r.l.
Samco Global Arms, Inc.
Sarco, Inc.
Scherer Supplies
Shockley, Harold H.
Shootin' Shack, Inc.
Silver Ridge Gun Shop
    (See Goodwin, Fred)
Simmons Gun Repair, Inc.
Smires, C. L.
Smith & Wesson
Southern Ammunition Co., Inc.
Sportsmen's Exchange & Western
    Gun Traders, Inc.
Springfield Sporters, Inc.
Springfield, Inc.
Steyr Mannlicher AG & CO KG
STI International
Strayer-Voigt, Inc.
Sturm Ruger & Co. Inc.
Sunny Hill Enterprises, Inc.
T&S Industries, Inc.
Tank's Rifle Shop
Tarnhelm Supply Co., Inc.
Terry K. Kopp Professional
    Gunsmithing
The A.W. Peterson Gun Shop, Inc.
The Gun Parts Corp.
The Gun Room Press
The Gun Shop
The Gun Shop
The Gun Works
The Southern Armory
The Swampfire Shop
    (See Peterson Gun Shop, Inc.)
VAM Distribution Co LLC
Vektor USA
Vintage Arms, Inc.
W. Waller & Son, Inc.
W.C. Wolff Co.
Walker Arms Co., Inc.
Weaver Arms Corp. Gun Shop
Wescombe, Bill (See North Star West)
Whitestone Lumber Corp.
Wild West Guns
Williams Mfg. of Oregon
Winchester Sutler, Inc., The
Wise Guns, Dale
Wisners Inc/Twin Pine Armory

GUNS & GUN PARTS, REPLICA & ANTIQUE

Ackerman & Co.
Ahlman Guns
Armi San Paolo
Auto-Ordnance Corp.
Ballard Rifle & Cartridge Co., LLC
Bear Mountain Gun & Tool
Billings Gunsmiths Inc.

Bob's Gun Shop
British Antiques
Buckskin Machine Works, A. Hunkeler
Cache La Poudre Rifleworks
Cash Mfg. Co., Inc.
CBC-BRAZIL
CCL Security Products
Chambers Flintlocks Ltd., Jim
Chicasaw Gun Works
Cogar's Gunsmithing
Cole's Gun Works
Colonial Repair
Colt Blackpowder Arms Co.
Colt's Mfg. Co., Inc.
Custom Riflestocks, Inc., Michael M.
    Kokolus
Custom Single Shot Rifles
David R. Chicoine
Delhi Gun House
Delta Arms Ltd.
Dilliott Gunsmithing, Inc.
Dixie Gun Works
Dixon Muzzleloading Shop, Inc.
Ed's Gun House
Flintlocks, Etc.
George E. Mathews & Son, Inc.
Getz Barrel Co.
Golden Age Arms Co.
Goodwin's Gun Shop
Groenewold, John
Gun Hunter Books
    (See Gun Hunter Trading Co)
Gun Hunter Trading Co.
Guns
Hastings Barrels
Hunkeler, A
    (See Buckskin Machine Works)
IAR Inc.
Imperial Miniature Armory
Ithaca Classic Doubles
Ken Starnes Gunmaker
Kokolus, Michael M.
    (See Custom Riflestocks)
L&R Lock Co.
Leonard Day
List Precision Engineering
Lock's Philadelphia Gun Exchange
Logdewood Mfg.
Lone Star Rifle Company
Lucas, Edward E
Mandall Shooting Supplies Inc.
Martin's Gun Shop
Mathews & Son, Inc., George E.
McKinney, R.P.
    (See Schuetzen Gun Co.)
Mid-America Recreation, Inc.
Mountain State Muzzleloading
    Supplies, Inc.
Mowrey Gun Works
Navy Arms Company
Neumann GmbH
North Star West
Parker & Sons Shooting Supply
Pasadena Gun Center
Pecatonica River Longrifle
PEM's Mfg. Co.
Peter Dyson & Son Ltd.
Pony Express Sport Shop
Quality Firearms of Idaho, Inc.
R.A. Wells Custom Gunsmith
Randco UK
Ravell Ltd.
Retting, Inc., Martin B
Rutgers Book Center
S&S Firearms
Samco Global Arms, Inc.
Sarco, Inc.
Shootin' Shack, Inc.
Silver Ridge Gun Shop
    (See Goodwin, Fred)
Simmons Gun Repair, Inc.
Sklany's Machine Shop
Southern Ammunition Co., Inc.
Starr Trading Co., Jedediah
Stott's Creek Armory, Inc.
Taylor's & Co., Inc.
Tennessee Valley Mfg.
The A.W. Peterson Gun Shop, Inc.
The Gun Parts Corp.
The Gun Room Press
The Gun Shop
The Gun Works

Tiger-Hunt Gunstocks
Turnbull Restoration, Doug
Uberti USA, Inc.
Upper Missouri Trading Co.
Vintage Industries, Inc.
Vortek Products, Inc.
Weber & Markin Custom Gunsmiths
Wescombe, Bill (See North Star West)
Whitestone Lumber Corp.
Winchester Sutler, Inc., The

GUNS, AIR

Air Arms
Air Rifle Specialists
Air Venture Airguns
AirForce Airguns
Airrow
Allred Bullet Co.
Arms Corporation of the Philippines
BEC, Inc.
Beeman Precision Airguns
Benjamin/Sheridan Co., Crossman
Brass Eagle, Inc.
Brocock Ltd.
Bryan & Assoc.
BSA Guns Ltd.
Compasseco, Ltd.
Component Concepts, Inc.
Conetrol Scope Mounts
Creedmoor Sports, Inc.
Crosman Airguns
Daisy Mfg. Co.
Daystate Ltd.
Diana
    (See U.S. Importer - Dynamit Nobel-
    RWS, Inc.)
Domino
Dynamit Nobel-RWS, Inc.
European American Armory Corp
    (See E.A.A. Corp)
FWB
Gamo USA, Inc.
Gaucher Armes, S.A.
Great Lakes Airguns
Groenewold, John
IAR Inc.
Interarms / Howa
J.G. Anschutz GmbH & Co. KG
Labanu, Inc.
Leapers, Inc.
List Precision Engineering
Mac-1 Airgun Distributors
Marksman Products
Maryland Paintball Supply
Merkuria Ltd.
Pardini Armi Srl
Precision Airgun Sales, Inc.
Precision Sales International, Inc.
Ripley Rifles
Robinson, Don
RWS
    (See US Importer-Dynamit Nobel-
    RWS, Inc.)
S.G.S. Sporting Guns Srl.
Savage Arms, Inc.
Smart Parts
Smith & Wesson
Steyr Mannlicher AG & CO KG
Stone Enterprises Ltd.
The A.W. Peterson Gun Shop, Inc.
The Gun Room Press
The Park Rifle Co., Ltd.
Tippman Pneumatics, Inc.
Tristar Sporting Arms, Ltd.
Trooper Walsh
UltraSport Arms, Inc.
Valor Corp.
Visible Impact Targets
Vortek Products, Inc.
Walther GmbH, Carl
Webley and Scott Ltd.
Weihrauch KG, Hermann
Whiscombe
    (See U.S. Importer-Pelaire
    Products)
World Class Airguns

GUNS, FOREIGN MANUFACTURER U.S. IMPORTER

Accuracy Internationl Precision Rifles
    (See U.S.)

Accuracy Int'l. North America, Inc.
Ad Hominem
Air Arms
Armas Kemen S. A.
    (See U.S. Importers)
Armi Perazzi S.p.A.
Armi San Marco
    (See U.S. Importers-Taylor's & Co)
Armi Sport
    (See U.S. Importers-Cape
    Outfitters)
Arms Corporation of the Philippines
Armscorp USA, Inc.
Arrieta S.L.
Astra Sport, S.A.
Atamec-Bretton
AYA
    (See U.S. Importer-New England
    Custom Gun Serv)
B.A.C.
B.C. Outdoors
BEC, Inc.
Benelli Armi S.p.A.
Benelli USA Corp
Beretta S.p.A., Pietro
Beretta U.S.A. Corp.
Bernardelli S.p.A., Vincenzo
Bersa S.A.
Bertuzzi
    (See U.S. Importer-New England
    Arms Co)
Bill Hanus Birdguns LLC
Blaser Jagdwaffen GmbH
Borovnik KG, Ludwig
Bosis
    (See U.S. Importer-New England
    Arms Co.)
Brenneke KG, Wilhelm
Browning Arms Co.
Bryan & Assoc.
BSA Guns Ltd.
Cabanas
    (See U.S. Importer-Mandall
    Shooting Supply
Cabela's
Cape Outfitters
CBC
Chapuis Armes
Churchill
    (See U.S. Importer-Ellett Bros.)
Cosmi Americo & Figlio s.n.c.
Crucelegui, Hermanos
    (See U.S. Importer-Mandall)
Cryo-Accurizing
Cubic Shot Shell Co., Inc.
Daewoo Precision Industries Ltd.
Dakota
    (See U.S. Importer-EMF Co., Inc.)
Dakota Arms, Inc.
Davide Pedersoli and Co.
Diana
    (See U.S. Importer - Dynamit Nobel-
    RWS, Inc.)
Domino
Dumoulin, Ernest
Eagle Imports, Inc.
EAW
    (See U.S. Importer-New England
    Custom Gun Serv)
Ed's Gun House
Effebi SNC-Dr. Franco Beretta
EMF Co., Inc.
Euro-Imports
Eversull Co., Inc.
F.A.I.R. Tecni-Mec s.n.c. di Isidoro
    Rizzini & C.
Fabarm S.p.A.
Fausti Cav. Stefano & Figlie snc
FEG
FERLIB
Fiocchi Munizioni S.p.A.
    (See U.S. Importer-Fiocch)
Firearms Co Ltd. / Alpine
    (See U.S. Importer-Mandall)
Firearms International
Flintlocks, Etc.
Franchi S.p.A.
FWB
Galaxy Imports Ltd., Inc.
Gamba S.p.A. Societa Armi Bresciane
    Srl

Gamo
   (See U.S. Importers-Arms United
   Corp, Daisy M)
Garbi, Armas Urki
Gaucher Armes, S.A.
Gibbs Rifle Co., Inc.
Glock GmbH
Goergen's Gun Shop, Inc.
Gonzalez Guns, Ramon B
Grulla Armes
Hammerli Ltd.
Hammerli USA
Hartford
   (See U.S. Importer-EMF Co. Inc.)
Hartmann & Weiss GmbH
Heckler & Koch, Inc.
Hege Jagd-u. Sporthandels GmbH
Helwan
   (See U.S. Importer-Interarms)
Holland & Holland Ltd.
Howa Machinery, Ltd.
I.A.B.
   (See U.S. Importer-Taylor's & Co.
   Inc.)
IAR Inc.
IGA
   (See U.S. Importer-Stoeger
   Industries)
Ignacio Ugartechea S.A.
Imperial Magnum Corp.
Imperial Miniature Armory
Import Sports Inc.
IMX, LLC
Inter Ordnance of America LP
Interarms / Howa
Intrac Arms International
J.G. Anschutz GmbH & Co. KG
John Rigby & Co.
JSL Ltd
   (See U.S. Importer-Specialty
   Shooters)
K. Eversull Co., Inc.
Kimar (See U.S. Importer-IAR, Inc)
Korth
Krico Deutschland GmbH
Krieghoff Gun Co., H.
KSN Industries Ltd
   (See U.S. Importer-Israel Arms)
Lakefield Arms Ltd
   (See Savage Arms Inc.)
Lapua Ltd.
Laurona Armas Eibar, S.A.L.
Lebeau-Courally
Lever Arms Service Ltd.
Llama Gabilondo Y Cia
London Guns Ltd.
M. Thys
   (See U.S. Importer-Champlin
   Firearms Inc)
Magtech Ammunition Co. Inc.
Mandall Shooting Supplies Inc.
Marocchi F.lli S.p.A
Mauser Werke Oberndorf
   Waffensysteme GmbH
McCann Industries
MEC-Gar S.r.l.
Merkel Freres
Miltex, Inc
Miroku, B C/Daly, Charles
   (See U.S. Importer)
Morini
   (See U.S. Importers-Mandall
   Shooting Supply)
New England Custom Gun Service
New SKB Arms Co.
Norica, Avnda Otaola
Norinco
Norma Precision AB
   (See U.S. Importers-Dynamit)
Northwest Arms
OK Weber,Inc.
Para-Ordnance Mfg., Inc.
Pardini Armi Srl
Perugini Visini & Co. S.r.l.
Peters Stahl GmbH
Pietta
   (See U.S. Importers-Navy Arms Co,
   Taylor's)
Piotti
   (See U.S. Importer-Moore & Co,
   Wm. Larkin)
PMC / Eldorado Cartridge Corp.

Powell & Son (Gunmakers) Ltd.,
   William
Prairie Gun Works
Ramon B. Gonzalez Guns
Rigby & Co., John
Rizzini F.lli
   (See U.S. Importers-Moore & C
   England)
Rizzini SNC
Robinson Armament Co.
Rossi Firearms
Rottweil Compe
Rutten
   (See U.S. Importer-Labanu Inc)
RWS
   (See US Importer-Dynamit Nobel-
   RWS, Inc.)
S.A.R.L. G. Granger
S.I.A.C.E. (See U.S. Importer-IAR Inc)
Sabatti S.r.l.
Sako Ltd
   (See U.S. Importer-Stoeger
   Industries)
San Marco
   (See U.S. Importers-Cape
   Outfitters-EMF)
Sarsilmaz Shotguns - Turkey
   (See B.C. Outdoors)
Sauer
   (See U.S. Importers-Paul Co., The,
   Sigarms I)
Savage Arms (Canada), Inc.
SIG
Sigarms, Inc.
SIG-Sauer
   (See U.S. Importer-Sigarms Inc.)
SKB Shotguns
Small Arms Specialists
Societa Armi Bresciane Srl
   (See U.S. Importer-Cape
Sphinx Systems Ltd.
Springfield, Inc.
Starr Trading Co., Jedediah
Steyr Mannlicher AG & CO KG
T.F.C. S.p.A.
Tanfoglio Fratelli S.r.l.
Tanner
   (See U.S. Importer-Mandall
   Shooting Supply)
Tar-Hunt Custom Rifles, Inc.
Taurus International Firearms
   (See U.S. Importer)
Taurus S.A. Forjas
Taylor's & Co., Inc.
Techno Arms
   (See U.S. Importer- Auto-Ordnance
   Corp)
The A.W. Peterson Gun Shop, Inc.
Tikka
   (See U.S. Importer-Stoeger
   Industries)
TOZ
   (See U.S. Importer-Nygord
   Precision Products)
Ugartechea S. A., Ignacio
Ultralux
   (See U.S. Importer-Keng's
   Firearms)
Unique/M.A.P.F.
Valtro USA, Inc
Voere-KGH m.b.H.
Walther GmbH, Carl
Weatherby, Inc.
Webley and Scott Ltd.
Weihrauch KG, Hermann
Westley Richards & Co.
Whiscombe
   (See U.S. Importer-Pelaire
   Products)
Wolf (See J.R. Distributing)
Zabala Hermanos S.A.

GUNS, FOREIGN-IMPORTER

Accuracy International
AcuSport Corporation
Air Rifle Specialists
American Frontier Firearms Mfg., Inc
Auto-Ordnance Corp.
B.A.C.
B.C. Outdoors
Bell's Legendary Country Wear

Benelli USA Corp
Big Bear Arms & Sporting Goods, Inc.
Bill Hanus Birdguns LLC
Bridgeman Products
British Sporting Arms
Browning Arms Co.
Cape Outfitters
Century International Arms, Inc.
Champion Shooters' Supply
Champion's Choice, Inc.
Chapuis USA
Cimarron F.A. Co.
CVA
CZ USA
Dynamit Nobel-RWS, Inc.
E&L Mfg., Inc.
E.A.A. Corp.
Eagle Imports, Inc.
Ellett Bros.
EMF Co. Inc.
Euroarms of America, Inc.
Eversull Co., Inc.
Fiocchi of America Inc.
Flintlocks, Etc.
Franzen International,Inc
   (See U.S. Importer for)
G.U. Inc
   (See U.S. Importer for New SKB
   Arms Co.)
Galaxy Imports Ltd., Inc.
Gamba, USA
Gamo USA, Inc.
Giacomo Sporting USA
Glock, Inc.
Gremmel Enterprises
Griffin & Howe, Inc.
GSI, Inc.
Guncraft Books
   (See Guncraft Sports Inc.)
Guncraft Sports Inc.
Gunsite Custom Shop
Gunsite Training Center
Hammerli USA
Hanus Birdguns Bill
I.S.S.
IAR Inc.
Imperial Magnum Corp.
Imperial Miniature Armory
Import Sports Inc.
IMX, LLC
Interarms / Howa
Intrac Arms International
K. Eversull Co., Inc.
K.B.I. Inc
Kemen America
Keng's Firearms Specialty, Inc. / US
   Tactical Systems
Krieghoff International,Inc.
Labanu, Inc.
Legacy Sports International
Lion Country Supply
London Guns Ltd.
Magnum Research, Inc.
Marx, Harry
   (See U.S. Importer for FERLIB)
MCS, Inc.
MEC-Gar U.S.A., Inc.
Navy Arms Company
New England Arms Co.
Nygord Precision Products, Inc.
OK Weber,Inc.
P.S.M.G. Gun Co.
Para-Ordnance, Inc.
Pelaire Products
Perazzi U.S.A. Inc.
Powell Agency, William
Precision Sales International, Inc.
Quality Arms, Inc.
Rocky Mountain Armoury
S.D. Meacham
Samco Global Arms, Inc.
Sanders Custom Gun Service
Savage Arms, Inc.
Schuetzen Pistol Works
Scott Fine Guns Inc., Thad
Sigarms, Inc.
SKB Shotguns
Small Arms Specialists
Southern Ammunition Co., Inc.
Specialty Shooters Supply, Inc.
Springfield, Inc.
Stoeger Industries

Stone Enterprises Ltd.
Swarovski Optik North America Ltd.
Tar-Hunt Custom Rifles, Inc.
Taurus Firearms, Inc.
Taylor's & Co., Inc.
The A.W. Peterson Gun Shop, Inc.
The Gun Shop
The Orvis Co.
The Paul Co.
Track of the Wolf, Inc.
Traditions Performance Firearms
Tristar Sporting Arms, Ltd.
Trooper Walsh
U.S. Importer-Wm. Larkin Moore
Uberti USA, Inc.
VAM Distribution Co LLC
Vektor USA
Vintage Arms, Inc.
Westley Richards Agency USA
   (See U.S. Importer)
Wingshooting Adventures
World Class Airguns

GUNS, SURPLUS, PARTS & AMMUNITION

Ahlman Guns
Alpha 1 Drop Zone
Armscorp USA, Inc.
Arundel Arms & Ammunition, Inc., A.
B.A.C.
Bondini Paolo
Cambos Outdoorsman
Century International Arms, Inc.
Cole's Gun Works
Conetrol Scope Mounts
Delta Arms Ltd.
Ed's Gun House
First Inc., Jack
Fleming Firearms
Forrest Inc., Tom
Garcia National Gun Traders, Inc.
Goodwin's Gun Shop
Gun City
Gun Hunter Books
   (See Gun Hunter Trading Co)
Gun Hunter Trading Co.
Hank's Gun Shop
Hege Jagd-u. Sporthandels GmbH
Interarms / Howa
Jackalope Gun Shop
Ken Starnes Gunmaker
LaRocca Gun Works
Lever Arms Service Ltd.
Log Cabin Sport Shop
Martin's Gun Shop
Navy Arms Company
Nevada Pistol Academy, Inc.
Northwest Arms
Oil Rod and Gun Shop
Paragon Sales & Services, Inc.
Parts & Surplus
Pasadena Gun Center
Power Plus Enterprises, Inc.
Quality Firearms of Idaho, Inc.
Ravell Ltd.
Retting, Inc., Martin B
Samco Global Arms, Inc.
Sanders Custom Gun Service
Sarco, Inc.
Shootin' Shack, Inc.
Silver Ridge Gun Shop
   (See Goodwin, Fred)
Simmons Gun Repair, Inc.
Sportsmen's Exchange & Western
   Gun Traders, Inc.
Springfield Sporters, Inc.
T.F.C. S.p.A.
Tarnhelm Supply Co., Inc.
The A.W. Peterson Gun Shop, Inc.
The Gun Parts Corp.
The Gun Room Press
The Gun Shop
Thurston Sports, Inc.
Vom Hoffe
   (See Old Western Scrounger, Inc.,
   The)
Williams Shootin' Iron Service, The
   Lynx-Line

GUNS, U.S. MADE

3-Ten Corp.
A.A. Arms, Inc.

Accu-Tek
Ace Custom 45's, Inc.
Acra-Bond Laminates
Ad Hominem
Airrow
Allred Bullet Co.
American Derringer Corp.
American Frontier Firearms Mfg., Inc
AR-7 Industries, LLC
ArmaLite, Inc.
Armscorp USA, Inc.
A-Square Company, Inc.
Austin & Halleck, Inc.
Autauga Arms, Inc.
Auto-Ordnance Corp.
Baer Custom, Inc, Les
Ballard Rifle & Cartridge Co., LLC
Barrett Firearms Manufacturer, Inc.
Bar-Sto Precision Machine
Benjamin/Sheridan Co., Crossman
Beretta S.p.A., Pietro
Beretta U.S.A. Corp.
Big Bear Arms & Sporting Goods, Inc.
Bond Arms, Inc.
Borden Ridges Rimrock Stocks
Borden Rifles Inc
Brockman's Custom Gunsmithing
Brown Co, E. Arthur
Brown Products, Inc., Ed
Browning Arms Co.
Bryan & Assoc.
Bushmaster Firearms
C. Sharps Arms Co. Inc./Montana
   Armory
Cabela's
Calico Light Weapon Systems
Cambos Outdoorsman
Cape Outfitters
Casull Arms Corp.
CCL Security Products
Century Gun Dist. Inc.
Charter 2000
Cobra Enterprises, Inc.
Colt's Mfg. Co., Inc.
Competitor Corp. Inc.
Conetrol Scope Mounts
Connecticut Shotgun Mfg. Co.
Connecticut Valley Classics
   (See CVC)
Cooper Arms
Crosman Airguns
Cryo-Accurizing
Cumberland Arms
Cumberland Mountain Arms
CVA
CVC
Daisy Mfg. Co.
Dakota Arms, Inc.
Dan Wesson Firearms
Dayton Traister
Dixie Gun Works
Downsizer Corp.
DS Arms, Inc.
E&L Mfg., Inc.
E. Arthur Brown Co.
Eagle Arms, Inc. (See ArmaLite, Inc.)
Emerging Technologies, Inc.
   (See Laseraim Technolo
Entre'prise Arms, Inc.
Essex Arms
Excel Industries Inc.
FN Manufacturing
Fort Worth Firearms
Freedom Arms, Inc.
Fulton Armory
Galena Industries AMT
Garcia National Gun Traders, Inc.
Gary Reeder Custom Guns
Genecco Gun Works
Gentry Custom Gunmaker, David
Gibbs Rifle Co. Inc.
Gil Hebard Guns Inc.
Gilbert Equipment Co., Inc.
Goergen's Gun Shop, Inc.
Gonzalez Guns, Ramon B
Goodwin's Gun Shop
Granite Mountain Arms, Inc
Grayback Wildcats
Griffin & Howe, Inc.
Gunsite Custom Shop
Gunsite Gunsmithy
   (See Gunsite Custom Shop)

H&R 1871, Inc.
Hammerli USA
Harrington & Richardson
(See H&R 1871, Inc.)
Harris Gunworks
Hart & Son, Inc.
Hatfield Gun
Hawken Shop, The
(See Dayton Traister)
Heritage Firearms
(See Heritage Mfg., Inc.)
Heritage Manufacturing, Inc.
Hesco-Meprolight
High Precision
Hi-Point Firearms/MKS Supply
HJS Arms, Inc.
H-S Precision, Inc.
Hutton Rifle Ranch
IAR Inc.
Imperial Miniature Armory
IMX, LLC
Israel Arms International, Inc.
Ithaca Classic Doubles
Ithaca Gun Company LLC
J.P. Enterprises Inc.
J.P. Gunstocks, Inc.
Jim Norman Custom Gunstocks
John Rigby & Co.
John's Custom Leather
K.K. Arms Co.
Kahr Arms
Kehr, Roger
Kelbly, Inc.
Kel-Tec CNC Industries, Inc.
Kimber of America, Inc.
Knight Rifles
Knight's Mfg. Co.
Kolar
KSN Industries Ltd
(See U.S. Importer-Israel Arms)
L.A.R. Mfg., Inc.
L.W. Seecamp Co., Inc.
LaFrance Specialties
Lakefield Arms Ltd
(See Savage Arms Inc.)
Laseraim Technologies, Inc.
Lever Arms Service Ltd.
Ljutic Industries, Inc.
Lock's Philadelphia Gun Exchange
Lomont Precision Bullets
Lone Star Rifle Company
M.O.A. Corp.
Mag-Na-Port International, Inc.
Magnum Research, Inc.
Mandall Shooting Supplies Inc.
Marlin Firearms Co.
Maverick Arms, Inc.
McBros Rifle Co.
McCann Industries
Mid-America Recreation, Inc.
Miller Arms, Inc.
MKS Supply, Inc.
(See Hi-Point Firearms)
Montana Armory, Inc
(See C. Sharps Arms Co. Inc.)
MPI Stocks
Navy Arms Company
NCP Products, Inc.
New England Firearms
New Ultra Light Arms, LLC
Noreen, Peter H.
North American Arms, Inc.
North Star West
Northwest Arms
Nowlin Mfg. Co.
Olympic Arms Inc.
Oregon Arms, Inc.
(See Rogue Rifle Co., Inc.)
P&M Sales & Services, LLC
Parker & Sons Shooting Supply
Phillips & Rogers, Inc.
Phoenix Arms
Precision Small Arms Inc.
Professional Ordnance, Inc.
ProWare, Inc.
Ramon B. Gonzalez Guns
Rapine Bullet Mould Mfg. Co.
Raptor Arms Co., Inc.
Remington Arms Co., Inc.
Rifles, Inc.
Rigby & Co., John
Robinson Armament Co.

Rock River Arms
Rocky Mountain Arms, Inc.
Rogue Rifle Co., Inc.
Rogue River Rifleworks
Rohrbaugh
Romain's Custom Guns, Inc.
RPM
Ruger (See Sturm, Ruger & Co., Inc.)
Russ Trading Post
Savage Arms (Canada), Inc.
Scattergun Technologies, Inc.
Searcy Enterprises
Sharps Arms Co., Inc., C.
Shiloh Rifle Mfg.
Sklany's Machine Shop
Small Arms Specialists
Smith & Wesson
Sound Technology
Springfield, Inc.
SSK Industries
STI International
Stoeger Industries
Strayer-Voigt, Inc.
Sturm Ruger & Co. Inc.
Sunny Hill Enterprises, Inc.
T&S Industries, Inc.
Taconic Firearms Ltd., Perry Lane
Tank's Rifle Shop
Tar-Hunt Custom Rifles, Inc.
Taurus Firearms, Inc.
Texas Armory (See Bond Arms, Inc.)
The A.W. Peterson Gun Shop, Inc.
The Gun Room Press
The Gun Works
Thompson / Center Arms
Tristar Sporting Arms, Ltd.
U.S. Fire Arms Mfg. Co., Inc.
U.S. Repeating Arms Co., Inc.
Visible Impact Targets
Volquartsen Custom Ltd.
Wallace, Terry
Weatherby, Inc.
Wescombe, Bill (See North Star West)
Wessinger Custom Guns & Engraving
Whildin & Sons Ltd, E.H.
Whitestone Lumber Corp.
Wichita Arms, Inc.
Wichita Arms, Inc.
Wildey, Inc.
Wilsom Combat
Winchester Consultants
Z-M Weapons

GUNSMITH SCHOOL

American Gunsmithing Institute
Bull Mountain Rifle Co.
Colorado Gunsmithing Academy
Colorado School of Trades
Cylinder & Slide, Inc., William R.
Laughridge
Lassen Community College,
Gunsmithing Dept.
Laughridge, William R
(See Cylinder & Slide Inc)
Log Cabin Sport Shop
Modern Gun Repair School
Montgomery Community College
Murray State College
North American Correspondence
Schools The Gun Pro
Nowlin Mfg. Co.
NRI Gunsmith School
Pennsylvania Gunsmith School
Piedmont Community College
Pine Technical College
Professional Gunsmiths of America
Smith & Wesson
Southeastern Community College
Spencer's Custom Guns
Trinidad St. Jr Col Gunsmith Dept.
Wright's Gunstock Blanks
Yavapai College

GUNSMITH SUPPLIES,
TOOLS & SERVICES

Ace Custom 45's, Inc.
Actions by "T" Teddy Jacobson
Alaskan Silversmith, The
Aldis Gunsmithing & Shooting Supply
Alley Supply Co.
Allred Bullet Co.
Alpec Team, Inc.

American Frontier Firearms Mfg., Inc
American Gunsmithing Institute
Baer Custom, Inc, Les
Bar-Sto Precision Machine
Bauska Barrels
Bear Mountain Gun & Tool
Bengtson Arms Co., L.
Biesen, Al
Biesen, Roger
Bill's Gun Repair
Blue Ridge Machinery & Tools, Inc.
Boyds' Gunstock Industries, Inc.
Break-Free, Inc.
Briley Mfg. Inc.
Brockman's Custom Gunsmithing
Brown Products, Inc., Ed
Brownells, Inc.
Bryan & Assoc.
B-Square Company, Inc.
Buffer Technologies
Bull Mountain Rifle Co.
Bushmaster Firearms
C.S. Van Gorden & Son, Inc.
Carbide Checkering Tools
(See J&R Engineering)
Carter's Gun Shop
Caywood, Shane J.
CBC-BRAZIL
Chapman Manufacturing Co.
Chem-Pak Inc.
Chicasaw Gun Works
Choate Machine & Tool Co., Inc.
Ciener Inc., Jonathan Arthur
Colonial Arms, Inc.
Colorado School of Trades
Colt's Mfg. Co., Inc.
Conetrol Scope Mounts
Craig Custom Ltd., Research &
Development
CRR, Inc./Marble's Inc.
Cumberland Arms
Cumberland Mountain Arms
Custom Checkering Service, Kathy
Forster
Custom Gun Products
D&J Bullet Co. & Custom Gun Shop,
Inc.
D'Arcy Echols & Co.
Decker Shooting Products
Dem-Bart Checkering Tools, Inc.
Dewey Mfg. Co., Inc., J.
Dixie Gun Works
Dixie Gun Works
Dremel Mfg. Co.
Du-Lite Corp.
Efficient Machinery Co
Entre'prise Arms, Inc.
Erhardt, Dennis
Evolution Gun Works Inc.
Faith Associates
Faloon Industries, Inc.
FERLIB
Fisher, Jerry A.
Forgreens Tool & Mfg., Inc.
Forkin, Ben (See Belt MTN Arms)
Forster, Kathy
(See Custom Checkering)
Gentry Custom Gunmaker, David
Goodwin's Gun Shop
Grace Metal Products
Greider Precision
GrE-Tan Rifles
Gruning Precision Inc
Gunline Tools
Half Moon Rifle Shop
Hammond Custom Guns Ltd.
Hastings Barrels
Henriksen Tool Co., Inc.
High Performance International
High Precision
Hoelscher, Virgil
Holland's Gunsmithing
Ironsighter Co.
Israel Arms International, Inc.
Ivanoff, Thomas G
(See Tom's Gun Repair)
J&R Engineering
J&S Heat Treat
Jantz Supply
Jenkins Recoil Pads, Inc.
JGS Precision Tool Mfg.
Jonathan Arthur Ciener, Inc.

Jones Custom Products, Neil A.
Kailua Custom Guns Inc.
Kasenit Co., Inc.
Kleinendorst, K. W.
Korzinek Riflesmith, J.
KSN Industries Ltd
(See U.S. Importer-Israel Arms)
LaBounty Precision Reboring, Inc
Laurel Mountain Forge
Lea Mfg. Co.
Lee Supplies, Mark
List Precision Engineering
London Guns Ltd.
Mahovsky's Metalife
Marble Arms
(See CRR, Inc./Marble's Inc.)
Mark Lee Supplies
Marsh, Mike
Martin's Gun Shop
McFarland, Stan
Menck, Gunsmith Inc., T.W.
Metalife Industries
(See Mahovsky's Metalife)
Metaloy, Inc.
Michael's Antiques
Micro Sight Co.
MMC
Mo's Competitor Supplies
(See MCS Inc)
Mowrey's Guns & Gunsmithing
Neil A. Jones Custom Products
New England Custom Gun Service
Ole Frontier Gunsmith Shop
P.M. Enterprises, Inc. / Precise
Metalsmithing
Parker & Sons Shooting Supply
Parker Gun Finishes
Paulsen Gunstocks
PEM's Mfg. Co.
Perazone-Gunsmith, Brian
Peter Dyson & Son Ltd.
Power Custom, Inc.
Practical Tools, Inc.
Precise Metalsmithing Enterprises /
P.M. Enterprises
Precision Specialties
R.A. Wells Custom Gunsmith
Ranch Products
Ransom International Corp.
Reardon Products
Rice, Keith
(See White Rock Tool & Die)
Robert Valade Engraving
Rocky Mountain Arms, Inc.
Romain's Custom Guns, Inc.
Roto Carve
Royal Arms Gunstocks
Scott McDougall & Associates
Sharp Shooter Supply
Shooter's Choice Gun Care
Simmons Gun Repair, Inc.
Smith Abrasives, Inc.
Southern Bloomer Mfg. Co.
Spencer Reblue Service
Spencer's Custom Guns
Spradlin's
Starr Trading Co., Jedediah
Starrett Co., L. S.
Stiles Custom Guns
Stoney Point Products, Inc.
Sullivan, David S .
(See Westwind Rifles Inc.)
Sunny Hill Enterprises, Inc.
T&S Industries, Inc.
T.W. Menck Gunsmith Inc.
Tank's Rifle Shop
Texas Platers Supply Co.
The A.W. Peterson Gun Shop, Inc.
The Dutchman's Firearms, Inc.
The Gun Works
The NgraveR Co.
The Robar Co.'s, Inc.
Theis, Terry
Tom's Gun Repair, Thomas G. Ivanoff
Track of the Wolf, Inc.
Trinidad St. Jr Col Gunsmith Dept.
Trulock Tool
Turnbull Restoration, Doug
United States Products Co.
Valade Engraving, Robert
Van Gorden & Son Inc., C. S.

Venco Industries, Inc.
(See Shooter's Choice)
W.C. Wolff Co.
Warne Manufacturing Co.
Washita Mountain Whetstone Co.
Weaver Arms Corp. Gun Shop
Wessinger Custom Guns & Engraving
White Rock Tool & Die
Wilcox All-Pro Tools & Supply
Wild West Guns
Will-Burt Co.
Williams Gun Sight Co.
Williams Shootin' Iron Service, The
Lynx-Line
Willow Bend
Windish, Jim
Winter, Robert M.
Wise Guns, Dale
Wright's Gunstock Blanks
Yavapai College
Ziegel Engineering

HANDGUN
ACCESSORIES

"Su-Press-On",Inc.
A.A. Arms, Inc.
Ace Custom 45's, Inc.
Action Direct, Inc.
ADCO Sales, Inc.
Adventurer's Outpost
Aimpoint c/o Springfield, Inc.
Aimtech Mount Systems
Ajax Custom Grips, Inc.
Alpha 1 Drop Zone
Alpha Gunsmith Division
American Derringer Corp.
American Frontier Firearms Mfg., Inc
Arms Corporation of the Philippines
Aro-Tek Ltd.
Astra Sport, S.A.
Autauga Arms, Inc.
Baer Custom, Inc, Les
Bagmaster Mfg., Inc.
Bar-Sto Precision Machine
Behlert Precision, Inc.
Berry's Mfg., Inc.
Bill's Custom Cases
Blue and Gray Products Inc
(See Ox-Yoke Originals
Bond Custom Firearms
Bowen Classic Arms Corp.
Bridgeman Products
Broken Gun Ranch
Brooks Tactical Systems
Brown Products, Inc., Ed
Bushmaster Hunting & Fishing
Butler Creek Corp.
Cannon Safe, Inc.
Centaur Systems, Inc.
Central Specialties Ltd
(See Trigger Lock Division
Charter 2000
Cheyenne Pioneer Products
Chicasaw Gun Works
Ciener Inc., Jonathan Arthur
Clark Custom Guns, Inc.
Classic Arms Company
Conetrol Scope Mounts
Craig Custom Ltd., Research &
Development
Crimson Trace Lasers
CRR, Inc./Marble's Inc.
Cylinder & Slide, Inc., William R.
Laughridge
D&L Industries (See D.J. Marketing)
D.J. Marketing
Dade Screw Machine Products
Delhi Gun House
DeSantis Holster & Leather Goods,
Inc.
Dixie Gun Works
Doskocil Mfg. Co., Inc.
E&L Mfg., Inc.
E. Arthur Brown Co.
E.A.A. Corp.
Ed Brown Products, Inc.
Essex Arms
European American Armory Corp (See
E.A.A. Corp.
Faloon Industries, Inc.
Federal Arms Corp. of America
Fisher Custom Firearms

PRODUCT & SERVICE DIRECTORY

Fleming Firearms
Flores Publications Inc, J
    (See Action Direct Inc.)
Freedom Arms, Inc.
Frielich Police Equipment
FWB
G.G. & G.
Galati International
GALCO International Ltd.
Garcia National Gun Traders, Inc.
Garthwaite Pistolsmith, Inc., Jim
Gil Hebard Guns Inc.
Gilmore Sports Concepts
Glock, Inc.
Goodwin's Gun Shop
Gould & Goodrich
Greider Precision
Gremmel Enterprises
Gun-Alert
Gun-Ho Sports Cases
H.K.S. Products
Hafner World Wide, Inc.
Hammerli USA
Heinie Specialty Products
Henigson & Associates, Steve
Hill Speed Leather, Ernie
Hi-Point Firearms/MKS Supply
Hobson Precision Mfg. Co.
Hoppe's Div. Penguin Industries, Inc.
H-S Precision, Inc.
Hunter Co., Inc.
Impact Case Co.
J.P. Enterprises Inc.
Jarvis, Inc.
JB Custom
Jeffredo Gunsight
Jim Noble Co.
John's Custom Leather
Jonathan Arthur Ciener, Inc.
K.K. Arms Co.
Kalispel Case Line
KeeCo Impressions, Inc.
King's Gun Works
KK Air International
    (See Impact Case Co.)
L&S Technologies Inc
    (See Aimtech Mount Systems)
Lakewood Products LLC
LaserMax, Inc.
Loch Leven Industries / Convert-A-Pell
Lohman Mfg. Co., Inc.
Mag-Na-Port International, Inc.
Magnolia Sports,Inc.
Mahony, Philip Bruce
Mandall Shooting Supplies Inc.
Marble Arms
    (See CRR, Inc./Marble's Inc.)
Markell,Inc.
McCormick Corp., Chip
MEC-Gar S.r.l.
Menck, Gunsmith Inc., T.W.
Merkuria Ltd.
Middlebrooks Custom Shop
Millett Sights
Mogul Co./Life Jacket
MTM Molded Products Co., Inc.
No-Sho Mfg. Co.
Omega Sales
Outdoor Sports Headquarters, Inc.
Ox-Yoke Originals, Inc.
Pachmayr Div. Lyman Products
Pager Pal
Palmer Security Products
Parker & Sons Shooting Supply
Pearce Grip, Inc.
Perazone-Gunsmith, Brian
Phoenix Arms
Practical Tools, Inc.
Precision Small Arms Inc.
Ram-Line Blount, Inc.
Ranch Products
Ransom International Corp.
Ringler Custom Leather Co.
RPM
Seecamp Co. Inc., L. W.
Simmons Gun Repair, Inc.
Sound Technology
Southern Bloomer Mfg. Co.
Springfield, Inc.
SSK Industries
Sturm Ruger & Co. Inc.
T.F.C. S.p.A.

TacStar
Tactical Defense Institute
Tanfoglio Fratelli S.r.l.
The A.W. Peterson Gun Shop, Inc.
The Concealment Shop, Inc.
The Gun Parts Corp.
The Gun Works
The Keller Co.
The Protector Mfg. Co., Inc.
Thompson / Center Arms
Trigger Lock Division / Central
    Specialties Ltd.
Trijicon, Inc.
Triple-K Mfg. Co., Inc.
Truglo, Inc
Tyler Manufacturing & Distributing
United States Products Co.
Universal Sports
Valor Corp.
Volquartsen Custom Ltd.
W. Waller & Son, Inc.
W.C. Wolff Co.
Wessinger Custom Guns & Engraving
Western Design
    (See Alpha Gunsmith Division)
Whitestone Lumber Corp.
Wild West Guns
Williams Gun Sight Co.
Wilsom Combat
Ziegel Engineering

HANDGUN GRIPS

A.A. Arms, Inc.
African Import Co.
Ahrends, Kim
    (See Custom Firearms, Inc)
Ajax Custom Grips, Inc.
Altamont Co.
American Derringer Corp.
American Frontier Firearms Mfg., Inc
American Gripcraft
Arms Corporation of the Philippines
Art Jewel Enterprises Ltd.
Baelder, Harry
Baer Custom, Inc, Les
Big Bear Arms & Sporting Goods, Inc.
Bob's Gun Shop
Boone Trading Co., Inc.
Boone's Custom Ivory Grips, Inc.
Boyds' Gunstock Industries, Inc.
Brooks Tactical Systems
Brown Products, Inc., Ed
Clark Custom Guns, Inc.
Cole-Grip
Colonial Repair
Crimson Trace Lasers
Custom Firearms (See Ahrends, Kim)
Dixie Gun Works
E.A.A. Corp.
EMF Co., Inc.
Essex Arms
European American Armory Corp (See
    E.A.A. Corp)
Faloon Industries, Inc.
Fibron Products, Inc.
Fisher Custom Firearms
Fitz Pistol Grip Co.
Forrest Inc., Tom
FWB
Garthwaite Pistolsmith, Inc., Jim
Goodwin's Gun Shop
Herrett's Stocks, Inc.
HIP-GRIP Barami Corp.
Hogue Grips
H-S Precision, Inc.
Huebner, Corey O.
Israel Arms International, Inc.
John Masen Co. Inc.
KeeCo Impressions, Inc.
Kim Ahrends Custom Firearms, Inc.
Korth
KSN Industries Ltd
    (See U.S. Importer-Israel Arms)
Lett Custom Grips
Linebaugh Custom Sixguns
Lyman Products Corp.
Mandall Shooting Supplies Inc.
Michaels Of Oregon
Millett Sights
N.C. Ordnance Co.
Newell, Robert H.

Northern Precision Custom Swaged
    Bullets
Pachmayr Div. Lyman Products
Pardini Armi Srl
Parker & Sons Shooting Supply
Perazone-Gunsmith, Brian
Pilgrim Pewter,Inc.
    (See Bell Originals Inc. Sid)
Precision Small Arms Inc.
Radical Concepts
Rosenberg & Son, Jack A
Roy's Custom Grips
Spegel, Craig
Stoeger Industries
Sturm Ruger & Co. Inc.
Sunny Hill Enterprises, Inc.
Tactical Defense Institute
Taurus Firearms, Inc.
The A.W. Peterson Gun Shop, Inc.
Tirelli
Triple-K Mfg. Co., Inc.
Tyler Manufacturing & Distributing
U.S. Fire Arms Mfg. Co., Inc.
Uncle Mike's
    (See Michaels of Oregon Co.)
Vintage Industries, Inc.
Volquartsen Custom Ltd.
Western Mfg. Co.
Whitestone Lumber Corp.
Wright's Gunstock Blanks

HEARING PROTECTORS

Aero Peltor
Ajax Custom Grips, Inc.
Brown Co, E. Arthur
Browning Arms Co.
David Clark Co., Inc.
Dillon Precision Products, Inc.
Dixie Gun Works
E-A-R, Inc.
Electronic Shooters Protection, Inc.
Gentex Corp.
Goodwin's Gun Shop
Gunsmithing, Inc.
Hoppe's Div. Penguin Industries, Inc.
Kesselring Gun Shop
Mandall Shooting Supplies Inc.
North Specialty Products
Parker & Sons Shooting Supply
Paterson Gunsmithing
Peltor, Inc. (See Aero Peltor)
R.E.T. Enterprises
Ridgeline, Inc
Rucker Dist. Inc.
Silencio/Safety Direct
Sound Technology
Tactical Defense Institute
The A.W. Peterson Gun Shop, Inc.
The Gun Room Press
Triple-K Mfg. Co., Inc.
Watson Trophy Match Bullets
Whitestone Lumber Corp.
Willson Safety Prods. Div.

HOLSTERS & LEATHER GOODS

A&B Industries,Inc
    (See Top-Line USA Inc)
A.A. Arms, Inc.
Action Direct, Inc.
Action Products, Inc.
Alessi Holsters, Inc.
Arratoonian, Andy
    (See Horseshoe Leather Products)
Autauga Arms, Inc.
Bagmaster Mfg., Inc.
Baker's Leather Goods, Roy
Bandcor Industries, Div. of Man-Sew
    Corp.
Bang-Bang Boutique
    (See Holster Shop, The)
Beretta S.p.A., Pietro
Bianchi International, Inc.
Brocock Ltd.
Brooks Tactical Systems
Brown, H. R.
    (See Silhouette Leathers)
Browning Arms Co.
Bull-X, Inc.
Cape Outfitters
Cathey Enterprises, Inc.
Chace Leather Products

Churchill Glove Co., James
Cimarron F.A. Co.
Classic Old West Styles
Clements' Custom Leathercraft, Chas
Cobra Sport S.r.l.
Colonial Repair
Counter Assault
Creedmoor Sports, Inc.
Delhi Gun House
DeSantis Holster & Leather Goods,
    Inc.
Dillon Precision Products, Inc.
Dixie Gun Works
Ekol Leather Care
El Paso Saddlery Co.
EMF Co., Inc.
Faust Inc., T. G.
Flores Publications Inc, J
    (See Action Direct Inc.)
Freedom Arms, Inc.
Gage Manufacturing
GALCO International Ltd.
Garcia National Gun Traders, Inc.
Gil Hebard Guns Inc.
Gilmore Sports Concepts
GML Products, Inc.
Goodwin's Gun Shop
Gould & Goodrich
Gun Leather Limited
Gunfitters
Hafner World Wide, Inc.
HandCrafts Unltd
    (See Clements' Custom Leather)
Hank's Gun Shop
Heinie Specialty Products
Henigson & Associates, Steve
Hill Speed Leather, Ernie
HIP-GRIP Barami Corp.
Hobson Precision Mfg. Co.
Hogue Grips
Horseshoe Leather Products
Hume, Don
Hunter Co., Inc.
Jim Noble Co.
John's Custom Leather
K.L. Null Holsters Ltd.
Kane Products, Inc.
Kirkpatrick Leather Co.
Kolpin Mfg., Inc.
Korth
Kramer Handgun Leather
L.A.R. Mfg., Inc.
Lawrence Leather Co.
Lock's Philadelphia Gun Exchange
Lone Star Gunleather
Magnolia Sports,Inc.
Mandall Shooting Supplies Inc.
Markell,Inc.
Marksman Products
Michaels Of Oregon
Minute Man High Tech Industries
Navy Arms Company
No-Sho Mfg. Co.
Null Holsters Ltd. K.L.
October Country Muzzleloading
Ojala Holsters, Arvo
Oklahoma Leather Products,Inc.
Old West Reproductions,Inc. R.M.
    Bachman
Pager Pal
Parker & Sons Shooting Supply
Pathfinder Sports Leather
PWL Gunleather
Renegade
Ringler Custom Leather Co.
Rogue Rifle Co., Inc.
Safariland Ltd., Inc.
Safety Speed Holster, Inc.
Scharch Mfg., Inc.
Schulz Industries
Second Chance Body Armor
Shoemaker & Sons Inc., Tex
Silhouette Leathers
Smith Saddlery, Jesse W.
Sparks, Milt
Stalker, Inc.
Starr Trading Co., Jedediah
Strong Holster Co.
Stuart, V. Pat
Tabler Marketing
Tactical Defense Institute
Ted Blocker Holsters, Inc.

Thad Rybka Custom Leather
    Equipment
The A.W. Peterson Gun Shop, Inc.
The Concealment Shop, Inc.
The Eutaw Co., Inc.
The Gun Works
The Keller Co.
The Outdoor Connection,Inc.
Top-Line USA, Inc.
Torel, Inc.
Triple-K Mfg. Co., Inc.
Tristar Sporting Arms, Ltd.
Tyler Manufacturing & Distributing
Uncle Mike's
    (See Michaels of Oregon Co.)
Valor Corp.
Venus Industries
Walt's Custom Leather, Walt Whinnery
Watson Trophy Match Bullets
Westley Richards & Co.
Whinnery, Walt
    (See Walt's Custom Leather)
Wild Bill's Originals
Wilsom Combat

HUNTING & CAMP GEAR, CLOTHING, ETC.

Ace Sportswear, Inc.
Action Direct, Inc.
Action Products, Inc.
Adventure 16, Inc.
Adventure Game Calls
All Rite Products, Inc.
Allen Co., Bob
Allen Sportswear, Bob
    (See Allen Co., Bob)
Alpha 1 Drop Zone
Armor (See Buck Stop Lure Co., Inc.)
Atlanta Cutlery Corp.
Atsko/Sno-Seal, Inc.
B.B. Walker Co.
Baekgaard Ltd.
Bagmaster Mfg., Inc.
Barbour, Inc.
Bauer, Eddie
Bear Archery
Beaver Park Product, Inc.
Beretta S.p.A., Pietro
Better Concepts Co.
Boss Manufacturing Co.
Browning Arms Co.
Buck Stop Lure Co., Inc.
Bushmaster Hunting & Fishing
Cambos Outdoorsman
Cambos Outdoorsman
Camp-Cap Products
Carhartt,Inc.
Churchill Glove Co., James
Clarkfield Enterprises, Inc.
Classic Old West Styles
Clements' Custom Leathercraft, Chas
Coghlan's Ltd.
Cold Steel Inc.
Coleman Co., Inc.
Coulston Products, Inc.
Counter Assault
Creedmoor Sports, Inc.
D&H Prods. Co., Inc.
Dakota Corp.
Danner Shoe Mfg. Co.
Deepeeka Exports Pvt. Ltd.
Dr. O's Products Ltd.
Duofold, Inc.
Dynalite Products, Inc.
E-A-R, Inc.
Ekol Leather Care
Flores Publications Inc, J
    (See Action Direct Inc.)
Forrest Tool Co.
Fox River Mills, Inc.
Frontier
G&H Decoys,Inc.
Gerber Legendary Blades
Glacier Glove
HandCrafts Unltd
    (See Clements' Custom Leather)
Hinman Outfitters, Bob
Hodgman, Inc.
Houtz & Barwick
Hunter's Specialties Inc.
James Churchill Glove Co.
John's Custom Leather

PRODUCT & SERVICE DIRECTORY

K&M Industries, Inc.
Kamik Outdoor Footwear
Kolpin Mfg., Inc.
L.L. Bean, Inc.
LaCrosse Footwear, Inc.
Langenberg Hat Co.
Leapers, Inc.
MAG Instrument, Inc.
Mag-Na-Port International, Inc.
Marathon Rubber Prods. Co., Inc.
McCann Industries
McCann's Machine & Gun Shop
Molin Industries, Tru-Nord Division
Mountain Hollow Game Calls
Murphy, R.R. Co., Inc.
Nelson/Weather-Rite, Inc.
North Specialty Products
Northlake Outdoor Footwear
Original Deer Formula Co., The.
Original Mink Oil, Inc.
Palsa Outdoor Products
Partridge Sales Ltd., John
Pointing Dog Journal, Village Press
  Publications
Powell & Son (Gunmakers) Ltd.,
  William
Pro-Mark Div. of Wells Lamont
Pyramid, Inc.
Ringler Custom Leather Co.
Robert Valade Engraving
Rocky Shoes & Boots
Russ Trading Post
Scansport, Inc.
Sceery Game Calls
Schaefer Shooting Sports
Servus Footwear Co.
Simmons Outdoor Corp.
Sno-Seal, Inc. (See Atsko/Sno-Seal)
Streamlight, Inc.
Swanndri New Zealand
T.H.U. Enterprises, Inc.
TEN-X Products Group
The A.W. Peterson Gun Shop, Inc.
The Eutaw Co., Inc.
The Orvis Co.
The Outdoor Connection,Inc.
Tink's Safariland Hunting Corp.
Torel, Inc.
Triple-K Mfg. Co., Inc.
United Cutlery Corp.
Valade Engraving, Robert
Venus Industries
Wakina by Pic
Walls Industries, Inc.
Wideview Scope Mount Corp.
Wilderness Sound Products Ltd.
Willson Safety Prods. Div.
Winchester Sutler, Inc., The
Wolverine Footwear Group
Woolrich, Inc.
Wyoming Knife Corp.
Yellowstone Wilderness Supply

KNIVES & KNIFEMAKER'S SUPPLIES

A.G. Russell Knives, Inc.
Action Direct, Inc.
Adventure 16, Inc.
African Import Co.
Aitor-Cuchilleria Del Norte S.A.
American Target Knives
Art Jewel Enterprises Ltd.
Atlanta Cutlery Corp.
B&D Trading Co., Inc.
Barteaux Machete
Belltown Ltd.
Benchmark Knives
  (See Gerber Legendary Blades)
Beretta S.p.A., Pietro
Beretta U.S.A. Corp.
Big Bear Arms & Sporting Goods, Inc.
Bill's Custom Cases
Blair Engraving, Jim
Boker USA, Inc.
Boone Trading Co., Inc.
Boone's Custom Ivory Grips, Inc.
Bowen Knife Co., Inc.
Brooks Tactical Systems
Browning Arms Co.
Buck Knives, Inc.
Buster's Custom Knives

Camillus Cutlery Co.
Campbell, Dick
Case & Sons Cutlery Co., W R
Chicago Cutlery Co.
Clements' Custom Leathercraft, Chas
Cold Steel Inc.
Coleman Co., Inc.
Colonial Knife Co., Inc.
Compass Industries, Inc.
Crosman Blades
  (See Coleman Co., Inc.)
CRR, Inc./Marble's Inc.
Cutco Cutlery
DAMASCUS-U.S.A.
Dan's Whetstone Co., Inc.
Deepeeka Exports Pvt. Ltd.
Degen Inc. (See Aristocrat Knives)
Delhi Gun House
DeSantis Holster & Leather Goods,
  Inc.
Diamond Machining Technology, Inc.
  (See DMT)
Dixie Gun Works
EdgeCraft Corp., S. Weiner
Empire Cutlery Corp.
Eze-Lap Diamond Prods.
Flitz International Ltd.
Flores Publications Inc, J
  (See Action Direct Inc.)
Forrest Tool Co.
Forthofer's Gunsmithing &
  Knifemaking
Fortune Products, Inc.
Frank Knives
Frost Cutlery Co.
Galati International
George Ibberson (Sheffield) Ltd.
Gerber Legendary Blades
Gibbs Rifle Co., Inc.
Glock, Inc.
Golden Age Arms Co.
GRS / Glendo Corp.
H&B Forge Co.
Hafner World Wide, Inc.
HandCrafts Unltd
  (See Clements' Custom Leather)
Harris Publications
High North Products, Inc.
Hoppe's Div. Penguin Industries, Inc.
Hunter Co., Inc.
Hunting Classics Ltd.
Imperial Schrade Corp.
J.A. Blades, Inc.
  (See Christopher Firearms Co.)
J.A. Henckels Zwillingswerk Inc.
Jackalope Gun Shop
Jantz Supply
Jenco Sales, Inc.
Jim Blair Engraving
Johnson Wood Products
KA-BAR Knives
Kasenit Co., Inc.
Kershaw Knives
Knifeware, Inc.
Koval Knives
Lamson & Goodnow Mfg. Co.
Lansky Sharpeners
Leapers, Inc.
Leatherman Tool Group, Inc.
Lethal Force Institute
  (See Police Bookshelf)
Lett Custom Grips
Linder Solingen Knives
Mandall Shooting Supplies Inc.
Marble Arms
  (See CRR, Inc./Marble's Inc.)
Matthews Cutlery
McCann Industries
McCann's Machine & Gun Shop
Molin Industries, Tru-Nord Division
Mountain State Muzzleloading
  Supplies, Inc.
Normark Corp.
October Country Muzzleloading
Outdoor Edge Cutlery Corp.
Pilgrim Pewter,Inc.
  (See Bell Originals Inc. Sid)
Plaza Cutlery, Inc.
Police Bookshelf
Queen Cutlery Co.
R&C Knives & Such
R. Murphy Co., Inc.

Randall-Made Knives
Ringler Custom Leather Co.
Robert Valade Engraving
Rodgers & Sons Ltd., Joseph
  (See George Ibberson)
Russ Trading Post
Scansport, Inc.
Schiffman, Mike
Sheffield Knifemakers Supply, Inc.
Smith Saddlery, Jesse W.
Spyderco, Inc.
T.F.C. S.p.A.
The A.W. Peterson Gun Shop, Inc.
The Creative Craftsman, Inc.
The Gun Room
The Gun Works
Theis, Terry
Traditions Performance Firearms
Traditions Performance Firearms
Tru-Balance Knife Co.
United Cutlery Corp.
Utica Cutlery Co.
Valade Engraving, Robert
Venus Industries
Washita Mountain Whetstone Co.
Weber Jr., Rudolf
Wells Creek Knife & Gun Works
Wenger North America/Precise Int'l
Western Cutlery
  (See Camillus Cutlery Co.)
Whinnery, Walt
  (See Walt's Custom Leather)
Wideview Scope Mount Corp.
Wostenholm
  (See Ibberson [Sheffield] Ltd.,
  George)
Wyoming Knife Corp.

LABELS, BOXES & CARTRIDGE HOLDERS

Ballistic Product, Inc.
Berry's Mfg., Inc.
Brocock Ltd.
Brown Co, E. Arthur
Cabinet Mtn. Outfitters Scents & Lures
Cheyenne Pioneer Products
Del Rey Products
DeSantis Holster & Leather Goods,
  Inc.
Fitz Pistol Grip Co.
Flambeau Products Corp.
Goodwin's Gun Shop
Hafner World Wide, Inc.
J&J Products, Inc.
Kolpin Mfg., Inc.
Liberty Shooting Supplies
Midway Arms, Inc.
MTM Molded Products Co., Inc.
Pendleton Royal, c/o Swingler
  Buckland Ltd.
Ziegel Engineering

LEAD WIRES & WIRE CUTTERS

3-D Ammunition & Bullets
Ames Metal Products
Big Bore Express
Bullet Swaging Supply Inc.
Goodwin's Gun Shop
Lightning Performance Innovations,
  Inc.
Montana Precision Swaging
Northern Precision Custom Swaged
  Bullets
Sport Flite Manufacturing Co.
Star Ammunition, Inc.
Unmussig Bullets, D. L.

LOAD TESTING & PRODUCT TESTING

Ballistic Research
Bitterroot Bullet Co.
Bridgeman Products
Briese Bullet Co., Inc.
Buckskin Bullet Co.
Bull Mountain Rifle Co.
CFVentures
Claybuster Wads & Harvester Bullets
Clearview Products
D&H Precision Tooling
Dead Eye's Sport Center
Defense Training International, Inc.

Duane's Gun Repair
  (See DGR Custom Rifles)
Gonzalez Guns, Ramon B
Gun Hunter Books
  (See Gun Hunter Trading Co)
Gun Hunter Trading Co.
H.P. White Laboratory, Inc.
Hank's Gun Shop
Henigson & Associates, Steve
Hoelscher, Virgil
Hutton Rifle Ranch
Jackalope Gun Shop
Jensen Bullets
L E Jurras & Assoc.
Liberty Shooting Supplies
Linebaugh Custom Sixguns
Lomont Precision Bullets
Maionchi-L.M.I.
MAST Technology
McMurdo, Lynn
  (See Specialty Gunsmithing)
Middlebrooks Custom Shop
Modern Gun Repair School
Multiplex International
Northwest Arms
Oil Rod and Gun Shop
Plum City Ballistic Range
R.A. Wells Custom Gunsmith
Ramon B. Gonzalez Guns
Rupert's Gun Shop
Small Custom Mould & Bullet Co.
SOS Products Co.
  (See Buck Stix-SOS Products Co.)
Spencer's Custom Guns
Trinidad St. Jr Col Gunsmith Dept.
Vancini, Carl (See Bestload, Inc.)
Vulpes Ventures, Inc. Fox Cartridge
  Division
W. Square Enterprises
X-Spand Target Systems

LOADING BLOCKS, METALLIC & SHOTSHELL

Battenfeld Technologies
Buffalo Arms Co.
Jericho Tool & Die Co., Inc.
Sinclair International, Inc.
The A.W. Peterson Gun Shop, Inc.

LUBRISIZERS, DIES & ACCESSORIES

Ballisti-Cast, Inc.
Ben's Machines
Buffalo Arms Co.
Cast Performance Bullet Company
Chem-Pak Inc.
Cooper-Woodward
GAR
Hart & Son, Inc.
Javelina Lube Products
Lee Precision, Inc.
Lithi Bee Bullet Lube
Lyman Products Corp.
Magma Engineering Co.
Redding Reloading Equipment
SPG LLC
The A.W. Peterson Gun Shop, Inc.
Thompson Bullet Lube Co.
United States Products Co.

MOULDS & MOULD ACCESSORIES

Ad Hominem
American Products, Inc.
Ballisti-Cast, Inc.
Buffalo Arms Co.
Cast Performance Bullet Company
GAR
Lee Precision, Inc.
Lyman Products Corp.
Magma Engineering Co.
NEI Handtools, Inc.
Old West Bullet Moulds
Penn Bullets
Rapine Bullet Mould Mfg. Co.
Redding Reloading Equipment
S&S Firearms
Small Custom Mould & Bullet Co.
The A.W. Peterson Gun Shop, Inc.
The Gun Works
Wolf's Western Traders

MUZZLE-LOADING GUNS, BARRELS & EQUIPMENT

Accuracy Unlimited
Ackerman & Co.
Adkins, Luther
Allen Mfg.
Armi San Paolo
Armoury, Inc., The
Austin & Halleck, Inc.
Bauska Barrels
Beaver Lodge (See Fellowes, Ted)
Bentley, John
Big Bore Express
Birdsong & Assoc., W. E.
Black Powder Products
Blount/Outers
Blue and Gray Products Inc
  (See Ox-Yoke Originals)
Bridgers Best
Buckskin Bullet Co.
Buckskin Machine Works, A. Hunkeler
Butler Creek Corp.
Cabela's
Cache La Poudre Rifleworks
California Sights
  (See Fautheree, Andy)
Cash Mfg. Co., Inc.
CBC-BRAZIL
Chambers Flintlocks Ltd., Jim
Chicasaw Gun Works
Cimarron F.A. Co.
Claybuster Wads & Harvester Bullets
Cogar's Gunsmithing
Colonial Repair
Colt Blackpowder Arms Co.
Conetrol Scope Mounts
Cousin Bob's Mountain Products
Cumberland Arms
Cumberland Mountain Arms
Curly Maple Stock Blanks
  (See Tiger-Hunt)
CVA
Dangler, Homer L.
Davide Pedersoli and Co.
Dayton Traister
deHaas Barrels
Delhi Gun House
Dixie Gun Works
Dixie Gun Works
Dixon Muzzleloading Shop, Inc.
EMF Co., Inc.
Euroarms of America, Inc.
Feken, Dennis
Fellowes, Ted
Flintlocks, Etc.
Fort Hill Gunstocks
Fowler, Bob
  (See Black Powder Products)
Frontier
Getz Barrel Co.
Goergen's Gun Shop, Inc.
Golden Age Arms Co.
Gonic Arms/North American Arm
Goodwin's Gun Shop
Green Mountain Rifle Barrel Co., Inc.
Hastings Barrels
Hawken Shop, The
  (See Dayton Traister)
Hege Jagd-u. Sporthandels GmbH
Hodgdon Powder Co.
Hoppe's Div. Penguin Industries, Inc.
Hornady Mfg. Co.
House of Muskets, Inc., The
Hunkeler, A
  (See Buckskin Machine Works
IAR Inc.
Impact Case Co.
Ironsighter Co.
J.P. Gunstocks, Inc.
Jamison's Forge Works
Jones Co., Dale
K&M Industries, Inc.
Kalispel Case Line
Kennedy Firearms
Knight Rifles
Knight Rifles
  (See Modern Muzzle Loading, Inc.)
Kolar
Kwik-Site Co.
L&R Lock Co.

PRODUCT & SERVICE DIRECTORY

L&S Technologies Inc
   (See Aimtech Mount Systems)
Lakewood Products LLC
Legend Products Corp.
Lodgewood Mfg.
Lothar Walther Precision Tool Inc.
Lyman Products Corp.
Markesbery Muzzle Loaders, Inc.
Marlin Firearms Co.
McCann's Muzzle-Gun Works
Michaels Of Oregon
Millennium Designed Muzzleloaders
MMP
Modern Muzzleloading, Inc
Mountain State Muzzleloading
   Supplies, Inc.
Mowrey Gun Works
MSC Industrial Supply Co.
Mt. Alto Outdoor Products
Navy Arms Company
Newman Gunshop
North Star West
October Country Muzzleloading
Oklahoma Leather Products,Inc.
Olson, Myron
Orion Rifle Barrel Co.
Ox-Yoke Originals, Inc.
Pacific Rifle Co.
Parker & Sons Shooting Supply
Parker Gun Finishes
Pecatonica River Longrifle
Peter Dyson & Son Ltd.
Pioneer Arms Co.
Prairie River Arms
Protektor Model
Rusty Duck Premium Gun Care
   Products
S&S Firearms
Selsi Co., Inc.
Shiloh Creek
Simmons Gun Repair, Inc.
Sklany's Machine Shop
Smokey Valley Rifles
South Bend Replicas, Inc.
Southern Bloomer Mfg. Co.
Splitfire Sporting Goods, L.L.C.
Starr Trading Co., Jedediah
Stone Mountain Arms
Sturm Ruger & Co. Inc.
Taylor's & Co., Inc.
Tennessee Valley Mfg.
The A.W. Peterson Gun Shop, Inc.
The Eutaw Co., Inc.
The Gun Works
Thompson / Center Arms
Thompson Bullet Lube Co.
Thunder Mountain Arms
Tiger-Hunt Gunstocks
Track of the Wolf, Inc.
Traditions Performance Firearms
Truglo, Inc
Uncle Mike's
   (See Michaels of Oregon Co.)
Upper Missouri Trading Co.
Venco Industries, Inc.
   (See Shooter's Choice)
Virgin Valley Custom Guns
Voere-KGH m.b.H.
W.E. Birdsong & Assoc.
Warne Manufacturing Co.
Warren Muzzleloading Co., Inc.
Wescombe, Bill (See North Star West)
White Shooting Systems, Inc.
   (See White Muzzleload
Woodworker's Supply
Wright's Gunstock Blanks
Young Country Arms
Ziegel Engineering

PISTOLSMITH

A.W. Peterson Gun Shop, Inc.
Acadian Ballistic Specialties
Accuracy Unlimited
Ace Custom 45's, Inc.
Actions by "T" Teddy Jacobson
Adair Custom Shop, Bill
Ahlman Guns
Ahrends, Kim
   (See Custom Firearms, Inc)
Aldis Gunsmithing & Shooting Supply
Alpha Precision, Inc.
Alpine Indoor Shooting Range

Armament Gunsmithing Co., Inc.
Aro-Tek Ltd.
Arundel Arms & Ammunition, Inc., A.
Baer Custom, Inc, Les
Bain & Davis, Inc.
Banks, Ed
Bar-Sto Precision Machine
Behlert Precision, Inc.
Ben William's Gun Shop
Bengtson Arms Co., L.
Bill Adair Custom Shop
Billings Gunsmiths Inc.
Bowen Classic Arms Corp.
Broken Gun Ranch
Cannon's
Caraville Manufacturing
Chicasaw Gun Works
Clark Custom Guns, Inc.
Cleland's Outdoor World, Inc
Colonial Repair
Colorado School of Trades
Colt's Mfg. Co., Inc.
Corkys Gun Clinic
Craig Custom Ltd., Research &
   Development
Curtis Custom Shop
Custom Firearms (See Ahrends, Kim)
Cylinder & Slide, Inc., William R.
   Laughridge
D&D Gunsmiths, Ltd.
D&L Sports
David R. Chicoine
Dayton Traister
Dilliott Gunsmithing, Inc.
Ellicott Arms, Inc. / Woods
   Pistolsmithing
F.I., Inc. - High Standard Mfg. Co.
Ferris Firearms
Fisher Custom Firearms
Forkin, Ben (See Belt MTN Arms)
Forkin Arms
Francesca, Inc.
Frielich Police Equipment
G.G. & G.
Garthwaite Pistolsmith, Inc., Jim
Gary Reeder Custom Guns
Genecco Gun Works
Gentry Custom Gunmaker, David
George E. Mathews & Son, Inc.
Greider Precision
Guncraft Sports Inc.
Guncraft Sports, Inc.
Gunsite Custom Shop
Gunsite Gunsmithy
   (See Gunsite Custom Shop)
Gunsite Training Center
Hamilton, Alex B
   (See Ten-Ring Precision, Inc)
Hammond Custom Guns Ltd.
Hank's Gun Shop
Hanson's Gun Center, Dick
Harris Gunworks
Harwood, Jack O.
Hawken Shop, The
   (See Dayton Traister)
Heinie Specialty Products
High Bridge Arms, Inc
Highline Machine Co.
Hoag, James W.
Irwin, Campbell H.
Island Pond Gun Shop
Ivanoff, Thomas G
   (See Tom's Gun Repair)
J&S Heat Treat
Jarvis, Inc.
Jeffredo Gunsight
Jensen's Custom Ammunition
Jungkind, Reeves C.
Kaswer Custom, Inc.
Ken Starnes Gunmaker
Ken's Gun Specialties
Kilham & Co.
Kim Ahrends Custom Firearms, Inc.
King's Gun Works
La Clinique du .45
LaFrance Specialties
LaRocca Gun Works
Lathrop's, Inc.
Lawson, John G
   (See Sight Shop, The)
Leckie Professional Gunsmithing
Linebaugh Custom Sixguns

List Precision Engineering
Long, George F.
Mag-Na-Port International, Inc.
Mahony, Philip Bruce
Mahovsky's Metalife
Mandall Shooting Supplies Inc.
Marent, Rudolf
Marvel, Alan
Mathews & Son, Inc., George E.
McCann's Machine & Gun Shop
MCS, Inc.
Middlebrooks Custom Shop
Miller Custom
Mitchell's Accuracy Shop
MJK Gunsmithing, Inc.
Modern Gun Repair School
Montgomery Community College
Mo's Competitor Supplies
   (See MCS Inc)
Mowrey's Guns & Gunsmithing
Mullis Guncraft
NCP Products, Inc.
Novak's, Inc.
Nowlin Mfg. Co.
Pace Marketing, Inc.
Paris, Frank J.
Pasadena Gun Center
Peacemaker Specialists
PEM's Mfg. Co.
Performance Specialists
Peterson Gun Shop, Inc., A.W.
Pierce Pistols
Piquette's Custom Engraving
Power Custom, Inc.
Precision Specialties
Randco UK
Ries, Chuck
Rim Pac Sports, Inc.
Rocky Mountain Arms, Inc.
RPM
Ruger's Custom Guns
Sanders Custom Gun Service
Score High Gunsmithing
Scott McDougall & Associates
Shooters Supply
Shootin' Shack, Inc.
Singletary, Kent
Springfield, Inc.
SSK Industries
Swenson's 45 Shop, A. D.
Swift River Gunworks
Ten-Ring Precision, Inc.
Terry K. Kopp Professional
   Gunsmithing
The A.W. Peterson Gun Shop, Inc.
The Gun Shop
The Gun Works
The Robar Co.'s, Inc.
The Sight Shop
Thompson, Randall
   (See Highline Machine Co.)
Thurston Sports, Inc.
Tom's Gun Repair, Thomas G. Ivanoff
Turnbull Restoration, Doug
Vic's Gun Refinishing
Volquartsen Custom Ltd.
Walker Arms Co., Inc.
Walters Industries
Wardell Precision Handguns Ltd.
Wessinger Custom Guns & Engraving
White Barn Wor
Wichita Arms, Inc.
Wild West Guns
Williams Gun Sight Co.
Williamson Precision Gunsmithing
Wilsom Combat
Wright's Gunstock Blanks

POWDER MEASURES, SCALES, FUNNELS & ACCESSORIES

4-D Custom Die Co.
Battenfeld Technologies
Buffalo Arms Co.
Dillon Precision Products, Inc.
Fremont Tool Works
Frontier
GAR
High Precision
Hoehn Sales, Inc.
Jones Custom Products, Neil A.
Modern Muzzleloading, Inc

Neil A. Jones Custom Products
Peter Dyson & Son Ltd.
Precision Reloading, Inc.
RCBS Div. of Blount
Redding Reloading Equipment
Sanders Gun and Machine Shop
The A.W. Peterson Gun Shop, Inc.
The Gun Works
Vega Tool Co.
VibraShine, Inc.

PRESS ACCESSORIES, METALLIC

Buffalo Arms Co.
Efficient Machinery Co
Hollywood Engineering
R.E.I.
Redding Reloading Equipment
The A.W. Peterson Gun Shop, Inc.
Thompson Tool Mount
Vega Tool Co.

PRESS ACCESSORIES, SHOTSHELL

Efficient Machinery Co
Hollywood Engineering
Lee Precision, Inc.
MEC, Inc.
Precision Reloading, Inc.
R.E.I.
The A.W. Peterson Gun Shop, Inc.

PRESSES, ARBOR

Blue Ridge Machinery & Tools, Inc.
Goodwin's Gun Shop
K&M Services
The A.W. Peterson Gun Shop, Inc.

PRESSES, METALLIC

4-D Custom Die Co.
Battenfeld Technologies
Dillon Precision Products, Inc.
Fremont Tool Works
Goodwin's Gun Shop
Hornady Mfg. Co.
Lee Precision, Inc.
RCBS Div. of Blount
Redding Reloading Equipment
The A.W. Peterson Gun Shop, Inc.

PRESSES, SHOTSHELL

Ballistic Product, Inc.
Dillon Precision Products, Inc.
Goodwin's Gun Shop
Hornady Mfg. Co.
MEC, Inc.
Precision Reloading, Inc.
The A.W. Peterson Gun Shop, Inc.

PRESSES, SWAGE

Bullet Swaging Supply Inc.
MAST Technology
The A.W. Peterson Gun Shop, Inc.

PRIMING TOOLS & ACCESSORIES

Goodwin's Gun Shop
Hart & Son, Inc.
K&M Services
RCBS Div. of Blount
Simmons, Jerry
Sinclair International, Inc.
The A.W. Peterson Gun Shop, Inc.

REBORING & RERIFLING

Ahlman Guns
Bauska Barrels
BlackStar AccuMax Barrels
BlackStar Barrel Accurizing
   (See BlackStar AccuMax
Buffalo Arms Co.
Champlin Firearms, Inc.
Ed's Gun House
Fred F. Wells / Wells Sport Store
H&S Liner Service
Ivanoff, Thomas G
   (See Tom's Gun Repair)
Jackalope Gun Shop
LaBounty Precision Reboring, Inc
Mandall Shooting Supplies Inc.
NCP Products, Inc.
Pence Precision Barrels
Pro-Port Ltd.
Redman's Rifling & Reboring

Rice, Keith
   (See White Rock Tool & Die)
Ridgetop Sporting Goods
Savage Arms, Inc.
Shaw, Inc., E. R.
   (See Small Arms Mfg. Co.)
Siegrist Gun Shop
Simmons Gun Repair, Inc.
Stratco, Inc.
Terry K. Kopp Professional
   Gunsmithing
The Gun Works
Time Precision
Tom's Gun Repair, Thomas G. Ivanoff
Turnbull Restoration, Doug
Van Patten, J. W.
White Rock Tool & Die
Zufall, Joseph F.
Reloading Tools and Accessories
4-D Custom Die Co.
Advance Car Mover Co., Rowell Div.
American Products, Inc.
Ammo Load, Inc.
Armfield Custom Bullets
Arms Corporation of the Philippines
Atlantic Rose, Inc.
Atsko/Sno-Seal, Inc.
Bald Eagle Precision Machine Co.
Ballistic Product, Inc.
Belltown Ltd.
Ben William's Gun Shop
Ben's Machines
Berger Bullets Ltd.
Berry's Mfg., Inc.
Blount, Inc., Sporting Equipment Div.
Blue Mountain Bullets
Blue Ridge Machinery & Tools, Inc.
Bonanza (See Forster Products)
Break-Free, Inc.
Brown Co, E. Arthur
BRP, Inc. High Performance Cast
   Bullets
Brynin, Milton
B-Square Company, Inc.
Buck Stix--SOS Products Co.
Buffalo Arms Co.
Bull Mountain Rifle Co.
Bullseye Bullets
C&D Special Products
   (See Claybuster Wads & Harves
Camdex, Inc.
Camp-Cap Products
Canyon Cartridge Corp.
Case Sorting System
CH Tool & Die Co
   (See 4-D Custom Die Co)
Chem-Pak Inc.
CheVron Bullets
Claybuster Wads & Harvester Bullets
CONKKO
Cook Engineering Service
Crouse's Country Cover
Cumberland Arms
Curtis Cast Bullets
Custom Products
   (See Jones Custom Products)
CVA
D.C.C. Enterprises
Davide Pedersoli and Co.
Davis, Don
Davis Products, Mike
Denver Instrument Co.
Dewey Mfg. Co., Inc., J.
Dillon Precision Products, Inc.
Dropkick
E&L Mfg., Inc.
Eagan, Donald V.
Eezox, Inc.
Eichelberger Bullets, Wm.
Enguix Import-Export
Euroarms of America, Inc.
E-Z-Way Systems
Federated-Fry (See Fry Metals)
Feken, Dennis
Ferguson, Bill
First Inc., Jack
Fisher Custom Firearms
Fitz Pistol Grip Co.
Flambeau Products Corp.
Flitz International Ltd.
Forster Products

Fremont Tool Works
Fry Metals
Gehmann, Walter
(See Huntington Die Specialties)
Graf & Sons
Graphics Direct
Graves Co.
Green, Arthur S.
Greenwood Precision
GTB
Gun City
Hanned Precision
(See Hanned Line, The)
Harrell's Precision
Harris Enterprises
Harrison Bullets
Haydon Shooters Supply, Russ
Heidenstrom Bullets
High Precision
Hirtenberger Aktiengesellschaft
Hoch Custom Bullet Moulds
(See Colorado Shooter's)
Hodgdon Powder Co.
Hoehn Sales, Inc.
Hoelscher, Virgil
Holland's Gunsmithing
Hondo Ind.
Hornady Mfg. Co.
Howell Machine
Hunters Supply, Inc.
Hutton Rifle Ranch
Image Ind. Inc.
Imperial Magnum Corp.
INTEC International, Inc.
Iosso Products
J&L Superior Bullets
(See Huntington Die Special)
Javelina Lube Products
JGS Precision Tool Mfg.
JLK Bullets
Jonad Corp.
Jones Custom Products, Neil A.
Jones Moulds, Paul
K&M Services
Kapro Mfg.Co. Inc. (See R.E.I.)
Knoell, Doug
Korzinek Riflesmith, J.
L.A.R. Mfg., Inc.
L.E. Wilson, Inc.
Lapua Ltd.
Le Clear Industries
(See E-Z-Way Systems)
Lee Precision, Inc.
Legend Products Corp.
Liberty Metals
Liberty Shooting Supplies
Lightning Performance Innovations, Inc.
Lithi Bee Bullet Lube
Littleton, J. F.
Lock's Philadelphia Gun Exchange
Lortone Inc.
Loweth, Richard H.R.
Lyman Instant Targets, Inc.
(See Lyman Products)
Lyman Products Corp.
MA Systems
Magma Engineering Co.
MarMik, Inc.
Marquart Precision Co.
MAST Technology
Match Prep--Doyle Gracey
Mayville Engineering Co.
(See MEC, Inc.)
MCS, Inc.
MEC, Inc.
Midway Arms, Inc.
MI-TE Bullets
Montana Armory, Inc
(See C. Sharps Arms Co. Inc.)
Mo's Competitor Supplies
(See MCS Inc)
Mountain South
Mountain State Muzzleloading
Supplies, Inc.
MTM Molded Products Co., Inc.
Multi-Scale Charge Ltd.
MWG Co.
Navy Arms Company
Necromancer Industries, Inc.
Newman Gunshop
North Devon Firearms Services

October Country Muzzleloading
Old West Bullet Moulds
Omark Industries,Div. of Blount,Inc.
Original Box, Inc.
Outdoor Sports Headquarters, Inc.
Paco's
(See Small Custom Mould & Bullet Co)
Paragon Sales & Services, Inc.
Pease Accuracy
Pinetree Bullets
Ponsness/Warren
Prairie River Arms
Prime Reloading
Professional Hunter Supplies
(See Star Custom Bull)
Pro-Shot Products, Inc.
R.A. Wells Custom Gunsmith
R.E.I.
R.I.S. Co., Inc.
Rapine Bullet Mould Mfg. Co.
Reloading Specialties, Inc.
Rice, Keith
(See White Rock Tool & Die)
Rochester Lead Works
Rooster Laboratories
Rorschach Precision Products
SAECO
(See Redding Reloading Equipment)
Sandia Die & Cartridge Co.
Saunders Gun & Machine Shop
Saville Iron Co.
(See Greenwood Precision)
Scot Powder Co. of Ohio, Inc.
Seebeck Assoc., R.E.
Sharp Shooter Supply
Sharps Arms Co., Inc., C.
Shiloh Creek
Shiloh Rifle Mfg.
Sierra Specialty Prod. Co.
Silver Eagle Machining
Skip's Machine
Small Custom Mould & Bullet Co.
Sno-Seal, Inc. (See Atsko/Sno-Seal)
SOS Products Co.
(See Buck Stix-SOS Products Co.)
Spencer's Custom Guns
SPG LLC
Sportsman Supply Co.
SSK Industries
Stalwart Corporation
Star Custom Bullets
Starr Trading Co., Jedediah
Stillwell, Robert
Stoney Point Products, Inc.
Stratco, Inc.
Tamarack Products, Inc.
Taracorp Industries, Inc.
TCCI
TCSR
TDP Industries, Inc.
Tetra Gun Lubricants (See FTI, Inc.)
The Hanned Line
The Protector Mfg. Co., Inc.
Thompson / Center Arms
Timber Heirloom Products
TMI Products
(See Haselbauer Products, Jerry)
Vega Tool Co.
Venco Industries, Inc.
(See Shooter's Choice)
VibraShine, Inc.
Vibra-Tek Co.
Vihtavuori Oy/Kaltron-Pettibone
Vitt/Boos
W.B. Niemi Engineering
W.J. Riebe Co.
Waechter
WD-40 Co.
Webster Scale Mfg. Co.
White Rock Tool & Die
Widener's Reloading & Shooting
Supply, Inc.
Wise Custom Guns
Woodleigh
(See Huntington Die Specialties)
Yesteryear Armory & Supply
Young Country Arms

RESTS BENCH, PORTABLE AND ACCESSORIES

Adventure 16, Inc.
Armor Metal Products
Bald Eagle Precision Machine Co.
Bartlett Engineering
Battenfeld Technologies
Blount/Outers
Browning Arms Co.
B-Square Company, Inc.
Bull Mountain Rifle Co.
Canons Delcour
Chem-Pak Inc.
Clift Mfg., L. R.
Clift Welding Supply & Cases
Decker Shooting Products
Desert Mountain Mfg.
Efficient Machinery Co
Greenwood Precision
Harris Engineering Inc.
Hidalgo, Tony
Hoehn Sales, Inc.
Hoelscher, Virgil
Hoppe's Div. Penguin Industries, Inc.
Keng's Firearms Specialty, Inc. / US
Tactical Systems
Kolpin Mfg., Inc.
Kramer Designs
Midway Arms, Inc.
Millett Sights
Protektor Model
Ransom International Corp.
Russ Haydon Shooters' Supply
Saville Iron Co.
(See Greenwood Precision)
Sinclair International, Inc.
Stoney Point Products, Inc.
T.H.U. Enterprises, Inc.
The A.W. Peterson Gun Shop, Inc.
The Outdoor Connection,Inc.
Thompson Target Technology
Tonoloway Tack Drives
Varmint Masters, LLC
Wichita Arms, Inc.
Zanotti Armor, Inc.
Ziegel Engineering

RIFLE BARREL MAKER

Airrow
American Safe Arms, Inc.
Bauska Barrels
BlackStar AccuMax Barrels
BlackStar Barrel Accurizing
(See BlackStar AccuMax
Border Barrels Ltd.
Brown Co, E. Arthur
Buchsenmachermeister
Bullberry Barrel Works, Ltd.
Bushmaster Firearms
Canons Delcour
Carter's Gun Shop
Christensen Arms
Cincinnati Swaging
Cryo-Accurizing
D&J Bullet Co. & Custom Gun Shop, Inc.
deHaas Barrels
Dilliott Gunsmithing, Inc.
DKT, Inc.
Donnelly, C. P.
Douglas Barrels Inc.
Fred F. Wells / Wells Sport Store
Gaillard Barrels
Gary Schneider Rifle Barrels Inc.
Getz Barrel Co.
Granite Mountain Arms, Inc
Green Mountain Rifle Barrel Co., Inc.
Gruning Precision Inc
Half Moon Rifle Shop
Harris Gunworks
Hart Rifle Barrels,Inc.
Hastings Barrels
Hoelscher, Virgil
Hofer Jagdwaffen, P.
H-S Precision, Inc.
Jackalope Gun Shop
Knippel, Richard
Krieger Barrels, Inc.
Lilja Precision Rifle Barrels
Lothar Walther Precision Tool Inc.

McGowen Rifle Barrels
McMillan Rifle Barrels
Mid-America Recreation, Inc.
Modern Gun Repair School
Morrison Precision
Obermeyer Rifled Barrels
Olympic Arms Inc.
Orion Rifle Barrel Co.
Pac-Nor Barreling
Pell, John T. (See KOGOT)
Pence Precision Barrels
Raptor Arms Co., Inc.
Rogue Rifle Co., Inc.
Sabatti S.r.l.
Sanders Custom Gun Service
Savage Arms, Inc.
Schneider Rifle Barrels, Inc, Gary
Shaw, Inc., E. R.
(See Small Arms Mfg. Co.)
Shilen, Inc.
Siskiyou Gun Works
(See Donnelly, C. P.)
Small Arms Mfg. Co.
Specialty Shooters Supply, Inc.
Spencer's Custom Guns
Strutz Rifle Barrels, Inc., W. C.
Swift River Gunworks
Terry K. Kopp Professional
Gunsmithing
The Gun Works
The Wilson Arms Co.
Turnbull Restoration, Doug
Unmussig Bullets, D. L.
Verney-Carron
Virgin Valley Custom Guns
W.C. Strutz Rifle Barrels, Inc.
Wiseman and Co., Bill

SCOPES, MOUNTS, ACCESSORIES, OPTICAL EQUIPMENT

A.R.M.S., Inc.
ABO (USA) Inc
Accu-Tek
Ackerman, Bill
(See Optical Services Co)
Action Direct, Inc.
ADCO Sales, Inc.
Adventurer's Outpost
Aimpoint c/o Springfield, Inc.
Aimtech Mount Systems
Air Rifle Specialists
Air Venture Airguns
All Rite Products, Inc.
Alley Supply Co.
Alpec Team, Inc.
Apel GmbH, Ernst
ArmaLite, Inc.
Arundel Arms & Ammunition, Inc., A.
B.A.C.
Baer Custom, Inc, Les
Bansner's Ultimate Rifles, LLC
Barrett Firearms Manufacturer, Inc.
Beaver Park Product, Inc.
BEC, Inc.
Beeman Precision Airguns
Ben William's Gun Shop
Benjamin/Sheridan Co., Crossman
BKL Technologies
Blount, Inc., Sporting Equipment Div.
Blount/Outers
Borden Rifles Inc
Brockman's Custom Gunsmithing
Brocock Ltd.
Brown Co, E. Arthur
Brownells, Inc.
Brunton U.S.A.
BSA Optics
B-Square Company, Inc.
Bull Mountain Rifle Co.
Burris Co., Inc.
Bushmaster Firearms
Bushnell Sports Optics Worldwide
Butler Creek Corp.
Cabela's
Carl Zeiss Inc.
Center Lock Scope Rings
Chuck's Gun Shop
Clark Custom Guns, Inc.
Clearview Mfg. Co., Inc.
Compass Industries, Inc.
Compasseco, Ltd.

Concept Development Corp.
Conetrol Scope Mounts
Creedmoor Sports, Inc.
Crimson Trace Lasers
Crosman Airguns
Custom Quality Products, Inc.
D&H Prods. Co., Inc.
D.C.C. Enterprises
Daisy Mfg. Co.
Del-Sports, Inc.
DHB Products
E. Arthur Brown Co.
Eclectic Technologies, Inc.
Ed Brown Products, Inc.
Edmund Scientific Co.
Ednar, Inc.
Eggleston, Jere D.
Emerging Technologies, Inc.
(See Laseraim Technolo
Entre'prise Arms, Inc.
Euro-Imports
Evolution Gun Works Inc.
Excalibur Electro Optics Inc
Excel Industries, Inc.
Faloon Industries, Inc.
Farr Studio, Inc.
Federal Arms Corp. of America
Freedom Arms, Inc.
Fujinon, Inc.
G.G. & G.
Galati International
Gentry Custom Gunmaker, David
Gil Hebard Guns Inc.
Gilmore Sports Concepts
Gonzalez Guns, Ramon B
Goodwin's Gun Shop
GSI, Inc.
Gun South, Inc. (See GSI, Inc.)
Guns
Guns Div. of D.C. Engineering, Inc.
Gunsmithing, Inc.
Hakko Co. Ltd.
Hammerli USA
Harris Gunworks
Harvey, Frank
Hertel & Reuss
Hiptmayer, Armurier
Hiptmayer, Klaus
HiTek International
Holland's Gunsmithing
Impact Case Co.
Ironsighter Co.
Jeffredo Gunsight
Jena Eur
Jerry Phillips Optics
Jewell Triggers, Inc.
John Masen Co. Inc.
John's Custom Leather
Kahles A Swarovski Company
Kalispel Case Line
KDF, Inc.
Keng's Firearms Specialty, Inc. / US
Tactical Systems
KenPatable Ent., Inc.
Kesselring Gun Shop
Kimber of America, Inc.
Kowa Optimed, Inc.
KVH Industries, Inc.
Kwik-Site Co.
L&S Technologies Inc
(See Aimtech Mount Systems)
L.A.R. Mfg., Inc.
Laser Devices, Inc.
Laseraim Technologies, Inc.
LaserMax, Inc.
Leapers, Inc.
Lee Co., T. K.
Leica USA, Inc.
Leupold & Stevens, Inc.
Lightforce U.S.A. Inc.
List Precision Engineering
Lohman Mfg. Co., Inc.
Lomont Precision Bullets
London Guns Ltd.
Mac-1 Airgun Distributors
Mag-Na-Port International, Inc.
Mandall Shooting Supplies Inc.
Marksman Products
Maxi-Mount Inc.
McBros Rifle Co.
McCann's Machine & Gun Shop
McMillan Optical Gunsight Co.

PRODUCT & SERVICE DIRECTORY

MCS, Inc.
MDS
Merit Corp.
Military Armament Corp.
Millett Sights
Mirador Optical Corp.
Mitchell Optics, Inc.
MMC
Mo's Competitor Supplies
   (See MCS Inc)
MWG Co.
Navy Arms Company
New England Custom Gun Service
Nightforce (See Lightforce USA Inc)
Nikon, Inc.
Norincoptics (See BEC, Inc.)
Olympic Optical Co.
Optical Services Co.
Orchard Park Enterprise
Oregon Arms, Inc.
   (See Rogue Rifle Co., Inc.)
Ozark Gun Works
P.M. Enterprises, Inc. / Precise
   Metalsmithing
Parker & Sons Shooting Supply
Parsons Optical Mfg. Co.
PECAR Herbert Schwarz GmbH
PEM's Mfg. Co.
Pentax Corp.
PMC / Eldorado Cartridge Corp.
Precise Metalsmithing Enterprises /
   P.M. Enterprises
Precision Sport Optics
Premier Reticles
R.A. Wells Custom Gunsmith
Ram-Line Blount, Inc.
Ramon B. Gonzalez Guns
Ranch Products
Randolph Engineering Inc.
Rice, Keith
   (See White Rock Tool & Die)
Robinson Armament Co.
Rogue Rifle Co., Inc.
Romain's Custom Guns, Inc.
S&K Scope Mounts
Sanders Custom Gun Service
Sanders Gun and Machine Shop
Schmidt & Bender, Inc.
Schumakers Gun Shop
Scope Control, Inc.
ScopLevel
Score High Gunsmithing
Seecamp Co. Inc., L. W.
Segway Industries
Selsi Co., Inc.
Sharp Shooter Supply
Shepherd Enterprises, Inc.
Sightron, Inc.
Simmons Outdoor Corp.
Six Enterprises
Southern Bloomer Mfg. Co.
Splitfire Sporting Goods, L.L.C.
Sportsmatch U.K. Ltd.
Springfield, Inc.
SSK Industries
Stiles Custom Guns
Stoeger Industries
Stoney Point Products, Inc.
Sturm Ruger & Co. Inc.
Sunny Hill Enterprises, Inc.
Swarovski Optik North America Ltd.
Swift Instruments, Inc.
T.K. Lee Co.
TacStar
Talley, Dave
Tasco Sales, Inc.
Tele-Optics
The A.W. Peterson Gun Shop, Inc.
The Outdoor Connection,Inc.
Thompson / Center Arms
Thompson Target Technology
Traditions Performance Firearms
Trijicon, Inc.
TruGlo, Inc
Ultra Dot Distribution
Uncle Mike's
   (See Michaels of Oregon Co.)
Unertl Optical Co., Inc.
United Binocular Co.
United States Optics Technologies,
   Inc.
Valor Corp.

Virgin Valley Custom Guns
Visible Impact Targets
Voere-KGH m.b.H.
Warne Manufacturing Co.
Warren Muzzleloading Co., Inc.
WASP Shooting Systems
Watson Trophy Match Bullets
Weaver Products
Weaver Scope Repair Service
Weigand Combat Handguns, Inc.
Wessinger Custom Guns & Engraving
Westley Richards & Co.
White Rock Tool & Die
White Shooting Systems, Inc.
   (See White Muzzleload)
Whitestone Lumber Corp.
Wideview Scope Mount Corp.
Wilcox Industries Corp
Wild West Guns
Williams Gun Sight Co.
York M-1 Conversions
Zanotti Armor, Inc.

SHELLHOLDERS

Fremont Tool Works
Goodwin's Gun Shop
Hart & Son, Inc.
Hollywood Engineering
K&M Services
King & Co.
Protektor Model
The A.W. Peterson Gun Shop, Inc.
Vega Tool Co.

SHOOTING/TRAINING
SCHOOL

Alpine Indoor Shooting Range
American Gunsmithing Institute
American Small Arms Academy
Auto Arms
Beretta U.S.A. Corp.
Bob's Tactical Indoor Shooting Range
   & Gun Shop
Bridgeman Products
Cannon's
Chapman Academy of Practical
   Shooting
Chelsea Gun Club of New York City
   Inc.
Cherry Creek State Park Shooting
   Center
CQB Training
Defense Training International, Inc.
Executive Protection Institute
Ferris Firearms
Front Sight Firearms Training Institute
G.H. Enterprises Ltd.
Gene's Custom Guns
Griffin & Howe, Inc.
Guncraft Books
   (See Guncraft Sports Inc.)
Guncraft Sports Inc.
Guncraft Sports, Inc.
Gunsite Training Center
Henigson & Associates, Steve
Jensen's Custom Ammunition
Jensen's Firearms Academy
Kemen America
L.L. Bean, Inc.
Lethal Force Institute
   (See Police Bookshelf)
Loch Leven Industries / Convert-A-Pell
Mandall Shooting Supplies Inc.
McMurdo, Lynn
   (See Specialty Gunsmithing)
Mendez, John A.
NCP Products, Inc.
Nevada Pistol Academy, Inc.
North American Shooting Systems
North Mountain Pine Training Center
   (See Executive)
Nowlin Mfg. Co.
Paxton Quigley's Personal Protection
   Strategies
Pentheny de Pentheny
Performance Specialists
Police Bookshelf
River Road Sporting Clays
SAFE
Shoot Where You Look
Shooter's World
Shooters, Inc.

Sigarms, Inc.
Smith & Wesson
Specialty Gunsmithing
Starlight Training Center, Inc.
Tactical Defense Institute
The Firearm Training Center
The Midwest Shooting School
The Shooting Gallery
Thunden Ranch
Western Missouri Shooters Alliance
Yankee Gunsmith
Yavapai Firearms Academy Ltd.

SHOTSHELL
MISCELLANY

American Products, Inc.
Ballistic Product, Inc.
Bridgeman Products
Goodwin's Gun Shop
Lee Precision, Inc.
MEC, Inc.
Precision Reloading, Inc.
R.E.I.
T&S Industries, Inc.
The A.W. Peterson Gun Shop, Inc.
The Gun Works
Vitt/Boos
Ziegel Engineering

SIGHTS, METALLIC

100 Straight Products, Inc.
Accura-Site
   (See All's, The Jim Tembelis Co.,
   Inc.)
Ad Hominem
Alley Supply Co.
All's, The Jim J. Tembelis Co., Inc.
Alpec Team, Inc.
Andela Tool & Machine, Inc.
AO Sight Systems
ArmaLite, Inc.
Aro-Tek Ltd.
Ashley Outdoors, Inc.
Aspen Outfitting Co.
Axtell Rifle Co.
B.A.C.
Baer Custom, Inc, Les
Ballard Rifle & Cartridge Co., LLC
BEC, Inc.
Bob's Gun Shop
Bo-Mar Tool & Mfg. Co.
Bond Custom Firearms
Bowen Classic Arms Corp.
Bradley Gunsight Co.
Brockman's Custom Gunsmithing
Brooks Tactical Systems
Brown Co, E. Arthur
Brown Dog Ent.
Brownells, Inc.
Buffalo Arms Co.
Bushmaster Firearms
C. Sharps Arms Co. Inc./Montana
   Armory
California Sights
   (See Fautheree, Andy)
Cape Outfitters
Cape Outfitters
Cash Mfg. Co., Inc.
Center Lock Scope Rings
Champion's Choice, Inc.
C-More Systems
Colonial Repair
CRR, Inc./Marble's Inc.
Davide Pedersoli and Co.
DHB Products
Dixie Gun Works
DPMS (Defense Procurement
   Manufacturing Services, Inc.)
E. Arthur Brown Co.
Evolution Gun Works Inc.
Faloon Industries, Inc.
Farr Studio, Inc.
G.G. & G.
Garthwaite Pistolsmith, Inc., Jim
Goergen's Gun Shop, Inc.
Goodwin's Gun Shop
Guns Div. of D.C. Engineering, Inc.
Gunsmithing, Inc.
Hank's Gun Shop
Heidenstrom Bullets
Heinie Specialty Products
Hesco-Meprolight

Hiptmayer, Armurier
Hiptmayer, Klaus
IMX, LLC
Innovative Weaponry Inc.
J.G. Anschutz GmbH & Co. KG
J.P. Enterprises Inc.
Keng's Firearms Specialty, Inc. / US
   Tactical Systems
Knight Rifles
Knight's Mfg. Co.
L.P.A. Snc
Leapers, Inc.
List Precision Engineering
London Guns Ltd.
Lyman Instant Targets, Inc.
   (See Lyman Products)
Mandall Shooting Supplies Inc.
Marble Arms
   (See CRR, Inc./Marble's Inc.)
MCS, Inc.
MEC-Gar S.r.l.
Meprolight (See Hesco-Meprolight)
Merit Corp.
Mid-America Recreation, Inc.
Middlebrooks Custom Shop
Millett Sights
MMC
Modern Muzzleloading, Inc
Montana Armory, Inc
   (See C. Sharps Arms Co. Inc.)
Montana Vintage Arms
Mo's Competitor Supplies
   (See MCS Inc)
Navy Arms Company
New England Custom Gun Service
Newman Gunshop
North Pass
Novak's, Inc.
OK Weber,Inc.
One Ragged Hole
P.M. Enterprises, Inc. / Precise
   Metalsmithing
Parker & Sons Shooting Supply
PEM's Mfg. Co.
Perazone-Gunsmith, Brian
Precise Metalsmithing Enterprises /
   P.M. Enterprises
RPM
Sharps Arms Co., Inc., C.
Slug Site
STI International
T.F.C. S.p.A
Talley, Dave
Tank's Rifle Shop
The A.W. Peterson Gun Shop, Inc.
The Gun Doctor
The Gun Works
Trijicon, Inc.
Truglo, Inc
United States Optics Technologies,
   Inc.
Warne Manufacturing Co.
WASP Shooting Systems
Wichita Arms, Inc.
Wild West Guns
Williams Gun Sight Co.
Wilsom Combat
Wilsom Combat

STOCK MAKER

Acra-Bond Laminates
Al Lind Custom Guns
Amrine's Gun Shop
Antique Arms Co.
Artistry in Wood
Aspen Outfitting Co.
Bain & Davis, Inc.
Bansner's Ultimate Rifles, LLC
Baron Technology
Belding's Custom Gun Shop
Billings Gunsmiths Inc.
Bob Rogers Gunsmithing
Boltin, John M.
Bone Engraving, Ralph
Borden Ridges Rimrock Stocks
Bowerly, Kent
Boyds' Gunstock Industries, Inc.
Brace, Larry D.
Briganti, A.J.
Brown Precision, Inc.
Buchsenmachermeister
Bull Mountain Rifle Co.

Burkhart Gunsmithing, Don
Cambos Outdoorsman
Cambos Outdoorsman
Caywood, Shane J.
Chicasaw Gun Works
Chuck's Gun Shop
Claro Walnut Gunstock Co.
Coffin, Charles H.
Colorado Gunsmithing Academy
Custom Riflestocks, Inc., Michael M.
   Kokolus
Custom Single Shot Rifles
Custom Stocking
D&D Gunsmiths, Ltd.
D.D. Custom Stocks, R.H. "Dick"
   Devereaux
Dangler, Homer L.
D'Arcy Echols & Co.
DGR Custom Rifles
DGR Custom Rifles
DGS, Inc., Dale A. Storey
Erhardt, Dennis
Eversull Co., Inc.
Fieldsport Ltd.
Fisher, Jerry A.
Forster, Larry L.
Fred F. Wells / Wells Sport Store
Gary Goudy Classic Stocks
Genecco Gun Works
Gene's Custom Guns
George E. Mathews & Son, Inc.
Gillmann, Edwin
Grace, Charles E.
Great American Gunstock Co.
Gruning Precision Inc
Gunsmithing Ltd.
Hank's Gun Shop
Harper's Custom Stocks
Harry Lawson Co.
Heilmann, Stephen
Hensley, Gunmaker, Darwin
Heydenberk, Warren R.
Hofer Jagdwaffen, P.
Huebner, Corey O.
Hughes, Steven Dodd
Island Pond Gun Shop
Jack Dever Co.
Jamison's Forge Works
Jay McCament Custom Gunmaker
Jim Norman Custom Gunstocks
John Rigby & Co.
K. Eversull Co., Inc.
Keith's Custom Gunstocks
Klein Custom Guns, Don
Knippel, Richard
L E Jurras & Assoc.
Larry Lyons Gunworks
Lind Custom Guns, Al
Mathews & Son, Inc., George E.
McGowen Rifle Barrels
Mercer Custom Guns
Mid-America Recreation, Inc.
Mitchell, Jack
Modern Gun Repair School
Morrow, Bud
Nelson's Custom Guns, Inc.
Nettestad Gun Works
Nickels, Paul R.
Oakland Custom Arms,Inc.
Paul and Sharon Dressel
Paul D. Hillmer Custom Gunstocks
Paulsen Gunstocks
Pawling Mountain Club
Pecatonica River Longrifle
Pentheny de Pentheny
Quality Custom Firearms
R&J Gun Shop
R.A. Wells Custom Gunsmith
Ralph Bone Engraving
Rigby & Co., John
Ron Frank Custom Classic Arms
Royal Arms Gunstocks
Ruger's Custom Guns
Sanders Custom Gun Service
Six Enterprises
Skeoch, Brian R.
Smith, Art
Smith, Sharmon
Speiser, Fred D.
Stott's Creek Armory, Inc.
Sturgeon Valley Sporters
Talmage, William G.

Taylor & Robbins
The Custom Shop
Tiger-Hunt Gunstocks
Trico Plastics
Tucker, James C.
Turnbull Restoration, Doug
Vest, John
Walker Arms Co., Inc.
Wayne E. Schwartz Custom Guns
Weber & Markin Custom Gunsmiths
Wenig Custom Gunstocks
Wiebe, Duane
Wild West Guns
Williamson Precision Gunsmithing
Winter, Robert M.
Working Guns

STOCKS (COMMERCIAL)

Accuracy Unlimited
Acra-Bond Laminates
Ahlman Guns
Arms Ingenuity Co.
Arundel Arms & Ammunition, Inc., A.
Aspen Outfitting Co.
B.A.C.
Baelder, Harry
Balickie, Joe
Bansner's Ultimate Rifles, LLC
Barnes Bullets, Inc.
Battenfeld Technologies
Beitzinger, George
Belding's Custom Gun Shop
Bell & Carlson, Inc.
Biesen, Al
Biesen, Roger
Blount, Inc., Sporting Equipment Div.
Blount/Outers
Bob's Gun Shop
Borden Ridges Rimrock Stocks
Borden Rifles Inc
Bowerly, Kent
Boyds' Gunstock Industries, Inc.
Brockman's Custom Gunsmithing
Brown Co, E. Arthur
Buckhorn Gun Works
Bull Mountain Rifle Co.
Bullberry Barrel Works, Ltd.
Butler Creek Corp.
Cali'co Hardwoods, Inc.
Cape Outfitters
Caywood, Shane J.
Chambers Flintlocks Ltd., Jim
Chicasaw Gun Works
Chuilli, Stephen
Claro Walnut Gunstock Co.
Cloward's Gun Shop
Coffin, Charles H.
Coffin, Jim (See Working Guns)
Colonial Repair
Colorado Gunsmithing Academy
Colorado School of Trades
Conrad, C. A.
Creedmoor Sports, Inc.
Curly Maple Stock Blanks
   (See Tiger-Hunt)
Custom Checkering Service, Kathy
   Forster
Custom Gun Products
Custom Riflestocks, Inc., Michael M.
   Kokolus
D&D Gunsmiths, Ltd.
D&G Precision Duplicators
   (See Greene Precision)
D&J Bullet Co. & Custom Gun Shop,
   Inc.
D.D. Custom Stocks, R.H. "Dick"
   Devereaux
David W. Schwartz Custom Guns
Devereaux, R.H. "Dick"
   (See D.D. Custom)
DGR Custom Rifles
Dillon, Ed
Duane's Gun Repair
   (See DGR Custom Rifles)
Duncan's Gun Works, Inc.
Eggleston, Jere D.
Erhardt, Dennis
Eversull Co., Inc.
Faloon Industries, Inc.
Faloon Industries, Inc.
Fibron Products, Inc.
Fieldsport Ltd.

Fisher, Jerry A.
Folks, Donald E.
Forster, Kathy
   (See Custom Checkering)
Forthofer's Gunsmithing &
   Knifemaking
Francotte & Cie S.A. Auguste
Game Haven Gunstocks
Gervais, Mike
Gillmann, Edwin
Giron, Robert E.
Goens, Dale W.
Golden Age Arms Co.
Goodwin's Gun Shop
Great American Gunstock Co.
Green, Roger M.
Greenwood Precision
Griffin & Howe, Inc.
Guns
Guns Div. of D.C. Engineering, Inc.
Gunsmithing Ltd.
Hammerli USA
Hanson's Gun Center, Dick
Harper's Custom Stocks
Harris Gunworks
Harry Lawson Co.
Hart & Son, Inc.
Harwood, Jack O.
Hecht, Hubert J, Waffen-Hecht
Hensley, Gunmaker, Darwin
High Tech Specialties, Inc.
Hiptmayer, Armurier
Hiptmayer, Klaus
Hoelscher, Virgil
Hoenig & Rodman
Hogue Grips
H-S Precision, Inc.
Huebner, Corey O.
Island Pond Gun Shop
Israel Arms International, Inc.
Ivanoff, Thomas G
   (See Tom's Gun Repair)
J.P. Gunstocks, Inc.
Jackalope Gun Shop
Jarrett Rifles, Inc.
Jay McCament Custom Gunmaker
Jim Norman Custom Gunstocks
John Masen Co. Inc.
Johnson Wood Products
KDF, Inc.
Keith's Custom Gunstocks
Kelbly, Inc.
Kilham & Co.
Klein Custom Guns, Don
Klingler Woodcarving
Knippel, Richard
Kokolus, Michael M.
   (See Custom Riflestocks)
KSN Industries Ltd
   (See U.S. Importer-Israel Arms)
Lawson Co., Harry
Lind Custom Guns, Al
Mandall Shooting Supplies Inc.
McBros Rifle Co.
McDonald, Dennis
McKinney, R.P.
   (See Schuetzen Gun Co.)
McMillan Fiberglass Stocks, Inc.
Michaels Of Oregon
Mid-America Recreation, Inc.
Miller Arms, Inc.
Mitchell, Jack
Morrison Custom Rifles, J. W.
MPI Stocks
MWG Co.
NCP Products, Inc.
Nelson's Custom Guns, Inc.
New England Arms Co.
New England Custom Gun Service
Newman Gunshop
Nickels, Paul R.
Oakland Custom Arms,Inc.
Oil Rod and Gun Shop
Old World Gunsmithing
One Of A Kind
Ottmar, Maurice
Pacific Research Laboratories, Inc.
   (See Rimrock)
Pagel Gun Works, Inc.
Paragon Sales & Services, Inc.
Parker & Sons Shooting Supply
Paul and Sharon Dressel

Paul D. Hillmer Custom Gunstocks
Paulsen Gunstocks
Pawling Mountain Club
Pecatonica River Longrifle
PEM's Mfg. Co.
Pohl, Henry A.
   (See Great American Gun Co.)
Powell & Son (Gunmakers) Ltd.,
   William
Precision Gun Works
R&J Gun Shop
R.A. Wells Custom Gunsmith
Ram-Line Blount, Inc.
Rampart International
Reagent Chemical & Research, Inc.
   (See Calico Hard)
Reiswig, Wallace E.
   (See Claro Walnut Gunstock)
Richards Micro-Fit Stocks
RMS Custom Gunsmithing
Robinson, Don
Robinson Armament Co.
Robinson Firearms Mfg. Ltd.
Romain's Custom Guns, Inc.
Ron Frank Custom Classic Arms
Roto Carve
Ryan, Chad L.
Sanders Custom Gun Service
Saville Iron Co.
   (See Greenwood Precision)
Schiffman, Curt
Schiffman, Mike
Schiffman, Norman
Score High Gunsmithing
Simmons Gun Repair, Inc.
Six Enterprises
Speiser, Fred D.
Stan De Treville & Co.
Stiles Custom Guns
Storey, Dale A. (See DGS Inc.)
Swann, D. J.
Swift River Gunworks
Szweda, Robert
   (See RMS Custom Gunsmithing)
T.F.C. S.p.A.
Talmage, William G.
Tecnolegno S.p.A.
The A.W. Peterson Gun Shop, Inc.
The Gun Shop
The Orvis Co.
Tiger-Hunt Gunstocks
Tirelli
Tom's Gun Repair, Thomas G. Ivanoff
Track of the Wolf, Inc.
Trevallion Gunstocks
Tuttle, Dale
Vic's Gun Refinishing
Vintage Industries, Inc.
Virgin Valley Custom Guns
Volquartsen Custom Ltd.
Walker Arms Co., Inc.
Weber & Markin Custom Gunsmiths
Weems, Cecil
Wenig Custom Gunstocks
Werth, T. W.
Western Mfg. Co.
Wild West Guns
Williams Gun Sight Co.
Windish, Jim
Winter, Robert M.
Working Guns
Wright's Gunstock Blanks
Zeeryp, Russ
Stuck Case Removers
Goodwin's Gun Shop
MarMik, Inc.
The A.W. Peterson Gun Shop, Inc.
Tom's Gun Repair, Thomas G. Ivanoff

TARGETS, BULLET & CLAYBIRD TRAPS

Action Target, Inc.
Air Arms
American Target
Autauga Arms, Inc.
Beeman Precision Airguns
Benjamin/Sheridan Co., Crossman
Beomat of America, Inc.
Birchwood Casey
Blount, Inc., Sporting Equipment Div.
Blount/Outers

Blue and Gray Products Inc
   (See Ox-Yoke Originals)
Brown Precision, Inc.
Bull-X, Inc.
Champion Target Co.
Crosman Airguns
D.C.C. Enterprises
Detroit-Armor Corp.
Diamond Mfg. Co.
Federal Champion Target Co.
G.H. Enterprises Ltd.
Hiti-Schuch, Atelier Wilma
H-S Precision, Inc.
Hunterjohn
J.G. Dapkus Co., Inc.
Kennebec Journal
Kleen-Bore,Inc.
Lakefield Arms Ltd
   (See Savage Arms Inc.)
Leapers, Inc.
Littler Sales Co.
Lyman Instant Targets, Inc.
   (See Lyman Products)
Marksman Products
Mendez, John A.
Mountain Plains Industries
MSR Targets
Muscle Products Corp.
N.B.B., Inc.
National Target Co.
North American Shooting Systems
Outers Laboratories Div. of Blount,
   Inc. Sporting
Ox-Yoke Originals, Inc.
Palsa Outdoor Products
Passive Bullet Traps, Inc.
   (See Savage Range)
PlumFire Press, Inc.
Precision Airgun Sales, Inc.
Quack Decoy & Sporting Clays
Remington Arms Co., Inc.
Rockwood Corp.
Rocky Mountain Target Co.
Savage Range Systems, Inc.
Schaefer Shooting Sports
Seligman Shooting Products
Shooters Supply
Shoot-N-C Targets
   (See Birchwood Casey)
Target Shooting, Inc.
The A.W. Peterson Gun Shop, Inc.
Thompson Target Technology
Trius Traps, Inc.
Universal Sports
Visible Impact Targets
Woods Wise Products
World of Targets
   (See Birchwood Casey)
X-Spand Target Systems
Zriny's Metal Targets
   (See Z's Metal Targets)

TAXIDERMY

African Import Co.
Kulis Freeze Dry Taxidermy
Montgomery Community College
World Trek, Inc.

TRAP & SKEET SHOOTER'S EQUIPMENT

Allen Co., Bob
Allen Sportswear, Bob
   (See Allen Co., Bob)
American Products, Inc.
Bagmaster Mfg., Inc.
Baker, Stan
Ballistic Product, Inc.
Beomat of America, Inc.
Beretta S.p.A., Pietro
Blount/Outers
Bridgeman Products
C&H Research
Cape Outfitters
Claybuster Wads & Harvester Bullets
Fiocchi of America Inc.
G.H. Enterprises Ltd.
Game Winner, Inc.
Hoppe's Div. Penguin Industries, Inc.
Hunter Co., Inc.
Jamison's Forge Works
Jenkins Recoil Pads, Inc.
Jim Noble Co.

Kalispel Case Line
Kolar
Lakewood Products LLC
Ljutic Industries, Inc.
Mag-Na-Port International, Inc.
Maionchi-L.M.I.
MEC, Inc.
Moneymaker Guncraft Corp.
MTM Molded Products Co., Inc.
NCP Products, Inc.
Pachmayr Div. Lyman Products
Palsa Outdoor Products
Perazone-Gunsmith, Brian
Pro-Port Ltd.
Protektor Model
Quack Decoy & Sporting Clays
Randolph Engineering Inc.
Remington Arms Co., Inc.
Rhodeside, Inc.
Shooting Specialties
   (See Titus, Daniel)
Shotgun Sports Magazine, dba
   Shootin' Accessories Ltd.
T&S Industries, Inc.
TEN-X Products Group
The Gun Works
Trius Traps, Inc.
Truglo, Inc
Universal Sports
Warne Manufacturing Co.
Weber & Markin Custom Gunsmiths
X-Spand Target Systems
Ziegel Engineering

TRIGGERS, RELATED EQUIPMENT

Actions by "T" Teddy Jacobson
B&D Trading Co., Inc.
Baer Custom, Inc, Les
Behlert Precision, Inc.
Bond Custom Firearms
Boyds' Gunstock Industries, Inc.
Bull Mountain Rifle Co.
Chicasaw Gun Works
Dayton Traister
Electronic Trigger Systems, Inc.
Eversull Co., Inc.
FWB
Gentry Custom Gunmaker, David
Goodwin's Gun Shop
Guns
Hart & Son, Inc.
Hawken Shop, The
   (See Dayton Traister)
Hoehn Sales, Inc.
Hoelscher, Virgil
Holland's Gunsmithing
Impact Case Co.
J.P. Enterprises Inc.
Jewell Triggers, Inc.
John Masen Co. Inc.
Jones Custom Products, Neil A.
K. Eversull Co., Inc.
KK Air International
   (See Impact Case Co.)
L&R Lock Co.
List Precision Engineering
London Guns Ltd.
M.H. Canjar Co.
Mahony, Philip Bruce
Master Lock Co.
Miller Single Trigger Mfg. Co.
NCP Products, Inc.
Neil A. Jones Custom Products
Nowlin Mfg. Co.
PEM's Mfg. Co.
Penrod Precision
Robinson Armament Co.
Schumakers Gun Shop
Sharp Shooter Supply
Shilen, Inc.
Simmons Gun Repair, Inc.
Spencer's Custom Guns
Tank's Rifle Shop
Target Shooting, Inc.
The A.W. Peterson Gun Shop, Inc.
The Gun Works
Watson Trophy Match Bullets

MANUFACTURER'S DIRECTORY

A

A Zone Bullets, 2039 Walter Rd., Billings, MT 59105 / 800-252-3111; FAX: 406-248-1961
A&B Industries,Inc (See Top-Line USA Inc)
A&W Repair, 2930 Schneider Dr., Arnold, MO 63010 / 617-287-3725
A.A. Arms, Inc., 4811 Persimmont Ct., Monroe, NC 28110 / 704-289-5356; or 800-935-1119; FAX: 704-289-5859
A.B.S. III, 9238 St. Morritz Dr., Fern Creek, KY 40291
A.G. Russell Knives, Inc., 1920 North 26th Street, Springdale, AR 72764 / 479-751-7341; FAX: 479-751-4520 ag@agrussell.com agrussell.com
A.R.M.S., Inc., 230 W. Center St., West Bridgewater, MA 02379-1620 / 508-584-7816; FAX: 508-588-8045
A.W. Peterson Gun Shop, Inc., 4255 W. Old U.S. 441, Mt. Dora, FL 32757-3299 / 352-383-4258; FAX: 352-735-1001
ABO (USA) Inc, 615 SW 2nd Avenue, Miami, FL 33130 / 305-859-2010; FAX: 305-859-2099
AC Dyna-tite Corp., 155 Kelly St., P.O. Box 0984, Elk Grove Village, IL 60007 / 847-593-5566; FAX: 847-593-1304
Acadian Ballistic Specialties, P.O. Box 787, Folsom, LA 70437 / 504-796-0078 gunsmith@neasoft.com
Accuracy International, Foster, PO Box 111, Wilsall, MT 59086 / 406-587-7922; FAX: 406-585-9434
Accuracy Internationl Precision Rifles (See U.S.)
Accuracy Int'l. North America, Inc., PO Box 5267, Oak Ridge, TN 37831 / 423-482-0330; FAX: 423-482-0336
Accuracy Unlimited, 16036 N. 49 Ave., Glendale, AZ 85306 / 602-978-9089; FAX: 602-978-9089 frankglenn@earthlink.net
Accuracy Unlimited, 7479 S. DePew St., Littleton, CO 80123
Accura-Site (See All's, The Jim Tembelis Co., Inc.)
Accurate Arms Co., Inc., 5891 Hwy. 230 West, McEwen, TN 37101 / 931-729-4207; FAX: 931-729-4211 email@accuratecompanies.com www.accuratepowder.com
Accu-Tek, 4510 Carter Ct, Chino, CA 91710
Ace Custom 45's, Inc., 1880 1/2 Upper Turtle Creek Rd., Kerrville, TX 78028 / 830-257-4290; FAX: 830-257-5724 www.acecustom45.com
Ace Sportswear, Inc., 700 Quality Rd., Fayetteville, NC 28306 / 919-323-1223; FAX: 919-323-5392
Ackerman & Co., Box 133 US Highway Rt. 7, Pownal, VT 05261 / 802-823-9874 muskets@togsther.net
Ackerman, Bill (See Optical Services Co)
Acra-Bond Laminates, 134 Zimmerman Rd., Kalispell, MT 59901 / 406-257-9003; FAX: 406-257-9003 merlins@digisys.net; www.acrabondlaminates.com
Action Bullets & Alloy Inc, RR 1, PO Box 189, Quinter, KS 67752 / 785-754-3609; FAX: 785-754-3629 bullets@ruraltel.net
Action Direct, Inc., PO Box 770400, Miami, FL 33177 / 305-969-0056; FAX: 530-734-3760 action-direct.com
Action Products, Inc., 22 N. Mulberry St., Hagerstown, MD 21740 / 301-797-1414; FAX: 301-733-2073
Action Target, Inc., PO Box 636, Provo, UT 84603 / 801-377-8033; FAX: 801-377-8096
Actions by "T" Teddy Jacobson, 16315 Redwood Forest Ct., Sugar Land, TX 77478 / 281-277-4008; FAX: 281-277-9112; tjacobson@houston.rr.com www.actionsbyt.com
AcuSport Corporation, 1 Hunter Place, Bellefontaine, OH 43311-3001 / 513-593-7010; FAX: 513-592-5625
Ad Hominem, 3130 Gun Club Lane, RR #3, Orillia, ON L3V 6H3 CANADA / 705-689-5303; FAX: 705-689-5303
Adair Custom Shop, Bill, 2886 Westridge, Carrollton, TX 75006
ADCO Sales, Inc., 4 Draper St. #A, Woburn, MA 01801 / 781-935-1799; FAX: 781-935-1011
Adkins, Luther, 1292 E. McKay Rd., Shelbyville, IN 46176-8706 / 317-392-3795
Advance Car Mover Co., Rowell Div., P.O. Box 1, 240 N. Depot St., Juneau, WI 53039 / 414-386-4464; FAX: 414-386-4416
Adventure 16, Inc., 4620 Alvarado Canyon Rd., San Diego, CA 92120 / 619-283-6314
Adventure Game Calls, R.D. 1, Leonard Rd., Spencer, NY 14883 / 607-589-4611
Adventurer's Outpost, P.O. Box 547, Cottonwood, AZ 86326-0547 / 800-762-7471; FAX: 602-634-8781
Aero Peltor, 90 Mechanic St, Southbridge, MA 01550 / 508-764-5500; FAX: 508-764-0188
African Import Co., 22 Goodwin Rd, Plymouth, MA 02360 / 508-746-8552; FAX: 508-746-0404
AFSCO Ammunition, 731 W. Third St., P.O. Box L, Owen, WI 54460 / 715-229-2516
Ahlman Guns, 9525 W. 230th St., Morristown, MN 55052 / 507-685-4243; FAX: 507-685-4280 www.ahlmans.com
Ahrends, Kim (See Custom Firearms, Inc) Box 203, Clarion, IA 50525 / 515-532-3449; FAX: 515-532-3926

Aimpoint c/o Springfield, Inc., 420 W. Main St, Geneseo, IL 61254 / 309-944-1702
Aimtech Mount Systems, PO Box 223, Thomasville, GA 31799 / 229-226-4313; FAX: 229-227-0222 aimtech@surfsouth.com; www.aimtech-mounts.com
Air Arms, Hailsham Industrial Park, Diplocks Way, Hailsham, E. Sussex, BN27 3JF ENGLAND / 011-0323-845853
Air Rifle Specialists, P.O. Box 138, 130 Holden Rd., Pine City, NY 14871-0138 / 607-734-7340; FAX: 607-733-3261 ars@stny.rr.com www.air-rifles.com
Air Venture Airguns, 9752 E. Flower St., Bellflower, CA 90706 / 310-867-6355
AirForce Airguns, P.O. Box 2478, Fort Worth, TX 76113 / 817-451-8966; FAX: 817-451-1613 www.airforceairguns.com
Airgun Repair Centre, 3227 Garden Meadows, Lawrenceburg, IN 47025 / 812-637-1463; FAX: 812-637-1463
Airrow, 11 Monitor Hill Rd, Newtown, CT 06470 / 203-270-6343
Aitor-Cuchilleria Del Norte S.A., Izelaieta, 17, 48260, Ermua, S SPAIN / 43-17-08-50 info@aitor.com; www.ailor.com
Ajax Custom Grips, Inc., 9130 Viscount Row, Dallas, TX 75247 / 214-630-8893; FAX: 214-630-4942
Aker International, Inc., 2248 Main St., Suite 6, Chula Vista, CA 91911 / 619-423-5182; FAX: 619-423-1363
Al Lind Custom Guns, 7821 76th Ave. SW, Lakewood, WA 98498 / 253-584-6361
Alana Cupp Custom Engraver, P.O. Box 207, Annabella, UT 84711 / 801-896-4834
Alaska Bullet Works, Inc., 9978 Crazy Horse Drive, Juneau, AK 99801 / 907-789-3834; FAX: 907-789-3433
Alaskan Silversmith, The, 2145 Wagner Hollow Rd., Fort Plain, NY 13339 / 518-993-3983 sidbell@capital.net www.sidbell.cizland.com
Aldis Gunsmithing & Shooting Supply, 502 S. Montezuma St., Prescott, AZ 86303 / 602-445-6723; FAX: 602-445-6763
Alessi Holsters, Inc., 2465 Niagara Falls Blvd., Amherst, NY 14228-3527 / 716-691-5615
Alex, Inc., Box 3034, Bozeman, MT 59772 / 406-282-7396; FAX: 406-282-7396
Alfano, Sam, 36180 Henry Gaines Rd., Pearl River, LA 70452 / 504-863-3364; FAX: 504-863-7715
All American Lead Shot Corp., P.O. Box 224566, Dallas, TX 75062
All Rite Products, Inc., 9554 Wells Circle, Suite D, West Jordan, UT 84088-6226 / 800-771-8471; FAX: 801-280-8302 www.allriteproducts.com
Allard, Gary/Creek Side Metal & Woodcrafters, Fishers Hill, VA 22626 / 703-465-3903
Allen Co., Bob, 214 SW Jackson, P.O. Box 477, Des Moines, IA 50315 / 515-283-2191; or 800-685-7020; FAX: 515-283-0779
Allen Co., Inc., 525 Burbank St., Broomfield, CO 80020 / 303-469-1857; or 800-876-8600; FAX: 303-466-7437
Allen Firearm Engraving, PO Box 155, Camp Verde, AZ 86322 / 928-567-3892; FAX: 928-567-3901 rosebudmkco@aol.com
Allen Mfg., 6449 Hodgson Rd., Circle Pines, MN 55014 / 612-429-8231
Allen Sportswear, Bob (See Allen Co., Bob)
Alley Supply Co., PO Box 848, Gardnerville, NV 89410 / 775-782-3800 FAX: 775-782-3827 jetalley@aol.com www.alleysupplyco.com
Alliant Techsystems Smokeless Powder Group, P.O. Box 6, Rt. 114, Bldg. 229, Radford, VA 24141-0096 www.alliantpowder.com
Allred Bullet Co., 932 Evergreen Drive, Logan, UT 84321 / 435-752-6983; FAX: 435-752-6983
All's, The Jim J. Tembelis Co., Inc., 216 Loper Ct., Neenah, WI 54956 / 920-725-5251; FAX: 920-725-5251
Alpec Team, Inc., 201 Ricken Backer Cir., Livermore, CA 94550 / 510-606-8245; FAX: 510-606-4279
Alpha 1 Drop Zone, 2121 N. Tyler, Wichita, KS 67212 / 316-729-0800
Alpha Gunsmith Division, 1629 Via Monserate, Fallbrook, CA 92028 / 619-723-9279; or 619-728-2663
Alpha LaFranck Enterprises, P.O. Box 81072, Lincoln, NE 68501 / 402-466-3193
Alpha Precision, Inc., 3238 Della Slaton Rd., Comer, GA 30629-2212 / 706-783-2131 jim@alphaprecisioninc.com www.alphaprecisioninc.com
Alpine Indoor Shooting Range, 2401 Government Way, Coeur d'Alene, ID 83814 / 208-676-8824; FAX: 208-676-8824
Altamont Co., 901 N. Church St., P.O. Box 309, Thomasboro, IL 61878 / 217-643-3125; or 800-626-5774; FAX: 217-643-7973
Alumna Sport by Dee Zee, 1572 NE 58th Ave., P.O. Box 3090, Des Moines, IA 50316 / 800-798-9899
Amadeo Rossi S.A., Rua: Amadeo Rossi, 143, Sao Leopoldo, RS 93030-220 BRAZIL / 051-592-5566

AmBr Software Group Ltd., P.O. Box 301, Reistertown, MD 21136-0301 / 800-888-1917; FAX: 410-526-7212
American Ammunition, 3545 NW 71st St., Miami, FL 33147 / 305-835-7400; FAX: 305-694-0037
American Derringer Corp., 127 N. Lacy Dr., Waco, TX 76705 / 800-642-7817; or 254-799-9111; FAX: 254-799-7935
American Display Co., 55 Cromwell St., Providence, RI 02907 / 401-331-2464; FAX: 401-421-1264
American Frontier Firearms Mfg., Inc, PO Box 744, Aguanga, CA 92536 / 909-763-0014; FAX: 909-763-0014
American Gas & Chemical Co., Ltd, 220 Pegasus Ave, Northvale, NJ 07647 / 201-767-7300
American Gripcraft, 3230 S Dodge 2, Tucson, AZ 85713 / 602-790-1222
American Gunsmithing Institute, 1325 Imola Ave #504, Napa, CA 94559 / 707-253-0462; FAX: 707-253-7149
American Handgunner Magazine, 591 Camino de la Reina, Ste 200, San Diego, CA 92108 / 619-297-5350; FAX: 619-297-5353
American Pioneer Video, PO Box 50049, Bowling Green, KY 42102-2649 / 800-743-4675
American Products, Inc., 14729 Spring Valley Road, Morrison, IL 61270 / 815-772-3336; FAX: 815-772-8046
American Safe Arms, Inc., 1240 Riverview Dr., Garland, UT 84312 / 801-257-7472; FAX: 801-785-8156
American Security Products Co., 11925 Pacific Ave., Fontana, CA 92337 / 909-685-9680; or 800-421-6142; FAX: 909-685-9685
American Small Arms Academy, P.O. Box 12111, Prescott, AZ 86304 / 602-778-5623
American Target, 1328 S. Jason St., Denver, CO 80223 / 303-733-0433; FAX: 303-777-0311
American Target Knives, 1030 Brownwood NW, Grand Rapids, MI 49504 / 616-453-1998
Americase, P.O. Box 271, 1610 E. Main, Waxahachie, TX 75165 / 800-880-3629; FAX: 214-937-8373
Ames Metal Products, 4323 S. Western Blvd., Chicago, IL 60609 / 773-523-3230; or 800-255-6937; FAX: 773-523-3854
Amherst Arms, P.O. Box 1457, Englewood, FL 34295 / 941-475-2020; FAX: 941-473-1212
Ammo Load, Inc., 1560 E. Edinger, Suite G, Santa Ana, CA 92705 / 714-558-8858; FAX: 714-569-0319
Amrine's Gun Shop, 937 La Luna, Ojai, CA 93023 / 805-646-2376
Amsec, 11925 Pacific Ave., Fontana, CA 92337
Analog Devices, Box 9106, Norwood, MA 02062
Andela Tool & Machine, Inc., RD3, Box 246, Richfield Springs, NY 13439
Anderson Manufacturing Co., Inc., 22602 53rd Ave. SE, Bothell, WA 98021 / 206-481-1858; FAX: 206-481-7839
Andres & Dworsky KG, Bergstrasse 18, A-3822 Karlstein, Thaya, AUSTRIA / 0 28 44-285; FAX: 02844 28619 andres.dnorsky@wvnet.as
Angelo & Little Custom Gun Stock Blanks, P.O. Box 240046, Dell, MT 59724-0046
Answer Products Co., 1519 Westbury Drive, Davison, MI 48423 / 810-653-2911
Antique American Firearms, PO Box 71035, Dept. GD, Des Moines, IA 50325 / 515-224-6552
Antique Arms Co., 1110 Cleveland Ave., Monett, MO 65708 / 417-235-6501
AO Sight Systems, 2401 Ludelle St., Fort Worth, TX 76105 / 888-744-4880; or 817-536-0136 FAX: 817-536-3517
Apel GmbH, Ernst, Am Kirschberg 3, D-97218, Gerbrunn, GERMANY / 0 (931) 707192 info@eaw.de www.eaw.de
Aplan Antiques & Art, James O., James O., HC 80, Box 793-25, Piedmont, SD 57769 / 605-347-5016
AR-7 Industries, LLC, 998 N. Colony Rd., Meriden, CT 06450 / 203-630-3536; FAX: 203-630-3637
Arizona Ammunition, Inc., 21421 No. 14th Ave., Suite E, Phoenix, AZ 85027 / 623-516-9004; FAX: 623-516-9012 www.azammo.com
Arkansas Mallard Duck Calls, Rt. Box 182, England, AR 72046 / 501-842-3597
ArmaLite, Inc., P.O. Box 299, Geneseo, IL 61254 / 800-336-0184; or 309-944-6939; FAX: 309-944-6949
Armament Gunsmithing Co., Inc., 525 Rt. 22, Hillside, NJ 07205 / 908-686-0960; FAX: 718-738-5019 armamentgunsmithing@worldnet.att.net
Armas Kemen S. A. (See U.S. Importers)
Armas Urki Garbi, 12-14 20.600, Eibar (Guipuzcoa), / 43-11 38 73
Armfield Custom Bullets, 10584 County Road 100, Carthage, MO 64836 / 417-359-8480; FAX: 417-359-8497
Armi Perazzi S.p.A., Via Fontanelle 1/3, 1-25080, Botticino Mattina, / 030-2692591; FAX: 030 2692594
Armi San Marco (See U.S. Importers-Taylor's & Co I
Armi San Paolo, 172-A, I-25062, via Europa, ITALY / 030-2751725

Armi Sport (See U.S. Importers-Cape Outfitters)

Armite Laboratories, 1560 Superior Ave., Costa Mesa, CA 92627 / 213-587-7768; FAX: 213-587-5075

Armoloy Co. of Ft. Worth, 204 E. Daggett St., Fort Worth, TX 76104 / 817-332-5604; FAX: 817-335-6517

Armor (See Buck Stop Lure Co., Inc.)

Armor Metal Products, PO Box 4609, Helena, MT 59604 / 406-442-5560; FAX: 406-442-5650

Armory Publications, 17171 Bothall Way NE, #276, Seattle, WA 98155 / 206-364-7653; FAX: 206-362-9413 armorypub@aol.com www.grocities.com/armorypub

Armoury, Inc., The, Rt. 202, Box 2340, New Preston, CT 06777 / 860-868-0001; FAX: 860-868-2919

Arms & Armour Press, Wellington House, 125 Strand, London, WC2R 0BB ENGLAND / 0171-420-5555; FAX: 0171-240-7265

Arms Corporation of the Philippines, Bo. Parang Marikina, Metro Manila, PHILIPPINES / 632-941-6243; or 632-941-6244; FAX: 632-942-0682

Arms Craft Gunsmithing, 1106 Linda Dr., Arroyo Grande, CA 93420 / 805-481-2830

Arms Ingenuity Co., P.O. Box 1, 51 Canal St., Weatogue, CT 06089 / 203-658-5624

Arms Software, 4851 SW Madrona St., Lake Oswego, OR 97035 / 800-366-5559; or 503-697-0533; FAX: 503-697-3337

Arms, Programming Solutions (See Arms Software)

Armscorp USA, Inc., 4424 John Ave., Baltimore, MD 21227 / 410-247-6200; FAX: 410-247-6205 info@armscorpusa.com www.armscorpusa.com

Arnold Arms Co., Inc., P.O. Box 1011, Arlington, WA 98223 / 800-371-1011; or 360-435-1011; FAX: 360-435-7304

Aro-Tek Ltd., 206 Frontage Rd. North, Suite C, Pacific, WA 98047 / 206-351-2984; FAX: 206-833-4483

Arratoonian, Andy (See Horseshoe Leather Products)

Arrieta S.L., Morkaiko 5, 20870, Elgoibar, SPAIN / 34-43-743150; FAX: 34-43-743154

Art Jewel Enterprises Ltd., Eagle Business Ctr., 460 Randy Rd., Carol Stream, IL 60188 / 708-260-0400

Artistry in Wood, 134 Zimmerman Rd., Kalispell, MT 59901 / 406-257-9003; FAX: 406-257-9167 merlins@digisys.net www.acrabondlaminates.com

Art's Gun & Sport Shop, Inc., 6008 Hwy. Y, Hillsboro, MO 63050

Arundel Arms & Ammunition, Inc., A., 24A Defense St., Annapolis, MD 21401 / 410-224-8683

Arvo Ojala Holsters, P.O. Box 98, N. Hollywood, CA 91603 / 818-222-9700; FAX: 818-222-0401

Ashby, David. See: ASHBY TURKEY CALLS

Ashby Turkey Calls, David L. Ashby, P.O. Box 1653, Ozark, MO 65721-1653

Ashley Outdoors, Inc., 2401 Ludelle St, Fort Worth, TX 76105 / 888-744-4880; FAX: 800-734-7939

Aspen Outfitting Co., Jon Hollinger, 9 Dean St, Aspen, CO 81611 / 970-925-3406

A-Square Company, Inc., 1230 S. Hurstbourne Parkway, Liberty Center II, Suite 220, Louisville, KY 40222 / 502-719-3006; FAX: 502-719-3030

Astra Sport, S.A., Apartado 3, 48300 Guernica, Espagne, SPAIN / 34-4-6250100; FAX: 34-4-6255186

Atamec-Bretton, 19 rue Victor Grignard, F-42026, St.-Etienne (Cedex 1, / 77-93-54-69; FAX: 33-77-93-57-98

Atlanta Cutlery Corp., 2143 Gees Mill Rd., Box 839 CIS, Conyers, GA 30207 / 800-883-0300; FAX: 404-388-0246

Atlantic Mills, Inc., 1295 Towbin Ave., Lakewood, NJ 08701-5934 / 800-242-7374

Atlantic Rose, Inc., P.O. Box 10717, Bradenton, FL 34282-0717

Atsko/Sno-Seal, Inc., 2664 Russell St., Orangeburg, SC 29115 / 803-531-1820; FAX: 803-531-2139

Auguste Francotte & Cie S.A., rue du Trois Juin 109, 4400 Herstal-Liege, BELGIUM / 32-4-248-13-18; FAX: 32-4-948-11-79

Austin & Halleck, Inc., 2150 South 950 East, Provo, UT 84606-6285 / 800-821-5783; or 801-374-9990; FAX: 801-374-9998

Austin Sheridan USA, Inc., P.O. Box 577, 36 Haddam Quarter Rd., Durham, CT 06422 / 860-349-1772; FAX: 860-349-1771; swalzer@palm.net

Autauga Arms, Inc., Pratt Plaza Mall No. 13, Prattville, AL 36067 / 800-262-9563; FAX: 334-361-2961

Auto Arms, 738 Clearview, San Antonio, TX 78228 / 512-434-5450

Automatic Equipment Sales, 627 E. Railroad Ave., Salesburg, MD 21801

Auto-Ordnance Corp., PO Box 220, Blauvelt, NY 10913 / 914-353-7770

Autumn Sales, Inc. (Blaser), 1320 Lake St., Fort Worth, TX 76102 / 817-335-1634; FAX: 817-338-0119

Avnda Otaola Norica, 16 Apartado 68, 20600, Eibar,

AWC Systems Technology, P.O. Box 41938, Phoenix, AZ 85080-1938 / 602-780-1050; FAX: 602-780-2967

Axtell Rifle Co., 353 Mill Creek Road, Sheridan, MT 59749 / 406-842-5814

AYA (See U.S. Importer-New England Custom Gun Serv

B

B & P America, 12321 Brittany Cir, Dallas, TX 75230 / 972-726-9069

B&D Trading Co., Inc., 3935 Fair Hill Rd., Fair Oaks, CA 95628 / 800-334-3790; or 916-967-9366; FAX: 916-967-4873

B.A.C., 17101 Los Modelos St., Fountain Valley, CA 92708 / 435-586-3286

B.B. Walker Co., PO Box 1167, 414 E Dixie Dr, Asheboro, NC 27203 / 910-625-1380; FAX: 910-625-8125

B.C. Outdoors, Larry McGhee, PO Box 61497, Boulder City, NV 89006 / 702-294-3056; FAX: 702-294-0413 jdalton@pmcammo.com www.pmcammo.com

B.M.F. Activator, Inc., 12145 Mill Creek Run, Plantersville, TX 77363 / 936-894-2397; or 800-527-2881; FAX: 936-894-2397

Badger Shooters Supply, Inc., P.O. Box 397, Owen, WI 54460 / 800-424-9069; FAX: 715-229-2332

Baekgaard Ltd., 1855 Janke Dr., Northbrook, IL 60062 / 708-498-3040; FAX: 708-493-3106

Baelder, Harry, Alte Goennebeker Strasse 5, 24635, Rickling, GERMANY / 04328-722732; FAX: 04328-722733

Baer Custom, Inc, Les, 29601 34th Ave, Hillsdale, IL 61257 / 309-658-2716; FAX: 309-658-2610

Baer's Hollows, P.O. Box 284, Eads, CO 81036 / 719-438-5718

Bagmaster Mfg., Inc., 2731 Sutton Ave., St. Louis, MO 63143 / 314-781-8002; FAX: 314-781-3363

Bain & Davis, Inc., 307 E. Valley Blvd., San Gabriel, CA 91776-3522 / 626-573-4241 baindavis@aol.com

Baker, Stan, 10000 Lake City Way, Seattle, WA 98125 / 206-522-4575

Baker's Leather Goods, Roy, PO Box 893, Magnolia, AR 71754 / 870-234-0344 pholsters@ipa.net

Bald Eagle Precision Machine Co., 101-A Allison St., Lock Haven, PA 17745 / 570-748-6772; FAX: 570-748-4443

Balickie, Joe, 408 Trelawney Lane, Apex, NC 27502 / 919-362-5185

Ballard, Donald. See: BALLARD INDUSTRIES

Ballard Industries, Donald Ballard Sr., PO Box 2035, Arnold, CA 95223 / 408-996-0957; FAX: 408-257-6828

Ballard Rifle & Cartridge Co., LLC, 113 W Yellowstone Ave, Cody, WY 82414 / 307-587-4914; FAX: 307-527-6097 ballard@wyoming.com

Ballistic Product, Inc., 20015 75th Ave. North, Corcoran, MN 55340-9456 / 763-494-9237; FAX: 763-494-9236 info@ballisticproducts.com www.ballisticproducts.com

Ballistic Research, 1108 W. May Ave., McHenry, IL 60050 / 815-385-0037

Ballisti-Cast, Inc., 6347 49th St. NW, Plaza, ND 58771 / 701-497-3333; FAX: 701-497-3335

Bandcor Industries, Div. of Man-Sew Corp., 6108 Sherwin Dr., Port Richey, FL 34668 / 813-848-0432

Bang-Bang Boutique (See Holster Shop, The)

Banks, Ed, 2762 Hwy. 41 N., Ft. Valley, GA 31030 / 912-987-4665

Bansner's Ultimate Rifles, LLC, P.O. Box 839, 261 E. Main St., Adamstown, PA 19501 / 717-484-2370; FAX: 717-484-0523 bansner@aol.com

Barbour, Inc., 55 Meadowbrook Dr., Milford, NH 03055 / 603-673-1313; FAX: 603-673-6510

Barnes, 4347 Tweed Dr., Eau Claire, WI 54703-6302

Barnes Bullets, Inc., P.O. Box 215, American Fork, UT 84003 / 801-756-4222; or 800-574-9200; FAX: 801-756-2465 email@barnesbullets.com barnesbullets.com

Baron Technology, 62 Spring Hill Rd., Trumbull, CT 06611 / 203-452-0515; FAX: 203-452-0663 dbaron@baronengraving.com www.baronengraving.com

Barraclough, John K., 55 Merit Park Dr., Gardena, CA 90247 / 310-324-2574

Barramundi Corp., P.O. Drawer 4259, Homosassa Springs, FL 32687 / 904-628-0200

Barrett Firearms Manufacturer, Inc., P.O. Box 1077, Murfreesboro, TN 37133 / 615-896-2938; FAX: 615-896-7313

Barry Lee Hands Engraving, 26192 E. Shore Route, Bigfork, MT 59911 / 406-837-0035

Bar-Sto Precision Machine, 73377 Sullivan Rd., PO Box 1838, Twentynine Palms, CA 92277 / 760-367-2747; FAX: 760-367-2407 barsto@eee.org www.barsto.com

Barta's Gunsmithing, 10231 US Hwy. 10, Cato, WI 54230 / 920-732-4472

Barteaux Machete, 1916 SE 50th Ave., Portland, OR 97215-3238 / 503-233-5880

Bartlett Engineering, 40 South 200 East, Smithfield, UT 84335-1645 / 801-563-5910

Basics Information Systems, Inc., 1141 Georgia Ave., Suite 515, Wheaton, MD 20902 / 301-949-1070; FAX: 301-949-5326

Bates Engraving, Billy, 2302 Winthrop Dr. SW, Decatur, AL 35603 / 256-355-3690 bbrn@aol.com

Battenfeld Technologies, 5875 W. Van Horn Tavern Rd., Columbia, MO 65203 / 573-445-9200; FAX: 573-447-4158 battenfeldtechnologies.com

Bauer, Eddie, 15010 NE 36th St., Redmond, WA 98052

Baumgartner Bullets, 3011 S. Alane St., W. Valley City, UT 84120

Bauska Barrels, 105 9th Ave. W., Kalispell, MT 59901 / 406-752-7706

Bear Archery, RR 4, 4600 Southwest 41st Blvd., Gainesville, FL 32601 / 904-376-2327

Bear Arms, 374-A Carson Road, St. Mathews, SC 29135

Bear Mountain Gun & Tool, 120 N. Plymouth, New Plymouth, ID 83655 / 208-278-5221; FAX: 208-278-5221

Beartooth Bullets, PO Box 491, Dept. HLD, Dover, ID 83825-0491 / 208-448-1865 bullets@beartoothbullets.com; beartoothbullets.com

Beaver Lodge (See Fellowes, Ted)

Beaver Park Product, Inc., 840 J St., Penrose, CO 81240 / 719-372-6744

BEC, Inc., 1227 W. Valley Blvd., Suite 204, Alhambra, CA 91803 / 626-281-5751; FAX: 626-293-7073

Beeks, Mike. See: GRAYBACK WILDCATS

Beeman Precision Airguns, 5454 Argosy Dr., Huntington Beach, CA 92649 / 714-890-4800; FAX: 714-890-4808

Behlert Precision, Inc., P.O. Box 288, 7067 Easton Rd., Pipersville, PA 18947 / 215-766-8681; or 215-766-7301; FAX: 215-766-8681

Beitzinger, George, 116-20 Atlantic Ave., Richmond Hill, NY 11419 / 718-847-7661

Belding's Custom Gun Shop, 10691 Sayers Rd., Munith, MI 49259 / 517-596-2388

Bell & Carlson, Inc., Dodge City Industrial Park, 101 Allen Rd., Dodge City, KS 67801 / 800-634-8586; or 620-225-6688; FAX: 620-225-6688 email@belland carlson.com www.belland carlson.com

Bell Reloading, Inc., 1725 Harlin Lane Rd., Villa Rica, GA 30180

Bell's Gun & Sport Shop, 3309-19 Mannheim Rd, Franklin Park, IL 60131

Bell's Legendary Country Wear, 22 Circle Dr., Bellmore, NY 11710 / 516-679-1158

Belltown Ltd., 11 Camps Rd., Kent, CT 06757 / 860-354-5750; FAX: 860-354-6764

Ben William's Gun Shop, 1151 S. Cedar Ridge, Duncanville, TX 75137 / 214-780-1807

Benchmark Knives (See Gerber Legendary Blades)

Benelli Armi S.p.A., Via della Stazione, 61029, Urbino, ITALY / 39-722-307-1; FAX: 39-722-327427

Benelli USA Corp, 17603 Indian Head Hwy, Accokeek, MD 20607 / 301-283-6981; FAX: 301-283-6988 benelliusa.com

Bengtson Arms Co., L., 6345-B E. Akron St., Mesa, AZ 85205 / 602-981-6375

Benjamin/Sheridan Co., Crossman, Rts. 5 and 20, E. Bloomfield, NY 14443 / 716-657-6161; FAX: 716-657-5405; www.crosman.com

Ben's Machines, 1151 S. Cedar Ridge, Duncanville, TX 75137 / 214-780-1807; FAX: 214-780-0316

Bentley, John, 128-D Watson Dr., Turtle Creek, PA 15145

Beomat of America, Inc., 300 Railway Ave., Campbell, CA 95008 / 408-379-4829

Beretta S.p.A., Pietro, Via Beretta, 18-25063, Gardone V.T., ITALY / 39-30-8341-1; FAX: 39-30-8341-421

Beretta U.S.A. Corp., 17601 Beretta Drive, Accokeek, MD 20607 / 301-283-2191; FAX: 301-283-0435

Berger Bullets Ltd., 5443 W. Westwind Dr., Glendale, AZ 85310 / 602-842-4001; FAX: 602-934-9083

Bernardelli, Vincenzo, P.O. Box 460243, Houston, TX 77056-8243 www.bernardelli.com

Bernardelli S.p.A., Vincenzo, 125 Via Matteotti, PO Box 74, Brescia, ITALY / 39-30-8912851-2-3; FAX: 39-30-8910249

Berry's Mfg., Inc., 401 North 3050 East St., St. George, UT 84770 / 435-634-1682; FAX: 435-634-1683 sales@berrysmfg.com www.berrysmfg.com

Bersa S.A., Benso Bonadimani, Gonzales Castillo 312, 1704, Ramos Mejia, ARGENTINA / 011-4656-2377; FAX: 011-4656-2093+

Bert Johanssons Vapentillbehor, S-430 20 Veddige, SWEDEN,

Bertuzzi (See U.S. Importer-New England Arms Co)

Better Concepts Co., 663 New Castle Rd., Butler, PA 16001 / 412-285-9000

Beverly, Mary, 3201 Horseshoe Trail, Tallahassee, FL 32312

Bianchi International, Inc., 100 Calle Cortez, Temecula, CA 92590 / 909-676-5621; FAX: 909-676-6777

Biesen, Al, 5021 Rosewood, Spokane, WA 99208 / 509-328-9340

Biesen, Roger, 5021 W. Rosewood, Spokane, WA 99208 / 509-328-9340

Big Bear Arms & Sporting Goods, Inc., 1112 Milam Way, Carrollton, TX 75006 / 972-416-8051; or 800-400-BEAR; FAX: 972-416-0771

Big Bore Bullets of Alaska, PO Box 521455, Big Lake, AK 99652 / 907-373-2673; FAX: 907-373-2673 doug@mtaonline.net ww.awloo.com/bbb/index.

Big Bore Express, 16345 Midway Rd., Nampa, ID 83651 / 208-466-9975; FAX: 208-466-6927 bigbore.com

Big Sky Racks, Inc., P.O. Box 729, Bozeman, MT 59771-0729 / 406-586-9393; FAX: 406-585-7378

Big Spring Enterprises "Bore Stores", P.O. Box 1115, Big Spring Rd., Yellville, AR 72687 / 870-449-5297; FAX: 870-449-4446

Bilal, Mustafa, 908 NW 50th St., Seattle, WA 98107-3634 / 206-782-4164

Bilinski, Bryan. See: FIELDSPORT LTD.

Bill Austin's Calls, Box 284, Kaycee, WY 82639 / 307-738-2552

Bill Adair Custom Shop, 2886 Westridge, Carrollton, TX 75006 / 972-418-0950

Bill Hanus Birdguns LLC, PO Box 533, Newport, OR 97365 / 541-265-7433; FAX: 541-265-7400 www.billhanusbirdguns.com

Bill Wiseman and Co., P.O. Box 3427, Bryan, TX 77805 / 409-690-3456; FAX: 409-690-0156

Billeb, Stephenn. See: QUALITY CUSTOM FIREARMS

Billings Gunsmiths Inc., 1841 Grand Ave., Billings, MT 59102 / 406-256-8390

Billingsley & Brownell, P.O. Box 25, Dayton, WY 82836 / 307-655-9344

Bill's Custom Cases, P.O. Box 2, Dunsmuir, CA 96025 / 530-235-0177; FAX: 530-235-4959 billscustomcases@mindspring.com

Bill's Gun Repair, 1007 Burlington St., Mendota, IL 61342 / 815-539-5786

Billy Bates Engraving, 2302 Winthrop Dr. SW, Decatur, AL 35603 / 256-355-3690 bbrn@aol.com

Birchwood Casey, 7900 Fuller Rd., Eden Prairie, MN 55344 / 800-328-6156; or 612-937-7933; FAX: 612-937-7979

Birdsong & Assoc., W. E., 1435 Monterey Rd, Florence, MS 39073-9748 / 601-366-8270

Bismuth Cartridge Co., 3500 Maple Ave., Suite 1650, Dallas, TX 75219 / 214-521-5880; FAX: 214-521-9035

Bison Studios, 1409 South Commerce St., Las Vegas, NV 89102 / 702-388-2891; FAX: 702-383-9967

Bitterroot Bullet Co., PO Box 412, 2001 Cedar Ave., Lewiston, ID 83501-0412 / 208-743-5635; FAX: 208-743-5635 brootbil@lewiston.com

BKL Technologies, PO Box 5237, Brownsville, TX 78523

Black Belt Bullets (See Big Bore Express)

Black Hills Ammunition, Inc., P.O. Box 3090, Rapid City, SD 57709-3090 / 605-348-5150; FAX: 605-348-9827

Black Hills Shooters Supply, P.O. Box 4220, Rapid City, SD 57709 / 800-289-2506

Black Powder Products, 67 Township Rd. 1411, Chesapeake, OH 45619 / 614-867-8047

Black Sheep Brand, 3220 W. Gentry Parkway, Tyler, TX 75702 / 903-592-3853; FAX: 903-592-0527

Blacksmith Corp., PO Box 280, North Hampton, OH 45349 / 800-531-2665; FAX: 937-969-8399 bcbooks@glasscity.net

BlackStar AccuMax Barrels, 11501 Brittmoore Park Drive, Houston, TX 77041 / 281-721-6040; FAX: 281-721-6041

BlackStar Barrel Accurizing (See BlackStar AccuMax

Blacktail Mountain Books, 42 First Ave. W., Kalispell, MT 59901 / 406-257-5573

Blair Engraving, Jim, PO Box 64, Glenrock, WY 82637 / 307-436-8115

Blammo Ammo, P.O. Box 1677, Seneca, SC 29679 / 803-882-1768

Blaser Jagdwaffen GmbH, D-88316, Isny Im Allgau, GERMANY

Bleile, C. Roger, 5040 Ralph Ave., Cincinnati, OH 45238 / 513-251-0249

Blount, Inc., Sporting Equipment Div., 2299 Snake River Ave., PO Box 856, Lewiston, ID 83501 / 800-627-3640; or 208-746-2351; FAX: 208-799-3904

Blount/Outers, PO Box 39, Onalaska, WI 54650 / 608-781-5800; FAX: 608-781-0368

Blue and Gray Products Inc (See Ox-Yoke Originals

Blue Book Publications, Inc., 8009 34th Ave. S. Ste. 175, Minneapolis, MN 55425 / 800-877-4867; or 612-854-5229; FAX: 612-853-1486 bluebook@bluebookinc.com www.bluebookinc.com

Blue Mountain Bullets, HC 77, PO Box 231, John Day, OR 97845 / 541-820-4594

Blue Ridge Machinery & Tools, Inc., PO Box 536-GD, Hurricane, WV 25526 / 800-872-6500; FAX: 304-562-5311 blueridgemachine@worldnet.att.net blueridgemachiney.com

BMC Supply, Inc., 26051 - 179th Ave. S.E., Kent, WA 98042

Bob Allen Co.214 SW Jackson, P.O. Box 477, Des Moines, IA 50315 / 800-685-7020; FAX: 515-283-0779

Bob Rogers Gunsmithing, PO Box 305, 344 S. Walnut St., Franklin Grove, IL 61031 / 815-456-2685; FAX: 815-456-2777

Bob's Gun Shop, P.O. Box 200, Royal, AR 71968 / 501-767-1970; FAX: 501-767-1970 gunparts@hsnp.com www.gun-parts.com

Bob's Tactical Indoor Shooting Range & Gun Shop, 90 Lafayette Rd., Salisbury, MA 01952 / 508-465-5561

Boessler, Erich, Am Vogeltal 3, 97702, Munnerstadt, GERMANY

Boker USA, Inc., 1550 Balsam Street, Lakewood, CO 80215 / 303-462-0662; FAX: 303-462-0668 sales@bokerusa.com bokerusa.com

Boltin, John M., PO Box 644, Estill, SC 29918 / 803-625-2185

Bo-Mar Tool & Mfg. Co., 6136 State Hwy 300, Longview, TX 75604 / 903-759-4784; FAX: 903-759-9141 marykor@earthlink.net bo-mar.com

Bonadimani, Benso. See: BERSA S.A.

Bonanza (See Forster Products), 310 E Lanark Ave, Lanark, IL 61046 / 815-493-6360; FAX: 815-493-2371

Bond Arms, Inc., PO Box 1296, Granbury, TX 76048 / 817-573-4445; FAX: 817-573-5636

Bond Custom Firearms, 8954 N. Lewis Ln., Bloomington, IN 47408 / 812-332-4519

Bondini Paolo, Via Sorrento 345, San Carlo di Cesena, ITALY / 0547-663-240; FAX: 0547-663-780

Bone Engraving, Ralph, 718 N Atlanta, Owasso, OK 74055 / 918-272-9745

Boone Trading Co., Inc., PO Box 669, Brinnon, WA 98320 / 800-423-1945; or 360-796-4330; FAX: 360-796-4511 sales@boonetrading.com boonetrading.com

Boone's Custom Ivory Grips, Inc., 562 Coyote Rd., Brinnon, WA 98320 / 206-796-4330

Boonie Packer Products, PO Box 12517, Salem, OR 97309-0517 / 800-477-3244; or 503-581-3244; FAX: 503-581-3191; booniepacker@aol.com booniepacker.com

Borden Ridges Rimrock Stocks, RR 1 Box 250 BC, Springville, PA 18844 / 570-965-2505; FAX: 570-965-2328

Borden Rifles Inc, RD 1 Box, 250BC, Springville, PA 18844 / 717-965-2505; FAX: 717-965-2328

Border Barrels Ltd., Riccarton Farm, Newcastleton, SCOTLAND UK

Borovnik KG, Ludwig, 9170 Ferlach, Bahnhofstrasse 7, AUSTRIA / 042 27 24 42; FAX: 042 26 43 49

Bosis (See U.S. Importer-New England Arms Co.)

Boss Manufacturing Co., 221 W. First St., Kewanee, IL 61443 / 309-852-2131; or 800-447-4581; FAX: 309-852-0848

Bostick Wildlife Calls, Inc., P.O. Box 728, Estill, SC 29918 / 803-625-2210; or 803-625-4512

Bowen Classic Arms Corp., PO Box 67, Louisville, TN 37777 / 865-984-3583 www.bowenclassicarms.com

Bowen Knife Co., Inc., P.O. Box 590, Blackshear, GA 31516 / 912-449-4794

Bowerly, Kent, 710 Golden Pheasant Dr, Redmond, OR 97756 / 541-595-6028

Boyds' Gunstock Industries, Inc., 25376 403RD AVE, MITCHELL, SD 57301 / 605-996-5011; FAX: 605-996-9878

Brace, Larry D., 771 Blackfoot Ave., Eugene, OR 97404 / 541-688-1278; FAX: 541-607-5833

Bradley Gunsight Co., P.O. Box 340, Plymouth, VT 05056 / 860-589-0531; FAX: 860-582-6294

Brass Eagle, Inc., 7050A Bramalea Rd., Unit 19, Mississauga,, ON L4Z 1C7 CANADA / 416-848-4844

Brauer Bros., 1520 Washington Avenue., St. Louis, MO 63103 / 314-231-2864; FAX: 314-249-4952 www.brauerbros.com

Break-Free, Inc., 1035 S Linwood Ave., Santa Ana, CA 92705 / 714-953-1900; FAX: 714-953-0402

Brenneke KG, Wilhelm, PO Box 1646, 30837 Langenhagen, GERMANY / 0511-97262-0; FAX: 0511-97262-62 info@brenneke.de; www.brenneke.com

Bridgeman Products, Harry Jaffin, 153 B Cross Slope Court, Englishtown, NJ 07726 / 732-536-3604; FAX: 732-972-1004

Bridgers Best, P.O. Box 1410, Berthoud, CO 80513

Briese Bullet Co., Inc., RR1, Box 108, Tappen, ND 58487 / 701-327-4578; FAX: 701-327-4579

Brigade Quartermasters, 1025 Cobb International Blvd., Dept. VH, Kennesaw, GA 30144-4300 / 404-428-1248; or 800-241-3125; FAX: 404-426-7726

Briganti, A.J., 512 Rt. 32, Highland Mills, NY 10930 / 914-928-9573

Briley Mfg. Inc., 1230 Lumpkin, Houston, TX 77043 / 800-331-5718; or 713-932-6995; FAX: 713-932-1043

British Antiques, PO Box 35369, Tucson, AZ 85740 / 520-575-9063 britishantiques@hotmail.com

British Sporting Arms, RR1, Box 130, Millbrook, NY 12545 / 914-677-8303

Broad Creek Rifle Works, Ltd., 120 Horsey Ave., Laurel, DE 19956 / 302-875-5446; FAX: 302-875-1448 bcrw4guns@aol.com

Brockman's Custom Gunsmithing, P.O. Box 357, Gooding, ID 83330 / 208-934-5050

Brocock Ltd., 43 River Street, Digbeth, Birmingham, B5 5SA ENGLAND / 011-021-773-1200; FAX: 011-021-773-1211 sales@brocock.co.un www.brocock.co.uk

Broken Gun Ranch, 10739 126 Rd., Spearville, KS 67876 / 316-385-2587; FAX: 316-385-2597

Brooker, Dennis, Rt. 1, Box 12A, Derby, IA 50068 / 515-533-2103

Brooks Tactical Systems, 279-C Shorewood Ct., Fox Island, WA 98333 / 253-549-2866 FAX: 253-549-2703 brooks@brookstactical.com www.brookstactical.com

Brown, H. R. (See Silhouette Leathers)

Brown Co., E. Arthur, 3404 Pawnee Dr, Alexandria, MN 56308 / 320-762-8847

Brown Dog Ent., 2200 Calle Camelia, 1000 Oaks, CA 91360 / 805-497-2318; FAX: 805-497-1618

Brown Precision, Inc., 7786 Molinos Ave., Los Molinos, CA 96055 / 530-384-2506; FAX: 916-384-1638 www.brownprecision.com

Brown Products, Inc., Ed, 43825 Muldrow Trail, Perry, MO 63462 / 573-565-3261; FAX: 573-565-2791 www.edbrown.com

Brownells, Inc., 200 S. Front St., Montezuma, IA 50171 / 641-623-5401; FAX: 641-623-3896 orderdesk@brownells.com; www.brownells.com

Browning Arms Co., One Browning Place, Morgan, UT 84050 / 801-876-2711; FAX: 801-876-3331

Browning Arms Co. (Parts & Service), 3005 Arnold Tenbrook Rd., Arnold, MO 63010 / 617-287-6800; FAX: 617-287-9751

BRP, Inc. High Performance Cast Bullets, 1210 Alexander Rd., Colorado Springs, CO 80909 / 719-633-0658

Brunton U.S.A., 620 E. Monroe Ave., Riverton, WY 82501 / 307-856-6559; FAX: 307-856-1840

Bryan & Assoc., R D Sauls, PO Box 5772, Anderson, SC 29623-5772 / 864-261-6810 bryanandac@aol.com www.huntersweb.com/bryanandac

Brynin, Milton, P.O. Box 383, Yonkers, NY 10710 / 914-779-4333

BSA Guns Ltd., Armoury Rd. Small Heath, Birmingham, ENGLAND / 011-021-772-8543; FAX: 011-021-773-084

BSA Optics, 3911 SW 47th Ave. Ste. 914, Ft Lauderdale, FL 33314 / 954-581-2144; FAX: 954-581-3165 4inforbasaoptics.com www.bsaoptics.com

B-Square Company, Inc., ;, P.O. Box 11281, 2708 St. Louis Ave., Ft. Worth, TX 76110 / 817-923-0964; or 800-433-2909; FAX: 817-926-7012

Buchsenmachermeister, P. Hofer Jagdwaffen, Buchsenmachermeister, Kirchgasse 24 A-9170, Ferlach, AUSTRIA / 43 4227 3683; FAX: 43 4227 368330 peterhofer@hoferwaffen.com www.hoferwaffen.com

Buck Knives, Inc., 1900 Weld Blvd., P.O. Box 1267, El Cajon, CA 92020 / 619-449-1100; or 800-326-2825; FAX: 619-562-5774 8

Buck Stix--SOS Products Co., Box 3, Neenah, WI 54956

Buck Stop Lure Co., Inc., 3600 Grow Rd. NW, P.O. Box 636, Stanton, MI 48888 / 517-762-5091; FAX: 517-762-5124

Buckeye Custom Bullets, 6490 Stewart Rd., Elida, OH 45807 / 419-641-4463

Buckhorn Gun Works, 8109 Woodland Dr., Black Hawk, SD 57718 / 605-787-6472

Buckskin Bullet Co., P.O. Box 1893, Cedar City, UT 84721 / 435-586-3286

Buckskin Machine Works, A. Hunkeler, 3235 S. 358th St., Auburn, WA 98001 / 206-927-5412

Budin, Dave, Main St., Margaretville, NY 12455 / 914-568-4103; FAX: 914-586-4105

Budin, Dave. See: DEL-SPORTS, INC.

Buenger Enterprises/Goldenrod Dehumidifier, 3600 S. Harbor Blvd., Oxnard, CA 93035 / 800-451-6797; or 805-985-5828; FAX: 805-985-1534

Buffalo Arms Co., 99 Raven Ridge, Sandpoint, ID 83864 / 208-263-6953; FAX: 208-265-2096 www.buffaloarms.com

Buffalo Bullet Co., Inc., 12637 Los Nietos Rd., Unit A, Santa Fe Springs, CA 90670 / 800-423-8069; FAX: 562-944-5054

Buffalo Rock Shooters Supply, R.R. 1, Ottawa, IL 61350 / 815-433-2471

Buffer Technologies, P.O. Box 104930, Jefferson City, MO 65110 / 573-634-8529; FAX: 573-634-8522

MANUFACTURER'S DIRECTORY

Bull Mountain Rifle Co., 6327 Golden West Terrace, Billings, MT 59106 / 406-656-0778

Bullberry Barrel Works, Ltd., 2430 W. Bullberry Ln. 67-5, Hurricane, UT 84737 / 435-635-9866; FAX: 435-635-0348

Bullet Metals, PO Box 1238, Sierra Vista, AZ 85636 / 520-458-5321; FAX: 520-458-1421 info@theantimonyman.com; bullet_metals.com

Bullet N Press, 1210 James St., Gastonia, NC 28052 / 704-853-0265 gnpress@nemaine.com www.nemaine.com/bnpress

Bullet Swaging Supply Inc., PO Box 1056, 303 McMillan Rd, West Monroe, LA 71291 / 318-387-3266; FAX: 318-387-7779; leblackmon@colla.com

Bullseye Bullets, 1808 Turkey Creek Rd. #9, Plant City, FL 33567 / 800-741-6343 bbullets8100@aol.com

Bull-X, Inc., 520 N. Main, Farmer City, IL 61842 / 309-928-2574; or 800-248-3845; FAX: 309-928-2130

Burkhart Gunsmithing, Don, PO Box 852, Rawlins, WY 82301 / 307-324-6007

Burnham Bros., P.O. Box 1148, Menard, TX 78659 / 915-396-4572; FAX: 915-396-4574

Burris Co., Inc., PO Box 1747, 331 E. 8th St., Greeley, CO 80631 / 970-356-1670; FAX: 970-356-8702

Bushmaster Firearms, 999 Roosevelt Trail, Windham, ME 04062 / 800-998-7928; FAX: 207-892-8068 info@bushmaster.com; www.bushmaster.com

Bushmaster Hunting & Fishing, 451 Alliance Ave., Toronto, ON M6N 2J1 CANADA / 416-763-4040; FAX: 416-763-0623

Bushnell Sports Optics Worldwide, 9200 Cody, Overland Park, KS 66214 / 913-752-3400; or 800-423-3537; FAX: 913-752-3550

Buster's Custom Knives, P.O. Box 214, Richfield, UT 84701 / 801-896-5319

Butler Creek Corp., 290 Arden Dr., Belgrade, MT 59714 / 800-423-8327; or 406-388-1356; FAX: 406-388-7204

Butler Enterprises, 834 Oberting Rd., Lawrenceburg, IN 47025 / 812-537-3584

Butterfield's, 220 San Bruno Ave., San Francisco, CA 94103 / 415-861-7500; FAX: 415-861-0183 arms@butterfields.com; www.butterfields.com

Buzz Fletcher Custom Stockmaker, 117 Silver Road, P.O. Box 189, Taos, NM 87571 / 505-758-3486

C

C&D Special Products (See Claybuster Wads & Harves

C&H Research, 115 Sunnyside Dr., Box 351, Lewis, KS 67552 / 316-324-5445 www.09.net(chr)

C. Palmer Manufacturing Co., Inc., P.O. Box 220, West Newton, PA 15089 / 412-872-8200; FAX: 412-872-8302

C. Sharps Arms Co. Inc./Montana Armory, 100 Centennial Dr., PO Box 885, Big Timber, MT 59011 / 406-932-4353; FAX: 406-932-4443

C.S. Van Gorden & Son, Inc., 1815 Main St., Bloomer, WI 54724 / 715-568-2612

C.W. Erickson's L.L.C., 530 Garrison Ave NE, PO Box 522, Buffalo, MN 55313 / 73-682-3665; FAX: 763-682-4328 www.archerhunter.com

Cabanas (See U.S. Importer-Mandall Shooting Supply

Cabela's, One Cabela Drive, Sidney, NE 69160 / 308-254-5505; FAX: 308-254-8420

Cabinet Mtn. Outfitters Scents & Lures, P.O. Box 766, Plains, MT 59859 / 406-826-3970

Cache La Poudre Rifleworks, 140 N. College, Ft. Collins, CO 80524 / 303-482-6913

Calibre Press, Inc., 666 Dundee Rd., Suite 1607, Northbrook, IL 60062 / 800-323-0037; FAX: 708-498-6869

Cali'co Hardwoods, 3580 Westwind Blvd., Santa Rosa, CA 95403 / 707-546-4045; FAX: 707-546-4027 calicohardwoods@msn.com

Calico Light Weapon Systems, 1489 Greg St., Sparks, NV 89431

California Sights (See Fautheree, Andy)

Cambos Outdoorsman, 532 E. Idaho Ave., Ontario, OR 97914 / 541-889-3135; FAX: 541-889-2633

Cambos Outdoorsman, Fritz Hallberg, 532 E. Idaho Ave., Ontario, OR 97914 / 541-889-3135; FAX: 541-889-2633

Camdex, Inc., 2330 Alger, Troy, ML 48083 / 810-528-2300; FAX: 810-528-0989

Cameron's, 16690 W. 11th Ave., Golden, CO 80401 / 303-279-7365; FAX: 303-628-5413

Camillus Cutlery Co., 54 Main St., Camillus, NY 13031 / 315-672-8111; FAX: 315-672-8832

Campbell, Dick, 20000 Silver Ranch Rd., Conifer, CO 80433 / 303-697-0150; FAX: 303-697-0150

Camp-Cap Products, P.O. Box 3805, Chesterfield, MO 63006 / 314-532-4340; FAX: 314-532-4340

Cannon, Andy. See: CANNON'S

Cannon Safe, Inc., 216 S. 2nd Ave. #BLD-932, San Bernardino, CA 92400 / 310-692-0636; or 800-242-1055; FAX: 310-692-7252

Cannon's, Andy Cannon, Box 1026, 320 Main St., Polson, MT 59860 / 406-887-2048

Canons Delcour, Rue J.B. Cools, B-4040, Herstal, BELGIUM / 32.(0)42.40.61.40; FAX: 32(0)42.40.22.88

Canyon Cartridge Corp., P.O. Box 152, Albertson, NY 11507 FAX: 516-294-8946

Cape Outfitters, 599 County Rd. 206, Cape Girardeau, MO 63701 / 573-335-4103; FAX: 573-335-1555

Caraville Manufacturing, P.O. Box 4545, Thousand Oaks, CA 91359 / 805-499-1234

Carbide Checkering Tools (See J&R Engineering)

Carhartt,Inc., P.O. Box 600, 3 Parklane Blvd., Dearborn, MI 48121 / 800-358-3825; or 313-271-8460; FAX: 313-271-3455

Carl Walther GmbH, B.P. 4325, D-89033, Ulm, GERMANY

Carl Zeiss Inc., 13005 N Kingston Ave, Chester, VA 23836 / 800-441-3005; FAX: 804-530-8481

Carlson, Douglas R, Antique American Firearms, PO Box 71035, Dept GD, Des Moines, IA 50325 / 515-224-6552

Carolina Precision Rifles, 1200 Old Jackson Hwy., Jackson, SC 29831 / 803-827-2069

Carrell, William. See: CARRELL'S PRECISION FIREARMS

Carrell's Precision Firearms, William Carrell, 10346 Shadybrook Dr., Boise, ID 83704-3942

Carry-Lite, Inc., 5203 W. Clinton Ave., Milwaukee, WI 53223 / 414-355-3520; FAX: 414-355-4775

Carter's Gun Shop, 225 G St., Penrose, CO 81240 / 719-372-6240

Cartridge Transfer Group, Pete de Coux, HC 30 Box 932 G, Prescott, AZ 86305-7447 / 928-776-8285; FAX: 928-776-8276; pdbullets@commspeed.net

Cascade Bullet Co., Inc., 2355 South 6th St., Klamath Falls, OR 97601 / 503-884-9316

Cascade Shooters, 2155 N.W. 12th St., Redwood, OR 97756

Case & Sons Cutlery Co., W R, Owens Way, Bradford, PA 16701 / 814-368-4123; or 800-523-6350; FAX: 814-768-5369

Case Sorting System, 12695 Cobblestone Creek Rd., Poway, CA 92064 / 619-486-9340

Cash Mfg. Co., Inc., P.O. Box 130, 201 S. Klein Dr., Waunakee, WI 53597-0130 / 608-849-5664; FAX: 608-849-5664

Caspian Arms, Ltd., 14 North Main St., Hardwick, VT 05843 / 802-472-6454; FAX: 802-472-6709

Cast Performance Bullet Company, PO Box 153, Riverton, WY 82501 / 307-857-2940; FAX: 307-857-3132 castperform@wyoming.com castperformance.com

Casull Arms Corp., P.O. Box 1629, Afton, WY 83110 / 307-886-0200

Cathey Enterprises, Inc., P.O. Box 2202, Brownwood, TX 76804 / 915-643-2553; FAX: 915-643-3653

Cation, 2341 Alger St., Troy, MI 48083 / 810-689-0658; FAX: 810-689-7558

Caywood, Shane J., P.O. Box 321, Minocqua, WI 54548 / 715-277-3866

CBC, Avenida Humberto de Campos 3220, 09400-000, Ribeirao Pires, SP, BRAZIL / 55-11-742-7500; FAX: 55-11-459-7385

CBC-BRAZIL, 3 Cuckoo Lane, Honley, Yorkshire HD7 2BR, ENGLAND / 44-1484-661062; FAX: 44-1484-663709

CCG Enterprises, 5217 E. Belknap St., Halton City, TX 76117 / 800-819-7464

CCI Ammunition, P.O. Box 856, Lewiston, ID 83501 / 208-746-2351 www.cci_ammunition.com

CCL Security Products, 199 Whiting St, New Britain, CT 06051 / 800-733-8588

Cedar Hill Game Calls, Inc., 238 Vic Allen Rd, Downsville, LA 71234 / 318-982-5632; FAX: 318-368-2245

Centaur Systems, Inc., 1602 Foothill Rd., Kalispell, MT 59901 / 406-755-8609; FAX: 406-755-8609

Center Lock Scope Rings, 9901 France Ct., Lakeville, MN 55044 / 612-461-2114

Central Specialties Ltd (See Trigger Lock Division

Century Gun Dist. Inc., 1467 Jason Rd., Greenfield, IN 46140 / 317-462-4524

Century International Arms, Inc., 1161 Holland Dr, Boca Raton, FL 33487

CFVentures, 509 Harvey Dr., Bloomington, IN 47403-1715

CH Tool & Die Co (See 4-D Custom Die Co), 711 N Sandusky St, PO Box 889, Mt Vernon, OH 43050-0889 / 740-397-7214; FAX: 740-397-6600

Chace Leather Products, 507 Alden St., Fall River, MA 02722 / 508-678-7556; FAX: 508-675-9666

Chadick's Ltd., P.O. Box 100, Terrell, TX 75160 / 214-563-7577

Chambers Flintlocks Ltd., Jim, 116 Sams Branch Rd, Candler, NC 28715 / 828-667-8361; FAX: 828-665-0852

Champion Shooters' Supply, P.O. Box 303, New Albany, OH 43054 / 614-855-1603; FAX: 614-855-1209

Champion Target Co., 232 Industrial Parkway, Richmond, IN 47374 / 800-441-4971

Champion's Choice, Inc., 201 International Blvd., LaVergne, TN 37086 / 615-793-4066; FAX: 615-793-4070

Champlin Firearms, Inc., PO Box 3191, Woodring Airport, Enid, OK 73701 / 580-237-7388; FAX: 580-242-6922 info@champlinarms.com www.champlinarms.com

Chapman Academy of Practical Shooting, 4350 Academy Rd., Hallsville, MO 65255 / 573-696-5544; or 573-696-2266

Chapman, J Ken. See: OLD WEST BULLET MOULDS

Chapman Manufacturing Co., 471 New Haven Rd., PO Box 250, Durham, CT 06422 / 860-349-9228; FAX: 860-349-0084 sales@chapmanmfg.com www.chapmanmfg.com

Chapuis Armes, 21 La Gravoux, BP15, 42380, St. Bonnet-le-Chatea, FRANCE / (33)77.50.06.96

Chapuis USA, 416 Business Park, Bedford, KY 40006

Charter 2000, 273 Canal St, Shelton, CT 06484 / 203-922-1652

Checkmate Refinishing, 370 Champion Dr., Brooksville, FL 34601 / 352-799-5774; FAX: 352-799-2986 checkmatecustom.com

Cheddite France S.A., 99 Route de Lyon, F-26501, Bourg-les-Valence, FRANCE / 33-75-56-4545; FAX: 33-75-56-3587; export@cheddite.com

Chelsea Gun Club of New York City Inc., 237 Ovington Ave., Apt. D53, Brooklyn, NY 11209 / 718-836-9422; or 718-833-2704

Chem-Pak Inc., PO Box 2058, Winchester, VA 22604-1258 / 800-336-9828; or 540-667-1341; FAX: 540-722-3993 info@chem-pak.com www.chem-pak.com

Cherry Creek State Park Shooting Center, 12500 E. Belleview Ave., Englewood, CO 80111 / 303-693-1765

Chet Fulmer's Antique Firearms, P.O. Box 792, Rt. 2 Buffalo Lake, Detroit Lakes, MN 56501 / 218-847-7712

CheVron Bullets, RR1, Ottawa, IL 61350 / 815-433-2471

Cheyenne Pioneer Products, PO Box 28425, Kansas City, MO 64188 / 816-413-9196; FAX: 816-455-2859 cheyennepp@aol.com www.cartridgeboxes.com

Chicago Cutlery Co., 1536 Beech St., Terre Haute, IN 47804 / 800-457-2665

Chicasaw Gun Works, 4 Mi. Mkr., Pluto Rd. Box 868, Shady Spring, WV 25918-0868 / 304-763-2848; FAX: 304-763-3725

Chipmunk (See Oregon Arms, Inc.)

Choate Machine & Tool Co., Inc., P.O. Box 218, 116 Lovers Ln., Bald Knob, AR 72010 / 501-724-6193; or 800-972-6390; FAX: 501-724-5873

Christensen Arms, 385 N. 3050 E., St. George, UT 84790 / 435-624-9535; FAX: 435-674-9293

Christie's East, 219 E. 67th St., New York, NY 10021 / 212-606-0406 christics.com

Chu Tani Ind., Inc., P.O. Box 2064, Cody, WY 82414-2064

Chuck's Gun Shop, P.O. Box 597, Waldo, FL 32694 / 904-468-2264

Chuilli, Stephen, 8895 N. Military Trl. Ste., Ste. 201E, Palm Beach Gardens, FL 33410

Churchill (See U.S. Importer-Ellett Bros.)

Churchill, Winston G., 2838 20 Mile Stream Rd., Proctorville, VT 05153 / 802-226-7772

Churchill Glove Co., James, PO Box 298, Centralia, WA 98531 / 360-736-2816; FAX: 360-330-0151

CIDCO, 21480 Pacific Blvd., Sterling, VA 22170 / 703-444-5353

Ciener Inc., Jonathan Arthur, 8700 Commerce St., Cape Canaveral, FL 32920 / 321-868-2200; FAX: 321-868-2201

Cimarron F.A. Co., P.O. Box 906, Fredericksburg, TX 78624-0906 / 210-997-9090; FAX: 210-997-0802

Cincinnati Swaging, 2605 Marlington Ave., Cincinnati, OH 45208

Clark Custom Guns, Inc., 336 Shootout Lane, Princeton, LA 71067 / 318-949-9884; FAX: 318-949-9829

Clark Firearms Engraving, P.O. Box 80746, San Marino, CA 91118 / 818-287-1652

Clarkfield Enterprises, Inc., 1032 10th Ave., Clarkfield, MN 56223 / 612-669-7140

Claro Walnut Gunstock Co., 1235 Stanley Ave., Chico, CA 95928 / 530-342-5188; FAX: 530-342-5199

Classic Arms Company, Rt 1 Box 120F, Burnet, TX 78611 / 512-756-4001

Classic Arms Corp., PO Box 106, Dunsmuir, CA 96025-0106 / 530-235-2000

Classic Old West Styles, 1060 Doniphan Park Circle C, El Paso, TX 79936 / 915-587-0684

Claybuster Wads & Harvester Bullets, 309 Sequoya Dr., Hopkinsville, KY 42240 / 800-922-6287; or 800-284-1746; FAX: 502-885-8088 50

Clean Shot Technologies, 21218 St. Andrews Blvd. Ste 504, Boca Raton, FL 33433 / 888-866-2532

Clearview Mfg. Co., Inc., 413 S. Oakley St., Fordyce, AR 71742 / 501-352-8557; FAX: 501-352-7120

Clearview Products, 3021 N. Portland, Oklahoma City, OK 73107
Cleland's Outdoor World, Inc, 10306 Airport Hwy, Swanton, OH 43558 / 419-865-4713; FAX: 419-865-5865
Clements' Custom Leathercraft, Chas, 1741 Dallas St., Aurora, CO 80010-2018 / 303-364-0403; FAX: 303-739-9824 gryphons@home.com kuntaoslcat.com
Clenzoil Worldwide Corp, Jack Fitzgerald, 25670 1st St., Westlake, OH 44145-1430 / 440-899-0482; FAX: 440-899-0483
Clift Mfg., L. R., 3821 hammonton Rd, Marysville, CA 95901 / 916-755-3390; FAX: 916-755-3393
Clift Welding Supply & Cases, 1332-A Colusa Hwy., Yuba City, CA 95993 / 916-755-3390; FAX: 916-755-3393
Cloward's Gun Shop, 4023 Aurora Ave. N, Seattle, WA 98103 / 206-632-2072
Clymer Mfg. Co., 1645 W. Hamlin Rd., Rochester Hills, MI 48309-3312 / 248-853-5555; FAX: 248-853-1530
C-More Systems, P.O. Box 1750, 7553 Gary Rd., Manassas, VA 20108 / 703-361-2663; FAX: 703-361-5881
Cobalt Mfg., Inc., 4020 Mcewen Rd Ste 180, Dallas, TX 75244-5090 / 817-382-8986; FAX: 817-383-4281
Cobra Enterprises, Inc., 1960 S. Milestone Drive, Suite F, Salt Lake City, UT 84104 FAX: 801-908-8301 www.cobrapistols@networld.com
Cobra Sport S.r.l., Via Caduti Nei Lager No. 1, 56020 San Romano, Montopoli v/Arno (Pi, ITALY / 0039-571-450490; FAX: 0039-571-450492
Coffin, Charles H., 3719 Scarlet Ave., Odessa, TX 79762 / 915-366-4729; FAX: 915-366-4729
Coffin, Jim (See Working Guns)
Coffin, Jim. See: WORKING GUNS
Cogar's Gunsmithing, 206 Redwine Dr., Houghton Lake, MI 48629 / 517-422-4591
Coghlan's Ltd., 121 Irene St., Winnipeg, MB R3T 4C7 CANADA / 204-284-9550; FAX: 204-475-4127
Cold Steel Inc., 3036 Seaborg Ave. Ste. A, Ventura, CA 93003 / 800-255-4716; or 800-624-2363; FAX: 805-642-9727
Cole-Grip, 16135 Cohasset St., Van Nuys, CA 91406 / 818-782-4424
Coleman Co., Inc., 250 N. St. Francis, Wichita, KS 67201
Cole's Gun Works, Old Bank Building, Rt. 4 Box 250, Moyock, NC 27958 / 919-435-2345
Collings, Ronald, 1006 Cielta Linda, Vista, CA 92083
Colonial Arms, Inc., P.O. Box 636, Selma, AL 36702-0636 / 334-872-9455; FAX: 334-872-9540 colonialarms@mindspring.com www.colonialarms.com
Colonial Knife Co., Inc., P.O. Box 3327, Providence, RI 02909 / 401-421-1600; FAX: 401-421-2047
Colonial Repair, 47 NAVARRE ST, ROSLINDALE, MA 02131-4725 / 617-469-4951
Colorado Gunsmithing Academy, RR 3 Box 79B, El Campo, TX 77437 / 719-336-4099; or 800-754-2046; FAX: 719-336-9642
Colorado School of Trades, 1575 Hoyt St., Lakewood, CO 80215 / 800-234-4594; FAX: 303-233-4723
Colorado Sutlers Arsenal (See Cumberland States
Colt Blackpowder Arms Co., 110 8th Street, Brooklyn, NY 11215 / 718-499-4678; FAX: 718-768-8056
Colt's Mfg. Co., Inc., PO Box 1868, Hartford, CT 06144-1868 / 800-962-COLT; or 860-236-6311; FAX: 860-244-1449
Compass Industries, Inc., 104 East 25th St., New York, NY 10010 / 212-473-2614; or 800-221-9904; FAX: 212-353-0826
Compasseco, Ltd., 151 Atkinson Hill Ave., Bardtown, KY 40004 / 502-349-0910
Competition Electronics, Inc., 3469 Precision Dr., Rockford, IL 61109 / 815-874-8001; FAX: 815-874-8181
Competitor Corp. Inc., Appleton Business Center, 30 Tricnit Road Unit 16, New Ipswich, NH 03071 / 603-878-3891; FAX: 603-878-3950
Component Concepts, Inc., 530 S Springbrook Road, Newberg, OR 97132 / 503-554-8095; FAX: 503-554-9370 cci@cybcon.com www.phantomonline.com
Concept Development Corp., 16610 E. Laser Drive, Suite 5, Fountain Hills, AZ 85268-6644
Conetrol Scope Mounts, 10225 Hwy. 123 S., Seguin, TX 78155 / 210-379-3030; or 800-CONETROL; FAX: 210-379-3030
CONKKO, P.O. Box 40, Broomall, PA 19008 / 215-356-0711
Connecticut Shotgun Mfg. Co., P.O. Box 1692, 35 Woodland St., New Britain, CT 06051 / 860-225-6581; FAX: 860-832-8707
Connecticut Valley Classics (See CVC)
Conrad, C. A., 3964 Ebert St., Winston-Salem, NC 27127 / 919-788-5469
Cook Engineering Service, 891 Highbury Rd., Vict, 3133 AUSTRALIA
Cooper Arms, P.O. Box 114, Stevensville, MT 59870 / 406-777-0373; FAX: 406-777-5228

Cooper-Woodward, 3800 Pelican Rd., Helena, MT 59602 / 406-458-3800 dolymama@msn.com
Corbin Mfg. & Supply., Inc., 600 Industrial Circle, P.O. Box 2659, White City, OR 97503 / 541-826-5211; FAX: 541-826-8669
Cor-Bon Bullet & Ammo Co., 1311 Industry Rd., Sturgis, SD 57785 / 800-626-7266; FAX: 800-923-2666
Corkys Gun Clinic, 4401 Hot Springs Dr., Greeley, CO 80634-9226 / 970-330-0516
Corry, John, 861 Princeton Ct., Neshanic Station, NJ 08853 / 908-369-8019
Cosmi Americo & Figlio s.n.c., Via Flaminia 307, Ancona, ITALY / 071-888208; FAX: 39-071-887008
Coulston Products, Inc., P.O. Box 30, 201 Ferry St. Suite 212, Easton, PA 18044-0030 / 215-253-0167; or 800-445-9927; FAX: 215-252-1511
Counter Assault, 120 Industrial Court, Kalispell, MT 59901 / 406-257-4740; FAX: 406-257-6674
Cousin Bob's Mountain Products, 7119 Ohio River Blvd., Ben Avon, PA 15202 / 412-766-5114; FAX: 412-766-5114
Cox, Ed. C., RD 2, Box 192, Prosperity, PA 15329 / 412-228-4984
CP Bullets, 1310 Industrial Hwy #5-6, South Hampton, PA 18966 / 215-953-7264; FAX: 215-953-7275
CQB Training, P.O. Box 1739, Manchester, MO 63011
Craftguard, 3624 Logan Ave., Waterloo, IA 50703 / 319-232-2959; FAX: 319-234-0804
Craig Custom Ltd., Research & Development, 629 E. 10th, Hutchinson, KS 67501 / 316-669-0601
Crandall Tool & Machine Co., 19163 21 Mile Rd., Tustin, MI 49688 / 616-829-4430
Creedmoor Sports, Inc., P.O. Box 1040, Oceanside, CA 92051 / 619-757-5529
Creek Side Metal & Woodcrafters, Fishers Hill, VA 22626 / 703-465-3903
Creighton Audette, 19 Highland Circle, Springfield, VT 05156 / 802-885-2331
Crimson Trace Lasers, 8090 SW Cirrus Dr., Beverton, OR 97008 / 800-442-2406; FAX: 503-627-0166 www.crimsontrace.com
Crit'R Call (See Rocky Mountain Wildlife Products)
Crosman Airguns, Rts. 5 and 20, E. Bloomfield, NY 14443 / 716-657-6161; FAX: 716-657-5405
Crosman Blades (See Coleman Co., Inc.)
Crouse's Country Cover, P.O. Box 160, Storrs, CT 06268 / 860-423-8736
CRR, Inc./Marble's Inc., 420 Industrial Park, P.O. Box 111, Gladstone, MI 49837 / 906-428-3710; FAX: 906-428-3711
Crucelegui, Hermanos (See U.S. Importer-Mandall)
Cryo-Accurizing, 2101 East Olive, Decatur, IL 62526 / 801-395-2796; FAX: 217-423-3075
Cubic Shot Shell Co., Inc., 98 Fatima Dr., Campbell, OH 44405 / 330-755-0349
Cullity Restoration, 209 Old Country Rd., East Sandwich, MA 02537 / 508-888-1147
Cumberland Arms, 514 Shafer Road, Manchester, TN 37355 / 800-797-8414
Cumberland Mountain Arms, P.O. Box 710, Winchester, TN 37398 / 615-967-8414; FAX: 615-967-9199
Cumberland States Arsenal, 1124 Palmyra Road, Clarksville, TN 37040
Cummings Bullets, 1417 Esperanza Way, Escondido, CA 92027
Cupp, Alana, Custom Engraver, PO Box 207, Annabella, UT 84711 / 801-896-4834
Curly Maple Stock Blanks (See Tiger-Hunt)
Curtis Cast Bullets, 527 W. Babcock St., Bozeman, MT 59715 / 406-587-8117; FAX: 406-587-8117
Curtis Custom Shop, RR1, Box 193A, Wallingford, KY 41093 / 703-659-4265
Curtis Gun Shop (See Curtis Cast Bullets)
Custom Bullets by Hoffman, 2604 Peconic Ave., Seaford, NY 11783
Custom Calls, 607 N. 5th St., Burlington, IA 52601 / 319-752-4465
Custom Checkering Service, Kathy Forster, 2124 S.E. Yamhill St., Portland, OR 97214 / 503-236-5874
Custom Chronograph, Inc., 5305 Reese Hill Rd., Sumas, WA 98295 / 360-988-7801
Custom Firearms (See Ahrends, Kim)
Custom Gun Products, 5021 W. Rosewood, Spokane, WA 99208 / 509-328-9340
Custom Gun Stocks, 3062 Turners Bend Rd, McMinnville, TN 37110 / 615-668-3912
Custom Products (See Jones Custom Products)
Custom Quality Products, Inc., 345 W. Girard Ave., P.O. Box 71129, Madison Heights, MI 48071 / 810-585-1616; FAX: 810-585-0644

Custom Riflestocks, Inc., Michael M. Kokolus, 7005 Herber Rd., New Tripoli, PA 18066 / 610-298-3013; FAX: 610-298-2431 mkokolus@prodigy.net
Custom Single Shot Rifles, 9651 Meadows Lane, Guthrie, OK 73044 / 405-282-3634
Custom Stocking, Mike Yee, 29927 56 Pl. S., Auburn, WA 98001 / 253-839-3991
Custom Tackle and Ammo, P.O. Box 1886, Farmington, NM 87499 / 505-632-3539
Cutco Cutlery, P.O. Box 810, Olean, NY 14760 / 716-372-3111
CVA, 5988 Peachtree Corners East, Norcross, GA 30071 / 800-251-9412; FAX: 404-242-8546
CVC, 5988 Peachtree Crns East, Norcross, GA 30071
Cylinder & Slide, Inc., William R. Laughridge, 245 E. 4th St., Fremont, NE 68025 / 402-721-4277; FAX: 402-721-0263
CZ USA, PO Box 171073, Kansas City, KS 66117 / 913-321-1811; FAX: 913-321-4901

D

D&D Gunsmiths, Ltd., 363 E. Elmwood, Troy, MI 48083 / 810-583-1512; FAX: 810-583-1524
D&G Precision Duplicators (See Greene Precision)
D&H Precision Tooling, 7522 Barnard Mill Rd., Ringwood, IL 60072 / 815-653-4011
D&H Prods. Co., Inc., 465 Denny Rd., Valencia, PA 16059 / 412-898-2840; or 800-776-0281; FAX: 412-898-2013
D&J Bullet Co. & Custom Gun Shop, Inc., 426 Ferry St., Russell, KY 41169 / 606-836-2663; FAX: 606-836-2663
D&L Industries (See D.J. Marketing)
D&L Sports, P.O. Box 651, Gillette, WY 82717 / 307-686-4008
D&R Distributing, 308 S.E. Valley St., Myrtle Creek, OR 97457 / 503-863-6850
D.C.C. Enterprises, 259 Wynburn Ave., Athens, GA 30601
D.D. Custom Stocks, R.H. "Dick" Devereaux, 5240 Mule Deer Dr., Colorado Springs, CO 80919 / 719-548-8468
D.J. Marketing, 10602 Horton Ave., Downey, CA 90241 / 310-806-0891; FAX: 310-806-6231
Dade Screw Machine Products, 2319 NW 7th Ave., Miami, FL 33127 / 305-573-5050
Daewoo Precision Industries Ltd., 34-3 Yeoeuido-Dong, Yeongdeungoo-GU 15th Fl., Seoul, KOREA
Daisy Mfg. Co., PO Box 220, Rogers, AR 72757 / 501-621-4210; FAX: 501-636-0573
Dakota (See U.S. Importer-EMF Co., Inc.)
Dakota Arms, Inc., 130 Industry Road, Sturgis, SD 57785 / 605-347-4686; FAX: 605-347-4459 info@dakotaarms.com; dakotaarms.com
Dakota Corp., 77 Wales St., P.O. Box 543, Rutland, VT 05701 / 802-775-6062; or 800-451-4167; FAX: 802-773-3919
Da-Mar Gunsmith's Inc., 102 1st St., Solvay, NY 13209
DAMASCUS-U.S.A., 149 Deans Farm Rd., Tyner, NC 27980 / 252-221-2010; FAX: 252-221-2009
Dan Wesson Firearms, 119 Kemper Lane, Norwich, NY 13815 / 607-336-1174; FAX: 607-336-2730
Danforth, Mikael. See: VEKTOR USA
Dangler, Homer L., 2870 Lee Marie Dr., Adrian, MI 49220 / 517-266-1997
Danner Shoe Mfg. Co., 12722 NE Airport Way, Portland, OR 97230 / 503-251-1100; or 800-345-0430; FAX: 503-251-1119
Dan's Whetstone Co., Inc., 130 Timbs Place, Hot Springs, AR 71913 / 501-767-1616; FAX: 501-767-9598 questions@danswhetstone.com danswhetstone.com
Danuser Machine Co., 550 E. Third St., P.O. Box 368, Fulton, MO 65251 / 573-642-2246; FAX: 573-642-2240
Dara-Nes, Inc. (See Nesci Enterprises, Inc.)
D'Arcy Echols & Co., PO Box 421, Millville, UT 84326 / 435-755-6842
Darlington Gun Works, Inc., P.O. Box 698, 516 S. 52 Bypass, Darlington, SC 29532 / 803-393-3931
Darwin Hensley Gunmaker, PO Box 329, Brightwood, OR 97011 / 503-622-5411
Data Tech Software Systems, 19312 East Eldorado Drive, Aurora, CO 80013
Dave Norin Schrank's Smoke & Gun, 2010 Washington St., Waukegan, IL 60085 / 708-662-4034
Dave's Gun Shop, 555 Wood Street, Powell, WY 82435 / 307-754-9724
David Clark Co., Inc., PO Box 15054, Worcester, MA 01615-0054 / 508-756-6216; FAX: 508-753-5827 sales@davidclark.com davidclark.com
David Condon, Inc., 109 E. Washington St., Middleburg, VA 22117 / 703-687-5642
David Miller Co., 3131 E Greenlee Rd, Tucson, AZ 85716 / 520-326-3117
David R. Chicoine, 1210 Jones Street, Gastonia, NC 28052 / 704-853-0265 gnpress@nemaine.com
David W. Schwartz Custom Guns, 2505 Waller St, Eau Claire, WI 54703 / 715-832-1735

MANUFACTURER'S DIRECTORY

Davide Pedersoli and Co., Via Artigiani 57, Gardone VT, Brescia 25063, ITALY / 030-8912402; FAX: 030-8911019 www.davide_pedersol.com
Davis, Don, 1619 Heights, Katy, TX 77493 / 713-391-3090
Davis Industries (See Cobra Enterprises, Inc.)
Davis Products, Mike, 643 Loop Dr., Moses Lake, WA 98837 / 509-765-6178; or 509-766-7281
Daystate Ltd., Birch House Lanee, Cotes Heath Staffs, ST15.022, ENGLAND / 01782-791755; FAX: 01782-791617
Dayton Traister, 4778 N. Monkey Hill Rd., P.O. Box 593, Oak Harbor, WA 98277 / 360-679-4657; FAX: 360-675-1114
DBI Books Division of Krause Publications, 700 E State St, Iola, WI 54990-0001 / 715-445-2214
D-Boone Ent., Inc., 5900 Colwyn Dr., Harrisburg, PA 17109
de Coux, Pete (See Cartridge Transfer Group)
Dead Eye's Sport Center, 76 Baer Rd., Shickshinny, PA 18655 / 570-256-7432 deadeyeprizz@aol.com
Decker Shooting Products, 1729 Laguna Ave., Schofield, WI 54476 / 715-359-5873; FAX: 715-355-7319
Deepeeka Exports Pvt. Ltd., D-78, Saket, Meerut-250-006, INDIA / 011-91-121-640363 or ; FAX: 011-91-121-640988 deepeeka@poboxes.com www.deepeeka.com
Defense Training International, Inc., 749 S. Lemay, Ste. A3-337, Ft. Collins, CO 80524 / 303-482-2520; FAX: 303-482-0548
Degen Inc. (See Aristocrat Knives)
deHaas Barrels, RR 3, Box 77, Ridgeway, MO 64481 / 816-872-6308
Del Rey Products, P.O. Box 5134, Playa Del Rey, CA 90296-5134 / 213-823-0494
Delhi Gun House, 1374 Kashmere Gate, Delhi, 0110 006 INDIA / 3940814; or 394-0974; FAX: 3917344 dgh@vsnl.com
Delorge, Ed, 6734 W. Main, Houma, LA 70360 / 985-223-0206
Del-Sports, Inc., Dave Budin, Box 685, 817 Main St., Margaretville, NY 12455 / 845-586-4103; FAX: 845-586-4105
Delta Arms Ltd., P.O. Box 1000, Delta, VT 84624-1000
Delta Enterprises, 284 Hagemann Drive, Livermore, CA 94550
Delta Frangible Ammunition LLC, PO Box 2350, Stafford, VA 22555-2350 / 540-720-5778; or 800-339-1933; FAX: 540-720-5667 dfa@dfanet.com www.dfanet.com
Dem-Bart Checkering Tools, Inc., 1825 Bickford Ave., Snohomish, WA 98290 / 360-568-7356; FAX: 360-568-1798
Denver Instrument Co., 6542 Fig St., Arvada, CO 80004 / 800-321-1135; or 303-431-7255; FAX: 303-423-4831
DeSantis Holster & Leather Goods, Inc., P.O. Box 2039, 149 Denton Ave., New Hyde Park, NY 11040-0701 / 516-354-8000; FAX: 516-354-7501
Desert Mountain Mfg., P.O. Box 130184, Coram, MT 59913 / 800-477-0762; or 406-387-5361; FAX: 406-387-5361
Detroit-Armor Corp., 720 Industrial Dr. No. 112, Cary, IL 60013 / 708-639-7666; FAX: 708-639-7694
Devereaux, R.H. "Dick" (See D.D. Custom)
Dewey Mfg. Co., Inc., J., PO Box 2014, Southbury, CT 06488 / 203-264-3064; FAX: 203-262-6907 deweyrods@worldnet.att.net www.deweyrods.com
DGR Custom Rifles, 4191 37th Ave SE, Tappen, ND 58487 / 701-327-8135
DGS, Inc., Dale A. Storey, 1117 E. 12th, Casper, WY 82601 / 307-237-2414; FAX: 307-237-2414 dalest@trib.com www.dgsrifle.com
DHB Products, P.O. Box 3092, Alexandria, VA 22302 / 703-836-2648
Diamond Machining Technology, Inc. (See DMT)
Diamond Mfg. Co., P.O. Box 174, Wyoming, PA 18644 / 800-233-9601
Diana (See U.S. Importer - Dynamit Nobel-RWS, Inc., 81 Ruckman Rd., Closter, NJ 07624 / 201-767-7971; FAX: 201-767-1589
Dibble, Derek A., 555 John Downey Dr., New Britain, CT 06051 / 203-224-2630
Dietz Gun Shop & Range, Inc., 421 Range Rd., New Braunfels, TX 78132 / 210-885-4662
Dilliott Gunsmithing, Inc., 657 Scarlett Rd., Dandridge, TN 37725 / 865-397-9204 gunsmithd@aol.com dilliottgunsmithing.com
Dillon, Ed, 1035 War Eagle Dr. N., Colorado Springs, CO 80919 / 719-598-4929; FAX: 719-598-4929
Dillon Precision Products, Inc., 8009 East Dillon's Way, Scottsdale, AZ 85260 / 480-948-8009; or 800-762-3845; FAX: 480-998-2786 sales@dillonprecision.com www.dillonprecision.com
Dina Arms Corporation, P.O. Box 46, Royersford, PA 19468 / 610-287-0266; FAX: 610-287-0266
Division Lead Co., 7742 W. 61st Pl., Summit, IL 60502
Dixie Gun Works, P.O. Box 130, Union City, TN 38281 / 731-885-0700; FAX: 731-885-0440

Dixon Muzzleloading Shop, Inc., 9952 Kunkels Mill Rd., Kempton, PA 19529 / 610-756-6271 dixonmuzzleloading.com
DKT, Inc., 14623 Vera Drive, Union, MI 49130-9744 / 800-741-7083 orders; FAX: 616-641-2015
DLO Mfg., 10807 SE Foster Ave., Arcadia, FL 33821-7304
DMT--Diamond Machining Technology Inc., 85 Hayes Memorial Dr., Marlborough, MA 01752 FAX: 508-485-3924
Dohring Bullets, 100 W. 8 Mile Rd., Ferndale, MI 48220
Dolbare, Elizabeth, P.O. Box 502, Dubois, WY 82513-0502
Domino, PO Box 108, 20019 Settimo Milanese, Milano, ITALY / 1-39-2-33512040; FAX: 1-39-2-33511587
Donnelly, C. P., 405 Kubli Rd., Grants Pass, OR 97527 / 541-846-6604
Doskocil Mfg. Co., Inc., P.O. Box 1246, 4209 Barnett, Arlington, TX 76017 / 817-467-5116; FAX: 817-472-9810
Douglas Barrels Inc., 5504 Big Tyler Rd., Charleston, WV 25313-1398 / 304-776-1341; FAX: 304-776-8560 www.benchrest.com/douglas
Downsizer Corp., PO Box 710316, Santee, CA 92072-0316 / 619-448-5510; FAX: 619-448-5780 www.downsizer.com
DPMS (Defense Procurement Manufacturing Services, Inc.), 13983 Industry Avenue, Becker, MN 55308 / 800-578-DPMS; or 763-261-5600 FAX: 763-261-5599
Dr. O's Products Ltd., P.O. Box 111, Niverville, NY 12130 / 518-784-3333; FAX: 518-784-2800
Drain, Mark, SE 3211 Kamilche Point Rd., Shelton, WA 98584 / 206-426-5452
Dremel Mfg. Co., 4915-21st St., Racine, WI 53406
Dri-Slide, Inc., 411 N. Darling, Fremont, MI 49412 / 616-924-3950
Dropkick, 1460 Washington Blvd., Williamsport, PA 17701 / 717-326-6561; FAX: 717-326-4950
DS Arms, Inc., P.O. Box 370, 27 West 990 Industrial Ave., Barrington, IL 60010 / 847-277-7258; FAX: 847-277-7259 www.dsarms.com
DTM International, Inc., 40 Joslyn Rd., P.O. Box 5, Lake Orion, MI 48362 / 313-693-6670
Duane A. Hobbie Gunsmithing, 2412 Pattie Ave, Wichita, KS 67216 / 316-264-8266
Duane's Gun Repair (See DGR Custom Rifles)
Dubber, Michael W., P.O. Box 312, Evansville, IN 47702 / 812-424-9000; FAX: 812-424-6551
Duck Call Specialists, P.O. Box 124, Jerseyville, IL 62052 / 618-498-9855
Duffy, Charles E (See Guns Antique & Modern DBA), Williams Lane, PO Box 2, West Hurley, NY 12491 /914-679-2997
Du-Lite Corp., 171 River Rd., Middletown, CT 06457 / 203-347-2505; FAX: 203-347-9404
Dumoulin, Ernest, Rue Florent Boclinville 8-10, 13-4041, Votten, BELGIUM / 41 27 78 92
Duncan's Gun Works, Inc., 1619 Grand Ave., San Marcos, CA 92069 / 760-727-0515
Duofold, Inc., RD 3 Rt. 309, Valley Square Mall, Tamaqua, PA 18252 / 717-386-2666; FAX: 717-386-3652
Dybala Gun Shop, P.O. Box 1024, FM 3156, Bay City, TX 77414 / 409-245-0866
Dykstra, Doug, 411 N. Darling, Fremont, MI 49412 / 616-924-3950
Dynalite Products, Inc., 215 S. Washington St., Greenfield, OH 45123 / 513-981-2124
Dynamit Nobel-RWS, Inc., 81 Ruckman Rd., Closter, NJ 07624 / 201-767-7971; FAX: 201-767-1589

E

E&L Mfg., Inc., 4177 Riddle By Pass Rd., Riddle, OR 97469 / 541-874-2137; FAX: 541-874-3107
E. Arthur Brown Co., 3404 Pawnee Dr., Alexandria, MN 56308 / 320-762-8847
E.A.A. Corp., P.O. Box 1299, Sharpes, FL 32959 / 407-639-4842; or 800-536-4442; FAX: 407-639-7006
Eagan, Donald V., P.O. Box 196, Benton, PA 17814 / 717-925-6134
Eagle Arms, Inc. (See ArmaLite, Inc.)
Eagle Grips, Eagle Business Center, 460 Randy Rd., Carol Stream, IL 60188 / 800-323-6144; or 708-260-0400; FAX: 708-260-0486
Eagle Imports, Inc., 1750 Brielle Ave., Unit B1, Wanamassa, NJ 07712 / 908-493-0333
E-A-R, Inc., Div. of Cabot Safety Corp., 5457 W. 79th St., Indianapolis, IN 46268 / 800-327-3431; FAX: 800-488-8007
EAW (See U.S. Importer-New England Custom Gun Serv
Eckelman Gunsmithing, 3125 133rd St. SW, Fort Ripley, MN 56449 / 218-829-3176
Eclectic Technologies, Inc., 45 Grandview Dr., Suite A, Farmington, CT 06034

Ed Brown Products, Inc., P.O. Box 492, Perry, MO 63462 / 573-565-3261; FAX: 573-565-2791 www.edbrown.com
Edenpine, Inc. c/o Six Enterprises, Inc., 320 D Turtle Creek Ct., San Jose, CA 95125 / 408-999-0201; FAX: 408-999-0216
EdgeCraft Corp., S. Weiner, 825 Southwood Road, Avondale, PA 19311 / 610-268-0500; or 800-342-3255; FAX: 610-268-3545 www.edgecraft.com
Edmisten Co., P.O. Box 1293, Boone, NC 28607
Edmund Scientific Co., 101 E. Gloucester Pike, Barrington, NJ 08033 / 609-543-6250
Ednar, Inc., 2-4-8 Kayabacho, Nihonbashi Chuo-ku, Tokyo, JAPAN / 81(Japan)-3-3667-1651; FAX: 81-3-3661-8113
Ed's Gun House, Ed Kukowski, PO Box 62, Minnesota City, MN 55959 / 507-689-2925
Eezox, Inc., P.O. Box 772, Waterford, CT 06385-0772 / 800-462-3331; FAX: 860-447-3484
Effebi SNC-Dr. Franco Beretta, via Rossa, 4, 25062, ITALY / 030-2751955; FAX: 030-2180414
Efficient Machinery Co, 12878 N.E. 15th Pl., Bellevue, WA 98005 / 425-453-9318; or 800-375-8554; FAX: 425-453-9311; priemc@aol.com www.sturdybench.com
Eggleston, Jere D., 400 Saluda Ave., Columbia, SC 29205 / 803-799-3402
Eichelberger Bullets, Wm., 158 Crossfield Rd., King Of Prussia, PA 19406
Ekol Leather Care, P.O. Box 2652, West Lafayette, IN 47906 / 317-463-2250; FAX: 317-463-7004
El Paso Saddlery Co., P.O. Box 27194, El Paso, TX 79926 / 915-544-2233; FAX: 915-544-2535
Eldorado Cartridge Corp (See PMC/Eldorado
Electro Prismatic Collimators, Inc., 1441 Manatt St., Lincoln, NE 68521
Electronic Shooters Protection, Inc., 11997 West 85th Place, Arvada, CO 80005 / 800-797-7791; FAX: 303-456-7179
Electronic Trigger Systems, Inc., PO Box 13, 230 Main St. S., Hector, MN 55342 / 320-848-2760; FAX: 320-848-2760
Eley Ltd., P.O. Box 705, Witton, Birmingham, B6 7UT ENGLAND / 021-356-8899; FAX: 021-331-4173
Elite Ammunition, P.O. Box 3251, Oakbrook, IL 60522 / 708-366-9006
Elk River, Inc., 1225 Paonia St., Colorado Springs, CO 80915 / 719-574-4407
Ellett Bros., 267 Columbia Ave., P.O. Box 128, Chapin, SC 29036 / 803-345-3751; or 800-845-3711; FAX: 803-345-1820
Ellicott Arms, Inc. / Woods Pistolsmithing, 8390 Sunset Dr., Ellicott City, MD 21043 / 410-465-7979
Elliott Inc., G. W., 514 Burnside Ave., East Hartford, CT 06108 / 203-289-5741; FAX: 203-289-3137
EMAP USA, 6420 Wilshire Blvd., Los Angeles, CA 90048 / 213-782-2000; FAX: 213-782-2867
Emerging Technologies, Inc. (See Laseraim Technolo
EMF Co., Inc., 1900 E. Warner Ave., Suite 1-D, Santa Ana, CA 92705 / 949-261-6611; FAX: 949-756-0133
Empire Cutlery Corp., 12 Kruger Ct., Clifton, NJ 07013 / 201-472-5155; FAX: 201-779-0759
English, Inc., A.G., 708 S. 12th St., Broken Arrow, OK 74012 / 918-251-3399 agenglish@wedzone.net www.agenglish.com
Engraving Artistry, 36 Alto Rd., Burlington, CT 06013 / 203-673-6837 bobburt44@hotmail.com
Enguix Import-Export, Alpujarras 58, Alzira, Valencia, SPAIN / (96) 241 43 95; FAX: (96) 241 43 95
Enhanced Presentations, Inc., 5929 Market St., Wilmington, NC 28405 / 910-799-1622; FAX: 910-799-5004
Enlow, Charles, 895 Box, Beaver, OK 73932 / 405-625-4487
Entre'prise Arms, Inc., 15861 Business Center Dr., Irwindale, CA 91706
EPC, 1441 Manatt St., Lincoln, NE 68521 / 402-476-3946
Epps, Ellwood/Isabella (See Gramps), Box 341, Washago, ON L0K 2B0 CANADA / 705-689-5348
Epps, Ellwood & Isabella. See: "GRAMPS" ANTIQUES
Erhardt, Dennis, 4508 N. Montana Ave., Helena, MT 59602 / 406-442-4533
Erma Werke GmbH, Johan Ziegler St., 13/15/FeldiglSt., D-8060 Dachau, GERMANY
Essex Arms, P.O. Box 363, Island Pond, VT 05846 / 802-723-6203; FAX: 802-723-6203
Essex Metals, 1000 Brighton St., Union, NJ 07083 / 800-282-8369
Estate Cartridge, Inc., 12161 FM 830, Willis, TX 77378 / 409-856-7277; FAX: 409-856-5486
Euber Bullets, No. Orwell Rd., Orwell, VT 05760 / 802-948-2621
Euroarms of America, Inc., PO Box 3277, Winchester, VA 22604 / 540-662-1863; FAX: 540-662-4464
Euro-Imports, 905 West Main Street, Suite E, El Cajon, CA 92020 / 619-442-7005; FAX: 619-442-7005
European American Armory Corp (See E.A.A. Corp)

57TH EDITION, 2003 • **543**

DIRECTORY

Evans Engraving, Robert, 332 Vine St, Oregon City, OR 97045 / 503-656-5693

Eversull Co., Inc., 1 Tracemont, Boyce, LA 71409 / 318-793-8728; FAX: 318-793-5483 bestguns@aol.com

Evolution Gun Works Inc., 4050 B-8 Skyron Dr., Doylestown, PA 18901 / 215-348-9892; FAX: 215-348-1056

Excalibur Electro Optics Inc, P.O. Box 400, Fogelsville, PA 18051-0400 / 610-391-9105; FAX: 610-391-9220

Excel Industries Inc., 4510 Carter Ct., Chino, CA 91710 / 909-627-2404; FAX: 909-627-7817

Executive Protection Institute, PO Box 802, Berryville, VA 22611 / 540-554-2540 rwk@crosslink.com personalprotecion.com

Eyster Heritage Gunsmiths, Inc., Ken, 6441 Bishop Rd., Centerburg, OH 43011 / 740-625-6131

Eze-Lap Diamond Prods., P.O. Box 2229, 15164 West State St., Westminster, CA 92683 / 714-847-1555; FAX: 714-897-0280

E-Z-Way Systems, PO Box 4310, Newark, OH 43058-4310 / 614-345-6645; or 800-848-2072; FAX: 614-345-6600

F

F.A.I.R. Tecni-Mec s.n.c. di Isidoro Rizzini & C., Via Gitti, 41 Zona Industrial, 25060 Marcheno (Bres, ITALY / 030/861162-8610344; FAX: 030/8610179 info@fair.it www.fair.it

F.I., Inc. - High Standard Mfg. Co., 5200 Mitchelldale St., Ste. E17, Houston, TX 77092-7222 / 713-462-4200; or 800-272-7816; FAX: 713-681-5665 www.highstandard.com

Fabarm S.p.A., Via Averolda 31, 25039 Travagliato, Brescia, ITALY / 030-6863629; FAX: 030-6863684

Fagan & Co.Inc, 22952 15 Mile Rd., Clinton Township, MI 48035 / 810-465-4637; FAX: 810-792-6996

Faith Associates, PO Box 549, Flat Rock, NC 28731-0549 FAX: 828-697-6827

Faloon Industries, Inc., PO Box 1060, Tijeras, NM 87059 / 505-281-3783

Far North Outfitters, Box 1252, Bethel, AK 99559

Farm Form Decoys, Inc., 1602 Biovu, P.O. Box 748, Galveston, TX 77553 / 409-744-0762; or 409-765-6361; FAX: 409-765-8513

Farr Studio, Inc., 1231 Robinhood Rd., Greeneville, TN 37743 / 615-638-8825

Farrar Tool Co., Inc., 12150 Bloomfield Ave., Suite E, Santa Fe Springs, CA 90670 / 310-863-4367; FAX: 310-863-5123

Faulhaber Wildlocker, Dipl.-Ing. Norbert Wittasek, Seilergasse 2, A-1010 Wien, AUSTRIA / OM-43-1-5137001; FAX: 43-1-5137001

Faulk's Game Call Co., Inc., 616 18th St., Lake Charles, LA 70601 / 318-436-9726; FAX: 318-494-7205

Faust Inc., T. G., 544 minor St, Reading, PA 19602 / 610-375-8549; FAX: 610-375-4488

Fausti Cav. Stefano & Figlie snc, Via Martiri Dell Indipendenza, 70, Marcheno, 25060 ITALY

Fauthrene, Andy, P.O. Box 4607, Pagosa Springs, CO 81157 / 970-731-5003; FAX: 970-731-5009

Feather, Flex Decoys, 4500 Doniphan Dr., Neosho, MO 64850 / 318-746-8596; FAX: 318-742-4815

Federal Arms Corp. of America, 7928 University Ave, Fridley, MN 55432 / 612-780-8780; FAX: 612-780-8780

Federal Cartridge Co., 900 Ehlen Dr., Anoka, MN 55303 / 612-323-2300; FAX: 612-323-2506

Federal Champion Target Co., 232 Industrial Parkway, Richmond, IN 47374 / 800-441-4971; FAX: 317-966-7747

Federated-Fry (See Fry Metals)

FEG, Budapest, Soroksariut 158, H-1095, HUNGARY

Feken, Dennis, Rt. 2, Box 124, Perry, OK 73077 / 405-336-5611

Felk Oil Gun Lube, 2121 Castlebridge Rd., Midlothian, VA 23113 / 804-794-3744; FAX: 208-988-4834

Fellowes, Ted, Beaver Lodge, 9245 16th Ave. SW, Seattle, WA 98106 / 206-763-1698

Ferguson, Bill, P.O. Box 1238, Sierra Vista, AZ 85636 / 520-458-5321; FAX: 520-458-9125

FERLIB, Via Costa 46, 25063, Gardone V.T., ITALY / 30-89-12-586; FAX: 30-89-12-586

Ferris Firearms, 7110 F.M. 1863, Bulverde, TX 78163 / 210-980-4424

Fibron Products, Inc., P.O. Box 430, Buffalo, NY 14209-0430 / 716-886-2378; FAX: 716-886-2394

Fieldsport Ltd., Bryan Bilinski, 3313 W South Airport Rd, Traverse Vity, MI 49684 / 616-933-0767

Fiocchi Munizioni S.p.A. (See U.S. Importer-Fiocch

Fiocchi of America Inc., 5030 Fremont Rd., Ozark, MO 65721 / 417-725-4118; or 800-721-2666; FAX: 417-725-1039

Firearms & Metal Engraving, P.O. Box 1255, Sierra Vista, AZ 85636 / 520-455-5541

Firearms Co Ltd. / Alpine (See U.S. Importer-Mandall

Firearms Engraver's Guild of America, 332 Vine St., Oregon City, OR 97045 / 503-656-5693

Firearms International, 5709 Hartsdale, Houston, TX 77036 / 713-460-2447

First Inc., Jack, 1201 Turbine Dr., Rapid City, SD 57701 / 605-343-9544; FAX: 605-343-9420

Fish Mfg. Gunsmith Sptg. Co., Marshall, Rd. Box 2439, Rt. 22 N, Westport, NY 12993 / 518-962-4897; FAX: 518-962-4897

Fisher, Jerry A., 631 Crane Mt. Rd., Big Fork, MT 59911 / 406-837-2722

Fisher Custom Firearms, 2199 S. Kittredge Way, Aurora, CO 80013 / 303-755-3710

Fitz Pistol Grip Co., P.O. Box 744, Lewiston, CA 96052-0744 / 916-778-0240

Fitzgerald, Jack. See: CLENZOIL WORLDWIDE CORP

Flambeau Products Corp., 15981 Valplast Rd., Middlefield, OH 44062 / 216-632-1631; FAX: 216-632-1581

Flannery Engraving Co., Jeff W, 11034 Riddles Run Rd, Union, KY 41091 / 606-384-3127

Flayderman & Co., Inc., PO Box 2446, Ft Lauderdale, FL 33303 / 954-761-8855

Fleming Firearms, 7720 E 126th St. N, Collinsville, OK 74021-7016 / 918-665-3624

Flintlocks, Etc., 160 Rossiter Rd., P.O. Box 181, Richmond, MA 01254 / 413-698-3822; FAX: 413-698-3866 flintetc@vgernet.net

Flitz International Ltd., 821 Mohr Ave., Waterford, WI 53185 / 414-534-5898; FAX: 414-534-2991

Flores Publications Inc, J (See Action Direct Inc.), PO Box 830760, Miami, FL 33283 / 305-559-4652; FAX: 305-559-4652

Fluoramics, Inc., 18 Industrial Ave., Mahwah, NJ 07430 / 800-922-0075; FAX: 201-825-7035

Flynn's Custom Guns, P.O. Box 7461, Alexandria, LA 71306 / 318-455-7130

FN Manufacturing, PO Box 24257, Columbia, SC 29224 / 803-736-0522

Folks, Donald E., 205 W. Lincoln St., Pontiac, IL 61764 / 815-844-7901

Foothills Video Productions, Inc., P.O. Box 651, Spartanburg, SC 29304 / 803-573-7023; or 800-782-5358

Foredom Electric Co., Rt. 6, 16 Stony Hill Rd., Bethel, CT 06801 / 203-792-8622

Forgett, Valmore. See: NAVY ARMS COMPANY

Forgreens Tool & Mfg., Inc., PO Box 955, Robert Lee, TX 76945 / 915-453-2800; FAX: 915-453-2460

Forkin, Ben (See Belt MTN Arms)

Forkin Arms, 205 10th Avenue S.W., White Sulphur Spring, MT 59645 / 406-547-2344

Forrest Inc., Tom, PO Box 326, Lakeside, CA 92040 / 619-561-5800; FAX: 619-561-0227

Forrest Tool Co., P.O. Box 768, 44380 Gordon Lane, Mendocino, CA 95460 / 707-937-2141; FAX: 717-937-1817

Forster, Kathy (See Custom Checkering)

Forster, Larry L., PO Box 212, 220 First St. NE, Gwinner, ND 58040-0212 / 701-678-2475

Forster Products, 310 E Lanark Ave, Lanark, IL 61046 / 815-493-6360; FAX: 815-493-2371

Fort Hill Gunstocks, 12807 Fort Hill Rd., Hillsboro, OH 45133 / 513-466-2763

Fort Knox Security Products, 1051 N. Industrial Park Rd., Orem, UT 84057 / 801-224-7233; or 800-821-5216; FAX: 801-226-5493

Fort Worth Firearms, 2006-B, Martin Luther King Fwy., Ft. Worth, TX 76104-6303 / 817-536-0718; FAX: 817-535-0290

Forthofer's Gunsmithing & Knifemaking, 5535 U.S. Hwy 93S, Whitefish, MT 59937-8411 / 406-862-2674

Fortune Products, Inc., 205 Hickory Creek Rd, Marble Falls, TX 78654 / 210-693-6111; FAX: 210-693-6394

Forty Five Ranch Enterprises, Box 1080, Miami, OK 74355-1080 / 918-542-5875

Foster. See: ACCURACY INTERNATIONAL

Fountain Products, 492 Prospect Ave., West Springfield, MA 01089 / 413-781-4651; FAX: 413-733-8217

4-D Custom Die Co., 711 N. Sandusky St., PO Box 889, Mt. Vernon, OH 43050-0889 / 740-397-7214; FAX: 740-397-6600; info@ch4d.com ch4d.com

Fowler Bullets, 806 Dogwood Dr., Gastonia, NC 28054 / 704-867-3259

Fowler, Bob (See Black Powder Products)

Fox River Mills, Inc., P.O. Box 298, 227 Poplar St., Osage, IA 50461 / 515-732-3798; FAX: 515-732-5128

Foy Custom Bullets, 104 Wells Ave., Daleville, AL 36322

Francesca, Inc., 3115 Old Ranch Rd., San Antonio, TX 78217 / 512-826-2584; FAX: 512-826-8211

Franchi S.p.A., Via del Serpente 12, 25131, Brescia, ITALY / 030-3581833; FAX: 030-3581554

Francotte & Cie S.A. Auguste, rue de Trois Juin 109, 4400 Herstal-Liege, BELGIUM / 32-4-248-13-18; FAX: 32-4-948-11-79

Frank Knives, 13868 NW Keleka Pl., Seal Rock, OR 97376 / 541-563-3041; FAX: 541-563-3041

Frank Mittermeier, Inc., P.O. Box 2G, 3577 E. Tremont Ave., Bronx, NY 10465 / 718-828-3843

Franzen International,Inc (See U.S. Importer for)

Fred F. Wells / Wells Sport Store, 110 N Summit St, Prescott, AZ 86301 / 520-445-3655

Freedom Arms, Inc., P.O. Box 150, Freedom, WY 83120 / 307-883-2468; FAX: 307-883-2005

Fremont Tool Works, 1214 Prairie, Ford, KS 67842 / 316-369-2327

French, Artistic Engraving, J. R., 1712 Creek Ridge Ct, Irving, TX 75060 / 214-254-2654

Frielich Police Equipment, 211 East 21st St., New York, NY 10010 / 212-254-3045

Front Sight Firearms Training Institute, P.O. Box 2619, Aptos, CA 95001 / 800-987-7719; FAX: 408-684-2137

Frontier, 2910 San Bernardo, Laredo, TX 78040 / 956-723-5409; FAX: 956-723-1774

Frontier Arms Co.,Inc., 401 W. Rio Santa Cruz, Green Valley, AZ 85614-3932

Frontier Products Co., 2401 Walker Rd, Roswell, NM 88201-8950 / 614-262-9357

Frontier Safe Co., 3201 S. Clinton St., Fort Wayne, IN 46806 / 219-744-7233; FAX: 219-744-6678

Frost Cutlery Co., P.O. Box 22636, Chattanooga, TN 37422 / 615-894-6079; FAX: 615-894-9576

Fry Metals, 4100 6th Ave., Altoona, PA 16602 / 814-946-1611

Fujinon, Inc., 10 High Point Dr., Wayne, NJ 07470 / 201-633-5600; FAX: 201-633-5216

Fullmer, Geo. M., 2499 Mavis St., Oakland, CA 94601 / 510-533-4193

Fulmer's Antique Firearms, Chet, PO Box 792, Rt 2 Buffalo Lake, Detroit Lakes, MN 56501 / 218-847-7712

Fulton Armory, 8725 Bollman Place No. 1, Savage, MD 20763 / 301-490-9485; FAX: 301-490-9547

Furr Arms, 91 N. 970 W., Orem, UT 84057 / 801-226-3877; FAX: 801-226-3877

FWB, Neckarstrasse 43, 78727, Oberndorf a. N., GERMANY / 07423-814-0; FAX: 07423-814-89

G

G C Bullet Co. Inc., 40 Mokelumne River Dr., Lodi, CA 95240

G&H Decoys,Inc., P.O. Box 1208, Hwy. 75 North, Henryetta, OK 74437 / 918-652-3314; FAX: 918-652-3400

G.G. & G., 3602 E. 42nd Stravenue, Tucson, AZ 85713 / 520-748-7167; FAX: 520-748-7583

G.H. Enterprises Ltd., Bag 10, Okotoks, AB T0L 1T0 CANADA / 403-938-6070

G.U. Inc (See U.S. Importer for New SKB Arms Co.)

G.W. Elliott, Inc., 514 Burnside Ave., East Hartford, CT 06108 / 203-289-5741; FAX: 203-289-3137

G96 Products Co., Inc., 85 5th Ave, Bldg. #6, Paterson, NJ 07544 / 973-684-4050; FAX: 973-684-3848; g96prod@aol

Gage Manufacturing, 663 W. 7th St., A, San Pedro, CA 90731 / 310-832-3546

Gaillard Barrels, P.O. Box 21, Pathlow, SK S0K 3B0 CANADA / 306-752-3769; FAX: 306-752-5969

Gain Twist Barrel Co. Rifle Works and Armory, 707 12th Street, Cody, WY 82414 / 307-587-4919; FAX: 307-527-6097

Galati International, PO Box 10, 616 Burley Ridge Rd., Wesco, MO 65586 / 573-775-2308; FAX: 573-775-4308 support@galatiinteenation.com www.galatiinternational.com

Galaxy Imports Ltd., Inc., P.O. Box 3361, Victoria, TX 77903 / 361-573-4867; FAX: 361-576-9622 galaxy@cox_internet.com

GALCO International Ltd., 2019 W. Quail Ave., Phoenix, AZ 85027 / 602-258-8295; or 800-874-2526; FAX: 602-582-6854

Galena Industries AMT, 5463 Diaz St, Irwindale, CA 91706 / 626-856-8883; FAX: 626-856-8878

Gamba S.p.A. Societa Armi Bresciane Srl, Renato, Via Artigiani 93, ITALY / 30-8911640; FAX: 30-8911648

Gamba, USA, P.O. Box 60452, Colorado Springs, CO 80960 / 719-578-1145; FAX: 719-444-0731

Game Haven Gunstocks, 13750 Shire Rd., Wolverine, MI 49799 / 616-525-8257

Game Winner, Inc., R 1 Box Industrial Park, Opp, AL 36467 / 770-434-9210; FAX: 770-434-9215

Gamebore Division, Polywad Inc, PO Box 7916, Macon, GA 31209 / 912-477-0669

Gamo (See U.S. Importers-Arms United Corp, Daisy M

Gamo USA, Inc., 3911 SW 47th Ave., Suite 914, Ft. Lauderdale, FL 33314 / 954-581-5822; FAX: 954-581-3165 gamousa@gate.net www.gamo.com

Gander Mountain, Inc., 12400 Fox River Rd., Wilmont, WI 53192 / 414-862-6848

GAR, 590 McBride Avenue, West Paterson, NJ 07424 / 973-754-1114; FAX: 973-754-1114 garreloading@aol.com

Garbi, Armas Urki, 12-14 20.600 Eibar, Guipuzcoa, SPAIN

Garcia National Gun Traders, Inc., 225 SW 22nd Ave., Miami, FL 33135 / 305-642-2355

Garrett Cartridges Inc., PO Box 178, Chehalis, WA 98532 / 360-736-0702 garrettcartridges.com

Garthwaite Pistolsmith, Inc., Jim, Rt 2 Box 310, Watsontown, PA 17777 / 570-538-1566; FAX: 570-538-2965

Gary Goudy Classic Stocks, 1512 S. 5th St., Dayton, WA 99328 / 509-382-2726 goudy@innw.net

Gary Reeder Custom Guns, 2601 7th Avenue East, Flagstaff, AZ 86004 / 928-526-3313; FAX: 928-527-0840 gary@reedercustomguns.com www.reedercustomguns.com

Gary Schneider Rifle Barrels Inc., 12202 N. 62nd Pl., Scottsdale, AZ 85254 / 602-948-2525

Gator Guns & Repair, 7952 Kenai Spur Hwy., Kenai, AK 99611-8311

Gaucher Armes, S.A., 46 rue Desjoyaux, 42000, Saint-Etienne, FRANCE / 04-77-33-38-92; FAX: 04-77-61-95-72

GDL Enterprises, 409 Le Gardeur, Slidell, LA 70460 / 504-649-0693

Gehmann, Walter (See Huntington Die Specialties)

Genco, P.O. Box 5704, Asheville, NC 28803

Genecco Gun Works, 10512 Lower Sacramento Rd., Stockton, CA 95210 / 209-951-0706; FAX: 209-931-3872

Gene's Custom Guns, P.O. Box 10534, White Bear Lake, MN 55110 / 612-429-5105

Gentex Corp., 5 Tinkham Ave., Derry, NH 03038 / 603-434-0311; FAX: 603-434-3002 sales@derry.gentexcorp.com www.derry.gentexcorp.com

Gentner Bullets, 109 Woodlawn Ave., Upper Darby, PA 19082 / 610-352-9396

Gentry Custom Gunmaker, David, 314 N Hoffman, Belgrade, MT 59714 / 406-388-GUNS davidgent@mcn.net gentrycustom.com

George & Roy's, PO Box 2125, Sisters, OR 97759-2125 / 503-228-5424; or 800-553-3022; FAX: 503-225-9409

George E. Mathews & Son, Inc., 10224 S. Paramount Blvd., Downey, CA 90241 / 562-862-6719; FAX: 562-862-6719

George Ibberson (Sheffield) Ltd., 25-31 Allen St., Sheffield, S3 7AW ENGLAND / 0114-2766123; FAX: 0114-2738465

Gerald Pettinger Books, see Pettinger Books, Rt. 2, Box 125, Russell, IA 50238 / 641-535-2239 gpettinger@lisco.com

Gerber Legendary Blades, 14200 SW 72nd Ave., Portland, OR 97223 / 503-639-6161; or 800-950-6161; FAX: 503-684-7008

Gervais, Mike, 3804 S. Cruise Dr., Salt Lake City, UT 84109 / 801-277-7729

Getz Barrel Co., P.O. Box 88, Beavertown, PA 17813 / 717-658-7263

Giacomo Sporting USA, 6234 Stokes Lee Center Rd., Lee Center, NY 13363

Gibbs Rifle Co., Inc., 211 Lawn St, Martinsburg, WV 25401 / 304-262-1651; FAX: 304-262-1658

Gil Hebard Guns Inc., 125 Public Square, Knoxville, IL 61448 / 309-289-2700; FAX: 309-289-2233

Gilbert Equipment Co., Inc., 960 Downtowner Rd., Mobile, AL 36609 / 205-344-3322

Gillmann, Edwin, 33 Valley View Dr., Hanover, PA 17331 / 717-632-1662

Gilman-Mayfield, Inc., 3279 E. Shields, Fresno, CA 93703 / 209-221-9415; FAX: 209-221-9419

Gilmore Sports Concepts, 5949 S. Garnett, Tulsa, OK 74146 / 918-250-3810; FAX: 918-250-3845 gilmore@webzone.net www.gilmoresports.com

Giron, Robert E., 12671 Cousins Rd.., Peosta, IA 52068 / 412-731-6041

Glacier Glove, 4890 Aircenter Circle, Suite 210, Reno, NV 89502 / 702-825-8225; FAX: 702-825-6544

Glaser Safety Slug, Inc., PO Box 8223, Foster City, CA 94404 / 800-221-3489; FAX: 510-785-6685 safetyslug.com

Glass, Herb, PO Box 25, Bullville, NY 10915 / 914-361-3021

Glimm, Jerome. See: GLIMM'S CUSTOM GUN ENGRAVING

Glimm's Custom Gun Engraving, Jerome C. Glimm, 19 S. Maryland, Conrad, MT 59425 / 406-278-3574 jandlglimm@mcn.net

Glock GmbH, P.O. Box 50, A-2232, Deutsch Wagram, AUSTRIA

Glock, Inc., PO Box 369, Smyrna, GA 30081 / 770-432-1202; FAX: 770-433-8719

Glynn Scobey Duck & Goose Calls, Rt. 3, Box 37, Newbern, TN 38059 / 901-643-6241

GML Products, Inc., 394 Laredo Dr., Birmingham, AL 35226 / 205-979-4867

Gner's Hard Cast Bullets, 1107 11th St., LaGrande, OR 97850 / 503-963-8796

Goens, Dale W., P.O. Box 224, Cedar Crest, NM 87008 / 505-281-5419

Goergen's Gun Shop, Inc., 17985 538th Ave, Austin, MN 55912 / 507-433-9280; FAX: 507-433-9280

GOEX Inc., PO Box 659, Doyline, LA 71023-0659 / 318-382-9300; FAX: 318-382-9303 mfahringer@goexpowder.com; www.goexpowder.com

Golden Age Arms Co., 115 E. High St., Ashley, OH 43003 / 614-747-2488

Golden Bear Bullets, 3065 Fairfax Ave., San Jose, CA 95148 / 408-238-9515

Gonic Arms/North American Arm, 134 Flagg Rd., Gonic, NH 03839 / 603-332-8456 or 603-332-8457

Gonzalez Guns, Ramon B, PO Box 370, 93 St. Joseph's Hill Rd, Monticello, NY 12701 / 914-794-4515

Goodling's Gunsmithing, 1950 Stoverstown Road, Spring Grove, PA 17362 / 717-225-3350

Goodwin, Fred. See: GOODWIN'S GUN SHOP

Goodwin's Gun Shop, Fred Goodwin, Sherman Mills, ME 04776 / 207-365-4451

Gotz Bullets, 11426 Edgemere Ter., Roscoe, IL 61073-8232

Gould & Goodrich, 709 E. McNeil, Lillington, NC 27546 / 910-893-2071; FAX: 910-893-4742

Gournet Artistic Engraving, Geoffroy Gournet, 820 Paxinosa Ave., Easton, PA 18042 / 610-559-0710 geoffroygournet.com

Gournet, Geoffroy. See: GOURNET ARTISTIC ENGRAVING

Grace, Charles E., 1305 Arizona Ave., Trinidad, CO 81082 / 719-846-9435

Grace Metal Products, PO Box 67, Elk Rapids, MI 49629 / 616-264-8133

Graf & Sons, 4050 S Clark St, Mexico, MO 65265 / 573-581-2266; FAX: 573-581-2875

"Gramps" Antiques, Ellwood & Isabella Epps, Box 341, Washago, ON L0K 2B0 CANADA / 705-689-5348

Granite Mountain Arms, Inc, 3145 W Hidden Acres Trail, Prescott, AZ 86305 / 520-541-9758; FAX: 520-445-6826

Grant, Howard V., Hiawatha 15, Woodruff, WI 54568 / 715-356-7146

Graphics Direct, P.O. Box 372421, Reseda, CA 91337-2421 / 818-344-9002

Graves Co., 1800 Andrews Ave., Pompano Beach, FL 33069 / 800-327-9103; FAX: 305-960-0301

Grayback Wildcats, Mike Beeks, 5306 Bryant Ave., Klamath Falls, OR 97603 / 541-884-1072

Graybill's Gun Shop, 1035 Ironville Pike, Columbia, PA 17512 / 717-684-2739

Great American Gunstock Co., 3420 Industrial Drive, Yuba City, CA 95993 / 530-671-4570; FAX: 530-671-3906

Great Lakes Airguns, 6175 S. Park Ave, New York, NY 14075 / 716-648-6666; FAX: 716-648-5279

Green, Arthur S., 485 S. Robertson Blvd., Beverly Hills, CA 90211 / 310-274-1283

Green, Roger M., P.O. Box 984, 435 E. Birch, Glenrock, WY 82637 / 307-436-9804

Green Head Game Call Co., RR 1, Box 33, Lacon, IL 61540 / 309-246-2155

Green Mountain Rifle Barrel Co., Inc., P.O. Box 2670, 153 West Main St., Conway, NH 03818 / 603-447-1095; FAX: 603-447-1099

Greenwood Precision, P.O. Box 407, Rogersville, MO 65742 / 417-725-2330

Greg Gunsmithing Repair, 3732 26th Ave. North, Robbinsdale, MN 55422 / 612-529-8103

Greg's Superior Products, P.O. Box 46219, Seattle, WA 98146

Greider Precision, 431 Santa Marina Ct., Escondido, CA 92029 / 619-480-8892; FAX: 619-480-9800

Gremmel Enterprises, 2111 Carriage Drive, Eugene, OR 97408-7537 / 541-302-3000

GrE-Tan Rifles, 29742 W.C.R. 50, Kersey, CO 80644 / 970-353-6176; FAX: 970-356-9133

Grier's Hard Cast Bullets, 1107 11th St., LaGrande, OR 97850 / 503-963-8796

Griffin & Howe, Inc., 36 W. 44th St., Suite 1011, New York, NY 10036 / 212-921-0980

Griffin & Howe, Inc., 33 Claremont Rd., Bernardsville, NJ 07924 / 908-766-2287

Grifon, Inc., 58 Guinam St., Waltham, MS 02154

Groenewold, John, PO Box 830, Mundelein, IL 60060 / 847-566-2365

GRS / Glendo Corp., P.O. Box 1153, 900 Overlander St., Emporia, KS 66801 / 316-343-1084 or 800-835-3519 glendo@glendo.com www.grstools.com

Grulla Armes, Apartado 453, Avda Otaloa 12, Eiber, SPAIN

Gruning Precision Inc, 7101 Jurupa Ave., No. 12, Riverside, CA 92504 / 909-689-6692; FAX: 909-689-7791

gruningprecision@earthlink.net www.gruningprecision.com

GSI, Inc., 7661 Commerce Ln., Trussville, AL 35173 / 205-655-8299

GTB, 482 Comerwood Court, San Francisco, CA 94080 / 650-583-1550

Guarasi, Robert. See: WILCOX INDUSTRIES CORP

Guardsman Products, 411 N. Darling, Fremont, MI 49412 / 616-924-3950

Gun Accessories (See Glaser Safety Slug, Inc.), PO Box 8223, Foster City, CA 94404 / 800-221-3489; FAX: 510-785-6685

Gun City, 212 W. Main Ave., Bismarck, ND 58501 / 701-223-2304

Gun Hunter Books (See Gun Hunter Trading Co), 5075 Heisig St, Beaumont, TX 77705 / 409-835-3006; FAX: 409-838-2266; gunhuntertrading@hotmail.com

Gun Hunter Trading Co., 5075 Heisig St., Beaumont, TX 77705 / 409-835-3006; FAX: 409-838-2266 gunhuntertrading@hotmail.com

Gun Leather Limited, 116 Lipscomb, Ft. Worth, TX 76104 / 817-334-0225; FAX: 800-247-0609

Gun List (See Krause Publications), 700 E State St, Iola, WI 54945 / 715-445-2214; FAX: 715-445-4087

Gun South, Inc. (See GSI, Inc.)

Gun Vault, 7339 E Acoma Dr., Ste. 7, Scottsdale, AZ 85260 / 602-951-6855

Gun-Alert, 1010 N. Maclay Ave., San Fernando, CA 91340 / 818-365-0864; FAX: 818-365-1308

Guncraft Books (See Guncraft Sports Inc.), 10737 Dutchtown Rd, Knoxville, TN 37932 / 865-966-4545; FAX: 865-966-4500 findit@guncraft.com www.usit.net/guncraft

Guncraft Sports Inc., 10737 Dutchtown Rd., Knoxville, TN 37932 / 865-966-4545; FAX: 865-966-4500 findit@guncraft.com www.usit.net/guncraft

Guncraft Sports, Inc., Marie C. Wiest, 10737 Dutchtown Rd., Knoxville, TN 37932 / 865-966-4545; FAX: 865-966-4500 www.guncraft.com

Gunfitters, PO Box 426, Cambridge, WI 53523-0426 / 608-764-8128 gunfitters@aol.com www.gunfitters.com

Gun-Ho Sports Cases, 110 E. 10th St., St. Paul, MN 55101 / 612-224-9491

Gunline Tools, 2950 Saturn St., "O", Brea, CA 92821 / 714-993-5100; FAX: 714-572-4128

Gunnerman Books, PO Box 217, Owosso, MI 48867 / 989-729-7018

Guns, 81 E. Streetsboro St., Hudson, OH 44236 / 330-650-4563 jcpevear@aol.com

Guns Antique & Modern DBA / Charles E. Duffy, Williams Lane, West Hurley, NY 12491 / 914-679-2997

Guns Div. of D.C. Engineering, Inc., 8633 Southfield Fwy., Detroit, MI 48228 / 313-271-7111; or 800-886-7623; FAX: 313-271-7112 guns@rifletech.com www.rifletech.com

GUNS Magazine, 591 Camino de la Reina, Suite 200, San Diego, CA 92108 / 619-297-5350; FAX: 619-297-5353

Gunsite Custom Shop, P.O. Box 451, Paulden, AZ 86334 / 520-636-4104; FAX: 520-636-1236

Gunsite Gunsmithy (See Gunsite Custom Shop)

Gunsite Training Center, P.O. Box 700, Paulden, AZ 86334 / 520-636-4565; FAX: 520-636-1236

Gunsmithing Ltd., 57 Unquowa Rd., Fairfield, CT 06430 / 203-254-0436; FAX: 203-254-1535

Gunsmithing, Inc., 30 West Buchanan St., Colorado Springs, CO 80907 / 719-632-3795; FAX: 719-632-3493

Gurney, F. R., Box 13, Sooke, BC V0S 1N0 CANADA / 604-642-5282; FAX: 604-642-7859

Gwinnell, Bryson J., PO Box 1307, Kilauea, HI 96754

H

H&B Forge Co., Rt. 2, Geisinger Rd., Shiloh, OH 44878 / 419-895-1856

H&P Publishing, 7174 Hoffman Rd., San Angelo, TX 76905 / 915-655-5953

H&R 1871, Inc., 60 Industrial Rowe, Gardner, MA 01440 / 978-632-9393; FAX: 978-632-2300

H&S Liner Service, 515 E. 8th, Odessa, TX 79761 / 915-332-1021

H. Krieghoff Gun Co., Boschstrasse 22, D-89079, Ulm, GERMANY / 731-401820; FAX: 731-4018270

H.K.S. Products, 7841 Founion Dr., Florence, KY 41042 / 606-342-7841; or 800-354-9814; FAX: 606-342-5865

H.P. White Laboratory, Inc., 3114 Scarboro Rd., Street, MD 21154 / 410-838-6550; FAX: 410-838-2802

Hafner World Wide, Inc., PO Box 1987, Lake City, FL 32055 / 904-755-6481; FAX: 904-755-6595 hafner@isgroupe.net

Hagn Rifles & Actions, Martin, PO Box 444, Cranbrook, BC V1C 4H9 CANADA / 604-489-4861

Hakko Co. Ltd., 1-13-12, Narimasu, Itabashiku Tokyo, JAPAN / 03-5997-7870/2; FAX: 81-3-5997-7840

Hale, Engraver, Peter, 800 E Canyon Rd., Spanish Fork, UT 84660 / 801-798-8215

Half Moon Rifle Shop, 490 Halfmoon Rd., Columbia Falls, MT 59912 / 406-892-4409

Hall Manufacturing, 142 CR 406, Clanton, AL 35045 / 205-755-4094

Hall Plastics, Inc., John, P.O. Box 1526, Alvin, TX 77512 / 713-489-8709

Hallberg, Fritz. See: CAMBOS OUTDOORSMAN

Hallowell & Co., PO Box 1445, Livingston, MT 59047 / 406-222-4770; FAX: 406-222-4792 morris@hallowellco.com; hallowellco.com

Hally Caller, 443 Wells Rd., Doylestown, PA 18901 / 215-345-6354

Hamilton, Alex B (See Ten-Ring Precision, Inc)

Hammans, Charles E., PO Box 788, 2022 McCracken, Stuttgart, AR 72160-0788 / 870-673-1388

Hammerli Ltd., Seonerstrasse 37, CH-5600, SWITZERLAND / 064-50 11 44; FAX: 064-51 38 27

Hammerli USA, 19296 Oak Grove Circle, Groveland, CA 95321 FAX: 209-962-5311

Hammets VLD Bullets, P.O. Box 479, Rayville, LA 71269 / 318-728-2019

Hammond Custom Guns Ltd., 619 S. Pandora, Gilbert, AZ 85234 / 602-892-3437

Hammonds Rifles, RD 4, Box 504, Red Lion, PA 17356 / 717-244-7879

HandCrafts Unltd (See Clements' Custom Leather), 1741 Dallas St, Aurora, CO 80010-2018 / 303-364-0403; FAX: 303-739-9824 gryphons@home.com kuntaoslcat.com

Handgun Press, PO Box 406, Glenview, IL 60025 / 847-657-6500; FAX: 847-724-8831 jschroed@inter-access.com

Hands Engraving, Barry Lee, 26192 E Shore Route, Bigfork, MT 59911 / 406-837-0035

Hank's Gun Shop, Box 370, 50 West 100 South, Monroe, UT 84754 / 801-527-4456

Hanned Precision (See Hanned Line, The)

Hansen & Co. (See Hansen Cartridge Co.), 244-246 Old Post Rd, Southport, CT 06490 / 203-259-6222; FAX: 203-254-3832

Hanson's Gun Center, Dick, 233 Everett Dr, Colorado Springs, CO 80911

Hanus Birdguns Bill, PO Box 533, Newport, OR 97365 / 541-265-7433; FAX: 541-265-7400

Hanusin, John, 3306 Commercial, Northbrook, IL 60062 / 708-564-2706

Hardin Specialty Dist., P.O. Box 338, Radcliff, KY 40159-0338 / 502-351-6649

Harford (See U.S. Importer-EMF Co. Inc.)

Harper's Custom Stocks, 928 Lombrano St., San Antonio, TX 78207 / 210-732-5780

Harrell's Precision, 5756 Hickory Dr., Salem, VA 24133 / 703-380-2683

Harrington & Richardson (See H&R 1871, Inc.)

Harris Engineering Inc., Dept GD54, Barlow, KY 42024 / 502-334-3633; FAX: 502-334-3000

Harris Enterprises, P.O. Box 105, Bly, OR 97622 / 503-353-2625

Harris Gunworks, 11240 N. Cave Creek Rd., Ste. 104, Phoenix, AZ 85020 / 602-582-9627; FAX: 602-582-5178

Harris Hand Engraving, Paul A., 113 Rusty Ln, Boerne, TX 78006-5746 / 512-391-5121

Harris Publications, 1115 Broadway, New York, NY 10010 / 212-807-7100; FAX: 212-627-4678

Harrison Bullets, 6437 E. Hobart St., Mesa, AZ 85205

Harry Lawson Co., 3328 N. Richey Blvd., Tucson, AZ 85716 / 520-326-1117

Hart & Son, Inc., Robert W., 401 Montgomery St, Nescopeck, PA 18635 / 717-752-3655; FAX: 717-752-1088

Hart Rifle Barrels,Inc., PO Box 182, 1690 Apulia Rd., Lafayette, NY 13084 / 315-677-9841; FAX: 315-677-9610 hartrb@aol.com hartbarrels.com

Hartford (See U.S. Importer-EMF Co. Inc.)

Hartmann & Weiss GmbH, Rahlstedter Bahnhofstr. 47, 22143, Hamburg, GERMANY / (40) 677 55 85; FAX: (40) 677 55 92

Harvey, Frank, 218 Nightfall, Terrace, NV 89015 / 702-558-6998

Harwood, Jack O., 1191 S. Pendlebury Lane, Blackfoot, ID 83221 / 208-785-5368

Hastings Barrels, 320 Court St., Clay Center, KS 67432 / 913-632-3169; FAX: 913-632-6554

Hatfield Gun, 224 N. 4th St., St. Joseph, MO 64501

Hawk Laboratories, Inc. (See Hawk, Inc.), 849 Hawks Bridge Rd, Salem, NJ 08079 / 609-299-2700; FAX: 609-299-2800

Hawk, Inc., 849 Hawks Bridge Rd., Salem, NJ 08079 / 609-299-2700; FAX: 609-299-2800

Hawken Shop, The (See Dayton Traister)

Haydel's Game Calls, Inc., 5018 Hazel Jones Rd., Bossier City, LA 71111 / 318-746-3586; FAX: 318-746-3711

Haydon Shooters Supply, Russ, 15018 Goodrich Dr NW, Gig Harbor, WA 98329-9738 / 253-857-7557; FAX: 253-857-7884

Heatbath Corp., P.O. Box 2978, Springfield, MA 01101 / 413-543-3381

Hecht, Hubert J, Waffen-Hecht, PO Box 2635, Fair Oaks, CA 95628 / 916-966-1020

Heckler & Koch GmbH, PO Box 1329, 78722 Oberndorf, Neckar, GERMANY / 49-7423179-0; FAX: 49-7423179-2406

Heckler & Koch, Inc., 21480 Pacific Blvd., Sterling, VA 20166-8900 / 703-450-1900; FAX: 703-450-8160 www.hecklerkoch-usa.com

Hege Jagd-u. Sporthandels GmbH, P.O. Box 101461, W-7770, Ueberlingen a. Boden, GERMANY

Heidenstrom Bullets, Urdngt 1, 3937 Heroya, NORWAY,

Heilmann, Stephen, PO Box 657, Grass Valley, CA 95945 / 530-272-8758; FAX: 530-274-0285 sheilmann@jps.net metalwood.com

Heinie Specialty Products, 301 Oak St., Quincy, IL 62301-2500 / 217-228-9500; FAX: 217-228-9502 rheinie@heinie.com www.heinie.com

Helwan (See U.S. Importer-Interarms)

Henigson & Associates, Steve, PO Box 2726, Culver City, CA 90231 / 310-305-8288; FAX: 310-305-1905

Henriksen Tool Co., Inc., 8515 Wagner Creek Rd., Talent, OR 97540 / 541-535-2309; FAX: 541-535-2309

Henry Repeating Arms Co., 110 8th St., Brooklyn, NY 11215 / 718-499-5600

Hensley, Gunmaker, Darwin, PO Box 329, Brightwood, OR 97011 / 503-622-5411

Heppler, Keith. See: KEITH'S CUSTOM GUNSTOCKS

Hercules, Inc. (See Alliant Techsystems, Smokeless)

Heritage / VSP Gun Books, PO Box 887, McCall, ID 83638 / 208-634-4104; FAX: 208-634-3101

Heritage Firearms (See Heritage Mfg., Inc.)

Heritage Manufacturing, Inc., 4600 NW 135th St., Opa Locka, FL 33054 or 305-685-5966; FAX: 305-687-6721 infohmi@heritagemfg.com www.heritagemfg.com

Herrett's Stocks, Inc., P.O. Box 741, Twin Falls, ID 83303 / 208-733-1498

Hertel & Reuss, Werk fr Optik und Feinmechanik GmbH, Quellhofstrasse 67, 34 127, GERMANY / 0561-83006; FAX: 0561-893308

Herter's Manufacturing Inc., 111 E. Burnett St., P.O. Box 518, Beaver Dam, WI 53916-1811 / 414-887-1765; FAX: 414-887-8444

Hesco-Meprolight, 2139 Greenville Rd., LaGrange, GA 30241 / 706-884-7967; FAX: 706-882-4683

Hesse Arms, Robert Hesse, 1126 70th Street E., Inver Grove Heights, MN 55077-2416 / 651-455-5760; FAX: 612-455-5760

Hesse, Robert. See: HESSE ARMS

Heydenberk, Warren R., 1059 W. Sawmill Rd., Quakertown, PA 18951 / 215-538-2682

Hickman, Jaclyn, Box 1900, Glenrock, WY 82637

Hidalgo, Tony, 12701 SW 9th Pl., Davie, FL 33325 / 954-476-7645

High Bridge Arms, Inc, 3185 Mission St., San Francisco, CA 94110 / 415-282-8358

High North Products, Inc., PO Box 2, Antigo, WI 54409 / 715-627-2331; FAX: 715-623-5451

High Performance International, 5734 W. Florist Ave., Milwaukee, WI 53218 / 414-466-9040

High Precision, Bud Welsh, 80 New Road, E. Amherst, NY 14051 / 716-688-6344; FAX: 716-688-0425

High Tech Specialties, Inc., P.O. Box 839, 293 E Main St., Rear, Adamstown, PA 19501 / 717-484-0405; FAX: 717-484-0523 bansner@aol.com

Highline Machine Co., Randall Thompson, 654 Lela Place, Grand Junction, CO 81504 / 970-434-4971

Hi-Grade Imports, 8655 Monterey Rd., Gilroy, CA 95021 / 408-842-9301; FAX: 408-842-2374

Hill, Loring F., 304 Cedar Rd., Elkins Park, PA 19027

Hill Speed Leather, Ernie, 4507 N 195th Ave, Litchfield Park, AZ 85340 / 602-853-9222; FAX: 602-853-9235

Hinman Outfitters, Bob, 107 N Sanderson Ave, Bartonville, IL 61607-1839 / 309-691-8132

Hi-Performance Ammunition Company, 484 State Route 366, Apollo, PA 15613 / 412-327-8100

HIP-GRIP Barami Corp., P.O. Box 252224, West Bloomfield, MI 48325-2224 / 248-738-0462; FAX: 248-738-2542 hipgripja@aol.com www.hipgrip.com

Hi-Point Firearms/MKS Supply, 8611-A North Dixie Dr., Dayton, OH 45414 / 877-425-4867; FAX: 937-454-0503 www.hi-pointfirearms.com

Hiptmayer, Armurier, RR 112 750, P.O. Box 136, Eastman, PQ JOE 1P0 CANADA / 514-297-2492

Hiptmayer, Heidemarie, RR 112 750, P.O. Box 136, Eastman, PQ JOE 1P0 CANADA / 514-297-2492

Hiptmayer, Klaus, RR 112 750, P.O. Box 136, Eastman, PQ JOE 1P0 CANADA / 514-297-2492

Hirtenberger Aktiengesellschaft, Leobersdorferstrasse 31, A-2552, Hirtenberg, / 43(0)2256 81184; FAX: 43(0)2256 81807

HiTek International, 484 El Camino Real, Redwood City, CA 94063 / 415-363-1404; or 800-54-NIGHT; FAX: 415-363-1408

Hiti-Schuch, Atelier Wilma, A-8863 Predlitz, Pirming, Y1 AUSTRIA / 0353418278

HJS Arms, Inc., P.O. Box 3711, Brownsville, TX 78523-3711 / 800-453-2767; FAX: 210-542-2767

Hoag, James W., 8523 Canoga Ave., Suite C, Canoga Park, CA 91304 / 818-998-1510

Hobson Precision Mfg. Co., 210 Big Oak Ln, Brent, AL 35034 / 205-926-4662; FAX: 205-926-3193 cahobbob@dbtech.net

Hoch Custom Bullet Moulds (See Colorado Shooter's)

Hodgdon Powder Co., 6231 Robinson, Shawnee Mission, KS 66202 / 913-362-9455; FAX: 913-362-1307

Hodgman, Inc., 1750 Orchard Rd., Montgomery, IL 60538 / 708-897-7555; FAX: 708-897-7558

Hodgson, Richard, 9081 Tahoe Lane, Boulder, CO 80301

Hoehn Sales, Inc., 2045 Kohn Road, Wright City, MO 63390 / 636-745-8144; FAX: 636-745-8144 hoehnsal@usmo.com

Hoelscher, Virgil, 1804 S. Valley View Blvd., Las Vegas, NV 89102 / 310-631-8545

Hoenig & Rodman, 6521 Morton Dr., Boise, ID 83704 / 208-375-1116

Hofer Jagdwaffen, P., Buchsenmachermeister, Kirchgasse 24, A-9170 Ferlach, AUSTRIA / 43 4227 3683; FAX: 43 4227 368330 peterhofer@hoferwaffen.com www.hoferwaffen.com

Hoffman New Ideas, 821 Northmoor Rd., Lake Forest, IL 60045 / 312-234-4075

Hogue Grips, P.O. Box 1138, Paso Robles, CA 93447 / 800-438-4747; or 805-239-1440; FAX: 805-239-2553

Holland & Holland Ltd., 33 Bruton St., London, ENGLAND / 44-171-499-4411; FAX: 44-171-408-7962

Holland's Gunsmithing, P.O. Box 69, Powers, OR 97466 / 541-439-5155; FAX: 541-439-5155

Hollinger, Jon. See: ASPEN OUTFITTING CO.

Hollis Gun Shop, 917 Rex St., Carlsbad, NM 88220 / 505-885-3782

Hollywood Engineering, 10642 Arminta St., Sun Valley, CA 91352 / 818-842-8376; FAX: 818-504-4168

Homak, 5151 W. 73rd St., Chicago, IL 60638-6613 / 312-523-3100; FAX: 312-523-9455

Home Shop Machinist The Village Press Publications, PO Box 1810, Traverse City, MI 49685 / 800-447-7367; FAX: 616-946-3289

Hondo Ind., 510 S. 52nd St., I04, Tempe, AZ 85281

Hoppe's Div. Penguin Industries, Inc., Airport Industrial Mall, Coatesville, PA 19320 / 610-384-6000

Horizons Unlimited, P.O. Box 426, Warm Springs, GA 31830 / 706-655-3603; FAX: 706-655-3603

Hornady Mfg. Co., P.O. Box 1848, Grand Island, NE 68802 / 800-338-3220; or 308-382-1390; FAX: 308-382-5761

Horseshoe Leather Products, Andy Arratoonian, The Cottage Sharow, Ripon, ENGLAND / 44-1765-605858 andy@horseshoe.co.uk www.horseshoe.co.uk

House of Muskets, Inc., The, PO Box 4640, Pagosa Springs, CO 81157 / 970-731-2295

Houtz & Barwick, P.O. Box 435, W. Church St., Elizabeth City, NC 27909 / 800-775-0337; or 919-335-4191; FAX: 919-335-1152

Howa Machinery, Ltd., Sukaguchi, Shinkawa-cho Nishikasugai-gun, Aichi 452, JAPAN

Howell Machine, 815 1/2 D St., Lewiston, ID 83501 / 208-743-7418

H-S Precision, Inc., 1301 Turbine Dr., Rapid City, SD 57701 / 605-341-3006; FAX: 605-342-8964

HT Bullets, 244 Belleville Rd., New Bedford, MA 02745 / 508-999-3338

Hubert J. Hecht Waffen-Hecht, P.O. Box 2635, Fair Oaks, CA 95628 / 916-966-1020

Huebner, Corey O., PO Box 564, Frenchtown, MT 59834 / 406-721-7168

Huey Gun Cases, PO Box 22456, Kansas City, MO 64113 / 816-444-1637; FAX: 816-444-1637 hueycases@aol.com www.hueycases.com

Hugger Hooks Co., 3900 Easley Way, Golden, CO 80403 / 303-279-0600

Hughes, Steven Dodd, PO Box 545, Livingston, MT 59047 / 406-222-9377; FAX: 406-222-9377

Hume, Don, P.O. Box 351, Miami, OK 74355 / 800-331-2686; FAX: 918-542-4340

Hungry Horse Books, 4605 Hwy. 93 South, Whitefish, MT 59937 / 406-862-7997

Hunkeler, A (See Buckskin Machine Works, 3235 S 358th St., Auburn, WA 98001 / 206-927-5412

Hunter Co., Inc., 3300 W. 71st Ave., Westminster, CO 80030 / 303-427-4626; FAX: 303-428-3980

Hunterjohn, PO Box 771457, St. Louis, MO 63177 / 314-531-7250

Hunter's Specialties Inc., 6000 Huntington Ct. NE, Cedar Rapids, IA 52402-1268 / 319-395-0321; FAX: 319-395-0326

Hunters Supply, Inc., PO Box 313, Tioga, TX 76271 / 940-437-2458; FAX: 940-437-2228 hunterssupply@hotmail.com hunterssupply.net

Hunting Classics Ltd., P.O. Box 2089, Gastonia, NC 28053 / 704-867-1307; FAX: 704-867-0491

Huntington Die Specialties, 601 Oro Dam Blvd., Oroville, CA 95965 / 530-534-1210; FAX: 530-534-1212

Hutton Rifle Ranch, P.O. Box 45236, Boise, ID 83711 / 208-345-8781

Hydrosorbent Products, PO Box 437, Ashley Falls, MA 01222 / 800-448-7903; FAX: 413-229-8743 orders@dehumidify.com; www.dehumidify.com

I

I.A.B. (See U.S. Importer-Taylor's & Co. Inc.)

I.D.S.A. Books, 1324 Stratford Drive, Piqua, OH 45356 / 937-773-4203; FAX: 937-778-1922

I.N.C. Inc (See Kickeez I.N.C., Inc.)

I.S.S., P.O. Box 185234, Ft. Worth, TX 76181 / 817-595-2090

I.S.W., 106 E. Cairo Dr., Tempe, AZ 85282

IAR Inc., 33171 Camino Capistrano, San Juan Capistrano, CA 92675 / 949-443-3642; FAX: 949-443-3647 sales@iar-arms.com www.iar-arms.com

Ide, K. See: STURGEON VALLEY SPORTERS

IGA (See U.S. Importer-Stoeger Industries)

Ignacio Ugartechea S.A., Chonta 26, Eibar, 20600 SPAIN / 43-121257; FAX: 43-121669

Illinois Lead Shop, 7742 W. 61st Place, Summit, IL 60501

Image Ind. Inc., 382 Balm Court, Wood Dale, IL 60191 / 630-766-2402; FAX: 630-766-7373

Impact Case Co., P.O. Box 9912, Spokane, WA 99209-0912 / 800-262-3322; or 509-467-3303; FAX: 509-326-5436 info@kkair.com www.kkair.com

Imperial (See E-Z-Way Systems), PO Box 4310, Newark, OH 43058-4310 / 614-345-6645; FAX: 614-345-6600 ezway@infinet.com www.jcunald.com

Imperial Magnum Corp., P.O. Box 249, Oroville, WA 98844 / 604-495-3131; FAX: 604-495-2816

Imperial Miniature Armory, 10547 S. Post Oak Road, Houston, TX 77035-3305 / 713-729-8428; FAX: 713-729-2274 miniguns@aol.com www.1800miniature.com

Imperial Schrade Corp., 7 Schrade Ct., Box 7000, Ellenville, NY 12428 / 914-647-7601; FAX: 914-647-8701 csc@schradeknives.com www.schradeknives.com

Import Sports Inc., 1750 Brielle Ave., Unit B1, Wanamassa, NJ 07712 / 908-493-0302; FAX: 908-493-0031

IMR Powder Co., 1080 Military Turnpike, Suite 2, Plattsburgh, NY 12901 / 518-563-2253; FAX: 518-563-6916

IMX, LLC, 2169 Greenville Rd., La Grange, GA 30241 / 706-812-9841; or 877-519-3473; FAX: 706-882-9050 mpatillo@crossfirellc.com

Info-Arm, P.O. Box 1262, Champlain, NY 12919 / 514-955-0355; FAX: 514-955-0357

Ingle, Ralph W., Engraver, 112 Manchester Ct., Centerville, GA 31028 / 478-953-5824 riengraver@aol.com www.fega.com

Innovative Weaponry Inc., 2513 E. Loop 820 N., Fort Worth, TX 76118 / 817-284-0099; or 800-334-3573

INTEC International, Inc., P.O. Box 5708, Scottsdale, AZ 85261 / 602-483-1708

Inter Ordnance of America LP, 3305 Westwood Industrial Dr, Monroe, NC 28110-5204 / 704-821-8337; FAX: 704-821-8523

Interarms / Howa, PO Box 208, Ten Prince St, Alexandria, VA 22313 / 703-548-1400; FAX: 703-549-7826

Intercontinental Distributors, Ltd., PO Box 815, Beulah, ND 58523

Intrac Arms International, 5005 Chapman Hwy., Knoxville, TN 37920

Ion Industries, Inc, 3508 E Allerton Ave, Cudahy, WI 53110 / 414-486-2007; FAX: 414-486-2017

Iosso Products, 1485 Lively Blvd., Elk Grove Village, IL 60007 / 847-437-8400; FAX: 847-437-8478

Iron Bench, 12619 Bailey Rd., Redding, CA 96003 / 916-241-4623

Ironside International Publishers, Inc., 3000 S. Eaos St., Arlington, VA 22202 / 703-684-6111; FAX: 703-683-5486

Ironsighter Co., PO Box 85070, Westland, MI 48185 / 734-326-8731; FAX: 734-326-3378 www.ironsighter.com

Irwin, Campbell H., 140 Hartland Blvd., East Hartland, CT 06027 / 203-653-3901

Island Pond Gun Shop, Cross St., Island Pond, VT 05846 / 802-723-4546

Israel Arms International, Inc., 1085 Gessner Rd., Ste. F, Houston, TX 77055 / 713-789-0745; FAX: 713-914-9515 iaipro@wt.net www.israelarms.com

Ithaca Classic Doubles, Stephen Lamboy, No. 5 Railroad St., Victor, NY 14564 / 716-924-2710; FAX: 716-924-2737 ithacadoubles.com

Ithaca Gun Company LLC, 901 Rt. 34 B, King Ferry, NY 13081 / 315-364-7171; FAX: 315-364-5134 info@ithacagun.com

Ivanoff, Thomas G (See Tom's Gun Repair)

J

J J Roberts Firearm Engraver, 7808 Lake Dr, Manassas, VA 20111 / 703-330-0448; FAX: 703-264-8600 james..roberts@angelfire.com www.angelfire.com/va2/engraver

J&D Components, 75 East 350 North, Orem, UT 84057-4719 / 801-225-7007

J&J Products, Inc., 9240 Whitmore, El Monte, CA 91731 / 818-571-5228; FAX: 800-927-8361

J&J Sales, 1501 21st Ave. S., Great Falls, MT 59405 / 406-453-7549

J&L Superior Bullets (See Huntington Die Special)

J&R Engineering, P.O. Box 77, 200 Lyons Hill Rd., Athol, MA 01331 / 508-249-9241

J&R Enterprises, 4550 Scotts Valley Rd., Lakeport, CA 95453

J&S Heat Treat, 803 S. 16th St., Blue Springs, MO 64015 / 816-229-2149; FAX: 816-228-1135

J. Dewey Mfg. Co., Inc., PO Box 2014, Southbury, CT 06488 / 203-264-3064; FAX: 203-262-6907 deweyrods@worldnet.att.net www.deweyrods.com

J. Korzinek Riflesmith, RD 2, Box 73D, Canton, PA 17724 / 717-673-8512

J.A. Blades, Inc. (See Christopher Firearms Co.)

J.A. Henckels Zwillingswerk Inc., 9 Skyline Dr., Hawthorne, NY 10532 / 914-592-7370

J.G. Dapkus Co., Inc., Commerce Circle, P.O. Box 293, Durham, CT 06422

J.G. Anschutz GmbH & Co. KG, Daimlerstr. 12, D-89079 Ulm, Ulm, GERMANY / 49 731 40120; FAX: 49 731 4012700 JGA-info@anschuetz-sport.com anschuetz-sport.com

J.I.T. Ltd., P.O. Box 230, Freedom, WY 83120 / 708-494-0937

J.J. Roberts / Engraver, 7808 Lake Dr., Manassas, VA 20111 / 703-330-0448 jjrengraver@aol.com www.angelfire.com/va2/engraver

J.P. Enterprises Inc., P.O. Box 378, Hugo, MN 55110 / 612-486-9064; FAX: 612-482-0970

J.P. Gunstocks, Inc., 4508 San Miguel Ave., North Las Vegas, NV 89030 / 702-645-0718

J.R. Williams Bullet Co., 2008 Tucker Rd., Perry, GA 31069 / 912-987-0274

J.W. Morrison Custom Rifles, 4015 W. Sharon, Phoenix, AZ 85029 / 602-978-3754

J/B Adventures & Safaris Inc., 2275 E. Arapahoe Rd., Ste. 109, Littleton, CO 80122-1521 / 303-771-0977

Jack A. Rosenberg & Sons, 12229 Cox Ln., Dallas, TX 75234 / 214-241-6302

Jack Dever Co., 8520 NW 90th St., Oklahoma City, OK 73132 / 405-721-6393 jbdever1@home.com

Jack First, Inc., 1201 Turbine Dr., Rapid City, SD 57701 / 605-343-9544; FAX: 605-343-9420

Jack Jonas Appraisals & Taki, 13952 E. Marina Dr., #604, Aurora, CO 80014

Jackalope Gun Shop, 1048 S. 5th St., Douglas, WY 82633 / 307-358-3441

Jaffin, Harry. See: BRIDGEMAN PRODUCTS

Jagdwaffen, P. See: BUCHSENMACHERMEISTER

James Calhoon Mfg., Shambo Rte. 304, Havre, MT 59501 / 406-395-4079 www.jamescalhoon.com

James Calhoon Varmint Bullets, Shambo Rt., 304, Havre, MT 59501 / 406-395-4079 www.jamescalhoon.com

James Churchill Glove Co., PO Box 298, Centralia, WA 98531 / 360-736-2816; FAX: 360-330-0151 churchillglove@localaccess.com

James Wayne Firearms for Collectors and Investors, 2608 N. Laurent, Victoria, TX 77901 / 361-578-1258; FAX: 361-578-3559

Jamison's Forge Works, 4527 Rd. 6.5 NE, Moses Lake, WA 98837 / 509-762-2659

Jantz Supply, 309 West Main Dept HD, Davis, OK 73030-0584 / 580-369-2316; FAX: 580-369-3082 jantz@brightok.net www.knifemaking.com

Jarrett Rifles, Inc., 383 Brown Rd., Jackson, SC 29831 / 803-471-3616 www.jarrettrifles.com

Jarvis, Inc., 1123 Cherry Orchard Lane, Hamilton, MT 59840 / 406-961-4392

JAS, Inc., P.O. Box 0, Rosemount, MN 55068 / 612-890-7631

Javelina Lube Products, PO Box 337, San Bernardino, CA 92402 / 714-882-5847; FAX: 714-434-6937

Jay McCament Custom Gunmaker, Jay McCament, 1730-134th St. Ct. S., Tacoma, WA 98444 / 253-531-8832

JB Custom, P.O. Box 6912, Leawood, KS 66206 / 913-381-2329

Jeff W. Flannery Engraving Co., 11034 Riddles Run Rd., Union, KY 41091 / 606-384-3127 engraving@fuse.net http://home.fuse.net/engraving/

Jeffredo Gunsight, P.O. Box 669, San Marcos, CA 92079 / 760-728-2695

Jena Eur, PO Box 319, Dunmore, PA 18512

Jenco Sales, Inc., PO Box 1000, Manchaca, TX 78652 / 800-531-5301; FAX: 800-266-2373

Jenkins Recoil Pads, Inc., 5438 E. Frontage Ln., Olney, IL 62450 / 618-395-3416

Jensen Bullets, RR 1 Box 187, Arco, ID 83213 / 208-785-5590

Jensen's Custom Ammunition, 5146 E. Pima, Tucson, AZ 85712 / 602-325-3346; FAX: 602-322-5704

Jensen's Firearms Academy, 1280 W. Prince, Tucson, AZ 85705 / 602-293-8516

Jericho Tool & Die Co., Inc., 2917 St. Hwy. 7, Bainbridge, NY 13733 / 607-563-8222; FAX: 607-563-8560 jerichotool.com www.jerichotool.com

Jerry Phillips Optics, P.O. Box L632, Langhorne, PA 19047 / 215-757-5037; FAX: 215-757-7097

Jesse W. Smith Saddlery, 0499 County Road J, Pritchett, CO 81064 / 509-325-0622

Jester Bullets, Rt. 1 Box 27, Orienta, OK 73737

Jewell Triggers, Inc., 3620 Hwy. 123, San Marcos, TX 78666 / 512-353-2999; FAX: 512-392-0543

J-Gar Co., 183 Turnpike Rd., Dept. 3, Petersham, MA 01366-9604

JGS Precision Tool Mfg., 100 Main Sumner, Coos Bay, OR 97420 / 541-267-4331; FAX: 541-267-5996

Jim Chambers Flintlocks Ltd., Rt. 1, Box 513-A, Candler, NC 28715 / 704-667-8361

Jim Garthwaite Pistolsmith, Inc., Rt. 2 Box 310, Watsontown, PA 17777 / 717-538-1566

Jim Blair Engraving, PO Box 64, Glenrock, WY 82637 / 307-436-8115

Jim Noble Co., 1305 Columbia St, Vancouver, WA 98660 / 360-695-1309; FAX: 360-695-6835 jnobleco@aol.com

Jim Norman Custom Gunstocks, 14281 Cane Rd., Valley Center, CA 92082 / 619-749-6252

Jim's Gun Shop (See Spradlin's)

Jim's Precision, Jim Ketchum, 1725 Moclips Dr., Petaluma, CA 94952 / 707-762-3014

JLK Bullets, 414 Turner Rd., Dover, AR 72837 / 501-331-4194

Johanssons Vapentillbehor, Bert, S-430 20, Veddige, SWEDEN

John Hall Plastics, Inc., P.O. Box 1526, Alvin, TX 77512 / 713-489-8709

John J. Adams & Son Engravers, 7040 VT Rt 113, Vershire, VT 05079 / 802-685-0019

John Masen Co. Inc., 1305 Jelmak, Grand Prairie, TX 75050 / 817-430-8732; FAX: 817-430-1715

John Norrell Arms, 2608 Grist Mill Rd, Little Rock, AR 72207 / 501-225-7864

John Partridge Sales Ltd., Trent Meadows Rugeley, Staffordshire, WS15 2HS ENGLAND

John Rigby & Co., 500 Linne Rd. Ste. D, Paso Robles, CA 93446 / 805-227-4236; FAX: 805-227-4723 jrigby@calinet www.johnrigbyandco.com

Johnny Stewart Game Calls, Inc., P.O. Box 7954, 5100 Fort Ave., Waco, TX 76714 / 817-772-3261; FAX: 817-772-3670

John's Custom Leather, 523 S. Liberty St., Blairsville, PA 15717 / 724-459-6802; FAX: 724-459-5996

Johnson Wood Products, 34897 Crystal Road, Strawberry Point, IA 52076 / 563-933-6504 johnsonwoodproducts@yahoo.com

Johnston Bros. (See C&T Corp. TA Johnson Brothers)

Jonad Corp., 2091 Lakeland Ave., Lakewood, OH 44107 / 216-226-3161

Jonathan Arthur Ciener, Inc., 8700 Commerce St., Cape Canaveral, FL 32920 / 321-868-2200; FAX: 321-868-2201

Jones, Co., Dale, 680 Hoffman Draw, Kila, MT 59920 / 406-755-4684

Jones Custom Products, Neil A., 17217 Brookhouser Rd., Saegertown, PA 16433 / 814-763-2769; FAX: 814-763-4228

Jones, J. See: SSK INDUSTRIES

MANUFACTURER'S DIRECTORY

Jones Moulds, Paul, 4901 Telegraph Rd, Los Angeles, CA 90022 / 213-262-1510
JP Sales, Box 307, Anderson, TX 77830
JRP Custom Bullets, RR2 2233 Carlton Rd., Whitehall, NY 12887 / 518-282-0084 or 802-438-5548
JSL Ltd (See U.S. Importer-Specialty Shooters)
Juenke, Vern, 25 Bitterbush Rd., Reno, NV 89523 / 702-345-0225
Jungkind, Reeves C., 5001 Buckskin Pass, Austin, TX 78745-2841 / 512-442-1094
Jurras, L. See: L E JURRAS & ASSOC.
Justin Phillippi Custom Bullets, P.O. Box 773, Ligonier, PA 15658 / 412-238-9671

K

K&M Industries, Inc., Box 66, 510 S. Main, Troy, ID 83871 / 208-835-2281; FAX: 208-835-5211
K&M Services, 5430 Salmon Run Rd., Dover, PA 17315 / 717-292-3175; FAX: 717-292-3175
K. Eversull Co., Inc., 1 Tracemont, Boyce, LA 71409 / 318-793-8728; FAX: 318-793-5483 bestguns@aol.com
K.B.I. Inc, PO Box 6625, Harrisburg, PA 17112 / 717-540-8518; FAX: 717-540-8567
K.K. Arms Co., Star Route Box 671, Kerrville, TX 78028 / 210-257-4718; FAX: 210-257-4891
K.L. Null Holsters Ltd., 161 School St. NW, Hill City Station, Resaca, GA 30735 / 706-625-5643; FAX: 706-625-9392 ken@klnullholsters.com www.klnullholsters.com
Ka Pu Kapili, P.O. Box 745, Honokaa, HI 96727 / 808-776-1644; FAX: 808-776-1731
KA-BAR Knives, 1125 E. State St., Olean, NY 14760 / 800-282-0130; FAX: 716-373-6245 info@ka-bar.com www.ka-bar.com
Kahles A Swarovski Company, 2 Slater Rd., Cranston, RI 02920 / 401-946-2220; FAX: 401-946-2587
Kahr Arms, PO Box 220, 630 Route 303, Blauvelt, NY 10913 / 845-353-7770; FAX: 845-353-7833 www.kahr.com
Kailua Custom Guns Inc., 51 N. Dean Street, Coquille, OR 97423 / 541-396-5413 kailuacustom@aol.com www.kailuacustom.com
Kalispel Case Line, P.O. Box 267, Cusick, WA 99119 / 509-445-1121
Kamik Outdoor Footwear, 554 Montee de Liesse, Montreal, PQ H4T 1P1 CANADA / 514-341-3950; FAX: 514-341-1861
Kamyk Engraving Co., Steve, 9 Grandview Dr, Westfield, MA 01085-1810 / 413-568-0457
Kane, Edward, P.O. Box 385, Ukiah, CA 95482 / 707-462-2937
Kane Products, Inc., 5572 Brecksville Rd., Cleveland, OH 44131 / 216-524-9962
Kapro Mfg.Co. Inc. (See R.E.I.)
Kasenit Co., Inc., 13 Park Ave., Highland Mills, NY 10930 / 914-928-9595; FAX: 914-928-7292
Kaswer Custom, Inc., 13 Surrey Drive, Brookfield, CT 06804 / 203-775-0564; FAX: 203-775-6872
KDF, Inc., 2485 Hwy. 46 N., Seguin, TX 78155 / 830-379-8141; FAX: 830-379-5420
KeeCo Impressions, Inc., 346 Wood Ave., North Brunswick, NJ 08902 / 800-468-0546
Keeler, R. H., 817 "N" St., Port Angeles, WA 98362 / 206-457-4702
Kehr, Roger, 2131 Agate Ct. SE, Lacy, WA 98503 / 360-491-0691
Keith's Bullets, 942 Twisted Oak, Algonquin, IL 60102 / 708-658-3520
Keith's Custom Gunstocks, Keith M. Heppler, 540 Banyan Circle, Walnut Creek, CA 94598 / 925-934-3509; FAX: 925-934-3143 kmheppler@hotmail.com
Kelbly, Inc., 7222 Dalton Fox Lake Rd., North Lawrence, OH 44666 / 216-683-4674; FAX: 216-683-7349
Kelley's, P.O. Box 125, Woburn, MA 01801-0125 / 800-879-7273; FAX: 781-272-7077 kels@star.net www.kelsmilitary.com
Kellogg's Professional Products, 325 Pearl St., Sandusky, OH 44870 / 419-625-6551; FAX: 419-625-6167
Kelly, Lance, 1723 Willow Oak Dr., Edgewater, FL 32132 / 904-423-4933
Kel-Tec CNC Industries, Inc., PO Box 236009, Cocoa, FL 32923 / 407-631-0068; FAX: 407-631-1169
Kemen America, 2550 Hwy. 23, Wrenshall, MN 55797 / 218-384-3670 patrickl@midwestshootingschool.com midwestshootingschool.com
Ken Eyster Heritage Gunsmiths, Inc., 6441 Bishop Rd., Centerburg, OH 43011 / 740-625-6131; FAX: 740-625-7811
Ken Starnes Gunmaker, 15940 SW Holly Hill Rd, Hillsboro, OR 97123-9033 / 503-628-0705; FAX: 503-628-6005
Keng's Firearms Specialty, Inc. / US Tactical Systems, 875 Wharton Dr., P.O. Box 44405, Atlanta, GA 30336-1405 / 404-691-7611; FAX: 404-505-8445

Kennebec Journal, 274 Western Ave., Augusta, ME 04330 / 207-622-6288
Kennedy Firearms, 10 N. Market St., Muncy, PA 17756 / 717-546-6695
Kenneth W. Warren Engraver, PO Box 2842, Wenatchee, WA 98807 / 509-663-6123; FAX: 509-665-6123
KenPatable Ent., Inc., PO Box 19422, Louisville, KY 40259 / 502-239-5447
Ken's Gun Specialties, Rt. 1, Box 147, Lakeview, AR 72642 / 501-431-5606
Ken's Kustom Kartridges, 331 Jacobs Rd., Hubbard, OH 44425 / 216-534-4595
Kent Cartridge America, Inc, PO Box 849, 1000 Zigor Rd, Kearneysville, WV 25430
Kent Cartridge Mfg. Co. Ltd., Unit 16 Branbridges Industrial Esta, Tonbridge, Kent, ENGLAND / 622-872255; FAX: 622-872645
Keowee Game Calls, 608 Hwy. 25 North, Travelers Rest, SC 29690 / 864-834-7204; FAX: 864-834-7831
Kershaw Knives, 25300 SW Parkway Ave., Wilsonville, OR 97070 / 503-682-1966; or 800-325-2891; FAX: 503-682-7168
Kesselring Gun Shop, 4024 Old Hwy. 99N, Burlington, WA 98233 / 360-724-3113; FAX: 360-724-7003 info@kesselrings.com kesselrings.com
Ketchum, Jim (See Jim's Precision)
Kickeez I.N.C., Inc., 301 Industrial Dr, Carl Junction, MO 64834-8806 / 419-649-2100; FAX: 417-649-2200 kickey@ipa.net
Kilham & Co., Main St., P.O. Box 37, Lyme, NH 03768 / 603-795-4112
Kim Ahrends Custom Firearms, Inc., Box 203, Clarion, IA 50525 / 515-532-3449; FAX: 515-532-3926
Kimar (See U.S. Importer-IAR,Inc)
Kimber of America, Inc., 1 Lawton St., Yonkers, NY 10705 / 800-880-2418; FAX: 914-964-9340
King & Co., PO Box 1242, Bloomington, IL 61702 / 309-473-2161
King's Gun Works, 1837 W. Glenoaks Blvd., Glendale, CA 91201 / 818-956-6010; FAX: 818-548-8606
Kingyon, Paul L. (See Custom Calls)
Kirkpatrick Leather Co., PO Box 677, Laredo, TX 78040 / 956-723-6631; FAX: 956-725-0672 mike@kirkpatrickleather.com www.kirkpatrickleather.com
KK Air International (See Impact Case Co.)
KLA Enterprises, P.O. Box 2028, Eaton Park, FL 33840 / 941-682-2829; FAX: 941-682-2829
Kleen-Bore,Inc., 16 Industrial Pkwy., Easthampton, MA 01027 / 413-527-0300; FAX: 413-527-2522 info@kleen-bore.com; www.kleen-bore.com
Klein Custom Guns, Don, 433 Murray Park Dr, Ripon, WI 54971 / 920-748-2931 daklein@charter.net
Kleinendorst, K. W., RR 1, Box 1500, Hop Bottom, PA 18824 / 717-289-4687
Klingler Woodcarving, P.O. Box 141, Thistle Hill, Cabot, VT 05647 / 802-426-3811
Knifeware, Inc., P.O. Box 3, Greenville, WV 24945 / 304-832-6878
Knight & Hale Game Calls, Box 468, Industrial Park, Cadiz, KY 42211 / 502-924-1755; FAX: 502-924-1763
Knight Rifles, 21852 hwy j46, P.O. Box 130, Centerville, IA 52544 / 515-856-2626; FAX: 515-856-2628
Knight Rifles (See Modern Muzzle Loading, Inc.)
Knight's Mfg. Co., 7750 Ninth St. SW, Vero Beach, FL 32968 / 561-562-5697; FAX: 561-569-2955
Knippel, Richard, 500 Gayle Ave Apt 213, Modesto, CA 95350-4241 / 209-869-1469
Knock on Wood Antiques, 355 Post Rd., Darien, CT 06820 / 203-655-9031
Knoell, Doug, 9737 McCardle Way, Santee, CA 92071 / 619-449-5189
Knopp, Gary. See: SUPER 6 LLC
Koevenig's Engraving Service, Box 55 Rabbit Gulch, Hill City, SD 57745 / 605-574-2239
KOGOT, 410 College, Trinidad, CO 81082 / 719-846-9406; FAX: 719-846-9406
Kokolus, Michael M. (See Custom Riflestocks)
Kolar, 1925 Roosevelt Ave, Racine, WI 53406 / 414-554-0800; FAX: 414-554-9093
Kolpin Mfg., Inc., P.O. Box 107, 205 Depot St., Fox Lake, WI 53933 / 414-928-3118; FAX: 414-928-3687
Korth, Robert-Bosch-Str. 4, P.O. Box 1320, 23909 Ratzeburg, GERMANY / 4541-8009; FAX: 451-4993230
Korth USA, 437R Chandler St., Tewksbury, MA 01876 / 978-851-8656 www.korthusa.com
Korzinek Riflesmith, J., RD 2 Box 73D, Canton, PA 17724 / 717-673-8512
Koval Knives, 5819 Zarley St., Suite A, New Albany, OH 43054 / 614-855-0777; FAX: 614-855-0945

Kowa Optimed, Inc., 20001 S. Vermont Ave., Torrance, CA 90502 / 310-327-1913; FAX: 310-327-4177
Kramer Designs, P.O. Box 129, Clancy, MT 59634 / 406-933-8658; FAX: 406-933-8658
Kramer Handgun Leather, P.O. Box 112154, Tacoma, WA 98411 / 206-564-6652; FAX: 206-564-1214
Krause Publications, Inc., 700 E. State St., Iola, WI 54990 / 715-445-2214; FAX: 715-445-4087
Krico Deutschland GmbH, Nurnbergerstrasse 6, D-90602, Pyrbaum, GERMANY / 09180-2780; FAX: 09180-2661
Krieger Barrels, Inc., N114 W18697 Clinton Dr., Germantown, WI 53022 / 414-255-9593; FAX: 414-255-9586
Krieghoff Gun Co., H., Boschstrasse 22, D-89079 Elm, GERMANY or 731-4018270
Krieghoff International,Inc., 7528 Easton Rd., Ottsville, PA 18942 / 610-847-5173; FAX: 610-847-8691
KSN Industries Ltd (See U.S. Importer-Israel Arms)
Kukowski, Ed. See: ED'S GUN HOUSE
Kulis Freeze Dry Taxidermy, 725 Broadway Ave., Bedford, OH 44146 / 216-232-8352; FAX: 216-232-7305 jkulis@kastaway.com kastaway.com
KVH Industries, Inc., 110 Enterprise Center, Middletown, RI 02842 / 401-847-3327; FAX: 401-849-0045
Kwik-Site Co., 5555 Treadwell St., Wayne, MI 48184 / 734-326-1500; FAX: 734-326-4120 kwiksiteco@aol.com

L

L E Jurras & Assoc., L. E. Jurras, PO Box 680, Washington, IN 47501 / 812-254-6170; FAX: 812-254-6170 jurasgun@rtcc.net
L&R Lock Co., 1137 Pocalla Rd., Sumter, SC 29150 / 803-775-6127; FAX: 803-775-5171
L&S Technologies Inc (See Aimtech Mount Systems)
L. Bengtson Arms Co., 6345-B E. Akron St., Mesa, AZ 85205 / 602-981-6375
L.A.R. Mfg., Inc., 4133 W. Farm Rd., West Jordan, UT 84088 / 801-280-3505; FAX: 801-280-1972
L.B.T., Judy Smith, HCR 62, Box 145, Moyie Springs, ID 83845 / 208-267-3588
L.E. Wilson, Inc., Box 324, 404 Pioneer Ave., Cashmere, WA 98815 / 509-782-1328; FAX: 509-782-7200
L.L. Bean, Inc., Freeport, ME 04032 / 207-865-4761; FAX: 207-552-2802
L.P.A. Snc, Via Alfieri 26, Gardone V.T., Brescia, ITALY / 30-891-14-81; FAX: 30-891-09-51
L.R. Clift Mfg., 3821 Hammonton Rd., Marysville, CA 95901 / 916-755-3390; FAX: 916-755-3393
L.S. Starrett Co., 121 Crescent St., Athol, MA 01331 / 617-249-3551
L.W. Seecamp Co., Inc., PO Box 255, New Haven, CT 06502 / 203-877-3429; FAX: 203-877-3429 seecamp@optonline.net
La Clinique du .45, 1432 Rougemont, Chambly,, PQ J3L 2L8 CANADA / 514-658-1144
Labanu, Inc., 2201-F Fifth Ave., Ronkonkoma, NY 11779 / 516-467-6197; FAX: 516-981-4112
LaBoone, Pat. See: THE MIDWEST SHOOTING SCHOOL
LaBounty Precision Reboring, Inc, 7968 Silver Lake Rd., PO Box 186, Maple Falls, WA 98266 / 360-599-2047; FAX: 360-599-3018
LaCrosse Footwear, Inc., P.O. Box 1328, La Crosse, WI 54602 / 608-782-3020; or 800-323-2668; FAX: 800-658-9444
LaFrance Specialties, P.O. Box 87933, San Diego, CA 92138-7933 / 619-293-3373; FAX: 619-293-7087
Lake Center Marina, PO Box 670, St. Charles, MO 63302 / 314-946-7500
Lakefield Arms Ltd (See Savage Arms Inc.)
Lakewood Products LLC, 275 June St., Berlin, WI 54923 / 800-872-8458; FAX: 920-361-7719 lakewood@dotnet.com; www.lakewoodproducts.com
Lamboy, Stephen. See: ITHACA CLASSIC DOUBLES
Lampert, Ron, Rt. 1, 44857 Schoolcraft Trl., Guthrie, MN 56461 / 218-854-7345
Lamson & Goodnow Mfg. Co., 45 Conway St., Shelburne Falls, MA 03170 / 413-625-6564; or 800-872-6564; FAX: 413-625-9816 www.lamsonsharp.com
Langenberg Hat Co., P.O. Box 1860, Washington, MO 63090 / 800-428-1860; FAX: 314-239-3151
Lansky Levine, Arthur. See: LANSKY SHARPENERS
Lansky Sharpeners, Arthur Lansky Levine, PO Box 50830, Las Vegas, NV 89016 / 702-361-7511; FAX: 702-896-9511
LaPrade, PO Box 250, Ewing, VA 24248 / 423-733-2615
Lapua Ltd., P.O. Box 5, Lapua, FINLAND / 6-310111; FAX: 6-4388991
LaRocca Gun Works, 51 Union Place, Worcester, MA 01608 / 508-754-2887; FAX: 508-754-2887
Larry Lyons Gunworks, 110 Hamilton St., Dowagiac, MI 49047 / 616-782-9478

Laser Devices, Inc., 2 Harris Ct. A-4, Monterey, CA 93940 / 408-373-0701; FAX: 408-373-0903

Laseraim Technologies, Inc., P.O. Box 3548, Little Rock, AR 72203 / 501-375-2227

Laserlyte, 2201 Amapola Ct., Torrance, CA 90501

LaserMax, Inc., 3495 Winton Place, Bldg. B, Rochester, NY 14623-2807 / 800-527-3703; FAX: 716-272-5427

Lassen Community College, Gunsmithing Dept., P.O. Box 3000, Hwy. 139, Susanville, CA 96130 / 916-251-8800; FAX: 916-251-8838

Lathrop's, Inc., Inc., 5146 E. Pima, Tucson, AZ 85712 / 520-881-0266; or 800-875-4867; FAX: 520-322-5704

Laughridge, William R (See Cylinder & Slide Inc)

Laurel Mountain Forge, P.O. Box 52, Crown Point, IN 46308 / 219-548-2950; FAX: 219-548-2950

Laurona Armas Eibar, S.A.L., Avenida de Otaola 25, P.O. Box 260, Eibar 20600, SPAIN / 34-43-700600; FAX: 34-43-700616

Lawrence Brand Shot (See Precision Reloading)

Lawrence Leather Co., P.O. Box 1479, Lillington, NC 27546 / 910-893-2071; FAX: 910-893-4742

Lawson Co., Harry, 3328 N Richey Blvd., Tucson, AZ 85716 / 520-326-1117; FAX: 520-326-1117

Lawson, John. See: THE SIGHT SHOP

Lawson, John G (See Sight Shop, The)

Lazzeroni Arms Co., PO Box 26696, Tucson, AZ 85726 / 888-492-7247; FAX: 520-624-4250

Le Clear Industries (See E-Z-Way Systems), PO Box 4310, Newark, OH 43058-4310 / 614-345-6645; FAX: 614-345-6600

Lea Mfg. Co., 237 E. Aurora St., Waterbury, CT 06720 / 203-753-5116

Leapers, Inc., 7675 Five Mile Rd., Northville, MI 48167 / 248-486-1231; FAX: 248-486-1430

Leatherman Tool Group, Inc., 12106 NE Ainsworth Cir., P.O. Box 20595, Portland, OR 97294 / 503-253-7826; FAX: 503-253-7830

Lebeau-Courally, Rue St. Gilles, 386 4000, Liege, BELGIUM / 042-52-48-43; FAX: 32-042-52-20-08

Leckie Professional Gunsmithing, 546 Quarry Rd., Ottsville, PA 18942 / 215-847-8594

Ledbetter Airguns, Riley, 1804 E Sprague St, Winston Salem, NC 27107-3521 / 919-784-0676

Lee Co., T. K., 1282 Branchwater Ln., Birmingham, AL 35216 / 205-913-5222 odonmich@aol.com www.scopedot.com

Lee Precision, Inc., 4275 Hwy. U, Hartford, WI 53027 / 262-673-3075; FAX: 262-673-9273 info@leeprecision.com; www.leeprecision.com

Lee Supplies, Mark, 9901 France Ct., Lakeville, MN 55044 / 612-461-2114

LeFever Arms Co., Inc., 6234 Stokes, Lee Center Rd., Lee Center, NY 13363 / 315-337-6722; FAX: 315-337-1543

Legacy Sports International, 10 Prince St., Alexandria, VA 22314

Legend Products Corp., 21218 Saint Andrews Blvd., Boca Raton, FL 33433-2435

Leibowitz, Leonard, 1205 Murrayhill Ave., Pittsburgh, PA 15217 / 412-361-5455

Leica USA, Inc., 156 Ludlow Ave., Northvale, NJ 07647 / 201-767-7500; FAX: 201-767-8666

LEM Gun Specialties Inc. The Lewis Lead Remover, PO Box 2855, Peachtree City, GA 30269-2024 / 770-487-0556

Leonard Day, 6 Linseed Rd Box 1, West Hatfield, MA 01088-7505 / 413-337-8369

Les Baer Custom,Inc., 29601 34th Ave., Hillsdale, IL 61257 / 309-658-2716; FAX: 309-658-2610

LesMerises, Felix. See: ROCKY MOUNTAIN ARMOURY

Lethal Force Institute (See Police Bookshelf), PO Box 122, Concord, NH 03301 / 603-224-6814; FAX: 603-226-3554

Lett Custom Grips, 672 Currier Rd., Hopkinton, NH 03229-2652 / 800-421-5388; FAX: 603-226-4580 info@lettgrips.com; www.lettgrips.com

Leupold & Stevens, Inc., 14400 NW Greenbrier Pky., Beaverton, OR 97006 / 503-646-9171; FAX: 503-526-1455

Lever Arms Service Ltd., 2131 Burrard St., Vancouver, BC V6J 3H7 CANADA / 604-736-2711; FAX: 604-738-3503

Lew Horton Dist. Co., Inc., 15 Walkup Dr., Westboro, MA 01581 / 508-366-7400; FAX: 508-366-5332

Liberty Metals, 2233 East 16th St., Los Angeles, CA 90021 / 213-581-9171; FAX: 213-581-9351

Liberty Safe, 1060 N. Spring Creek Pl., Springville, UT 84663 / 800-247-5625; FAX: 801-489-6409

Liberty Shooting Supplies, P.O. Box 357, Hillsboro, OR 97123 / 503-640-5518; FAX: 503-640-5518 info@libertyshootingsupplies.com www.libertyshootingsupplies.com

Lightforce U.S.A. Inc., 19226 66th Ave. So., L-103, Kent, WA 98032 / 208-476-9814; FAX: 208-476-9814

Lightning Performance Innovations, Inc., RD1 Box 555, Mohawk, NY 13407 / 315-866-8819; FAX: 315-867-5701

Lilja Precision Rifle Barrels, PO Box 372, Plains, MT 59859 / 406-826-3084; FAX: 406-826-3083 lilja@riflebarrels.com www.riflebarrels.com

Lincoln, Dean, Box 1886, Farmington, NM 87401

Lind Custom Guns, 7821 76th Ave SW, Lakewood, WA 98498 / 253-584-6361 lindcustguns@worldnot.att.net

Linder Solingen Knives, 4401 Sentry Dr., Tucker, GA 30084 / 770-939-6915; FAX: 770-939-6738

Lindsay, Steve, RR 2 Cedar Hills, Kearney, NE 68847 / 308-236-7885

Lindsley Arms Cartridge Co., P.O. Box 757, 20 College Hill Rd., Henniker, NH 03242 / 603-428-3127

Linebaugh Custom Sixguns, P.O. Box 455, Cody, WY 82414 / 307-645-3332 sitgunner.com

Lion Country Supply, P.O. Box 480, Port Matilda, PA 16870

List Precision Engineering, Unit 1 Ingley Works, 13 River Road, Barking, ENGLAND / 011-081-594-1686

Lithi Bee Bullet Lube, 1728 Carr Rd., Muskegon, MI 49442 / 616-788-4479

"Little John's" Antique Arms, 1740 W. Laveta, Orange, CA 92668

Little Trees Ramble (See Scott Pilkington)

Littler Sales Co., 20815 W. Chicago, Detroit, MI 48228 / 313-273-6889; FAX: 313-273-1099 littlerptg@aol.com

Littleton, J. F., 275 Pinedale Ave., Oroville, CA 95966 / 916-533-6084

Ljutic Industries, Inc., 732 N. 16th Ave., Suite 22, Yakima, WA 98902 / 509-248-0476; FAX: 509-576-8233 ljuticgun.net www.ljuticgun.com

Llama Gabilondo Y Cia, Apartado 290, E-01080, Victoria, spain, SPAIN

Loch Leven Industries / Convert-A-Pell, PO Box 2751, Santa Rosa, CA 95405 / 707-573-8735; FAX: 707-573-0369

Lock's Philadelphia Gun Exchange, 6700 Rowland Ave., Philadelphia, PA 19149 / 215-332-6225; FAX: 215-332-4800

Lodewick, Walter H., 2816 NE Halsey St., Portland, OR 97232 / 503-284-2554

Lodgewood Mfg., P.O. Box 611, Whitewater, WI 53190 / 262-473-5444; FAX: 262-473-6448 lodgewd@idcnet.com www.lodgewood.com

Log Cabin Sport Shop, 8010 Lafayette Rd., Lodi, OH 44254 / 330-948-1082; FAX: 330-948-4307

Logan, Harry M., Box 745, Honokaa, HI 96727 / 808-776-1644

Logdewood Mfg., PO Box 611, Whitewater, WI 53190 / 262-473-5444; FAX: 262-473-6448 lodgewd@idcnet.com

Lohman Mfg. Co., Inc., 4500 Doniphan Dr., P.O. Box 220, Neosho, MO 64850 / 417-451-4438; FAX: 417-451-2576

Lomont Precision Bullets, 278 Sandy Creek Rd, Salmon, ID 83467 / 208-756-6819; FAX: 208-756-6824 klomont.com

London Guns Ltd., Box 3750, Santa Barbara, CA 93130 / 805-683-4141; FAX: 805-683-1712

Lone Star Gunleather, 1301 Brushy Bend Dr., Round Rock, TX 78681 / 512-255-1805

Lone Star Rifle Company, 11231 Rose Road, Conroe, TX 77303 / 936-856-3363

Long, George F., 1500 Rogue River Hwy., Ste. F, Grants Pass, OR 97527 / 541-476-7552

Lortone Inc., 2856 NW Market St., Seattle, WA 98107

Lothar Walther Precision Tool Inc., 3425 Hutchinson Rd., Cumming, GA 30040 / 770-889-9998; FAX: 770-889-4919 lotharwalther@mindspring.com www.lothar-walther.com

Loweth, Richard H.R., 29 Hedgegrow Lane, Kirby Muxloe, Leics, LE9 2BN ENGLAND / (0) 116 238 6295

LPS Laboratories, Inc., 4647 Hugh Howell Rd., P.O. Box 3050, Tucker, GA 30084 / 404-934-7800

Lucas, Edward E, 32 Garfield Ave., East Brunswick, NJ 08816 / 201-251-5526

Lupton, Keith. See: PAWLING MOUNTAIN CLUB

Lyman Instant Targets, Inc. (See Lyman Products)

Lyman Products Corp., 475 Smith Street, Middletown, CT 06457-1541 / 860-632-2020; or 800-225-9626; FAX: 860-632-1699 lymansales@cshore.com www.lymanproducts.com

M

M. Thys (See U.S. Importer-Champlin Firearms Inc)

M.H. Canjar Co., 6510 Raleigh St., Arvada, CO 80003 / 303-295-2638; FAX: 303-295-2638

M.O.A. Corp., 2451 Old Camden Pike, Eaton, OH 45320 / 937-456-3669

MA Systems, P.O. Box 1143, Chouteau, OK 74337 / 918-479-6378

Mac-1 Airgun Distributors, 13974 Van Ness Ave., Gardena, CA 90249 / 310-327-3581; FAX: 310-327-0238 mac1@maclairgun.com mac1airgun.com

Macbean, Stan, 754 North 1200 West, Orem, UT 84057 / 801-224-6446

Madis Books, 2453 West Five Mile Pkwy., Dallas, TX 75233 / 214-330-7168

Madis, George. See: WINCHESTER CONSULTANTS

MAG Instrument, Inc., 1635 S. Sacramento Ave., Ontario, CA 91761 / 909-947-1006; FAX: 909-947-3116

Magma Engineering Co., P.O. Box 161, 20955 E. Ocotillo Rd., Queen Creek, AZ 85242 / 602-987-9008; FAX: 602-987-0148

Mag-Na-Port International, Inc., 41302 Executive Dr., Harrison Twp., MI 48045-1306 / 586-469-6727; FAX: 586-469-0425 email@magnaport.com www.magnaport.com

Magnolia Sports,Inc., 211 W. Main, Magnolia, AR 71753 / 501-234-8410; or 800-530-7816; FAX: 501-234-8117

Magnum Power Products, Inc., P.O. Box 17768, Fountain Hills, AZ 85268

Magnum Research, Inc., 7110 University Ave. NE, Minneapolis, MN 55432 / 800-772-6168; or 763-574-1868; FAX: 763-574-0109 magnumresearch.com

Magnus Bullets, P.O. Box 239, Toney, AL 35773 / 256-420-8359; FAX: 256-420-8360

Mag-Pack Corp., P.O. Box 846, Chesterland, OH 44026

MagSafe Ammo Co., 4700 S US Highway 17/92, Casselberry, FL 32707-3814 / 407-834-9966; FAX: 407-834-8185

Magtech Ammunition Co. Inc., 837 Boston Rd #12, Madison, CT 06443 / 203-245-8983; FAX: 203-245-2883 rfine@mactechammunition.com www.mactech.com.br

Mahony, Philip Bruce, 67 White Hollow Rd., Lime Rock, CT 06039-2418 / 203-435-9341

Mahovsky's Metalife, R.D. 1, Box 149a Eureka Road, Grand Valley, PA 16420 / 814-436-7747

Maine Custom Bullets, RFD 1, Box 1755, Brooks, ME 04921

Maionchi-L.M.I., Via Di Coselli-Zona, Industriale Di Guamo 55060, Lucca, ITALY / 011 39-583 94291

Makinson, Nicholas, RR 3, Komoka, ON N0L 1R0 CANADA / 519-471-5462

Malcolm Enterprises, 1023 E. Prien Lake Rd., Lake Charles, LA 70601

Mallardtone Game Calls, 2901 16th St., Moline, IL 61265 / 309-762-8089

Mandall Shooting Supplies Inc., 3616 N. Scottsdale Rd., Scottsdale, AZ 85251 / 480-945-2553; FAX: 480-949-0734

Marathon Rubber Prods. Co., Inc., 1009 3rd St, Wausau, WI 54403-4765 / 715-845-6255

Marble Arms (See CRR, Inc./Marble's Inc.)

Marchmon Bullets, 8191 Woodland Shore Dr., Brighton, MI 48116

Marent, Rudolf, 9711 Tiltree St., Houston, TX 77075 / 713-946-7028

Mark Lee Supplies, 9901 France Ct., Lakeville, MN 55044 / 612-461-2114

Markell,Inc., 422 Larkfield Center 235, Santa Rosa, CA 95403 / 707-573-0792; FAX: 707-573-9867

Markesbery Muzzle Loaders, Inc., 7785 Foundation Dr., Ste. 6, Florence, KY 41042 / 606-342-5553; or 606-342-2380

Marksman Products, 5482 Argosy Dr., Huntington Beach, CA 92649 / 714-898-7535; or 800-822-8005; FAX: 714-891-0782

Marlin Firearms Co., 100 Kenna Dr., North Haven, CT 06473 / 203-239-5621; FAX: 203-234-7991

MarMik, Inc., 2116 S. Woodland Ave., Michigan City, IN 46360 / 219-872-7231; FAX: 219-872-7231

Marocchi F.lli S.p.A, Via Galileo Galilei 8, I-25068 Zanano, ITALY

Marquart Precision Co., P.O. Box 1740, Prescott, AZ 86302 / 520-445-5646

Marsh, Mike, Croft Cottage, Main St., Derbyshire, DE4 2BY ENGLAND / 01629 650 669

Marshall Enterprises, 792 Canyon Rd., Redwood City, CA 94062

Martin B. Retting Inc., 11029 Washington, Culver City, CA 90232 / 213-837-2412

Martin Hagn Rifles & Actions, P.O. Box 444, Cranbrook, BC V1C 4H9 CANADA / 604-489-4861

Martin's Gun Shop, 937 S. Sheridan Blvd., Lakewood, CO 80226 / 303-922-2184

Martz, John V., 8060 Lakeview Lane, Lincoln, CA 95648 FAX: 916-645-3815

Marvel, Alan, 3922 Madonna Rd., Jarretsville, MD 21084 / 301-557-6545

Marx, Harry (See U.S. Importer for FERLIB)

Maryland Paintball Supply, 8507 Harford Rd., Parkville, MD 21234 / 410-882-5607

MAST Technology, P.O. Box 60969, Boulder City, NV 89006

Master Lock Co., 2600 N. 32nd St., Milwaukee, WI 53245 / 414-444-2800

Match Prep--Doyle Gracey, P.O. Box 155, Tehachapi, CA 93581 / 661-822-5383; FAX: 661-823-8680

Mathews & Son, Inc., George E., 10224 S Paramount Blvd, Downey, CA 90241 / 562-862-6719; FAX: 562-862-6719

Matthews Cutlery, 4401 Sentry Dr., Tucker, GA 30084 / 770-939-6915

Mauser Werke Oberndorf Waffensysteme GmbH, Postfach 1349, 78722, Oberndorf/N., GERMANY

Maverick Arms, Inc., 7 Grasso Ave., P.O. Box 497, North Haven, CT 06473 / 203-230-5300; FAX: 203-230-5420

Maxi-Mount Inc., P.O. Box 291, Willoughby Hills, OH 44096-0291 / 440-944-9456; FAX: 440-944-9456 maximount454@yahoo.com

Mayville Engineering Co. (See MEC, Inc.)

Mazur Restoration, Pete, 13083 Drummer Way, Grass Valley, CA 95949 / 530-268-2412

McBros Rifle Co., P.O. Box 86549, Phoenix, AZ 85080 / 602-582-3713; FAX: 602-581-3825

McCament, Jay. See: JAY MCCAMENT CUSTOM GUNMAKER

McCann Industries, P.O. Box 641, Spanaway, WA 98387 / 253-537-6919; FAX: 253-537-6919 mccann.machine@worldnet.att.net www.mccannindustries.com

McCann's Machine & Gun Shop, P.O. Box 641, Spanaway, WA 98387 / 253-537-6919; FAX: 253-537-6993 mccann.machine@worldnet.att.net www.mccannindustries.com

McCann's Muzzle-Gun Works, 14 Walton Dr., New Hope, PA 18938 / 215-862-2728

McCluskey Precision Rifles, 10502 14th Ave. NW, Seattle, WA 98177 / 206-781-2776

McCombs, Leo, 1862 White Cemetery Rd., Patriot, OH 45658 / 614-256-1714

McCormick Corp., Chip, 1715 W. FM 1626 Ste. 105, Manchaca, TX 78652 / 800-328-CHIP; FAX: 512-462-0009

McDonald, Dennis, 8359 Brady St., Peosta, IA 52068 / 319-556-7940

McFarland, Stan, 2221 Idella Ct., Grand Junction, CO 81505 / 970-243-4704

McGhee, Larry. See: B.C. OUTDOORS

McGowen Rifle Barrels, 5961 Spruce Lane, St. Anne, IL 60964 / 815-937-9816; FAX: 815-937-4024

Mchalik, Gary. See: ROSSI FIREARMS

McKenzie, Lynton, 6940 N. Alvernon Way, Tucson, AZ 85718 / 520-299-5090

McKinney, R.P. (See Schuetzen Gun Co.)

McMillan Fiberglass Stocks, Inc., 1638 W. Knudsen Dr. #102, Phoenix, AZ 85027 / 602-582-9635; FAX: 602-581-3825

McMillan Optical Gunsight Co., 28638 N. 42nd St., Cave Creek, AZ 85331 / 602-585-7868; FAX: 602-585-7872

McMillan Rifle Barrels, P.O. Box 3427, Bryan, TX 77805 / 409-690-3456; FAX: 409-690-0156

McMurdo, Lynn (See Specialty Gunsmithing), PO Box 404, Afton, WY 83110 / 307-886-5535

MCS, Inc., 34 Delmar Dr., Brookfield, CT 06804 / 203-775-1013; FAX: 203-775-9462

McWelco Products, 6730 Santa Fe Ave., Hesperia, CA 92345 / 619-244-8876; FAX: 619-244-9398

MDS, P.O. Box 1441, Brandon, FL 33509-1441 / 813-653-1180; FAX: 813-684-5953

Measurement Group Inc., Box 27777, Raleigh, NC 27611

Measures, Leon. See: SHOOT WHERE YOU LOOK

MEC, Inc., 715 South St., Mayville, WI 53050 / 414-387-4500; FAX: 414-387-5802 reloaders@mayul.com www.mayvl.com

MEC-Gar S.R.l., Via Madonnina 64, Gardone V.T. Brescia, ITALY / 39-30-8912687; FAX: 39-30-8910065

MEC-Gar U.S.A., Inc., Hurley Farms Industr. Park, 115, Hurley Road 6G, Oxofrd, CT 06478 / 203-262-1525; FAX: 203-262-1719 mecgar@aol.com www.mec-gar.com

Mech-Tech Systems, Inc., 1602 Foothill Rd., Kalispell, MT 59901 / 406-755-8055

Meister Bullets (See Gander Mountain)

Mele, Frank, 201 S. Wellow Ave., Cookeville, TN 38501 / 615-526-4860

Menck, Gunsmith Inc., T.W., 5703 S 77th St, Ralston, NE 68127

Mendez, John A., P.O. Box 620984, Orlando, FL 32862 / 407-344-2791

Men-Metallwerk Elisenhuette GmbH, P.O. Box 1263, Nassau/Lahn, D-56372 GERMANY / 2604-7819

Meprolight (See Hesco-Meprolight)

Mercer Custom Guns, 216 S Whitewater Ave, Jefferson, WI 53549 / 920-674-3839

Merit Corp., PO Box 9044, Schenectady, NY 12309 / 518-346-1420 sales@meritcorporation.com www.meritcorporation.com

Merkel Freres, Strasse 7 October, 10, Suhl, GERMANY

Merkura Ltd., Argentinska 38, 17005, Praha 7 CZECH, REPUBLIC / 422-875117; FAX: 422-809152

Metal Merchants, PO Box 186, Walled Lake, MI 48390-0186

Metalife Industries (See Mahovsky's Metalife)

Metaloy, Inc., Rt. 5, Box 595, Berryville, AR 72616 / 501-545-3611

Metals Hand Engraver/European Hand Engraving, Ste. 216, 12 South First St., San Jose, CA 95113 / 408-293-6559

Michael's Antiques, Box 591, Waldoboro, ME 04572

Michaels Of Oregon, PO Box 1690, Oregon City, OR 97045 www.michaels-oregon.com

Micro Sight Co., 242 Harbor Blvd., Belmont, CA 94002 / 415-591-0769; FAX: 415-591-7531

Microfusion Alfa S.A., Paseo San Andres N8, P.O. Box 271, Eibar, 20600 SPAIN / 34-43-11-89-16; FAX: 34-43-11-40-38

Mid-America Recreation, Inc., 1328 5th Ave., Moline, IL 61265 / 309-764-5089; FAX: 309-764-2722

Middlebrooks Custom Shop, 7366 Colonial Trail East, Surry, VA 23883 / 757-357-0881; FAX: 757-365-0442

Midway Arms, Inc., 5875 W. Van Horn Tavern Rd., Columbia, MO 65203 / 800-243-3220; or 573-445-6363; FAX: 573-446-1018

Midwest Gun Sport, 1108 Herbert Dr., Zebulon, NC 27597 / 919-269-5570

Midwest Sport Distributors, Box 129, Fayette, MO 65248

Mike Davis Products, 643 Loop Dr., Moses Lake, WA 98837 / 509-765-6178; or 509-766-7281

Military Armament Corp., P.O. Box 120, Mt. Zion Rd., Lingleville, TX 76461 / 817-965-3253

Millennium Designed Muzzleloaders, PO Box 536, Routes 11 & 25, Limington, ME 04049 / 207-637-2316

Miller Arms, Inc., P.O. Box 260 Purl St., St. Onge, SD 57779 / 605-642-5160; FAX: 605-642-5160

Miller Custom, 210 E. Julia, Clinton, IL 61727 / 217-935-9362

Miller Single Trigger Mfg. Co., Rt. 209, Box 1275, Millersburg, PA 17061 / 717-692-3704

Millett Sights, 7275 Murdy Circle, Adm. Office, Huntington Beach, CA 92647 / 714-842-5575; or 800-645-5388; FAX: 714-843-5707

Mills Jr., Hugh B., 3615 Canterbury Rd., New Bern, NC 28560 / 919-637-4631

Milstor Corp., 80-975 Indio Blvd., Indio, CA 92201 / 760-775-9998; FAX: 760-775-5229 milstor@webtv.net

Miltex, Inc, 700 S Lee St, Alexandria, VA 22314-4332 / 888-642-9123; FAX: 301-645-1430

Minute Man High Tech Industries, 10611 Canyon Rd. E., Suite 151, Puyallup, WA 98373 / 800-233-2734

Mirador Optical Corp., P.O. Box 11614, Marina Del Rey, CA 90295-7614 / 310-821-5587; FAX: 310-305-0386

Miroku, B C/Daly, Charles (See U.S. Importer)

Mitchell, Jack, c/o Geoff Gaebe, Addieville East Farm, 200 Pheasant Dr, Mapleville, RI 02839 / 401-568-3185

Mitchell Bullets, R.F., 430 Walnut St, Westernport, MD 21562

Mitchell Optics, Inc., 2072 CR 1100 N, Sidney, IL 61877 / 217-688-2219; or 217-621-3018; FAX: 217-688-2505 mitche1@attglobal.net

Mitchell's Accuracy Shop, 68 Greenridge Dr., Stafford, VA 22554 / 703-659-0165

MI-TE Bullets, 1396 Ave. K, Ellsworth, KS 67439 / 785-472-4575; FAX: 785-472-5579

Mittermeier, Inc., Frank, PO Box 2G, 3577 E Tremont Ave, Bronx, NY 10465 / 718-828-3843

Mixson Corp., 7635 W. 28th Ave., Hialeah, FL 33016 / 305-821-5190; or 800-327-0078; FAX: 305-558-9318

MJK Gunsmithing, Inc., 417 N. Huber Ct., E. Wenatchee, WA 98802 / 509-884-7683

MKS Supply, Inc. (See Hi-Point Firearms)

MMC, 5050 E. Belknap St., Haltom City, TX 76117 / 817-831-9557; FAX: 817-834-5508

MMP, 518 Buck Hollow Lane, Harrison, AR 72601 / 870-741-5019; FAX: 870-741-3104 mmp@alltel.net www.mmpsabots.com

Modern Gun Repair School, PO Box 846, Saint Albans, VT 05478 / 802-524-2223; FAX: 802-524-2053 jfwp@dlilearn.com; www.mgsinfoadlifearn.com

Modern Muzzleloading, Inc, PO Box 130, Centerville, IA 52544 / 515-856-2626

Moeller, Steve, 1213 4th St., Fulton, IL 61252 / 815-589-2300

Mogul Co./Life Jacket, 500 N. Kimball Rd., Ste. 109, South Lake, TX 76092

Molin Industries, Tru-Nord Division, P.O. Box 365, 204 North 9th St., Brainerd, MN 56401 / 218-829-2870

Monell Custom Guns, 228 Red Mills Rd., Pine Bush, NY 12566 / 914-744-3021

Moneymaker Guncraft Corp., 1420 Military Ave., Omaha, NE 68131 / 402-556-0226

Montana Armory, Inc (See C. Sharps Arms Co. Inc.), 100 Centennial Dr., PO Box 885, Big Timber, MT 59011 / 406-932-4353; FAX: 406-932-4443

Montana Outfitters, Lewis E. Yearout, 308 Riverview Dr. E., Great Falls, MT 59404 / 406-761-0859

Montana Precision Swaging, PO Box 4746, Butte, MT 59702 / 406-494-0600; FAX: 406-494-0600

Montana Vintage Arms, 2354 Bear Canyon Rd., Bozeman, MT 59715

Montgomery Community College, PO Box 787-GD, Troy, NC 27371 / 910-576-6222; or 800-839-6222; FAX: 910-576-2176; hammondp@mcc.montgomery.cc.nc.us www.montgomery.cc.nc.us

Morini (See U.S. Importers-Mandall Shooting Supply)

Morrison Custom Rifles, J. W., 4015 W Sharon, Phoenix, AZ 85029 / 602-978-3754

Morrison Precision, 6719 Calle Mango, Hereford, AZ 85615 / 520-378-6207 morprec@c2i2.com

Morrow, Bud, 11 Hillside Lane, Sheridan, WY 82801-9729 / 307-674-8360

Morton Booth Co., P.O. Box 123, Joplin, MO 64802 / 417-673-1962; FAX: 417-673-3642

Mo's Competitor Supplies (See MCS Inc)

Moss Double Tone, Inc., P.O. Box 1112, 2101 S. Kentucky, Sedalia, MO 65301 / 816-827-0827

Mountain Hollow Game Calls, Box 121, Cascade, MD 21719 / 301-241-3282

Mountain Plains Industries, 244 Glass Hollow Rd., Alton, VA 22920 / 800-687-3000; FAX: 540-456-8134

Mountain South, P.O. Box 381, Barnwell, SC 29812 / FAX: 803-259-3227

Mountain State Muzzleloading Supplies, Inc., Box 154-1, Rt. 2, Williamstown, WV 26187 / 304-375-7842; FAX: 304-375-3737

Mountain View Sports, Inc., Box 188, Troy, NH 03465 / 603-357-9690; FAX: 603-357-9691

Mowrey Gun Works, P.O. Box 246, Waldron, IN 46182 / 317-525-6181; FAX: 317-525-9595

Mowrey's Guns & Gunsmithing, 119 Fredericks St., Canajoharie, NY 13317 / 518-673-3483

MPC, P.O. Box 450, McMinnville, TN 37110-0450 / 615-473-5513; FAX: 615-473-5516

MPI Stocks, PO Box 83266, Portland, OR 97283 / 503-226-1215; FAX: 503-226-2661

MSC Industrial Supply Co., 151 Sunnyside Blvd., Plainview, NY 11803-9915 / 516-349-0330

MSR Targets, P.O. Box 1042, West Covina, CA 91793 / 818-331-7840

Mt. Alto Outdoor Products, Rt. 735, Howardsville, VA 24562

MTM Molded Products Co., Inc., 3370 Obco Ct., Dayton, OH 45414 / 937-890-7461; FAX: 937-890-1747

Mulberry House Publishing, P.O. Box 2180, Apache Junction, AZ 85217 / 888-738-1567; FAX: 480-671-1015

Mulhern, Rick, Rt. 5, Box 152, Rayville, LA 71269 / 318-728-2688

Mullins Ammunition, Rt. 2, Box 304K, Clintwood, VA 24228 / 540-926-6772; FAX: 540-926-6092

Mullis Guncraft, 3523 Lawyers Road E., Monroe, NC 28110 / 704-283-6683

Multiplex International, 26 S. Main St., Concord, NH 03301 FAX: 603-796-2223

Multipropulseurs, La Bertrandiere, 42580, FRANCE / 77 74 01 30; FAX: 77 93 19 34

Multi-Scale Charge Ltd., 3269 Niagara Falls Blvd., N. Tonawanda, NY 14120 / 905-566-1255; FAX: 905-276-6295

Mundy, Thomas A., 69 Robbins Road, Somerville, NJ 08876 / 201-722-2199

Murmur Corp., 2823 N. Westmoreland Ave., Dallas, TX 75222 / 214-630-5400

Murphy, R.R. Murphy Co., Inc. See: MURPHY, R.R. CO., INC.

Murphy, R.R. Co., Inc., R.R. Murphy Co., Inc. Murphy, P.O. Box 102, Ripley, TN 38063 / 901-635-4003; FAX: 901-635-2320

Murray State College, 1 Murray Campus St., Tishomingo, OK 73460 / 508-371-2371

Muscle Products Corp., 112 Fennell Dr., Butler, PA 16002 / 800-227-7049; or 724-283-0567; FAX: 724-283-8310 mpc@mpc_home.com www.mpc_home.com

Muzzleloaders Etcetera, Inc., 9901 Lyndale Ave. S., Bloomington, MN 55420 / 612-884-1161 muzzleloaders-etcetera.com

MWG Co., P.O. Box 971202, Miami, FL 33197 / 800-428-9394; or 305-253-8393; FAX: 305-232-1247

N

N.B.B., Inc., 24 Elliot Rd., Sterling, MA 01564 / 508-422-7538; or 800-942-9444

N.C. Ordnance Co., P.O. Box 3254, Wilson, NC 27895 / 919-237-2440; FAX: 919-243-9845

Nagel's Custom Bullets, 100 Scott St., Baytown, TX 77520-2849

Nalpak, 1937-C Friendship Drive, El Cajon, CA 92020 / 619-258-1200

Nastoff, Steve. See: NASTOFFS 45 SHOP, INC.

Nastoffs 45 Shop, Inc., Steve Nastoff, 1057 Laverne Dr., Youngstown, OH 44511

National Bullet Co., 1585 E. 361 St., Eastlake, OH 44095 / 216-951-1854; FAX: 216-951-7761

National Target Co., 4690 Wyaconda Rd., Rockville, MD 20852 / 800-827-7060; or 301-770-7060; FAX: 301-770-7892

Naval Ordnance Works, Rt. 2, Box 919, Sheperdstown, WV 25443 / 304-876-0998

Navy Arms Company, Valmore J. Forgett Jr., 815 22nd Street, Union City, NJ 07087 / 201-863-7100; FAX: 201-863-8770 info@navyarms.com www.navyarms.com

NCP Products, Inc., 3500 12th St. N.W., Canton, OH 44708 / 330-456-5130; FAX: 330-456-5234

Necessary Concepts, Inc., P.O. Box 571, Deer Park, NY 11729 / 516-667-8509; FAX: 516-667-8588

Necromancer Industries, Inc., 14 Communications Way, West Newton, PA 15089 / 412-872-8722

NEI Handtools, Inc., 51583 Columbia River Hwy., Scappoose, OR 97056 / 503-543-6776; FAX: 503-543-7865 nei@columbia-center.com www.neihandtools.com

Neil A. Jones Custom Products, 17217 Brookhouser Road, Saegertown, PA 16433 / 814-763-2769; FAX: 814-763-4228

Nelson, Gary K., 975 Terrace Dr., Oakdale, CA 95361 / 209-847-4590

Nelson, Stephen. See: NELSON'S CUSTOM GUNS, INC.

Nelson/Weather-Rite, Inc., 14760 Santa Fe Trail Dr., Lenexa, KS 66215 / 913-492-3200; FAX: 913-492-8749

Nelson's Custom Guns, Inc., Stephen Nelson, 7430 Valley View Dr. N.W., Corvallis, OR 97330 / 541-745-5232 nelsons-custom@home.com

Nesci Enterprises Inc., P.O. Box 119, Summit St., East Hampton, CT 06424 / 203-267-2588

Nesika Bay Precision, 22239 Big Valley Rd., Poulsbo, WA 98370 / 206-697-3830

Nettestad Gun Works, 38962 160th Avenue, Pelican Rapids, MN 56572 / 218-863-4301

Neumann GmbH, Am Galgenberg 6, 90575, GERMANY / 09101/8258; FAX: 09101/6356

Nevada Pistol Academy, Inc., 4610 Blue Diamond Rd., Las Vegas, NV 89139 / 702-897-1100

New England Ammunition Co., 1771 Post Rd. East, Suite 223, Westport, CT 06880 / 203-254-8048

New England Arms Co., Box 278, Lawrence Lane, Kittery Point, ME 03905 / 207-439-0593; FAX: 207-439-0525 info@newenglandarms.com www.newenglandarms.com

New England Custom Gun Service, 438 Willow Brook Rd., Plainfield, NH 03781 / 603-469-3450; FAX: 603-469-3471 bestguns@cyborportal.net www.newengldandcustom.com

New England Firearms, 60 Industrial Rowe, Gardner, MA 01440 / 508-632-9393; FAX: 508-632-2300

New Orleans Jewelers Supply Co., 206 Charters St., New Orleans, LA 70130 / 504-523-3839; FAX: 504-523-3836

New SKB Arms Co., C.P.O. Box 1401, Tokyo, JAPAN / 81-3-3943-9550; FAX: 81-3-3943-0695

New Ultra Light Arms, LLC, 1024 Grafton Rd., Morgantown, WV 26508 / 304-292-0600; FAX: 304-292-9662 newultralightarm@cs.com www.NewUltraLightArm.com

Newark Electronics, 4801 N. Ravenswood Ave., Chicago, IL 60640

Newell, Robert H., 55 Coyote, Los Alamos, NM 87544 / 505-662-7135

Newman Gunshop, 119 Miller Rd., Agency, IA 52530 / 515-937-5775

Nicholson Custom, 17285 Thornlay Road, Hughesville, MO 65334 / 816-826-8746

Nickels, Paul R., 4328 Seville St., Las Vegas, NV 89121 / 702-435-5318

Nicklas, Ted, 5504 Hegel Rd., Goodrich, MI 48438 / 810-797-4493

Niemi Engineering, W. B., Box 126 Center Rd, Greensboro, VT 05841 / 802-533-7180; FAX: 802-533-7141

Nightforce (See Lightforce USA Inc)

Nikon, Inc., 1300 Walt Whitman Rd., Melville, NY 11747 / 516-547-8623; FAX: 516-547-0309

Nitex Gun Shop, P.O. Box 1706, Uvalde, TX 78801 / 830-278-8843

Noreen, Peter H., 5075 Buena Vista Dr., Belgrade, MT 59714 / 406-586-7383

Norica, Avnda Otaola, 16 Apartado 68, Eibar, SPAIN

Norinco, 7A Yun Tan N, Beijing, CHINA

Norincoptics (See BEC, Inc.)

Norma Precision AB (See U.S. Importers-Dynamit)

Normark Corp., 10395 Yellow Circle Dr., Minnetonka, MN 55343-9101 / 612-933-7060; FAX: 612-933-0046

North American Arms, Inc., 2150 South 950 East, Provo, UT 84606-6285 / 800-821-5783; or 801-374-9990; FAX: 801-374-9998

North American Correspondence Schools The Gun Pro, Oak & Pawney St., Scranton, PA 18515 / 717-342-7701

North American Shooting Systems, P.O. Box 306, Osoyoos, BC V0H 1V0 CANADA / 604-495-3131; FAX: 604-495-2816

North Devon Firearms Services, 3 North St., Braunton, EX33 1AJ ENGLAND / 01271 813624; FAX: 01271 813624

North Mountain Pine Training Center (See Executive

North Pass, 1418 Webster Ave, Fort Collins, CO 80524 / 970-407-0426

North Specialty Products, 10091 Stageline St., Corona, CA 92883 / 714-524-1665

North Star West, P.O. Box 488, Glencoe, CA 95232 / 209-293-7010 northstarwest.com

North Wind Decoy Co., 1005 N. Tower Rd., Fergus Falls, MN 56537 / 218-736-4378; FAX: 218-736-7060

Northern Precision Custom Swaged Bullets, 329 S. James St., Carthage, NY 13619 / 315-493-1711

Northlake Outdoor Footwear, P.O. Box 10, Franklin, TN 37065-0010 / 615-794-1556; FAX: 615-790-8005

Northside Gun Shop, 2725 NW 109th, Oklahoma City, OK 73120 / 405-840-2353

Northwest Arms, 26884 Pearl Rd., Parma, ID 83660 / 208-722-6771; FAX: 208-722-1062

No-Sho Mfg. Co., 10727 Glenfield Ct., Houston, TX 77096 / 713-723-5332

Nosler, Inc., P.O. Box 671, Bend, OR 97709 / 800-285-3701; or 541-382-3921; FAX: 541-388-4667

Novak's, Inc., 1206 1/2 30th St., P.O. Box 4045, Parkersburg, WV 26101 / 304-485-9295; FAX: 304-428-6722

Now Products, Inc., PO Box 27608, Tempe, AZ 85285 / 800-662-6063; FAX: 480-966-0890

Nowlin Mfg. Co., 20622 S 4092 Rd, Claremore, OK 74017 / 918-342-0689; FAX: 918-342-0624 nowlinguns@msn.com; nowlinguns.com

NRI Gunsmith School, 4401 Connecticut Ave. NW, Washington, DC 20008

Nu-Line Guns, Inc., 1053 Caulks Hill Rd., Harvester, MO 63304 / 314-441-4500; or 314-447-4501; FAX: 314-447-5018

Null Holsters Ltd. K.L., 161 School St NW, Resaca, GA 30735 / 706-625-5643; FAX: 706-625-9392

Numrich Arms Corp., 203 Broadway, W. Hurley, NY 12491

NW Sinker and Tackle, 380 Valley Dr., Myrtle Creek, OR 97457-9717

Nygord Precision Products, Inc., P.O. Box 12578, Prescott, AZ 86304 / 928-717-2315; FAX: 928-717-2198

O

O.F. Mossberg & Sons, Inc., 7 Grasso Ave., North Haven, CT 06473 / 203-230-5300; FAX: 203-230-5420

Oakland Custom Arms, Inc., 4690 W. Walton Blvd., Waterford, MI 48329 / 810-674-8261

Oakman Turkey Calls, RD 1, Box 825, Harrisonville, PA 17228 / 717-485-4620

Obermeyer Rifled Barrels, 23122 60th St., Bristol, WI 53104 / 262-843-3537; FAX: 262-843-2129

October Country Muzzleloading, P.O. Box 969, Dept. GD, Hayden, ID 83835 / 208-772-2068; FAX: 208-772-9230 ocinfo@octobercountry.com www.octobercountry.com

Oehler Research, Inc., PO Box 9135, Austin, TX 78766 / 512-327-6900; or 800-531-5125; FAX: 512-327-6903

Oil Rod and Gun Shop, 69 Oak St., East Douglas, MA 01516 / 508-476-3687

Ojala Holsters, Arvo, PO Box 98, N Hollywood, CA 91603 / 503-669-1404

OK Weber, Inc., P.O. Box 7485, Eugene, OR 97401 / 541-747-0458; FAX: 541-747-5927 okweber@pacinfo okweber.com

Oker's Engraving, PO Box 126, Shawnee, CO 80475 / 303-838-6042

Oklahoma Ammunition Co., 3701A S. Harvard Ave., No. 367, Tulsa, OK 74135-2265 / 918-396-3187; FAX: 918-396-4270

Oklahoma Leather Products, Inc., 500 26th NW, Miami, OK 74354 / 918-542-6651; FAX: 918-542-6653

Old Wagon Bullets, 32 Old Wagon Rd., Wilton, CT 06897

Old West Bullet Moulds, J Ken Chapman, P.O. Box 519, Flora Vista, NM 87415 / 505-334-6970

Old West Reproductions, Inc. R.M. Bachman, 446 Florence S. Loop, Florence, MT 59833 / 406-273-2615; FAX: 406-273-2615

Old Western Scrounger, Inc., 12924 Hwy. A-I2, Montague, CA 96064 / 916-459-5445; FAX: 916-459-3944

Old World Gunsmithing, 2901 SE 122nd St., Portland, OR 97236 / 503-760-7681

Old World Oil Products, 3827 Queen Ave. N., Minneapolis, MN 55412 / 612-522-5037

Ole Frontier Gunsmith Shop, 2617 Hwy. 29 S., Cantonment, FL 32533 / 904-477-8074

Olson, Myron, 989 W. Kemp, Watertown, SD 57201 / 605-886-9787

Olson, Vic, 5002 Countryside Dr., Imperial, MO 63052 / 314-296-8086

Olympic Arms Inc., 620-626 Old Pacific Hwy. SE, Olympia, WA 98513 / 360-456-3471; FAX: 360-491-3447

Olympic Optical Co., P.O. Box 752377, Memphis, TN 38175-2377 / 901-794-3890; or 800-238-7120; FAX: 901-794-0676 80

Omega Sales, P.O. Box 1066, Mt. Clemens, MI 48043 / 810-469-7323; FAX: 810-469-0425

100 Straight Products, Inc., P.O. Box 6148, Omaha, NE 68106 / 402-556-1055; FAX: 402-556-1055

One Of A Kind, 15610 Purple Sage, San Antonio, TX 78255 / 512-695-3364

One Ragged Hole, P.O. Box 13624, Tallahassee, FL 32317-3624

Op-Tec, P.O. Box L632, Langhorn, PA 19047 / 215-757-5037

Optical Services Co., P.O. Box 1174, Santa Teresa, NM 88008-1174 / 505-589-3833

Orchard Park Enterprise, P.O. Box 563, Orchard Park, NY 14127 / 616-656-0356

Oregon Arms, Inc. (See Rogue Rifle Co., Inc.)

Oregon Trail Bullet Company, PO Box 529, Dept. P, Baker City, OR 97814 / 800-811-0548; FAX: 514-523-1803

Original Box, Inc., 700 Linden Ave., York, PA 17404 / 717-854-2897; FAX: 717-845-4276

Original Deer Formula Co., The., PO Box 1705, Dickson, TN 37056 / 800-874-6965; FAX: 615-446-0646 deerformula1@aol.com

Original Mink Oil, Inc., 10652 NE Holman, Portland, OR 97220 / 503-255-2814; or 800-547-5895; FAX: 503-255-2487

Orion Rifle Barrel Co., RR2, 137 Cobler Village, Kalispell, MT 59901 / 406-257-5649

Otis Technology, Inc., RR 1 Box 84, Boonville, NY 13309 / 315-942-3320

Ottmar, Maurice, Box 657, 113 E. Fir, Coulee City, WA 99115 / 509-632-5717

Outa-Site Gun Carriers, 219 Market St., Laredo, TX 78040 / 210-722-4678; or 800-880-9715; FAX: 210-726-4858

Outdoor Edge Cutlery Corp., 6395 Gunpark Dr., Unit Q, Boulder, CO 80301 / 303-652-8212; FAX: 303-652-8238

Outdoor Enthusiast, 3784 W. Woodland, Springfield, MO 65807 / 417-883-9841

Outdoor Sports Headquarters, Inc., 967 Watertower Ln., West Carrollton, OH 45449 / 513-865-5855; FAX: 513-865-5962

Outers Laboratories Div. of ATK, Route 2, P.O. Box 39, Onalaska, WI 54650 / 608-781-5800; FAX: 608-781-0368

Ox-Yoke Originals, Inc., 34 Main St., Milo, ME 04463 / 800-231-8313; or 207-943-7351; FAX: 207-943-2416

Ozark Gun Works, 11830 Cemetery Rd., Rogers, AR 72756 / 479-631-1024; FAX: 479-631-1024 ogw@hotmail.com www.eocities.com/ocarkgunworks

P

P&M Sales & Services, LLC, 4697 Tote Rd. Bldg. H-B, Comins, MI 48619 / 989-848-8364

P.A.C.T., Inc., P.O. Box 531525, Grand Prairie, TX 75053 / 214-641-0049

P.M. Enterprises, Inc. / Precise Metalsmithing, 146 Curtis Hill Rd., Chehalis, WA 98532 / 360-748-3743; FAX: 360-748-1802 precise1@quik.com

P.S.M.G. Gun Co., 10 Park Ave., Arlington, MA 02174 / 617-646-8845; FAX: 617-646-2133

Pace Marketing, Inc., P.O. Box 2039, Stuart, FL 34995 / 561-871-9682; FAX: 561-871-6552

Pachmayr Div. Lyman Products, 475 Smith St., Middletown, CT 06457 / 860-632-2020; or 800-225-9626; FAX: 860-632-1699 lymansales@cshore.com www.pachmayr.com

Pacific Armament Corp, 4813 Enterprise Way, Unit K, Modesto, CA 95356 / 209-545-2800 gunsparts@att.net

Pacific Cartridge, Inc., 2425 Salashan Loop Road, Ferndale, WA 98248 / 360-366-4444; FAX: 360-366-4445

Pacific Research Laboratories, Inc. (See Rimrock)

Pacific Rifle Co., PO Box 1473, Lake Oswego, OR 97035 / 503-538-7437

Pac-Nor Barreling, 99299 Overlook Rd., PO Box 6188, Brookings, OR 97415 / 503-469-7330; FAX: 503-469-7331

Paco's (See Small Custom Mould & Bullet Co)

Page Custom Bullets, P.O. Box 25, Port Moresby, NEW GUINEA

Pagel Gun Works, Inc., 1407 4th St. NW, Grand Rapids, MN 55744 / 218-326-3003

Pager Pal, 200 W Pleasantview, Hurst, TX 76054 / 800-561-1603; FAX: 817-285-8769 www.pagerpal.com

Paintball Games International Magazine Aceville, Castle House 97 High St., Essex, ENGLAND / 011-44-206-564840

Palmer Security Products, 2930 N. Campbell Ave., Chicago, IL 60618 / 773-267-0200; FAX: 773-267-8080 info@palmersecurity.com www.palmersecurity.com

Palsa Outdoor Products, P.O. Box 81336, Lincoln, NE 68501 / 402-488-5288; FAX: 402-488-2321

Paragon Sales & Services, Inc., 2501 Theodore St, Crest Hill, IL 60435-1613 / 815-725-9212; FAX: 815-725-8974

Para-Ordnance Mfg., Inc., 980 Tapscott Rd., Scarborough, ON M1X 1E7 CANADA / 416-297-7855; FAX: 416-297-1289

Para-Ordnance, Inc., 1919 NE 45th St., Ste 215, Ft. Lauderdale, FL 33308

Pardini Armi Srl, Via Italica 154, 55043, Lido Di Camaiore Lu, ITALY / 584-90121; FAX: 584-90122

Paris, Frank J., 17417 Pershing St., Livonia, MI 48152-3822

Parker & Sons Shooting Supply, 9337 Smoky Row Road, Strawberry Plains, TN 37871 / 865-933-3286; FAX: 865-932-8586

Parker Gun Finishes, 9337 Smokey Row Rd., Strawberry Plains, TN 37871 / 423-933-3286

Parker Reproductions, 114 Broad St., Flemington, NJ 08822 / 908-469-0100; FAX: 908-469-9692

Parsons Optical Mfg. Co., PO Box 192, Ross, OH 45061 / 513-867-0820; FAX: 513-867-8380 psscopes@concentric.net

Partridge Sales Ltd., John, Trent Meadows, Rugeley, ENGLAND

Parts & Surplus, P.O. Box 22074, Memphis, TN 38122 / 901-683-4007

Pasadena Gun Center, 206 E. Shaw, Pasadena, TX 77506 / 713-472-0417; FAX: 713-472-1322

Passive Bullet Traps, Inc. (See Savage Range)

Paterson Gunsmithing, 438 Main St., Paterson, NJ 07502 / 201-345-4100

Pathfinder Sports Leather, 2920 E. Chambers St., Phoenix, AZ 85040 / 602-276-0016

Patrick W. Price Bullets, 16520 Worthley Drive, San Lorenzo, CA 94580 / 510-278-1547

Pattern Control, 114 N. Third St., P.O. Box 462105, Garland, TX 75046 / 214-494-3551; FAX: 214-272-8447

Paul A. Harris Hand Engraving, 113 Rusty Lane, Boerne, TX 78006-5746 / 512-391-5121

Paul and Sharon Dressel, 209 N. 92nd Ave., Yakima, WA 98908 / 509-966-9233; FAX: 509-966-3485 dressels@nwinfo.net www.dressels.com

Paul D. Hillmer Custom Gunstocks, 7251 Hudson Heights, Hudson, IA 50643 / 319-988-3941

Paul Jones Moulds, 4901 Telegraph Rd., Los Angeles, CA 90022 / 213-262-1510

Paulsen Gunstocks, Rt. 71, Box 11, Chinook, MT 59523 / 406-357-3403

Pawling Mountain Club, Keith Lupton, PO Box 573, Pawling, NY 12564 / 914-855-3825

Paxton Quigley's Personal Protection Strategies, 9903 Santa Monica Blvd., 300, Beverly Hills, CA 90212 / 310-281-1762 www.defend-net.com/paxton

Payne Photography, Robert, Robert, P.O. Box 141471, Austin, TX 78714 / 512-272-4554

PC Co., 5942 Secor Rd., Toledo, OH 43623 / 419-472-6222

Peacemaker Specialists, PO Box 157, Whitmore, CA 96096 / 530-472-3438

Pearce Grip, Inc., PO Box 40367, Fort Worth, TX 76140 / 206-485-5488; FAX: 206-488-9497

Pease Accuracy, Bob, P.O. Box 310787, New Braunfels, TX 78131 / 210-625-1342

PECAR Herbert Schwarz GmbH, Kreuzbergstrasse 6, 10965, Berlin, GERMANY / 004930-785-7383; FAX: 004930-785-1934 michael.schwart@pecar-berlin.de www.pecar-berlin.de

Pecatonica River Longrifle, 5205 Nottingham Dr., Rockford, IL 61111 / 815-968-1995; FAX: 815-968-1996

Pedersen, C. R., 2717 S. Pere Marquette Hwy., Ludington, MI 49431 / 231-843-2061; FAX: 231-845-7695 fega@fega.com

Pedersen, Rex C., 2717 S. Pere Marquette Hwy., Ludington, MI 49431 / 231-843-2061; FAX: 231-845-7695 fega@fega.com

Peet Shoe Dryer, Inc., 130 S. 5th St., P.O. Box 618, St. Maries, ID 83861 / 208-245-2095; or 800-222-PEET; FAX: 208-245-5441

Peifer Rifle Co., P.O. Box 192, Nokomis, IL 62075-0192 / 217-563-7050; FAX: 217-563-7060

Pejsa Ballistics, 1314 Marquette Ave., Apt 807, Minneapolis, MN 55403 / 612-374-3337; FAX: 612-374-5383

Pelaire Products, 5346 Bonky Ct., W. Palm Beach, FL 33415 / 561-439-0691; FAX: 561-967-0052

Pell, John T. (See KOGOT)

Peltor, Inc. (See Aero Peltor)

PEM's Mfg. Co., 5063 Waterloo Rd., Atwater, OH 44201 / 216-947-3721

Pence Precision Barrels, 7567 E. 900 S., S. Whitley, IN 46787 / 219-839-4745

Pendleton Royal, c/o Swingler Buckland Ltd., 4/7 Highgate St., Birmingham, ENGLAND / 44 121 440 3060; or 44 121 446 5898; FAX: 44 121 446 4165

Pendleton Woolen Mills, P.O. Box 3030, 220 N.W. Broadway, Portland, OR 97208 / 503-226-4801

Penn Bullets, P.O. Box 756, Indianola, PA 15051

Pennsylvania Gun Parts Inc, PO Box 665, 300 Third St, East Berlin, PA 17316-0665 / 717-259-8010; FAX: 717-259-0057

Pennsylvania Gunsmith School, 812 Ohio River Blvd., Avalon, Pittsburgh, PA 15202 / 412-766-1812; FAX: 412-766-0855 pgs@pagunsmith.com www.pagunsmith.com

Penrod Precision, 312 College Ave., PO Box 307, N. Manchester, IN 46962 / 260-982-8385; FAX: 260-982-1819

Pentax Corp., 35 Inverness Dr. E., Englewood, CO 80112 / 303-799-8000; FAX: 303-790-1131

Pentheny de Pentheny, 2352 Baggett Ct., Santa Rosa, CA 95401 / 707-573-1390; FAX: 707-573-1390

Perazone-Gunsmith, Brian, Cold Spring Rd, Roxbury, NY 12474 / 607-326-4088; FAX: 607-326-3140

Perazzi U.S.A. Inc., 1010 West Tenth, Azusa, CA 91702 / 626-334-1234; FAX: 626-334-0344 perazziusa@aol.com

Performance Specialists, 308 Eanes School Rd., Austin, TX 78746 / 512-327-0119

Perugini Visini & Co. S.r.l., Via Camprelle, 126, 25080 Nuvolera, ITALY / 30-6897535; FAX: 30-6897821

Pete Elsen, Inc., 1529 S. 113th St., West Allis, WI 53214 / 414-476-4660; FAX: 414-476-5160

Pete Mazur Restoration, 13083 Drummer Way, Grass Valley, CA 95949 / 530-268-2412

Pete Rickard, Inc., 115 Roy Walsh Rd, Cobleskill, NY 12043 / 518-234-2731; FAX: 518-234-2454 rickard@telenet.net peterickard.com

Peter Dyson & Son Ltd., 3 Cuckoo Lane, Honley Huddersfield, Yorkshire, HD7 2BR ENGLAND / 44-1484-661062; FAX: 44-1484-663709 info@peterdyson.co.uk www.peterdyson.com

Peter Hale/Engraver, 800 E. Canyon Rd., Spanish Fork, UT 84660 / 801-798-8215

Peters Stahl GmbH, Stettiner Strasse 42, D-33106, Paderborn, GERMANY / 05251-750025; FAX: 05251-75611

Petersen Publishing Co. (See Emap USA), 6420 Wilshire Blvd., Los Angeles, CA 90048 / 213-782-2000; FAX: 213-782-2867

Peterson Gun Shop, Inc., A.W., 4255 W. Old U.S. 441, Mt. Dora, FL 32757-3299 / 352-383-4258; FAX: 352-735-1001

Petro-Explo Inc., 7650 U.S. Hwy. 287, Suite 100, Arlington, TX 76017 / 817-478-8888

Pettinger Books, Gerald, Rt. 2, Box 125, Russell, IA 50238 / 641-535-2239 gpettinger@lisco.com

Pflumm Mfg. Co., 10662 Widmer Rd., Lenexa, KS 66215 / 800-888-4867; FAX: 913-451-7857

PFRB Co., PO Box 1242, Bloomington, IL 61702 / 309-473-3964; FAX: 309-473-2161

Philip S. Olt Co., P.O. Box 550, 12662 Fifth St., Pekin, IL 61554 / 309-348-3633; FAX: 309-348-3300

Phillippi Custom Bullets, Justin, P.O. Box 773, Ligonier, PA 15658 / 724-238-2962; FAX: 724-238-9671 jrp@wpa.net http://www.wpa.net~jrphil

Phillips & Rogers, Inc., 100 Hilbig #C, Conroe, TX 77301 / 409-435-0011

Phoenix Arms, 1420 S. Archibald Ave., Ontario, CA 91761 / 909-947-4843; FAX: 909-947-6798

Photronic Systems Engineering Company, 6731 Via De La Reina, Bonsall, CA 92003 / 619-758-8000

Piedmont Community College, P.O. Box 1197, Roxboro, NC 27573 / 336-599-1181; FAX: 336-597-3817 www.piedmont.cc.nc.us

Pierce Pistols, 55 Sorrellwood Lane, Sharpsburg, GA 30277-9523 / 404-253-8192

Pietta (See U.S. Importers-Navy Arms Co, Taylor's

Pilgrim Pewter,Inc. (See Bell Originals Inc. Sid)

Pilkington, Scott (See Little Trees Ramble)

Pine Technical College, 1100 4th St., Pine City, MN 55063 / 800-521-7463; FAX: 612-629-6744

Pinetree Bullets, 133 Skeena St., Kitimat, BC V8C 1Z1 CANADA / 604-632-3768; FAX: 604-632-3768

Pioneer Arms Co., 355 Lawrence Rd., Broomall, PA 19008 / 215-356-5203

Piotti (See U.S. Importer-Moore & Co, Wm. Larkin)

Piquette, Paul. See: PIQUETTE'S CUSTOM ENGRAVING

Piquette's Custom Engraving, Paul R. Piquette, 80 Bradford Dr., Feeding Hills, MA 01030 / 413-789-4582; FAX: 413-786-8118 ppiquette@aol.com www.pistoldynamics.com

Plaza Cutlery, Inc., 3333 Bristol, 161 South Coast Plaza, Costa Mesa, CA 92626 / 714-549-3932

Plum City Ballistic Range, N2162 80th St., Plum City, WI 54761 / 715-647-2539

PlumFire Press, Inc., 30-A Grove Ave., Patchogue, NY 11772-4112 / 800-695-7246; FAX: 516-758-4071

PMC / Eldorado Cartridge Corp., PO Box 62508, 12801 U.S. Hwy. 95 S., Boulder City, NV 89005 / 702-294-0025; FAX: 702-294-0121 kbauer@pmcammo.com www.pmcammo.com

Poburka, Philip (See Bison Studios)

Pohl, Henry A. (See Great American Gun Co.

Pointing Dog Journal, Village Press Publications, P.O. Box 968, Dept. PGD, Traverse City, MI 49685 / 800-272-3246; FAX: 616-946-3289

Police Bookshelf, PO Box 122, Concord, NH 03301 / 603-224-6814; FAX: 603-226-3554

Polywad, Inc., P.O. Box 7916, Macon, GA 31209 / 912-477-0669 polywadmpb@aol.com www.polywad.com

Ponsness/Warren, P.O. Box 8, Rathdrum, ID 83858 / 208-687-2231; FAX: 208-687-2233

Pony Express Reloaders, 608 E. Co. Rd. D, Suite 3, St. Paul, MN 55117 / 612-483-9406; FAX: 612-483-9884

Pony Express Sport Shop, 16606 Schoenborn St., North Hills, CA 91343 / 818-895-1231

Potts, Wayne E., 912 Poplar St., Denver, CO 80220 / 303-355-5462

Powder Horn Ltd., PO Box 565, Glenview, IL 60025 / 305-565-6060

Powell & Son (Gunmakers) Ltd., William, 35-37 Carrs Lane, Birmingham, B4 7SX ENGLAND / 121-643-0689; FAX: 121-631-3504

Powell Agency, William, 22 Circle Dr., Bellmore, NY 11710 / 516-679-1158

Power Custom, Inc., 29739 Hwy. J, Gravois Mills, MO 65037 / 573-372-5684; FAX: 573-372-5799 rwpowers@laurie.net www.powercustom.com

Power Plus Enterprises, Inc., PO Box 38, Warm Springs, GA 31830 / 706-655-2132

Powley Computer (See Hutton Rifle Ranch)

Practical Tools, Inc., 7067 Easton Rd., P.O. Box 133, Pipersville, PA 18947 / 215-766-7301; FAX: 215-766-8681

Prairie Gun Works, 1-761 Marion St., Winnipeg, MB R2J 0K6 CANADA / 204-231-2976; FAX: 204-231-8566

Prairie River Arms, 1220 N. Sixth St., Princeton, IL 61356 / 815-875-1616; or 800-445-1541; FAX: 815-875-1402

Pranger, Ed G., 1414 7th St., Anacortes, WA 98221 / 206-293-3488

Precise Metalsmithing Enterprises / P.M. Enterprises, 146 Curtis Hill Rd., Chehalis, WA 98532 / 360-748-3743; FAX: 360-748-8102 precise1@quik.com

Precision Airgun Sales, Inc., 5247 Warrensville Ctr Rd, Maple Hts., OH 44137 / 216-587-5005; FAX: 216-587-5005

Precision Cast Bullets, 101 Mud Creek Lane, Ronan, MT 59864 / 406-676-5135

Precision Delta Corp., PO Box 128, Ruleville, MS 38771 / 662-756-2810; FAX: 662-756-2590

Precision Firearm Finishing, 25 N.W. 44th Avenue, Des Moines, IA 50313 / 515-288-8680; FAX: 515-244-3925

Precision Gun Works, 104 Sierra Rd Dept. GD, Kerrville, TX 78028 / 830-367-4587

Precision Munitions, Inc., P.O. Box 326, Jasper, IN 47547

Precision Reloading, Inc., PO Box 122, Stafford Springs, CT 06076 / 860-684-7979; FAX: 860-684-6788 info@precisionreloading.com www.precisionreloading.com

Precision Sales International, Inc., PO Box 1776, Westfield, MA 01086 / 413-562-5055; FAX: 413-562-5056 precision-sales.com

Precision Shooting, Inc., 222 McKee St., Manchester, CT 06040 / 860-645-8776; FAX: 860-643-8215 www.precisionshooting.com

Precision Small Arms Inc., 9272 Jeronimo Rd, Ste 121, Irvine, CA 92618 / 800-554-5515; or 949-768-3530; FAX: 949-768-4808 www.tcbebe.com

Precision Specialties, 131 Hendom Dr., Feeding Hills, MA 01030 / 413-786-3365; FAX: 413-786-3365

Precision Sport Optics, 15571 Producer Lane, Unit G, Huntington Beach, CA 92649 / 714-891-1309; FAX: 714-892-6920

Premier Reticles, 920 Breckinridge Lane, Winchester, VA 22601-6707 / 540-722-0601; FAX: 540-722-3522

Prescott Projectile Co., 1808 Meadowbrook Road, Prescott, AZ 86303

Preslik's Gunstocks, 4245 Keith Ln., Chico, CA 95926 / 916-891-8236

Price Bullets, Patrick W., 16520 Worthley Dr., San Lorenzo, CA 94580 / 510-278-1547

Prime Reloading, 30 Chiswick End, Meldreth, ROYSTON UK / 0763-260663

Primos, Inc., P.O. Box 12785, Jackson, MS 39236-2785 / 601-366-1288; FAX: 601-362-3274

PRL Bullets, c/o Blackburn Enterprises, 114 Stuart Rd., Ste. 110, Cleveland, TN 37312 / 423-559-0340

Pro Load Ammunition, Inc., 5180 E. Seltice Way, Post Falls, ID 83854 / 208-773-9444; FAX: 208-773-9441

Professional Gunsmiths of America, Rt 1 Box 224, Lexington, MO 64067 / 660-259-2636

Professional Hunter Supplies (See Star Custom Bull), PO Box 608, 468 Main St, Ferndale, CA 95536 / 707-786-9140; FAX: 707-786-9117 wmebride@humboldt.com

Professional Ordnance, Inc., 1070 Metric Drive, Lake Havasu City, AZ 86403 / 928-505-2420; FAX: 928-505-2141 www.professional-ordnance.com

PrOlixr Lubricants, PO Box 1348, Victorville, CA 92393 / 760-243-3129; FAX: 760-241-0148 prolix@accex.net prolixlubricant.com

Pro-Mark Div. of Wells Lamont, 6640 W. Touhy, Chicago, IL 60648 / 312-647-8200

Proofmark Corp., PO Box 610, Burgess, VA 22432 / 804-453-4337; FAX: 804-453-4337 proofmark@rivnet.net

Pro-Port Ltd., 41302 Executive Dr., Harrison Twp., MI 48045-1306 / 586-469-6727; FAX: 586-469-0425 e-mail@magnaport.com www.magnaport.com

Pro-Shot Products, Inc., P.O. Box 763, Taylorville, IL 62568 / 217-824-9133; FAX: 217-824-8861

Protektor Model, 1-11 Bridge St., Galeton, PA 16922 / 814-435-2442 hrk@penn.com www.protektormodel.com

Prototech Industries, Inc., 10532 E Road, Delia, KS 66418 / 785-771-3571; prototec@grapevine.net

ProWare, Inc., 15847 NE Hancock St., Portland, OR 97230 / 503-239-0159

PWL Gunleather, P.O. Box 450432, Atlanta, GA 31145 / 800-960-4072; FAX: 770-822-1704 covert@pwlusa.com www.pwlusa.com

Pyromid, Inc., PO Box 6466, Bend, OR 97708 / 503-548-1041; FAX: 503-923-1004

Q

Quack Decoy & Sporting Clays, 4 Ann & Hope Way, P.O. Box 98, Cumberland, RI 02864 / 401-723-8202; FAX: 401-722-5910

Quaker Boy, Inc., 5455 Webster Rd., Orchard Parks, NY 14127 / 716-662-3979; FAX: 716-662-9426

Quality Arms, Inc., Box 19477, Dept. GD, Houston, TX 77224 / 281-870-8377; FAX: 281-870-8524 arrieta2@excite.com www.gunshop.com

Quality Custom Firearms, Stepehn Billeb, 22 Vista View Drive, Cody, WY 82414 / 307-587-4278; FAX: 307-587-4297 stevbilleb@wyoming.com

Quality Firearms of Idaho, Inc., 659 Harmon Way, Middleton, ID 83644-3065 / 208-466-1631

Que Industries, Inc., PO Box 2471, Everett, WA 98203 / 425-303-9088; FAX: 206-514-3266 queinfo@queindustries.com

Queen Cutlery Co., PO Box 500, Franklinville, NY 14737 / 800-222-5233; FAX: 800-299-2618

R

R&C Knives & Such, 2136 CANDY CANE WALK, Manteca, CA 95336-9501 / 209-239-3722; FAX: 209-825-6947

R&D Gun Repair, Kenny Howell, RR1 Box 283, Beloit, WI 53511

R&J Gun Shop, 337 S. Humbolt St., Canyon City, OR 97820 / 541-575-2130 rjgunshop@highdestertnet.com

R&S Industries Corp., 8255 Brentwood Industrial Dr., St. Louis, MO 63144 / 314-781-5400 polishingcloth.com

R. Murphy Co., Inc., 13 Groton-Harvard Rd., P.O. Box 376, Ayer, MA 01432 / 617-772-3481

R.A. Wells Custom Gunsmith, 3452 1st Ave., Racine, WI 53402 / 414-639-5223

R.E. Seebeck Assoc., P.O. Box 59752, Dallas, TX 75229

R.E.I., P.O. Box 88, Tallevast, FL 34270 / 813-755-0085

R.E.T. Enterprises, 2608 S. Chestnut, Broken Arrow, OK 74012 / 918-251-GUNS; FAX: 918-251-0587

R.F. Mitchell Bullets, 430 Walnut St., Westernport, MD 21562

R.I.S. Co., Inc., 718 Timberlake Circle, Richardson, TX 75080 / 214-235-0933

R.T. Eastman Products, P.O. Box 1531, Jackson, WY 83001 / 307-733-3217; or 800-624-4311

Rabeno, Martin, 92 Spook Hole Rd., Ellenville, NY 12428 / 845-647-2121; FAX: 845-647-2121 fancygun@aol.com

Radack Photography, Lauren, 21140 Jib Court L-12, Aventura, FL 33180 / 305-931-3110

Radiator Specialty Co., 1900 Wilkinson Blvd., P.O. Box 34689, Charlotte, NC 28234 / 800-438-6947; FAX: 800-421-9525

Radical Concepts, P.O. Box 1473, Lake Grove, OR 97035 / 503-538-7437

Rainier Ballistics Corp., 4500 15th St. East, Tacoma, WA 98424 / 800-638-8722; or 206-922-7589; FAX: 206-922-7854

Ralph Bone Engraving, 718 N. Atlanta St., Owasso, OK 74055 / 918-272-9745

Ram-Line Blount, Inc., P.O. Box 39, Onalaska, WI 54650

Ramon B. Gonzalez Guns, PO Box 370, 93 St. Joseph's Hill Road, Monticello, NY 12701 / 914-794-4515

Rampart International, 2781 W. MacArthur Blvd., B-283, Santa Ana, CA 92704 / 800-976-7240; or 714-557-6405

Ranch Products, P.O. Box 145, Malinta, OH 43535 / 313-277-3118; FAX: 313-565-8536

Randall-Made Knives, P.O. Box 1988, Orlando, FL 32802 / 407-855-8075

Randco UK, 286 Gipsy Rd., Welling, DA16 1JJ ENGLAND / 44 81 303 4118

Randolph Engineering Inc., 26 Thomas Patten Dr., Randolph, MA 02368 / 781-961-6070; FAX: 781-961-0337

Randy Duane Custom Stocks, 7822 Church St., Middletown, VA 22645-9521

Range Brass Products Company, P.O. Box 218, Rockport, TX 78381

Ranger Shooting Glasses, 26 Thomas Patten Dr., Randolph, MA 02368 / 800-541-1405; FAX: 617-986-0337

Ransom International Corp., 1027 Spire Dr, Prescott, AZ 86302 / 520-778-7899; FAX: 520-778-7993 ransom@primenet.com www.ransom-intl.com

Rapine Bullet Mould Mfg. Co., 9503 Landis Lane, East Greenville, PA 18041 / 215-679-5413; FAX: 215-679-9795

Raptor Arms Co., Inc., 273 Canal St, #179, Shelton, CT 06484 / 203-924-7618; FAX: 203-924-7624

Ravell Ltd., 289 Diputacion St., 08009, Barcelona, SPAIN / 34(3) 4874486; FAX: 34(3) 4881394

Ray Riling Arms Books Co., 6844 Gorsten St., Philadelphia, PA 19119 / 215-438-2456; FAX: 215-438-5395 sales@rayrilingarmsbooks.com www.rayrilings.com

Ray's Gunsmith Shop, 3199 Elm Ave., Grand Junction, CO 81504 / 970-434-6162; FAX: 970-434-6162

Raytech Div. of Lyman Products Corp., 475 Smith Street, Middletown, CT 06457-1541 / 860-632-2020; or 800-225-9626; FAX: 860-632-1699 lymansales@cshore.com www.lymanproducts.com

RCBS Div. of Blount, 605 Oro Dam Blvd., Oroville, CA 95965 / 800-533-5000; or 916-533-5191; FAX: 916-533-1647 www.rcbs.com

Reagent Chemical & Research, Inc. (See Calico Hard)

Reardon Products, P.O. Box 126, Morrison, IL 61270 / 815-772-3155

Red Diamond Dist. Co., 1304 Snowdon Dr., Knoxville, TN 37912

Redding Reloading Equipment, 1089 Starr Rd., Cortland, NY 13045 / 607-753-3331; FAX: 607-756-8445 techline@redding-reloading.com www.redding-reloading.com

Redfield Media Resource Center, 4607 N.E. Cedar Creek Rd., Woodland, WA 98674 / 360-225-5000; FAX: 360-225-7616

Redman's Rifling & Reboring, 189 Nichols Rd., Omak, WA 98841 / 509-826-5512

Redwood Bullet Works, 3559 Bay Rd., Redwood City, CA 94063 / 415-367-6741

Reed, Dave, Rt. 1, Box 374, Minnesota City, MN 55959 / 507-689-2944

Reiswig, Wallace E. (See Claro Walnut Gunstock

Reloaders Equipment Co., 4680 High St., Ecorse, MI 48229

Reloading Specialties, Inc., Box 1130, Pine Island, MN 55463 / 507-356-8500; FAX: 507-356-8800

Remington Arms Co., Inc., 870 Remington Drive, P.O. Box 700, Madison, NC 27025-0700 / 800-243-9700; FAX: 910-548-8700

Remington Double Shotguns, 7885 Cyd Dr., Denver, CO 80221 / 303-429-6947

Renato Gamba S.p.A.-Societa Armi Bresciane Srl., Via Artigiani 93, 25063 Gardone, Val Trompia (BS), ITALY / 30-8911640; FAX: 30-8911648

Renegade, P.O. Box 31546, Phoenix, AZ 85046 / 602-482-6777; FAX: 602-482-1952

Renfrew Guns & Supplies, R.R. 4, Renfrew, ON K7V 3Z7 CANADA / 613-432-7080

Reno, Wayne, 2808 Stagestop Road, Jefferson, CO 80456

Republic Arms, Inc. (See Cobra Enterprises, Inc.)

Retting, Inc., Martin B, 11029 Washington, Culver City, CA 90232 / 213-837-2412

RG-G, Inc., PO Box 935, Trinidad, CO 81082 / 719-845-1436

RH Machine & Consulting Inc, PO Box 394, Pacific, MO 63069 / 314-271-8465

Rhino, P.O. Box 787, Locust, NC 28097 / 704-753-2198

Rhodeside, Inc., 1704 Commerce Dr., Piqua, OH 45356 / 513-773-5781

Rice, Keith (See White Rock Tool & Die)

Richard H.R. Loweth (Firearms), 29 Hedgegrow Lane, Kirby Muxloe, Leics. LE9 2BN, ENGLAND

Richards Micro-Fit Stocks, 8331 N. San Fernando Ave., Sun Valley, CA 91352 / 818-767-6097; FAX: 818-767-7121

Rickard, Inc., Pete, RD 1, Box 292, Cobleskill, NY 12043 / 800-282-5663; FAX: 518-234-2454

Ridgeline, Inc, Bruce Sheldon, PO Box 930, Dewey, AZ 86327-0930 / 800-632-5900; FAX: 520-632-5900

Ridgetop Sporting Goods, P.O. Box 306, 42907 Hilligoss Ln. East, Eatonville, WA 98328 / 360-832-6422; FAX: 360-832-6422

Ries, Chuck, 415 Ridgecrest Dr., Grants Pass, OR 97527 / 503-476-5623

Rifles, Inc., 873 W. 5400 N., Cedar City, UT 84720 / 801-586-5996; FAX: 801-586-5996

Rigby & Co., John, 500 Linne Rd. Ste. D, Paso Robles, CA 93446 / 805-227-4236; FAX: 805-227-4723 jrigby@calinet www.johnrigbyandco.com

Riggs, Jim, 206 Azalea, Boerne, TX 78006 / 210-249-8567

Riley Ledbetter Airguns, 1804 E. Sprague St., Winston Salem, NC 27107-3521 / 919-784-0676

Rim Pac Sports, Inc., 1034 N. Soldano Ave., Azusa, CA 91702-2135

Ringler Custom Leather Co., 31 Shining Mtn. Rd., Powell, WY 82435 / 307-645-3255

Ripley Rifles, 42 Fletcher Street, Ripley, Derbyshire, DE5 3LP ENGLAND / 011-0773-748353

River Road Sporting Clays, Bruce Barsotti, P.O. Box 3016, Gonzales, CA 93926 / 408-675-2473

Rizzini F.lli (See U.S. Importers-Moore & C England)

Rizzini SNC, Via 2 Giugno, 7/7Bis-25060, Marcheno (Brescia), ITALY

RLCM Enterprises, 110 Hill Crest Drive, Burleson, TX 76028

RMS Custom Gunsmithing, 4120 N. Bitterwell, Prescott Valley, AZ 86314 / 520-772-7626

Robert Evans Engraving, 332 Vine St., Oregon City, OR 97045 / 503-656-5693

Robert Valade Engraving, 931 3rd Ave., Seaside, OR 97138 / 503-738-7672

Robinett, R. G., P.O. Box 72, Madrid, IA 50156 / 515-795-2906

Robinson, Don, Pennsylvaia Hse, 36 Fairfax Crescent, W Yorkshire, ENGLAND / 0422-364458

Robinson Armament Co., PO Box 16776, Salt Lake City, UT 84116 / 801-355-0401; FAX: 801-355-0402 zdf@robarm.com; www.robarm.com

Robinson Firearms Mfg. Ltd., 1699 Blondeaux Crescent, Kelowna, BC V1Y 4J8 CANADA / 604-868-9596

Robinson H.V. Bullets, 3145 Church St., Zachary, LA 70791 / 504-654-4029

Rochester Lead Works, 76 Anderson Ave., Rochester, NY 14607 / 716-442-8500; FAX: 716-442-4712

Rock River Arms, 101 Noble St., Cleveland, IL 61241

Rockwood Corp., Speedwell Division, 136 Lincoln Blvd., Middlesex, NJ 08846 / 800-243-8274; FAX: 980-560-7475

Rocky Mountain Armoury, Mr. Felix LesMerises, 610 Main Street, P.O. Box 691, Frisco, CO 80443-0691 / 970-668-0136; FAX: 970-668-4484 felix@rockymountainarmoury.com

Rocky Mountain Arms, Inc., 1813 Sunset Pl, Unit D, Longmont, CO 80501 / 800-375-0846; FAX: 303-678-8766

Rocky Mountain Target Co., 3 Aloe Way, Leesburg, FL 34788 / 352-365-9598

Rocky Mountain Wildlife Products, PO Box 999, La Porte, CO 80535 / 970-484-2768; FAX: 970-484-0807 critrcall@earthlink.net www.critrcall.com

Rocky Shoes & Boots, 294 Harper St., Nelsonville, OH 45764 / 800-848-9452; or 614-753-1951; FAX: 614-753-4024

Rodgers & Sons Ltd., Joseph (See George Ibberson)

Rogue Rifle Co., Inc., P.O. Box 20, Prospect, OR 97536 / 541-560-4040; FAX: 541-560-4041

Rogue River Rifleworks, 500 Linne Road #D, Paso Robles, CA 93446 / 805-227-4706; FAX: 805-227-4723 rrrifles@calinet.com

Rohner, Hans, 1148 Twin Sisters Ranch Rd., Nederland, CO 80466-9600

Rohner, John, 186 Virginia Ave., Asheville, NC 28806 / 303-444-3841

Rohrbaugh, P.O. Box 785, Bayport, NY 11705 / 631-363-2843; FAX: 631-363-2681 API380@aol.com

Romain's Custom Guns, Inc., RD 1, Whetstone Rd., Brockport, PA 15823 / 814-265-1948 romwhetstone@penn.com

Ron Frank Custom Classic Arms, 7131 Richland Rd., Ft. Worth, TX 76118 / 817-284-9300; FAX: 817-284-9300 rfrank3974@aol.com

Rooster Laboratories, P.O. Box 412514, Kansas City, MO 64141 / 816-474-1622; FAX: 816-474-1307

Rorschach Precision Products, 417 Keats Cir., Irving, TX 75061 / 214-790-3487

Rosenberg & Son, Jack A, 12229 Cox Ln, Dallas, TX 75234 / 214-241-6302

Ross, Don, 12813 West 83 Terrace, Lenexa, KS 66215 / 913-492-6982

Rosser, Bob, 1824 29th Ave. So., Suite 214, Homewood, AL 35209 / 205-870-4422; FAX: 205-870-4421 bob@hand_engravers.com handengravers.com
Rossi Firearms, Gary Mchalik, 16175 NW 49th Ave, Miami, FL 33014-6314 / 305-474-0401; FAX: 305-623-7506
Roto Carve, 2754 Garden Ave., Janesville, IA 50647
Rottweil Compe, 1330 Glassell, Orange, CA 92667
Roy Baker's Leather Goods, PO Box 893, Magnolia, AR 71754 / 870-234-0344
Royal Arms Gunstocks, 919 8th Ave. NW, Great Falls, MT 59404 / 406-453-1149; FAX: 406-453-1194 royalarms@lmt.net; lmt.net/~royalarms
Roy's Custom Grips, Rt. 3, Box 174-E, Lynchburg, VA 24504 / 804-993-3470
RPM, 15481 N. Twin Lakes Dr., Tucson, AZ 85739 / 520-825-1233; FAX: 520-825-3333
Rubright Bullets, 1008 S. Quince Rd., Walnutport, PA 18088 / 215-767-1339
Rucker Dist. Inc., P.O. Box 479, Terrell, TX 75160 / 214-563-2094
Ruger (See Sturm, Ruger & Co., Inc.)
Ruger, Chris. See: RUGER'S CUSTOM GUNS
Ruger's Custom Guns, Chris Ruger, 1050 Morton Blvd., Kingston, NY 12401 / 845-336-7106; FAX: 845-336-7106 rugerscustom@outdrs.net rugergunsmith.com
Rundell's Gun Shop, 6198 Frances Rd., Clio, MI 48420 / 313-687-0559
Runge, Robert P., 1120 Helderberg Trl. #1, Berne, NY 12023-2909
Rupert's Gun Shop, 2202 Dick Rd., Suite B, Fenwick, MI 48834 / 517-248-3252
Russ Haydon Shooters' Supply, 15018 Goodrich Dr. NW, Gig Harbor, WA 98329 / 253-857-7557; FAX: 253-857-7884
Russ Trading Post, William A. Russ, 23 William St., Addison, NY 14801-1326 / 607-359-3896
Russ, William. See: RUSS TRADING POST
Rusteprufe Laboratories, 1319 Jefferson Ave., Sparta, WI 54656 / 608-269-4144; FAX: 608-366-1972 rusteprufe@centurytiel.net rusteprufe.com
Rusty Duck Premium Gun Care Products, 7785 Foundation Dr., Suite 6, Florence, KY 41042 / 606-342-5553; FAX: 606-342-5556
Rutgers Book Center, 127 Raritan Ave., Highland Park, NJ 08904 / 908-545-4344; FAX: 908-545-6686
Rutten (See U.S. Importer-Labanu Inc)
RWS (See US Importer-Dynamit Nobel-RWS, Inc.), 81 Ruckman Rd, Closter, NJ 07624 / 201-767-7971; FAX: 201-767-1589
Ryan, Chad L., RR 3, Box 72, Cresco, IA 52136 / 319-547-4384

S

S&K Scope Mounts, RD 2 Box 72E, Sugar Grove, PA 16350 / 814-489-3091; or 800-578-9862; FAX: 814-489-5466 comments@scopemounts.com www.scopemounts.com
S&S Firearms, 74-11 Myrtle Ave., Glendale, NY 11385 / 718-497-1100; FAX: 718-497-1105
S.A.R.L. G. Granger, 66 cours Fauriel, 42100, Saint Etienne, FRANCE / 04 77 25 14 73; FAX: 04 77 38 66 99
S.C.R.C., PO Box 660, Katy, TX 77492-0660 FAX: 713-578-2124
S.D. Meacham, 1070 Angel Ridge, Peck, ID 83545
S.G.S. Sporting Guns Srl., Via Della Resistenza, 37 20090, Buccinasco, ITALY / 2-45702446; FAX: 2-45702464
S.I.A.C.E. (See U.S. Importer-IAR Inc)
Sabatti S.r.l., via Alessandro Volta 90, 25063 Gardone V.T., Brescia, ITALY / 030-8912207-831312; FAX: 030-8912059
SAECO (See Redding Reloading Equipment)
Safari Press, Inc., 15621 Chemical Lane B, Huntington Beach, CA 92649 / 714-894-9080; FAX: 714-894-4949
Safariland Ltd., Inc., 3120 E. Mission Blvd., P.O. Box 51478, Ontario, CA 91761 / 909-923-7300; FAX: 909-923-7400
SAFE, PO Box 864, Post Falls, ID 83877 / 208-773-3624; FAX: 208-773-6819 staysafe@safe-llc.com; www.safe-llc.com
Safety Speed Holster, Inc., 910 S. Vail Ave., Montebello, CA 90640 / 323-723-4140; FAX: 323-726-6973 e-mail@safetyspeedholster.com www.safetyspeedholster.com
Saf-T-Lok, 5713 Corporate Way, Suite 100, W. Palm Beach, FL 33407
Sako Ltd (See U.S. Importer-Stoeger Industries)
Sam Welch Gun Engraving, Sam Welch, HC 64 Box 2110, Moab, UT 84532 / 435-259-8131
Samco Global Arms, Inc., 6995 NW 43rd St., Miami, FL 33166 / 305-593-9782; FAX: 305-593-1014 samco@samcoglobal.com; www.samcoglobal.com
Sampson, Roger, 2316 Mahogany St., Mora, MN 55051 / 612-679-4868
San Marco (See U.S. Importers-Cape Outfitters-EMF

Sanders Custom Gun Service, 2358 Tyler Lane, Louisville, KY 40205 / 502-454-3338; FAX: 502-451-8857
Sanders Gun and Machine Shop, 145 Delhi Road, Manchester, IA 52057
Sandia Die & Cartridge Co., 37 Atancacio Rd. NE, Auqerque, NM 87123 / 505-298-5729
Sarco, Inc., 323 Union St., Stirling, NJ 07980 / 908-647-3800; FAX: 908-647-9413
Sarsilmaz Shotguns - Turkey (see B.C. Outdoors)
Sauer (See U.S. Importers-Paul Co., The, Sigarms I
Sauls, R. See: BRYAN & ASSOC.
Saunders Gun & Machine Shop, R.R. 2, Delhi Road, Manchester, IA 52057
Savage Arms (Canada), Inc., 248 Water St., P.O. Box 1240, Lakefield, ON KOL 2HO CANADA / 705-652-8000; FAX: 705-652-8431
Savage Arms, Inc., 100 Springdale Rd., Westfield, MA 01085 / 413-568-7001; FAX: 413-562-7764
Savage Range Systems, Inc., 100 Springdale RD., Westfield, MA 01085 / 413-568-7001; FAX: 413-562-1152
Saville Iron Co. (See Greenwood Precision)
Savino, Barbara J., P.O. Box 51, West Burke, VT 05871-0051
Scansport, Inc., P.O. Box 700, Enfield, NH 03748 / 603-632-7654
Scattergun Technologies, Inc., 620 8th Ave. South, Nashville, TN 37203 / 615-254-1441; FAX: 615-254-1449
Sceery Game Calls, P.O. Box 6520, Sante Fe, NM 87502 / 505-471-9110; FAX: 505-471-3476
Schaefer Shooting Sports, P.O. Box 1515, Melville, NY 11747-0515 / 516-643-5466; FAX: 516-643-2426 rschaefe@optonline.net www.schaefershooting.com
Scharch Mfg., Inc., 10325 Co. Rd. 120, Salida, CO 81201 / 719-539-7242; or 800-836-4683; FAX: 719-539-3021 scharch@chaffee.net www.scharch.com
Scherer, Liz. See: SCHERER SUPPLIES
Scherer Supplies, Liz Scherer, Box 250, Ewing, VA 24248 FAX: 423-733-2073
Schiffman, Curt, 3017 Kevin Cr., Idaho Falls, ID 83402 / 208-524-4684
Schiffman, Mike, 8233 S. Crystal Springs, McCammon, ID 83250 / 208-254-9114
Schiffman, Norman, 3017 Kevin Cr., Idaho Falls, ID 83402 / 208-524-4684
Schmidt & Bender, Inc., PO Box 134, Meriden, NH 03770 / 603-469-3565; FAX: 603-469-3471 scopes@cyberportal.net; schmidtbender.com
Schmidtke Group, 17050 W. Salentine Dr., New Berlin, WI 53151-7349
Schneider Bullets, 3655 West 214th St., Fairview Park, OH 44126
Schneider Rifle Barrels, Inc, Gary, 12202 N 62nd Pl, Scottsdale, AZ 85254 / 602-948-2525
Schroeder Bullets, 1421 Thermal Ave., San Diego, CA 92154 / 619-423-3523; FAX: 619-423-8124
Schuetzen Pistol Works, 620-626 Old Pacific Hwy. SE, Olympia, WA 98513 / 360-459-3471; FAX: 360-491-3447
Schulz Industries, 16247 Minnesota Ave., Paramount, CA 90723 / 213-439-5903
Schumakers Gun Shop, 512 Prouty Corner Lp. A, Colville, WA 99114 / 509-684-4848
Scope Control, Inc., 5775 Co. Rd. 23 SE, Alexandria, MN 56308 / 612-762-7295
ScopLevel, 151 Lindbergh Ave., Suite C, Livermore, CA 94550 / 925-449-5052; FAX: 925-373-0861
Score High Gunsmithing, 9812-A, Cochiti SE, Albuquerque, NM 087123 / 800-326-5632; or 505-292-5532; FAX: 505-292-2592
Scot Powder, Rt.1 Box 167, McEwen, TN 37101 / 800-416-3006; FAX: 615-729-4211
Scot Powder Co. of Ohio, Inc., Box GD96, Only, TN 37140 / 615-729-4207; or 800-416-3006; FAX: 615-729-4217
Scott Fine Guns Inc., Thad, PO Box 412, Indianola, MS 38751 / 601-887-5929
Scott McDougall & Associates, 7950 Redwood Dr., Suite 13, Cotati, CA 94931 / 707-546-2264; FAX: 707-795-1911 www.colt380.com
Searcy Enterprises, PO Box 584, Boron, CA 93596 / 760-762-6771; FAX: 760-762-0191
Second Chance Body Armor, P.O. Box 578, Central Lake, MI 49622 / 616-544-5721; FAX: 616-544-9824
Seebeck Assoc., R.E., P. O. Box 59752, Dallas, TX 75229
Seecamp Co. Inc., L. W., PO Box 255, New Haven, CT 06502 / 203-877-3429; FAX: 203-877-3429
Segway Industries, P.O. Box 783, Suffern, NY 10901-0783 / 914-357-5510
Seligman Shooting Products, Box 133, Seligman, AZ 86337 / 602-422-3607
Sellier & Bellot, USA Inc, PO Box 27006, Shawnee Mission, KS 66225 / 913-685-0916; FAX: 913-685-0917

Selsi Co., Inc., P.O. Box 10, Midland Park, NJ 07432-0010 / 201-935-0388; FAX: 201-935-5851
Semmer, Charles (See Remington Double Shotguns), 7885 Cyd Dr, Denver, CO 80221 / 303-429-6947
Sentinel Arms, P.O. Box 57, Detroit, MI 48231 / 313-331-1951; FAX: 313-331-1456
Service Armament, 689 Bergen Blvd., Ridgefield, NJ 07657
Servus Footwear Co., 1136 2nd St., Rock Island, IL 61204 / 309-786-7741; FAX: 309-786-9808
Shappy Bullets, 76 Milldale Ave., Plantsville, CT 06479 / 203-621-3704
Sharp Shooter Supply, 4970 Lehman Road, Delphos, OH 45833 / 419-695-3179
Sharps Arms Co., Inc., C., 100 Centennial, Box 885, Big Timber, MT 59011 / 406-932-4353
Shaw, Inc., E. R. (See Small Arms Mfg. Co.)
Shay's Gunsmithing, 931 Marvin Ave., Lebanon, PA 17042
Sheffield Knifemakers Supply, Inc., PO Box 741107, Orange City, FL 32774-1107 / 386-775-6453; FAX: 386-774-5754
Sheldon, Bruce. See: RIDGELINE, INC
Shepherd Enterprises, Inc., Box 189, Waterloo, NE 68069 / 402-779-2424; FAX: 402-779-4010 sshepherd@shepherdscopes.com www.shepherdscopes.com
Sherwood, George, 46 N. River Dr., Roseburg, OR 97470 / 541-672-3159
Shilen, Inc., 205 Metro Park Blvd., Ennis, TX 75119 / 972-875-5318; FAX: 972-875-5402
Shiloh Creek, Box 357, Cottleville, MO 63338 / 314-925-1842; FAX: 314-925-1842
Shiloh Rifle Mfg., 201 Centennial Dr., Big Timber, MT 59011 / 406-932-4454; FAX: 406-932-5627
Shockley, Harold H., 204 E. Farmington Rd., Hanna City, IL 61536 / 309-565-4524
Shoemaker & Sons Inc., Tex, 714 W Cienega Ave, San Dimas, CA 91773 / 909-592-2071; FAX: 909-592-2378
Shoot Where You Look, Leon Measures, Dept GD, 408 Fair, Livingston, TX 77351
Shooters Arms Manufacturing Inc., Rivergate Mall, Gen. Maxilom Ave., Cebu City 6000, PHILIPPINES / 6332-254-8478; www.shootersarms.com.ph
Shooter's Choice Gun Care, 15050 Berkshire Ind. Pky., Middlefield, OH 44062 / 440-834-8888; FAX: 440-834-3388; www.shooterschoice.com
Shooter's Edge Inc., 3313 Creekstone Dr., Fort Collins, CO 80525
Shooters Supply, 1120 Tieton Dr., Yakima, WA 98902 / 509-452-1181
Shooter's World, 3828 N. 28th Ave., Phoenix, AZ 85017 / 602-266-0170
Shooters, Inc., 5139 Stanart St., Norfolk, VA 23502 / 757-461-9152; FAX: 757-461-9155 gflocker@aol.com
Shootin' Shack, Inc., 357 Cypress Drive, No. 10, Tequesta, FL 33469 / 561-842-0990; FAX: 561-545-4861
Shooting Chrony, Inc., 3269 Niagara Falls Blvd., N. Tonawanda, NY 14120 / 905-276-6292; FAX: 416-276-6295
Shooting Specialties (See Titus, Daniel)
Shooting Star, 1715 FM 1626 Ste 105, Manchaca, TX 78652 / 512-462-0009
Shoot-N-C Targets (See Birchwood Casey)
Shotgun Sports, PO Box 6810, Auburn, CA 95604 / 530-889-2220; FAX: 530-889-9106
Shotgun Sports Magazine, dba Shootin' Accessories Ltd., P.O. Box 6810, Auburn, CA 95604 / 916-889-2220
Shotguns Unlimited, 2307 Fon Du Lac Rd., Richmond, VA 23229 / 804-752-7115
Siegrist Gun Shop, 8752 Turtle Road, Whittemore, MI 48770 / 989-873-3929
Sierra Bullets, 1400 W. Henry St., Sedalia, MO 65301 / 816-827-6300; FAX: 816-827-6300
Sierra Specialty Prod. Co., 1344 Oakhurst Ave., Los Altos, CA 94024 FAX: 415-965-1536
SIG, CH-8212 Neuhausen, SWITZERLAND
Sigarms, Inc., Corporate Park, Exeter, NH 03833 / 603-772-2302; FAX: 603-772-9082 www.sigarms.com
Sightron, Inc., 1672B Hwy. 96, Franklinton, NC 27525 / 919-528-8783; FAX: 919-528-0995 info@sightron.com www.sightron.com
Signet Metal Corp., 551 Stewart Ave., Brooklyn, NY 11222 / 718-384-5400; FAX: 718-388-7488
SIG-Sauer (See U.S. Importer-Sigarms Inc.)
Silencio/Safety Direct, 56 Coney Island Dr., Sparks, NV 89431 / 800-648-1812; or 702-354-4451; FAX: 702-359-1074
Silent Hunter, 1100 Newton Ave., W. Collingswood, NJ 08107 / 609-854-3276
Silhouette Leathers, PO Box 1161, Gunnison, CO 81230 / 303-641-6639 oldshooter@yahoo.com

Silver Eagle Machining, 18007 N. 69th Ave., Glendale, AZ 85308
Silver Ridge Gun Shop (See Goodwin, Fred)
Simmons, Jerry, 715 Middlebury St., Goshen, IN 46528-2717 / 574-533-8546
Simmons Gun Repair, Inc., 700 S. Rogers Rd., Olathe, KS 66062 / 913-782-3131; FAX: 913-782-4189
Simmons Outdoor Corp., PO Box 217, Heflin, AL 36264
Sinclair International, Inc., 2330 Wayne Haven St., Fort Wayne, IN 46803 / 260-493-1858; FAX: 260-493-2530 sales@sinclairintl.com www.sinclairintl.com
Singletary, Kent, 2915 W. Ross, Phoenix, AZ 85027 / 602-526-6836 kentscustom@hotmail.com
Siskiyou Gun Works (See Donnelly, C. P.)
Six Enterprises, 320-D Turtle Creek Ct., San Jose, CA 95125 / 408-999-0201; FAX: 408-999-0216
SKB Shotguns, 4325 S. 120th St., Omaha, NE 68137 / 800-752-2767; FAX: 402-330-8029 skb@radiks.net skbshotguns.com
Skeoch, Brian R., PO Box 279, Glenrock, WY 82637 / 307-436-9655; FAX: 307-436-9034
Skip's Machine, 364 29 Road, Grand Junction, CO 81501 / 303-245-5417
Sklany's Machine Shop, 566 Birch Grove Dr., Kalispell, MT 59901 / 406-755-4257
Slezak, Jerome F., 1290 Marlowe, Lakewood (Cleveland), OH 44107 / 216-221-1668
Slug Site, Ozark Wilds, 21300 Hwy. 5, Versailles, MO 65084 / 573-378-6430 john.ebeling.com
Small Arms Mfg. Co., 5312 Thoms Run Rd., Bridgeville, PA 15017 / 412-221-4343; FAX: 412-221-4303
Small Arms Specialists, 443 Firchburg Rd, Mason, NH 03048 / 603-878-0427; FAX: 603-878-3905 miniguns@empire.net miniguns.com
Small Custom Mould & Bullet Co., Box 17211, Tucson, AZ 85731
Smart Parts, 1203 Spring St., Latrobe, PA 15650 / 412-539-2660; FAX: 412-539-2298
Smires, C. L., 5222 Windmill Lane, Columbia, MD 21044-1328
Smith & Wesson, 2100 Roosevelt Ave., Springfield, MA 01104 / 413-781-8300; FAX: 413-731-8980
Smith, Art, 230 Main St. S., Hector, MN 55342 / 320-848-2760; FAX: 320-848-2760
Smith, Mark A., P.O. Box 182, Sinclair, WY 82334 / 307-324-7929
Smith, Michael, 2612 Ashmore Ave., Red Bank, TN 37415 / 615-267-8341
Smith, Ron, 5869 Straley, Ft. Worth, TX 76114 / 817-732-6768
Smith, Sharmon, 4545 Speas Rd., Fruitland, ID 83619 / 208-452-6329 sharmon@fmtc.com
Smith Abrasives, Inc., 1700 Sleepy Valley Rd., P.O. Box 5095, Hot Springs, AR 71902-5095 / 501-321-2244; FAX: 501-321-9232
Smith, Judy. See: L.B.T.
Smith Saddlery, Jesse W., 0499 County Road J, Pritchett, CO 81064 / 509-325-0622
Smokey Valley Rifles, E1998 Smokey Valley Rd, Scandinavia, WI 54977 / 715-467-2674
Snapp's Gunshop, 6911 E. Washington Rd., Clare, MI 48617 / 989-386-9226
Sno-Seal, Inc. (See Atsko/Sno-Seal)
Societa Armi Bresciane Srl (See U.S. Importer-Cape)
SOS Products Co. (See Buck Stix-SOS Products Co.), Box 3, Neenah, WI 54956
Sotheby's, 1334 York Ave. at 72nd St., New York, NY 10021 / 212-606-7260
Sound Technology, Box 391, Pelham, AL 35124 / 205-664-5860; or 907-486-2825 rem700P@sprintmail.com; www.soundtechsilencers.com
South Bend Replicas, Inc., 61650 Oak Rd.., South Bend, IN 46614 / 219-289-4500
Southeastern Community College, 1015 S. Gear Ave., West Burlington, IA 52655 / 319-752-2731
Southern Ammunition Co., Inc., 4232 Meadow St., Loris, SC 29569-3124 / 803-756-3262; FAX: 803-756-3583
Southern Bloomer Mfg. Co., P.O. Box 1621, Bristol, TN 37620 / 615-878-6660; FAX: 615-878-8761
Southern Security, 1700 Oak Hills Dr., Kingston, TN 37763 / 423-376-6297; FAX: 800-251-9992
Sparks, Milt, 605 E. 44th St. No. 2, Boise, ID 83714-4800
Spartan-Realtree Products, Inc., 1390 Box Circle, Columbus, GA 31907 / 706-569-9101; FAX: 706-569-0042
Specialty Gunsmithing, Lynn McMurdo, P.O. Box 404, Afton, WY 83110 / 307-886-5535
Specialty Shooters Supply, Inc., 3325 Griffin Rd., Suite 9mm, Fort Lauderdale, FL 33317
Speer Bullets, PO Box 856, Lewiston, ID 83501 / 208-746-2351; www.speer-bullets.com
Spegel, Craig, PO Box 387, Nehalem, OR 97131 / 503-368-5653

Speiser, Fred D., 2229 Dearborn, Missoula, MT 59801 / 406-549-8133
Spencer Reblue Service, 1820 Tupelo Trail, Holt, MI 48842 / 517-694-7474
Spencer's Custom Guns, 4107 Jacobs Creek Dr, Scottsville, VA 24590 / 804-293-6836; FAX: 804-293-6836
SPG LLC, PO Box 1625, Cody, WY 82414 / 307-587-7621; FAX: 307-587-7695
Sphinx Systems Ltd., Gesteigtstrasse 12, CH-3800, Matten, BRNE, SWITZERLAND
Splitfire Sporting Goods, L.L.C., P.O. Box 1044, Orem, UT 84059-1044 / 801-932-7950; FAX: 801-932-7959 www.splitfireguns.com
Sport Flite Manufacturing Co., PO Box 1082, Bloomfield Hills, MI 48303 / 248-647-3747
Sporting Clays Of America, 9257 Bluckeye Rd, Sugar Grove, OH 43155-9632 / 740-746-8334; FAX: 740-746-8605
Sports Innovations Inc., P.O. Box 5181, 8505 Jacksboro Hwy., Wichita Falls, TX 76307 / 817-723-6015
Sportsman Safe Mfg. Co., 6309-6311 Paramount Blvd., Long Beach, CA 90805 / 800-266-7150; or 310-984-5445
Sportsman Supply Co., 714 E. Eastwood, P.O. Box 650, Marshall, MO 65340 / 816-886-9393
Sportsman's Communicators, 588 Radcliffe Ave., Pacific Palisades, CA 90272 / 800-538-3752
Sportsmatch U.K. Ltd., 16 Summer St., Leighton, Buzzard Beds, Bedfordshire, LU7 8HT ENGLAND / 01525-381638; FAX: 01525-851236 info@sportsmatch-uk.com www.sportsmatch-uk.com
Sportsmen's Exchange & Western Gun Traders, Inc., 560 S. C St., Oxnard, CA 93030 / 805-483-1917
Spradlin's, 457 Shannon Rd, Texos Creek, CO 81223 / 719-275-7105; FAX: 719-275-3852 spradlins@prodigy.net; www.spradlins.net
Springfield Sporters, Inc., RD 1, Penn Run, PA 15765 / 412-254-2626; FAX: 412-254-9173
Springfield, Inc., 420 W. Main St., Geneseo, IL 61254 / 309-944-5631; FAX: 309-944-3676
Spyderco, Inc., 20011 Golden Gate Canyon Rd., Golden, CO 80403 / 800-525-7770; or 800-525-7770; FAX: 303-278-2229; sales@spyderco.com www.spyderco.com
SSK Industries, J. D. Jones, 590 Woodvue Lane, Wintersville, OH 43953 / 740-264-0176; FAX: 740-264-2257
Stackpole Books, 5067 Ritter Rd., Mechanicsburg, PA 17055-6921 / 717-796-0411; FAX: 717-796-0412
Stalker, Inc., P.O. Box 21, Fishermans Wharf Rd., Malakoff, TX 75148 / 903-489-1010
Stalwart Corporation, PO Box 46, Evanston, WY 82931 / 307-789-7687; FAX: 307-789-7688
Stan De Treville & Co., 4129 Normal St., San Diego, CA 92103 / 619-298-3393
Stanley Bullets, 2085 Heatheridge Ln., Reno, NV 89509
Stanley Scruggs' Game Calls, Rt. 1, Hwy. 661, Cullen, VA 23934 / 804-542-4241; or 800-323-4828
Star Ammunition, Inc., 5520 Rock Hampton Ct., Indianapolis, IN 46268 / 800-221-5927; FAX: 317-872-5847
Star Custom Bullets, PO Box 608, 468 Main St., Ferndale, CA 95536 / 707-786-9140; FAX: 707-786-9117 wmebridge@humboldt.com
Star Machine Works, PO Box 1872, Pioneer, CA 95666 / 209-295-5000
Starke Bullet Company, P.O. Box 400, 605 6th St. NW, Cooperstown, ND 58425 / 888-797-3431
Starkey Labs, 6700 Washington Ave. S., Eden Prairie, MN 55344
Starkey's Gun Shop, 9430 McCombs, El Paso, TX 79924 / 915-751-3030
Starlight Training Center, Inc., Rt. 1, P.O. Box 88, Bronaugh, MO 64728 / 417-843-3555
Starline, Inc., 1300 W. Henry St., Sedalia, MO 65301 / 660-827-6640; FAX: 660-827-6650 info@starlinebrass.com; http://www.starlinebrass.com
Starr Trading Co., Jedediah, PO Box 2007, Farmington Hills, MI 48333 / 810-683-4343; FAX: 810-683-3282
Starrett Co., L. S., 121 Crescent St, Athol, MA 01331 / 978-249-3551; FAX: 978-249-8495
State Arms Gun Co., 815 S. Division St., Waunakee, WI 53597 / 608-849-5800
Steelman's Gun Shop, 10465 Beers Rd., Swartz Creek, MI 48473 / 810-735-4884
Steffens, Ron, 18396 Mariposa Creek Rd., Willits, CA 95490 / 707-485-0873
Stegall, James B., 26 Forest Rd., Wallkill, NY 12589
Steve Henigson & Associates, P.O. Box 2726, Culver City, CA 90231 / 310-305-8288; FAX: 310-305-1905
Steve Kamyk Engraver, 9 Grandview Dr., Westfield, MA 01085-1810 / 413-568-0457
Steves House of Guns, Rt. 1, Minnesota City, MN 55959 / 507-689-2573

Stewart Game Calls, Inc., Johnny, PO Box 7954, 5100 Fort Ave., Waco, TX 76714 / 817-772-3261; FAX: 817-772-3670
Stewart's Gunsmithing, P.O. Box 5854, Pietersburg North 0750, Transvaal, SOUTH AFRICA / 01521-89401
Steyr Mannlicher AG & CO KG, Mannlicherstrasse 1, A-4400, Steyr, AUSTRIA / 0043-7252-78621; FAX: 0043-7252-68621
STI International, 114 Halmar Cove, Georgetown, TX 78628 / 800-959-8201; FAX: 512-819-0465 www.stiguns.com
Stiles Custom Guns, 76 Cherry Run Rd, Box 1605, Homer City, PA 15748 / 712-479-9945
Stillwell, Robert, 421 Judith Ann Dr., Schertz, TX 78154
Stoeger Industries, 17603 Indian Head Hwy., Suite 200, Accokeek, MD 20607-2501 / 301-283-6300; FAX: 301-283-6986; www.stoegerindustries.com
Stoeger Publishing Co. (See Stoeger Industries)
Stone Enterprises Ltd., 426 Harveys Neck Rd., PO Box 335, Wicomico Church, VA 22579 / 804-580-5114; FAX: 804-580-8421
Stone Mountain Arms, 5988 Peachtree Corners E., Norcross, GA 30071 / 800-251-9412
Stoney Point Products, Inc., PO Box 234, 1822 N Minnesota St, New Ulm, MN 56073-0234 / 507-354-3360; FAX: 507-354-7236 stoney@newulmtel.net www.stoneypoint.com
Storage Tech, 1254 Morris Ave., N. Huntingdon, PA 15642 / 800-437-9393
Storey, Dale A. (See DGS Inc.)
Storm, Gary, P.O. Box 5211, Richardson, TX 75083 / 214-385-0862
Stott's Creek Armory, Inc., 2526 S. 475W, Morgantown, IN 46160 / 317-878-5489; FAX: 317-878-9489 www.sccalendar.com
Stratco, Inc., P.O. Box 2270, Kalispell, MT 59901 / 406-755-1221; FAX: 406-755-1226
Strayer, Sandy. See: STRAYER-VOIGT, INC.
Strayer-Voigt, Inc., Sandy Strayer, 3435 Ray Orr Blvd, Grand Prairie, TX 75050 / 972-513-0575
Streamlight, Inc., 1030 W. Germantown Pike, Norristown, PA 19403 / 215-631-0600; FAX: 610-631-0712
Strong Holster Co., 39 Grove St., Gloucester, MA 01930 / 508-281-3300; FAX: 508-281-6321
Strutz Rifle Barrels, Inc., W. C., PO Box 611, Eagle River, WI 54521 / 715-479-4766
Stuart, V. Pat, Rt.1, Box 447-S, Greenville, VA 24440 / 804-556-3845
Sturgeon Valley Sporters, K. Ide, PO Box 283, Vanderbilt, MI 49795 / 517-983-4338
Sturm Ruger & Co. Inc., 200 Ruger Rd., Prescott, AZ 86301 / 928-541-8820; FAX: 520-541-8850 www.ruger.com
"Su-Press-On",Inc., PO Box 09161, Detroit, MI 48209 / 313-842-4222
Sullivan, David S .(See Westwind Rifles Inc.)
Summit Specialties, Inc., P.O. Box 786, Decatur, AL 35602 / 205-353-0634; FAX: 205-353-9818
Sun Welding Safe Co., 290 Easy St. No.3, Simi Valley, CA 93065 / 805-584-6678; or 800-729-SAFE; FAX: 805-584-6169; sunwelding.com
Sunny Hill Enterprises, Inc., W1790 Cty. HHH, Malone, WI 53049 / 920-795-4722; FAX: 920-795-4822
Super 6 LLC, Gary Knopp, 3806 W. Lisbon Ave., Milwaukee, WI 53208 / 414-344-3343; FAX: 414-344-0304
Sure-Shot Game Calls, Inc., P.O. Box 816, 6835 Capitol, Groves, TX 77619 / 409-962-1636; FAX: 409-962-5465
Survival Arms, Inc., 273 Canal St., Shelton, CT 06484-3173 / 203-924-6533; FAX: 203-924-2581
Svon Corp., 2107 W. Blue Heron Blvd., Riviera Beach, FL 33404 / 508-881-8852
Swann, D. J., 5 Orsova Close, Eltham North Vic., 3095 AUSTRALIA / 03-431-0323
Swanndri New Zealand, 152 Elm Ave., Burlingame, CA 94010 / 415-347-6158
Swanson, Mark, 975 Heap Avenue, Prescott, AZ 86301 / 928-778-4423
Swarovski Optik North America Ltd., 2 Slater Rd., Cranston, RI 02920 / 401-946-2220; or 800-426-3089; FAX: 401-946-2587
Sweet Home, Inc., P.O. Box 900, Orrville, OH 44667-0900
Swenson's 45 Shop, A. D., 3839 Ladera Vista Rd, Fallbrook, CA 92028-9431
Swift Bullet Co., P.O. Box 27, 201 Main St., Quinter, KS 67752 / 913-754-3959; FAX: 913-754-2359
Swift Instruments, Inc., 952 Dorchester Ave., Boston, MA 02125 / 617-436-2960; FAX: 617-436-3232
Swift River Gunworks, 450 State St., Belchertown, MA 01007 / 413-323-4052
Szweda, Robert (See RMS Custom Gunsmithing)

T

T&S Industries, Inc., 1027 Skyview Dr., W. Carrollton, OH 45449 / 513-859-8414

T.F.C. S.p.A., Via G. Marconi 118, B, Villa Carcina 25069, ITALY / 030-881271; FAX: 030-881826

T.G. Faust, Inc., 544 Minor St., Reading, PA 19602 / 610-375-8549; FAX: 610-375-4488

T.H.U. Enterprises, Inc., P.O. Box 418, Lederach, PA 19450 / 215-256-1665; FAX: 215-256-9718

T.K. Lee Co., 1282 Branchwater Ln., Birmingham, AL 35216 / 205-913-5222 odonmich@aol.com www.scopedot.com

T.W. Menck Gunsmith Inc., 5703 S. 77th St., Ralston, NE 68127

Tabler Marketing, 2554 Lincoln Blvd., Suite 555, Marina Del Rey, CA 90291 / 818-755-4565; FAX: 818-755-0972

Taconic Firearms Ltd., Perry Lane, PO Box 553, Cambridge, NY 12816 / 518-677-2704; FAX: 518-677-5974

TacStar, PO Box 547, Cottonwood, AZ 86326-0547 / 602-639-0072; FAX: 602-634-8781

Tactical Defense Institute, 574 Miami Bluff Ct., Loveland, OH 45140 / 513-677-8229; FAX: 513-677-0447

Talley, Dave, P.O. Box 821, Glenrock, WY 82637 / 307-436-8724; or 307-436-9315

Talmage, William G., 10208 N. County Rd. 425 W., Brazil, IN 47834 / 812-442-0804

Talon Industries Inc. (See Cobra Enterprises, Inc.)

Tamarack Products, Inc., PO Box 625, Wauconda, IL 60084 / 708-526-9333; FAX: 708-526-9353

Tanfoglio Fratelli S.r.l., via Valtrompia 39, 41, Brescia, ITALY / 30-8910361; FAX: 30-8910183

Tanglefree Industries, 1261 Heavenly Dr., Martinez, CA 94553 / 800-982-4868; FAX: 510-825-3874

Tank's Rifle Shop, PO Box 474, Fremont, NE 68026-0474 / 402-727-1317; FAX: 402-721-2573 jtank@mitec.net www.tanksrifleshop.com

Tanner (See U.S. Importer-Mandall Shooting Supply)

Taracorp Industries, Inc., 1200 Sixteenth St., Granite City, IL 62040 / 618-451-4400

Target Shooting, Inc., PO Box 773, Watertown, SD 57201 / 605-882-6955; FAX: 605-882-8840

Tar-Hunt Custom Rifles, Inc., 101 Dogtown Rd., Bloomsburg, PA 17815 / 570-784-6368; FAX: 570-784-6368 www.tar-hunt.com

Tarnhelm Supply Co., Inc., 431 High St., Boscawen, NH 03303 / 603-796-2551; FAX: 603-796-2918 info@tarnhelm.com www.tarnhelm.com

Tasco Sales, Inc., 2889 Commerce Pky., Miramar, FL 33025

Taurus Firearms, Inc., 16175 NW 49th Ave., Miami, FL 33014 / 305-624-1115; FAX: 305-623-7506

Taurus International Firearms (See U.S. Importer)

Taurus S.A. Forjas, Avenida Do Forte 511, Porto Alegre, RS BRAZIL 91360 / 55-51-347-4050; FAX: 55-51-347-3065

Taylor & Robbins, P.O. Box 164, Rixford, PA 16745 / 814-966-3233

Taylor's & Co., Inc., 304 Lenoir Dr., Winchester, VA 22603 / 540-722-2017; FAX: 540-722-2018

TCCI, P.O. Box 302, Phoenix, AZ 85001 / 602-237-3823; FAX: 602-237-3858

TCSR, 3998 Hoffman Rd., White Bear Lake, MN 55110-4626 / 800-328-5323; FAX: 612-429-0526

TDP Industries, Inc., 606 Airport Blvd., Doylestown, PA 18901 / 215-345-8687; FAX: 215-345-6057

Techno Arms (See U.S. Importer- Auto-Ordnance Corp

Tecnolegno S.p.A., Via A. Locatelli, 6 10, 24019 Zogno, I ITALY / 0345-55111; FAX: 0345-55116

Ted Blocker Holsters, Inc., 9396 S.W. Tigard St., Tigard, OR 97223 / 800-650-9742; FAX: 503-670-9692 www.tedblocker.com

Tele-Optics, 630 E. Rockland Rd., PO Box 6313, Libertyville, IL 60048 / 847-362-7757

Tennessee Valley Mfg., 14 County Road 521, Corinth, MS 38834 / 601-286-5014

Ten-Ring Precision, Inc., Alex B. Hamilton, 1449 Blue Crest Lane, San Antonio, TX 78232 / 210-494-3063; FAX: 210-494-3066

TEN-X Products Group, 1905 N Main St, Suite 133, Cleburne, TX 76031-1305 / 972-243-4016; or 800-433-2225; FAX: 972-243-4112

Tepeco, P.O. Box 342, Friendswood, TX 77546 / 713-482-2702

Terry K. Kopp Professional Gunsmithing, Rt 1 Box 224, Lexington, MO 64067 / 816-259-2636

Testing Systems, Inc., 220 Pegasus Ave., Northvale, NJ 07647

Tetra Gun Lubricants (See FTI, Inc.)

Tex Shoemaker & Sons, Inc., 714 W. Cienega Ave., San Dimas, CA 91773 / 909-592-2071; FAX: 909-592-2378

Texas Armory (See Bond Arms, Inc.)

Texas Platers Supply Co., 2453 W. Five Mile Parkway, Dallas, TX 75233 / 214-330-7168

Thad Rybka Custom Leather Equipment, 134 Havilah Hill, Odenville, AL 35120

Thad Scott Fine Guns, Inc., P.O. Box 412, Indianola, MS 38751 / 601-887-5929

The A.W. Peterson Gun Shop, Inc., 4255 West Old U.S. 441, Mount Dora, FL 32757-3299 / 352-383-4258

The Accuracy Den, 25 Bitterbrush Rd., Reno, NV 89523 / 702-345-0225

The Ballistic Program Co., Inc., 2417 N. Patterson St., Thomasville, GA 31792 / 912-228-5739; or 800-368-0835

The BulletMakers Workshop, RFD 1 Box 1755, Brooks, ME 04921

The Competitive Pistol Shop, 5233 Palmer Dr., Ft. Worth, TX 76117-2433 / 817-834-8479

The Concealment Shop, Inc., 617 W. Kearney St., Ste. 205, Mesquite, TX 75149 / 972-289-8997; or 800-444-7090; FAX: 972-289-4410 concealmentshop@email.msn.com www.theconcealmentshop.com

The Country Armourer, P.O. Box 308, Ashby, MA 01431-0308 / 508-827-6797; FAX: 508-827-4845

The Creative Craftsman, Inc., 95 Highway 29 North, P.O. Box 331, Lawrenceville, GA 30246 / 404-963-2112; FAX: 404-513-9488

The Custom Shop, 890 Cochrane Crescent, Peterborough, ON K9H 5N3 CANADA / 705-742-6693

The Dutchman's Firearms, Inc., 4143 Taylor Blvd., Louisville, KY 40215 / 502-366-0555

The Ensign-Bickford Co., 660 Hopmeadow St., Simsbury, CT 06070

The Eutaw Co., Inc., 7522 Old State Rd., Holly Hill, SC 29059 / 803-496-3341

The Firearm Training Center, 9555 Blandville Rd., West Paducah, KY 42086 / 502-554-5886

The Fouling Shot, 6465 Parfet St., Arvada, CO 80004

The Gun Doctor, 435 East Maple, Roselle, IL 60172 / 708-894-0668

The Gun Parts Corp., 226 Williams Lane, West Hurley, NY 12491 / 914-679-2417; FAX: 914-679-5849

The Gun Room, 1121 Burlington, Muncie, IN 47302 / 765-282-9073; FAX: 765-282-5270 bshstleguns@aol.com

The Gun Room Press, 127 Raritan Ave., Highland Park, NJ 08904 / 732-545-4344; FAX: 732-545-6686 gunbooks@rutgersgunbooks.com www.rutgersgunbooks.com

The Gun Shop, 716-A South Rogers Road, Olathe, KS 66062

The Gun Shop, 62778 Spring Creek Rd., Montrose, CO 81401

The Gun Shop, 5550 S. 900 East, Salt Lake City, UT 84117 / 801-263-3633

The Gun Works, 247 S. 2nd St., Springfield, OR 97477 / 541-741-4118; FAX: 541-988-1097 gunworks@worldnet.att.net; www.thegunworks.com

The Gunsight, 1712 North Placentia Ave., Fullerton, CA 92631

The Gunsmith in Elk River, 14021 Victoria Lane, Elk River, MN 55330 / 612-441-7761

The Hanned Line, P.O. Box 2387, Cupertino, CA 95015-2387 smith@hanned.com www.hanned.com

The Keller Co., 4215 McEwen Rd., Dallas, TX 75244 / 214-790-8585

The Lewis Lead Remover (See LEM Gun Specialties)

The Midwest Shooting School, Pat LaBoone, 2550 Hwy. 23, Wrenshall, MN 55797 / 218-384-3670 shootingschool@starband.net

The NgraveR Co., 67 Wawecus Hill Rd., Bozrah, CT 06334 / 860-823-1533

The Ordnance Works, 2969 Pidgeon Point Road, Eureka, CA 95501 / 707-443-3252

The Orvis Co., Rt. 7, Manchester, VT 05254 / 802-362-3622; FAX: 802-362-3525

The Outdoor Connection,Inc., 7901 Panther Way, Waco, TX 76712-6556 / 800-533-6076; or 254-772-5575; FAX: 254-776-3553 floyd@outdoorconnection.com www.outdoorconnection.com

The Park Rifle Co., Ltd., Unit 6a Dartford Trade Park, Power Mill Lane, Dartford DA7 7NX, ENGLAND /011-0322-222512

The Paul Co., 27385 Pressonville Rd., Wellsville, KS 66092 / 785-883-4444; FAX: 785-883-2525

The Protector Mfg. Co., Inc., 443 Ashwood Place, Boca Raton, FL 33431 / 407-394-6011

The Robar Co.'s, Inc., 21438 N. 7th Ave., Suite B, Phoenix, AZ 85027 / 623-581-2648 www.robarguns.com

The School of Gunsmithing, 6065 Roswell Rd., Atlanta, GA 30328 / 800-223-4542

The Shooting Gallery, 8070 Southern Blvd., Boardman, OH 44512 / 216-726-7788

The Sight Shop, John G. Lawson, 1802 E. Columbia Ave., Tacoma, WA 98404 / 206-474-5465

The Southern Armory, 25 Millstone Road, Woodlawn, VA 24381 / 703-238-1343; FAX: 703-238-1453

The Surecase Co., 233 Wilshire Blvd., Ste. 900, Santa Monica, CA 90401 / 800-92ARMLOC

The Swampfire Shop (See Peterson Gun Shop, Inc.)

The Wilson Arms Co., 63 Leetes Island Rd., Branford, CT 06405 / 203-488-7297; FAX: 203-488-0135

Theis, Terry, 21452 FM 2093, Harper, TX 78631 / 830-864-4438

Thiewes, George W., 14329 W. Parada Dr., Sun City West, AZ 85375

Things Unlimited, 235 N. Kimbau, Casper, WY 82601 / 307-234-5277

Thirion Gun Engraving, Denise, PO Box 408, Graton, CA 95444 / 707-829-1876

Thomas, Charles C., 2600 S. First St., Springfield, IL 62794 / 217-789-8980; FAX: 217-789-9130

Thompson / Center Arms, P.O. Box 5002, Rochester, NH 03866 / 603-332-2394; FAX: 603-332-5133 tech@tcarms.com; www.tcarms.com

Thompson Bullet Lube Co., PO Box 409, Wills Point, TX 75169 / 866-476-1500; FAX: 866-476-1500 thomlube@flash.net www.thompsonbulletlube.com

Thompson Precision, 110 Mary St., P.O. Box 251, Warren, IL 61087 / 815-745-3625

Thompson, Randall. See: HIGHLINE MACHINE CO.

Thompson Target Technology, 4804 Sherman Church Ave. S.W., Canton, OH 44710 / 330-484-6480; FAX: 330-491-1087; www.thompsontarget.com

Thompson Tool Mount, 1550 Solomon Rd., Santa Maria, CA 93455 / 805-934-1281 ttm@pronet.net thompsontoolmount.com

Thompson, Randall (See Highline Machine Co.)

3-D Ammunition & Bullets, PO Box 433, Doniphan, NE 68832 / 402-845-2285; or 800-255-6712; FAX: 402-845-6546

3-Ten Corp., P.O. Box 269, Feeding Hills, MA 01030 / 413-789-2086; FAX: 413-789-1549

Thunden Ranch, HCR 1, Box 53, Mt. Home, TX 78058 / 830-640-3138

Thunder Mountain Arms, P.O. Box 593, Oak Harbor, WA 98277 / 206-679-4657; FAX: 206-675-1114

Thurston Sports, Inc., RD 3 Donovan Rd., Auburn, NY 13021 / 315-253-0966

Tiger-Hunt Gunstocks, Box 379, Beaverdale, PA 15921 / 814-472-5161 tigerhunt4@aol.com www.gunstockwood.com

Tikka (See U.S. Importer-Stoeger Industries)

Timber Heirloom Products, 618 Roslyn Ave. SW, Canton, OH 44710 / 216-453-7707; FAX: 216-478-4723

Time Precision, 640 Federal Rd., Brookfield, CT 06804 / 203-775-8343

Tinks & Ben Lee Hunting Products (See Wellington)

Tink's Safariland Hunting Corp., P.O. Box 244, 1140 Monticello Rd., Madison, GA 30650 / 706-342-4915; FAX: 706-342-7568

Tioga Engineering Co., Inc., PO Box 913, 13 Cone St., Wellsboro, PA 16901 / 570-724-3533; FAX: 570-724-3895 tiogaeng@epix.net

Tippman Pneumatics, Inc., 3518 Adams Center Rd., Fort Wayne, IN 46806 / 219-749-6022; FAX: 219-749-6619

Tirelli, Snc Di Tirelli Primo E.C., Via Matteotti No. 359, Gardone V.T. Brescia, I ITALY / 030-8912819; FAX: 030-832240

TM Stockworks, 6355 Maplecrest Rd., Fort Wayne, IN 46835 / 219-485-5389

TMI Products (See Haselbauer Products, Jerry)

Tom Forrest, Inc., P.O. Box 326, Lakeside, CA 92040 / 619-561-5800; FAX: 619-561-0227

Tombstone Smoke'n' Deals, PO Box 31298, Phoenix, AZ 85046 / 602-905-7013; FAX: 602-443-1998

Tom's Gun Repair, Thomas G. Ivanoff, 76-6 Rt. Southfork Rd., Cody, WY 82414 / 307-587-6949

Tom's Gunshop, 3601 Central Ave., Hot Springs, AR 71913 / 501-624-3856

Tonoloway Tack Drives, HCR 81, Box 100, Needmore, PA 17238

Top-Line USA, Inc., 7920-28 Hamilton Ave., Cincinnati, OH 45231 / 513-522-2992; or 800-346-6699; FAX: 513-522-0916

Torel, Inc., 1708 N. South St., P.O. Box 592, Yoakum, TX 77995 / 512-293-2341; FAX: 512-293-3413

TOZ (See U.S. Importer-Nygord Precision Products)

Track of the Wolf, Inc., P.O. Box 6, Osseo, MN 55369-0006 / 612-424-2500; FAX: 612-424-9860

Traditions Performance Firearms, P.O. Box 776, 1375 Boston Post Rd., Old Saybrook, CT 06475 / 860-388-4656; FAX: 860-388-4657 trad@ctz.nai.net www.traditionsmuzzle.com

Trafalgar Square, P.O. Box 257, N. Pomfret, VT 05053 / 802-457-1911

Trail Visions, 5800 N. Ames Terrace, Glendale, WI 53209 / 414-228-1328

MANUFACTURER'S DIRECTORY

Trax America, Inc., PO Box 898, 1150 Eldridge, Forrest City, AR 72335 / 870-633-0410; or 800-232-2327; FAX: 870-633-4788 trax@ipa.net www.traxamerica.com

Treadlok Gun Safe, Inc., 1764 Granby St. NE, Roanoke, VA 24012 / 800-729-8732; or 703-982-6881; FAX: 703-982-1059

Treemaster, P.O. Box 247, Guntersville, AL 35976 / 205-878-3597

Trevallion Gunstocks, 9 Old Mountain Rd., Cape Neddick, ME 03902 / 207-361-1130

Trico Plastics, 28061 Diaz Rd., Temecula, CA 92590 / 909-676-7714; FAX: 909-676-0267 ustinfo@ustplastics.com; www.tricoplastics.com

Trigger Lock Division / Central Specialties Ltd., 220-D Exchange Dr., Crystal Lake, IL 60014 / 847-639-3900; FAX: 847-639-3972

Trijicon, Inc., 49385 Shafer Ave., P.O. Box 930059, Wixom, MI 48393-0059 / 810-960-7700; FAX: 810-960-7725

Trilux, Inc., P.O. Box 24608, Winston-Salem, NC 27114 / 910-659-9438; FAX: 910-768-7720

Trinidad St. Jr Col Gunsmith Dept., 600 Prospect St., Trinidad, CO 81082 / 719-846-5631; FAX: 719-846-5667

Triple-K Mfg. Co., Inc., 2222 Commercial St., San Diego, CA 92113 / 619-232-2066; FAX: 619-232-7675 sales@triplek.com www.triplek.com

Tristar Sporting Arms, Ltd., 1814 Linn St. #16, N. Kansas City, MO 64116-3627 / 816-421-1400; FAX: 816-421-4182 tristar@blity-it.net www.tristarsportingarms

Trius Traps, Inc., P.O. Box 25, 221 S. Miami Ave., Cleves, OH 45002 / 513-941-5682; FAX: 513-941-7970 triustraps@fuse.net triustraps.com

Trooper Walsh, 2393 N Edgewood St, Arlington, VA 22207

Trotman, Ken, 135 Ditton Walk, Unit 11, Cambridge, CB5 8PY ENGLAND / 01223-211030; FAX: 01223-212317

Tru-Balance Knife Co., P.O. Box 140555, Grand Rapids, MI 49514 / 616-453-3679

True Flight Bullet Co., 5581 Roosevelt St., Whitehall, PA 18052 / 610-262-7630; FAX: 610-262-7806

Truglo, Inc, PO Box 1612, McKinna, TX 75070 / 972-774-0300; FAX: 972-774-0323 www.truglosights.com

Trulock Tool, PO Box 530, Whigham, GA 31797 / 229-762-4678; FAX: 229-762-4050 trulockchokes@hotmail.com; trulockchokes.com

Tru-Square Metal Products Inc., 640 First St. SW, P.O. Box 585, Auburn, WA 98071 / 253-833-2310; or 800-225-1017; FAX: 253-83-2349 t-tumbler@qwest.net

Tucker, James C., PO Box 1212, Paso Robles, CA 93447-1212

Tucson Mold, Inc., 930 S. Plumer Ave., Tucson, AZ 85719 / 520-792-1075; FAX: 520-792-1075

Turnbull Restoration, Doug, 6680 Rt. 5 & 20, PO Box 471, Bloomfield, NY 14469 / 585-657-6338; FAX: 585-657-6338; turnbullrest@mindspring.com www.turnbullrestoration.com

Tuttle, Dale, 4046 Russell Rd., Muskegon, MI 49445 / 616-766-2250

Tyler Manufacturing & Distributing, 3804 S. Eastern, Oklahoma City, OK 73129 / 405-677-1487; or 800-654-8415

U

U.S. Fire Arms Mfg. Co., Inc., 55 Van Dyke Ave., Hartford, CT 06106 / 877-227-6901; FAX: 800-644-7265 usfirearms.com

U.S. Importer-Wm. Larkin Moore, 8430 E. Raintree Ste. B-7, Scottsdale, AZ 85260

U.S. Repeating Arms Co., Inc., 275 Winchester Ave., Morgan, UT 84050-9333 / 801-876-3440; FAX: 801-876-3737

U.S. Tactical Systems (See Keng's Firearms Specialty)

U.S.A. Magazines, Inc., P.O. Box 39115, Downey, CA 90241 / 800-872-2577

Uberti USA, Inc., P.O. Box 469, Lakeville, CT 06039 / 860-435-8068; FAX: 860-435-8146

Ugartechea S. A., Ignacio, Chonta 26, Eibar, SPAIN / 43-121257; FAX: 43-121669

Ultra Dot Distribution, 2316 N.E. 8th Rd., Ocala, FL 34470

Ultralux (See U.S. Importer-Keng's Firearms)

UltraSport Arms, Inc., 1955 Norwood Ct., Racine, WI 53403 / 414-554-3237; FAX: 414-554-9731

Uncle Bud's, HCR 81, Box 100, Needmore, PA 17238 / 717-294-6000; FAX: 717-294-6005

Uncle Mike's (See Michaels of Oregon Co.)

Unertl Optical Co., Inc., 103 Grand Avenue, P.O. Box 895, Mars, PA 16046-0895 / 724-625-3810; FAX: 724-625-3819; unertl@nauticom.net

Unique/M.A.P.F., 10 Les Allees, 64700, Hendaye, FRANCE / 33-59 20 71 93

UniTec, 1250 Bedford SW, Canton, OH 44710 / 216-452-4017

United Binocular Co., 9043 S. Western Ave., Chicago, IL 60620

United Cutlery Corp., 1425 United Blvd., Sevierville, TN 37876 / 865-428-2532; or 800-548-0835; FAX: 865-428-2267

United States Optics Technologies, Inc., 5900 Dale St., Buena Park, CA 90621 / 714-994-4901; FAX: 714-994-4904 www.usoptics.com

United States Products Co., 518 Melwood Ave., Pittsburgh, PA 15213-1136 / 412-621-2130; FAX: 412-621-8740 sales@us-products.com www.us-products.com

Universal Sports, PO Box 532, Vincennes, IN 47591 / 812-882-8680; FAX: 812-882-8680

Unmussig Bullets, D. L., 7862 Brentford Dr., Richmond, VA 23225 / 804-320-1165

Upper Missouri Trading Co., PO Box 100, 304 Harold St., Crofton, NE 68730-0100 / 402-388-4844

USAC, 4500-15th St. East, Tacoma, WA 98424 / 206-922-7589

Utica Cutlery Co., 820 Noyes St., Utica, NY 13503 / 315-733-4663; FAX: 315-733-6602

V

V.H. Blackinton & Co., Inc., 221 John L. Dietsch, Attleboro Falls, MA 02763-0300 / 508-699-4436; FAX: 508-695-5349

Valade Engraving, Robert, 931 3rd Ave, Seaside, OR 97138 / 503-738-7672

Valor Corp., 5555 NW 36th Ave., Miami, FL 33142 / 305-633-0127; FAX: 305-634-4536

Valtro USA, Inc, 1281 Andersen Dr., San Rafael, CA 94901 / 415-256-2575; FAX: 415-256-2576

VAM Distribution Co LLC, 1141-B Mechanicsburg Rd., Wooster, OH 44691 www.rex10.com

Van Gorden & Son Inc., C. S., 1815 Main St., Bloomer, WI 54724 / 715-568-2612

Van Horn, Gil, P.O. Box 207, Llano, CA 93544

Van Patten, J. W., P.O. Box 145, Foster Hill, Milford, PA 18337 / 717-296-7069

Vancini, Carl (See Bestload, Inc.)

Vann Custom Bullets, 330 Grandview Ave., Novato, CA 94947

Van's Gunsmith Service, 224 Route 69-A, Parish, NY 13131 / 315-625-7251

Varmint Masters, LLC, Rick Vecqueray, PO Box 6724, Bend, OR 97708 / 541-318-7306; FAX: 541-318-7306 varmintmasters@bendcable.com www.varmintmasters.net

Vecqueray, Rick. See: VARMINT MASTERS, LLC

Vega Tool Co., c/o T.R. Ross, 4865 Tanglewood Ct., Boulder, CO 80301 / 303-530-0174

Vektor USA, Mikael Danforth, 5139 Stanart St, Norfolk, VA 23502 / 888-740-0837; or 757-455-8895; FAX: 757-461-9155

Venco Industries, Inc. (See Shooter's Choice)

Venus Industries, P.O. Box 246, Sialkot-1, PAKISTAN FAX: 92 432 85579

Verney-Carron, B.P. 72, 54 Boulevard Thiers, 42002, FRANCE / 33-477791500; FAX: 33-477790702

Vest, John, 1923 NE 7th St., Redmond, OR 97756 / 541-923-8898

VibraShine, Inc., PO Box 577, Taylorsville, MS 39168 / 601-785-9854; FAX: 601-785-9874

Vibra-Tek Co., 1844 Arroya Rd., Colorado Springs, CO 80906 / 719-634-8611; FAX: 719-634-6886

Vic's Gun Refinishing, 6 Pineview Dr., Dover, NH 03820-6422 / 603-742-0013

Victory Ammunition, PO Box 1022, Milford, PA 18337 / 717-296-5768; FAX: 717-296-9298

Victory USA, P.O. Box 1021, Pine Bush, NY 12566 / 914-744-2060; FAX: 914-744-5181

Vihtavuori Oy, FIN-41330 Vihtavuori, FINLAND, / 358-41-3779211; FAX: 358-41-3771643

Vihtavuori Oy/Kaltron-Pettibone, 1241 Ellis St., Bensenville, IL 60106 / 708-350-1116; FAX: 708-350-1606

Viking Video Productions, P.O. Box 251, Roseburg, OR 97470

Vincent's Shop, 210 Antoinette, Fairbanks, AK 99701

Vincenzo Bernardelli S.p.A., 125 Via Matteotti, P.O. Box 74, Gardone V.T., Bresci, 25063 ITALY / 39-30-8912851-2-3; FAX: 39-30-8910249

Vintage Arms, Inc., 6003 Saddle Horse, Fairfax, VA 22030 / 703-968-0779; FAX: 703-968-0780

Vintage Industries, Inc., 781 Big Tree Dr., Longwood, FL 32750 / 407-831-8949; FAX: 407-831-5346

Viper Bullet and Brass Works, 11 Brock St., Box 582, Norwich, ON N0J 1P0 CANADA

Viramontez Engraving, Ray Viramontez, 601 Springfield Dr., Albany, GA 31707 / 229-432-9683 sgtvira@aol.com

Viramontez, Ray. See: VIRAMONTEZ ENGRAVING

Virgin Valley Custom Guns, 450 E 800 N #20, Hurricane, UT 84737 / 435-635-8941; FAX: 435-635-8943 vvcguns@infowest.com www.virginvalleyguns.com

Visible Impact Targets, Rts. 5 & 20, E. Bloomfield, NY 14443 / 716-657-6161; FAX: 716-657-5405

Vitt/Boos, 1195 Buck Hill Rd., Townshend, VT 05353 / 802-365-9232

Voere-KGH m.b.H., PO Box 416, A-6333 Kufstein, Tirol, AUSTRIA / 0043-5372-62547; FAX: 0043-5372-65752

Volquartsen Custom Ltd., 24276 240th Street, PO Box 397, Carroll, IA 51401 / 712-792-4238; FAX: 712-792-2542 vcl@netins.net www.volquartsen.com

Vom Hoffe (See Old Western Scrounger, Inc., The), 12924 Hwy A-12, Montague, CA 96064 / 916-459-5445; FAX: 916-459-3944

Vorhes, David, 3042 Beecham St., Napa, CA 94558 / 707-226-9116; FAX: 707-253-7334

Vortek Products, Inc., P.O. Box 871181, Canton, MI 48187-6181 / 313-397-5656; FAX: 313-397-5656

VSP Publishers (See Heritage/VSP Gun Books), PO Box 887, McCall, ID 83638 / 208-634-4104; FAX: 208-634-3101

Vulpes Ventures, Inc. Fox Cartridge Division, PO Box 1363, Bolingbrook, IL 60440-7363 / 630-759-1229; FAX: 815-439-3945

W

W. Square Enterprises, 9826 Sagedale Dr., Houston, TX 77089 / 281-484-0935; FAX: 281-464-9940 lfdwcpdq.net www.loadammo.co,

W. Waller & Son, Inc., 2221 Stoney Brook Rd., Grantham, NH 03753-7706 / 603-863-4177 wallerandson.com

W.B. Niemi Engineering, Box 126 Center Road, Greensboro, VT 05841 / 802-533-7180 or 802-533-7141

W.C. Strutz Rifle Barrels, Inc., PO Box 611, Eagle River, WI 54521 / 715-479-4766

W.C. Wolff Co., PO Box 458, Newtown Square, PA 19073 / 610-359-9600; or 800-545-0077; mail@gunsprings.com www.gunsprings.com

W.E. Birdsong & Assoc., 1435 Monterey Rd., Florence, MS 39073-9748 / 601-366-8270

W.E. Brownell Checkering Tools, 9390 Twin Mountain Cir, San Diego, CA 92126 / 858-695-2479; FAX: 858-695-2479

W.J. Riebe Co., 3434 Tucker Rd., Boise, ID 83703

W.R. Case & Sons Cutlery Co., Owens Way, Bradford, PA 16701 / 814-368-4123; or 800-523-6350; FAX: 814-768-5369

Waechter, 43 W. South St. #1FL, Nanticoke, PA 18634 / 717-864-3967; FAX: 717-864-2669

Wagoner, Vernon G., 2325 E. Encanto St., Mesa, AZ 85213-5917 / 480-835-1307

Wakina by Pic, 24813 Alderbrook Dr., Santa Clarita, CA 91321 / 800-295-8194

Waldron, Herman, Box 475, 80 N. 17th St., Pomeroy, WA 99347 / 509-843-1404

Walker Arms Co., Inc., 499 County Rd. 820, Selma, AL 36701 / 334-872-6231; FAX: 334-872-6262

Walker Mfg., Inc., 8296 S. Channel, Harsen's Island, ML 48028

Wallace, Terry, 385 San Marino, Vallejo, CA 94589 / 707-642-7041

Walls Industries, Inc., P.O. Box 98, 1905 N. Main, Cleburne, TX 76031 / 817-645-4366; FAX: 817-645-7946

Walters Industries, 6226 Park Lane, Dallas, TX 75225 / 214-691-6973

Walters, John. See: WALTERS WADS

Walters Wads, John Walters, 500 N. Avery Dr., Moore, OK 73160 / 405-799-0376; FAX: 405-799-7727 www.tinwadman@cs.com

Walther GmbH, Carl, B.P. 4325, D-89033 Ulm, GERMANY

Walther USA, PO Box 2208, Springfield, MA 01102 / 413-747-3443 www.walther-usa.com

Walther USA, PO Box 208, Ten Prince St., Alexandria, VA 22313 / 800-372-6454; FAX: 413-747-3592

Walt's Custom Leather, Walt Whinnery, 1947 Meadow Creek Dr., Louisville, KY 40218 / 502-458-4361

WAMCO--New Mexico, P.O. Box 205, Peralta, NM 87042-0205 / 505-869-0826

Ward & Van Valkenburg, 114 32nd Ave. N., Fargo, ND 58102 / 701-232-2351

Ward Machine, 5620 Lexington Rd., Corpus Christi, TX 78412 / 512-992-1221

Wardell Precision Handguns Ltd., 48851 N. Fig Springs Rd., New River, AZ 85027-8513 / 602-465-7995

Warenski, Julie, 590 E. 500 N., Richfield, UT 84701 / 801-896-5319; FAX: 801-896-5319

Warne Manufacturing Co., 9039 SE Jannsen Rd., Clackamas, OR 97015 / 503-657-5590 or 800-683-5590; FAX: 503-657-5695

Warren & Sweat Mfg. Co., P.O. Box 350440, Grand Island, FL 32784 / 904-669-3166; FAX: 904-669-7272

Warren Muzzleloading Co., Inc., Hwy. 21 North, P.O. Box 100, Ozone, AR 72854 / 501-292-3268

Washita Mountain Whetstone Co., P.O. Box 378, Lake Hamilton, AR 71951 / 501-525-3914

Wasmundt, Jim, P.O. Box 511, Fossil, OR 97830

MANUFACTURER'S DIRECTORY

WASP Shooting Systems, Rt. 1, Box 147, Lakeview, AR 72642 / 501-431-5606

Watson Bros., 39 Redcross Way, SE1 1H6, London, ENGLAND FAX: 44-171-403-336

Watson Trophy Match Bullets, 467 Pine Loop, Frostproof, FL 33843 / 863-635-7948; or 864-244-7948 cbestbullet@aol.com

Wayne E. Schwartz Custom Guns, 970 E. Britton Rd., Morrice, MI 48857 / 517-625-4079

Wayne Firearms For Collectors & Investors

Wayne Specialty Services, 260 Waterford Drive, Florissant, MO 63033 / 413-831-7083

WD-40 Co., 1061 Cudahy Pl., San Diego, CA 92110 / 619-275-1400; FAX: 619-275-5823

Weatherby, Inc., 3100 El Camino Real, Atascadero, CA 93422 / 805-466-1767; FAX: 805-466-2527 weatherby.com

Weaver Arms Corp. Gun Shop, RR 3, P.O. Box 266, Bloomfield, MO 63825-9528

Weaver Products, P.O. Box 39, Onalaska, WI 54650 / 800-648-9624; or 608-781-5800; FAX: 608-781-0368

Weaver Scope Repair Service, 1121 Larry Mahan Dr., Suite B, El Paso, TX 79925 / 915-593-1005

Webb, Bill, 6504 North Bellefontaine, Kansas City, MO 64119 / 816-453-7431

Weber & Markin Custom Gunsmiths, 4-1691 Powick Rd., Kelowna, BC V1X 4L1 CANADA / 250-762-7575; FAX: 250-861-3655; www.weberandmarkinguns.com

Weber Jr., Rudolf, P.O. Box 160106, D-5650, GERMANY / 0212-592136

Webley and Scott Ltd., Frankley Industrial Park, Tay Rd., Birmingham, B45 0PA ENGLAND / 011-021-453-1864; FAX: 021-457-7846

Webster Scale Mfg. Co., P.O. Box 188, Sebring, FL 33870 / 813-385-6362

Weems, Cecil, 510 W Hubbard St, Mineral Wells, TX 76067-4847 / 817-325-1462

Weigand Combat Handguns, Inc., 685 South Main Rd., Mountain Top, PA 18707 / 570-868-8358; FAX: 570-868-5218; sales@jackweigand.com www.scopemount.com

Weihrauch KG, Hermann, Industriestrasse 11, 8744 Mellrichstadt, Mellrichstadt, GERMANY

Welch, Sam. See: SAM WELCH GUN ENGRAVING

Wellington Outdoors, P.O. Box 244, 1140 Monticello Rd., Madison, GA 30650 / 706-342-4915; FAX: 706-342-7568

Wells, Rachel, 110 N. Summit St., Prescott, AZ 86301 / 520-445-3655

Wells Creek Knife & Gun Works, 32956 State Hwy. 38, Scottsburg, OR 97473 / 541-587-4202; FAX: 541-587-4223

Welsh, Bud. See: HIGH PRECISION

Wenger North America/Precise Int'l, 15 Corporate Dr., Orangeburg, NY 10962 / 800-431-2996; FAX: 914-425-4700

Wenig Custom Gunstocks, 103 N. Market St., PO Box 249, Lincoln, MO 65338 / 660-547-3334; FAX: 660-547-2881 gustock@wenig.com www.wenig.com

Werth, T. W., 1203 Woodlawn Rd., Lincoln, IL 62656 / 217-732-1300

Wescombe, Bill (See North Star West)

Wessinger Custom Guns & Engraving, 268 Limestone Rd., Chapin, SC 29036 / 803-345-5677

West, Jack L., 1220 W. Fifth, P.O. Box 427, Arlington, OR 97812

Western Cutlery (See Camillus Cutlery Co.)

Western Design (See Alpha Gunsmith Division)

Western Mfg. Co., 550 Valencia School Rd., Aptos, CA 95003 / 831-688-5884 lotsabears@eathlink.net

Western Missouri Shooters Alliance, PO Box 11144, Kansas City, MO 64119 / 816-597-3950; FAX: 816-229-7350

Western Nevada West Coast Bullets, PO BOX 2270, DAYTON, NV 89403-2270 / 702-246-3941; FAX: 702-246-0836

Westley Richards & Co., 40 Grange Rd., Birmingham, ENGLAND / 010-214792953

Westley Richards Agency USA (See U.S. Importer for Westwind Rifles, Inc., David S Sullivan, P.O. Box 261, 640 Briggs St., Erie, CO 80516 / 303-828-3823

Weyer International, 2740 Nebraska Ave., Toledo, OH 43607 / 419-534-2020; FAX: 419-534-2697

Whildin & Sons Ltd, E.H., RR 2 Box 119, Tamaqua, PA 18252 / 717-668-6743; FAX: 717-668-6745

Whinnery, Walt (See Walt's Custom Leather)

Whiscombe (See U.S. Importer-Pelaire Products)

White Barn Wor, 431 County Road, Broadlands, IL 61816

White Pine Photographic Services, Hwy. 60, General Delivery, Wilno, ON K0J 2N0 CANADA / 613-756-3452

White Rock Tool & Die, 6400 N. Brighton Ave., Kansas City, MO 64119 / 816-454-0478

White Shooting Systems, Inc. (See White Muzzleload

Whitestone Lumber Corp., 148-02 14th Ave., Whitestone, NY 11357 / 718-746-4400; FAX: 718-767-1748

Wichita Arms, Inc., 923 E. Gilbert, P.O. Box 11371, Wichita, KS 67211 / 316-265-0661; FAX: 316-265-0760

Wick, David E., 1504 Michigan Ave., Columbus, IN 47201 / 812-376-6960

Widener's Reloading & Shooting Supply, Inc., P.O. Box 3009 CRS, Johnson City, TN 37602 / 615-282-6786; FAX: 615-282-6651

Wideview Scope Mount Corp., 13535 S. Hwy. 16, Rapid City, SD 57701 / 605-341-3220; FAX: 605-341-9142 wvdon@rapidnet.com ww.jii.to

Wiebe, Duane, 5300 Merchant Cir. #2, Placerville, CA 95667 / 530-344-1357; FAX: 530-344-1357 wiebe@d-wdb.com

Wiest, Marie. See: GUNCRAFT SPORTS, INC.

Wilcox All-Pro Tools & Supply, 4880 147th St., Montezuma, IA 50171 / 515-623-3138; FAX: 515-623-3104

Wilcox Industries Corp, Robert F Guarasi, 53 Durham St, Portsmouth, NH 03801 / 603-431-1331; FAX: 603-431-1221

Wild Bill's Originals, PO Box 13037, Burton, WA 98013 / 206-463-5738; FAX: 206-465-5925

Wild West Guns, 7521 Old Seward Hwy, Unit A, Anchorage, AK 99518 / 800-992-4570; or 907-344-4500; FAX: 907-344-4005

Wilderness Sound Products Ltd., 4015 Main St. A, Springfield, OR 97478 / 800-47-0006; FAX: 541-741-0263

Wildey, Inc., 45 Angevine Rd, Warren, CT 06754-1818 / 203-355-9000; FAX: 203-354-7759

Wildlife Research Center, Inc., 1050 McKinley St., Anoka, MN 55303 / 612-427-3350; or 800-USE-LURE; FAX: 612-427-8354

Wilhelm Brenneke KG, PO Box 1646, 30837 Langenhagen, Langenhagen, GERMANY / 0511/97262-0; FAX: 0511/97262-62; info@brenneke.com www.brenneke.com

Will-Burt Co., 169 S. Main, Orrville, OH 44667

William Fagan & Co., 22952 15 Mile Rd., Clinton Township, MI 48035 / 810-465-4637; FAX: 810-792-6996

William Powell & Son (Gunmakers) Ltd., 35-37 Carrs Lane, Birmingham, B4 7SX ENGLAND / 121-643-0689; FAX: 121-631-3504

William Powell Agency, 22 Circle Dr., Bellmore, NY 11710 / 516-679-1158

Williams Gun Sight Co., 7389 Lapeer Rd., Box 329, Davison, MI 48423 / 810-653-2131; or 800-530-9028; FAX: 810-658-2140 williamsgunsight.com

Williams Mfg. of Oregon, 110 East B St., Drain, OR 97435 / 503-836-7461; FAX: 503-836-7245

Williams Shootin' Iron Service, The Lynx-Line, Rt. 2 Box 223A, Mountain Grove, MO 65711 / 417-948-0902; FAX: 417-948-0902

Williamson Precision Gunsmithing, 117 W. Pipeline, Hurst, TX 76053 / 817-285-0064; FAX: 817-280-0044

Willow Bend, PO Box 203, Chelmsford, MA 01824 / 978-256-8508; FAX: 978-256-8508

Willson Safety Prods. Div., PO Box 622, Reading, PA 19603-0622 / 610-376-6161; FAX: 610-371-7725

Wilson Combat, 2234 CR 719, Berryville, AR 72616-4573 / 800-955-4856; FAX: 870-545-3310

Wilson Case, Inc., PO Box 1106, Hastings, NE 68902-1106 / 800-322-5493; FAX: 402-463-5276 sales@wilsoncase.com www.wilsoncase.com

Winchester Consultants, George Madis, P.O. Box 545, Brownsboro, TX 75756 / 903-852-6480; FAX: 903-852-3045; gmadis@prodigy.com

Winchester Div. Olin Corp., 427 N. Shamrock, E. Alton, IL 62024 / 618-258-3566; FAX: 618-258-3599

Winchester Sutler, Inc., The, 270 Shadow Brook Lane, Winchester, VA 22603 / 540-888-3595; FAX: 540-888-4632

Windish, Jim, 2510 Dawn Dr., Alexandria, VA 22306 / 703-765-1994

Wingshooting Adventures, 0-1845 W. Leonard, Grand Rapids, MI 49544 / 616-677-1980; FAX: 616-677-1986

Winkle Bullets, R.R. 1, Box 316, Heyworth, IL 61745

Winter, Robert M., PO Box 484, 42975-287th St., Menno, SD 57045 / 605-387-5322

Wise Custom Guns, 1402 Blanco Rd, San Antonio, TX 78212-2716 / 210-828-3388

Wise Guns, Dale, 333 W Olmos Dr, San Antonio, TX 78212 / 210-828-3388

Wiseman and Co., Bill, PO Box 3427, Bryan, TX 77805 / 409-690-3456; FAX: 409-690-0156

Wisners Inc/Twin Pine Armory, P.O. Box 58, Hwy. 6, Adna, WA 98522 / 360-748-4590; FAX: 360-748-1802

Wolf (See J.R. Distributing)

Wolfe Publishing Co., 6471 Airpark Dr., Prescott, AZ 86301 / 520-445-7810; or 800-899-7810; FAX: 520-778-5124

Wolf's Western Traders, 1250 Santa Cora Ave. #613, Chula Vista, CA 91913 / 619-482-1701 patwolf4570book@aol.com

Wolverine Footwear Group, 9341 Courtland Dr. NE, Rockford, MI 49351 / 616-866-5500; FAX: 616-866-5658

Wood, Frank (See Classic Guns, Inc.), 5305 Peachtree Ind. Blvd., Norcross, GA 30092 / 404-242-7944

Woodleigh (See Huntington Die Specialties)

Woods Wise Products, P.O. Box 681552, Franklin, TN 37068 / 800-735-8182; FAX: 615-726-2637

Woodstream, P.O. Box 327, Lititz, PA 17543 / 717-626-2125; FAX: 717-626-1912

Woodworker's Supply, 1108 North Glenn Rd., Casper, WY 82601 / 307-237-5354

Woolrich, Inc., Mill St., Woolrich, PA 17701 / 800-995-1299; FAX: 717-769-6234/6259

Working Guns, Jim Coffin, 1224 NW Fernwood Cir, Corvallis, OR 97330-2909 / 541-928-4391

World Class Airguns, 2736 Morningstar Dr., Indianapolis, IN 46229 / 317-897-5548

World of Targets (See Birchwood Casey)

World Trek, Inc., 7170 Turkey Creek Rd., Pueblo, CO 81007-1046 / 719-546-2121; FAX: 719-543-6886

Worthy Products, Inc., RR 1, P.O. Box 213, Martville, NY 13111 / 315-324-5298

Wostenholm (See Ibberson [Sheffield] Ltd., George)

Wright's Gunstock Blanks, 8540 SE Kane Rd., Gresham, OR 97080 / 503-666-1705 doyal@wrightsguns.com www.wrightsguns.com

WTA Manufacturing, PO Box 164, Kit Carson, CO 80825 / 800-700-3054; FAX: 719-962-3570

Wyant Bullets, Gen. Del., Swan Lake, MT 59911

Wyant's Outdoor Products, Inc., PO Box 9, Broadway, VA 22815

Wyoming Custom Bullets, 1626 21st St., Cody, WY 82414

Wyoming Knife Corp., 101 Commerce Dr., Ft. Collins, CO 80524 / 303-224-3454

X

X-Spand Target Systems, 26-10th St. SE, Medicine Hat, AB T1A 1P7 CANADA / 403-526-7997; FAX: 403-528-2362

Y

Yankee Gunsmith, 2901 Deer Flat Dr., Copperas Cove, TX 76522 / 817-547-8433

Yavapai College, 1100 E. Sheldon St., Prescott, AZ 86301 / 520-776-2353; FAX: 520-776-2355

Yavapai Firearms Academy Ltd., PO Box 27290, Prescott Valley, AZ 86312 / 928-772-8262 info@yfainc.corn www.yfainc.com

Yearout, Lewis E. (See Montana Outfitters), 308 Riverview Dr E, Great Falls, MT 59404 / 406-761-0859

Yee, Mike. See: CUSTOM STOCKING

Yellowstone Wilderness Supply, P.O. Box 129, W. Yellowstone, MT 59758 / 406-646-7613

Yesteryear Armory & Supply, P.O. Box 408, Carthage, TN 37030

York M-1 Conversions, 12145 Mill Creek Run, Plantersville, TX 77363 / 936-894-2397; FAX: 936-894-2397

Young Country Arms, William, 1409 Kuehner Dr #13, Simi Valley, CA 93063-4478

Z

Zabala Hermanos S.A., Lasao, 6-20690, Elgueta, Guipuzcoa, 20600 SPAIN / 943-768076; FAX: 943-768201

Zander's Sporting Goods, 7525 Hwy 154 West, Baldwin, IL 62217-9706 / 800-851-4373; FAX: 618-785-2320

Zanotti Armor, Inc., 123 W. Lone Tree Rd., Cedar Falls, IA 50613 / 319-232-9650

Zeeryp, Russ, 1601 Foard Dr., Lynn Ross Manor, Morristown, TN 37814 / 615-586-2357

Zero Ammunition Co., Inc., 1601 22nd St. SE, PO Box 1188, Cullman, AL 35056-1188 / 800-545-9376; FAX: 205-739-4683

Ziegel Engineering, 2108 Lomina Ave., Long Beach, CA 90815 / 562-596-9481; FAX: 562-598-4734 ziegel@aol.com www.ziegeleng.com

Zim's, Inc., 4370 S. 3rd West, Salt Lake City, UT 84107 / 801-268-2505

Z-M Weapons, 203 South St., Bernardston, MA 01337 / 413-648-9501; FAX: 413-648-0219

Zriny's Metal Targets (See Z's Metal Targets)

Zufall, Joseph F., P.O. Box 304, Golden, CO 80402-0304

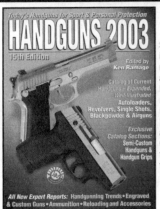

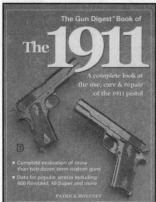
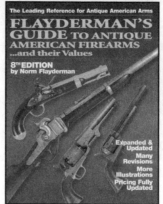
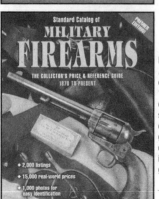

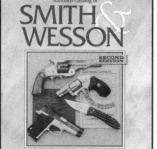